DATE DUE

CORRECTIONS

A Comprehensive View

SECOND EDITION

Ira J. Silverman
University of South Florida

WADSWORTH

THOMSON LEARNING

Australia • Canada • Mexico • Singapore • Spain • United Kingdom • United States

WADSWORTH

★

THOMSON LEARNING ™

To the important women in my life: Happy Silverman, Lilyan Silverman, Ruth Glick, and my newest treasure, Sidney Hannah Martenfelt

Executive Editor, Criminal Justice: Sabra Horne
Development Editor: Terri Edwards
Editorial Assistant: Cortney Bruggink
Marketing Manager: Jennifer Somerville
Marketing Assistant: Karyl Davis
Project Editor: Jennie Redwitz
Print Buyer: Karen Hunt
Permissions Editor: Joohee Lee
Text Designer: Christy Butterfield
Photo Researchers: Meyers Photo-Art

Copy Editor: Lura Harrison
Illustrator: Lotus Art
Cover Designer: Joan Greenfield
Cover Image: Chain gang—Underwood Photo Archives/ Superstock; Cell block—Superstock; Watch tower— Chris Salvo/FPG International; Tatooed man— Douglas Kent Hall; Group therapy—Robert Maass
Cover Printer: Phoenix Color Corp.
Compositor: R&S Book Composition
Printer: Courier Westford

Printed in the United States of America
1 2 3 4 5 6 7 04 03 02 01 00

Library of Congress Cataloging-in-Publication Data
Silverman, Ira J.
    Corrections: a comprehensive view/Ira J. Silverman.— 2nd ed.
        p. cm.
    Includes bibliographical references and index.
    ISBN 0-534-54648-X
    1. Corrections—History. 2. Punishment—Philosophy.
3. Criminal justice, Administration of—History.
4. Corrections—United States—History. 5. Punishment— United States—Philosophy. 6. Criminal justice, Administration of—United States—History.   I. Title.
HV8705 .S55   2000
365′.9—dc21   00-043620

Wadsworth/Thomson Learning
10 Davis Drive
Belmont, CA 94002-3098
USA

For more information about our products, contact us:
Thomson Learning Academic Resource Center
1-800-423-0563
http://www.wadsworth.com

International Headquarters
Thomson Learning
International Division
290 Harbor Drive, 2nd Floor
Stamford, CT 06902-7477
USA

UK/Europe/Middle East/South Africa
Thomson Learning
Berkshire House
168-173 High Holborn
London WC1V 7AA
United Kingdom

Asia
Thomson Learning
60 Albert Street, #15-01
Albert Complex
Singapore 189969

Canada
Nelson Thomson Learning
1120 Birchmount Road
Toronto, Ontario M1K 5G4
Canada

Brief Contents

Contents

PART 4 The Contemporary Prison: Its Administration and Management

Chapter 10 The Contemporary Prison: Beginning the 21st Century 223

Preface

During the last years of the 20th century, a parade of events and changes in the United States has had a major impact on correctional systems. A perception exists that violence is increasing despite Uniform Crime Report data showing a drop in both adult and juvenile crime. The movement of crime out of the inner city and into the suburbs and the randomness of victimization (e.g., carjackings, the Oklahoma City bombing, home invasions, and student shootings on school sites) have led to a growing public hatred and intolerance for criminals, creating a demand for immediate solutions to the crime problem (e.g., mandatory sentencing, three strikes laws, harsh treatment for those convicted). This backlash has caused massive increases in prison populations, requiring more funding for prison construction and inmate services, straining budgets to the point that prison funding grew at the expense of higher education funding. Other trends included increasing numbers of women, older individuals, and juveniles in prisons.

Corrections is the term that describes the official responses to the punishment of convicted offenders in the United States. It encompasses the broad range of facilities, programs, and services that deal with these offenders. Because corrections is under intense scrutiny, it is important for students to know and understand the many aspects of this field. Thus, these are the primary goals of this book:

- To provide students with an accurate, detailed, and up-to-date account of the development of correctional practices.
- To show how historical events and social issues have helped to shape today's correctional systems.
- To describe objectively and in detail contemporary corrections in the United States in terms of its present structure, clients, management and personnel, and programs.
- To provide a historical perspective of prisoners' rights and the current constitutional guarantees to which inmates are entitled.

Numerous references and sources have been used to provide a well-rounded and broad presentation of the information that constitutes this intrinsically interesting topic.

Organization of the Text

Part One introduces the student to the correctional system, its relationship to the other segments of the criminal justice system, and the role of sentencing. Chapter 1 deals with the place of corrections in the criminal justice system. Chapter 2 considers the various justifications, aspects, and strategies surrounding sentencing. Chapter 3 examines the ultimate sentence—the death penalty.

Part Two provides a four-chapter picture of the historical development of corrections from ancient times (Chapter 4) through the development of U.S. prisons during the 19th century (Chapter 5), the approaches taken in the Deep South (Chapter 6), and the Big House prisons of the first half of the 20th century (Chapter 7). The latter chapter also looks at the emergence of modern prisons and the factors that influenced them. This includes the development of rehabilitative institutions, the massive social changes that occurred during the 1960s and their impact on race relations, and the environment of contemporary prisons.

Part Three contains two chapters which focus on issues of classification and custody and correctional clientele. Chapter 8 details the history of classification and examines the modern classification system and custody. It also examines changes in prison demographics and offers a look at special category offenders. Chapter 9 profiles female offenders and discusses the special problems of incarcerated women and their adaptations to prison life.

Part Four comprises four chapters, which deal with a variety of issues related to prison administration and management. Chapter 10 opens with a look at the social environment of contemporary prisons and the subsequent problems it presents to administrators. Chapter 11 discusses correctional administrators and managers and the organizational contexts in which they work. Chapter 12 examines disruptive inmate groups and gangs that are classified as security threats. Chapter 13 focuses on line correctional officers and their roles, work environment, training, and relations with inmates.

Part Five is concerned with correctional law and inmates' rights and the ways in which these factors impact the operation of prisons. Chapter 14 examines the history of prisoners' rights and current laws protecting their access to law libraries, attorneys, and the courts. It also analyzes the impact of the Prisoner Litigation Reform Act, which restricts prisoners' access to the courts. Chapter 15 studies prisoners' constitutional, substantive, and procedural rights.

Part Six, which includes two chapters, focuses on the basic programs and services that must be maintained by correctional institutions to provide for inmates' needs. Educational, work, and recreational programs and their role in diminishing inmates' life skills deficits are examined in Chapter 16. Health, mental health, food, and religious services are discussed in Chapter 17. The chapter also looks at the importance of food services, the problems and issues associated with providing these services, and the role played by chaplains in the prison environment.

Part Seven describes American jails, probation, intermediate sanctions, and parole. Chapter 18 deals with jails and the role they play in the criminal justice and correctional processes. Chapter 19 describes and discusses probation programs. Chapter 20 treats the various intermediate sanctions that fall between standard probation and incarceration. Chapter 21 takes a detailed look at parole, including the impact of prelease visitations on later parolee behavior and the special problems presented by paroled sex offenders.

An epilogue that deals with our perceptions of the future of corrections is available on the Wadsworth Criminal Justice Web site: http://cj.wadsworth.com.

Special Features of This Text

This book presents a comprehensive treatment of correctional history, issues, and practices. This treatment is necessary if the reader is to understand the contemporary state of corrections, especially the growing emphasis on punishment. The views of those who lived or worked in corrections during earlier times can make the past come alive for students and will help them analyze the issues and problems in the field today and to think critically about solutions. Much of this research is supported by the extensive use of primary references. The inclusion of various chapters not usually found in other texts (e.g., southern prisons, gangs) can enhance students' understanding of differences existing in the various state systems. The following is a list of the special chapters that emphasize aspects of corrections not usually found in other corrections texts:

- Chapter 3 is new to this edition. It takes a detailed look at the death penalty.
- Chapter 4 examines the historical evolution of the punishments used to deal with rule or law violators.
- Chapter 6 traces correctional practices developed in the various southern states.
- Chapter 7 examines the Big House prisons that existed in northern states during the first half of the 20th century. It also deals with the rehabilitative type of prison that existed during the 30-year period following World War II. The chapter further details the sociopolitical developments of the 1960s and their impact on American corrections.
- Chapter 12 examines the development of prison gangs and their impact on the environment of the contemporary prison.
- Chapters 14 and 15 review a large number of cases and issues dealing with legal issues germane to corrections.
- Part Six covers in some detail the programs and services necessary in modern correctional facilities.

Several boxed features (called Close-Up, Historical Perspective, Consider This, Program Focus, or In Their Own Words) highlight actual events, unique and controversial programs and issues, personal experiences by inmates and their family members, personal experiences by correctional staff and others associated with the criminal justice process, and important court cases. Many conclude with questions challenging students to think about the issues presented.

The References and Table of Cases include both primary and secondary sources as well as an extensive compilation of books, monographs, and articles on historical and contemporary aspects of corrections. Also included is a list of court cases dealing with inmates' constitutional rights and other major correctional legal issues.

The Glossary provides students with definitions of the important terms found throughout the text. This serves as an excellent reference source and can also be used to review important concepts discussed in the text.

Learning Tools

The text contains the following features, which are designed to help the student learn, organize, and understand the material:

- *Key Terms and Concepts* at the beginning of each chapter alert students to important material.
- *Learning Objectives* open each chapter.
- *Topical headings and subheadings* provide students with a clear idea of the content that follows.
- Each chapter concludes with a *Summary* that recaps the chapter.
- *Critical Thinking Questions* and *Test Your Knowledge* sections are presented at the end of each chapter.

Acknowledgments

The preparation of this text was immeasurably enhanced by the help of a number of academic colleagues and professionals in the field of corrections. They contributed to one or both editions by providing information and material to update chapters or reading and critiquing chapters. I particularly wish to thank Mike Gilbert, Jo Gustafson, Harvey Landress, and Linda Breakall. Mike, a friend and colleague, was always available as a sounding board for my ideas and thoroughly reviewed chapters 11 and 13 several times. Jo, a corrections information specialist at the National Institute of Corrections, has been a continuing source of information whose help and support went above and beyond the call of duty. Harvey, a friend and colleague, provided continuing support and contributed many hours reading, writing, and revising parts of the manuscript, particularly the material on health care, AIDS drugs, and other infectious diseases; he provided invaluable insights and information. Linda, a member of the USF library staff, was extremely helpful in obtaining reference materials. Others at USF who were very helpful include Norm Voissem and members of the USF library staff: Susan Silver, Larry Heilos, and Marilyn Burke.

I wish also to acknowledge the expertise of the authors who contributed chapters to the First Edition of this book: Gerasimos (Gerry) Gianakis, Correctional Administration; Larry R. Ard and Ken Kerle, The American Jail; and Linda Smith, Intermediate Sanctions: Getting Tough in the Community. This First Edition was written with my co-author Manuel Vega, whose contributions were most appreciated. Further, I am grateful to Richard Rison for his reviews, insightful comments, and assistance in preparing material for many chapters. Moreover, I am thankful to Judi Benestante not only for her review of the education section but also for increasing the clarity of many chapters that she read. Finally, I wish to express my eternal gratitude to William Blount—"older brother," friend, colleague, and former chair of our department—for all his support and encouragement throughout both editions.

Typing and other related clerical services were provided by many people. I would like to especially thank Vicki Andrews who provided word processing assistance (many times overnight) and without whose help I would not have been able to complete the Second Edition in a timely fashion. I am also grateful to Marianne Bell and Carol Rennick, of the College of Arts and Sciences Information Processing Center, who typed numerous drafts of my chapters and assisted me in numerous related tasks that were necessary to complete this project. I wish to acknowledge Shirley Latt, office manager of the Department of Criminology, who also provided assistance. I also wish to express my appreciation to Jennifer Stauffer Walgren, who has just completed her MA in Criminology at USF, for her assistance in writing drafts of segments for many chapters and for her work on the initial update of chapters 14 and 15. Last, I wish to acknowledge the assistance of my graduate students who read several chapters and provided a "consumer's" perspective. For the work they have done, they all have my undying gratitude.

This text has not only benefited from scholarly literature, as noted by our extensive list of references, but also from materials and comments supplied by those working in corrections or related fields. The following individuals made special contributions to this text by reviewing chapters; providing expertise, materials, and comments; and writing special features that improved the real-world picture this text has endeavored to furnish: *Leslie Acoca, director, Women's and Girl's Institute, National Council on Crime and Delinquency; David Agresti, former director of programs, PRIDE of Florida; *Mary Alley, parenting program coordinator, Nebraska Department of Corrections, Nebraska Correctional Center for Women; Jaye Anno, private consultant and co-founder, National Commission on Correctional Health Care; *Pat Arvonio, warden (retired), East Jersey State Prison, New Jersey State Department of Corrections; *Chris Athey, chaplain, Death Row Unit, Chaplaincy Programs, Texas Department of Criminal Justice; Kay Wood Bailey, president, International Corrections Art Network; Ann Bartolo, unit manager, FCI-Morgantown, Federal Bureau of Prisons; *Gordon Bazemore, associate professor, Florida Atlantic University, Community Justice Institute; Allen Beck, BJS statistician, Office of Justice Programs, Bureau of Justice Statistics; *John Benestante, assistant director, Texas Correctional Industries, Texas Department of Criminal Justice; *Judi Benestante, educational specialist, Federal Programs and Grants, Windham School District, Texas Department of Criminal Justice; Fred Berlin, director, National Institute for the Study, Prevention, and Treatment of Sexual Trauma, and associate professor, School of Medicine, Johns Hopkins University; *Barbara Bloom, assistant professor, Administration of Justice, San Jose State University; John Boston, project director, Criminal Appeals Bureau, Prisoners' Rights Project, Legal Aid Society, New York City; *Jim Brazzil, chaplain, Walls Unit, Chaplaincy Programs, Texas Department of Criminal Justice; Peter Breen, director, CenterForce, San Quentin, California; *Tim Brennan, research associate professor, Department of Psychology, University of Colorado; *Steve Bright, director, Southern Center for Human Rights; Robert A. Buchanan, president, Correctional Services Group Inc., Kansas City, Missouri; Sammy Bunetello, assistant director, Security Threat Group Man, Texas Department of Criminal Justice; *Sherry Burt, information officer, Minnesota Department of Corrections; *Redonna Chandler, coordinator, Drug Abuse, Federal Medical Center, Lexington, Kentucky; Darryl Cheatwood, professor of criminal justice and sociology, University of Texas–San Antonio; Russell Clemens, American Federation of State, County, and Municipal Employees; *William Collins, attorney at law, co-editor, *Correctional Law Reporter*; *Georgia Comming, director, Vermont Center for Prevention and Treatment of Sexual Abuse; *Larry Cothran, executive officer, Technology and Transfer, California Department of Corrections; *Stephanie Covington, co-director, Institute for Relational Development; *Brian Cox, specialist, School Psychology, Windham School District, Texas Department of Criminal Justice; *Todd Craig, former chief information officer, Office of Public Affairs, Federal Bureau of Prisons; Kristina R. Crisafulli, project manager, Bureau of Justice Statistics Clearinghouse, Rockville, Maryland; *Frank Cullen, professor, Division of Criminal Justice, University of Cincinnati; Terry Danner, associate professor, Division of Social Science, St. Leo College; *Tony D'Cunha, operations manager, Texas Correctional Industries, Texas Department of Criminal Justice; Mike Deutsch, attorney at law, People's Law Center (involved in the defense of Attica inmates); Joel DeVolentine, Florida Department of Juvenile Justice; Richard Dieter, executive director, Death Penalty Information Center; *Simon Dinitz, professor emeritus, Department of Sociology, Ohio State University; Jack E. Dison, associate professor, Department of Criminology, Arkansas State University; *Don Drennon, classification officer, Federal Bureau of Prisons; *Alice Fins, managing editor, Publications, American Correctional Association; *Catherine Fogel, associate professor, School of Nursing, University of North Carolina; Robert Fong, associate professor, Department of Criminal Justice, California State University–Long Beach; Mike Gilbert, associate professor, Division of Social Policy, University of Texas–San Antonio Downtown Campus; *Cory Godwin, vice chair, State Classification Committee, Florida Department of Corrections; *Jim Gondles, executive director, American Correctional Association; *Kara Gotsch, editor, National Prison Project Journal, American Civil Liberties Union; *Robert Greiser, manager, Federal Prison Industries, Planning, Research, and Activation; * Jerry Groom, administrator of chaplaincy services, Texas Department of Criminal Justice; Casey F. Hairston, vice president, Parents Inc., and professor and associate dean, Indiana University School of Social Work, Indianapolis; Abdul Hafiz, chaplain, Chaplaincy Programs, FCI Terminal Island, Federal Bureau of Prisons; *Terry Hammons, retired classification manager, Federal Bureau of Prisons; *Steve Hart, reception services coordinator, Programs and Administration, Florida Department of Corrections; *Carl Hawkins, captain, Inspectional Services, Hillsborough County Sheriff's Office, Tampa, Florida; *Dana Hold, teacher, Windham School District, Texas Department of Criminal Justice; *Winston Hold, chaplaincy regional coordinator, Chaplaincy Programs, Texas Department of Criminal Justice; Gwyn Ingley, executive director, Correctional Industries Association; *John Irwin, professor emeritus, Department of Sociology, San Francisco State University; Mike Israel, member, Lifers Board of Directors, Rahway Prison, New Jersey, and criminal justice director, Kean College, Union, New Jersey; Cheryl Johnson, former director of instructional services, Windham School District, Texas Department of Criminal Justice; *Levinia Johnson, training development director, Academy for Staff Development, Food Service Specialty, Virginia Department of Corrections; *Sam Jordan, director, Program to Abolish the Death Penalty, Amnesty International USA; *George Kendall, NAACP Legal Defense Fund; Ken Kerle, managing editor, *American Jails,* American Jail Association; *Bob Kirchner, chapter president, Camps Division, California Peace Officers Association; *Steve Kramer, psychologist, Benchmark Behavioral Systems, Draper, Utah; Harvey Landress, vice president for planning, Gulf Coast Jewish and Family Services; Janice LaRosa, Unlimited Gravel Club sponsor, and psychological specialist, Tomoka Correctional Institution, Daytona Beach, Florida; Renee M. Legrand, former executive director, Louisiana Junior Chamber of Commerce; Kraig Libstag, former psychologist at the Vermont Treatment Program for Sexual Offenders; *Robert Levinson, special projects administrator, American Correctional Association; *Robert Lucas, captain, Detention Department, Hillsborough County Sheriff's Office; *Dorris MacKenzie, professor, Department of Criminology, University of Maryland–College Park; Jess Maghan, retired executive director, Forum for Comparative Corrections, Office of International Criminal Justice, Chicago, Illinois; *Tim Mann, general manager, Labor Line Services, An Affiliate of PRIDE Enterprises; Mark Mauer, assistant director, The Sentencing Project; Gail McCall, associate professor, Department of Recreation, University of Florida; Howard McClish, lieutenant, recreational specialist, Minnesota Correctional Facility, Oak Park Heights; *Jerry McClone, superintendent, Ohio Central School System, Ohio Department of Corrections; *Sylvia McCollum, inmate placement administrator, Federal Bureau of Prisons; *Rod Miller, president and publisher, *Detention and Corrections Reporter,* CRS, Inc; *Merry Morrash, director, School of Criminal Justice, University of Michigan; *Steve Morrison, Office of Science and Technology, National Law Enforcement and Technology Center, National Institute of Justice (NIJ); *Marilyn Moses, Social Science Program Analyst, Office of Justice Program, Department of Justice; Dana Murray, graphics manager, American Correctional Association; Lane Murray, retired superintendent, Windham School District, Texas Department of Criminal Justice; James W. Mustin, director, Family and Corrections Network; David Nunnellee, former public information officer, Texas Department of Criminal Justice; Joe Papy, region IV director, Community Corrections, Florida Department of Corrections; Barbara Parrer, executive director, Institutional Programs (in Arts, Crafts, Humanities), Oklahoma City, Oklahoma; *David Parrish, colonel/commander, Jail Division, Hillsborough County Sheriff's; *Joan Petersilia, professor of criminology and law, University of California, Irvine School of Social Ecology; Tom Pospichal, private consultant and former division manager, UNICOR, Federal Bureau of Prisons; *Mike Power, executive assistant, East Jersey State Prison, New Jersey State Department of Corrections; *Kay Pranis, restorative justice planner, Sentencing to Service, Minnesota Department of Corrections; *Christine Rasche, professor, University of North Florida, Department of Criminal Justice; *Blossom Regan, director of program development, New York Therapeutic Communities, Stay'n Out and Serendipity; *Mack Reynolds, information officer, Camps Program Unit, California Department of Corrections; Charles Riggs, former chaplaincy administrator, Chaplaincy Programs, Federal Bureau of Prisons; *Richard Rison, retired warden, Federal Bureau of Prisons; Martin Salisbury, former director of education, Patuxent Institute, Maryland; *Vincent Schiraldi, president, Justice Policy Institute; Pat Scholes, correctional information specialist, National Institute of Corrections; Robert R. Schulze, former assistant chaplaincy administrator, Federal Bureau of Prisons; *Michael Shannon, assistant director, Standards and Accreditation, American Correctional Association; Richard Shaw, chaplain, Albany, Rensselaer, and Schenectady County jails, and instructor; David

Shellner, corrections specialist, Information Center, National Institute of Corrections; *Brenda Smith, senior counsel/director, Women in Prison Project, National Women's Law Center; *Tracy Snell, BJS statistician, Bureau of Justice Statistics, U.S. Department of Justice, Office of Justice Programs; *Emmett Solomon, administrator of chaplaincy programs, Texas Department of Criminal Justice; Steve Steurer, executive director, Correctional Education Association; *Don Steward, senior psychologist, Corrections Mental Institution, Chattahoochee, Florida; Judy Ford Stokes, president, Food Management/Design, Judy Ford Stokes & Associates; *Victor Streib, dean and professor of law, Claude W. Pettit College, Ohio Northern University; Bill Taylor, professor, Department of Criminal Justice, University of Southern Mississippi; *Larry Todd, information officer, Texas Department of Criminal Justice; Alice Tracy, assistant director, Correctional Education Association; Chris Tracy, superintendent, Windham School District, Texas Department of Criminal Justice; *Susan Van Baalan, chaplaincy administrator, Chaplaincy Programs, Federal Bureau of Prisons; *Bob Verdeyen, director, Standards and Accreditation, American Correctional Association; Glenn Walters, Psychology Services, FCI, Schuylkill, Pennsylvania; Dale Welling, executive director, National Major Gangs Task Force; *Harry Wilhelm, marketing manager, American Correctional Association; *Ron Williams, executive director, New York Therapeutic Communities, Stay'n Out and Serendipity; Frank Wood, retired corrections commissioner, Minnesota Department of Corrections; *Nancy Zang, special administrator, Executive Division, Michigan Department of Corrections; *Ruth Zaplan, management consulting director, KPMG Peat Marwick; *Jason Ziedenburg, senior policy analyst, Justice Policy Institute; and *Judy Ziegler, administrative manager, CenterForce.

I am also grateful to the staff at Wadsworth Publishing for their invaluable assistance and support. I wish to especially thank Dan Alpert, developmental editor, for his unflagging support, without which this project would not have been completed, and Sabra Horne for her continuing support throughout this project. Jennie Redwitz, overall production editor for this edition also deserves my gratitude for the superb job she did in managing all that is involved in bringing a book to press. Lura Harrison, copyeditor, expertly edited the manuscript, improving its readability and correcting errors in it. This expertly produced text was the result of the efforts of all of these people.

This book went through a number of meticulous reviews for both content and style. The comments and suggestions of the following reviewers has enhanced the focus and presentation of the material: Kelly J. Asmussen, Peru State College; Elizabeth McConnell, Valdosta State University; Mary Finn, Georgia State University; and James L. Jengeleski, Shippensburg University.

Finally, I would like to thank the most important person in my life, my wife of 33 years Happy, for her support throughout both of these editions. It is impossible to put into words the feeling of gratitude I have for all of the sacrifices she made and for the extraordinary forbearance, love, and tireless support that she provided during the more than 15 years that both editions were in preparation. Further, when deadlines were nearing and time was tight she also read and critically edited portions of the manuscript. Were it not for her continuing love, nurturing, and support and concern for my well-being I could never have completed either of these projects.

*The names with an asterisk are new to the second edition.

The Correctional Process

1

LEARNING OBJECTIVES

After completing this chapter, you should be able to:

1. Define the terms *corrections* and *penology* and discuss the place of corrections within the criminal justice system.

2. Comment on the hidden nature of corrections and on its role in the solution of the crime problem.

3. Describe the organization of corrections within the United States.

4. Specify the relationship between the police and corrections and describe the correctional functions performed by the police.

5. Discuss the impact of prosecutorial discretion on corrections and describe the correctional functions performed by prosecutors.

6. Describe the relationship between sentencing and corrections.

7. Discuss the courts' role in correcting unconstitutional conditions within prisons.

8. Discuss the importance of history and social issues in the evolution of corrections.

Introduction

Nearly 150 people had gathered from three suburban neighborhood associations in the elementary school cafeteria. Most had noticed that the graffiti had first appeared about a year ago on traffic signs, on a wall behind the subdivision, and on a solid wooden fence. Then they noticed it by the school and then the mall. Now, it was everywhere—drawings of crowns, crosses, and arrows, with nicknames repeated over and over.

The police lieutenant told them that in the last 6 months at least four gangs had become organized in their part of town, mostly made up of 12- to-20-year-olds. Police intelligence clearly showed that, although some gang members came from other parts of town, many came from *their* neighborhoods. By the end of the year, the lieutenant said, there would likely be 10 gangs, all contributing to escalating crime. Their community was becoming more dangerous—first graffiti, then vandalism, and now car break-ins. Where would it stop? Robbery? Assault? Even murder? The people in the room were angry. They demanded that the police arrest and lock up the gang members.

The lieutenant told the assembly that even though at least half a dozen gang members had been arrested for the recent rash of car break-ins and petty vandalism, and the police soon expected to make additional arrests for drug sales and stolen property, none of the gang members were likely to serve any "time." Most were juveniles, and none had serious prior offenses, even though one or two were on probation. It would take a "serious" crime to possibly put them away, the officer said—and being a member of a gang is not a crime.

"What's gone wrong that we can't get these hoodlums locked up? Why can't we be safe in our own neighborhood? Can't we get rid of the vermin before we're robbed and beaten up?" one resident loudly complained. The audience broke into applause (Landress, 1999).

Official responses to the punishment of convicted offenders in the United States are collectively referred to as **corrections.** Currently and historically, the system of institutions, programs, and services that makes up corrections in this country has been under fire for not adequately protecting the community. Much of the current public dissatisfaction with corrections seems to focus on the "lenient treatment" received by convicted criminals (e.g., they do not serve long enough terms, not enough of them are incarcerated, most prisons are too soft on them). Generally, the public feels that prisons are not punitive enough. Many people feel that if more money were spent on incarcerating all criminals in harsh prisons for the full term of their sentences, crime would be diminished (Federal Probation, 1996). Do you think this would be an appropriate solution? If so, why?

This text attempts to answer this and other questions about convicted offenders by first examining historical events and the social changes that led to developments in correctional, or penal, responses to criminal behavior. In this way, current approaches to reducing criminal behavior may be better understood. One of the insights we will gain is that corrections can provide only part of the solution to the high level of crime in the United States.

Corrections

Technically, the term *corrections* has been applied only to actions taken by agencies to deal with convicted offenders. Today, however, it is typically defined in broader terms, including all agencies, programs, and organizations on the local, state, and federal levels that deal with both those accused of crimes (e.g., pretrial detainees) and those convicted of them. Of course, there are limitations on what can be done to those who have only been indicted for crimes.

Efforts directed at convicted offenders involve a variety of methods and approaches that include punishment, treatment (e.g., for drug addiction), and the improvement of academic and job skills. The objectives of these efforts include returning offenders who will lead productive lives to society and protecting society from criminal acts. However, historically, many have believed that retribution should be the primary correctional response to convicted offenders; that is, those who victimize others should suffer (Federal Probation, 1996). Methods of meeting correctional objectives typically translate into some restriction or deprivation of liberty, such as placing convicted offenders on some form of probation or parole, or imprisoning them. With pretrial detainees and those in pretrial diversion programs, the criminal justice system attempts to meet these objectives (except retribution) by placing some limitations on them.

"Corrections" replaced the older term **penology,** which came from a Latin word meaning punishment. Penology encompasses an organized body of concepts, theories, and approaches centered around the prison and the institutional experience; it signifies "the study of punishment." The term *corrections* describes the broad range of facilities, programs, and services dealing with convicted offenders. It also places less emphasis on punishment. This has created a dilemma in determining the right methods of dealing with criminals. Should criminals be punished, or should we also attempt to rehabilitate them? Insightful readers are likely to ask themselves, "Can't you rehabilitate through punishment?" Although the answer is a qualified "yes," the beneficial results of punishing criminals have not been amply demonstrated, because punishment, alone, does not rehabilitate. It does not effectively address the structural limitations that manifest themselves in fewer educational, vocational, and residential opportunities.

Our historical review of corrections will show that most U.S. correctional systems have had an underlying

The Pitfalls of Early and Mandatory Release

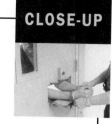

CLOSE-UP

Although the early and mandatory releases of inmates are necessary and often harmless, they are nevertheless very risky, particularly to the communities into which these offenders are released. This is a risk that most people do not want to take. The cases that follow illustrate their argument.

Garrett Johns

Garrett Johns spent much of his adult life either on probation or in prison. In 1994, he spent time in jail for exposing himself. That same year, he grabbed a 12-year-old girl, shocking her with a stun gun before she was able to escape. Following convictions for false imprisonment and battery, he was sentenced to community control followed by probation. He then spent almost 2 years in state prison for violating the terms of his probation. Within 3 years of his 1997 release, Johns was found guilty of rape in Hillsborough County, Florida, and faces two sexual battery charges in Pinellas County, Florida. He faces a mandatory 15-year sentence for the rape conviction (Lima, 1998, August 15).

Arthur Evans

Arthur Evans, a former professional boxer, spent the past two decades in prison in Wisconsin for armed robbery and in New York for a fatal mugging. He was released to a halfway house in Buffalo, and within 7 hours, he engaged in the brutal sexual assault of a Buffalo woman. He was convicted of second-degree rape and assault, and his sentence may range anywhere from 15 years to life in prison (Gryta, 1998, October 28).

Demeris Tolbert

Demeris Tolbert served 2½ years of a 54-month to 9-year sentence for a drug conviction. Although he should have served at least two thirds of his sentence, which would have meant a 2003 release year, Tolbert was released on parole in January 1998, following a 5-minute parole hearing, during which he promised to obey the law. After failing to appear at a mandatory weekly parole meeting on September 24, 1998, a warrant was issued for his arrest. After he opened fire on two cops, wounding one, Tolbert was captured. He was questioned about two murders in the area that police believed were committed by the same person. Shockingly, he confessed to five, two of which he committed following his release from prison (Marzulli, 1999, January 3).

---

punitive orientation. Yet, one of the original goals of imprisonment was reformation, which has been pursued in a variety of ways, often with limited success. Beginning with the penitentiary, the objectives of punishment and reform have generally been combined and have become a source of friction, making it difficult to fully realize either of them. The difficulty of imposing harsh sanctions on most convicted offenders is that they are not in prisons but, rather, under some form of community supervision. This makes it impossible to maintain a rigid punitive regimen. In contrast, most prisons are not structured or organized to facilitate rehabilitation.

The Low Visibility of Corrections

An important characteristic of the formal corrections process compared with other criminal justice system components is its low visibility. Prisons are the least visible of the components because most of them, particularly the older "fortress"-type institutions, are located in isolated, thinly populated rural areas or in remote parts of urban counties. Visits by community leaders, politicians, or judges who routinely sentence offenders to these facilities have, until recently, been a rarity. This has also imposed hardships on many families of inmates who want to remain in close touch. Finally, the public is typically denied access due to security and liability issues.

Within the community, correctional services become visible only in a few instances, such as when an attempt is made to locate a probation office (or some similar service center or facility for offenders) in a specific area of the community. Although they recognize the need for these facilities, citizens often take the position of "not in my backyard" (NIMBY). The furor is even greater when an area is proposed as a site for a prison or jail (McShane, Williams, & Wagoner, 1992; Rogers & Haimes, 1987). The exceptions to NIMBY are communities that have lost a major industry who view the building of a prison as a source of jobs and a means of improving the area's economy. They fight to get new prisons built in their area (Brooks, 1997).

Frequently, the public only becomes aware of correctional institutions when adverse publicity occurs, as in the case of a riot, an escape, a guard or an inmate slaying, or a dramatic event such as the execution of an infamous criminal or the commission of a heinous crime by an ex-convict. This is particularly true if the criminal was released prior to the expiration of his or her sentence as a consequence of overcrowded prisons. Our Close-Up, "The Pitfalls of Early and Mandatory Release," reflects public concern over the implications of early release. These news stories tend to validate the public view of offenders as inherently bad, brutal, or beyond change, which, in turn, may contribute to a more punitive public attitude.

Unconstitutional conditions (such as poor medical care) and reduced services and programs, often due to overcrowding and budgetary constraints, have also kept prisons in the public eye. However, there is less concern about the loss or reduction of programs and services, because large segments of the population feel that inmates are not entitled to them.

Racial conflicts present another source of attention for correctional institutions. In facilities where the population is composed of a disproportionate number of minorities, the animosities between different ethnic groups are magnified by the nature of institutional life. Self-preservationist instincts in this tense atmosphere are manifested in the formation of prison gangs and cliques and in "veneers of toughness by inmates" (Silberman, 1995). Bottled-up anger and frustration can be seen in gang rapes and assaults, intensified racial conflicts between inmates, and hostile inmate-guard relations.

This situation has been further aggravated by **prison overcrowding,** because when institutions are filled beyond capacity, an inmate cannot escape the inherent dangers of prison life by taking refuge in a safe single cell. A prison too crowded to restrain its most dangerous and aggressive inmates is likely to generate high levels of anxiety and violence, which further aggravate both individual and group conflict. Overcrowding occurred in spite of the fact that the number of prison beds doubled during the 1980s.

Public Opinion and Policy

Regardless of the specific factors that raise public fears about crime, the bottom line is that these fears are influencing criminal justice policy. Polls from 1994 to 1998 indicate that crime, violence, and drugs combined have become the primary concern of Americans, substantially outweighing concerns about the economy and health care. Despite the fact that crime has been dropping since 1992, almost 50 percent of the respondents in a 1998 Gallup Poll believed that crime in the United States was greater than the previous year, and almost 50 percent believed that this was the case in their own area. The fears and concerns about crime have affected public attitudes toward the performance of the various segments of the criminal justice system. For example, a 1998 survey showed that although almost 60 percent of the respondents had a great deal of confidence in the police, only one fourth had this level of faith in corrections (Maguire & Pastore, 1999).

Public perceptions of the purpose of imprisonment are somewhat inconsistent with their general punitive attitudes. A 1995 survey that asked whether the government needed to make a greater effort in punishing or rehabilitating convicted offenders found that almost 6 out of 10 opted for greater punishment (see Figure 1.1). However, Americans have different views about what needs to be done once convicted offenders are imprisoned (Flanagan & Longmire, 1996; Maguire & Pastore, 1998). Specifically, once an individual is confined, the public places greater emphasis on programs and services that increase the odds that he or she will become a law-abiding and productive member of society upon release (Maguire & Pastore, 1998; see Figure 1.2). There is also strong support for making inmates productive in ways that benefit society, including constructing buildings and performing services for the state that would otherwise require hiring citizens. Although controversial, there is strong public support for paying inmates to work with the stipulation that they return two thirds of their income to their victims (see Chapter 16; see also Figure 1.3). Further, the public recognizes the value of allowing inmates to earn their way out of prison through good behavior and program participation. Finally, 90 percent of the public supports the reduction of overcrowding through the development of vocational programs in the community for nonviolent and first-time offenders.

Such evidence suggests that public standards for corrections are extremely

A New York Police officer escorts the wife and brother of slain officer Anthony Mosomillo into the church for Mosomillo's funeral. Mosomillo was shot to death by a parolee wanted on drug charges.

high. They want correctional priorities to include placing offenders in facilities that provide sufficient surveillance and control to protect the public from being victimized. These facilities also should provide programs and services that increase the offender's potential for becoming a productive member of society. This latter view flies in the face of what politicians have argued the public wants—namely, the no-frills/get-tough approach to corrections. This has included the reintroduction of chain gangs, longer sentences, and tougher prisons that offer fewer programs, services, and amenities (e.g., the removal of televisions, the reduction of educational and work programs, and the removal of most recreation equipment). In fact, some politicians appear to want to return to the punitive and inhumane conditions that characterized 19th-century prisons (see Chapters 4, 5, and 6). However, public opinion does not appear to be as punishment oriented. This raises the question, "Who is leading and who is following?" (Flanagan & Longmire, 1996, p. 92).

Although politicians who argue for tougher prisons claim to have public support, evidence shows that they may have misperceived public attitudes toward corrections. Some research has concluded that most Americans believe prisons should be tough while also providing opportunities for rehabilitation. Such research recognizes that most inmates will be released at some point, and that without appropriate programs and services they will likely return to a life of crime. However, until political perceptions are changed, there is little hope that the funding to make effective reintegration into the community possible will be forthcoming. Instead, we see funding cuts in these areas, as well as legislation requiring all offenders to serve a greater portion of their sentence before being eligible for release.

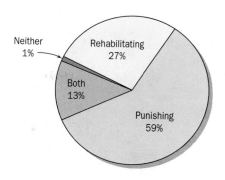

Figure 1.1 *Should the Government Put Greater Effort into Punishing or Rehabilitating Offenders?*

Source: Adapted from K. Maguire and K. Pastore (Eds.) (1997). *Sourcebook 1996*. Washington, DC: Bureau of Justice Statistics.

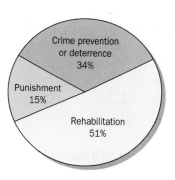

Figure 1.2 *What Is the Most Important Goal of Prison?*

Source: Adapted from K. Maguire and K. Pastore (Eds.) (1998). *Sourcebook 1997*. Washington, DC: Bureau of Justice Statistics.

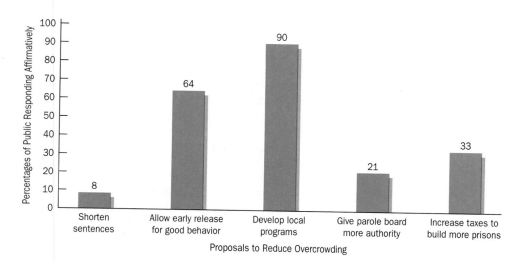

Figure 1.3 *Public Views on Proposals to Reduce Prison Overcrowding*

Source: Adapted with permission from T. J. Flanagan and D. R. Longmire (Eds.) (1996). *Americans View Crime and Justice: A National Public Opinion Survey*. Thousand Oaks, CA: Sage Publications, p. 88.

Recent polls indicate that crime, violence, and drugs combined have become the primary concern of Americans. This concern has affected public attitudes toward the criminal justice system.

Corrections and the Criminal Justice System

Although the problems currently facing corrections are of great concern, they are not unique to corrections. For reasons that are implicit in the dilemmas faced by a democratic society that has groups with differing values and concerns, it is difficult to find a time when corrections has not experienced a significant number of problems in dealing with crime, criminals, and criminal behavior. Some of these factors are explored in the following chapters, which examine the historical background and systematic developments that have helped to shape corrections. However, to place contemporary corrections in the proper perspective, we begin by examining its place in the criminal justice system. Specifically, we focus on the complex and often conflicting relationships between corrections and other components of the system. Further, we examine the correctional functions performed by these other components either in addition to, or as part of, their regular responsibilities.

The Criminal Justice Process

The activities of the criminal justice system form a continuum, which includes a series of steps and potential exit points (see Figure 1.4). Felonies, misdemeanors, and juvenile cases receive different dispositions within the criminal justice system and thus follow separate paths in the process. Apprehended offenders may be screened out of the system at various points along the way; this is pictorially presented as a **correctional funnel** (see Figure 1.5), through which most cases "leak" out before the sentencing.

Organization of the Correctional System

No single system of corrections exists in this country; instead, there are numerous correctional systems: a federal system, 50 state systems, and several thousand local systems. Therefore, we need to provide a brief overview of corrections in general prior to examining the interrelationships between it and the other justice system components. One key distinction in corrections is the difference between jails and prisons. Jails are almost always local—although several federal jails do exist—and they are used primarily to detain pretrial arrestees and convicted misdemeanants. Prisons are state or federal facilities that typically hold convicted felons who have been sentenced to more than one year of incarceration.

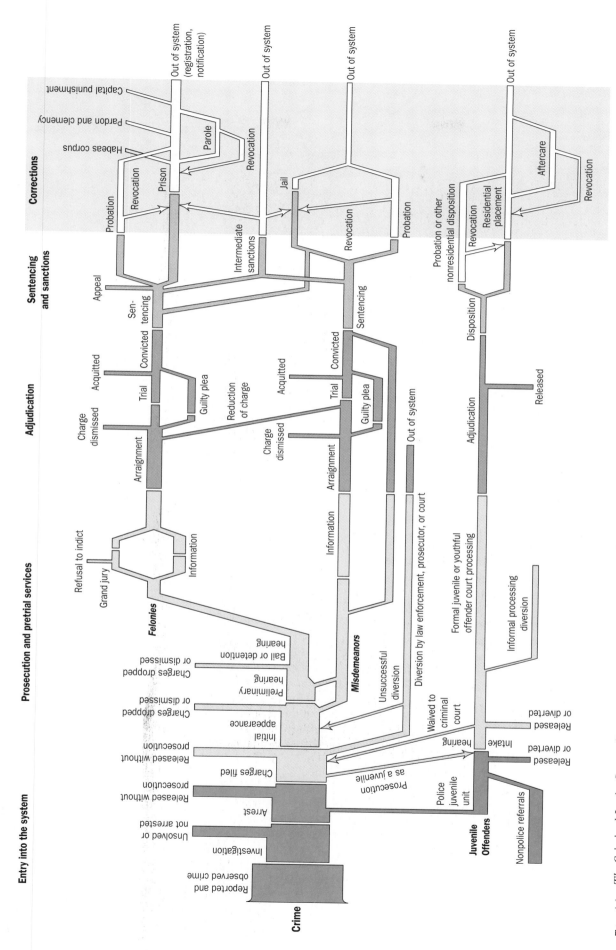

Figure 1.4   *The Criminal Justice System Sequence*

Source: Adapted from the President's Commission on Law Enforcement and Administration of Justice (1967). *The Challenge of Crime in a Free Society*. This revision, a result of the Symposium on the 30th Anniversary of the President's Commission, was prepared by the Bureau of Justice Statistics in 1997.

Note: This chart gives a simplified view of caseflow through the criminal justice system. Procedures vary among jurisdictions. The weights of the lines are not intended to show actual size of caseloads.

Figure 1.5 *The Correctional Funnel: Felony Convictions and Sentences Relative to the Number of Arrests, 1996*

Source: Adapted from Jodi M. Brown and Patrick A. Langan (1999). *Felony Sentences in State Courts, 1996*. Washington, DC: Bureau of Justice Statistics.

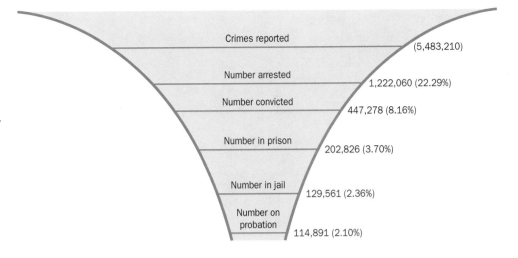

Crimes reported — (5,483,210)
Number arrested — 1,222,060 (22.29%)
Number convicted — 447,278 (8.16%)
Number in prison — 202,826 (3.70%)
Number in jail — 129,561 (2.36%)
Number on probation — 114,891 (2.10%)

The federal system, administered by the Bureau of Prisons, consists of 94 prisons, 6 jails, and 1 probation and parole service division. It deals with offenders who are accused or convicted of breaking federal laws. Federal prisons are divided into six levels of security ranging from minimum security camps to a supermaximum security prison in Florence, Colorado.

Each state correctional system is organized according to the wishes of its governor and legislature, which means they vary widely (see Chapter 11). State prisons typically house convicted felons who have received sentences of more than one year or who are awaiting execution; these prisons are usually divided into three or four levels of security. Both state and federal correctional systems also include probation, other community correctional services (e.g., halfway houses), and some form of parole or postrelease supervision.

Jails are the major **local correctional** facilities; they usually house convicted misdemeanants and pretrial detainees. Some local systems also place these offenders on probation, on work release, or in boot camps. At this level, terms are normally short—averaging a little over 100 days. Thus, the turnover in clientele is extremely large (Camp & Camp, 1997). Most local correctional programs are at the county level, but larger cities across the country (e.g., New York City) may also have their own programs. Additionally, jails in six states are run on a statewide basis. (Local programs are more fully discussed in Chapter 18.)

The Four Components of Criminal Justice

The criminal justice system is composed of four major subsystems: police, prosecutors, courts, and corrections, each with different responsibilities. Often forgotten is that none of these subsystems is mutually exclusive of the others; what is done in one has an effect on all the others. Each component provides clientele to the next one in the process:

police → prosecutors   prosecutors → courts
courts → corrections

The cycle is often repeated when released offenders recidivate and, again, become police "clientele." Increased efforts by the police, such as drug sweeps, produce an immediate impact on the other subsystems by overloading what are already heavy work schedules. Finally, if corrections is forced to release potential recidivists because of overcrowding from the increased activity of other subsystems, then they may, in turn, produce an increase in the workload of the police and courts.

Unlike justice systems in other parts of the world, the American criminal justice process is not composed of a single system, but includes numerous, relatively independent systems and subsystems of institutions and procedures. In all of the thousands of towns, cities and counties and 50 fifty states—and even in the federal government—there are criminal justice "systems." All apprehend, prosecute, convict, and punish or attempt to rehabilitate lawbreakers; yet, no two are exactly alike, and few are linked in any systematic way. We will look at how the first three components impact corrections.

The Role of Police in Corrections

An increase in the social agencies dealing with the offender has increased the direct **role of the police in corrections.** This is, in part, reflected in the interactions between the police and community-based corrections. The neutral ground where the probation or parole officer and the police first meet is usually the court and involves the probation officer's (PO's) presentation of the presentence investigation report (PSI). The PO may make a sentencing recommendation with which the police officer disagrees because he or she has seen first-hand the harm done by the offender. This disagreement could adversely affect the relationship between the police officer and the PO.

Relations between police and probation or parole personnel in the urban setting also tend to be adversely affected by the size of the respective departments and high turnover rates among personnel. POs in many urban areas are not highly visible and may be strictly limited in their mobility as a consequence of excessive paperwork or administrative responsibilities. However, the increasing use of community control and other intensive supervision programs, which require more face-to-face contacts between POs and offenders in the community, has increased interaction between POs and law enforcement. This has been further enhanced by POs assuming, in a number of states, a greater law enforcement/surveillance role in offender management. Police also serve as a valuable source of information for various correctional agencies. This includes providing probation or parole officers with a more comprehensive picture of the offender to be used in preparing a PSI.

Because of their uniforms, weapons, hardware, and traditional roles (i.e., law enforcement, crime control), it may be difficult to conceive of the police as the point at which corrections begins. The most visible corrections function by local law enforcement agencies is the operation of short-term detention and post-adjudication facilities (i.e., jails) that (1) hold offenders awaiting trial and convicted felons awaiting transfer to state institutions; and (2) punish convicted misdemeanants. Also, many county correctional agencies provide limited duration drug treatment, industry, and work release programs. Participation in these programs may have some correctional benefits. In addition, the jail experience may have some deterrent effect because individuals given a taste of incarceration may recognize the potential costs of continued criminal activity.

Some police departments operate programs directed toward the prevention, control, and treatment of delinquency. Police departments with special juvenile units may place youths on informal probation. This typically involves an agreement between the police, the adolescent, and his or her parents to meet certain conditions, which may include attending school and restricted after-school activities. Some police departments also operate delinquency programs that work directly with juvenile authorities for transitioning youths from detention facilities back into their communities. Officers are assigned a minimum number of at-risk youths, and they provide mentoring, counseling, and monitoring as the juveniles move back into their neighborhoods where their delinquent acts occurred. These programs attempt to stem the recidivism rate of juvenile crime (Hawkins, 1999).

Police in some jurisdictions operate community-based intervention programs that enable youths at risk of joining gangs to spend their time more productively. Such programs are an attractive alternative to traditional approaches such as curfews.

Many police departments also assign school resource officers (SROs) to junior and senior high schools, as one of their roles is preventing and diverting youths from contact with the juvenile justice system. SROs counsel students and their parents and provide lectures on law enforcement and related topics. These activities have led many SROs, who are often better educated than their counterparts (many have BA degrees), to a deeper understanding of the limited influence that corrections has in deciding which offenders to release (Florida Department of Law Enforcement, 1990).

Police departments in some jurisdictions operate community-based intervention programs such as the Neutral Zone in Mound Terrace, Washington, in cooperation with other multiagency local groups. The Neutral Zone offers youths at risk of joining a gang, or those already affiliated with one, a safe area for productively spending their time. Staffed on Friday and Saturday nights by police officers, recreation specialists, community alcohol and drug service providers, and others, the Neutral Zone provides an attractive alternative to traditional law enforcement approaches, which typically rely on police arrests and curfews to regulate gang behavior (Thurman, Giacomazzi, Reisig, & Mueller, 1996, p. 279).

A less visible police corrections function involves their discretionary arrest authority. This **gatekeeper function** allows police to determine whether formal action should be taken against an offender. When an offender is not taken into custody, the police have several options—all of which may involve a correctional function: (1) they can warn offenders and release them; (2) in dealing with juveniles, police can take the youngster home and confer with the family; or (3) they can refer the adult or juvenile to a diversion program, such as pretrial intervention or community mental health (Finn & Sullivan, 1988). For some first-time offenders, the only correctional action necessary may be a reprimand, a warning, or a referral.

With the movement toward **community policing** in America and the federal expenditures authorized in 1994 to pay to put more police officers on the streets, police agencies are systematically moving toward increased collaboration with the community on how to identify and solve problems (Gaffigan, 1994, p. 13). "Police use a wide range of methods—formal and informal—in getting their job done [of which] law enforcement is only one method among many" (Goldstein, 1990, p. 11).

The multidimensional approach that police must take in problem solving suggests that they should be creative in their techniques; they should look at the underlying conditions that contribute to the problem and consider a broad range of responses, rather than invoking only the criminal justice process. If the goal is to effectively prevent recidivism, arrest is one option, but there are often more effective ways to address the problem. For example, a certain bar has several fights every Friday and Saturday night; frequently someone is hit with a glass bottle or a pool cue. By the time the police arrive, the suspect is usually gone, and the injured person is on his or her way to the hospital. Traditionally, the police response was to take a report and try to identify the suspect. Often, the suspect is never identified, though, and the police and the bar continue to have the same problem. Even if a subject is identified, other persons may engage in physical altercations, and the cycle continues.

A problem-solving officer would look at the underlying conditions that contribute to the problem and suggest such solutions as (1) serving beer in plastic cups rather than glass bottles; or (2) keeping pool cues in the back room and instituting a checkout process that requires a deposit on the pool cue secured by a driver's license or another form of identification. If another fight occurs, the harm from the plastic cup may reduce injury to the face or parts of the body. The checkout policy provides the bar owner with reimbursement for the broken pool cue, and the officer can easily identify a suspect from his identification card. Although the problem was not entirely eliminated, the size, scope, and harm it created has been reduced. Further, this is likely to deter some patrons from involvement in such activity because their identities would be known and arrest is more likely (Hawkins, 1999).

A review of research in this area suggests that while it is too soon to draw unqualified conclusions about the success of community policing programs, the most consistent are

> (1) efforts to achieve a strong police presence in communities are likely to result in some fear reduction but not necessarily crime reduction itself; (2) efforts to aggressively police communities, through enforcement of minor disorder and incivilities as well as interrogations of persons that appear to be "suspicious," seem to be associated with lower crime rates. These results suggest that there are interesting possibilities for [effective] and proactive prevention-oriented policing. (Brame & Piquero, 1998, p. 195)

Community policing changes the gatekeeper function by diverting the person from the criminal justice process to the problem-solving process to reduce the recurrence of problems. It changes the role from reactive to proactive, in which the focus is to reduce the number of crime incidents. The problem-solving process in community policing provides officers with a wider range of ways to reduce the number of future problems. Reducing the number of offenders entering the criminal justice system probably decreases the number entering the corrections system. Our Close-Up, "The Police-Corrections Link," looks at some further aspects of the relationship between police and corrections.

The Role of Prosecutors in Corrections

Prosecutors impact corrections in various ways. The **discretionary authority** exercised by the office of the prosecutor has indirect, but extremely important, conse-

The Police-Corrections Link

A final link between police and corrections that deserves attention is their mutual collaboration, referred to as *police-corrections partnerships*. Although these partnerships are a contemporary development, several have developed in recent years, and they appear to be rapidly increasing. According to a study conducted by The National Institute of Justice (Parent & Snyder, 1999), police-corrections partnerships can be divided into one of five categories:

1. *Enhanced Supervision Partnerships* Police and corrections officers jointly supervise offenders who are on probation or parole. They provide interagency support through information sharing and training. This is the largest category of police-corrections partnerships.
2. *Fugitive Apprehension Units* Police and corrections officers (COs), together, attempt to locate offenders who have escaped from probation or parole supervision.
3. *Information Sharing Partnerships* Police and COs exchange information about offenders in whom they share a mutual interest.

4. *Specialized Enforcement Partnerships* Police, COs, and, often, members of other organizations and programs in the community unite to resolve specific problems in the area (e.g., gang activity reduction, curbing violence from firearms, etc.).
5. *Interagency Problem-Solving Partnerships* Police and COs collaborate to identify problems in the community and designate resources to resolve them.

Although a full discussion of the pros and cons of police-corrections partnerships is beyond the scope of this text, it is important to recognize that, despite their reported benefits and rapid increase, there are issues that will need to be dealt with. These alliances, for example, create numerous legal questions, including liability issues during probation and parole searches, authority regarding search and seizure, and so on.

One example of a police-corrections partnership is Operation Night Light in Boston, Massachusetts. As one of the oldest Enhanced Supervision Partnerships, Operation Night Light was formally

created in 1992, following a discussion between probation officers and the gang unit of the Boston Police Department that led to the realization that they were dealing with the same offenders. The implementation of Operation Night Light included joint patrols, curfew checks, and information sharing (e.g., with the DEA, INH, etc.) about offenders in the community, particularly gang members. Although no empirical data have been gathered, more than 5,000 contacts with gang member probationers have been made, and the levels of homicide and firearm assaults in Boston have declined over the past decade. Additionally, "police and probation officers reportedly have developed new respect for one another and recognize that they can use their formal powers in complementary ways in the pursuit of a common purpose" (Parent & Snyder, 1999, p. 13).

quences for corrections. Decisions by prosecutors affect the size and the nature of the prison population, because they can decide whether to initiate prosecution against those arrested by the police and the specific charges that will be brought against them.

Prosecutors have the broadest discretion when making a determination of whether a case merits prosecution (Miller et al., 1991).[1] Some prosecutors have developed administrative procedures to assist them in making these decisions. For example, the Prosecutors Information System uses computers to generate ratings that help attorneys decide which cases to prosecute. Second, prosecutors can screen out defendants who have been charged by requesting that the judge or magistrate enter a **nolle prosequi** (i.e., a formal decision by the prosecutor not to prosecute further) for a case at the preliminary hearing (Black, Nolan, & Nolan-Haley, 1991).[2] From a prosecutor's standpoint, screening out questionable cases as early as possible conserves scarce resources. The prosecutor's right to decide not to prosecute despite

sufficient evidence to do so is one of the broadest, most powerful examples of discretionary authority available to anyone in the criminal justice system (Miller et al., 1991; Richardson, 1998). Such broad discretion is permitted on the grounds that near autonomy is a fundamental prerequisite for safeguarding the integrity of the prosecutor in the decision-making process. Third, prosecutors can remove cases from the system by requesting that the offender be declared incompetent to stand trial. However, the Supreme Court has ruled that if there is no substantial possibility that these individuals can be restored to competency in a reasonable period of time through treatment, they must either be institutionalized through civil commitment proceedings or released (*Jackson v. Indiana*, 1997). Most states require that this determination be made within a 6-month period (Bonnie; Coughlin; Jefferies, Jr.; & Low, 1997).

Prosecutors may decide not to take official action in a particular case for a variety of reasons. Staff and budget limitations may restrict their ability to prosecute all

Table 1.1

Programs Provided by the Jacksonville Florida State Attorney's Office

Name of Program	Type of Program	Program Design
Youth Offender Program (YOP)	Diversion program for juveniles administered by the state attorney's office	Involves three programs designed to provide consequences and meet various needs of offenders
First Offender Program (FOP)	State attorney diversion program for first-time misdemeanor arrests	Juveniles pay restitution, perform community service hours, and participate in counseling
Junior FOP	Designed for extremely young offenders	Juveniles and parents brought in to meet staff; counseling referrals if necessary
Juvenile Alternative Services Program	Grant program administered by the state attorney's office for minor offenses diverted out of court	Juveniles are assigned sanctions by volunteer mediators and are monitored by state attorney case managers
Multiagency Assessment Program (MAAP)	Grant program administered by the state attorney's office for juveniles exhibiting multiple risk factors for reoffending	Juveniles are intensely monitored at home and at school by state attorney case managers
Focus on Females (FOF)	A delinquency prevention class for females in a state attorney diversion program	A collaborative effort with social service agencies that addresses issues that affect females and possibly contribute to crime
Early Delinquency Intervention Program (EDIP)	Utilized by the state attorney's office as a diversion program	A juvenile sanction designed for second offenders
Kids in Distress (KIDS)	State attorney's office diversion program	Designed for juvenile sexual offenders not needing court action
School Outreach Program (SORP)	State attorney program assigning assistant state attorneys to middle schools	Attorneys visit schools regularly and speak to students, staff, and teachers
Truancy Arbitration Program (TAP)	Grant program administered by the state attorney's office	Designed to compel children to attend school and used as a diversionary program for parents facing prosecution for failing to send their kids to school
Conflict Resolution Training		State attorney staff work with schools to institute peer mediation
Program for At-Risk Students (PAS)	State attorney program	Designed to educate at-risk students not currently in the system about the importance of staying in school and the consequences of criminality
Juvenile Drug Court	Diversion program for juveniles whose criminal activity is driven by substance abuse	Kids participate in a multiphased treatment program and have regular status hearings before a judge

(continued)

criminal violations, which requires the establishment of priorities. Also, charges may be dropped in cases where the offense is minor and a criminal charge would result in severe embarrassment or possible injury to the accused or his or her family. For example, if a well-known sports celebrity were arrested for indecent exposure, the prosecutor might drop charges if the defendant agreed to seek professional help. Charges may also be dropped in cases where available alternatives to a criminal proceeding would achieve the same purposes as prosecution. These include (1) invoking a civil sanction (e.g., revocation of a license), (2) institutionalizing mentally disturbed or retarded individuals in a treatment facility through civil commitment, and (3) revoking probation or parole rather than initiating new charges. The characteristics of the defendant—such as age, sex, prior record, or family situation—may also influence the prosecutor to treat him or her leniently, by reducing or dismissing the charge or referring the person to a pretrial diversion program (Whitehead & Bloom, 1993). Reduction or dismissal of charges may occur because the victim either precipitated the offense by his or her own conduct or was unwilling to cooperate with the prosecutor. Finally, charges may be reduced or dismissed for individuals who testify for the prosecution or act as informers for the prosecutor or the police.

Table 1.1

Programs Provided by the Jacksonville Florida State Attorney's Office *(continued)*

Name of Program	Type of Program	Program Design
Drug Free Youth Incentive Program (D-FY-INCE)	State attorney program	Uses community incentives and peer pressure to influence youths not to use drugs
Victim Impact Panels	State attorney program	Victims tell juveniles the effect the crimes had on their lives
First-Step for Teens	Program for domestic violence offenders, run by Hubbard House	Used as a condition of community control
Helping At-Risk Kids (HARK)	Hubbard House Program; juveniles are identified through a state attorney's office computer program	Designed for juveniles who witness domestic violence; used as a condition of community control or probation
Shoot Baskets Not Brothers	Summer program run by the Jacksonville Sheriff's Office	Can be mandated for appropriate juveniles as a condition of community control or probation in adult court, or as part of a diversion contract
Toastmasters International/ Boys and Girls Club	Youth leadership programs in the jail	Designed to help juveniles develop effective communication skills, self-esteem; focuses on leadership skills and cultural enrichment, as well
Excel Program	Sponsored by the Duval County School District	A jail school served by a full-time counselor; working on computers at their own pace, juveniles can earn up to 12 credits per year
Learn to Read	Partnership with state attorney's office	Volunteers tutor juveniles with particularly poor reading skills
Jailed Juvenile Mentor Program	Organized by staff at the state attorney's office	Volunteer mentors are recruited from throughout the country; they visit inmates regularly to form positive bonds
Youth On Guard Program	State attorney's office program	Includes minicamps for previously jailed juveniles and their mentors; activities are oriented toward teamwork and leadership skills
Inside/Outside	State attorney's office mentor program	Volunteers associated with local churches and synagogues meet with juveniles in jail, as well as after they are released
Prerelease Staffing	Occasional services offered by the state attorney's office	Provide atypical services, such as having staff find doctors or dentists to improve a juvenile's well-being
Youth Employment Service (YES)	Collaborative effort of several social service agencies	Designed to increase employment opportunities for at-risk youths
Jailed Juvenile Program	Collaborative effort with the Urban League	Urban League staff provide employability skills to juveniles in jail and upon their release

Source: Harry Shorstein (1998). State Attorney, Fourth Judicial Circuit. Personal communication.

Direct involvement by the prosecutor's offices in intervention programs places prosecutors in the more direct role of correctional agents. The Office of the State Attorney in Duval County, Florida, operates 19 distinctive pretrial diversion programs and 5 habilation and aftercare programs for juveniles incarcerated as adults (see Table 1.1). An evaluation of the Program for At-Risk Students (PAS) found that it may have averted as many as 1,500 property crimes (Shorstein, 1998). Shorstein further argued that efforts to prevent juvenile crime will not succeed if juveniles who break the law face no punitive consequences; habitual and violent juvenile criminals should be treated like adults. Since 1992, his office has prose-

cuted over 1,900 juvenile cases in adult court. He concluded that aggressive prosecution did make a difference:

From 1993 to 1997, the number of juveniles arrested in Jacksonville for violent felonies, weapons offenses, and vehicle thefts dropped by an average of forty-five percent. Dr. Rasmussen concluded in his evaluation of our juvenile justice innovations that over 7,200 robberies, burglaries, and motor vehicle thefts were prevented by incarcerating habitual juvenile offenders as adults during his study period of 1992–1995. (p. 7)

Conservatively, the public benefit of this reduction in property crime is about $6 million per year or $21,000 per offender (Rasmussen & Yu, 1996). By taking a tough stance against habitual offenders, who account for a substantial amount of the crime, Shorstein can simultaneously provide intervention programming, which includes intervention habilitation and aftercare. Such programs serve both at-risk and convicted juvenile offenders. They also represent a means of strengthening families, which may be a significant factor in the long-term reduction of criminality among youths (Rasmussen and Yu, 1996).

The Role of the Court in Corrections

Courts determine guilt or innocence, which, along with sentencing, impacts corrections. Additionally, the courts review the constitutionality of prison conditions, mandating changes when necessary. They also operate some correctional programs.

The most obvious relationship between the courts and corrections involves sentencing. For adults, the correctional process formally begins when a court finds an offender guilty of violating a criminal law. Sentencing is among the most crucial stages of the court procedure because a wide range of sanctions can be imposed on the convicted offender. Historically, discretion has played a varying role in sentencing, but recently this has been consistently limited by state statutory changes, including the increased use of determinate sentences, sentencing guidelines, and mandatory sentencing. (For an expanded discussion of sentencing, see Chapter 2.) Sentencing determines whether offenders will be referred or committed to a particular agency, institution, or facility, as well as the conditions under which they will serve their term.

Sentencing also affects the correctional process on a more subtle level. The extent to which a defendant regards his sentence as fair may influence his willingness to participate in correctional programs. Moreover, certain sentencing practices give correctional officials authority to detain an offender until his chances of successful integration into the community are maximized; other sentencing practices may require earlier release or detention beyond that point. Sentencing is related to community security insofar as it affects the ability of correctional agencies to change the behavior of convicted offenders. It may also help curtail crimes by persons other than the offender being sentenced. This may occur through *deterrence*—the creation of conscious fear of swift and certain punishment— or through more complex means, such as reinforcing social norms by the

imposition of severe penalties (Task Force on the Courts, 1973, p. 109).

There is not a collective community view as to how the justice system should deal with specific offenses or individual offenders. The level of public support for different approaches to controlling and correcting crime varies over time; at any given point, one or more approaches will receive public endorsement. Although the most vocal members of the community have frequently supported punishment as the major objective of sentencing, other segments have considered rehabilitation, reformation, or reintegration to be the most important objective. The question facing legislators who pass laws and judges who impose them is which view to consider. However, the creation of sentencing guidelines and mandatory sentencing laws increasingly appears to be reducing judicial discretion.

Many elements influence the sentence(s) that individual offenders receive. Several of the dominant factors are listed in Table 1.2.

Initially, the thrust of sentencing reform revolved around changes in procedures and decision making, which were intended to result in dispositions that were more fair, rational, humane, open to inspection, subject to accountability, and—however measured—more effective. However, in the 1980s and early 1990s, an explosion of drug-related crime and violent crime, as well as a high level of media exposure to these offenses, resulted in intense pressure on judges to impose longer sentences. This has continued, despite a falling crime rate since 1992, because, believing that crime is still rising, the public favors harsher sentences. Elected judges often feel compelled to take a hard stance on crime.

Courts affect the correctional process through sentencing, which determines whether offenders will be committed to a particular institution or facility and the conditions under which they will serve their term.

Table 1.2

Factors Affecting an Offender's Disposition

1. The statutory sanctions mandated for the offense.
2. The judge's perceptions of the community's view of the purpose of corrections. These perceptions are impacted by the community's social structure and conditions, such as increasing crime or the recent occurrence of particularly brutal or heinous offenses.
3. Judges' personalities and their own perceptions of the offense, the place where it occurred, the way in which it was perpetrated, and the offender.
4. The presentence investigation report usually influences the judge's perception of the offender because it provides, to some extent, the probation officer's view of the offender and the crime. It may emphasize (or exclude) certain information and recommendations.
5. The attitude of the victim, which in recent years has been more often taken into consideration in sentencing.
6. The viewpoint of the police, which is either presented to the prosecutor who, in turn, presents it to the judge or is expressed directly by the police in open court.
7. The persuasiveness of counsel at the sentencing hearing.
8. The political climate of the community in which the judge presides.
9. The limitations imposed by the lack of appropriate correctional facilities.
10. The plea-bargaining process, which in most instances influences the sentence that the defendant will receive. This plea agreement is usually negotiated before a guilty plea is made. Judges can reject a plea bargain, but this is not done frequently because it would clog an already overburdened system.

Judges' Impact on Prisons   Until the mid-1960s, most state and federal courts refused to consider prisoner complaints concerning prison conditions, a position referred to as the **hands-off doctrine** (Branham & Krantz, 1997; Singer & Statsky, 1974). This de facto procedure changed for several reasons. After visiting many prisons, a number of judges recognized the need for **court intervention in prison operations** to correct major deficiencies they noted. They were also frustrated by the failure of the legislative and executive branches to correct these conditions. Historically, on the federal level, precedents existed—regardless of their popularity—to support court intervention to ensure that basic constitutional rights were accorded to a variety of groups. This was exemplified by cases involving changes in criminal procedure, civil rights, and women's rights. Federal judges are appointed for life, so they are free to render decisions without fear of political repercussions.

Chapters 14 and 15 will discuss the changes relating to corrections made by the courts. Since the mid-1960s, the courts have taken the position that people entering our jails and prisons are not deprived of all their constitutional rights.

The Courts' Correctional Programs   The courts operate correctional programs with judges performing correctional functions as part of their authority. For example, Florida employs **probation without adjudication,** which allows judges to withhold sentencing in the interest of reducing the penetration of offenders into the criminal justice system. This approach is similar to the use of deferred prosecution in the federal courts, where it has been applied since 1946 to youthful offenders.

Judges have also developed special **drug courts** that focus on giving offenders an opportunity to deal with their drug problems and related issues. Our Program Focus, "Drug Courts," presents a description of these programs.

A study of court processing by the Vera Institute of Justice found that in 56 percent of all felony arrests for crimes against persons, the victim had been in a previous relationship with the accused. The report concluded:

> Because our society has not found adequate alternatives to arrest and adjudication for coping with interpersonal anger publicly expressed, we pay a price. The price includes large court caseloads, long delays in processing and, ultimately, high dismissal rates. These impose high financial costs on taxpayers and high personal costs on defendants and their families. The public pays in another way, too. The congestion and drain on resources caused by an excessive number of such cases in the courts weakens the ability of the criminal justice system to deal quickly and decisively with the "real" felons, who may be getting lost in the shuffle. The risk that they will be returned to the street increases, as does the danger to law-abiding citizens on whom they prey. (Vera Institute of Justice, 1977, p. xv)

In many cases, victims who had a prior relationship with their perpetrators are usually not interested in having them prosecuted once they have cooled off. Some may also fear for their safety, or even their lives, if they proceed with legal recourse. Thus, initial court time spent on these cases is wasted and makes an alternative process more practical and economical. In a society drowning in litigation, neighborhood dispute settlement programs are a valuable alternative to the courts.

Finally, in some states, the courts' involvement in the correctional process is very direct, often including, on a county level, direct responsibility for probation services for both juvenile and adult offenders. In these jurisdictions, the county's chief judge has administrative

PROGRAM FOCUS

Drug Courts

In the traditional court process, drug offenders are often cycled in and out repeatedly at taxpayers' expense. Drug courts use the authority of the court to reduce crime by changing the defendants' drug-using behavior. Almost 300 of these programs are currently in operation and an additional 17 are either about to start or are being planned. Drug courts offer defendants the possibility of dismissed charges or reduced sentences, if they choose to be diverted to drug court programs by judges who preside over the drug court proceedings, monitor the progress of defendants through frequent status hearings, and prescribe sanctions and rewards.

Drug court programs generally accept defendants with substance abuse problems who are being charged with drug possession and/or other nonviolent offenses such as property crimes. They generally supervise these defendants for a period of 12 to 15 months, during which they are required to attend treatment sessions, undergo frequent and random urinalyses, and appear before judges on a regular and frequent basis.

Sanctions for failing to abide by drug court program rules may include (1) verbal warning from the judge; (2) transfer to an earlier stage of the program; (3) incarceration for several days or weeks; or (4) more frequent status hearings, treatment sessions, or drug tests. Such intensive supervision is designed to intervene in the indefinite cycle of rehabilitation to relapse, which is often followed by a new arrest that triggers either probation revocation and the imposition of the original sentence or an arrest for a new offense and an additional sentence of incarceration. The impact of more intensive supervision is reflected in reduced drug use for most participants.

Defendants who fail to complete the treatment program have their charges adjudicated. Defendants who complete the treatment program are not prosecuted further, and most have their charges dismissed.

Drug courts developed primarily as a response to the high recidivism rate among drug offenders. Their effectiveness may be assessed by the benefits they have offered, both to the community, as well as to individual offenders.

For the community, drug courts offer better supervision for offenders in the area. They require more responsibility and greater accountability of offenders to act in accordance with the special conditions of their release. They also provide greater coordination and account-

ability, including a reduction in the duplication of services, which saves taxpayers money. While the treatment component of drug court costs ranges from $1,200 to $3,000 per participant, this pales in comparison with average jail costs of $5,000 per defendant. Other cost savings include reduced police overtime, witness costs, and grand jury costs where applicable. There has also been a reduction in other types of crime, as drug users typically engage in theft and other types of criminal activity to support their drug habits. These benefits, alone, would likely make drug courts a worthwhile approach for some offenders. There are, however, additional benefits of drug courts, which have had a powerful impact on the individuals involved in them. (Drug Courts Program Office and Technical Assistance Project–DCPOTAP, 1998).

Almost 100,000 people have entered drug court programs in the past decade, and over 70 percent have either graduated or are still patients (DCPOTAP, 1998). This represents twice the retention rate of traditional drug treatment programs. Once they become drug clean, most programs require their participants to obtain a high school diploma or its equivalent. Also, many of these offenders were either unemployed or on public assis-

oversight for the probation department but usually delegates its management to a chief probation officer.

Effects on Corrections

The preceding discussion emphasized that the correctional process cannot be understood apart from its relationship to the other components of the criminal justice system. We have stressed that these criminal justice subsystems affect corrections in several ways. First, they control the intake process of offenders into the system

and, thus, determine the level, quality, and extent of the services that corrections can offer. Some examples include jail and prison overcrowding caused by the harsh drug policies of the late 1980s and early 1990s, mandatory sentences, and requirements that inmates serve a higher proportion of their sentence before being released. These policies resulted in a glut of arrests and subsequent convictions of large numbers of drug offenders, which have strained correctional budgets. Second, the other subsystems in the criminal justice system perform a variety of correctional functions, some indepen-

tance due to their drug problems. Once in the program, these participants are required to obtain jobs and become self-supporting. Further, about two thirds of drug court participants are parents of minority children. The program has helped many to either retain or regain their children upon completion. Moreover, more than 500 babies of program participants were born drug free while in the program, thus minimizing substantial medical and service costs (amounting to a minimum of $250,000 per baby) required for the care of drug-addicted infants. Several programs also mandate that their participants perform community service activities.

Given the benefits of the drug court to the community and to its members, one would expect recidivism rates among these offenders to decline—and they have. Recidivism rates range from 5 to 28 percent for program participants and less than 4 percent for graduates. Further, among defendants in the program who are tested with urinalysis, less than 10 percent test positive—a figure substantially lower than the rate of offenders who are not in drug court programs (DCPOTAP, 1998).

Miami's Drug Court

One of the oldest drug courts in the United States is in Miami. The Felony Drug Court program was implemented in 1989. It focuses on treating and directing nonviolent drug users into an alternative program that is aimed at providing treatment for drug addiction. Dade County's drug court program has three phases: detoxification, stabilization, and aftercare.

During the detoxification phase, the goals include stopping drug use as well as eliminating the physical dependence on drugs (Goldkamp & Weisland, 1993). Urine samples at this phase are taken daily and the defendant's treatment plan is implemented. The treatment plan is designed by both the counselor and the defendant, and it is composed of both short-term and long-term goals. The average length of time spent in this phase ranges from 2 to 6 weeks.

The next phase is stabilization. During this phase, the goal is to continue to abstain from the use of drugs. A variety of services are offered to the defendant to accomplish this goal, including individual and group counseling, wellness programs, and fellowship meetings. During this phase, which generally ranges from 3 to 6 months, urine testing as well as court appearances occur periodically.

The last phase is aftercare; it lasts from 8 to 12 months. The goals of aftercare include teaching the de-

fendant the necessary skills to obtain employment upon release, obtaining employment, and abstaining from drug use. The services offered during this phase include educational programs, such as literacy programs, GED programs, and vocational training. The two following interactions from the judge running this program show that he has dual objectives: encouraging offenders to comply with the rules and reprimanding those who fail to comply.

"John! Looking good, John! Come over here! . . . You going to school still? Get your GED yet? All right, seven out of seven clean, good attendance. You in phase III now? Okay. See me back here in 30 days." . . .

[To another participant] "What are you doing here? You've got two out of five dirty, and you've missed your last five sessions. What are you spending your money on, anyway? It can't be food." . . . [He orders the client to return in 2 weeks, so his progress can be monitored more closely.] (Finn & Newlyn, 1993, pp. 9, 10)

dent of and some related to the formal correctional system. These functions occur throughout the entire criminal justice process, from offenders' initial police contact to their conviction, after which they become clients of the correctional system. A third effect is the control that is exerted over the correctional system by court mandates and legislative actions. These actions affect correctional policies, as well as day-to-day operating procedures.

The correctional subsystem has been plagued by a variety of problems throughout its history, many of which can be traced to overcrowding. Indeed, the present array

of problems within the correctional subsystem are attributable to a variety of social changes, many of which began in the 1960s. These changes contributed to higher levels of drug use and related crime, as well as increasing violent crime. Reactions to these problems by the criminal justice system resulted in severe prison overcrowding, leading to community placement and early releases for many inmates. These effects have contributed to a hardening of public attitudes toward the goals of the correctional process. The move toward harsher punishment has weakened the "correctional/reform" aspects of corrections, sparking controversy among corrections professionals and criminologists about the purposes of sanctions.

Organization of the Text

One inescapable fact is that criminals are human beings who, like law-abiding citizens, are part of society. Thus, the treatment to which they are and have been subjected when convicted is better understood when examined in relation to the societal conditions in which it has occurred. Many of the events, social issues, and philosophies that have been important throughout the history of humanity (e.g., the Enlightenment, the industrial revolution, religious movements, the civil rights movement) have affected the manner in which criminals have been treated. One easily discernible pattern is that as we have become more civilized, our treatment of criminals has become more humane.

This text is divided into seven parts. Part One examines correctional issues, the interface between corrections and components of the criminal justice system, and the issues that relate to the death penalty. Part Two examines various historical events and trends that have produced different reactions to criminal behavior over time. To understand the historical antecedents of contemporary corrections, it is necessary to focus on the eras during which these reactions occurred and the social conditions that produced them. This serves as a foundation for understanding current responses to dealing with criminals and the conditions that characterize our contemporary corrections system. Thus, during any given time period, the sanctions imposed on apprehended offenders and the conditions they experience are a function of an evolutionary process. This process is a blend of historical events and trends as well as specific current social conditions. The historical overview presented covers many of the things that human societies have done in their attempts to deal with criminal behavior as well as the reasons for these practices. This covers a vast period of time and requires a relatively lengthy account, especially as these events pertain to the United States.

This, then, is the backdrop against which contemporary corrections exists. The remainder of the text is organized around specific aspects of the contemporary corrections system. Part Three examines classification and different correctional populations. It looks at issues relating to classification, custody security, and the characteristics of male and female offenders and special category offenders (e.g., elderly and long-term offenders). Part Four focuses on the contemporary prison and its administration and management. The discussion centers on the structure, management, and control of prisons and the key role of custodial personnel. Security threat groups and inmate gangs are also examined.

Part Five focuses on prisoner rights. This discussion centers on the history of prisoners' rights, their access to the courts and their substantive rights, and procedural issues.

Part Six discusses vital institutional programs and services, including education, vocational training and work, medical and psychological services, food, religion, and recreation. Additionally, related problems and issues, such as mental health, drug treatment, and contagious diseases (including HIV/AIDS, tuberculosis, and hepatitis), are examined.

Part Seven deals with community-based programs, including jails that house substantial numbers of pretrial detainees and convicted misdemeanants; probation; parole or supervised community release, sex offender registration, and civil commitment programs. These represent front-end and back-end correctional programs, which oversee three quarters of those under correctional supervision. We also look at intermediate sanctions, which have expanded to accommodate the increasing number of convicted offenders for whom there is no room in prison but who need more intensive supervision than can be provided by traditional probation. Finally, in Chapter 21 we discuss parole and other methods that enable inmates to maintain community ties. An epilogue that deals with our perceptions of the future of corrections is available on the Wadsworth Criminal Justice Web site: http://cj.wadsworth.com. This discussion includes a look at restorative justice, privatization, and how The Americans for Disabilities Act affects corrections.

Summary

Although corrections has traditionally dealt with the punishment of convicted offenders, its meaning has evolved to include both those accused and convicted of criminal offenses. Corrections has generally had low visibility among the public, but public attitudes toward crime and justice have had a powerful influence on correctional policies.

One aspect of the interdependent nature of the criminal justice system is the role of other agents in the correctional system. The police act as gatekeepers in their arrest decisions, as well as informal influences on community-based corrections. Prosecutors conserve resources by screening out cases at the formal charging phase. They may also be directly involved as supervisors in pretrial diversion programs. The courts make a determination of guilt or innocence, thereby deciding whether to proceed to the sentencing phase. They also establish and change constitutional standards regarding prisoners' rights and sometimes operate correctional programs.

This has been a brief overview of the correctional process. Its history and development may only be well understood in a broad historical context. The remainder of the textbook focuses on the history and evolution of corrections, discussing, in detail, several important issues in the field.

Critical Thinking Questions

1. Discuss the nature of public opinion as it relates to corrections. What is the primary source of information upon which the public bases its opinion? How is public opinion reflected in correctional policies? Provide specific examples from the text.

2. Discuss the interdependent nature of the four major components of the criminal justice system, focusing specifically on how corrections fits into this context. How do other aspects of the justice system affect corrections? How does corrections affect the other three components?

3. Why does corrections have such a low visibility?

4. Using specific examples from the text, discuss several benefits and drawbacks associated with the interdependent structure of our justice system. Given unlimited money and resources, would you change the system? How, or why not?

5. A sociohistorical examination of corrections reflects a strong association between the social climate of the time period and the focus of corrections. Provide a few examples that support this claim. If this continues to be the case, what do you think the future of corrections holds? Why? (Provide specific examples from contemporary American society that might directly or indirectly affect corrections.)

Test Your Knowledge

1. Attitude surveys conducted show that about what percentage of the American public feels that the government should deal more strictly with criminals?
   a. Less than 50%
   b. 60
   c. 84
   d. 98

2. Correctional functions are performed by:
   a. the police.
   b. the courts.
   c. prosecutors.
   d. all of the above.
   e. none of the above.

3. Choose the true statement.
   a. The courts still view inmates as slaves of the state.
   b. The courts continue to refuse to deal with prison conditions because judges feel that they lack the expertise to determine their constitutionality.
   c. People beginning sentences in our jails and prisons are not deprived of all their constitutional rights.
   d. None of the above.

4. In general, prisons are:
   a. the most visible component of the criminal justice system.
   b. as visible as other components of the criminal justice system.
   c. less visible than other components of the criminal justice system.
   d. None of the above reflects an accurate statement about prisons in general.

5. Which of the following reflects the most accurate statement about victims?
   a. They have been given less attention during the sentencing process because of their extremely biased views against defendants.
   b. They have usually not wanted to testify during the sentencing process.
   c. Their attitudes have been increasingly taken into consideration during the sentencing phase.
   d. Their attitudes have received some attention over the last decade.

Endnotes

1. The preliminary hearing and the grand jury, where applicable, are designed to place limitations on a prosecutor's discretion. The Glossary provides a brief discussion of these processes.

2. Another limitation on prosecutorial discretion used by some jurisdictions involves a requirement that prosecutors prepare a written report that specifies the reasons that they are requesting that a case be nolle prosequi (i.e., the indictment be dropped).

Sentencing: Imposing Correctional Sanctions

LEARNING OBJECTIVES

After completing this chapter, you should be able to:

1. Specify and discuss the role of sentencing in the correctional process.

2. Define, describe, and discuss retribution, deterrence, incapacitation, and rehabilitation as rationales for the sanctions applied to criminals.

3. List and describe the various monetary sanctions that may be applied to convicted criminals.

4. Specify and discuss the various community sanctions (e.g., probation) that may be applied to convicted criminals.

5. Describe the sanction of incarceration, and specify the factors that affect the nature of this sentence.

6. Compare and contrast indeterminate and determinate sentences and the sentencing justifications of each.

7. Define and describe mandatory and presumptive sentences and the problems they appear to be engendering for corrections.

8. Describe and discuss sentencing guidelines as a manner of reforming the sentencing process.

9. Define "truth-in-sentencing laws" and "three strikes laws." Specify the impact of these sentencing strategies.

KEY TERMS AND CONCEPTS

Chronic offenders
Day fines
Determinate sentences
Deterrence
Good time
Incapacitation
Incarceration
Indeterminate sentences
Just deserts
Mandatory sentences
Probation
Rational choice theory

Reformation
Rehabilitation
Reintegration
Restitution
Restorative justice
Retribution
Sentence
Sentencing guidelines
Three strikes laws
Truth-in-sentencing
    laws

Introduction

Offenders enter the correctional system either when they plead guilty or when they are convicted of one or more crimes at a trial. A judge or jury then imposes a sentence on them, one of the most important decisions made in the criminal justice system. It is of primary concern to all major parties associated with any criminal event: offenders and their families; victims and their families; prosecutors; defense counsel; and the correctional personnel who will carry it out. A sentence represents the punishment specified for a given crime by the legislature of a given political jurisdiction; it is imposed by one of its courts and carried out by its correctional system.

Justifications for Punishing Offenders

Each society develops justifications for the punishments imposed on criminals, and these justifications have varied over time. However, some suffering has almost always been a part of the sanctions imposed on offenders. Ever since this country's birth, many reformative and rehabilitative roles have been sought for our penal systems, even when these roles clashed with the objective of social defense and the maintenance of public order. The punishment of criminal behavior has been the paramount purpose, however, and is justified on several grounds:

- *Retribution/Just deserts:* "You're going to get what's coming to you."
- *Deterrence:* "We're going to punish you so that you will not do it again." A variation is, "We're going to punish you so that you will serve as an example to others, and they will not do it."
- *Incapacitation:* "We're going to punish you in such a way that you will be physically unable to victimize us."
- *Rehabilitation:* "We're going to place you under correctional supervision so that we can find out what your problems are and solve them."
- *Restorative justice:* "We're going to put you under supervision in the community so that you can make things right between yourself and the community by repairing the harm that your actions caused to the victim and the community" (Minnesota Department of Corrections-MDOC, 1997).

These justifications overlap considerably, because they all involve some element of offender suffering. We will look at each, along with the concept of community *reintegration*.

Retribution: Just Deserts

The punitive response to criminal behavior is rooted in tradition. **Retribution,** defined as "deserved punishment for evil done," is a relatively primitive human reaction. It is not difficult to understand why this justification for the use of punishment (**just deserts**) has received a high level of public support throughout history. For example, during the Iran hostage crisis when 49 hostages were held at the American embassy by Iranians, most newspapers received letters suggesting that the United States round up an equal number of Iranian students here on visas and keep them under the same conditions that our hostages were enduring in Tehran. Some of the religious and philosophical justifications used to support retribution follow:

1. It fulfills a religious mission through retaliation. There are biblical sanctions for the punishment of transgressors, so society is doing God's work by carrying out His punishment.

2. It removes the tension in society caused by the criminal act, creating harmony through retaliation.

3. It washes the guilt of the criminal away through suffering and expresses society's disapproval of the behavior.

4. It makes victims whole again by making the offender suffer as they did.

Although *just deserts* and *retribution* are often used interchangeably, there are some distinctions between them. Just deserts can be viewed as the modern reformulation of the retributive view. Its primary emphasis is on what offenders fairly merit for their crimes. Its central organizing principle is proportionality—the severity of the penalty should be proportional to the gravity of the offense. This position is distinct from retribution in two ways. First, whereas retribution relies on the doctrine "an eye for an eye" and has been criticized for its highly abstract concept of the punishment of evil by evil, just deserts emphasizes the idea of penal censure of the defendant. This requires that the nature of the punishment be consistent with the offender's criminal conduct. Second, the retribution approach has been objected to on the grounds that it generally requires harsh punishment. Just deserts, on the other hand, sees the punishment as being proportional to the seriousness of the crime, even if it does not impose harm on the offender. In fact, just deserts proponents have advocated a substantial reduction in the penalty levels for all crimes (Von Hirsch, 1998).

Deterrence

Deterrence is a justification for punishment based on the belief that the pain caused by punishment will *deter* future criminal actions by the individual and others. In

John King, front, and Lawrence Brewer were charged with first-degree murder in the death of James Byrd, Jr., who was tied to a truck and dragged to his death along a rural East Texas road. Punishments for such crimes may include the death penalty; it is hoped that the severity of the sentence will deter others from committing similar offenses.

this section, we look at theories of deterrence, types of deterrence, deterrence research, and factors that affect deterrence.

Theories of Deterrence   The concept of deterrence as a means of controlling crime dates back over 200 years to the work of Beccaria and Bentham. Referred to as *classical theory,* the deterrence position assumes that human beings have free will, and they engage in a rational cost-benefit analysis of the risks and rewards associated with a behavior and its consequences prior to engaging in it. This means that people will not act impulsively, out of the need for money, or as the result of any social or psychological problem. This assumption of deterrence theory is, at best, hypothetical.

One problem the theory does not address is, "How does one determine the optimal sentence that will produce a deterrent effect for any given offense?" (Rossi & Beck, 1997, p. 22). What type of punishment, and how much of it, will deter offenders from recidivating and serve as an example that will deter others, as well?

Deterrence now tends to be reflected in choice theory, or **rational choice theory** (Abell, 1991; Cornish & Clarke, 1986). Although rational choice theory focuses on the rational decision-making elements that contribute to the decision of whether or not to engage in criminal activity, it recognizes that the degree of reasoning involved varies from offender to offender and from crime to crime. For example, some criminologists have focused on the factors burglars consider when deciding which homes to target: Are the residents home? Are the homes open to public view? Is there easy availability to escape routes? (Cromwell, Marks, Olson, & Avary, 1991; MacDonald & Gifford, 1989). Other factors reported to motivate their involvement in crime included obtaining money, impressing friends, and the excitement of the acts (Marshall & Horney, 1991). Finally, some research has focused on factors influencing offenders to desist from crime. These have been found to include shock (e.g., seeing a friend shot or killed during his or her last crime) or the cumulative effects of factors, such as recognition of the inevitability of capture, a reduced ability to do time, fear of incarceration, and general anxiety over a life of crime (Cusson & Pinsonneault, 1986).

Types of Deterrence   The imposition of punishment for its deterrent effect is based on the belief that these sanctions will prevent future crime because of the painful consequences suffered by convicted offenders. There are two types of deterrence. *Specific deterrence* occurs when offenders do not recidivate because they do not want to face further sanctions. *General deterrence* occurs when other potential offenders do not engage in criminal activity because they want to avoid penalties that others have received.

Deterrence Research   There have been several approaches to deterrence research. One approach examines general deterrence by measuring the relationship between the probability of being punished (i.e., getting arrested, convicted, and incarcerated or otherwise punished) and the rate of crime. If deterrence works, then, as the probability of punishment rises, arrests should go down. However, there is no consistent evidence showing this to be true. Although some studies (e.g., Gibbs, 1968; Tittle & Rowe, 1974) have shown that certainty of punishment resulted in reduced crime rates, others[1] have shown an inconsistent relationship or none at all.

Another approach to deterrence research is to determine whether the threat of punishment reduces illegal behavior. The best known of these studies examined the effects of toughened anti–drunk-driving laws and found that they had a short-term deterrent effect but a negligible long-term effect (Ross, McCleary, & LaFree, 1990).

A third approach uses what is referred to as *perceptual research*. Here, subjects are asked to determine how certain they are that they might get caught and punished if they break a specific law. They are then asked whether they actually would commit that crime. If deterrence works, those who feel that they would get caught and punished should be the least likely to engage in the crime. The research tends to show that the more certain the perceived punishment, the less likely individuals are to say that they would engage in the crimes (see Grasmick & Bursik, 1990; Klepper & Nagin, 1989).

Finally, deterrence research has examined the effect of punishment on those who receive it. The results of this line of research are inconsistent. Some studies indicate that a majority of inmates have a history of previous arrests, convictions, and even incarcerations (e.g., Greenfeld, 1985). Beck and Shipley (1989) found that just under two thirds of convicted felons are rearrested within 3 years of their release from prison, and those with the most extensive criminal records are the most likely to recidivate. Other studies, however, have shown that punishment may have a suppressor effect on some forms of criminal behavior. Severely punished delinquents, arrested spouse abusers, arrested drunk drivers, and arrested novice offenders were less likely to commit future offenses when compared with offenders who were treated more leniently.[2]

Factors Affecting Deterrence   Although there is no consensus on the deterrent effect of punishment, there is some agreement that three factors may significantly affect its success or failure: the certainty, the severity, and the swiftness of the punishment. Research conducted thus far has typically failed to examine all of these factors together, thus making it difficult to determine their relative efficacy. The low crime clearance rate (only 22% for all Uniform Crime Report [UCR] index offenses[3] [Federal Bureau of Investigation, 1998]), the relatively slow rate at which the courts operate, and the perceived leniency of the system (in the early 1990s it was expected that prison inmates would only serve about one third of their sentences [Langan & Dawson, 1993; Langan & Solari, 1993]), arguably, interact to reduce the deterrent effects of criminal justice system actions.

A second issue is the impact of **truth-in-sentencing laws,** which now require offenders to serve a substantial portion of their sentence (most require 85%), on deterrence (Ditton & Wilson, 1999).

Interviews with 589 incarcerated property offenders provided insight into their perceptions of the deterrent impact of various sanctions, programs, and other criminal justice system actions (Dinitz & Huff, 1988). These offenders indicated that criminal justice system actions that increased the chances of imprisonment or the sentence length were perceived to have the highest deterrent effect (see Figure 2.1). More recently, Nagin (1998) has raised some interesting questions about the deterrence issue. First, in considering the impact that sanctions have on deterring a potential offender, one must ask whether that offender is aware of the penalty associated with the behavior he or she is considering. To date, there is a paucity of research on this topic. Other relevant questions include:

> How do would-be offenders combine prior experience with the criminal justice system and new information on penalties? How long does it typically take for persons to become aware of new [sentencing systems]? How do they become aware of changes in penalties, and what information source do they use in updating their impressions? How do [first-time offenders] form impressions of sanctions? (Nagin, 1998, p. 351)

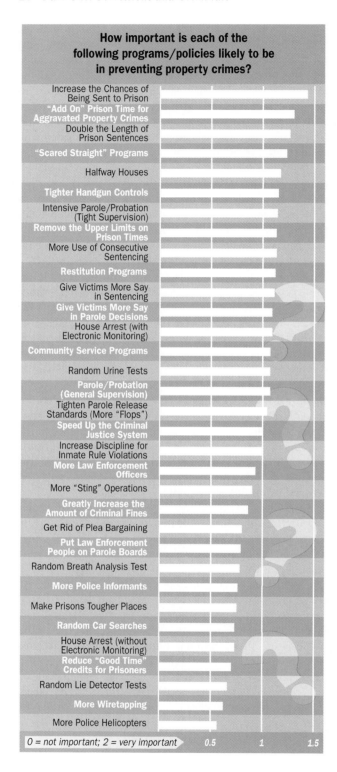

How important is each of the following programs/policies likely to be in preventing property crimes?

- Increase the Chances of Being Sent to Prison
- "Add On" Prison Time for Aggravated Property Crimes
- Double the Length of Prison Sentences
- "Scared Straight" Programs
- Halfway Houses
- Tighter Handgun Controls
- Intensive Parole/Probation (Tight Supervision)
- Remove the Upper Limits on Prison Times
- More Use of Consecutive Sentencing
- Restitution Programs
- Give Victims More Say in Sentencing
- Give Victims More Say in Parole Decisions
- House Arrest (with Electronic Monitoring)
- Community Service Programs
- Random Urine Tests
- Parole/Probation (General Supervision)
- Tighten Parole Release Standards (More "Flops")
- Speed Up the Criminal Justice System
- Increase Discipline for Inmate Rule Violations
- More Law Enforcement Officers
- More "Sting" Operations
- Greatly Increase the Amount of Criminal Fines
- Get Rid of Plea Bargaining
- Put Law Enforcement People on Parole Boards
- Random Breath Analysis Test
- More Police Informants
- Make Prisons Tougher Places
- Random Car Searches
- House Arrest (without Electronic Monitoring)
- Reduce "Good Time" Credits for Prisoners
- Random Lie Detector Tests
- More Wiretapping
- More Police Helicopters

0 = not important; 2 = very important   0.5   1   1.5

Figure 2.1 *Perceived Effectiveness of Actions in Preventing Property Crimes*

Source: S. Dinitz and R. Huff (1988). *The Figgie Report Part VI. The Business of Crime: The Criminal Perspective.* Richmond, VA: Figgie International, Inc., p. 39. Reprinted with permission of the publisher.

Incapacitation

Incapacitation refers to the prevention of potential crime by physically restraining the offender. Historically, efforts at permanent prevention have involved capital punishment and dismemberment. Today, in most parts of the world, these punishments have been replaced by incarceration. Incapacitation is still used to justify imprisonment; proponents argue that as long as offenders are in confinement, they are not free to commit further crimes. This is true, of course, only if offenders do not commit offenses while they are in prison. Incapacitation also assumes that the offender who is confined (or dead) would have otherwise recidivated.

Although relatively infrequently imposed, our most severe punishments—capital punishment and life imprisonment without parole—continue to be supported, because they appear to represent a means of totally incapacitating the most serious offenders. This is generally regarded, by both supporters and critics of the punitive approach, as the most plausible utilitarian argument for punishment.

Incapacitation has been suggested as a possible answer to the problem of **chronic offenders** (i.e., those arrested for five or more offenses) who, although small in number, account for a disproportionate share of serious crime (Petersilia, Greenwood, & Lavin, 1978; Wolfgang, Figlio, & Sellin, 1972). Wolfgang's research on two cohorts of juveniles from Philadelphia—one born in 1945 and the other in 1958—found that chronics, who represented 6 to 7 percent of the males in these cohorts, committed more than half of the delinquent behaviors and at least two thirds of the index offenses (Tracy, Wolfgang, & Figlio, 1985). Further, Miller, Dinitz, and Conrad (1982) studied a cohort of adults with at least one arrest for a violent offense. They found that there was an 80 percent chance of these offenders committing an additional offense after each arrest. For those convicted of rape, murder, and assault, there was a 50 percent chance that this offense would be violent.

Incapacitation strategies have taken three approaches. The first is *collective incapacitation*, which would mandate that all individuals convicted of a certain offense (e.g., robbery) receive the same sentence (e.g., 5 years). Although research has shown that this strategy would have only a modest impact (10 to 20%) on crime reduction, it might double, triple, or even more dramatically affect the size of the prison population, depending on which categories of offenders were chosen for incapacitation (Cohen, 1983).

Selective incapacitation would base sentences on predictions that certain offenders will commit serious offenses at higher rates than others convicted of the same types of crimes. These predictions are based primarily on the offender's prior record, age, and juvenile and adult drug use (Greenwood, 1982). This approach suffers from the fact that we can only correctly identify at most 45 percent of those who will engage in future offenses. Thus, if existing scales to identify high-rate offenders were used for purposes of incapacitation, 55 out of every 100 people that would be imprisoned would not have committed an offense had they remained free (Cohen, 1983). Obviously, this level of accuracy is unethical and unacceptable. A similar issue is raised with regard to both "truth-in-sentencing laws" and "three strikes laws": How many offenders will be imprisoned for an unnecessarily long period of time to prevent some from reoffending (Shichor & Sechrest, 1996)? It is also important to realize that, except in the cases of life without parole and capital punishment, incapacitation is only temporary.

Criminal career incapacitation avoids many of the problems associated with selective incapacitation (Cohen, 1983). This involves the identification of classes of criminals who typically have active high rates of crime. Cohen's research in Washington, DC, led to two important conclusions. First, individuals convicted of robbery and burglary were prime candidates for incapacitation, because they often committed these offenses at relatively high rates and had relatively short careers. Second, prison sentences for these offenders might shorten their expected careers and thus reduce robbery and burglary rates. Further, Cohen found that a 2-year prison sentence imposed on convicted robbers would reduce robberies by 8 percent and only increase the total prison population by 7 percent.

Rehabilitation

The concept of **reformation** can be traced back to the early European antecedents of the prison system. In the United States, the development of the penitentiary was based on the idea that imprisonment would "reform" inmates by instilling in them a new sense of morality and purpose. This original notion was later modified in response to a growing belief, espoused primarily by positivists, that criminal behavior was caused by traits within the offender, as well as conditions in their environment. Many felt that providing inmates with a variety of services and programs (e.g., education, job training, psychological assistance), labeled as **rehabilitation,** during their incarceration would improve their ability to cope with the external conditions and thereby reduce the probability of future criminality. After World War II, rehabilitation became an increasingly dominant approach, which reached its height in the 1960s. Rehabilitation was emphasized as a justification for imprisonment programs with an emphasis on providing offenders with opportunities to deal with their problems and improve their academic and work

Rehabilitation may include a variety of services and programs. Here inmates in the Lifeline Program participate in a group therapy session.

skills. These programs still exist in contemporary prisons (see, e.g., Chapters 16 and 17); however, their survival is continually threatened by pressure from those who believe that inmates are not deserving of these "benefits."

Contemporary research on rehabilitation programs has identified a new set of principles that reflect the rejuvenation of the reformation approach. These principles include:

- Treat only those human deficits that are directly related to the propensity to commit crimes. These factors may include attitudes directly related to the commission of crime, criminal associates, impulsivity, weak socialization, and below average intelligence.

- Treat all deficits simultaneously—if an offender has multiple deficits—that increase the likelihood that he or she will reoffend.

- Match offenders' learning styles to particular teaching styles; that is, programs must fit the specific needs of and learning styles of their participants.

- Use the highest level of treatment intensity for those clients who are predicted to be the most likely to recidivate.

- Use programs that teach clients skills that enable them to understand and resist antisocial behavior. This means that we may need to use effective social learning principles to model and shape socially acceptable behavior.

- Treat offenders in well-supported programs. The best intervention will fail with insufficient funding or lack of commitment from treatment staff, administrators, or support staff. This can be a problem in facilities that are primarily designed for custody purposes.

- Use treatment that involves research in both the design and the evaluation of the program. Use high doses of intervention, because this method is related to lower recidivism rates (Gaes, 1998, pp. 715–716).

Restorative Justice

Restorative justice is a new criminal justice framework that emerged in the 1990s as a method for reforming our entire justice system (Brathwaite, 1998; MDOC, 1997). It has gained acceptance and support by many criminal justice professionals and community groups across the nation. Instead of viewing crime as violations of state law, restorative justice focuses on the harm that crime creates for the victim and the community. It further emphasizes active victim, offender, and community participation in repairing the harm caused to the victim and the community. In Minnesota, restorative justice programs include victims' services; restitution; face-to-face meetings between victims, offenders, and their support systems; victim impact panels; and skill-building classes for offenders (MDOC, 1997, p. 1). Restorative justice will be discussed further in the Epilogue.

Reintegration

Although imprisonment has been touted as serving one or more of these sanctioning functions, its critics point to the debilitating and sometimes destructive effects that it may have on inmates. These effects are described in the chapters that follow. Some of these critics have suggested that **reintegration,** an approach that emphasizes community-based residential and nonresidential alternatives to incarceration, may be a solution to these problems. Supporters argue that only hard-core offenders require imprisonment and that nondangerous offenders can be effectively and more economically supervised in the community. This allows these offenders to maintain ties with family and friends and benefit from community programs and services not available in prisons. These programs also help to relieve prison overcrowding, and they are less costly to operate.

Types of Dispositions

Judges may impose one or more of a variety of dispositions on convicted offenders. One decision is to impose a **sentence,** a punishment specified for a given crime by the legislature of that state. Another option is suspending the sentence, a procedure that can be accomplished in two ways: deferring the pronouncement of a sentence or suspending its implementation. Postponement of sentencing allows the judge to create potential substitutes for the sentence (e.g., offender must successfully complete a specific program). In a nationally representative sample, two thirds of the probation sentences involved the judge suspending the prison sentence (Bonczar, 1997). It is presumed that offenders would be more motivated to comply with the conditions of their probation knowing that, if they failed to, they could go to prison (Petersilia, 1998).

Other types of dispositions include monetary sanctions, community programs, and incarceration. We will look at each.

Monetary Sanctions

Fines *Fines* are monetary sanctions that are usually assessed in the case of minor misdemeanor offenses. They may be the only sanction imposed, or they may be combined with other sentencing alternatives, such as probation, restitution, or confinement. The statutes specifying criminal fines tend to be inconsistent and chaotic, and they provide judges with little guidance as to the appropriate monetary amounts to be assessed.

We do not know if fines are effective tools in controlling criminal behavior. Some critics of fines argue that they cannot incapacitate; others maintain that fines have a detrimental effect on defendants who are poor. Many offenders are confined in local jails for nonpayment of criminal fines, because this is the standard sanction. The Supreme Court, in *Tate v. Short* (1971), ruled that imprisoning people who are unable to pay a fine discriminates against the poor, and is, therefore, unconstitutional. Courts, however, can constitutionally incarcerate offenders for nonpayment when jail time was a sentence option.

Day Fines The **day fine** is an innovation proposed to reduce the economic inequities resulting from fines (Hillsman & Greene, 1988). This practice, which originated in Scandinavia, has been adopted in other European countries and was first tested in Staten Island, New York, and Milwaukee, Wisconsin (Greene, 1992; McDonald, 1992; Worzella, 1992). Day fines allow judges to impose monetary sanctions that are commensurate with the seriousness of the offense, while tying the amount of the fine to the offender's income and assets. Thus, a day fine equalizes the monetary burden on offenders from different socioeconomic levels.

To establish a day fine, the courts typically go through a two-step process (McDonald, 1992). First, they determine the monetary units assigned to the offense (the more serious the crime, the higher the number of units). The next step is to calculate the dollar value of each monetary unit based on the economic circumstances of the offender. For example:

> [Joseph Burke] pled guilty to attempted unauthorized use of an auto (a class B misdemeanor). . . . Mr. Burke is 21 years old . . . single and lives with his mother, to whom he contributes support. He works at a restaurant and reports take-home pay of $180 per week. He was sentenced to pay a ten-unit day fine and his unit value was set at $11.78. His fine totaled $117.80 [which he was allowed to pay in five payments over three months].

> [Mr. Smith] pled guilty to disorderly conduct. He is a 20-year-old Transit Authority employee, with no dependents and income of $800 every 2 weeks. He was sentenced to pay a five-unit day fine. Each unit was fixed at $32 for a total of $160—which he paid in full at sentencing. (Greene, 1992, p. 36)

One problem associated with the day-fine system is the difficulty and expense involved in establishing the true economic circumstances of each offender.

McDonald (1992) concluded that the day-fine programs in Milwaukee and Staten Island increased the proportion of fines collected within those jurisdictions. An evaluation of the Staten Island program concluded that judges have become comfortable with this approach to levying fines (Winterfield & Hillsman, 1991). However, overall, the Staten Island project demonstrated modest success. An assessment of four other day-fine programs in Arizona, Connecticut, Iowa, and Oregon found only limited success, which led to this conclusion: "Given [the] limited reach of these projects, however, even more positive results would not have demonstrated that day fines show promise of becoming an intermediate sanction capable of diverting large numbers of felony offenders from prison" (Tonry, 1998, p. 699).

The future of day fines seems relatively weak. As of mid-1997, only one project in Phoenix remained in operation. The Bureau of Justice Assistance (BJA) (1996) cautioned that, "much careful thought must be given to making day fines an option in specific jurisdictions" (p. 5). Tonry (1998) further noted that any new day-fine projects should consider problems that led to their abandonment in England. Such problems included (1) if the per-day or per-week cost is too high, then the amount of the fine becomes based on the offenders' means rather than the seriousness of the offense; and (2) all of the parties involved must accept and understand both its principles and practical applications, because, in England, there was speculation that some magistrates disapproved of this system, because it took away their discretion and thereby deprived them of some of their authority (Tonry, 1997, 1998).

Restitution **Restitution,** as a sentence or part of a sentence, requires offenders to repay their victims (or the community) money or services to restore the losses caused by the criminal act. Restitution is usually imposed as a condition of another sanction, such as probation or incarceration. It suffers from the same problems as fines; that is, lower-income offenders, who compose the vast majority of the offenders processed through the courts, are the least likely and the least able to pay. Some jurisdictions may have restitution centers with programs that require offenders to work to help them meet these obligations. Additionally, most prisons that pay inmates for their work require that a portion of their income go toward restitution (see Chapter 16). Victim restitution has become an integral part of restorative justice, and it will be dealt with more extensively in the Epilogue.

Community Programs

In between fines or unsupervised suspended sentences and incarceration lies another option judges can use: to allow convicted offenders to remain in the community under some form of correctional supervision and control. This punishment usually takes the form of probation or placement in a residential community program.

Probation The most common sentence in the American judicial system is **probation.** This involves placing the offender under community supervision by a probation agency and usually requires compliance with special conditions, such as a curfew or restrictions on personal acquaintances. A new series of options—intensive probation supervision, house arrest, or community control—has been designed for offenders who require more intensive supervision. Forms of intensive supervision vary and may involve confinement to one's residence (except to go to work, attend school, or engage in some other mandated activity) and/or more intensive surveillance by probation officers. Programs for higher-risk offenders may require them to wear an electronic bracelet that helps to monitor their whereabouts during the times they are supposed to be at home, thus increasing the intensity of supervision.

Residential Community Programs Halfway houses and other residential programs provide more intensive supervision than probation and can furnish specific treatment programs for adjudicated individuals. These facilities have been used both as an intermediate step between the community and prison (halfway-in houses) and between prison and the community (halfway-out houses).

The halfway house serves as an intermediate step between prison and reintegration into the community.

Incarceration

Incarceration, or a sentence to jail or prison, is imposed when there is a perceived need to crack down on the offender (e.g., when the offender is habitual, a threat to the community). To the American public, it represents the most commonly deserved sanction for criminal behavior and is used more often and with longer terms in the United States than anywhere else in the Western world. In 1990, 46 percent of convicted felons served an average of 72 months; this dropped to an average of 68 months in 1996. Figure 2.2 shows the changes in the mean minimum and the mean maximum sentences to state prisons between 1990 and 1996. Figure 2.3 shows the average length of felony state court sentences of those committed to prison throughout the United States (Ditton & Wilson, 1999). Figure 2.4 shows the mean minimum sentences for 1990 and 1996.

Although the cost of imprisonment can be a limiting factor in its use, some feel that imprisonment can save money (Reynolds, 1992). One study indicated that the average offender commits 187 crimes per year, costing an average of $430,000 per year in lost property, police investigations, and so on. Thus, keeping that inmate in prison at a cost of $25,000 per year represents a substantial savings. Zedlewski (1987) concludes that even when considering prison construction costs, "given the large number of crimes averted by imprisonment . . . incapacitating prison-eligible offenders now crowded out of today's [prisons], construction would likely cost communities less than they now pay in social damages and prevention" (p. 6).

Sentencing Categories

In the United States, sentencing policies typically fall into one of two distinct categories: indeterminate or determinate sentences. A third category is mandatory sentences, which can be indeterminate or determinate. Another form of sentences, usually administered for misdemeanors, can at best be described as "creative sentences."

Indeterminate Sentences

Indeterminate sentences are defined in terms of a minimum period to be served before release can be considered and a maximum period, after which the inmate must be released. A period of parole supervision is generally required following release; this is supposed to consolidate the benefits of treatment while in prison and assist inmates in adjusting to the community.

Each penal code specifies the minimum and maximum time frames to be imposed for each offense, known as **sentencing guidelines.** They limit some, but not all, judicial discretion in sentencing. Most states

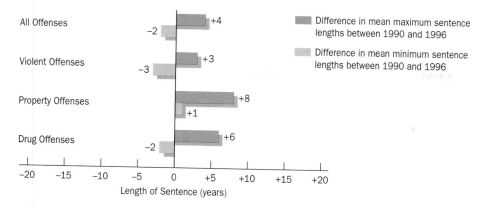

Figure 2.2 *Changes in Mean Minimum and Maximum Sentences to State Prisons Between 1990 and 1996*

Source: P. M. Ditton and D. J. Wilson (1999). *Truth in Sentencing in State Prisons*. Washington, DC: Bureau of Justice Statistics.

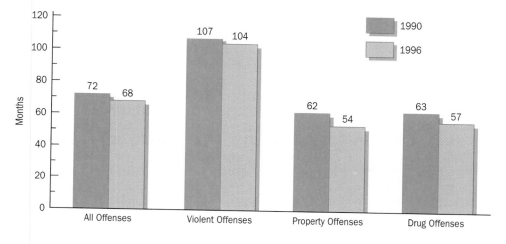

Figure 2.3 *Average Maximum Sentence Length* (1990, 1996)*

*Maximum sentence length an offender may be required to serve for the most serious offense.
Source: P. M. Ditton and D. J. Wilson (1999). *Truth in Sentencing in State Prisons*. Washington, DC: Bureau of Justice Statistics.

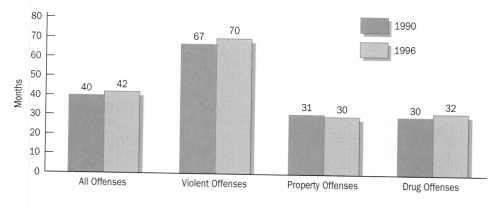

Figure 2.4 *Mean Minimum Sentences* (1990, 1996)*

*Minimum time served is the jurisdiction's estimate of the shortest time each admitted prisoner must serve before becoming eligible for release.
Source: P. M. Ditton and D. J. Wilson (1999). *Truth in Sentencing in State Prisons*. Washington, DC: Bureau of Justice Statistics.

limit the minimum sentence to no more than one half of the maximum (e.g., 5 to 10 years). Some states permit wider discretion, allowing sentences to range from very low minimums, such as 6 months, to an unrealistic maximum, such as 200 years. Although these absurdly long sentences create the appearance of toughness, parole commissions are able to make release decisions independent of the courts, which may negate these harsh sentences. The discretion at both ends of this process creates severe discrepancies in the sentences given to, and the time served by, individuals with similar offenses.

This has led to much criticism and inmate dissatisfaction. Also, the uncertainties over the length of time to be served generate stress among some inmates, which could lead to psychological problems and increased hostility toward the corrections system (Mason, 1990).

Indeterminate sentencing is a reflection of the rehabilitation philosophy. It is not surprising then that, given the decrease in public support for rehabilitation, the use of indeterminate sentencing has also declined. Many jurisdictions have moved to *determinate sentencing* practices and truth-in-sentencing laws. In 1998, 27 states' practices met federal truth-in-sentencing requirements (Ditton & Wilson, 1999).

Determinate Sentences

A **determinate sentence** imposes a fixed term on an offender based on explicit statutory standards that specify the exact length of punishment with no review by an administrative agency (parole board). Postincarceration supervision may be part of the sentence (BJA, 1996, p. 2). Determinate sentences are fixed, but in practice they may be reduced by **good time,** a statutory provision for the reduction of time served through the accumulation of automatic or earned credits. Statutory or automatic good time is now available in 34 states (*Corrections Compendium,* 1997, July). Some states base their good-time laws solely on the length of the sentence. Indiana, for example, allows the sentence to be reduced by good-time credits. This, by far, is the most controversial type of good time, because it significantly affects an inmate's sanction by automatically deducting days from his or her term; this does not sit well with the public.

Administrative *gain time* is even more controversial, because, in states like Florida it was used primarily to ease prison overcrowding; it is typically implemented when prison populations reach a certain level. Gain time is often added to regular good time, and, in Florida, it resulted in all types of offenders being released early. This led to public outrage when any of these early releasees, particularly violent offenders, committed new crimes.

Earned credits, which are available in 29 states and range from 1 day per month up to 44 days per year, are usually given for participation in programs (e.g., work, education, or treatment programs) and for exceptional conduct (e.g., heroic deeds). Inmates may lose any or all of their good time as the result of rule violations.

The net result of good-time provisions considerably reduces the time served by most inmates incarcerated under determinate sentences. However, as a result of the support for truth-in-sentencing legislation, which generally requires that inmates serve 85 percent of their sentence, at least 15 states either have eliminated good time altogether or have made inmates eligible for it only after they have completed at least 85 percent of their sentence. Nevertheless, the use of good time is likely to continue because it is perceived as an incentive to both reinforce positive behavior and to encourage participation in rehabilitative programs.

Mandatory Sentences

Despite good-time provisions, sentencing trends in the United States are generally of a punitive nature. A number of U.S. jurisdictions have enacted reforms in their sentencing policies that reflect the retributive doctrine of punishment, with varying results. The objective of most of these reforms has been to greatly restrict or eliminate parole and the broad discretion that judges are afforded under indeterminate sentencing.

These reforms have generally taken one of four forms: mandatory minimum sentences, presumptive sentencing guidelines, truth-in-sentencing laws, or three strikes laws. All of these reforms are variations of **mandatory sentences,** which require incarceration for certain types of offenses for specified lengths of time. All 50 states and the District of Columbia employ mandatory sentences. It is important to understand that mandatory sentences may be determinate, as are the ones discussed in this section; or they may be indeterminate, as reflected in sentencing guidelines discussed earlier (see pp. 28–30). The following explains the general differences between the two forms:

> "A minimum sentence is specified by statute for offenders convicted of a particular crime or particular crime with specified circumstance (e.g., robbery with a firearm or selling drugs to a minor within 1,000 feet of a school)." Mandatory minimum sentences can be used in indeterminate and determinate sentencing structures. . . . In indeterminate sentencing the mandatory minimum requires the inmate serve a fixed amount of prison time in prison before being eligible for discretionary release. Under a determinate sentence, the offender is required to serve a fixed amount of time in prison before being eligible for discretionary release without the approval of the parole board. (BJA, 1998, p. 2)

Mandatory Minimum Sentences Mandatory minimum sentences generally require judges to impose mandatory sentences of incarceration, often of a specified length, for certain crimes and categories of offenders. Mandatory minimum sentences have been used in spite of evidence that they do not work. In passing this legislation, elected officials wanted to assure the public that their fears were being addressed. Judges must impose these sentences unless there are aggravating or mitigating circumstances, in which case they may lengthen or shorten them within narrow boundaries and with written justification. Rather than being tailored to fit the offender, this type of sentence is designed to fit the offense (BJA, 1998, p. 2). Typically, politicians who pass these laws do so more for symbolic reasons than practical ones.

Many public officials who must administer sentences with mandatory minimum requirements oppose them for both instrumental and moral reasons. From an instrumental perspective, mandatory minimum laws increase the cost to the public as a result of rising trial rates and case-processing time. One study conducted by the U.S. Sentencing Commission found that trial rates were 2.5 times greater for offenses imposing mandatory minimum penalties than for those without them (i.e., 30% vs. 12%) (Tonry, 1992). The reason is that offenders who are looking at long prison sentences have little to lose and a lot to gain by going to trial.

For moral reasons, mandatory minimum statutes are widely detested by federal judges across the political spectrum. The primary reason is that these laws prescribe identical mandatory minimum sentences for every convicted participant in a drug transaction, from the leaders down to the lowest participant, based solely on the type of drug and the weight of any "mixture or substance containing a detectable amount" of the drug. The bottom line is that the average length of stay in prison for drug offenders has more than tripled, from 23.1 months to 71.8 months, since Congress adopted the first broad mandatory minimum statute in 1986 (Taylor, 1993).

Evaluations of mandatory minimum penalties have generally indicated that some judges and prosecutors have devised ways to avoid their use. Some prosecutors have refused to file charges bearing mandatory penalties, and some judges have acquitted factually guilty defendants. In other cases, prosecutors and judges have developed new plea-bargaining practices to avoid mandatory sentencing (e.g., let the offender plead guilty to a lesser charge that has no mandatory minimum requirement). Further, to avoid imposing penalties with a mandatory minimum, some judges have altogether ignored statutory requirements and imposed sentences inconsistent with them (Tonry, 1996).

Another consideration is the impact of mandatory minimum sentences on imprisonment rates (Caulkins, Rydell, Schwabe, & Chiesa, 1997). We need to look not only at those being incarcerated under these requirements but also those being freed. The adoption of determinate sentencing practices, including mandatory minimum guidelines, has made it necessary to release some offenders early to make room for the new ones. Thus, mandatory minimum sentences give newly convicted offenders what is tantamount to a priority reservation on prison beds.

Presumptive Sentencing   Presumptive sentencing procedures are characterized by the following:

1. The appropriate sentence for an offender in a specific case is presumed to fall within a given range of sentences that have been created by a sentencing authority (e.g., the sentencing commission) and adopted by the legislature.

2. Sentencing judges are expected to sentence within the range of sentences or provide written justification, citing aggravating or mitigating circumstances, for going above or below the range (BJA, 1998, p. 2).

3. Presumptive sentences typically provide for some review, usually appellate, for any departure from the predetermined sentence range.

There are several reasons for providing this review:

- to ensure that the punishment is proportionate to the seriousness of the offense and the of-

fender's prior criminal history. Murder is more serious than burglary, so it receives a higher point score.

- to deal with prison overcrowding and strained state budgets and to assess correctional resources. Thus, even while building more prisons, states still face growing prison populations and rising budgets, which require them to look for ways to reduce this problem. Many states require that priority be given to the incarceration of convicted felons committing the most severe offenses, possessing criminal histories showing a clear disregard for the law, and exhibiting a failure of past efforts to rehabilitate them. A further caveat is the requirement that convicted offenders should receive the least restrictive penalty that is necessary to achieve the purpose of the sentence.

- to provide the offender with needed educational or vocational training, medical care, and other correctional treatment in the most effective manner (BJA, 1996, pp. 32–41).

Figure 2.5 presents a sentencing grid with two axes, adapted from Minnesota's sentencing procedures. The horizontal axis contains criminal history scores, based on offender characteristics, which attempt to predict recidivism; the vertical axis contains the list of offenses, listed in decreasing seriousness. The offender's criminal history score is obtained by summing points assigned to a variety of factors, including juvenile and adult convictions, previous incarcerations, supervisory status at the time of the offense (probation or parole; escape), employment status, and educational achievement. Once the offender's score has been determined, the judge can locate the recommended sentence by finding the cell that contains the intersection of the criminal history score with the appropriate offense. The cell lists the sentence to be given (along with its permissible range) in months. Thus, an individual who has a criminal history score of 3 and has been convicted of a Level VII offense should be sentenced to 78 months in prison. Judges have some leeway though and can impose sentences from 74 to 82 months, depending on each offender's circumstances.

As of 1996, 19 states had a sentencing commission and 17 had sentencing guidelines; 10 of these were presumptive and 7 were voluntary, meaning that the legislature had not mandated their use. They were based on past sentencing practices and were to serve only as a guide.

Truth in Sentencing   To ensure that violent offenders serve a large portion of their sentences, in 1994 Congress authorized additional funding for states and jails to increase secure confinement under the Violent Crime Control and Law Enforcement Act (Office of Justice

CONVICTION OFFENSE (Common offenses listed in italics)		0	1	2	3	4	5	6 or more
Murder, 2nd Degree (intentional murder, drive-by-shootings)	X	306 299–313	326 319–333	346 339–353	366 359–373	386 379–393	406 399–413	426 419–433
Murder, 3rd Degree Murder, 2nd Degree (unintentional murder)	IX	150 144–156	165 159–171	180 174–186	195 189–201	210 204–216	225 219–231	240 234–246
Criminal Sexual Conduct, 1st Degree Assault, 1st Degree	VIII	86 81–91	98 93–103	110 105–115	122 117–127	134 129–139	146 141–151	158 153–163
Aggravated Robbery 1st Degree	VII	48 44–52	58 54–62	68 64–72	78 74–82	88 84–92	98 94–102	108 104–112
Criminal Sexual Conduct, 2nd Degree (a) & (b)	VI	21	27	33	39 37–41	45 43–47	51 49–53	57 55–59
Residential Burglary Simple Robbery	V	18	23	28	33 31–35	38 36–40	43 41–45	48 46–50
Nonresidential Burglary	IV	12[1]	15	18	21	24 23–25	27 26–28	30 29–31
Theft Crimes (over $2,500)	III	12[1]	13	15	17	19 18–20	21 20–22	23 22–24
Theft Crimes ($2,500 or less) Check Forgery ($200-$2,500)	II	12[1]	12[1]	13	15	17	19	21 20–22
Sale of Simulated Controlled Substance	I	12[1]	12[1]	12[1]	13	15	17	19 18–20

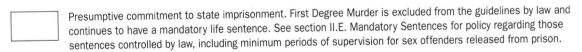

Presumptive commitment to state imprisonment. First Degree Murder is excluded from the guidelines by law and continues to have a mandatory life sentence. See section II.E. Mandatory Sentences for policy regarding those sentences controlled by law, including minimum periods of supervision for sex offenders released from prison.

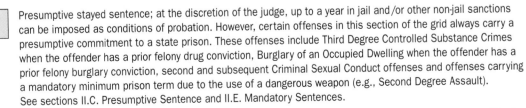

Presumptive stayed sentence; at the discretion of the judge, up to a year in jail and/or other non-jail sanctions can be imposed as conditions of probation. However, certain offenses in this section of the grid always carry a presumptive commitment to a state prison. These offenses include Third Degree Controlled Substance Crimes when the offender has a prior felony drug conviction, Burglary of an Occupied Dwelling when the offender has a prior felony burglary conviction, second and subsequent Criminal Sexual Conduct offenses and offenses carrying a mandatory minimum prison term due to the use of a dangerous weapon (e.g., Second Degree Assault). See sections II.C. Presumptive Sentence and II.E. Mandatory Sentences.

Effective August 1, 1996

[1]One year and one day

Figure 2.5 *Minnesota Sentencing Guidelines Grid (Presumptive Sentence Lengths in Months)*

Note: Italicized numbers within the grid denote the range within which a judge may sentence without the sentence being deemed a departure. Offenders with nonimprisonment felony sentences are subject to jail time according to law.
Source: State of Minnesota (1998, August). IV Sentencing Guidelines Grid. Retrieved September 13, 1999, from the World Wide Web: www.corr.state.mn.us.

Programs [OJP], 1997). To qualify for grants—known as Truth In Sentencing (TIS) grants—states must require offenders who are convicted of UCR Part I violent offenses[4] to serve approximately 85 percent of their sentence. In states with indeterminate sentencing, offenders convicted of Part I offenses must serve 85 percent of the maximum time allowed within their sentence.

By 1998, 27 states and Washington, DC, met the requirements of TIS grants.[5] As of 1999, 14 states[6] had abolished discretionary parole for all offenders, while others[7] had abolished it for certain offenses. Finally, 23 states chose not to enact legislation meeting TIS grant requirements. Their reasons included (1) prison construction and/or operations costs would be too high, even with the federal grant money [16 states]; (2) current sentencing practices appeared to be working well [15 states]; and various other reasons [2 states and Washington, DC] (GAO, 1998, p. 3).

Three Strikes and You're Out   The high level of public concern with crime in the 1990s led many states to consider statutes that mandated life without parole for repeat

felony offenders. Such policies have been referred to as **three strikes laws,** because they dictate that offenders be put away for life after being convicted of their third felony. Although three strikes laws are designed to deal with dangerous offenders who have committed violent crimes, there is evidence that this may not always be the case.

One case that provided a major impetus for three strikes laws involved a repeat violent offender, Richard Allen Davis, who abducted Polly Klaas from her home and then murdered her. Klaas's family lobbied for tougher sentences for repeat violent offenders that would incapacitate them for life. However, 6 years after their inception, Klaas's grandfather spoke out against three strikes laws:

> "[A]dded to the grief that Polly's death has caused, my family now regrets that the law passed in her name casts too wide a net [i.e., ensnares many low-level property and drug offenders, contrary to its original objective], fails to target hard-core offenders it set out to reach, and has diverted critical funds from crime prevention and education." (Klaas, 1999, Sept. 3, p. 15)

Washington enacted the nation's first three strikes law in 1993, followed closely by California. Their laws

One impetus for three strikes laws, which mandate life imprisonment for repeat offenders, was the case of Richard Allen Davis, who abducted Polly Klaas and murdered her. Here her father, Marc Klaas, and other activists speak with the media about the search for another missing child, Xiana Fairchild.

differ in three important ways. First, in Washington, all three strikes must fall under specific felony offenses as listed in the legislation. Under California law, only the first two convictions must be from the state's list of "strikeable" offenses—any subsequent felony can count as the third strike. Second, the California law contains a two-strikes feature in which the prior conviction for a strikeable offense requires an enhanced sentence of twice what the offender would have otherwise received. The Washington law contains no such second-strike provision. Third, the sanctions for a third strike differ. Washington law requires a life term in prison without the possibility of parole for a person convicted for the third time of any of the "most serious offenses" listed in the law. In California, a "third striker" has the potential to be released after serving a minimum of 25 years (Clark, Austin, & Henry, 1997).

When the three strikes laws were initially implemented in Washington and California, some analysts projected that, because of its broader scope, the law enacted in California would have a much greater impact on the local criminal justice system than the law passed in Washington (Austin, 1994). The profiles of inmates sentenced under the three strikes laws in Washington and California do differ and may be reflective of their legislative differences. The majority of California inmates sentenced to life under three strikes legislation were sent to prison for a nonviolent third offense, whereas, with the exception of one inmate, all Washington three-strikers were sentenced for crimes against persons. The Washington inmates were also older, which is probably reflective of the state's narrower "strike zone" (Clark, Austin, & Henry, 1997). Such evidence demonstrates that, although the statutes share the same title, "three strikes and you're out," they can have dramatically different meanings and implications.

A review of the provisions of the 24 states that have enacted three strikes legislation has revealed several differences, including distinctions in how a "strike zone" is defined, the number of strikes required to be "out," and what it means to be "out" (Clark, Austin, & Henry, 1997). The *strike zone*—what constitutes a strike and under what conditions—varies from state to state. Although violent felonies, such as murder, rape, robbery, arson, aggravated assault, and carjacking, are typically included as strike offenses in most states, some have included other charges, such as the sale of drugs (Indiana), the sale of drugs to minors (California), escape (Florida), treason (Washington), and embezzlement and bribery (South Carolina), among their strikeable offenses (Clark, Austin, & Henry, 1997).

There are also variations between states in the number of strikes needed to be *out*. Three strikes are required to be out in 20 states, but 7 of them—Arkansas, California, Connecticut, Kansas, Montana, Pennsylvania, and Tennessee—also have enhanced penalties for two strikes, depending on the offense (Clark, Austin, & Henry, 1997). Finally, states differ as to what sanction

will be imposed when sufficient strikes have accumulated. Most three strikes laws involve mandatory minimum sentences, but some states impose mandatory life sentences with no possibility of parole.

Despite the fact that 24 states and the federal government have enacted some variation of three strikes, several questions arise about the need for these laws, because both state and federal laws had previously provided severe penalties for dangerous or violent offenders. About two thirds of the states had habitual offender statutes, which provided for harsher penalties for repeat, as opposed to first-time, offenders.

Proponents of three strikes laws contend that they deter crime. They point to a 4-year drop in crime, as measured by the California Crime Index, which they believe is a direct result of the three strikes law. Despite such claims, some research has reported results to the contrary. For example, Ambrosio and Schiraldi (1997) found that, from 1994 to 1995, violent crime in non-three-strikes states fell nearly three times more rapidly than it did in three strikes states. Another California study examined the impact through studying the 3-year periods before and after three strikes went into effect. The researchers expected to find a drop in crime among those over the age of 30, because three strikes disproportionately targeted this population. Instead, they found that there was a drop in crime for the 20- to 24-year-old group; this was contrary to what arguments for three strikes based on selective incapacitation and deterrence would have led them to expect (Males, Macular, & Taq-Eddin, 1997).

Critics have argued that defendants facing lengthy mandatory sentences would be more likely to demand trials, thereby slowing down the processing of cases and adding to the problem of court delay and jail crowding (Clark, Austin, & Henry, 1997). For example, in 1994, the Los Angeles jail population classified as high security increased from 35 percent to 62 percent of the total inmate population (Campaign for Effective Crime Policy [CFECP], 1998, November). An additional, more long-term concern was that once more offenders began to serve longer terms of incarceration, prison overcrowding (already at crisis levels in many states) would grow even worse (Austin & James, 1997). The California Department of Corrections estimated that the three strikes law would add 275,000 new inmates by the year 2028, at an annual cost of $5.7 billion. These additional inmates would require new prison construction costing $21 billion. Further, sentencing offenders to longer prison terms without the possibility of release will add to the already high cost of caring for geriatric inmates (CFECP, 1998, November).

Critics have also raised the issues of uneven application and racial disparity. Uneven application derives from prosecutorial discretion and plea bargaining. Data from California, Georgia, and Washington have shown that three strikes laws result in racial disparities in sentencing. For example, a 1997 California report found that, al-

Three Strikes Applied to Minor Offenses

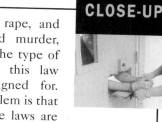

CLOSE-UP

In Washington, a 35-year-old small-time offender, Larry Fisher, was sentenced to life. His first strike involved pushing his grandfather down and taking $390 from him; his second strike involved robbing a pizza parlor in which he concealed his finger so it looked like a gun and made off with $100. For his final strike, he again used his finger and held up a sandwich shop for $150. Conviction for his third offense would have resulted in a 22-month sentence, but under the three strikes law he faces life in prison.

The most ludicrous example involves Jerry Williams, who grabbed a slice of pizza from a group of children. This offense was his third strike. Under California law, because he had a prior record of two felonies, including robbery and attempted robbery, he was sentenced to 25 years to life.

Others sentenced under this law, like Cecil Davis, charged with kidnapping, rape, and attempted murder, are just the type of offenders this law was designed for. The problem is that unless the laws are specific or allow some discretion in applying them, they will ensnare people like Larry Fisher and Jerry Williams.

---

though blacks compose 7 percent of the population and account for 20 percent of the felony arrests and 31 percent of state prisoners, they make up 43 percent of those incarcerated for a third strike (Schiraldi & Ambrosio, 1997).

One argument advanced by critics is that the statutory language allows the laws to be applied to relatively minor offenders. See our Close-Up, "Three Strikes Applied to Minor Offenses."

Two recent court cases have had a significant impact on the three strikes law in California. California judges have expressed some opposition to the three strikes law. This issue was addressed by the California Supreme Court in *People v. Romero* (1996), which allowed for judicial discretion in deciding to dismiss a prior conviction. The California Supreme Court limited the judicial discretion to dismiss a prior strike by placing a number of restrictions on the dismissals, such as "dismissals must truly be in furtherance of justice, the court may not dismiss a prior conviction because it disagrees with the three strikes law, the court may not dismiss in order to ease the court congestion, and dismissal must truly be reasonable" (Assembly Committee on Public Safety, 1997). This ruling may well further limit the use of the three strikes law, but it could create a major logjam of appeals for the nearly 26,000 inmates sentenced under the law who may be eligible for resentencing (Clark, Austin, & Henry, 1997). Additional judicial discretion was granted in *People v. Alvarez* (1997), which allowed for judicial discretion in declaring a crime a misdemeanor. The court ruled that where a current conviction could be filed as either a misdemeanor or a felony, the trial court could declare the crime to be a misdemeanor at sentencing.

However, a 1998 decision *(People v. Williams)* appeared to have narrowed the *Romero* ruling by limiting the power of the court to disregard convictions, not only based on the letter of the law but also its spirit. Judges are required to consider the nature and circumstances of the defendant's present felony, and his or her prior serious, or violent, felony convictions, and the particulars of the person's background and prospects for change. Further, in disregarding a felony as a "strike" the trial court must set forth its reasons in writing, which are reviewable by higher courts. In the *Williams* case, he had previous convictions for attempted robbery and rape. His current conviction was for driving under the influence of PCP (i.e., DUI), which indicated to the judge that he had not followed through on treatment efforts. This was preceded by three previous convictions for the same offense.

The most recent data from the Los Angeles Sheriff's Department have suggested that the pace of three strikes cases coming into the system may be slowing. The number of two-strikes cases filed by the Los Angeles district attorney declined by 15 percent between the second quarter of 1995 and the second quarter of 1996. Likewise, there was a 28 percent decline between the two periods in the number of three strikes cases filed. The Los Angeles County Sheriff's Department (1996) considered it too early to say whether these findings suggest a trend or whether there is another possible cause. In addition, the impact on the state prison systems has not been as severe as projected in either Washington or California (Clark, Austin, & Henry, 1997).

Creative Sentences

Some judges impose sentences that might be described as creative or offbeat (indeed, some people might describe them as off the wall). There is some question as to whether some of these sentences are unconstitutional. Judges typically impose creative sentences on misdemeanants. Our Close-Up, "Judges Who Create Sentences," illustrates the ingenuity of some judges.

CONCLUSION

It is clear that the sentence, which starts convicted offenders into the correctional process, has immense

Judges Who Create Sentences

Judge Joe B. Brown [a controversial Memphis, Tennessee, jurist, once sentenced a convicted] drug offender to stand in front of a gorilla cage for an hour. [Brown said,] "I wanted him to get the idea that could be him locked up and confined, and see how bad that was." He did get this man's attention. Brown stated that his approach to sentencing is not to hand out easier punishments but to devise those that have special meaning to each individual lawbreaker. His goal is to make the punishment fit the offender, more so than the offense. Thus, his typical sentences for first-time nonviolent offenders include probation and community work, like washing police cars or clearing weed-filled lots. Other probation conditions also require that offenders complete a job training course or school.

Perhaps the most controversial aspect of Judge Brown's sentences has been allowing burglary victims, accompanied by a sheriff's deputy or bailiff, to visit the burglar's home and take something of equal value while the burglar watches. These visits are made without warning so as not to allow burglars to hide their most valuable possessions. This practice troubles many people. Scott Wallace of the Criminal Justice Policy Foundation says, "I don't think it's a good idea, to involve the victim in a face-to-face intimidating confrontation." Paul Levine, director of public affairs with the National Association of Criminal Defense Lawyers, questioned the constitutionality of the practice. In contrast, others have applauded his approach. For example, Leslie Balin, a defense lawyer in Memphis

stated that "It's my firm belief that these sentences are not done just for the purpose of being different, but for the purpose of turning individual lives around." According to Judge Brown, the objective of his approach is to "use the coercive power of the court to do a bit of social engineering" (Finger, 1993, p. 10).

Judge Howard Boardman, of Visalia, California, has also dispensed creative and controversial sentences. In his most controversial sentence, he gave a woman convicted of severely abusing her children a choice: four years in prison or probation with the condition that she use Norplant, the long-term subcutaneous contraceptive. The woman originally accepted the probation sentence with the Norplant condition but later reversed herself and sued the judge for violating her "reproductive rights." The suit was dismissed about a year later when her probation was revoked and she was sent to prison (she tested positive for cocaine). As a result of the Norplant sentence, an individual who violently opposed its use entered Judge Boardman's court and tried to shoot him. The judge was not injured in the incident (Castro, 1992; Southwick, 1992).

Other judges have also imposed creative sentences. A common innovation is shaming, whereby the judge requires the offender to do something in public that will bring disgrace to him or her. This has included:

1. An offender was required to wear a sign while standing on a street corner for 3 hours 3 days a week, saying "I'm a thief."
2. A Philadelphia butcher was fined $10,000 for selling rotting meat and required to place an ad in the paper confessing to the sale of

"filthy, putrid and contaminated meat."
3. Shoplifters were required to wear signs confessing their crime while parading in front of the store they stole from (Allwen-Mills, 1997).
4. Child molesters have been required to post signs on their doors warning children to keep away or wear T-shirts advertising their conviction.
5. A daughter was required to be chained to her mother for a month.
6. A petty thief was forced to shovel horse manure for a month (Kising, 1996).
7. An 18-year-old who spray painted swastikas, ethnic slurs, and anarchist messages on five schools was required to pay $9,115, serve a term of probation, perform 100 hours of community service, and write a 500-page essay on cultural diversity (Klein, 1997).

Although there is no scientific evidence that shaming works, there are some compelling arguments for its use:

> "Shaming is a potentially cost-effective, politically popular method of punishment," said Professor Dan Kahan, of the University of Chicago Law School. He concluded that a public sick of the rampant crime that plagues their communities "wants more from criminal punishment. They want a message. They want moral condemnation of the offender." (Allen-Mills, 1997, April 20)

Do you think that judges should be allowed the type of discretion to hand down sentences like those described? Do you think that these sentences can accomplish any of the goals of sentencing that we discussed earlier? Which ones, if any, and why?

implications for them. At the very least, the sentence will set the tone for their immediate futures and perhaps much longer. For better or worse, usually the latter, if the offenders are incarcerated, they will be thrown into an environment that will totally dominate their lives. In the chapters that follow, we will try to convey a picture of how correctional sanctions, and the processes that accompany them, have evolved into their present form.

Summary

The justifications for sentences given to offenders in the United States include retribution or just deserts; deterrence; incapacitation; and rehabilitation. Despite their differences, all of these sentencing philosophies involve punishing the offender. One or more sentencing justifications are reflected in such sanctions as monetary payment (e.g., day fines, restitution), community programs (e.g., probation, residential), and incarceration.

Sentencing policies in the United States typically fall into one of two categories: determinate (fixed) or indeterminate (a range). Determinate sentences may be reduced through such mechanisms as good time and administrative gain time. Recently, though, corrections has been becoming more punitive, with determinate sentences often taking the form of a mandatory sentence. Specifically, sanctions may have a mandatory minimum time to be served; they may be presumptive; or offenders may be required, through a truth-in-sentencing statute, to serve about 85 percent of the given sentence. For second or third felonies, offenders may be sentenced to very lengthy prison terms, or even life in prison, under a three strikes law. Finally, some judges have imposed creative sentences, the future of which remains to be seen.

Critical Thinking Questions

1. Define the four major sentencing philosophies. How are they similar to and different from one another? What do you perceive as the three biggest benefits and drawbacks of each justification, in terms of its implications for the correctional system?

2. Discuss the major types of dispositions. What do they involve? For which types of offenders are they used? Discuss your feelings about each. Do you support them? Why or why not?

3. What is the primary distinction between determinate and indeterminate sentencing? Discuss the pros and cons of each. How are mandatory sentences a form of determinate sentencing?

4. Provide four examples of mandatory sentences. Compare and contrast each of them. What are the benefits of each for corrections? The drawbacks? What are the benefits of each for the community? The drawbacks?

5. Analyze the "truth-in-sentencing" and the "three strikes" laws for their benefits and drawbacks. How can these sentencing strategies be modified to more closely meet their original objectives?

Test Your Knowledge

1. As a justification for the imposition of a penal sanction, retribution specifies that:
   a. the pain of punishment will discourage further criminal behavior.
   b. while being punished, the criminal will not be able to further victimize society.
   c. the criminal is getting what he or she deserves.
   d. society is getting revenge for the harm it has suffered.

2. Restitution can be thought of as:
   a. deserved punishment.
   b. a form of nonmonetary punishment.
   c. payment for harm done to the victim.
   d. a sentence that requires the offender to perform community service.

3. Indeterminate sentences:
   a. require that a specific number of years be served.
   b. are typically associated with some form of parole.
   c. were developed to implement the modern form of retribution.
   d. are none of the above.

Endnotes

1. See Bursik, Grasmick, & Chamlin, 1990; Chiricos & Waldo, 1970; and Zedlewski, 1987.

2. Murray & Cox, 1979; Shapiro and Votey, 1984; Sherman & Berk, 1984; Smith & Gartin, 1989.

3. Index crimes include Part I property crimes (burglary, larceny, and motor vehicle theft).

4. Part I violent crimes include murder and non-negligent manslaughter, forcible rape, aggravated assault, arson, and robbery. For definitions of these crimes see any Uniform Crime Report.

5. Arizona, California, Connecticut, Delaware, Florida, Georgia, Iowa, Kansas, Louisiana, Maine, Michigan, Minnesota, Mississippi, Missouri, New Jersey, New York, North Carolina, North Dakota, Ohio, Oklahoma, Oregon, Pennsylvania, South Carolina, Tennessee, Utah, Virginia, Washington, and Washington, DC. Illinois qualified in 1996 only (Ditton & Wilson, 1999).

6. Arizona, Delaware, Florida, Illinois, Indiana, Kansas, Maine, Minnesota, Mississippi, New Mexico, North Carolina, Ohio, Oregon, Washington, and Wisconsin. Further, California allows discretionary release only for offenders with indeterminate life sentences (Ditton & Wilson, 1999).

7. Alaska, New York, Tennessee, and Virginia (Ditton & Wilson, 1999).

The Death Penalty: The Ultimate Sanction

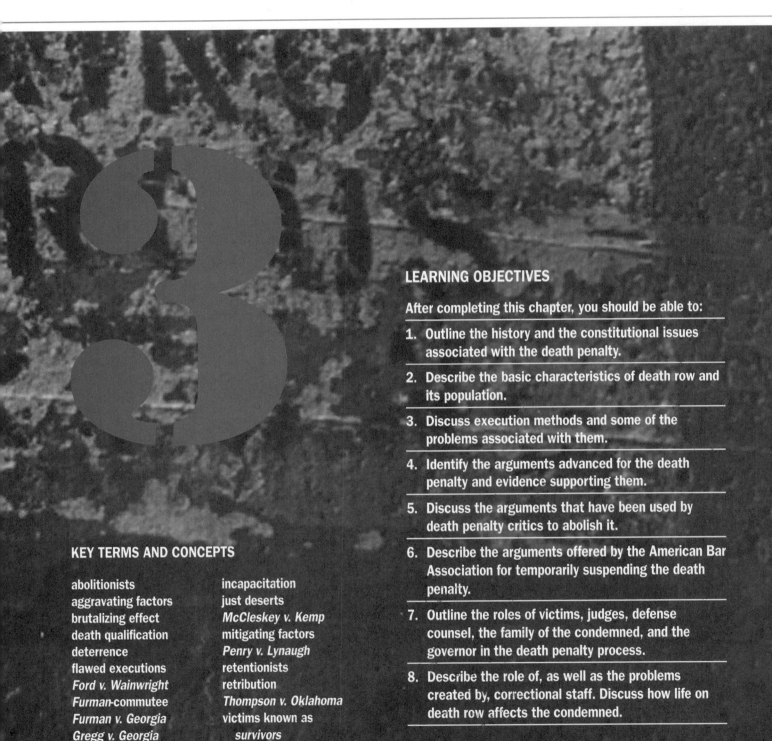

LEARNING OBJECTIVES

After completing this chapter, you should be able to:

1. Outline the history and the constitutional issues associated with the death penalty.

2. Describe the basic characteristics of death row and its population.

3. Discuss execution methods and some of the problems associated with them.

4. Identify the arguments advanced for the death penalty and evidence supporting them.

5. Discuss the arguments that have been used by death penalty critics to abolish it.

6. Describe the arguments offered by the American Bar Association for temporarily suspending the death penalty.

7. Outline the roles of victims, judges, defense counsel, the family of the condemned, and the governor in the death penalty process.

8. Describe the role of, as well as the problems created by, correctional staff. Discuss how life on death row affects the condemned.

KEY TERMS AND CONCEPTS

abolitionists
aggravating factors
brutalizing effect
death qualification
deterrence
flawed executions
Ford v. Wainwright
Furman-commutee
Furman v. Georgia
Gregg v. Georgia

incapacitation
just deserts
McCleskey v. Kemp
mitigating factors
Penry v. Lynaugh
retentionists
retribution
Thompson v. Oklahoma
victims known as
   survivors

Introduction

Capital punishment is our most extreme sanction, and in the United States it is generally reserved for only the most heinous first-degree murderers. However, this is not always the case; for example, the federal government has over 60 capital offenses outside of first-degree murder, including carjackings involving murder and drive-by shootings (Harries & Cheatwood, 1997, p. 4). Although the death penalty is rarely imposed (about 300 death sentences are imposed annually), its highly controversial nature and irreversible consequences require that arguments for and against its use be discussed. Between 1930 and March 2000, 4,483 prisoners in the United States were executed (see Figure 3.1; DPIC, 2000).

In colonial days, executions were well-attended public events. Sermons were given, not only to preach to the condemned, but also to reinforce the importance of godly behavior and retribution for the disobedient to the assembled public. However, by the 19th century, middle-class America had become dissatisfied with the public display of suffering: "It had become for them a source of distress, a cruel event to be avoided at all costs" (Johnson, 1998, p. 29). In the South, public executions—both legal and illegal—continued for some time. After the abolition of slavery, many southern whites sought alternative ways to control the black population (Johnson, 1998). Racial fear and hatred led to many lynchings, which were considered noble acts of "popular justice" well into the 20th century (Johnson, 1998).

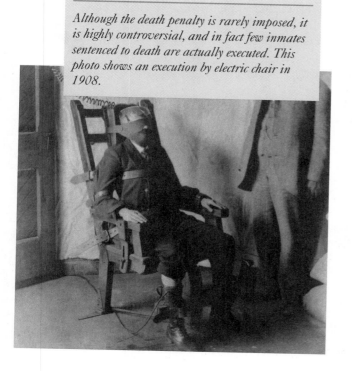

Although the death penalty is rarely imposed, it is highly controversial, and in fact few inmates sentenced to death are actually executed. This photo shows an execution by electric chair in 1908.

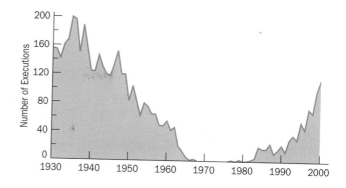

Figure 3.1   *Executions in the U.S. from 1930 to 2000**

*This includes the period through March 3, 2000.
Sources: T. Snell (1999, December). *Capital Punishment 1997*. Washington, DC: Bureau of Justice Statistics; Amnesty International USA (AIUSA), 2000a, March; Death Penalty Information Center (1999, March—www.essential.org/dpic).

Capital Punishment

In this section, we will take a closer look at capital punishment, examining issues of its constitutionality, death row statistics, execution procedures, and arguments for and against the death penalty.

Constitutionality

In *Furman v. Georgia* (1972), the Supreme Court struck down existing capital punishment statutes. Two of the five concurring justices ruled that the death penalty violated the equal protection clause of the Fourteenth Amendment and the cruel and unusual punishment clause of the Eighth Amendment, whereas the other two justices did not object to the death penalty per se, but rather to its arbitrary application which discriminated against the poor and powerless.

After the *Furman* decision, several states reformed their judicial system in response to the faults sited by the Court. Four years later in 1976, the Supreme Court responded in *Gregg v. Georgia,* permitting the reinstatement of capital punishment in states that had rewritten their statutes to reflect the constitutional standards established in *Furman*. Table 3.1 highlights the changes made to the Georgia statute following *Furman*.

Following the *Gregg* decision, many states modeled their statutes to conform to constitutional standards required by this case. Most approved statutes permitted the death penalty after the consideration of mitigating and aggravating circumstances (which will be discussed later).

Executions began again in 1977, and by March 2000, 624 offenders, including 4 women, had been put to death (Death Penalty Information Center [DPIC], 2000; see Figure 3.2). Following the reinstatement of the death penalty, many appeals were filed to establish the boundaries of capital punishment statutes. In 1977, the Court held in *Coker v. Georgia* that the death penalty was an excessive and disproportionate penalty for the rape of an adult. As of 1986, seven states had death penalty statutes with capital crimes that did not involve murder. They include California, for train-wrecking, treason, and perjury causing an execution; Florida, for capital drug

---

Table 3.1

New Rules for Capital Trials in Georgia Following *Furman*

- The death penalty is reserved for specific crimes.
- The trial is bifurcated—that is, divided into two phases, one for determination of guilt and the other for consideration of sentence.
- Lesser offenses are included when supported by the evidence.
- Once found guilty, a hearing is held in which the judge or jury hears about mitigating and aggravating circumstances.
- At least 1 of 10 specified aggravating circumstances must be found to exist beyond a reasonable doubt and designated in writing before a death sentence can be imposed.
- In jury cases, the trial judge is bound by the recommended sentence.
- In its review of a death sentence (which is automatic), the state supreme court must consider whether the sentence was influenced by passion, prejudice, or any other arbitrary factor; whether the evidence supports the finding of a statutory aggravating circumstance; and whether the death sentence "is excessive or disproportionate to the penalty imposed in similar cases, considering both the crime and the defendant."
- If the court affirms the death sentence, it must include in its decision reference to similar cases that it has considered.

Source: *Gregg v. Georgia* (1976) 428 U.S. 153 96 S.Ct.

trafficking; Kentucky, for kidnapping with aggravating factors; Louisiana, for aggravated rape of a victim under 12 and treason; Mississippi, for aircraft piracy; New Jersey, for furthering a narcotics conspiracy by commanding or threatening others to gain their involvement; and Utah, for aggravated assault by a prisoner serving a life sentence if serious bodily injury is intentionally caused. Their constitutionality remains uncertain because no one has been sentenced to death for them (Bohm, 1999).

Death Row Statistics

Annual executions peaked in the 1930s, with 197 executions in 1935. Executions then declined dramatically from the 1940s until they halted altogether in 1967. Since the death penalty was reinstated in 1976, executions have risen unsteadily (see Figure 3.2). A new post-*Furman* high of 98 executions was reached in 1999. In 2000, by March 22, 26 people had been executed (Amnesty International USA [AIUSA], 2000a, March; DPIC, 2000).[1] Interestingly, Harries and Cheatwood (1977) found a positive correlation between execution rates and homicide rates; homicides rose as executions rose.

Before 1976, death row inmates waited an average of 13 months for their executions. Between 1977 and 1984, the average stay on death row rose to 6 years. Throughout the rest of 1980s, waiting time grew to almost 8 years, and by the end of 1998, the average stay on death row extended over 9 years (American Correctional Association, 1989; Snell, 1999). As of January 2000, a record high of 3,659 inmates, all convicted of murder, were on death row in 39 (including the federal government and the military) of the 40 jurisdictions that had death penalties (see Figure 3.3).

Figure 3.4 shows the racial makeup of the 624 defendants executed between January 17, 1977, and March 22,

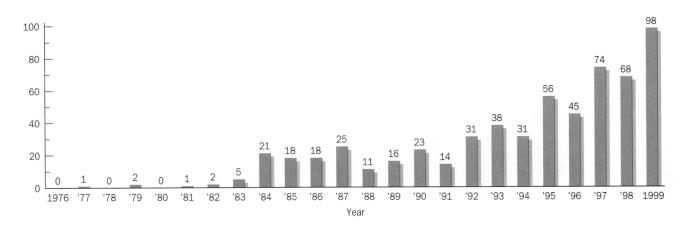

Figure 3.2 *Executions from 1976 to 1999**

*As of March 22, there were 26 executions in 2000.
Source: DPIC (2000), www.essential. org/dpic/dpicexecoo.html. Reprinted by permission of the Death Penalty Information Center.

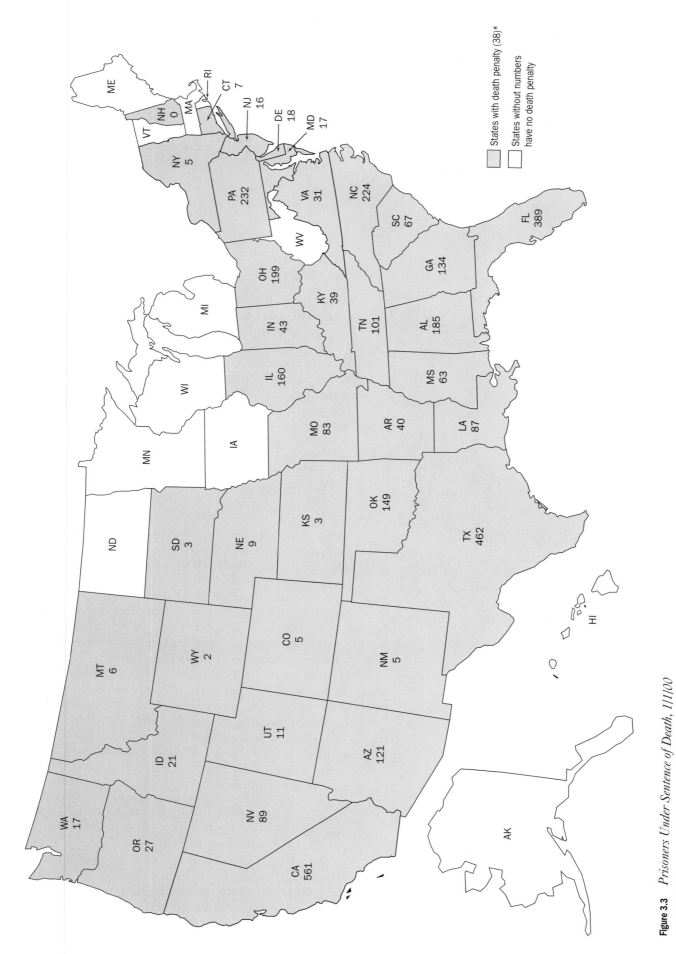

Figure 3.3 *Prisoners Under Sentence of Death, 1/1/00*

*Thirty-eight states have the death penalty. The 40 jurisdictions noted in the text include the federal government and the military.

Source: NAACP Legal Defense Fund (2000, January). "Death Row USA." New York: Author, pp. 24–25.

States with death penalty (38)*

States without numbers have no death penalty

Figure 3.4 *Race of Defendants Executed Since 1977 (as of March 22, 2000)*

Source: DPIC (2000). Reprinted by permission of the Death Penalty Information Center.

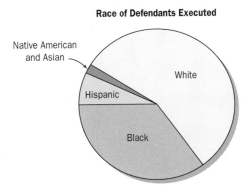

Race of Defendants Executed

Defendant Race	Number Executed	Percent of Total Executed
Black	219	35%
Hispanic	42	7%
White	351	56%
Native American and Asian	12	2%

2000. Figure 3.5 gives a breakdown of the racial makeup of their victims. From 1930 to 1967 (when executions were halted), the racial breakdown of those executed was 45 percent white, 53 percent black, and 2 percent other races. From January 17, 1977 (when executions resumed), to March 22, 2000, the breakdown was 56 percent white, 35 percent black, 7 percent Hispanic, and 2 percent Asian and Native American. More than 80 percent of the executions occurred in southern states. Figure 3.6 provides a picture of the demographic makeup of death row inmates. The average death row inmate was a never married, white male, who was either a high school graduate or had earned his GED. Figure 3.7 gives a breakdown of defendant versus victim racial demographics. Those who murdered white victims were far more likely to be executed (DPIC, 2000).

Finally, it is important to note that few inmates sentenced to death are actually executed. Between 1973 and 1998, 6,431 entered state and federal prisons under a death sentence. There where 500 executed, and 2,479 other inmates were removed, otherwise, from death row (Snell, 1999). Figure 3.8 gives a breakdown of the reasons for death sentence turnarounds for inmates between 1973 and 1998.

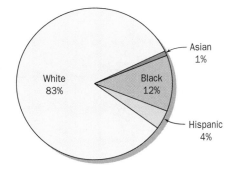

Figure 3.5 *Race of Victims of Those Executed* (as of March 22, 2000)*

*About 84% of the victims in death penalty cases are white, even though only 50% of murder victims are white.
Source: DPIC (2000). Reprinted by permission of the Death Penalty Information Center.

Executions

The methods of execution, as of March 2000, included lethal injection (36 states), electrocution (11 states), lethal gas (7 states), hanging (4 states), and firing squad (3 states) (see Figure 3.9). The total is more than 38 states, because several states authorize more than one method. Arizona, Arkansas, Delaware, and Nebraska authorize the choice of a second method for those sentenced before a given date. Several states authorize two methods of execution.[2] In January 2000, Illinois placed a moratorium on executions in that state; between 1987 and 2000, 13 prisoners were released from death row in Illinois because of wrongful convictions.

Table 3.2 discusses some of the procedures different states use.

Flawed Executions Technically **flawed executions** include those where the equipment or method of execution malfunctions. From 1983 to 1999, there were 25 "botched" executions (DPIC, 2000b, March). Electrocution has become controversial, both because of flawed executions and the fact that it is considered inhumane, cruel, and unusual despite court rulings to the contrary. "Old Sparky," Florida's electric chair, came under considerable scrutiny following unexpected complications during electrocutions. During the 1997 execution of Pedro Medina, "a mask covering his face burst into foot-long blue and orange flames which flickered for about 6 to 10 seconds, filling the execution chamber with smoke" (*New York Times*, 3-25-97, p. A12). On July 8, 1999, following the reconstruction of "Old Sparky," blood appeared on Allen Lee "Tiny" Davis' shirt during his execution, again raising the issue of the constitutionality of the method of electrocution. Our Close-Up, "A Shocking Way to Go," on page 46 describes another flawed execution. Lethal injection is now the primary method of execution in Florida; prisoners can choose between the two methods.

Even lethal injection, which is considered the most humane method of execution, has gone awry. In several cases, where the convict had been a drug abuser, technicians found it difficult to locate suitable veins into which

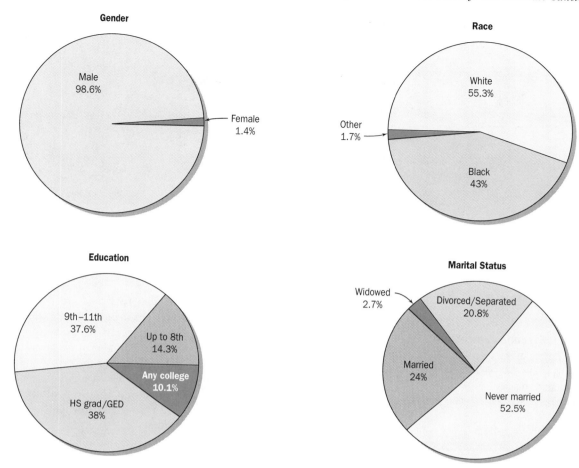

Figure 3.6 *Demographics of Death Row*

Source: T. Snell (1999, December). *Capital Punishment 1998*. Washington, DC: Bureaus of Justice Statistics, p. 8.

	White Victim	Black Victim	Hispanic Victim	Asian Victim	Total
White Defendant	312 (52.17%)	11 (1.84%)	3 (.50%)	3 (.50%)	329
Black Defendant	142 (23.75%)	55 (9.20%)	5 (.84%)	5 (.84%)	207
Hispanic Defendant	21 (3.51%)	2 (.33%)	15 (2.51%)	1 (.17%)	39
Asian Defendant	1 (.17%)	0 (0%)	0 (0%)	4 (.67%)	5
Native American	8 (1.34%)	0 (0%)	0 (0%)	0 (0%)	8
Total	484 (80.94%)	68 (11.37%)	23 (3.85%)	13 (2.18%)	

Figure 3.7 *Defendant-Victim Racial Combinations**

*Note: In addition, there were 10 defendants executed for the murders of multiple victims of different races. Of those, 5 defendants were black, 4 white, and 1 Hispanic (1.67%). These figures account for the period from 1977 through December 1999.
Source: NAACP Legal Defense and Education Fund (2000). "Death Row USA: Winter 2000." New York: Author, p. 9.

to insert catheters, delaying the process for up to 45 minutes. In the case of Raymond Landry, the tube carrying the drugs sprang a leak, which halted the process while the catheter was reinserted. Stephen McCoy's violent reaction to the drugs caused him to gag, contort, and cough violently. One witness fainted (Haines, 1992).

There have also been instances of botched gassing. Jimmy Lee Gray was put to death in the Mississippi gas chamber, and shortly after the cyanide pellets were re-leased he began to convulse. Gray's gasps and contortions lasted for more than 8 minutes (Haines, 1992).

Arguments For and Against the Death Penalty

There are many opinions on capital punishment, ranging from individuals who feel that criminals, especially violent ones, are not deserving of public support in what they perceive as "country club" prisons and should be

Outcomes for Those Sentenced to Death (*N* = 6,431)

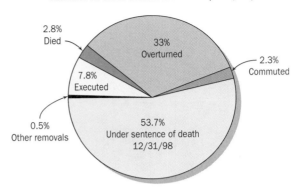

Breakdown of Removals from Death Row (*N* = 2,979)

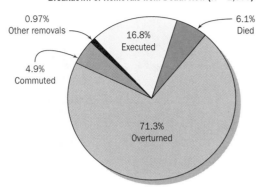

Figure 3.8 *Dispositions of Death Sentences, (1973–1998)*

Source: T. Snell (1999, December). *Capital Punishment 1998.* Washington, DC: Bureau of Justice Statistics, p. 15.

Table 3.2

Facts about Execution Procedures

- Almost all states surveyed have written procedures regarding the execution process.
- Electric chairs were built by either inmates or an outside contractor.
- States using the electric chair use natural sponges soaked in a brine (not just saline) solution. Copper devices are prevalent in headgear, ranging from mesh, to solid, to perforated devices.
- The most common reason stated for changing from electrocution to lethal injection was that it is considered [a] "more humane method of electrocution."
- All states surveyed utilizing lethal injection as a method of execution administered the drugs manually and do not utilize a machine. States cited the possibility of malfunctioning machinery as the reason why drugs are administered manually.
- The most commonly used drugs for the lethal injection procedure are sodium Pentothal (puts the inmate to sleep); second, pancurium bromide (stops respiration); and, third, potassium chloride (stops the heart). Usually, between each drug, a saline wash is used.
- Virginia has a mandatory 10 mg intramuscular injection of thyroxine because the inmate is more relaxed, and it makes it easier for the technician to insert the IV. Other states offer a sedative injection as an option.
- Most execution teams are made up of department of corrections personnel; however, Arkansas used community-based medical personnel in its lethal injection procedure. Team members are either voluntary or appointed. Several states cited screening and evaluation of members, postexecution debriefing sessions, and the availability of counseling.
- States cited the need for statutory provisions regarding protection of medical personnel from censure from professional associations for their involvement in the execution process.

Source: "Execution Methods Used by States"; Supplemental Report, Florida Corrections Commission, June 1997, p. 10.

---

executed to those who feel that life is sacred and the government has no right to execute offenders, regardless of the crimes committed. In between these extremes lies the majority of individuals whose views are affected by such factors as the nature of the crime and the degree to which the system provides assurances that the offender will not be released. Those favoring capital punishment are referred to as **retentionists;** those against it are called **abolitionists.**

The Pro–Death Penalty Position Retentionists justify the death penalty with the same arguments used to support other penal sanctions:

1. **Retribution** is deserved: "An eye for an eye."
2. The offender must "pay" for what he has done (**just deserts**).
3. Executing the offender, or **incapacitation,** will prevent him from ever committing murder again.
4. Executions serve as a **deterrence** to others who may be dissuaded from committing murder, knowing the potential consequences.
5. There is a high level of public support for the death penalty.

1. and **2.** Retribution is rooted in two attitudes: revenge, in which the offender is paid back for his wrongful behavior, and "just deserts," which demands that the offender be punished to repay society for the harm done (Fickenauer, 1988). Revenge is further based on an emotional, "get even" feeling and a belief that "taking a life deserves execution" (Bohm, 1992).

3. For many, execution represents total incapacitation; this criminal will never kill again. However, although recidivism is certainly a concern in all areas of corrections, research does not support hypotheses that predict the future dangerousness of murderers, particularly death row inmates (Marquart & Sorenson, 1989;

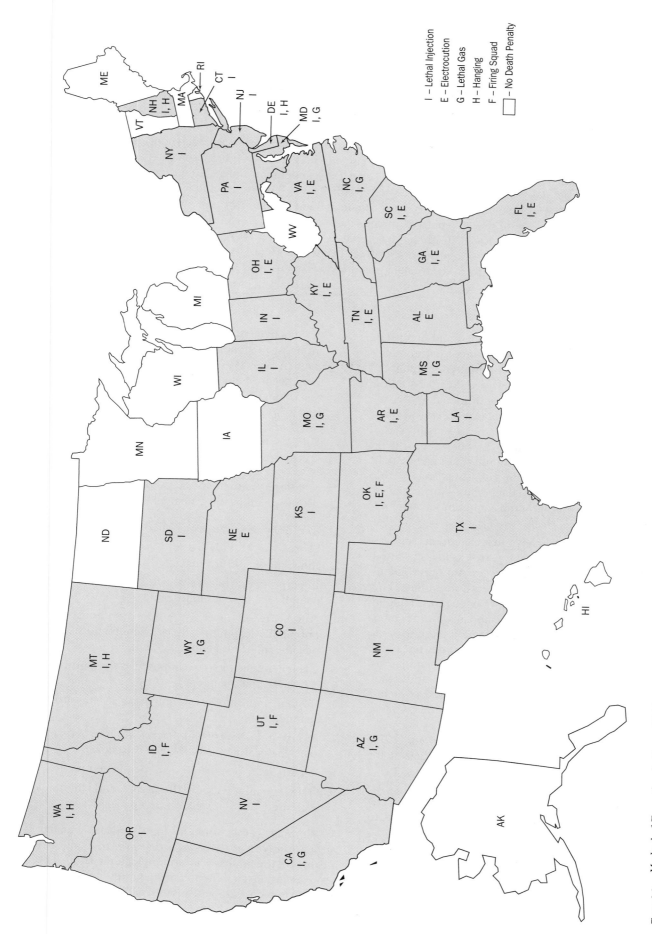

Figure 3.9 *Method of Execution by State, 2000*

Sources: AIUSA (2000b, March). Methods of Execution in the USA, www.amnestyusa.org/abolish/methus.html.

A Shocking Way to Go

CLOSE-UP

The electric chair is supposed to be a quick and humane way to put a criminal to death. But when the executioner at the Florida State Prison threw the switch on cop killer Jessie Tafero, it seemed anything but. To the horror of spectators, fire and smoke shot out from the headpiece strapped to Tafero's skull. He nodded and gurgled for four minutes as his eyebrows burned and ashes fell from his head to his shoulders. The 2,000 volt current had to be turned off twice to keep the whole metal-and-leather headgear from bursting into flames.

"Torture," said the condemned man's lawyer, Mark Olive. "Barbarous," said Thomas Horkan, executive director of the Florida Catholic Conference. Last week, prison officials explained that an overzealous maintenance man had replaced the natural sponge in the headpiece with a synthetic sponge which had been purchased at a local store. When tested in a toaster, the synthetic sponge started to smoke. Tafero, officials insisted, was braindead after the first shock of electricity, and felt no pain.

Source: "A Shocking Way to Go," TIME, *May 21, 1990. © 1990 TIME, Inc. Reprinted by permission.*

Sorenson & Wrinkle, 1996). Marquart and Sorensen (1989) found that less than 1 percent of the murderers who had their sentences commuted committed another murder after being released. Several studies have been conducted on the institutional and post-release behavior of **Furman-commutees** (inmates who were released from death row as a result of the *Furman* decision) (Marquart & Sorensen, 1989). None of the studies found significant evidence that the former death row inmates—presumably the most dangerous of the dangerous—presented a greater threat to prisons or the community than other inmates.

4. The public tends to believe that executions serve as a deterrence. Not only is the person who is executed unable to commit another murder, but other potential killers may also be dissuaded from killing. The deterrent effects of executions have been studied in several ways. One approach compares murder rates in states with capital punishment with those without it. Another strategy compares the murder rates in a given jurisdiction before and after executions. A third approach examines murder rates and other crime rates in a specific state before and after the abolition or institution of capital punishment. Only a few of these studies found evidence that capital punishment was a deterrence (e.g., Ehrlich, 1975; Layson, 1986), and they have been criticized for methodological errors. Zimring and Hawkins (1973) indicated that punishment was likely to be an effective deterrence for individuals who are generally law abiding, but not for those who are predisposed to commit crimes.

5. There is strong public support for the death penalty, with an estimated 71 percent of the public showing support in 1999 (Maguire & Pastore, 1999). A Gallup Poll released in February 2000 found that support was 66 percent, still a clear majority. Among the strongest proponents of the death penalty is Ernest van den Haag (1975), who contends that the punishment for misbehavior must fit the crime, a *proportionality* argument. Van den Haag feels that the death penalty is particularly appropriate for heinous murders, because it protects society more than other possible sanctions. By imposing capital punishment, the scales of justice are balanced.

The Anti–Death Penalty Position Abolitionists' arguments against the death penalty include:

1. Executions are state-sanctioned murder; no killing is right.
2. Innocent people are convicted and executed.
3. It perpetrates violence and may contribute to the commission of other murders.
4. Not everyone receives competent representation, potentially leading to the conviction and execution of some innocent people.
5. Capital punishment is imposed disproportionately on blacks and the poor.
6. Capital punishment is imposed in an arbitrary manner.
7. Many Americans would prefer "life without parole" over the death penalty if given the choice.
8. It costs more to execute than to imprison for life.
9. The mentally retarded, the insane, and children are executed; this is not right (see pp. 64–65).

Although public support for the death penalty is strong, the vast majority of articles on the subject appearing in the professional criminological and legal literature are against it. The following represents a summary of the common arguments used by abolitionists.

1. Executions by the state are morally repugnant to some individuals and groups; they feel that life is sacred and not to be taken by man. They also note that the biblical admonition "Thou shalt not kill" applies to the state as well as to the individual.

2. Many abolitionists believe the death penalty should not be applied because of its finality. Once carried out, there is no way to reverse its effects if a mistake was made and an innocent person was executed. There is no doubt that mistakes are made, and there are a number of case studies to support this argument. Bedau and Radelet (1987) maintained that, of the thousands of persons sentenced to death in the United States from 1900 to 1985, 350 were erroneously convicted. Of these, 23 were executed, and 21 others narrowly won reprieves. The Death Penalty Information Center (2000c) has identified 87 persons who have been released from death row since 1973, once evidence of their innocence emerged. The DPIC further estimates that for every 100 inmates under death sentences, 1 is innocent (1997, 2000). Some common reasons found in these studies are shown in Figure 3.10 and in Table 3.3.

3. Abolitionists argue that the death penalty has a **brutalizing effect;** that is, it may cause an increase in the number of murders because it reinforces violence (Bowers & Pierce, 1980). The research on the deterrent effects of capital punishment provides no consistent evidence for this position (e.g., Peterson & Bailey, 1988, 1991). Peterson and Bailey (1998) found "no consistent evidence that the availability of capital punishment, number of executions, the amount nor type of television coverage received by executions were significantly associated with rates for total and different types of felony murder" (p. 388).

In a 1994 study of the impact of the reinstatement of capital punishment in Oklahoma, Cochran, Chamlin and Seth found "no evidence that Oklahoma's reintroduction of execution produced a significant decrease in the level of criminal homicides during the period under investigation." Moreover, their results suggested that the reintroduction of

Table 3.3

Reasons for Increased Risk of Error in Capital Cases

General Reasons
1. Overall expansion of the death penalty
2. More political now

Investigation
1. Pressure on police/prosecutors to "solve" murders
2. Lack of eyewitness testimony
3. Limited resources of the defense attorney

Trial (Very Risky)
1. Factors that increase the likelihood of conviction:
   a. Publicity-influenced juries
   b. Death-qualified juries more likely to convict and in error
   c. Fear of death
   d. Heinousness of death penalty cases
2. Factors that decrease the likelihood of conviction
   a. More thorough representation
   b. A more careful review of the case on appeal

Plea Bargaining and Dismissal
1. Guilty pleas by innocent defendants
2. Failure to dismiss charges against innocent defendants

Sources: Adapted from R. Dieter (1997). *Innocence and the Death Penalty: The Increasing Danger of Executing the Innocent.* Washington, DC: The Death Penalty Information Center; S. R. Gross (1966). The risk of death: Why erroneous convictions in capital cases. *Buffalo Law Review,* 44(2), 469–500.

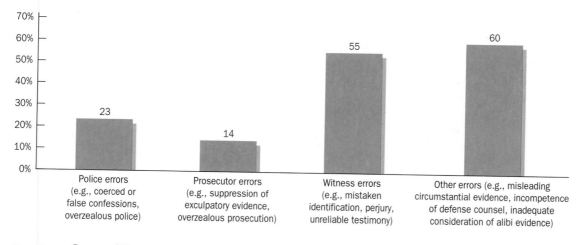

Figure 3.10 *Causes of Erroneous Convictions*

Source: H. A. Bedau and M. L. Radelet (1987). Miscarriages of justice in potentially capital cases. *Stanford Law Review, 40,* 21.

The Death Penalty Brings Justice

IN THEIR OWN WORDS

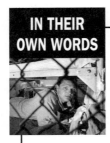

by Governor George E. Pataki

On March 7, 1995, I fulfilled a major campaign promise and signed legislation reinstating the death penalty in New York. For eighteen years, the Legislature—the people's voice—overwhelmingly supported capital punishment. For eighteen years, New Yorkers' demands were thwarted by gubernatorial veto.

Under this legislation, those who murder a police officer, a probation, parole, court or corrections officer, a judge, a witness or member of a witness' family are subject to the death penalty. Someone who murders while already serving life in prison or while escaping from prison, or who murders while committing other serious felonies also is eligible. Contract killers, serial murderers, those who torture their victims or those who have murdered before can also be sentenced to death.

In determining whether juries should impose the death penalty on anyone convicted of first-degree murder, the bill expressly authorizes them to hear and consider additional evidence whenever the murder was committed as part of an act of terrorism or committed by someone with two or more prior serious felony convictions. This is an important step toward ensuring that the law is applied to criminals who commit crimes such as two-time convicted killer Thomas Grasso, the World Trade Center bombers, or Colin Ferguson of the Long Island Railroad massacre. This law is balanced to safeguard defendants' rights while ensuring that the state of New York has a fully credible and enforceable death penalty statute.

The most important characteristic of government is the service and protection of its members from enemies, both foreign and domestic. In the United States, government is an instrument of the people. Therefore, legislation must reflect the will of those who entrust representatives to create the laws of society. In New York, the overwhelming majority of voters demanded the death penalty.

The relationship between a government and its people is referred to as a social contract. The notion of a social contract dates back to when our ancestors first started to live in groups, but became a formal political theory with Thomas Hobbes. The concept is simple. We relinquish a little bit of our autonomy in exchange for safety, security and a sense of community for the greater good. Hobbes proclaimed that, without this arrangement, life would be "poor, nasty, brutish and short."

As societies developed, governments were created, and the people in the United States created the government to enforce the rules they had established. These rules, or laws, protect us and give a sense of safety that allows us to be concerned with more than survival. Those who kill violate the most sacred of understandings that we as a society embrace. With this violation comes the legitimate demand on our government to provide justice for wrongs committed against us. The death penalty is society's way of telling its members that when you commit a crime as horrendous as murder, you are not fit to live among us.

The death penalty will not bring back the victims of violent crime, but I am confident that it will act as a deterrent of crime and it will save lives. Those who disagree only need to look to the account of the August 1977 riot at Eastern Correctional Facility, where correctional officers being held hostage overheard inmates deciding against executing the hostages because, at the time, it was a capital offense. The deterrent saved lives. Without the death penalty as a tool for jurists, a murderer can kill again without consequence.

Another flawed position held by death penalty opponents is that once a criminal is behind bars he or she no longer is a threat to society. Consider the case of Corey Jackson, an inmate who was serving a 25-years-to-life sentence for a 1994 homicide. On May 9, 1996, he was convicted of executing three teens, on a drug dealer's orders, and was sentenced to three more life sentences. While awaiting transfer to a state prison from the Brooklyn House of Detention, Jackson slashed a handyman at that facility, Robert Manning, in the face with a razor. The attack on Manning left him with 60 stitches and a permanent scar. Manning was lucky to escape with his life. What makes this case even more disturbing is the fact that Manning sat on the jury that found Jackson guilty of the teen murders, and after Jackson's savage attack on Robert Manning, he yelled "You thought I couldn't get you, but I got you." It is evident that Jackson has no regard for the rules of our society.

For too many years Americans have lived in fear of crime. This New York law alone will not stop crime, but it is an important step in the right direction. The citizens of New York have spoken loudly and clearly in their call for justice for those who commit the most serious of crimes by depriving other citizens of their lives. New Yorkers are convinced that the death penalty will deter these vicious crimes. I agree, and as their governor, I acted accordingly.

George E. Pataki is the governor of the State of New York.

Source: Corrections Today, *August 1996. Reprinted with permission of the American Correctional Association, Lanham, MD.*

Protesters demonstrate against the impending execution of Mumia Abu-Jamal, who was convicted of killing a Philadelphia police officer in 1981. Opinions on capital punishment vary widely, ranging from full support to total opposition.

capital punishment produced a brutalizing effect in situations in which the perpetrator's perceived sense of being wronged was enhanced (e.g., an argument precipitated a stranger's homicide). This situation "weakens socially based inhibitions against the use of lethal force to settle disputes. [This] allows the offender to kill strangers who threaten the offender's sense of self or honor" (p. 129).

Finally, as a result of the 1972 Supreme Court decision in *Furman v. Georgia*, more than 600 death row inmates across the country had their sentences commuted to life imprisonment. Marquart and Sorenson (1988) found that the executions of the 47 Texas inmates whose sentences were commuted by *Furman* would not have greatly protected society, as they were no more dangerous than other inmates.

4. Another issue involves the constitutionality of the death penalty when the competence of the attorneys defending the accused is questionable. Failure to fully present available evidence has resulted in death sentences for individuals who have either been potentially innocent, not guilty by reason of insanity, or guilty of a lesser crime. Our Close-Up, "Indigents Don't Usually Get the 'Dream Team' in Capital Cases," examines this problem.

5. A major issue surrounding the death penalty is its biased application; that is, it appears to be employed in a racially and class-biased, and, arguably, gender-discriminatory manner. Historically, more than 50 percent of those executed between 1930 and 1967 in the United States were black (U.S. Department of Justice, 1978). More recently, blacks constituted 43 percent of those on death row, compared with whites, who constituted 55 percent of death row inmates (NAACP, 2000; Snell, 1999). Blacks' representation on death row is still disproportionate to their representation in the general population (12%) and to their representation among death-eligible homicide offenders. Although blatant racism was the norm in the application of the death penalty until the middle of the 20th century, since 1976, the issue of its discriminatory imposition has largely shifted to the race of the victim. Statistics show that 52 percent of white victims are killed by other whites, while blacks commit about 24 percent of these murders (NAACP, 2000). With few exceptions, blacks on death row are there for killing a white, even though homicide is largely an intraracial crime.

State	Race of Victim Disparities	Race of Defendant Disparities
Alabama	✓	✓
Arizona	✓	
Arkansas	✓	✓
California	✓	
Colorado	✓	
Connecticut	✓	
Delaware	✓	
Florida	✓	✓
Georgia	✓	
Idaho*		
Illinois	✓	
Indiana	✓	
Kansas**		
Kentucky	✓	✓
Louisiana	✓	
Maryland	✓	✓
Mississippi	✓	✓
Missouri	✓	
Montana*		

State	Race of Victim Disparities	Race of Defendant Disparities
Nebraska	✓	
Nevada		
New Hampshire**		
New Jersey	✓	✓
New Mexico		
New York**		
North Carolina	✓	
Ohio	✓	
Oklahoma	✓	✓
Oregon		
Pennsylvania	✓	
South Carolina	✓	
South Dakota		
Tennessee	✓	✓
Texas	✓	✓
Utah*		
Virginia	✓	
Washington	✓	✓
Wyoming*		

Figure 3.11 *Data on Racial Discrimination in Death Penalty States*

*No death race data are available.

**No death sentences imposed as January 1, 1998.

Only studies whose results were statistically significant, or where the ratio between death sentencing (or prosecutors charging) rates (e.g., between white victim and black victim cases) was 1.5 or larger and with a sample size of at least 10 cases in each group, were included. The disparities in nine states (CA, CO, GA, KY, MS, NJ, NC, PA, and SC) are based on well-controlled studies. The results in other states are from less well-controlled studies and are only suggestive.

All of the race of victim disparities except in Delaware were in the direction of more death sentences in white victim cases.

All of the race of defendants disparities except two (Florida and Tennessee) were in the direction of more death sentences for blacks.

Source: Death Penalty Information Center (1998, June). *The Death Penalty in Black and White: Who Lives, Who Dies, Who Decides—New Studies on Racism in Capital Punishment.* Washington, DC: Author. Adapted with permission of the Death Penalty Information Center.

Twenty-three of 28 studies conducted between 1976 and 1990 indicated that murderers who killed whites were more likely to be sentenced to death than those who killed blacks (General Accounting Office, 1990a; see Figure 3.5). Further, many of these studies showed that black defendants were more likely than whites to get the death penalty. These data suggest that black victims' lives may be less valued than those of whites and that discrimination still results in the proportionately high percentage of blacks receiving the death penalty. This argument is further underscored by an American Bar Association report that examines disparities in both the race of the victim and the defendants (see Figure 3.11; Baldus & Woodworth, 1998). However, despite a pattern of racial bias in death penalty sentencing, the Supreme Court ruled in *McCleskey v. Kemp* (1987) that only evidence of racial bias particular to the case at hand was relevant.

Finally, racially biased prosecutors who are able to seek the death penalty represent another way that racism can influence the application of the death penalty. The Death Penalty Information Center (1998, June) found that, although race is not supposed to be a factor that influences the prosecutor's decision to seek the death penalty, for black defendants it is the most important one. Research by Baldus and Williams (1971, 1997) found support for this view in 75 percent of the states with death row inmates. In 93 percent of these states, race of victim disparities were found; offenders with white victims were significantly more likely to receive the death penalty than those with black victims. In about half of these cases, the race of the defendant was a significant predictor of who received the death penalty. This may be due to the fact that 98 percent of the prosecutors who sought the death penalty were white, whereas black and Hispanic prosecutors each made up 1 percent (DPIC, 1998).

6. Because a very small number of those charged with murder actually are sentenced to death, its use is seen as arbitrary by critics. Although 8,564 offenders are convicted of murder annually, only 4.3 percent receive the death penalty; 31 percent are sentenced to life in prison (Brown, Langan, & Levin, 1999). Findings in a three-state survey appear to support the position that its application is arbitrary. The survey found that 80 percent of respondents agreed strongly with the statement "the death penalty is too arbitrary because some people are executed and others go to prison" (Bowers, 1993, p. 166).

7. Many abolitionists favor a life without parole (LWOP) sentence, a relatively new innovation available in 37 states and the federal government, as an alternative to a death sentence or a regular life sen-

Convicted by a Jury, Exonerated by DNA: The Kirk Bloodsworth Case

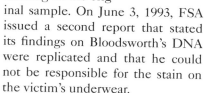

CLOSE-UP

Factual Background

On July 25, 1984, a 9-year-old girl was found dead in a wooded area. She had been beaten with a rock, sexually assaulted, and strangled. Kirk Bloodsworth was convicted on March 8, 1985, of sexual assault, rape, and first-degree murder. A Baltimore County judge sentenced Bloodsworth to death.

Prosecutor's Evidence

The prosecution based its case on several points:

- An anonymous caller tipped police that Bloodsworth had been seen with the girl earlier in the day.
- A witness identified Bloodsworth from a police sketch compiled by five witnesses.
- The five witnesses testified that they had seen Bloodsworth with the little girl.
- Bloodsworth had told acquaintances he had done something "terrible" that day that would affect his marriage.
- In his first police interrogation, Bloodsworth mentioned a "bloody rock," even though no weapons were known of at the time.
- Testimony was given that a shoe impression found near the victim's body was made by a shoe that matched Bloodsworth's size.

Postconviction Challenges

In 1986 Bloodsworth's attorney filed an appeal contending the following: Bloodsworth mentioned the bloody rock because the police had one on the table next to him while they interrogated him; the terrible thing mentioned to friends was that he had failed to buy his wife a taco salad as he had promised; and police withheld information from defense attorneys regarding the possibility of another suspect.

The Maryland Court of Appeals overturned Bloodsworth's conviction in July 1986 because of the withheld information. He was retried, and a jury convicted him a second time. This time Bloodsworth was sentenced to two consecutive life terms.

After an appeal of the second conviction was denied, Bloodsworth's lawyer moved to have the evidence released for more sophisticated testing than was available at the time of trial. The prosecution agreed, and in April 1992, the victim's panties and shorts, a stick found near the murder scene, reference blood samples from Bloodsworth and the victim, and an autopsy slide were sent to Forensic Science Associates (FSA) for Polymerase Chain Reaction (PCR) testing.

DNA Results

The FSA report, issued on May 17, 1993, stated that semen on the autopsy slide was insufficient for testing. It also stated that a small semen stain had been found on the panties. The report indicated that "the majority of DNA associated with the epithelial fraction* had the same genotype as the semen. . . . It was an expected result, according to the report." Finally, the report concluded that Bloodsworth's DNA did not match any of the evidence received for testing. FSA did, however, request a fresh sample of Bloodsworth's blood for retesting in accord with questions about proper labeling on the original sample. On June 3, 1993, FSA issued a second report that stated its findings on Bloodsworth's DNA were replicated and that he could not be responsible for the stain on the victim's underwear.

Conclusion

On June 25, 1993, the FBI conducted its own test of the evidence and obtained the same results as FSA. In Maryland, new evidence can be presented no later than one year after the final appeal. Prosecutors joined a petition with Bloodsworth's attorneys to grant him a pardon. A Baltimore County circuit judge ordered Bloodsworth released from prison on June 28, 1993. Maryland's governor pardoned Bloodsworth in December 1993. Bloodsworth served almost 9 years of the second sentence, including 2 years on death row.

Epithelial tissue covers most internal surfaces and organs of the body, as well as the outer surfaces. Before conducting DNA testing on sperm this tissue is removed.
Source: E. Connors, T. Lundregan, N. Miller, & T. McEwen (1996). Convicted by Juries, Exonerated by Science: Case Studies in the Use of DNA Evidence to Establish Innocence After Trial. *Washington, DC: U.S. Department Justice, Office of Justice Programs, National Institute of Justice.*

tence with the possibility of parole (DPIC, 2000e). Of the 37 states that offer LWOP, 33 (as well as the federal government) also have the death penalty (DPIC, 2000e). This sentence can be used to incapacitate career criminals.

A Gallop Poll released in February 2000 found that although a majority of Americans still favored the death penalty, support was dropping; 66 percent favored the death penalty, down from a high of 75 percent in 1981. However, when offered the alternative

CLOSE-UP

Indigents Don't Usually Get the "Dream Team" in Capital Cases

The world watched in awe as the expert defense and strategies employed by O. J. Simpson's "dream team" of lawyers in the 1995 double murder case won him an acquittal. Although there has been public debate about his guilt in the case, few would deny that if a poor man with no resources, represented by an overworked public defender, had been tried for the same case he probably would have been found guilty.

Unless you have money, the legal representation you receive may be underpaid; be unable to afford a thorough investigation, expert witnesses, and research; and lack the skills and even the interest to defend you in court. Yet, for those facing the death penalty, most of whom are either poor, uneducated, mentally retarded, or mentally ill, that is the risk they face.

Stephen Bright, director of the Southern Center for Human Rights, notes that you get "the death sentence not for the worst crime, but for the worst lawyer" (Bright, 1994). He provides several examples. In the case of George McFarland, tried for capital murder in Houston, his defense attorney, John Benn, could

not stay awake during his trial. Asked what the problem was, 72-year-old Benn said it (the trial) was boring. Benn is not the only Houston defense lawyer to fall asleep during a defendant's fight for life; Joe Frank Cannon dozed during the trials of at least 2 of his clients who subsequently received the death penalty (10 of his past clients have been sent to death row). Despite appeals for new trials, the Texas Court of Criminal Appeals decided the constitutional right of counsel was being met, whether or not the attorney was asleep (Bright, 1997a).

Exzavious Gibson, during a habeas corpus appeal from his conviction and death penalty, faced the court without a lawyer. When the judge asked him if he wanted to proceed, he told the court he did not have an attorney. "The state was represented by an assistant Attorney General who specialized in capital habeas corpus cases" (Bright, 1997a). With an I.Q. of about 80, and no training in court procedures, Gibson was not able to adequately represent himself. He offered no evidence, questioned no witnesses, and never made an objection. He lost his appeal.

In the case of James Messer, his court-appointed defense lawyer

gave no opening statement, presented no evidence or defense case, raised no objections, and then "emphasized the horror of the crime in some brief closing remarks." Although there was much evidence to present, he had not taken the trouble to do so. During the closing remarks, "he repeatedly hinted that death was the most appropriate punishment for his own client," who was later executed (Bright, 1997a).

Appointed defense lawyers are typically paid little, sometimes not even enough to pay the overhead on their offense. In fact, court-appointed attorneys are paid less than attorneys doing any other kind of legal work. In many states there is a limit, as well. For example, in Alabama, defense attorneys are paid only $20 an hour for out-of-court time in capital cases, with a limit of $1,000 per case. In many southern states, private practice attorneys, many of whom do not normally practice criminal law, are used to represent defendants facing death.

How do you feel about the fact that individuals who are tried for a capital crime may receive less than adequate legal representation? Should this be a constitutional basis for an appeal?

---

of LWOP, support for the death penalty dropped to 52 percent. Also, 91 percent of respondents said they believed that at least one innocent person had been executed in the previous 20 years (DPIC, 2000f).

The LWOP sentence seems to ensure that offenders will remain in prison for the rest of their lives (Cheatwood, 1996). However, there are loopholes that might result in the release of these inmates. LWOP statutes are usually written to exclude common methods of release such as parole and expiration of sentence due to the accumulation of good-time credit. However, sometimes placement in a work release program or being released on home fur-

loughs can permit access to the community. With the exception of Washington, no state forbids all of these forms of release (Cheatwood, 1988).

These LWOP statutes rarely address whether governors, through executive clemency, can pardon LWOP inmates. Executive clemency may be the only way governors can deal with two unpleasant realities; the increasing number of lifers who tend not to have more serious prior adult convictions and substantially more preprison drug use and the increasing health costs for aging inmates—25 percent require almost round-the-clock care and 95 percent require medication (Cheatwood, 1996).

8. There is also evidence that LWOP is more cost effective than execution because of the high cost of capital trials and the cost of appeals, which can run into the millions of dollars. Research done at Duke University found that it costs North Carolina taxpayers $163,000 more, on average, to try, convict, and execute a murderer than it does to keep him or her in prison for life (Cook & Slawson, 1993). Studies in various states have found the cost from arrest to execution ranges between $1.6 and $3.2 million (Costanzo, 1997). Another study found that the elimination of the death penalty in California would save the state "at least several tens of millions of dollars annually," and that local governments would save "in the millions to tens of millions of dollars on a statewide basis" (DPIC, 2000f).

There are several reasons for the higher cost of capital trials, including more time for pretrial preparation and jury selection, bifurcated capital trials, ap-

A strong argument against the death penalty is that its effects cannot be reversed if it is later discovered that an innocent person was executed. Shown here is Rubin "Hurricane" Carter, a former middleweight boxer who spent 19 years in prison wrongly accused of murder. Carter came close to being on death row.

peals, and the cost of the execution itself (Costanzo, 1997). Interestingly, with the exception of the appellate process, the process of death-qualifying juries is the number 1 factor in making capital cases more expensive (Garey, 1985; Kaplan, 1983). (For a synopsis of the death qualification process, see the Juries section in this chapter, pp. 55–56.)

Organized Opposition   Several major organizations have expressed opposition to the death penalty in different ways. The American Medical Association has opposed any physician participation in executions, including their presence and pronouncement of death. This is primarily because of their oath to "preserve life when there is hope of doing so." In reality, however, doctors have continued to be involved in executions, and most states that impose capital punishment require a physician to be present. This has spurred ethical debate within the medical profession (The American College of Physicians et al., 1994).

The American Bar Association at its meeting in 1997 passed a resolution that called upon jurisdictions with capital punishment "to refrain from its use until greater fairness and due process are assured" (Harris, 1997, p. 2). Although not taking a position on the death penalty, the ABA invokes previously adopted policies (e.g., reducing the risk that innocent people may be executed).

There are, of course, many other national organizations that have declared their opposition to the death penalty, including the American Civil Liberties Union, the National Coalition to Abolish the Death Penalty, and the NAACP Legal Defense and Educational Fund.

Amnesty International (AI) (1989a; 1998) is the most well-known international organization that has pursued a continuing fight to abolish executions. AI argues that fundamental human rights, including the right to life, are protected by the United Nations' Universal Declaration of Human Rights, which limits what a state may do to a human being. AI asserts that "no matter what reason a government gives for executing prisoners and what method of execution is used, the death penalty cannot be separated from the issue of human rights" (p. 1).

In 1998, 53 percent of the countries in the world had abolished the death penalty by law, or by not using it (AI, 1999; see Figure 3.12). Further, of the Western, or industrialized, countries, only the United States retains capital punishment. Abolitionists question why, of the more socially advanced countries of the world, only we continue to execute people. In 1997, a UN monitor, Bacre Waly Ndiaye, visited the United States to monitor the use of the death penalty. Ndiaye commented that, after China, where he estimates that 60 percent of crimes are now death-eligible, the United States has done more than any other society to expand the use of the death penalty (Crossette, 1997).

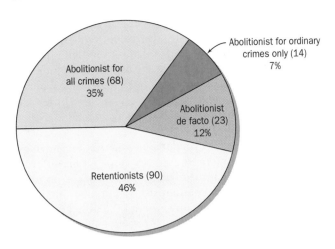

Figure 3.12   *Number of Countries That Abolished the Death Penalty*

Source: Amnesty International–USA (1999, April 1). "Abolitionist and Retentionist Countries." Washington, DC: Author. (www.amnestyusa.org/abolish/abret.html)

Participants in the Death Penalty Process

Participants in the process include both those outside and inside of death row. These include the sentencing judge, the defense counsel, juries, the victims, the family of the condemned, the governor, the condemned, the death row staff, and the media.

Judges and the Politics of Death

Politics and the death penalty have become intertwined. Judges have come under increasing pressure to impose capital punishment. Some feel that unless an elected judge is willing to take a strong pro–death penalty stance, remaining on the bench is unlikely. This is illustrated in our Close-Up, "Killing for Votes."

Defense Counsel

Calvin Burdine, 46, on trial for the stabbing death of his roommate, had his murder conviction thrown out because his lawyer allegedly slept during long segments of his 1984 trial. The prosecution failed to meet the 120-day limit set by the trial judge for giving Burdine a new trial, so a U.S. district judge ordered him set free. (Stack, 2000, March 2)

Poor people accused of capital crimes are often defended by lawyers who lack the skills, resources, and commitment to handle serious cases. In these cases, it is not the facts of the crime but the quality of legal representation that often determines which cases will result in the imposition of the death penalty. A Georgia Board of Pardons and Paroles member contended that if the

files of 100 cases punished by death and 100 punished by life were shuffled, it would be impossible to sort them out by sentence based upon information in the files about the crime and the offender. (Bright, 1994)

The basic reason most capital defendants receive inadequate representation at trial and on appeal is because of poor public funding for theses cases. For example, Alabama limits compensation for out-of-court preparation to $20 per hour up to a limit of $1,000; in Kentucky, the limit is $2,500. Yet, it takes an average of 500 hours to prepare for a capital trial, making it difficult to find attorneys willing to take these cases. In other cases, it is too expensive for some counties to pay the defense costs of trying a capital case. The Louisiana Supreme Court solved this problem by creating a "presumption of incompetence of counsel" under which the state in death penalty cases must be able to prove at the pretrial hearing that counsel for the defense is "competent" or the judge will not let the prosecution go forward until the defendant is provided with reasonably effective counsel. This idea has not been adopted widely. In other jurisdictions:

> A poor person facing the death penalty may be assigned an attorney who has little or no experience in the defense of capital or even serious criminal cases, one reluctant or unwilling to defend him, one with little or no empathy or understanding of the accused or his particular plight, one with little or no knowledge of criminal or capital punishment law, or one with no understanding of the need to document and present mitigating circumstances. (Bright, 1994, pp. 1845–1846)

In practice the mirror test is too often the one used to determine adequate counsel, as explained by the vice president of the Georgia trial lawyers association. "You put a mirror under the court-appointed lawyer's nose, and if the mirror clouds up, that's adequate counsel" (as cited by Bright, 1994, p. 1852).

This situation is not a consequence of a lack of money but of the failure of the political system to recognize the need for not only paying prosecutors but also defense counsel. The defense also requires adequate funds to hire expert witnesses.

As inadequate as defense counsel can be at trial, the situation can worsen during the postconviction process. Here, there is no obligation for states to provide counsel. Even if the defendant is represented by a lawyer during the appeals process, the attorney may have "little or no appellate experience, no knowledge of capital punishment law, and little or no incentive or inclination to provide vigorous advocacy" (Bright, 1997, p. 1848). One judge in Georgia appointed a lawyer newly admitted to the bar, with five days of experience, to handle the appeal of a capital case. With this kind of representation, defendants under a death sentence have little chance to

Killing for Votes

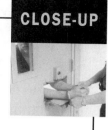

In Mississippi, Supreme Court Justice James Robertson was removed from office following a recall election in 1992 in which his opponent attacked Robertson's decisions in death penalty cases. Robertson was even criticized for ruling that executions were not permitted for the crime of rape, a position directly mandated by U.S. Supreme Court rulings. Nevertheless, Robertson was opposed by the Mississippi Prosecutors Association and was voted off the court. One example of the patently false advertising directed against Justice Robertson read:

"Vote against Robertson because he's opposed to the death penalty, and *he wants to let all these people go.*"

In Texas, Judge Charles Campbell was voted off the Texas Court of Criminal Appeals in 1994 following the reversal of a highly publicized capital murder case. Judge Campbell had served on the bench for 12 years and previously had been a conservative prosecutor. He was succeeded by Stephen Mansfield, who misrepresented his own qualifications, had been fined for practicing law without a license, and had virtually no criminal law experience. But he promised to uphold more death sentences. Judge Mansfield is now among the judges responsible for reviewing every death penalty case that comes before the court. *Source: R. Dieter (1996).* Killing for Votes: The Dangers of Politicizing the Death Penalty Process. *Washington, DC: Death Penalty Information Center.*

---

rectify the errors made by their trial counsel. One solution to this problem used in states, such as Florida, is to establish a centralized, truly independent capital defender office staffed by experienced capital trial counsel.

The role of counsel during the appeals process is to re-examine the evidence presented at trial, or to find new evidence that may not have been presented at trial as a result of it being withheld by prosecutors or because there was insufficient investigation to uncover it. Counsel also needs to assess whether there were any prosecutorial or judicial errors (e.g., inadequate jury instructions). This process requires the preparation of appeals on the state and federal levels, a long and time-consuming process.

During the last days leading up to the execution, good attorneys look for reasons why the execution should be stayed to present to both federal and state courts and to the governor. To file these motions, attorney(s) must travel to the location of the appropriate federal and state appeals courts; this requires funding. With only one attorney, which is often the case in the appellate process, it is extremely difficult to file all these motions and at the same time try to plead with the governor for clemency. Even the Supreme Court appoints one of its members on a rotating basis to be available just before an execution to review a motion for a stay of execution.

Finally, a good attorney is often at the prison during the hours before execution, if not otherwise occupied working for a stay, to console the inmate's family and to be present at the execution to provide support for his or her client.

Juries

Juries play a role in determining whether inmates are to be sentenced to death. In some states, the jury recommends a sentence to the judge, who decides whether to take the recommendation. In other states, the jury's decision is binding on the court.

Death qualification of jurors is the process of pre-qualifying jurors by having them answer questions about their attitudes toward capital punishment. Research has shown that the death qualification process tends to bias jurors against the defendant, thus making them more likely to impose a death sentence (see Haney, 1984 for a more comprehensive discussion). In *Witherspoon v. Illinois* (1968), the Supreme Court ruled that expressing a general anti–death penalty sentiment was not a valid reason for removing a potential juror from the pool.

In Texas, the deciding factor between life and death is essentially assessing whether the offender is likely to commit further criminal acts of violence, thereby becoming a continuing threat to society. One study of Texas sentencing looked at two groups: prisoners sentenced to death whose sentences were later commuted or reversed, and inmates who had committed capital murder, but who were sentenced by juries (who had the choice between life and death) to life in prison. In Texas, juries are asked to predict the potential for violence of the defendant being sentenced. The study concluded "that jurors err in the direction of predicting future dangerousness, i.e., they predicted that the defendant would be violent when in fact he/she was not" (Marquart, Ekland-Olson, & Sorenson, 1989, p. 486).

During the penalty phase, some jurors consider in their deliberations both **aggravating factors** (e.g., commission of murder during a felony, multiple victims) that made the crime more heinous and **mitigating factors** (e.g., no prior criminal record, offender is a juvenile) that might demonstrate that imposition of the death sentence is unwarranted.

Another juror issue involves the extent to which they understand the instructions judges give them prior to their deliberations. Research has suggested that juror comprehension is substantially limited and varies widely depending on the legal issue being examined. One study found that less than 13 percent of the Texas jurors studied were able to paraphrase, in their own words, the court's instruction in a technically accurate fashion (Steele & Thornburg, 1988).

Frank and Applegate (1998) conducted a more recent study of jurors' understanding of sentencing instructions. They divided their sample of 258 prospective jurors into two groups. Both groups viewed a videotape that contained facts of an actual homicide case followed by sentencing instructions given by the judge. Both groups received the same questionnaire, which contained items asking the subjects to (1) evaluate whether a hypothetical juror in the scenario had acted in accordance with the law and (2) note whether various statements were consistent with the law, and, if not, to choose the correct statement. The two distinctions upon which the groups were compared included (1) whether they received a written copy of the instructions and (2) whether the instructions were written in laypersons' or legal terms. Overall, juror comprehension of the sentencing instructions was low, with the prospective jurors answering less than 60 percent of the items correctly. Further, the highest comprehension level was among those who had received written instructions. Their results suggested that both written instructions and instructions written in laypersons' terms had a significant influence on jurors' understanding of sentencing instructions.

Victims Known as *Survivors*

Victims known as *survivors,* those who survived a crime when other(s) did not, and family members and friends of deceased victims are understandably stressed by the often lengthy court procedures, delays, and media exposure to what they suffered, during the time preceding an execution. In the past, victims have often been largely forgotten by the system. Many have been traumatized by finding out important news of their cases from reporters or the television. With the increased sensitivity to victims' needs, states have provided *victim advocates* to help lessen the stress for victims. Victim advocates console, inform, and spend time with the victims; they explain the process, find community resources for them, and attend important meetings and hearings with survivors (Zelenka, 1993).

The next of kin of the victim also have the right to make a statement at the sentencing hearing. An example of a state's policy on victim impact evidence establishes:

> Once the prosecution has provided evidence of the existence of one or more aggravating circumstances as described in subsection (5), the prosecution may introduce, and subsequently argue, victim impact evidence. Such evidence shall be designed to demonstrate the victim's uniqueness as an individual human being and the resultant loss to the community's members by the victim's death. Characterizations and opinions about the crime, the defendant, and the appropriate sentence shall not be permitted as a part of victim impact evidence. (Florida Statute ss. 921.142, 1998)

The Family of the Condemned

Family members of the condemned suffer from prolonged grief often characterized by self-accusation, social isolation, and fear, among other emotions. One disturbing effect found in a study by Smykla (1987) is medical illnesses, including depression. Reactions of death row family members who attempt to hide their feelings sometimes resemble schizophrenia (Smykla, 1987).

The Governor

In fictional stories, the governor often steps in and grants clemency to the condemned man at the last minute. In real life, this rarely happens. In the early part of the 20th century, clemencies were granted in about 20 percent of capital cases, but in recent years, clemency has been seldom used. Between 1976 and 1999, only 41 inmates were granted clemency (DPIC, 2000e, Jan.). As in the case of elected judges, a governor's attitude toward the death penalty is often an important determinant in his or her election to office. The American public strongly favors capital punishment, and they generally support candidates who do the same (Dieter, 1996).

The Condemned

Daily life on death row is characterized largely by isolation—imposed by both the state and the inmate. The condemned are provided with the basic necessities to keep them alive but nothing else. The ongoing surveillance and close confinement preclude inmate privacy. Occasional callouts and mealtimes are the only contact the inmates have with one another. They may also interact during outdoor exercise time, but many opt not to go. The prison staff largely ignores death row inmates and many make their lives more miserable by imposing strict rules on visitation and subjecting them to body searches following visitations, despite the fact that no physical contact is permitted between inmates and their guests.

There are many implications of the routinized lifestyle and isolation that inmates are subjected to on death row. Because prisoners spend about 23 hours a day alone in their cells, many feel vulnerable to possible harm that staff members may inflict on them. Many also experience intense fear with their impending execution. Physical deterioration, depression, and other psychiatric disorders characterize some inmates who cannot deal with life on death row. Our Program Focus, "Making the Life of the Condemned More Humane," provides some alternatives to this dreary existence (Johnson, 1998).

Staff: Working on Death Row

Issues that need to be addressed by officials managing death row are similar to general population issues and include housing, personnel administration, custody and security procedures, orientation of new inmates, personal hygiene and property, records, food service, medical service, legal services and access to a law library, recreation, visitation, and counseling services (American Correctional Association, 1989).

Officers Working on death row is a stressful assignment that readily lends itself to indifferent and abusive treatment of the prisoners. The death row guard's role has been likened to that of an intrusive waiter and an unwanted escort. Relations between guards and inmates are frequently either hostile or impersonal. Tension as well as fear of violence affects officers and inmates alike.

Death row presents unique problems for both staff and the condemned. Inmates must cope with their impending death and the hopes and disappointments associated with their appeals. This creates intense stress and may result in acting out and even mental illness. For the staff, this creates an emotionally charged situation that can erupt into violence. They must deal with the problems these inmates face. The officers work under constant pressure. The prisoners, they believe, are violent men determined to escape. As one said, "They will hurt you to get away. You've got to watch them all the time. They'll kill you. They've all killed before." The fearful eventuality of being taken hostage preoccupies a number of officers.

Remarkably, some officers are able to suppress their fears and take a broader view of their jobs. These officers see themselves as correctional professionals who must go about their work in a civil and responsive but fundamentally businesslike way. They see themselves as figures of authority whose job it is to help the prisoner cope with the pains of imprisonment. These more responsive officers belief that their objective is to be a concerned professional who can "deal with them on a one-to-one basis but not get emotionally involved with them" (Johnson, 1998).

Death row officers are normally not involved in executions; the execution team is assembled from officers who have had little or no contact with the prisoner prior to the deathwatch. Nevertheless, prisoners tend to hold each and every officer accountable. "You can feel the tension in the air after an execution," observed one officer. "I think that they are angry at anybody with a (correctional) uniform."

Anger is not the only emotion to follow in the wake of an execution. Prisoners may also feel a sense of loss, a reinforcement of their own feelings of powerless and vulnerability, and a heightened recognition of the fate that may await them.

Some of the death row officers also feel a genuine sense of loss with the execution of a prisoner they have come to know and like. Others remain aloof, cognizant of the emotional hurt that involvement with prisoners would bring. "You can't be buddy-buddy," said one, "you've got to keep it business. This business is a matter of life and death, killing and dying."

One approach to helping those involved in the execution, is the pre-trauma prevention and post-trauma intervention programs put into effect at California San Quentin Prison more than 10 years ago. Its goal is to protect staff so that the only person who will not survive the execution is the condemned inmate. This pre-trauma strategy is designed to help those involved comprehend the post-trauma syndrome and its normal course of development (e.g., loss of appetite, nightmares). It is sort of a "stress inoculation" following the execution post-trauma phase, including an initial "critical incident debriefing." The team helps those experiencing post-trauma syndrome to cope with the stress until arrangements can be made for professional help. Three weeks later a psychological briefing is held for the execution team that deals with the delayed effects of the execution. Another session several weeks later is a psychological debriefing, which focuses on the strategies for stress management.

The warden supervises numerous activities related to an execution. Some wardens pray with inmates prior to their deaths, or arrange for a chaplain to do so.

Making the Life of the Condemned More Humane

Conventional correctional practice was based on the idea that death-sentenced inmates were dangerous offenders with little or nothing to lose. They were seen as extreme escape risks and assault risks to staff and other inmates. Thus, they were typically housed in separate areas of the prison known as "death rows." Whereas in the past, the time between the imposition and the execution of a capital sentence was measured in weeks or months, today it is measured in years. Moreover, the number of individuals sentenced to death has increased substantially. Some states provide alternatives to solitary confinement on death row: mainstreaming and work programs.

Mainstreaming Death Row Inmates

An early example of mainstreaming death-sentenced inmates into the general inmate population occurred under the leadership of Tom Murton at Tucker Prison Farm in Arkansas in 1968. Under Murton's leadership, death row inmates were fully integrated into the regular prison population over a 10-month period. However, the program was subsequently dismantled by the Arkansas Board of Corrections.

In 1989, Missouri began this practice. Prior to this, death-sentenced prisoners were housed in the state's major maximum security prison, which was constructed before 1900, on a "death row" completely segregated from the main prison population. Following a 1986 class action suit, the Department of Corrections entered into a consent decree that resulted in broad changes in the management of death row.

In April 1989, a new 500-bed maximum security facility was opened and the 70 death-sentenced inmates were transferred there. Using a revised classification system, which afforded inmates more privileges, inmates were housed in one of four levels: minimum custody, medium custody, close custody, and administrative segregation. Nevertheless, they remained completely isolated from the general population inmates.

Changes, which led to mainstreaming, began within a few months after these inmates filed a motion for contempt, challenging several conditions of their confinement. Staff were required to escort "capital punishment" (CP) inmates to the facility dining room for meals. Thereafter, CP inmates were permitted to visit the law library and the facility gym, and they were given work assignments in the prison laundry. Based on the successes of these and other changes, preparations were made to fully integrate CP inmates with the general population inmates. This was achieved by January 1991.

There were many benefits to integration. First, there was a significant monetary savings because several special posts and functions were eliminated, and staff positions could be reallocated. Second, there was a substantial reduction in legal expenses because CP inmates were afforded the same benefits that the general population received. This minimized litigation. Third, there was greater flexibility in the use of bed space at this facility.

Inmates benefited from these changes in many ways. Access to the law library and attorney visitation provided better opportunities for successful appeals. Recreation, visitation opportunities, and the commissary made life more bearable. Health care was improved. Equal work opportunities became available, and the difficulties of providing psychological services were minimized.

In general, the mainstream program provided the CP inmates with a web of incentives to conform with regulations and a "humanized" environment. Further, disciplinary actions, grievances, and inmate-on-inmate violence decreased, minimizing a number of difficulties for staff.

Although historically, isolating capital offenders on death row may have been warranted when there was a relatively short period of time between sentencing and imposition of the penalty, this is no longer the case. Liberalized mainstreaming programs of the past 15 years suggest that the integration of death-sentenced inmates into the general inmate population is an idea whose time has come.

Death Row Work Programs

Other states have given some inmates the opportunity to work while on death row.

The Texas Death Row Garment Factory opened on July 1, 1986. Initial training started with 6 men on each of the two shifts, gradually working up to a full force of 100 men (50 on each shift). Since most of the them had never operated a sewing machine before, we commenced sewing items such as sheets, pillowcases, napkins, and cook caps for departmental use along with diapers and aprons for contract sales. By 1989, while still maintaining a 100-man death row workforce, the operation was expanded to include a separate garment factory on the back side of the unit, which was manned by the general population. In late 1990, the mission was changed, and they retooled for the production of officer's gray pants. All remaining production items were moved to other garment facilities within the system and to enable the death row factory to produce all the officer's gray pants needed within the system.

In subsequent years, as the warehouse stock of pants was large enough to meet demand, the factory expanded to produce a lumbar support belt for officers, specialty bookbags for school-children, and a high-visibility safety vest for highway workers. Over its years of operation, the factory grew from 5,000 to 10,000 square feet.

In its $11\frac{1}{2}$ years of operation, the Death Row Garment Factory has risen from an average of 100 inmates working per day to 134. During this period, 95 percent of the inmates turned out for work each day, with the remaining 5 percent absent due to visits, medical, interviews, and short-term bench warrants. This factory has trained 430 inmates, 90 of whom have been executed, and 45 of whom have left death row for various reasons (released, life sentence, time, etc.). From the beginning participation in the Death Row Work Capable Program has been voluntary, with men coming in and out of the program regularly due to personal, legal, and medical reasons, as well as the ever present possibility of bench warrants. Further, an additional 35 to 40 death row inmates have worked on the housing unit in support jobs such as porters and barbers. Finally, the production of officer uniform pants at this facility resulted in a savings of $500,000.00 yearly since the system did not have to purchase the items from the outside.

This, like any other program, reduced idle time and resulted in a more manageable population on Texas' death row. Violent instances at the factory were minimal (less than five in almost twelve years) which was substantially less than other factories staffed by the general population inmates. None of these involved tools used as weapons or resulted in any injuries. Tools (scissors, clippers, tweezers, rulers, and cutting machines) are checked out to inmates by his number at the start of the shift, and returned at the completion of the shift. No tools were ever lost.

Death row inmates worked voluntarily in this program despite the fact that they received no rewards like salary or good-time credit. While each inmate had his own personal reasons for working in the factory, they generally fit into three categories. First, with time spent on death row averaging $8\frac{1}{2}$ years, some just want to keep busy doing something other than sleeping, eating, or playing basketball. Working a four hour shift does not take up that much of the day, and besides, the plant is air-conditioned in the summer, which contributes to a positive work attitude. Secondly, some work for the limited privileges that being a work-capable inmate brings which included additional work time in a climate-controlled environment, visitation in a less restrictive environment, permission to go to the commissary, meals served on hot carts (allowing inmates to prepare his own tray and choice of eating in cell or day room), relaxed recreation and shower schedules, out-of-cell time each day with relaxed security measures like not being handcuffed while on the wing and when being transported to and from visitation, the commissary, and medical. Lastly, some inmates work just to prove to themselves, and others, that they still have some socially redeeming value as human beings. If the inmate's case was to be overturned, their work record while in the program could be used as evidence that imposing another death sentence is unnecessary, and that the inmate can function in the general population just as well while serving their sentence.

Of course, there are any number of combinations of these three areas, but at the very root of their reasoning is the fact that "they can," and have done so very successfully for over $11\frac{1}{2}$ years. There seems to be no evidence that this feeling will change during the coming years as new inmates enter the program.

In conclusion, Tony D'Cuna (1999) Special Programs Manager at Texas Correctional Industries provides the following assessment and update on this factory:

In my visits to this facility, a sense of self-esteem, pride in workmanship, a conducive work environment, a chance to be away from the "row," having a work ethic and relief from the monotony were some of the reasons I heard from Death Row individuals at our factory. Overall, the atmosphere in this factory was always relaxed and resembled any other of our facilities.

[In December 1998, due to a high-profile escape by a death row inmate working in maintenance, not in the factory, the Texas Board of Criminal Justice decided to temporarily suspend the Death Row Work Program. As of March 2000, the Board had not decided whether to reinstate it. This factory is currently staffed by the general population inmates.]

Do you think death row inmates should be allowed to work in industry and other work programs? Why or why not?

Sources: Adapted from G. Lombardi, R. D. Sluder, and D. Wallace (1997, June). Mainstreaming death-sentenced inmates: The Missouri experience and its legal significance. Federal Probation, 61(2), 3–10; and from material specially prepared for this text by Tony D'Cuna (1999), Special Programs Manager, Texas Correctional Industries.

A Warden's Reflection on the Execution Process

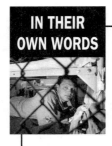

Connie Evans should have meant no more to me than any other condemned prisoner on "the row," as inmates and staff call death row, but it was not that way. In the course of almost four years, during my many visits as warden to death row, we had developed something of a relationship. Getting to know him had been a rewarding experience, and our communications with each other was something I believed we both genuinely looked forward to. Now it was all rapidly coming to an end, as the time arrived for me to give the order that would put him to death.

. . . With the appointed execution time of one minute past midnight just seconds away, I knocked on the metal door twice. The lock turned and the door swiftly swung open. Chaplain Padgett and I somberly escorted Connie Ray Evans the final few feet from the last-night cell to the execution chamber. Entering the room, the condemned man exchanged a few words with several of the officers, his voice still clear and natural.

. . . [T]he officers swiftly immobilized Evans's head with the harness and chinstrap that protruded from the headrest. I silently prayed for a quick and painless death for my prisoner, and a process free of mechanical failure or human error for me. There were so many things that could go wrong.

. . . Despite being immobilized from head to toe, Connie Evans was visibly shaking. His face was etched in fear, and his large, dark brown eyes moved rapidly from side to side, trying to comprehend what was happening. The chaplain stepped into the chamber to exchange some last words with him. Feeling helpless and out of place, I marveled at the calm with which Connie had walked the steps taking him to his fate, something like the feelings experienced by the terminally ill. I had reflected often on such a scenario, concluding that if I faced the executioner I would either slip into unconsciousness out of absolute terror, or have to be dragged, kicking and screaming, to my death.

. . . When Childs and Barry Parker left the gas chamber, Connie asked how much longer we had to wait. Still lost in thought, I collected myself and gently recited the explanation I had offered earlier. I had to await a telephone call from the attorney general. He would either clear the way to proceed with the execution or notify me that a reprieve had been granted. It was a sobering explanation to be sure, but I wanted no secrets, no misunderstandings between us. Connie had a right to know everything that was going to happen, and I had a responsibility to be honest and forthright with him. At that late hour no one, least of all my prisoner, expected any legal relief. Although we both knew that courts had granted many last-minute stays of execution, Connie Ray Evans had run out of legal arguments. At a few minutes past midnight, after six years on Mississippi's death row, he would also run out of time.

. . . I ordered the curtains screening the gas chamber to be opened. The telephone rang almost immediately in the witness room as Dwight Presley relayed my order (though not my anger) to Steve Puckett. Even before Presley hung up, the curtains opened quickly, and the witnesses stared at the sight of the prisoner already strapped in the chair.

. . . Standing in front of the observation window that occupied the right side of the chamber, I haltingly held up two fingers for Connie to see, indicating it would be a few minutes yet before his life would be extinguished.

How long the final minutes would be for both of us! I turned to speak to one of the physicians, but I was interrupted by the shrill ring of the red telephone on the wall behind me. The sound came without warning, and it instantly drowned out all other noise in the room. Instinctively, I spun around to the observation window of the gas chamber. Our eyes met and locked in an embrace of fear and anticipation that only a warden and his condemned prisoner could understand.

. . . The telephone was still ringing, but somehow it sounded far away. Feeling a tugging at my shoulder, I turned to see Dwight Presley motioning for me to take the phone from him. I stepped away, as if I could somehow postpone the inevitable by not answering. Finally, I took a deep breath and slowly lifted the phone to my ear. . . .

. . . At last, on an oppressively hot, muggy July night in the flat emptiness that is the Mississippi Delta, the time had arrived to exact justice from Connie Ray Evans. Handing the telephone to someone behind me, I knew that I had nothing left to say to my prisoner. Our eyes had never strayed from each other, and my expression conveyed the message—there would be no reprieve this night. I slowly shook my head, and Connie closed his eyes. A lone tear streamed down his cheek.

Although this was to be my second execution in less than two months, there was no way I could have prepared myself for the difficult task of sending a young man whom I had grown to know and like to his death. In the nearly four years since our first meeting, I had concluded on numerous occasions that I would gladly swap Connie Ray Evans's date with the gas chamber with that of any one of dozens of other prisoners—not all of them on death row.

. . . Staring blankly into the witness room, I felt dulled by the terrible reality that was now upon me. The witnesses, too, had been interrupted by the sudden ringing of the telephone in the execution room. They were waiting—waiting for my order to kill another human being. Stepping into the chamber, I felt the hair on the back of my neck stand up. Positioning myself directly in front of my prisoner, fumbling with the death warrant in shaking hands, I slowly began to read the document. In a quivering, staccato voice, I read for what seemed an eternity. Gazing into Connie's eyes, I stumbled through the closing chapter of this bizarre ritual, asking him if he wished to make a final public statement. His eyes welled with tears now, and I was struck by his childlike appearance. This was not the same cold-blooded murderer who had arrived on death row six years before. His tears were not just those of a young man fearful of what lay beyond death's door; I was convinced they were also tears of genuine sorrow and pain for the tragic hurt and sadness he had caused so many people.

. . . Try as I might, I was unable to tear my eyes from his. He gazed up at me, as if in shock. His eyes were wet, with a glassy appearance that conveyed a chilling acceptance of his impending death. Connie spoke quietly, haltingly. He wanted to whisper his final words to me privately, he said, and I leaned down so I could hear him. He thanked me for being his friend. I started to speak, but he asked me to wait, and then told me softly, "From one Christian to another, I love you." I wanted to respond, but no words would come. Now I was the one in shock, shaken to my very soul. We had talked so much in the final weeks and days, our conversations always relaxed and easy; yet now, when it seemed most important, I was at a complete loss for words. What does one say to a man who has told his executioner that he loves him? The question hurtled through my mind, seeking answers that were not there. In the weeks since the most recent execution, I had slept with troubled dreams, fitfully trying to make sense of the whole thing. Looking at the man in front of me, I wondered if I would ever sleep peacefully again. I reached down and placed my hand on Connie's arm, gently squeezing for what seemed a very long time. As I stood up and prepared to leave him, for some mysterious reason I felt as if all my tensions had dissipated. The fear inside me released its icy grip, and I knew that I would fulfill my responsibilities. Connie had indeed forgiven me.

Quickly turning around and stepping out of the chamber, I ordered it sealed, even while realizing that some of my self remained inside. There is a part of the warden that dies with his prisoner. Nobody else can suffer the intimacy of impending death, or experience the pitiable helplessness involved, in the same way as the warden and his condemned prisoner.

. . . Executions strip away the veneer of life for both warden and prisoner. Connie Ray Evans and I transcended our environment, and the roles in which we had been cast. The two of us had somehow managed to become real people to each other. There were no more titles or social barriers behind which either of us could hide—I was no longer a prison warden, and he had become someone other than a condemned prisoner. We were just two ordinary human beings caught up in a vortex of events that neither of us could control.

. . . The moment had arrived and could be delayed no longer. I looked into the chamber, my attention again focused on the chair. An old inmate who had escaped its clutches years before, when his death sentence was commuted, once referred to it as the "black death." How appropriate a name, I thought. My eyes shifted quickly to the lever. The executioner's hand was gripping it firmly, ready to drop its deadly cargo.

. . . Prepared to utter the words that would execute Connie Ray Evans, I looked into his eyes, drawn by the need for one last glimpse of him alive. Our eyes met for the final time. How, I asked aloud, had we traveled such different paths, only to be brought together in the dark confines of Mississippi's death row? *Source: Donald A. Cabana, (1996). Death at Midnight: The Confession of an Executioner. Boston: Northeastern University Press. Copyright © 1996 by Donald A. Cabana. Reprinted with permission of Northeastern University Press.*

Preparing the Condemned for Execution

IN THEIR OWN WORDS

The execution process is just that, a process leading to the conclusion of a person's life by execution. Along this difficult path, the condemned offender has many years to live with the consequences that led him or her to death row. During these years of introspection, offenders are exposed to religious programming from both the unit chaplains and volunteers. The chaplains work with the death row offender by the same means that they try to touch other offenders, including prayer, Bible study, religious services, and spiritual counseling.

Although the unit chaplains approach their duty to death row offenders with the same fervor as they do regular offenders, the condemned have unique spiritual needs and considerations. Many death row offenders, both male and female, must deal with their crime, while also dealing with what led them to enact the crime. Some offenders project that anger onto the unit chaplain, as that chaplain is an employee of the system. Therefore, unit chaplains utilize volunteers and spiritual advisors in conjunction with their own council as a means to minister.

The death row chaplain tries, by whatever means available, to be of service to the offender. When Chaplain Athey at the Ellis Unit receives a notice of execution date, he begins to pray, often including the approximately twenty volunteers and their affiliated churches. As the date for the execution grows nearer, the chaplain tries to prepare the offender for death, whether she or he has professed a belief in God or not. As the execution approaches, more and more effort is made to provide for the offender's needs (e.g., frequent pastoral visits, contact with attorneys and family). With the offender's permission, the chaplain also holds special prayer sessions, communion or other pastoral events.

About two weeks before a scheduled execution, the death row chaplain begins to make daily contact with the two other chaplains. They try to convey the emotional state of the offender, along with the well-being and concerns of the family. The death row chaplain has made special efforts to meet with the offender family away from the condemned in order to respond to the families' unique needs and concerns. Often, the family has issues to deal with regarding their own emotions over the forthcoming execution.

In Huntsville, Chaplain Brazzil prepares for the last day by staying in touch with the warden and staff on the Huntsville unit. He is careful to meet any needs the staff may have at this time. He is also in contact with the regional chaplain, Alex Taylor, in the office of the Director of Chaplains for any developments with the offender's family and witnesses coming for the execution.

The evening before the execution, Chaplain Brazzil uses the time to prepare himself for the upcoming emotional event. He spends time in prayer both that night and the next morning. When he arrives at the unit, he reviews the packet of information with background data on the offender, security issues, and witness information. He also spends time with the security personnel that will be involved in the process.

After an early lunch, Chaplain Brazzil takes his Bible and information packet back to the death house to await the arrival of the condemned. He makes a point to be there before the offender arrives, so that he can speak immediately to him upon entry.

The offender is taken into the death house and strip-searched, fingerprinted, and then contained in a holding cell. Generally, this is the only activity throughout the afternoon. The chaplain and two guards remain in the cell. Chaplain Brazzil utilizes this time to develop a rapport, allowing a deeper ministry during the last few critical hours.

This recognizes the emotionally charged nature of officially sanctioned death and provides a means for those involved to deal with it (Vasquez, 1993).

The Warden

Although the warden's specific duties in the execution process vary, they are generally consistent and include a wide range of activities. Prior to the execution, the warden supervises the execution team in the preparation and "practice" of the upcoming execution. She or he may also select the witnesses to the execution. As the inmate nears death, the warden spends a lot of time answering his questions and addressing his concerns. Such issues range from attire to "How much longer?" Some wardens even pray with the inmates prior to their deaths. Wardens also follow the inmate through his ritual to and from the last night cell and into the death chamber. During the execution, the warden is the overseer. She or he takes the phone call from the attorney general, either giving the go-ahead or the message that a reprieve was granted. Once the order to continue has been given, the warden reads the death warrant to the inmate and then gives the signal to the executioner to proceed. After the execution, the warden must deal with the media. This means that if there was a mechanical or

Near 3:00 P.M., the offender's spiritual advisor arrives for a thirty-minute visit. At this time Chaplain Brazzil joins the witness support liaison and together they visit the offender's family at the Hospitality House, or sometimes a local motel as necessary for the convenience of the family. They try to prepare the family of the offender for the events they will experience over the next several hours. The liaison chaplain stays with the family and later accompanies them to the viewing room, staying with them during the execution and then returning with them to the Hospitality House afterward for prayer, sharing, and closure with the family members.

At approximately 4:00 P.M., Chaplain Brazzil returns to the unit, remaining by the side of the offender for the remainder of time, including the last meal and the last telephone calls to family who are not in attendance. The offender is offered a shower and change of clothes, if desired. Next, they discuss the execution procedure, and the chaplain assists the offender with the preparation of any final statements.

Tension mounts at this point, usually allowing the opportunity for prayer, communion, confessions or any other needs. This time is unstructured and led by the offender.

When the Warden arrives to announce it is time for the final stage, the offender is escorted into the death chamber and strapped onto the gurney. Once the offender is secure, the officers leave and the medical team arrives to start the IV solutions in both arms. Chaplain Brazzil makes a point to talk with the offender to distract him or her from the process, allowing the offender to talk as desired. The chaplain uses touch to reassure the condemned person that he will be there through each step. As witnesses are brought in, they continue to talk or pray. Usually near 6:00 P.M., everyone is assembled and the procedure begins. Chaplain Brazzil remains beside the offender until the execution is complete. [Keep in mind that the actual time frames and procedure vary by state and method of execution.]

After the offender is pronounced dead, several activities happen simultaneously. The witnesses are escorted back to the Hospitality House. Chaplain Brazzil gives the family any possessions and last thoughts from the offender. A chaplain liaison then "debriefs" the family, allowing Chaplain Brazzil to return to the unit to gauge the staff's response. Another TDCJ chaplain and a psychologist debriefs the victim's family, aiding them with closure in their lives. This debriefing takes place within the walls of the TDCJ facility. At no time is there contact between the offender and victim witnesses.

In the aftermath of an execution, the role of the chaplain is still an ongoing process. If the body is not claimed, Chaplain Brazzil buries the offender in the Joe Byrd Memorial Cemetery in Huntsville, Texas.

Other members of the Witness Support Liaison Team continue to offer assistance to both the families of the executed and the victim. Usually, this follow-up ministry involves varied roles, such as aiding with information as to how to obtain a death certificate, or guiding them to other sources for assistance either in the legalistic or pastoral realm. The liaison also follows up by calling the victim's and the executed offender's family periodically, sending letters and cards, and offering emotional support.

This system, involving many years of ministry to the condemned on the unit, transferring the process to the Huntsville Unit for the final day, and providing council to both the victims and condemned families is a system that is still evolving. The intent is to provide the best possible assistance and support in the worst possible circumstances.

Source: Prepared by Chaplains Atley and Brazzil (1999) especially for the 2nd edition of Corrections: A Comprehensive View. *Chaplaincy Programs, Texas Department of Criminal Justice.*

human error that caused the execution to go awry, the warden must deal with the aftermath. The feature In Their Own Words, "A Warden's Reflection on the Execution Process," describes one warden's experience with carrying out an execution.

The Chaplain

Chaplains minister to the needs of inmates on death row, which include working with inmate families and assisting inmates in making final decisions before their execution (e.g., disposal of personal property and trust fund money). They may also help them deal with the pain and myriad emotions they may experience during their last day (Marble, 1988). Our feature In Their Own Words, "Preparing the Condemned for Execution," provides the views of two chaplains on the execution process.

The Media

One issue prison officials must deal with during the execution process is how to handle the media. There can be massive media interest, especially in a high-profile execution. Decisions must be made regarding whether or not cameras will be allowed onto prison grounds, whether live broadcasts from prison grounds will be allowed, whether an area or building will be offered to accommodate the media, and how media representatives will be chosen to witness the execution. Security is the biggest concern, though some argue that if reporters, journalists, photographers, producers, engineers, and all their heavy equipment, cables, and trucks are not allowed on prison grounds, security issues would be best served. Further, officials could do without the additional burdens of handling a media frenzy. Others, including Tipton Kindel of the California Department of Corrections, argue that "In the end, we decided the public interest would be served best by the widest news coverage possible" (Kindel, 1993).

Women, Juveniles, and the Mentally Retarded on Death Row

This section takes a look at three smaller populations on death row. It also examines the issue of mental competency and execution.

Women on Death Row

Three percent of all prisoners executed since the colonial period have been women (Streib, 1999). Although relatively rare, the number of women on death row is increasing. Eleven percent of murder arrestees in 1998 were women, and 2 percent of them received the death penalty (AIUSA, 2000a; FBI, 1999). As of March 2000, there were 47 women on death row, about 1.3 percent (or 1 in 77) of the death row population. They accounted for about 0.1 percent of the approximately 50,000 women imprisoned in the United States (DPIC, 2000a; NAACP, 2000; Streib, 1999).

From 1973 through March 2000, 126 death sentences were imposed on women; 4 were executed, and 76 had their sentences reversed or commuted to life imprisonment. The four executions constituted approximately 0.6 percent of all executions since 1976, when executions resumed in the United States. Of the four executions, one took place in 1984 (Velma Barfield in North Carolina), two in 1998 (Karla Faye Tucker in Texas and Judy Buenoano in Florida), and one in February 2000 (Betty Lou Beets in Texas) (DPIC, 2000a). Women are unlikely to be arrested for murder, even less likely to be sentenced to death, and almost never executed. Our Close-Up, "Karla Faye Tucker: A Tale of Two Women," details a 1998 high-profile case.

Executing Juveniles

The United States has executed more juveniles than any other nation in the world. In 1989, the Supreme Court ruled in *Thompson v. Oklahoma* that the execution of juveniles under 16 at the time of the offense is cruel and unusual punishment and therefore unconstitutional. The Court offered two reasons for its decision. First, executing juveniles would be contrary to societal standards of decency, because no state that has considered a minimum age included youths under 16. Second, executing youths for crimes committed when they were under 16 "represents no more than purposeless and needless imposition of pain and suffering." Thus, this would be inconsistent with the retributive purpose of the death penalty, because, due to their immaturity, juveniles are not held to the same level of culpability as adults when committing crimes. Twelve states have a minimum age of 16 for the imposition of the death penalty, 4 others set 17 as the minimum, and 15 require a minimum age of 18 (AIUSA, 2000; DPIC, 2000). Between 1976 and March 2000, seven states[3] carried out 16 executions of juveniles; all were under 18 at the time they committed their crimes (AIUSA, 2000; DPIC, 2000g).

With the increase in violent crime by juveniles in recent years, many have called for increasingly severe punishment, including the death penalty. Eighteen percent of those arrested for murder are juveniles, but only 2 percent of death sentences handed out are to juveniles. As of March 2000, 70 juveniles, all male, were on death row. Juveniles represent 2 percent of the death row population and 2.6 percent of those executed (NAACP, 2000). The reversal rate of juvenile execution is 88 percent, which also suggests that the execution of a juvenile is a rare event.

Executing juveniles appears to be all but abandoned internationally, because almost all nations except the United States are signatories to the UN covenant on the Rights of the Child, which expressly forbids the execution or life imprisonment without parole for juveniles who were under 18 at the time they committed a crime. Nevertheless, between 1985 and 1997, 23 juveniles were executed abroad. Known executions of minors during this period were carried out in Bangladesh, Iran, Iraq, Nigeria, Pakistan, Saudi Arabia, and Yemen (Streib 1998; Amnesty International, 1998).

The Mentally Retarded on Death Row

Executing the mentally retarded has been a controversial issue. The problem, in part, is finding a consensus as to what constitutes mental retardation. The American Association on Mental Retardation defines it, in part, as "substantial limitations in present functioning . . . characterized by significantly subaverage intellectual functioning, existing concurrently with related limitations in two or more [defined areas]." Through testing, an individual can be assessed and a score assigned for each of several areas of intellectual functioning. The outcome results in the assignment of a "mental age," which yields a comparison between the offender's level of functioning and a "normal" level of functioning for individuals that age.

Karla Faye Tucker: A Tale of Two Women

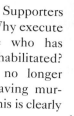

CLOSE-UP

On February 3, 1998, pickax murderer Karla Faye Tucker became the first woman to be executed in Texas since the Civil War. Fifteen years earlier, after becoming angry at a workman, Tucker and her boyfriend decided to break into the man's apartment to steal motorcycle parts. While there, they killed the workman and a woman with him. Tucker was an out-of-control, violent, thieving drug-addict. She had been addicted to drugs since she was 8 years old; she had been sexually active since 11 or 12, and she had later prostituted herself. Tucker admitted she was strung out on numerous drugs and boasted, just after the killings, that she had experienced a surge of sexual pleasure every time she swung the 3-foot pickax (Verhovek, 1998a).

Flash forward to 1998. Karla Faye Tucker sits in prison awaiting death. In a lengthy letter to Governor Bush, Tucker repents and requests commutation. She writes:

When I did give my heart to Jesus and repent for what I had done, that night and all of my life from the time I knew right from wrong, my whole outlook on life radically changed. I no longer was influenced by peer pressure or a need for acceptance. In my trial I did plead not guilty to capital murder. If I had it to do all over again I would not do it the same way. . . . I am asking you to commute my sentence and allow me to pay society back by helping others and helping to prevent crimes and suicides. I can't bring back the lives I took. But I can, if I am allowed, now help save lives. That is the only real restitution I can give, and I am willing to do that in any way someone may ask it of me. If you believe that executing me is the only answer and the only solution, then I will accept that. But if, by some small chance, you believe I can actually help others keep from doing what I did, by me sharing Jesus with them and sharing about what I did and what my choices led to, then I am asking you to please commute my sentence to life and give me a chance to help you in making a difference in our society. (Tucker, 1998, pp. 6, 10)

She is not the same woman who entered prison 15 years earlier. The gentle, soft-spoken young woman is a born-again Christian, no longer high on narcotics, and seemingly reformed. Supporters asked, Why execute someone who has been rehabilitated? This is no longer a stark-raving murderer—this is clearly a loving woman, who would no longer be a threat to society. Cynics commented that it is easier to execute a scary-looking ugly man than it is to execute a lovely young woman, but would that not be gender discrimination? Others claimed, "They all find Christ in prison."

Toward the end, Tucker accepted her fate calmly, professing a faith that would carry her to Heaven. Hundreds of reporters, supporters with anti–death penalty placards, and death penalty advocates converged at the prison on the day of her execution. When her completed execution was announced, "a loud cheer went up from the crowd" (Verhovek, 1998b).

Should society allow no room for the rehabilitation of those on death row? Is it fair to condemn a youthful inmate, and execute him or her 15 years later, when time has honed the individual into someone very different? Do you think Karla Faye Tucker should have been executed?

Many defenses have presented the argument that because an inmate functions at the mental age of a 12-year-old (for example), his or her sentence should correspond with that of a 12-year-old under similar circumstances. The Supreme Court disagreed, upholding the executions of the mentally retarded in ***Penry v. Lynaugh*** (1989). It reasoned that, "there is not full equivalence between a child and a mentally disabled adult" (Streib, 1996). As of March 2000, 34 offenders with mental retardation had been executed since 1977 (DPIC, 2000f). Only 12 states[4] forbid execution of the mentally retarded.

Competency to Be Executed

The Supreme Court prohibited the execution of the insane in ***Ford v. Wainwright*** (1986). Even prior to this case, however, no state allowed the insane to be executed. Since the *Ford v. Wainwright* decision, several unresolved issues regarding the execution of the insane have emerged, including the legality of medicating-to-execute and the establishment of criteria for what constitutes insanity.

Medicating-to-execute, thus far, has typically involved the forcible prescription of antipsychotic drugs to make an offender competent enough to be executed. Although there has not been a U.S. Supreme Court ruling on the prescription of antipsychotic drugs specifically for the purpose of making an offender competent to be executed, the Court has ruled that the forced medical treatment of antipsychotic drugs may only occur when it is in the inmate's best medical interest (*Washington v. Harper*, 1990). The Louisiana State Supreme Court applied this ruling to Michael Owen Perry, a paranoid schizophrenic sentenced to death for the multiple murders of five family members (*Perry v. Louisiana*, 1992). Without antipsychotic drugs, Perry would remain incompetent to be executed for the rest of his life. The Court ruled that forcible medication for the purpose of punishment, not medical treatment, was unconstitutional. This is an issue that will likely reach the Supreme Court in the near future.

Several controversial cases have emerged in the past few decades that have raised the question, "What constitutes incompetent to be executed?" One such case is the "Unabomber," David Kaczynski.

When Attorney General Janet Reno decided to seek the death penalty for Kaczynski, who had been sought for close to 20 years for a series of bombings, many officials and legal ethicists, even some who supported capital punishment, objected. Many believed that Kaczynski, a former math professor, was insane. Although he refused psychiatric testing, former U.S. Attorney and death penalty advocate Joseph diGenova observed, "He may not be legally insane, but . . . no jury is ever going to give him the death penalty if they get a look at him." Complicating the controversy was the report that federal prosecutors promised Kacznyski's brother, who turned him in, that they would not seek the death penalty. Ultimately, a plea bargain was struck, and Kaczynski was sentenced to life without parole (Sniffen, 1998, p. 4).

Interestingly, in a somewhat similar case, Manuel ("Manny") Babbit was convicted and sentenced to death for the robbery-murder of an 87-year-old woman in California. Babbit appealed his death sentence based on the grounds that he suffered from post-traumatic stress disorder (PTSD), a consequence of his service in Vietnam. Despite numerous supporters and a purple heart for saving a life, the courts rejected his appeals, and Governor Davis refused to grant clemency. Babbit was executed on May 4, 1999. Although the issue here is insanity during the commission of the crime, the question is still raised, "What constitutes insanity?"

Summary

Following a de facto and a de jure decade-long moratorium, the death penalty was reinstated as a result of the 1976 *Gregg v. Georgia* decision. Since then, men and women have been executed by firing squad, electrocution, gas, and lethal injection, each of which has had its own "mishap" during an execution. Arguments for the death penalty are primarily related to retribution and proportionality of punishment, although some cite public opinion and deterrence, even though there is no scientific evidence to support the deterrence position. There are numerous anti–death penalty arguments, including its arbitrary application; its irrevocability, particularly with regard to executing the innocent; cost; and the fact that there are alternatives (e.g., life without parole) that are just as effective.

Judges, prosecutors, defense attorneys, and juries all play a unique role in the sentencing phase of a capital case. The victim's family and the family of the condemned are also deeply and personally affected by the death penalty, particularly when an execution is carried out. Additional participants in the execution process include the prison staff (e.g., the warden, the guards, the chaplain), the media, and the execution team, which is assembled just prior to an execution.

Death row comprises primarily adults, males, and a disproportionate number of blacks. Women are almost never executed, and the execution of juveniles is also relatively rare; although the United States has executed more juveniles than any other nation in the world. No one under 16 may be executed according to the 1989 Supreme Court decision *Thompson v. Oklahoma*. Executing individuals who are incompetent also raises several legal and ethical issues. To date, the Supreme Court has resolved them to the extent that it is unconstitutional to execute a special class of defendants with mental illnesses. It is not, however, unconstitutional to execute the mentally retarded, although juries must consider it when they make their sentencing decisions.

Critical Thinking Questions

1. Discuss the arguments for and against capital punishment.

2. The debate surrounding the death penalty involves both moral and legal issues. How do these issues overlap in public opinion polls? In what other aspects of arguments for and against capital punishment do the moral and legal issues coincide? How?

3. Numerous legal issues surround capital punishment, from prosecutorial discretion to charging the defendant with a capital offense to the execution itself. Place yourself in the following positions and describe your role with respect to a capital case: the trial prosecutor; the trial defense counsel; the trial judge; an appellate defense lawyer.

4. You are a juror in a capital case in which you now are deliberating the verdict. Place yourself in the position of both a juror that believes the defendant is innocent and one who believes he or she is guilty. Describe how you would handle each role. Also, discuss how you would handle the latter role during the penalty stage, in which you are given two alternatives: a death sentence or life without parole.

5. How would you feel about assuming the following roles that relate to post-trial supervision of and actual

execution of inmates sentenced to death: a CO on duty in death row; a chaplain; a warden; a member of the execution team; a governor.

6. How would you deal with the stress of being on death row if you were (1) innocent of charges or (2) guilty of charges that resulted in a death sentence?

Test Your Knowledge

1. With regard to the deterrence-brutalization research, what do the findings show?

   a. Support for the brutalization argument—executions generally lead to a higher homicide rate

   b. Support for the deterrence argument—executions generally lead to a lower homicide rate

   c. That executions and homicide rates are unrelated

   d. Mixed support for both deterrence and brutalization

2. Which Supreme Court case in 1972 abolished capital punishment, as it was then practiced?

   a. *Gregg v. Georgia*

   b. *Furman v. Georgia*

   c. *McCleskey v. Kemp*

   d. *Coker v. Georgia*

3. Which participant's role in the execution process includes giving the proceed order to the executioner?

   a. The attorney general

   b. The governor

   c. The warden

   d. The chaplain

4. In *Penry v. Lynaugh*, the Supreme Court upheld execution of:

   a. juveniles.

   b. the insane.

   c. the incompetent.

   d. the mentally retarded.

5. Post-*Furman* studies generally show:

   a. The incapacitation argument is accurate—those who should have been executed were indeed more dangerous than those sentenced to life.

   b. The incapacitation argument is not accurate—those who should have been executed were no more dangerous than those sentenced to life.

   c. Mixed support for the incapacitation argument—in some states *Furman*-commutees were more dangerous, whereas in others, lifers were more dangerous.

   d. The incapacitation argument is wrought with methodological errors. No conclusions may be drawn at this time.

Endnotes

1. See www.essential.org/dpic/dpicexecoo.html.

2. These states include Arizona, California, Idaho, Kentucky, Missouri, Montana, North Carolina, Ohio, South Carolina, Tennessee, Utah, Virginia, and Washington. New Hampshire, Idaho, Oklahoma, and Wyoming authorize another method (legal injection) if their primary method is found unconstitutional. On March 22, 2000, the Georgia legislature voted to make lethal injection the primary means of execution in that state; electrocution will be phased out (AIUSA-www.amnestyusa.org/abolish/methus.html; DPIC, 2000f).

3. The seven states were Georgia, Louisiana, Missouri, Oklahoma, South Carolina, Texas, and Virginia (DPIC, 2000f).

4. The 12 states are Arkansas, Colorado, Georgia, Indiana, Kansas, Kentucky, Maryland, Nebraska, New Mexico, New York (except for murder by prisoners), Tennessee, and Washington (DPIC, 2000f).

The Evolution of Punishment

LEARNING OBJECTIVES

After completing this chapter, you should be able to:

1. Differentiate between the early notions of public and private wrongs.

2. Describe the role of retaliation against offenders in early societies and how compensation developed as an alternative to blood feuds.

3. Give examples of some early forms of corporal punishment and public ridicule for criminal offenders.

4. Discuss the use of whipping as a punishment for criminal behavior, and identify and refute the arguments advanced to justify its continued use.

5. Discuss the use of capital punishment through the ages.

6. Describe the imposition of galley servitude as a punishment for crime.

7. Identify and discuss the role of bagnes in galley servitude and in the subsequent development of prisons.

8. Describe the early practices of banishment and transportation.

9. Compare the indenture system with slavery, and describe its use in the development of the American colonies in contrast to the system used in Australia.

10. Discuss the development of workhouses as forerunners of prisons.

KEY TERMS AND CONCEPTS

Amsterdam Workhouse	Maison de Force
Bagnes	Outlawry
Banishment	Pillories
Blood feud	Private wrongs
Branding	Public humiliation
Bridewell	Public wrongs
Bridles	Russian knout
Compensation	Spin House
Ducking stool	Stocks
Gags	Ticket of leave
Galleys	Transportation
Hospice of San Michele	Wergild
Hulks	Whipping
Lex talionis	Workhouses

Introduction

Before discussing the evolution of punishment, it is important to note that methods employed historically to punish offenders do not change abruptly (Spierenburg, 1991). Instead, they evolve gradually and unevenly, especially when comparing different countries. For long periods, capital punishment, dismemberment, and banishment were used to some degree followed by transportation and long-term imprisonment. Although many forms of punishment were eventually abandoned in most countries, some are still used in several parts of the world today.

Punishment of Early Criminal Behavior

Early groups had no written laws, but most had norms or customs that regulated behavior. In ancient times the power of control rested with the father as head of the basic social unit, the family. This authority was so absolute that it included the power of life and death. Clans and tribes had two classes of wrongful acts: *public wrongs* and *private wrongs*. The whole social group was obligated to take repressive action to control public wrongs, whereas individuals and blood relatives dealt with private wrongs (Wines, 1895).

Public Wrongs

Preliterate societies had six basic categories of **public wrongs,** crimes against society or the group: sacrilege and other offenses against religion, treason, witchcraft, incest and other sex offenses, poisoning, and violations of the hunting rules. Religious offenses were the most heinous because they were believed to expose not only offenders but the entire group to untold disasters because this angered their gods (Oppenheimer, 1913/1975). An offender might be hacked or stoned to death or suffer some equally gruesome punishment. Today, some religious offenses continue to be punished by extreme fundamentalist nations. In 1989, the Ayatollah Khomeini of Iran called for Muslims to execute Salman Rushdie, offering a reward which was recently raised to $2.5 million, because of statements in his book *The Satanic Verses* that were alleged to insult the Islamic prophet Muhammad. To survive, Rushdie was forced into hiding and continues to be protected by the British government (Pertman, 1997).

Incest was believed to offend the spirits and to bring disaster on the land. Witchcraft or sorcery was thought to involve the use of magical powers for individual revenge or advancement or to bring disaster to the group. Poisoning was seen as witchcraft because the effect of the drugs on the body was believed to involve the manipulation of supernatural powers. Treason usually involved rendering assistance to an enemy at war with the tribe (e.g., joining the opponent or revealing military secrets)

and sometimes included refusal to fight against an enemy. These violators were customarily executed. Even today, these actions are subject to severe punishment. Finally, those breaching the hunting and fishing rules (e.g., those guilty of frightening off the herd before the hunt could be executed) were punished by the group because of its need to protect sources of food (Oppenheimer, 1913/1975).

Private Wrongs

In primitive groups, private revenge was the only means victims had to deal with most **private wrongs**—cases of physical injury, property damage, or theft. Striking back was also a way to prevent future attacks on self and property. Of course, the original aggressor defended against a victim's retaliation by reattacking, thereby setting the stage for perpetual conflict (Schafer, 1976).

As tribal societies became more advanced, the responsibility for punishing major crimes shifted from individuals of different clans or tribes to the entire group. It was during this time that the **blood feud** developed, under which acts against one individual were viewed as acts against that person's entire kinship group and required the victim's family, tribe, or community to take action. Revenge was directed at restoring the balance of power between groups and was really a response to the perpetrator's group rather than to the injury suffered by the victim (Schafer, 1969). Blood feud retaliation was customarily carried out by *lex talionis,* the principle of an eye for an eye. This meant that if a man knocked out the tooth of someone of his own rank, the victim's kinship group was permitted to knock out his tooth. Several ancient codes, such as the Babylonian Code of Hammurabi (about 2500 B.C.) and the Indian Manama Dharma Astra, carefully regulated the extent of the revenge (Schafer, 1976). In Europe, between the Roman period and the start of the Middle Ages (the 5th to 11th centuries), society was composed largely of feuding families and tribes (Johnson, 1996; Schafer, 1976).

Since blood feuds could start a perpetual vendetta that made life perilous for both feuding clans, one widely used solution, though not universal, was the system of **compensation,** or **wergild.** Typically, tribes creating cities and towns adopted a compensation system that became an acceptable alternative to retaliation because payment subjected the criminal to humiliation and appeased the victim's desire for revenge. Even homicide could be atoned for by paying a fine in cattle and sheep (Schafer, 1977). The amount of reparations depended on such factors as the age, rank, sex, and influence of the victim. "A free man was worth more than a slave, a grown-up more than a child, a man more than a woman, and a person of rank more than a freeman" (Barnes, 1930/1972, p. 49).

This system ultimately led to the concept of **outlawry** (Schafer, 1977); those who would not or could not pay the necessary reparations were declared outlaws and ostracized by the group. Outlaws who did not escape could be killed or sold into slavery (Ives, 1914/1970). Only those criminals who paid their blood fines could remain in the community (Schafer, 1977).

The practice of granting sanctuary or protection to those accused of crimes, dating back to the time of Moses, was also an outgrowth of blood feud retaliation (Wines, 1895). Most countries had a city or a special building, such as a temple or a church, where the accused could flee and stay for a certain period until the alleged "wrong" could be resolved through mediation and concession. Until the 13th century, a criminal in England could claim refuge in a church for 40 days, after which he had to surrender or admit guilt and forfeit his property. Following this, he was afforded safe passage out of the realm (Ives, 1914/1970). This practice was abandoned in England by the mid-17th century.

When compensation replaced private revenge, disputes over the amount of payment were resolved at periodically held tribal assemblies. These assemblies were an example of early judicial proceedings. The growth of a central authority (e.g., a king) in the fifth and sixth centuries led to the first Anglo-Saxon laws known as "the dooms" in 601 to 604 to control violence. These laws provided evidence of the custom of the "king's peace," under which the king extended his protection to those in his presence and in the local area where he was currently staying. Those breaching the king's peace were fined in addition to paying the victim's compensation (Johnson, 1996; Oppenheimer, 1913/1975).

By the mid-14th century kings had gained absolute power and gradually extended their peace to more areas, and when they became strong enough they proclaimed the entire country under their control. With the development of a strong central authority, the definition of crime and its resolution was altered. Private wrongs became offenses against the king's peace, and breaches of public order and the compensation system changed. Eventually, all compensation went to the state. Viewed as acts against both the divine and temporal powers of the king, crime now represented an act of revolt against a king's omnipotence. Harsh punishments served multiple objectives: to deter those who might challenge the ruler's position; to control violent behavior; and to deter the rest of society. Criminals were subjected to corporal or capital punishment and sometimes both (i.e., torture preceded execution) (Barnes, 1930/1972; Johnson, 1996).

Historical Types of Punishment

From early times, the most common forms of punishment were exile, corporal punishment, capital punishment, and, less often, public ridicule. In some cases,

punishment may have been twofold (e.g., mutilation sometimes accompanied placement in the pillories).

Humiliation

Public humiliation, or shame, has been used as a punishment from primitive times to the present. In ancient Greece, army deserters were publicly displayed in women's clothes. In England during the Middle Ages, public humiliation was used to deal with fraud by merchants; for example, a baker selling short-weighted loaves of bread might be forced to walk through the streets with bread tied around his neck (Ives, 1914/1970).

Gags consisted of devices that were used to shame and constrain "scolds" who openly, habitually, and abusively found fault, unjustly criticized, or lied about others. A **bridle** was an iron cage that fit over the head and had a front plate that was sharpened or covered with spikes designed to fit into the mouth of the offender, making movement of the tongue very painful. Its more common use against women reflected sexist views of the volatility of women's words. In England, it was most commonly used until the late 1800s by husbands to keep their wives subservient (Andrews, 1899). In colonial America, it was employed against both sexes to control such behaviors as swearing and drunkenness (Newman, 1978).

The **ducking stool** was used as a punishment as early as the 11th century. Those sentenced to be "ducked" were placed on a chair and suspended over a body of water and plunged into it. This was customarily reserved for females who continually nagged and used abusive language (Earle, 1896/1969). In England, it was also used for brawlers, slanderers, prostitutes, quarrelsome married couples (tied back to back and ducked), wife beaters, male scolds, and sellers of bad beer or bread. Occasionally, offenders were dipped too often and died. The last ducking in England occurred in 1820 (Wilson, 1931). In pre-19th century America, its use was widespread in the colonies outside of New England (Earle, 1896/1969). During the 1800s it was used infrequently, and by the end of the century it was no longer employed (Andrews, 1899).

Stocks were used as outside jails to punish the idle prior to the construction of houses of correction in England. In Europe, from the Reformation until the 19th century, they were used for offenses such as swearing, Sabbath breaking, wife abuse, and petty forms of theft. In colonial America they were used for similar crimes. For example, a Boston carpenter hired to construct a set of stocks for the city in 1639 was confined in them for charging too much to build them (Wilson, 1931).

The use of **pillories** dates to the pre-Christian era. In England, they were commonly employed during the Tudor period, but their peak use was during the 17th

Stocks were a form of public humiliation used to punish a variety of offenses in Europe and colonial America.

century (Newman, 1978). Like stocks, pillories occupied a prominent place in English towns and villages and served to show offenders the community's disapproval while advertising their guilt. Pillories were used for a variety of offenses, ranging from blasphemy to treason, to pickpocketing and drunkenness. Some offenders were secured to them by having their ears nailed to the frame and released by having their ears cut off. While secured, they were defenseless against the missiles the crowd might throw (including stones), which could result in serious injury or death. Their use was abolished in the 1830s in both England and France (Earle, 1896/1969). In colonial America, the use of the pillory followed the same pattern as in England and continued until 1803. However, as the population of towns grew and the nature of social relationships became more impersonal, the stigmatizing power of this punishment declined. With the declining use of the pillory and stocks, the ancient practice of **branding** became the means, at least temporarily, for offenders to be identified and stigmatized.

Branding was employed primarily for making offenders, slaves, and prisoners of war recognizable. Offenders were typically branded on their thumb with a letter denoting their offense (e.g., "M" for murderer; "T" for thief). Hawthorne's 1850 book, *The Scarlet Letter*, immortalized the requirement in many American colonies that offenders wear letters sewn on their outer garments specifying their crimes. Another practice in both England and the American colonies was to require offenders to hang a paper around their necks or pinned to their chest describing their offenses.

New elements of branding are reflected in some contemporary penal policies. In the late 1980s, a county judge in Sarasota, Florida, ordered those she found guilty of drunk driving to put bumper stickers on their cars identifying themselves as drunk drivers. Moreover, the new sex offender registration legislation ("Megan's Law") resurrects the public exposure of identification of released sex offenders (see Chapter 21). The Internet is also a medium for publicizing offenders of certain crimes. Thus, today we have seen an evolution of the purpose of this punishment from humiliation to community protection. It is believed that the public will be better protected if the serious offenders are known in their communities.

Corporal Punishments

Until the end of the 18th century, corporal punishment represented the most universally employed method of punishing offenders (Barnes & Teeters, 1943). It was typically imposed in public as a means of setting an example for other potential offenders (deterrence), and it inflicted pain on the offender as well, serving a retributive function.

Whipping, also known as flogging or scourging, is one of the oldest, most widely employed means of corporal punishment, dating back to ancient Egyptian times. Its extensive use as a punishment has no equal. Although whipping was common in England before the 16th century, it was not until 1530 that the Whipping Act was passed to deter and punish those who were not productive members of society. This law ordered vagrants (men, women, or children) to be tied to the tail end of a cart, stripped naked, and beaten until their bodies were bloody as they were pulled through the town or village (Newman, 1978; Parry, 1934/1975). Many offenders subjected to this type of brutality died (Scott, 1938). Under Queen Elizabeth in 1597, the cart was replaced by the whipping post and offenders were only stripped to the waist.

The most extensive use of whipping occurred in Europe during a 300-year period that began in 1600 (Newman, 1978). Its demise in England began in the early 1800s with the abolition of flogging for women. Whipping men became less frequent and was carried out inside prisons. It was not until 1948 that it was abolished as a punishment for crimes. In Russia it was quite common for servants, serfs, workers, and even women of rank to be brought to police stations to be whipped. Russia also invented what Cooper (1870) called the "most formidable punisher ever devised," the **Russian knout.** This instrument was a wooden-handled whip that typically consisted of several rawhide thongs twisted together, terminating in a single strand that projected about 18 inches beyond the body of the knot. The strand sometimes had hooks or rings attached to the ends (Scott, 1938). To spare an offender a painful death, his family sometimes bribed the executioner to wield the knout like an axe and inflict the fatal blow on the first stroke (deLangy, 1854).

In the American colonies flogging and other forms of corporal punishment were as frequently employed as in England for such offenses as lying, swearing, perjury, selling rum to Indians, sleeping rather than attending church on the Sabbath, drunkenness, and stealing. These punishments were also used to preserve the virtue of young unmarried women (Earle, 1896/1969; Newman, 1978).

After the Revolution, imprisonment gradually replaced corporal and capital punishment. Pennsylvania abolished whipping in 1786, and in 1790 the federal government prohibited it, as well as the use of the pillory for federal offenses. Several states continued to use whipping during the 19th century, but by the 20th century only two states retained it (Sutherland, 1924). In Maryland, the last known flogging took place in 1949, while in Delaware it occurred in 1952, although the law was not repealed until 1972 (Rubin, 1973; Burns, 1975). The use of whipping in Delaware past the second half of the 20th century provided Caldwell (1947) with an opportunity to examine the arguments used to support flogging (see Table 4.1).

Amnesty International (AI) (1997) reports that whipping is still legal in at least 8 countries.[1] In Singapore, caning is a mandatory penalty for 20 crimes. In 1994, an 18-year-old American youth living in Singapore confessed to vandalizing several vehicles. He was sentenced to 4 months in prison and was given four lashes

Table 4.1

For and Against Whipping

Proponents	Opponents
Violent offenders must suffer pain.	Whipping puts a premium on violence and aligns the criminal against society.
Whipping is cheaper than imprisoning an offender.	Only the most hardened criminals were flogged and then were placed in prison.
Whipping reforms the offender.	The human being is too complex an organism to assume that so simple a thing as a lash will reform those seeking to adjust to the intricate play of biological, geographical, and social forces.
"Spare the rod, spoil the child."	This confuses childhood spanking within the context of a continuing, loving family unit valued by the child with an impersonal whipping by the criminal justice system.
Whipping prevents further criminal acts.	Studies conducted in Great Britain, Canada, and Delaware revealed that whipping has not reformed offenders. In Delaware 320 offenders were whipped between 1920 and 1939; by 1942 61.9% that had been whipped once were convicted of a subsequent offense, and 65.1% that had been whipped twice were convicted of another offense. In comparison, of the 516 offenders not whipped who could have been, during 1928, 1932, 1936, and 1940, only 52.3% were convicted of some offense before 1945.
Whipping is only effective when the lashes are laid on with sufficient force to make an impression on the offender.	Recidivism data on 106 offenders whipped by Warden Wilson, known to lay the lashes on "hard," showed that between 1935 and 1942, two thirds had subsequently recidivated by 1945 (45% committing a major crime).

Source: Compiled from R. G. Caldwell (1947). *Red Hannah*, Philadelphia: University of Pennsylvania Press.

with an inch-thick rattan cane (Shenon, 1994). In spite of the publicity describing the brutality of this punishment, a *USA Today* poll found that 53 percent of the American public favored whipping and other harsh punishments as deterrents to crime (Stone, 1994). In the Sudan many people, including women, are publicly flogged after summary trials (AI, 1997).

Capital Punishment

From ancient times to the present, execution has represented the most extreme reaction to criminal behavior in almost all societies. In many cultures, death was the most frequently used means to punish offenders. As communities developed, it seemed to provide the only definite means of ridding the community of troublesome and offensive characters, while at the same time satisfying the desire for vengeance. Additionally, it displayed the power of the rulers and what would happen to those who challenged their authority (Laurence, 1960).

Among the earliest recorded laws in ancient China, beheading was the prescribed method. The oldest recorded death sentence can be found in the Amherst papyri, which included an account of the trial of a state criminal in Egypt in 1500 B.C.; the condemned offender was found guilty of using "magic" and sentenced to death. In England, capital punishment emerged in about 450 B.C. (Laurence, 1960).

From the Norman Conquest in the 11th century through the 17th century, the death penalty was frequently combined with estate forfeiture, thereby impoverishing the offender's family. All felonies and high and petty treasons were capital crimes. From 1688 to 1820 the number of capital offenses in England soared from 50 to over 200. Many of these were implemented to protect property (Mackay, 1985). Early on, there were two ways to escape the death penalty. First, one could refuse to go to trial and be pressed to death by giant stones. This saved the family's property from forfeiture. Second, one could have the case transferred to an ecclesiastical court (benefit of clergy[2]), which could not impose the death penalty except in cases of heresy (Greek, 1992). Over time, crimes designated as "felonies without benefit of clergy" diminished.

During this era, the large number of capital crimes led England's criminal code to be called the "Bloody Code." However, the death sentence was not meted out to all individuals convicted of capital crimes, because it would have been socially and politically unacceptable, and this could have threatened public acceptance of

the law (Ekirch, 1987). Therefore, the courts circumvented the severity of these laws by using discretion in implementing the death sentence and *transportation* (discussed later in this chapter) to apportion sentences so as to achieve the proper mixture of deterrence and retribution.

Historically, methods of execution have been limited only by human imagination and ingenuity and have included flaying or burying alive, boiling in oil, crushing beneath the wheels of vehicles or feet of elephants, throwing to wild beasts, forcing combat in the arena, blowing from the mouth of a cannon, impaling, piercing with javelins, starving to death, poisoning, strangling, suffocating, drowning, shooting, beheading, and, more recently, electrocuting, using the gas chamber, and giving a lethal injection. The severity of the execution was often based on factors such as the social class of the offender and the degree to which the crime offended the ruling powers.

During the Middle Ages, an offender's death would often be preceded by excruciating torture, including drawing and quartering, being dragged to the gallows tied to the tail of a horse, having bellies slit open and entrails cut out, and being burned by the executioner (Laurence, 1960). The most widely used form of execution has been hanging, which has been used from ancient times to the present.

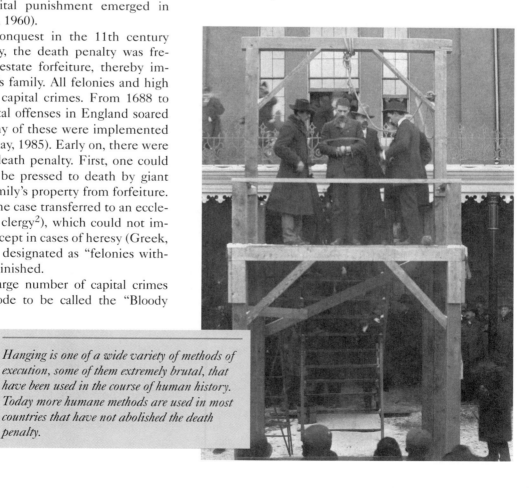

Hanging is one of a wide variety of methods of execution, some of them extremely brutal, that have been used in the course of human history. Today more humane methods are used in most countries that have not abolished the death penalty.

With the "progress" of humankind, there has been a demand for more humane methods of execution. The invention of the electric chair in the late 1800s was one such innovation. Today, as noted in Chapter 3, the death penalty has been abolished in law or in practice in 98 of the world's countries with only 95 retaining it (AI, 1997).

Banishment

Banishment was an acceptable alternative to the death penalty because it had the same effect of ridding the community of the offender (Wines, 1895). Among the oldest forms of punishment, **banishment** has historically included both temporary and permanent exclusion from the community and enslavement or exile of offenders to a penal colony (Oppenheimer, 1913/1975).

The practice of outlawry dates back to the fourth century in England. Outlaws were men and women who either fled from justice (failed to appear in court to face the charges against them) or had been banished to the wilderness, which became their "penal colony" (Ives, 1914/1970). Their property was forfeited to the king, they could be killed by anyone, and their children were also viewed as outlaws. They could only return to the community by securing a royal pardon (Bellamy, 1973). During medieval times, outlaws banded together for both camaraderie and to accomplish their criminal objectives. When pursued by sheriffs and bounty hunters, outlaws were allowed by medieval kings to purchase a pardon either by a monetary payment or performance of some service.

By the 1400s, being declared an outlaw became less of a hardship. Instead of taking to the woods and becoming professional robbers, some hid out with friends until a pardon could be secured, whereas others moved away and continued their trades. Outlawry was not abolished in England until 1938; in the United States, North Carolina had an outlaw statute until 1970 (Walker, 1973).

Slavery as Banishment
Slaves in ancient civilizations were acquired as prisoners of war, as defaulters on debts, and as criminals. In the Greek city-state of Athens, serious offenders could be banished and enslaved if they failed to pay a required tax. In the Roman Empire, most lower-class offenders were sentenced for life at hard labor in the imperial mines, which, in effect, made them slaves. The more fortunate worked on public projects, such as building and repairing roads or in state factories (Sellin, 1976). During the Middle Ages penal servitude was revived to relieve labor shortages, to reduce the more brutal punishments used to control crime, and to go beyond merely punishing offenders.

Penal Slavery at the Oars
Galleys were oar-driven ships used in commerce and warfare for hundreds of years until the 17th century by Mediterranean nations. Galley slaves sat four to six per seat in the waist of the boat on benches, chained to their places sometimes for days at a time, manning large oars that required much strength and skill. The food provided was sometimes barely adequate for subsistence and during battles overseers used whips to maintain the pace (Ives, 1914/1970; Sellin, 1976). In Europe during the Middle Ages, the galley was a widely used major repository for convicts and other undesirables.

Bagnes were secure stockades established at seaports to house slaves and others. By the 1600s, bagnes began to be used to hold crippled galley convicts while they were in port (Bamford, 1973).[3] Some were transformed into **workhouses,** penal facilities where work was required, so these convicts could contribute to their self-support. However, physical problems did not allow many of these men to work effectively. The government had contracted with businesses to provide workers in these facilities, so galley oarsmen who were in port began to be pressed into service and these bagnes became workhouse prisons. The facilities operated on a lease arrangement with businesses, with the state providing the factory building, inmate housing, food, and clothing. Convict labor solved the industrialist's two major problems: absenteeism and discipline. These were the antecedents of industrial prisons.

Although convicts in the bagnes worked daily from dawn to dusk, conditions had significantly improved since the galleys and jails. By the time bagnes developed, galley use was decreasing and had all but disappeared by 1800 in France, Italy, and Spain. In these countries, bagnes served as a transition from the galleys to prisons.

French Bagnes: Forerunners of Industrial Prisons
In France by the mid-1700s, most convicts were sent to one of four bagnes. Although most confinement conditions during this era were poor, the bagnes cared for their inmates because they needed them to work. At two of the French facilities in the late 1700s, Toulon (2,500 inmates) and Rochefort (1,000+ inmates), inmates were housed on decommissioned galleys or hulks. However, at Brest, a large three-story prison building was constructed that held 1,880 inmates. By comparison, the largest American prisons, Auburn and Sing-Sing, had each held fewer than 700 inmates as late as 1850. Although some textbooks, notably Barnes and Teeters (1943), have viewed the prison as an American invention, this is a gross oversimplification of its historical origins. The characteristics of the bagnes, particularly the one at Brest, were similar to American industrial prisons in that they employed inmates for state profit as well as to reform them; however, they differed in that bagnes housed inmates in dormitories, not cells, and there was no rule of silence (Bamford, 1973).

Transportation, the practice of transporting offenders to remote locations, replaced bagnes in France by the mid-1800s as the method of punishment. Italy had no colonies to which to transport its offenders, so bagnes were used there until 1889, when they were replaced by cellular prisons (Sellin, 1976).

Transportation: An Intermediate Punishment

As early as the 15th century, Spain and Portugal shipped convicts to colonies and distant military settlements; however, this practice was abandoned because these men were needed on the galleys (Rusche & Kirchheimer, 1939/1957). England became the first country during the early modern period, which dates from the 16th century onward, to systematically ship offenders to its colonies. France and Russia also used this practice.

England pioneered the establishment of workhouses, but rather than adapt this system to incarcerate felons, it chose to transport them to its new American colonies. Magistrates were given the authority to exile rogues and vagabonds, and by 1615 less serious offenders who were sentenced to death were also eligible. Thus, transportation served as an intermediate punishment between execution and lesser sanctions such as whipping or pillorying.

The widespread use of this sanction began with the Transportation Act of 1718, which was passed to deal with an alarming increase in crime caused by the disorganizing effects of the transition from medieval to modern times (Linebaugh, 1992). The reduced need for farm workers, along with insufficient industrial development and a doubling of the population during a 100-year period, produced high unemployment. These displaced workers were responsible for increased crime (Ekirch, 1987).[4] Parliament, pressured to do something about crime, chose transportation rather than expanding their workhouses or increasing their use of capital punishment. Imprisonment did not gain favor because of its high costs and the fear that it might be used by a tyrant to subjugate the nation. Capital punishment also declined in favor (Hughes, 1987).

Transportation was the ideal solution because it had none of the drawbacks of other alternatives: undesirables were not supposed to be able to return; the costs were minimal; it provided a source of labor for the new developing colonies; and it might serve as a means for reforming these offenders (Ekirch, 1987). From 1718 to 1769, 69.5 percent of the almost 17,000 felons convicted at the Old Bailey in London were sentenced to transportation, 15.5 percent were executed, and the remainder were given lesser punishments. Capital felons subjected to transportation served 14-year terms; other felons served 7 years. Of the convicts, 70 to 80 percent were male, were unskilled, were from the lower classes, and probably had been driven to crime by economic necessity (Blumenthal, 1962; Ekirch, 1987).

The Indenture System

Before proceeding, we need to clarify the system of white servitude prevailing in the colonies prior to the Revolution because transported convicts were part of this population. The system of indentured servitude provided colonists with a needed labor force at about one quarter of the cost of a free man. Indentured servants also tended to be more obedient and dependable workers, because the penalties for sassing a boss or running away were severe (Van der Zee, 1985). Indentured servants comprised two types of individuals: those who came voluntarily and exchanged their labor for the benefit of being transported to the Americas, and criminals and others (e.g., those who were shanghaied—kidnapped) who were involuntarily sentenced (Ives, 1914/1970; Smith, 1947/1965). Regardless of how they came, all were considered "slaves" for the term of their indenture. In total, indentured servants represented half (30,000 to 50,000) of all the colonists coming to this country from the early 1600s to the 1700s (Blumenthal, 1962; Van der Zee, 1985).

Convicts awaiting shipment to the colonies were detained in gaols (jails) for up to 6 months or more under notoriously unhealthy conditions (Ekirch, 1987). Their voyage to America differed little from that experienced by African slaves. They were chained below deck in damp, cramped quarters with little fresh air or light, and disease was rampant.

The sale of convicts and other servants upon their arrival was likened to cattle auctions. Convicts were purchased for all types of agricultural, retail, and industrial work. Women were considered less valuable because they could not perform heavy labor; however, the colonies had a shortage of females, so they "contributed to make life a bit more tolerable by becoming the wives, mistresses, or simply adding an amiable dimension to colonial life" (Smith, 1947/1965). The life of indentured servants was harsh because, like slaves, they were the private property of their masters and could be bought and sold, treated harshly, whipped, or placed in iron collars and chains when unruly. Numerous servants attempted to escape, and most were successful; however, if apprehended, they were punished by having their servitude extended (Ekirch, 1987). If women became pregnant, either by liaisons with other servants or by submitting to their masters' sexual demands, their servitude was increased by up to a year to compensate their masters for lost time due to childbearing.

For the British, the transportation of convicts provided a cheap and easy means of dealing with their criminal population. Despite colonists' fears of the dangers posed by these criminals, life in America provided many fewer opportunities for property crime. This probably meant that these felons rarely ran afoul of the law (Smith, 1947/1965).

The outbreak of the American Revolution had a devastating effect on English corrections. It meant that fewer convicts could be shipped to the American colonies, and other methods of dealing with the convict population were not in place. Although more than 200 offenses still carried the death penalty, its implementation was still not tolerated in large numbers (Ekirch,

Lemain: The Historical Antecedent of *Escape from New York*

The 1981 movie *Escape from New York* was set in 1997. The movie centers around the hijacking and crash of Air Force One—with the president on board—into the middle of Manhattan Island, which had been converted into a top-security penal colony. A 400 percent increase in crime prompted its establishment as a permanent prison for recalcitrant offenders unable to live in society. Those entering were given a choice of death or placement on the island for life. There were no guards; the only system of control was that developed by the inmates. Escape was prevented by a 50-foot-high wall surrounding the island, and all bridges and waterways were mined. A federal police force patrolled the island's perimeter and anyone attempting to escape that failed to heed the warning to return was shot.

Although the plot is fictional, in 1785 a plan was advanced to place convicts on the island of Lemain—known today as MacCarthy Island—which was 400 miles up the Gambia River in what was then the British West African colony of Gambia. The plan was to transport 150 convicts with enough provisions for 6 months and some goods to be used for trading. To prevent escape, a private armed ship was to be stationed downriver to provide security. The island was fertile and crops could be produced within 4 months of occupancy. The premise was that if the convicts were left to their own devices, and prevented from escaping, they would quickly become planters of cotton, tobacco, indigo, and yams. Although realizing that in the first year many convicts would die due to the change of climate, it was believed that as the colony became more stable and more convicts arrived, the food supply would improve and eventually 4,000 transportees could be accommodated. As the settlement developed the convicts would form their own government, grow prosperous, and therefore become honest and ultimately return home reformed and upstanding citizens. Thus, in the same way that their old lifestyle in England had corrupted these offenders, exposure to this pristine environment would have a purifying effect. The economics of this solution favored its initiation; however, it was never implemented due to the potentially high death rate resulting from the region's unhealthy climate and the fear that landing criminals among the African natives would trigger a massacre—who died would depend on if the convicts were armed (Ekirch, 1987; Mackay, 1985). One wonders if this idea would have been initiated if Australia had been unavailable as a depository for convicts.

The idea of isolating convicts on a deserted island continues to be raised. Reflect for a moment on the pros and cons of this arrangement as a permanent placement for recalcitrant offenders, those to be executed, or serial sex offenders.

1987). However, judges still viewed it as an effective deterrence for serious offenders, and as robberies and burglaries mounted so did the execution of the most recalcitrant (Beattie, 1987).

Floating Prisons

With transportation to the colonies a dwindling option, the Hulks Act of 1776 specified that convicts were to be put to work at hard labor on the Thames River. They were to be housed in **hulks** (broken-down and abandoned war vessels and transport ships) that were transformed into nautical prisons. Starting with two hulks that quickly became overcrowded, the English government was forced to use gaols and workhouses, which were unsuited for long-term imprisonment. The construction of prisons was too costly, so the government continued to put more hulks into service despite death rates of up to one third of 5,792 inmates aboard these vessels between 1776 and 1795. At their peak in the early 1800s, there were 10 of these vessels holding 5,000 convicts. Conditions aboard these hulks (e.g., poor sanitation and ventilation, a starvation diet, harsh discipline, overcrowding) led convicts to use the phrase "hell upon earth" to describe them (Branch-Johnson, 1957). Their demise, like other punishments, was gradual and primarily due to the discovery of Australia.

During the late 1700s, while hulks were being stuffed with convicts, transportation of convicts to a remote location was still being sought with cost as the key factor in site selection. Various West African locations were suggested as was Australia, which was later chosen. However, as our Consider This, "Lemain: The Historical Antecedent of *Escape from New York*" suggests, other ideas were considered first.

Transportation to Australia

After rejecting various African locations, the newly discovered Australia was chosen as the destination for transported convicts. Australia was chosen because of its healthy climate, of conditions suitable to agricultural

development, and it was too far for felons to return to England easily (Mackay, 1985). Whereas convicts were shipped to America to assist in developing existing colonies, in Australia the majority of colonists were to be convicts.

The first shipment of convicts was transported under government control in the late 1780s, but private contractors were subsequently used and paid per convict transported. This made the 3-to-8-month trip disastrous because contractors were initially permitted to carry as many convicts as possible, and there was no incentive to keep the convicts healthy. Thus, a large number of them died. To improve convict conditions, some ships had government-appointed doctors to supervise convict health. A payment plan was also initiated, under which three quarters of the fee was paid on embarkation and the rest when convicts landed in decent health. Subsequently, the death rate dropped to about 1 percent (Hughes, 1987).

In 1788, after an 8-month, 15,000-mile journey, the first fleet arrived in Australia. Trouble began immediately, because most convicts were unskilled and unable to perform the tasks necessary to develop a colony. The military also refused to supervise them (Hirst, 1983; Hughes, 1987). A structure for convict labor and status evolved over the next 6 months. Convicts were employed on government projects (e.g., road building, farming) under convict overseers. Others were assigned to free settlers who started to develop private farms. Under the Australian system, convicts served a fixed term and then became free. Those serving the majority of their sentences on the hulks before shipment to Australia were eligible for release after a year. If they wanted to farm they were granted 30 or more acres of land and convicts to help them. In time, no distinction was made between those settlers who had been convicts and those who had always been free (Hirst, 1983).[5]

The key to development of the colony was the convict assignment system. It was economical because it shifted the responsibilities of feeding, clothing, and housing convicts from the government to private citizens. It also induced prosperous free settlers to consider immigrating because of the lure of free convict labor. Nevertheless, 10 to 20 percent of the convicts were incorrigible and were controlled by flogging or by placement on chain gangs or in penal colonies (Hirst, 1983).

A New Society About 24,000 women were transported to Australia between 1788 and 1852. No formal policy prescribed that women were sent for breeding and sexual conveniences; however, this was implicit in the colony's first governor's request for more women convicts. He wanted them for purposes of marrying and raising

Transportation was an intermediate punishment between execution and lesser sanctions. Shown here are caged prisoners on a transport ship bound for Australia.

native-born families who would then provide the base for an agricultural society of small farms. Initially, women were assigned as mistresses, which was akin to a "mail-order bride" system. However, pressure from the evangelical lobby eventually ended this practice.

Despite the unfavorable portrait of convict women, many were able to raise children who benefited the community. The population of native-born children grew rapidly, and schools were established to facilitate their development. The first generation of native children were the most law-abiding, morally conservative people in the country. The legacy of the convict system was not criminality but its opposite—repulsion of it. Thus, a new society developed from what was largely a convict population. Ex-convicts held positions of trust in both the government and the private sector. They were lawyers, teachers, magistrates, constables, superintendents, and owners of large enterprises and farms (Hirst, 1987).

Rewards and Punishment The most enticing reward for convicts was to be released from their sentences, which, in Australia, occurred in one of three ways: (1) an absolute pardon—rarely given—from the governor, which restored all rights including to return to England; (2) a conditional pardon, which gave the convict citizenship in the colony but no right to return to England; and (3) a **ticket of leave,** which did not end their sentence, but freed convicts from their obligation to work for the government or a master. They could work as free agents for wages, as long as they remained in the colony until their sentences ended and they committed no crimes. In time, the "ticket" was considered a reward and issued for various types of good behavior until about 1820 when a more structured system was initiated. The worst thing a master could do to convicts was to stop them from getting their tickets (Hirst, 1983). However, at the expiration of their sentence they were still not free to return to England (Mudie, 1964).

Many convicts lacked the self-restraint to resist the temptations of working in an open confinement setting. Several lash and penal colonies were established both on the mainland and offshore as a sanction to motivate the lazy and disobedient and as a deterrent to potential reoffending (Hirst, 1983; Hughes, 1986). Short of execution, assignment to these brutal colonies was the most dreaded punishment for crimes committed in Australia. Norfolk Island was the penal colony of last resort; it was used for the absolute worst convicts, because its location 400 miles from New Zealand made it escape-proof. Commandants were granted absolute control over the lives of all convicts, who were required to serve a minimum of 10 years. (In Chapter 5, we will see how Alexander Maconochie transformed this prison into a model institution in 1840.)

The end of England's use of transportation began in the 1830s, prompted by growing propaganda in England that it was not punitive enough and had minimal deterrent effect. In 1847, England began incarcerating offenders, who were then transferred to public work gangs. Ultimately, they were exiled to Western Australia to fulfill acute labor needs. Pressure from other colonies forced Britain to discontinue this practice entirely in 1868. More than 160,000 convicts and exiles were shipped to Australia in the 80-year period during which transportation was in effect.

Transportation to Australia had its virtues and defects. Historically, it represented an early attempt to employ an intermediate punishment in a country where the only other alternative was execution, as there was an unwillingness to fund long-term prisons (Shaw, 1966). Although much of the treatment of convicts was cruel and often barbaric, what happened in Australia was truly remarkable. An almost exclusively convict population took an undeveloped land and created a functional society.

The French also developed penal colonies in Guiana, on the northeast coast of South America; the most infamous was Devil's Island where convicts were shipped from the 1850s until World War II (Rickards, 1968). Conditions at these colonies were incredibly brutal due to location and climatic conditions of high temperature and tropical rains. Inmates were plagued by yellow fever, marsh fevers, fatal anemia, and dysentery. This, combined with the work in the jungles from dawn to dark, produced a death rate averaging from 25 to 32 percent (Wines, 1895). The Russians finally established major penal colonies in Siberia. They had the most brutal and degrading system of transportation—largely due to Siberia's frigid location—and they were the only major nation to continue this practice into the 1990s (Burke, 1992).

The Continued Support for Transportation

Today transportation is infrequently used to deal with offenders. However, there continue to be occasional proponents for resurrecting this practice despite its checkered history of brutality, inhumane conditions, and servitude. In the United States, Alaska and other island outposts have been mentioned as potential penal colonies. As space travel becomes more common, it is likely that someone will suggest establishing a penal colony on another planet or on the moon (a similar idea appears in some *Star Trek* episodes). Adherents argue that penal colonies give offenders a chance to start new lives, to live with their families, and to support themselves and their dependents (Caldwell, 1965). Objections include (1) finding a suitable location for penal colonies; (2) citizens' resistance to penal colonies in their areas; (3) the difficulties of establishing a normal community made up of criminals; (4) the advisability of raising children in this environment; and (5) the concern

Banished as Punishment

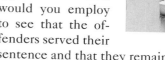
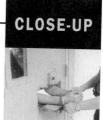

Two 17-year-old Alaskan Indian boys, visiting Seattle, pleaded guilty to robbing and beating a pizza delivery man with a baseball bat (Akre, 1994). These first-time offenders were allowed by a Washington State judge to face a tribal court rather than go to prison. The tribal court banished the boys to separate isolated Alaskan islands for 12 to 18 months. Each boy "would be given forks for digging up clams, axes and saws for cutting firewood, and some food to carry them through the first five days. [Also] a sleeping bag and shelter, which would be equipped with a wood stove for cooking and heat" (p. 70).[6] The boys would be checked on regularly but in emergencies would have no means of contacting the outside world.

If you view this punishment as appropriate, what types of first-time offenders should be subjected to this punishment? What types of controls would you employ to see that the offenders served their sentence and that they remained in good health?

---

that their isolation encourages the use of brutal and sadistic practices (Caldwell, 1965). Thus, unless someone can develop a plan offsetting the extremely negative aspects of using penal colonies, this practice should remain a sordid facet of correctional history. However, as our Close-Up, "Banished as Punishment," shows, history tends to repeat itself.

Forerunners of Long-Term Imprisonment

Long-term prisons as facilities for punishing and reforming large numbers of convicted offenders are a relatively recent development. Although prisons, jails, and dungeons existed for thousands of years, they were not a primary means of punishing offenders. Instead, prior to the 1800s, they served almost exclusively as detention facilities. In examining the evolution of punishment, it is important to recognize that there was no abrupt transition from corporal and capital punishment to imprisonment, as some authors have implied. Change was gradual and uneven, and in the Western world, this transition spanned the period from the 16th to the middle of the 19th century (Barnes, 1930/1972; Spierenburg, 1991).

Monasteries and asylums were the earliest facilities resembling prisons (Spierenburg, 1991).[7] The regimented discipline employed at monasteries led them to be viewed as models for prisons and as residence facilities for parents with children unfit for life outside. Medieval hospitals may also have been used for incarceration (Spierenburg, 1991). These hospitals typically functioned as a refuge for the sick, aged, homeless, and others. Dating back to the 12th century, hospitals with detention areas usually housed the insane. By the 15th century, separate institutions—known as asylums—which resembled prisons were built to confine the insane for relatively long periods of time. However, they were not viewed as our first prisons because of their charitable purposes and their clientele (people not considered responsible for their actions). That "honor" instead went to workhouses, which were developed a century later.

Workhouses and Houses of Correction

Workhouses and houses of correction are viewed as the forerunners of the modern prison. Their development and growth can be traced to long-term social and cultural changes, which included efforts to alter the behavior of offenders through punishment or reformation (Spierenburg, 1991). Workhouses were first established to reform those who were immoral or living in sin. This involved efforts to regulate and control bad habits—drinking, gambling, and immoral sexual behavior—through the criminalization of offenses against morality. There was also a change in attitudes toward the able-bodied poor who were now seen as undeserving. This led to restrictions on the punishment of beggars, beginning with their being chased away. After workhouses developed, they were confined in them and subjected to forced labor (Spierenburg, 1991). The Protestant reformation also facilitated the acceleration of the emergence of workhouses because its tenets required that "everyone should work." This norm came to be accepted in Catholic countries as well. This fit in well with the workhouse regimen of forcing the able-bodied poor to work.

These combined developments occurred between the 12th and 15th centuries and were accompanied by increased stability, peace, and the gradual development of centralized governments and justice systems. This reinforced the focus on the poor and other marginals because they became a threat to this new social order. Banishment to another area became impossible because magistrates were now concerned about how these people would affect neighboring towns. Although workhouses were developed to control and reform the undeserving poor, early on they were also used to incarcerate some convicted criminals. Given the apparent refusal of criminals to work, depriving them of their liberty and reforming them through forced labor was deemed appropriate.

The first workhouse in England was **Bridewell,** an old palace donated to the city of London by Edward VI. It was renovated and opened about 1556 to deal with the increasing number of public nuisances (including beggars, prostitutes, con artists, and other petty offenders).[8] Work was the chief mode of reformation, and the profits from this went toward making the facility self-sufficient. Initially, inmates were paid for their work and charged for their meals. Other English counties eventually built workhouses, often also called Bridewells.

In line with the thinking of the times, "correction" of inmates was also achieved by physical punishment. Thus, at the London Bridewell both males and females were flogged twice a week until each had received what was deemed punishment proportionate to their crimes. Flogging, restriction of diet, and placement in stocks were used to punish rule violators and those not meeting work quotas (Ives, 1914/1970; Sellin, 1976; Van der Slice, 1936). As with many such experiments, the Bridewells achieved varying levels of success in reforming inmates.

Because there was no central government oversight, local authorities were left to manage and fund them. As a result their quality and effectiveness varied tremendously.

By the late 1600s, these institutions had deteriorated and become overcrowded places of detention indistinguishable from gaols. Men, women, children, the old, the young, and serious and minor offenders were housed together indiscriminately. Inmates made their own rules and predators preyed on the weak and innocent. Ruthless cruelty was compounded by unhygienic conditions that produced serious epidemics of gaol fever—mostly typhus—or malignant forms of dysentery. Also, food was not provided, forcing inmates to depend on the charity of family and friends to avoid starvation (Grunhut, 1948/1972; Ives, 1914/1970).

European Workhouses[9]

In Europe, the **Amsterdam Workhouse** for men opened in 1596 and the **Spin House** for women was established a year later. They served as models for other workhouses developed throughout Holland and other northern European areas during the 17th and 18th centuries.[10] When the Amsterdam Workhouse opened, weaving was the primary type of work. By 1700, it was replaced by rasping, which involved reducing a hardwood log to dust and then boiling it to extract the pigment used in dying cloth. Accordingly, these facilities were known as "Rasphouses." Workers had quotas to

The use of forced labor as a means of reforming those who were considered immoral dates from the 15th century. In this scene at the Vagrants' Prison in Coldbath Fields, prisoners in the upper part of the picture are working on a tread-wheel, a device used to operate machinery; those in the lower part of the picture are exercising.

Early Workhouses: Multifaceted

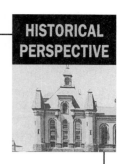

HISTORICAL PERSPECTIVE

The management of workhouses approximated a household or family model. The offenders sent to these facilities were viewed as having broken away from the disciplinary restraints of family control. Thus, to reform them required a more structured environment.

To accommodate these views, management involved four levels. At the top were the town's magistrates who established the facilities and appointed a board of administrators (the second level), who managed finances and served as an internal court to judge and punish inmate rule violators. The operational administrator occupied the third level. It is here that we can use the family analogy. Known as the "indoor father," he and his wife were considered the heads of this household and were viewed as surrogate parents to the inmates. The indoor father had from one to three assistants who were responsible for providing discipline, maintenance, food, other necessities, and supervision of inmates at work. On the fourth level were minor personnel, typically servants and assistants. There were no guards.

Inmates were rarely separated on arrival, suggesting they were not viewed as predisposed to aggressive behavior. Although those who conceived of these facilities felt they had the best interest of the inmates in mind, the number of attempted and completed escapes suggests that inmates did not feel the same way. For example, at the Delft facility, 28 percent of the inmates absconded and remained at large. The frequency of escapes led Spierenburg (1991) to conclude that no day passed without some inmates thinking about it.

Subcultures typically develop whenever individuals interact in groups for any length of time. Data are scant, but there were some aspects of prison subculture reported, including the use of argot (special words and phrases), graffiti, and tattooing. Additionally, professional criminals were accorded high status. This was possible because their extended terms enabled them to become well-acquainted with all aspects of the institutions. Also, as professional criminals, they were viewed as leaders and were respected by other offenders. Their frequent escapes may have also added to their status. When you read Chapter 7, compare the subculture of the Big House with that of these early workhouses.

---

produce each day. Those not meeting them were punished; overproduction was rewarded with special prison coins, which could be used to buy items in the prison store. This represented the first use of prison script and of a token economy. A policy of sentence reductions was also initiated, primarily to reward inmates who snitched (accused and testified against others involved in crimes). Good behavior could also earn an inmate early release.

The Spin House for women was initially more like a charitable asylum than a prison. However, over time it became a penal facility to punish professional beggars, prostitutes, and other petty criminals. Most women initially labored at spinning, but by the 18th century most worked sewing linen.

Our Historical Perspective, "Early Workhouses: Multifaceted," examines the characteristics of early workhouses, many of which have survived over time.

At the beginning of the 1600s, workhouses were used primarily for beggars and vagabonds. By the mid-1600s, they were used for criminals, and the public viewed them as places for the punishment of convicts. Thus, according to Spierenburg, the birth of the prison can be traced to the middle of the 17th century, specifically to two institutions: one in Amsterdam and another in Hamburg, Germany. Although small, rarely holding more than 100 inmates, their importance was symbolic, because they were the first facilities to imprison offenders exclusively to punish them. Their prominence also reflected the public's acceptance of this method of dealing with offenders. However, it was not until prisons developed in the United States that incarceration as penal philosophy became widespread.

The Hospice of San Michele

The **Hospice of San Michele** was a composite social welfare facility that developed over several hundred years. The juvenile facility, initiated by Pope Clement XI, is historically important because many of its ideas anticipated features that became an integral part of early adult and juvenile systems in the United States.

The institution for juvenile males housed (1) youths under age 20 convicted of crimes, who were funded by the sale of inmate-produced goods to the church and government, and (2) incorrigible youths inclined toward vice or incorrigibility, who were sent and paid for by their parents—this was a cross between a military school and a juvenile institution for these youths.

The design of this facility, which resembled a cell block, represents its most lasting contribution. Along each wall there were three tiers with 10 cells per tier. The space running through the middle of the two rows of cells was used as a workshop. This design influenced the Maison de Force (to be discussed next) and became, in a modified form, one primary architectural model for prison cell blocks (e.g., Auburn) in the United States (Sellin, 1930). A vocational training program, directed by skilled artisans was developed to teach incarcerated youths a trade to prepare them to earn a legitimate living upon release. Religious and moral instructions were also an integral part of this program.

The two groups of youths were subjected to different programs. Those convicted of crimes worked together in silence, chained to the workbench in the central hall, dedicated to spinning and knitting tasks. Sometimes they were forced to listen to the monks reading the Bible. At night they were separately confined in small brick cells. These were the essential features of the Auburn system, which (as noted in Chapter 5), became the dominant model for prisons in the United States 50 years later (Sellin, 1930; Wines, 1895).

The incorrigible group was individually confined in cells day and night without labor; this resembled an early version of the Pennsylvania system. These youths had visits from clergy, who lectured them and attempted to teach them Christian doctrine. Finally, whipping was used to punish youths who disobeyed the rules. It is interesting that St. Michele recognized that delinquent and incorrigible youths required distinct programs. It took until the 1960s for our juvenile justice system to realize this fact.

The Maison de Force

Established in 1773 by Vilain in Ghent, Belgium, the **Maison de Force** was clearly ahead of its time. It had a rudimentary classification system that separated felons from misdemeanants and vagrants and provided separate sections for women and for children. Vilain believed that offenders should be sentenced to a minimum of one year so that they could learn a trade and felt that they should be able to have their sentences reduced as a reward for good conduct. This was an early form of "good time" (Wines, 1895).

Work was the primary method of reform, and it offered inmates opportunities to engage in productive occupations (e.g., weaving, shoemaking, tailoring). As incentives, inmates were allowed to keep a portion of their earnings and to work overtime. However, a portion of this money had to be saved for the inmate's release so that he would not be forced to return to a life of crime. Inmates worked together during the day but were housed separately at night. This facility also had a resident chaplain and a physician. Discipline was maintained by guards who used a system of graduated punishments, ranging from warnings to whippings to solitary confinement and finally to the extension of the inmate's sentence (1 week was added for each day spent in the dungeon). This enlightened perspective earned Vilain the title of "father of modern penitentiary science" (Wines, 1895).

By 1783, what was once a remarkable establishment had lost much of its reformative value due to opposition from private industry, which believed the prison's manufacturing operations had injured their business. Persuading the monarch to terminate the prison meant that inmates were no longer fully employed nor able to learn marketable skills that would enable them to secure jobs upon release (Howard, 1791). (About 150 years after the termination of work at this facility—during the Big House era—the United States succumbed to the same pressures and closed most prison industries, with similar consequences.) Under the mistaken belief that disagreeable conditions discouraged inmates from future criminal acts, the monarch reduced the quality and quantity of food served to them and lowered the maintenance in the housing units. Instead, such measures tended to alienate inmates.

Summary

The punishment of early criminal behavior included sanctions for both public and private wrongs. Public wrongs consisted of religious offenses, treason, witchcraft, incest and other sex offenses, poisoning, and violations of hunting rules. Violations were typically punished through torture and/or death. Private wrongs, including personal physical injury, property damage, and theft were retaliated against with private vengeance, which was often a catalyst for perpetual conflict. Compensation became a widely accepted alternative to private revenge, as it humiliated the offender while also appeasing the victim's desire for retribution.

Historically, offenders were punished in various ways. Such humiliation and shame tactics as gags, the ducking stool, stocks, pillories, and branding were widely employed on many types of offenders. Corporal punishment, most commonly whipping, was the most universal means of inflicting punishment on offenders. Capital punishment was and continues to be the most extreme response to crime. From ancient times to the present, it has provided the only certain method for ridding the community of the offender, while simultaneously appeasing the community's desire for vengeance.

Banishment became an acceptable alternative to the death penalty because it had the same effect of ridding the community of the offender. This was done through exiling or enslavement. Maritime nations subjected criminals to penal slavery at the oars. Slaves sat four to six per seat on the oar ships, called galleys, which were used in trade and warfare. Secure stockades, called bagnes, were initially established at seaports to house slaves. Over time, they developed into facilities that were the forerunners of industrial prisons.

Transportation was an intermediate punishment first used by England when they transported convicts to American colonies. Indentured servants—either those who voluntarily exchanged their labor for transportation to America or offenders who were involuntarily sentenced to servitude composed half of the colonial population. The American Revolution had a devastating effect on English corrections, particularly transportation, as fewer convicts could be shipped to America. No alternative mechanism for dealing with offenders was in place, so hulks were substituted for transportation. Hulks were overcrowded nautical prisons with death rates as high as one third. Upon the discovery of Australia, it became the new destination for transported convicts. From 1788 to 1852, 24,000 women were transported to Australia for the implicit purpose of reproducing. Many raised law-abiding children, and a new colony developed from a colony of convicts. In Australia, convicts were released from their sentences in one of three ways: an absolute pardon, a conditional pardon, or a ticket of leave. Punishments, particularly the lash and penal colonies, were sanctions for nonconformists. Transportation was abandoned in stages, although its use has never been entirely discontinued. People continue to advocate variations of it today.

Workhouses and houses of correction were the forerunners of the modern prison. Bridewells were the first institutions to attempt reform, and they achieved varying levels of success. The Amsterdam workhouses for men and women served as models for other European workhouses. The Hospice of San Michele was an early juvenile reformatory, which developed over several hundred years. The design of the facility, which resembled a cell block, was its most lasting contribution. It influenced the Maison de Force, which had many other innovative features, as well.

Critical Thinking Questions

1. What were the differences between public and private wrongs, and how were these handled in early societies?
2. What role did compensation play in the reduction of blood feuds?
3. For what offense would you be placed in the stocks and pillories? What types of punishment might you expect?
4. Discuss the use of whipping as a punishment for criminal behavior. If you were debating the question, "Should whipping be retained or abolished?" which side would you take? What justifications would you use to support your position, and how would you rebut the arguments of your opponent?

5. Discuss galley servitude and the subsequent development of the bagnes.
6. If you had a choice of whether to be sent as a convict to the American colonies or to be transported to Australia, which would you choose? Justify your choice by comparing the strengths and weaknesses of the place you choose.
7. Imagine yourself as a convict in Europe during the early development of prisons. Which of these institutions would you prefer to be in? Justify your choice.

Test Your Knowledge

1. Early preliterate societies brutally punished taboo violators primarily to:
   a. placate supernatural powers.
   b. rehabilitate offenders.
   c. deter future deviance.
   d. make an example of nonconformists.
2. An early practice wherein an offender or his clan offered an economic settlement to the victim to avoid revenge was known as:
   a. retribution.
   b. compensation.
   c. *lex talionis.*
   d. endogamy.
3. Bridles were used primarily as punishments for:
   a. drunkards.
   b. vagabonds.
   c. scolds.
   d. prostitutes.
4. The early British practice of sending convicts to the American colonies came to an end as a result of:
   a. the War of 1812.
   b. the increasing African slave trade.
   c. the increasing use of capital punishment in England.
   d. the American Revolution.
5. Which of the following institutions had juvenile programs?
   a. Maison de Force
   b. Bagnes
   c. Hospice of St. Michele
   d. All of them

Endnotes

1. Pakistan, Iran, Sudan, Singapore, Trinidad and Tobago, United Arab Emirates, Yemen, and Saudi Arabia.

2. See the Glossary.

3. P. W. Bamford (1973). *Fighting Ships and Prisons: The Mediterranean Galleys of France in the Age of Louis XIV.* Minneapolis: University of Minnesota Press. Excerpts used with the permission of the publisher.

4. A. R. Ekirch (1987). *Bound for America: The Transportation of British Convicts to the Colonies, 1718–1775.* Oxford: Oxford University Press Inc. © 1987. Reprinted by permission of Oxford University Press.

5. J. B. Hirst (1983). *Convict Society and its Enemies.* Sydney, Australia: George Allen and Unwin. © 1983. Reprinted with the permission of the publisher.

6. This experiment came to an end in September 1995, when problems with the tribal court and reports of inadequate supervision prompted the sentencing judge to recall the boys from the two islands to which they had been banished. One of the boys was sentenced to 55 months in prison and the other to 31 months and both received credit for 12 months on the islands. They were also required to pay restitution of $35,000 to the pizza driver they injured (Banished tribal teens, 1995). Even if this experiment had been managed appropriately, the use of this form of punishment today is highly questionable.

7. Pieter Spierenburg (1991). *The Prison Experience.* © 1991 by Pieter Spierenburg. Reprinted by permission of Rutgers University Press.

8. It is important to note that Bridewells were only used for misdemeanants because at this time more serious offenders were subject to corporal and capital punishment.

9. Except where otherwise noted, the discussion of the workhouse on the continent is drawn from the work of Spierenburg (1991).

10. The use of galley servitude in Southern Europe for marginals precluded the development of these facilities in these countries with the exceptions of the appearance in 1622 of a workhouse in Lyon, France, and one in Madrid, Spain. This, along with the use of transportation and the employment of offenders in public works, resulted in a delay in the adoption of imprisonment as a means of dealing with both marginal and other offenders until the later part of the 18th, and in some cases well into the 19th, century (Spierenburg, 1991).

The Development of Prisons in the United States

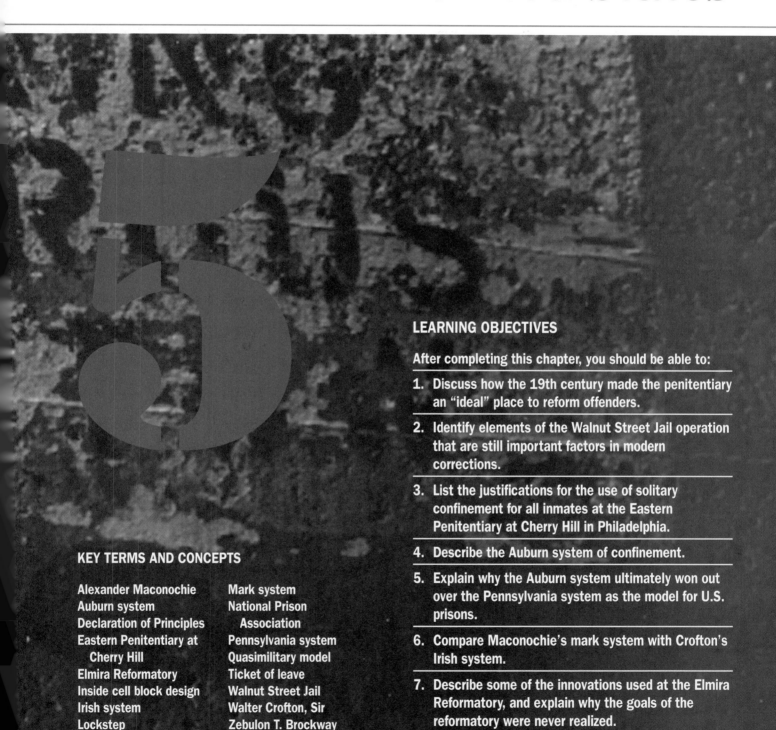

5

KEY TERMS AND CONCEPTS

Alexander Maconochie
Auburn system
Declaration of Principles
Eastern Penitentiary at
Cherry Hill
Elmira Reformatory
Inside cell block design
Irish system
Lockstep

Mark system
National Prison
  Association
Pennsylvania system
Quasimilitary model
Ticket of leave
Walnut Street Jail
Walter Crofton, Sir
Zebulon T. Brockway

LEARNING OBJECTIVES

After completing this chapter, you should be able to:

1. Discuss how the 19th century made the penitentiary an "ideal" place to reform offenders.

2. Identify elements of the Walnut Street Jail operation that are still important factors in modern corrections.

3. List the justifications for the use of solitary confinement for all inmates at the Eastern Penitentiary at Cherry Hill in Philadelphia.

4. Describe the Auburn system of confinement.

5. Explain why the Auburn system ultimately won out over the Pennsylvania system as the model for U.S. prisons.

6. Compare Maconochie's mark system with Crofton's Irish system.

7. Describe some of the innovations used at the Elmira Reformatory, and explain why the goals of the reformatory were never realized.

Introduction

Chapter 4 traced the development and employment of different forms of punishment through the 18th century. Although imprisonment was used for some offenders, its development as a primary means of punishment did not occur until after the American Revolution. This chapter traces the evolution of imprisonment in the United States to the end of the 19th century. To set the stage for this discussion, we briefly examine the forms of punishment employed in colonial America.

Punishment During the Colonial Period

Corporal and capital punishment were commonly employed for most offenses. During the 1700s, criminal codes specified a variety of punishments including fines and whippings, banishment, and hanging. Branding was also used (e.g., having a letter burned on a visible part of the body) to identify strangers and community members who had committed crimes. This, along with forms of public ridicule (e.g., stocks, pillory), served as an important social control mechanism in tight-knit communities where people were concerned about their reputations with their neighbors (Rothman, 1971).[1]

Incarceration was an uncommon practice and was never used as the sole form of punishment. Jails held people awaiting trial, those who were sentenced but not punished, and debtors. A few workhouses also existed but were used primarily as a deterrence to idle strangers, beggars, and pilferers, who, if apprehended, could also be whipped and put to hard labor.

Post-Revolution Methods of Social Control

Following the American Revolution, which ended in 1783, the social, economic, and intellectual forces that created this nation led to a reassessment of British methods of social control (Rothman, 1971). New ideas of penal reform, espoused by Cesare Becarria, founder of the classical school of criminology, were adopted. He asserted that the causes of crime could be traced to the antiquated colonial criminal codes. Beccaria (1764/1963) felt that to prevent crimes

> laws must be clear . . . ; punishment should be based on the extent of harm that the act causes society . . . [and] used only . . . on the supposition that it prevents crime. . . . Punishment for each crime should be inevitable, prompt and public [and it] . . . should be severe enough to override any pleasure that accrues from the criminal acts. (p. 94)

Many reformers embraced the idea of imprisonment simply because it was more humane than hanging and whipping (Rothman, 1971). Other reformers instrumental in developing the *Pennsylvania system* believed in the reformative value of prison. In either case, prison allowed for matching the seriousness of the crime to an appropriate level of punishment.

By the early 19th century, convicts were thought of as victims of faulty upbringing and community corruptions. Many believed that they could be reeducated and rehabilitated in a well-ordered institutional setting organized around the principles of separation, obedience, and labor. Thus, a prison free of corrupting community influences that provided appropriate training could resocialize offenders. Moreover, in the same way that the "criminal environment led him into crime, the institutional environment would lead him out of it" (Rothman, 1971, p. 83).

These premises were put to the test with the *Pennsylvania* and *Auburn systems*, which developed an institutional environment and program directed at reforming offenders. These systems were to serve as the foundation for our new system of social control.

The Pennsylvania System

In 1787, penal reformers formed the Philadelphia Society for Alleviating the Miseries of Public Prisons. This group was instrumental in persuading the legislature to designate the **Walnut Street Jail** as a temporary state prison and change its orientation toward reformation.

The Walnut Street Jail The reformers who planned the Walnut Street Jail, which is considered our first prison, faced the same problems that we grapple with today: (1) Should prisoners be housed separately or in association? and (2) Should it be for the purpose of punishment (Lewis, 1922/1996)? The Quakers wanted to develop a program that reformed offenders while also providing humane treatment. To accomplish this, the Walnut Street Jail was remodeled in 1790 to provide for the confinement of two classes of offenders.

More serious offenders, previously subjected to corporal or capital punishment, were confined in a newly built penitentiary house containing 16 solitary cells called *punishment cells*. After a period of time, these inmates could earn the privilege of working while still confined to their cells, and after completing a portion of their sentence, they could be released into the general population of the prison. Less serious offenders were congregately housed in eight large rooms and were permitted to work at occupations basic to the economy of the period (Lewis, 1922/1996).

The prisoner labor system presented authorities with the issue of which incentives are effective in encouraging inmate production. The same two incentives that are typically used today were used then. Inmates were paid wages with deductions made for daily maintenance, tools, court costs, and fines. Most left with money in their pockets. However, the major incentive was not the money but the hope of a pardon, which might be awarded for their good work. Discipline of inmates was humane—prisoners were not shackled and corporal punishment was not used. However, disobedient offenders could be put in solitary cells and still be charged daily maintenance expenses (Lewis, 1922/1996).

During its first decade of operation, the program at the Walnut Street Jail appeared to be successful. Street crime dropped to a point where people felt secure on the streets as well as in their homes and businesses. Despite its great promise, by 1800, a number of factors contributed to its downfall. Discipline at the institution became lax; pardons were issued to placate convicts and achieve order. However, the primary factor causing Walnut Street's failure was its inability to handle the increasing inmate population. This resulted from (1) Pennsylvania's growing population, and (2) the increased substitution of solitary confinement for capital punishment, which resulted in more commitments and longer prison terms.

Recognizing that reform was impossible under overcrowded conditions, the Pennsylvania legislature authorized the construction of two penitentiaries, the Western Penitentiary at Pittsburgh and the Eastern Penitentiary at Cherry Hill. The Western Penitentiary was demolished because poor planning and construction made it impossible to utilize its goals of solitary confinement or work. It was replaced with a facility similar in design to the one at Cherry Hill, which could meet these objectives.

The Eastern Penitentiary Opened in 1829, the **Eastern Penitentiary at Cherry Hill** was the first facility to put into effect the **Pennsylvania system,** or "separate system." It was designed so inmates would not have to be removed from their cells except when sick. Inmates ate, slept, read their Bibles, received moral instruction, and worked in their cells. Their only interpersonal contact was with the warden, guards, the chaplain, and members of some Philadelphia organizations interested in inmate care and welfare. Inmates were not permitted to receive or send letters to family or anyone on the outside (Barnes & Teeters, 1951; Lewis, 1922/1996).

The Cherry Hill facility had seven wings, resembling the spokes of a wheel and extending from a hub-like center with a total of 252 cells. Each cell block had a passage running down the center with 21 spacious cells—each 12 feet wide by 7 feet long by 16 feet high—on either side of the outside wall. All inmates were allowed one hour of exercise per day; those in first floor cells had individual walled exercise yards,

The Walnut Street Jail in Philadelphia was the first prison in the United States. There serious offenders were confined in solitary cells instead of being subjected to corporal or capital punishment.

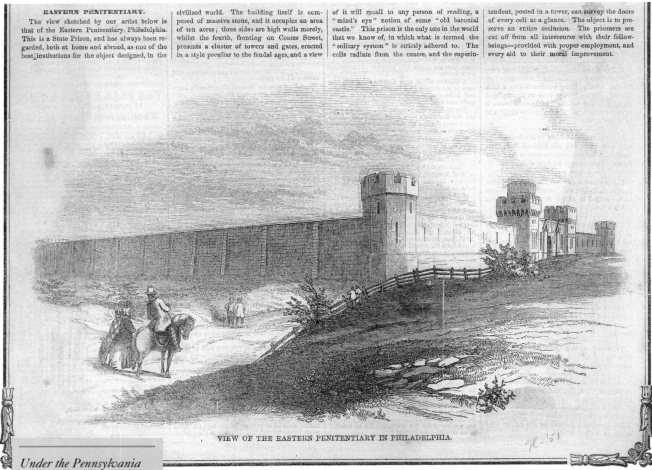

EASTERN PENITENTIARY.

The view sketched by our artist below is that of the Eastern Penitentiary, Philadelphia. This is a State Prison, and has always been regarded, both at home and abroad, as one of the best institutions for the object designed, in the civilized world. The building itself is composed of massive stone, and it occupies an area of ten acres; three sides are high walls merely, whilst the fourth, fronting on Coates Street, presents a cluster of towers and gates, erected in a style peculiar to the feudal ages, and a view of it will recall to any person of reading, a "mind's eye" notion of some "old baronial castle." This prison is the only one in the world that we know of, in which what is termed the "solitary system" is strictly adhered to. The cells radiate from the centre, and the superintendent, posted in a tower, can survey the doors of every cell at a glance. The object is to preserve an entire seclusion. The prisoners are cut off from all intercourse with their fellow-beings—provided with proper employment, and every aid to their moral improvement.

VIEW OF THE EASTERN PENITENTIARY IN PHILADELPHIA.

Under the Pennsylvania system that was first put into effect at the Eastern Penitentiary, shown here, inmates were not removed from their cells unless they were sick.

whereas those on the second floor were given an extra cell for exercise purposes. The institutional program was based on solitary confinement, work, and penitence and was justified on the grounds that

1. Communication in any [form] contributed to the contamination of the less hardened by the vicious.

2. Solitary confinement without the opportunity of communication with fellow prisoners would stop all such contamination.

3. Living in silence day and night, [the inmate] would inevitably reflect upon his sins and resolve to forever abandon such activity.

4. Labor in the cell would enable him to contribute to his support and at the same time would relieve the dreadful monotony of solitary confinement (Gillin, 1935, p. 282).

In this country, this system did not receive wide acceptance.[2] However, many European countries adopted it as a model for their own penal systems.

The Auburn System

Although Auburn Prison in New York eventually became the model for prisons throughout the United States, its initial construction and administration in 1816 followed traditional patterns of the period. At first, it followed a system of congregate work and confinement. However, disorders at this prison and another New York prison prompted authorities to search for better methods of prison management (Lewis, 1922/1996).

A commission devised a plan employing a threefold classification system of assigning inmates to one of three programs. The first group, the least serious criminals, were to work in silence in the prison shops during the day and be confined in separate cells at night. The second group, the more serious and hardened criminals, were to alternate between solitary confinement and

Did Auburn Test the Pennsylvania Model?

Despite the fact that Auburn was not designed for total solitary confinement, on Christmas Day in 1821, as mandated by the New York State legislature, 80 of the "worst inmates" being held at this prison were placed in total solitary confinement. Except for a Bible to read, they had no work, no contact with visitors, nor any other methods for passing the lonely hours. The legislature failed to anticipate the disastrous consequences of solitude (e.g., attempted suicides, mental breakdowns, and deaths) without anything to do. After 18 months, the increasing number of convict deaths led the governor to visit the prison. Shocked by what he observed, he terminated the program and pardoned most of the survivors (Lewis, 1922/1996; McKelvey, 1977).

CONSIDER THIS

Assume you were an evaluator asked to consider whether this experiment was a test of the Pennsylvania system. What factors would you consider in your evaluation?[3]

work as recreation. The third group, vicious and hardened criminals, were to be confined in their cells without labor. This plan embodied the views of the period, which held that prisoners could be reformed through penitence and that imprisonment was to be for punishment (Lewis, 1922/1996).

Unlike the cells at Eastern Penitentiary, which occupied the outside wall of the prison, these newly built solitary confinement cells—for reasons of economy—were built back to back, five tiers high in a hollow building. They were very small (7 ft. long, 4 ft. wide, and 7 ft. high), and their doors opened onto galleries or walkways 8 to 10 feet from the outer wall of the building—which had small barred windows. This made them dark, dreary, and devoid of much fresh air (Lewis, 1922/1996). Despite its many faults, this pattern of **inside cell blocks** was adopted by most states that built prisons during the next century. The high cost of prison construction assured that prisons built according to this plan are still being used today. Our Consider This examines the Auburn experiment with the Pennsylvania model.

The Auburn Plan With no existing acceptable prison regimen at this point, at Auburn, under the guidance of Warden Elam Lynds, a new system was evolving. It was a compromise between solitary confinement and the congregate confinement of earlier facilities. By 1823, this new **Auburn system** was in full operation. It included (1) separate confinement of each inmate at night, (2) work in groups in the prison shops and yards during the day, which paid inmate imprisonment costs, and (3) rigidly enforced silence day and night, which prevented inmates from corrupting each other or plotting escapes and riots. This system met the objectives of imprisonment and provided an economical system of management and strict discipline, allowing for the safe and efficient functioning of the prison (Lewis, 1922/1996).

Inmates received no inducements to comply with the system's rigid requirements. Obedience was obtained by a prompt, severe system of punishment, which inmates dreaded, known as the "stripes"—flogging. Disobedient inmates were taken from the work area and flogged with a rawhide whip in a way that would not endanger their health or ability to work. Thus, the key features of the Auburn system were silence, hard congregate labor, and corporal punishment for rule violators.

The Auburn-Pennsylvania Controversy

By the 1830s, the two American penitentiary systems had achieved worldwide recognition, and attention began to focus on which provided the best model for future prisons.

The Pennsylvania camp insisted that the separate design (1) eliminated contamination and plotting by inmates, (2) did not require well-trained guards because contact with inmates was minimal, and (3) allowed convicts, once isolated, to immediately begin the reformation process. There was little need for the whip because isolation provided few chances to violate the rules. In short, it was secure, quiet, humane, efficient, and reformative.

Pennsylvania supporters criticized the Auburn system on the basis that it was nearly impossible to enforce silence when inmates worked, ate, and exercised together. Further, inmate contact for long periods without talking was cruel and unenforceable as shown by the frequency with which inmates were punished. Auburn advocates criticized the Pennsylvania system, saying that prolonged isolation was cruel, dangerous, and unnatural, as proven by its trial at Auburn, which bred insanity and suicide.

The most persuasive arguments for the Auburn system were that (1) Auburn-type institutions were less costly to construct because cells could be smaller because inmates only slept in them, and (2) profits were

Under the Auburn system, inmates were confined separately at night and worked in groups during the day; a rule of silence was strictly enforced at all times.

greater due to the greater efficiency resulting from the variety and quantity of products produced when convicts worked together. In fact, in 1828 Auburn's warden announced he no longer needed state funds to run the prison (Lewis, 1922/1996). Indeed, the Auburn system eventually prevailed in the United States due to cost issues.

As we note in our Close-Up, "The Real Versus Ideal Pennsylvania System," some key goals of this system could not be realized even during the early "honeymoon" years. Even its basic tenet of completely separating inmates was not initially possible (Teeters, 1970). Eventually, this system was abandoned for practical reasons, including overcrowding (Wines, 1895). Cherry Hill then became just another Auburn-type prison, existing as a maximum security facility until 1970.

The Auburn Model Prevailed

The Auburn system became the model for United States prisons primarily because of its economic advantages. Further, doctrines of separation, obedience, labor, and silence were consistent with the values of the time regarding reformation. Maintaining a daily routine of

hard work was consistent with views on the causes and results of crime; those not willing to work were seen as prone to commit crime. Idleness also gave inmates opportunities to teach each other the values and techniques of crime. Thus, the tougher the regimen, the greater the possibilities of successful reformation.

To achieve these goals a **quasimilitary model** was adopted. This included a daily schedule that was organized around a military routine. Convicts were marched in striped uniforms from place to place in "close-order single file," each looking over the next man's shoulder with their faces pointed to the right to prevent conversation and their feet moving in unison. This type of formation, known as the **lockstep,** became a hallmark of American prisons well into the 1930s. The dominance of the Auburn model can be seen (Table 5.1) from the 29 prisons built throughout the country between 1825 and 1869 that followed this design (McKelvey, 1977; Morse, 1940).

Although many states embraced the Auburn model, their institutions failed to follow its rigid standards. The degree to which the model was followed depended largely on the varying skills and concerns of those running these prisons. Generally, the farther west the state, the more loosely enforced were the model's rigid rules of discipline (Rothman, 1971). Finally, it is important to note that many elements of this system (including the lockstep, silent system, regimented routines, and

The Real Versus Ideal Pennsylvania System

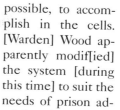

This Close-Up focuses on the first seven years of Eastern Penitentiary's operation. Typically, if a program is going to adhere to its operational plan it will do so in its early years.

The Disciplinary System Failures

Developers of the Pennsylvania system were convinced they could use solitude to change the offender's behavior without "assailing his flesh." This was the way the system was supposed to work and how it was officially portrayed. Under this system punishment involved restricting privileges, including work and moral and religious instruction books. At the outset this plan was flawed because half of the inmates were illiterate, so depriving them of books was meaningless punishment; viewing work as a privilege was also questionable because it sent mixed messages as to the purpose of work.

Because those who established and ran this program considered it the most enlightened system of incarceration, they were unwilling to admit it was not a total success. Public pronouncements tended to obscure the fact that from the beginning some inmates had behaved as they did in other prisons.

By 1835, the facility had its first 300 inmates. Upon arrival these offenders spent their "first few days in contemplation" (Thibaut, 1982, p. 194). The warden's journal indicated that about one fifth of the first inmates committed disciplinary infractions or displayed mental disturbances. This figure is probably underestimated because the warden was often away from the prison, and no official records of infractions or punishments were required. The punishments imposed on inmates were supposed to be of a nonviolent nature, but the staff soon learned

these methods were ineffective with more rebellious prisoners. What developed was a system of graded punishments, starting with those publicly acknowledged and moving to those that were more severe (Thibaut, 1982).

The first and mildest punishment was a deprivation of the use of the exercise yard by the convict for a given period. The second stage of punishment included a serious reduction in rations. For severe cases, the dark cell was employed . . . often . . . [inmates were . . . denied . . . [a blanket]. The next degree of punishment . . . was the absolute deprivation of food, for a period of not over three days. A further stage [involved] . . . the infliction of "ducking," in which . . . convict[s were] suspended from the yard wall by the wrists, and drenched with buckets of cold water, the degree of severity . . . depended on [the temperature]. [Other punishments included] the "mad or tranquilizing chair" . . . [that] was a large box-chair made of planks . . . [in which] the convict was strapped . . . and his hands were handcuffed. . . . It was not possible to move body or limbs, and the consequent pain was intense. Arms and legs swelled frightfully. (Lewis, 1922/1996, pp. 221–222)

The Work Requirement Failures

The determination of the [Prison Board] . . . to occupy every prisoner with some form of work, while at the same time maintaining isolation, presented the prison staff with serious organizational difficulties. [Divergence from this ideal was evident at the outset.] Dyeing, blacksmithing, carriage-making, cooking, and washing were difficult, if not im-

possible, to accomplish in the cells. [Warden] Wood apparently modif[ied] the system [during this time] to suit the needs of prison administration. In fact, men were working all about the premises, some of them in the doubtless convivial company of men brought in to work on prison construction. . . .

Wood's administration, through 1833, was relaxed to the extent that the separate system was certainly in jeopardy. While [t]he Board of Inspectors acknowledged the deterioration of the system in . . . when they ordered . . . "all the prisoners be confined to the cells in accordance with their sentences. . . . Clearly, Warden Wood accepted a much less stringent application of . . . [their] mandate (Thibaut, 1982, pp. 210–212). . . .

In summary, it is clear that in several important respects the designs of the reformers of the Philadelphia Society for Alleviating the Miseries of Public Prisons had succumbed, during the first years of [operation of] the Eastern State Penitentiary, to compelling forces that reshaped the separate system in practice (p. 221).

Our point in presenting this discussion is to show that (1) public pronouncements regarding the success of a program may gloss over deficiencies to demonstrate its success; and (2) no matter how well-intentioned program planners and administrators are there will always be some prisoners who will not conform to program rules and who may be controlled by methods that are outside approved policies.

Table 5.1
Auburn-Type Prisons Built Between 1825 and 1869

New York (Sing Sing)	1825	Maine (Thomaston)	1845
Connecticut (Wethersfield)	1827	New York (Clinton)	1845
Maryland (Baltimore)	1829	Minnesota (Stillwater)	1849
Vermont (Windsor)	1831	Texas (Huntsville)	1851
Tennessee (Nashville)	1831	California (San Quentin)	1852
New Hampshire (Concord)	1832	Wisconsin (Waupun)	1852
Illinois (Alton)	1833	Illinois (Joliet)	1858
Ohio (Columbus)	1834	Indiana (Michigan City)	1860
Louisiana (Baton Rouge)	1835	Idaho (Boise)	1863
Missouri (Jefferson City)	1836	Kansas (Lansing)	1864
Michigan (Jackson)	1838	Nevada (Carson City)	1864
Iowa (Ft. Madison)	1840	South Carolina (Columbia)	1865
Alabama (Wetumpka)	1841	West Virginia (Moundsville)	1866
Indiana (Jeffersonville)	1842	Nebraska (Lincoln)	1869
Mississippi (Jackson)	1842		

fortress prisons) evolved over time and remained part of our penal system well into the 20th century.

Antecedents of the Reformatory Movement

By the end of the Civil War, the inadequacies of both the Pennsylvania and Auburn systems were abundantly clear. The rigid discipline of both systems had degenerated to more or less corrupt, lax, and brutal routines (Rothman, 1980).[4] Further, overcrowding and under-staffing made the silence system unenforceable (Wines & Dwight, 1867).

In their place, prison industries run by private contractors, who leased inmate labor, became the major focus of institutional operations because they were so profitable (Wines & Dwight, 1867). Although benefiting the state, this diminished the authority of prison staff over inmates because during work hours contractors had control of the inmates. Discipline was used to maintain production, and its use for reformative purposes became secondary.

Taken together, these circumstances created turmoil in the prisons. Wardens resorted to a variety of harsh and bizarre punishments to regain control, including flogging and placing inmates in solitary confinement—dungeons—on a bread and water diet. The most horrendous punishment was the Kansas "water crib," where an inmate was placed face down in the crib with hands cuffed behind his back. As the water rose, the inmate, slowly drowning, fought to keep his head above the rising water. Whereas in solitary it took days to bring a man

around, this torture was said to get his cooperation immediately (Rothman, 1980).

Reformers were appalled by these forms of torture and punishment. In searching for programs that could be used to develop a new prison system, reformers were heavily influenced by the work of Captain Alexander Maconochie and Sir Walter Crofton.

Alexander Maconochie's Mark System

While serving as a young naval officer in 1810, **Alexander Maconochie** was captured by the French and became a prisoner of war; this made him sensitive to the brutalities of prisons. Later, he investigated the convict transportation system as the lieutenant governor of a prison colony off the coast of Australia. This led him to develop a revolutionary plan for penal reform (Barry, 1972).

Maconochie believed that pain and suffering were an essential part of any penal system, because they deterred others from violating the law and reinforced in the offender's mind the wrongfulness of his behavior. However, he felt its major objective should be to reform offenders. This required a prison program that emphasized persuasion, not coercion, and included (1) punishment for past behavior and (2) training to prepare offenders to return to society as useful, honest, and trustworthy citizens. He also felt that a system of reformation needed trained personnel. This required the formation of a Prison Service Career Tract, which should have a distinct status for prison administrators and a career ladder with promotion based on their success in reforming offenders.[5]

Maconochie believed that to change an offender, his sentence should be "task oriented"—that is, based on good conduct and performance of a specified quantity of labor rather than on a period of time. This came to be known as the **mark system,** because sentences were to consist of a specified number of marks or points based on the seriousness of the offense. Rather than a 10-year term for burglary, an offender's sentence might be 10,000 marks. The offender had to earn enough marks to pay off the debt to be released. Maconochie's system consisted of four stages that provided convicts with tangible goals and rewards to strive for (Taylor, 1978).

Penal Stage Upon entering prison, the inmate would be exposed to a short but severe penal stage designed to punish him for his past offenses. This included placement in solitary confinement, on a diet of bread and water, and moral instruction to instill in him a feeling of remorse for his past actions.

Associational Stage Felons then entered a second stage, which provided more freedom and allowed association between inmates. They were also given the opportunity to earn marks to reduce those assigned by the court. However, they could choose to do nothing and remain in prison indefinitely on a diet of bread and water. Marks were viewed as wages and could be earned by working, participation in educational programs, and good behavior. They could also be used to buy better clothing and food, deposited in a prison bank to be redeemed for cash upon discharge, or used toward obtaining an earlier release.

Finally, punishment for prison violations was imposed by adding marks to an offender's sentence. Maconochie felt this placed offenders' fate in their own hands. This was the first system to employ a form of indeterminate sentencing.[6]

Social Stage Inmates entered this third stage when the marks they earned had been reduced to those owed by a given percentage. This was labeled the "social stage," because inmates with common interests could organize into groups of six. Daily earnings were awarded to the group with each inmate receiving one sixth of the total, and conversely, individual fines and expenses were deducted from the group's total. This made each inmate responsible for the conduct of all group members. This taught inmates a sense of social responsibility, which Maconochie felt was required to live in society.

Ticket of Leave Finally, convicts earning a sufficient number of marks to offset those debited to them at sentencing were entitled to a conditional pardon known as a **ticket of leave.** Maconochie felt that once released, offenders should be able to feel totally free. They should not be subjected to police questioning, summary jurisdiction (the power to arrest and imprison them), or any other special conditions. Only a new conviction for a crime justified imprisonment (Barry, 1958). This is in contradiction to those who credit him with contributing to the development of parole,[7] because parole has always involved supervision.

Application of the Mark System In 1840, as the administrator of Norfolk Island penal colony off the coast of Australia, Maconochie first applied his system. This was one of Britain's worst colonies because it held "the twice-condemned"—criminals sent from England to penal colonies in Australia, where they committed new offenses. He was only able to implement a modified version of his program; it included an initial penal stage (and two others), in which progress was based on the acquisition of marks (Barry, 1958). He was unable to release offenders earning enough marks to offset those owed but did issue an "island ticket of leave," allowing them to live outside the main barracks and use their leisure time to work for themselves.

Despite these limitations, Maconochie was able in four short years to transform Britain's most dreaded penal colony into a modern, open institution. He dismantled the gallows, and almost totally eliminated whipping and confinement in irons. He also established schools, encouraged reading, and allowed convicts to eat with forks and knives instead of their fingers.

Maconochie recognized the importance of being open and available to talk to inmates and of treating them with dignity. He managed by walking around, which more than 100 years later came to be viewed as a key element in effective prison management (see Chapter 11):

> I encouraged all to address me with freedom. I would not even listen to a man unless he stood up and spoke to me like one. . . . I encouraged all, if they wanted to come to myself with their request, instead of seeking to make friends among those more immediately about me. To facilitate this I walked and rode about the island quite alone, and rather invited, than discouraged, conversation with any. . . . (Maconochie, 1859, as cited by Barry, 1958, p. 116)

Maconochie's Recall Maconochie found Norfolk Island a turbulent, brutal hell, and left it a peaceful, well-ordered community. However, English society still associated imprisonment with punishment and misery, which made many of his superiors hostile to his views. When word reached London that he had allowed inmates the luxury of celebrating the Queen's birthday with games and dinner, he was removed (Barry, 1958). He also was recalled because under his regime inmate costs increased by 21 percent, which contradicted his claims that his program would be less expensive. What he meant was that, in the long run, if offenders were reformed this system would save the government money. This is a problem that has continually plagued corrections; institutions with good programs will invariably cost more to operate. However, if these programs reduce recidivism rates, their higher short-term costs will be offset by long-term savings. Maconochie's superiors apparently ignored evidence that his program was successful; under 3 percent of 1,450 inmates discharged from the penal colony were convicted of new crimes, and only 20 of the 920 doubly convicted and "allegedly irreclaimable" were reconvicted (Barry, 1958). This is quite remarkable given the high unemployment rate in the areas where these inmates were released. Any warden today would be pleased with results of this kind, given the 62.3 percent recidivism rates of prison inmates during the late 1990s (Greenfield & Snell, 1999).

In 1849, Maconochie was appointed governor of the new Birmingham Borough Prison, but again, he was unable to fully implement his system (Barry, 1972). Maconochie failed in both cases because of the legally entrenched sentencing system, the inability to recruit a staff that subscribed to his principles, and the outward hostility of public officials.

Sir Walter Crofton's Irish System

The penal philosophy of Alexander Maconochie would have died if **Sir Walter Crofton** had not been appointed chairman of the board of directors of the Irish convict prisons. In 1854 when he assumed this position his most pressing problem was overcrowding (Dooley, 1978). He solved this by developing a new system that was labeled the **Irish system.** Like Maconochie's, Crofton's system (1) punished convicts for their past crimes and (2) prepared them for release by giving them the opportunity to earn increased responsibility and privileges while progressing through a four-stage system. Its basic facets are described in Table 5.2.

A variety of measures was used to gauge the success of this system. Among the most reliable was the decline in the prison population from 3,933 in 1854 when Crofton took office to 1,314 by 1862. Equally impressive

---

Table 5.2
Stages of the Irish System

Solitary Confinement Stage   Entrance phase
1. Entering offenders were incarcerated in a conventional prison (for about 9 months)
2. *Regimen:* Silence and solitary confinement, except during school, exercise, chapel, and work

Associational Stage   Commenced after successful completion of solitary confinement
1. Convicts were transferred to prisons where they worked on public works projects
2. Had to progress through three conduct classes, which required the accumulation of 108 marks and took about 12 months. Progress up the class structure brought rewards of better clothes and more privileges

Intermediate Stage   Crofton's unique contribution; entered after the accumulation of 108 marks
1. About three quarters of all convicts entered this stage.
2. *Rational:*
    a. Inmates had to prove to society that they were reformed by showing they had developed sufficient powers of self-control to resist temptation under circumstances of relative freedom
    b. Training under conditions of partial freedom prepared offenders for full freedom on release; thus, inmates were minimally supervised
3. *Uniqueness:* Represented an early antecedent of current prerelease centers
4. *Objections:*
    a. The requirement that prisons had to be built where the work was performed
    b. High cost of supervising the inmates
        (1) Solution: Build two portable huts that housed guards and inmates that could be dismantled and moved to another location when a project was completed

Conditional Release Stage   Entered upon completion of intermediate stage
1. Inmates granted a conditional pardon (ticket of leave) for the remainder of their sentence; represented first use of parole as the term is applied today
    a. Inmates were under supervision, and those disobeying regulations could be charged with a misdemeanor, summarily tried, and, if convicted, have their tickets of leave revoked

---

Sources: Barnes & Teeters, 1951; Dooley, 1978; Wines, 1895.

was the number of convicts who were successfully discharged from conditional release as compared with those returned to prison. Between 1856 and 1861, 1,227 tickets of leave were issued, of which only 5.6 percent were revoked (Dooley, 1978).

The Reformatory System

In the United States, the Irish system was a rallying point for penal reformers. They organized to translate these new principles of reform into practice. From this emerged the reformatory movement. In 1870, reformers developed a model for a new prison system at a conference in Cincinnati—the National Congress on Penitentiary and Reformatory Discipline—at which the **National Prison Association** (NPA) was organized[8] (Wines, 1895). The leading reform ideas of the era were discussed and incorporated into a **Declaration of Principles** that was adopted by the conference (see Table 5.3). It advocated "a philosophy of reformation as opposed to the adoption of punishment, progressive classification of prisoners based on the mark system, the indeterminate sentence, and the cultivation of the inmate's self-respect" (Barnes & Teeters, 1951, p. 524). The adoption of these principles was truly remarkable considering the brutal conditions of prisons during this era (Barnes & Teeters, 1951; McKelvey, 1977).

The Elmira Reformatory

The first reformatory, **Elmira Reformatory** in New York, opened in 1877 and was headed by **Zebulon T. Brockway.** For the next 20 years he made one of the most ambitious attempts to put the Declaration of Principles into effect at Elmira.

Judges sentenced first-time felons, ages 16 to 30, capable of being reformed to Elmira (Rothman, 1980). These offenders received modified indeterminate sentences, under which they were incarcerated until they were reformed or served their maximum term.

Upon entering the institution, inmates were placed in Grade 2. If they behaved acceptably and successfully completed their work or school assignments, they received 3 marks per month in each of these three areas (for a total of 9 marks per month). They needed 54 marks (which could be earned in as few as 6 months) to be promoted to Grade 1. Six additional months of good behavior in Grade 1, which yielded an additional 54 marks, entitled the inmate to parole. Thus "an obedient inmate could . . . earn release after just one year of confinement irrespective of his minimum sentence" (Pisciotta, 1994, p. 21). Uncooperative inmates were punished by being demoted to Grade 3. Promotion from Grade 3 to Grade 2 required 3 months of satisfactory behavior.

Table 5.3
Basic Tenets of the Declaration of Principles

1. Reformation, not vindictive suffering, should be the purpose of penal treatment of prisoners.
2. Classification should be made on the basis of a mark system, patterned after the Irish system.
3. Rewards should be provided for good conduct.
4. The prisoner should be made to realize that his destiny is in his own hands.
5. The chief obstacles to prison reform are the political appointment of prison officials, and the instability of management.
6. Prison officials should be trained for their jobs.
7. Indeterminate sentences should be substituted for fixed sentences, and the gross disparities and inequities in prison sentences should be removed. Also, it should be emphasized that repeated short sentences are futile.
8. Religion and education are the most important agencies of reformation.
9. Prison discipline should be such as to gain the will of the prisoner and conserve his self-respect.
10. The aim of the prison should be to make industrious freemen rather than orderly and obedient prisoners.
11. Industrial training should be fully provided for.
12. The system of contract labor in prisons should be abolished.
13. Prisons should be small, and there should be separate institutions for different types of offenders.
14. The law should strike against the so-called higher-ups in crime, as well as against the lesser operatives.
15. There should be indemnification for prisoners who are later discovered to be innocent.
16. There should be revision of the laws relating to the treatment of insane criminals.
17. There should be a more judicious exercise of the pardoning power.
18. There should be established a system for the collection of uniform penal statistics.
19. A more adequate architecture should be developed, providing sufficiently for air and sunlight, as well as for prison hospitals, school rooms, etc.
20. Within each state, prison management should be centralized.
21. The social training of prisoners should be facilitated through proper association and the abolition of the silence rules.
22. Society at large should be made to realize its responsibility for crime conditions (Wood & Waits, 1941, pp. 532–533).

Brockway's Innovative Programs

Brockway established a school program that enabled inmates to progress from learning basic arithmetic, reading, and writing skills to classes in psychology, ethics, and other studies. He also developed an industrial arts

At the Elmira Reformatory in New York, first-time felons between the ages of 16 and 30 were incarcerated until they were reformed or served their maximum time. The inmates participated in a school program in which they received training in trades such as drafting.

program that transformed Elmira into a truly industrial "reformatory." By the late 1880s, inmates could choose from more than 20 trades, and within the next 10 years 36 were available (e.g., shoemaker, fresco painter, blacksmith, carpenter, tailor). In 1888 when inmate labor was abolished because of business and labor pressure, Brockway established a military system, which included dressing inmates in uniforms, assigning them ranks, and dividing them into companies. This early precursor to *boot camps* involved inmate-soldiers marching 5 to 8 hours per day under military discipline that paralleled that at West Point. This was also one of the first prisons to use recreation (e.g., track, basketball) as a method of treatment (Pisciotta, 1983, 1994).

Brockway is also credited with developing the first parole system in the United States. Inmates successfully completing the grade system could request a hearing before the parole board, called the board of managers, who would determine their suitability for release after consulting with the superintendent. To be eligible they had to have a job and a place to live. While under supervision, they were required to (1) remain employed for 6 months, (2) submit monthly reports, cosigned by their employers, stating they were maintaining good work habits, (3) keep the same job, and (4) behave—that is, avoid alcohol use and association with undesirables. There were no paid parole officers, so Brockway had to rely on volunteers to supervise parolees during the 6-month parole period. Inmates violating the conditions of

their parole were returned to Elmira and placed in the second or third grade at Brockway's discretion and given another chance at reform (Pisciotta, 1994).

Finally, despite his progressive ideas for reform, Brockway's disciplinary methods were more severe than those advocated in the Declaration of Principles; however, he considered these punishments therapeutic. This position was consistent with his belief that inmates were disobedient patients and punishment was an interview process. One inmate who worked outside an "interview room" and observed inmates after they left related:

> He not alone paddles, but pounds, stamps, kicks, not alone the kidneys but all over the head and body. To be cut, scarred, marred, and beaten entirely out of shape is a frequent occurrence, and very often with a wide red mark across the face . . . which originated from Brockway's oiled strap. (Pisciotta, 1994, p. 37)

Brockway also employed other disciplinary methods, including (1) solitary confinement in what he called rest cure cells where inmates were placed on a restrictive diet of bread and water, sometimes put in restraints so they could not sit for hours; (2) administering a quick slap or punch in the face; and (3) whipping with a rubber hose. Apparently, Brockway considered these types of discipline appropriate because he never denied administering them and, in fact, argued they were for the inmates' own good (Pisciotta, 1983).

Reformatory Models Fell Short

Between 1877 and 1913 reformatories were established in 17 states. These institutions failed to socialize their inmates and mold them into obedient citizens-workers. Inmates at all these facilities rejected the authority of their custodians and, responding to the deprivations of prison life (see Chapter 7), coped by

> "resorting to...violence, revolts, escapes, drugs, arson, homosexuality [and] suicide" [which] forced reformatory [staff] to focus [on] custody and control in the interest of personal and organizational survival....[Thus] America's adult reformatories [including Elmira] were...ineffective and brutal prisons [rather than institutions of benevolent reform]. (Pisciotta, 1994, p. 103)

By 1910, the reformatory movement had reached its peak and was on the decline (Morse, 1940).

Although reformatories failed in practice, they crystallized progressive correctional thought. During the Big House Era—discussed in Chapter 7—which spanned the first half of the 20th century, there continued to be sporadic attempts to introduce bits and pieces of the Declaration of Principles into juvenile programs and even into adult institutions. However, it was not until after World War II, that the necessary support became available to create a new type of prison—the "rehabilitative institution" (see Chapter 7)—in which these ideas could be tested more fully.

Summary

Corporal and capital punishment were the most widely used methods of punishment during the colonial period; however, the social, economic, and intellectual forces of the American Revolution led to a reevaluation of these methods of social control.

The Pennsylvania and Auburn systems offered the most well known institutional changes in corrections at that time. The Pennsylvania reformers experimented with different systems, including the Walnut Street Jail, which was designed as a temporary state prison with a reformation orientation. The Eastern Penitentiary adopted a vastly different treatment approach characterized by solitary confinement, work, and penitence. The system devised at Auburn became the model for U.S. prisons. Auburn experimented with a threefold inmate classification system. Depending on the severity of their offense, inmates either worked together in silence, worked part-time alone and part-time together, or had no contact with one another. This plan of congregate work, silence, and separate cell confinement was adopted as an acceptable confinement method. Both the Auburn and Pennsylvania systems achieved worldwide recognition, which fostered a debate over which was the better model for future prisons. Ultimately, the Pennsylvania model was used by only a few jurisdictions in the United States; the Auburn system prevailed, primarily for economic reasons.

By the end of the Civil War, weaknesses in both systems were clear, suggesting the need for further reform.

Alexander Maconochie and Sir Walter Crofton heavily influenced the reformation movement. Maconochie's mark system was structured toward the goal of reformation. The mark system enabled inmates to work their way out of prison. Its first application at Norfolk Island was successful, but punitive public views resulted in Maconochie's recall. Crofton's Irish system was also designed to reform inmates, but the means to achieve this goal involved increasing privileges and phased release.

The reformatory movement directly emerged from the principles of the Irish system. Reformers developed a rehabilitative model for a new prison system, the first of which was Elmira Reformatory. Inmates in Elmira could progress through a "grade" system, which resulted in early release for the successful. Warden Brockway established a number of innovative programs, including educational and military systems. Elmira also had the first parole system in the United States. Despite his liberal reformation ideas, Brockway regressed to earlier disciplinary techniques, which he believed were therapeutic. Reformatories were established in 17 states, but their goals were never achieved.

Critical Thinking Questions

1. What was the importance of the Walnut Street Jail? Describe its program.
2. If you were given a choice of being sent as an inmate to Cherry Hill (Pennsylvania system) or Auburn Prison, which would you choose? Justify your answer by discussing the strengths of the system you choose and why you would find the other less attractive.
3. Why was the Auburn model adopted by most states in the United States?
4. What caused the failure of the Auburn and Pennsylvania models?
5. Detail the roles of Maconochie and Crofton in the development of the reformatory. Discuss why you would find these systems more attractive as an inmate than the other alternatives available at the time.
6. What were the advantages and disadvantages of being an inmate at the Elmira Reformatory?
7. Why did the reformatory movement fail?

Test Your Knowledge

1. Which of the following was a characteristic of the Walnut Street Jail?
   a. pay for work
   b. leg irons and chains
   c. guards that carried weapons
   d. frequent corporal punishment

2. Various alternatives were tried before the Auburn system was finally developed. Which of the following methods was experimented with at Auburn but did not become part of the system?

   a. silence

   b. 24-hour-a-day solitary confinement

   c. congregate labor

   d. severe corporal punishment

3. Which of the following modern correctional practices was foreshadowed by Maconochie's mark system?

   a. disciplinary hearings

   b. inmate vocational training

   c. indeterminate sentencing

   d. prison boot camps

4. Which of the following is *not* a key element of the 1870 National Prison Association's Declaration of Principles?

   a. solitary confinement

   b. indeterminate sentencing

   c. the mark system

   d. classification

Endnotes

1. David J. Rothman. *The Discovery of the Asylum.* Copyright ©1971 by David J. Rothman. By permission Little, Brown and Company.

2. A number of other states experimented with solitary confinement for short periods of time during the first third of the 19th century, but only New Jersey and Rhode Island systematically tested the Pennsylvania model. These other states included Maryland, Virginia, Massachusetts, and Maine.

3. As an evaluator you would have to determine if the conditions at Auburn were the same as those at Cherry Hill. A comparison of these conditions would reveal that Auburn lacked the larger, more roomy cells and failed to provide inmates with productive labor.

4. David J. Rothman. *Conscience and Convenience: The Asylum and Its Alternatives in Progressive America.* Copyright ©1980 by David J. Rothman. By permission Little, Brown and Company.

5. This was to be modeled after Britain's Foreign Service. England today does have a professional prison service with two distinct career tracks, one involving those seeking to be governors and the other for prisoner officers (correctional officers). While visiting English institutions, I was impressed with both groups.

6. See Chapter 2. Chapter 7 also examines indeterminate sentencing with a specific focus on its use as a part of a rehabilitation program.

7. For example, see Burns, 1975.

8. In 1941 the NPA was renamed the American Prison Association, and in 1954 it became the American Correctional Association.

Southern Penal Systems

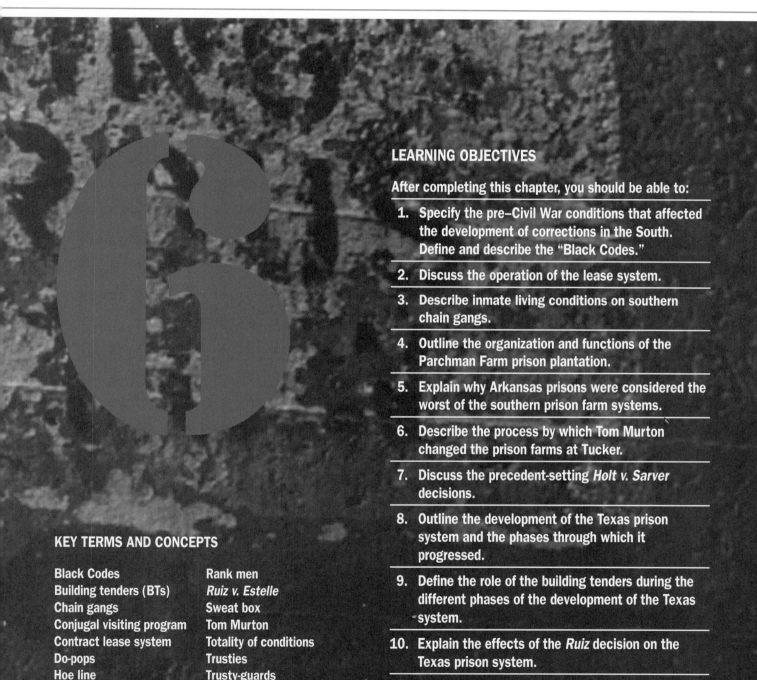

KEY TERMS AND CONCEPTS

Black Codes
Building tenders (BTs)
Chain gangs
Conjugal visiting program
Contract lease system
Do-pops
Hoe line
Lease system
Parchman Farm
Penal slavery

Rank men
Ruiz v. Estelle
Sweat box
Tom Murton
Totality of conditions
Trusties
Trusty-guards
Tucker telephone
Yard man

Introduction

Popular views of southern prison systems have been influenced by movies such as *Cool Hand Luke* and *Brubaker.* We have chosen to examine the southern system in a separate chapter because the different social and economic factors in this region produced methods of handling prisoners that were distinct from those in other parts of the country. The reader should remember that until the 1950s, southern states[1] were segregated by law and could generally be characterized as strongly racist. However, we do not wish to imply that the contemporary South is any more racist than the rest of the country.

Punishment in the Pre–Civil War South

Slave owners had traditionally dominated southern legislatures and protected their slave interests. Recognizing that both slaves and free men needed to be punished for their crimes, they felt separate laws were required to keep their slaves docile and to prevent them from running away. These laws, called **Black Codes,** inflicted more severe punishments on slaves than on whites for many offenses and defined certain acts as crimes only when committed by slaves. For example, in Virginia slaves could be executed for rape or buying or receiving stolen property, whereas whites received only prison sentences. In Louisiana, slaves could be executed for striking their owners for the third time. Imprisonment was not imposed on slaves because it deprived owners of their labor.

The population of pre–Civil War prisons was composed almost solely of white males and a few free blacks with the exception of Virginia and Maryland, where free blacks composed one third to one half of the prison population. Generally, the racial groups were segregated, but sometimes whites and blacks had to be housed in the same facilities. This "problem" was solved in 1858 when blacks began being leased to private contractors for work outside prisons on canals, roads, and bridges (Ayers, 1984).[2]

Women represented a small proportion of the prison population during this era. They were generally housed in small, dirty, and unventilated buildings within the prison. Many were also sexually abused, often resulting in pregnancy. However, because so few were imprisoned, their plight was generally ignored. Their best chance was to gain early release through a pardon, which governors, sensitive to their plight, often granted (Ayers, 1984).

Auburn-type prisons in the South were initially established to reform offenders through compulsory labor. Like prisons in the North, they established industrial shops that produced goods for sale on the open market to pay operating costs. However, these industries failed to produce enough revenue to pay for prison operations. To remedy this, some states experimented with the lease system. Under this system, in some cases, a private company was contracted to control and operate prison shops, with the warden retaining overall control of inmates (Ayers, 1984). In others, the entire prison operation was handed over to a company for a fee or a portion of the profits from the convict labor. Because lessees wanted to maximize their profits, they fed and clothed inmates as cheaply as possible, used guards willing to work for substandard wages, or used inmates in this capacity and worked them from dawn to dusk for punishment. Rule violations were severe and included solitary confinement on bread and water (Sellin, 1976).

The Post–Civil War Period

After the Civil War, the economy and the infrastructure of the southern states were in shambles and heavy taxes were required to rebuild them. At the same time they still had to deal with those convicted of crimes. Several factors led most southern states to choose a lease system to deal with inmates (Ayers, 1984). Despite its popularity in the South (96 percent of all leased convicts were in the South), the lease system was actually invented in Massachusetts in 1798. Its widespread use in the post–Civil War South was primarily a function of the political economy following military defeat and the termination of slavery (Myers, 1998).

The Lease System

The lease system gained popularity in the post–Civil War period for a number of reasons. After the war, large numbers of free blacks began to be arrested as criminals, soon constituting 90 percent of those incarcerated. Because of deep racist beliefs, the crime problem became confused with "the negro problem." For these racists, this was "proof" of the inherent criminality of blacks and of their "inferiority." A more accurate characterization of southern blacks was that most were disorganized, uneducated, and poverty stricken—a legacy of their former slave status. In one rare instance, Aure Aranud, a courageous Louisiana legislator, offered a remarkably frank explanation of the criminal motives of blacks:

> Can you not see that [the fact that black tenant farmers or laborers rarely had incomes exceeding $40 per year] is not sufficient to support [them]? And every day you divest him from a chance of earning something is a robbery of his daily bread? Should any one . . . be surprised to hear that negroes steal? I am surprised that they do not steal more. (cited in Hair, 1962, as quoted by Carleton, 1971, pp. 44–45)

Arguments like Aranud's fell on deaf ears; the problem focused on how to deal with this expanding inmate population.

A second factor was the combination of bad economic times and the run-down condition of many state prisons. Because states could not afford to build enough new prisons to house an escalating convict population, many turned to leasing as a temporary solution.

Third, the change from an agricultural slave economy to the beginnings of industrial development created a demand for labor. This was in short supply in many parts of the region, especially in dangerous jobs such as mining, building railroads, and turpentine production. Convicts provided a reliable workforce: they could not get whiskey; they were not allowed to brawl; and they were chained together and guarded by men ordered to shoot anyone attempting to escape or to whip those not keeping up the work pace. Mississippi's experience in using inmates to build a railroad through the Canay Swamps illustrates these conditions:

> [Inmates] were placed in the swamp in water ranging to their knees, and in almost nude state they spaded caney and rooty ground, their bare feet chained together by chains that fretted the flesh. They were compelled to attend to the calls of nature in line as they stood day in and day out, their thirst compelling them to drink the water in which they were compelled to deposit their excrement. (Foreman & Tatum, 1938, p. 260, cited by Sellin, 1976, p. 148)

There was a bright side and a dark side to the lease system. It gave impetus to industrial development in the South, which would not have been possible for many years. However, it did so at a terrible cost to those inmates who were involved in it (Ayers, 1984).

A fourth reason for its popularity was that law-abiding citizens had no concern for the welfare of criminals despite the documented horrendous and inhumane conditions under which leased convicts worked. Added to this was the fact that most lessees were free blacks and this returned them to a condition of servitude.

Fifth, this system was justified on the grounds that it reformed its charges. Claims were made that it taught work and discipline. Indeed, the system gained a reputation, even among foreign visitors, of turning out good workers (Ayers, 1984).

Sixth, there were major economic incentives for maintaining the lease system. It was ideally suited for industrialists whose only concern was making money and for the states who benefited from fees paid by contractors (Ayers, 1984). Further, the lease system provided a constant pool of labor that could be used at any type of job.

A final factor making this system attractive to contractors was that convicts could be forced to work under conditions that free laborers would not tolerate. In many camps, guards would wake up convicts at 4:30 A.M. and work them until nightfall with only a 40-minute dinner break. With the exception of Sundays and holidays, they worked every day regardless of the weather.

This system of **penal slavery** made both black and white convicts the temporary or lifelong "slaves" of their employers. Under most leases, convicts were turned over to contractors who were responsible for feeding, clothing, disciplining, and sometimes housing them. Contractors also paid annual fees, providing added revenue, which sometimes constituted sizable portions of a state's budget. In Alabama and Tennessee this amounted to about 10 percent of these states' incomes (Ayers, 1984).

Under the lease system, convicts were turned over to private contractors in return for the payment of an annual fee. The lease system provided a labor supply to penal farms such as this one in Mississippi, but convicts were often subjected to harsh discipline and unsanitary living conditions.

Living conditions in the work camps were scarcely above subsistence level (McKelvey, 1977). Inmates lived in grossly overcrowded foul smelling huts that were completely closed up at night. They also slept on crude bunks; sanitary conditions were abysmal and rampant disease was common. A glimpse of these conditions is provided by our Historical Perspective feature: "The American Siberia: Life Under the Florida Lease System."

Discipline in the work camps was quite severe. Although whipping was the usual punishment, some guards devised ingenious forms of torture or reinstituted others dating from the Middle Ages. These included the "ordeal by water," where prisoners had a funnel forced in their mouth, into which a steady stream of water was poured. Also used was the medieval practice of "hanging by the thumbs," which produced great agony and even death. Many convicts were also subjected to as many as 10 hours or more in the **sweat box:**

> [which was] a coffin like cell with just enough space to accommodate a man standing erect. Generally made of wood or tin it was completely closed except for a hole two inches in diameter at nose level. When placed under the blistering southern sun, the temperature inside becomes unbearable. In a few hours, a man's body swells and occasionally bleeds. (Moos, 1942, p. 18)

To prevent escape, convicts wore striped uniforms, were usually shackled, and sometimes had heavy iron balls attached to the chains. Dogs and armed guards provided added security measures. The escape attempts, harsh

discipline, and barbaric and unsanitary conditions produced very high convict mortality rates.

In the South after the Civil War, this new form of penal slavery for blacks, which was worse than the plantation system, enabled the state to transfer its responsibility for convicts to a private authority that also paid for it (Sellin, 1976). This era represents one of the low points in American corrections.

The lease system was also employed in several western states and territories—Washington territory, Montana, Wyoming, Nebraska, and Oregon (McKelvey, 1977). It was not until 1936 that the system was finally abolished in every state (Barnes & Teeters, 1951). We will see in the Epilogue that overcrowding and the high cost of prison construction and operation in the 1980s prompted states and local jurisdictions to reconsider the involvement of private contractors in managing prisons and prisoners.

Chain Gangs

The term **chain gang** has been used to refer to all southern prison camps that employed inmates at hard labor. We will employ it only to refer to the use by counties and states of chained convicts to build railroads and levees and to construct and maintain county roads and state highways.[3] Many jurisdictions viewed this as an excellent way to improve roads required by the advent of the automobile and to avoid building expensive prisons. To maximize output and minimize escapes, armed guards and shackles were used. Whipping and other harsh practices were used to discipline those who were unruly or

---

HISTORICAL PERSPECTIVE

The American Siberia: Life Under the Florida Lease System

The line of the proposed railroad was through a virgin wilderness; there seems to have been no attention whatever paid to proper equipment, and the story of that terrible journey stands unparalleled in criminal annals. Dozens of those who went into the tropical marshes and palmetto jungles of Lake Eustace went to certain death. There was no provision made for either shelter or supplies. Rude huts were built of whatever material

came to hand, and in the periods of heavy rain it was no unusual thing for the convicts to awake in the morning half submerged in mud and slime. The commissary department dwindled into nothing . . . there was no food at all. . . . [T]he convicts were driven to live as the wild beasts, except that they were only allowed the briefest intervals from labor to scour the woods for food. They dug up roots and cut the tops from "cabbage" palmetto trees. Noble Hawkins, a ten-year Nassau convict, lived for fourteen days on nothing but palmetto tops and a

little salt, and his case was but one of many. . . . It was not long before the camp was ravaged by every disease induced by starvation and exposure. The pestilential swamps were full of fever, and skin maladies; scurvy and pneumonia ran riot. Dysentery was most common, and reduced the men to a point of emaciation difficult to describe or to credit. Every stopping-place was a shambles, and the line of survey is punctuated by grave-yards (Powell, 1891/1970, pp. 10–13).

Southern prison camps used "chain gangs" of convicts to build railroads and maintain roads and highways. The shackles were never removed, and the men slept chained together in cages.

unwilling to work. Our Historical Perspective feature, "Life on the Chain Gang: Even Circus Animals Lived Better," on page 104 provides a perspective on conditions prevailing in some camps (Tannenbaum, 1924).

Convicts on the chain gang worked 10- to 12-hour days, depending on the season. The guards overseeing these inmates were poorly paid, were usually illiterate, and could only control the inmates by resorting to brute force (Sellin, 1976). Flogging was the most common form of punishment until it was abolished in most states just prior to World War II. Despite the efforts of reformers in some states, few if any, changes were made in the terrible conditions on chain gangs until the mid-1950s.

Prison Farming in the 1900s

When some southern states abolished leasing, they developed large prison farms and plantations for those convicts who were not employed on the roads. These institutions operated primarily to maximize profits and reduce or eliminate the costs of imprisoning convicted offenders. The treatment inmates received was not much better than that received by inmates on the chain gangs. The Carolinas were the first states to initiate penal farming on a large scale, and afterward the concept was followed to some extent in all the southern states. By the 1930s, the major southern penal farms were An-

gola in Louisiana and Cummins in Arkansas. No southern state, however, developed penal farming to a greater extent than Mississippi, where the state penitentiary, **Parchman Farm,** became the prototype. The work of William Banks Taylor (1984, 1993,[4] 1997, 1998) provides an excellent history of the Mississippi penal system. Drawing on his work, we briefly examine the development of this system as an example of the prison farm concept.

The Parchman Penal Farm in Mississippi

The penal farm organization followed a plantation model under which each farm was divided into essentially autonomous field camps for purposes of crop rotation, accountability, self-sufficiency, simplified management, and the dispersal of laborers. By 1917, 13 camps were operating, producing cotton and their own food (Taylor, 1984, 1993).

Labor on these farms, which was "under the gun," began at sunrise, 6 days a week. Convicts were marched to the fields under the supervision of an unarmed sergeant—who ran the camp—and his unarmed assistants and several armed **trusty-guards.** They were the only armed men on the farms. They functioned as the camp security force both in the fields and at night and could

HISTORICAL PERSPECTIVE

Life on the Chain Gang: Even Circus Animals Lived Better

Frank Tannenbaum (1924) provides a rare glimpse of life at a camp that employed cages to house its convicts.

As soon as a man comes to a chain gang camp he is shackled. That shackle generally stays put as long as he is there—and that may be a life-time. The chain is riveted to both ankles.... A dozen men and more will be chained to each other when they are asleep in their beds [at night, all day Sunday, when it rains—which can last for two weeks—and sometimes during the day. This means they have no freedom of movement]. Thus, they lie in their beds on Sundays... [and f]requently, when it rains [they] may be [there]....The typical cages [they sleep in] are small. They stand on wheels...[and] range from seven by seven [to]...nine by twenty. The[y have] 18 beds,...nine beds on each side of the cage... [stacked] three... high...other....They lie on their beds, their faces almost touching the bed above them. The cage frequently has tin roofing. On hot days—Sundays, Saturday afternoons, holidays—the sun streams down on the cage and makes an oven of the place, and the human beings in it roast. These cages are not cleaned. Under this crowding it would be impossible to keep them sanitary... [These] steel road cage[s were] similar to those used for circus animals, except they did not have the privacy which would be given to a respectable lion, tiger, or bear. (pp. 84–86)

shoot escaping convicts. Using convict trustees to perform most guard, service, and support functions kept the prison's payroll quite low. Trusty status was also a powerful reward for good behavior (Taylor, 1993). They worked as staff sergeants, cooks, hospital orderlies, and skilled artisans. This system's cost effectiveness and efficiency, which was an outgrowth of the pre–Civil War slave structure on plantations, allowed it to continue until a federal court finally intervened in 1972 (*Gates v. Collier*, 1972).

Parchman's system of convict discipline reflected the principles advanced by Alexander Maconochie, Sir Walter Crofton, and Zebulon Brockway (discussed in Chapter 5), which advocated progressive penal stages for convicts based on adherence to fixed rules of behavior. A reasonable schedule of rewards and punishments encouraged adherence to rules. All convicts began their sentence in the cotton rows, manning the "long line" under the gun from dawn until dusk. This was Parchman's version of Maconochie's old penal system. Encouraging productive labor in the rows provided both negative and positive behavioral stimuli. A number of indulgences—splendid food, mash liquor produced by convicts, gambling privileges, and participation in sports—were made available to productive and well-behaved gunmen.

The **conjugal visiting program** was another major incentive for black inmates. Its origins are unclear; initially it was neither legislatively sanctioned nor concerned with maintaining marital relationships. As early as 1918, this system provided black convicts access to both prostitutes and visiting spouses. Authorities viewed sexual favors as valuable in the management of black convicts (Taylor, 1998). By the 1930s, black inmates could take their wives or girlfriends to their sleeping quarters where privacy was secured by hanging up blankets (Hopper, 1969). In 1940, some camps constructed a makeshift building, known as the red house for its color, to be used for conjugal visiting. Camp sergeants viewed this as an effective motivational tool, but there is little doubt it had negative effects on white prisoners who were denied this privilege initially.[5] By the early 1950s, most black and white male camps had "red houses," although prostitutes were now excluded from the camps (Hopper, 1969). It was not until 1957 that the conjugal visiting program was formally recognized when a reform-oriented warden officially established what he called his "family day program." Thus, the oldest conjugal visiting system in the nation was initially racially motivated, but by the time it was officially recognized, it had a more humanistic basis. (Chapter 21 discusses further the issues regarding conjugal visits.)

The reward system also included early release. Pardons and early release were granted for good behavior, meritorious conduct (usually given to a trusty-shooter who prevented escapes by shooting the escapees), and general clemency on major holidays (e.g., Christmas) or when a governor left office (Taylor, 1993).

Convicts refusing to obey the rules were whipped with a wide belt known as "Black Annie" and/or transferred to a maximum security unit known as "Little Alcatraz." Isolation on a restricted diet was rarely used because it weak-

At a chain gang work camp, portable wagons were used to house inmates.

ened convicts, enabling them to escape work. All forms of corporal punishment were finally banned by a federal court in 1972 (*Gates v. Collier*, 1972; Taylor, 1998).

Growth of the Prison Farm Complex

Governor James K. Vardaman was responsible for legislation defining Parchman as Mississippi's primary prison facility in 1906 (Taylor, 1993). He felt that institutions should be self-sufficient, make a profit, and reform inmates by providing job skills. Between 1906 and 1933, while other systems operated at a loss, Mississippi prisons made $4 million above their operating costs. The self-sufficiency of the farm operations created opportunities for inmates to learn trades and provided housing, food, and medical care up to the standards of the period (Taylor, 1993). By 1933, with the Great Depression in full swing, the system experienced declining revenues. The legislature was unwilling to fund the prison adequately, resulting in a deterioration of the physical plant and living conditions for inmates. To increase revenues, superintendents diversified prison operations at Parchman by establishing new canning and shoe factories and a modern slaughterhouse. This helped to pump huge revenues into the state treasury and to provide work for those displaced from farms because of mechanization.

During the 1940s and 1950s, there were improvements in health care, living conditions, and in the food inmates received. Educational programming was also initiated along with a new classification system under which tests determined work and educational placements. However, declining revenues from a depressed cotton market forced an increasing number of pardons and the early release of better inmates—including many trusty-shooters who really controlled the camps—to save money. This worsened the system's security problems (Taylor, 1993). Despite some improvements in working conditions and medical care, by 1956 Mississippi prisons were being targeted by the civil rights movement for their racist policies. A new superintendent was brought in to change the system's image. He initiated several programs, but the real change involved the abolition of the prison's "money-making" philosophy in favor of an approach emphasizing the rehabilitation and welfare of prisoners and the protection of society (Taylor, 1993).

This approach was short-lived. In the early 1960s, through better management and increasing mechanization, an attempt was made to restore Parchman's to the "good old days" when the farm was making money. Continuing deficits forced cuts in staff, medical and food services, and even in inmate clothing. However, the real problems resulted from a change in the inmate population. This system was established to handle a largely black, illiterate, unskilled, and rural population, but by the mid-1960s the offenders admitted were 40 percent white and almost 90 percent literate. These white inmates were more unmanageable and often from urban backgrounds, which made them less willing to do farm work. Further, the civil rights movement inspired blacks to resist their "oppressive" treatment, and the probation and parole systems removed the most easily managed inmates. Finally, agricultural mechanization increased inmate idleness, because new programs were insufficient to absorb those previously involved in farm work.

Security then became a critical problem, which was further aggravated by a short-staffed civilian workforce. Trusty-shooters continued to be the primary security force, because the legislature refused to fund a civilian guard system. By the late 1960s, inmates complained about being mistreated, overworked, fed terribly, and forced to endure merciless whippings and other tortures by guards and trusties.

The Courts Intervene

After a U.S. Circuit Court finding in 1970 that the totality of conditions in Arkansas prisons violated Eighth Amendment protections against cruel and unusual punishment, the Mississippi legislature acted to protect itself. It hired a qualified superintendent but failed to fund newly established staff positions to replace the inmate guards, to ban the lash, and to solve the question of racial inequities. This led to an inmate class action lawsuit filed in 1971, seeking relief from alleged unconstitutional conditions and practices at Parchman. The judge found that confinement at the prison deprived inmates of their basic constitutional rights (*Gates v. Collier*, 1972). He ordered immediate changes, including the elimination of segregation of inmates by race, mail censorship, and confinement of inmates under improper conditions in solitary confinement. The prison was also required to adopt a meaningful classification system, provide inmates better protection and medical care, phase out the trusty-shooters, and improve physical facilities. Finally, the judge ordered the state to devise a plan to improve inmate housing, water, treatment, medical services, and firefighting facilities.

Although the unconstitutional conditions that existed and the problems addressed by the inmate suit have largely been corrected, Taylor (1993) asserts that the Mississippi penal system remains an "ongoing problem" plagued by a number of problems, including a lack of political support, poor morale, increasing inmate-on-inmate violence, racially based gangs, inmate idleness, and reduced participation in programs. Nevertheless, Taylor (1999) contends that, historically, the Parchman Farm was among the most effective penal institutions in the United States. It was the last revenue-generating prison in the nation, recording a net profit of over half a million dollars as late as 1955 to 1956. It was a "prison administrator's dream come true": a place that promoted incredible security and uncommonly close relationships between the keepers, the kept, and the families of the kept (Cabana, 1996).

The anonymous veteran employees interviewed by Taylor (1999) contributed some profoundly ironic reflections on Parchman Farm prior to court intervention:

> Just maybe, the failure of convicts to return constituted a rare triumph for convict rehabilitation . . . old Parchman Farm, after all, was much more than a cotton plantation: it was a largely self-sufficient community, a place where convicts worked in a wide variety of very practical jobs, many of them managerial positions, and a number of the jobs taught skills that were as marketable outside the prison as within it. . . . [Also the institution was secure in that it had few attempted escapes and of these, few were successful. And was not . . . plagued by horrible riots many other prisons were.] . . . also [it had better] food, better health, and a much smaller number of deaths. . . . [It would be possible to conclude, they suggested, that by most objective standards the old penal farm was remarkably successful.] (Taylor, 1999, pp. 5–6)

Nonetheless, in 1996 a scholar revisited Parchman Farm and offered another view, labeling the regime as "worse than slavery" (Oshinsky, 1996).

Arkansas: The Worst of the Southern Systems

Although many prison farms such as Angola in Louisiana have vied for the honor of the "worst" prison farm, the Arkansas system appears to win the prize. The horrendous conditions at the two prison farms composing this system were brought to public attention by an official investigation released to the press in January 1967, when newly elected Governor Winthrop Rockefeller was about to take office. In his inaugural address, Rockefeller described this prison system as the "worst in the nation." He appointed a reform warden, **Tom Murton,** to bring these institutions, still operating using 18th-century methods, up to mid-20th-century standards (Murton & Hyams, 1969). The system consisted of the Cummins Farm (16,000 acres) and the Tucker Farm (4,500 acres), each producing rice, cotton, vegetables, and livestock. The combined inmate population was close to 2,000, with only 34 civilian employees at the two facilities.

The Pre-Murton Arkansas System In the Arkansas system an inmate's status was very important, because it determined his living conditions, treatment, and privileges.

Trusties were at the top of the inmate hierarchy. With only three civilian employees, trusties were responsible for operating most facets of the prison, including serving as guards and operating prison services (e.g., food, medical, farm). They had their own dormitory, the most freedom, and the best food and were in the best position to extort money and goods from inmates. The middle-status group, half-trusties or **do-pops,** were so named because they had duties that included popping doors open for superiors, cleaning buildings, waiting tables, and caring for the animals. They had their own dormitory, ate almost as well as the trusties, and were one step from trusty status.

Rank men, or farm laborers, were on the lowest level in the inmate classification system. In the barracks, they were subjected to being kicked and walked on by trusties. They could be forced to sweep all night and at daybreak be marched to the fields where the trusty-guard could beat them all day. They had no socks, underwear, t-shirts, or outerwear to protect them against the cold. They worked the hardest, ate the worst food, and lived in abysmal conditions.

Although all prisons have sub-rosa economies and power structures, inmate control of these farms led to a system of extreme corruption, brutality, and deprivation. Trusties frequently deprived incoming inmates of their money or property by threats or with promises of better treatment. Inmates without outside resources were forced to bargain with their bodies, which included selling their blood (blood-sucking program).[6] Powerful inmates victimized younger and weaker ones. Arkansas had no minimum age for prison confinement, so there were many 14-year-olds in the system who were ripe for "punking" (being made into passive homosexual partners for other inmates).

Whereas most rank men ate poorly, those with money could buy extra food from the inmate serving it. Trustees sold "good beds" for $1 to $3; the right to receive medical care also had its price (*Holt v. Sarver*, 1970; Murton & Hyams, 1969). To survive, inmates developed various rackets. Laundry workers charged a $2 fee to clean clothes, and they sold food. Kitchen workers bought food from the commissary and prepared it using the prison kitchen. Gambling flourished. Trusties profited most because they controlled everything in the prison, including jobs, discipline, housing, food, and access to services and administration. The trusties' freedom to leave the farm to go to town meant they could bring back free-world items, such as weapons, liquor, and drugs, to sell to other inmates at a considerable profit. The most incredible aspect of this system was the inmate shacks. A trusty with power and money could obtain lumber to build a shack. Appropriate payoffs to facility technicians would get him water, electricity, and gas. He then bought a television, a gas range, and a refrigerator and became a squatter. When he left, he could sell his job, house, and personal property to his successor. These "squatters" were even allowed to bring women to these "homes." Some trusties did so well they did not want to leave the prison (*Holt v. Sarver*, 1970).

Although the prison superintendent was responsible for seeing that there were no inmate escapes, his major function was to operate the farm at a profit. This required the planting and harvesting of 56 different crops. To achieve this, he made a deal with the **yard man**—the chief trusty—who really ran the prison:

> He told them, "Get the crops in and keep the men quiet, I will give you extra privileges. I don't care how you manage. Use a lead pipe, anything. Just do it. And keep anything you make on the side." (Murton & Hyams, 1969, pp. 42–43)

The control of men who were cold, hungry, tired, and hopeless required a brutal system of punishment. This included whipping and torture that ranged from inmates having their fingers, toes, noses, ears, or genitals pinched with pliers to having needles inserted under their fingernails. The most dreaded and vicious torture was the **Tucker telephone,** which is profiled with other punishments in our Close-Up, "Corporal Punishment Arkansas Style."

As late as 1966, the Arkansas parole system was an extension of the system of penal slavery. As a parolee, an inmate became an indentured slave; that is, to be paroled, an inmate had to be sponsored for a job. Sponsorship was usually accorded to people who had contacts

Corporal Punishment Arkansas Style

Whipping—Oh, Captain!

LL-34 said that in April 1966 he was whipped for not picking enough "pickles," and Mr. Bruton ordered his head peeled [shaved] and he was given ten more lashes on the bare buttocks. He refused to cry out "Oh, Captain!" and was locked up for another hour, then given twenty more lashes by Mr. Bruton (Murton & Hyams, 1969, p. 11).

The Infamous "Tucker Telephone"

The telephone designed by prison superintendent Jim Bruton consisted of an electric generator taken from a crank-type telephone and wired in sequence with two dry-cell batteries. An undressed inmate was strapped to the treatment table at Tucker Hospital while electrodes were attached to his big toe and to his penis. The crank was then turned, sending an electrical charge into his body. [This was known as being "rung up" in contrast to receiving a "long distance call," which involved the infliction of several charges.] . . . Sometimes the "telephone" operator's skill was defective, and the sustained current not only caused the inmate to lose consciousness but resulted in irreparable damage to his testicles. Some men were literally driven out of their minds (Murton & Hyams, 1969, p. 7). [The Tucker telephone was not only used to punish inmates but also for getting them to provide information.]

CLOSE-UP

with the parole board. Thus, parolees could be worked like slaves because if they complained or tried to get another job, the employer could call their parole officer, who would send them back to prison.

The Murton System Murton decided to change this system by first assuming control of Tucker Farm, the smaller of the two farms. Taking charge of an institution that was almost entirely run by inmates was extremely difficult, because it was impossible to eliminate past practices and abuses without their cooperation. To win their cooperation, he set up an educational program with the help of the school district and a vocational training program that provided marketable skills and jobs on release with the local gas company. He also guaranteed the rank men that they would be coming back at night and not mysteriously disappearing in the fields. Murton instituted controls to reduce gambling and the production of alcohol. He improved food, clothing, and working conditions and replaced the system of purchasing jobs with one based on merit. He established an elected camp council, formed a disciplinary committee that heard all complaints against inmates, decided guilt or innocence, rendered judgment, and determined punishment. Murton reserved the right to veto any action and gave inmates the option of having their cases heard only by him. The strap and the other barbaric punishments were replaced with solitary confinement of one to two days.

Farm operations and food service were reorganized and a new doctor was hired who was concerned about inmate welfare. Inmates were given footlockers with padlocks, and a recreation program was established. Within 10 months, Murton felt he had accomplished enough at Tucker to assume control of Cummins and began making changes similar to those at Tucker. However, his tenure was cut short as a result of a controversial investigation in which Murton brought to light the high number of inmates who had disappeared—most of whom were listed as escapees or who had died under questionable circumstances. He concluded that some, if not most, of these inmates had been murdered by prison officials or other inmates. In the controversy following these revelations, Murton was fired in 1968, ostensibly for being "incapable of and insensitive to the requirements of operating in harmony with his associates in a government structure" (Murton & Hyams, 1969, p. 191).

The Courts Intervene When Murton left Arkansas, conditions basically reverted to the way they were before his arrival. Fortunately for the inmates, beginning in the late 1960s the federal courts adopted a "hands-on approach to prisons," which opened the way for inmates to challenge unconstitutionally harsh practices. In *Jackson v. Bishop* (1968), the federal Appeals Court ruled that whipping for disciplinary purposes violated Eighth Amendment protections against cruel and unusual pun-

ishment. Further, in *Holt v. Sarver*, 1969, and in *Holt v. Sarver*, 1970, the federal court instituted the concept of a **totality of conditions** as proof. Thus, taken individually, conditions cited may not have represented constitutional violations, but taken in "their totality" (i.e., together) they did constitute cruel and unusual punishment and violated the Eighth Amendment. The court found inadequate medical and dental facilities and inmate access to them and unsanitary kitchen facilities. The court went to on say that:

> For the ordinary convict a sentence to the Arkansas Penitentiary today amounts to a banishment from civilized society to a dark and evil world completely alien to the free world, a world that is administered by criminals under rules and customs completely foreign to free world culture. . . . A convict . . . has no assurance whatever that he will not be killed, injured or sexually assaulted . . . confinement involves living under degrading and disgusting conditions. . . . However constitutionally tolerable the Arkansas system may have been in former years, it simply will not do today as the Twentieth Century goes into its eighth decade. (*Holt v. Sarver*, 1970, p. 381)

The judge ruled that if the state wanted to continue confining inmates at these prison farms it had to eliminate the trusty and field guard system, ensure inmate safety, change the barracks system, and eliminate the isolation cells. It deemed these conditions so intolerable that it required these changes be made in months rather than years.

Our Close-Up, "The Arkansas Prison System in the 1990s," provides a brief look at how this system has changed since the 1970s.

The Texas System

No discussion of southern penal systems would be complete without including the Texas prison system, which was and still is the largest in the region. In 1849, the first Texas penitentiary based on the Auburn model was opened in Huntsville. Its inmates were expected to produce sufficient quantities of goods to make it self-supporting. The history of how Texas dealt with inmates can be divided into several periods, including the 1871 to 1876 early contract period and the 1876 to 1909 contract lease system; the agricultural expansion period or the era of the plantation farm (1910–1947); the period of reform and stability (1948–1971); and the period of court intervention (1972–1990).

The Contract Period and Contract Lease System In the decades following the Civil War, and after failing to operate a profitable prison manufacturing program, Texas officials decided to lease the entire prison operation to private businesses. Thus, convicts were housed, fed,

The Arkansas Prison System in the 1990s

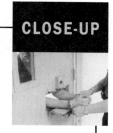

The legal dispute regarding the constitutionality of the Arkansas prison system lasted for 13 years. By 1982, Arkansas had convinced the court that its prisons met "minimal constitutional standards." Only a very few people associated with Arkansas corrections (e.g., a few inmates with long sentences) saw the case through from its initiation until it was settled.

During the 13 years the federal courts were involved in Arkansas corrections many changes occurred, including replacing inmate trusty supervisors with trained staff; establishing inmate rights through formalized disciplinary and grievance processes; creating sanitary and humane living and working conditions; improving medical care; and constructing new facilities costing millions of dollars. Staff increased from 35 to more than 1,000 during this period, and budgets increased accordingly.

By 1980 the Arkansas system had left behind its 19th-century approach and become a relatively conventional system. However, problems remain and Arkansas faces the same major issues as most other systems. After implementing tougher sentencing laws, the demand for prison bed space increased dramatically. Between the early 1970s and 1997 the Arkansas prison population increased from about 2,000 to over 10,000 inmates. Despite budget increases (e.g., $6 million in 1977 to $178 million in 1997), the system still struggles to accommodate a rising inmate population. It is not unusual to have hundreds of convicted offenders in county jails waiting for prison space.

By the mid-1990s, all units owned by the Department of Corrections, including Cummins, were accredited by the American Correctional Association. Further, the number of offenders sent to community correctional programs (primarily probation) increased strikingly. In 1993 the state created a separate Department of

Community Punishment—with an annual budget of approximately $30 million—which administers probation, parole, and nontraditional residential centers for offenders. During 1997, construction of new units and the expansion of existing facilities continued; and by the summer there were about 25,000 felons on probation. Two private prisons were to receive their first inmates in January 1998. Thus, correctional expansion and reform in Arkansas continue to unfold.

Source: Prepared especially for Corrections: A Comprehensive View, *2nd ed., by Jack E. Dison, Associate Professor, Department of Criminology, Arkansas State University.*

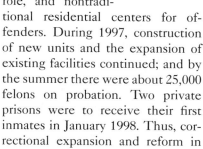

worked, and cared for by contractors whose only concern was profit. Although the state saved money, the brutality and neglect to which the inmates were subjected was extreme and ranged from poor clothing and food to beatings and murder (Copeland, 1980; Crouch & Marquart, 1989).[7]

Between 1876 and 1883, the state assumed more supervisory control over Huntsville prison and its inmates. The result was a **contract lease system** under which prison officials were responsible for supervising, disciplining, and housing the inmates while inmates worked for private contractors. In 1885, to make its prisons more self-sufficient, the state purchased its first prison farm. This established an agricultural component, which in the next era became its major aspect. The contract lease system failed to improve inmate conditions substantially, leading to continued criticism; yet it persisted for over 25 years (Crouch & Marquart, 1989; Martin & Eckland-Olson, 1987).

The Plantation Farm Period Around 1880, the prison system began to buy thousands of acres of farmland around Huntsville and Houston. With the demise of the contract lease system, the prisons entered into the agricul-

tural business in a big way. Although not economically successful, these farms provided work for a large proportion of the inmates, who continued to be harshly treated. By 1947, conditions were so bad that the Texas prisons were labeled as among the nation's worst.

The prison farms were so spread out and remotely located that they required no fencing. Remoteness also made their wardens essentially autonomous with each viewing his farm as his own private kingdom (Copeland, 1980). Living conditions at these farms were poor and overcrowded as illustrated by the following news account:

> [T]he stench is awful for they get soap enough for only one fourth of the men in the tanks to get a soap and water bath every three weeks and at this farm there is no provision for the prisoners to wash their clothing. . . . In rainy weather, the prisoners are unable to wash their own clothing, even in plain water. (*Houston Chronicle,* December 14, 1947, as cited by Copeland, 1980, p. 64)

There was not enough to eat, and some food was spoiled and unfit for human consumption. These terrible conditions led to frequent inmate work strikes. This led the guards to appoint **building tenders** (BTs), typically long-term inmates who were chosen for their superior intelligence or physical prowess and given the authority to maintain order within the tanks. From the outset they were described as a plague on the system. BTs performed functions similar to trusty-guards in Mississippi and Arkansas, except that they did not carry firearms (Copeland, 1980). BTs also controlled the gambling, access to contraband such as narcotics, and such things as putting an inmate on the sick list, which meant he could rest for the day (Copeland, 1980). They maintained order through violence and carried weapons such as knives and clubs. Thus, tank society was dominated by the strong and vicious with the weak being constantly victimized physically and/or sexually. Also, a substantial number of inmates died from the harsh working conditions, from poor sanitation and medical care, and at the hands of civilian prison guards.

On the farms everyone worked. The majority of inmates were assigned to the **hoe line,** carrying hoes and other tools, and marching to work sites up to 5 miles away where they were supervised by armed guards on horseback. There were also dog packs and other armed officers on the work perimeter to prevent escapes. Inmate workers were driven mercilessly by the guards, who used rubber hoses, chains, bullwhips, and even their horses to bully inmates to work, including those unable to work due to heat exhaustion or for other physical reasons. This caused some to try to escape work by self-mutilation. This included amputations (of a foot, hand, or of several fingers), cuts into which lye or some infection-causing materials were placed, fracturing of arms or legs, and severing of the Achilles tendon. Amputating three fingers from one hand was the "million dollar" injury because this made wielding a hoe or other similar tools impossible (Copeland, 1980; Crouch & Marquart, 1989).

The state's concern for guards was no better than for the inmates. Guards worked from 12 to 14 hours a day without hope of any vacations, and even sickness was no excuse for missing work. They paid for their own uniforms and weapons, lived in a room in the inmates barracks, and ate food almost as bad as the inmates'. Many were illiterate, and the system provided no formal training. Thus, many inmates found it easy to manipulate their guards.

Like the previous period in Texas prison history, the plantation farm era finally succumbed to external criticism. With the election of a reform governor in 1947, efforts toward making major changes in the system began.

The Period of Reform and Stability This period saw many system changes and improvements. A newly elected governor who ran on a platform of prison reform hired an experienced prison administrator, O. B. Ellis, to manage Texas prisons (Crouch & Marquart, 1989). Under Ellis and his successor George Beto, the Texas system went from worst to best in the nation by the 1960s. The reforms effected during this approximately 20-year period created an "orderly, steady and philosophically consistent" system, the hallmark of which was the degree of control exerted over the inmates (Krajick, 1978). In addition to tightened security and control, there were improvements in inmate conditions. Incorrigible inmates were removed from the farms and placed in isolation, and self-mutilators were no longer "rewarded" by being removed from the farms. Although extremely flagrant abuses were eliminated and some staff were fired, Ellis was unable to change the use of physical punishment to control inmates, including handcuffing inmates to cell bars. Despite continuing criticism, neither Beto, nor W. J. Estelle—Beto's successor—eliminated the building tender system; rather, they modified it to exert more control over inmates. It was not abolished until the 1980s, and then it was by court order.

Typically, all able-bodied inmates worked during this era. About 50 percent of the inmates did agricultural work. However, all inmates spent their first 6 months on the hoe line doing *stoop* agricultural work. This involved using their hands or hand tools to plow, plant seed, and maintain and harvest the crops. After this period, some were rewarded for good behavior and employed in modern dairies, raising livestock and chickens, and running farm machinery. Other inmates were given a chance to work in programs where they could learn a skill that might lead to employment upon release. Our Close-Up, "Texas Inmates Learn Marketable Skills," looks at two of the most distinctive programs operating during this era. About 10 percent of the inmate workforce built and maintained all prison buildings. Using inmate labor, Texas could build facilities at about two thirds of their free-world cost.

Toward the end of this period, the Texas system was reputed to be the safest, most orderly, and most economically run in the nation. This was largely attributed to its full employment system, which, based on the goal of self-sufficiency, also served as a mechanism of control and may have been a vehicle for rehabilitation. However, order and control in this system were achieved through brutal means.

Education was another important facet of the Texas Department of Corrections (TDC) program during this era. Academic and vocational classes were offered through the Windham School District, which was established by the state legislature in 1969 to conduct educational programs at TDC. New inmates with less than a fifth-grade equivalency were required to attend school; others could attend one day a week (Gettinger, 1978). A junior college program offered academic and vocational training leading to an associate of arts degree, and courses leading to a bachelor's degree were also available.

Texas Inmates Learn Marketable Skills

CLOSE-UP

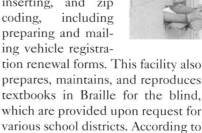

Visitors to the Ellis unit bus repair facility and the Wayne and Coffield records conversion facilities cannot help but be impressed with these programs because of the extent to which they parallel those on the outside.

The bus repair plant renovates and repairs buses for schools throughout the state at a cost of approximately half their replacement value. The inmates can take a school bus that has been in an accident or has deteriorated to a point where it is no longer functional and completely renovate it—including painting the interior and exterior, re-pairing the frame, replacing the engine, replacing the seats, and so on—so that it looks and performs as well as a new one. They also repair and construct bodies for fire engines. This plant is operated by 150 inmates who are supervised by eight employees. (This shop still exists today.)

Equally impressive are two records conversion facilities, which employ more than 1,300 inmates who work three shifts a day. These facilities place such records as vehicle registrations, traffic tickets, and other records on microfilm, magnetic computer tape, or punch cards. They also provide services such as file maintenance, mail inserting, and zip coding, including preparing and mailing vehicle registration renewal forms. This facility also prepares, maintains, and reproduces textbooks in Braille for the blind, which are provided upon request for various school districts. According to the supervisors of these programs, inmates that work in these programs have little difficulty obtaining jobs upon release.

The Trusty-Guard System As in the past, a hierarchical trusty-guard system was the backbone of the Texas prisons that kept inmates under tight control. At the top were head building tenders, who were in charge of the inside of a particular cell block and accountable for all inmate behavior in it. They were the most powerful inmates in the prisoner society. Next were rank-and-file building tenders, who assisted the head BT in controlling the cell block; turnkeys, who opened and closed riot gates; and bookkeepers, who kept prison records. On the third rung were runners, strikers, or hitmen who kept the cell block clean, dispensed supplies, and provided BTs with physical backup when necessary (Crouch & Marquart, 1989; Marquart & Crouch, 1984).

Inmates who became BTs were given status and power as well as tangible rewards. They had freedom of movement within the prison, their own showers, access to food as often as they wanted, freedom to carry weapons, immunity from punishment, and access to gifts and bribes from inmates for helping them with their problems. As the staff depended on the BTs, they in turn depended on their own network of stool pigeons. Force was frequently used and often involved the weapons that BTs were allowed to possess. BTs controlled the tanks (cell blocks) through fear, intimidation, and physical force. From the standpoint of prison officials, the inmate elite, and many average inmates, this made prison life more stable and predictable. However, for inmates disliked by BTs or considered problems, life in the tanks was tense and often not safe.

Officials controlled BTs by a policy of divide and conquer. While united when confronting other inmates, BTs regularly snitched on each other for revenge or to help "the man." When they became too abusive, got involved in drugs, or got into the protection rackets, they were fired if the staff found out about it. This system worked until the early 1970s when the guard force remained the same but the prison population almost doubled. Officials became increasingly dependent on BTs to control inmates but were less able to control them. As a result BTs wielded even more discretionary power, and they used it routinely to punish inmates physically. Under these circumstances, staff lost control of the prisons.

The Courts Intervene: *Ruiz v. Estelle* By the mid-1970s, the once solid support that the TDC had enjoyed from the press and the legislature began to crack. The death knell for the TDC was ***Ruiz v. Estelle*** (1980). David Ruiz was an inmate with a 25-year sentence for armed robbery when he began to file writs and write letters complaining about conditions in the Texas prisons. A federal judge, William Justice, combined his petition with six similar civil actions filed by other Texas inmates against Wayne Estelle, director of the Texas Department of Corrections, and several of his wardens.

The *Ruiz* case, the most far-reaching in correctional legal history, lasted for 9 months and involved 349 witnesses and 1,600 exhibits. Judge Justice issued the most sweeping and detailed order in the history of prison litigation, finding that the conditions in almost every part of this prison system violated minimum constitutional standards. His opinion covered overcrowding, security and supervision, health care, discipline, access to the courts, fire safety and sanitation, work safety and hygiene, unit size, structure, and location. Part of his order mandated the elimination of the "unlawfully maintained building tender" system (p. 1298). To ensure that the changes either ordered or mutually agreed to in a consent decree between the prison officials and the plaintiffs were implemented, he appointed Vincent M. Nathan to act as Special Master in the case.[8]

Although the state initially resisted the orders to change, it began to comply in late 1983. Restrictions were imposed on guards using physical force to control inmates. The BT system was abolished, which created a power vacuum because it dissolved the inmate power structure that had defined and governed the nature of inmate relations for many years. A surge of inmate violence and aggression resulted. One veteran guard explained it in this way:

> The inmates know they're not going to get their asses whipped by nobody. They know there's no BTs to whip their ass. So they do what they want to do. You know, "F**k TDC." There is nobody to stop them from killing somebody. They're trying to stake their claim now that the BTs are gone. (as cited by Crouch & Marquart, 1989, p. 198)

Other changes in the control system also had negative effects. The imposition of new restrictions on the use of force without creating effective alternatives of control meant inmates could act out with impunity. Additionally, from 1979 to 1985 the TDC staff increased from about 2,500 to 9,000, creating a disaster because there were not enough experienced personnel to socialize new corrections officers (COs). Many COs were receiving money or loans from inmates for performing favors (e.g., giving them a copy of their file) or bringing in contraband (e.g., drugs and weapons) (Crouch & Marquart, 1989). In an environment without any controls, "survival of the fittest" became the norm. By the mid-1980s TDC prisons, particularly the hard-core units, had become very dangerous places.

The crisis in self-protection—created by the removal of the BTs and greater restrictions on guards—was further aggravated by racial tensions. Many inmates joined gangs for self-protection. Gangs also offered their members access to contraband and vied for control of these illicit markets. Gang conflict during this era accounted for a disproportionate amount of violence. (See Chapter 12 for a detailed discussion of gang development and activities.)

To regain stability, TDC's governing board came to grips with the requirements of the *Ruiz* decision in the mid-1980s. Under the new leadership of Raymond Procunier,[9] an outsider with no commitments to its tradition, a new legalistic order was developed. Following a mandate to transform the system as rapidly as possible into a constitutionally acceptable operation, he centralized decision making and expanded rules. He formal-ized accountability procedures to standardize operations and to maximize compliance with rules by all staff. This placed major constraints on official staff discretion in rewarding and punishing inmates. The use of force (except in well-defined situations) was banned. Control was to be achieved by legal devices (including the write-up or report of rule violations, which could affect an inmate's good time and eventual release), administrative segregation, and, when necessary, lock-down, especially to control gang-affiliated or assaultive inmates. Initially 1,700 inmates were locked down. This rose to more than 3,000 and hovered between this figure and 2,500 until the late 1980s. The lockdown policy was successful, and both guards and inmates reported that this was the major reason the prisons became safer.

As these changes took hold and the system approached compliance with the *Ruiz* requirements, a new bureaucratic order emerged. Court oversight declined and TDC's central office gained greater autonomy in managing the prison, particularly in control issues. In turn, the central office relaxed bureaucratic control over prison operations, believing that new compliance policies were sufficiently institutionalized and that greater prison unit autonomy would not jeopardize inmate rights (Crouch & Marquart, 1989).

The Value of Work Camps and Prison Farms

This discussion of southern prisons may appear to suggest that work camps or prison farms should not be part of a modern corrections system. However, it is not the model that is objectionable but the abuses that have characterized it. There appears to be real value in the employment of inmates in agricultural activities and other outdoor programs, for example, forestry camps and road crews. These programs give inmates opportunities to work in the fresh air, engage in productive labor, and get some exercise. Further, it tires them out and minimizes problems generated by idleness in the prisons. Placing minimum-security inmates serving long sentences in small work camps reduces incarceration costs, gives them freedom of movement not available in larger facilities, and provides an alternative placement for inmates who want to avoid gang involvement or disengage from it. Agricultural programs also provide food for the prison system and for sale to other state agencies, which helps to reduce imprisonment costs. Finally, given the high cost of constructing and operating traditional prisons, these facilities deserve a place, at least in major state correctional systems.

There are some disadvantages in small work camps. They lack special programs and services because they cannot be cost-effectively maintained in these settings. Additionally, the work opportunities at these camps may not result in many future job skills.

Today, prisons in the South face the same problems as those in the North: They must deal with an escalating prison population.

Summary

Punishment in the pre–Civil War South was characterized by de jure (the Black Codes) and de facto racism. States typically used Auburn-type prisons to reform offenders, but when the industry failed to cover operating costs of the prisons, some experimented with the lease system. Following the Civil War, the lease system continued to solve several problems faced by American corrections; however, it turned offenders into penal slaves. Some jurisdictions used chain gangs, as this was an excellent means by which to build railroads and levees and maintain county roads and state highways.

Upon the abolition of leasing, many southern states developed large prison farms and plantation prisons for convicts who were not part of chain gangs. Parchman's penal farm, which evolved over time, became the main prison in Mississippi. It was founded on the goals of profit and reformation, and it reflected many of the principles that had been employed by Maconochie, Crofton, and Brockway. A federal court discontinued the prison in 1972.

Arkansas had the worst prison farm of the southern systems. When Warden Murton took over standards resembled those from the 18th century, and its inmates were running the prison. Murton attempted to improve the conditions and bring them up to contemporary standards. Despite progress, Murton's stay was short-lived, and once he was fired conditions again regressed. By the precedent "totality of conditions," conditions at Arkansas prisons were ruled unconstitutional.

The Texas system was the last major prison system to change. It was initially based on the Auburn model, but subsequently changed to a contract system where the prison operation was leased to private businesses. Between 1876 and 1883, the contract lease system was employed. Prison officials were responsible for supervising, disciplining, and housing the inmates, but inmates worked for private contractors. With the demise of the contract lease system, the Texas prison bought numerous acres of farmland and went into the business of agriculture. The state assumed total control over the inmates, and conditions on the remote prison farms were harsh. By the 1960s, with the election of a new governor and the appointment of a new prison administrator, Texas' prison system went through a period of reform and stability, and gained a reputation as the best system in the South. Trusty-guards had an important role in the new system, as they maintained control over the inmates. However, *Ruiz v. Estelle* revealed that conditions were quite inhumane in the TDC, and Judge Justice mandated numerous changes in the system to bring it up to modern standards.

Although the problems with southern prisons seem to indicate that work camps and prison farms are barbaric, it is important to recognize that the systems have been largely abused. Some of the ideas behind work camps and prison farms as forms of corrections are very valuable. For example, the employment of inmates in various outdoor activities accomplishes productive labor, while tiring the inmates out and occupying them in legitimate activity, thereby inhibiting them from engaging in criminal behavior. Also, as Bill Taylor asserts, these conditions were not much worse than conditions in most other prisons in the U.S. before the 1950s.

Critical Thinking Questions

1. As a southerner living in the pre–Civil War South, why would you support the Black Codes? Define and describe the Black Codes.

2. Discuss the operation of the lease system.

3. As an inmate on a southern chain gang after the Civil War, what would be the state of your living conditions?

4. Outline the organization and functions of the Parchman Farm prison plantation. What would it be like living as an inmate at one of the camps?

5. Explain why Arkansas prisons were considered the worst of the southern prison farm systems. Describe the process by which Tom Murton changed the prison farm at Tucker.

6. Discuss the precedent-setting *Holt v. Sarver* decisions.

7. Describe your life at Cummins Prison farm if you were a trusty versus a "rank man."

8. Outline the development of the Texas prison system and the phases through which it progressed.

9. If you were serving time during the era in which the building tenders ran the tanks, would you become a building tender? Include in your response advantages of this status during the different periods of evolution of the Texas prison system.

10. What were the effects of the *Ruiz* decision on the Texas prison system? If you had been an inmate in this system during this time period how would you have survived?

11. Suggest some reasons why work camps or prison farms could still be beneficial to corrections. See the Program Focus, "Prisons Without Walls," in Chapter 16.

Test Your Knowledge

1. The early practice of handing prisons over to an individual or company who took responsibility for its

operation and usually paid the state a fee or a portion of the profits that were derived from the labor of the convicts was known as the:

a. chain gang.

b. lease system.

c. lease camp.

d. plantation prison.

2. The main goal that the lease system, chain gangs, and prison plantations had in common was to:

a. hold prisoners awaiting trial.

b. rehabilitate offenders.

c. develop inmate job skills.

d. maximize profits from convict labor.

3. The Mississippi prison system followed:

a. the Auburn model.

b. a chain gang model.

c. a plantation model.

d. a contract system model.

4. Conditions in the Arkansas prison system were finally challenged by the courts because they were:

a. unconstitutional.

b. inefficient.

c. immoral.

d. not cost-effective.

5. Building tenders in the Texas prison were:

a. paid trusties.

b. armed with shotguns.

c. trusties who performed maintenance duties such as repairing the plumbing.

d. trusty-guards.

e. none of the above.

Endnotes

1. The southern states include Mississippi, Louisiana, Alabama, Georgia, Florida, South Carolina, North Carolina, Arkansas, Tennessee, Texas, Kentucky, and Virginia.

2. Excerpted from *Vengeance and Justice: Crime and Punishment in the 19th-Century American South,* by Edward L. Ayers. Copyright © 1984 by Oxford University Press, Inc. Reprinted by permission.

3. Camps of this kind were established in Arkansas, Alabama, Florida, Louisiana, Mississippi, and Texas.

4. Material from *Brokered Justice: Race, Politics, and Mississippi Prisons, 1798–1992,* by William Banks Taylor, is used by permission. © 1993 by the Ohio State University Press. All rights reserved.

5. Hopper (1969, 1989) offers a somewhat different interpretation of the development of this system. He contends that the small rural nature of these camps and the plantation mind-set of those who ran them helped to maintain a view of workers, whether they were slaves or inmates, as not willing to work productively through punishment alone. Moreover, the small rural nature of these camps allowed for a more informal visiting system without the attendant security problems and supervision that would be necessary at large prison complexes. Also the small size of these camps enabled sergeants to get to know the inmates and their families more personally. This, he feels, fostered a greater concern for the physical and emotional needs of their charges. Thus, for Hopper this more liberal visiting program, along with the home furlough program, seemed to be designed to help inmates maintain contacts with their families.

6. Inmates were actually paid $5 per pint of blood; however, $1 went to the Officers' Welfare Fund and another $1 went to the Inmate Welfare Fund—from which inmates derived little benefit. Thus, all the inmate got was $3. The real beneficiary of this system was the doctor who had the contract to sell the blood to Cutter Laboratories. He made between $130,000 and $150,000 per year from these donations.

7. From *An Appeal to Justice: Litigated Reform of Texas Prisons* by Ben M. Crouch and James W. Marquart, copyright © 1989. Reprinted by permission of the authors and the University of Texas Press.

8. It was not until March 31, 1990, that he finally completed his role as master in this case. At that point the burden for overseeing compliance shifted to System's Assistant Director for Compliance Charles Smith and his staff members. He had to oversee compliance in 10 areas for an additional 2 years.

9. Raymond Procunier was a prison administrator with experience in New Mexico, California, Utah, and Virginia. He resigned after a year and was succeeded by his deputy, Lane McCotter—an army colonel with experience running the stockade at Fort Leavenworth—who had been hired at the same time as Procunier.

The Big House, the Rehabilitative Institution, and the Prisoner Movement Eras

LEARNING OBJECTIVES

After completing this chapter, you should be able to:

1. Describe the basic characteristics of a typical Big House prison and the factors that shaped its social environment.

2. Outline the basic features of a total institution and their impact on the prison social environment.

3. Contrast the three common modes of adapting to prison life: doing time, jailing, and gleaning.

4. Describe some creative ways inmates developed to adapt to the deprivations of prison life.

5. Discuss the problems faced by guards in the Big House and the solutions they developed.

6. Describe the social changes that preceded and gave rise to the rehabilitative institution.

7. Describe the roles of the following factors in the rehabilitative institution: indeterminate sentencing, classification and its shortcomings, and treatment in a correctional setting.

8. Outline the basic features of prison life at the Soledad Correctional Institution.

9. Specify the reasons that the transformation of prisons into "correctional facilities" was doomed to failure.

10. Describe the social changes that occurred in the United States from the mid-1950s to the late 1960s that had a major impact on prisons and inmates.

11. Explain the factors that caused the demise of the traditional prison stratification system and changed the nature of race relations in the prison.

12. Discuss the factors that influenced the development of the "prisoner movement" during the 1970s and the different groups involved in the prisoner movement.

13. Discuss the phases of the Attica revolt, the retaking of the prison, and the cover-up that followed.

Introduction

This chapter focuses on three eras of the 20th century that are important for understanding contemporary corrections. The first section examines the *Big House* era, which lasted from about 1900 to 1950. During this period, prison populations grew from about 50,000 to 163,000 inmates (Barnes & Teeters, 1943; Bureau of Justice Statistics, 1982). The second examines the emergence of the *rehabilitative institution*, including the social conditions conducive to its development, the basic components characterizing these new types of prisons, and the factors that led to their demise. The final section traces the impact of the sociopolitical conditions of the 1960s and 1970s on prisons, including the conditions that changed the inmate social structure and heightened levels of inmate violence. Further, some inmates began to define themselves as political prisoners which, along with the social turmoil of this era, contributed to the development of the third era, the *prisoner movement*. We also look at the groups involved in this movement and their impact on the prison environment. Keep in mind that any attempt to portray prisons during a given period is hampered by variations between states in policies, practices, and facilities.

However, first, we examine the inmate social world and how prisoners are socialized into it.

The Inmate Social World

The social patterns that develop in a prison result from the interaction between the prison's environmental characteristics and inmate characteristics. Inmates bring to prison the values and attitudes developed in their free-world lives and their prior experiences in other facilities (Irwin & Cressey, 1962). Other inmate characteristics that shape the prison world include (1) population characteristics such as age, race/ethnic origin, rural versus urban background, and educational level; (2) the extent of an inmate's identification with outside subcultures; and (3) how they adapt to the dehumanizing conditions and deprivations of prison life. Prevailing societal attitudes and values also influence prison socialization. These factors produce an inmate world that includes several subcultures, adaptations to prison life, and a status system.

The Inmate Subculture

The inmate subculture helps inmates cope with the special circumstances of prison life by providing ways of thinking, feeling, and acting for all aspects of prison life. Much research and debate has centered on the factors influencing the development of this subculture (Thomas & Petersen, 1977). One position, the **deprivation model,** argues that the inmate culture is a collective response to the deprivations imposed by prison life—for example, lack of heterosexual relations (Sykes, 1958). In contrast, the **importation model** asserts that it is shaped by a socialization process involving preprison exposure to and adoption of a criminal value system (Irwin & Cressey, 1962). Rather than arguing over which model is valid, it is more appropriate to understand the inmate subculture as a dynamic system affected by a variety of factors both within and outside the prison (Thomas & Petersen, 1977).

The Prison as a Total Institution

The term **total institution** refers to such places as custodial hospitals, military training bases, and prisons, where (1) large groups of people (2) live and work together around the clock (3) within a circumscribed space and (4) under a rigid schedule of activities (Goffman, 1961). Prison, like other total institutions, (5) subjects inmates to deprivation and (6) limits their freedom. Sykes (1958) called this the "pains of imprisonment." These features apply to all prisons, from early penitentiaries to contemporary prisons.

As total institutions, prisons have several distinctive characteristics. Life activities in these facilities are carried out within a very circumscribed area; this does not allow inmates to avoid continuing contact with people they find distasteful. Moreover, inmates are deprived of their autonomy as a result of the imposition of a highly routinized schedule. This discourages individuality and subjects inmates to an extensive system of formal rules. For example, during the Big House era the Iowa State Penitentiary had 105 rules governing inmate behavior (Wickersham Commission, 1931). The following excerpt illustrates the frustration felt by inmates who were deprived of opportunities to exercise initiative under this regime:

> *Aurn:* No feeling of being able to say anything about your life. It is like everything is shoveled to you. You know, you are in this hole, and everything that you need—your room, your board, your house—is shoved through a hole at you. That takes all the responsibility away from a person, and then X amount of years later you are out in the streets again, and then you will be responsible, which you never had to be, and it is like being in the other world. . . . And you come in here, and you are given your sheets, and you are given your room to sleep in, and they try to make you as comfortable as they can within security, you know, which is another trick. And then you go out in the street, like I said before, and then you have got a whole different ball game. (Toch, 1977a, pp. 121–122)[1]

Deprivation of privacy also occurs. Not only are inmates subject to random cell searches, pat-down body searches, strip searches, and sometimes body cavity examinations, but showering and toilet use may be watched by a guard of the opposite sex.[2]

Deprivation of Security The most disturbing feature of prison life is that inmates are deprived of security. Danger permeates the institutional environment. The levels of violence during different eras have been influenced by various factors, including the number of violence-prone inmates entering the system and the ability of more experienced inmates to control them, the ethnic/racial makeup of the prison population, and the extent of staff control over inmates. In every era, there have been enough "thugs" or outlaws to threaten many inmates' sense of security:

> While . . . every prisoner does not live in constant fear of being robbed or beaten, the constant companionship of thieves, rapists, murderers, and aggressive homosexuals is far from reassuring. . . . [Further,] inmate[s] have always been acutely aware that sooner or later [they] will be "tested"—that someone will "push" [them to] see how far they can go and [they] must be prepared to fight for the safety of [their] person and possessions. (Sykes, 1958, p. 77)

Toch (1977a) offers:

> [While prisons protect the public from inmates they] . . . often fail to protect inmates from each other. Individuals who cannot overcome aggressors are in constant danger of being attacked; persons who successfully defend themselves may find themselves constantly "tested."

> *Cox R 6:* They told me that you can't run away from it. You have to knock them down, face up to them. The first person that you knock out, you get locked up for three or four days, and then you come out and come back down, and you're going to get a lot more respect. (p. 158)

Chronic understaffing continues to contribute to the problem of prison security, which is further aggravated by an increasingly violent-prone inmate population. In some prisons, contact with the outside world is restricted by security concerns. This includes restrictions on visitors and the number of permissible visits per month, further isolating many inmates. Big Houses usually prohibited contact visits with outsiders and restricted the correspondence and reading material that inmates could receive (Sykes, 1958). Despite more liberal visiting and correspondence policies today, contact with family and friends is still difficult for many inmates.[3] Some inmates view the restrictive visitation policies as a moral rejection by society. Hence, many identify with the prison subculture, which provides a new reference group, social relationships, and rationalizations that help neutralize their feelings of isolation and rejection (Korn & McCorkle, 1954).

Standard of Living Inmates are also stripped of many goods and services upon admission; most personal property is confiscated. Beyond basic necessities, inmates are neither provided with nor can they buy many amenities taken for granted on the outside. Even though some inmates live better in prison because they have "three hots (meals) and a cot," clothing, and basic medical care, most, if given a choice, would prefer "to be on their own" on the outside.

Many problems emerge when comparing the standard of living of inmates with people on the outside (Sykes, 1958). How does one compare wearing ill-fitting clothing and living in a cell where inmates share a chair with cellmates and use a scrap of old blanket as a rug with living in a spartan home or apartment and having a minimal wardrobe on the outside? How can the bland, poor quality of prison food compare with the variety of food choices on the outside? Although prison services and the items available in the commissary have dramatically improved, most inmates still live under impoverished conditions compared with life outside.

Deprivation of Opportunity On top of their poor quality of life, inmates are deprived of opportunities for meaningful work. Even though prisons were built on the idea that work would reform offenders, by the middle of the Big House era, few opportunities for meaningful work existed. This meant idleness for many, and for others it involved "make work" tasks using more inmates than a job required.

Prison also deprives inmates of normal heterosexual outlets and denies them the civilizing influence of intimate contact with the opposite sex. Language in prison is coarse, profane, obscene, and brutal; manners are almost nonexistent; personal hygiene is poor; and emotions are often experienced and expressed in the extreme. Finally, the prison world is split by a wall that separates correctional workers, who occupy a superordinate status, from inmates, who occupy a subordinate status (Goffman, 1961). In this world, inmates can never achieve equal status with staff. Social distance is typically great and often formally mandated. Whereas staff members usually refer to inmates by their first name, last name, or nickname, inmates are required to address staff as "Mister," "Officer," or some other title, along with their surnames. Nevertheless, some corrections officers (COs) manage to develop interpersonal relationships with some prisoners.

Prisonization

Clemmer (1940/1958) used the term **prisonization** to describe the socialization process by which inmates take on the norms, customs, and culture of the penitentiary. He described the process as follows:

> Every man who enters the penitentiary undergoes prisonization to some extent. The first . . . step concerns his status. He becomes at once an anonymous figure in a subordinate group. A number replaces a name. He wears the clothes of the other members of the subordinate group. He is questioned and admonished. He soon learns . . . the warden is all-powerful . . . [and] the ranks, titles, and authority of various officials. And whether he uses the prison slang and argot or not, he comes to know its meanings. Even though a new man may hold himself aloof from other inmates and remain a solitary figure, he finds himself within a few months referring to or thinking of keepers as "screws," the physician as the "croaker" and using the local nicknames to designate persons. . . . He learns to eat in haste and in obtaining food he imitates the tricks of those near him. (p. 299)

Various factors affect the extent to which inmates assimilate into the prison culture (Clemmer, 1940/1958; Johnson & Toch, 1982; Thomas & Petersen, 1977). These factors include personal characteristics such as age, race, marital status, socioeconomic status, educational attainment, and extent of criminal involvement. Inmates incarcerated for short periods, such as a year or so, neither adopted the prison culture nor became prisonized (Clemmer, 1940/1958). Most people can endure deprivations for short periods of time because they see an end to their torment. For those facing long sentences, prison becomes home. Some inmates who are imprisoned for many years and have the opportunity to be released refuse, because they fear they cannot adjust to society and have no family to assist them.

Involvement in the prison world and its subculture is more likely if inmates (1) have little or no contact with the larger society, (2) feel they are unlikely to be reunited with their family and friends and obtain some meaningful job on release, or (3) are habitual, professional, and gang-involved offenders expecting upon release to return to criminal activities (Thomas & Petersen, 1977). Finally, where an inmate is in his or her sentence may determine that individual's commitment to the prison subculture. At the start, outside values, experiences, and associations may be prominent; after a few months or a year, prison subcultural values, experiences, and friendships may be more important; near release—if they intend "to go straight," get a job, and be reunited with family—they may adopt more conventional values and behavior.

The Process of Role Dispossession

Entering prison can be a terrifying experience, particularly for first timers, resulting in a state of shock. Role disposition occurs as inmates are separated from the outside world. They undergo **role dispossession** (Goffman, 1961); that is, they lose the opportunity to play certain roles—including workers and lovers—and certain rights, such as the right to freely marry, vote, and contest a divorce. Married men often lose their status as heads of households, because they are not at home when day-to-day decisions are made and no longer support their families. Women, while still mothers, cannot care for their children and may lose them if no relative is willing to care for them.

Admission processing procedures deprive individuals of key elements that are important for maintaining their self-concept. This begins the **mortification process** (Goffman, 1961). These include getting fingerprinted, being photographed, handing over cash and personal belongings, being bathed and getting thoroughly searched, receiving ill-fitting prison clothing, getting a prison haircut and a medical examination, and having prison regulations explained.

As soon as inmates arrive, they receive an identification number. Their first socialization experience in prison may involve an obedience test or even a will-breaking contest. This, along with feelings of humiliation felt by inmates, is well illustrated in our Close-Up, "The Admission Process."

The ability to adapt to prison varies. Every **fish** (newcomer) faces the same question: "How am I going to do my time?" Preprison orientation affects how individuals cope with the prison experience. Some offenders know what to expect in prison, either because they have served time before or because they have acquired knowledge about prison life from the streets.

Big House Prisons

Resembling military fortresses, **Big House** prisons were usually surrounded by thick concrete walls with towers at each corner. They averaged populations of 2,500 men, housed in large cell blocks with up to six tiers of one- or two-man cells. As newer units were added, they were usually more spacious, cleaner, and better ventilated and heated, with toilets and small sinks. Many of the prisons allowed inmates to decorate their cells with paintings, rugs, and furniture, which made their cramped spaces more accommodating. Still, they were harsh, oppressive worlds of concrete and steel, which subjected inmates to the chilling cold in the winter, oppressive heat and stench in the summer, and constant unnerving levels of noise.

Other distinctive features included a mess hall, workshops and industrial facilities, an administration building, and a recreation yard. Some recreation yards had baseball diamonds, tables and benches, and basketball and handball courts. The better known of the Big House

The Admission Process

Barbara Deming (1966), a pacifist arrested for demonstrating against nuclear testing, gives us a rare glimpse of how this process affects the newly admitted inmate. Then, an excerpt from the Malcolm Braly (1967) novel *On the Yard*, based upon 17 years as an inmate beginning in 1943, captures the essence of obedience testing to which inmates often are subjected as part of their initiation into the prison.

Barbara Deming describes her experience as follows:

> At the House of Detention, a . . . guard empties the bags [and] keeps every . . . article. We . . . packed a . . . comb, toothbrush, deodorant, a change of underclothes. She takes them all— even . . . some pieces of Kleenex. And if I have to blow my nose? "Find something else to do it on," she tells me cheerfully. She explains then: I might be smuggling in dope this way. I am led into a large shower room and told to strip . . . and I struggle hard now for self-possession. Her stance reminds me a little of that of an animal trainer. Now she asks me to hold my arms wide for a moment, turn my back and squat. I ask the reason. She, too, is searching for dope—or for concealed weapons. One of my companions has been led in by another woman and has stripped and is sitting on the toilet there. Her face is anguished. She explains her predicament to the guard: she is menstruating, but her extra sanitary napkins have been taken from her. "Just don't think about it," the woman tells her. I don't know how to help her; catch her eye and look away. I am given a very short hospital gown and led now into a small medical-examination room. . . . I climb up on the table. I assume

that the examination performed is to check for venereal disease. The woman in the white smock grins at me and then her assistant, who grins back. No, this too is a search for concealed dope or dangerous weapons. . . . They wouldn't be able to admit it to themselves, but their search, of course [is not for drugs but for] something else, and is efficient: their search is for our pride. . . . (pp. 3–4)

Braly shows what happens to a newly admitted inmate who fails to comply with a guard's request during the admission process.

> When they had all been photographed, the sergeant ordered them to strip down and throw their coveralls into a canvas laundry basket, and their shoes, socks and underwear into a cardboard box next to it. "You take nothing—nothing—inside the walls. . . ."
>
> [Stick] . . . stepped in front of the sergeant. . . . He lifted his arms when he was told to, but he hesitated before opening his mouth, and then only parted his lips. "Much wider," the sergeant said. "Show some tonsil." Stick thrust his head forward and jerked his mouth open inches from the sergeant's face, who swayed back and looked at Stick thoughtfully. "All right, lift your nuts." Stick thrust his pelvis forward and exposed his scrotum. The sergeant's eyes flickered. . . . "All right, son," he said softly, "let's have a look at your a**." Stick stood rigid. "Don't you hear well?" Still Stick didn't move. "Don't be modest. I see a lot of a**holes. They all look the same." "F**k you," Stick said. The sergeant nodded with the appearance of satisfaction, and

pressed a button set in the base of his phone. "This is a place," he told Stick, "where you can buy a great deal of trouble very cheaply. . . ." In less than a minute the door flew open and three guards entered on the double. The goon squad [included guards called] Farmer . . . the Indian . . . a small Negro—the Spook. . . .

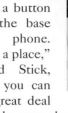

> The sergeant nodded at Stick, who hadn't moved, and told the Spook he had refused to bend over. . . . The Farmer and the Indian closed on Stick like fingers of the same hand as they armlocked him from either side. They raised him straining to his tiptoes. The Spook looked up at him. "You see, you've aroused our curiosity." The Indian and the Farmer bent Stick as easily as they would break a shotgun. The Spook pried open his clamped rump. Stick jerked wildly and made a hissing noise. "My, my," the Spook murmured, "not a feather on him. Some jocker's due to score." He looked up at the sergeant. "You think he might have something keister stashed? We can X-ray." "No," the sergeant said. "He's just some kind of nut." The Spook studied Stick knowingly. "Yes, he's some kind of nut. Yes, put him in a holding cell. I'll think up some charge before I go off duty."

Sources: B. Deming, (1966). Prison Notes. *Boston: Beacon Press, pp. 3–4. Reissued as* Prisons That Could Not Hold. *Athens, GA: University of Georgia Press, 1995. Used with permission.* M. Braly (1967).[4] On the Yard. © *1967, 1995 Malcom Braly. Reprinted by permission of Knox Burger, in association with Harold Ober Associates, Inc.*

The "Big House" prison resembled a military fortress. Convicts were housed in cell blocks with up to six tiers of one- or two-man cells, where they were subject to a highly routinized schedule.

prisons included Stateville in Illinois, Sing Sing in New York, the Ohio Penitentiary in Columbus, and Canyon City in Colorado.

The Big House also saw the collapse of prison industry and the emergence of prison idleness. Full employment for inmates extended over a 70-year period, lasting into the 20th century. However, both the **state-use system,** which restricted the sale of prison-made goods to only state and local governments, and the overabundance of men to do a shrinking pool of jobs led to idleness and such attendant problems as riots and inmate schemes. The only stable prison industry was making license plates.[5] As a result, by the mid-1930s, relatively harsh punishments and strict custody functions were used to control inmates (Morse, 1940).

The Big House Inmate System

The Big House had its own subculture, status system, and ways of adjusting to prison deprivations.

Inmate Subculture In the Big House, two factors produced the inmate subculture: the convict code and the conditions of confinement.

The **convict code,** influenced by the thieves code, was the dominant value system in the Big House. The inmates' loyalty to one another, their strong commitment to thief values, and their communication network placed them in a superior role in the inmate world (Irwin, 1980; Irwin & Cressey, 1962) (see Table 7.1). Not all inmates abided by its rules, yet many gave lip service to its values and evaluated each other based on its core value—rightness or solidness, which meant someone who could be trusted and, more important, relied on not to rat on another offender.

For thieves, imprisonment was a recurring problem. Their subculture provided ways of doing time designed

Table 7.1

The Convict Code

Values	Norms
Convict loyalty to one another	Do your own time
Loyalty to thief values	Don't rat on other inmates
Emphasis on trustworthiness	Maintain dignity and respect
Utilitarian behavior	Help other thieves
Manipulation/exploitation of others	Leave (most) inmates alone
	Manifest no weakness
	Don't openly help staff/ administration
	Avoid fights
	Settle conflict within

Sources: Irwin, 1980; Irwin & Cressey, 1962.

to reduce the discomfort and time in prison. When they came to prison, they brought a code that emphasized trustworthiness, which translated into "Do your own time" and "Don't rat on another prisoner." It also expected thieves to (1) maintain dignity and respect, (2) help other thieves, (3) leave most other inmates alone, (4) manifest no weaknesses, and (5) not openly cooperate with staff or administration. These norms formed the convict code. It also admonished inmates to avoid fights, but expected even weaker inmates who were beaten, raped, or deprived of property to settle conflicts among themselves and not seek help from prison officials. It created a system of mutual aid for a small number of prisoners, produced patterns of exploitation among others, and helped create a hierarchy among the prisoners (Sykes & Messinger, 1960). Finally, the convict code

was influenced by the deprivations and limitations on freedom associated with prison life. Its core values stressed utilitarian and manipulative behavior. Those who could function in this manner were best able to acquire available wealth and positions of influence in the prison (Irwin & Cressey, 1962).

Inmate Status System Big Houses were dominated by white, lower class individuals, many with reform school experience who lacked job skills. Blacks and other minorities were usually segregated by being housed and fed separately and delegated to menial jobs (Clemmer, 1940/1958).[6] Table 7.2 examines the inmate status system that characterized these institutions. Much like status systems in a free society, it was based on prestige, privilege, and power.

Table 7.2

The Inmate Status System in the Big House

Upper Class Status	Right Guys	"Do right according to the inmate code"
		Had high prestige as thieves
		Tended to cooperate with each other
		Had a tough/cool demeanor
		Did not cooperate with officials to obtain favors
Upper Middle Class Status	Merchants	Obtained and/or manufactured scarce luxury items—legal or illegal, e.g., cigarettes, alcohol, weapons, porno
	Politicians	Formed special relationships with officials
		Influenced inmate assignments and jobs
		Had advanced information on shakedowns and parole decisions
	Gamblers	Obtained economic power through their wagering skills
	Characters	Provided humorous diversion through personality or talent
	Prison Toughs	Operated in cliques and manifested hostility toward society, most inmates, and prison staff
		Earned respect by virtue of their willingness to use violence
Middle Class Status	"Typical" Prisoners	"The undistinguished majority"
		Had little or no criminal skill
		Got no respect
	Square Johns	Were accidental offenders
		Were oriented to conventional society
		Included embezzlers and "heat of argument" homicides
Lower Class Status	Hoosiers	Were dullards from rural areas with little knowledge of crime
	Prison Queens	Were openly homosexual
		Appeared feminine in dress and in manner
	Punks	Were youths coerced into providing sexual favors
	Rats	Informed on others to staff
	Rapos/Abnormal Sex Offenders	Were child molesters
		Ignored and excluded from informal inmate activities
	Dingbats	Seen as crazy but harmless
	Crazies	Considered dangerous and unpredictable

Sources: Clemmer, 1940/1958; Irwin, 1980; Korn & McCorkle, 1959. Prepared by J. W. Silverman.

The Upper Class included **right guys,** who were the sophisticated, intelligent, and urbanized inmates. They could always be depended on "to do right according to the inmate code" (Korn & McCorkle, 1959). Their high prestige as thieves, their tendency to cooperate with one another, and their demeanor of toughness and coolness further enhanced their position.

On the next level were those of Upper Middle Class status: merchants, politicians, gamblers, characters, and prison toughs.

Merchants' status was based on their ability to obtain or manufacture scarce luxury items, both legal and illegal (e.g., cigarettes), to be sold or traded in the inmate economy. **Politicians** generally occupied positions in the administrative offices or worked for key officials, which gave them access to files and other sources of information. They knew about key decisions before other inmates as a result of their special relationships with key officials (e.g., serving as a captain's clerk). This enabled them to influence job and cell assignments and obtain special privileges. **Gamblers** acquired substantial winnings gambling within the inmate economy. **Characters** were good at providing humorous diversions by virtue of their storytelling abilities, dress, or general behavior. **Prison toughs** manifested a constant hostility toward prison officials, conventional society, and most other prisoners. Cliques of these toughs occasionally hurt or killed other inmates, usually those without prestige or power.

Most inmates fell into the Middle Class; they failed to distinguish themselves as either criminals or characters (Clemmer, 1940/1958). **Typical prisoners** were lower and working class individuals with little or no criminal skill and, as a result, they got no respect. **Square Johns,** also in this group, were accidental offenders, who were not considered criminals by the inmate population and were oriented to conventional society. Their crimes included homicides committed in the heat of an argument or embezzlement.

The lowest stratum included **Hoosiers,** dull, backward individuals with little knowledge of crime who came from rural areas; openly homosexual **prison queens; punks,** young inmates forced to provide sexual favors; informers, or **rats; rapos,** or abnormal sex offenders, sentenced for incest and child molesting and considered repulsive by most inmates; **dingbats,** considered crazy but harmless; and **crazies** who, due to their unpredictable behavior, were considered extremely dangerous and to be treated with caution.

Adapting to Prison Life   Inmates chose one of three prison adaptations based on their preprison activities and commitment to either a free-world orientation or to criminal values. **Doing time,** the most frequent adaptation, involved avoiding trouble and getting out fast with a minimum of pain (Irwin, 1980). It was adopted by thieves and most other inmates who shared these concerns. These offenders avoided situations that might extend or intensify their punishment. **Jailing** involved becoming immersed in the prison world. It was generally adopted by **state-raised youths,** inmates who had spent a major part of their lives in juvenile institutions, jails, or prisons beginning in their early teens or before (Irwin, 1980). These prisoners almost completely oriented themselves to the prison, which became the world around which their lives revolved.

For many state-raised youths, prison was better than life on the outside, because in prison they could manipulate the system. Some occupied high-status positions in the inmate hierarchy (e.g., secretary to the captain or warden), which enhanced their power and provided income. Working in the laundry enabled inmates to give special attention to the clothing of paying customers. For many of these inmates the prison became their "home," and some inmates caused problems before release to have their sentences extended, whereas others committed crimes after release to be recommitted. In the movie *The Shawshank Redemption* the librarian, when released after 50 years, was unable to make it on the outside and hanged himself. **Gleaning** was adopted by a small number who wanted to use available prison resources to improve their minds and postprison employment potential (Irwin, 1980). They spent their time reading, attending the prison's education programs, and learning trades either through the few vocational training programs or from prison job assignments.

Coping with Prison Deprivation   The scarcity of goods and services in prison led many inmates to improvise substitutes to make prison life more bearable. One example was the brewing of prison alcohol, called *pruno* or *raisin jack.* It was made by accumulating sugar, grains, fruit or potatoes, and yeast and fermenting them for several days to a few weeks. Although foul tasting and highly impure, it was intoxicating, providing inmates the outlet for which they were looking. Some prisoners also made weapons, usually *shivs* (knives made from materials available in the prison, including kitchen utensils, metal from the shops, and even from seemingly harmless items such as toothbrushes).

Inmates also made adaptations to the prison's single-sex world. One adaptation involved homosexual patterns, a form of improvisation in the Big House. Nelson (1933), an ex-long-term inmate, indicated the emotional consequences of the deprivation of heterosexual contact:

> For all the possible forms of starvation, surely none is more demoralizing than sexual starvation . . . to be starved for month after weary month, year after endless year . . . this is the secret quintessence of human misery. Is it any wonder . . . that the prisoner should seek relief in any available form? . . . [I]t makes little

difference to the average prisoner that the only available means of sexual satisfaction are abnormal... [Inmates have] a hunger not only for sexual intercourse, but... for the voice... touch... laugh... tears of a woman; and women themselves. (p. 143)

Prisons deprive men of opportunities for normal sexual and affectionate relations, which promotes conditions for homosexual behavior. This underscores the almost totally womanless environment of Big Houses. Inmate contact with women was limited to the few female employees and visits from wives or girlfriends.

Homosexual encounters involved two distinctive role patterns. **Jockers, wolves,** or **daddies** performed the traditional masculine role in oral or anal intercourse, except the object of their gratification was a male rather than a female. This was a more accepted role. Other inmates felt that, if desperate enough for sexual satisfaction, they too would assume this role (Nelson, 1933; Sykes, 1958).

The "female" role was often assumed by younger, weaker, more naive, and more effeminate-appearing inmates. They were "turned out," by being seduced or tricked by an experienced wolf who supplied them with gifts and kindness and provided protection from other inmates; sometimes they became the "girlfriend" of a tough wolf to avoid victimization from other inmates. Punks were also trapped into playing the female role, because in other institutions they were homosexual prostitutes, serving inmates in exchange for luxuries like tobacco and candy. Inmates, beginning as wolves might, after a period of continued homosexual activity, change their sexual orientation and continue their homosexuality after being released.

Opportunities for normal sexual relations were restricted, because few women worked in these prisons and visits were tightly controlled. A few inmates still found ways to have sexual liaisons with women (usually in poorly managed prisons or large city jails where guards got jobs through political influence) (Fishman, 1934). At these facilities, for a price, inmates were permitted to have sexual relationships with wives or mistresses, and some managed to manipulate female staff. At Leavenworth, a group of inmates even managed to smuggle in some prostitutes to service inmates for a price (Wilson, 1948).

Prison stupor, or prison psychosis, was a form of psychological escape from the deprivations of prison life. The Big Houses were not a stimulating environment; most inmates spent much of their time in small, poorly ventilated cells and had little opportunity for sunshine, fresh air, or contact with persons of their choosing except for a short time in the prison yard. Meals were depressing events during which inmates ate poorly cooked food of inferior quality under unpleasant conditions. They had a short time to eat—sometimes only 20 minutes—and no talking was allowed. Limited visits failed to provide inmates the kind of mental and emotional stimulation to keep their minds and emotions active and enable them to remain well balanced (Nelson, 1933). Lack of normal sexual outlets, combined with long periods of dead time spent in cells, generated erotic and other sexual fantasies among inmates. They also had almost no responsibility for meeting their own needs (e.g., planning a day's work or budgeting for necessities like food). The result was often a loss of physical or mental alertness and initiative resulting in prison stupor. In the advanced stages inmates usually walked around with an expression of total indifference on their faces, and their eyes were glazed with absentmindedness.

Big House Prison Guards

Big House prison guards were referred to as **hacks, screws,** or **bulls;** they "did time" like the inmates. The following description captures the essence of a Big House guard's life:

The life of the guard, except for his privilege of leaving at night after his twelve hour shift, is in many cases more unpleasant than that of the convict.... The guards are politically appointed, untrained for their work by even an institutional school of instruction, with no assurance of tenure or pension, underpaid, many physically unfit for the crises (escapes, mutiny, pursuit, and supervision), [and] inexperienced in prison conditions. (Jacobs, 1977,[7] p. 21)

Guards functioned in a hostile environment because of the inmate code's admonition not to cooperate or interact openly with them or the administration. This made their jobs difficult because most of their contact was with inmates during the workday. They were responsible for supervising inmate activities and for preventing problems (e.g., fights and escapes, prison rule violations, infrequent riots). Also, some inmates were particularly problematic for their keepers as a result of their deprived circumstances.

The guards also had to enforce an incredibly large number of arbitrary and inclusive prison rules, including such trivial violations as forbidding loud talking in the cells, not getting in or out of bed promptly, and not wearing an outside shirt (Wickersham Commission, 1931). The guards were scarcely freer than the prisoners because the rules they worked under were sometimes as oppressive and imprecise as those for inmates (Rothman, 1980; Wickersham Commission, 1931). They were often prohibited from doing anything except watching and talking to inmates, which essentially involved giving them orders (Rothman, 1980). Stateville guards were subjected to the most stringent controls. They could be disciplined for not saluting a captain and for reading a

Big House prison guards were responsible for supervising inmate activities and preventing problems such as fights and escapes. They also enforced rules governing inmate behavior.

newspaper, and their barracks could be searched by their superiors for contraband items (e.g., radios) or to expose gambling (Jacobs, 1977; Kantrowitz, 1996).

The multiplicity of rules that guards had to enforce, and those under which they operated, placed them in a catch-22 position. Guards could enforce the rules rigidly; however, this had practical drawbacks. They required inmate cooperation to operate and maintain the prison, and they were evaluated based on their ability to control inmates. Thus, a noisy, troublesome, dirty cell block adversely reflected on a guard's ability to handle inmates.

Guards used several disciplinary methods to control inmates, some of which were brutal (e.g., beatings). This was the least effective and most exaggerated control strategy, because the guards were greatly outnumbered by inmates. Although guards could call for backup from other guards, this was not well received by administration because of understaffing at most prisons.

Officially, until the 1930s, inmate rule violators could be whipped in many prisons or subjected to two kinds of isolation. **Administrative segregation** involved placing inmates in regularly equipped and ventilated cells where three meals a day were provided and they could be confined for many months (Rothman, 1980). **Solitary confinement** cells, often called the hole, were also used as punishment. These were frequently bare, unlighted, and unventilated, causing them to be extremely hot in sum-

mer and cold in winter. Inmates received only buckets for bodily needs, and they were sometimes stripped and not given blankets, leaving them to sleep naked on the stone floor. Fed only bread and water, some inmates lost up to 15 pounds in a short time. By the late 1930s, there were improvements in the treatment of inmates in solitary, which limited confinement to a short duration, usually a week or two. Wardens often circumvented this rule by confining inmates for the maximum period, releasing them for a day, and then confining them again. This cycle could be repeated for months (Rothman, 1980).

Guards developed several informal methods of controlling inmates by obtaining their cooperation. Some were implicit, like ignoring minor offenses or avoiding positions where they would discover rule infractions. Others involved special agreements with key inmates not to break certain rules in exchange for some special treatment. Inmates lost privileges, such as attending movies or ball games, for minor rule violations, but major violations could result in loss of good time or an additional sentence, both of which extended the period of their confinement. **Corrupt favoritism** involved arrangements by guards to grant special privileges to certain key inmates in exchange for their assistance in maintaining order. An inmate would take certain liberties such as obtaining more food or cell changes for himself or others. If guards failed to act, he would continue the practice. These inmates not only kept their own violations within acceptable limits and supported the prison value system—which indirectly supported conformity—but also controlled by coercion and violence inmates who threatened the prison routine and their privileged arrangements (Korn & McCorkle, 1959). Also, by not strictly enforcing the rules, guards could build a fund of goodwill, which proved valuable during riots when the tables were turned (Sykes, 1956).

Finally, the guards' authority was eroded by their tendency to transfer many responsibilities to trusted inmates, including allowing them to assume responsibility for minor chores such as preparing reports, locking and unlocking doors, and making cell checks at periodic counts. These inmates had positions such as that of an administrative assistant, which gave them power and influence in the prison. Even when a guard was transferred to another position, he would find this arrangement already in operation. The risks of changing an existing arrangement were more than many guards were willing to take, since they knew that inmates could send a *snitch* or *kite*—an anonymous note—to a guard's superior detailing past derelictions of duty. This was often enough to sustain the existing balance of power.

Disturbances and Riots

The Big Houses were occasionally rocked by disturbances, but they were relatively peaceful places because the control strategies employed by the guards and administration were generally effective, and inmates wanted to do their time peacefully and quickly and knew that participation in disturbances could result in longer sentences. However, inmates were far from content and satisfied. The deprivations, tensions, and pressures of prison life created pent-up feelings that could not be expressed. The riots and disturbances that occurred were unpredictable and spontaneous, often erupting over minor incidents that disturbed the fragile peace and set off an explosion of suppressed feelings. Bad food was a frequent precipitating cause of riots in these institutions because this represented one of the few pleasures inmates had. Other inflammatory factors included administrative changes in prison routines that resulted in the loss of privileges, upsetting the precarious balance between prison leaders and inmates, or increased punishment and deprivation. Overcrowding heightened tensions because it resulted in hastily prepared food and reduced privileges, yard time, privacy, and individual attention to inmates (Bates, 1936). Their seriousness should not be overlooked, as our Close-Up "Prison Riots During the Big House Era" shows.

Conflicts for Administrators

Big House administrators and their staffs were responsible for maintaining order (e.g., preventing escapes and controlling internal disruption and violence) and providing prisoners with the necessities of life—usually on a meager budget. In most Big Houses, there was a constant

Prison Riots During the Big House Era

CLOSE-UP

The greatest loss of life reported from a prison uprising was the Ohio Penitentiary fire on Monday, April 21, 1930. The fire began at 6:00 in the evening and was set by inmates apparently intending to create confusion and then escape. Two thousand prisoners were loose in the yard and were threatening violence, which did not materialize. Guards would not open the cells in and near burning buildings. Guard Watkins held the keys, insisting that he did it on orders of [the] Deputy . . . who later denied any such orders. By the time other officers wrested the keys from Watkins and opened the cells, 317 inmates were reported to have died. It is surprising that the property damage resulted in but $11,000 (Fox, 1956, p. 22). . . .

In Colorado, on Friday, October 3, 1929, 150 inmates . . . obtained four guns and barricaded themselves in cell-house No. 3 holding seven guards hostage. Prison officers attacked the cell-house and the inmates felled three officers in the first rush. . . . They demanded that the prison gates . . . be [opened] and they be allowed to escape. [They also] . . . threatened to kill a hostage each hour . . . as long as their demands were ignored. The administration demanded unconditional surrender. The body of [the] guard . . . hangman was the first to be thrown from the cell-house. . . . Armed guards had been able to isolate the riot to the cell-house. National guardsmen were called, bringing in one airplane and several three-inch field pieces. [The] Warden . . . was shot seriously, but recovered. The Catholic chaplain . . . set the charge of dynamite at the cell-house and exploded it, after which the cell-house was sprayed with machine gun fire. . . . Prisoners retreated to the undamaged part of the cell-house and continued their fight. [Inmates drove back an advancing militia]. . . . As their ammunition ran out, inmate leader Danny Daniels shot his lieutenants and then shot himself. The toll was seven guards killed, five inmates killed, $500,000 in property damage, a new record, and an escape prevented (Fox, 1956, pp. 26–27).

conflict between advocates of humane treatment and those who were punitively oriented.

Pressures for harsh treatment came from external and internal sources. The Wickersham Crime Commission (1931) viewed a prison's major function as suppressing and controlling dangerous offenders. Humane treatment and rehabilitation required experimentation and administrative flexibility, which created custodial problems. These included increasing the risk of disturbances and escapes, which the press was quick to report (Barnes & Teeters, 1951). However, a warden's efforts to introduce humane practices and reform programs for offenders rarely received any positive attention and often left him open to accusations of coddling convicts or running a country club. Most prison officials were political appointees who wanted job security, which meant they did not experiment with risky practices.

Several other factors also fostered a tendency to employ forceful and harsh control measures. Many inmates were considered violent and presented escape risks. Most wardens were inexperienced, and guards were usually individuals of low caliber who relied upon the most expedient control methods (Wickersham Commission, 1931). The geographic isolation of prisons, the autonomy of prison administrators, and the authoritarian paramilitary organizational structure of prisons were additional contributing factors.

Pressures for humane practices and programs came from reformers. The "new penology" movement, which was rooted in the principles passed in 1870 at the National Congress on Penitentiary and Reformatory, was a persistent force for change (Barnes & Teeters, 1951). Most states, except many in the South, went through periods when a governor supporting reform appointed a progressive warden. In more humane prisons, inmates spent more time outside their cells, had better food, and ate it under more normal conditions (i.e., at small tables). Also, visiting was less restricted and discipline was less cruel.

The new penology influenced prison design by rejecting old fortress-type prisons that caged inmates like animals. Thus, new prisons like the federal facility at Lewisburg implemented this philosophy, which called for security without depressing restraint, the circulation of light and air within the facility, a library, hospital facilities, and a mess hall. The Historical Perspective, "Progressive Developments During the Big House Era," looks at progressive developments during this era and the impediments to their full realization.

The End of an Era

The changes that took place in the treatment of offenders from 1900 to 1950 were characterized by a gradual and uneven movement toward less brutality and puni-

tiveness, combined with more humane routines. At the beginning of this era, the "silent system" was in effect. Inmates could be routinely whipped for violating prison rules, and they often spent over two thirds of their sentences in their cells. As this era progressed, treatment personnel entered prisons, and their rehabilitative emphasis brought them into conflict with the punitive-oriented views of custodial staff. So began the struggle between these groups, which became more pervasive in the next era as more systems established treatment departments.

Finally, not all institutions during this era could be described as "Big Houses." Southern prisons were different from Big House–type prisons. Also, each state had a small population of female inmates housed in small, separate institutions, often known as reformatories, or, in special sections of male prisons (Barnes & Teeters, 1951). These differed from Big Houses in their size and population and the offenses and social patterns of female inmates (see Chapter 9).

The Rehabilitative Institution

This section examines the emergence of the rehabilitative institution, which spanned the period between 1950 and the early 1970s, including the social conditions conducive to its development, the basic components that characterized this new type of prison, and the factors that contributed to its demise.

Social Change and the Rehabilitative Era

The term **rehabilitative institution** refers to a prison with a major focus on treating and "curing" the offender. The blueprint for this institution was developed at the National Congress on Penitentiary and Reformatory Discipline (1870) and was followed by a Progressive Movement aimed at the reformation of inmates. These newly constructed institutions were not constructed in many states until after World War II. They had a different appearance, organization, type of prisoner, and most important, impact on offenders from Big Houses. By the 1950s, the rehabilitative philosophy dominated corrections, at least in the sense that penologists regarded it as embracing the goals toward which corrections should work (Irwin, 1980).

The change from a system of warehousing and punishing offenders to one of rehabilitating them occurred during an era when our society was undergoing many social changes. The period following World War II was characterized by economic growth, increasing urbanization, and mobility. However, those in the lower socioeconomic classes found it difficult to move up the social ladder through hard work as many immigrant groups

Progressive Developments During the Big House Era

Progressive Developments Initiated by Some States

- Efforts were made to classify inmates, paving the way for treatment programs and different custody and security considerations.

- Inmates were grouped by the need for supervision and the risk of escape. This separated younger offenders from more hardened, older ones and gave more freedom to those who could be trusted.

- The construction of medium and minimum security facilities was begun.

- A centralized, governmental authority for operating an integrated prison system was created.

- Institutional specialization began with the establishment of prisons for the criminally insane, reformatories for those ages 16 to 25, and separate institutions for women.

- Reflecting the new influence of the social sciences, classification teams were augmented by psychologists and social workers concerned with understanding human behavior

and attempting to unravel the individual causes of criminal behavior (Hippchen, 1978).

- A period of isolation and classification for newly admitted inmates prior to their being placed in the general population was established.

- Centralized receiving and diagnostic centers were established. At these classification facilities, inmates were evaluated and a treatment plan was developed that included placement in an appropriate facility and in work or education programs (if needed and available).

Impediments to Their Realization

By 1940 a national survey found that 45 of the 88 institutions polled had classification procedures. Impediments to their realization included:

- No prison or system of prisons could provide the treatment necessary to correct all of the problems that were diagnosed.

- One half of the states offered educational programs, but only one quarter had programs based on professional educational standards.

- Vocational training, involving more than just on-the-job instruction, was available in only about one fifth of the prisons.

- A custody/system needs vs. treatment conflict emerged. Both concerns were to be given equal voice in programming decisions, but custody/system needs weighed more heavily and usually prevailed over treatment considerations.

- If a low-risk inmate wanted to learn printing, and the print shop was at a maximum security facility, he would likely be sent to a minimum security farm if the system needed inmates to produce food. If he was a high-risk inmate and the print shop was at a minimum security facility or outside the prison walls, he would be denied access.

Sources: Bates, 1936; Barnes & Teeters, 1943, 1951; Morse, 1940.

---

had done in the past because this, now, was based increasingly on education and occupational skills. Most immigrants and migrants arriving in the cities lacked the skills to compete for better jobs, which frequently meant they were unable to improve their economic situation. This led to the development of hard-core slums that produced enduring lower class subcultures. These areas included:

1. second- and third-generation lower class whites who remained in the slum (because of physical, mental, or other adverse circumstances)

2. a disproportionate number of blacks, whose lower socioeconomic position was also a result of racial prejudice and discrimination

3. Puerto Ricans, whose problems were similar to blacks and who also were hampered by a language barrier

4. Mexicans, with similar problems to Puerto Ricans

5. whites from depressed rural areas of Appalachia who had difficulty in adjusting to an urban environment. Other contributing factors were the low quality of schools in the slums and the subcultural value systems that neglected education.

This lack of mobility facilitated the development of subcultures heavily involved in delinquency and crime, which had several implications for the prison system. First, the prison population of this era was largely composed of the preceding urban groups. This contributed to a more diverse ethnic mix in the prison population; this is not surprising because the criminal justice system tends to deal most strictly with street crime, which is overwhelmingly perpetrated by those in the lower class. Second, the street norms of many youth groups in these subcultures contained antisocial dimensions that shaped the inmate world. Third, frustration and hostility were generated when many individuals in these groups, particularly blacks, tried to improve their circumstances and met with blatant discrimination. This also made them susceptible to explosive violence and ripe for participation in the prisoner revolution (discussed in the final part of the chapter).

This time period also saw changes in approaches to social problems, such as family disorganization, race relations, juvenile delinquency, and urban crime, which affected the criminal justice system (Irwin, 1980). The Depression of the 1930s and World War II changed perceptions about how to deal with these problems from an isolationist and individualistic orientation to one that involved government intervention and empowerment of government agencies to deal with conditions needing to be rectified.

Although the rehabilitation of offenders was not a new idea, society was not prepared to entertain the idea of correcting offenders until after World War II when the G.I. Bill provided college funds to former soldiers, creating a pool of college-educated professionals who could be employed in these programs. Also, in the early 1950s, prisons were disrupted by a series of riots. Richard McGee, chairman of the American Prison Association's committee to study inmate violence, concluded that inmate violence was caused by a failure of the public and inmates to understand the rehabilitative functions and purposes of prisons. In 1954, the American Prison Association, in support of the rehabilitation ideal, changed its name to the American Correctional Association (ACA) and its primary publication to *The American Journal of Corrections*. It also issued a revised *Manual of Correctional Standards* (MCS) (McKelvey, 1977). Further, a new group of penal specialists referred to by Irwin (1980) as **correctionalists** emerged. It included college-educated administrators and employees of prisons, probation and parole officers, and a few academic penologists. Their objective was to reduce the rapidly increasing crime problem by persuading state governments and concerned segments of the population that it could be reduced by identifying and "curing" offenders of their criminality. Thus, the primary function of prisons was to be *rehabilitation*, which was a new form of reformation based on scientific methods (Irwin, 1980).

Some states, like Wisconsin and Minnesota, responded by reorganizing institutional staff structures and introducing new programs into old prisons. Others, like New York and California, constructed new facilities to more adequately test this orientation. Some merely gave lip service to the correctional ideal by relabeling key aspects of the prison environment. Prisons became known as correctional institutions, guards as correctional officers, prisoners as inmates, and solitary confinement as the adjustment center. Thus, Warden Joe Ragen, who ran a strict, punitive prison, simply renamed his system of total control at Stateville in Illinois "rehabilitation" (Jacobs, 1977).

The Rise and Fall of the Rehabilitative Institution

The *Manual of Correctional Standards* of the American Correctional Association (Committee for the Revision of the 1954 Manual [CRTM], 1959) viewed rehabilitation as the basic aim of an institution. Toward this end, inmates were to receive indeterminate sentences, and be classified to receive appropriate institutional programming and treatment.

Indeterminate Sentencing Indeterminate sentencing was a critical component of rehabilitation, because it was impossible to determine in advance the length of imprisonment necessary to rehabilitate an offender. This reflects a reliance on the assumptions of the **medical model**—that is, that problems would be dealt with as illnesses by diagnosing and treating them (Rothman, 1980). Thus, just as it is impossible to predict how long it will take to cure someone hospitalized for a physical illness, no prediction could be made on the time it would take for inmates to respond to treatment programs in a correctional institution.

Further, despite their offenses, inmates amenable to treatment were to be paroled when they were "cured," whereas those who were unwilling to change their criminal lifestyles remained in prison; this assured that real criminals were not "coddled" (Rothman, 1980).

The indeterminate sentence was based on many faulty assumptions. It presupposed that correctional professionals had the knowledge to develop programs to "reform" many offenders. It assumed they (1) were skillful enough to determine the crucial factors behind the criminality of specific inmates; (2) had or could develop programs that would improve an offender's behavior or personality (i.e., cure them); and (3) had the tools and diagnostic instruments to determine when an offender was ready for release. In fact, correctional administration had none of these skills (Irwin, 1980).

Implementation of the indeterminate sentence also created problems. First, it gave correctional administrators and parole board members considerable discretionary authority, including the opportunity to avoid unfavorable criticism by keeping "notorious" and heinous offenders in prison while giving preferential treatment to high-status offenders. This generated a great deal of hostility among inmates. Second, it was criticized because it resulted in longer prison sentences and less parole flexibility than determinate sentencing (Rubin, 1973). This was because many jurisdictions only employed a modified indeterminate sentence, which required inmates to serve from half to most of their maximum sentence before being eligible for parole. This was often longer than the one third required for parole eligibility in determinate sentencing states (Rubin, 1973). Inmates were never sure exactly how much time they had to serve before they were eligible for parole or release (Irwin, 1980).

> I was sentenced to San Quentin on an indefinite term. The prisoner there has no notion of the term the parole board will set until the end of the first year [when the] board fixes his maximum, and may reduce it. The first year is a perfect hell for a prisoner. He keeps asking others who were convicted of a similar offense about details of their crime and of their maximum sentence [so as to get some idea of his potential sentence]. I kept thinking and worrying about it, for every year in prison makes a difference. My worry interferes with my work, and I get sent to the "hole" for inefficiency in work. That looks bad on my record and I wonder whether it will increase my maximum sentence. This worry drives a person mad. [When] . . . the sentence is fixed the prisoner can settle down to serve his time and it is a great relief to have it settled. (Sutherland & Cressey, 1966, pp. 635–636)

Inmate Classification Ideally, **classification** in a correctional institution was to parallel the process physicians use to diagnose and treat physical illnesses. Thus, a team of correctional professionals was designated to discover the nature of an inmate's criminality and to prescribe a program to cure these deficiencies. This plan, however, was tentative because classification was viewed as a dynamic process to be modified continually according to the inmate's changing needs (CRTM, 1959). Unfortunately, classification never operated as it was intended because social scientists were neither able to develop valid diagnostic instruments nor programs that "cured" criminality. Moreover, security and management concerns dominated offender placement (Irwin, 1980; Sutherland & Cressey, 1966).

Correctional Treatment Programs In a correctional institution, all aspects of the facility's milieu were to be directed toward changing the offender. This included having adequate buildings, equipment, and resources for treatment staff to achieve their program objectives. It also meant staffing the facility with adequate and competent personnel, selected and trained to operate under conditions that would promote a high degree of efficiency and morale (CRTM, 1959). Obviously, much variation existed in the extent to which correctional institutions met these criteria.

Therapeutic programs were to include individual and group therapy and counseling, under the direction of psychologists and psychiatrists (or other trained counselors and therapists). However, low salaries and undesirable working conditions made it almost impossible to hire these professionals (Irwin, 1980).

Group counseling usually involved 10 to 12 inmates (and a staff member) meeting at least weekly for a 1- or 2-hour session to discuss their problems. These groups were supposed to develop sufficient confidence and cohesiveness to enable participants to express true feelings without fear of any adverse repercussions. As it was, many inmates felt compelled to attend because they were led to believe by treatment staff and parole board members that their parole was contingent on participation. The following comments by inmates further suggest why these sessions were not very effective:

> The counseling leader is usually an incompetent member of the staff, especially when dealing with socially maladjusted people. Groups, as they stand, don't have any leadership to prod inmates toward areas requiring attention. Consequently, many hours are spent just bitching about this bull [correctional officer] or that bull and nothing concrete is really established.

> In eighteen months of group counseling, I've only learned more ways to commit crimes—heard all about other inmates' crimes and all they had—new cars, etc.—and yet they bummed cigarettes—it's just a process of wasting time and attempted brainwashing. (Kassebaum, Ward, & Wilner, 1971, pp. 137–139)

The effectiveness of these treatment sessions was jeopardized by participants who were adept at "conning"; that is, inmates learned what the therapist expected of them and then went through the process of "being cured."

> In California, one formula (believed to be foolproof by inmate adherents) prescribed a short period of intense "messing up" upon entering prison followed by a mixture of half group therapy and half group vocational training. This was followed with a gradual reduction of prison behavior and a few carefully written letters to close kin. (Martinson, 1972, as cited by Prettyman, 1981, p. 79)

Thus, for some inmates, involvement in treatment and other programs was not aimed at self-improvement but part of "playing the game" necessary to be released (Conrad, 1965).

Synanon at the Nevada State Prison

Synanon was an early drug treatment program that appeared to be successful. It consisted of former addicts living together in a drug-free environment. Life in this community centered on educational, therapeutic, and work activities designed to maintain abstinence. Addicts entering the program progressed through three stages. The first stage restricted them to the "house" with participation in all aspects of the program. The therapeutic program consisted of three weekly group meetings intended to help individuals discover and deal with the problems underlying their addiction. This group process provided support and created a feeling of mutual dependency. After developing sufficient confidence and maturity, residents entered the second stage. They could now work outside the "house" but were required to return after work and participate in the therapeutic process. In the third stage, individuals left the house, returning only for occasional visits. One criticism of this program was that only a very small proportion of its participants ever reached the third stage. Nevertheless, this approach was seen as very successful in treating drug addiction (*Time*, 1963; Yablonsky, 1965).

Synanon Moves into Prison

After hearing a presentation on Synanon, the prison psychologist at the Nevada State Prison was so impressed he asked Chuck Dederich, Synanon's founder, to set up a group in the prison. A contingent of Synanon people from California (including several ex-cons) went to Reno to assist in developing a program. A tier of cells was set aside in the prison for the program, and the Synanon people began to visit the prison to try to sell the program. Initially, both inmates and guards were unreceptive; however, under the leadership of ex-cons from the Synanon group, the program took hold. At first, it only attracted addicted inmates; later, it also drew some nonaddicts also.

When some inmates who participated in the early sessions began to dramatically change their behavior, the resisting factions started to reappraise their initial negative reactions. Inmates who at first blasted Synanon people as "do gooders" and "snitches" began to reverse their field and many joined Synanon. This accelerated when they saw some "big-yard tough guys" responding with enthusiasm. The guards, who at first feared that Synanon would produce a laxness in security, later revised their opinion in the light of a sharp reduction in fighting and other inmate problems. . . .

The new dimension that Synanon added . . . was a change of behavior within the walls. . . . [Inmates still swore to] reverse their criminal and deviant pattern when they left the institu-

tion . . . but [this was not the major change] . . . [what staff began to see] was fewer . . . "black eyes on the big yard . . ." meaning that the fighting problem had decreased. Many former hard-core candidates for solitary confinement began to work, maintained self-discipline, and became concerned with the fate of their Synanon "brothers." From the inmates' point of view, for the first time, many saw the vague possibility of a future without crime. . . .

[M]any Synanon members reported their feeling that Synanon's complex of activities and thought patterns gave them a hook for transcending the grim environment of the prison. In one seminar discussion that [Yablonsky] directed in the cell-block, the men told [him] that Synanon stimulated their otherwise vegetable-like existence. They began to read more, think more, and "moved toward life rather than away from it." [It] also provided a connection for many of the men with the outside world. . . . (Yablonsky, 1965, pp. 338–339)

Yablonsky, in discussing the problems that the Synanon program needed to deal with in the prison setting, focused on the "doing time" mentality as a serious obstacle to rehabilitation.

Inmates adopting a doing-time orientation emphasized criminal values and associations in prison.

Group counseling was the dominant form of treatment in adult correctional settings because it was inexpensive and easy to implement. By the end of the 1950s, prisons began to experiment with the more intense therapy technique of *milieu therapy*. This involved the conversion of prisons or units within prisons into "therapeutic communities." Our Program Focus, "Synanon at the Nevada State Prison," provides a brief description of this process.

Academic and vocational programs typically offered more substance than therapeutic treatment programs (Irwin, 1980). By the 1950s, innovative facilities had elementary and high school programs and had arrangements with colleges for inmates to take advanced courses on a correspondence basis. However, few facilities had accredited teachers, which meant that inmate teachers conducted most classes. Vocational training

This, along with a rejection of the society that placed them in prison, also resulted in a strong aversion to treatment. This was reinforced by staff attitudes that saw inmates as unable to "change their stripes." To shake up the antitreatment, doing-time structure that surrounds the inmate, the Synanist is required, according to Yablonsky (1965), to:

almost automatically [inject] . . . a disturbing abrasive[ness] into the "doing-time" con culture. He is inviting the criminal to change, and he provides for him an "in-person" example of the fact that this is possible. The Synanist is "walking the [w]alk." He hobnobs with the prison administration and is apparently enjoying the rewards of his changed way of life. This is disconcerting to all segments of the inmate system, since it begins to crack up many long-established rationalizations and beliefs about being a con "forever." (p. 344)

Synanon attack therapy sessions were effective in changing behavior because they constantly required participants to face their problems. From the start, individuals recognized that criminal or other unacceptable behavior would bring harsh criticism rather than praise.

Candy: What do you want in here, Shotgun?
Shotgun: Well, and, I thought I might change myself, you know—do the thing. I know there's something wrong with me. [Shotgun's comments are accompanied by the snarl and shoulder-shrugging of the "hip" tough guy.]
Synanist: Well, what's wrong with you, man?
Shotgun: I don't know—you know, I'm pretty crazy sometimes.
Synanist: Yeah, we know that, but what's wrong with you?
Shotgun: Well, I figured I could do something for myself. But if you don't want me here, well, I'll just go.
Synanist: No one said they didn't want you here. We want to know what you want to do.
Shotgun: Well, I'm always getting in trouble—and I want to do something about it.
Candy: Why do they call you Shotgun?
Shotgun: [brightening up] Well, I pulled lots of robberies with a shotgun. . . .

The Synanon group then moves to another level of attack and appraisal.

Who do you hang with in the yard?
    Well, my best buddy is Joe.
    Why do you hang with Joe?
    Well, he's a pretty good guy; he's a good thief.
    What is a good thief?

Shotgun falls back on his criminal track and says,

A good thief is a guy who knows how to rob and will burn through anyone that gets in his way.

The group begins to ridicule his relationship with "good-thief" Joe.

They again allude to robbery of this sort as "insanity." Shotgun becomes increasingly hostile under the attack. . . . This may have been the first time in his life that he had experienced an attack of this kind from his criminal peer group. The attack was a double whammy, because it was against the very basis of his "reputation." (Yablonsky, 1965, pp. 348–349)

Judging from Yablonsky's comments, the Synanon program at the Nevada State Prison was successful. However, in 1964 it was terminated when a new governor, who did not support the program, was elected. Therapeutic community programs were established in other prisons. However, they failed for a variety of reasons (e.g., the programs were poorly conceived, lack of support from prison personnel). Recently, a number of therapeutic community programs, like Stay'n Out, have been established successfully and, like Synanon, have been found to reduce recidivism (see Chapter 19) (Mullen, 1991).
Source: L. Yablonsky (1965). The Tunnel Back: Synanon. New York: Macmillan. Reprinted with permission of the author.

programs were available in all correctional institutions, but these programs suffered from many problems, including (1) not having enough openings for the demand, (2) failure to prepare participants adequately for a trade upon release, and (3) obsolete equipment, inadequate techniques, and lack of skilled instructors with up-to-date knowledge. Nevertheless, these educational programs still benefited inmates more than the ineffectual and sometimes harmful therapy programs directed by unskilled staff.

Treatment and custody staff were supposed to be treated equally in correctional facilities, unlike in Big Houses, where the authority of custodial staff was unchallenged due to the emphasis on custodial concerns. However, the "rehabilitation emphasis" of correctional facilities required a new role for treatment staff, who

Soledad: An Exemplary Rehabilitative Institution

PROGRAM FOCUS

During the era of rehabilitation California had the most progressive program. Even before other states embraced the rehabilitative ideal, this state had begun to establish these programs in the mid-1940s (Sullivan, 1990). John Irwin, who spent 5 years at Soledad Correctional Institution in California as an inmate during its "golden age," provides an excellent portrait of it as a typical rehabilitation facility. We summarize his work below.

The Physical Plant

At Soledad, perimeter security consisted of a high fence and a gun tower. Inmates were housed in cells arranged around the outside walls of each wing, giving each an unbarred outside window. With the exception of one unit housing reception, segregation, and isolation, all cells had solid doors with small screened inspection windows. At the outset, inmates were housed in single cells with each unit containing a desk, a bunk, and a chair. In the five medium security wings, inmates had keys to their own cell doors. The prison's inside walls were painted in pastel colors (e.g., pale green, pale blue) rather than drab colors. Soledad also had two dining rooms with tiled floors and octagonal oak tables and a well-equipped gym, several shops, a spacious library, and an education building.

The Routine and Programs

The routine at Soledad was more relaxed, giving inmates opportunities to make choices such as whether to go to breakfast or sleep an extra hour before going to work. For most of the day and on weekends, the cell blocks were open and inmates were free to go to the yard, library, or gym. At night they could leave their units for scheduled activities (e.g., gym, school, library).

Reflecting the emphasis on rehabilitation, programming included a broad selection of vocational training and good elementary and high school programs. Therapy for most inmates involved weekly group counseling sessions (although these were usually conducted by poorly trained guards and other staff). Participation was all but mandatory because parole was dependent on program involvement. By the late 1950s, sessions were held daily in an effort to intensify the treatment program.

The Population

In the 1950s, California experienced a major shift in the percentage of its nonwhite inmate population. By then nonwhites composed more than 40 percent of the population, including approximately 25 percent Mexican-Americans and 15 percent blacks. The Mexican-American population was composed of two groups—one raised in Texas (Tejanos) and the other primarily from Los Angeles (Chicanos). Although both groups came to be

called Chicanos, there was hostility between them that sometimes resulted in fights. Many also harbored hostility toward white inmates because of the discrimination they had experienced from whites, particularly in the public schools. Most white prisoners had come from lower and working-class urban areas, and some were state-raised youths—individuals literally raised by state agencies because they had spent most of their youth in one or more institutions. Black offenders were from Los Angeles or San Francisco or were migrants from the South and Southwest. Figure 7.1 portrays the relationships among these groups.

The Prison Atmosphere

Due to the diverse subcultural orientations, no single inmate code developed, nor did a single cohort of leaders dominate the prison. The prison was a relatively calm and orderly place. Despite racial hostility and the formation of separate groups, there were friendships and interaction among the different ethnic groups. Most prisoners came to believe that staff members were sincere in their efforts to help offenders and would discover their basic psychological, vocational, and physical defects or problems and correct them.

Tips and cliques were a major factor in maintaining the peace at Soledad. **Tips** were crowds or extended social networks of people whose association was based on

were charged with discovering and correcting the inmate's "defects." This also involved viewing inmates as having the potential for change—not as "bad people," but as those whose social circumstances caused them to commit crimes. On the other hand, custodial staff were responsible for maintaining internal control and preventing escapes (Irwin, 1980). Thus, although all institution staff members were to be part of an integrated treatment team whose primary objective was the rehabilitation of inmates, in reality the treatment component had to be

merged into an existing prison organization long dominated by a custody orientation (Cressey, 1965, as cited by Irwin, 1980). However, custody staff views continued to dominate decision making, with support by the administration who also voiced concern about avoiding dangerous outcomes and any adverse publicity. To maintain their integrity, treatment staff often developed a therapeutic rationale for the custodial decisions they made and continued their involvement in this charade to maintain the appearance that the institution was operating a humane

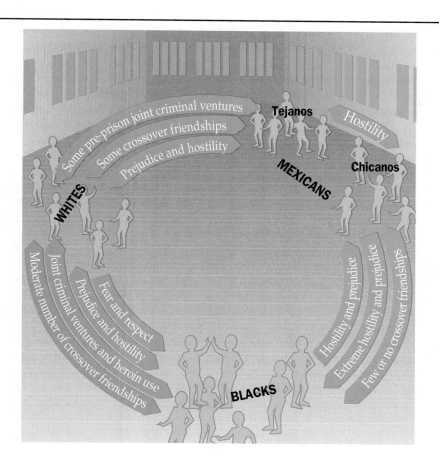

Figure 7.1 *Interethnic Relationships at Soledad*

Source: Material compiled from J. Irwin (1980). *Prisons in Turmoil.* Boston: Little, Brown, pp. 50–51.

several tips. Cliques were composed of people who had regular contact (e.g., at work or in the yard) and shared an interest in some prison activity, subcultural orientation, or preprison experience. The interconnections between cliques and tips, and tips and other tips, produced extensive and overlapping networks involving bonds of friendship, communication, and obligation. This facilitated cooperative enterprises involving contraband and scarce commodities. It also was a major factor in reducing open confrontations, which were often avoided by settling disputes through indirect negotiations between tips and cliques.

Although few in number, "deviants" existed in the correctional institution; they were inmates who were not convinced of the value of rehabilitation programs and were also not deterred from violating prison rules, even though this behavior could extend their term in prison. Persistent troublemakers were placed in special units called **adjustment centers,** segregation units that detained inmates for indefinite periods of time with reduced privileges and virtually no mobility. The rehabilitation rationale for the adjustment center was that some prisoners required more intensive therapy in a more restrictive setting.

Sources: J. Irwin (1986). Prisons in Turmoil. *Boston: Little, Brown; L. E. Sullivan (1990).* The Prison Reform Movement. *Boston: Twayne Publishers.*

preprison contacts or common subcultural involvement. These networks of people were typically interracial, overlapping, and connected. For example, Irwin was a member of a tip of Los Angeles young people involved in heroin use and theft that was connected to a tip from San Francisco through prior relationships in youthful institutions. Although not all tip members knew each other, membership involved certain obligations and provided the basis for casual associations that increased the likelihood of friendship.

Cliques were smaller primary and semiprimary groups formed by prisoners from the same tip or from

and individualized treatment program (Irwin, 1980). Our Program Focus, "Soledad: An Exemplary Rehabilitative Institution," profiles a model correctional facility.

The Failure of Rehabilitative Institutions

The idea that prisons could be transformed into hospitals for curing offenders was unrealistic. Corrections professionals did not understand the causes of criminal behavior, so they could not develop diagnostic instruments and programs that identified or changed offender behavior. Also, the view that all offenders could be sufficiently motivated to take full advantage of high-quality treatment programs was highly questionable. Although many offenders did so voluntarily, some were only motivated by desire for early release. It would not have mattered if a sufficient number of offenders had successfully been reintegrated on release, but this was not the case. Those returning to prison became increasingly disillusioned with the rehabilitation ideal and again blamed their involvement in crime on their life circumstances rather than on their individual problems (Irwin, 1980). However, these programs were not a total loss because many inmates, like Irwin, did successfully complete them.

A paradoxical outcome of the rehabilitative ideal of self-improvement was the emergence of a **prison intelligentsia,** composed of newly literate inmates who, as a result of participation in the educational programs, developed their reading skills so that this became an informative and enjoyable pastime. They served as the focal point for criticism of the rehabilitation approach. Many developed an expanded view of society, our culture, the prison system, and even their own criminal careers. This new intelligentsia of ex-offenders and inmates and returning offenders continued to critically examine the correctional system and to disseminate their views. Those returning to prison were a strong force in fostering inmate disillusionment with rehabilitation. However, this was not the only factor that shattered the fragile peace in the rehabilitative institution and hastened the demise of this approach. Continuing changes in the ethnic/racial composition of the prison population, along with its politicization and the administrative reaction to these changes, all hastened the death of this noble experiment (Irwin, 1980). Several other factors, among them public outrage with crime and criminals, struck the final blow in the mid-1970s. These changes are discussed in more detail in the final part of the chapter.

The Prisoner Movement

From the mid-1950s to the early 1970s, the United States underwent major social and cultural changes. These changes led to a **prisoner movement,** in which prisoners and others fought to reform prison conditions. Here we will discuss some of the changes that profoundly affected corrections.

Factors Leading to the Prisoner Movement

The **authority revolution** was manifested in decreasing respect for tradition. Not only were average citizens increasingly beginning to question the legitimacy of rules and customs once thought to be sacred, but oppressed classes relegated to second-class status were no longer willing to accept a subservient position. Moreover, the youth culture became a major socializing force and adults became distrusted. This, coupled with more than a 50 percent increase in the youth population, strained both formal and informal mechanisms of social control.

In the mid-1950s, as a result of the **civil rights movement,** blacks began to achieve greater equality in American society. In 1954, the Supreme Court, in *Brown v. Board of Education,* struck down the "separate but equal" doctrine that had supported segregation. The in-

creasing size of the northern black vote made civil rights a key issue in national elections, resulting in the establishment of the Federal Civil Rights Commission in 1957. Martin Luther King, Jr. rose to national prominence and gained support for the civil rights movement through nonviolent, but direct, action protests against segregation and discrimination. As blacks intensified their expectations and dissatisfaction with their current circumstances, the result was a rising tempo of nonviolent action culminating in the student sit-ins of the 1960s and the birth of the civil rights revolution (National Advisory Commission on Civil Disorders, 1968). Yet, by 1964, some movement leadership concluded that nonviolent direct action was of limited usefulness despite major victories. Subsequently, blacks took to the streets rioting to express dissatisfaction with their current circumstances.

From the mid-1960s to early 1970s, the United States also experienced both violent and nonviolent reactions to the **Vietnam War.** The widespread opposition involved a variety of individuals and social groups (e.g., youths and students, prestigious leaders, academic and literary figures, radical groups, and religious groups) (Brooks, 1969). Resistance to the war escalated to a point where a large part of the population opposed it, with some radical opponents questioning the legitimacy of the political system conducting the war and using violence to oppose it.

The prison system did not escape the influence of these events. Inmates had been exposed to them through the mass media. Prior to imprisonment, many had been involved in riots or political movements, and they had been exposed to civil rights leaders (Jacobs, 1977). Politically active inmates continued their civil rights struggle from their cells by emulating outside groups and by protesting the conditions of their confinement. Some rejected the legitimacy of the prison system itself.

Changes in the traditional prison stratification system resulted from a shift in the racial/ethnic makeup of the prison population and the development of a new sense of pride and self-respect by minority inmates. The black prisoner movement resulted from the same conditions that precipitated the black civil rights movement (e.g., mistreatment by superiors, mandated segregation policies, etc.). Moreover, as this movement achieved prominence, the proportion of blacks in prison was growing to a point where they were becoming the dominant group. Blacks developed a new self-image based on a new perception of their identity and heritage. Some inmates adopted African names, wore African clothing and jewelry, changed to a natural or "Afro" hairstyle, and adopted the view that "black is beautiful" (Carroll, 1974; Irwin, 1980; Silberman, 1978).

Until the emergence of the **Black Muslims,** religious groups had not typically served as a basis for col-

The rise of the black power movement had a major impact on prison life. Racial hostility increased, creating a pattern of informal segregation and increased racial violence.

lective black inmate behavior in prison (Jacobs, 1976). The Black Muslims represented the largest, best organized, and most articulate militant group on the radical side of the political spectrum. During the 1950s and 1960s, under the leadership of Elijah Muhammad, the Black Muslims strove to become a broad-based mass movement and did considerable recruiting in the jails and prisons (Lincoln, 1973). Black inmates joined this group because it gave them an opportunity for involvement in something uniquely black that enhanced their self-identity. It also helped members break the drug-crime cycle by requiring them to take vows to avoid involvement in both upon their release. Muslim temples helped released offenders keep their vows by assisting them in getting housing and jobs.

During the 1960s, Black Muslims became a sizable faction in many prisons, organizing themselves into distinctive groups characterized by a high degree of commitment and discipline (Irwin, 1980; Jacobs, 1977). Although adopting a hostile stance, Muslims rarely initiated violence and generally reacted violently only to protect a group member. However, both prison administrators and white inmates felt threatened and antagonized by Muslim statements that condemned whites and white society (Irwin, 1980). This organized group of blacks now threatened whites who were not organized and who still controlled the best positions in the prison. Whites in some prisons responded by developing activist groups (New York State Special Commission on Attica, 1972).[8]

Instead of recognizing the Black Muslims' potential for maintaining peace and for reforming offenders,

prison administrators reacted only to its rhetoric, refusing their demands for basic rights (Jacobs, 1977). Some even prohibited membership in the group. Court rulings eventually forced prison administrators to recognize the Muslims as a religious organization and to allow them to practice their religion in prison because none of their activities presented a clear and present danger. Over time, the Muslims modified their more extreme black supremacy and nationalistic doctrines and became less politically and more religiously oriented. Some black inmates, dissatisfied with their conservative position, joined more violent radical groups emerging during the late 1960s (e.g., the Black Panthers).

During the 1960s, several factors sparked changes that transformed racial/ethnic relations in our prisons. Black inmates viewed both white inmates and correctional officers (COs)—most were white—as a threat. Racial hostility in prisons was further aggravated by the prejudices and sometimes discriminatory behavior of COs. Black solidarity represented not only a desire to cultivate the unique aspects of black culture but also a response to the perceived threat of an alliance between white staff and prisoners based on racial identification.

This created a pattern of informal racial segregation, which was inconsistent with the outside move toward racial equality and eliminating segregation. Thus, white and black inmates often worked side by side and shared cell blocks, but communication was almost exclusively limited to official matters. Social interaction was limited to one's own ethnic/racial group in dining rooms, day rooms, and at informal gatherings (Attica Commission, 1972; Carroll, 1974; Irwin, 1980). Figure 7.2 provides some examples of inmate social interaction.

The composition of the prison population not only affected how well a given group fared but the overall environment of the institution. In California, an alliance between whites and Chicanos placed blacks in an unfavorable position in prisons where they were outnumbered by this coalition (Irwin, 1980). In facilities where blacks were in the majority, they claimed the "best spots" in formal gathering areas (such as the yard), and whites had to accept inferior locations. With the increasing racial hostility, there was a sharp increase in racial violence.

The disintegration of the tip and clique network (discussed in the Program Focus feature on page 132), facilitated the newfound prominence of state-raised youths in prison. They hung out in the prison yard, boasting about their exploits and exaggerating their abilities.

Until the racial hostility of the 1960s, their power had been curtailed by two factors: a fear that older and more respected inmates would become violent and murderous when pushed too far and the solidarity of other inmates against them (Irwin, 1980). State-raised youths always displayed a high level of prejudice, even during the era of racial tolerance (Irwin, 1980). When the prison's climate was changed by racial conflict and violence, they openly displayed racist attitudes by calling themselves Nazis and tattooing their bodies with swastikas. Similarly, cliques of black youths manifested open racial hostility. Their position was further enhanced when both black and white prisoners, even respected and older inmates who felt threatened by rising racial hostilities, joined or associated with these cliques in self-defense. The ranks of white groups were further swelled by the imprisonment of increasing numbers of outlaw motorcycle gang members who held extreme racist views and sometimes assumed leadership of these groups.

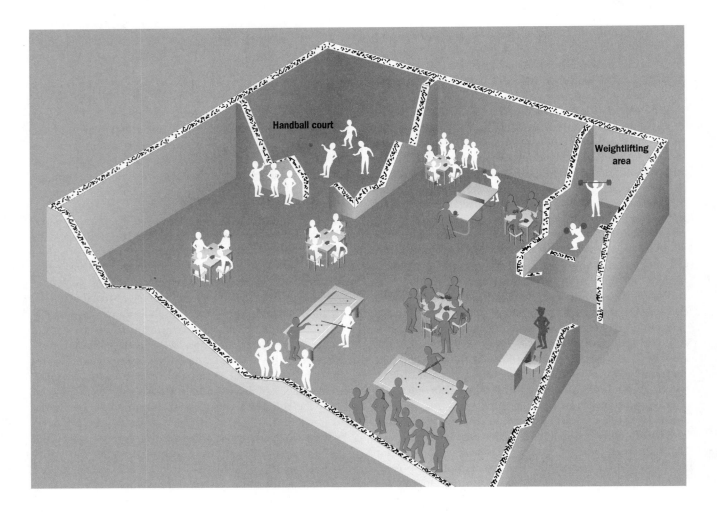

Figure 7.2 *Racial Segregation of Prisoners in the Gym*
Source: L. Carroll (1974). *Hacks, Blacks, and Cons.*

Chicano inmates formed neighborhood-based cliques whose major concern was controlling drug trafficking rather than racial hatred and violence. These groups fought among themselves to achieve dominance in this area, but it was not until the demise of the prisoner movement in the 1970s that these violent cliques and gangs became a major force in prisons (see Chapter 12).

The Emergence of the Prisoner Movement

The prisoner movement spanned the period from 1970 to 1975 and included the following features: (1) it provided a basis for inmate harmony by redirecting the violence and hostility toward each other toward other forces (e.g., prison administration) and toward society, which temporarily halted the trend toward racial/ethnic division; (2) it involved a change in inmate self-concept from subservient participant to active reformer; and (3) it focused on reforming prison conditions through both free-world and inmate groups (Irwin, 1980).

The early 1970s also saw inmates critically examining their position in society and in prison. The Attica Commission (1972) noted that many prisoners viewed themselves as **political prisoners** and blamed society for victimizing them by failing to give them a chance to compete effectively or to provide equal educational opportunities and adequate housing. They claimed correctional rehabilitation efforts were misdirected because it was not them, but society, that needed to be reformed. Inmates' views of themselves as political prisoners sentenced for crimes having political motivation was alien to American corrections (Attica Commission, 1972). This changed with the civil rights movement in the 1950s and continued with the Vietnam War protests in the 1960s (Glaser, 1971). Those movements considered the crimes of their members to be morally justified because they were motivated by political objectives and did not victimize others. "Victimless" crimes included the use of narcotics and acts involving resistance to oppressive government policies. Officials refused to consider this view, and when these offenders were incarcerated, they were treated no differently from other criminals.

Left-wing political groups formed in the 1960s attempted to persuade individuals that the solution to existing problems was to destroy the existing system and start over. They focused on prisons because they incarcerated predominantly lower class minorities, which they felt presented a clear and glaring manifestation of the inequities, injustices, and prejudices that "characterized" U.S. society (Irwin, 1980). Their involvement included providing leaders and workers for both old and new inmate organizations, lawyers to develop the new area of prison law, and citizens to actively participate at movement conferences, rallies, and other organized events (Irwin, 1980).

By 1970, black inmates became more attracted to radical groups because neither the civil rights movement nor the Muslims provided any potent strategies for dealing with their problems. During this period, Puerto Rican and Chicano inmates also began to develop an ethnic consciousness and promoted their own special interests. Moreover, a new type of white inmate was entering prison. This inmate was younger, better educated, and more involved in drugs and felt the criminal justice system discriminated against him because of his lower class status (Attica Commission, 1972).

A much smaller group adopted a class-oriented Marxist position that espoused a revolutionary political ideology (Berkman, 1979). It argued that the ruling elite, by controlling government and the workplace, effectively set one group of exploited people against another in the same way prison officials turned blacks against whites to maintain control (Berkman, 1979). However, the elite's major strategy was dominating the means of production and controlling the wealth of society. In this way, the capitalist elite controlled the labor force and dictated the terms under which they worked. Workers either endured exploitation or were excluded from the workplace. Prisoners were one segment of the working class who were excluded from participation in the economic system.

Prisoner Movement Organizations

The prisoner movement consisted of many groups, running the gamut from revolutionary groups to those that tried to operate within the current system. The widespread publicity associated with the prisoner movement, along with its lofty goals, brought together and radicalized all the organizations working on prison issues. Most groups still maintained their own philosophies, identities, strategies, goals, and memberships.

Self-Help Groups **Self-help groups** emerged several years before the prisoner movement and were primarily concerned with the improvement of the life circumstances of ex-prisoners. Seven Steps, one of the earliest of these organizations, was founded by Bill Sands, a former inmate at San Quentin. Modeled after the 12 steps of the Alcoholics Anonymous program, these 7 steps were developed to guide inmates in maintaining their freedom (Sands, 1964). This group spread to prisons in other parts of the country, and it is currently one of the largest inmate self-help organizations. It sparked the development of many other self-help groups; some were broad-based (e.g., the Fortune Society), others were racially and ethnically based (e.g., SATE for black inmates).

Ethnically based self-help groups typically emphasized ethnic themes to attract and motivate individual prisoners (Moore, 1978). For example, the Chicano cultural group EMPLEO operated on the principle that by awakening the group identity of Mexican-Americans and establishing a sense of obligation toward their group, constructive change for ex-convicts and addicts could be achieved. It also maintained contact with outside community groups to provide inmates with motivational models and resources to assist them upon their release.

Self-help groups were important for the prisoner movement because they were the largest inmate organizations (Irwin, 1980). Prison administrators accepted and frequently encouraged these organizations, because they represented a safer alternative to the more radical political groups. Many inmates also preferred these organizations because their orientation was more to self-advancement than political change.

Prisoner Rights Groups **Prisoner rights groups** began to increase in number just before the emergence of the prisoner movement (Irwin, 1980). In the 1960s, their goal was to reduce the disparities between the legal and social circumstances of prisoners and members of conventional society. They directed their efforts toward increasing inmate constitutional rights and developing meaningful prison industries programs with reasonable wages. For released offenders they sought to restore the full rights and privileges accorded to all citizens (Irwin, 1980).

Radical Groups **Radical groups** were concerned with changing society rather than helping individual inmates or changing prison conditions (Irwin, 1980). Outside groups focused on prisons because they were an example of the oppression and exploitation of the poor and nonwhites by a capitalist economic system. The Black Panthers and the National Lawyers Guild were two radical groups who held differing perspectives.

The Black Panthers originated in 1966 in Oakland, California, in reaction to police brutality in the black community (Stratton, 1973). Representing themselves as a Marxist-Leninist revolutionary party directed toward freeing blacks from their current state of suppression by corporate capitalism, Black Panther leaders saw inmates as embittered and disgruntled and thus ripe for involvement in revolutionary political activity (Jacobs, 1976). George Jackson, an inmate and Black Panther leader, argued: "I feel that the building of revolutionary consciousness of the prisoner class is paramount in the overall development of a hard left revolutionary cadre" (Committee on Internal Security, 1973a, p. 181). They appealed to apolitical prisoners by offering them the more positive status of political prisoner. This enabled them to redefine their status from offender to victim and view prison and its administration as a manifestation of the repressive organizations characteristic of American society. Their objective was to unite all prisoner move-

ment groups through an inclusive ideology emphasizing their similarities and minimizing their differences. At Attica Prison in New York, prior to the riot (discussed later in the chapter) between 200 and 300 inmates were estimated to be members, and at San Quentin in California a similar number were involved. Former members of the Black Panthers from New York State prisons reported joining for several reasons including status, protection, and a search for identity (Hankins, 1973; Hughes, 1973; Stratton, 1973).

The **National Lawyers Guild,** which was established in 1936, extended its activities in the 1970s to include initiating class action suits in instances where it felt prisoners' rights were violated; providing legal representation for prisoners involved in revolutionary activity; and negotiating with prison administrators to achieve inmate objectives. They first played an open role in the Folsom Prison strike of 1970 by holding press conferences and contacting the news media in support of the strike and being present during picketing and demonstrations. Also, during the Attica riot, members served on the observation committee and provided defense attorneys for inmates involved in the riot.

Most radical groups were established outside the prisons, because prison administrators typically banned them, forcing the few inmates who joined them to keep their membership a secret. Inmate membership was limited primarily to nonwhite inmates, because whites had more politically conservative ideas and resented the attention these groups gave to racism and black prisoners. Only a few black inmates were true revolutionaries (Carroll, 1974; Irwin, 1980). Most leaned toward revolutionary ideas but were unwilling to adopt the true lifestyle of revolutionaries. They were what the movement described as *half-steppers* (Carroll, 1974). Table 7.3 shows the difference between them and true revolutionaries.

Prisoner Movement Activities

Prisoner movement activities included those inside the prisons, ranging from inmate strikes to sporadic violence and riots. Nevertheless, outside organizations and individuals provided the actual major support base for movement activities because inmates were essentially limited in their influence on criminal justice policy.

Strikes Inmate strikes occurred in many states. Groups of inmates prepared a list of grievances directed at making changes in existing relationships and structures. They then developed a coalition from major inmate racial groups who supported their demands and strategies and attempted to obtain outside support from area prisoner groups. These coalitions sought to organize collective protests (such as strikes) to pressure the prison

Table 7.3

A Comparison of Dedicated and Pseudo Revolutionaries

	True Black Revolutionaries	Half-Steppers
Orientation	Oriented toward the future revolution	Oriented toward the present but manifested public commitment to the future revolution
Real Objective	To prepare themselves for the future revolution	To use the revolutionary organization to do easier time and "keep them whities off their backs."
Lifestyle	Spartan lifestyle—their cells were typically devoid of decorations, containing only necessities such as a desk, bed, typewriter, radio, and revolutionary books	Unwilling to adopt spartan lifestyle, yet decorated their cells with revolutionary posters to give illusion of commitment to the revolution, publicly denounced the "racist pigs," and advocated revolution
Participation in Inmates' Economy	Did not participate—felt sign of weakness to deal with the deprivations of prison life (e.g., by obtaining extra food from the kitchen, using drugs, being involved in homosexuality)	Did participate—unwilling to defer gratification of their needs
Other Activities	Pursued self-improvement activities that could result in an outside job or an early parole; developed positive identity by learning about black culture	Involvement gave them opportunity to engage in jam sessions, have occasional banquets, meet girls from the outside, and rap with each other

Source: L. Carroll (1974). *Hacks, Blacks, and Cons.* Reprinted by permission of L. Carroll.

administration into negotiations and to attract public attention and sympathy for their grievances and circumstances (Irwin, 1980) (see our Close-Up, "The Folsom Prison Strike," on page 141).

Riots The **Attica revolt** occurred in August 1971. It was characterized by rising inmate expectations based on improving prison conditions and increasing tensions between inmates and COs. The COs were all white, primarily from rural areas, and not trained to deal with the new breed of young, urban, minority black and Puerto Rican inmates who did not blindly accept their authority without question (Attica Commission, 1972). The riot was not planned but rather sparked by a rebellion against disciplinary actions by COs.

During the first phase of the riot, hundreds of prisoners went on a 3-hour rampage, destroying and stealing property, taking over parts of the prison, and taking 50 officers and civilians hostage. The Muslims assumed the responsibility of protecting the hostages and releasing the seriously injured. Recognizing the disastrous consequences of the escalating situation, one inmate attempted to establish order by developing a tenuous coalition between leaders of the various prison factions. This group developed a policy for treatment of hostages, formulated rules governing inmate activities, and formed a security force to assure compliance. They also developed the demands put forth to Commissioner of Corrections Russell Oswald; the demands included a request for the formation of a negotiating committee comprising people from groups that the inmates trusted.

The final committee consisted of 30 members, some from the requested inmate groups and others chosen by Governor Nelson Rockefeller. They met with the inmates and developed a list of proposals to submit to Commissioner Oswald. The only demands Oswald rejected were for the removal of the superintendent, inmate transportation to a foreign country, complete amnesty, unconditional release of inmates eligible for parole, and the release of the remaining 1,200 inmates so that they could join the rioting group. The observers' committee presented the inmates with the 28 points to which Commissioner Oswald had agreed. The inmates rejected his offer for the following reasons:

1. They did not trust Oswald's promises of no physical or administrative reprisals or criminal charges for property damage.

2. The inmates wanted amnesty (immunity) from prosecution, because they feared mass prosecutions for all crimes relating to the riot.[11]

3. Many inmates approved the 28 points, but they felt obligated to support their leaders and feared the harsh discipline they might receive from other inmates for nonsupport.

4. There was a sense of unreality based on their sudden freedom, prominence, and power, leading many to believe that by holding out they would be granted all their demands.

> Many of the men in D-yard probably did not believe the 28 points really represented the best deal they could make. . . . They had hostages; the state had not moved against them. If they could [pry] . . . those 28 points out of the state, might they not yet get more—even amnesty? (Wicker, 1975, p. 175)

When the compromise proposal was rejected on the fourth day of the riot, some negotiating committee members asked that Governor Rockefeller come to the prison to meet with them to avert a bloodbath if the prison was taken by force. He refused, feeling the key issue was amnesty, which was beyond his power to grant.[12] On the night of the fourth day, with negotiations at an impasse, Commissioner Oswald, with Rockefeller's approval, decided to take the prison by force the next morning. The state police major who briefed the troops before the assault admonished them not to turn this into a "turkey shoot"—that is, a game where people are rewarded for drawing blood.[13] Although most men involved in retaking the prison acted with restraint, three state investigations and one trial concluded that the force used was excessive (*Jones v. State*, 1983).

The shooting was done in the midst of clouds of tear gas by troopers wearing gas masks, making it difficult for officers to see and know what they were aiming at (Deutsch, Cunningham, & Fink, 1991). The shooting was unnecessary, because the gas was expected to immobilize the inmates and force them to the ground within seconds; the inmates only had knives and clubs, and there was no evidence of inmate attacks (Bell, 1985). Even when no one was left standing, the indiscriminate shooting continued (Glaberson, 1991). It is amazing that only 39 persons (10 hostages and 29 inmates) died of state-inflicted bullet wounds, and 3 hostages and 85 inmates suffered nonlethal gunshot wounds. Despite the inmates' warning, *no hostages were killed by inmates during the assault,* and some hostages were protected from injury by inmate guards throwing their bodies on top of them. The tragedy of Attica did not end when the shooting stopped. Despite promises of no reprisals, inmates continued to be kicked, prodded, beaten, and subjected to verbal abuse after the revolt was crushed.

Whereas 62 inmates were indicted for 1,289 crimes arising out of the Attica riot, only one state trooper was indicted for murder despite evidence that troopers killed 10 hostages and inmates killed 1 (before the retaking of the prison). This apparent injustice may be related to a public view that inmates brought this on themselves and thus deserved what was done to them. To make matters worse, the state police were given the pivotal responsibility of investigating whether their own officers used excessive force in bringing the prison under control. State investigative prosecutors blamed the offi-

Inmates of Attica State Prison raise their hands in clenched fist salutes during a negotiating session with Commissioner Russell Oswald. Although Oswald subsequently agreed to some of the prisoners' demands, the inmates rejected his offer and the commissioner decided to retake the prison by force.

The Folsom Prison Strike

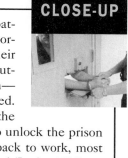

The Folsom prison strike in 1968 was the longest of these strikes, lasting 19 days and involving nearly all 2,400 inmates at Folsom. It began when inmates refused to go to work or to the yard after having smuggled out a list of 29 demands. These demands were for (1) constitutional rights, such as changing policies to reflect federal court decisions (e.g., due process in disciplinary sentencing), and (2) political freedom (e.g., ending persecution or segregation of inmates because of political beliefs).[10]

The warden locked down the prison, which meant keeping inmates in their cells. Outside groups provided support by organizing picket lines at the Folsom Prison entrance and supplied the media with a description of the strike and its issues. At the outset inmate enthusiasm was high; however, it dropped off dramatically after two weeks as supplies of cigarettes, food, and radio batteries for their portable radios—their only means of outside information— were consumed. Thus, when the warden offered to unlock the prison if inmates went back to work, most of them acquiesced (Irwin, 1980).
Source: J. Irwin (1980). Prisons in Turmoil. *Boston: Little, Brown.*

---

cers who collected the evidence for tampering with it, and "concluded their effort was not to enforce the law but to protect their own" (Bell, 1985, p. 202).[14]

Despite the fact that a special state grand jury was impaneled to reexamine this case and the continued allegations of a cover-up, a new governor decided to close the book on Attica, which had become one of New York's more embarrassing blunders. He then pardoned inmates convicted of crimes during the riot and closed the investigation. Although this appeared fair and equitable, it actually put culpable police officers and state officials beyond the reach of the law (Bell, 1985). Our Close-Up, "Attica Civil Rights Case and Its Legacy," by Michael Deutsch (1998), one of the attorneys for the inmate plaintiffs in the civil rights suit brought against the state, provides another chapter in the continuing Attica saga.

Escalating Violence   Increasing defiance and violence followed the Attica rebellion and was indicative of a general escalation of prison violence in the 1970s. Along with other social changes, the prisoner movement created an atmosphere charged with hostility in many prisons. Many young inmates entering prison, particularly minorities, were belligerent and rejected traditional norms regarding respect for institutional authority (Irwin, 1980). This—along with the prisoner movement view that inmates had rights, could not be treated arbitrarily, and were victims rather than perpetrators—produced inmates prone to challenge staff authority and to attack them. In the past, violence against guards had been relatively rare, usually occurring after a hostile confrontation. However, in the 1970s attacks reached their highest level in prison history and occurred randomly without provocation. Violence, particularly in its ex-

treme forms (e.g., the killing of COs), was an extension of the revolutionary activities advocated by more radical groups who considered themselves a part of the forthcoming revolution (Irwin, 1980). Violence and other incidents of defiance negatively influenced administrative reactions to the prisoner movement because they represented a serious threat to prison control.

Outside Support   Most organized activities outside the prison associated with the prisoner movement were controlled and supported by persons not in prison because prisoners did not possess the mobility, resources, or access to channels of communication necessary to plan and execute successful movement activities. Not surprisingly, prison administrators were threatened and irritated by outside scrutiny of prison activities and practices because their authority had never been previously questioned. Outsiders associated with the prison movement were involved in three basic types of activities. First, numerous attorneys were involved in the litigation of prisoner rights cases, which afforded inmates certain constitutional protections. Second, involvement in the publicized trials of a few well-known political prisoners rallied support for the movement by focusing attention on unethical and illegal procedures employed in the investigation and prosecution of these cases. Finally, from 1968 to 1975, conferences were held to call attention to prison problems and issues ("prisoner rights," "racism in prison," "abolishing prisons") (Irwin, 1980).

This third part of this chapter has examined how changes in the ethnic/racial composition of the prison population, along with the prisoner movement and its accompanying politicization of inmates, changed the nature of the prison environment. These and other external

Attica Civil Rights Case and Its Legacy*

CLOSE-UP

Incredible as it may seem, the Attica class-action civil rights suit brought in 1974, on behalf of the protesting prisoners who were killed, shot, beaten, and tortured when state law enforcement stormed the Attica New York State Prison on September 13, 1971, is still fighting its way through the federal courts. On July 16, 1998, the U.S. Court of Appeals for the Second Circuit, sitting in New York City, heard oral arguments in the appeal by former Assistant Deputy Warden, Karl Pfeil. He had been found liable by a jury in Buffalo, New York, in February 1992, to all the prisoners, for failing to prevent the systematic beatings and torture against them as reprisals after the prison was retaken. The Appeals Court was also reviewing two subsequent money damage awards against Pfeil for allowing the reprisals, returned by two other juries in 1997, on behalf of two class members, Frank BB Smith and David Brosig, for $4,000,000 and $75,000, respectively.

After the February 1992 liability verdict, a long process of negotiations toward possible settlement was entered into, with the intervention of the court and the assistance of detailed written responses from each class member. The process was finally abandoned when it was disclosed that then governor, Mario Cuomo, refused to agree to any settlement. As a result of the liability verdict however, each member of the class, over 1,200 prisoners, was entitled to an individual damages trial to determine the amount of money to be awarded to compensate them for their injuries.

After further delays caused by the defendant Pfeil and the State of New York, finally, in June 1997, two damage trials were held in Buffalo. The first plaintiff, Frank Big Black Smith, who was the head of security during the 4-day rebellion and had been one of the main spokespersons for the Attica Brothers after he was released from prison in 1974, was brutally tortured after the prison guards had circulated a false rumor that he had castrated a hostage. Smith had been held nude on a table with a football under his chin, told that if he dropped it he would be killed, and then was repeatedly smashed in the testicles, spit upon, and had cigarettes put out on his body. He was kept on the table for over 5 hours and then made to run through the gauntlet and taken to another room where he was beaten to near unconsciousness by four guards while he begged for his life. Smith testified to 26 years of pain in his testicles, legs, and wrists; nightmares; recurrent fears; and other continuing suffering. After hearing all of the testimony, a Buffalo working-class jury (six whites and one black) awarded him $4 million in compensatory damages. The second plaintiff, David Brosig, beaten while being taken through the prison yard and in the gauntlet was awarded $75,000. Another 500 prisoners in the class suit experienced similar treatment.

The state still refused to talk about a settlement and bankrolled and assisted Karl Pfeil in his appeal to the Second Circuit. In his appeal, Pfeil raised numerous legal issues, arguing that the verdicts against him should be thrown out, that the Attica Brothers should not have been permitted to proceed as a class, and that after 27 years the case should begin all over again with each of the 1,000 plus plaintiffs required to bring their case individually.

Before a packed courtroom filled with Attica Brothers and their supporters, counsel for the plaintiff class argued that the evidence against Karl Pfeil was overwhelming, that the case was properly a class, that the verdicts were proper in all respects, and that it was time to end the delays and obfuscation and finally force the state to com-

---

factors shaped the nature of the contemporary prison to be examined in Chapter 10.

Summary

The Big House era was characterized by harsh conditions and inmate idleness. The inmate subculture was the result of the convict code and conditions of confinement, which were reflected in the prison as a total institution. Inmates lived a life of deprivation, which influenced the degree to which they underwent prisonization. Prison adaptation took one of three forms: doing time, jailing, or gleaning. To cope with deprivations, inmates improvised. Big House prison guards also had to function in an oppressive environment. They used disciplinary and nonpunitive methods to maintain inmate control. Although the Big Houses were usually peaceful, there were occasional disturbances. The movement toward rehabilitation between 1900 and 1950 conflicted with the punitiveness of the custodial staff. Changes in social conditions after World War II were conducive to development of treatment-oriented prisons.

The rehabilitative institutions prevailed from the 1950s to the early 1970s. The indeterminate sentence

pensate the victims of state terror and violence at Attica. All concerned now await the decision by the Court of Appeals.

If the appeal is successful, under the indemnity law, the state will have to immediately pay on the two verdicts, and the remaining plaintiffs would be entitled to their own individual damage trials. Facing this prospect, the state might well come in good faith to the settlement table, which could result in finally getting compensation for all those killed, shot, and beaten at Attica.

Special recognition should be given to the lawyers who have fought this case with almost no compensation for over 28 years: Liz Fink, Michael Deutsch, Joe Heath, Dan Meyers, and Dennis Cunningham as well as Attica Brothers, Frank Big Black Smith, Akil Al-Jundi, and Herbert X. Blyden (the latter two have passed away), who have valiantly kept the meaning of Attica alive in the public arena.

In almost every prison rebellion since Attica, and there have been many, the lesson of avoiding the use of deadly force and keeping communication going has been followed. Attica has taught state authorities that the use of deadly force, even against convicted criminals, will have serious political fallout and must be avoided. In prison hostage situations waiting the prisoners out is clearly the course that Attica has established. Prisoner hostage taking is caused by legitimate prisoner grievances that result in desperate acts to gain the attention of the authorities and the public. Although the acts are desperate, the underlying issues are real and must be addressed.

The agreements reached with the prisoners involved in the Lucasville, Ohio,[15] riot in 1993 were vague and depend on the good faith of the authorities. The willingness of the Lucasville prisoners, however, to accept more promises and end the stalemate, may also have been a lesson that they have learned from Attica. The Attica prisoners refused to accept less than all their demands. They wanted the warden fired, something the officials refused to consider. The Lucasville prisoners also wanted the warden fired, but by the 11th day, they surrendered without obtaining that demand. Further, these inmates of the 1990s, not infused with the revolutionary rhetoric and hopes of the 1960s, may well have realized that certain things were possible and certain demands were not. Even at Attica, however, the prisoners' nonnegotiable demands to replace the warden or for passage out of the prison to a nonimperialist country, may well have been forgotten after 11 days of waiting.

One lesson that clearly has not been learned from Attica is that prisoners must be treated with human dignity, respect, and with basic standards. Additionally, if you deny prisoners fairness and humane treatment you will cause rebellion, violence, and hostage taking. One can only wonder how long prison rebellions caused by inhumane and degrading treatment will go on before those in authority learn this most important lesson.

On January 4, 2000, the state of New York agreed to pay $8 million to 1,280 inmates who were plaintiffs in the class-action suit. The state did not admit to wrongdoing or liability, but agreed to set aside the funds to settle the ongoing suit, filed in 1974 (ABCNews.com, 2000, Jan. 4—more.abcnews.go.com/sections/us/dailynews/attica000104.html).

Source: Prepared especially for Corrections: A Comprehensive View, *2nd ed., by Michael E. Deutsch, Attorney at Law. Deutsch has been active in the defense of Attica prisoners for over 20 years.*

and inmate classification were two major elements in the rehabilitative institutions. Therapeutic programs involved individual and group therapy. Other rehabilitative efforts included academic and vocational programs. Treatment and custody staff had both disciplinary and treatment functions. The failure of rehabilitative institutions can be traced to a lack of understanding by professionals of the causes of criminal behavior. Thus, they were unable to develop the diagnostic instruments or the programs that could change current behavior. Changes in the demographic composition of the inmate population, as well as administrative reactions to these changes, also contributed to the demise of the rehabilitative institution.

The prisoner movement from 1970 to 1975 was characterized by inmates who strove to reform prison conditions. Many of these inmates defined themselves as political prisoners and blamed society for victimizing them by failing to provide the opportunities necessary for becoming upstanding citizens. They viewed society rather than themselves as requiring reform. The groups involved in the prison movement ran the spectrum from self-help to radical groups. The objective was improving themselves and prison conditions and expanding inmate rights. To get attention these groups were involved in strikes, sporadic violence, and riots, the most serious being the Attica revolt. Increasing violence followed, creating hostility toward the prisoner movement. The prisoner movement, along with other factors (e.g., changes in the ethnic/racial composition of the prison population), influenced contemporary prisons.

Critical Thinking Questions

1. As an inmate entering a Big House prison, describe your reactions to the prison environment. Choose a role in the inmate status hierarchy and one of the adaptations to prison life. Indicate why you chose each.

2. Analyze the pros and cons of transforming our prison system back into the Big House–type prison.

3. You are a young inmate entering a rehabilitative institution after serving time in a Big House. Compare your past experiences in the Big House with your new experiences in a rehabilitative institution like Soledad.

4. As a guard in a Big House prison, what difficulties would you face in carrying out your delegated responsibilities, and what methods would you develop to handle these problems?

5. What are some of the solutions that inmates improvise to cope with the deprivations of prison?

6. Identify the factors that led to the development of the correctional institution.

7. What role did the following play in the rehabilitative institution: indeterminate sentencing, classification, and treatment in a correctional setting? What were some of the problems associated with implementing them?

8. What were the social changes on the outside and the changes on the inside that influenced the development of the prisoner movement? Also, identify the major groups involved in the prisoner movement and the role they played. Which of these groups would you be associated with, and why would you choose it?

9. As an inmate at Attica during the pre- and post-riot periods, describe your experience. What role did you play during the riot? Discuss the cover-up that followed.

10. Should inmates be allowed to demonstrate peacefully when they have legitimate grievances that are not being resolved? If not, how should they express the failure by the prison to deal with their legitimate grievances?

Test Your Knowledge

1. According to the text, what is the best way to describe the development of the inmate subculture?

   a. It is a collective response to the deprivations imposed by prison life.

   b. It is a dynamic system affected by the historical development of the prison, outside social and political developments, criminal values, and conditions within the prison.

   c. It is shaped by a socialization process involving the adoption of a criminal value system to which the inmate is exposed prior to confinement.

   d. It is based on economic considerations.

2. Which of the following is a subtle but important attitude change that results as part of the prisonization process?

   a. the recognition that nothing is owed to the environment for the supplying of needs

   b. a slowly developing respect for the prison administration

   c. disregard for the moral wrongness of crime

   d. an increasing emphasis on the need for self-rehabilitation

3. The elite group of inmates who were more sophisticated, tended to cooperate with each other, and whose demeanor was characterized by toughness and coolness were known as:

   a. accomplished characters.

   b. right guys.

   c. Hoosiers.

   d. dingbats.

   e. hard rocks or tush hogs.

4. The mode of adaptation to prison life in which an inmate used available prison resources to better himself for life on the outside was known as:

   a. just doing time.

   b. jailing.

   c. gleaning.

   d. role dispossession.

5. Under the concept of indeterminate sentencing, an inmate's release from prison was contingent on:

   a. serving the entire sentence.

   b. the inmate's rehabilitation.

   c. the determination of when justice had been served.

   d. when overcrowding required more cell space.

6. Within the context of the correctional institution, classification would ideally serve as a means of:

a. diagnosis.

b. security.

c. punishment.

d. treatment.

7. The relatively peaceful coexistence between inmates at Soledad Prison was a result of

   a. the structure of tips and cliques.

   b. the brutality of the guards.

   c. the Big House–type inmate structure.

   d. the success of the rehabilitative programs.

8. When extended tip networks declined in prisons because of increasing interracial hostilities, what became the main purpose of inmate cliques?

   a. self-defense

   b. rehabilitation

   c. keeping inmates in touch with the free world

   d. racial integration

9. The prisoner self-help group Seven Steps:

   a. focuses on awakening the identity of Chicano inmates.

   b. is modeled after Alcoholics Anonymous.

   c. is an inmate subgroup of the Black Muslims.

   d. focuses on raising the political awareness of white inmates.

Endnotes

1. H. Toch (1977). *Living in Prison: The Ecology of Survival.* New York: The Free Press, Div. of Macmillan. Reproduced by permission of the American Psychological Association.

2. This only applies to the contemporary prison. Prior to this there were no female guards in male prisons.

3. See Chapter 21 for a discussion of the issue of approved visiting lists and other rules relating to visiting.

4. © 1967, 1995. Malcolm Braly. Reprinted by permission of Knox Burger, in association with Harold Ober Associates, Inc.

5. Chapter 16 provides a more detailed discussion of the history and development of prison industry programs.

6. D. Clemmer et al. (1958). *The Prison Community.* © 1958 by Donald Clemmer. Reprinted with the permission of Holt, Rinehart & Winston, Inc. Copyright renewed 1986 by Rose Emelia Clemmer.

7. J. Jacobs (1977). *Stateville: The Penitentiary in Mass Society.* Chicago: University of Chicago Press. Reprinted by permission.

8. *Banks v. Hanvener,* 1964; *Knuckles v. Prasse,* 1969; Jacobs, 1980. Prison regulations related to the practice of religion are discussed in Chapter 17.

9. Reprinted by permission of L. Carroll (1974/1988). *Hacks, Blacks, and Cons.* Prospect Heights, IL: Waveland Press, Inc.

10. This is only a partial list of demands included in the Folsom Manifesto. For a complete list, see Irwin (1980).

11. The local district attorney promised no mass prosecutions and that charges would only be brought if there was substantial evidence to link specific inmates with a specific crime. Although amnesty was a major concern, a poll found that more than two thirds of the inmates would have given up this demand to get out of the yard safely.

12. Bell (1985) asserts that if Rockefeller had come and assured the inmates that only those involved in the death of the one guard would be prosecuted, the inmates might have surrendered peacefully.

13. A turkey shoot is a contest in which the first shooter to draw blood from the head or neck of the turkey gets the animal. Special Prosecutor Malcolm Bell, writing after years of investigating the revolt, entitled his book on the revolt *The Turkey Shoot.*

14. © 1985 by Malcolm Bell. Reprinted by permission of Knox Burger Associates.

15. See Chapter 11 for a further discussion of this riot.

Classification, Custody, and Special Category Offenders

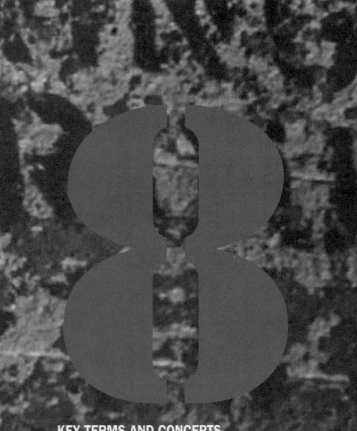

KEY TERMS AND CONCEPTS

Administrative facility
Administrative segregation (AS)
Career criminals
Classification
Classification committee
Community custody
Cottage industries
Criminally insane
Custody levels
Disciplinary detention (DD)
High-security institution
In custody
Long-term offenders
Low-security institution
Mainstreaming
Management variables
Mature offenders
Maximum custody
Medium security institution

Mentally disordered
Mentally handicapped
Minimum security institution
Objective classification systems
Organic disorders
Out custody
Overclassification
Protective custody (PC)
Psychotic disorders
Reception and diagnostic centers
Reclassification
Security
Special management
Supermax
Underclassification
Youthful offender

LEARNING OBJECTIVES

After completing this chapter, you should be able to:

1. Outline the history of classification as it developed in the United States.

2. Define classification and discuss its purposes.

3. List the characteristics of objective classification systems.

4. Describe the benefits of an objective classification system.

5. Explain the process of meeting inmate programs, services, and housing.

6. Describe the reclassification process and discuss its functions.

7. Identify the steps of the Federal Bureau of Prisons' classification system.

8. Describe several major background characteristics that are common among prison inmates.

9. Identify the problems that special category offenders pose for correctional institutions.

10. Outline the major issues involved in the treatment of mentally disordered inmates.

11. Define the label *mentally handicapped,* and explain the problems associated with inmates who have this condition.

12. Explain why the sex offender presents such a difficult problem for the correctional system.

13. Contrast the characteristics and special needs of mature and youthful offenders.

14. Explain how the characteristics and problems of long-term offenders differ from those of other inmates.

Introduction

Whenever people are placed in an institution, it is necessary to obtain certain information about them to integrate them into the organization. Corrections systems accomplish this task through **classification,** a process that attempts to match inmates with the appropriate level of supervision, security, programs, and services to fit his or her needs. Although classification has a long history, its effectiveness as a tool for correctional management can be tied to the more recent development of objective diagnostic and placement systems.

Inmates are often classified and assigned to a facility by community programs staff immediately after sentencing. Then after arrival at a facility they are reclassified later to confirm the initial classification. In some systems, inmates are assessed and classified at central **reception and diagnostic centers** and then transferred to appropriate facilities. In other systems, the process is carried out in a prison reception unit where inmates are kept until it is completed. Inmates are then placed into the facility's general population. Regardless of the approach used, certain procedures need to be followed before the offender's first institutional placement.

Smooth and well-organized admission procedures make the offender's transition from the free world to institutional life less traumatic. The American Correctional Association (ACA, 1981a) recommends that admissions procedures facilitate the adjustment of inmates to the system and reduce their anxiety. This can be accomplished by having staff explain to the offender each step in the admissions process.

Classification and Custody

How do inmates get assigned to a particular institution after they are sentenced? Institutions employ **objective classification systems,** which provide more accurate information on inmates' characteristics through using evaluation instruments containing explicit criteria. The key principle in assigning an inmate to a facility is to match the inmate's needs and the need to protect the community with a facility designed to meet these goals—no more, no less (Rison, 2000). Custody classification focuses on facility control issues—that is, "How much supervision do inmates need so that they do not represent a danger to staff and inmates?" Inmates' program needs must also be assessed. Finally, a good classification system makes more efficient use of prison resources and guides future planning (Rison, 2000). We turn now to a brief look at the roots and development of classification.

History of Classification

The history of classification dates back to the mid-1500s when workhouses and houses of correction were first opened in England and Europe. Initial forms of classification resulted from demands of reformers who were trying to eliminate prisoners' vices (e.g., gambling, drinking) and reduce the mistreatment and corruption of younger and weaker offenders (Sutherland & Cressey, 1966; Wines, 1895). These early classification systems separated juveniles from adults, first offenders from repeaters, and men from women. Classification was also used for making work assignments. However, overcrowding made separation of offenders less feasible. This simple system served these institutions because they functioned as pretrial and presentence facilities.

When prisons developed in the United States, classification was not a major factor. In the Pennsylvania system inmates were completely separated from one another, so classification was not necessary. At Auburn-type prisons little classification was needed because offenders were housed similarly, they worked at productive labor, and harsh discipline was used to maintain order [National Institute of Corrections (NIC), 1981a]. By the mid-1850s, several factors (e.g., changing views about the causes and treatment of deviant behavior, increasing humanitarian concerns) led to the removal of certain groups of offenders from jails and prisons for placement in specialized institutions. Facilities were established for juvenile delinquents, insane offenders, young adults, blacks, women, defective delinquents, and the sick or infirm.

Our discussion of the Big House in Chapter 7 focused briefly on the roots of the contemporary classification process and the important role played by the development of the social sciences in this process. By 1950, with the emergence of rehabilitative institutions, there was a general focus on treatment, and most jurisdictions had developed systems for classifying inmates for unit and work assignments. Further, rehabilitation-oriented facilities developed elaborate classification systems centering around the placement of offenders into treatment programs. In other correctional systems, systematic program planning was done by **classification committees,** which consisted of staff members with responsibility for classifying inmates (Rison, 2000).

Through the mid-1970s most classification in the United States was based on subjective judgments by correctional practitioners, with experience, intuition, and "clinical" skills being the basis of these decisions. The general lack of documentation and accountability of these systems led to many inappropriate inmate program and housing assignments, inconsistent classification of offenders in similar situations, high levels of **overclassification**—placement of inmates under more supervision (custody) and control (security) than required—and inefficient use of facilities (Solomon & Camp, 1993. Used with permission). These *subjective systems* also were potentially unconstitutional (the misclassification of inmates might place them at risk for potential injury) and raised issues of their validity; it is impossible to test the validity of subjective systems (Austin, 1993).

Enthusiasm for rehabilitation declined in the early 1970s because prisons were not succeeding in their attempts to rehabilitate criminals. Also, rising crime rates and violence resulted in public disillusionment with the effort. Many states passed legislation that increased the number of offenders sent to prison and the length of their sentences. Growing populations strained existing facilities, many of which were outdated and designed to warehouse offenders. These overcrowded and increasingly dangerous institutions were subjected to court scrutiny that often found them violating constitutional standards of confinement. This combination of pressures required correctional systems to plan new facilities and to make more efficient use of existing ones. *Classification* was recognized by both prison administrators and the courts as a major tool for making decisions about facility planning, managing violence and overcrowding, and making institutions constitutionally acceptable (Austin, 1994; Correctional Services Group, 1985; NIC, 1981a; Solomon & Camp, 1993). The recognition by the courts of the importance of classification is best expressed in *Palmigiano v. Garrahy* (1977):

> Classification is essential to the operation of an orderly and safe prison. It is a prerequisite for rational allocation of whatever program opportunities exist within the institution. It enables the institution to gauge the proper custody level of an inmate, to identify the inmate's educational, vocational, and psychological needs, and to separate nonviolent inmates from the more predatory. . . . Classification is also indispensable for any coherent future planning. (p. 22)

Modern Classification Systems

Prison classification is the sorting out procedure that results in matching a prisoner to the appropriate level of supervision (**custody level**), institutional protective barriers (**security**), programs, and services to meet his or her needs. This process periodically reviews the inmate's placement to achieve the most appropriate assignments possible (NIC, 1981a, p. 2).

On any given day about 2 million people are incarcerated in our prisons and jails (Justice Policy Institute, 2000, February 15). These people come from all sectors of society and represent a broad spectrum of educational, social, and economic levels. They range from the scholarly to the illiterate, the unskilled worker to the professional, the psychotic to the well-adjusted, the minor offender to the career criminal, nonviolent property offenders to serial murderers, and prison-wise offenders with extensive involvement in the criminal or prison subcultures to "naive" first offenders.

Classification is the primary mechanism for categorizing and ordering this diverse inmate population so that inmates can be dealt with efficiently. Jails and prisons transform citizens into inmates through the classification process. This process assesses their risks and needs and enables them to be assigned to appropriate institutions, housing units, and programs (Brennan, 1987, 1993; NIC, 1981a). Moreover, from a management perspective, a classification system that is acceptable and useful to administrators and is based on a system's resources can be a significant factor in helping that system achieve its correctional objectives (Burke & Adams, 1991).

Classification Objectives

Classification serves five main objectives: protecting inmates from violence committed by other inmates, protecting the public, maximizing efficient use of resources, controlling inmate behavior, and providing planning information.

Protecting Inmates

A safe environment is a high-priority objective for both jails and prisons (Austin, 1994; Brennan; 1987, 1993). Although effective classification cannot totally eliminate prison violence, it can influence the factors that aggravate it. These include failure to separate predators from victims, placement of severely disturbed inmates into the general population, and failure to separate rival gang members. Screening for special risk offenders (e.g., those with suicidal tendencies, the aged, substance abusers) identifies inmates who require special monitoring, treatment, or program assignments (Austin, 1994). In using this knowledge, prisons can become constitutionally acceptable by giving inmates reasonable protection from assault and services for medical, substance abuse, and psychiatric problems.

Protecting the Public

Classification also helps to protect the public from high-risk offenders (Solomon & Camp, 1993). This requires valid methods of determining levels of dangerousness. When coupled with appropriate assignments relating to security, custody, and release recommendations, classification can reduce the probability of escape, erroneous community placement, and serious crimes against the public. Decisions that release high-risk offenders into the community can generate adverse media attention, public outrage, strong criticism of the prison system, and possibly adverse political consequences. Generally, risky decisions to place certain inmates into the community by furlough or release to a halfway house are not a classification decision problem. Rather, they are administrative decisions that deviate from the classification system recommendations. This moves the decision from an objective classification decision back to a subjective decision that overrides sound classification.

Misclassification is generally a human error; frequently, the error lies in completing classification without all of the information necessary to make a rational decision. This is often the case with new commitments; files containing vital classification information may not be received for weeks or months after sentencing. To illustrate this point, about 1991, the first successful helicopter escape from the federal correctional institution in Pleasanton, California, occurred. The helicopter pilot was taken hostage by the inmates' girlfriend and forced to land inside the fence on the recreation area of the facility. A close review of the case determined serious **underclassification** of the inmate, who had been incorrectly scored as a low-level medium security offender. Reclassification after the escape revealed information on the inmate reflecting multiple escapes (nine) and other outstanding charges that were not available when the classification decision and transfer to the Pleasanton facility was approved. The inmate should have been reclassified as a level 6 inmate as opposed to a level 3. Policy must complement classification (Rison, 2000).

Predicting Dangerousness   The prediction of dangerousness is not an exact science, and its use is very controversial. A review of studies on the accuracy of prediction in corrections and human behavior concludes that the value of "prediction of unusual human behavior such as serious crime is limited" (Clear, 1988, p. 9). Nevertheless, in a prison setting, staff must make determinations of an inmate's "public risk"—the potential that he or she will commit a crime, particularly a violent one, upon escape or release. Typically, past violent behavior figures prominently in assessing an inmate's risk potential; this is used to make decisions about institutional placement and release.

When a decision about the risk posed by an inmate is made, it can be either right or wrong. If the decision is to declare the inmate too much of a risk for release or reduction in custody, he or she will remain within the present status. Under this condition it will be impossible to know whether the right or wrong decision was made because the error is invisible and the inmate's behavior will not be "tested" under the appropriate conditions (she will not be in the community). Only if the inmate is released or given a reduction in custody and/or security level can we know if an error was made—*if* she victimizes someone after release or reduction in security. This type of mistake is very visible and can have severe consequences for the corrections system.

When correctional practitioners are concerned about this latter type of error, they generally require high cutoff scores on risk assessment scales, ensuring that a high proportion of offenders are placed in the high-risk category. This reduces the potential visible errors—that is, escapes and subsequent offenses by releasees—but drastically increases the invisible ones; that is, many inmates may be overclassified and kept in expensive higher security facilities. These inmates may resort to violent behavior to protect themselves or be victimized as a result of their overclassification situation. Thus, this system suffers because expensive space is being misused, and there may be control problems.

As we increase our use of sophisticated management information systems, Brennan (1993) asserts there will be "a quantum leap in predictive accuracy." Yet, he argues, even these new tools should still be advisory because: "The human judge must always have an override capacity to introduce the intuitive, holistic, integrative role and take into account any extraneous issues" (p. 66. Used with permission).

Maximizing Efficient Use of Resources

The growth of prison populations has strained corrections, requiring more efficient distribution of resources. Effective classification can maximize efficiency and provide inmates with the most impartial, consistent, and equitable placements.

New classification systems use criteria that determine inmates' custody needs and place them at appropriate levels. Their goal, including those currently in use in Minnesota, Tennessee, New York, and other states, is the elimination of overclassification (NIC, 1981a). A review of studies by NIC (1981a) of older classification systems revealed that many systems held 40 to 50 percent of their inmates in maximum custody. However, when objective criteria on the danger posed by these inmates were used, only 8 to 15 percent of them were found to require this placement. This type of overclassification can cause a shortage of expensive high-security or custody placements for inmates who require them. Valid placements are the primary means of protecting inmates and staff from violent assaults and reducing the anxiety caused by unanticipated victimizations. This allows for the development of a more orderly, predictable, and controlled prison environment (Brennan, 1987).

Classification and security systems save taxpayers money. For instance, in Florida placing an inmate with a risk threat classification calls for housing him at a level 4 facility, which would cost $13,400 a year. If the same inmate were overclassified and placed in a prison cell at a level 7 facility, the cost would rise to $25,800 a year. It is clear that a good classification system can save taxpayers money by placing inmates at an appropriate classification level.

Controlling Inmate Behavior

Classification assists in several social control functions. Specifically, it is linked to the control of inmate behavior because it can be used to reward or punish. Inmates who frequently break prison rules can be reclassified to a custody status with fewer privileges and job opportunities.

Those with a good record can be rewarded by placement in an honor unit or in a community program. Appropriate security and custody assignments can also help to reduce fear, violence, escapes, abuse, and litigation (Austin, 1994; Solomon & Camp, 1993).

Providing Planning Information

Objective classification systems are invaluable for coherent planning of budgets, the types of institutions that need to be built, staffing, programs, and services. Growing prison populations have forced most states to make decisions about constructing new facilities. Formerly, planning was often based only on projected trends of prison population increases. However, objective classification systems can provide more accurate information on the characteristics of the prison population, which can be used to project security, custody, and staffing needs for new institutions and to provide input on whether to expand existing prisons (Austin, 1994).

They also help assess medical, mental, substance abuse, and educational program and service needs. For example, the number of sex offenders, older offenders, and long-term offenders seems to be increasing. This type of information can assist correctional systems in planning for the special needs of these inmates (see the Special Offender Categories section later in Chapter 17; Solomon & Camp, 1993). This avoids the types of errors made by planners in the past who overestimated the need for expensive maximum security cells while underestimating the need for less expensive minimum security ones (Brennan, 1987). It can also assist systems in avoiding unnecessary litigation (Austin, 1994). Classification is not a panacea for all institutional problems, but it can satisfy various needs of corrections systems, inmates, staff, courts, and the public.

Elements of the Classification Process

Classification can be divided into two phases: (1) initial determinations of the level of security and custody needed and program recommendations and (2) periodic reclassification. Both phases require that appropriate scales be used to measure inmates' need; we will look at each by examining the Federal Bureau of Prisons' (BOP) classification models. Next, we look at evaluations of the federal classification system and its impact.

Security and Custody

The level of *security* (physical barriers to escape) and *custody* (degree of staff supervision needed) are two classification decisions that must be made for each inmate. Currently, there is a lack of consistency in how the two are designated from facility to facility. Many states and

the federal government currently employ objective classification systems but may have different names for their main adult facilities. In California major adult facilities are called *prisons* (e.g., California State Prison, San Quentin Prison), whereas in New York these same institutions are called *correctional facilities* (e.g,. Auburn Correctional Facility) (ACA, 1999). Some jurisdictions even fail to distinguish between security and custody levels in their facilities. For example, the federal institutions at Alderson, West Virginia, and El Reno, Oklahoma, were formerly labeled *reformatories*. However, Alderson was a minimum security facility for women, and El Reno was a youthful offender institution with a perimeter security that included a double fence and towers with armed guards. Conversely, two facilities can have identical architectural plans and the same security levels.

A review of the ACA directory found that adults and juveniles in the 50 states, the federal system, and the District of Columbia are sent to 29 "different" types of confinement (Levinson & Gerard, 1986). Failure to distinguish between security features with standardized labels can be confusing within a given correctional system, can adversely affect the ability to use a sophisticated classification system, and can result in serious management problems and wasted resources (Levinson & Gerard, 1986).

As a result of *Ruiz v. Estelle* (1980), the BOP was ordered to transfer the 81 plaintiffs into federal custody for protective custody reasons. Warden R. H. Rison captained a team to classify and transfer each inmate to a federal facility. This team attempted to apply the federal classification guidelines to the Texas sentencing laws. Unfortunately, the low-custody Texas inmates all scored at the super-maximum BOP level, illustrating that one system generally cannot be transposed to another system. Each local, state, or federal correctional system must be individually designed (Rison, 1981).

To solve these problems and eliminate confusion, the ACA and the National Institute of Corrections recommend that all jurisdictions make a distinction between *custody* and *security* and develop uniform criteria distinguishing between levels for each. Henderson, Rauch, and Phillips (1997) have provided the following two core definitions for these concepts:

Facility Security Level The nature and number of physical design barriers available to prevent escape and control inmate behavior. Typical security categories are maximum, medium, and minimum.

Inmate Custody Category The degree of staff supervision necessary to ensure adequate control of the inmate (NIC, 1987). These designations include close, in, out, and community. An inmate's designation determines the types of privileges he or she will have.

Table 8.1

Initial Security and Custody Levels

Levels of Institution	Levels of Custody
Level I **Minimum security institutions,** also known as federal prison camps, have dormitory housing, a relatively low staff-to-inmate ratio, and no fences. These institutions are work and program oriented, and many are located adjacent to larger institutions or on military bases, where inmates help serve the labor needs of the larger institution or the base.	**Out custody** The second lowest custody level assigned to an inmate, requiring the second lowest level of security and staff supervision. An inmate who has *out* custody may be assigned to less secure housing and may be eligible for work details outside the institution's secure perimeter with a minimum of 2-hour intermittent staff supervision.
Level II **Low-security** federal correctional **institutions** (FCIs) have double-fenced perimeters, mostly dormitory housing, and strong work and program components. The staff-to-inmate ratio in these institutions is higher than in minimum security facilities.	**In custody** The second highest custody level assigned to an inmate, it requires the second highest level of security and staff supervision. An inmate who has *in* custody is assigned to regular quarters and is eligible for all regular work assignments and activities under a normal level of supervision. Inmates with *in* custody are not eligible for work details or programs outside the institution's secure perimeter.
Level III **Medium security** FCIs have strengthened perimeters (often double fences with electronic detection systems), cell-type housing, a wide variety of work and treatment programs, and an even higher staff-to-inmate ratio than low-security FCIs.	**In custody** This is the same as in a low-security facility, except that it provides an opportunity for inmates to be transferred from a medium security to a low-security facility without a custody change.
Level IV **High-security institutions,** also known as U.S. penitentiaries (USPs), have highly secure perimeters (featuring walls or reinforced fences), multiple- and single-occupant cell housing, and close staff supervision and movement controls.	**Maximum custody** The highest custody level assigned to an inmate, requiring the highest level of security and staff supervision. An inmate with maximum custody requires ultimate control and supervision. This classification is for individuals who, by their behavior, have been identified as assaultive, predacious, riotous, serious escape risks, or seriously disruptive to the orderly running of an institution. Accordingly, quarters and work assignments are assigned to ensure maximum control and supervision.
Level V **Administrative facilities** are institutions with special missions, such as the detention of noncitizen or pretrial offenders, the treatment of inmates with serious or chronic medical problems, or the containment of extremely dangerous, violent. or escape prone inmates. Administrative facilities include Metropolitan Correctional (MCCs) and Detention Centers (MDCs), Federal Medical Centers (FMCs), and U.S. penitentiaries. Administrative facilities are capable of holding inmates in all security categories.	**In custody** This is unless the inmate has a minimum security level and designation was not for security reasons, in which case the initial custody assignment is *out*.

Source: BOP, 1998, p. 23

It would be impossible to discuss all of the different inmate classification systems in use in this country, so we will focus on the BOP system.[1] This will provide an example of how an objective classification system operates.

Initial Classification

Under this system a new inmate's initial classification (designation) is based on security considerations. Classification is carried out by community corrections staff prior to the inmates' arrival at the institution, generally immediately following sentencing. The federal system specifies four distinct levels of security, based on such features as the presence of external patrols, gun towers, security barriers, or detection devices; the type of housing within the institution; internal security features; and the staff-to-inmate ratio. Table 8.1 shows the levels of institution and the custody designations to which new inmates can be assigned.

An inmate's security level is decided by the range within which his or her total score falls. Within security levels, such factors as offender's residence, level of overcrowding, age, racial balance, and need to separate certain inmates from each other are important. Our Program Focus, Initial Security Designation, on page 152, provides an example of how a determination is made about what type of security-level institution an inmate will be housed in.

Initial Security Designation

PROGRAM FOCUS

John Smith is convicted of armed bank robbery. He is sentenced to 240 months. He has a detainer[2] for an assault that resulted in serious bodily injury. He has prior convictions that resulted in commitments for armed robbery, burglary, possession of drugs for sale, and domestic violence on a spouse. His presentence report indicates he has a record of drug and alcohol problems. Based on these factors, he classifies for placement in a high security level institution (Hammons, 2000; see Figure 8.1).

The assignment of an inmate to a particular institution is initially based on:

- the level of security and supervision the inmate requires
- the level of security and staff supervision the institution is able to provide

New commitments are scored on 14 items (see Figure 8.1, items 1–14, Security Designation Data). We describe the ones requiring explanation in Table 8.2 on page 154.

Inmate Programs, Services, and Housing Needs

Assessment of an inmate's program and service requirements is one of the initial decisions made in the classification process. The needs of inmates are almost as diverse as those of the free-world population. This has led to confusion about the most effective programs for inmate populations. When coupled with traditionally meager correctional budgets, this has curtailed programming dealing with inmate problems or providing them marketable skills (NIC, 1981a). This problem has been further aggravated by an increasing prison population, which is straining resources and placing major emphasis on simply providing bed space.

State correctional systems have different procedures for screening and placing inmates. Many systems make distinctions between available programs and the security levels appropriate for placement in them. In some systems, an inmate's cell block assignment may impose restrictions on program placement. In others, the availability of programs is extremely limited. Programming is discussed in more detail in Chapters 16 and 17, but two points need to be made here. First, inmate idleness has been a key factor in institutional disturbances. Second, it is indisputable that most inmates lack marketable skills and have other problems and deficits contributing to their involvement in crime. Denying them an opportunity to remedy these problems while in prison and expecting them to "go straight" upon release is ludicrous.

Appropriate placement of inmates should involve a balance between security, inmate needs, and program availability. One reason states consider inmate needs in their classification schemes is to avoid lawsuits. To settle these suits, states with few programs have often had to spend considerable money to develop even minimal programming. Systems and institutions should strive to achieve a balance between the resources used for inmate programs and the inmates' legitimate needs.

Determining an inmate's programming and housing needs requires information from various sources. A medical screening of each new inmate is done within 24 hours of arrival to determine if there are medical reasons for housing inmates away from the general population. The BOP also does a social interview to determine if there are any nonmedical reasons for not placing the inmate in the general population. This interview is conducted in private so that the inmate can feel free to provide sensitive information. This screening process also includes a review of the inmate's Presentence Investigation Report and SENTRY (the BOP's on-line information system, which stores inmate information) for any documentation indicating the inmate has a history of sexually aggressive behavior or has recently been the victim of a sexual assault. Also evaluated are inmates' general physical appearance (this is done to protect those with youthful or feminine characteristics from being sexually assaulted) and their emotional condition. Further, during this process an inmate will be informed about prison rules, including correspondence, disposition of funds, and monitoring of inmate telephone calls. The results of the intake screening process will be used by BOP staff in making housing assignments.

BOP classification teams are headed by a unit manager and include a case manager, a counselor, and usually an education advisor, a psychology services representative, and health services staff. They all are required to interview new arrivals within 5 days. The functions of team members include:

- The education advisor is the consultant and expert on all education, recreation, and vocational training matters.
- Unit psychologists are responsible for providing written psychological reports for inmates scheduled for a team meeting.

INMATE LOAD DATA	1. REG NO **08794-2638**		2. LAST NAME **SMITH**	

3. FIRST NAME **JOHN**	4. MIDDLE **X**	5. SUFFIX

6. RACE **White**	7. SEX **Male**	8. ETHNIC ORIGIN **White**	9. DATE OF BIRTH **2-22-70**

10. OFFENSE/SENTENCE **Armed Robbery**

11. FBI NUMBER **8767423**	12. SOCIAL SECURITY NUMBER **567-62-5027**	
13. STATE OF BIRTH **CALIFORNIA**	14. OR COUNTRY OF BIRTH	15. CITIZENSHIP

16. ADDRESS - STREET **3901 KLEIN BLVD**	17. CITY **LOMPOC**

18. STATE **CALIFORNIA**	19. ZIP CODE **93436**	20. OR FOREIGN COUNTRY	
21. HEIGHT - FT: **5** IN: **8**	22. WEIGHT **170**	23. HAIR **BLACK**	24. EYES **BROWN**

25. ARS ASSIGNMENT

SECURITY DESIGNATION DATA ///

1. PUBLIC SAFETY FACTORS	A - NONE B - DISRUPTIVE GROUP **C - GREATEST SEVERITY OFFENSE**	F - SEX OFFENDER G - THREAT GOVT OFFICIAL H - DEPORTABLE ALIEN	I - SENTENCE LENGTH L - SERIOUS ESCAPE M - PRISON DISTURBANCE	C

2. USM OFFICE	3. JUDGE	4. REC FACILITY	5. REC PROGRAM

6. TYPE OF DETAINER	0 - NONE 1 - LOWEST/LOW MODERATE	3 - MODERATE 5 - HIGH	**7 - GREATEST**	7

7. SEVERITY OF CURRENT OFFENSE	0 - LOWEST 1 - LOW MODERATE	3 - MODERATE 5 - HIGH	**7 - GREATEST**	7

8. MONTHS TO RELEASE **204**

9. TYPE OF PRIOR COMMITMENT	0 = NONE	1 = MINOR	**3 = SERIOUS**	3

10. HISTORY OF ESCAPE OR ATTEMPTS		NONE	>15 YEARS	10–15 YEARS	5–10 YEARS	<5 YEARS	0
	MINOR	0	1	1	2	3	
	SERIOUS	0	3	3	3	3	

11. HISTORY OF VIOLENCE		NONE	>15 YEARS	10–15 YEARS	5–10 YEARS	<5 YEARS	6
	MINOR	0	1	1	3	5	
	SERIOUS	0	2	4	6	7	

12. PRECOMMITMENT STATUS	**0 = NOT APPLICABLE**	−3 = OWN RECOGNIZANCE OR VOLUNTARY SURRENDER	0

13. VOLUNTARY SURRENDER DATE **N/A**	14. VOLUNTARY SURRENDER LOCATION **N/A**

15. CRIM HX PTS _____	16. SECURITY POINT TOTAL	23

17. OMDT REFER (Y/N) **N**

18. REMARKS: DESIGNATE TO USP LOMPOC; CLASSIFIES FOR PLACEMENT IN A HIGH SECURITY FACILITY BECAUSE HE ROBBED A BANK WITH A 45 CALIBER GUN, HAS PRIOR ARMED ROBBERIES, ASSAULTS, AND DRUG OFFENSES

Figure 8.1 *Inmate Load and Security Designation Form—Male (BP-337)*

Table 8.2

Factors in Determining Initial Security Classification

1. *Public Safety Factors* (1)   These ensure increased security concerns to protect society. Ordinarily, public safety factors require confinement in a facility with more security.
   a. *Disruptive group membership*   Gang members require validation. Once validated, these inmates will remain confined in a high security level institution.
   b. *Greatest severity offenses*   Offenses such as robbery, aircraft piracy, serious assaults, serious escapes, kidnapping, and sexual offenses fall into this category. The criterion is the offense posed a serious threat to the victim or society.
   c. *Sex offenders*   These include those sentenced for attempted forcible rape, sexual contact with a minor, rape, or use of a minor for prostitution purposes.
   d. *Sentence length*   This figures in the percent of time served out of the projected period of incarceration.
   e. *History of escapes or attempts*   The degree of seriousness of the escape or attempt and how long ago it occurred is a factor.
   f. *Prison disturbances*   Involvement in a series of violent incidents, for which the inmate was guilty of engaging, encouraging, or furthering institutional disturbances, is added to the score.
2. *Type of Detainer*[2] (6)   Officials score the severity of the lodged detainer, which is based on the seriousness of the offense for which the offender was convicted.
3. *Severity of the Current Offense* (7)   Officials score the most serious offenses resulting in the current incarceration (this is determined by a severity-of-offense scale).
   a. *Lowest*   This category includes drugs for personal use, gambling, liquor violations, traffic offenses, vagrancy, vandalism, and property offenses under $2,000.
   b. *Low moderate*   This includes drugs, indecent exposure, property offense totaling $2,000 to $250,000, postrelease violations, and indecent exposure.
   c. *Moderate*   This includes auto theft, breaking and entering, burglary, drugs, escape by walking away from an open institution, property offenses over $250,000, and child abandonment.
   d. *High*   This includes cruelty to children, drugs, involuntary manslaughter, residential burglary, and sexual offenses.
   e. *Greatest*   This includes arson, assault, robbery, carjacking, drugs in which the offender was part of a network, sexual offenses, weapons, homicide, kidnapping, treason, and escapes from closed institutions.
4. *Type of Prior Commitment* (9)   The seriousness of the offenses resulting in the prior imprisonment is scored.
5. *History of Violence* (11)   The seriousness of any act against a person or property resulting in a fine or conviction, and when it happened, is another factor.

Note: The numbers in parentheses represent top point score associated with each factor.

- Health services staff ensure that accurate and current medical information is forwarded to the unit classification team.
- The unit manager supervises the other primary team members (the case manager, the counselor, and the unit secretary), directs the housing unit activities, and is responsible for the unit's operation and quality control of all correspondence and programs.

Initial classification occurs within 4 weeks of the inmate's arrival at the designated institution following sentencing, initial commitment to BOP custody, and interviews by classification teams. All subsequent reviews of an inmate's status or progress are considered *program reviews*. When an inmate is *predesignated*—that is, his or her security level is determined by community corrections personnel—a program review is held within 4 weeks of his or her arrival at the new institution. Each inmate receives a program review at least once every 180 days. Within 12 months of the inmate's projected release date, program reviews are conducted at least once every 90

days. At these program reviews updated information on inmates is provided:

- The counselor summarizes the inmate's work performance and participation in individual or group counseling.
- The education advisor provides a summary of the inmate's education test results, recommended educational program needs, and progress toward completion of education and other applicable release readiness programs.
- The health services staff provide a report on the medical or psychological/psychiatric conditions that may affect the inmate's security, custody, or program participation.

Reclassification

Initially, a new inmate's custody status is determined by the custody levels available at the institution to which he or she is assigned; these may include maximum, in, out, and community. The lowest level of custody, **com-**

Minimum security institutions like the Laconia State Prison in New Hampshire, shown here, have dormitory housing, a relatively low staff-to-inmate ratio, and no fences.

munity, is ordinarily reserved for those inmates who meet the qualifications for participation in community activities. An inmate who has community custody may be eligible for the least secure housing—including outside the institution's perimeter—may work on outside details with minimal supervision, and may participate in community-based program activities if other eligibility requirements are satisfied.

The initial review (**reclassification**) for a possible custody-level change normally does not occur earlier than 6 months after institutional placement; subsequent reviews depend on custody status. An inmate's score on the custody classification form (see Figure 8.2) may suggest a reduced or increased security requirement based on consideration of both precommitment and postcommitment variables.

Factors Affecting Reclassification   Each time inmates are reclassified,[3] they are rated on the security factors in Table 8.2 and escapes, which are now included as a separate factor in the base score (see Figure 8.2). They are also scored on the following custody factors:

1. *Percent of time served*   The portion of the projected period of incarceration that the inmate has already served. This is calculated by:

$$\frac{\text{Actual time served (months)}}{\text{Anticipated time of confinement (months)}} = \%$$

2. *Involvement with drug/alcohol abuse*   Any history or current indications of dependency on drugs or alcohol (includes drug trafficking) is scored.

3. *Mental/psychological stability*   This is broken down as follows: (a) an "unfavorable report" means that the individual shows evidence of serious mental instabil-

ity; (b) a "favorable report" means no finding of serious mental instability; and (c) "no referral" means the case was not referred for evaluation. The conclusion should be interpreted in light of whether or not the inmate is appropriate for a lower custody or security status.

4. *Type and number of the most serious incident report*   This could span a period of 10 years, depending on the severity of the disciplinary reports (Hammons, 2000).

5. *Frequency of disciplinary reports in the past year*   The score is determined by giving points to the number of reports received over the last year (e.g., six plus reports = 0; two to five = 1; etc.).

6. *Responsibility demonstrated by the inmate*   This is based on the inmate's general demeanor as reflected in peer group associates, degree of program involvement, level of dependability, and nature of interaction with staff and other inmates.

7. *Family and community ties*   This takes into consideration marital status or common-law relationships, family support, regularity of visits, correspondence, family stability in the community, and the stability of relationships that the inmate has with nonfamily members in the community.

Reclassification-Based Transfers   The classification system is what triggers inmate transfers to lower or higher security institutions following reclassifications. The system is intended to assign inmates to an institution commensurate with their custody and security needs; thus, inmates need to be continually evaluated (reclassified).

A. IDENTIFYING DATA	1. INSTITUTION CODE	2. UNIT	3. DATE

4. NAME **JOHN SMITH**	5. REGISTER NUMBER **08794-2638**

6. CRIMINAL HISTORY POINTS _____

7. MANAGEMENT VARIABLES	A - NONE B - JUDICIAL RECOMMENDATION D - RELEASE RESIDENCE/PLANNING E - POPULATION MANAGEMENT G - CIMS	I - MED/PSYCH TREATMENT N - PROGRAM PARTICIPATION R - WORK CADRE S - PSF WAIVED U - MARIEL CUBAN	V - GREATER SECURITY W - LESSER SECURITY	

8. PUBLIC SAFETY FACTORS	A - NONE B - DISRUPTIVE GROUP **C - GREATEST SEVERITY OFFENSE**	F - SEX OFFENDER G - THREAT GOVT OFFICIAL H - DEPORTABLE ALIEN	I - SENTENCE LENGTH L - SERIOUS ESCAPE M - PRISON DISTURBANCE	C

B. BASE SCORING //

1. TYPE OF DETAINER	0 = NONE 1 = LOWEST/LOW MODERATE 3 = MODERATE 5 = HIGH **7 = GREATEST**	7

2. SEVERITY OF CURRENT OFFENSE	0 - LOWEST 1 - LOW MODERATE	3 - MODERATE 5 - HIGH	**7 - GREATEST**	7

3. MONTHS TO RELEASE **204**	

4. TYPE OF PRIOR COMMITMENT	0 - NONE	1 - MINOR	**3 - SERIOUS**	3

5. HISTORY OF ESCAPE OR ATTEMPTS		NONE	>15 YEARS	10–15 YEARS	5–10 YEARS	<5 YEARS	0
	MINOR	**0**	1	1	2	3	
	SERIOUS	0	3	3	3	3	

6. HISTORY OF VIOLENCE		NONE	>15 YEARS	10–15 YEARS	5–10 YEARS	<5 YEARS	6
	MINOR	0	1	1	3	5	
	SERIOUS	0	2	4	**6**	7	

7. PRECOMMITMENT STATUS	**0 = NOT APPLICABLE** −3 = OWN RECOGNIZANCE OR VOLUNTARY SURRENDER	0

8. BASE SCORE	23

C. CUSTODY SCORING //

1. PERCENTAGE OF TIME SERVED	3 = 0–25% **4 = 26–75%** 5 = 76–90% 6 = 91+%	4

2. DRUG/ALCOHOL ABUSE	2 = WITHIN PAST 5 YEARS 3 = MORE THAN 5 YEARS AGO **4 = NEVER**	4

3. MENTAL/PSYCHOLOGICAL STABILITY	2 = UNFAVORABLE **4 = NO REFERRAL OR FAVORABLE**	4

4. TYPE & NO OF MOST SERIOUS INCIDENT RPT	0 = ANY GREAT (100) IN PAST 10 YR 2A = ONLY 1 HIGH (200) IN PAST 2 YR 3A = ONLY 1 MOD (300) IN PAST YR 4 = ONLY 1 LOW MOD (400) IN LAST YR	1 = MORE THAN 1 HIGH (200) IN PAST 2 YR 2B = MORE THAN 1 MOD (300) IN PAST YR 3B = MORE THAN 1 LOW MOD (400) IN PAST YR **5 = NONE**	5

5. FREQUENCY OF DISCIPLINARY REPORTS (IN PAST YEAR)	0 = 6+ 1 = 2 THRU 5 2 = ONE **3 = NONE**	3

6. RESPONSIBILITY DEMONSTRATED	0 = POOR 2 = AVERAGE **4 = GOOD**	4

7. FAMILY/COMMUNITY TIES	3 = NONE OR MINIMAL **4 = AVERAGE OR GOOD**	4

8. CUSTODY TOTAL	28

9. CUSTODY VARIANCE	CUSTODY TOTAL (SECTION C, ITEM 8) A	28

BASE SCORE		10	11	12	13	14	15	16	17	18	19	20	21	22	23	24	25	26	27	**28**	29	30
	0–6 PTS	+8	+7	+6	+5	+5	+4	+3	+2	+2	+1	0	0	0	−1	−2	−2	−3	−4	−5	−5	−6
	7–9 PTS	+8	+7	+6	+5	+5	+4	+3	+2	+2	+1	0	0	0	0	−1	−2	−2	−3	−4	−5	−5
	10–13 PTS	+8	+7	+6	+5	+5	+4	+3	+2	+2	+1	0	0	0	0	0	−1	−2	−2	−3	−4	−5
	14–22 PTS	+8	+7	+6	+5	+5	+4	+3	+2	+2	+1	0	0	0	0	0	0	0	−1	−2	−2	−3
	23–27 PTS	+8	+7	+6	+5	+5	+4	+3	+2	+2	+1	0	0	0	0	0	0	0	0	**−1**	−2	−2

10. SECURITY TOTAL—ADD OR SUBTRACT CUSTODY VARIANCE (ABOVE) TO BASE SCORE (SECTION B, 8)	−1

CUSTODY CLASSIFICATION - PAGE 2		
11. SCORED SECURITY LEVEL _____	12. MANAGEMENT SECURITY LEVEL Medium	19

13.   CUSTODY CHANGE CONSIDERATION

A.   IF CUSTODY VARIANCE SCORE (SECTION C, ITEM 9) IS IN THE (+) RANGE, CONSIDER A CUSTODY INCREASE

B.   IF CUSTODY VARIANCE SCORE (SECTION C, ITEM 9) **IS IN THE (−) RANGE, CONSIDER A CUSTODY DECREASE**

C.   IF CUSTODY VARIANCE SCORE (SECTION C, ITEM 9) IS ZERO, THE PRESENT CUSTODY SHOULD CONTINUE

D.   INSTITUTION ACTION

1. TYPE OF REVIEW:	(EXCEPTION OR **REGULAR**)		R
2. CURRENT CUSTODY:	(MAXIMUM, IN, OUT, COMMUNITY)		MAXIMUM
3. NEW CUSTODY:	(MAXIMUM, IN, OUT, COMMUNITY)		IN
4. ACTION:	(APPROVE, DISAPPROVE)		APPROVE
5. DATE OF NEXT REVIEW			
6. CHAIRPERSON'S NAME AND SIGNATURE			
7. FOR EXCEPTION REVIEW NAME (WARDEN OR DESIGNEE) AND SIGNATURE			
8. SUMMARY OF FINAL ACTION:		SECURITY LEVEL	HIGH
		CUSTODY	**IN**

Figure 8.2   *Custody Classification Form—Male (BP-338)*

Any changes in the inmate's custody or security level most likely will necessitate transferring the inmate to an institution consistent with reclassification mandates. For example, each institution level is designed to incarcerate inmates with certain custody levels. If an inmate scores at a custody level not authorized at the current designated institution, a transfer must be made to an institution that is authorized to confine inmates with that particular custody level. Thus, if an inmate confined in a maximum security facility is reclassified as a medium custody inmate, he or she must be transferred to an institution authorized to house inmates with medium custody.

Inmates may systematically progress from high-security facilities to lower security facilities as their behavior and sentence length warrant a change in custody. Ideally, inmates should progress from maximum security facilities to minimum security facilities over the course of their incarceration. This maintains the proper balance of inmates confined in facilities (Rison, 2000).

Figure 8.2 shows how our hypothetical inmate, John Smith, is adapting to prison life. Based on his custody scoring (section C8) and the resulting custody variance table (section C9), John Smith's security total (section C10) may make him eligible for reclassification to a lower custody level (section D3).

Management Variables   Another factor in making security-classification changes is the use of **management variables.** These are applied to ensure that inmates are placed in the most appropriate security level institution. Management variables temper computer scores with human decision making.[4] These variables include:

1. *Judicial Recommendations*   Assignment to a drug or boot camp program may be recommended.

2. *Inmate's Release Residence*   Placing inmates who are close to release in institutions within 500 miles of their release area is desirable. This is an overriding factor at that time and may cause placement outside normal guidelines.

3. *Population Management*   Overcrowding may affect an institution's designated security level to the extent that it does not provide an appropriate security for certain inmates.

4. *Medical or Psychiatric*   Inmates who are presently exhibiting psychiatric problems may need an initial referral to a psychiatric center. Likewise, inmates

requiring medical or surgical treatment may need to be placed at a medical center.

5. *Program Participation*   Current or desired participation in a unique and/or limited program may (1) delay an inmate's transfer to a lower security level facility pending program completion, or (2) require a facility placement not commensurate with the inmate's security level. Thus, this variable can justify an inmate's placement, due to program participation, outside of normal guidelines.

6. *Separation Needs*   Separating certain types of inmates (e.g., rival gang members; weak inmates who have been sexually assaulted) helps manage security.

7. *Escape Risk*   An inmate's security score may not reflect the need for greater security due to impending charges or an escape risk that is not supported by a finding of guilt.

Under the BOP system the final score on the Custody Classification Form is only a guideline in deciding an inmate's custody. The unit management team or the warden is the final review authority. The intent of the custody classification system is to permit staff to use professional judgment within specific guidelines. Custody changes are not dictated by the point total. However, when the unit team decides not to follow the recommendation of the point total, they must document the reason(s) for this decision in writing on the custody review form and inform the inmate.

Generally, if the Custody Variance score (section C10) is:

■ in the plus (+) range, authorities will consider a custody increase.

■ 0, the inmate's present custody is continued.

■ in the minus (–) range, authorities will consider a custody decrease.

The custody variance table (C9) intersects Smith's initial classification score (base score = 23, B8) with his custody score (C8 = 28), resulting in a –1 variance (C10). The custody level is normally changed by only one level; the authorities decided to decrease Smith's custody level by one from maximum to in.

Evaluations of the Federal System

The acid test of any classification system is whether it improves efficiency and reduces management problems. In studies, the federal model succeeded in several areas:

1. It confined more inmates in less secure facilities with no concurrent increases in assaults or escapes.

2. It better balanced each facility's racial composition.

3. It curtailed the number of transfers between institutions (this system removed a warden's transfer authority, eliminating preferential transfers).

4. It provided more current, consistent, and relevant information, enabling determination of the types of facilities that were needed, adjustment of staffing patterns, and more specific budget justifications.

5. It found there was a need for fewer secure beds, which enabled the postponement of the building of another administrative maximum security prison; instead, a new nonsecure facility was built at a savings of $13 million.

Only in the area of *protective custody* did this system not have any positive impact (i.e., the number of inmates in this status was not reduced) (Levinson, 1980).

A study by Kane and Saylor (1983) found that the items used to assign inmates to different security-level institutions were also related to postadmission behavior; that is, inmates who were classified by this method were distinguishable from one another in terms of their institutional behavior, justifying their assignment to different security-level institutions.

There are several reasons inmates create management problems when inappropriately classified. Inmates placed in less secure facilities than they require may exploit the less aggressive and unsophisticated inmates in these facilities. Conversely, the inmates assigned to higher security institutions than they require may act out in response to pressure from the more sophisticated and aggressive inmates at these custody levels. They may need to be more violent to be accepted by peers in these facilities or to avoid being exploited (i.e., for self-protection). Inmates who are unable to protect themselves may need to be transferred (Buchanan & Whitlow, 1987; Correctional Services Group, 1985). Currently, the need for appropriate placement is particularly critical because it is important to eliminate as many management problems as possible under the current overcrowded prison conditions.

The Impact of Objective Classification Systems

Although research is limited, a review of 18 studies on systems employing objective classification suggests that overall this method had a positive impact on these systems:[5]

1. Significant decreases in overclassification were seen. The proportion of inmates classified at minimum or lower custody levels was much higher than previously believed. Most systems found that 25 to 40 percent of their inmates could be safely housed in minimum custody.

2. There were increases in the consistency of classification decision making, and staff errors and misinterpretations of classification policy were reduced.

3. No increases, and even some reductions, were seen in rates of escapes and institutional misconduct.

4. There were modest but important improvements in a system's ability to house inmates according to level

of risk; but, there continued to be difficulties in developing criteria that are predictive of risk.

5. There has been staff acceptance of objective classification instruments as useful tools in managing a rapidly increasing prison population.

6. While there is evidence that inmate misconduct is predicted by classification criteria, there is evidence from a California study that the institutional environment may be an equally or more important contributor to inmate misconduct.

7. The ability to more effectively determine future resource needs, including staffing levels, inmate programs, and types of facilities has been enhanced; most systems are automated (Alexander & Austin, 1992).

Special Housing and Management Units

Prisons use several forms of segregation, in which classification plays a part, to deal with certain categories of inmates.

Protective Custody

Protective custody (PC) did not become a discernible correctional format until the 1960s; now about 10,000 inmates are housed in PC units in state and federal facilities (BJS, 1997, May). PC involves the segregation of a variety of inmates who are in serious danger of being harmed for reasons that include their offense (e.g., child molestation), gambling debts, sexual orientation, being identified as a snitch, being notorious but naive criminals, and being victims of vendettas. Inmates placed in protective custody include:

1. Victims of inmate assaults

2. Inmate informants

3. Inmates pressured to participate in sexual activity

4. Inmates who seek protection through detention, claiming to be former law enforcement officers, informants, or others in sensitive law enforcement positions, whether or not there is official information to verify the claim

5. Inmates who refuse to enter the general population for unspecified reasons

6. Inmates whom staff feel are in serious danger of bodily harm

Although conditions of confinement for PC and *administrative segregation* inmates are usually more restrictive than for the general population, more programs and services have become available for them during the 1980s and 1990s.

The role of classification in PC is threefold. First, a good classification system can help reduce the conditions that spawn the need for PC. This can be accomplished by "preventing an unmanageable combination of weak and strong, sophisticated and unsophisticated, old and young inmates from coming into contact with each other" (Henderson & Phillips, 1990, pp. 21–22). Good classification resulted in a lowering of the proportion of PC inmates during the 1980s and the 1990s. Nevertheless, PC units are becoming more difficult to manage because of the varied backgrounds and behaviors of those placed in them. In some facilities, it is necessary to protect PC cases from each other (Angelone, 1999).

Second, the classification process can identify verified and unverified PC cases. In verified cases, the victim's attacker or the source of the threat can be identified and the need for protection established. Verified cases receive top priority for PC program resources. Protection can be for either the short or long term, depending on the nature of the threat. Unverified PC cases involve inmates who refuse to disclose the source of the alleged threat. They may do this to manipulate the system (e.g., get a transfer to another institution) or to get at a PC inmate whom they may want to harm. Thus, proper screening is very important. The Virginia Department of Corrections requires inmates to name the source of a threat and explain the circumstances behind the problem before considering a transfer into PC. This has reduced their unverified PC cases (Angelone, 1999).

A third classification function involves the continuing evaluation of these inmates both in terms of their confinement status and for participation in programs. For inmates in protective custody, and even for those in administrative segregation and on death row, the courts have required reasonable levels of programs and services, in some cases comparable to those available to the general population (Johnson, 1990; NIC, 1981a). ACA (1990b) standards stipulate that inmates in PC and administrative segregation should have access to programming and activities that include library, educational, religious guidance, social, and recreational services. With the courts deferring to prison administrators, it would not be surprising to see a reduction in the privileges that inmates on these units receive (see Chapter 14). Our Program Focus, "Conditions of PC Confinement" on page 160 describes a case dealing with this problem.

Disciplinary and Administrative Segregation

Administrative segregation (AS) is a form of nonpunitive separation from the general population sometimes imposed by classification committees for inmates who pose serious threats to themselves, staff, or other inmates or to institutional security; are under investigation for serious rule violations; or are awaiting transfer. **Disciplinary detention** (DD) involves separation of inmates who have been found guilty of serious rule violations and

Conditions of PC Confinement

PROGRAM FOCUS

[In] *Williams v. Lane* [(1989), an appeals court] strongly affirmed correctional administrators' responsibility to provide substantially equivalent programs in many areas to inmates in protective custody. . . . the court held that restrictions placed on the opportunity of protective custody inmates to attend religious services, use the law library, and participate in vocational, educational, and recreational programs were unreasonable. . . . The appeals court [also] affirmed the general principles of equal access to truly equivalent programs [for PC inmates].

Williams provides an interesting indication of the direction in which protective custody programs may be headed, and of solutions that may be worthy of consideration by other agencies. . . . [T]he parties in that case developed a two-tiered system of PC . . . which . . . provid[es] access to equivalent programs for [legitimate] . . . long-term PC [inmates] . . . without creating a system that is unduly attractive to spurious cases.

In the system devised as a remedy in this case, an inmate requesting PC placement is held for 30 days in what may be characterized as the "brief" PC program, pending evaluation of the actual protective needs the case presents. During that 30-day period, the inmate is held in relatively spartan circumstances and is provided only basic services and privileges, generally comparable to those offered any inmate in administrative segregation. An inmate whose claimed need for protection cannot be verified is returned to the general population. If that individual makes subsequent requests for protection, another 30-day evaluation period commences each time. By not making a full panoply of PC programs available during this evaluation period, there is less motivation for inmates to seek this status without true need.

In each case of an inmate seeking protection, staff first consider other available methods for problem resolution, such as transfer to another housing unit or to another facility. Reliance on these alternate solutions is the first and best course of action, in order to continue to provide the inmate with typical access to a general population.

The second tier, or "full" program status, is entered only when it is clear that a verified protection case cannot be re-introduced into a general population setting. In these cases, the strategy is to offer a full range of programs and services comparable to those offered in the general population. This is done through a wide range of program offerings that are comparable [in quality, although they may be customized as to form, location, or times offered. This program is used only when it is clear that long-term PC status is the only viable option for a given offender.]

As a final note on conditions of confinement, there have been a number of cases in which PC inmates have challenged double-celling in a PC unit. The general principles to keep in mind are that as long as internal screening ensures reasonable precautions against housing together inmates who pose a potential threat to each other, and as long as reasonably equivalent access is provided to necessary programs, there is no constitutional right to a single cell in PC status.

In summary, there are clearly a number of potentially serious legal problems in the area of managing PC cases. Specific state laws and agency regulations will inevitably shape the individual application of the broad legal principles discussed above. Clearly defined, consistently implemented procedures that cover day-to-day facility management, the screening of prospective PC cases, and operation protections against liability [are necessary].

Source: J. Henderson & R. L. Phillips (November 1990). Protective Custody Management in Adult Correctional Facilities. *Washington, DC: pp. 19–20. National Institute of Corrections.*

---

are punished by being segregated in special secure units for limited periods of time. They are typically housed in single cells or rooms and receive basic necessities and services such as food, clothing, showers, medical care, and visitation by the prison chaplain; they are allowed limited exercise, reading materials, and mail. However, they may be deprived of visitation privileges, participation in work and education programs, other privileged activities (e.g., TV), and personal items that might be fashioned into weapons (ACA, 1990b). Inmates with a disciplinary status generally receive regular reviews to determine if their behavior has improved to the extent that they can be returned to the general population.

Supermaxes

There is no agreed-on definition of **supermax** facilities. A survey[6] conducted by LIS (1997) of supermax housing defined it as:

> a free-standing facility, or a distinct unit within a facility, that provides for the management and secure control of inmates who have been officially designated as

exhibiting violent or seriously disruptive behavior while incarcerated. Such inmates have been determined to be a threat to safety and security in traditional high-security facilities, and their behavior can be controlled only by separation, restricted movement, and limited direct access to staff and other inmates.

Supermax housing, for purposes of this survey, did not include maximum or close custody facilities or units that are designated for routine housing of inmates with high custody needs, inmates in disciplinary segregation or protective custody, or other inmates requiring segregation or separation for other routine purposes. (p. 1)

Based on this survey it was found that there were at least 57 supermax facilities nationwide (13,500 beds). An additional 10 DOCs are pursuing the development of 3,000 additional beds. Some of the variations between these facilities include:

- Allowing inmates to have physical contact with one another
- Out-of-cell versus in-cell programming
- Physical contact with staff (limited to recreational and security staff and caseworkers)

Some of the other features found in these facilities include:

1. requiring inmates to spend most of their day, usually 23 hours, in their cells
2. the development of selection procedures and special training for new staff
3. a set of criteria under which inmates can earn transfer out of the supermax
4. an objective instrument or procedure for determining which inmates need to be placed in these facilities

Our Program Focus, "Florence, Colorado: A Consolidation Model," on page 162, profiles the development by the BOP of the supermax concept and its newest facility.

The Future of Classification

Classification and security systems are paramount to good prison management. They are not perfect systems, but they do keep like offenders together. They also place prisoners in facilities with only the necessary amount of security to keep the inmates safe and the community well protected (Rison, 2000). However, Austin (1993) suggests that if objective classification is to be improved and more widely used in the future, there is a need for more refined classification procedures, data, and instruments to deal with a variety of changes in corrections.

First, prison systems are not only receiving more inmates, but these inmates are more diverse. Systems are seeing a rapid growth in the number of African Americans, Hispanics, gang members, and women.

Second, many jurisdictions are moving toward eliminating early release procedures. While this will increase the time served by inmates, some inmates will still have relatively short sentences. This, coupled with mandatory and habitual offender laws may create two distinct populations: a short-term group with relatively rapid turnover and a growing group of long-term offenders who will spend the rest of their lives in prison. Classification, programming, and work assignments for short- and long-term inmates will present major challenges to correctional systems. Although current attitudes do not favor a return to the rehabilitation philosophy, there is a continued recognition of the need for prison programming to deal with special offender groups, such as drug addicts, sex offenders, the seriously disturbed, the chronically unemployed, and the illiterate. However, given limited resources and the view that the criminal justice system cannot break the crime cycle for all offenders, there is a need for "corrections and classification to do a better job of identifying those who can best benefit from [programming] and intervention" (Austin, 1993, p. 121).

A third issue involves improving system efficiency in the placement of inmates in the community. This is important from the standpoint of reducing overcrowding in the prisons and protecting the community from victimization.

A final issue is that of internal classification. Besides system-level classification, Austin (1993) suggests the need for a second layer of classification at the institution level that guides housing, work, and program assignments. These procedures are designed to be used in conjunction with an objective classification system to deal with issues such as compatibility and degree of risk presented by inmates who share a common custody designation. This helps improve the management of these groups. This second layer of classification further groups inmates at a given custody level, based on their personalities, and then devises specific housing placement and programming for them within a given facility. Austin (1993) feels that, despite the fact this requires additional staff, this layer of classification will soon become a regular part of the next generation of objective prison classification systems.

Most major prison systems use an objective classification system. For those who want to implement this type of system a plan is needed that includes:

1. A systemwide classification advisory committee composed of respected individuals to design and set up the new program
2. Pilot testing of the new system using a representative sample of inmates to determine the probable effect on facility functions

Historically, Alcatraz was the first supermax facility in the Federal Bureau of Prisons. Closed in 1963, Alcatraz was replaced by the Marion facility located in Marion, Illinois. This was the first of the modern supermax facilities in the United States. The main facility had an average population of 350 male inmates,[7] all of whom exhibited extreme antisocial behavior (50% had murder records and 79% assault records), were serious escape risks (36% had escaped or attempted it), or had lengthy, complex sentences. In 1978, prompted by the need to deal with the most violent and disruptive inmates, the federal system decided to "concentrate" these inmates in one place (a consolidation model) and to designate this a Level VI (most secure) facility. Marion was chosen because it was more suitable for high-security operations than other federal prisons. In 1994, the administrative maximum facility in Florence, Colorado, replaced Marion. Marion was downgraded to a U.S. penitentiary, or a Level V facility.

Florence: An Administrative Maximum Facility

The Administrative Maximum Facility (ADX), which opened in 1994, is one of four federal institutions that make up the Federal Correctional Complex in Florence, Colorado. This facility is the first specifically designed maximum security penitentiary built by the BOP. It houses adult male offenders who require an uncommon level of security. The institution's modern design enhances the safety of staff and inmates and improves living conditions and program opportunities for the inmate population. The systems of inmate housing, programs, security, and control in the ADX meet legal and constitutional requirements as well as sound correctional practices.

As of January 1, 2000, there were 346 inmates with an average age of 40.1 years, serving an average sentence of 40.3 years. The primary reasons for referral are

- murder/attempted murder of an inmate (22.9%)
- assaulting inmates (19.21%)
- assaults on staff (15.5%)
- greater security–increased monitoring needs (13.6%)
- escape behavior (9.6%)
- court commitment (4.5%)
- rioting (3.7%)

Other reasons for transfer are

- attempted murder of staff
- taking staff hostage
- participation as a leader in a work and/or food strike
- introduction of narcotics
- gang leadership

Housing A stratified system of housing provides inmates with incentives to adhere to the standards of conduct associated with a high-security/maximum custody program. As inmates demonstrate periods of clear conduct and positive institutional adjustment, they progress from the General Population Units to the Intermediate Unit/Transitional Unit and ultimately to the Pre-Transfer Unit. Those successful in the Pre-Transfer Unit will move out to other BOP high-security facilities. The types of privileges afforded to the inmates are determined by their housing unit assignment in this stratified program.

The institution has nine housing units, ranging from most to least restrictive:

- *The Control Unit* is a special long-term detention unit, housing 78 inmates. Its 85 square feet of living space house the most dangerous and assaultive inmates in BOP custody. Prior to placement in the Control Unit a due process hearing is conducted.

- *The Special Housing Unit* is a short-term unit, housing 68 inmates in 90-square-foot cells. It houses both inmates in Disciplinary Segregation, who have been found guilty of prohibited acts while at the ADX, and those in Administrative Detention, who are pending internal investigations or transfer or who have other temporary administrative needs.

- *The High-Security Unit* houses inmates with greater security needs. There are 64 cells in the unit, which are 85 square feet each.

- *General Population Unit(s)* house 64 inmates in 85-square-foot cells. J unit has a total of 64 cells: The (A) side of J unit has 32 cells and houses inmates in the Transitional program. The (B) side of J unit has 32 cells and houses inmates in the Intermediate program. The Pre-Transfer Unit is the most open population unit and houses 64 inmates. The cells in the last three units are 79 square feet. It will take an inmate a minimum of 36 months to work his way through the stratified system of housing. The minimum stay in a General Population Unit is 12 months, the Intermediate program 7 months, the Transitional program 5 months, and the Pre-Transfer Unit 12 months.

Programs and Services

- *Education Programming* This is provided via closed-circuit television and one-to-one assistance by education staff. Programs include adult basic education, general equivalency diploma, English as a second language, parenting, self-study courses, and leisure library.

- *Religious Programs* The ADX respects and honors the religious beliefs of all offenders and provides appropriate opportunities for religious activities while maintaining a safe environment for staff and inmates. Two chaplains tour each housing unit weekly and are assisted by contract religious leaders to address the religious concerns of specific inmate groups. A closed-circuit television system augments these services.

- *Psychological Services* Two full-time psychologists tour the housing units weekly attending to the personal concerns of each inmate. Additionally, substance abuse counseling, stress management courses, and other forms of counseling are provided via closed-circuit television. Inmates diagnosed as suffering chronic or problematic psychological problems or who require in-depth treatment or medication are transferred to the BOP's medical facility at Springfield, Missouri. There is also one contract psychiatrist.

- *Recreation* Each unit has indoor and outdoor recreation facilities. Inmates in a General Population Unit have recreation in groups of up to 12 for at least 12 hours per week. High-Security Unit inmates have recreation individually for 7½ hours a week, those in the Intermediate, 28½ hours weekly, Transitional, 28½ hours, and Pre-Transfer unit inmates are out of their cells virtually all day and have recreation outside of the unit for 21 hours a week.

- *Control Unit and Special Housing* Units there are smaller, more secure, and provide individual recreation areas. While in Disciplinary Segregation status inmates have recreation for 5 hours weekly; those in Control Unit and in Administrative Detention status units have recreation for 7 hours per week. Recreational opportunities will also be offered via the closed-circuit television and commercial broadcasts.

- *Food Services* The method of serving three meals per day depends on the type and security of the unit. Inmates in the Control, Special Housing, General Population, and High-Security units eat meals in their cells. Inmates in the Intermediate and Transitional units eat their meals together in a common area of the unit, and Pre-Transfer Unit inmates eat in a separate common dining room.

- *Visiting* All social visits are conducted in noncontact visiting booths. Inmates are permitted to have five social visits per month, which last up to 7 hours and can include up to three visitors per visit.

- *Commissary Services* are available to all inmates except those in Disciplinary Segregation status. Available items include limited clothing, snack foods, stamps, and so on.

- *Medical Services* ADX has health services consistent with community health-care standards for outpatient care. Hospital staff make daily rounds to attend to the medical concerns of the prisoners and, when clinically warranted, escort inmates to the medical department for treatment.

- *Laundry and Clothing* Inmates are provided with bedding, towels, pants, shirts, jumpsuits, undergarments, and socks. They may also purchase from the commissary such items as shorts, T-shirts, and tennis shoes.

- *Legal Services* All inmates are afforded access to the courts. Legal access is assisted through the location of basic law libraries within each unit and a main law library, from which inmates can have current legal periodicals delivered. Inmates are permitted to contact outside counsel or petition the courts for appointed counsel whenever necessary.

Public Controversy The Alcatraz, Marion, and Florence models reflect specific principles for control. The use of physical punishment was never allowed at Alcatraz and is strictly prohibited at Marion and Florence. The punishment in all lockdowns was, and is, restraint on activities and the limited number of privileges and amenities inmates have.

Conditions at Marion have been challenged by inmate suits alleging "cruel and unusual punishment" (e.g., *Bruscino v Carlson*, 1988; *Hewitt v. Helms*, 1983), but the institution's policies have been upheld by the courts. The high-security system has reduced the level of violence. In the 43 months before implementing the high-security operation, six inmates and two COs were killed in the prison. In the 43 months after its implementation three inmates were killed (Karacki, 1987).

The use of maximum coercive authority by the government always attracts the attention of the press, and since the 1960s, the electronic media, as well as prison reform groups and inmates' rights organizations. Operations at Alcatraz, Marion, and Florence produced similar concerns from critics. Each system has attracted national attention, and each is the object of heated controversies. Arguments that oppose the new breed of ADX facilities and programs include:

- Inmates are psychologically disabled as a result of serving long years under such highly restrictive regimes [Human Rights Watch (WTS), 1997].

- Some of these facilities, particularly those in Indiana, are used to house the mentally ill (HWS, 1997).

(continued)

163

Florence, Colorado: A Consolidation Model

(continued)

- Inmates from these prisons transferred back to penitentiaries are so filled with rage at being kept "like animals in a cage" that they strike out against other prisoners and particularly against employees of the system that so confined them.
- When they are finally released to the "free world" their postrelease criminal conduct will demonstrate that the anger engendered by their experiences in Alcatraz, Marion, or Florence will be taken out in the form of assaults on the citizens (Rison, 2000).

- "Choosing to subject hundreds of prisoners to prolonged periods in extremely harsh and potentially harmful conditions cannot be justified as necessary to ensure security or to serve legitimated goals of punishment" (HWS, 1997, p. 11).

Conversely, prison administrators recognize the importance of special interest groups, such as the National Prison Project and Amnesty International, that oppose these strict conditions of confinement. They represent a system of checks and balances for the proper care and control of inmates. For prison managers working with a difficult, extremely aggressive offender another position takes precedence, "Some prisoners will always need incarceration, will always be a threat to other prisoners and staff, and will always be a threat to the community." This position begs the question, "Is 70 inmates in the Control Unit at Florence out of a population of 130,000 inmates confined in the BOP an abuse of control?"

Source: Prepared by Richard Rison (2000) for the 2nd edition of this text. Rison is a retired prison warden, with 35 years of experience; he administered five federal prisons.

3. Provision for automation and inclusion in the department's management information system, which helps to reduce errors in scoring inmates and to monitor them better

4. A highly trained classification staff to smoothly implement the program and keep it running

5. A monitoring or evaluation plan to ensure that it works as planned and continued monitoring to determine its impact on inmate management

There is evidence that an increasing number of jurisdictions are employing objective classification systems. Not only has this occurred in prison systems but also at the local level where new-generation jails have been built and direct supervision programs have been instituted. Progress has also been noted in the reduction of overclassification. Austin (1993), in commenting on the status of classification, states:

Despite dramatic advances much work still remains. In particular, new classification systems that govern the internal movement of inmates within a facility are required. Prison classification systems also need to better interface with jail, probation, and parole classification systems so that critical information about offenders follows them as they move through the correctional system. Finally, considerable experimentation and research are needed to better understand the influence of the prison environment as it relates to inmate behavior. (p. 123)

Prison Population Changes

The rate of incarceration for males sentenced to state or federal correctional institutions in 1925 was 149 per 100,000 U.S. residents; by 1998, it was 866 per 100,000. (See Chapter 9 for a discussion of female prisoners.) Figures 8.3 and 8.4 depict the pattern of growth in the population. Since 1970, there has been a dramatic increase in the male inmate population,[8] reflecting the public's disenchantment with the rehabilitation approach to corrections and the drug epidemic in the United States.

Sex and Age Changes

Historically, incarcerated males have vastly outnumbered incarcerated females, constituting between 94 and 97 percent of the inmate population. However, although women remain a small part of the inmate population, their rate of incarceration has been growing steadily since 1974, when it rose from 7 per 100,000 to 57 per 100,000 in 1998 (Beck & Mumola, 1999, p. 5). Female inmate rates have been growing at a much faster rate than males since 1990, at 8.5 percent versus 6.6 percent growth for males (p. 5). During this same period, while the female inmate population nearly doubled, the male population grew only by a little over two thirds.[9] In the United States, as in other countries, men are arrested far more frequently than women. This disparity has existed historically and has been true for almost all offenses. Current statistics show that men account for 7 out of 10 persons arrested for index crimes (FBI, 1998).

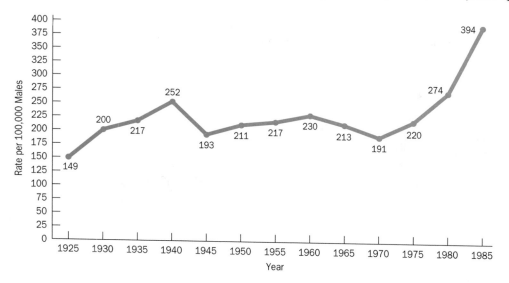

Figure 8.3 *Male Rates of Incarceration (1925–1985)*

Source: *State and Federal Prisoners, 1925–85* (1986). Washington, DC: BJS.

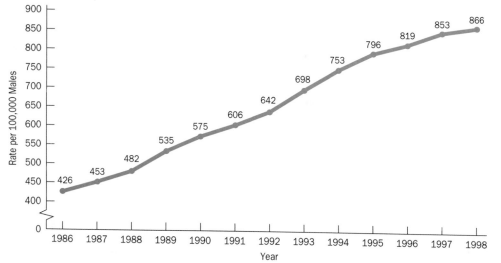

Figure 8.4 *Male Rates of Incarceration (1986–1998)*

Source: R. Cohen (1991). *Prisoners in 1990.* Washington, DC: Author; BJS (1989). *Prisoners in 1988.* Washington, DC: Author; T. L. Snell & D. C. Morton (1992). *Prisoners in 1991.* Washington, DC: BJS; D. Gillard (1993). *Prisoners in 1992.* Washington, DC: BJS; D. Gillard & A. Beck (1994). *Prisoners in 1993.* Washington, DC: BJS; A. Beck & D. Gillard (1995); D. Gillard & A. Beck (1996); C. J. Mumola & A. Beck (1997); D. Gillard & A. Beck (1998); A. Beck & C. J. Mumola (1998); K. Maguire & A. L. Pastore (1999).

There was also a noticeable increase in the age of the prison population between 1991 and 1997. Despite the tougher stance on imprisoning young offenders, their proportion in the prison population dropped steadily between 1991 and 1997 (see Figure 8.5). In 1997, the percentage of those 17 and younger held in state or federal prisons had dropped from 0.6 percent in 1991 to 0.4 percent; the rates for rates for those 18 to 19 dropped from 2.9 to 2.6 percent; rates for those 20 to 24 dropped from 17.4 to 15.8 percent. By contrast, we have seen growth in most age groups beginning at 35, probably indicative of more prisoners serving more of their sentence length. Also, the age distribution of the inmate population in the adult prison system is truncated because many offenders under 18 are housed in juvenile institutions. However, with the increasingly violent nature of juvenile crime and a growing public intolerance of it, many

violent juveniles will likely be tried as adults and sent to adult prisons. However, at this point juveniles have had a limited effect on the prison population.

Arrests provide a different picture. FBI data show that 42 percent of all persons arrested for serious (index) crimes in 1997 were under 21. Arrest rates in general peak at an early age and then decline precipitously; this occurs earlier for property offenses than for violent offenses. In 1998, for offenders under 21, arrest figures for property crimes peaked at 13 to 14, but arrests for violent crimes did not peak until 18 (see Figure 8.6; FBI, 1997). Historically, as offenders grow older, they commit proportionally fewer crimes and present less of a threat to society than younger criminals. Both violent and property crimes begin to drop from age 30 onward, with a precipitous drop beginning at 40 (see Figure 8.6; FBI, 1998). Ironically, the popular "three strikes and you're

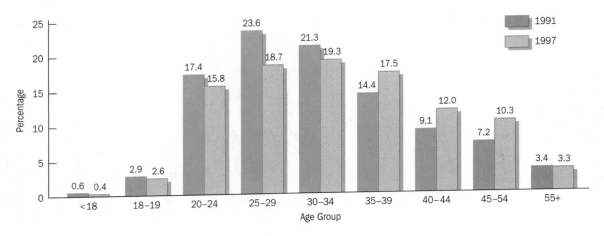

Figure 8.5 *Percent of Inmates Held in State or Federal Prison by Age (1991 and 1997)*

Source: A. J. Beck & C. J. Mumola (1999). *Prisoners in 1998.* Washington, DC: BJS, p. 10.

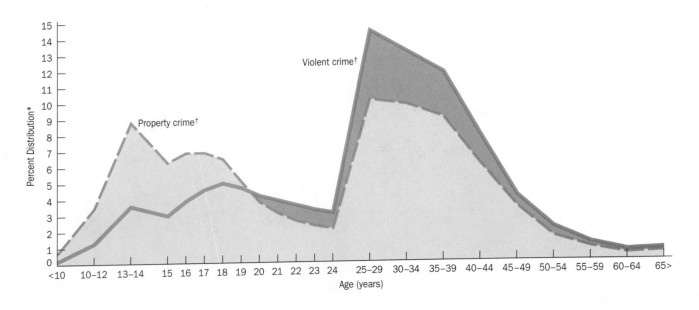

Figure 8.6 *Arrest Rates for Male Inmates by Age (1998)*

*Because of rounding, the percentages may not add to total.
†Violent crimes are offenses of murder, forcible rape, robbery, and aggravated assault.
†Property crimes are offenses of burglary, larceny-theft, motor vehicle theft, and arson.
Source: Federal Bureau of Investigation (1999). *Crime in the United States, 1998.* Washington, DC: U.S. Department of Justice.

out" laws are more likely to be applied to the older age group, having little immediate impact on younger (and much more criminally active) offenders.

Changes in Sentencing

Between 1988 and 1996, the average imposed prison sentence length decreased. From 1992 to 1996, the length of sentences imposed for robbery, aggravated assault, burglary, larceny, and drug trafficking also dropped. However, sentences imposed for murder increased (see Figure 8.7). The actual time served also decreased for these crimes (except for larceny—which stayed the same—and murder—which increased); however, inmates were serving a greater proportion of their sentences (see Figure 8.8). For example, inmates released from state prison in

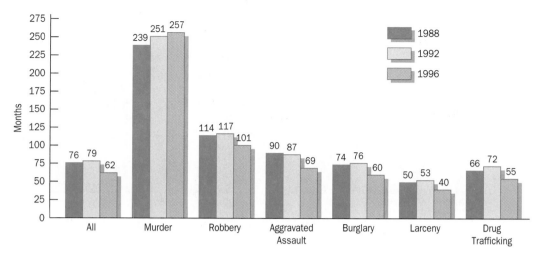

Figure 8.7 *Average Imposed Sentence Length (months)*

Source: D. J. Levin, P. A. Langan, & J. M. Brown (2000, February). *State Court Sentencing of Convicted Felons, 1996.* Washington, DC: BJS.

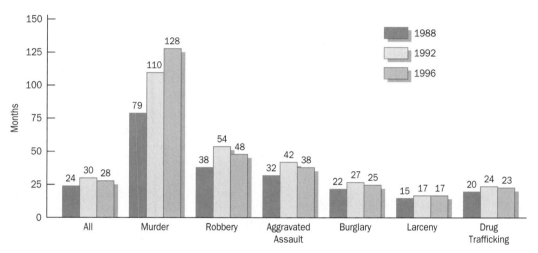

Figure 8.8 *Actual Time to Be Served (months)*

Source: Levin, Langan, & Brown (2000, February).

1988 served only about one third of their sentences, whereas those sentenced in 1996 will serve almost half of their term. Thus, by 1996, we had begun to see the impact of standardized sentencing guidelines.

Prisoner Demographics

In this section, we look at the impact of race, family structure, work history and economic status, education, and other factors on the makeup of the prison population.

Racial and Ethnic Differences

Any casual observer of American prisons would be struck by the disproportionate percentage of blacks and other minorities housed there. Blacks accounted for 41 percent of the jail inmates in 1998 (Gillard, 1999). Relative to their numbers in the population, this means that they were six times more likely than white non-Hispanics to be held in local jails and twice as likely as Hispanics. In prisons, blacks constituted 49.4 percent of the inmate population (Beck & Mumola, 1999).

Table 8.3

Inmates Admitted to State and Federal Prisons (by race)

	1926	1986	1996
White	37,734	122,483	185,700
Black	12,075	98,519	163,900
Other	503	2,881	4,300

Sources: P. A. Langan (1991). Race of Prisoners Admitted to State and Federal Institutions, 1926–1986, Washington, DC: BJS; Bureau of Justice Statistics (1999, April). Correctional Populations in the United States, 1996. Washington, DC: BJS, Table 1.20.

Table 8.3 shows that there was an 8-fold increase in black admissions to prisons between 1926 and 1986, which increases to more than 13-fold if we include 1996. This increase cannot be explained by changes in the size of the black population. During the 10-year period between 1986 to 1996 black admissions increased by 1.7 times (BJS, 1999; Langan, 1991, May). By contrast, white admissions increased by 1.5 times.

Figure 8.9 *Race of New Court Commitments to State and Federal Prison (1930–1996)*

Sources: P. A. Langan (1991). *Race of Prisoners Admitted to State and Federal Institutions, 1926–1986.* Washington, DC: BJS; BJS (1999, April). *Correctional Populations in the United States, 1996.* Washington, DC: Author.

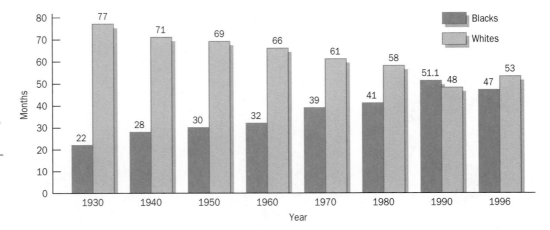

Another important trend was the steady increase of the proportion of blacks entering prisons, from 21 percent in 1926 to more than half of the inmates admitted in 1996 (see Figure 8.9). Black admissions rates to prisons (i.e., per 100,000 blacks in the population) almost tripled between 1926 and 1996, while their numbers in prisons grew almost fourfold. In comparison the white admissions rates dropped during this time, and numerically the increase was not as great. This obviously raises some questions about the role played by discrimination in these population increases. Is justice racially blind?

Mauer and Huling (1995) found that the proportion of blacks between the ages of 20 and 29 under some form of correctional supervision—in prison or jail or on probation parole—went from one in four to one in three over a 5-year period. Black women have experienced the largest increase of all groups under correctional supervision, rising by 78 percent between 1989 and 1994. Drug policies were found to be the most significant factor in a decade-long increase in young African Americans under correctional supervision. This is not surprising because African Americans and Hispanics account for almost 90 percent of those sentenced to prison for drug possession (Mauer & Huling, 1995). We also need to consider the impact of the "baby boomerang" on the offender population. It is estimated that by the year 2005, the number of teens between the ages of 14 and 17 will increase by 20 percent, but the increase among blacks will be even larger—26 percent (Fox, 1996). Some of the unanticipated consequences of ever-increasing black incarceration rates are

1. loss of voting rights for an estimated 1.4 million black males

2. a 7 percent drop in income for 18- to 30-year-olds after arrest, and a 10 percent drop in earnings for disadvantaged youths, which led to a 6 percent increase in crime between 1988 and 1994

3. a drop in community cohesion, which adversely affects an area's ability to fight crime and to form the

human capital necessary to sustain social norms, provide role models, and encourage productive activities

4. the removal of potential wage earners, which disrupts family relations and increases a community's alienation from the larger society. (Mauer, 1997, p. 14)

To deal with the escalating numbers of black offenders entering the criminal justice system, Mauer and Huling (1995) suggest an intermediate strategy that would reduce the severity of criminal control by creating a broader number of sentencing options for nonviolent offenders who would otherwise be sentenced to prison. Another alternative may be to address this problem at the front end. For example, Florida has established an aggressive Minority Over Representation project, which targets a higher proportion of this group for diversion and prevention programs. This is designed to have a positive effect in reducing minority group representation in the prison population (DeVolentine, 1996–1997).

Other Sociodemographic Factors

Although the impact of some sociodemographic factors (e.g., disrupted families, abuse, family criminality, educational insufficiency) on criminal behavior is controversial, it is probably fair to say that individuals with many of these characteristics are at high risk for involvement in crime. Studies of inmate populations reflect that their backgrounds generally deviate from the general public in areas of education, economic status or work history, and victimization.

Just over one third of the inmate population had completed high school compared with 85 percent of U.S. males between the ages of 20 and 29 (Beck et al., 1993). Another one fourth reported having received a general equivalency diploma, but one fifth had not gone beyond the eighth grade.

Four out of 10 reported a monthly income of less than $600; almost 6 out of 10 had incomes of less than $1,000 (see Figure 8.10b). Six out of 10 had never married (see

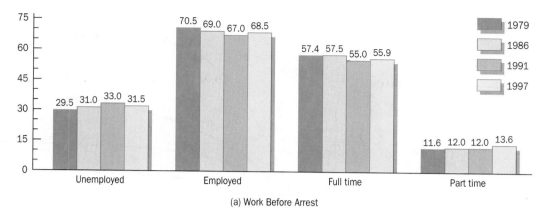

(a) Work Before Arrest

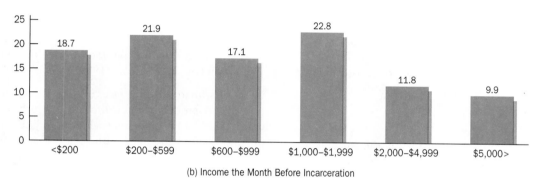

(b) Income the Month Before Incarceration

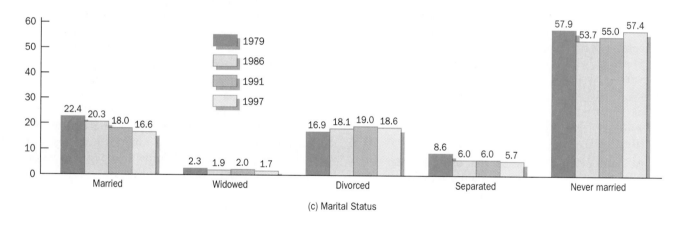

(c) Marital Status

Figure 8.10 *Inmate Sociodemographic Summaries*

Source: Adapted from C. J. Mumola (2000, January). *Veterans in Prison or Jail*. Washington, DC: BJS.

Figure 8.10c) (Beck et al., 1993). Other research found that 40 percent of the inmates had either never worked or had held a variety of short-term jobs (Rolph & Chaikin, 1987). On average, this group had committed more crimes than groups with a more stable employment history.

Finally, an estimated 38 percent of the women and 13 percent of the male inmate population in 1991 reported receiving some type of support from social security, welfare, or charity before being admitted to prison. More than half of these inmates had a preprison income of less than $10,000 (Beck et al., 1993).

Several studies show that many inmates report having been abused extensively as children (Mouzakitis, 1981; Straus, Gelles, & Steinmetz, 1980). Females are more likely to report being victimized than males, and this abuse occurred both before and after age 17 (Harlow, 1999). Inmates reported higher levels of abuse (1) if they grew up with foster as opposed to biological parents, (2) if their parents were heavy drug or alcohol abusers or (3) if a family member had been in prison or jail. Thus, the role models provided by family members also appear to play a part in an individual becoming a

Figure 8.11 *Percentage of U.S. Males Likely to Ever Go to Prison*

Source: T. P. Bonczar & D. J. Beck (1997). *Lifetime Likelihood of Going to State or Federal Prison.* Washington, DC: Bureau of Justice Statistics.

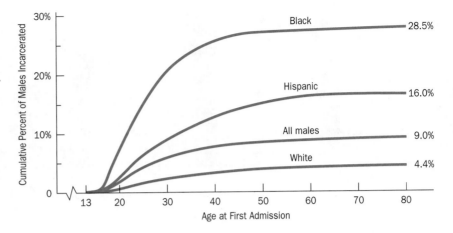

criminal (Glueck & Glueck, 1974). Abused state prisoners were also more likely to be serving time for a violent crime than those not abused (Harlow, 1999).

Recidivism

Recidivism is often used to measure the success of prison programs, or even imprisonment, itself. Recidivism patterns show that:

- Close to two thirds were rearrested during the 3-year period after their release, with 46 percent reconvicted and 41 percent returned to prison or jail. Fifteen percent of these were for violent crimes.

- Sixty percent had been incarcerated in the past, and for the vast majority this had been within 5 years prior to their current offense (Beck et al., 1993; Needels, 1996).

- At least one study indicates that using a 3-year vs. a longer period of time provides more accurate data on reincarceration. At the 3-year cutoff, only 41 percent of the sample had been reincarcerated, while after 17 years the rate rose to 61 percent.

- Most offenders are rearrested for crimes similar to those for which they had been previously imprisoned (Beck & Shipley, 1989).

- The factors most likely to predict return to prison recidivism rates in the early years included being young, black, and high school dropouts. Over a longer period of time, the criminal history variables—such as the number of property offenses convictions, type of prison from which the offender was released, and first offender status—were strongly predictive of future recidivism. This suggests that a follow-up of prison release for more than the standard 3-year cutoff point provides more re-

liable information on determining reincarceration (Beck & Shipley, 1989; Needels, 1996).

It is estimated that 1 in every 20 persons will serve time in prison during their lifetime. Figure 8.11 shows that black and Hispanic males are more likely to be imprisoned than white males (Bonczar & Beck, 1997).[10]

Special Category Offenders

Many inmates have characteristics, problems, and/or needs that set them apart from others in the prison population. This section provides an in-depth look at five inmate groups that represent significant challenges for corrections: (1) inmates with mental illnesses or retardation; (2) sex offenders; (3) mature inmates; (4) long-term offenders; and (5) youthful offenders. We recognize that we are not covering all special inmate categories, but these five groups enable us to provide a perspective on the management approaches used to deal with special types of inmates, the problems they pose to prison personnel, and the adjustments and accommodations they make to prison life.

Mentally Ill Offenders

Inmates in this category, including the psychologically disturbed and the retarded, often require some form of **special management** (programs specifically designed for them), because many may act unpredictably or in bizarre ways. These offenders suffer from disorders that have emotional, intellectual, cognitive, or behavioral ramifications. Their disorders result in behavior or mental states that tend to place them at a higher risk of being victimized or otherwise getting into trouble (e.g., disregarding rules or not understanding rules or instructions) (DeVolentine, 1999). They may also engage in unpredictable or violent behavior, placing other inmates and

The Treatment of the Mentally Disordered

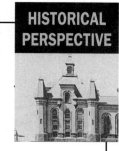

HISTORICAL PERSPECTIVE

The treatment of mentally disordered individuals has varied throughout American history. The nature of the treatment is usually due to some combination of the treatment philosophy and the economics of the era. This is reflected in the fact that, historically, the mentally ill and the retarded were housed without any differentiation, despite significant differences in their disorders (DeVolentine, 1999). In the 1700s, families tried to keep disordered individuals at home, sending them to almshouses when they became too unmanageable. In these facilities, they were likely to be locked in cellars or attics (Rothman, 1971). During the 1800s, Dorothea Dix toured prisons and other institutions that held the mentally disordered and concluded they could not receive appropriate care in prisons. Her efforts resulted in the development of institutions specifically for the mentally disordered. From 1860 until approximately 1970, there were separate institutions for the severely mentally disordered and often for those who were **criminally insane.** The criminally insane included those individuals who were found incompetent to stand trial, acquitted by reason of insanity, and inmates who became mentally ill while in prison.

In the 1950s, the development of antipsychotic drugs eventually led to an emphasis on community-based treatment, and many mental hospitals were closed or reduced their services and patient caseloads.

One outcome of this has been that many former mental patients became homeless street people. When not taking their medication, some engaged in behavior that made them public nuisances (e.g., screaming, starting fires, urinating and defecating on the street, and accosting and assaulting people). As a result, this has sometimes brought them into contact with the criminal justice system, with placement in jails or prisons.
Sources: DeVolentine, 1999; Rothman, 1971.

---

staff at risk of injury or worse. Thus, they may need specialized help and programs to function within the prison.

We will use the term **mentally disordered** to describe those individuals who are classified as mentally or emotionally disturbed. Public attitudes toward these individuals have changed over the years (see our Historical Perspective feature).

Types of Mental Disorders   In the *Diagnostic and Statistical Manual* (DSM-IV), published by the American Psychiatric Association (1994), mental disorders can roughly be divided into **psychotic disorders,** including the various forms of schizophrenia and severe mood disorders; **organic disorders,** caused by damage to the central nervous system; less serious disorders (e.g., anxiety, depression), and a variety of other disorders that include personality disorders, sexual disorders, and adjustment disorders. The psychotic disorders represent the most serious psychological disturbances, whereas antisocial personality disorders pose the greatest crime problems.

Jemelka, Rahman, and Trupin (1993) reviewed studies on the incidence of mental disorders among inmates and found two that directly assessed the extent of mental illness through diagnostic interviews. The first, which was based on a sample of 413 California inmates, estimated that 14.1 percent of them could be diagnosed as having severe organic brain syndrome, schizophrenia, a major depressive disorder, or a bipolar disorder. Some-

what over half of this group were showing symptoms of their disturbances at the time of the study, while the rest were not actively symptomatic (Independent Research Consortium, 1989).

A second study of 3,332 inmates found that 8 percent had severe psychiatric disabilities that required mental health treatment. An additional 16 percent were diagnosed as having significant psychiatric disabilities needing periodic services (Steadman, Fabisiak, & Dvoskin, 1987). Jemelka et al. (1993) concluded that "it is clear . . . that at any given time 10 to 15 percent of state prison populations are suffering from a major mental disorder and are in need of the kinds of psychiatric services associated with these illnesses" (p. 11). These rates are five to six times higher than those found in the general population.

In the first comprehensive study on mental illness in corrections, BJS estimated that 283,800 mentally ill inmates were held in state and federal prisons, with an additional 547,800 on probation. Figure 8.12 shows the percentage of inmates under correctional supervision that have mental or emotional problems (Ditton, 1999, July). Characteristics of this population include the following:

- They are more likely than other inmates to have committed violent crimes.

- They are more likely than other inmates to have been homeless a year prior to arrest and more likely to be unemployed.

Figure 8.12 *Mental Condition and Treatment of Correctional Populations*

Source: R. M. Ditton (1999, July). *Mental Health and Treatment of Inmates and Probationers.* Washington, DC: Bureau of Justice Statistics, p. 46.

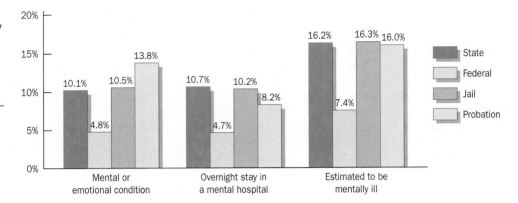

- Whites have a higher rate of illness than blacks or Hispanics.

- Offenders between 45 and 54 are the most likely to be identified as mentally ill.

- Unlike inmates in prisons, those in jail and on probation are more likely to report being under supervision for property and public-order offenses.

- A family history of incarceration or alcohol and drug abuse is more prevalent among this group.

- They report higher rates of past physical and sexual abuse—1 in 10 females and almost 50 percent of the males report abuse.

- Six in 10 report being under the influence of alcohol or drugs at the time of their current offense.

- Six in 10 receive treatment while incarcerated; this drops to 1 in 4 for jail inmates and 1 in 5 for probationers.

- Many have disciplinary problems: involvement in fights and being charged with breaking prison rules or jail rules.

- Mentally ill inmates report negative life experiences related to drinking (e.g., losing a job, being held at a police station, prior stays in detoxification units). (Ditton, 1999, July)

Our Close-Up, "Challenges of the Mentally Ill in Prison vs. in the Community," discusses the kinds of adjustments faced by the mentally ill in prison versus in the community, as well as the management problems they create for prison staff.

Mentally Handicapped Inmates

The **mentally handicapped** (retarded) constitute another group who may require special services and programs in or out of prison. As a group, they appear to commit crimes at about the same rate as nonhandicapped people. Approximately 2.3 percent of the general population of the United States is identified as retarded. Four levels of retardation[11] are recognized, but only individuals from the highest two levels—the mildly retarded (IQs 55–69) and the moderately retarded (IQs 55–69)—are usually found in correctional institutions (Garcia & Steele, 1988). This is because the limited mental capacity of the lowest two categories makes it difficult to prove criminal intent (DeVolentine, 1993).

Overrepresented in the Prison Population About 2 percent of the prison population (14,500) is retarded, while 12,550 other retarded criminals are held in facilities for the retarded (Conley, Luckasson, & Bouthilet, 1992). Thus, proportionally, there are about 1½ times as many retarded offenders in prisons and other facilities as are found in the general population. The major reasons for the overrepresentation of the retarded in correctional populations include the higher likelihood of being impoverished and residing in high-crime areas; their inability to think quickly, making them more likely to be caught; their higher rates of confession and lower rates of plea bargaining, which contribute to higher sentences; and their lower chances of being paroled given their poor candidacy for jobs (Santamour, 1990).

Retarded individuals are not likely to be treated with sympathy or understanding by other inmates. Instead, they are likely to be ridiculed or sexually assaulted, have their commissary items taken, or otherwise be victimized. Often, they do not understand the consequences of their actions and break rules continually or become involved in altercations. They also tend to have difficulties adjusting to regular prison programs, because even though they are able to understand concrete instructions, many struggle with abstract concepts. Thus, abbreviated instructions or allegedly understood norms of behavior cause the retarded individuals extreme difficulties (DeVolentine, 1999). Such difficulties suggest the need for special placement and programs for many of the retarded inmates.

Challenges of the Mentally Ill in Prison vs. in the Community

While it is true that there are many unique aspects about the culture and life on the "inside," entering the gate of a correctional facility does not place the traveler in a completely different world from the "free world." Many of the values, attitudes, and beliefs of the culture at large continue to exist behind the walls and razor wire of prisons.

Thus, the challenges mental illness presents for the mentally ill offender and the staff responsible for them are both similar to and different from the challenges for the mentally ill, their caretakers, their employees, and neighbors living in the "free world" community. Just as in the larger community, mentally ill inmates who are living in an outpatient setting (i.e., among other non-mentally ill inmates) often face the stigma of mental illness. They may be referred to as "bugs" by non-mentally ill inmates and are often viewed as less desirable associates. Custodial staff may also perceive them as less capable or reliable, preferring not to have them assigned to their work squads.

However, the same unusual behavior that results in the identification of an inmate as mentally ill sometimes may have a positive result not observed in the community at large. Many younger or more physically capable inmates who are prone to preying on others may avoid teasing or preying on a less capable mentally ill inmate because of the perception he may "bug out" and become unexpectedly violent. Thus, these often ungrounded fears serve the mentally ill inmate by determining potential predators.

Toch (1982) and Toch and Adams (1987) characterized mentally ill inmates as either disturbed-non-disruptive or disturbed-disruptive.

Disturbed-nondisruptive mentally ill inmates usually provide little challenge for the staff. However, it is with the disturbed-disruptive inmate in the outpatient setting that security goals and treatment goals may clash and where the contrast with the larger community is most obvious. Mentally ill inmates who display low-level threatening behaviors, such as refusing verbal orders or showing verbal disrespect, are still subject to the consequences of the institutional disciplinary system and disciplinary confinement (see Chapter 13). As a consequence, they may be restricted to a one- or two-person cell in a separate confinement unit for 15, 30, or more days. Although many mentally ill inmates tolerate this without problems, some experience acute exacerbation of their symptoms.

For mentally ill inmates treated with psychotropic medication a major challenge faced by mental health staff is treatment compliance. Between 2 to 30 percent of people who take psychotropic medication experience undesirable side effects, such as blurred vision, tremors, dry mouth, constipation, increased sensitivity to sunlight, or decreased libido. Most side effects can be adequately addressed by the addition of medication (e.g., Cogentin) to counter these effects. However, this is not always effective, and the inmate may begin to refuse his medication; this almost always results in a deterioration of his mental status.

Profile of a Mentally Ill Inmate

William is a 34-year-old male serving a 99-year sentence for sexual battery with a deadly weapon. He has been in prison for 13 years. During that time he has had an extensive history of being treated for paranoid schizophrenia, with the most consistent symptoms being delusions of grandeur, hallucinations, and bizarre self-neglectful behaviors. He has been hospitalized three times and responds quickly to psychotropic medication. Although he is heterosexual and expresses no interest in sex with other inmates, he continues to have sexual urges which he normally relieves through masturbation. He recognizes the benefit of medication but has complained that all medications tried thus far have made him unable to obtain an erection. He states that his peers in the outpatient setting often say, "Man, if that stuff is doing that to you, I wouldn't take it." Upon discharge, he has continued to take his medication for a year or more. However, despite medication compliance counseling, he eventually becomes preoccupied with his erectile dysfunction, refuses his medication, and again becomes severely psychotic. Now, in his third hospitalization, his attending psychiatrist changed him to a new medication. After one week, he elatedly reported that he was again able to obtain an erection, and his mental status continues clear. His treatment team is hopeful that this will result in continued compliance upon discharge and no further need for hospitalization.

Source: Prepared by Don J. Stewart, especially for the 2nd edition of Corrections: A Comprehensive View. *He is a senior psychologist at Corrections Mental Health Institution in Chattahoochee, Florida.*

Experts differ as to whether to place these offenders in segregated institutions and housing or to mainstream them with the general population. Whatever the approach taken, there is a need to protect their safety (Anno, 1991a) and to teach them the rudimentary social, daily living, and work skills that they may lack. Achieving these skills may allow many of them to become independent and avoid being reincarcerated. Unfortunately, most prisons do not have special programs to deal with these inmates' problems, and without them they will likely regress and lose some vital life skills (Ellis & Luckasson, 1985).

Sex Offenders

Although sex offenders can be classified in a variety of ways, the FBI system presents an easy way to distinguish them. This system divides major sex offenders into two categories, child molesters and rapists. In prison, these offenders present a variety of management problems, many of which are discussed in this chapter.

Characteristics   Because sexual offenses are committed in private and many are unreported, numerous sex offenders do not enter the criminal justice system. Characteristically, although sex offenders seem ordinary in most other respects (e.g., they have a family, hold jobs, play sports, and maintain friendships), the majority were themselves victims of sexual molestation (Lotke, 1996; Schwartz, 1995). Moreover, although most sex offenders exhibit symptoms of personality disorders (e.g., antisocial personality disorder), most do not have major psychiatric disorders.

Currently, the enforcement of sex offender laws is more aggressive, and definitions of sex offenses are expanding more rapidly than ever before. Thus, acts that were tolerated before are now criminally prosecuted. This gives the appearance of increased criminal sexual activity; however, the changes may largely be in the official response to lower grades of sexual assault (Lotke, 1996).

In 1980, sex offenders constituted 6.9 percent of the prison population. This rose to a high of 9.7 percent in 1994, at which point it began dropping, and by 1997, sex offenders composed 8.5 percent of the prison population. The actual number of sex offenders may be underestimated, though, because many of these offenders are strongly motivated to seek plea bargains that allow them to plead guilty to non-sex offenses (Vaughn & Sapp, 1990). In this way, they avoid the low status given these offenders in the prison hierarchy and the potential violence directed toward them, particularly child sexual abusers. However, by entering prison as non-sex offenders, they are unlikely to receive any treatment and will likely relapse upon their release. A good classification system (as discussed earlier in this chapter) can identify these offenders and provide treatment for them.

Treatment Options   A study of inmate attitudes toward sexual behavior found that sexual offenders attribute lower harm to having sex with children than other inmates, and those who rated this activity low harm were more likely to be sex offenders. This seems to indicate that sex offender treatment should focus on developing empathy for victims (Winfree, Awmiller, & Devenny, 1996).

Forty-four states offer prison programming for sex offenders.[12-13] Over half the states have special facilities, including therapeutic communities and advanced-level program sites for multiphasic treatment programs for sex offenders. Other available programs include individual and group counseling, inmate support groups, medical treatment, and even victim-offender reconciliation, which is rare. Additional treatments include relapse prevention, Depo-Provera, aversion therapy, victim empathy, and anger management (Lillis, 1993a; Wees, 1996).

Treatment of sexual offenders is controversial because much of the public believes they should be punished, not treated. However, the maladaptive behaviors of sex offenders are likely to be further aggravated, rather than deterred, by imprisonment alone. While sex offenders generally have lower recidivism rates than other offenders, those who receive treatment have even lower rates (10.9%) (Lotke, 1996). Research by Cummings and Pithers (1992) that evaluated the Vermont Treatment Program for Sexual Aggressors indicated that offender treatment should become a priority for corrections, as the recidivism rate for offenders in the program was under 10 percent. Our Program Focus examines the Vermont Treatment Program for Sexual Aggressors (VTPSA).

A variety of approaches are employed in treating sex offenders. Most programs include both individual and group psychotherapy, but individual therapy is not used as extensively, because sex offenders tend to engage in a great deal of denial and secrecy. Several behavioral techniques are used to reduce the deviant sexual arousal experienced by many sexual offenders (Krauth & Smith, 1988). The penile plethysmograph, a pressure-sensitive device that attaches to the penis to detect erections, is used to identify an offender's deviant sexual interests. Behavior therapy is used to recondition an offender's arousal patterns, "increasing arousal to nondeviant adult stimuli while decreasing arousal to deviant stimuli, such as children or of aggression toward women" (Marques, Day, Nelson, & Miner, 1989, p. 28).

Our Program Focus, "12 Measures of Recidivism," on page 179 looks at a study of 407 adult sex offenders conducted over a 10-year period. It further examines recidivism.

A final issue in treating sexual offenders involves those who deny committing their offense or greatly minimize their deviant sexual acts. Although most sex offenders take this stance at least until conviction, many

VTPSA Program Description

Harvey Doe, age 35, raped four women in a suburban neighborhood over a one-month period of time. All the rapes occurred in the victims' homes after 11 P.M.; all the women lived alone. Doe was arrested during the fourth rape when the victim's brother unexpectedly dropped by after a night on the town. When interviewed by the police, Doe gave a complete confession. Harvey Doe's wife was shocked when she received a phone call from her husband saying he had been arrested for sexual assault.

The Does had three school-age children. Harvey was a steady worker, having worked for the same company for 10 years. He rarely drank, and his wife had never seen him intoxicated during their 11-year marriage. Mrs. Doe later told the probation officer who was preparing the presentence investigation report that they had been experiencing marital difficulties over the past year, and Harvey had started to take long walks after the kids were put to bed. Harvey told police that he had cased out an entire neighborhood during his walks choosing his future victims.

Is Harvey Doe a typical rapist? Many people think rapists are sick men who are dysfunctional in all areas of their life. And yet Harvey led an otherwise normal life; he didn't even have a speeding ticket on his record. Many people think that sex offenders can't change and the only way to protect society is to lock them up for the rest of their natural life. And yet Harvey entered a treatment program in prison stating he wanted to get help with his problems.

What should happen to people like Harvey Doe? Do they need to spend the rest of their lives in prison to protect the community from them? Are they ever able to live their lives in society without hurting others? How does society balance punishment, rehabilitation, and restitution?

The Vermont Department of Corrections started the Vermont Treatment Program for Sexual Aggressors (VTPSA) in 1982 for men just like Harvey Doe. VTPSA began as a 16-bed unit in a regional correctional facility. It has grown over the years and now includes two incarcerated programs and community-based programs in almost every Vermont county. The intensive incarcerated program is located on the grounds of the Northwest State Correctional Facility in Swanton and currently houses 36 offenders for an average length of stay of 2 to 3 years. The less intensive incarcerated program for the lower risk sex offender is located on the grounds of the Southeast State Correctional Facility in Windsor and currently houses 24 offenders for an average length of stay of 12 to 18 months. The community-based programs are for sex offenders who are assessed at time of sentencing as low risk, amenable for treatment, and exhibiting the self-control to manage their deviant behavior under a probationary sentence. The community-based programs are also for those sex offenders who have completed one of the incarcerated treatment programs.

Entrance criteria for all of the programs require the offender to take responsibility for his offense and express an interest in treatment. If placed on probation, the offender is mandated into one of the specialized community programs. If sentenced to prison, the offender will not be recommended for parole until successfully completing the incarceration program. The treatment programs are based on a cognitive-behavioral and relapse prevention model of treatment and supervision. The clinicians are licensed at a masters level or Ph.D level. All clinicians from the community-based treatment programs attend monthly supervision meetings. Clinicians in the incarcerated programs meet on a weekly basis. Probation and parole officers receive specialized training on the supervision of sex offenders. The collaboration between clinicians and correctional staff is an essential part of the VTPSA.

Harvey was referred to the intensive sex offender program because he was a rapist. He was transferred to NWSCF to undergo a psychosexual evaluation to assess his treatment needs and amenability to treatment. The evaluation consisted of a clinical interview, paper and pencil tests, and a plethysmograph* to assess his deviant arousal. During the evaluation Harvey was placed on the treatment unit. This allowed Harvey to talk to other men in the treatment program about their views on the program. Some of his anxiety was relieved by talking to other men in his situation. Up to that time he had never talked to another sex offender about his problems; in fact, aside from the investigating police officer and his attorney he had not discussed his crimes with anyone.

Harvey was found appropriate for treatment and upon entering the program was assigned to a core group. This core group had seven other sex offenders in it; there were both rapists and child molesters in the group. Harvey

(continued)

(continued)

remained in this core group for the 2.5 years he was in treatment, and the group met twice a week for a total of 5 hours. Harvey also participated in up to two specialty groups during each week. The focus of the specialty groups changed every 4 to 8 months. One of the first groups Harvey participated in was a behavior therapy group. The penile plethysmograph had shown Harvey to be aroused to coercive and aggressive sex. His deviant arousal increased during times he was angry. In the behavior therapy group Harvey learned to reduce and manage his deviant sexual arousal. Because anger was so tied to his deviant arousal, Harvey also participated in two anger management groups. One group dealt with the immediate management of anger, and the other group dealt with the more long-term chronic anger that Harvey had struggled with since childhood when he was physically abused by his father.

It took Harvey a long time to sincerely empathize with his victims. Similar to many sex offenders, at the start of the treatment process, Harvey felt remorse for himself and guilt for what he had put his family through. His victims came in third. This changed over the course of treatment. To feel empathy for his victims, Harvey needed to really look at the harm he caused, not only his four victims, but also their families and friends. Harvey was very self-absorbed when he entered treatment, and he repeated the victim empathy group twice before the treatment staff felt he had gained sufficient skills from the group. The last assignment in the victim empathy group is for the offender to role play his

offense first as himself and then as his victim. If a victim wants to meet with his or her abuser that meeting would be arranged by the treatment staff. The most common meeting in recent years is for parents of child victims to meet with the abuser. These meetings are facilitated by a therapist, and the emphasis is that the meeting is for the benefit of the victim and/or family members not the offender. Harvey wanted to meet with his victims, but they did not want to meet with him. Instead, two of them met with his parole officer prior to his parole to discuss his risk factors, his parole conditions, and his progress in treatment.

Five basic treatment goals form the framework for both the incarcerated and community-based programs:

- Offenders must accept full responsibility for their sexually aggressive behavior and modify the cognitive distortions they use to justify their offending behaviors.

- Offenders must develop victim empathy and understand the consequences of their sexually aggressive behavior toward their victims.

- Offenders must learn to control their deviant sexual arousal.

- Offenders must improve social competence, particularly in the areas that appear to be most directly related to their sexual-offending patterns.

- Offenders must develop relapse prevention skills[†] that will provide them with the skills to identify risk factors and in turn develop strategies for interrupting or exiting from their cycle.

Before entering any of the VTPSA treatment programs offenders sign a limited confidentiality waiver to facilitate communication

among clinicians and the Department of Corrections. Offenders also are given a treatment agreement that informs them of the treatment procedures, risks, and benefits of treatment and limits on confidentiality. The program employs a closely monitored transition process as the offender moves from the incarcerated program to a community-based treatment program. Parole officers use relapse prevention strategies in their supervision and work closely with family members, employers, and other people who support the offender's reentry into the community. Support teams of volunteers who are specially trained also work with offenders who have little or no family support systems to return to when paroled.

Harvey completed the sex offender program while in prison. The treatment staff relied not only on their own observations but also on those of the correctional officers who observed Harvey in his daily interactions with other inmates. The first year in treatment Harvey was observed quietly strongarming other more vulnerable inmates to get his needs met. An important change in treatment occurred when Harvey stopped this behavior on the unit. Harvey also underwent another psychosexual evaluation prior to his community release.

Before his transition back into the community, Harvey and his therapist met with his parole officer. Harvey discussed his offenses in detail, outlined his risk factors,[‡] and discussed his relapse prevention plan. The parole officer talked to Harvey about the requirements on parole. The therapist was there to ensure that all relevant information on Harvey's progress in treatment was discussed. Potential problem areas were also discussed along with Harvey's coping strategies. The parole officer had already met with his wife and children. A later meeting took place between Harvey, his therapist, and the three volunteers who had chosen to support him during his transition back into the community. Although Harvey's wife had stayed with Harvey during his incarceration, there was concern the marriage might fail, and if so Harvey would need added support. His in-laws were particularly upset that their daughter had elected to stay with Harvey and would have preferred a divorce.

Upon release, Harvey participated in a weekly treatment group and every 2 weeks saw a marriage counselor with his wife. The first 3 months on parole were hard for Harvey. His wife was more independent. His children, although glad to have him back home, had very active school and social lives. He was insecure about seeing old friends. Working a 40-hour week, attending his therapy sessions, and making his weekly meeting with his parole officer had him exhausted and resentful by the weekend. And yet the structure was also reassuring. Meeting the men in his treatment group was particularly helpful as three of the men had been through the same program at NWSCF. They had experienced many of the same problems and anxieties that Harvey was talking about.

The treatment program did not cure Harvey, but it did give him the skills to handle difficulties in a responsible manner without hurting others. He began to see himself as a recovering sex offender (similar to a recovering alcoholic)—he might have urges to lose his temper or be abusive to another person, but

he had a choice as to how he would respond. He also had acquired skills to respond in a way that would not hurt others. Anger continued to be Harvey's most significant risk factor, but he now had tools to either resolve or lower his feelings of anger. He no longer denied his feelings of anger; he had learned that feeling anger was not the problem, it was his response to anger. Now when he felt anger, he knew it was time to use the relapse prevention tools he learned in treatment. He also discovered how important it was to talk over even the smallest problem with people who knew about his sexually abusive history.

There is an ongoing debate on the issue of treatment effectiveness and whether it is cost effective. McGrath (1995) analyzed the cost effectiveness of outpatient treatment. He used Vermont salaries to estimate the average cost of one reoffense. The costs included pretrial investigation, court costs, incarceration, incarcerated treatment, parole supervision, and victim-related costs. The average cost of a reoffense came to $138,828. McGrath then estimated the costs of outpatient treatment in Vermont. With offenders paying on an ability-to-pay basis and the Department of Corrections supplementing the difference, the cost to the Department of Corrections is on average, $346 per offender per year. The total cost of treatment per offender, based on 3 years of weekly treatment, is $1,038. Using a cost-benefit model, McGrath examined savings for 100 treated versus 100 untreated sex offenders. The conclusions were that when there is no difference in the recidivism rate between treated and untreated offenders, the cost to the state is the additional $103,800 of treatment funds ($1,038 × 100) that

the Department of Corrections spends to supplement the treatment groups. The savings start if recidivism is reduced by as little as 1 percent when the offender engages in treatment.

The penile plethysmograph is used to measure erectile response in males. During this procedure the client is instructed, in the privacy of the laboratory room, to place a gauge onto the shaft of his penis. The gauge is connected to the chart, which is in the adjoining room as is the evaluator who has verbal contact with the client during the evaluation. The client, seated in a recliner, is presented with both deviant and nondeviant sexual stimuli, and the gauge detects the change in the size of the penis. The erectile response, which is recorded on a strip chart operated by the evaluator, provides a record of the client's arousal pattern. The stimuli typically used are audiotapes and slides.

When audiotapes are used, the client is given a set of earphones. The audiotapes include both normal and deviant sexual activity of both sexes. When slides are used, the image is projected on the wall or screen in front of the client. The typical slides include both nude and clothed poses of males and females of varying ages.

†*Relapse prevention is a self-management program designed to teach individuals who are trying to change their behaviors to identify problems early on and to develop strategies to avoid or cope more effectively with their problems to avoid a relapse (Marlatt & Gordon, 1980).*

‡*Risk factors are a set of internal stimuli or external circumstances that threaten the offender's sense of self-control and thus increase the risk of reoffending. For example, risk factors for a child molester may include having a job that allows access with minor children such as being a janitor at a elementary school or dating a woman who has children.*

Source: Georgia Cumming is the Director of VTPSA. She prepared this program focus especially for the 2nd edition of Corrections: A Comprehensive View.

subsequently admit their guilt. The rationale for working with deniers is twofold: (1) if these offenders fail to receive treatment they will reoffend; and (2) if offered in a community setting, this saves the money associated with their incarceration. Most programs have allowed those in complete denial to participate in programs for a certain period of time after which, if there is no change, they will be terminated. One other option is a pretreatment program that can be used both in prison or as part of community-based programs (see Table 8.4).

Table 8.4
Stages of Pretreatment

Stage 1 Showing offenders that the therapist respects them by recognizing that while they have done bad things, they are not bad people

Stage 2 Dealing with the offenders' discomfort, giving them hope by telling them that treatment offers a good chance for positive change; making offenders recognize the sooner they are honest, the faster they will receive treatment

Stage 3 Assisting offenders to understand the protective function of denial; make them understand that other people have inappropriate sexual feelings, and that they have the power to not act on these feelings; make them realize that despite the fact that they committed inappropriate sex acts they are not monsters

Stage 4 At this point offenders may be ready to risk abandoning old defensive measures and to accept accountability and appropriate forms of sexual behavior. This includes inviting thoughts and actions that emphasize that offenders can make choices about what they do and be accountable for their behavior by focusing on how the offenders' behavior has resulted in their current predicament.

Stage 5 Here the focus is on enhancing empathy by forcing offenders to take responsibility for their actions. This includes providing examples of empathetic behavior, such as the therapist recognizing the hurt the offender is feeling, acknowledging the offenders' own sexual victimizations, and using hypothetical questions.

Stage 6 At this point, offenders may be ready to gradually confront their behavior. This may start with confrontation about previous similar acts and make offenders more willing to deal with their instant offenses.

Finally, it is suggested that offenders be allowed to participate in this program for 6 months, after which if they show only minimal change in their denial or resistance to acknowledging their guilt, the program should be terminated.

What do you think? Should we focus on trying to help those that deny their involvement in their sexual offense and fail to acknowledge their responsibility, or should we just deal with those who recognize and take responsibility for their deviant sexual behavior?

Source: S. C. Brake & D. Shannon (1997). Using Pretreatment to Increase Admission in Sex Offenders. In B. K. Schwartz & H. R. Cellini (eds.). *The Sex Offender: New Insights, Treatments, Innovations, and Legal Developments*. Kingston, NJ: Civic Research Institute.

Child Molesters   Vaughn and Sapp (1990) surveyed adult sex offender treatment administrators to obtain a perspective on the position of sex offenders in the inmate status hierarchy. They reported that sex offenders were on the lower end of the hierarchical spectrum. However, there is a distinction made between rapists and child molesters, with rapists ranking higher. Child molesters are perceived as socially degraded by their fellow inmates, and they are fair game for violence-prone inmates (see Figure 8.13) (Toch, 1978, pp. 23–24). Vaughn and Sapp (1990) relate this, in part, to molesters' passive personalities.

Mature Inmates

Inmates who are older or younger than their fellow prisoners present unique challenges to the corrections system. Both the proportion of older Americans in the U.S. population and the average age of the general population have been increasing dramatically since the end of the Baby Boom. We will use the term **mature offenders** to describe this population, because it avoids some semantic baggage associated with the terms *older* and *elderly*. This commonly includes those 45 to 65, with most authors deciding to use ages 50 or 55 as the lower cutoff age. The rationale for this, as Anno (1991a) notes, is that "experienced correctional health practitioners have argued for a lower age definition of elderly as applied to those incarcerated on the grounds that . . . inmates' biological ages frequently are considerably higher than their chronological ages owing to substance abuse, smoking, poor nutrition and lack of prior care, among other factors" (p. 145). We are designating as older or mature those inmates who are age 50 or over simply because this is the

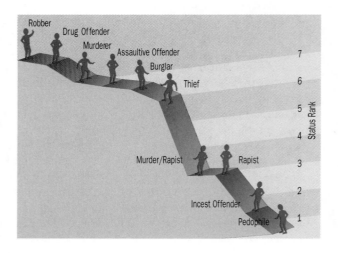

Figure 8.13   *Correctional Status Hierarchy*

Source: M. S. Vaughn and A. D. Sapp (1990). Less than utopian: Sex offender treatment in a milieu of power struggles, status positioning, and inmate manipulation in state correctional institutions, pp. 73–89, *The Prison Journal*, July. Reproduced with permission of Sage Publications, Inc.

12 Measures of Recidivism

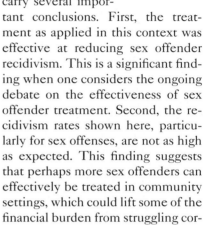

Four hundred seven adult sex offenders in a community residential treatment facility were divided into control groups as follows: treatment completers (*n* = 167), passive failure to complete (*n* = 107), and treatment failures (*n* = 133). Twelve measures of recidivism were collected on each offender through the National Center on the Identification of Criminals and the Utah Bureau of Criminal Identification. The recidivism measures were as follows: probation revoked, parole revoked, warrant issued for nonsex offense, warrant issued for sex offense, rearrested for misdemeanor nonsex offense, rearrested for misdemeanor sex offense, convicted of misdemeanor nonsex offense, convicted of misdemeanor sex offense, rearrested for felony nonsex offense, rearrested for felony sex offense, convicted of felony nonsex offense, and convicted of a felony sex offense. The time at risk of the offenders in this population was 4 years with a standard deviation of 2.4 years. The median number of years at risk was 3, and the range was up to 10 years.

The data show that for all categories of recidivism, the more treatment completed, the less recidivism. For rule violations (failure to report, drinking, curfew, etc.), there was 67 percent recidivism for the treatment failures, 38 percent for the passive failures, and 21 percent for the treatment completers (chi square $p \leq .001$). For non-sex offenses, the recidivism rate was 32 percent for treatment failures, 20 percent for passive failures, and 16 percent for the treatment completers (chi square $p \leq .05$). For sex offenses, the recidivism rate was 28 percent for treatment failures, 19 percent for passive failures, and 13 percent for the treatment completers (chi square $p \leq .05$). Across all definitions of recidivism, the result was similar. The treatment failures reoffended at a 71 percent rate, the passive failures at a 48 percent rate, and the treatment completers at a 31 percent rate (chi square $p \leq .001$).

These results carry several important conclusions. First, the treatment as applied in this context was effective at reducing sex offender recidivism. This is a significant finding when one considers the ongoing debate on the effectiveness of sex offender treatment. Second, the recidivism rates shown here, particularly for sex offenses, are not as high as expected. This finding suggests that perhaps more sex offenders can effectively be treated in community settings, which could lift some of the financial burden from struggling correctional systems.

Source: Prepared by S. P. Kramer, L. Bench, Ph.D., & S. Erickson (1999) for the 2nd edition of this text.

most commonly used age and provides us with a greater range of information.

It is no surprise that the average age of prison inmates has also increased, along with the number of inmates over age 50. During the 11 years from 1986 to 1997, the proportion of inmates 55 and over increased by 300 percent (American Correctional Association, 1986, 1997). Further, the Florida Department of Corrections reported that, in 1990, the proportion of inmates over 50 was increasing faster than the total inmate population. By 2025, it is estimated that mature inmates will compose 25 percent of the inmate population (Joinovich, 1997).

Types of Older Offenders   Mature offenders can be classified into three groups based on their incarceration histories (Dugger, 1988; Flynn, 1992; Morton, 1992a). The first group consists of offenders who have usually committed and were imprisoned for their first crime after age 50. Their crimes typically involve murder, manslaughter, rape, or other sexual offenses. Nevertheless, they are likely to see their crimes as spontaneous and perceive themselves as noncriminals (Teller & Howell, 1981). As newcomers to prison, they are naive about prison life, which often makes them easy prey for more prisonwise inmates. Thus, they may find adjustment to prison difficult. Frequently, they have community ties, making placement easier for them on release than the other two groups of older inmates.

The second group is part of the **long-term offender (LTO)** group. This group consists of individuals who committed very serious crimes at an early age, were sentenced to long terms, and have grown old in prison. Although their adjustment to prison is often relatively successful, their extended sentences often weaken or destroy their ties with family and friends. This, combined with a lack of appropriate work experience, makes their readjustment to the community upon release difficult. The LTO group is discussed in more detail in the next section.

The third group consists of **career criminals,** or habitual offenders who serve life in prison in installments (i.e., they are in and out of prison all of their lives). They usually adjust well to prisons and present few management problems. Frequently, they have substance abuse problems—usually alcohol addiction—which becomes more serious as they age. They also lack the necessary social, life, and coping skills to be successful on the outside, which contributes to their recidivism. Their community ties are weak or nonexistent, and their poor employment records make it difficult for them to obtain meaningful jobs. Thus, reintegration into the community is a difficult experience for many of these inmates.

The Integration of Mature Inmates   Although it seems obvious that because of their age and other factors mature inmates should be segregated from the general prison population, there are many issues that must be considered when making this decision. First, although they are chronologically 50 or over, this group is far from uniform. Like the general population, the mental and physical condition of older inmates varies widely, with some being both mentally and physically old at age 50, whereas others are young in body and mind at 60, 70, or even older (White & Abeles, 1990). Second, placement and programming of these inmates must be consistent with the Federal Rehabilitation Act of 1973 and the Americans with Disabilities Act of 1990. Both acts prohibit discrimination against people with disabilities, which are more often found in the older population. These pieces of legislation call for mainstreaming people with these disabilities whenever possible and require that they have equal access to all services and programs (Flynn, 1992; Morton, 1992a).

Mainstreaming, or the placement of mature inmates in the general population, has historically had a stabilizing effect on prisons, because mature inmates have had a calming and settling effect on younger inmates (Flynn, 1992; Kratcoski & Babb, 1990). However, a decline in the respect for elders by inmates has reduced this effect. One solution to keeping older inmates in the general population is to cluster them in their own living units. Not only do older inmates prefer this, but it also provides them more safety. This also gives them a respite from the loud and more physically active younger inmates. Mainstreaming also ensures that mature inmates have the same access to programming and services as younger inmates and allows placement at a prison closer to the inmate's home community, which facilitates visits from family and friends.

There are also persuasive arguments for establishing special units to house and provide programming for older inmates. First, many existing physical plants often fail to meet the needs of older inmates. Historically, prisons have been designed to accommodate healthy, young, dangerous, and violent offenders. These large institutions have multitiered cell blocks that are poorly equipped to deal with aging inmates who may be impaired in some way (Flynn, 1992). Second, even though many elderly inmates are serving time for serious violent crimes, a large proportion do not present high security risks and could be placed in less secure settings, allowing the expensive facilities to be used for those who really require them (Flynn, 1992; Vito & Wilson, 1985). Finally, there is a need to provide for the special health requirements of this group, including identifying, monitoring,

and treating chronic ailments and geriatric medical problems as they develop (Flynn, 1992; Lipson, 1990).

Systems with sizable numbers of older inmates "should provide a flexible continuum of care and services from inmate admission to release that will ensure that older offenders are managed in the most effective way" (Morton, 1999, p. 5). Thus, most older inmates should be mainstreamed. Recognizing that the level of functioning of these inmates varies, a good classification system helps because it offers the maximum degree of flexibility in inmate placement (Morton, 1992a). These inmates also need to be reassessed more often than the general population. Staff need training in recognizing problems of the elderly, and health services staff must be cognizant of their needs as well (Morton, 1999). Others who cannot function effectively in the general population should be placed in special units that can provide a protected environment and the medical care they need. With continued public intolerance of crime and such bills as "three strikes and you're out" and "truth-in-sentencing laws," requiring inmates to serve 85 percent of their sentences, it is likely that sizable numbers of inmates will be growing old in our state and federal prison systems (Camp & Camp, 1994a; Flynn, 1992).

Finally, the pursuit of early release programs for older inmates, based on such risk factors as potential recidivism and other considerations, appears to be desirable. Age is an extremely reliable predictor of recidivism, because, generally, younger males are 4.8 times more likely to be rearrested than those 45 and over. Also, on humanitarian grounds the early release of older inmates, particularly the infirm and terminally ill, gives them the opportunity to spend their last months or years with family and friends or at least provides a more normal living setting. Cost is also a factor. Nationally, it costs an average of $67,000 annually to incarcerate one elderly inmate; this is three times the cost for younger inmates (Turley, 1990).

However, transitioning into the community presents a challenge because these inmates have frequently outlived or alienated any family they have, they may require skilled home nursing care for medical problems, and the placement of older inmates in the community is difficult. Some of these inmates even refuse parole because they have no place to go. Also, it is frightening for someone who has spent 20 years or more in prison to be released without a support system. This requires that correctional systems develop working relationships with outside agencies that can provide the necessary support, housing, and medical care (Morton, 1999).

Programming for Older Offenders   Although many institutions have programs that mature inmates may attend, only a few have programs designed specifically for them (Voinovich et al., 1997). The most extensive of these types of programs was called The Pennsylvania Project, which began in 1973 and ended in 1982 due to

Programs for mature inmates vary from one institution to another and may focus on sports and recreation, education, arts and crafts, or other types of activities.

overcrowding and lack of finances. The Pennsylvania Project provided educational and counseling opportunities that focused on life skills, remedial education, and communication and recreational skills (Harter & Oehler, 1997).

Existing programs for older offenders vary. Ten institutions have sports and recreation programs for inmates 40 and older. Other institutions that offer services specifically for mature offenders provide several opportunities. Programs may include lifestyle alternatives in exercise, nutritional, or medical needs, therapeutic arts and crafts, issues surrounding incarceration, and educational programs on the aging process (Voinovich et al., 1997). Although most older inmates work, many do face age-related limitations. Some may not be able to work full time and those working outside may require more breaks or may be more susceptible to dehydration. Another solution is to follow the BOP system, which gives the aged and the infirm opportunities to work by bringing the work to their units and allowing them to work at their own pace (Morton, 1999).

Recommendations for future programs and resources to assist mature inmates in prison include adequate clothing and supplies (e.g., geriatric furniture, walkers, dentures, warmer clothing, etc.); the development of an interagency agreement with the Department of Aging; the employment of rehabilitation specialists and occupational and physical therapists; and more innovative programming (e.g., health education, spiritual programming, estate/wills/funeral planning, establishment of a hospice unit) (Voinovich et al., 1997). Such programs may face problems. Table 8.5 presents several issues that may emerge with mature inmate programming.

Long-Term Offenders

It is difficult to define the *long-term offenders* population (LTOs) because there is no agreement about what constitutes "long term." Some scholars have suggested that the term should be applied to offenders who have received a sentence of 5 years, some 7 or more, and some 10 or more. Regardless of the minimum amount of time required to qualify as a long-termer, inmates serving long sentences require increasing attention simply because there are greater numbers of them. They are also likely to cause unique management problems and require different programming approaches from short-term inmates.

Since the late 1970s, sentencing patterns emphasizing determinate and mandatory minimum sentences

---

Table 8.5

Issues in Mature Inmate Programming

---

1. *Health Care* The greatest contributor to the high cost of aging inmates is medical expenses. Given the increasing number of inmates with noncommutable sentences, correctional health care is going to require a geriatric specialization. Specific problems include cost (e.g., hospice, chronic illness treatment, etc.) as well as other issues (e.g., compassionate release for the terminally ill).
2. *Depression* Elderly inmates are substantially more likely to experience depression than their younger counterparts. The cause of their depression may stem from deterioration brought on by long confinement, loss of family or friends, etc.
3. *Nutrition* Elderly inmates have unique dietary needs. For example, because of their sedentary lifestyle, as well as their reduction in muscle tissue, older inmates need fewer calories and less protein.
4. *Staff* A major issue in many prisons is the lack of effectively trained staff to deal with mature offenders. Further, even with training, some correctional staff may lack the interpersonal skills and/or aptitude to deal with elderly inmates.

Sources: T. Edwards (1999). The Aging Inmate Population, *SLC Special Series Report.* Longmont, CO: The National Institute of Corrections; S. M. Hunter and M. L. Thigpen (1997). Prison Medical Care: Special Needs Populations and Cost Control, *Special Issues in Corrections.* Longmont, CO: NIC.

Table 8.6
Profile of Long-Term Inmates

- *Age* Thirty-five percent of long-term inmates are currently age 40 years or older as compared with 19 percent of inmates sentenced to less than 15 years.
- *Race* Blacks (52.5%) and Hispanic (27.3%) are overrepresented in the long-term inmate population.
- *Gender* Males account for 97.6 percent of the 7,987 long-term inmates.
- *Education* Long-term inmates were more likely to have been a high school graduate (53%) than shorter-term inmates (44%).
- *Time Remaining* The majority of inmates (60%) serving long sentences have at least 10 years remaining on their sentence; nearly 10 percent of 792 inmates have 25 years or more left to serve before being eligible for parole.
- *Crime Category* Ninety percent (N = 7,186) of long-term inmates are incarcerated for violent felony offenses (VFOs); most are incarcerated for murder (68%). An additional 9 percent of long-term inmates are serving sentences of at least 15 years for drug crimes.
- *Security* LTOs are usually imprisoned at maximum security prisons.

This study shows the diversity of LTOs. Further, it concludes that while most young inmates eventually will return to communities within the state, many other inmates will grow old and die in prison. Of long-term inmates currently incarcerated, 704 will not be eligible for release until they are more than 70 years old.

Source: J. Lyons (1996). *Research in Brief: Long-Term Inmates*. Albany, NY: New York State Department of Corrections.

have resulted in an increasing number of inmates being imprisoned for longer periods of time.[14] As of 1997, at least 10 percent of the prison population had served 10 years or more. This represented a 4 percent increase from 1991 (Beck & Mumola, 1999). Moreover, 32.4 percent of inmates in adult correctional facilities were serving 20 years or more, life, or natural life (Camp & Camp, 1998). Federal Truth-in-Sentencing grants have provided financial incentives to be used for building or expanding new or temporary facilities to increase the number of beds for inmates required to serve at least 85 percent of their sentences. Mauer (1995), however, contends that operating and construction costs associated with increasing bed space will result in states spending between two and seven dollars for each dollar they receive in federal funds.

Table 8.6 shows the results of a New York State study on the characteristics of LTOs based on using a sentence of 15 years as the definitional criterion.

Differences from Other Inmates Although LTOs are far from a homogeneous group, their lengthy confinement has resulted in the development of similar attitudes and coping strategies (Cowles, 1990a; Flanagan, 1990; Gaes, 1990a). They seemed to shift their orientation from the outside world to the world inside the prison because of the difficulties that they face in maintaining outside relationships (Cowles, 1990b). Family and friends cannot expect to resume normal relationships with them in the near future, so this tends to reduce their motivation to continue relationships (Cowles, 1990b; Flanagan, 1990). Thus, a vital link is lost with the outside world (Flanagan, 1990). This usually means a loss of financial resources as well, which may force many LTOs to depend on illegitimate activities for their money. One way of providing legitimate outside contact for LTOs is through citizen volunteers who can help them maintain a connection with the outside and reduce feelings of abandonment. This may be one way of educating the public about these forgotten inmates (McGinnis, 1990).

Phases of Adjustment to Prison Life Upon entering prison, LTOs manifest certain problem behaviors and attitudes that typically change over time. Those with longer criminal records are more likely to be violent, particularly during the early part of their sentences; they are also more likely to have procriminal attitudes. This places them at higher risk for suicide than their short-term inmate counterparts (Porporino, 1990). However, as LTOs get older in prison, their criminal attitudes diminish regardless of their previous criminality.

LTOs first entering prison are typically in a state of denial. They work on and file appeals and try to figure out other ways of getting out of prison. At some point, most of them accept their imprisonment and begin to look for ways to make it on a daily basis. They develop a perspective that involves focusing on the "here and now." This is often reinforced by associating with other LTOs. This coping strategy takes the form of doing one's own time, which involves avoiding trouble (e.g., minding your own business); using time profitably (involvement in work, education, etc.); and, where possible, maintaining interaction with outsiders (Gaes, 1990a, 1990b). LTOs who establish close friendships face the devastation of having these relationships severed by transfers and releases (Flanagan, 1990). To avoid this pain, they may either develop guarded relationships with other inmates or adopt a solitary lifestyle, labeled the "behavioral deep freeze of incarceration" (Gaes, 1990a; Zamble & Porporino, 1988). Another problem faced by LTOs is separation from their family and friends. Possible ways of dealing with the issue of separation include allowing these inmates to have larger visiting lists to facilitate visits with their extended families and allowing more time for visitation and privileges such as home visits, furlough day visits, and family visitations, including conjugal visits (Santos, 1995).

Special Services It is important to consider how LTOs perceive the prison and its services because of the permanency of their confinement. Most people can tolerate unpleasant conditions for short periods of time, but this ability to cope can change when the conditions have to be endured for a lifetime. Many persons reading this book are students who may currently live under unfavorable conditions and eat food in a college cafeteria that is not particularly to their liking. All inmates find prison conditions, such as crowding, noise, and lack of privacy distasteful; however, for LTOs these discomforts are magnified, because this is their long-term home. LTOs expressed some concern about food quality, but Sabath and Cowles (1990) found that their greatest services-related concern was about medical treatment. They found that treatment professionals also had concerns about the quality of medical care received by LTOs. Both felt this was a consequence of the generally slow and inefficient state of service delivery in prison.

Management Challenges Consistent responses from LTOs about their incarceration include hopelessness, despondency, boredom, despair, and idleness. Such attitudes and feelings may present a challenge, because inmates who have nothing to lose are dangerous. Prison managers have agreed that, without incentives, there is little reason for inmates to follow the rules. Further, they have reported that managing such individuals is impossible unless you have something that they want.

Some have claimed that the management of difficult LTOs requires an "Earned Privileges Behavioral Management Philosophy," which is based on the premise that no inmate privilege should be viewed as a right. Access to physical fitness equipment, sources of entertainment, employment, and educational programs should be contingent on positive inmate behavior. Available good time must be earned and not given away. Moreover, sources of positive behavioral incentives, such as weights and televisions should not be eliminated. The elimination of positive behavioral motivators removes potentially critical management tools. Underlying this management model is a true "carrot and stick" approach to inmate behavioral management. Positive inmate behavior must be acknowledged and rewarded within standards that are clearly communicated to inmates. Punishment for rule infractions must be swift and certain and administered fairly and within the law. Sufficient beds in "segregation" must be available to punish rule breakers.

Each long-term inmate must understand his or her specific set of sanctions, as well as the possibilities to gain (limited) release time and improved living conditions. This educational process could begin with a personal explanation of the incentives for positive behavior and the sanctions for those who want to test the system. This must be reinforced for new inmates with actual experience to show how those with positive motivation

live in contrast to how others who choose not to participate positively live. There should be a clear distinction between the two possibilities (Hunter, Crew, Sexton & Lutz, 1997).[15]

Classification System Because LTOs are initially considered escape risks, they are usually assigned to more secure institutions and classified as close custody on admission. However, their classification should be reviewed every 6 months. If they demonstrate that they have made a successful adjustment, they can be moved to a less secure institution and after several years of good behavior have their custody status reduced. There are many views on LTO housing, but there is some consensus on placing those who are performing acceptably in discrete units within an institution as opposed to developing a special prison (Palmer, 1995). Mainstreaming this population may seem like a way of dispersing stable inmates throughout an institution, but it may have negative consequences for LTOs. In discrete units, LTOs are able to live in a quiet trouble-free environment where each inmate respects the others' rights, while at the same time offering one another both understanding and support. Feelings of isolation and alienation are virtually unknown. Friendships are typically maintained for the duration of inmates' sentences and beyond. As Palmer (1995) states: "Those paroled earliest help their friends still inside with financial assistance and vocationally and with general moral support."

Many LTOs may qualify behaviorally for movement to minimum security prisons, but the high level of integration between these facilities and the community makes these assignments extremely unlikely for the majority of LTOs. In light of this, an alternative living environment should be available as an incentive for good behavior. Special housing units for LTOs should look like contemporary homes and be built using the cottage-style model for housing juveniles in residential treatment. They could be in a secure perimeter but would resemble a cottage-type boardinghouse and cost about one fifth of traditional cells. Inside, inmates would be permitted to have items such as furniture, personal clothing, and gardens and plants. Another privilege could include allowing inmates to have pets. Pets have been shown to combat depression and provide inmates with renewed interest in their surroundings (Palmer, 1995).

However, whereas some states have made efforts toward creating more flexible programming and have dealt with some issues related to classification, most of the 24 jurisdictions in the Iowa study had not developed a new classification system for LTOs. This may be related to the fact that the full impact of truth-in-sentencing laws has not been felt (i.e., the anticipated increase in the number of inmates has not yet occurred). If states fail to recognize the potential effects of truth-in-sentencing and other such punitive policies, they will likely find themselves with overcrowded prisons, placing both staff and inmates in peril.

Management Plans for Individual LTOs   LTOs need to have their prison careers structured rather than just being assigned to jobs or programs, or worse, being idle (Hunter et al., 1996).[16] This type of career planning can be accomplished by a system of individualized management plans that match each inmate's needs with the best available programs. Such plans would provide each inmate with a guide for organizing his or her life according to special activity needs based on that inmate's psychological and physical health conditions. The plans must be individualized; all long-term inmates will follow different paths of adjustment and interaction during their inmate career. To succeed in fulfilling their purposes, while also maintaining security, programs must be "owned" by the long-term inmates—individual management plans will do this. These plans can, and should be, implemented in accordance with the more general management strategy of making privileges contingent on behavior. Thus, for example, participation in educational and employment programs should be tied to such behaviors as staying out of gangs, not confronting correc-

Correctional institutions may have to make special provisions to meet the needs of physically or medically handicapped offenders, such as this inmate with AIDS.

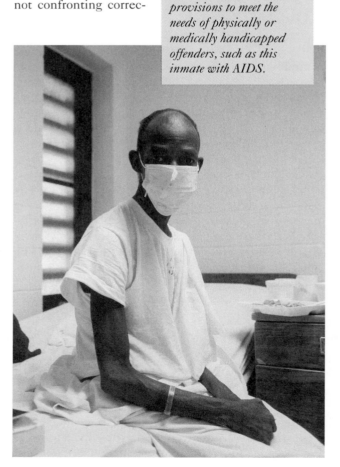

tional officers, and performing to a high standard on a work assignment. Inmate idleness, coupled with overcrowding, poses a significant threat to the safety of both inmates and correctional employees. This combination is a priority issue that must be addressed (Hunter et al., 1997). One approach involves offering inmates the opportunity for education and vocational training. This training is then related to the requirements of a job in an industry program that has promotion possibilities (Gaes, 1990b; McGinnis, 1990).

Another option that has been successful is to involve LTOs in high-technology kinds of programs that require long-term skill development. For example, in a Missouri facility, Cowles (1990a) experimented successfully with a program involving LTOs in video production. Although there were initial reservations about bringing expensive video equipment into the prison, he reported that the inmates maintained the equipment, created viable products, and behaved maturely and responsibly.

Another option for LTOs is to legitimize the prison's **cottage industries,** such as tailoring, legal research, and correspondence, which are currently part of the illegitimate prison economy. Cottage industries are work that inmates can do alone or in their cells. If these activities are legitimized and put under the control of prison administration, they can provide LTOs with viable and meaningful jobs, while facilitating a more functional facility (Cowles, 1990a).

Finally, LTOs should be encouraged to obtain the education required for such jobs as clerks, accountants, vocational counselors, health-care assistants, life-skill coaches, and lead workers in industrial shops. A rather unique idea would be to create institutional research positions where inmates would engage in activities such as monitoring the institutional environment, planning programs, and solving grievances (Palmer, 1995).

The Youthful Offender

There is no universally agreed-on definition of a **youthful offender.** However, generally those between the ages of 13 and 24 fall into discussions of this offender group. Juvenile violence, coupled with the transformation of criminal justice legislation, has blurred the separation between juveniles and adults. The result is that more youths are being tried in adult courts. Although the modal age for adulthood is 18, the lower age range for transferring a juvenile to adult court ranges from 10 to 14.

Between 1980 and 1997, violent arrests for offenders between 10 and 17 peaked in 1994 and then dropped steadily; however, they were still above their 1980 rates. Further, the percentage of those under 18 who were arrested rose 48 percent for violent index offenses and 7 percent for property offenses between 1988 and 1997 (FBI, 1998). Figure 8.14 shows the increase in the number of those 18 and under in prison for different time pe-

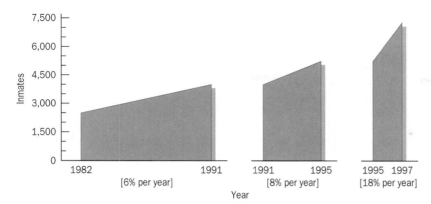

Figure 8.14 *Number of Inmates Under 18*

Source: R. B. Levinson & J. J. Green, III (1998). New Boys on the Block: Under-18-Year-Olds in Adult Prisons. Lanham, MD: American Correctional Association. Reprinted with permission.

riods between 1982 and 1997 (Levinson & Green, 1998). Although youth offenders are increasing numerically, their percentage of the prison population still is less than half of 1 percent (Beck & Mumola, 1999).

Housing and Programming of Youth Offenders   Most adults corrections systems believe that they can simply use existing adult classification systems on violent youths now entering prison (Glick & Sturgeon, 1998.)[17] Even though they have committed heinous crimes, they are still in the middle of their adolescent development. Juveniles "still require teaching, training, and loving" (Gondles, 1997). Youths are often in situations where they are targets of

aggression, and they also receive rewards for engaging in it. Moreover, adolescents, by definition, usually lack the appropriate prosocial skills and information-processing skills to deal with such problems.

Table 8.7 looks at trends in remanding juveniles to adult systems and co-mingling them with adults in jails and prison.

Another area of concern with a youthful offenders population is their greater likelihood of being victims of sexual and other types of assaults. The prototype prison rape victim in these facilities is young, if not the youngest in the facility; they are very small in stature relative to the other adults, which makes them subject to attack. These prisoners are characterized as inexperienced "lambs," unable to cope with predator inmates (Maitland

Youthful offenders are more likely than older inmates to be victims of sexual and other types of assaults. Their fear of further victimization can give rise to anxiety, depression, and other psychological disturbances.

Table 8.7

Trends in Remanding Juveniles to Adult Courts

1. There was an increase in transfers and remands of juveniles to adult jurisdictions and facilities.
2. The age categories being applied to juveniles to transfer them to adult jurisdictions increasingly are blurring the lines separating the child from the juvenile and from the adult. The juvenile age category (for juvenile delinquents) slowly is being eroded.
3. Younger juveniles increasingly are being remanded to adult facilities.
4. Most jurisdictions responding to this survey relied upon a transfer hearing process.[18] However, there is an increasing trend toward (a) transferring juveniles automatically; (b) employing discretionary adjudication in juvenile cases (i.e., imposing mandatory minimum sentences); (c) extending juvenile court jurisdiction to beyond the age of majority; and (d) employing split sentences that mix both juvenile and adult sanctions. Added to this is what appears to be a new juvenile "three strikes" approach. This means that most juveniles convicted of two or three offenses in the same year will upon a subsequent conviction be deemed serious juvenile repeat offenders and automatically be tried in adult court. This type of leeway has resulted in some jurisdictions criminalizing the young offender beyond the scope of their crimes.
5. Imposing adult norms on juveniles eventually will create hybrid inmates with more social, emotional, and interpersonal problems.
6. Offense categories for which a juvenile may be transferred to an adult jurisdiction may be expanded as age categories are lowered.
7. Juveniles are committing more violent offenses against persons.
8. Young black men and women disproportionately are transferred to adult jurisdictions and remanded to adult facilities.
9. More young offenders potentially could be locked up in adult facilities than in juvenile facilities.
10. Over 50 percent of those responding to the study by Glick and Sturgeon indicated that youth offenders should be placed in juvenile facilities until they reach the age of majority or until they start presenting problems for the facility. For those jurisdictions housing juveniles 18 to 21 in adult facilities, 1 in 3 keeps them separated from adult contact.
11. Young offenders' safety in adult facilities appears to be the major problem challenging officials in adult facilities. Safety concerns are caused by rival gang violence and higher potential for sexual assault.
12. There does not seem to be a concerted effort to develop innovative programming for remanded juveniles. These youths require special programming that includes:
    - an assessment process that focuses on diagnosing learning disabilities, mental retardation, and emotional disturbances and then providing these youths with an immediate and positive experience that enhances their learning.
    - vocational training programs that are designed to meet individual needs and special disabilities. For youths it is critical to provide job training and marketable skills; many will be released while they are young and able to work.
    - intensive drug and alcohol treatment programs; improvements in food menus that meet the needs of a youthful population; and improved medical and dental care.
13. The boundaries of the adult, as a "reasoning and responsible" individual, are being consistently redrawn to encompass increasingly younger persons.

Sources: Adapted from B. Glick & W. Sturgeon (1998). *No Time to Play: Youth Offenders in Adult Correctional Systems.* Lanham, MD: American Correctional Association; P. Torbet, R. Gable, H. Hurst, I. Montgomery, L. Szymanski, & D. Thomas (1996, July). *State Responses to Serious and Violent Juvenile Crime.* Washington, DC: National Center for Juvenile Justice.

& Sluder, 1996). This makes them prime targets for becoming someone's "girlfriend" (Ziedenberg, 1997).

Fear of victimization can be devastating and affect an inmate's feeling of well-being:

> Fearful inmates experience a multitude of psychological disturbances. The inmate has difficulty working and satisfying the few practical demands of his environment. He is frequently anxious and depressed . . . has a low level of energy [and has feelings of hopelessness]. Fearful inmates are also more likely to report physical health problems and to express an overall concern about their physical well-being. (Ziedenberg, 1997, p. 24)

The differences between inmates who adjust well and those who do not are germane, given the potential implications for each. Inmates with adjustment problems have few inmate friends, and others would not aid them if they were attacked. They are often victimized in prison, and thus have high fear of further victimization. As a consequence, they are more likely to be anomic— that is, to feel that the guidelines for acceptable behavior are absent, unclear, or confusing.

The most healthy inmates, on the other hand, believe that other inmate friends would come to their defense if they were attacked, and accordingly, they have little fear of being victimized. Furthermore, these inmates have inmate friends to confide in about personal problems, and thus, they have low levels of anomie. These inmates may present problems classified as aggressors or be affiliated with gangs (Maitland & Sluder, 1996).

Table 8.8
Desirable Characteristics of Youthful Offender Staff

- Staff should have special training or education in adolescent development.
- Working with youthful offenders requires a great deal of patience. Unlike their adult counterparts, youthful offenders cling to staff. They require an explanation (as do most adolescents) for every order or request. They question everything they are asked to do and as one group of correctional staff said, "they (youthful offenders) whine more than adults do."
- Youthful offenders require staff to listen much more than the adult population does. Some staff feel it is because they spend more time with the staff than adults do. "They are talking constantly. Listening to what they have to say provides significant insights into the individual and to the entire youthful offender population as a whole." Relatedly, it is equally as important for staff to communicate effectively with inmates. Although this may be frustrating, it is fundamental for staff-inmate relations.
- Youthful offenders need stability in their lives. It is incumbent upon the staff to create a consistent environment that is constant, safe, and secure. Staff attendance is an important ingredient of that stability. One group of correctional supervisors observed that the youthful offenders know staff's days off, and when someone takes an unscheduled day off, it can be a source of disruption to the stability of the unit.
- Employees working with youthful offenders must have a positive attitude and be able to demonstrate that attitude in consistent and predictable behaviors. Youthful offenders, as a rule, have been exposed to a great deal of negativity and look to staff for positive reinforcement in their lives.
- To work effectively in youthful offenders programs, staff must be part of an overall team effort.
- To work effectively with this population, staff should have the physical ability to physically control a youthful offender. Also, working with youthful offenders is physically demanding because "they never stop." Correctional officers report that working with youthful offenders requires stamina because they constantly are occupied and actively doing something.

Source: Adapted from B. Glick & W. Sturgeon, with C. R. Venator-Santiago (1998). *No Time to Play: Youth Offenders in Adult Correctional Systems.* Lanham, MD: American Correctional Association.

Both custody and program staff may find these profiles of interest in identifying inmates who are likely to have difficulties in adjusting to the prison environment and treating them. The profiles may also be useful to medical and counseling staff to begin to explore whether inmate complaints are tied to individual and social factors rather than physiological problems. Inmate education and reception programs are suggested, in which inmates are more fully informed of the peculiarities of institutional life and afforded opportunities to de-

velop ties within their social settings. The prison staff has absolute control over vital decisions that directly impact inmates. Properly informed of the effects of various factors on inmate general well-being, corrections officials should be better positioned to make decisions involving inmate needs.

Finally, we examine the role of staff in dealing with youthful offenders. Two things are clear about youthful offenders: (1) they offer special challenges for staff; and (2) they require a special type of corrections staff that have traits and skills to work effectively with violent youthful offenders. Table 8.8 provides a more in-depth insight into the general requirements of staff who deal with youthful offenders.

Staff Training Ideally, these qualifications should exist before the correctional staff actually begins to work with the youthful offender population, but usually this is not practical. Instead, the training they receive is piecemeal. More important, however, is the content of the training. Training should focus on developing and/or improving the qualities noted in Table 8.8. It should not be restricted to just line staff who have direct contact with youthful offenders but also include key administrators, managers, and ancillary staff. Other important areas that all staff should be continually trained in include:

- *Conflict Resolution* These techniques are essential because youthful offenders constantly observe how staff deal with conflict. Staff should become masterful at practicing conflict resolution. Conflict resolution also plays an important part in the overall modeling that all staff who work with youthful offenders should display.
- *Role Modeling* This is important in working with youthful offenders because sometimes the correctional staff with whom they come into contact are the only stable adults that they have had in their lives. So correctional staff should present to these youth an impeccable role model.
- *Self-Defense* A course should teach a few basic self-defense techniques where mastery of the martial arts techniques is required. Staff who work with youthful offenders should have the ability to physically control those who act out violently, using the minimal amount of force to gain control effectively and efficiently.
- *Adolescent Behavior Patterns* Knowing and understanding the stages of adolescent behavior is critically important in discerning what is a rule violation and what is just part of growing up. The official disciplinary system should only be used for serious rule violations, and

the sanctions should be those geared toward things that youthful offenders do not want to lose, such as television privileges, recreation yard, or phone privileges. Often, they use the disciplinary system by committing rule violations to fulfill their own needs, such as getting a lockdown so that they do not have to go to school or getting placed in administrative segregation so that they will get a single cell. They use the system to escape reality. "They turn what the system considers a negative into a positive," one manager explained during a recent training session.

- *Security* Staff must be taught that working with youthful offenders requires increased security, vigilance, and strict adherence to basic security practices.
- *Supervision* Staff should be trained in understanding how adolescents recreate and spend their leisure time. It is critically important to be able to supervise youthful offenders both in group and individual activities so that they will use their free time constructively. (Glick & Sturgeon, 1998)

Summary

Prison classification is the sorting out procedure that results in matching a prisoner to the appropriate level of supervision (custody level), institutional protective barriers (security), programs, and services to meet his or her needs. This process periodically reviews the inmate's placement to achieve the most appropriate assignments possible. A good classification system protects inmates from one another, protects the public, makes efficient use of prison resources, controls inmates, and is a source of planning.

Classification can be divided into two phases: (1) initial determinations of the level of security and custody needed and program recommendations; and (2) periodic reclassification. Both phases require that appropriate scales be used to measure inmates' needs. In classifying inmates, it is important to make distinctions between security and custody.

The Bureau of Prisons uses objective criteria to classify inmates but also allows staff overrides. Initial classification considers the following items: public safety factors, types of detainers, severity of the current offense, expected length of incarceration, history of violence, and type of prior commitment. Based on an inmate's total score on the initial classification form he or she is placed in one of the following types of institutions: minimum security, low security, medium security, high security, or an administrative facility.

An inmate's initial review (reclassification) for a possible custody-level change uses the custody classification form. This may suggest reduced or increased security requirements based on the consideration of both precommitment and postcommitment variables. Each time inmates are reclassified, they are rated on the factors used for initial designation; escapes are now being included as a separate factor in the evaluation. These factors are percent of time served, involvement with drug/alcohol abuse, mental/psychological stability, type and number of the most serious incident report, frequency of disciplinary reports in the past year, family or community ties, and responsibility demonstrated by the inmate. Management variables are also considered in determining appropriate inmate placement.

Assessment of an inmate's program and service requirements is the third facet of the classification process. This involves a balance between security, inmate needs, and program availability. The BOP uses classification teams that include the unit manager, a case manager, a counselor, and usually an education advisor, a psychology services representative, and health services staff.

The U.S. prison population differs from the general population in several ways. For example, inmates are disproportionately young, male, and from minority groups. However, the proportions of female inmates and older inmates are increasing. The impact of objective classification can be seen in (1) more inmates being confined in less secure facilities with no concurrent increases in assaults or escapes; (2) a better balance in each facility's racial composition; (3) fewer transfers between institutions; (4) more current, consistent, and relevant information, enabling determination of the type of facilities that were needed, adjustment of staffing patterns, and more specific budget justifications; (5) the need for fewer secure beds, which saves scarce resources; and (6) more effectively planning to determine future resource needs, including staffing levels, inmate programs, and types of facilities.

Prisons use several forms of segregation, in which classification plays a part, to deal with certain categories of inmates. PC involves the segregation of a variety of inmates who are in serious danger of being harmed for reasons that include their offense (e.g., child molestation), gambling debts, sexual orientation, being identified as a snitch, being naive, and vendettas. One way to reduce the number of inmates in PC is to require that they identify enemies and verify their claims.

Supermax facilities are freestanding facilities, or distinct units within a facility, that provide for the management and secure control of inmates who have been officially designated as exhibiting violent or seriously disruptive behavior while incarcerated. Such inmates have been determined to be a threat to safety and security in traditional high-security facilities, and their behavior can be controlled only by separation, restricted movement, and limited direct access to staff and other inmates. To meet court requirements, these facilities must create means by which inmates can earn their way out. The BOP uses a three-tiered system of improving privileges as an incentive for inmates to adhere to standards of conduct.

Many inmates have unique characteristics and needs that separate them from others in the prison population. Examples of such "special categories" offenders include the mentally retarded, mature inmates, long-term offenders, youthful offenders, and sex offenders.

Inmates with psychological or behavioral disorders present management problems to the prison staff. Mentally handicapped inmates also require special programming, which may be difficult given that there are different levels of retardation. Retarded individuals are often ridiculed and abused, which raises issues about whether they should be segregated or mainstreamed.

Sex offenders present problems for both the community and corrections. Treatment of sexual offenders is controversial because the public generally feels that they should be punished, not treated. A variety of approaches are employed in treating sex offenders. Most programs incorporate both individual and group therapy, with a focus on group therapy. Research has shown that those who receive treatment have a lower rate of recidivism than those who go untreated.

Mature inmates also present unique challenges to corrections. Categorizations of older offenders include mature inmates, long-term offenders, and career criminals. Classification of older offenders should include both mainstreaming and segregation for those who need a protected environment. Existing programs for mature inmates are few in number but provide necessary special services, such as alternatives in exercising, geriatric furniture, walkers, health care, and so on.

The number of long-term offenders is increasing. They are different from other inmates in that they must adjust to the permanency of prison life. Most LTOs go through phases of this adjustment. Because they are a high-escape risk, LTOs require a stricter classification policy. These inmates do undergo regular reviews to determine whether they are eligible for a less stringent classification. Special precautions should also be taken to deal with feelings such as hopelessness, boredom, and idleness that are common among LTOs.

Finally, youthful offenders, even though they have committed "adult" crimes, still have adolescent needs—such as the needs to be taught, trained, and loved. Prisons must take special precautions because of their vulnerability to being victimized. Staff who deal with youthful offenders require unique training (e.g., in conflict resolution, role modeling, and so on). It is preferable that youth offenders under 18 first be placed in juvenile facilities and then be transferred to adult facilities. Another option is to have special facilities for those 14 to 18 and 19 to 24.

Critical Thinking Questions

1. Explain the major functions of classification.

2. If you were the commissioner of corrections for a state, would you choose an objective or subjective classification system? Justify your answer in terms of benefits to the inmates and the corrections system.

3. Analyze the differences between *security* and *custody*.

4. If you were a classification officer working for the BOP, what factors would you consider in initially classifying an inmate and in reclassifying an inmate?

5. Describe the reasons that prison systems use protective custody and supermax facilities.

6. Analyze the characteristics of prison inmates versus the general population. Why do these differences occur?

7. Discuss the changes that have occurred in the prison population. What are the main categories of offenders who require special programs or management in a correctional setting?

8. As a superintendent of a correctional mental health facility, what kinds of mental disorders would you be dealing with and what problems would you face in dealing with this population?

9. As a mentally retarded offender in prison, what problems would you face in adjusting to institutional life that are different from those faced by other inmates?

10. You are a consultant asked to recommend whether a state should begin providing sex offender treatment. What recommendations would you include in your report? Also, what type of programming would you provide?

11. What issues should be considered when planning for dealing with older offenders?

12. What are the problems associated with placing youths under 18 in adult facilities? Discuss some solutions to these problems.

13. You are asked to plan programming for long-term offenders. What issues would you have to consider in designing long-term programming for this group?

Test Your Knowledge

1. Through the mid-1970s, most classification decisions were based on:

   a. custody concerns.

   b. subjective judgment.

c.   convenience.

d.   objective tests.

2. Which of the following is true of classification?

a.   Inmates are only classified when they are in a correctional system.

b.   Inmates are only classified once to determine their appropriate security and custody levels and then regularly classified only with respect to changes in programming.

c.   Classification only deals with changes in inmate programming.

d.   Inmates receive an initial classification and then are reclassified regularly to determine if changes in custody, security, or programming are warranted.

3. The degree of staff supervision necessary to ensure adequate control of an inmate and minimize the danger that inmate may pose to the staff and other inmates is known as:

a.   security level.

b.   custody category.

c.   jurisdictional label.

d.   classification status.

4. Which of the following trends is/are occurring in the U.S. inmate population?

a.   There are proportionately more female inmates.

b.   The inmate population is getting older.

c.   There are proportionately more Hispanic inmates.

d.   All of the above are true.

5. Which of the following occurrences was apparently *most responsible* for the present volume of mentally disordered individuals in prison?

a.   the abolishment of the insanity defense

b.   new laws passed against erratic behavior in public

c.   the development of antipsychotic drugs

d.   the rapid spread of psychiatric therapy programs inside prisons

6. The Americans with Disabilities Act (ADA) of 1990

a.   applies to staff but not inmates.

b.   applies to mature and handicapped offenders but not others.

c.   applies to all inmates, staff, and visitors.

d.   does not apply within a correctional institution.

Endnotes

1. The material dealing with the BOP classification system was drawn from bureau policy statements, including PS#5100.07; 5270.07; 5290.10; 5290.12; and 53222.10. Dick (2000), a retired BOP warden, provided comments, interpretation, and concrete examples that greatly clarified this material. He also wrote the Supermax Program Focus, which deals with the history of federal supermaxes, and provides a detailed description of the new supermax at Florence.

Terry Hammons, a retired BOP classification manager, provided the case example used on the scoring forms, did the actual scoring and interpretation of initial classification and reclassification, and assisted in interpreting this material.

2. A warrant placed against a person incarcerated in a correctional facility, notifying the holding authority of the intention of another jurisdiction to take custody of that individual when released.

3. In instances in which an action pending on an incident and a resulting conviction would change the inmate's custody or program placement, it is suggested that inmates be maintained in their current status and that a review be scheduled following the action of the disciplinary committee.

4. Other factors considered are that past behavior is a predictor of future behavior and that recent behavior is a better predictor of future actions than far distant behavior.

5. Although many of the studies were methodologically weak, they contributed knowledge on the limitations and merits of this approach (Alexander & Austin, 1992).

6. Responses were received from corrections departments (DOCs) in 50 states; the District of Columbia; New York City, New York; Cook County (Chicago), Illinois; the Federal Bureau of Prisons; and the Correctional Service of Canada.

7. Although Marion has a rated capacity of 440 (i.e., the number of inmates it was designed to hold) and contains over 500 cells, the nature of the inmate population has led the BOP to restrict the number of inmates placed there to about 350.

8. Beck & Mumola, 1999; BJS, 1983, 1984; Cohen, 1990.

9. Beck, Gillard, Greenfeld, Harlow, Hester, Jankowski, Snell, Stephan, & Morton, 1993; Innes, 1988; Snell, 1993.

10. Other studies have also examined recidivism. Beck and Shipley (1989) followed more than 108,000 state prisoners for 3 years after they were released in 1983. They found that close to two thirds were rearrested during that period, with 46 percent reconvicted and 41 percent returned to prison or jail. Fifteen percent of these were for violent crimes. The majority had been repeat offenders before their release. Recidivism rates were highest in the first year and among males, blacks, Hispanics, high school dropouts, younger releasees, and those with extensive priors. A more recent self-report survey of inmates in 1991 found that 60 percent had been incarcerated in the past, and for the vast majority this had been within 5 years prior to their current offense (Beck et al., 1993).

11. We should note that there is some controversy about the use of intelligence tests as definitive measures of intellectual potential, especially with minority group individuals.

12. Arizona reports beginning a program for women (Lillis, 1993a).

13. Fifty states, the Federal Bureau of Prisons, and the District of Columbia were surveyed. Only Ohio and Montana failed to respond (Lillis, 1993a).

14. Dugger, 1990; Flanagan, 1990; Porporino, 1990.

15. Unless otherwise noted, this material was adapted from Hunter et al. (1997).

16. The General Well-Being (GWB) assesses self-representations of subjective well-being. It comprises 19 items that, when combined, produce an overall score measuring well-being. Cumulative scale scores range from 19 (highest well-being) to 130 (lowest well-being). In addition, six subscales can be derived from the GWB scale that measure an individual's health worry, energy level, the extent to which one believes he or she has a satisfying and interesting life, depression/cheerfulness, the extent of emotional-behavioral control, and whether a person is relaxed or tense/anxious (Maitland & Sluder, 1996).

17. Unless otherwise noted, this material was adapted from Glick and Sturgeon (1998).

18. Under this transfer or judicial waiver process the juvenile judge has the authority to waive jurisdiction and transfer the case to criminal court. Key criteria in this process include consideration of the following: age, current offense, criminal history, and amenability to rehabilitation. This process only occurs after a motion by the prosecutor.

The Female Offender in Prison and in the Community

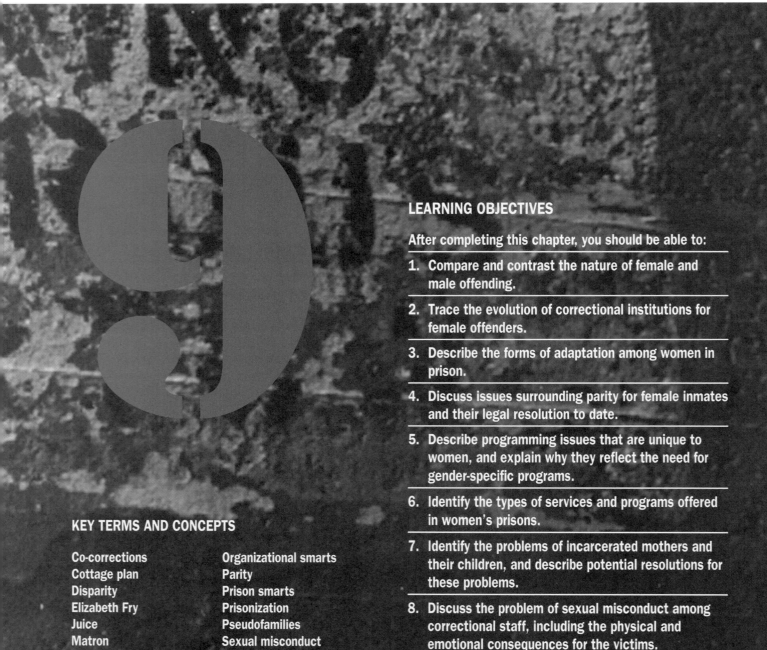

9

LEARNING OBJECTIVES

After completing this chapter, you should be able to:

1. Compare and contrast the nature of female and male offending.

2. Trace the evolution of correctional institutions for female offenders.

3. Describe the forms of adaptation among women in prison.

4. Discuss issues surrounding parity for female inmates and their legal resolution to date.

5. Describe programming issues that are unique to women, and explain why they reflect the need for gender-specific programs.

6. Identify the types of services and programs offered in women's prisons.

7. Identify the problems of incarcerated mothers and their children, and describe potential resolutions for these problems.

8. Discuss the problem of sexual misconduct among correctional staff, including the physical and emotional consequences for the victims.

9. Evaluate the advantages and disadvantages of co-corrections.

KEY TERMS AND CONCEPTS

Co-corrections
Cottage plan
Disparity
Elizabeth Fry
Juice
Matron
Mix

Organizational smarts
Parity
Prison smarts
Prisonization
Pseudofamilies
Sexual misconduct

Introduction

The image most commonly evoked by the word *prisoner* is that of a minority male, but the reality is that the faces of prisoners increasingly belong to women, especially women of color (Acoca & Austin, 1996). This chapter examines trends in female imprisonment and offending. We will look at profiles of incarcerated women; trace the history of female penal institutionalization; go inside the social world of female inmates; examine the special problems created in the mother-child bond when the parent is incarcerated; look at programs and services for female inmates, including issues of parity with programs for male inmates; and study community-based alternative programs for women.

Female Arrest Profiles

In 1998, women constituted approximately 20 percent of the arrests by law enforcement agencies. Specifically, they were about 17 percent of those arrested for Part I violent crimes and 29 percent of those arrested for Part I property crimes (Greenfeld, 1999). Female arrest rates were highest for minor property crimes (e.g., larceny)

and for substance abuse offenses. Between 1960 and 1998, the female percentage of total arrest rates rose from 11 percent to 22 percent because of the sharp increase in their arrests for minor property crimes (FBI, 1998; Steffensmeier & Allan, 1998).

Still, for every woman in prison there are approximately 16 men. As a result, women's prisons are fewer in number and usually smaller than the average prison for men, and they are likely to be different in structure and programming. Consequently, this segment of the corrections system has not received much attention until recently as the number of women incarcerated has skyrocketed. The female rate of imprisonment grew from 6 per 100,000 women in 1925 to 57 per 100,000 women in 1998 (see Figures 9.1 and 9.2). (The rates for men went from 149 (1925) to 866 (1998) per 100,000 U.S. males) (BJS, 1986). A consistent growth rate began in the early 1980s, but the sprint occurred between 1986 and 1998 when it went from 20 to 57 per 100,000 (Figure 9.2). However, although the female inmate population increased substantially, their percentage of the inmate population did not rise as steadily (see Table 9.1). In 1925, women represented 3.7 percent of the total inmate population. By 1985, this had risen to 4.4 percent. Since then it has risen steadily, but slowly; in 1998 women

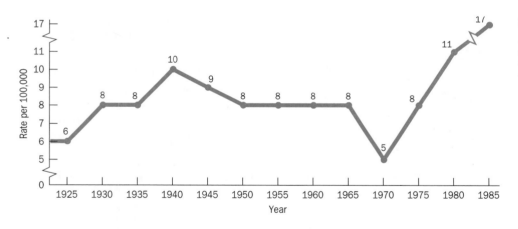

Figure 9.1 *Female Rate of Incarceration (1925–1985)*

Source: *State and Federal Prisoners, 1925–85.* (1986). Washington, DC: BJS.

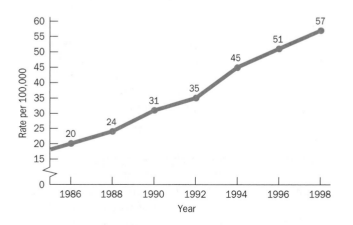

Figure 9.2 *Female Rate of Incarceration (1986–1998)*

Sources: A. J. Beck (1999). *Prisoners in 1998.* Washington, DC: Bureau of Justice Statistics; D. K. Gillard & A. Beck (1999). *Prisoners in 1997.* Washington, DC: BJS; C. J. Mumola & A. Beck (1997). *Prisoners in 1996;* D. K. Gillard & A. Beck (1996). *Prisoners and Jail Inmates in 1995.* Washington DC: BJS; A. Beck & D. K. Gillard (1995). *Prisoners in 1994;* D. K. Gillard & A. Beck (1994). *Prisoners in 1993;* D. K. Gillard (1993). *Prisoners in 1992;* T. L. Snell & D. K. Morton (1992). *Prisoners in 1991;* R. Cohen (1991). *Prisoners in 1990;* BJS (1990). *Prisoners in 1989;* BJS (1989). *Prisoners in 1988;* BJS (1988). *Prisoners in 1987;* BJS (1987). *Prisoners in 1986.*

Table 9.1

Numbers of Women in Prison (1925–1998)

Year	Women	Total Inmates	% Women
1925	3,438	91,669	3.7
1930	4,668	129,453	3.6
1935	4,902	144,180	3.4
1940	6,361	173,706	3.7
1945	6,040	133,649	4.5
1950	5,814	166,165	3.5
1955	7,125	185,780	3.8
1960	7,688	212,953	3.6
1965	7,568	210,895	3.6
1970	5,635	196,441	2.9
1975	8,675	240,593	3.6
1980	12,331	315,974	3.9
1985	21,406	418,616	4.4
1986	26,610	544,972	4.9
1987	28,839	585,084	4.9
1988	32,691	627,600	5.2
1989	40,556	712,364	6.0
1990	43,845	773,919	5.7
1991	47,691	825,559	5.8
1992	50,409	882,500	5.7
1993	55,409	970,444	5.7
1994	64,403	1,054,702	6.1
1995	68,544	1,125,874	6.1
1996	74,730	1,183,368	6.3
1997	79,624	1,244,554	6.4
1998	84,427	1,302,019	6.5

Sources: A. J. Beck (1999). *Prisoners in 1998.* Washington, DC: BJS; D. K. Gillard & A. Beck (1998). *Prisoners in 1997;* C. J. Mumola & A. Beck (1997). *Prisoners in 1996;* D. K. Gillard & A. Beck (1996). *Prisoners and Jail Inmates in 1995;* A. Beck & D. K. Gillard (1995). *Prisoners in 1994; D.K. Gillard & A. Beck (1994). Prisoners in 1993;* D. K. Gillard (1993). *Prisoners in 1992;* T. L. Snell & D. K. Morton (1992). *Prisoners in 1991;* R. Cohen (1991). *Prisoners in 1990;* BJS (1990). *Prisoners in 1989;* BJS (1989). *Prisoners in 1988;* BJS (1988). *Prisoners in 1987;* BJS (1987). *Prisoners in 1986;* BJS (1986). *State and Federal Prisoners, 1925–85.* Washington, DC: Author.

were 6.5 percent of the inmate population (Beck, 1999, p. 5; BJS, 1986). In contrast, the number of women incarcerated has risen sharply. In 1925 there were 3,438 females in prison; by 1950 this number had grown to almost 6,000. This population increased steadily from 1975 to 1998, with the real growth occurring between 1986 (26,610) and 1998 (84,427). Annual growth from 1990 to 1998 averaged about 8.5 percent (vs. 6.6 percent for men); total numbers rose 92.6 percent (vs. 67 percent for men) (Beck, 1999, p. 5; BJS, 1986). Although women still represent only a minority of the prison population, there is a significant difference in the requirements for managing a population of 20,000 versus 84,000.

Female prisoners generally had more difficult economic circumstances than male inmates prior to entering prison. Only about 4 in 10 women in state prisons reported that they had been employed full-time prior to their arrest in contrast to nearly 6 in 10 male inmates. About 37 percent of women and 28 percent of men had incomes of less than $600 per month prior to arrest. However, 30 percent of female inmates reported receiving welfare assistance just before their arrest compared with 8 percent of the males (Greenfeld & Snell, 1999).

The characteristics of female inmates included:

1. Typically, they were over age 30 and a member of a racial or ethnic minority.

2. A large percentage of them had abused drugs and had experienced physical or sexual abuse. For example, in 1997, almost three fourths of female inmates in state prisons said they had used drugs regularly at some time in the past, and slightly over one half reported a prior history of physical or sexual abuse.

3. A large majority of them were unmarried.

4. Almost two thirds had at least one minor child (under age 18).

   a. The total number of minor children whose mothers were in federal and state prisons increased from about 61,000 in 1991 to about 110,000 in 1997.

   b. After the mother entered prison, the vast majority of minor children lived with their grandparent, another relative, a friend, or the father.

5. They committed violent crimes at a six times lower per-capita rate than males.

6. The average sentence and time served for women were shorter than for males with equivalent offenses.

7. Three out of four violent female offenders committed simple assault.

8. In nearly two out of three cases, they had a prior relationship with their victims.

9. Their proportion of convictions for violent and property crimes has been decreasing while their proportion of drug and public-order offenses has been increasing.

Thus, women in prison typically committed more nonviolent offenses, had a tendency to be substance abusers, served shorter sentences than their male counterparts, were likely to be mothers, were older than males, and tended to victimize people they knew.

A History of Female Prison Programs

When compared with the treatment of male offenders, the history of the incarceration of women shows a pattern of neglect toward managing this small portion of offenders. Houses of correction were the first confinement facilities and were intended for the idle, destitute, and criminals of both sexes. With some exceptions (e.g., the Maison de Force and the Amsterdam Spinhouse), these early facilities housed men and women together in large rooms where the survival of the strongest was the norm. One real implication of this structure was that women were often victimized by male inmates (Grunhut, 1972).

In colonial America, as in England, provisions were not usually made for separating women from men in county jails. This pattern continued even after the Revolution at such facilities as Walnut Street Jail in 1790. Shocked by this and other factors, reformers of the Philadelphia Society devised a new plan for the Walnut Street Jail (see Chapter 5). Women at this newly designed facility were housed in a separate section (Barnes, 1927/1968; Lewis, 1922/1967). However, the reformist zeal that characterized the birth of the penitentiary did not benefit women. This was reflected in the fact that men were housed in single cells, whereas women generally continued to be housed congregately in large cells in separate sections of men's prisons. Rafter (1985) painted this picture: "Whereas male prisoners were closely supervised, women seldom had a **matron** (the chief supervisor of women's units). Often idleness rather than hard labor was their curse" (p. 4).

Reformation Programs

Elizabeth Fry, an English Quaker, began a movement in England in 1813 to improve the conditions under which women were incarcerated. She traveled widely, both in Europe and the United States, campaigning for separate female facilities, to be supervised and staffed by women. Women also would be classified into specific treatment groups, provided with religious instruction, work, education, and preparation for employment after release (Feinman, 1986).

Reformers in the United States moved to adopt Fry's program. In 1825, when the New York House of Refuge for juveniles was opened, a separate building was set aside for female delinquents who were to be supervised by two women. This was the first institution based on the idea that females could be reformed. In 1839, New York State opened the Mount Pleasant Female Prison, a separate institution for women, which was attached to and administratively dependent on Sing Sing, a men's facility. The women were housed in cells modeled after those in Auburn. Additionally, the institution had a nursery for children, which meant that women did not have to be separated from their babies or care for them in their single cells (Rafter, 1990).

In 1863, the House of Shelter was opened as a section of the Detroit House of Corrections under the superintendence of reformer Zebulon T. Brockway. He hired female officers to serve as role models and divided the women into small family groups in which they received domestic training. He also used a graded system by which obedient inmates were rewarded by promotion to better living conditions (Rafter, 1990).

Following the Cincinnati meeting of the National Prison Association in 1870, major correctional reforms were called for, including separate institutions for women. In 1873, the first of these facilities, the Indiana Reformatory for Women and Girls, was opened. It duplicated some features of the Detroit House of Corrections, including its employment of female personnel.

In the late 19th century, three independent women's prisons were built—one in Massachusetts and two in New York. Based on the idea that females could be reformed through domestic training, an architectural modification of the **cottage plan** was slowly incorporated into the newer adult institutions. Under the cottage plan, these institutions consisted of several small units, each housing approximately 30 inmates, surrounding a central building that had regular cells. The cells were used to hold inmates until they were ready to be moved into the cottages. These institutions, which provided a more relaxed disciplinary atmosphere, were used for females under 30 who had committed minor crimes. Between 1900 and 1939, 25 of these facilities for women were built, primarily in the Northeast and Midwest (Freedman, 1981).

In the South, because private prison industry contractors did not want women prisoners, they were kept in central prisons, which also held old and sick males who were unable to work (see Chapter 6). After World War II, a few reformatories were built in this region, which terminated the co-correctional arrangements in most early women's prisons. Many facilities built during this era are still in use today. Their outdated architecture lacks many of the amenities present in more modern construction, imposing program and treatment limitations that make it difficult to meet the needs of today's female inmates and also increasing the likelihood of litigation (Chesney-Lind, 1986, 1987).

Parity

Recent correctional reform efforts involving women have focused on gaining *parity* with male prisoners. Do women receive **parity,** or equal treatment, in sentencing, programming, and other resources? Based on a Pennsylvania study, Steffensmeier, Kramer, and Streifel (1993) contend that men and women appearing in court under similar circumstances and charged with similar offenses are likely to be treated in basically the same way. However, Fogel (1998) contends that this is not the case in North Carolina or in other southern states. Zang (1998) adds that, if the court has flexibility, they tend to give women shorter sentences.

The impetus for these reforms has come from three sources. First, feminist criminologists have exposed the disparities in the treatment received by women and

Recent reform efforts have attempted to correct disparities between the resources and programs available to male and female inmates.

have been instrumental in initiating changes.[1] Second, the American Correctional Association developed guidelines and recommendations for providing programs for female offenders, including programs for pregnant women, and establishing sound family relationships, nontraditional vocational training and career counseling, child and family services, and a range of diversionary and other community correctional services. The third major source of these reforms was inmate litigation.

Beginning in the mid-1970s, legal challenges by female inmates to conditions of confinement resulted in some significant changes. One area that was addressed was the **disparity,** or lack of equal resources, in the programs in women's institutions as compared with those for men. In *Barefield v. Leach* (1974), a New Mexico court found that the state had failed to provide parity in its vocational programming and its paid work for inmates. The court ruled that this could not be justified simply because it cost more to provide programs in the smaller female facilities (see also *Canterino v. Wilson*, 1989). The courts also rendered several decisions supporting adequate and appropriate medical care and parity with men's institutions in programming, conditions, and opportunities in women's prisons.[2] These decisions have reflected a proportional approach to equality. Our Close Up, "The Resolution of Parity," shows how a system's

positive reaction to parity issues can result in an amicable settlement.

Rather than examine the parity between programs available to female inmates and their male counterparts, the courts have taken the position that gender differences in institutional programming, alone, are not necessarily unconstitutional. In *Pargo v. Elliot* (1995), the Eighth Circuit Court adopted five criteria for analyzing discrimination claims in penal institutions:

1. population of the facility
2. security level
3. types of crimes
4. lengths of sentences
5. special characteristics (which the court did not define)

The *Pargo* test has been adopted in other decisions, which have found that the equal protection clause is no longer an effective mechanism for improving programs and conditions for female offenders. "By the time one finds groups of male and female inmates suitable for an equal protection comparison using the five factors quoted above, the groups may be too small to be worth comparing" (*Correctional Law Reporter*, Feb./Mar., 1997, p. 76).

One requirement for women to receive equal educational, vocational, and work opportunities and services is a female-based classification system. Our In Their Own

The Resolution of Parity

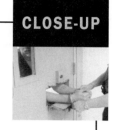

Judy Butler, a minimum security prisoner confined at the Federal Correctional Institution, Fort Worth, Texas, filed suit in 1984 against the Bureau of Prisons (BOP). She was one of 10 women who joined in this class action lawsuit against the attorney general of the United States, William F. Smith, and Norman A. Carlson, director of the Federal Bureau of Prisons. This case was instituted by the American Civil Liberties Union based on a concern that the BOP had no camp facilities for female inmates. The case went to trial in 1989 and was settled in 1996. The BOP responded to the court by establishing a female camp system. A court-appointed master evaluated female governance practices at five female camp facilities. At issue was equality and parity for camp-eligible men and women. It concluded that some practices for females differed from those for males.

Findings inconsistent with BOP values were identified as follows:

1. Fewer female camps than male camps
2. Lower staff-to-inmate ratio
3. More strip searching and less privacy
4. Longer waits for job assignments
5. More female issues in jobs with lower-paying grades
6. No more female camps on military bases, just fewer job opportunities
7. Women not allowed to wear civilian clothing during visits
8. Sexual harassment

The Butler case was settled by the BOP's implementing criteria to bring parity between female and male policies. This included (1) transferring women to minimum security facilities closer to home; (2) making classifications to institutions utilizing the least restrictive means test, and (3) establishing female camps that provided them with opportunities and programs that the male population was receiving. One result was the acquisition and opening of the major primary care hospital and female complex at Carswell. Warden Richard Rison (now retired), who opened this new facility reported that the females involved in the Butler suit were absolutely no problem at Carswell. Their grievances about female prison practices in the Butler case were legitimate and a common problem that administrators face when there is massive growth in the prison population.

This discussion of the Butler case emphasizes the importance of equity and parity when developing prison policies and practices for the activation of a facility.

Source: This was prepared by Richard Rison (2000) for the 2nd edition of this text. Rison is a retired prison warden with 35 years of experience, who administered five federal prisons.

Words feature, "The Need for a Distinctive Female Classification System," discusses the current state of female classification.

Co-Correctional Facilities

With the opening of the **co-correctional** program at the Federal Correctional Institution in Fort Worth, Texas, in 1971, the housing of females in the same prison with men had come full circle. As noted earlier, women had been housed in male facilities during most of the 19th century. Although a few states housed some women in male facilities prior to the 1970s, there were few or no shared programs in these facilities. The increasing pressure on many systems to achieve some kid of parity, particularly in providing programs and services, prompted some systems to experiment with co-correctional programs because this offered a cost-effective solution to this problem. They also offered a normal environment, enabling both men and women to be more easily reintegrated into society (Davis, 1998).

Presently, there are nine co-correctional institutions in the United States.[3] In contemporary co-correctional institutions, men and women are housed separately but normally participate in most programs and share services. The public has many misconceptions about co-correctional institutions, among which are that there is extreme promiscuity, the two sexes share sleeping quarters, and there are many illegitimate births (Halford, 1984). Rules in these institutions prohibit male-female contact beyond holding hands and the supervision is relatively strict. Illicit sexual activity and some pregnancies do occur, but these behaviors are not common.

Supporters of co-corrections assert that it benefits both men and women. The more relaxed atmosphere decreases tension and violence and reduces or eliminates homosexual behavior among men. Studies have found that bringing female inmates into an all-male institution brings about many improvements, including better personal sanitation, decreased vandalism, and increased educational competency among students. Further, co-corrections produces a more balanced and normal prison

IN THEIR OWN WORDS

The Need for a Distinctive Female Classification System

Prisoner classification is crucial for female offenders to receive appropriate treatment, for safety reasons, and to avoid biased decisions. This technique is used to address the diversity among female prisoners and to bring order, discipline, fairness, and a degree of rationality to decisions affecting these inmates. Classification decisions place prisoners into various security levels, programs, services, and treatment options. All institutional processing decisions regarding the prisoner depend on a preliminary act of classification. Thus, the new female prisoner cannot be effectively processed, housed, or treated until a classification (or diagnosis) is conducted.

For both male and female prisoners, classification systems are based on two broad principles: (1) prisoners can be classified according to risk prediction regarding their potential for violence, suicide, and the danger they present to the community if they escape; and (2) treatment and rehabilitation can be provided by assessing the social, psychological, medical, and treatment needs of the new prisoner (e.g., drug problems, sexual abuse, employment history, education, financial problems, family history, etc.). This assessment provides guidance in treating the prisoner, in designing rehabilitation programs, and in identifying any special needs that the female inmate may have during incarceration.

Classification has important implications for the life of a female inmate. It governs the security level in which she is placed (e.g., maximum, medium, or minimum security), which in turn will determine the type of detainee with whom she is housed (e.g., drug offenders, prostitutes, first-time offenders, etc.). The consequences of classification extend to several other key areas, including eligibility and access to needed programs, early release to community placements, and visitation arrangements. It can also profoundly influence how a prisoner is viewed and understood by both staff and other inmates.

During the 1980s new objective data-based classification procedures emerged. These statistical classification methods were, perhaps naively, offered as being both "gender-neutral" and objective. They were presented as having equal applicability to male and female detainees, yet, they were designed largely using male samples, and focused almost exclusively on the risk and needs factors identified for male prisoners. In recent years, it has become increasingly obvious that these methods have very poor validity or relevance for women prisoners. Their use with female prisoners may result in different and often unfair treatment. It is well established that violence among women prisoners is much lower than among males. Consequently, the likelihood of overclassification errors (i.e., falsely labeling the female prisoner as a high-risk case) using a male-based classification model is very high for female inmates. Additionally, these male risk–based classification systems have been found to have very low predictive accuracy for women prisoners. Yet, their widespread use for classifying women prisoners continues.

In the last several years a number of researchers have called for classification methods to be specifically designed for women prisoners, to address their specific needs and increase the validity of classifications for risk and rehabilitation. Currently, there is a critical need for more research in this area. However, this research continues to be meagerly supported and as a result little progress has been made.

Source: This was prepared by Tim Brennan for the 2nd edition of this text. Brennan is a research associate professor in the Psychology Department at the University of Colorado.

environment, emphasizing personal responsibility and positive interaction between a sexually integrated staff and inmate populations. These facilities also have better living conditions, more freedom, and fewer grievances than single-sex facilities (Davis, 1998).

Women tend to benefit from greater availability of medical, psychological, legal, and social services and educational and vocational programs. Some drawbacks for women include increased control and security (to control sexual activity), less opportunity for leadership, and more avoidance of nontraditional programs because of the perception that they are unfeminine (Schweber, 1984). Other problems include higher costs due to increased surveillance and security measures, pregnancies, prostitution, and pimping (Davis, 1998). Smykla (1980) also feels that women may be exploited in cocorrectional facilities because they continue to be seen as men's sexual objects.

Thus, the question is, Considering the advantages and disadvantages of coed facilities is there a place for them in modern corrections? If coed facilities are to be successful they require special programs for females and a period of prior admission for women to be placed in a single-sex facility so that they have time away from men. Who should be assigned to a coed facility? They are inappropriate for highly criminalized predatory offenders. By the same token their more relaxed atmosphere suggests they can be used as a reward for prosocial inmates (e.g., those who choose not to join or choose to leave gangs), who are good candidates for a prison directed toward transition and integration of the offender into the community (Davis, 1998).

The Social World of the Female Inmate

Inmate adaptations to prison vary from facility to facility, depending on such factors as institutional and administrative programs, prison personnel, the physical layout of the institutions, and inmate characteristics. These adaptations can be grouped under the concept of **prisonization,** which describes the degree to which inmates participate in and adopt the prison subculture. Research related to female adaptations has been criticized for focusing principally on homosexuality and for

tending to assume that the variables involved in male prison subcultures are applicable to women's prisons (Giallombardo, 1966; Pollock-Byrne, 1990).

The differences between how men and women "do time" is largely a function of gender role socialization; men typically "do their own time," whereas women's lives remain integrated with those of significant others (e.g., parents, children, spouses) on the outside. Another difference is that men tend to act out and be more aggressive in a prison setting; women do not. This is reflected in the observation by criminologist Cris Rasche (2000) that in prison, "Men go bad, women go mad." Women do time and deal with the isolation of imprisonment by looking for and establishing support systems, a **pseudofamily.** Men, in contrast, involve themselves in gang relationships, usually more often for protection (Zang, 1998). This section draws heavily from Barbara Owen's (1998) study of the California Central Women's Facility (CCWF) to provide a description of life in a female prison.[4]

Prison Relationships at CCWF

The pseudofamily is the basic form of relationship in women's prisons. Some have the misconception that these are homosexual in nature, but most are based on asexual pairing and participation is not associated with a greater likelihood of homosexual experience (Propper, 1982, p. 128).

Either the play family or one's role as "homosexual partner" forms the basis for a woman's role and status

Many female inmates form close friendships, which sometimes develop into intense physical or emotional relationships.

within the prison culture. These complicated personal relationships provide emotional, practical, and material connections, as well as sexual and familial ties. These relationships reflect the dominant roles played by women in the free world and continue to find expression in prison life. Although the basis of some families may be the romantic dyad or couple, families can also be formed by individual women developing close ties. In such families, an older and definitely "prisonwise" woman takes on the role of a "mom," with younger, or at least naive, women taking on the roles of daughters, or in cases where the women take on a male identity, sons. Some women who take on the "butch" or the aggressive role may be a dad, a son, or a brother, but these designations are often fluid.

Women adopting male identities and roles almost always wear pants, men's boxer shorts, hard work boots, and extremely short hair. They also may mimic the male habit of grabbing (groping) one's crotch. As one woman says, "I got a roommate now, she's grabbing down between her legs and to this day I don't know what she thinks she has down there." These women also may modify their first names to more masculine names (e.g., from Kathleen to Charlie).

Same-sex relationships are a constant feature of women's prisons. Lesbian relationships are known as "homo-secting" in the prison argot. They are more observable in the female prisons because they are less frowned upon. While some women find these relationships unnatural, a portion of them change their views over time. "Zoom," who was heterosexual on the streets describes her transition to homosexuality in prison:

> The person I met was first a friend. However, in a close environment like this a bond becomes more important. Women are very emotional, and we build little families and what have you. And one thing leads to another. You know, it is not force. There is no rapes and all that shit they have in the movies. (p. 138)

Although a significant number of women in prison seem to be involved in these same-sex relationships, there are many women at CCWF who "do not play"— that is, become involved with another prisoner in a physically intimate relationship. The fear of same-sex advances was voiced by many women prior to entering the prison. However, Owen found force was rarely used in recruiting individuals for relationships. The standard disclaimer "I don't play" or "I don't use" was sufficient declaration of one's desire to stay out of these arrangements.

The close tie or emotional relationship is another distinguishable type. Some of these are based on gender identities and family structure, whereas others are similar to mentoring roles. Laura, who is at the end of her 5-year sentence, provides an example of a mentoring relationship with a young first-termer:

> I am Sally's best friend. She has never been in trouble before and I need to protect her. People will take advantage of her; they just might want her canteen. Sally . . . she is not con-wise. . . . She does not know the prison rules and I have to be on her. She doesn't know that there are things you write or say on the phone that can make you be under investigation. She has learned to be more careful in approaching people, in being kind. We are really more like sisters and I look after her. (p. 141)

Another inmate, Randi, explains another form of these relationships, the "dog" relationship, [which] is based more on equality and reciprocity and is fundamentally characterized by its dependability. "You can go from friend to friend, but you always have that one to fall back on . . . the one you always go back to. This is your dog" (p. 139).

Outside Family Relationships

Most women in prison are mothers. Children are part of the prison culture because they are a part of the present and the future plans of the offender. For almost half of these women reunification with their children upon release was their primary goal. The primacy of these relationships impacts the values shaping prison culture in several ways. Conversations about children become sacred, as does acknowledging the intensity and grief attached to the isolation of the women with histories of child abuse.

For women, the physical separation of imprisonment is often accompanied by emotional estrangement from their children as well as other relatives. Thus, family relationships form the foundations for the substitute play family, or the pseudofamily. Prison affects family relationships in different ways:

- For many women their family provides support.
- For some, their relationships are negative because of the family's strong reaction to their arrest and subsequent imprisonment.
- Some women feel abandoned by their families.
- Some women experience a reconciliation with their parents and/or their spouse.

Although most women value their relationships with their free-world family, particularly their children, keeping these relationships for many makes it harder for them to do their time. "Divine" reflects a common inmate sentiment:

> You cannot do your time here and out on the streets at the same time. That makes you do hard time. You just have to block that out of your mind. You can't think about what is going on out there and try to do [your time]. (p. 129)

The Female Inmate Subculture

As in the free world, the life experiences of incarcerated women differ greatly from those of men. Their complex and diverse histories produce a prison culture that is itself complex and diverse. Prison smarts, organizational smarts, mentoring, race, the convict code, and "the mix" all interact to create the female prison culture.

The Prison-Smart Offender Women entering the prison world must learn a unique set of strategies, behaviors, and meanings. Their success in negotiating this world is dependent on two key factors. First, their past criminal behavior, jail and prison experiences, and experiences with the street culture provide some indication of what they can expect in prison. Second, interpersonal coping skills, cleverness, and an understanding of the prison bureaucracy also determine a woman's success in negotiating this new terrain. Women who are **prison smart** have learned through experience how to manage the prison community's resources and members in a way that allows them to "do their own time." They cultivate relationships with both staff and other prisoners that allow them some measure of freedom and autonomy in their everyday life. They also operate narrowly within the prison's rules and regulations, sometimes outside their specific intent. In this way they can build a personal world and stay out of the **mix,** the underground behavior that brought them to prison in the first place. This involves maintaining personal relationships that are constructive and unlikely to bring trouble and creating a daily program that meets their personal and material needs without drawing any negative attention to themselves or their activities.

One key aspect of "prison smarts" is the ability to get things done. This means having the **juice**—that is, possessing information and influence that come through a job or relationships with authority figures. This enables the prisoner to get things done, legally or illegally, often by circumventing the rules or avoiding the delays experienced by the "nobody" or the "nondescript." Other prisoners will come to the prisoner with the juice with questions and requests for advice because of her reputation.

Critical aspects of prison smarts are respect and reputation. Respect is based on past offense history and interaction with staff and prisoners. It can be gained by standing one's ground and maintaining a positive reputation in dealing with other prisoners. Directly related to respect is reputation. Being known and being recognized lifts an individual out of the faceless crowd and gives a woman an elevated prison identity. For those tied to the mix, this type of reputation becomes a centerpiece to prison identity and survival.

The Organizationally Smart Offender Some women enter prison with skills in interpersonal relations, managing bureaucracies, and recognizing reciprocity in terms of "common courtesy"; they have **organizational smarts.** These women also carve out a social existence that meets their needs and minimizes the deprivations of imprisonment.

Relying on their cleverness and ability, these women survive without having a commitment to a prison identity. The more-educated learn early on to apply skills obtained in their preprison life through schooling, employment, experience, or intelligence to get better jobs. These women learn that getting along with officers is a key to negotiating the prison world and that officers tend to reciprocate attitudes and behavior.

The Role of Mentoring Some newcomers learn to negotiate the prison world by being mentored by someone who "knows what is happening." At CCWF, most of the older prisoners discuss the fact that "in the old days, someone would take you under their wing and tell you how to do time, [but] not anymore. These youngsters don't listen to anybody. I guess they have to learn the hard way." Other women develop nonromantic close relationships with their roommates and take on the responsibility of setting them straight.

As a woman learns the prison culture, she is exposed to a variety of styles of doing time. In some sense, doing time is related to the day-to-day business of developing a program and settling into a satisfying routine. Two of the most significant factors in how a female inmate does time are her degree of commitment to a deviant identity, particularly a criminal identity, and the stage she is in in her prison sentence.

The Convict Code Although the convict code among women is not nearly as important as that among men, there is a female version; it includes:

- "Mind your own business."
- "The police are not your friend; stay out of their face."
- "Take care of one another."
- "If asked something (by staff), you do not tell."
- "Do not allow rat-packing; fight one-on-one only."

There was universal agreement among the old-timers that the code has changed as a result of the influx of younger prisoners. Victoria, a lifer in her late forties, notes:

These youngsters are rude, disrespectful, and inconsiderate. They have never been taught. Even when they get locked up, they are back on the yard, harder than before. They always say so many youngsters come to prison and they think they are going "to kick it on the yard." Youngsters want to be noticed, to put their stuff out. They can be loud and obnoxious. . . . You didn't bring nobody down with you. "Do your own time." That was the rule. (p. 176)

Achieving respect in a female prison not only involves adhering to the convict code but guarding one's behavior toward other prisoners and staff. A respected prisoner does not cause trouble for other prisoners and is not "messy." Being messy generally involves gossip and less-than-truthful behavior, but it can be extreme and involve more serious trouble too. A minor dimension of respect involves responding to physical challenges. Although fights are not an everyday occurrence, being ready to defend oneself contributes to such a reputation.

However, unlike the male code its female counterpart tolerates higher levels of informing on other prisoners to the staff, known as "telling," "ratting," or "snitching." In male prisons, not only is snitching not tolerated it can get an inmate killed. A few women have borrowed elements of the male code and avoid interaction with officers at all times. This is one distinction between "inmates" (who sometimes inform) and "convicts" (who take their problems to their pseudofamily).

Race Among the women at CCWF, race is deemphasized in the everyday life and is not seen as a critical factor in the inmate subculture. Race, however, did not disappear in the lives of the women at CCWF. It was most likely to emerge during times of specific confrontations, such as interpersonal conflict or competition over a scarce resource, or in cultural expressions (songs, movies, or slang) where racial content was brought out. However, "Chicago" cites racism at CCWF, especially among the staff.

I never saw such prejudice until I came here. As far as the white people staff, I think they are KKK. I have white friends [among the prisoners] but here the staff will call you niggers. They do it and get away with it. . . . The prison is fucked up and the staff is fucked up. . . . Like I said, babe, there is a lot of prejudice that goes on in here. Their attitudes, you can tell when a person doesn't want to speak to you because you are black. They are mean. And they just look at you like ogh, you are black and, I don't want to look at a nigger. I don't want to look at you. Or they will tell you to get up on the wall and be rough with you and kick your legs open with their knees. Like they did me. . . . They said, "You fucking nigger, I ought to body slam you." I looked at him like he was crazy. The black officers don't like it, but they (the officers) back each other up. They are co-workers and they are going home and we are staying here. They are going home and they get paid. It is part of the system; they

can't front off each other. The black staff are in a no-win situation. The black staff know it is wrong. (pp. 154–155)

The Mix A final dimension of prison culture found at CCWF is the amorphous concept of "the mix." Most see the mix as something to avoid. As Mindy describes it, "The mix is continuing the behavior that got you here in the first place" (p. 179). Few women claimed to be presently involved in the mix, but many claimed previous involvement. The majority of women at CCWF receive material support through "putting money on the books" or quarterly packages from family members. Those that do not have two options: they must rely on in-prison hustles to supply their material needs or obtain prison jobs. Still others connect with people on the street, known as tricks and runners. These are usually older males that the inmates either knew prior to their incarceration, met through mutual friends, or contacted through magazines or other publications soliciting pen pals. In one Florida prison a female offender was able to build up an account of $12,000 by writing letters to outside males on the pretense that she would be with them when she was released. She also told many that she was about to be released and asked them to send airline tickets so that she could be with them more easily. Some of these men actually showed up at the prison on the day of her supposed release.

Being in the mix can cause you to have your days taken (meaning reducing good-time credits) or to go to "jail" (administrative segregation). The most frequently involved behavior relates to "homo-secting–homosexual relationships," involvement in drugs, fights, and "being messy." Most women in the CCWF study said that going home is their first priority, but they pointed out that some women are more at home in prison and do not seem to care if they "lose time." Those in the mix do not act as if they have an outside orientation; instead they devote their time to in-prison pursuits, such as drugs, girlfriends, and fighting, while risking their days. There was a general consensus that the yard was the primary location for activities composing the mix. The mix has three major components: the drug mix, the homosexual mix, and the fighting and being messy mix.

The Drug Mix For many women, the risks involved in obtaining and using drugs, the expense of drug use in the inflated market of the prison, and the ultimate loss of time due to sanctions attached to the drug mix are the embodiment of trouble in prison. The use of drugs and the risk attached to this use are also related to changes in the content of the prisoner culture. According to Randi: "When you are in the mix, you are always in debt (strung out, scared), worrying that you will not get your money on time. You have to rely on friends (from the streets) for money." Most women report that cash money is rarely used; instead dealers have the money placed on their books by someone from the outside. Those in the mix also sell their jewelry, clothes, canteen, and the box (quarterly package). These women possess an inside orientation and seem to show little regard for returning to the street.

The Homosexual Mix One woman, who describes herself as an "assertive lesbian on the streets," says:

> Most of the femmes are confused [about this] in here. They want that touch, that feeling. But girlfriends can get you in trouble. You have to be careful. It took me a long time to learn this. Now this place scares me. It used to be fun, a playground. No more. When I was involved with women, I used to beat them, and talk trash to them. In lesbian life you do it to get affection. I am still hurt about the way I treated them in the past. [I acknowledge that] I did all those things, my crimes, hurting my woman but it is all over now. . . . They don't understand anything but being treated bad. I think there is some abuse in the homosexual culture on the streets. . . . Now it is too hard to get sexually involved with someone in here; there is so much switching. (pp. 184–185)

The Fighting Mix and Being Messy Although few women take on the role of enforcer—collecting drug debts or "evening the score"—conflict can still exist in the prison setting. Most conflict is verbal, involving a disagreement over behavior, an interpretation of bad will, or a personality clash. Women in the "fighting mix" often use force or coercion as a way of bullying other prisoners. They feel they have a right to take advantage of a woman if she can't "stand for her own." Fights usually occur as lover's quarrels, unsuccessful drug deals, and sometimes assaults on strangers.

Final Thoughts on CCWF

The majority of the women at CCWF serve their sentences, survive the mix, and return to society, resuming their lives in the free community. Many return to circumstances not of their making, such as abuse and economic marginality, which re-create the conditions of their original offense. Others continue making self-destructive choices of drug use and other criminal behavior. However, for some women incarceration has positive results. It provides an opportunity for them to think about what they were doing to themselves and their children. For others, prison gives them "time out" from their self-destructive behavior on the streets and provides an incentive not to return to their previous lives.

It is also important to emphasize the damage that imprisonment does to women. Morgan, a long-termer serving both time for violence and an SHU term for continued violence inside states:

> Prison makes you very bitter [and] you become dehumanized. I've been in prison since I was seventeen. I have been abandoned by my family members and anyone else who knew me out there. Being in prison forces you to use everything that you have just to survive. . . . It's difficult to show compassion or to have it when [there is no reciprocation]. Being in prison all this time, I didn't feel like I belonged; I didn't feel adequate enough to deal with the inadequacies I felt were inside. . . .
>
> But I am finally to a point that I am really in tune with myself. I detached myself as far as socializing and being in crowds and different things that made me very uncomfortable or paranoid.
>
> I feel that, in society as a whole, women are subject to being made the victim. I was a victim that turned perpetrator, but everybody has an instinct of survival for themselves. You understand what I'm sayin'. Because I was a woman in society, I was put in the situation where it was a do or die thing, and I did. . . . Now that I'm older, . . . I recognize what I want to happen in the future. It is up to me. (p. 190)

Once a woman organizes her program and life in the prison, some women begin to think about their lives and what brought them to prison.

Pregnancy, Motherhood, and Female Incarceration

In the words of an inmate mother, "Being a mother in prison is worse than losing a child . . . it's a kind of continuous grief" (Fogel, 1998). This section examines the special needs of pregnant inmates and means of strengthening mother-child bonds strained by the mother's incarceration.

Pregnancy

One in four women entering prison is either pregnant or has recently delivered a child (Church, 1990; Fogel, 1998). Moreover, 7 out of 10 women under some form of correctional supervision have minor children (Greenfeld and Snell, 1999). According to a *Corrections Compendium* study (1999), there were about 1,900 pregnant inmates entering prison in 1998, and more than 1,400 gave birth during that year. Bloom and Steinhart (1993) estimated that 9 percent of all incarcerated women were pregnant. Using this percentage and an estimated 120,000 women in jails and prisons in 1995, they determined that approximately 10,800 of these women were pregnant during that time period.

Pregnant prisoners represent a unique group among childbearing women. By virtue of their unfavorable past and present life circumstances, pregnant prisoners have been found to be more prone to smoking, drug and alcohol abuse, and late entry into prenatal care than their matched controls and are more vulnerable to negative birth outcomes than women in the general population (Egley, Miller, Granados, & Fogel, 1992). Nevertheless, at least one study has documented better pregnancy outcomes among prisoners than in women with similar characteristics (Egley et al., 1992).

Incarcerated pregnant women have many lifestyle behaviors that can jeopardize their pregnancy, most notably substance abuse and poor nutrition (Fogel, 1993, 1996). Many are underweight when they become pregnant and gain less than the recommended weight during pregnancy. Pregnant prisoners also have high incidences of past and current sexually transmitted diseases and are less likely to have received adequate prenatal care prior to being imprisoned, which is linked to premature birth or low birthweight babies.

The many risk factors associated with this group suggest that they can benefit from intensive prenatal education. Of particular concern is the level of substance abuse reported by pregnant inmates. Although many prisons offer substance abuse treatment programs, they are not tailored to the needs of pregnant women. Further, stopping smoking is not a focus of substance abuse programs in prisons.

Prenatal classes that prepare inmates for birth and parenting and peer group and group counseling sessions may increase pregnant prisoners' available sources of much needed social support while incarcerated. Prisons that house all pregnant and newly postpartum women together also facilitate peer support.

Comprehensive maternity care for the pregnant prisoner should be part of the rehabilitative environment of incarceration. The problems of incarcerated pregnant women pose great challenges for those in corrections.

Incarcerated Mothers

More than 7 out of 10 incarcerated women are mothers of minor children (Greenfeld & Snell, 1999). The vast majority of female prisoners want to maintain relationships with their children and plan to resume care for them upon release. One of the most stressful conditions of incarceration for women is separation from their children. Many imprisoned mothers never see their children or see them infrequently (Baunach, 1993; Fogel, 1991, 1996).

Although there is limited research on the effects of mother-child separation on the children, existing evidence suggests that children with incarcerated mothers do suffer. These children may experience financial hardship, decreased quality of care, weakening of family bonds, and multiple-home placements and live apart from their siblings (Beatty, 1997; U.S. Department of Justice, 1994). The repeated alternative placement of children, particularly when it involves unfamiliar surroundings and people or further segregation from other family members, may create insecurities and emotional problems for them (Johnston, 1995; Sharp & Marcus-Mendoza, 1998). Other research has linked mothers' incarceration to children's poor school performance, aggressive behavior, teen pregnancy, and psychological problems (Beatty, 1997; Kampfer, 1995; Moses, 1995). However, in some instances, the mother's behavior may adversely affect her children, and her incarceration may actually benefit them. Specifically, drug use in the home and associations with other offenders may create a dangerous environment for the children; incarceration may remove this influence (Clear, 1996; Sharp & Marcus-Mendoza, 1998).

Spending time with their children is the most important concern of most female inmates because they fear that their younger children will not know them and their older children will reject them. However, visits have been limited by prison rules and other factors, including inadequate family transportation, lack of family financial resources, and long distances between the prison and the family. Over the past few decades, correctional facilities have begun to recognize the need to establish programs that facilitate the maintenance and strengthening of the parent-child bond.

In the mid-1980s, as a consequence of concerns voiced by female inmates and staff, programs were established to target very specific needs of female inmates. These include

- child abuse education services
- parenting classes
- legal aid (which addresses such topics as foster care, legal guardianship, family custody, etc.)
- substance abuse intervention
- family advocacy programs (which typically integrate several types of services)
- prenatal care
- recreation programs
- college parenting classes

The objective is to enable inmates to interact with their children while in prison and to make the transition from prison back into the community (Fogel, 1998).

More important, visitation programs affect the reunification of incarcerated mothers with their children. Most female correctional institutions offer some type of visitation during the day, while almost half offer overnight visitation opportunities. Many institutions also provide special day events and weekend activities for women who qualify. Although day and weekend services are brief in duration, they may be critical in fostering the parent-child bond. As one mother stated in her diary:

> Words cannot express my appreciation for allowing me to do this. I think I got a breakthrough with him. I am the only one he trusts right now and he needed to hear a message of hope. He was even thinking of suicide, because he felt no one cared. This weekend our talks have given him some real issues to consider. Lots of times the choices we make are because we are not aware of the options. I needed time to let him know that there are options available to him other than the streets! (Stumbo & Little, 1990, p. 9)

Nevertheless, although various programs have improved the means by which mother and child can bond, visits and other forms of communication are still not what they should be. Less than half the women in prison in 1997 reported receiving visits from their children, with 23 percent seeing their children monthly. Additionally, 37 percent of these women received phone calls on a weekly basis and 45 percent received mail (Snell, 2000).

Programs for Incarcerated Mothers The past few decades have witnessed a rapid increase in the number of programs for incarcerated mothers. Many require screening for those mothers who wish to participate. This screening is designed to exclude mothers who have a history of violence, child abuse or neglect, and those with a poor prison record (Bloom, 1988). Recently, there have been some positive changes in these programs. An increasing number of states have support organizations that facilitate visitations by providing travel, as well as other services, such as sponsored bus trips, family day trips, and escort services. One program that was initially established as a result of collaboration between an organization (National Institute of Justice) and a community group was the Girl Scouts Beyond Bars Program. Our Program Focus provides an in-depth view of the goals and characteristics of this program.

Although the strong punitive sentiment among the general public is inconsistent with rehabilitative and reintegrative efforts, it is critical to recognize that, for all but violent inmates, incarceration is an ineffective crime control strategy. Punishment is by no means a substitute for proactive intervention, which is essential for inmates to live productive lives. Many programs, in spite of their institutional location, maintain progressive philosophies and goals that are directly opposed to those reflected in the subcultural and structural elements of a correctional facility. To allow incarcerated women and their children to make meaningful contributions to their families, communities, and society as a whole means not only

Some prisons have developed programs that allow mothers to live full-time with their children while serving their sentence.

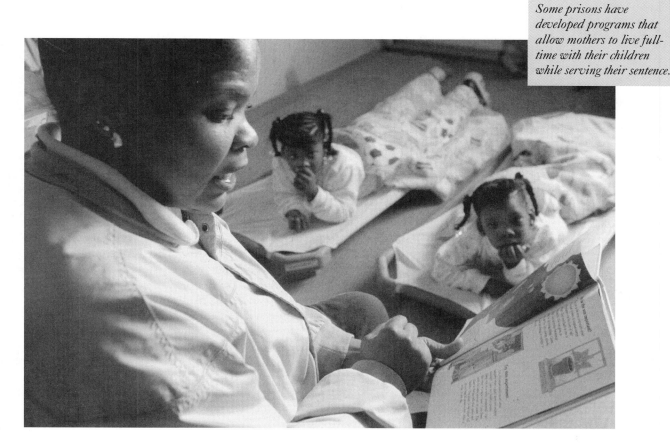

Girl Scouts Beyond Bars Program

PROGRAM FOCUS

A result of the joint efforts of Carol A. Smith, a Baltimore circuit court judge, and Marilyn Moses, an NIJ program manager, a Girl Scout troop was established in 1992 for daughters of women incarcerated at Maryland Correctional Institute for Women (MCIW). The proposed troop would hold meetings in the correctional facility and involve the mothers as adult troop members.

The designed goals, structure, membership, and activities of the Girl Scouts Beyond Bars Program combined traditional scouting with the needs and requirements of incarcerated mothers and their daughters. The program objectives for mothers were to enhance visitation; to preserve or enhance the mother-daughter bond; to reduce the stress of separation; to reduce reunification problems following release; and, ultimately, to help decrease failure following release. For daughters, the objectives were to preserve or enhance the mother-daughter bond; to enhance the daughter's sense of self; to reduce the daugh-

ter's school and home behavior problems; and to reduce reunification problems following the mother's release from MCIW.

The Girl Scouts Beyond Bars Program opened its troop membership to mothers of daughters between the ages of 7 and 17 who resided in the city of Baltimore. Membership criteria included being infraction free for 30 days, remaining infraction free, and not having a conviction for an offense against children. Once the mothers were released from MCIW, the daughters were permitted to remain in the community program or transfer to another troop.

On alternate Saturday mornings, twice per month, the troop held 2-hour meetings in the MCIW gymnasium. During the troop meetings, the mothers and daughters engaged in a variety of activities following 15 minutes of private conversation between the mothers and daughters and the traditional recitation of the Girl Scout pledge. They worked on scout badges, developed special educational projects over the course of several weeks, and focused on issues confronting today's girls, such as teen pregnancy and drug use, discussed through role-playing skits.

Separate mothers' meetings were held in the morning on the same day as the general GSBB meetings. For the most part, they were devoted to general discussions of child-rearing issues and GSBB Program plans. A licensed social worker led many of the meetings and directed the discussion toward parenting issues. On the other occasions, a GSBB staff member or volunteer led the discussion.

On alternate Saturdays, the girls met in community troop meetings in Baltimore. They worked on projects begun in MCIW or initiated projects to take into MCIW and enjoyed many regular Girl Scout activities, including sleepovers, field trips, and multitroop Girl Scout gatherings. They also went skating and lunched at restaurants, which donated their food and service. Cost factors precluded full involvement in the total Girl Scout experience. The girls were provided transportation to and from the meetings.

Source: K. J. Block & M. Potthast (1997). "Inmate Mothers and Enhanced Visitation Through Girl Scouts." Paper presented at the Annual Meetings of the Academy of Criminal Justice Sciences.

allocating resources but also understanding their dilemmas. Our Program Focus, "The Nebraska MOLD and Nursery School Programs," on page 208 provides some insight into how women's prisons can maintain the bond between mother and child.

Reunification after Release

The postrelease reunification of mother and child brings about new challenges that are not directly dealt with in an institutional setting. These are both psychological and practical in nature and are often associated with events and circumstances that occurred while the mother was incarcerated (Henriques, 1996). For example, the resumption of parental responsibility may be difficult if previous bonds were not established or if they

were insufficiently strong. A positive reunion is often contingent upon the opportunities for continued contact between mothers and children during the mother's incarceration. Lack of support from correctional institutions, including preplanning and postplanning, may also inhibit the reunion between mothers and their children.

Once children are returned to mothers who were incarcerated, both face considerable challenges. Guilt and shame often make it difficult for mothers to discipline and set limits for their children. Further, in their mothers' absence the children may have developed friends, new interests, and activities that make them unwilling to invest time in building a relationship with a mother who has been absent or is no longer as important to them. For mothers, their children's unwillingness to rearrange their priorities may be viewed as a form of rejection. Some mothers may also blame themselves and society for their current circumstances. This is further aggravated by the fact that following their incarceration, mothers have to deal with the stigma of being an ex-offender. Children too may be angry at themselves or at their mothers for leaving them. Some may also fear that their mothers will be sent away again (Henriques, 1996).

Those needing temporary financial aid can apply for welfare, but they will need to find a job soon; this may be a condition of their release. For mothers who lose custody of their children while in prison, the inability to provide support may make regaining custody a more difficult task. As a single parent employment may enable her to support her children, but she may be faulted for not providing adequate supervision while she is working (Pollock-Byrne, 1990).

The establishment of meaningful relationships between mother and child is difficult if drug involvement continues after release. While in prison drug intervention programs are essential to ensure that mothers deal with their addiction problems; for some, it is also necessary that they be required, as a condition of their release, to participate in community drug treatment programs as well.

To prepare women to reunite with their children, prison programs need to focus on helping women deal with these issues. Specifically, programs need to focus on three areas: initial separation, maintaining and strengthening ties during the separation, and the issues related to reuniting mother and child after release (Henriques, 1998).

Sexual Misconduct by Correctional Staff

Sexual misconduct by correctional staff generally refers to any type of improper conduct of a sexual nature directed at prisoners (GAO, 1999). Specifically, sexual misconduct may include:

- Any sexual advance made by staff members, agents, or volunteers of the corrections department
- Requests for sexual favors by staff members, agents, or volunteers of the corrections department
- Verbal or physical conduct of a sexual nature in prison toward a prisoner by staff members, agents, or volunteers of the corrections department

Specific behaviors may include touching, kissing, walking in on an inmate who is dressing, inappropriate body or cavity searches, inappropriate comments about an inmate's personal appearance, and language of a sexual nature (Smith, 1998). Some concrete examples include:

- A prison guard walks in on you while you are changing your clothes and tells you that you are "what he likes."
- The food service worker tells you he can get you cigarettes if you "flash" him.
- You fall in love with a staff member and agree to get married as soon as you are released.
- You begin a sexual relationship with him while in prison.
- The chaplain comforts you when you receive bad news from home. She keeps asking you to come by and see her even when nothing is wrong. She begins to write you letters telling you how much she loves you.
- You were an exotic dancer before being incarcerated. Three officers on the midnight shift pay you to dance for them. (Smith, 1998)

Although there has been a growing recognition that staff-on-inmate sexual misconduct is a problem, only 41 states, the federal government, and the District of Columbia have passed laws criminalizing it. The increased concern over the problem has largely been driven by two sources:

1. At least 23 departments of corrections have faced class action or individual damage suits related to sexual misconduct.
2. Most state legislatures have passed laws criminalizing certain types of sexual misconduct or increasing the penalty for the offense. (NIC, 1996)

According to data provided by the Bureau of Prisons (BOP) and Texas and California officials, female inmates in those jurisdictions made at least 506 allegations of staff-on-inmate sexual misconduct between 1995 and 1998. Of these allegations, 18 percent resulted in staff resignations, employment terminations, or other administrative sanctions. The vast majority of claims were not sustained due to lack of physical and medical evidence. Thus, according to correctional officials, they were faced with instances of "he said versus she said."

The individual effects of sexual misconduct on inmates are both physical and emotional, and devastate those women who experience them. These include:

- She may contract HIV virus or other sexually transmitted diseases.
- She may become pregnant.
- She may feel trapped in her situation and powerless to change it.
- She may suffer emotional trauma.

These are repercussions that will affect her long after she has left prison (Smith, 1998, p. 11). For women who

PROGRAM FOCUS

The Mother/Offspring Life Development (MOLD) Program was started in the early 1970s at the Nebraska Correctional Center for Women (NCCW) in York, Nebraska. Initially, it was funded by a federal grant, and later the department of corrections assumed financial responsibility for the program.

The basic tenets of MOLD follow:

1. Children are allowed to stay on grounds with their mothers for 5 days each month. One child is allowed to stay with his or her mother in her room. If the mother has a roommate, mother and child can be asked to stay in another room for the length of the visit.

2. To participate in the visiting program, mothers must have a good institutional record, attend a class on rules and regulations, and pass a test on that material. They must also participate in one other MOLD class.

3. The mother must submit a child visitation contract 15 days in advance of the visit. The children's meals must be paid for in advance, by the mother. Transporters and caregivers must have confirmed the visit by returning the transportation papers to the Parenting Program Coordinator before the visit is approved. The mother is removed from her regular work schedule while her children are visiting; however, she is responsible for completing any school make-up work on her own time.

4. Classes in parenting, child development, money management, and personal development are available to all on a voluntary basis.

5. Mothers are asked to handle their own babies. One visiting problem has been the children making contact with a large number of inmates on grounds. This is especially true with infants. Infant visits are held in the MOLD area. In general, the behavior of the inmate population tends to improve when children are on grounds.

Children of incarcerated parents can be deeply affected by their absence. Our goal is to provide the opportunity for incarcerated mothers to have quality time with their children. Our hope is to lessen the impact of her being away, while keeping the mother-child relationship intact and growing.

Advantages of Prison Parenting Programs

Aside from the altruistic values of the parenting programs at NCCW, there are some very practical administrative advantages. First, mothers wanting to participate in any of the mother-child programs must have good conduct records. This is a tremendous incentive for these women to avoid poor decision making and acting out or irresponsible behavior in the prison setting. The result is a very significant and appropriate incentive to maintain a positive institutional adjustment.

Second, all inmate mothers wishing to participate in the MOLD or nursery programs are required to successfully complete parenting classes. Inmates who are involved in self-betterment programming, particularly instruction, are less idle, are more productive, and have higher self-esteem.

The impact of an infant or child's presence in the facility has an overall "calming" effect on the total prison environment. Because most of the inmates are mothers themselves, there is a self-imposed and

significantly higher expectation of good conduct from all inmates when the children are present. Her peers would ostracize a woman for contributing to a less-than-ideal environment by being argumentative or using profanity. Because there is such great value and ownership placed on the parenting programs here at NCCW, the inmate mothers "police" themselves to ensure the program's continued success. They are acutely aware that significant problems occurring within these programs could lead to increased public/media/political scrutiny and a termination of the programs. The women realize these programs are progressive and "fly in the face" of current penological philosophy, which is considerably more punitive in nature.

Finally, there is a considerable fiscal advantage to the nursery program in particular. It has been previously estimated that the cost per infant in this program averages out to approximately $11,000 per year. The cost for an infant who is placed from birth by welfare agencies into a foster home is approximately $17,000 annually. This is a fiscal impact that quickly gains the attention of policy makers.

Warden Wayne's objective was to try and sustain families as humanely as the law allows during their time of separation. "That flies in the face of the 'throw 'em in a cage, poke 'em with a sharp stick once a day, and make 'em so miserable they won't ever want to come back here again' philosophy," he says. "But these people will get out and move in next door. Your son or your daughter could be in here" (Dowing, 1997, October).

The Nursery School Program

In 1994, MOLD at NCCW was expanded to include a nursery. This nursery was modeled after the program at the Bedford Hills Correctional Facility, in New York. We are the only facility in the country to have both an overnight visiting program for older children and an on-grounds nursery. The objective of this program is to develop a bond between mother and child, in a learning environment. I feel this could make or break the relationship between mother and child, especially for first-time mothers; prior to this their only alternative was to hand the baby over to Grandma or put it in foster care. We are trying to build confidence in these women as mothers. I have also heard all the reasons why these programs are wrong; I couldn't disagree more. I will suffice it to quote my friend Sister Elaine Roulet of the Bedford Hills, NY Nursery, "A prince does not know he is born in a palace, our babies don't know they were born in prison; they both only know they are with their mothers."

A committee of staff members considers an inmate's eligibility for the nursery program; length of sentence, nature of the offense, criminal history, and institutional record are considered. The inmate must be within a timeframe in her sentence where she and the baby will leave the institution together, by the time, or before, the baby is 18 months old.

The participating mothers attend all classes offered through the MOLD and nursery programs. These include parenting, child development, infant-child CPR, and many others. Lamaze and breast-feeding classes, which prepare the mother for the experience of labor and the birth of her baby are also offered. The nursery instructor, or the parenting program coordinator, will go with the mother and coach her through labor.

The mother is the primary care provider for her baby. She is responsible for all of her child's emotional and physical needs. This includes feeding, bathing, play time, quiet time, laundry, etc. Proper personal hygiene is a must for both the mother and the infant. The State of Nebraska will provide the mother and child with medical care and with the necessary supplies needed to raise her child. The philosophy of the nursery is to encourage nurturing and to provide a secure environment for the infant. No physical, sexual, mental, or verbal punishment or abuse will be tolerated. In the event this does occur, the mother may be terminated from the program and the infant released to a pre-approved caregiver.

The program also provides opportunities for mothers to do things that promote both bonding and responsibility. The child may sleep with the mother to be comforted or if he or she is restless. Other times the program encourages that the child sleep in its crib. Mothers also have 2 hours to take their children outside and have the responsibility of checking on their children during breaks from work. Infants accompany their mothers to the prison dining room for all meals. Additionally, mothers have the opportunity to take pictures of and with their infants.

The mother must fulfill a half-time work assignment along with her nursery school assignment. Part of the mother's job assignment is to clean the nursery unit. To continue in the program mothers must maintain a good conduct record. Confinement to the segregation unit may result in their termination in the nursery program. Each case is evaluated on its own merit.

The MOLD and nursery programs at NCCW have had a very positive effect on inmate morale. The inmates take ownership and are very protective of this wonderful privilege. They watch their language and the nature of their conversations around the children. The programs also promote good behavior, because a good institutional record is imperative to having overnight visits or participating in the nursery program.

Inmate Views of Both Programs

Speaker 1 Hi, I'm an inmate at the Nebraska Correctional Center for Women and I've been participating in the MOLD program since 1975 when my daughter was 18 months old. She is now 24 years old. I've participated in day visits with my son. However, he is 12 now, which makes him too old to come on grounds. I've participated in day visits with my grandson, I've had overnights with my grandson and during 1975 to 1998 I've had a lot of overnight visits with my daughter who is now 24 and my son that's not old enough to come. I've had two children here in the hospital at York. . . . A lot of people like having children in a prison, and I think it makes it a better atmosphere altogether; the women act different when children are on the grounds. It's not a prison atmosphere like everybody thinks it is; all the women enjoy the children. Thank you very much.

Speaker 7 My name is Debra. I'm an inmate at the Nebraska Correctional Center for Women, serving a 3- to 5-year sentence for shoplifting. I'm a relapsed drug addict and having my son here for the 5-day overnight visit or the weekend visit at Wesley House, a program that helps us with our children in Omaha, Nebraska, has been a real joy to me. It eases my son's mind and before he got to come for his first visit he thought that I was dead because I had never left him. And, on the first visit that he had here at the Nebraska Center for Women with me, we were playing in the MOLD area and he touched my

(continued)

(continued)

face with both of his hands and he said, "Mommy I'm so glad you aren't dead, now we can play all day." And it just means a lot to me that it eases his mind and it helps him to be able to adapt and to accept the fact that I have done something wrong and there is always a consequence for negative behavior. And because of that I have been set aside and I cannot come home when I want to come home, and it's easier to get in trouble than it is to get out of trouble.

Speaker 11 Hi, my name is Sherri and I have participated in the MOLD Program as well as the Nursery Program. . . . Okay, I also was in the Nursery Program. I came in when I was 1-month pregnant and I was offered to go to the nursery. I went to the nursery and I loved the nursery, the bond with my child, it was fantastic, I mean it's so wonderful how they let you keep your child with you, you know, and the bond that me and my child had got, you know, it's unbreakable and the Nursery Program is wonderful. It helps mothers when they leave here, you know, to get on their feet, you know, with a little milk, clothing, Pampers, you know. They also take pictures of our kids and ahh . . . it's just a wonderful program to have your child in if you're in prison and you are pregnant.

Interviewer Questions (I = Interviewer. The other letters identify inmates.)

I: What does the playground consist of?

K: There's swings and a slide, a merry-go-round. There is this little spider thing that my kids really like that they climb through it, it's a metal thing, it's kind of like monkey bars that they can play on. And there's like a little bouncy teeter-totter type thing, my little boy always says, "Let's go see Mickey Mouse," and that's what he's talking about.

I: What is it that means most to you about having your overnights and day visits with your children?

K: The time with them, we call that our cutchie time. They get to tell me what's happening at home; they live with my mom. They tell me what happens at home and what they don't like about the new rules and basically the rules that I lived by and it helps me to show them that . . . this is not what they want to end up being like. They don't want to be here. It helps us to bond a lot. . . . we color a lot down here and do a lot of different stuff and they get to see that it's not really like they see on TV. It's not the hardcore door slamming, people getting shot and all that stuff. They see that it's a normal functioning place where Mom is getting help with her addiction.

I: What are the eating arrangements?

L: He gets to eat everything I eat, he gonna eat. I don't know, we pay $6 for 5 days. . . . They just come over and eat with me. It isn't all the junk he eats.

I: What do you think is the most important benefit of the MOLD Program?

L: I think it gives me a chance to know my [child] and it gives him a chance. Okay, before he started staying with me I wasn't Mom because he didn't know me as Mom. And now he comes up to me and says, "Mommy" and grabs my leg, and you know, that feels good because it never was like that. Now he knows who I am, he knows my voice, he knows me a lot better than he would have ever known me. Only 4 hours isn't enough, and this program is really good for not just me but everybody.

I: Do you feel like you would have the bonds that you have with him now if it wasn't for the MOLD Program?

L: I wouldn't have any kind of bond with him if it wasn't for me being able to keep him.

I: Does it take him a while to get used to being around you, or do you feel that your bond has stayed strong with him?

L: Well, I've been gone since he was 6 weeks and this program helped me to get to know my baby better. He really wasn't too used to me because I had only seen him for 4 hours, like in visiting. And then I started keeping him up here, I kept him for maybe 2 days at a time because he really wasn't used to being around me, so when I started keeping him he got used to me. Then I could keep him . . . I started keeping him just like 2 days and then I went to 3 days. . . .

I: And what does it mean for you to be able to have him up here?

L: It's really important to me because I haven't had a chance to be a mother to him, and if it wasn't for this program he wouldn't know me as well as he does now.

I: What are the nursery rooms like?

L: Well in the nursery they're smaller than the ones like the MOLD room and our rooms, but they're comfortable; there's room for us to play and stuff.

I: So, it doesn't make him feel insecure or like it's a jail that he's in?

L: No, it doesn't look like a jail; it's just a room like any other room. It's just . . . there's just more of them, I don't know, I don't think the kids know the difference.

Speaker 14 My name is Goldie Fisher. I have been participating in the MOLD Program for the last 10 years. I was incarcerated in 1988. My children were little . . . one was a little over 1 year and the other one was a little over 3 years. They used to come and spend the night. We would stay over in North Hall either in my room or in the MOLD room. We would play games. We would go outside and play basketball, soccer, or whatever they wanted to play. We would go over to the dining room to eat at scheduled times. I would read books to them at nighttime before going to bed, we'd color, do puzzles, ummm. Just . . . we could do about anything that they wanted to do.

Now they're over the age limit so they just come for day visits. I've been able to celebrate every birthday with them. I'm allowed to buy a cake and the MOLD building provides ice cream sometimes for them. I can make them a birthday box and buy canteen items and put it in . . . put in it, like candy, chips, personals. My oldest one, which is 14 now, he loves to come and just for me to make him nachos and sit around and watch movies and talk. My youngest one, he likes to watch movies and play games, and they like to wrestle and we talk. . . . I also work down here at the MOLD building and . . . the kids are happy, the parents are happy, it's a very positive environment down here. We have games, we have a little kitchenette, we have a little reading center, we have a play when they come down here to make cookies or bake with their kids or read them a story, and how much the kids really enjoy it.

You know, I hear . . . all the time you see the kids huggin' their moms or telling them, "I love you" and "I miss you" and I think it benefits the children as much as it benefits us moms. And also I think that the women here really give the mothers that have their children on grounds a lot of respect. A lot of your friends that are here doing time with you they come down here to see your kids or tell them hi! or they get them stuff from the canteen or make them things.

It's really a pull together situation when kids are here and I think it eases a lot of the tensions that sometimes arise when you're in prison. It just gives everybody a chance to put down all their differences and come together, and the kids really enjoy it. The rooms that we stay in up in the nursery aren't like the rooms you expect to see in a prison. It's more of a college dormitory type of room where you can have an extra cot for your daughter or son, or they can sleep with you in the bed, or you can have them in your room with you.

Would you develop a nursery program and/or an overnight program for mothers and children at a female institution? Discuss the reasons for and against developing these programs.

Source: Adapted from materials and personal viewpoints provided by Mary Alley (2000), parenting coordinator, State of Nebraska, Nebraska Correctional Center for Women, York, Nebraska, and former warden, Larry Wayne.

become pregnant while in prison this is very stressful because:

1. They may become afraid to tell anyone about the pregnancy and to seek medical attention.

2. Prenatal care in many facilities is inadequate and it may be difficult to receive medical care and nutrition necessary to have a healthy baby.

3. Few prisons will allow women to keep their babies, which means placing the baby up for adoption.

4. If they decide to terminate the pregnancy it can be difficult to obtain an abortion while in prison. Many states do not allow public funds to be used for abortions, so the woman is forced both to arrange for and pay a private agency to do the procedure.

5. They may be punished for becoming pregnant, be denied parole, receive a disciplinary report, lose work or visiting privileges, or be charged with separate criminal offenses. (Smith, 1998, p. 14)

Victims of sexual misconduct by correctional staff often feel trapped and powerless to change their situations, and they also suffer from severe emotional trauma. On the other hand, some women feel a misguided sense of power if they believe the relationship is meeting their financial and emotional needs. Regardless, women in both circumstances can feel fear of being caught and be ashamed of their involvement with staff.

These repercussions affect women for the rest of their lives—even after they are released. Indeed, the initial psychological trauma may manifest itself in such behaviors and feelings as alcohol and drug use, suicidal or homicidal feelings, panic attacks, insomnia, and fits of rage and anger (Smith, 1998).

In focus groups women inmates were asked, "Why are women vulnerable to sexual abuse in prison?" They responded:

- "Sex, just like drugs, is a part of being in prison. There has to be a certain amount of that going on. What's important is what the prison does when they discover someone having sex."

- "If we had more jobs in here, we wouldn't have to have sex just to get a candy bar, some street food, or a perm."

- "Cops should act like cops. They should stay in their place so that we can stay in ours."

- "A lot of these women have low self-esteem. They don't think a lot of themselves, so they'll settle for a soda, candy, or some cigarettes."

- "A lot of the girls that the officers bother are slow (have mental health problems). They can prey on these women because they don't know any better."

Beyond individual effects, sexual misconduct harms all women, including female correctional employees. First, many correctional staff offenders believe that all women, including inmates and female employees, are available for sex, and they treat them accordingly. Second, sexual misconduct shifts boundaries that are critical for security, as well as other prison functions, such as rehabilitation and participation in organized programs. Third, women who are not compliant with correctional employees' wishes (i.e., sexual talk or physical sexual relationships) may be sanctioned by being denied opportunities or privileges that women who participate receive (Smith, 1998).

Programming and Services for Female Inmates

Several factors have contributed to female inmates having needs and interests that differ from male inmates, particularly with regard to services and programming. These include:

- Women's disproportionate victimization from sexual or physical abuse

- Women's responsibility for children

- Women's higher likelihood of drug addiction

- Women's higher likelihood of mental illness

- Women's higher likelihood of being unemployed prior to incarceration (Belknap, Dunn, & Holsinger, 1997, p. 23)

These circumstances, coupled with the overall increase in the number of females incarcerated in jails and prisons, reflect the need for different programming to ensure parity and to provide structured intervention that decreases the likelihood of recidivism (Morash, Bynum, & Koons, 1998).

However, creating effective services for women requires that programs be designed and developed based on the reality of their lives, including recognizing the differences between male and female growth and development (Covington, 1998). Equality is not about providing the same programs, treatment, and opportunities for girls and boys; equality is about providing opportunities that mean the same to each gender (Belknap et al., 1997, p. 23). To have successful gender-specific programming and services, the following criteria need to exist:

- Meet the unique needs of females.

- Acknowledge the female perspective.

- Support the female experience through positive female role models.

- Listen to the needs and experiences of adolescent females.

- Recognize the contributions of girls and women.

- Respect female development.

- Empower young girls and women to reach their full potential.

- Work to change established attitudes that prevent or discourage young women from recognizing their potential. (p. 23)

Program initiatives and innovations are continually growing to meet the unique needs of female inmates. Corrections officials in the United States and Canada have described several categories of programs that offered a wide variety of opportunities. The most common offerings for female inmates included institutional work and adult basic education/General Equivalency Degree (GED) classes, life skills training, vocational training, prerelease programs, and prison industry (see Figure 9.3). Many also offered college classes, and some offered substance abuse treatment programs (*Corrections Compendium*, 1998, March).

In this section, we will look at a variety of programs and services for female inmates, including educational, vocational, recreational, and substance abuse programs and medical services.

Educational Programs

As with males, a majority of female inmates are undereducated. Only 39 percent had finished high school or received a GED (Greenfeld & Snell, 1999); many functioned at a much lower level. For example, data on a sample of female inmates, constituting 89 percent of the

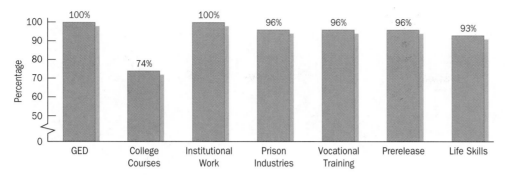

Figure 9.3 *Percentage of States Offering Programming for Female Inmates**

*Forty-seven states responded to the survey.

Source: Corrections Compendium (1998, March). Female Offenders: Their Numbers Grow, So Does the Need for Gender-Specific Programming, *CC, 23*(3): 8–23. Reprinted with permission, American Correctional Association.

women incarcerated in Florida between 1985 and 1987, found that the average reported grade level was 10.1, but the tested level was 7.4 (Blount, Danner, Vega, & Silverman, 1991).

Another part of the educational programming is life skills and related courses. These courses are very popular in women's prisons, particularly those dealing with parenting, visitation, and other family relations skills. Their popularity stems from the fact that they are perceived to have a direct positive impact on the inmates' abilities to maintain family relationships. The Michigan Department of Corrections, under the leadership of Nancy Zang, designed and implemented a voluntary life skills program especially for female inmates. Fifteen weeks are needed to complete the program; sessions are held three times a week for 2 hours. Participation usually involves 12 to 18 students per group; all start and typically graduate together. Chairs and tables are arranged in horseshoe fashion to allow participants to have eye contact, while promoting discussion. The curriculum includes units on:

- Self-awareness
- Communication
- Problem solving
- Stress management
- Anger management
- Employability skills
- Time and money management
- Family and community living

Vocational Programs

Most female inmates have minimal or no work experience, along with academic deficiencies. Effective programming for female inmates, then, needs to address their educational needs before offering opportunities to develop practical skills through vocational programs or prison industry assignments. Reading and writing skills, for example, are fundamental for inmates to get a job and lead an autonomous life outside the institution. A Florida study found this lack of educational skills to be a problem in qualifying for vocational training. This is not

surprising given that a national literacy study found 43 percent of female inmates as compared with 23 percent of women in the general population performed at the lowest level. This meant at best some (but not all) of these inmates were able to read short pieces of text to find a single fact, enter personal information in a document, or add numbers set up in a column. This was further confirmed by a Florida study that found three quarters of the inmates could not perform simple tasks necessary for any job, and more than one fourth had language skills at or below the third-grade level.[5]

This study also found that only three of the eight vocational training programs provided jobs where there was a substantial demand for workers and a livable wage. This led to the recommendation that the state discontinue the five programs not meeting this criterion and reallocate funds to increase basic education offerings for programs in the areas of commercial vehicle driving, print and graphic arts, technical illustration, and air conditioning and refrigeration mechanics.

For women to succeed on the outside, vocational programs must provide them with marketable skills. Partnerships, both public and private, that may result in employment upon release are optimal and may also facilitate the transition from the institution into the community.

Despite several suggestions to improve vocational programs for females, most are still behind the standards they can and should provide. Generally, Winifred (1996) found that vocational programs for women fall into five categories:

1. institutional maintenance (clerical work, food service for the institution, and general cleaning and maintenance of the grounds)
2. education (mostly remedial)
3. vocational training (primarily traditional cosmetology, sewing, food service, and clerical skills)
4. treatment (AA, NA)
5. medical care

Another important issue related to parity involves types of vocational training that should be available to women. A prevailing view is that women should be

These female inmates in California have been trained to fight fires. While it is widely believed that women should be offered the same programs as men, many female inmates are not interested in traditionally male programs.

offered the same programs as males. This fails to recognize that women are not men and may not have any interest in many traditionally male programs. Nancy Zang provides a perspective on this issue in our In Their Own Words feature, "Nontraditional vs. Traditional Programming for Women."

Based on a national study of innovative and promising programs for female offenders, Morash and Bynum (1996) reported that several state-level administrators recognized a connection "between low self-esteem, victimization, and other problems" (p. 45). Further, less than 20 percent of the programs identified by state- and institutional-level administrators as promising or innovative were work programs. Vocational programs provide an effective and widely used mechanism to release offenders through "good time" (e.g., work release and earned good time through prison jobs).

Recommendations for future vocational programs for female inmates include:

- certifying programs by the appropriate industry or state board and allowing inmates to take required exams while still incarcerated
- equal pay for women and men in comparable jobs
- new and/or updated equipment in instances where existing machinery and equipment are no longer adequate (e.g., computers)
- increased interaction with employers in the community

- stronger partnerships between the department of corrections and the department of education or other educational suppliers
- encouraging women to enroll in nontraditional programs
- coordinated moves and transfers in states that have multiple facilities, enabling inmates to complete training courses (Winifred, 1996)

Like vocational education programs, prison industries have had to face concerns of parity and the changes in the job sector from hard industries to more emphasis on technical and service jobs. To provide for the interests and needs of female inmates, Carp and Davis (1989) suggested that women's prisons need to develop work programs that include a garment shop, food service, and a data entry or telemarketing shop. In this regard, several jurisdictions have used female inmates to staff information lines that answer questions from callers about state tourism opportunities and as reservations agents for TWA and Best Western motels. Additionally, to increase work opportunities for women, some jurisdictions allow female inmates to work in programs with males (Davis, 1992a). Women who participate in occupational rehabilitation programs tend to earn more money and stay out of prison longer than those who do not (Bartolo, 1991).

Nontraditional vs. Traditional Programming for Women

IN THEIR OWN WORDS

Michigan is under a federal mandate to develop three nontraditional training programs. The reason for this is because the skilled trades tend to pay more. There are many reasons why women have not enrolled in these programs. First, when their interests were evaluated, it was found that these jobs were not the highest-ranking type of work that the women wanted. Second, an apprenticeship program in this state requires that the prisoner have functional reading and math levels, at no less than eighth grade level. If they can't read the electrical code they will not be able to do the job. Based on this criterion, it is hard to fill these programs; but, this is true of all of our vocational programs requiring a minimum of an eighth-grade reading level. Third, many women are in prison for short terms. Rather than invest hundreds of thousands of dollars in vocational programs that many will be unable to complete, it is better that they be persuaded to enroll in a trade program they can learn before they leave.

Michigan's experience with its three nontraditional programs rep-

resents a method to gauge the success of these types of nontraditional programs. For example, the auto mechanics program has probably the best auto mechanic teacher in the state of Michigan. Nevertheless, although the program has a capacity for 15 students, they have never had more than 3 women at a time interested in auto mechanics. Similarly, it took 4 years to find a woman interested in the electronics program. This is not to say that Michigan has not been successful in its apprenticeship programs. In five areas, including landscape gardener, computer operator, and food technician, there has never been a problem filling available slots. When we started a denture production program, "we had candidates coming out of the walls." For 13 slots there were over 85 women applicants.

On the other hand, every time I'm in a prison women want to know why we don't have a cosmetology program. Additionally, the programs with the biggest interest are those involving food service and domestic types of things. It may well be that what determines the program preferences for a woman

relates to how she was raised and what she is most comfortable doing.

The question is how do you expand female inmates' knowledge of the nature, requirements, and pay scales of different jobs? I think career exploration is probably needed much more in programming for women than it is with men. With men, we rarely have a problem finding some who want to work on a maintenance crew, or with at least a baseline knowledge of the difference between a hammer and a wrench. With women, we start out with the basics (i.e., identify tools). Thus, what is needed in the area of female programming is to provide these inmates with an opportunity to explore or learn about a variety of programs so that they can choose the one that best fits their interests and also pays a living wage.

Source: Adapted from a teleconference between Nancy Zang, program administrator for the Michigan Department of Corrections, and Ira J. Silverman on female inmate–related issues (1998).

Recreational Programs

Women's prisons lag behind men's facilities with regard to recreational activities. Even though appropriate recreation and exercise are seen as healthy and important activities, most women engage in leisure activities that are sedentary (e.g., watching television and playing board games) (Mann, 1984). Alternative activities found to be successful at women's facilities include aerobics classes and exercise rooms with stationary bicycles, treadmills, and weight equipment. One Minnesota prison had a bowling alley. Also popular are hobby and craft programs, featuring macramé, ceramics, and jewelry making (Carp & Davis, 1989).

Zang (1998) argues that women tend to respond to the opportunity to help others. She considers the At-Risk Babies Quilts Program at Crane Michigan's Women Facility to be a good example. Most female inmates are not quil-

ters, but those that could quilt taught the others. When the quilts were finished they were distributed to hospitals for HIV-positive infants and those with fetal drug or alcohol syndrome. After seeing a video about this nationwide program the women were enthusiastic about helping these babies because many were abandoned. As Assistant Warden Dan Hawkins notes, "These babies didn't have anybody in their lives, so we decided to help" (FYI, 1996).

Substance Abuse Treatment Programs

On every measure of drug use women offenders report higher usage than males (40% vs. 32%). Further, nearly one in three women serving in state prisons indicated that they had committed the offense that resulted in their incarceration to obtain money to support their drug habit. Even though the need for drug treatment is evident, its availability for women is not sufficient. A BJS survey found that only one in four state inmates is receiving treatment for an alcohol or drug problem. This treatment can range from short-term drug education or self-help groups to long-term treatment (Mumola, 1999). A Florida survey reported that substance abuse treatment for women was widely identified by correctional officials as being insufficiently provided (Morash et al., 1998).

Another theme in literature on female substance abuse focuses on providing an integrated program that considers all related factors. As noted, a high proportion of the female inmate population have been traumatized by being physically and/or psychologically abused or have witnessed violence. Thus, "most female offenders are trauma survivors and when they enter prisons they are at risk for being retraumatized by their experience in correctional facilities. Moreover, drugs or alcohol are used by women to mediate the pain of trauma" (Bloom & Covington, 1999, pp. 12–13). Further, these women often grow up in areas where drug dealing and addiction are a way of life. Finally, almost one fourth of the women in prison suffer from mental illness compared with 15 percent of the males. Previously,

> women were expected to seek help for addiction, psychological disorders, and trauma from separate sources and to incorporate what they learned from a recovery group, a counselor, and a psychologist into their own lives. This expectation has placed an unnecessary burden on recovering females. A gender responsive treatment program needs to integrate all three approaches. (Bloom & Covington, 1999, p. 13)

Thus, there is need to establish a substance abuse program that encompasses all these needs. Further, these programs must be developed in an environment where women can experience healthy relationships with counselors. Safety is another factor that must be considered. For many of these women their first experience of safety is in a prison setting. However, for the healing process to be successful they need to be assured of a safe environment. This means keeping female facilities free of physical and sexual harassment and abuse (Bloom & Covington, 1999).

Medical Services

The quality and quantity of health care received by all inmates have been questioned and generally found wanting (see Chapter 17). However, women commonly need and avail themselves of more medical services than men; as a result, the problem of poor medical services is greater for the female inmate. The street lifestyle of many female inmates (e.g., long histories of drug and alcohol abuse, poor diet, possibly indiscriminate sexual behavior, restricted access to medical services, and the tendency to neglect medical problems) means that women entering prison are likely to require medical attention and education to help them take better care of themselves on release to the community (Fogel, 1998). Generally, their access to

community-based health care is minimal. In prison they face disparity in medical care, which has been justified by the smaller size of many women's prisons.

Typically, female inmate medical problems include asthma, diabetes, HIV/AIDS, TB, hypertension, pregnancy, chlamydia, herpes, chronic pelvic inflammatory disease, and anxiety neurosis and depression (Acoca, 1998; Fogel, 1998; Ross & Lawrence, 1998). Further, a greater percentage of females than males (3.5% vs. 2.2%) were known to be HIV-positive. In the majority of states and in every region in the United States except the West, female inmates had a higher HIV-positive infection rate than male inmates (Maruschak, 1999). Drug use, trading sex for drugs and money, sexual abuse, living under conditions of poverty, and other gender-specific conditions of their lives make them more prone to HIV infection (De Groot, Leibel, & Zierler, 1998).

A barrier to treating women for HIV is their reluctance to participate in treatment and prevention strategies. This is due to fear of stigmatization upon disclosure of HIV status and the resulting stigmatization, negative experiences, and associations with correctional medical care that can be heightened by sexual abuse and apprehensions about HIV testing (De Groot et al., 1998).

An HIV program that meets these needs and concerns would include the following elements:

- voluntary HIV testing
- on-site HIV care from nurses and HIV specialists who were available several times weekly to respond to the needs of HIV-infected and at-risk women
- state-of-the-art drug treatments, which include access to a combination of drug therapy, antiviral medication monitoring—because HIV lowers the resistance to viruses—and postexposure to prophylactic (prevention) methods (e.g., condoms, bleach). All three of the facilities reported offering on-site gynecological and obstetric care.
- AIDS Education and Counseling (ACE)
- safer sex negotiation, skill-building, and self-esteem workshops to improve their abilities to make intelligent sexual choices
- peer-led counseling groups, drug treatment and AIDS education, and counseling
- discharge programming planning that includes (1) educational and marketable skills development to provide women with the wherewithal to stay out of prison, (2) the coordination of child care with drug abuse treatment services, safe housing, and medical and educational services (De Groot et al., 1998)

Acoca and Austin (1996) conducted interviews with 151 female inmates and found that 61 percent required medical treatment for physical problems and 45 percent required treatment for mental health issues. The women who were interviewed reported that their access to services—particularly psychological, substance abuse, and acute medical services—was limited. Further, they asserted that, in cases where they received initial medical treatment, continued medical treatment and follow-up appointments were lacking.

Research on gynecological services for women in prison has consistently suggested that these services are inadequate; gynecological exams are not conducted upon admission into institutions, nor are they provided annually. Screening questions are typically not asked, and, in many prisons, there are no doctors who are qualified to provide necessary obstetrics and gynecological care for female inmates. The implications of these inadequacies are life-threatening. Women in prison risk overlooking breast cancer, ovarian cancer, HIV, and abnormal Pap smears (Fink, Goodman, Hight, Miller-Mack, & De Groot, 1998; NIC, 1995).

To deal with this inadequate health care for women, the National Commission on Correctional Health (1995) mandates that:

1. Comprehensive services for women's unique problems should be provided in prisons, jails, and juvenile detention and confinement.

2. Correctional institutions should provide intake examinations that include

   a. breast exams and—depending on the patient's age, sexual history, and past medical history—a pelvic exam, Pap smear, and baseline mammogram.

   b. Correctional facilities should take histories on menstrual cycles, pregnancies, and gynecological problems, and make a nutrition assessment.

3. Institutions should provide laboratory tests to detect sexually transmitted diseases, including gonorrhea, syphilis, and chlamydia. Also, pregnancy tests should be done at admission, and if the results are positive those women who are also infected with HIV should be treated with AZT so they are less likely to transmit the disease to their new babies.

Correctional systems failing to comply with these standards can expect litigation on these issues, especially with the growing numbers of women entering prison.

Community Corrections for Females

The call for more community-based programs for women should not interfere with a commitment to equitable sentencing of male and female offenders. To the extent that mitigating and aggravating factors may be considered in sentencing, these should also be consistently applied across all offenders (Kenney, 1999). However, according to Morton (1998):

> Women represent less of a physical threat to the community than do men. Sentencing practices that mandate institutionalization for women for minor property offenses and drug use serve no meaningful societal or public safety benefits and are a waste of valuable resources that could be used for alternative punishments. Thus, incarceration should be the last option to be considered in sanctioning women offenders and invoked only when the woman is a danger to herself or others. (p. 15)

Nine out of 10 states report using some alternative to prison for female offenders after their commitment to prison. Figure 9.4 shows that the largest number of states use work release and that a high proportion of

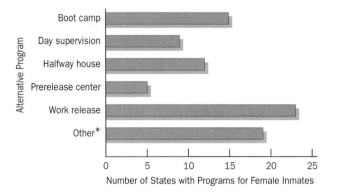

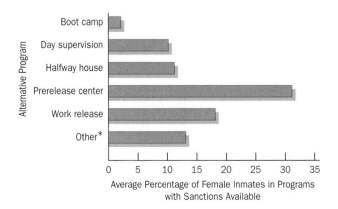

Figure 9.4 *Women in Alternative Sanctions After Commitment*

*Other programs include transition and aftercare programs, educational programs, and mental health programs.

Source: M. Morash, T. S. Bynum, & B. A. Koons (1998). *Women Offenders: Programming Needs and Promising Approaches.* Washington, DC: U.S. Department of Justice, Office of Justice Programs.

female inmates use prerelease centers and work release. Although boot camps are used by 15 states, they affect a very small percentage of the committed women. Even though community corrections and alternatives to prison are considered to be the best types of settings for female offenders, states vary greatly in the proportion of women they assign to these incarceration alternatives.

Boot Camp for Women

Since the development of boot camp prisons, the large majority of participants have been male. However, from a legal perspective, women are entitled to the same programming opportunities offered to male boot camp participants (Rafter, 1990). Although many correctional systems have strived for gender equality in prison programming, research has shown that unless the specific needs of female offenders are taken into account, negative consequences may result from women participating in programs originally developed for men (Gover, Styve, & MacKenzie, 1999).

On January 1, 1998, 15 states had boot camps that were either coed or only for women. There were 508 women participating in these programs, which represented 7.4 percent of the inmate boot camp population (Camp & Camp, 1998). In about half the programs female inmates are integrated into programs with male boot camp inmates (ACA, 1999). MacKenzie and Donaldson (1996) studied six boot camps with female participants. The women reported difficulties keeping up with the physical demands of the program. This is no surprise; "since these programs were originally designed for male participants, physical activity levels in most programs were determined according to the average male inmate's physical stamina" (p. 6).

Women also experienced added emotional stress because the majority of the boot camp staff and inmates were men. Additional difficulties were reported by women with past histories of abuse because the confrontation with the drill instructors reminded them of the past abusive situations (Gover, Styve, & MacKenzie, 1999). The highly confrontational environments of boot camps triggered emotions associated with past mental and physical abuse. The negative consequences of integrating males and females in these programs is clearly demonstrated by the fact that women in the separate programs reported less emotional and physical stress. The authors recommended that during the early stages of program development consideration be given to the potential effects of gender integration on program participants.

Community-Based Parenting Programs

As noted, more than two thirds of female inmates in federal and state prisons had at least one minor child. More than one half of female inmates in state prisons in 1997 were never visited by their minor children. A GAO (1999) study found the primary reasons for infrequent visitation are travel distances and related travel costs. They also found that the visitation policies and schedules in the three jurisdictions studied were the same for female and male inmates. However, given the fact that there are fewer women in prison than men the placement of female offenders, according to the BOP, presents unique challenges. It would be prohibitively expensive to establish facilities (relatively close to their families or community ties) for small numbers of women in every state. The BOP, in 1999, had 14 female facilities in operation, at which 30 percent of the inmates were assigned to prisons more than 500 miles from their release residences compared with 24 percent of male inmates (GAO, 1999).

Given the importance of maintaining the bond between mother and child and the lower security risk posed by most female offenders—whose crimes are nonviolent—what might be the most effective programming? One reasonable suggestion would be to follow the example of the California Department of Corrections (CDC). In 1980, California incarcerated roughly 1,000 women; this number rose to over 11,000 in 1999. In the early 1990s, the CDC recognized that any estimate of the fiscal and social costs of incarcerating mothers must include the cost of placing their children in foster or kinship care (Acoca & Raeder, 1999). In 1994, California legislators passed, and the governor signed, the "Pregnant and Parenting Women's Alternative Sentencing Program Act." This bill requires that the CDC design and fully implement intensive substance abuse and parenting programs in lieu of state prison commitments for pregnant and parenting women offenders and their children 0 to 6 years old. Accompanying this was an appropriation of $15 million for the design and construction of three residential mother-child treatment facilities that will serve a total of 120 women offenders and their children.

This represented two critically important advances. First, this program functions as a true alternative sentencing program for women offenders, because, with the agreement of the sentencing judge, district attorney, and probation department, they will go directly into residential treatment with their children rather than to prison. Second, the program, which is based on maternal and child health research, is designed not only to treat the mother's drug dependence but to maximize her child's development potential by enhancing the mother-child relationship. As Acoca and Raeder (1999) indicated, this emphasis on intensively treating the mother-child pair is rare in correctional settings, yet essential for interrupting the intergenerational cycle of family fragmentation and criminal activity. We end the chapter with our Program Focus, "Summit House," a model that embodies the elements of an effective community-based program for nonviolent female offenders and their children.

Summit House

The Summit House program strengthens the family by intervening in the lives of nonviolent women offenders and their children. Comprehensive services are administered to the women and their children through the efforts of a public-private partnership in a highly structured and controlled environment. The program, which opened in 1987, strives to break the cycle of crime.

The Day-Reporting Center

With over 1,400 women incarcerated in North Carolina on any day, and over 3,000 children without their mothers, Summit House expanded in 1994 to include a day-reporting center. This provides a structured case management approach in a nonresidential program for women on probation and parole in the Guilford area. With over 725 women on probation and probation officers averaging 150 caseloads, there were too few POs to provide the individual attention needed by these women. Instead of revoking a mother's probation, the probation officer and the courts now have an alternative to incarceration with the inception of the Resource Center.

Summit House

The new sentencing guidelines, passed in 1994, placed more nonviolent offenders in our communities across the state and violent and repeat offenders in prison for the full length of their sentence. Summit House operates programs—in four areas of the state—considered intermediate sanctions within sentencing guidelines.

Mothers are referred to the program by alternative sentencing centers, attorneys, judges, and probation officers throughout North Carolina. Most of the mothers are between the ages of 18 and 35, have not completed high school, have two children, are long-term substance abusers (cocaine/crack), and have been convicted of felonious forgery, uttering (putting a forged check into circulation), credit card fraud, or trafficking/sales of drugs.

These programs operate in a homelike setting. Dwellings with multiple bedrooms in residential communities provide women and children with housing in a neighborhood setting. A sense of community and cooperation is fostered by women and their children sharing meal preparation, chores, and other day-to-day responsibilities. The major goal of these programs is to empower mothers to make responsible life choices in order to be competent, productive members of society. To attain this goal Summit House has developed three primary subgoals:

1. To improve parenting skills
2. To identify and manage self-defeating behaviors
3. To practice self-supporting behaviors through developing long-term goals, life planning, education and training, financial management/budgeting, and employment

Program Success

The success of these programs can be measured in a variety of ways:

- *Economics* The average annual cost of incarcerating a woman in North Carolina is $33,000 ($90 per day). The cost of building a new prison cell ranges from $13,000 to $46,000. Foster care of at-risk children ranges from $26,000 to $56,000 per year ($73 to $154 per day). The annual capitalized cost to provide services to a mother and child at Summit House programs is $74 per day.

- *Future Savings* Female juveniles account for about 25 percent of

juvenile arrests. The children of imprisoned parents have been found to be much more likely to be incarcerated themselves.

- *Recidivism* A study of the residents in Summit House programs between 1990 and 1995 found that only 20 percent were reincarcerated as compared with a rate of 40 percent for those that were released from prison during this same period.

The Human Element

I came to Summit House in January 1988. I was 5 months pregnant, strung out on heroin, and had no idea about what was going on in my life. . . . I certainly hadn't planned on having a baby. I couldn't even take care of the child I already had. I couldn't even take care of myself. I had been living wherever I could, not working, stealing and forging checks to keep up my drug habit. . . . Anything else wasn't important. I'd even tried to get an abortion while I was in jail, with no luck. . . .

I was one of the first residents at Summit House. My daughter, who had been living with my ex-in-laws, came with me. She was 5 years old then. Sometime during the year and 2 months I was at Summit House, I got to know and love her very much. It was very hard trying to learn how to be a mother to her. No more were drugs and myself the center of my universe. That helped also when my son was born. . . . I was so terrified that something would be wrong with him . . . because of my drug addiction. He was born healthy and so beautiful. . . .

We were all like family there, and that's what I remember most *(continued)*

Summit House

(continued)

about the people who lived and worked at Summit House. We had problems, big and small, but we stuck it out.... I learned about compassion, unconditional love, and respect. They treated all of us just like they would treat their own friends and family. There was a lot of emphasis put on raising children. We went to a lot of classes on parenting, and the staff helped me learn new behaviors to replace the inappropriate ones I was used to. I use what I learned there now with my children, and it's made a big difference in their lives.

I was released in March of 1989. I was terrified of leaving and going back to the "real world." My life at Summit House had been very safe, and I didn't want to mess up again. I was really very scared. I got an apartment with my sister, got involved in a 12-step recovery program, got a job, and started school at a 4-year college [at which I currently work]. It's been almost 8 years to the day that I walked out of Summit House a frightened woman, unsure of my future, and terrified of my past. Today, ... I'm one year away from graduating with a degree in Public Relations and English.... Both of my children are with me. Ashley is now almost 14 years old and Stephen, ..., will be 9 in April. They both act like children their age act and I love it. They bring the kid out in me. We live [although] not perfect, but we do it.

I've had a few relapses since leaving Summit House, but I have managed to pull myself back up and keep going forward. I owe that to Summit House. They taught me to keep believing in myself and keep going, no matter what happens.

Source: Adapted from materials provided to The National Institute of Corrections in 1997 by Summit House, Greensboro, NC.

Summary

Female criminality is on the rise for two reasons: (1) the substantial increase in female property and substance abuse offenses, and (2) as a result of changes in sentencing laws, a more determinate sentencing model was instituted, which has resulted in a substantial increase in general prison populations. The overall percentage of females may not be increasing in all systems but the numbers of incarcerated females are steadily rising (e.g., from 26,610 in 1986 to 84,427 in 1998). The typical female inmate commits nonviolent offenses, is a substance abuser, serves shorter sentences than her male counterparts, is a mother, and is older than male inmates.

When compared with the treatment of male offenders, the history of the incarceration of women shows a pattern of neglect. During the colonial period men and women were housed together in county jails. This changed gradually, and in the 19th century, three independent women's prisons were built based on the idea that females could be reformed through domestic training. Throughout the years, further reforms and legal challenges by inmates led to continued improvement of female prisons.

Still, several problems remain. One of the major issues in female prisons is that they often lack parity with male facilities. General types of programs and services where parity has not existed include educational, vocational, recreational, substance abuse, and medical programs. Further female prison reform must focus on the special needs of females to include the same opportunities offered to the male population.

Women also adapt to prison differently from men. Men express their emotions and hostility through aggressive behavior; women generally express their troubles emotionally (Rasche, 2000). Women "do time" and deal with the isolation of imprisonment by looking for and establishing support systems, a pseudofamily.

Women entering prison may or may not have the experiential background or knowledge necessary to interpret or predict their day-to-day life in confinement. The prison-smart woman has learned through experience how to manage the prison community's resources and members in a way that allows her to "do her own time." The organizationally smart woman, in contrast, is skilled at interpersonal relations, managing bureaucracies, and common courtesy. She also carves out a social existence that meets her needs and minimizes the deprivations of imprisonment. Some newcomers learn to negotiate the prison world by being mentored by someone who "knows what is happening." Most see "the mix," a continuation of behavior that led to imprisonment, as something to avoid.

Pregnancy presents unique dilemmas for both incarcerated women and the corrections system. Incarcerated pregnant women have many lifestyle behaviors that can jeopardize their pregnancy, most notably substance abuse, poor nutrition, and high incidences of past and current sexually transmitted diseases. They are also less likely to have received adequate prenatal care prior to being imprisoned, which is linked to premature birth or low birthweight babies.

Recently, parent-child programs have been established in many institutions to foster mother-child relations. However, only three institutions have nursery programs that allow women to keep their newborns for a period of time. Incarcerated mothers who return to the community face several difficulties when they are reunited with their children. Once children are returned to mothers who were incarcerated, both face considerable challenges. Guilt and shame often make it difficult for mothers to discipline and set limits for their children. Further, in their mothers' absence, children may have developed friends, new interests, and activities that make them unwilling to invest time in building a relationship with a mother who has been absent.

Sexual harassment by correctional staff is also a large problem in female institutions. Sexual misconduct by correctional staff generally refers to any type of improper conduct of a sexual nature directed at prisoners. The individual effects of sexual misconduct on inmates are both physical and emotional and devastate those women who experience them.

Co-correctional institutions house men and women in the same prison. Sleeping arrangements are separate, but men and women participate in the same programs and receive similar services. The programs have advantages and disadvantages for both sexes. Supporters of co-corrections assert that it benefits both men and women by providing a more relaxed atmosphere, decreasing tension and violence, and reducing or eliminating homosexual behavior among men. Bringing female inmates into an all-male institution brings about many improvements, including better personal sanitation, decreased vandalism, and increased educational competency among students. Some drawbacks for women include increased control and security to control sexual activity, less opportunity for leadership, and avoidance of nontraditional programs because of the perception that they are unfeminine.

Sentencing practices that mandate institutionalization for women for minor property offenses and drug use serve no meaningful societal or public safety benefits and are a waste of valuable resources that could be used for alternative punishments. Thus, incarceration should be the last option to be considered in sanctioning women offenders and invoked only when the woman is a danger to herself or others. Given the importance of maintaining the bond between mother and child and the lower security risk posed by most female offenders—whose crimes are nonviolent—community-based programs that allow mothers to keep their children would be optimum.

Critical Thinking Questions

1. Provide a comprehensive discussion of the history of women in corrections. What general trends occurred? Describe the legal challenges that emerged in the 1970s.

2. Discuss all the issues you would have to deal with if you were placed in a female correctional institution.

3. If you were assigned to plan a new women's facility what issues relating to programming and services for females would you consider? What security designation would this facility have?

4. What are some of the major dilemmas that mothers in prison face? How do visitations contribute to or minimize the problems mothers have in prison? If you were the warden of a female prison, what types of programs, services, and policies would you establish to alleviate the problems associated with pregnancy and/or motherhood in your institution?

5. What are the advantages and disadvantages associated with co-corrections for both men and women? Do you advocate co-corrections? Why or why not?

6. Discuss the advantages and disadvantages associated with placing women in community corrections programs.

Test Your Knowledge

1. Which of the following is not characteristic of female offenders?
   a. Almost two thirds have minor children.
   b. Most of their violent offenses involve simple assaults.
   c. Their rate of violent crimes is only slightly less than males.
   d. The average sentence and time served for women were shorter than for males with equivalent offenses.

2. Co-corrections is:
   a. the housing of men and women in the same prison.
   b. the sentencing of offenders to both jail time and community-based programs.
   c. the use of male correctional officers in women's prisons.
   d. a radical new prison plan where male and female inmates share sleeping quarters.

3. Incarcerated women are characterized by:
   a. a history of abuse.
   b. drug dependency.
   c. poor education and work skills.
   d. all of the above.

4. Pseudofamilies in the women's prisons:
   a. are primarily based on homosexual relationships.

   b. heighten women's likelihood of involvement in homosexual relationships.

   c. no longer exist.

   d. are a basic form of relationship in women's prisons.

5. Vocational training programs in women's prisons:

   a. generally offer a greater variety than men's prisons.

   b. attract women mostly to nontraditional types of work.

   c. generally offer access to low-paying "women's work."

   d. should be developed based on the interests of women rather than simply mirroring male programs.

Endnotes

1. See e.g., Adler, 1975; Chesney-Lind, 1982; Feinman, 1986; Simon, 1975; Smart, 1979.

2. *Estelle v. Gamble,* 1976; *Glover v. Johnson,* 1991; *Molar v. Gates,* 1979; *Moorhead v. Lane,* 1991.

3. Chittenden Community Correctional Center, Vermont; Correctional Institution for Women, New Jersey; Lois Deberry Special Needs Facility, Nashville, Tennessee; Federal Correctional Institution, Lexington, Kentucky; Federal Correctional Institution, Pleasanton, California; Maine Correctional Center; Muncy State Correctional Institution, Pennsylvania; North Idaho Correctional Institution; and Rinz Correctional Center, Missouri.

4. Adapted form B. Owen (1998). *In the Mix: Struggle and Survival in a Women's Prison.* New York: State University of New York Press.

5. Economic and Demographic Research Division, Joint Legislative Management Committee for the Florida Legislature, 1995.

The Contemporary Prison: Beginning the 21st Century

10

LEARNING OBJECTIVES

After completing this chapter, you should be able to:

1. Identify the factors that gave rise to the contemporary prison and its present population characteristics.

2. Discuss the factors that contribute to overcrowded prisons and the consequences of working and living in this type of environment.

3. Specify the various factors that gave rise to ethnic hostility within contemporary prisons and the different reactions of the major ethnic groups to this prison situation.

4. Discuss aspects of ethnicity that have a definitive impact on the adaptation of blacks, Hispanics, and whites to prison.

5. Enumerate the major types of formal prisoner organizations in today's prisons, and discuss the roles they play.

6. List, describe, and discuss the various roles played by inmates in the prison social structure.

7. Contrast and discuss the prisons' legal and illicit economies, their currencies, and the effects on inmates and the administration.

8. List the various forms of inmate contraband, and describe the major ways they are made or brought into prisons.

9. Discuss the nature of sexual assault in the modern prison and the precautions that can be taken to protect potential inmate victims.

Introduction

The turmoil in contemporary prisons has its roots in events discussed in the preceding chapters. Surging crime rates during the 1960s and 1970s escalated the public's fear of being victimized and hardened attitudes toward punishment. These factors resulted in growing pressure to imprison more offenders. By the late 1980s, prison construction could not keep up with the increasing number of offenders entering these facilities. This led to **overcrowding,** which forced the early release of serious offenders, a process that increased public frustration.

Crime continued to be among top public concerns in the 1990s despite a 5-year drop in the crime index from 1991 to 1998 (Maguire & Pastore, 1999). Nevertheless, America's fear of crime has prompted:[1]

- Strong pressure on lawmakers to get tougher on crime.
- Statues mandating increased rates of incarceration and longer sentences (e.g., "three strikes and you're out").
- Truth-in-sentencing legislation, mandating that offenders serve 85 percent of their time.
- Changes in the manner of dealing with habitual and violent juvenile offenders.
- The building of more prisons.

The "war" on drugs and the changes in incarceration policies caused the U.S. prison population to rise from approximately 329,821 in 1980 to 1.3 million by the end of 1998 (Beck & Mumola, 1999).

These issues affected the nature of prisons and the composition of their populations. The major factors contributing to these changes included the increasing proportion of minority inmates, the increased court oversight of prisons, and the reaction of prison staff and administration to radical inmates.

Overcrowding

Overcrowding has plagued American corrections from its Walnut Street Jail beginnings. Almost every era has had too many inmates for the available space, programs, and resources. The present costs of dealing with overcrowding have caused correctional systems to struggle with supervising and controlling offenders. National data suggest that the recent increases in state prison populations may be the result of the increasing time served by state inmates. From 1990 to 1997, the average time served by inmates rose from 22 months to 27 months (Beck & Mumola, 1999). However, these data tend to underestimate the time to be served by incoming inmates because they are based on averages that fail to consider that some inmates will never be released, and others will not be released for a very long time (see Table 10.1). When minimum projections of time to be served include parole eligibility, good-time credits, and early release allowances, it is estimated that inmates entering state prison can be expected to serve an average of 43 months. Another indicator that time served in prison has been increasing is the drop in inmate release rates from 37 percent in 1991 to 31.2 percent in 1997 (Beck & Mumola, 1999).

Overcrowded prisons have plagued American corrections throughout its history. In this photo inmates' beds, stacked two high, fill a gymnasium at Corcoran State Prison in California.

Table 10.1

Time to Be Served on Current Sentences*

Months	1991	1997
<24	17.5	25.8
24–47	20.6	23.5
48–71	15.1	12.7
72–119	16.4	12.5
120–179	9.3	7.4
180–239	5.0	3.5
240+	7.0	4.0
Life	3.2	2.2
Don't know	5.9	8.4
	100%	100%

*Includes time served in local jails that was credited to the prison sentence and prior prison time served by returned parole violators.
Source: Data are based on the 1991 and 1997 "Survey of Inmates in State Correctional Facilities."
A. Beck & C. J. Mumola (1999). *Prisoners in 1998.* Washington, DC: Bureau of Justice Statistics.

The increasing number of prison inmates toward the end of the 20th century was due, not only to the hard line taken toward criminals in this era, but to other factors as well, including societal changes, the demographic makeup of the U.S. population, social attitudes, and criminal justice policy.

The "baby boom" made the most significant demographic impact on the U.S. prison population. A large number of males born between 1945 and 1960 reached their most crime-prone ages during the 1960s and 1970s. A number of this group became career criminals. Additionally, many poor and minority youths became increasingly alienated and angry. This anger, combined with the greater availability of weapons (from trafficking in drugs), created a lethal mixture.

Although more people were being sent to prison for longer periods of time, court decisions restricted the number of offenders who could be housed in existing facilities. The resulting early release of large numbers of offenders created a major public outcry. However, by the mid-1990s new prison construction had caught up with the increasing prison population and early release was no longer a major problem. During this period, 24 states instituted three strikes laws, and 27 states passed some form of truth-in-sentencing laws requiring offenders to serve up to 85 percent of their time before being eligible for good time; 15 states ended good time [Austin, Clark, & Henry, 1997; *Corrections Compendium* (CC), 1998, May]. In 1998, state prisons were estimated to be operating at an average of 13 percent above capacity, and the federal system was 27 percent over its stated capacity (Beck & Mumola, 1999).

Perhaps an even more accurate assessment of overcrowding comes from a 1997/98 *Corrections Compendium*

(1998, May) survey, which found that 84 percent of the states viewed prison overcrowding conditions as ranging from serious to very serious to critical. Of the four states and the federal government that account for 44 percent of the prison population, New York, Florida, California, and the federal government are operating above capacity, while only Texas is operating under capacity (Beck & Mumola, 1999). Of these jurisdictions, only Florida indicated that overcrowding is not a problem (*CC*, 1998, May). The number of inmates in state and federal facilities is expected to increase by 43 percent by the year 2004.

Almost three fourths of the jurisdictions responding to the survey reported they did not have adequate construction plans to meet these projected population increases. Further, most projected actions for meeting the need for new prisons involve having convicted felons serve some of their time in county or local jails; sending offenders to other jurisdictions; and converting gymnasiums, lounges, hallways, classrooms, and common areas into sleeping areas (*CC*, 1998, May). This may also create potential problems, though, because it reduces the areas where inmates spend their free time, thereby increasing idleness. This may lead to an increased potential for violence and other illicit inmate activities. Moreover, about 80 percent of the 46 jurisdictions responding to the survey indicated that they expected recent laws to increase the use of incarceration. Thus, corrections administrators and officers will be dealing with overcrowded prisons for some time to come because construction budgets are insufficient to meet the escalating demand for new prison beds. The group that will be most affected is "line officers [who face] the prospect of handling even more charges, more of whom are being put away for violent crimes, with the same human resources and reduced program with which to occupy idle hands" (Wees, 1996a, p. 2).

Overcrowding is not only a problem for the staff but for the inmates as well. Hassine (1999), an inmate at a maximum security facility in Pennsylvania, summarizes many of the harmful effects of overcrowding on inmate life:

- Prisons become less secure, facilitating the operation of the black market.
- Prisons are characterized by lawlessness, which makes life fearful for inmates on a day-to-day basis.
- Inmate programming is minimized.
- Some inmates are denied jobs.
- Arguments about daily life (e.g., bunk beds, property, storage) increase.
- Overworked staff tend to work odd shifts and, thus, behave erratically at times. Inmates are no longer able to expect uniform treatment or predictable behavior. Working relationships between inmates and staff often become strained.

Victor Hassine on Overcrowding

IN THEIR OWN WORDS

With the arrival of that "guy" who was overcrowding us, suddenly nothing worked right. Our lives became a daily challenge to avoid injury and stay out of trouble, which left us little time to reflect on the errors of our ways. In essence, the penitentiary evolved into a ghetto.

Once its prison population exceeded design capacity, Graterford became overcrowded. This numerical imbalance forced officials to institute double-celling or barracks-styled housing in order to accommodate the surplus population, despite the fact that the prison's cell blocks were not built for that kind of traffic.

While much can be argued about the psychological and physical dangers of squeezing two men into a poorly lit, poorly ventilated, bathroom-sized cell, the true evil of overcrowding has very little to do with crowded living space. Human beings, if they must, can and have lived in caves and tunnels. The destructive nature of prison overcrowding stems from the fact that it came unplanned, and was imposed on a system specifically created to discourage the confinement of too many inmates in one place.

Suddenly we inmates found ourselves at odds with our own rigidly designed environment. Furthermore, while inmate populations skyrocketed, the hiring of staff to support them did not increase proportionately. In Graterford, and in many other prisons, the hiring of treatment staff (e.g., teachers, counselors, and vocational instructors) was in fact frozen—while an endless number of illiterate and needy inmates stormed the prison gates.

Overcrowding as a Personal Experience

As an inmate confined to one Pennsylvania prison or another since 1981, I have experienced what overcrowding has done, is doing, and threatens to do. By the mid-1980s, I was fairly well dug into my prison routine, working, obeying, and vegetating. I had a single cell, and for better or worse, the prison system was functioning at an adequate level.

Then one day, my cell door opened and another man was shoved inside. My world was suddenly turned upside-down.

My first argument with my new co-tenant was, of course, over who got the top or bottom bunk. Then we fought over lights on or lights off, hygiene habits, toilet-use etiquette, cell cleaning, property storage, and whose friends could visit. Then there was missing property,

accusations of thievery, snoring, farting, and smoking. As these arguments raged on every day, new ones would arise to make things worse.

Since the prison staff was somewhat taken by surprise by this sudden overpopulation, there was no time to plan or screen double-celling. Inmates were shoved together solely on the basis of race, age, or cell availability. Nor did an inmate have any opportunity to screen potential cellmates. If you didn't voluntarily find someone to move in with you, one would be picked for you at random. This practice immensely compounded the problems associated with double-celling. It was bad enough living with a stranger in such close quarters without having to worry about whether he was a Jeffrey Dahmer.

As my day-to-day struggle with my cellmate became a fact of life, I realized just how much this guy Mr. Overcrowding was causing me serious problems in every aspect of my prison life. [Further], the possibility of one day waking up to a cannibal beside me, while certainly a cause for alarm, proved to be the least of my concerns.

Source: This material was adapted from Victor Hassine (1999). Life Without Parole: Living in Prison Today. *Los Angeles: Roxbury.*

Our In Their Own Words feature, "Victor Hassine on Overcrowding," provides a unique and in-depth account of the implications of overcrowding on an inmate.

The Inmate Racial Divide

The behaviors of black, Hispanic, and white inmates are so diverse that it is difficult to imagine any overall code of inmate solidarity that could span the social distance between inmates in these different groups (Carroll, 1990). Additionally, although black males represent

about 6 percent of the general population, they constituted almost 50 percent of the inmate population in 1997 (Beck & Mumola, 1999).

Pervasive racism suffered by blacks has generated deep-seated feelings of rage against whites who have contributed to their oppression.[2] **Black rage,** repressed in the past, is now being expressed through violence and aggression. Moreover, blacks who previously feared whites have now learned that whites are intimidated by and actually fear them. This revelation had an extraordinary impact on black expression of antiwhite feelings and has had dramatic repercussions

There is an immense social divide between inmates in different racial groups.

Others have argued that white officers' conceptions and fears may result in their discriminating against blacks by misunderstanding their behavior (e.g., horseplay may be seen as fighting, subjecting them to greater surveillance) (Carroll, 1990; Silberman, 1995). Hassine (1999) asserts that new white guards who have little experience interacting with different races tend to be much stricter with those of their own race. This view may reflect different periods, prison locations, and/or staff diversity. Silberman (1995), in his study of a maximum security prison, cited three factors that he felt had lessened discrimination against black and other minority inmates: court actions, professionalization of COs, and increasing numbers of minorities as COs and in positions of responsibility.

The prison behavior of Hispanic inmates (Puerto Ricans, Chicanos, etc.) is most influenced by the family. Their reliance on family for nurturing and support creates a dependency that influences their identity and self-esteem (Carroll, 1990). Thus, family separation while in prison can create problems for them. The barrio culture also has had important implications for their adaptation to imprisonment.[4] Barrio gangs remain a primary reference group into adulthood. Hispanic inmates spend much of their time interacting within their gangs, which become a surrogate family, offering support and helping them deal with problems. Because Hispanic gangs arise from territorial conflicts, they engage in much conflict and violence within the prison, often resulting from their drug trafficking in the prison. Thus, both Hispanics and blacks import their barrio or ghetto cultures into the prison, which helps them to maintain strong solidarity (Carroll, 1990).

The prison experience is painful for white inmates, primarily because they are more likely than blacks or Hispanics to blame themselves for their predicament in prison. One result is an almost "psychotic attempt to reside physically in the prison while living psychologically in the free community" (Johnson, 1976, p. 122). Until recently, their position in society has not allowed them to develop a class or ethnic consciousness, so there was little basis for promoting solidarity. Consequently, their fear of victimization at the hands of blacks and Hispanics led many to retreat into protective custody. White inmates, who may not have been prejudiced when they entered prison, tend to develop racist views after experiencing the hate, hostility, and violence directed against them by black inmates. In the 1990s, this contributed to the development of white supremacist, right-wing, sometimes "religiously" based, militant racist groups like the Aryan Brotherhood. This appears to have led to greater solidarity among whites.[5] Our In Their Own Words feature, "Race Relations in Prison: An Inmate's Perspective," provides insight on this issue.

on the social environment of the prison (Johnson, 1996; Silberman, 1978).

Although violence is not restricted to blacks (significant numbers of Hispanic and white inmates are also predisposed to use violence), Harer and Steffensmeir (1996a) found that blacks had significantly higher rates of violent behavior, based on guilty verdicts in disciplinary hearings, but lower rates of alcohol or drug use than whites.[3] They believe that this was a result of preprison exposure to a violent subculture, suggesting the role of the importation model in shaping the inmate culture (see Chapter 7):

> The inner city (from where most blacks come) and the prison both constitute settings . . . [that elicit] expectations of danger that evoke predatory behavior as well as protective violent responses. Particularly important . . . is the role of respect [which is earned through violence] and backing down from a confrontation not only is the ultimate loss of face but may actually increase future vulnerability. [For hard-core street-oriented youths, the risk of death is preferable to being disrespected by another.] (p. 343)

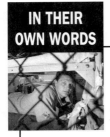

Race Relations in Prison: An Inmate's Perspective

Though the prison had been desegregated since the late 1960s, the inmates of Graterford continued to impose their own form of segregation. For example, it was an unspoken rule that the dining hall be divided into a black section and a white section. The administration did its part as well, for example, by refusing to double-cell white inmates with black inmates. De facto segregation was very much alive in those days, as it is today.

During my initial classification period at Graterford, I was required to identify myself as either black or white. There were no other options. Hispanics and Native Americans were classified as black or white, depending on their choice. It wasn't until the mid-1980s that the racial classification process at Graterford allowed inmates to designate themselves as anything other than black or white.

Among the African-American population at Graterford was a large and well-established Black Muslim community, the vast majority of which came from Philadelphia. On the other hand, most of the white prison staff were Christians, many of whom were raised in the rural communities around the prison. This extreme imbalance between the racial, regional, and religious composition of staff and inmates vividly reflected the general dysfunction of the prison that prevailed throughout my years there.

Though non-white inmates were usually embraced by the prison population, they were often viewed with suspicion by the white staff, who seemed to believe that only white inmates could be reformed into law-abiding citizens. This racial bias at Graterford did not result in favoritism by staff, but rather provoked a divisive and relentless competition between the inmates themselves for the staff's favor. Everyone in the prison system was forced to play the bias game, because the only group identity available to inmates was based on skin color.

Source: Victor Hassine (1999). Life Without Parole: Living in Prison Today. *Los Angeles: Roxbury.*

The Prison Social Environment

The prisoner movement affected the status quo of prison life in several ways. Inmates were provided with basic constitutional protections, and prisons were no longer subject to continued court oversight. However, COs felt that this curtailed their ability to maintain order and made it more difficult to find inmates guilty of infractions and to impose sanctions (Irwin, 1980). Additional problems included administrative and CO backlash, prompted by unprovoked inmate attacks and verbal harassment directed at them. This frequently came from radical inmates, and it aggravated racial tensions in some prisons.

To reassert authority, some states abolished or greatly restricted the formation of any group, particularly ethnic and racial groups, that made critical statements or were involved in political activities. Individuals suspected of political activities also found their behaviors restricted (Irwin, 1980). However, this suppression, in the 1970s, resulted in the breakdown of the informal inmate system of social control because it was no longer relevant. Irwin contended that although these groups may have presented problems, they would have caused far less turmoil than the violent cliques and gangs that developed and replaced them. More recently, Hassine (1999) asserted that the current reluctance of prison administrators to allow group activity is from fear that the groups may evolve into gangs. Thus, although social and religious groups are permitted to operate in the prison, the administration may discourage inmate involvement by making the rules of participation cumbersome. One unintended consequence of limiting these prosocial groups is racial polarization.

Another factor changing the prison environment is the criminal orientation of new inmates, who now resort to violence more quickly (Hassine, 1999). Given the fragmented social structure, it is surprising that prisons are not characterized by total chaos.[6] To survive in these violent, racially divided, hate-filled environments, most inmates limit their interactions to small cliques of friends or units such as gangs. These groups usually attract members of their own ethnic or racial type. Segregation pervades all aspects of group interactions. Even though prisons today are integrated, when given a choice, inmates choose to segregate themselves along ethnic or racial lines (Silberman, 1995). Inmate associations are also determined by such factors as proximity (based on work or cell assignments), shared prison interests, similar criminal orientations, and shared preprison

Table 10.2

Self-Reported Memberships by Organization and Site

Soledad (CTF—Central)	Stillwater	Rahway	Oregon State Prison	Bedford Hills
Alcoholics Anonymous	Advisory Council	Alcoholics Anonymous	Alcoholics Anonymous	Committee Against
Aryan Brotherhood*	Afro-American Culture	Forum	Bible Club	Life for Drugs
Black Guerilla	Education, Inc.	Lifers Group, Inc.	Car Club (Racing)	Hispanic Committee
Crypts*	Alcoholics Anonymous	Muslims	Gavel Club	Inmate Liaison Council
Family*	Asklepieion	NAACP	Jaycees	Lifers
Hell's Angels*	Atlantis		Keen Club	New Directions
Inmate Committee on	Aztalan (Hispanics)		Lakota (Native American)	Parent Awareness
Higher Education	Insight		Lifeline	Reality House
(ICHE)	Jaycees		Lifers	South Forty Program
Men's Advisory Council	Muslims		Masters Men (Chess Club)	Violence Alternative
Mexican Mafia*	Native American Culture		Motorcycle Club	
Muslims	Sounds Incarcerated, Inc.		Muslims	
Nuestra Familia*	Worker's Council		Seventh Club	
			Slot Car Club	
			Toastmasters	
			Uhuru (Black Culture)	

*Self-reported membership in unauthorized organizations.
Source: Adapted from J. G. Fox (1982). *Organizational and Racial Conflict in Maximum-Security Prisons*. Lexington, MA: Lexington Books, p. 142. With the permission of the author.

experiences, such as being "homeboys."[7] A **homeboy orientation** is based on sharing some common experiences like coming from the same town or neighborhood or having the same ethnic background. Another factor is street gang affiliation, which can increase the level of trust between inmates because it provides a common basis of experience and makes establishment of social relationships more comfortable and less threatening.

Prison Prosocial Organizations

These changes are not found in all prisons. There are many variations in systems across the country; for example, gangs do not exist in all prisons, or they may not be large or well-organized enough to dominate institutional life. In some prisons, the number of minority groups may be very small or nonexistent. Thus, the structure of the inmate world in a given facility is influenced by its demographic and institutional characteristics and its formal and informal prisoner organizations. Some of these groups are approved by the institutions and others operate underground (Berkman, 1979; Fox, 1982).

The prison environment of the contemporary inmate social world is best characterized as **pluralistic,** evidenced by the variety of existing authorized ethnic, religious, self-help, special interest, and other groups as well as unauthorized groups. A study of four men's and one woman's maximum security prisons, found that in

three (Stillwater, Oregon, Bedford Hills), approximately 50 percent of the inmates were members of at least one organization. Across the five prisons, minority inmates were more often members of prisoner organizations than whites (see Table 10.2) (Fox, 1982).

Prisoner organizations present a unique opportunity to channel inmate energies and use their talents in meaningful and beneficial ways (Fox, 1982). For some inmates, they provide an alternative to involvement in gangs. Inmates with potential leadership skills may be able to channel their energies and talents in a positive direction and still earn the respect of their fellow inmates. Others may disdain gang association yet still want to participate in a group to reduce their dead time (Irwin, 1980). The key to the development of these groups and inmate participation in them is a prison administration that supports these organizations and encourages membership in them.

Despite these advantages, positive prison organizations place a burden on institutional managers because their presence adds to the number of entities to be regulated. Most inmate groups are considered potential security risks for two reasons: they might, and some do, develop organized opposition to official policies and goals, or they are used as fronts by prison gangs for contraband trafficking. Thus, in controlling these groups staff have to walk a tightrope. They must supervise these groups and prevent their takeover by inmates with ulterior motives yet not impose excessive restrictions that

A Look at Prison Jaycees

IN THEIR OWN WORDS

The Junior Chamber of Commerce, commonly known as the Jaycees, is a leadership training organization through community service. There are some 154 institutional chapters within the United States and many more internationally.

The aims of these young men and women are developing personal growth and undertaking leadership training while providing solutions to community problems. The Jaycee process offers a threefold benefit to its members. Through the Individual Development program, Jaycees are helped to realize improved family communications, leadership skills, human relations, and public and spiritual development. The Management Development programs offer Jaycees opportunities to study and develop actual skills in personnel management, financial management, planning, and organization. Through community development programs, Jaycees gain needed leadership experience and become more sensitive to the needs of those around them. These three aspects of the organization combine to form what is known as the "Total Jaycee Concept."

Because of the Jaycees' excellent training programs, inmates often join because it will some day look impressive on their resume presented to the parole or pardon board. After joining, many truly become involved in the true Jaycee spirit. In this the whole prison population reaps the rewards because they truly service the community within the institution.

Do inmates provide service to their community? Yes. Most people do not realize an institutional facility is a community in itself, and our institutional chapters service that community. They also sometimes service the surrounding community as well. In Louisiana, most of our prison facilities are located in very rural areas with only a very small village or town located nearby. These communities are usually too small to support a regular Jaycee chapter. It is in these instances that I have seen institutional chapters step in and service the surrounding community as well as the prison facility—projects such as needy assistance in the case of a family's home burning; craft sales to benefit a cancer victim; and beautification projects in small towns badly needing a facelift. I have personally seen Jaycees work alongside local community residents in times when we have had severe hurricane or storm damage. They were working as volunteers, not a work release program.

One of the main keys to the success of an institutional chapter of the Junior Chamber depends upon the support they receive from the prison administration. Officials within prisons have no idea how just the delay of processing paperwork can be a detriment to the Junior Chamber chapter. Usually, the more successful chapters come from institutions that have support from the warden to the clerical worker that processes the paperwork.

In working with institutional chapters for the past 15 years as Ex-

---

might prompt inmates to quit and join groups such as gangs (Fox, 1982; Irwin, 1980).

Blacks, Native Americans, and Hispanics have formed **ethnic/racial organizations** that concentrate on cultural awareness and education. The number and proportion of inmates involved in these groups tend to vary according to the proportion of these inmates in each facility. The smaller the group is proportionally, the greater the likelihood these inmates will be members of an ethnic or racial organization. At institutions where these groups were predictable and enhanced prison stability, COs were more positive and supportive of them; at institutions plagued by racial and ethnic conflict or violence, COs were more concerned with personal safety and stressed the need for greater control over the formation of these organizations (Fox, 1982).

Religious organizations included only formal groups that existed apart from regularly scheduled religious programs. Silberman (1995) found that one quarter of the inmates at the maximum security prison he studied considered religious affiliation a major basis of association and identification. Involvement in these groups helped African Americans adjust to prison life. White Protestant inmates were found to be associated with religious groups like the Yokefellows. However, ethnic pride among some whites has led to affiliation with white supremacist groups. As with other religious groups, the courts have used the same rules to establish the rights of Native Americans to follow traditional practices as long as they do not interfere with legitimate correctional goals (Silberman, 1995).

Self-help organizations accounted for 27 percent of all prison organization memberships in Fox's study. Eighty-one percent of the inmates in these groups were white. Whites do not share a similar cultural background and need some basis other than ethnicity around which they can form groups. This may explain their attraction to these organizations, which include Alcoholics Anonymous and Narcotics Anonymous.

Special interest organizations involved a greater range of activities than any other type of prison group.

ecutive Director of the Louisiana Junior Chamber I have personally witnessed the evolution of many troubled people. One of the personal gains from this position is to watch the growth of individuals. Through working with these persons, I have watched what society would consider the worst that we have to offer become a successful, well-rounded individual. I have personally testified on behalf of some institutional Jaycee members at board hearings. I might add that I have also written or testified in protest when they were either not rehabilitated or had attempted to use the Jaycee organization as a reference and had not truly utilized the training offered.

I have also witnessed firsthand the impact of many factions, gangs, and other disruptive groups. Inmates have become entangled in the power of these groups, resulting in their wives calling me at home because their husband had been "set up" and thrown in solitary confinement as a result of the latest struggle. These have occurred al-most in all of the maximum security institutional chapters that I have worked with.

Most of our chapters attract "better inmates"—that is, those that know they need the kind of help the Jaycees have to offer. Most assuredly I am biased, but then again, I have seen the results. In the years in working with the Jaycees, I have seen very few repeat offenders, a record which, I feel can speak for itself.

Some of these people have no family and no future. Most of the time they are pleased to have something to do and that they can personally excel in. Often, their Jaycee career is the first time they have ever achieved any type of success. Needless to say, they are not going to jeopardize their contact with that success. Therefore, in working with these chapters, they have often been some of the easiest to service and by far the most appreciative of that service.

In Louisiana, we are very proud of our institutional chapters. We have at least one or more of our chapters recognized each year by the U.S. Junior Chamber of Commerce for outstanding achievements. We have members that were active in their institutional chapter now serving the Louisiana Jaycees as active members after release.

We believe in our institutional chapters and members. We also work very hard to service these chapters because of the need. Every institution would benefit from a Jaycee chapter—from the persons who would benefit from the self-help and training programs the Junior Chamber offers to the institutional community as a whole.

Source: Especially prepared by Renee M. LeGrande, Executive Director, Louisiana Junior Chamber of Commerce, for Corrections: A Comprehensive View, *2nd ed.*

Groups in various prisons were involved in cleanups, fund-raising, lobbying, and even in maintaining a stock car on the Pacific Northwest racing circuit (Fox, 1982). Overall, special interest groups received more official support from management than other organizations but not from most COs, who were nearly unanimous in rejecting any extension of their activities on the grounds that it might compromise their ability to control the inmate population. Nevertheless, legitimate nondisruptive groups that are appropriately supervised provide important viable alternatives to inmate involvement in prison gangs or threatening groups.

Also included in this category are organizations involved in providing input on resolving prison problems and changing prison conditions. Fox (1982) found that prison administrators were very reluctant to give these groups the kind of power to make changes, because they feared inmates would abuse it and cause serious problems. The In Their Own Words feature, "A Look at Prison Jaycees," profiles an inmate special interest group that has outside support. Then, in another In Their Own Words feature, inmates discuss "Peer Group Counseling at Rahway," examining a program designed to enable more experienced inmates to assist their fellow inmates in adjusting to prison and to release. Finally, the lifers program, an inmate-based group featured in three television films is described in the feature "Mike Israel, on 25 Years of 'Scared Straight'" on page 234.

The Changing Convict Code

Changes in the prison social world have reduced the importance of the **convict code** (described in Chapter 7) and created new inmate roles. This has complicated the lives of independent inmates, leading many to withdraw from normal prison activities. The new prison subculture is characterized by a disrespect for authority, illiteracy, and welfare mentality. This subculture has transformed the prison into an overcrowded, decaying inner city ghetto with its associated evils (Hassine, 1999).

Peer Group Counseling at Rahway

IN THEIR OWN WORDS

Program Description

The peer group counseling program began in 1987 when a group of inmates approached Associate Administrator Patrick Arvonio with an idea of offering small group counseling to newly incarcerated inmates. The initial topics were to focus upon an inmate's adjustment to incarceration and involved role-playing techniques and confrontational therapy by the peer (inmate) facilitators. The groups would be co-facilitated, by two trained inmates with staff supervision. The sessions would last 1½–2 hours over 12 weeks. The first group of eight inmate facilitators went through a 4-month training process by a member of the professional staff, who used a form of reality therapy as the principal treatment modality.

In December 1987, the inmates who completed the training began conducting the counseling groups. Since its inception the program has served over 1,500 inmates, many of whom now have the unique ability to provide perspectives from both sides, having been both participants and facilitators.

In 1990, a modification to one of the groups was made with the addition of a long-term offenders group. This group was designed to deal with issues that related to extended incarceration (more than 15 years). Issues discussed included the aging of some offenders, loss of family and friends, and dealing with younger offenders. The group also examined the prospect faced by some long-term offenders of never being released and dying incarcerated.

Role of Facilitators

Umi Khari and Benjamin Balisnomo The essence of the peer group counseling program is to defuse problems and possible negative reactions. The group has become a vehicle not unlike a mirror that we all must look into; each session is an open forum for the discussion of problems. Each member does have the opportunity to discuss topics that may be important to him and his family or close relationships. We all share problems that are not unique, isolated, or restricted to us alone, more often than not the very same problem.

Participation is critical in all peer groups if anything is to be achieved. For one to change he must choose to learn and thereby grow; each group member can be a part of the solution to another member's problem. We consider this to be the heart of the peer group program. Each way that a member grows from participation in the group can be considered part of that person's ongoing life's education. You see education isn't just about learning as much as it is a component of growing and living in reality.

I think that each facilitator has his own reasons for working with the groups; most of us want to give others a chance to understand that they are not alone. Some of the problems they are dealing with we are dealing with or have dealt with. Who can better understand why someone would do some of the things that men in prison have done in their life, but one who has been there. And this is what makes the peer group counseling program so unique. We have the ability to reach an individual that may not respond to a conventional counseling program; I believe it's the no-nonsense approach the group facilitators have.

And putting in work means to begin to help yourself and others within the group; putting in work also means being honest about your own feelings and emotions and giving truthful answers and caring. And hopefully, each member will develop an ability to really hear, versus just listening, and develop the ability to hear what another person is really saying.

Rashan Karim Ali I call counseling "work" because it is work at times to listen to others air their problems. They'll beat you in the head with a lot of nonsense. And you got to be able to share intelligent rhetoric. Facilitators do not have all the answers or the answer at all. But we have to have some solutions. This work requires extensive efforts by any facilitator; it's taxing, you can get burnt out just like professionals. But the results are well worth it when you can see a distinguishing difference in the prisoners who successfully complete their phase of counseling.

When I started counseling as a participant over 10 years ago, I was somewhat introverted—kept a lot in. I could not express myself to identify my problems. And one of

---

Although the convict code has retained many of its facets in the contemporary prison, there are at least three major changes (Silberman, 1995):

1. Toughness has become a central focus of inmate identity.

2. Loyalty has shifted from the inmate population as a whole to one's group (usually the ethnic or racial group).

3. Violence, once an administrative tool of control, is now being used by inmates to send the prison hurling out of control.

the facilitators asked me a question I will always remember. He confronted me hard. And he asked did I love myself. And I could not answer immediately. And being naive as I was I did not realize that he gave me "a set-up question." And I took it hook, line, and sinker. . . . I tried to answer. My answer of course was that indeed, I loved and did love myself. He jumped up and got in my face and shot back, how could I love myself when a few minutes earlier I told the group that I "stole, robbed, and beat and conned family." "How do you love yourself and smoke crack and sniff dope and abuse yourself?" "You did not wash your ass in weeks, how did you love yourself? Tell us." I was totally speechless. But it was a turning point in my life.

Being a facilitator, a prisoner who counsels prisoners, has been a very unique experience. And it affords the participant and myself the atmosphere of opportunity to be more real with ourselves in dialogue. Whereas, with the prison staff facilitating participants are more apt to be less expressive and the enthusiasm is not there at times.

This time of my incarceration most of my family have abandoned or alienated themselves from me. They have their own problems that I do understand. So I move on because I am very optimistic about all the strives I have made as a person and a man. They have simply gotten tired of me coming to prison. It has been rough, the loneliness and anxiety. This time in prison for myself has been a very humbling experience, a soul-searching journey. The majority of group participants do not relish this status of helplessness and the melancholiness that is so prevalent. So many of us are realizing that we failed a lot of people. But most of all we failed ourselves.

Personal Experiences of Facilitators

Umi Kari The peer group counseling program gave me a better perspective of the person I once was, as well as the person I am today. The peer group challenged me to look at the things that led me to prison and the things that may keep me out of prison if I am ever released.

They challenged me to look at my drug problem from the perspective that the drug is only a symptom of the problem and that I myself was the real problem. The problems that came about from my drug addiction would continue to make me act out in a self-destructive manner. You see by challenging me to look at myself I also had to look at those excuses I used for getting high. And once they got me to look at me and not the drug, I found out that I am a very insecure person, that I also have a very low opinion of myself, and a number of other things that I believe may have led me to do some of the things I have done in my life. The group also challenged me to look at how I would do all this TIME I have to do.

Fred Bowers I was open to receiving counseling but did not necessarily look to participate in a group setting at first. With some encouragement I agreed to go through a session of peer group counseling. Through this I was able to listen to and learn quite a bit from older prisoners, and at the same time share a lot of my experiences with them. The more we opened up and shared, the more the bridge and gap was closed between the younger and older prisoners. It gave me a sense of understanding and helped me further adjust to this weird, wild atmosphere called prison. It was weird because Rahway was unlike any other prison I had experienced.

Through this peer group I was able to spend time relating with others who could rationalize and make some sense out of what we were going through in prison. I learned a lot about confrontational experiences without violence (or resorting to violence). During group sessions we often dealt with topics such as family relationships, love relationships, hatred for the penal system, and updates on what is happening with the parole board. I gained a sense of brotherhood from others involved in peer group and learned to appreciate the confidentiality we committed ourselves to keep. Because of this ongoing experience with peer groups I talk more openly about my strengths, my weaknesses, and of course some of my hang-ups.

Source: Dr. Silverman would like to thank Mike Power, executive assistant at East Jersey State Prison, for providing the program overview and obtaining the inmate statements for the second edition of this text. He is also extremely grateful to the inmates for their frank and insightful comments.

Inmates resort to extreme violence to protect or maintain self-respect and punish snitches, even to the point of killing them; snitching is viewed as one of the worst things an inmate can do. The rise in violence can be further attributed to an increasing number of **state-raised youths,** who have graduated from youthful offender or juvenile facilities, which are usually permeated by violence and degradation and are controlled by the strongest and most aggressive youths. We will examine some of the social roles and adaptations that have developed in response to the contemporary prison environment.

Mike Israel, on 25 Years of "Scared Straight"

IN THEIR OWN WORDS

East Jersey State Prison is a mustard yellow nineteenth century fortress prison housing about 2,000 inmates in the middle of the urban sprawl of north-central New Jersey. The old building has four wings extending from a central domed pivot, and under that faded gold dome is a rather large, round room, with a stage and rows of iron bench seats bolted to the floor. Movies are shown there in the evening. By day, however, several times a week, the stage is used for an encounter that has been going on since 1975.

In the middle of the stage stand 12 adolescent males. They are at awkward attention, their arms straight at their sides, fists clenched in nervousness. They have all had encounters with the juvenile courts in the northeast and have been bused into the prison by an agency, and as the press would put it, they are being "scared straight."

In front of them paces a muscle-bound black inmate with a stocking cap who is yelling at them how stupid they are for being caught. A white inmate, not quite so fierce, walks up to a trembling kid standing at the end of the line and speaks to him confidentially. The kid steps out of the line to speak to the white inmate.

The muscle builder in the stocking cap barks at him to get back in line. He does. Then stocking cap demands of him, "Who told you to get out of line?"

The kid points to the white inmate.

Stocking cap pauses a moment, then looks at the kid, and says, "Do you know what you are?" No answer. "You're dead. You're meat."

All 12 of the juveniles are surprised. They don't understand. Then stocking cap tells them why. "Because you're the worst thing there is in this shit hole of a place. You're a snitch. You know what happens to snitches? If you die, you're lucky."

Then just slightly the tense mood changes while both the black and white inmates join each other in a clear comradeship in front of the line of kids. The men tell them what they consider a harmless gesture can be interpreted inside a prison as the worst of all iniquities, with terrible retribution, the reality they will fear if they end up where they are.

Fifty thousand juveniles have stood on that stage and have been manipulated by the Lifers Group in a series of creative game playing encounters to reach their deepest consciousness about the consequences of a criminal life. The best evaluative study was an experiment that tracked two comparable groups of 66 and 65 juveniles for 22 months after the experimental group experienced Scared Straight. Both groups continued delinquency patterns for about six months, but the experimental group's criminality began to decline over the next year-and-a-half. The maturation process was accelerated.

In spite of interminable obstacles, including political and interest group criticism, inmate turnover, and Department of Correction's imposed limits, the Lifers Group still goes on. One evening a month the Lifers meet with some of their juvenile clients and their parents in a follow-up discussion. They also meet with a Parental Awareness group, and with college students for tours of the prison and rap sessions. They are busy.

These men share a kinship and loyalty that is exceptional. Although there are no studies of the program's effect on the inmates themselves, professionals who have worked with them invariably believe that this program is to many of the Lifers their salvation.

The men talk of how, for the first time in their lives, they experience what it feels like to selflessly give of

Social Roles and Adaptations

New inmate social roles include the tough inmate and independents. Adaptations to prison life include numerous forms of withdrawal. State-raised youths, also known as *hogs*, *outlaws*, or **convicts,** are the most respected figures in contemporary prisons and dominate the inmate world through violence.[8] Arvonio (1997) describes the emergence of this new type of inmate:

Over the past several years many corrections professionals have been talking about a "different inmate." They say they are dealing with a new convict in their institutions. Believe it or not, many of the inmates, the so-called old timers are complaining about them too. They say this new breed is hard to reach. Many have gang affiliations. They don't respect any inmates outside of their gang. They don't have any need for the older, seasoned inmate's wisdom. They feel no remorse about their crimes in the street or those perpetuated on their fellow convicts. As the warden of a new federal penitentiary put it, even they are getting a lower class of inmate.

Perhaps most disturbing to staff and other inmates alike is that they have no fear. Prison just moves the street inside. They don't have any expectation of living very long due to what they see going on daily with

themselves to people who need them for no immediate personal gain. And give of themselves they do! After sessions they are drained and exhausted in ways they have never known before. They learn how to feel good about themselves, a new maturity.

"I know kids will listen," says Calvin Bass, the President, "if you show interest in them."

"If you let them know, 'I want to get down with y'all.'" These guys feel, 'if somebody would sit down and tell us.' Guys (that age) don't know anything! Most of us couldn't read or write."

"Maybe some 14-year-old kid won't have to experience the bull-shit I went through—you know—growing up in the ghetto, not knowing anything."

The Lifers Group is the most stable organization in the prison. In a culture without loyalties, these men share an uncommon solidarity. On the outside, their bond is continued with a group called "Friends of the Lifers," where they visit youth groups and speak to school classes. Corrections authorities generally do not want former inmates to associate with each other, but the Lifers are an exception.

Despite the popular conception that "Scared Straight is designed to literally scare juveniles into obeying the law," the focus of the group is actually on the verbal and written counseling that follows the activities on stage. Lifers group members speak to a group of juveniles:

> You dress up your hair—but there's nothing in the mind. The mind is not dressed up. You live in the ghetto, but the ghetto is your head. You've got to take the graffiti of prejudice out of your mind. You've got to take the graffiti of degradation and oppression out of your mind and work toward your potential. You still have a chance to be anything you want to be. Doctors, lawyers, judges. But if you want to be a convict, you can be that, too. We're trying to wake you up to the reality that you could do more with your life than what you are doing. (Wormser, 1991, p. 67)*

The benefits that the Lifers Group provides for its members are also largely ignored. Harvey George summarizes the sentiments of many lifers:

> For many of us, the group is our life inside prison. We live for this program. This is our chance to do something that we know is good, that we know is right, that we know will benefit some children, that we know will benefit us. You should understand that there are men in here, some of whom have committed terrible crimes, who want to do the right thing, but are afraid to or don't have the strength to. This does not excuse what they did, that doesn't mean that what they did must deny them the chance to do something for themselves and for others. The program gives all of us the chance. It not only helps children change their lives for the better. It helps us, too. (Wormser, 1991, p. 43)

This material is taken from R. Wormser (1991). Lifers: Learn the Truth at the Expense of Our Sorrow. Englewood Cliffs, NJ: Julian Messner, a Division of Burdett Press Inc., Simon & Schuster, Inc.
Source: Especially prepared for Corrections, 2nd ed. by Mike Israel, director of Criminal Justice at Kean University in Union, NJ, which is near the prison. He has been on the Lifers Group Advisory Board since its inception and is its former chair.

fellow members and others being killed so early in their lives. They don't expect to "see 20." The acceptance that that's the way it is, that to be in a gang is to risk dying young, means they do not fear death as others do.

The distinctive feature of these inmates is their emphasis on toughness and willingness to use violence (even committing murder) to maintain their status and honor. They are able to take care of themselves, whether as a part of a predatory clique or alone, and they have the guts to victimize and sexually exploit weaker inmates and members of other ethnic groups.[9] They succeed in the prison environment because it is the only world they know. These inmates wear society's rejection of them as a badge of honor (Irwin & Austin, 1994). As Jack Abbott, a self-defined state-raised inmate, relates, they are willing to callously use violence for a variety of purposes:

> [T]he high esteem we naturally have for violence, force . . . is what makes us effective, men whose judgment impinges on others, on the world: Dangerous killers who act alone and *without* emotion, who act with calculation and principles to avenge themselves, establish and defend their principles with acts of murder that usually evade prosecution by law; this is the state-raised convicts' conception of manhood, in the highest sense. (Abbott, 1982, p. 15)

Inmates like this one in a juvenile prison in Los Angeles may join the growing number of "state-raised youths." These youths have spent many of their formative years in an environment characterized by violence and degradation.

This is reinforced from the time a young inmate enters prison. "[He] either must kill or turn the tables on anyone who propositions him with threats of force . . . [if not, at some point he will become someone's *punk*—homosexual slave]. In doing so, it becomes known to all that you are a man, regardless of your youth" (Abbott, 1981, p. 94). Thus, one inmate bragged to a television reporter how he had chosen a guard at random and brutally killed him to gain admittance into the Aryan Brotherhood:

> I killed him about four different ways. I stabbed him, cut his eyes out, . . . [and] throat, strangled him, beat him with a fire extinguisher and flashlight, and stuck a ring of keys down his mouth. . . . looking into the camera [he] said, "This has just begun for me, I'm thirty-one years old. I got a lot of bodies to collect yet." (Earley, 1992, p. 265)

Today's younger inmate population is angry, alienated, lacking in remorse, and easily provoked by the stressors of prison life. Moreover, the prison culture has no mechanism that allows inmates to make peace with one another and learn a nonviolent response pattern. The inmate code of violence dictates that, when in doubt, inmates should hurt or kill a neighbor to avoid becoming a victim (Johnson, 1987, 1996). Weapons are preferred over fists because if one's opponent is not dead, "He might come back on you later" (Silberman, 1995, p. 37).

To survive in this environment, those who choose to move freely in the public areas of the prison adopt aggressive precautions that include "keeping a weapon (shank) on them or nearby, lifting weights to build up strength and talking and acting tough when the situation called for it" (McCorkle, 1992).

Independents **Independents** represent a unique category of inmates who may circulate freely within the contemporary prison (Irwin, 1980). In gang-controlled prisons, some maintain loose friendships with a major group, which protects them from other groups. Others can move freely in these prisons because they have been victorious in many confrontations. However, in gang-dominated prisons, these inmates must be cautious in their contacts with more powerful gang members, because no inmate is likely to survive the attacks of a gang that is determined to murder him. Black independents function better than whites in gang-dominated prisons, because there is a greater sense of solidarity among blacks. Hispanics, at least in California, must have a token affiliation with one of the Hispanic gangs (Irwin, 1980).

Some independents are able to move freely in the prison world because they present no threat to convict leaders, or they provide some valuable service. Included in this group are "jailhouse lawyers," characters, dings (who may be a source of amusement), and less desirable homosexuals. More desirable younger homosexuals must be attached to powerful groups or individuals to remain free from attack. In larger prisons, some politically oriented inmates who pursue goals such as prisoner rights may develop coalitions between warring gangs on prisoner issues. They are safe as long as they avoid conflicts with inmate leaders, violent activities, and involvement in the prison economic system (Irwin, 1980).

Withdrawal Many inmates in more violent prisons, rather than become associated with a gang or adopt a "hog" or convict identity, choose a more limited style of life referred to as **withdrawal,** or finding a "niche." The inmate withdraws, which usually guarantees his survival in the larger prison world (Johnson, 1997; Seymour, 1988). Both Earley (1992) and McCorkle (1992) found that roughly 80 percent of inmates reduced the risk of violent encounters by keeping to themselves. Other passive precautions included avoiding certain areas in the prison—the chow hall, recreational areas, housing units, and the yard where the presence of large numbers of inmates preclude close supervision—and spending more time in one's cell. Thus, McCorkle (1992) found that almost 4 out of every 10 inmates spend considerable time in their cells to avoid being victimized, and they were not very active players in the *sub-rosa,* illicit, *inmate economy.* They also tried to avoid responding violently to any provocations by aggressive inmates. These inmates maintain close contact with a few friends—individuals they know from the outside or have met in their units through work or shared interests.

A variation of this is what Silberman (1995) calls **prop friendships,** which involve a close relationship between two inmates, one of whom may be stronger than the other, who will back one another up in violent confrontations. This lifestyle is very attractive to first-term inmates who lack gang affiliations, connections, and the benefit of experience in prison.[10] It is also attractive to older, long-term inmates, because it provides a safer and more stable lifestyle.

"Convicts" usually disrespect and ignore those who withdraw from the prison world. Inmates who choose to cope with the prison world in this way may have to be deferential in subtle ways when they come in contact with convicts. By behaving this way, they place themselves in minimal danger of attack and robbery (Irwin, 1980).

Black dominators of the prison community may mark whites as targets. Moreover, young whites may be caught without a support system; new to the prison, they are often friendless, and other inmates avoid them for fear of being targeted themselves. Although they could develop a clique for self-protection, fear leads them to maintain a low profile. The convict code admonishes the vulnerable from seeking staff protection, and short of protective custody, staff are often not in a position to provide protection (Johnson, 1996). One option may be to join a gang, but this only limits their victimization to the gang. Even inmates joining formal organizations like the Jaycees may not be shielded because members may not protect them against predatory inmates. Joining formal inmate groups that meet in closed rooms is one way to avoid the general population for a while. For some of these inmates, the only other option may be to request a transfer to a protective custody unit (Irwin, 1980). This lack of alternatives may explain the significant rise in requests for transfers to these units.

Inmates choosing to withdraw may receive other tangible benefits as well (Irwin, 1980). By maintaining clean disciplinary records for a specified time, they can request transfer to honor blocks that usually house other inmates who have also withdrawn. Access to these units is more restricted than regular housing and inmates there usually have more privileges.

Inmate Violence

The changing roles and adaptations to the inmate world we have just described have had a major impact on prison violence and suicide. Major changes began to appear in the 1990s when prisons began to receive "young bloods" (i.e., teenagers who grew up in an America different from older cons). This new breed of inmates grew up on tougher and meaner streets, experienced more devastating poverty, were more poorly educated, and felt the destructive influence of the crack epidemic and the futility of believing that their conditions will ever improve. Their mode of settling even minor disputes involved the use of guns rather than face-to-face confrontations involving fistfights. Thus, when they arrived in prison, weapons became the common mode of settling arguments. Making matters worse is the fact that these "young bloods" are routinely looking at sentences of 60, 90, 120, and even 200 years. With the prospect of spending most or all of their lives behind bars, they have nothing to lose by impulsively responding to monotony, anger, boredom, and frustration with violence. Further, programs that were already serving only a small proportion of the inmate population are now being scaled back, while the inmate population is increasing, giving inmates fewer positive activities to occupy their time (Taylor, 1996).

There are several indicators that the level of violence in prison has increased. Assaults by inmates on other inmates rose by 20 percent in state and federal facilities—from 21,500 in 1990 to 25,948 in 1995—while assaults on staff increased by one third—from 10,371 in 1990 to 14,165 (Stephan, 1997).[11] The number of state facilities that reported inmate-related deaths rose from 65 to 74 from 1990 to 1995.

The Prison Economy

As in most eras, inmates in contemporary prisons are deprived of many luxuries that outsiders take for granted. The state takes care of inmates' basic needs, but the quality and quantity of the items furnished are often insufficient. As Sheehan (1978) found from her research at Greenhaven prison in New York:

> There are many things not provided by the state that most prisoners regard as even more necessary than people on the outside do—for example, talcum powder and deodorant, because of the prisoners' more limited bathing facilities. Store-bought cigarettes, instant coffee, and immersion coils for heating water help to fill the empty spaces of prison life. (p. 90)

The Legal Economic System

The legitimate prison economic system consists of inmate funds and goods obtained through approved channels, such as having relatives and friends make deposits to their prison accounts or send them goods that can be sold or traded. Policies vary with regard to their access to funds from an outside bank account. Work assignments can be another source of legal funds. Typically, inmates employed by private prison industries are paid the highest followed by agency-operated industries and at the bottom are nonindustry jobs (Camp & Camp, 1998). Table 10.3 shows typical low-end and high-end pay rates for prisoners.

Fifty percent of inmates are involved in nonindustry work, whereas only 6 percent are employed in industry work (Camp & Camp, 1998). Other sources of income include receiving veterans' benefits for those enrolled in educational programs (Gleason, 1978), managing the inmate welfare fund, and serving as staff barber (Kalinich, 1986). Inmates may also earn money through their hobbies, by making such items as belts, wallets, or paintings, which can be sold at gift shops located outside the prison or in the visitors' area. They may also enter these items

Table 10.3

Average Rate of Pay per Day

	Low		High	
	Actual Pay*	Average Pay	Actual Pay*	Average Pay
Private industries	$.20	$24.27	$49.20	$38.23
Agency-operated industries	.15	1.60	48.75	7.06
Nonindustry work	.10	.99	13.50	3.13

*Low Actual Pay is the lowest amount any system pays; High Actual Pay is the highest amount.
Source: Camp & Camp, 1998.

in outside crafts and art contests (Davidson, 1983). One inmate, for example, received $1,500 for winning first prize in an art contest (Welch, 1990).

Although there is no current empirical data on what it costs an inmate to survive, anecdotal information suggests that inmates need at least $20 to $40 per week to live above prison subsistence level. Data on inmate accounts from the state of Florida indicate the average inmate has about $10 per week in his or her canteen account, and that about 30 percent of inmates are indigent. Thus, unless they have either outside assistance or some nonlegal means of acquiring money, most inmates will not live well in prison. At the facility studied by Gleason (1978), gifts and government transfer payments accounted for three quarters of an average inmate's income. The only inmates living comfortably on income from legal sources were those who worked in prison industries, received veterans' benefits, or had family and friends willing and able to provide support.[12]

Desirable allowed commodities, such as cigarettes, stereos, books, and toiletries, can only be acquired through the canteen (at free-world prices) or from friends and relatives. Recently, some jurisdictions have ruled money contraband and issued **inmate credit cards** for making commissary purchases. These usually consist of ID badges with electronically sensitive tape that is used to scan inmate accounts and deduct the appropriate amount when purchases are made. Some prison systems issue **script** (nonlegal tender or "money" created for a special situation).

The Illegal Economy

The **sub-rosa,** or illegal, **inmate economy** thrives because it satisfies inmates' needs and contributes to their psychological well-being (Davidson, 1983; Kalinich, 1986). It provides illegal goods and services not available through normal channels. For inmates without any resources, where institutional pay is low, or when legitimate employment is limited, the sub-rosa system represents a means for improving an otherwise depressing existence. Even inmate nonparticipants take pleasure in the fact that it defeats, through inmate ingenuity and wit, a system designed to suppress them.

Though many prisons use credit card systems or script to try to limit economic activity to legal purchases from the prison store, these restrictions have had a negligible impact. The working capital of the prison economy includes cigarettes, "green" (real money), prison script, and goods and services that may be bartered.[13] Cigarettes have commonly been the basic prison currency. Normally, they are not contraband so inmates can legally have them. They have a standard value; loose cigarettes and packs are used as coins and dollar bills, while cartons serve as larger bills. However, cash is used in transactions approaching 20 to 25 cartons because the bulk of that many cartons could attract attention. Even inmates who are nonsmokers keep cartons for trading purposes. Vaughn and del Carmen (1993) reported that 90 percent of state correctional facilities now restrict smoking and a number of county jails ban it (LIS, 1991). Eleven states,[14] including Texas, Connecticut, Idaho, Utah, and Minnesota, have totally banned smoking in their state correctional facilities, and all but five others have partially banned it (Tischler, 1998).

In some facilities where cigarettes are banned, candy and other consumables from the canteen have replaced them (Knowles, 1994). In these facilities, cigarettes are now selling for between $40 to $60 per package. Finally, although having cash is illegal in many prison systems, this has not deterred its possession. Inmates prefer $10s and $20s because they are easier to handle, count, and conceal (Buentello, 1997).

By **hustling,** or wheeling and dealing, many inmates earn enough money to meet their needs and wants. There is a "hustle" in any prison job that places inmates in a position to obtain sellable goods (i.e., food, clothing), to provide services such as custom pressing, or to obtain information (Davidson, 1983).

> The swag man who sold me and others his sandwiches became my friend. But if it hadn't been so easy and profitable to steal from the kitchen, he probably would have ended up stealing from me. The more he provided his clandestine services, the more he created a demand, which in turn ensured him a steady income that was far less risky than breaking into another man's cell. (Hassine, 1999, p. 52)

According to Hassine (1999), the illegal economy functioned to control violence and support the inmate code, which included the following "rules": "Don't gamble, don't mess with drugs, don't mess with homosexuals, don't borrow or lend money and you might survive" (p. 52). It provided an incentive for inmates not to kill each other and to abide by the code. Overcrowding and failed security facilitated the growth of the black market, which, in turn, created a stable class of merchants and customers. If there were no rules to follow and continual conflict, the profits would drop because this unstable environment would substantially reduce the economy's ability to function.

Contraband

Contraband, anything that is declared illegal by the prison authorities, can be smuggled into institutions in a variety of ways. Liberal visiting policies allowing contact visits have made it easier for visitors to transfer contraband, particularly small quantities of drugs. To bring drugs into the prison, visitors must first get past the staff assigned to process them. Visitors, inmates, and even personnel who bring drugs into the prison rely on staff

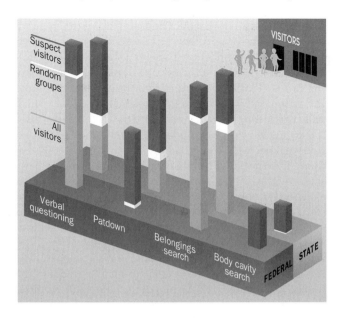

Figure 10.1 *Categories of Visitor Groups Selected for Different Types of Drug Control Activities*

Source: Adapted from C. W. Harlow (1992), *Drug Enforcement and Treatment in Prisons, 1990,* Washington, DC: U.S. Department of Justice.

searches to be quick, cursory, and superficial. Figure 10.1 shows the criteria for searches. About 9 out of 10 of the federal facilities and state institutions search visitors' belongings for drugs. Pat-down searches are conducted at 83 percent of the federal and 57 percent of the state facilities. In the case of body cavity searches, traffickers rely on the staff's natural reluctance and distaste for doing them. Nevertheless, these searches are usually conducted if visitors are suspected of smuggling drugs. Facilities using these intrusive searches report lower positive tests among inmates for drugs than those employing other methods (Harlow, 1992). Like the "mules" (people that bring drugs from South America), some visitors will swallow balloons with drugs, regurgitate them in the visitor's room bathroom, and then pass them on.

Experience shows that visitors can conceal drugs, and more recently cigarettes, anywhere on their person, in clothing like running shoes or in food items like potato chip bags, which may be resealed to look factory sealed (Chastang, 1993). Once brought in and passed, the inmate must then conceal the contraband because inmates are searched when leaving the visiting area. Inmates can hide drugs on their person but are safer from detection during strip searches if they hide them in a body cavity (Gunn, 1979; Kalinich, 1986).

Some correctional staff are also involved in introducing drugs and other contraband (e.g., money, escape tools, liquor, and cigarettes in facilities that have banned them) into the prison and smuggling things out—usually cash.[15] The sale of narcotics and now cigarettes is so lucrative that inmate dealers can pay staff well for their efforts. A typical connection involves a staff member meeting inmate contacts on the outside to pick up or purchase the drugs. The staff member then brings the drugs into the prison on his person or in a personal item like a lunch pail (Davidson, 1983; Kalinich, 1986). On a yearly basis, these guards could earn about $10,000 of undeclared tax-free income, with some making more than $50,000. Although the irregular timing of this activity makes it fairly safe, roughly 10 percent of the staff who run drugs get caught (Davidson, 1983). Reluctantly, recognizing that staff can be the only source of regular and large quantities of drugs and other types of contraband, some facilities have begun to subject staff to interdiction procedures. Usually, this only occurs when there is a suspicion of drug smuggling. Table 10.4 shows that about 54 percent of the federal and more than 43 percent of the state facilities question staff suspected of bringing in drugs. States were more likely to use more intrusive procedures at confinement facilities, with 23 percent reporting random staff frisking (Harlow, 1993).

Occasionally, staff who are too naive to recognize that many inmates are the masters of manipulation are duped or intimidated into bringing contraband into prison. Kalinich (1986) suggests how this can occur:

> [An inmate] becomes friendly with a guard or a professional staff member and asks the staff member to do simple favors for him; in return the . . . [inmate] provides some kind of service for the staff member, for example, giving him contraband food. After developing this relationship, the resident continues to request favors, and each favor becomes larger, with respect to rule violation, than the last one. At some point, the resident simply advises the staff member that he is now in violation of a law. The [inmate]

threatens to inform someone higher up about the illegal activity of the staff member, unless he provides favors to a greater extent. From this time, the staff member is in the resident's "pocket" and can be continually coerced into smuggling contraband. (p. 68)

There are many concerns about policies banning smoking from state correctional systems. A 1993 Supreme Court decision concluded that an inmate's exposure to environmental smoke could amount to cruel and unusual punishment. Reducing health-care cost and safety are other concerns. Many note that smoking has been banned in other state buildings.[16] However, smoking is viewed as an important tool in prison management. It provides a major incentive without which inmates have less motivation to cooperate and staff have fewer rewards at their disposal. Moreover, a high percentage of the prison staff smoke and, Warden Pat Koehene[17] notes, "You have to be sensitive to your staff, too" (Tischler, 1998, p. 1).

On the black market a skinny, hand-rolled cigarette costs $5 (Turner, 1997). Unlike drugs, cigarettes can be bought legally on the outside, which makes them more profitable than narcotics. A 0.65-ounce package of Bugler tobacco can be bought for $0.99 at any store. However, Texas Department of Criminal Justice (TDCJ) officials reported that it sells for $25 on the inside, and if split into fistfuls of cigarettes, it is worth even more.

Like narcotics, COs and other staff have the most opportunities for smuggling tobacco products into prison. Since the ban, in Texas tobacco has become the number one contraband item. Moreover, many COs and other staff members are smokers, and some do not feel that bringing tobacco in is "really a violation," because they disagree with the ban. For some, throwing a carton of cigarettes over the wall to make an extra $100 is more of a game than a law violation. It presents staff with an easy way to supplement their income without really feeling guilty or that they are violating the law.

Joe Fernald, warden of the Walls unit at TDCJ, stated that, "Anyone in prison with 200 bags of tobacco has power" (Turner, 1997, p. 1a). In Texas, staff caught trafficking in cigarettes can be subject to felony charges, and those guilty of lesser offenses may be forced to resign. In 1996, 40 employees at TDCJ were caught in tobacco violations. Although officials at TDCJ insisted the contraband problem was diminishing, Barbara Owens, a regional director, indicated that tobacco offenses occur daily (Turner, 1997). Inmates in Texas who violate the tobacco ban are subject to disciplinary action that includes loss of good time, trustee status, or the privilege of attending classes. Enforcing the ban on smoking is far from easy. COs who smell smoke in the cell blocks find that it is difficult to pinpoint its location in time to nab the violator. Trustees and work crews often are unsupervised for hours, giving them ample opportunities to light up. There is far from a consensus as to the effectiveness

Table 10.4

Drug Interdiction for Prison Staff by Type of Facility

Interdiction Activity*	Federal Confinement	State Confinement	State Community-Based
No reported interdiction activity	17.5%	23.4%	42.0%
Verbal questioning	53.8	43.3	45.2
Patdown	21.3	49.3	24.4
Other†	35.0	25.0	11.6
Number of facilities	80	957	250

*Interdiction activities are overlapping categories.
†Includes such measures as drug testing, belongings search, and visual inspection.
Source: Adapted from C. W. Harlow (1992). *Drug Enforcement and Treatment in Prisons, 1990*. Washington, DC: U.S. Department of Justice.

of the Texas ban, which involves the second largest prison population in the United States.

However, Vermont, the first state to ban smoking in 1992, revoked its edict because it had inadvertently created a huge illegal black market. A cigarette was selling for $3; inmates were lining up to pay $1 a drag; many were getting strong-armed and beaten for not paying on tobacco deals; and some were so desperate that they were smoking the instant drink mix Tang (Cain, 1996; Mooney, 1996). Finally, the ban on smoking has even extended to death row in California, which bans smoking inside, and Texas, with a total ban. Thus, inmates who are about to be executed are not permitted to have a final smoke (Cain, 1996).

Sex in Male Prisons

Sexual activities in prison can involve consensual and nonconsensual encounters or relationships, almost exclusively with males, although the presence of females and more liberal visiting programs have added an additional dimension. The values of the inmate population—including a strong masculine image, dominance and aggressiveness in sexual interactions, and a general propensity toward violence—affect the nature of sexual activity in the prison. These values are intensified in prison by racial hatred, the sexual deprivation brought about by incarceration, inaction on the part of correctional officers, and the failure of some administrators to segregate potential victims from predators.

There are no accurate estimates regarding the extent of homosexual behavior in contemporary prisons (Fagan, Wennerstrom, & Miller, 1996). One survey of a sample of 330 federal prison inmates found that 30 percent reported a homosexual experience in prison; most of those inmates admitted playing the dominant partner (Nacci & Kane, 1983, 1984). Less than 1 percent admitted to being forced, while 7 percent reported that they were seduced by inmates bearing gifts. Further, 3 out of 10 reported that they were propositioned while in prison. Of these targeted inmates, about two thirds reported that (1) staff did learn about the assault, and (2) these inmates did nothing "official" to remedy the situation. Our In Their Own Words feature, "From Thief to Cell Block Sex Slave" provides unique testimony on one man's victimization experience.

Offender Characteristics

Research suggests the following profile of sexual aggressors, often known as **jockers,** *wolves,* or *pitchers.* These inmates are older, heavier, and taller than their victims; may have histories of childhood sexual and/or physical abuse; are confident of their physical strength; have the ability to control others yet are deficient in controlling anger; have poor coping and problem-solving skills; are

often heterosexual in identity, preference, and practice on the outside; and use sexual threats and aggressiveness as a means of establishing their dominance over weaker inmates. Also, state-raised youths are more likely than others to assume an aggressive role and engage in prison sexual activities.[18]

There are many variants on patterns used by sexual aggressors to overcome the resistance of their targets, but in essence these tactics take three basic forms;

1. Some inmates use ploys, such as promises of protection or gifts, to entrap or persuade their victims into providing sex.[19] After the victim becomes dependent, the aggressor demands sex for continued assistance.

2. Less subtle, some aggressors pressure their victims over time by use of threats or intimidation (e.g., stalking) until their victim gives in.

3. The most aggressive, hostile inmates dispense with subtleties and simply take by force whatever sexual favors they want without regard for the victim (Fagan et al., 1996; Nacci & Kane, 1983).

Date rape, involving homosexuals as targets in a courting ritual that is a prelude to rape, has increased due to dormitory housing, double celling, and inmate idleness. In the courting ritual the inmate suitor contrives to be constantly with his homosexual target. This is a sign to the prison population that a romance is brewing and that other suitors should stay clear. The suitor's objective is to share a cell with his love interest—for them to live as a couple. However, the date rape rapist's underlying goal is to seek sexual gratification by dominating his target. The romance is one ploy that is used to ensnare the victims. "Date rapists usually focus their attention on inmates who are physically and psychologically weak because the hope is that these inmates will not report the crime" (Hassine, 1999, p. 141). The motivations behind sexual conquests satisfy a number of psychological motives for the offender. See Table 10.5 on page 244.

Victim Characteristics

A review of literature by Fagan et al. (1996) provides the following profile of the victims of sexual assaults in prison: typical victims, known in prison slang as *punks, kids,* or **catchers,** are smaller in stature, lighter in weight, younger than their aggressors (usually 18 to 30), and seen as weak, passive, and easily intimidated by other inmates. They also tend to engage in solitary activities, isolate themselves from other inmates, and ordinarily are not members of prison groups. They are often unsophisticated first-time offenders or nonviolent offenders whose lack of street smarts makes them unfamiliar with the appropriate tactics of self-defense or the operating strategies of gangs. Also vulnerable are racial

From Thief to Cell Block Sex Slave

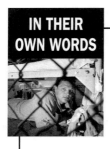

Two months ago in federal court in East St. Louis, Illinois, Michael Blucker, 28, a paroled thief, sued Illinois state prison guards and other employees whom he accused of ignoring his requests for help when he was allegedly raped and treated as a "sex slave" by gang members while behind bars. Mr. Blucker, who is HIV-positive, says he was infected as a result of the sexual abuse.

After a week long trial, the jury rejected claims against five of the seven defendants but was unable to reach a verdict on the other two—a prison psychiatrist and the prison's head of internal investigations. Mr. Blucker's claims against those two are scheduled to be retried this week.

As in many instances in which rape is alleged, the truth in Mr. Blucker's case is sharply disputed. Prison officials say Mr. Blucker prostituted himself while in prison to get drugs and is now lying to win money damages in court.

His testimony in the first trial echoes what prisoner advocates call a culture of rape in American prisons, in which weaker inmates are typically assaulted. Excerpts follow.

Questioned by his attorney, Joseph Condon, Mr. Blucker said the first rape occurred within ten days of his arrival as a gangly 24-year-old at Menard Correctional Center in Chester, Ill., in 1993. Mr. Blucker, who is white, said his assailants were black gang members. Authorities on prison rape say those outside the dominant inmate racial group are commonly victimized:

Q. When you arrived at 10 Gallery, East House, what if anything unusual happened to you?

A. I was celled with another inmate whose race wasn't the same as mine.

Q. What was the inmate's name?

A. I only know him by his gang name, and it was Tyboo at that time, T-y-b-o-o.

Q. What if anything unusual happened to you at the hands of Tyboo?

A. A few days after being celled with this person, the doors were rolled open for us to move to chow. I'm not sure if it was breakfast, lunch, and Tyboo was speaking to his bodyguard.... His name was Prince Mike. And they were talking about just subjects, whatever, and the subject of he needed a wife came up. I—it didn't register to me what he was referring to.... I was sitting down on the bed waiting.... Tyboo and Prince Mike had left.... I had to wait until after the other gang members left. Tyboo, Prince Mike and another individual came back into the room....

Q. What happened?

A. Tyboo went behind me in the back half, and ... I focused my attention on Prince Mike for something that he had said, and ... a stinger cord was placed around my neck from behind.

Q. What is a stinger?

A. A stinger is a device which Menard penitentiary sells in place of a hot pot. It heats up cups of water.

Q. Is it an electrical device?

A. Correct.

Q. What was done with the stinger cord?

A. It was wrapped around my neck.

Q. What happened next?

A. I was pulled back basically a little bit off my balance, told to remove my clothes or they would be removed for me, and I guess there really wasn't no

time to decide too much of anything because Prince Mike helped himself to removing my clothes. Trying to fight and breathe at the same time is a little hard. But when I tried doing it, the guy at the door showed me two homemade knives that were stuck in his waistband.

Using a prison vulgarism, the inmate with the knives said Mr. Blucker's choice was to submit to rape or be stabbed, Mr. Blucker testified. After providing graphic details of rape, he continued:

A. When they were done, they cleaned themselves off and left the gallery and closed the door.

Q. What did you do?

A. Cried, brushed my teeth, tried cleaning up what I could....

Prisoner advocates say that once an inmate has been "turned out"—raped—he is subject to repeated assaults. Mr. Blucker affirmed this:

Q. How many separate occasions were you sexually assaulted?

A. I can't number that....

Q. Did you resist any of these assaults?

A. Tried to....

Q. What did you do?

A. You can verbally say no until it gets physical, and then you have to fight back as much as you can until there is no more fighting.

Q. And when there is no more fighting, what happens?

A. You get raped.

Q. How tall are you?

A. Believe it or not, I'm not sure. Some people say I'm 6-foot-1½, some people say I'm 6-foot-3½.

Q. How much do you weigh?

A. Approximately 160 pounds.

Mr. Blucker said he was turned over to another cellmate, a gang leader nicknamed Johnny Cross, who then sold him off for the sexual pleasure of other inmates. Liaisons were typically arranged during the noise and bustle when cells were opened and inmates were marched to meals:

Q. How many times were you sold to another inmate?

A. Several.

Q. Did you resist any of those efforts to sell you?

A. Not to Johnny, but to the people in which I was being sent to. . . .

Q. Would you travel to the cells of these other inmates?

A. Yes. . . .

Q. Escorted by whom?

A. Inmates.

Q. Names?

A. Just whoever he, Johnny Cross, called . . . to take me down there to make sure I got there and to make sure I did what I was supposed to do and for them to collect the payment and to bring it back to them.

Q. The escorts were to collect the payment?

A. Yes.

Q. What did you see given in payment?

A. Marijuana or things that they call honey bears, which is homemade alcohol, soap, sometimes cash. . . . whatever it was he needed.

Mr. Blucker said he was ordered to become a drug courier for the gang, smuggling in marijuana passed on by a visiting gang accomplice:

Q. What happened in the visiting room between you and this woman?

A. I was assigned to the table, sat down across from her. She sat with her back to the officer, and she handed me two condoms with two cylinders of highly compressed marijuana inside which I was to insert right there at the table, insert into my anus.

Q. How were you to do that without being seen by the officers who were present?

A. Johnny Cross prior to the visit made me clean myself out, lubricate myself, and wear baggy pants without a belt so I could do so without actually going to the washroom to cause any suspicion upon myself.

Q. Having made the insertion, did you then leave the woman unknown to you and walk back into the prison?

A. Well, we had to make it look like we knew each other, so we held hands a minute. . . .

Q. Was it painful to carry that substance in your body?

A. It hurt, yeah.

Q. Were you frightened?

A. I was scared that it could possibly rip open or break open or something.

Q. What did you do with those drugs when you got back into the prison?

A. I didn't get that far.

Mr. Blucker said suspicious guards strip-searched him and placed him in a room without a toilet or water, so that when he needed to go the bathroom guards could accompany him and check his stool:

A. It was three days before I even had a bowel movement. But in between time I had inmates delivering me trays and messages from Johnny Cross that if I didn't bring it, the marijuana, back that I might as well stay there, not leave. In my food trays there was extra cellophane to re-wrap the packages, and I did. I re-wrapped 22 of them and swallowed them. Then I hollowed out an apple, and I hid the rest of it there. I had a bowel movement in front of the officers, they checked it, they shook me down, and I left.

Q. And how did you get the drugs out of your bowel?

A. I vomited what I could up. I ended up having a bowel movement . . . one of them didn't come out until like a week later.

Mr. Blucker said that after he told prison authorities of his abuse he was offered transfer to protective custody, special cells for inmates at risk of harm by others. But Mr. Blucker declined:

Q. What is the danger in protective custody?

A. Basically it's not protective custody. . . . If they want, they being gang members, to have something done to another individual in another part of the prison, whether it be segregation, P.C., or another building, all they have to do is send word to their other gang members, and it will be done regardless. . . .

Mr. Blucker was asked how he had changed:

Q. How are you different now that you've been through the experience of Menard, if you are?

A. I don't trust, not even my own family members. . . . I like to sit with my back to the wall and turn the chair out. . . . I know for a fact that myself I've got a lot of anger, a lot of hate and a really short temper. . . .

Q. Anything else?

A. Besides the fact I'm HIV-positive and that it doesn't sit well with me nor my family and that it bears a lot on whether or not I can get a job.

Q. Anything else?

(continued)

From Thief to Cell Block Sex Slave

(continued)

A. Fear.

Q. Of what?

A. A lot of people. I—my wife tried taking me through a mall, but there was too many people there. And I'm sorry to say it, black people, too. And it scared me. I had to leave....

Q. Anything else you notice about yourself?

A. No.

Q. No other questions.

Publicity about the case has prompted Illinois to start some prison AIDS-testing programs and other measures to prevent the spread of the disease, the leading cause of death among Illinois inmates. Mr. Blucker, paroled in 1996, lives with his wife in Crystal Lake, Illinois.

Source: From thief to cellblock sex slave: A convict's testimony (1997, Oct. 19), New York Times, Section 4, p. 7. Copyright © 1997 by The New York Times, Co. Reprinted by permission.

Table 10.5

Primary Motives for Sexual Assault among Men

1. Conquest and control as their primary motive
   Controlling the victim's sexual responses, even against his will, is the ultimate form of power over another individual. It may assure the offender of his strength and authority and compensate feelings of inadequacy or vulnerability.

2. Revenge or retaliation
   The offender was angry at the victim and used sexual assault as a means of retaliation.

3. Sadism and degradation
   Aggression becomes eroticized, and the offender derives excitement and gratification through the sexual abuse and humiliation of his victim. It may also be a means for some offenders experiencing conflict regarding their sexual identity. They are unable to admit their interest in sexual contacts with men, yet cannot abandon these interests. They punish their victims to deal with their unresolved and conflicting sexual interests.

4. Status and affiliation needs
   For some offenders, mutual participation in an assault serves to strengthen and confirm the social bond among offenders. It also serves as a means to demonstrate superiority and masculinity to group members in an effort to show their worthiness for group membership.

5. Establish and maintain social hierarchy in prison
   Inmates often use sexual threats, intimidation, or assault as a way of demonstrating who has control and dominance.

Source: Compiled from: T. J. Fagan, D. Wennerstrom, & J. Miller (1996). Sexual assault of male inmates: Prevention, identification, and intervention. *Journal of Correctional Health Care 3*(1), 49–63.

and ethnic groups who are in a minority in an institution or housing unit. Based on this profile, several groups are more prone to victimization by aggressive males:

- The mentally ill, mentally retarded, and elderly inmates who may not possess the cogni-

tive or physical strength to recognize and cope with sexual aggressors

- Effeminate-acting male inmates, because of their perceived weakness

- Homosexually oriented inmates who exhibit exaggerated feminine characteristics

- Child molesters

Once victimized, inmates who have been sexually assaulted become targets for repeated abuse and must overcome physical and psychological trauma. Compared with female victims, they often suffer greater physical injury and are the victims of multiple assaults by multiple assailants. These men also come to question their ability to defend themselves, their self-confidence, their masculinity, and their sense of personal dignity. Many victims also come to believe that being sexually abused compromises their manhood or sexual identity as men, and they change their sexual orientations (Fagan et al., 1996, p. 56). To cope, victims may choose self-defeating mechanisms that include substance abuse, suicide, and aggressive actions toward staff and more defenseless inmates (this is particularly true of adolescents). They also suffer a loss of status among inmates and staff. According to Dallao (1996):

> [N]on-violent inmates who are sexually assaulted may become violent and angry.... Without counseling, dealing with the feelings associated with ... rape trauma syndrome ... known as Post-Traumatic Stress Disorder, can be overwhelming, and an inmate who has been raped often is at high risk for suicide. (p. 106)

Taking a proactive approach to dealing with sexual assaults has many advantages. Correctional systems have an obligation to provide inmates with a safe and human environment. There are legal ramifications for both systems and individual staff for failing to take adequate precautions to prevent sexual assaults when staff hear, witness, or should be aware of an inmate's vulner-

Michael Blucker, shown here with his wife Laura, successfully sued the Menard Correctional Center in St. Louis for not protecting him from being repeatedly raped by other inmates. Blucker, who contracted HIV as a result of the rapes, was awarded $1.5 million in damages.

well, with more inmates joining an increasing number of organizations. The scope of inmate organizations has grown to include ethnic and racially based, religious, self-help, and special interest organizations. The convict code has also changed in several ways, and a new "tough" inmate role has emerged.

The changes within contemporary prisons have had a detrimental effect on inmates and their lives within the institution. There are high levels of inmate violence and suicide. Also, because the legal economic system does not meet inmates' needs, the illegal economy, fueled by contraband, helps to fill the void.

Sexual activity involves both consensual and nonconsensual relationships, almost exclusively among males, although with the increasing presence of females and more liberal visiting policies, this is not always the case. Sexual aggressors tend to differ from their victims in physical stature and character, with aggressors more likely to be older, heavier, taller, more confident in their strength, and less likely to control their anger. Being sexually victimized in prison often has detrimental psychological effects, which may manifest themselves within and outside the institution. There are also serious health risks among all inmates who engage in sexual activity in prison, including sexually transmitted diseases (STDs) and AIDS.

Critical Thinking Questions

1. Discuss how the prison environment has changed over the past several decades, particularly with regard to overcrowding and inmate demography. Why have these changes occurred, and what are some of their potential implications?

2. How are various prosocial organizations in prison evidence of its pluralistic structure? Discuss the major types of prosocial organizations in contemporary prisons.

3. Describe the "new tough inmate role." How are some groups of inmates able to avoid taking on this role or being victimized by tougher inmates? How does the tough inmate role perpetuate inmate violence in prison?

4. Compare and contrast the legal and illegal prison economies. What is contraband, and how and why is it the driving force behind the illegal economy?

5. How does sex in male prisons characterize the contemporary prison environment? In nonconsensual sexual encounters, who are typically the aggressors? The victims?

6. Discuss the primary motivations for sexual assault among men, as well as prevention and intervention strategies that may be employed to minimize coercive sexual encounters.

ability (Fagan et al., 1996) (see Chapter 15). Proactive precautions may include prevention, intervention, or prosecution (Dumond, 1992; Eigenburg, 1994; Fagan et al., 1996) (see Table 10.6).

Summary

Several social and demographic changes contributed to an increasing prison population, beginning in the 1960s. With the increasing prison population, contemporary prisons changed in other ways, as well. The character and demographics of the inmates have changed to reflect an increasing proportion of minorities and minority violence. The social environment of prisons changed, as

Table 10.6

Rape Prevention and Intervention Strategies

1. Sensitivity training for staff:
   a. *Incident-related* Sensitize staff to the fact that all homosexual behavior in prison is not consensual. They may not be skilled in distinguishing between coercive and consensual sexual behavior. Initially, this requires the rigorous enforcement of disciplinary sanctions against sexual activity between inmates.
   b. *Victim-related* COs should receive sensitivity training for responding to sexual assault victims in a compassionate, professional way.
      1. Educate new inmates about the risks.
      2. Provide crisis intervention.
      3. Provide protection for victims.
      4. Ensure that victims get appropriate medical and mental health care and the offer of pastoral care.
2. Improving safety features: Identify "blind spots" where sexual assaults may occur and improve surveillance and provide better lighting in these areas.
3. Careful screening and placement at admission of potential victims (See Chapter 15, *Farmer v. Brennan*): Staff, particularly medical and mental health staff, should be trained to recognize the characteristics of potential sexual assault victims and perpetrators.
4. Potential offenders: They need to be monitored carefully and housed with individuals possessing similar aggressive tendencies whenever feasible.
5. Prosecution:
   a. The objective is to ensure compliance and deter potential offenders.
   b. Both a disciplinary hearing and criminal justice prosecution are required as is the inmate victim's participation, which places the inmate at risk; ratting violates the inmates' code.
   c. To be successful requires specially trained correctional staff who are certified to collect physical and other evidence in a timely fashion.
   d. Correctional staff should be specially trained to deal with victim advocacy issues to help educate and support the victim during the process.

The Federal policy on dealing with sexual assault, prevention, and intervention provides a good model for a comprehensive policy dealing with this issue. This is illustrated by the requirement that the staff take seriously all statements from inmates that they have been victims of sexual assault and respond supportively and nonjudgmentally (Federal Bureau of Prisons, 1995, p. 41).

Test Your Knowledge

1. By 1998, the prison population in the United States had risen to _____ inmates.
   a. 565,000
   b. 1.3 million
   c. over 1.5 million
   d. 900,000

2. The type of formal organization within the prison to which the largest proportion of white inmates belong can be categorized as:
   a. ethnic.
   b. religious.
   c. self-help.
   d. special interest.

3. The members of which of the ethnic groups listed below are most likely to best function as independents?

   a. whites
   b. blacks
   c. Hispanics
   d. all of the above

4. Which of the items below is most likely to be used as "money" in the prison sub-rosa economy?
   a. prison script
   b. real money
   c. cigarettes
   d. candy

Endnotes

1. Ambrosio & Schiraldi, 1997; LIS, 1995; *What Are Prisons For?* 1982; Egan, 1994; *Wall Street Journal*, 12/96; *Americans View Crime and Justice*, 1996.

2. Grier & Cobbs, 1969; Silberman, 1978; Carroll, 1990.

3. The findings by Harer and Steffensmeir (1996a) of a significant race effect on prison violence is particularly significant because of the sophisticated statistical controls they

employed to rule out the role of other factors. They do note, however, that they did control for the effect of an inmate's race on staff decisions to file disciplinary reports. However, previous research has shown that this was not a factor in the federal system. Also, their measure of gang involvement was not sufficient to determine how the specific features of gangs contribute to prison violence and racial differences.

4. Carroll, 1990; Moore, 1978; Suttles, 1968.

5. Johnson, 1976; Jones, 1976; Carroll, 1990; Silberman, 1995.

6. Irwin, 1980; Irwin & Austin, 1994, 1997; Hassine, 1997.

7. Irwin, 1980; Silberman, 1995; Irwin & Austin, 1994, 1997.

8. Irwin, 1980; Irwin & Austin, 1994; Silberman, 1995; Johnson, 1996.

9. Irwin, 1980; Silberman, 1995; Johnson, 1996.

10. Irwin, 1980; Irwin & Austin, 1994; McCorkle, 1992; Sheehan, 1978; Johnson, 1996.

11. We should note that overall rates per 1,000 inmate assaults dropped slightly between 1990 and 1995 (31.3 to 27.0). However, whereas state rates dropped from 31.3 to 27.0, federal rates rose from 7.4 to 12.4. Regarding assaults on staff, a similar trend occurred for the states, where rates decreased from 15.5 to 14.7, whereas federal-level rates rose from 3.1 to 14.1 (Stephan, 1997). One possible explanation for slight decreases in assaults on state levels is that a sufficient proportion of older, more settled inmates are offsetting the newer, more volatile population. We may not yet have fully felt the impact of these new young bloods on the corrections system, and as their proportion in the prison population increases, the assaults will probably rise.

12. Gleason, 1978; Kalinich, 1986; Sheehan, 1978.

13. Davidson, 1983; Gleason, 1978; Irwin, 1980; Kalinich, 1986.

14. The others include Alabama, Indiana, Montana, North Dakota, Virginia, and Michigan.

15. Former prison guard, 1993; Herbeck, 1993; Three guards, 1993; Delguzzi, 1993; York, 1992.

16. Cain, 1996; *Helling v. McKinney*, 1993; Turner, 1997.

17. Pat Koehene is the president of the North American Association of Wardens. Further, inmates in Massachusetts are arguing that smoking bans constitute an Eighth Amendment violation (i.e., they cause "needless and unnecessary pain and suffering) (Tischler, 1998).

18. Cotton & Groth, 1982, 1984; Dumont, 1992; McCorkle, 1992; Nacci & Kane, 1983, 1984a; Wright, 1991; and Fagan et al., 1996.

19. Burgess, 1980; Fagan et al., 1996; Lockwood, 1980.

Correctional Administration

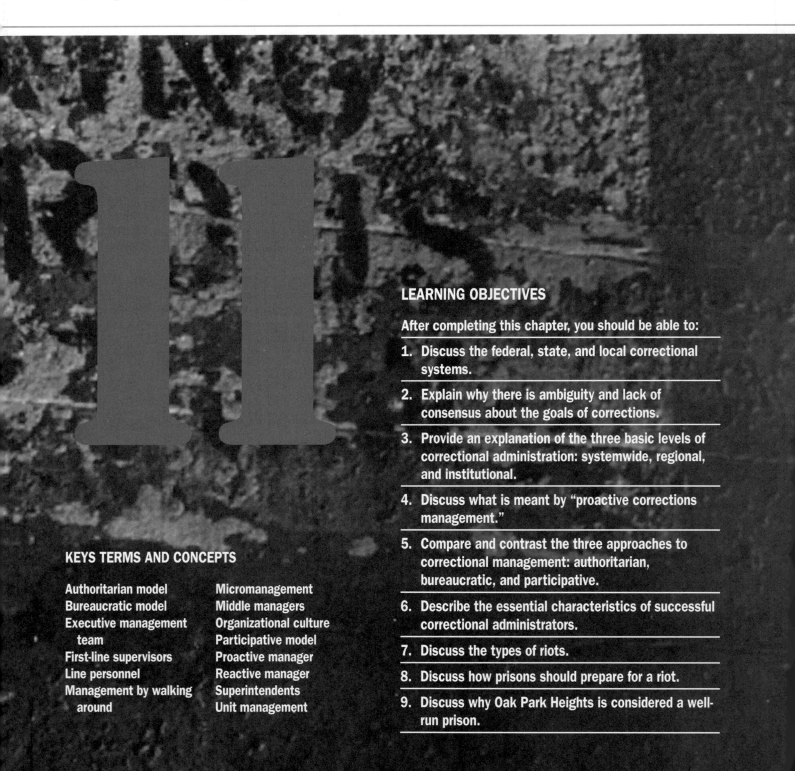

11

KEYS TERMS AND CONCEPTS

Authoritarian model
Bureaucratic model
Executive management
 team
First-line supervisors
Line personnel
Management by walking
 around

Micromanagement
Middle managers
Organizational culture
Participative model
Proactive manager
Reactive manager
Superintendents
Unit management

LEARNING OBJECTIVES

After completing this chapter, you should be able to:

1. Discuss the federal, state, and local correctional systems.

2. Explain why there is ambiguity and lack of consensus about the goals of corrections.

3. Provide an explanation of the three basic levels of correctional administration: systemwide, regional, and institutional.

4. Discuss what is meant by "proactive corrections management."

5. Compare and contrast the three approaches to correctional management: authoritarian, bureaucratic, and participative.

6. Describe the essential characteristics of successful correctional administrators.

7. Discuss the types of riots.

8. Discuss how prisons should prepare for a riot.

9. Discuss why Oak Park Heights is considered a well-run prison.

Introduction

"[W]hether prisons and jails are safe and civilized, on the one hand, or riotous and wretched, on the other, depends mainly on how they are organized and managed" (DiIulio, 1991, p. 33).[1] The most important factors in the success of any enterprise are the manner in which it is structured and the qualities of the people who run it (DiIulio, 1991). In prison, it is that structure and the individuals who manage it that create the environment in which all interactions among staff and between staff and inmates take place. It is imperative that administrators and managers and those who work under them hold similar views of the mission of the prison and its achievement. It is their task to provide the leadership by which this unity of purpose is defined and attained. In the correctional setting, this leads to prisons in which staff and inmates can work or do their time in safety and with dignity.

Because corrections is primarily a governmental rather than a private enterprise function, there are many ways in which it differs from a commercial enterprise. Both public and private organizations function most effectively under professional managers who recognize and react to environmental pressures, coordinate organizational relationships, manage and motivate people, and apply technologies germane to their fields.

U.S. Correctional Systems

Governmental functions and responsibilities in the United States are divided among federal, state, and local entities. Each of these levels of government generally operates and maintains its own correctional programs and facilities. As a result, corrections in the United States is divided into many different systems and programs and has diverse goals. This makes it difficult to describe.

The Federal Correctional System

Before 1895, federal prisoners were held in state and local facilities. Between 1895 and 1930, the Department of Justice acquired or constructed four federal penitentiaries, but there was little central leadership and each was run according to the whims of its warden. In 1930, Congress created the Federal Bureau of Prisons (BOP) and made it responsible for supervising those individuals who were convicted of violating federal laws. The BOP grew steadily and presently consists of facilities that include halfway houses, prison camps, correctional institutions, penitentiaries, and detention centers. Because the BOP currently has only a few detention facilities, it uses state and local jails to house most federal pretrial detainees. The organization of the BOP is centralized, but because of the tremendous size of the country, it is broken down into six regions to make the system more responsive to the central office (DiIulio, 1991). The map in Figure 11.1 shows the six regions and the location of BOP facilities in 1992.

Since its inception, the BOP has provided stable and innovative career service leadership in the correctional field. The National Institute of Corrections (NIC) was created as a division of the BOP to provide state and local correctional systems with information and technical assistance. One of the innovations developed by the BOP in the early 1970s was **unit management,** a form of correctional administration in which a team of correctional workers takes responsibility for managing a unit, or a cell block, of a facility. In our In Their Own Words feature on page 251, "Unit Management," Bob Levinson, an expert in this area, profiles this approach to inmates and institutional design.

State Correctional Systems

Each of the 50 states has developed and operates its own correctional system. These systems run the gamut from the massive California system with its many facilities and over 161,000 inmates to the very small North Dakota system with its few facilities and about 915 inmates (Beck & Mumola, 1999). With these differences, there is considerable variation in the organization of these systems. Although varying in complexity and the types of programs they have, almost all state systems consist of a department of corrections, headed by a politically appointed state director who develops policy and oversees the operation of state-mandated facilities and programs. The structure of the Minnesota system is presented in Figure 11.2 and can serve as an organizational example. Also in some states like Minnesota, the corrections department is responsible for inspecting, monitoring, and approving local (county and city) facility construction and operations (Wood, 1998). All states also have local detention facilities, and in a few states these are operated by states' department of corrections (see Chapter 18).

Local Correctional Systems

Approximately 3,300 jails and stockades in the United States make up the local correctional systems (Harlow, 1998). Each jurisdiction, which maintains facilities for holding pretrial detainees and convicted misdemeanants, is thus operating a "correctional system." More than 80 percent of these are operated by counties in 44 states. Almost all of these are operated by elected sheriffs. The rest are operated by municipalities, some are administered by police, and others are run by a locally constituted corrections department. (Six states— Alaska, Connecticut, Delaware, Hawaii, Rhode Island, and Vermont—administer their jails at the state level.)

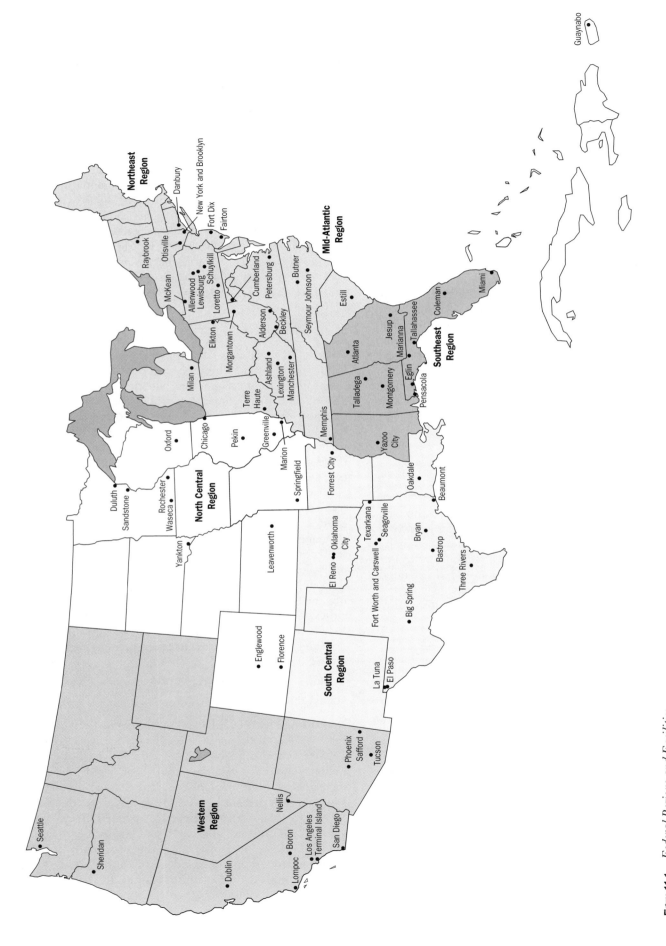

Figure 11.1 *Federal Regions and Facilities*

Source: U.S. Department of Justice (1997). *BOP/NIC Directory*. Washington, DC: Author, p. 4.

Unit Management

The Federal Bureau of Prisons began the systemwide implementation of unit management in the early 1970s. This more effective approach to managing inmates started in the 1960s at the National Training School for Boys, a federal institution for juvenile delinquents in Washington, D.C. The original Demonstration Counseling Project was funded, initially, by a special grant from then Attorney General Robert F. Kennedy. The first secure, adult facility built around the unit management concept was the Federal Correctional Institution in Butner, N.C., which opened in 1975. By 1996 two-thirds of the states responding to a Wisconsin Department of Corrections' survey (27 of 41) indicated that they were using unit management. Additionally, as of 1999, unit management is operational in the prison systems of Australia, Canada, Denmark, Israel, New Zealand, Sweden, the United Kingdom, and the Union of South Africa.

Truly, the unit management concept has spread around the world. But, what is *unit management*?

Unit Management Defined

Unit management has been called many things—some of which should not be repeated in polite society. More officially,

> Unit Management is an approach to inmate and institutional administration designed to improve control and relationships by dividing a large institution into smaller, more manageable groups, in order to improve the delivery of correctional services.
>
> —Roy E. Gerard,
> Assistant Director, BOP

Other definitions include an Ohio warden's: "A method to control inmate behavior," and the sign in the office of the superintendent of Alaska's Palmer Correctional Institution:

> Unit Management is NOT a program; it is a more effective way to manage programs.

Unit management has not only changed the way the Federal Bureau of Prisons (and everyone else) builds prisons, it also has altered how jails are constructed. The federal prison system's Metropolitan Correctional Centers—the first jails designed around the Unit Management concept—demonstrated that these places for detention and short-term incarceration could be more than facilities that warehouse people while they undergo the trial process.

In brief, it has been suggested that in many respects prisons and jails are like small cities—required to provide all of life's sustaining services—and in this context, units are like "neighborhoods."

Components of Unit Management— The "Ten Commandments"

One of the primary missions of corrections is to develop and operate facilities that balance the concepts of punishment, deterrence, incapacitation, and rehabilitation. Unit management helps provide this balance. It incorporates the notion that cooperation is most likely in small groups that have lengthy interactions. Other key ingredients are decentralization and delegated authority. This approach relies on constant communication among staff and between staff and inmates. Clearly written policies and procedures, participatory management, and an emphasis on teamwork are integral to unit management.

To the degree that the ten attributes listed in Table 11.1 are *absent*, unit management will fail. These requisites encompass two major goals unit management is designed to help attain:

- Establish a safe, humane environment (for both staff and inmates),

which minimizes the detrimental effects of incarceration; and

- Deliver a wide variety of counseling, social, educational, and vocational training programs designed to aid offenders to make a successful return to the community.

Does Unit Management Work?

How does one decide whether a particular correctional program "works"? Typically, testimonials and research. Unit management has both types of "evidence" at the international, federal, state, and local levels. Studies reveal that this approach to managing inmates in a wide variety of institutions and settings leads to less inmate-on-inmate and inmate-on-staff violence and a better facility and interpersonal climate—one which is safe and humane and minimizes the detrimental effects of confinement for both staff and inmates.

Both staff and inmates gain many benefits from adopting the procedures integral to unit management:

- Unit management fosters the development of correctional and managerial skills;

- The use of multidisciplinary teams improves communication and cooperation with other institutional departments throughout the facility;

- It increases the frequency or intensity of positive relationships between inmates and staff, which results in better communication and program planning;

- Decentralized management results in decisions about inmates being made more quickly by people who really know them; and

(continued)

Unit Management

Table 11.1

Unit Management's Ten Commandments

1. Unit management must be understood by, and have the support of, the top-level administration.
2. Unit management requires three sets of written guidelines:
   - a *policy statement* issued by the central office,
   - an institution *procedures manual,* and
   - a *unit plan* for each unit.
3. In the Table of Organization, unit managers are at the department head level, giving them responsibility for both the staff and inmates assigned to their unit; and, the organizational chart shows them and the head of security reporting to the same supervisor (usually a deputy warden).
4. Each unit's population size is based on its mission:
   - *General Unit*—150–250 inmates; in other words, two caseloads;
   - *Special Unit*—75–125 inmates (with a special problem and for which there is an *in-unit* treatment program).
5. Inmates and unit staff are permanently assigned to the unit; correctional officers are stationed in the unit for a minimum of 9 months.
6. Unit staffing consists of:

	General Unit	Special Unit
Unit manager	1	1
Case manager	2	1
*Correctional counselor	2	1
Unit secretary	1	1
Mental health staff	½	1
Correctional officers	24-hour coverage	24-hour coverage
Part-time staff	**	**

7. In addition to correctional officer coverage, unit staff provide 12-hour supervision Monday through Friday and 8 hours on each weekend day.
8. Staff offices are located on the unit (or as near to it as possible).
9. Unit personnel receive initial, and ongoing, formal training regarding their roles and responsibilities.
10. Unit management audits (conducted by knowledgeable central office or regional office staff) occur on a regularly scheduled basis—minimum, once a year.

*Correctional officers, usually at the sergeant level, who have been given special training.
**Education, recreation, volunteers, etc.
Source: This feature was especially prepared for *Corrections: A Comprehensive View,* 2nd ed., by Bob Levinson, author of *Unit Management in Prisons and Jails* (1999). Lanham, MD: American Correctional Association.

(continued)

- It results in increased program flexibility, because each unit can develop the type of program most appropriate for its own inmate population.

A correctional professional from North Carolina recently remarked: "If it wasn't for unit management, we wouldn't know how else to run a large institution." An administrator at a detention center in New York City stated:

Nobody thought it [unit management] would work. The institution's architecture was against it working; so was the idea of trying it on adolescents. Now even the bad inmates want it. They see it as being fairer. Among the staff there is less "ducking and hiding," which was the traditional way of handling problems. . . . The good guys won.

Source: This feature was especially prepared for Corrections: A Comprehensive View, *2nd ed., by Bob Levinson, author of* Unit Management in Prisons and Jails *(1999). Lanham, MD: American Correctional Association.*

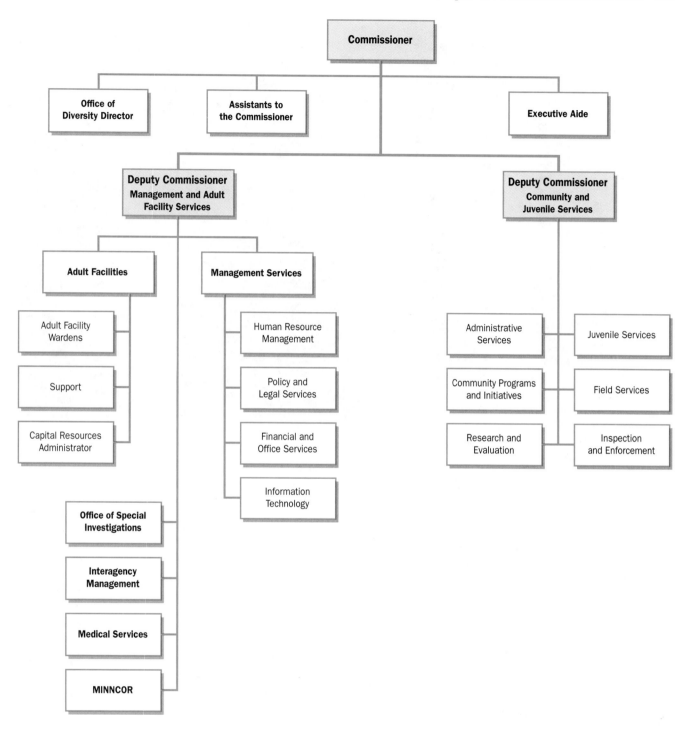

Figure 11.2 *Minnesota Department of Corrections Organization Chart—February 2000*

Source: Minnesota Department of Corrections (2000). "Organizational Profile—February 2000." St. Paul, MN: Author, p. 2; www.corr.state.mn.us/pdf/profile.pdf, p. 2.

Local systems also range from very large—for example, Los Angeles or New York City, which may have daily inmate populations that surpass 20,000—to those whose daily population may not reach 10. The administrative organization of larger systems may resemble that of state corrections while that of the smallest may be quite different and perhaps even informal. Jails and local corrections are more fully discussed in Chapter 18.

Del Norte County Assessor Donald Cochran (right) and Robert Presley, head of the California State Corrections Agency, tour the Pelican Bay State Prison after a riot in the exercise yard in February 2000. Almost all state correctional systems are headed by a politically appointed director who oversees the operation of state facilities.

Components of a Well-Run System

The well-run corrections system begins with a clearly developed and written mission statement that specifies the goals and objectives of the system. Then, it must be structurally sound, organized to efficiently carry out its mandate. Last, the administration must be sensitive to legislative mandates and consist of personnel capable of providing leadership and creating a humane environment.

Incarceration with a Mission

Incarceration (deprivation of liberty) is the sanction imposed for convicted offenders sentenced to a correctional facility. Incarceration represents a modern version of banishing offenders; prisons are designed to separate inmates from the outside community but do not have the power to punish inmates. The U.S. Constitution mandates that this separation occur under relatively humane conditions with respect for the fundamental human rights of the banished. Because incarceration is

usually for a limited time, there is an implicit concern that the government entity responsible for imprisonment not make inmates less fit for society than they were when they entered the prison. There is a tendency to forget that imprisonment itself exerts a very powerful influence on inmates and in essence defines them.

This spotlights the importance of having the purpose and direction of the correctional enterprise stated in specific terms. Thus, a mission statement, which delineates the purpose, goals, and objectives of the organization, should be in place before it begins operation. The federal BOP views its mission as:

> [protecting] society by confining offenders in controlled environments of prisons and community-based facilities that are safe, humane, and appropriately secure, and which provide work and other self-improvement opportunities to assist offenders in becoming law-abiding citizens. (Federal Bureau of Prisons, 1998, p. 5)

This statement suggests that the organization has responsibilities to its dual constituencies—protecting citizens and inmates through the governmental entities that are directly responsible for its functioning. Its mission is to release inmates who are prepared to be law-abiding. Table 11.2 on page 256 highlights the values that guide the BOP's operations, programming, and budgeting.

Wood (1998) asserts that

It is imperative that in addition to a clearly defined mission statement, an effective prison organization must put in place precise and succinct policies, procedures, job descriptions, and orders that relate each post in a correctional facility. All of this should be incorporated into pre-service and in-service training curriculums and reinforced by guiding staff in their supervisory contacts. It is also crucial that all policy and procedures be reviewed by employee groups that include correctional officers at regular intervals to insure that they reflect the dynamic and changing environment in which we work.

Structural Concepts

Much of what is involved in organizing correctional systems or institutions requires grouping various activities into separate units to carry out the work of the organization (e.g., recreation includes inside and outside activities, movies, sports, and arts and crafts activities). However, it is also important to recognize that an organizational structure is necessary to ensure that the various tasks needed to accomplish the missions and goals of the organization are performed. The structure represents the formal hierarchical network of relationships that exists among the various components, units, and positions of authority within the organization. Generally, this network is represented by an organizational table, which graphically presents these aspects of the institution as seen earlier in Figure 11.2. Several concepts helpful in defining how these organizations work are associated with hierarchically structured organizations.

Unity of command refers to the view that workers should only have to report directly to one boss. The ra-

tionale for this type of command structure is that it reduces the confusion for workers.

The second concept, *chain of command*, is related to the first. This recognizes that to maintain control of a large organization a leader must delegate oversight of its many workers and activities to executive managers who, in turn, delegate authority to middle managers, and they give authority to first-line supervisors. Traditionally, orders flow downward and information about performance flows upward. But if management staff do not spend time in the housing units and other facilities, there is a likelihood that they will not hear about problems that may affect security and control. This is because unfavorable information tends not to move up the hierarchy because staff are afraid that this will reflect poorly on their job performance.

However, when a prevention-oriented warden of a prison wants a particular action implemented, such as a change in the time inmates are to be locked down for the night, he or she involves staff in dialogue to get their input on any changes that might affect them. The warden and the staff would then develop contingency plans for implementation of any major changes. This permits staff at all levels to educate staff and inmates about the implications of the change prior to the actual implementation. With the exception of surprise searches, lockdowns, or other preventative initiatives where the element of surprise is critical to their objective, a good warden operates on the philosophy of no surprises for staff. This is the best way to avoid a disaster. At the very least wardens should instruct the appropriate assistant warden, who should pass the order to the appropriate middle manager, and so on down the line so that all staff

Table 11.2

Core Values of the Federal Bureau of Prisons

1. *Bureau Family*   The Bureau of Prisons recognizes that staff are the most valuable resource in accomplishing its mission and is committed to the personal welfare and professional development of each employee. A concept of "family" is encouraged through healthy, supportive relationships among staff and organization responsiveness to staff needs. The active participation of staff at all levels is essential to the development and accomplishment of organizational objectives.
2. *Promotes Integrity*   The Bureau of Prisons firmly adheres to a set of values that promotes honesty and integrity in the professional efforts of its staff to ensure public confidence in the Bureau's prudent use of its allocated resources.
3. *Recognizes the Dignity of All*   Recognizing the inherent dignity of all human beings and their potential for change, the Bureau of Prisons treats inmates fairly and responsively and affords them opportunities for self-improvement to facilitate their successful re-entry into the community. The Bureau further recognizes that offenders are incarcerated as punishment, not for punishment.
4. *Career Service Orientation*   The BOP is a career-oriented service, which has enjoyed a consistent management philosophy and a continuity of leadership, enabling it to evolve as a stable, professional leader in the field of corrections.
5. *Sound Correctional Management*   The BOP maintains effective security and control of its institutions utilizing the least restrictive means necessary, thus providing the essential foundation for sound correctional management programs.
6. *Community Relations*   The BOP recognizes and facilitates the integral role of the community in effectuating the Bureau's mission and works cooperatively with other law enforcement agencies, the courts, and other components of government.
7. *Correctional Workers*   All Bureau of Prisons staff share a common role as correctional workers, which requires a mutual responsibility for maintaining safe and secure institutions and for modeling society's mainstream values and norms.
8. *High Standards*   The BOP requires high standards of safety, security, sanitation, and discipline, which promotes a physically and emotionally sound environment for both staff and inmates.

are aware of intended actions in advance and can plan for them.

Span of control defines the limits of supervision by one person; that is, the number of programs or personnel that can be effectively supervised by one person is limited. Thus, managers at each level have a relatively small number of subordinates directly responsible to them (Fayol, 1916/1996).

Influence of the Legislative Branch

In the broadest sense, correctional policy is set by legislators who often lack correctional expertise to write laws that contain detailed instructions on correctional operations. Instead, they often specify that something be done and then authorize the correctional agency to figure out exactly what to do and how to do it (Meier, 1987). This is made more difficult by the fact that there is no consensus on what a successful corrections system should be doing aside from banishing offenders. Thus, the environment in which much corrections policy (i.e., missions and goals) is developed contains much public ignorance, emotion, and apathy, and disagreements among the experts and politicians. In our In Their Own Words feature, Richard Rison, a retired prison warden with 35 years of experience who administered five federal prisons, discusses the problems of *micromanagement* of correctional systems by legislative bodies.

Heads of state correctional systems are usually correctional professionals, normally appointed by the gov-

ernor, who have titles like director, commissioner, administrator, or secretary. The head of a department of corrections is usually selected on the basis of the fact that his or her corrections philosophy coincides with that of the governor. The department head's duties are to provide expert advice to the governor and legislature on correctional policy, implement the correctional policy that emerges from this political process, secure sufficient resources to operate the system effectively, and coordinate the corrections system with other interdependent agencies such as law enforcement, courts, and human welfare services. The problem system chiefs face in doing their jobs is highlighted by Frank Wood (1998), retired commissioner for the Minnesota Department of Corrections:

The problem in the field is that Correctional Administrators are hired and serve at the pleasure of Governors who in some cases are demagogues and political opportunists whose only interest is remaining in office or enhancing their visibility and name recognition for higher office. They hire administrators who will publicly support and carry out their misguided Criminal Justice policies. It should not be a revelation to anyone that when these Administrators come together they are unable to work out any consensus on what is enlightened Criminal Justice Policy. Whether that's the death penalty, three strikes you're out, mandatory minimum sentences, boot camps, housing inmates in tents, essential elements of Prison Pro-

A Retired Warden on the Pitfalls of Micromanagement

Policy set by legislative entities creates no problems when it is global and the organization has the latitude to implement it. The problem occurs when they start **micromanaging** (i.e., telling the experienced correctional officials how to implement a particular policy). For example, when governing bodies tell them that recreational activities—leisure time activities—are a luxury, when they don't have a clue that these are management tools. Thus, a warden trying to run a maximum security facility, where life safety is on his mind every single day, gets incredibly anxious and uptight when outsiders with little or no correctional knowledge tell the organization how they will implement a policy. Legislators can contribute to prison riots by passing legislation that angers inmates or or-

dering a warden to do things that can disrupt the prison community.

Another issue is the "get tough on crime" policies. Although some may see this as a return to a policy of prisons imposing harsh conditions on inmates, today contemporary systems cannot punish, violate the constitutional rights of, or treat inmates without dignity. [Rison notes based on his research and experience that although the public talks about the frills of a prison and what they would like to see done—get tough—they also are the first ones to let you know if your conditions are reaching the point of inhumane treatment.] So, what I think I hear the public saying, even though there is a lot of emotion in the crime issue, is that they still expect administrators to do the right thing. And some of the talk may be related

to getting things off their chest, but on the other hand I've never had anybody tell me that they expect inmates to be beaten, or have their rights violated. Although legislators may get tough on crime because it is a very popular notion that appeases the public, the public has no knowledge of what the cost is and what they're paying as we go to determinate sentencing models. However, the public clearly expects managers to do things right and leaders to do the right thing.

Source: Richard Rison (2000), a retired prison warden with 35 years of experience who administered five federal prisons, prepared this especially for Corrections: A Comprehensive View, *2nd ed.*

gramming, the quality of life for inmates in Prison, and the list goes on. In the American Medical Association, independent doctors come together and adopt positions like smoking is not conducive to good health. Administrators who serve at the pleasure of Governors cannot endorse enlightened Criminal Justice Policy because some are working for individuals who are out arousing the prejudices and fears of the public for their own political reasons and self-interest. [Wood was the exception in that he resisted attempts by politicians to use the latest "crime de jour, jump on the lockup, build more prisons" bandwagon. Instead he urged lawmakers and others to consider the long-term consequences of increasing the Minnesota inmate population.] (*Star Tribune,* Editorial, 1996, May 30).

The structure of state correctional systems is strongly influenced by the structure of state government. Political pressures not only come from the governor and legislators but also from the media and special interest groups (e.g., the American Civil Liberties Union; the NAACP). Also, court oversight and audits by outside groups have an impact. Although the formulation of corrections policy is mainly the responsibility of elected legislators, corrections administrators should lend their

expertise to this process. A good correctional administrator attempts to bring rationality and knowledge of what works to the legislative policy-making process.

Administrative Personnel

Various groups of administrators and managers exist within correctional systems. First, systemwide administrators and their staff are charged with operating the entire system. Next, institutional and field service (probation and parole) administrators (superintendents/wardens and regional parole administrators) run individual institutions or supervise regional offices. Middle-level managers are educational administrators or security personnel of the rank of captain or higher and parole and probation office managers. Finally, first-line supervisors oversee the day-to-day activities of personnel who work directly with inmates or ex-offenders on conditional release.

Levels of System Administration

There are three levels of system supervision. They include system administrators, regional administrators, and institutional administrators.

Level I   System Administrators

The department of correction's (DOC's) chief executive officer, along with his or her deputies, implements the correctional policy that emerges from the political process (see Table 11.3). These administrators also secure sufficient resources to operate the system effectively and coordinate the corrections system with other interdependent agencies, such as law enforcement, courts, and human welfare services.

State correctional departments may perform a variety of functions. For example, they may only oversee adult prisons, administer all adult services—including probation and parole field services—or supervise all correctional functions for both adults and juveniles. In some states even the local jails are controlled at the state level.

Level II   Regional Administrators

If an organization is big enough, it may break the system down into smaller units to ensure a unity of command. If a DOC commissioner has oversight responsibilities for 100 institutions, he or she may then break these down into 10 regions, each with a regional administrator supervising 10 institutions. This is an efficiency model.

A warden's influence depends to a great extent on his/her ability to develop a strong management team and practice a hands-on style of management.

Level III   The Institution

The institution, the third level, is also hierarchical. Although the philosophy of the management of prisons has evolved from authoritarian to bureaucratic to participative (greater involvement of COs and other staff in planning and policy development), the general administrative structure of prisons has remained the same for a long time. This structure normally includes a top administrator, an executive management team, department heads, and supervisors of line staff.

Institutional Administrators   The top administrator of a prison (i.e., the superintendent or warden) is typically appointed by the head of the department of corrections (see Table 11.3). **Superintendents** are responsible for running the entire prison (e.g., implementation of policy and responsibility for all personnel, fiscal management, security, control, and accountability of all inmates, programs, and activities within the prison). Wardens frequently must also spend time dealing with matters external to the direct management of their facility.

In some instances, they may be involved in the development of the system's master plan for the year. For example, on a yearly basis federal BOP wardens are asked to review current goals and identify strategies to submit to their regional administrators. The results of these re-

Table 11.3

System Administrators

Level	Supervision	Title	Description
I	System	Director, Commissioner	The central office or headquarters is housed at the system level. The chief executive of the system is the Director or Commissioner.
II	Regional	Regional Director	Large systems are broken down into smaller units of measurement for efficiency. Each region is geographically located and all facilities with each region are supervised by the Regional Director. The RD reports to the Director in Level I.
III	Institutional	Warden, Facility Director, Superintendent, Facility Administrator	This administrator supervises the institution or facility. He or she reports to the RD in Level II. If the system does not have a Level II, the Warden (or similar title) reports to the Director in Level I.

Table 11.4

The Executive Management Team

Warden

Associate Warden	Associate Warden	Associate Warden
Operations	Programs	Custody
Fiscal management	Inmate management	Security and control
Personnel	Education	Receiving and discharge
Training and development	Recreation	Inmate mail
Building and safety codes	Vocational training	Confidential investigations
Environmental conditions	Citizen involvement	Disturbance control
Food service	Volunteers	Emergency response
Medical services	Case management	Inmate discipline
Facility maintenance	Unit management	Special inmate management

gional meetings are, in turn, passed up the chain of command to the BOP's Executive Staff Strategic Planning Group. This, in turn, is used to identify strategic issues and to develop the BOP's overall goals for the coming year. At these regional meetings wardens also provide input for tentative budgets for funding for the next 2 years. Once yearly system goals are developed, divisions like health services, industries, education, and vocational training identify specific objectives they hope to achieve during the next year. Wardens, along with their executive staffs, formulate specific local objectives that will facilitate the achievement of systemwide goals. For example, in 1997 one of the BOP's strategic goals was to proactively manage its offender population to ensure a safe and secure population. To accomplish this, some new specialized or different facilities were built or added to existing facilities, community programs were expanded, classification programs were adjusted, and stressing the importance of communication skills was continued (Federal Bureau of Prisons, 1994; Houston, 1999).

Superintendents also often have to serve as a spokesperson for their facility, which means they often speak at

local civic organizations about the general problem of crime and try to allay the security-related fears of community groups. Encouraging local citizens to visit the prison is another way of maintaining good community relations. Retired Warden Rison (1996) asserts that "I do not believe I ever had a visitor to an institution that didn't leave with a more positive perception of federal prison management." He goes on to say, "We should consider community feedback as an essential of prison governance" (pp. 115–116).

It is in the oversight of programs, activities, and personnel that wardens can have the greatest impact on the atmosphere of the prison. Their influence is likely to depend on the extent to which they are fair, tough-minded, and able to develop a strong management team and practice a hands-on style of management. These characteristics also determine the extent to which the goals that have been set will be achieved.

Executive Management Team The **executive management team** selected by the warden is very important (see Table 11.4). At the top of this team are two associate

Figure 11.3   *Middle Managers*

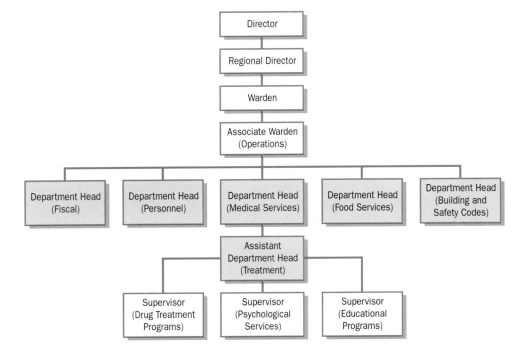

wardens (AWs). Large prisons have three AWs who divide the prison's departments between them. One AW is responsible for operations, which typically includes facilities, personnel, the business office, medical services, and food. In smaller facilities with only two AWs this may also include custody. The second AW controls programs, which include education, various psychological services, case management, recreation, and prison industries. The third AW controls custody (see Table 11.4).

Middle Managers   **Middle managers** occupy a variety of positions in the prison. They carry such titles as department head, captain, assistant department head, and coordinator (see Figure 11.3). They oversee the delivery of specific services in the prison. For instance, a prison's operations may include specialized units such as custody, medical services, and food services. These may be further divided with a manager for each subdivision. For example, medical services may include a subunit of treatment programs. The assistant superintendent for treatment may have individuals who supervise drug treatment programs, psychological services, or educational programs reporting to him or her. These individuals as heads of departments occupy leadership positions.

Department heads have full supervisory authority that allows them to do anything from rating employees to recommending disciplinary action. Other subunits with managers may include construction, fiscal, case management, religion, health services, security, administrative systems, management information systems, and facilities maintenance.

Supervisors of Line Staff   Most departments include supervisors. Employing the one-plus-one management principle, most have two levels of supervision for checks and balances. Captains supervise lieutenants (in some departments called correctional supervisors, watch commanders, or shift supervisors), and lieutenants supervise correctional officers (line staff).

First-line supervisors (lieutenants) generally have day-to-day designated duties in their department (Figure 11.4) Unlike managers, they can report things but cannot evaluate employees. Specifically, they are involved in:

- *Directing*   Assigning responsibility on a day-to-day basis, so all employees know what has to be done and when to do it.

- *Controlling*   Evaluating progress against objectives and making adjustments or decisions as needed.

- *Coordinating*   Making sure that facilities, supplies, and services are available when needed (e.g., they cannot schedule inmates for a movie if there is no facility available to show it in or if there are insufficient staff to supervise inmates). (Phillips & McConnell, 1996, pp. 46–47)

First-line supervisors translate organizational policy directly into action through their influence on line personnel. In personnel, a lieutenant may supervise a section with three employees that does background investigations; another lieutenant may manage training and

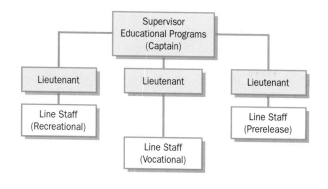

Figure 11.4 *Supervisors*

development. In other departments, such as facilities maintenance and construction, they may supervise both staff and inmates (Rison, 2000).

Finally, there are **line personnel;** they include (1) staff working in departments that support prison operations (e.g., food service, educational programs, medical services) and (2) COs, who are responsible for accomplishing the main work of the prison—controlling inmates (Phillips & McConnell, 1996). Even though they supervise inmates, these personnel are not considered part of the administrative hierarchy (although they may be seen by inmates in that capacity). Chapter 13 describes the functions of COs and the problems they face.

The Professional Administrator

The lack of scientific knowledge about what constitutes successful corrections management has hampered rational decision making about correctional practices and policies. Policy debates have tended to focus on the nature of crime and the role of public institutions in crime control, but rarely has the organization of these institutions been examined. Alvin Cohn (1973, 1979, 1981, 1991) argued that corrections administrators did not learn management theory and practice but rather applied techniques learned as they rose through the ranks. This view of administrators, which assumes that they rarely possess professional managerial skills that allow them to anticipate and plan for the future, is much less true today. This is probably due to the increased complexity of the entire correctional process, its legal implications, and internal and external standards (Rison, 2000). As a result, many prison administrators are professionals who, although they may have risen through the ranks, have earned college degrees (including PhDs) and also taken training programs sponsored by professional organizations (e.g., the ACA or the National Institute of Justice).

Characteristics of Successful Correctional Administrators

There is no overall agreement about the precise approach to good prison administration or the ideal management style. At the beginning of this chapter, we quoted John DiIulio on the importance of good management in the operation of safe and civilized penal institutions. We shall lean heavily on his findings and conclusions in this section (DiIulio, 1987, 1991). He cites a number of individuals who have managed or are presently managing safe, high–quality-of-life prisons but whose management styles differ. In evaluating the success of their management approaches he concluded that they share one common trait: devotion to the building and maintenance of an **organizational culture,** which is defined by Wilson (1989) as "a persistent, patterned way of thinking about the central tasks of, and human relationships in, an organization" (p. 91). This culture is to the organization what personality is to the individual. Once the culture develops it is passed from one managerial "generation" to the next (Wilson, 1989). Obviously, once that happens, the culture becomes a highly unifying force within the organization.

DiIulio has further identified six key behavioral patterns that characterize the organizational culture of a well-managed prison system or institution. These are things that successful leaders do to make their institutions or systems operate more effectively.

1. Successful leaders focus on outcomes by establishing an overall mission statement for the organization that specifies its primary objectives. For example, under James Bennett and Norman Carlson, the mission of the federal Bureau of Prisons was safety, humanity, and opportunity (DiIulio, 1991). In this system, institutions were organized around meeting these objectives. Good leaders inspire their subordinates to focus on actually producing measurable results and rewarding them for accomplishing specific tasks or goals (e.g., whether inmates are safe, whether prison industries have reached production goals). Excuses for failing (e.g., too few resources, overcrowding) are not accepted.

2. Institutional security and custody are viewed as the top priorities. This means that *all* workers within the institution (e.g., teachers, doctors, secretaries) are given the necessary skills and trained to think of themselves as correctional officers first. This is referred to as the correctional worker concept (Hambrick, 1992). Because they all share a similar viewpoint, there is a strengthening of morale. Although this strong sense of mission may sometimes impede needed changes, DiIulio and Hambrick believe that the net effect of this "togetherness" is positive.

characteristic is the MBWA principle: **management by walking around.** This involves administrators going out into the institution(s) to obtain a "first hand" look at and a real feel for what is actually going on in the institution(s). This keeps them from having to rely on secondhand, possibly distorted and incomplete reports from subordinates. MBWA allows leaders to be seen by both line officers and inmates, to interact with them, and to answer directly any questions staff might have. Frank Wood, a former warden of Oak Park Heights, a high-risk, maximum security Minnesota correctional facility, reported spending about one fourth of his time "eyeball-to-eyeball" with inmates and employees. This included his conducting the last meeting of each orientation for new inmates, so that they could understand their responsibilities while at Oak Park Heights and the facility's responsibilities to them (Ward, 1987). It also included staff meetings every morning to assess the previous day and take immediate action and follow up on any emerging problem, issue, or repair. Wood (1998) insisted that staff treat inmates the way they would want their father, brother, or son treated if they were in prison.

He also expected staff at all levels to be responsive to both real and imagined concerns of inmates. This proactive approach reduces the potential for any single or accumulated group of issues to be exploited by negative inmates or used to rally support for disruptive action on the part of the inmates. Information sharing and communication reduce the potential for surprises, incidents, major disturbances, or riots.

4. Successful administrators also make strong alliances with powerful figures in the world outside of the organization. Thus, they will have to develop relationships with individuals who can affect the institution's resources, legal standing, and public image (i.e., key politicians, judges, journalists, and reformers). A common strategy is to invite these movers and shakers, and other interested people, to visit their institutions so that they can see for themselves the conditions (both good and bad) that exist within these facilities.

5. Successful leaders do not often innovate, but when they do, the changes they make are likely to be far-reaching. To prepare inmates and staff for these changes, they are made slowly so that both can be told about them and have plenty of time to "learn the new ways." It is important when making changes in a correctional setting to be sensitive to the fact that correctional officers often look at impending changes in terms of how they will affect them rather than how they will benefit inmates. For example, providing inmates with opportunities to take college courses may be opposed unless staff have opportunities for advanced education.

6. A final characteristic is longevity; good leaders remain in their positions long enough to understand and to make necessary changes in the organization's internal operations and its relationships with outsiders. DiIulio indicates that most of the successful leaders have served at least 6 years. This length of tenure is sometimes difficult to achieve in political organizations that change leadership based on elections and political appointments.

Based on his experience Frank Wood, former corrections commissioner for Minnesota, considers the following important for effective leadership:

The most effective Prison Administrators anticipate problems, are responsive, pro-active, engage in strategic planning—which is long range in scope and in focus, systemwide and involves formulating, implementing, and evaluating actions that will enable a system to achieve its objectives—and tactical planning—which is short range, focuses on identifying current problems (e.g., crowding, developing solutions for them—building or renovating a housing unit), and places a high priority on prevention initiatives which reduce the need for after-the-fact crisis management. The end result, using this approach, is the reduction in the frequency, scope, and seriousness of the inevitable incidents in a maximum security prison. (1998)

Proactive Corrections Management

Managers can respond to organizational problems in one of two ways: reactively or proactively. A **reactive manager** waits until a problem manifests itself before taking action, whereas a **proactive manager** tries to anticipate and correct problems before they develop. Styles (1991) asserts that the federal BOP has avoided many inmate lawsuits by continually evaluating programs. Wardens and their executive staff are responsible for regularly monitoring their own facilities, and the bureau's Program Review Division conducts periodic inspections of each facility. If a reviewer finds a problem (e.g., an inoperative thermostat subjecting inmates to extreme temperatures), he or she immediately reports the problem while on site so that it can be fixed immediately. Inmates can thus see problems being dealt with rapidly and may be less likely to file lawsuits.

Access to information provides the basis for proactive organizational action. Normally, prison managers react to problems as they occur. When this is the case, problem inmates initiate managerial action and the organizational environment is reactive. Reactive organizations often do not have an open flow of information, particularly that which details problems, from the bottom of the chain of command. If there are problems, managers do not want to hear about them. This reduces the effectiveness of planning and proactive problem solving. In contrast, proactive anticipatory management requires open relationships between management and staff so that subordinates feel free to communicate problems without fear they will be evaluated negatively. It also requires that the warden routinely see and be seen in the institution. There must also be policies, procedures, and forums in place to ensure that communication is timely, intelligence is accurate, and critical information reaches the management team to ensure that decisions reflect the best information available in the organization (Wood, 1998).

In addition to anticipating problems, proactive administrators also plan for and create opportunities for the organization to develop its capacity to pursue its mission. This includes creation of goals and objectives, ongoing evaluation of the progress being made to achieve them, and the communication of the outcomes of these evaluations to all organizational members. This approach was illustrated in our earlier discussion of the wardens at the BOP who helped to develop system plans for the next year (see p. 258).

Three Major Management Models

Organizational theory concerns the manner in which power and authority within an organization are distributed and used to accomplish organizational objectives. The models we will examine also deal with management styles used to get workers to achieve organizational goals.

Organizations range from those whose structure is idiosyncratic and totally dependent on the characteristics of their leaders to those whose structure is determined by a set of very specific rules and regulations. We will examine three different organizational models: authoritarian, bureaucratic, and participative. It is important to remember that these models do not typically exist in their "pure form." Instead, it is likely that a given correctional organization will contain elements of at least two of these approaches. Nearly all contemporary organizations use some form of the bureaucratic model. This organizational approach can accommodate a variety of managerial styles and, therefore, provides the basic structure for contemporary corrections.

The Authoritarian Model

In authoritarian organizations, decision-making power lies in the hands of one person or a small number of high-level bosses. The authoritarian style dominated corrections management in the United States from the birth of prisons until the middle of the 20th century

(Barak-Glantz, 1986). It was associated with a correctional policy characterized by harshness and punishment. This organizational arrangement was first employed by Elam Lynds, often considered the architect of the Auburn correctional model (Lewis, 1922/1996).

The principal feature of the **authoritarian model** is strict control over both the inmates and staff (Barak-Glantz, 1986). Further, this model does not consider input from those outside of the system or facility or the views of lower-level institutional staff. All power and authority rests in the hands of the boss. Historically, authoritarian correctional administrations had goals that were quite simple: the temporary incarceration of offenders and the avoidance of critical incidents. This was done by creating a very repressive internal environment. However, when correctional goals became more complicated (e.g., rehabilitation and court mandates regarding prisoner rights), the authoritarian style could not deal effectively with this more complex organizational environment.

In theory, this arrangement can yield a safe and orderly institution in which both officers can work and inmates can "do their time" in relative security, if everyone "plays the game." However, the present level of politicization of both staff and inmates has decreased the chances that this will happen. The banishment goal of corrections is likely to be achieved through the authoritarian approach, but other goals (e.g., reintegration; opportunities for inmates to change through drug programs, education, and work programs) are less likely to be realized. In this environment, inmates are little more than "products" of the organization and often come out of the prison more bitter and crime-prone than when they entered it. Our Close-Up, "Joe Ragen," profiles this type of manager. One of the other problems associated with the authoritarian model is that it tends to revolve around "the beliefs and practices" that are unique to a particular leader. Once the leader leaves, dies, or is absent such organizations tend to rapidly decline in their ability to carry out their responsibilities. This is because it is a closed system isolated from the outside and also from feedback from lower-level staff on the inside (Gilbert, 1999).

The Bureaucratic Model

The **bureaucratic model** establishes a formal organizational structure that permits smooth changes in leadership. This structure avoids the major disruptions that often occur when there are leadership changes in an authoritarian organization. The essential elements of a bureaucratic organization include a hierarchical structure (positions with varying levels of authority) with a formal chain of command; a vertical authority and communication structure that flows from the top of the hierarchy to

Joe Ragen—The Ultimate Authoritarian

CLOSE-UP

The authoritarian style was found in its purest form in the classic Big House prison. This model was demonstrated most clearly by Joe Ragen, the warden of the Stateville (Illinois) Penitentiary from 1936 to 1961 (Jacobs, 1977). Ragen operated under a system of innumerable and very detailed rules. However, it was he, and not the rules, who was the source of authority, and he refused to share that authority with anyone. As James Jacobs (1977) notes, Ragen established a patriarchal organization based on his own charismatic author-

ity. He ran an autonomous institution that was not accountable to other public agencies nor the public at large and which had no contact with outside groups concerned about prison conditions. He demanded absolute personal loyalty from his subordinates, but neither the guards nor the inmates had any real rights under Ragen's stewardship. He believed that the inmates were only due the bare necessities of life. However, both the inmates and guards were relatively secure at Stateville.

In his classic study of Stateville, Jacobs (1977) characterized Ragen's rule as a prebureaucratic form of administration in that his power was

based on his personal charisma. When Ragen retired, he took the authority that held the prison together with him, and the fabric of the Stateville organization began to unravel. The organization's personnel had formed working relationships only through Ragen and his departure led to a loss of their authority. The conditions at Stateville following Ragen's departure were chaotic and the inmates "ran" the prison for more than a decade. The organization was so dependent on Ragen's idiosyncratic power that it had no structure to continue functioning in any effective way.

the bottom—that is, there are clearly defined power relationships between subordinates and superiors (e.g., sergeants and COs) and strict channels of communication; and written job descriptions and standard operating procedures that describe the specific duties and responsibilities for each position in the organization. In its purest form, a bureaucratically structured prison is run in terms of standard operating procedures defined by "the book." The functions and authority vested in each position are based on that position's job description.

The ideal type of bureaucratic prison organization is similar to a military unit. Rules and procedures direct the flow of all operations, and authority is legitimized by the power of the state. Further, "legislators and governors demand that principles, rules, and regulations be formulated to rationalize . . . correctional policy and practice" (Barak-Glantz, 1986, p. 45). See our Close-Up, "George Beto."

In reality, both authoritarian and bureaucratic approaches rely on control for the maintenance of social order inside the prison. Under the authoritarian model control is maintained by fear of the warden's response to disobedience. Within a bureaucratic system, control will most likely be maintained by the rules under which the institution is organized. In theory, these standardized policies should result in consistency and fairness, but in practice, because the correctional environment is very complicated, they usually do not. Although COs enforce rules and regulations in terms of their position rather than their relationship to the warden, their ability to obtain cooperation from inmates may be based on the individual bargains they make with inmates. Thus, in bu-

reaucratic organizations COs may use their discretion in applying the rules to achieve fairness. The rules may dictate that all cases be treated the same, but because the rules can never anticipate all contingencies, "going by the book" does not always guarantee fairness and the CO's discretion allows some equalization. Institutions where there is only rigid adherence to regulations are paralyzed by the inability to do anything creative or adapt to change (Burrell & Morgan, 1979; Gilbert, 1999).

DiIulio suggests that rules and formal organization are particularly necessary when people cannot be expected to cooperate spontaneously, as in prisons. Gilbert (1999) argues that this view is overly simplistic in an increasingly complex and changing corrections environment. Instead, what is required is the participation of members of the organization in solving the management problems. This forms the basis of the *participative model*, which we examine next. In our In Their Own Words feature on page 266, Michael Gilbert discusses two "Management Styles Inconsistent with the Realities of Prison."

However, it should be noted that even if a warden is working under a strict bureaucratic model or a strict authoritarian model this does not necessarily mean that he or she has adopted an authoritarian or bureaucratic style of management (Rison, 2000). In other words, management styles can overcome the problems of working in institutions with these management structures.

The Participative Model

"The control dilemma faced by prison authorities is that they can neither expect cooperation from inmates nor

George Beto and the Texas System

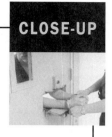
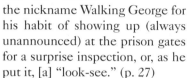

The Texas prison system under the direction of Dr. George Beto from 1962 to 1972 was considered the quintessential bureaucratic corrections organization (Barak-Glantz, 1986; DiIulio, 1987). In one sense, the inmates were part of the organization because they were treated as if they occupied a position in the bureaucratic hierarchy. The responsibility and duty of the inmate was to "do his own time," and he was rewarded for following the rules and punished for "messing up." A few carefully selected inmates had formal positions in the organization by being appointed "building tenders" (BTs). Their job was to help the guards control the other inmates in that particular unit. This system was intended to co-opt the process by which inmates select their own leaders and to replace them with ones less likely to be violent or exploitative. In spite of these precautions, BTs used violence and intimidation to control their units. Unlike other systems that reward powerful inmates for their help in maintaining order, the building tenders were rewarded openly rather than secretly, and their actions were presumed to be more subject to administrative controls.

The Texas system gained the reputation of being among the safest and best run in the nation during Beto's tenure. However, during the tenure of his successor, W. J. Estelle, the system deteriorated and became chaotic and violent. There were several reasons for this change for the worse (DiIulio, 1987). First, the population of the system nearly doubled in a very short time. Second, and more important, Estelle was not able to maintain the close working relationships and support that Beto had cultivated with powerful Texas legislators. Finally, and perhaps most important, Estelle managed the prisons from a distance. He was "an office-bound executive" in contrast to the close, hands-on management style that Beto had developed. As DiIulio notes:

Inmates came to know him [Beto] as the "preacher with a baseball bat in one hand and a bible in the other." Wardens and division heads came to respect (and fear) "Dr. Beto," as they called him, and he earned the nickname Walking George for his habit of showing up (always unannounced) at the prison gates for a surprise inspection, or, as he put it, [a] "look-see." (p. 27)

Under Beto, the central goal was control. Reintegration of inmates into the community and rehabilitation were important, but Beto believed that these latter goals could only be achieved in stable and safe prisons. After Beto's departure, his carefully crafted control system began to disintegrate and neither inmates nor guards felt safe. Thus, there was a reversion to a repressive authoritarian model to keep inmates from attaining control of the prison. At its worst, the bureaucratic prison can become as punitive as an authoritarian one.

---

govern without it" (Silberman, 1978, p. 392). This appears to be at the heart of the problems experienced in prison management and seems to pave the way for the coercive and harsh approach to control prisoners. The **participative model** is one approach that explicitly allows for input from staff and inmate components in the way it is run. Inmates can thus be treated as a formal component of the organization and, thus, have some input. This is important because formal inmate organizations are believed easier to deal with than informal ones. Although the administration may not be able to get the spontaneous cooperation of all the inmates, a measure of formal cooperation may be a realistic goal. The fact that informal bargaining goes on between inmates and guards shows that some basis for cooperation exists.

Similarly, the participative approach gives entry-level correctional workers the opportunity to contribute ideas to the solution of organizational problems. This increases their commitment to helping meet organizational goals. Advocates of the participative approach believe it is more consistent with the nature of prison work and can improve conditions for staff and inmates by providing for meaningful interaction between them and administration.

The participative model is based on the assumption that organizational goals are best achieved when all of the groups having a stake in their achievement contribute to the means by which they are accomplished. It recognizes that within any organization there are conflicting values and goals. There are three ways to deal with these conflicts: attempting to resolve them, ignoring them, or neutralizing them by appealing to individuals' self-interests as an alternative to collective goal-seeking. The traditional approach to correctional administration has almost always employed the latter two options.

The ideal participative organization is based on formal and open negotiations that include all organizational components (e.g., managers, treatment staff, COs). Thus, instead of depending on a set of inflexible rules for dealing with problems, those most closely involved

Management Styles Inconsistent with the Realities of Prison

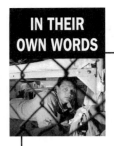

IN THEIR OWN WORDS

The autocratic (authoritarian) management style relies heavily on the values and attitudes exhibited by the leader, while the bureaucratic style relies heavily on hierarchical authority and rules enforced by top-down communication to control employees. These models differ in some respects, but they share enough common characteristics to be viewed as classical models of organization. These common characteristics are embodied in the paramilitary structure found in most correctional agencies.

Nevertheless, the autocratic and bureaucratic models are basically inconsistent with the nature of the work performed by correctional officers, because both are based on faulty beliefs about correctional work and line officers. They presume that correctional officers are strictly governed by formal rules and exercise little on-the-job discretion; yet, correctional officers use discretion in hundreds of decisions each day when dealing with inmates. The classical model also assumes that line officers hold little power compared with supervisory staff. This assumption ignores the power of the informal organization (i.e., the locker room) among employees that insulates them from what they perceive as unreasonable management expectations. It is this informal subculture that socializes new employees into the organization; it provides them with a body of beliefs and models of coping with the institutional environment held and practiced by the vast majority of COs. Often, the informal subculture is as powerful as the formal organization hierarchy.

The classical model also assumes that line officers will faithfully implement rules and regulations developed by management directives. However, this is dependent upon the ability of line officers to convert written policy and procedure into concrete actions and services. This is less likely to occur when these rules and regulations are seen by line officers as inconsistent with their own values, interests, beliefs, and experiences. These types of organizations also assume: (1) that formal rules and regulations, policies, and procedures can adequately guide officers in dealing with the range of situations they encounter on the job, and (2) that "by the book" responses ensure security and control. This might be true in theory, but in practice, officers routinely encounter situations and circumstances that require flexibility, sensitivity to the human condition of inmates, reasonable judgment, and exceptions to rules when "by the book" responses are unreasonable, inappropriate, or likely to decrease security and control.

Finally, it is assumed that discretionary power is controlled by formal policy when it is actually based on individual judgments. Thus, COs can comply, resist, subvert, or

with these problems (e.g., COs, teachers) are asked to recommend solutions for them. This can result in increased feelings of solidarity among all components and less likelihood of their being tied to groups outside the organization such as unions, prison reform groups, or legislatures. A presumed effect of this scenario is that the morale (and productivity) of correctional workers will be raised. However, this only holds true if management actually uses some of the recommendations made by employees. If employee input is ignored, or worse, discarded in a way that demonstrates that management was insincere and never intended to listen to employees, morale will erode sharply and the willingness of employees to invest themselves in helping manage the organization will cease (Gilbert, 1999).

Ideally, a participative organization should include all groups (including inmates in a prison). However, prisons in which this has been tried have experienced problems. These have generally occurred when prison administration or COs did not buy into the notion of inmate participation. They may also have failed because of the way in which inmate participation was allowed. Wood (1998) asserts that inmates should never be led to believe that they are a self-governing entity. It is healthy to set up a system and a forum where inmates' representatives, selected by staff and serving staggered, short terms, can provide input or make comments and suggestions in a respectful forum. In that forum when suggestions are rejected staff should articulate an intelligent, reasonable, and logical rationale. Suggestions that have merit should be reflected in implemented changes and made obvious to the inmates by virtue of their enactment. Of course, the participative approach can be used without inmate input.

All three models described in this section have had both successes and failures. Douglas McGregor (1960), an early proponent of participative management, contends that one's managerial style ultimately rests on his or her assumptions about human nature, and to an extent his or her system of management encourages behavior consistent with these assumptions. McGregor's (1960) concept of management by integration and self-control rather than by direction and control is based on the idea that an organization should create the condi-

openly oppose management directives. Simply stated, the discretionary power of employees cannot be taken away by management. In the final analysis, management is limited to disciplinary threats if line officers do not go by the book and are discovered. Unfortunately, this places officers in a no-win situation. If they go by the book, they will often undermine security, control, and their own safety. If they innovate, they run the risk of being disciplined or terminated.

Traditional authoritarian and bureaucratic styles of prison management do not recognize that line officers are only able to manage inmates when the contacts they have with inmates develop mutual consideration, respectful treatment, and two-way communication. The safety, security, and control sought by management are largely the results of these informal contacts between individual officers and inmates. Correctional officers are social service personnel who provide safety, security, control, and public safety through individual decision making; exercise flexible, reasonable, sensitive, and appropriate control behaviors; and make exceptions to rules consistent with the situations and human conditions encountered. Yet, this reality of prison work is largely ignored by traditional authoritarian and bureaucratic management styles typically adopted by prison management.

If this view is correct, it suggests the need for new management structures that are consistent with the realities of prison work. This means that management must be

- less authoritarian, autocratic, or bureaucratic;
- more democratic and less hierarchical;
- more participatory by involving staff at all levels in organizational management decision-making processes.

Furthermore, the importance of the role of discretionary decision making by line officers must be formally acknowledged and encouraged. Training programs and routine discussion of ethical issues and the predicaments routinely faced by officers will guide individual decision making more effectively than rigid adherence to rules. The participative and proactive models discussed in the next sections represent initial steps in the direction of realizing a management style that is more conducive to the institutional environment.

Source: Prepared especially for the second edition of this book by Michael J. Gilbert, associate professor of Criminal Justice, University of Texas at San Antonio. He has over 20 years of experience working with the military and civilian correctional systems in executive level positions and as a consultant. For a more thorough discussion of these issues, see M. J. Gilbert (1997), The illusion of structure: A critique of the classical model and the discretionary power of correctional officers. Criminal Justice Review, *22(1): 49–64.*

tions that allow employees to realize that they can best achieve their own goals by pursuing the goals of the organization. Recognition needs to be given to the fact that staff, reasonable inmates, and administrators all have the same expectations. They want to be treated fairly, they expect their work to be rewarded, and they expect opportunities for advancement to be provided to those who have demonstrated ability to lead and treat people with respect and dignity (Wood, 1998).

The bureaucratic and authoritarian approaches can work, but they tend to result in organizations with little flexibility or potential for improvement. The participative model allows for adaptive growth because it builds the necessary values as the participants demonstrate their capacity to act responsibly. Thus, it would appear that administrators, COs, and inmates can find enough common ground to reach a negotiated accommodation on most issues.

In the 1990s, there was a movement toward using the team concept of management within corrections. The team concept is an offshoot of participative management and stresses the need for correctional leaders to build stable management teams that are spirited, cohesive, and actively involved in planning and decision making. However, leaders should not abdicate responsibility for what happens within the prisons but instead should facilitate the participation and involvement of others in their search for solutions to the problems they face. Thus, encouraging participation increases trust and effectiveness, helps to train future managers, and reduces turnover (Wright, 1991).

Participatory management requires stressing that input from all workers is critical, because line workers (officers) can be your best "idea" people for solving real problems. The model also empowers employees so that they feel they are part of the team and can offer solutions. Another key for the administrator is that he or she offers participation to employees, even if they only wish to complain. As one correctional manager put it, "I believe and need the participatory management model, because I recruit talented people who know more about their jobs than I do. I need their thoughts, ideas and commitment. However, we are not a democracy, I reserve 51% of the vote on issues I feel I cannot totally delegate. My staff and I are clear on which issues are participatory vs. non-negotiable" (DeVolentine, 1993).

Finally, this model tends to look for a solution to problems with the people that are closest to the problems. Rison (2000) asserts

> that wardens don't run institutions; associate wardens don't run institutions. So, you've got to go to the staff who are working the areas everyday and find out if you have a problem, what it is that they would recommend, and get them involved. The line staff are the closest to the inmates and are the first to spot problems, but they are often the last to know about policy changes. New directives are handed down through the chain of command to put into practice whether or not they make any sense to line personnel. (personal communication)

Prison Disorder

The importance of good management in the maintenance of prison order prompts us to include a discussion of prison riots in this chapter. Correctional systems in the United States have experienced major disturbances since 1774 when a riot occurred at a facility built around an abandoned mine in Simsbury, Connecticut. Riots reflect a breakdown in control of the prison. Most prison riots have resulted from some combination of mismanagement and poor conditions. These disturbances have tended to become more frequent and destructive since the 1950s (American Correctional Association, 1981, 1990a; Martin & Zimmermann, 1990). Whereas the riots during the 1950s tended to be in protest of specific prison conditions, most of those occurring in the 1960s and 1970s had racial overtones and began to reflect the politicalization associated with the civil rights movement (see Chapter 7).

Management of the environment of the prison (i.e., the manner in which inmates are dealt with or controlled) plays a significant role in the occurrence of riots. Thus, poorly managed prisons with weak or changing leadership are most likely to have riots.

The best known prison disturbances since 1970 have been those at Attica, New York, and Santa Fe, New Mexico, where many lives were lost and extensive damage was done to the facilities. The riot at Attica, discussed in Chapter 7, involved many conditions and issues that have since been addressed by the courts and resolved in favor of the inmates. In our discussion of the New Mexico, Camp Hill, and Lucasville riots we focus on the management problems that existed at the time of their occurrence.

The New Mexico Riot

The factors that precipitated the riot at the Penitentiary of New Mexico at Santa Fe were enunciated by Raymond Procunier, a former prison administrator in California and Texas, who evaluated the institution just 3 weeks before the riot (Serrill & Katel, 1980). He reported the prison was overcrowded and understaffed and that many of its COs were untrained. Mr. Procunier was prophetic in saying that New Mexico state officials were "playing Russian roulette with the lives of inmates, staff and the public" (as cited in Serrill & Katel, 1980, p. 7). This riot, which occurred in February 1980, was one of the most savage in U.S. penal history.

Colvin (1982) argued that the riot was a product of changes in the control structure of the prison and the inmate social structure that had begun 5 years before. Prior to 1975, control had been maintained by accommodating two powerful groups of inmates. The first group controlled inmate selection for participation in educational programs and an outside contact program. This group helped to maintain order in these programs to ensure that they continued to operate. The second group controlled drug trafficking in the prison. This group also realized that if order broke down it would jeopardize their sources of supply and bring the heat down on traffickers.

This changed with a new administration, which in late 1975 began to wrestle control of the prison from the inmates. Inmate protests quickly followed these changes. In this environment, inmates' willingness to engage in violence grew, which encouraged formation of cliques for self-protection. These cliques adopted an ideology based on a willingness to use violence against other inmates, to confront and resist guards, and to "tough it out" in disciplinary confinement. The combative relations led staff to develop a system of snitches whose information was virtually unquestioned. Consequently, many inmates spent up to 6 months in segregation based on another inmate's unproven allegations (Hirliman, 1982). These tactics increasingly created a climate of suspicion and isolation among inmates in the period leading up to the riot.

Other factors contributing to the riot included (1) security lapses (e.g., the renovation of a high-security cell block during which dangerous inmates were transferred to a less secure dormitory); (2) gross understaffing (it was estimated that the prison had only about 50 percent of the staff required to operate it safely); and (3) a modification of the control center where steel grillwork windows were replaced with windows that were bulletproof and shatterproof, but breakable. These factors merely helped spark what was already an explosive prison atmosphere (Colvin, 1982).

W. G. Stone, an inmate at the time of the riot, provided an eyewitness account of the events in the book *The Hate Factory*. He reported that several inmates, drunk on home brew, hatched a plan to overpower the guards when they came for the nighshift. At 1:30 A.M., when the guards arrived, they were overpowered. To get to the north wing of the prison, inmates attacked the control center, breaking the recently installed glass windows and gaining control of the prison nerve center and

Security lapses at the State Penitentiary of New Mexico enabled inmates to gain control of the prison. This scene in the aftermath of the riot shows the extent of the damage caused by roaming bands of inmates.

the keys to the entire prison. Leaderless and uncontrolled, various groups of inmates roamed the prison, looting and destroying almost everything in sight (Hirliman, 1982; Serrill & Katel, 1980).

The rampaging inmates directed their fury and violence against both guards and inmates. Eleven of the 14 staff inside were taken hostage. None of these guards was killed, but they did not escape injury. Some were brutally assaulted. According to Stone, the most severely assaulted were three members of the guard "goon squad" who were beaten and repeatedly sodomized. However, some officers were protected by other inmates, and four officers escaped with the help of some inmates.

Inmate violence against one another was even more brutal. Inmates killed 30 of their fellow inmates, and some 200 others were beaten and raped. The killings were reportedly carried out by about 25 to 50 inmates. Some organized into "death squads," whereas others acted alone. Thirteen of the slain inmates were identified as snitches, but the motives for the rest of the killings could not be officially determined. Stone asserts that many were in retaliation for old injuries. Many inmates who died were not only killed but were horribly tortured and mutilated as well.

Unlike the Attica riot, there were no clear-cut leaders who took control of all the inmates at any point during this insurrection. Nevertheless, several inmates contacted authorities and began negotiating for better food; federal oversight to ensure no retaliation; improved visiting, educational, and recreational programs; an end to harassment; and the opportunity to talk to the press. Prison officials agreed to some of these demands, and in return hostages were gradually released. In the end, the

inmates got their news conference at which they told of conditions in the prison. The negotiators were promised that they would be transferred out of state because they feared for their safety. After 36 hours the riot ended. State police SWAT teams entered and without resistance assumed control.

In addition to the carnage and pain, the damages incurred by the state because of the riot were well over $100 million (Saenz & Reeves, 1989; Serrill & Katel, 1980). In the aftermath of the riot it was acknowledged that the New Mexico corrections system had been neglected, and the New Mexico penitentiary had been dangerously overcrowded and understaffed. The prison had had five wardens in the preceding 5 years, a strong indication that leadership in dealing with existing problems was essentially lacking (Serrill & Katel, 1980).

The Riot at Camp Hill

One of the last major disturbances of the 1980s occurred in October 1989, at the Camp Hill Correctional Institution (CHCI) in Pennsylvania. Two policy changes served to hasten the riot: (1) food could no longer be brought in by inmates' relatives on "Family Day" and (2) inmates' access to the "sick line" was restricted to every other day. These changes created a high level of inmate resentment because they were issued in an already tense prison. Inmates perceived these changes to be an arbitrary exercise of power by prison management. The riot began on October 25, when inmates stopped an inmate who attacked a correctional officer to keep from being taken into "custody." This disturbance was quelled that evening but erupted again the next morning. The second disturbance lasted until October 27. During the 3 days of the disturbance, 120 inmates and staff were injured and 12 buildings were destroyed.

After the riot, the Judiciary Committee of the Pennsylvania Senate suggested that two clusters of factors had contributed to the disturbance. First, there were systemic and institutional factors that included overcrowding, idleness, inadequate security, lack of staff, poor staff training, substandard facilities, and lack of programs. Second, there were poor administrative practices that included vague lines of authority and administrative responsibility; absence of clearly defined and easily understood rules and regulations; poor communication, particularly in dealing with inmates and staff; lack of familiarity by top staff with the institution, its staff, and inmates; and indecisive action on legitimate grievances (Adams Commission, 1989).

The Lucasville Riot

The 11-day riot at the Southern Ohio Correctional Facility at Lucasville, Ohio, continued the trend of bloody riots sparked by management problems. The riot, in which nine inmates and one correctional officer were killed, was touched off on Easter Sunday, 1993, when two guards were attacked by inmates at the end of the afternoon recreation period. Previously, tension within the prison had escalated when Warden Arthur Tate decided to force 159 Muslim inmates to take a TB skin test, which they refused to take on religious grounds.

A report issued by the Ohio Department of Rehabilitation and Correction showed that the prison had a long history of violence and security problems. It faulted prison staff for responding too slowly to the Easter disturbance in that they took too long to establish a command post; they did not respond to calls for help from COs trapped inside the prison; and the warden did not arrive at the prison until 3 hours after the riot had begun.

The Department of Corrections reports indicated that many long-standing problems also contributed to the uprising:

1. Warden Tate did not have confidence in his administrative and middle-management staff. This resulted in a disruptive tension among prison workers.

2. The practice of double celling (due to overcrowding) was seen by most prison staff to be a cause of the disturbance.

3. Force had been frequently used to control inmates. This was particularly true for black inmates, who made up 57 percent of the inmate population.

4. There was a lack of communication between staff and inmates resulting from racial and cultural differences.

5. The security of the institution was diminished by having inmate clerks who had access to sensitive personnel, disciplinary, and operational information. This included inmate assignment to the area in which Warden Tate had a confidential meeting to discuss a lockdown plan during which the TB tests would be completed.

Our In Their Own Words feature, "The Problems of Double Celling," looks in more detail at this issue. These problems are examples of things that can lead to dangerous levels of tension. With unabated tension, almost any spark can set off a major disturbance. The prison disorders discussed demonstrate the importance of adequate management in maintaining control in prisons. Later in this chapter, we present an example of a well-managed prison to serve as a contrast.

Control of Group Violence

Dealing with riots and other forms of group violence requires a relatively precise set of responses from correctional personnel. Prevention begins with good management (American Correctional Association [ACA], 1990a). This means that the institutional environment must be safe, sanitary, and humane, and the administration must be respectful of the rights of both staff and inmates. However, it is dangerous to assume that good inmates will remain good inmates in an emergency. In our Close-Up, "Prison Riots," on page 272 we draw on the work of Useem, Camp and Camp (1996) and the ACA (1990c) to describe different types of riots and the requirements for riot preparedness.

Wood (1998) provides some features that are critical to riot prevention, particularly in a maximum security prison. He asserts that the ideal form of staff supervision in this level of security is a combination of direct and indirect supervision. Staff should also be in a secure control station with a full view of the cell block and the staff on the floor in direct contact with the inmates. The cell block should be equipped with camera monitors. Staff working in secure control stations should be rotated every couple of hours with the staff on the floor. Staff in the secure control station are in a position to report any escalation of tension or call for assistance. With all staff in direct contact, a cell block takeover can happen and go undetected by those outside the block. Staff in the control station can also identify specific inmate actions and infractions for later accountability or prosecution.

A Well-Run Prison: Oak Park Heights

There is no question that safe, orderly prisons are a necessity for society, the prison staff, and the inmates. The basic features required to achieve this include appropriately designed institutions, decisive but humane administrators, well-trained correctional personnel, sensible

The Problems of Double Celling

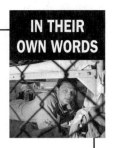

IN THEIR OWN WORDS

The real implications of this practice are not always understood by even some experienced corrections professionals. Putting high-risk persons in multioccupancy cells essentially removes from staff a major element of control in a maximum security prison. Politicians and some naive corrections administrators have accepted double celling as a cost-effective way of addressing the overcrowding problem caused by legislative decisions to create new felonies and enhance other felony sentences. What they are oblivious to is the fact that double celling a maximum security prison, which houses high-risk prisoners, gives the predatory inmate leadership substantial control over the entire inmate population of that facility. They can intimidate, extort, threaten, assault, and punish inmates with little chance of anyone reporting the activity. With all maximum security inmates double celled, there is no safe place in the prison. Inmates know staff cannot protect them. Unfortunately, some

administrators accept the notion that because reported behavior decreases with double celling that it translates into decreased violence and rule infractions. Inmates don't have to settle scores in the yard, the gym, the dining hall, school, or industry or on the cell block floor. This can all be handled at night in the cell or the dormitory when staffing is minimal. Sexual predators can direct that life be made so miserable for an attractive inmate in another cell that he will eventually end up where the predator wants him. Most inmates will not report threatening behavior or assaults when it is apparent staff have diminished capacity to protect them.

The problems at Lucasville and Santa Fe started with the decision to double cell or place high-risk prisoners in 100-man dormitories. For prison staff to maintain control of maximum security prisons that house high-risk offenders, they must have single cells for control. Predator inmates require intensive surveillance, supervision, accounta-

bility, and control. That is not possible in multioccupancy cells or dormitories.

Double celling works well in less secure facilities because inmates in these facilities are nearing the end of their sentences and are attempting to avoid any behaviors that interfere with their release dates or loss of good time. [One wonders if the Supreme Court thoroughly understood these issues when they ruled that double celling was constitutional at this prison (*Rhodes v. Chapman*, 1981; also see chapter 15).]

Consider whether the short-term savings that result from the double celling of violent inmates actually save money in the long run.
Source: F. Wood (1998), retired commissioner of the Minnesota Department of Corrections and former warden of Oak Park Heights Correctional Facility. Personal communication.

---

rules, and well-planned programs. As described next, an important factor in the running of safe, orderly prisons lies in the leadership and type of approach used in managing them.

The Oak Park Heights facility, a maximum security prison in Minnesota designed to hold 406 inmates, was an example of a well-run institution under the leadership of Warden Frank Wood. Put into service in 1982 it was billed as a "new generation" prison. It employs high-tech security combined with a tough code of discipline, a highly trained corps of correctional officers, and a personal and direct management style that extends to interactions with inmates. The essence of "new generation" architecture is that it keeps prisoners in small groups under close and constant surveillance in single cells. Small distinct housing areas allow inmates considerable freedom of movement. The architecture resembles a podular direct supervision type of structure and design (see Chapter 18) (Rutherford, 1985).

Oak Park Heights housed extremely dangerous inmates. Eighty-five percent had records of violence, and

many were transferred from other prisons where they had caused problems. The mission of the prison, according to Wood (1985), was

> to accept from the other adult male facilities, all inmates classified as maximum custody, or categorized as risks to the public. . . . Our program is designed to control, evaluate and facilitate the transfer of inmates to less secure facilities after they have demonstrated a satisfactory adjustment over an established time period at Oak Park Heights. (p. 3)

It has been very successful in controlling these inmates.

The institution is renowned worldwide for its earth-shelter design; the facility is built into a hillside. It has a sophisticated computerized security system that makes escape virtually impossible, a strict but direct and humane approach to management, and a well-trained staff. It is the latter two features that appear to make the major difference. Warden Wood strongly disapproved of staff

Prison Riots

CLOSE-UP

It is important for prison staff to be prepared before a riot occurs because they may have to make instantaneous decisions and rapidly mobilize forces. This is irrespective of whether or not the disturbance comes as a complete surprise. Riots can be divided into three categories: (1) riots that occur without warning, (2) riots that occur as a result of snowballing events, and (3) riots that occur after a significant amount of warning.

Riots Without Warning

Riots that occur without warning typically happen in high-security institutions where violent and rebellious inmates are concentrated. To deal with this prison officials rely on security measures, such as restricting inmates to their cells, using handcuffs, and not allowing inmates to congregate. The disturbances that occur in these facilities may be intense. These riots usually result from a lack of proper security (e.g., inmates taking advantage of a momentary facility weakness). Inmates can then spread the disturbance by defeating other security systems.

For prisons to overcome security problems there needs to be a continual presence of experienced staff. Also, each staff member must know his or her duties or this can

lead to security problems (e.g., security gates accidentally being left open and keys being left near control panels where inmates may have access to them).

Further, riots are more likely in facilities with deteriorating conditions, such as breakable windows, hiding places, and unsecured tables and chairs. Malfunctioning locks may provide inmates with the opportunity to start or expand a disturbance. So in older correctional facilities, it is prudent to correct some design flaws and do such things as painting, improving lighting, and soundproofing in areas with excessive noise.

Further, facilities need to collect reliable intelligence on a routine but systematic basis, particularly from respected inmates. The intelligence information should be regularly disseminated to top staff so that decision makers can keep a constant finger on the pulse of the institution.

Finally, it is important to

1. reduce units to a manageable size
2. have a well-designed classification system
3. have good tool, key, and contraband control procedures
4. have effective search procedures for both persons and areas
5. create systems of effective inspections of all physical security aspects

6. have effective systems of communication, including personal body alarms
7. create effective inmate programs

Snowballing Events

Some riots occur as a result of a snowballing set of events. These typically follow a common pattern.

1. Tensions usually exist within a group, and personal disputes among inmates inflame the pre-existing problems.
2. Conflicts gain momentum by inmates trying to retaliate or seek revenge.
3. The mutually hostile groups then mobilize their forces by fighting along racial lines or congregating in the yard.
4. As officers intervene, inmates redirect their hostility against the prison staff. In this case, the inmates may take officers hostage, signaling the beginning of a disturbance.

Avoiding riots in these situations does not so much require physical security as it does managing the escalating disturbance.

Riots with Warning

Finally, riots may occur after a significant amount of warning (e.g., inmate complaints about food and overcrowding). Correctional officials should not just ignore these or other warning signs, such as

---

violence toward inmates unless their own safety was threatened. He dealt directly with cases of staff violence, requiring that closely monitored incident reports be filed in all cases in which staff-inmate violence occurred. He believed that inmates will only be reinforced in their violent behavior if they are reacted to violently. Thus, staff were trained to resolve problems by nonphysical means, and those unable to deal with inmates on that basis were not retained. Wood believed that staff were the key ingredient of inmate control and insisted that they be in constant and direct contact with inmates (Northam, 1985).

Wood placed a heavy emphasis on full programming that included work, education and training, treatment, and recreation. Many inmates had jobs that paid from $0.40 to more than $2 per hour. Other inmates were assigned to an education unit. If inmates refused to work or participate in their assigned activities, they were locked in their cells. The focus of this programming was to keep inmates as busy as possible (Bottoms & Light, 1987). The incidence of violence by inmates, against one another and toward staff, was low at Oak Park Heights. Interviews with inmates indicated that they

- an increase in lockups and disciplinary cases
- a decline in attendance for popular events
- an increase in excessive or specific demands by inmates
- inmates stockpiling food
- an increase in demands by employees for greater safety
- an increase in employee turnover

If a riot appears to be imminent, prison officials may either take administrative or diplomatic actions:

1. *Administrative Actions* Locking down the unit or the entire facility, transferring the suspected instigators, canceling activities that allow inmates to congregate, and increasing the number of correctional officers on duty
2. *Diplomatic Actions* Making efforts to convince inmates that a riot would be costly to them personally and unnecessary because their complaints will be addressed in the future

Preparation for a riot includes having the required resources for use in a riot situation, developing a strategy, and having the mental readiness to respond to a disturbance. Of equal importance is having a strong organizational "core" (i.e., a group of individuals who have internalized the values and mission of the agency). Training and practice are needed to ensure that each member knows what to do and is prepared to act. Good preparation also includes having a set of predetermined guidelines for handling inmates' demands, such as requests for immunity from prosecution, control of keys, and use of force. Finally, each facility should have comprehensive riot plans that describe staff responsibilities (i.e., which staff are in charge, and how they will work together with other agencies that get involved).

Good training is another important aspect of riot preparation and prevention. Training enables staff to be more attentive to the signs of disorder among inmates, reduces their anxiety, and increases their alertness and perceptiveness. Mental, physical, and emotional readiness can only be achieved through field practice and instruction. This should also include training with other agencies that might be involved (e.g., state police and negotiating and tactical teams). This creates greater coordination and lessens the likelihood of miscommunication during a riot.

The more prepared a facility is for a disturbance, the less likely a riot will occur. Inmates are often aware of the preparedness of prison officials and may be deterred from starting a disturbance if they know they will be met quickly with an organized counterforce. Preparedness also increases the likelihood of containing an incident quickly, so that it does not evolve into a full-scale riot.

After a riot is over, it is necessary to help inmates and staff deal with the disturbance. As Freeman (1997) notes about the Camp Hill riot: "Each employee and inmate who was present at Camp Hill knows with absolute certainty that his or her work can collapse at any time without warning, or mercy." Employee reaction to this riot included anxiety over a recurrence, which resulted in sleep anxiety for some. Others contemplated or attempted suicide, drank, or took out their fears on their family. Those who could no longer live with the possibility of another riot left corrections. To help staff and their families deal with this trauma, some agencies like the one in Oklahoma established teams, composed of staff psychologists, case managers, and senior staff. In Oklahoma, inmates were also able to request assistance.

Source: Adapted from B. Useem, C. G. Camp, & G. M. Camp (1996). Resolution of Prison Riots: Strategies and Policies. *New York: Oxford University Press; R. M. Freeman (1997). Remembering the Camp Hill riot.* Corrections Today, 59(1): 56–59; *American Correctional Association (1990c).* Causes, Preventive Measures, and Methods of Controlling Riots and Disturbances in Correctional Institutions, *3rd ed. Washington, DC: Author.*

perceived this prison as a safe place (Northam, 1985; Wood, 1985).

A Poorly Run Prison: Mecklenburg Correctional Center

The Mecklenburg Correctional Center, a state prison in southern Virginia, serves as a comparison for Oak Park Heights. Mecklenburg, built in 1977, was architecturally designed as a "new generation" institution with a podular structure. Although it was billed as an "escape-proof" prison capable of segregating inmates into small groups to enable them to live and work together, it was beset by continual control problems. There were numerous reports of staff brutality (many of which were corroborated), and six death row inmates successfully escaped. Further, this prison was characterized by a management style that minimized staff contact with inmates and did not discourage staff brutality (Rutherford, 1985). It is no surprise that from the early to the mid-1980s, the National Prison Project of the ACLU received more inmate complaints from here than from any other U.S. prison.

This culminated in nine guards being held hostage for 20 hours in 1984. A statement by inmates described the takeover "as a quest to bring to light [the] inhuman, cruel, barbaric treatment at this institution." Al Bronstein of the ACLU was able to persuade the inmates to release their hostages and surrender, which avoided "a bloodbath of Attica dimensions" (Rutherford, 1985, p. 410). This comparison points out very clearly that it is management and not architecture that is important in running a safe, violence-free prison.

Toward Sound Management Principles

Changes in the orientation of corrections administration are essential if prisons are to develop into truly adaptive and effective organizations. The findings and concepts of organizational theory can be employed to highlight the role of management in this regard. An active corrections management team can also serve to deflect some of the instability in its environment through the development of managerial technologies and the opening of the organization to environmental groups. A science of corrections administration would also serve to better inform the political process about the development of correctional policy.

An examination of three different perspectives on correctional administration (DiIulio, 1991; Duffee, 1980; Kalinich, Stojkovic, & Klofas, 1988) yields similar conclusions about the key factors in developing a sound approach to correctional management:

1. The workings of the correctional institution must be approached holistically. This means that the functioning of all the components that interact within the institution must be considered, because that is the only way a complex system can be understood.

2. The study of prisons as organizations must include relevant groups outside the organization (e.g., the legislature), because it is impossible to understand an organization apart from its environment.

3. The managerial roles of correctional administrators must be reexamined, because the ultimate role of management is to ensure that the various components of the organization operate with minimum conflict in pursuit of compatible goals. If managers are to function effectively in the correctional environment, they must be armed with knowledge that includes sound methods that can be taught to both subordinates and peers.

4. We cannot know what managerial methods will best work within correctional organizations until we know how corrections itself works. Thus, corrections must use the information generated by its successes and failures to increase its effectiveness.

Given the importance of these aspects of the correctional enterprise, it is surprising that so little attention has been devoted to the topic of correctional organization and administration.

Summary

Organization and management are the determining factors in whether prisons and jails are safe and civilized, or riotous and wretched. Thus, it is imperative that administrators and managers and those who work under them hold similar views of the mission of the prison and its achievement.

The well-run corrections system begins with a clearly developed and written mission statement that specifies the goals and objectives the system needs to achieve. Correctional policy created by legislatures should avoid micromanaging—that is, telling experienced correctional officials how to implement a particular policy.

Various groups of administrators and managers exist within correctional systems. First, system administrators and their staff are charged with operating the entire system. Next, regional administrators supervise regional offices. Institutional administrators, such as wardens, oversee entire institutions. Middle managers—department heads and captains—oversee the delivery of specific services within the institution. Finally, first-line supervisors (lieutenants) oversee the day-to-day activities of line staff, or personnel who work directly with inmates or ex-offenders on conditional release.

Traditionally, in this structure orders flow downward and information about performance flows upward. But, if management staff do not spend time in the housing units and other facilities there is a likelihood that they will not hear about problems that may affect security and control. This is because unfavorable information tends not to move up the hierarchy because staff are afraid that it will reflect poorly on their job performance. Also, for change to be successful a prevention-oriented warden seeks advice from those on the line that are going to implement a particular action.

There are three major organizational management models. Under an authoritarian model, decision-making power lies in the hands of one person or a small number of high-level "bosses." Its principal feature is strict control over both inmates and staff. Authoritarian models fell out of favor when court mandates upholding prisoner rights were rendered. The bureaucratic model establishes a formal organizational structure that permits smooth changes in leadership and avoids the major disruptions that often occur when there are leadership changes in an authoritarian organization. The essential elements of a bureaucratic organization include a hierarchical structure (positions with varying levels of authority) with a formal chain of command—a vertical authority and communication structure that flows from top to bottom. The participative model allows for input from inmates and staff. An important aspect of the participative approach is that even entry-level correctional workers are given the opportunity to contribute ideas to the solution of organizational problems. Advocates believe it can better conditions for staff by providing meaningful interaction between them and administration.

Key behavioral patterns that characterize the organizational culture of a well-managed prison system or institution include focusing on outcomes; making security and custody top priorities; managing by walking around; developing relationships with those outside the institution who can impact its future; smoothing the way for far-reaching changes by involving concerned parties early on; and encouraging longevity in the leadership to ensure continuity.

It is important for prison staff to be prepared before a riot occurs because they may have to make instantaneous decisions and rapidly mobilize forces. Riots can be divided into three categories: (1) riots that occur without warning, (2) those that occur as a result of a snowballing set of events, and (3) riots that occur after a significant amount of warning. Preparation for a riot includes having the required resources for use in a riot situation, development of a strategy, and the training and practice in responding to a disturbance. Of equal importance is having a strong organizational core of individuals who have internalized the values and mission of the agency. Finally, each facility should have comprehensive riot plans that describe staff responsibilities.

Well-run prisons are further characterized by constant and direct contact with inmates, appropriately designed institutions, decisive but humane administrators, well-trained correctional personnel, sensible rules, and well-planned programs.

Critical Thinking Questions

1. Examine the issues involved with the development of correctional policy. In this area what presents the greatest problem to prison administrators?

2. If you were given the responsibility for reorganizing a corrections system, what rules would you follow in establishing a system that is safe and secure for both inmates and staff?

3. Identify the structure of correctional system administration.

4. Critically examine the authoritarian, bureaucratic, and participatory models. If you were given the authority to organize an institution, which of these models would you use to structure the institution?

5. You have just been assigned as warden for a facility that will open in a new correctional institution in a few months. What procedures would you establish to most effectively control riots?

Test Your Knowledge

Match the following:

____ **1.** Bureaucratic management

____ **2.** Authoritarian management

____ **3.** Proactive management

____ **4.** Participative management

____ **5.** Unit management

    a. management by an idiosyncratic manager

    b. management by the book

    c. giving teams responsibility for managing housing units

    d. management by shared responsibility

    e. management by anticipation of problems

6. Autocratic and bureaucratic models:

    a. are the best possible administrative models to use in a correctional system.

    b. are not as effective as paramilitary models.

    c. are inconsistent with the nature of the work performed by correctional officers.

    d. assume that discretionary power is controlled by formal policy.

7. Which of the following does not represent a category of riots?

    a. those that occur without warning

    b. those that occur as a result of a snowballing set of events

    c. those that occur after a significant amount of warning

    d. those that occur after a state of emergency has been declared

8. Which of the following represents an important characteristic of successful correctional administrators?

    a. They focus on outcomes.

    b. They develop an organizational culture.

    c. They use a direct, hands-on approach.

    d. They create alliances.

    e. All of the above.

Endnote

1. Selected excerpts from *No Escape: The Future of American Corrections,* by John H. DiIulio, Jr. Copyright © 1991 by Basic Books, Inc. Basic Books, Inc. Reprinted by permission of Perseus Books Group.

Security Threat Groups and Inmate Gangs

12

LEARNING OBJECTIVES

After completing this chapter, you should be able to:

1. Describe the development of gangs in U.S. prisons.

2. List the criteria developed by the National Institute of Corrections for identifying disruptive groups.

3. Discuss the extent of contemporary gangs in U.S. prisons.

4. Describe and discuss the five patterns of prison gang development.

5. Identify the various patterns of gang structure, categories of gang membership, and the gang recruitment process.

6. Discuss symbols and benefits associated with gang membership, and describe gang "business" activities.

7. Discuss the types and nature of problems that gangs pose for staff and other inmates.

8. Enumerate and describe the factors involved in strategies for gang control.

9. Discuss the alternatives available for nongang inmates in a gang-dominated system.

KEY TERMS AND CONCEPTS

Aryan Brotherhood
Associate members
Black Guerrilla Family
Bloods
Crips
Disruptive groups
General members
Hard-core members
Hierarchical model
Homeboy connection
Homeboy pattern
Intelligence
La Nuestra Familia
Mexican Mafia
Mexikanemi
Paramilitary model
Peripheral members

Potential members
Security threat groups (STGs)
Security threat individuals
Steering committee model
Strategic intelligence
Suspected members
Sympathizers
Tactical intelligence
Texas Syndicate
Throwaways
Unit management
Validated members
Wanna-be's

Introduction

Prisons have always contained a certain number of violence-prone individuals—typically graduates of juvenile institutions, or lower-class unskilled criminals—who held little respect for older offenders and "regular convicts." Although they posed a constant threat to prison stability, if they went too far, the older prison regulars would use force to bring them back into line. Historically, prisons have also held inmates who formed groups to intimidate weaker inmates or to disrupt the prison. These early groups were relatively ineffectual, though, because they could usually be dismantled by transferring known leaders to other prisons. Thus, they lacked any real permanence beyond the presence of a few core members (Buentello, 1999).

The baby boom substantially increased the youthful population of our urban ghettos, which, in turn, contributed to the growing juvenile population during the 1960s and 1970s. By the 1970s and 1980s, these youths had graduated to the adult system, increasing the number of more aggressively and criminally unskilled urban toughs in the system. As the number of these inmates increased, the ability of more stable elements in the prison community to control them diminished. Drawing on their street and institutional experience, they formed racially or ethnically based cliques which, in some cases, developed into gangs (Irwin, 1980). The growing number of gangs became a problem in the 1970s and 1980s.

McConville (1985) has argued that gangs would not have been able to flourish and dominate prisons if the following conditions had not been present:

1. Inmates were allowed to move relatively freely in the cell blocks and in other parts of the institution, including the dining hall, the yard, and workshops, which facilitated communication and intimidation.

2. Staff supervision was remote rather than direct; COs spent most of their time in control rooms rather than interacting with the inmates.

3. COs were unable to adequately protect general population inmates, which pushed them to join existing groups.

4. Poor control of profitable contraband, such as drugs, encouraged gangs to monopolize their trafficking activities.

5. Inmates had relatively easy communication with the outside as a result of less restrictive policies (e.g., regarding visiting, mail).

McConville (1985) has also maintained that longer prison sentences are another factor contributing to the persistence of prison gangs. There is evidence that some prison gangs have had stable leadership for 10 to 15 years (Camp & Camp, 1985). Also, prisons provide few rewards for following the rules, particularly for long-term

The proportion of gang members in prison populations has increased significantly since the 1960s. These inmates form cliques that identify themselves by specific colors, symbols, or hand signs and they often engage in disruptive or violent behavior.

inmates, because most privileges are now a matter of institutional or court-mandated policy. In some instances, the only incentive institutions offer is early release. This matters little to inmates facing 20 years or more prior to being eligible for release. New laws, such as "truth-in-sentencing" and "three strikes" statutes, will increase the number of inmates looking at more time spent in prison and, without other incentives or control strategies, will result in more inmates joining gangs. Inmates have ambitions and desires, and they require an environment that provides both challenges and opportunities to meet their needs. Gang membership provides them with opportunities for achieving power and acquiring many comforts that make a long stay in prison more tolerable.

Disruptive Inmate Groups

A variety of terms have been employed to describe groups that create problems for prison officials. Most recently, **security threat group** (STG) has become the general label for inmate gangs and other disruptive prison groups. The American Correctional Association (ACA, undated) defined these groups as:[1]

> Two or more inmates, acting together, who pose a threat to the security or safety of staff/inmates and/or are disruptive to programs and/or to the orderly management of the facility/system. (p. 1)

The STG designation is meant to include both small and less well organized groups, as well as more organized groups. Some of these are self-perpetuating groups; they continue to exist beyond the life of their leaders, with chapters in more than one prison and street affiliates. These more organized or larger groups have been referred to as **disruptive groups** or inmate disruptive groups; they are defined as:

> Any organization, association or groups of persons, either formal or informal, that may have a common name or identifying sign or symbol, or colors whose members or associates engage in or have engaged in activities that include, but are not limited to, planning, organizing, threatening, financing, soliciting or committing unlawful acts that violate the policies, rules, and regulations of the [corrections] department or the state code. (Welling, 1999)

The strength of these groups depends on their structure and leadership style, as well as on the size of its membership list. Nevertheless, poorly organized groups with a large number of members will not be strong, because size alone does not result in a better criminal organization. Finally, it is interesting to note that past distinctions between street and prison gangs no longer apply. These groups do not differ with regard to structure, leadership style, and age of gang members. Classic street gangs like the Gangster Disciples and Latin Kings are just as dangerous on the street as the Mexican Mafia and Texas Syndicate are in prison. Likewise, those gangs with street affiliates like the Gangster Disciples and Latin Kings are often as dangerous inside prison as they are in the urban areas in which they operate (Fleisher & Rison, 1999).

Because all prisons have numerous formal and informal inmate groups, it is important to distinguish between these groups. Although both types of groups may be organized along racial, ethnic, or cultural lines, nondisruptive groups are less regimented and organized and consequently, they are overlooked by prison staff (Buentello, 1999). However, like gangs, legitimate groups can create problems by demanding special privileges. For example, if a group can have itself defined as a religion, it can demand special diets or special rooms to conduct religious services.[2] There is evidence that some groups claiming religious status have used it as a front to cover their drug trafficking operations (ACA, undated; McConville, 1985).

In our discussion, we will use the terms *STG* and *gang* interchangeably. We recognize that the term *gang* may be used to describe groups commonly understood to limit their illicit activities to criminal pursuits, but some groups designated as gangs also pursue political objectives.

Finally, there are **security threat individuals**—any individual who has the potential to or has committed acts that threaten the safety of others and the orderly operations and security of the institution (Hart, 1999).

Criteria for Identifying Gangs or STGs

The National Institute of Corrections (NIC, 1991) has identified five criteria for determining if an inmate group is a gang or a security threat group:

1. Does the group have an organized leadership with a clear-cut chain of command?
2. Does the group remain unified through good times and bad and during conflict in the institution?
3. Does the group demonstrate its unity in obvious, recognizable ways?
4. Does the group engage in activities that are criminal or otherwise threatening to institutional operations?
5. Does the group place emphasis on member loyalty and group unity and identity; does it reward members for their criminal or antisocial activity? (pp. 1–2)

Although inmate groups may have some of these characteristics in common, the importance of legitimate inmate groups for prison stability requires the administration to differentiate between gangs and legitimate nondisruptive groups. Examples of recognizable nondisruptive groups include prison fellowship, "lifer" organizations, peer counseling groups, and the Jaycees (discussed in Chapter 10). Although members of these groups exhibit loyalty, identity, and unity, they should not be viewed or treated as gangs unless they engage in criminal activities. Moreover, groups such as the Cuban Marielitos may engage in criminal activity without a leadership structure. They may come together to commit one or a series of crimes, but they are less dangerous than gangs because their criminal group activities are short lived and, once over, they disband. This group falls within the broader category of STGs.

Nevertheless, inmates are generally predisposed to manipulate the prison environment to their advantage. This means that all inmate groups, even those that lack a gang structure, require consistent observation, because all have the potential to become disruptive and may even change their focus and structure to operate as gangs.

Organization and Development of STGs

Until about 1980, our knowledge of prison gangs was based on a few isolated studies and newspaper and mag-

Table 12.1

STGs in Prisons (1992)

State	Inmate Population*	STG Members	%	State	Inmate Population*	STG Members	%
Alabama	17,000	275	1.6	Nebraska	3,173	98	3.1
Alaska	2,298	NA†	NA	Nevada	6,069	272	4.5
Arizona	16,200	200	1.2	New Hampshire	1,500	36	2.4
Arkansas	7,731	213	2.7	New Jersey	23,600	6,000	24.4
California	105,602	3,384	3.2	New Mexico	3,229	100	3.1
Colorado	7,300	508	6.9	New York	61,000	NA	NA
Connecticut	10,832	1,070	9.8	N. Carolina	20,000	NA	NA
Delaware	1,649	56	3.4	N. Dakota	560	NA	NA
D.C.	10,500	125	1.2	Ohio	33,469	1,200	3.6
Florida	47,300	1,101	2.3	Oklahoma	13,660	675	4.9
Georgia	24,561	NA	NA	Oregon	6,500	300	4.6
Hawaii	2,774	NA	NA	Pennsylvania	22,175	2,181	9.8
Idaho	2,140	268	12.5	Rhode Island	3,000	20	0.7
Illinois	31,000	14,900	48.1	S. Carolina	16,500	800	4.9
Indiana	13,500	215	1.6	S. Dakota	1,500	43	2.7
Iowa	4,476	357	8.0	Tennessee	8,889	724	8.1
Kansas	6,054	NA	NA	Texas	51,619	2,720	5.3
Kentucky	9,787	NA	NA	Utah	3,024	NA	NA
Louisiana	15,000	NA	NA	Vermont	1,175	NA	NA
Maine	1,000	NA	NA	Virginia	16,876	894	5.3
Maryland	NAR†	NAR	NAR	Washington	10,032	275	2.7
Massachusetts	9,000	465	5.2	West Virginia	1,867	47	6.9
Michigan	34,383	1,500	4.4	Wisconsin	8,040	1,369	17.0
Minnesota	3,777	686	18.2	Wyoming	723	NA	NA
Mississippi	6,195	379	6.1	Subtotal	724,696	43,756	6.0
Missouri	15,240	300	2.0	FBOP	66,144	2,434	3.7
Montana	1,217	NA	NA	Total	790,840	46,190	5.9

*This is the inmate population as reported by survey respondents.

†NA: Information not available

‡NAR: Information not authorized for release

Source: ACA (undated). Gangs in Correctional Facilities: A National Assessment (Contract No. 91-IJ-CS-0026) (Unpublished report). Washington, DC: U.S. Department of Justice.

azine reports.[3] However, beginning in the mid-1980s and continuing during the 1990s, many studies gathered nationwide data.[4] The growing interest in prison gangs is an indicator of the problems they are posing for corrections. These studies have provided a better perspective on the nature, extent, and effects of these groups, as well as strategies that have been used to deal with them.

The ACA (undated) surveyed the 50 states and the federal system in 1992. Forty jurisdictions, including the federal system, reported the presence of one or more STGs. These agencies identified 1,153 individual STGs with a total membership of 46,190. The percentage of an institution's inmate population in these groups ranged from as little as 0.1 percent in Massachusetts and North Carolina to as much as 48.1 percent in Illinois among states that responded to the survey. The average STG had 40 members. Illinois reported the largest gang membership (14,900), followed by New Jersey (6,000), Cali-

fornia (3,384), and Texas (2,720). In 1992, 6 percent of the prison inmates were STG members—twice as many as Camp and Camp found in 1985. Table 12.1 presents the percentage of inmates in each STG and the prison population in each jurisdiction at the time of the survey in 1992. Finally, 50 different STGs were identified as being present in two or more systems nationwide.[5] Eleven states reported no gangs.[6]

Future estimates of the number of identified STGs and members in given jurisdictions will increase. More inmates with street gang and prior prison gang affiliations are entering prison. For many of these youths, reared in an environment in which their fathers, brothers, uncles, and cousins are all gang members, joining a gang is the natural thing to do. These individuals are the ones that generally become the hard-core members, both on the street and in prison (Buentello, 1999). However, in 1999, the National Youth Gang Survey reported that there were an estimated 31,000 street gangs nation-wide with 846,000 members. This represents more than a 7 percent drop in each since 1996 (Cook, 1999). There is little doubt that some of these youths have already entered the correctional system.

The Rise of Inmate Gangs

Five distinct patterns of gang development emerged, creating the widespread involvement seen in today's prisons. Initially, there did not appear to be a connection between the development of prison gangs in different states. The first gangs appeared in the State of Washington in 1950, then in California in 1957, and in Illinois in 1969. The isolated and sporadic development of gangs changed in the 1970s with the emergence of gangs in Utah, Texas, and Arizona. These gangs were tied to gangs in California, and in Wisconsin and Iowa, which were tied to groups in Illinois. In the 1980s, gang development continued in states around Illinois and began to form in the Northeast and in the South, as well. (See Figure 12.1.) The five patterns follow.

1. Gang development in prisons has taken several forms. The emergence of the original **Mexican Mafia**—also known as the EME—the first gang in California, illustrates the **homeboy pattern.** This gang formed from a nucleus of seven to eight Mexican-American inmates, from the Marvilla section of East Los Angeles at Duel Vocational Institution. These "homeboys" shared a distinctive ethnic minority status, subculture, and membership in youth gangs (Moore, 1978). Around 1956 to 1957, they banded together for self-protection, controlling other inmates, and operating illicit prison enterprises (e.g., narcotics, gambling). Initially, this group grew by recruiting the most violent Chicano inmates. Recognizing they posed a threat to prison control, the administration dispersed their members to other institutions. This gave the gang new recruiting grounds that resulted in its spread throughout the California system. They also began to assault and rob other Hispanics, mainly from rural Northern California.

2. Conflict between groups and the need for self-protection spawned new gangs. To defend themselves, some Northern Hispanics formed **La Nuestra Familia** (NF). The NF, recognizing the potential profits and other advantages from domination of the prison economy, particularly narcotics, began to compete with the Mexican Mafia for control of these markets. This struggle resulted in other gangs forming and alliances developing between blacks and the NF, and whites and the Mexican Mafia. The white inmate gangs eventually coalesced

in the California system and became known as the **Aryan Brotherhood** (AB). Members adopted a philosophy of white pride and used a shamrock with three sixes as their symbol (Welling, 1999). Black inmates formed the **Black Guerrilla Family** (BGF) to protect and advance the position of their race. Their philosophy, drawn from the radical black political groups of the mid-1960s, advocated violence to achieve their objectives. They also had a criminal faction that assisted in financing the political activities of the organization (Camp & Camp, 1985; Kahn, 1978; Welling, 1999).

Gang formation in California illustrates several factors that contribute to prison gang development including ethnic/racial division, self-protection, common cultural and homeboy backgrounds, and the transfer of gang members from one institution to another.

3. Outside gang members entered into Illinois prisons, forming gangs on the inside. Gangs in this system developed, particularly at Stateville and Pontiac, as a result of the incarceration of large numbers of inmates affiliated with four[7] of what have been called supergangs. The major gangs have an organizational structure similar to a corporation, including a president or leader, vice president, supervisors or others who make sure the orders are carried out, and street members who carry out the orders of the leaders (Welling, 1999). These street affiliations provided a natural basis for these gangs to establish organizations in the prison. They quickly gathered strength and power by vigorously recruiting inmates who were not members on the outside.

The **Crips** and **Bloods,** California street gangs, are not as highly organized as the Chicago street gangs. Their organizational structure is best described as a large circle surrounding numerous smaller circles. Each Blood and Crip "set" has its own leader and organizational structure, but not all "sets" interact or work for a common goal. Thus, when they enter prisons, they develop loosely organized cliques if other homeboys are present in the facility. However, they do not have the power base to achieve the organizational level of gangs like the Mexican Mafia (Welling, 1999). When they enter prisons, they create serious problems; they rape, assault, and kill nongang members to establish turf or deal drugs (Godwin, 1999). Facilities for self-protection against the Bloods and the Crips, and the Nortenos and the Surenos, have now formed in adult prisons for the same reasons. The youths forming these new gangs have been referred to as the "Pepsi Generation." These youths walk around "sagging their pants below their ass," and show little respect for older inmates. They are also seen as needlessly violent, and as not thinking before they speak or act.

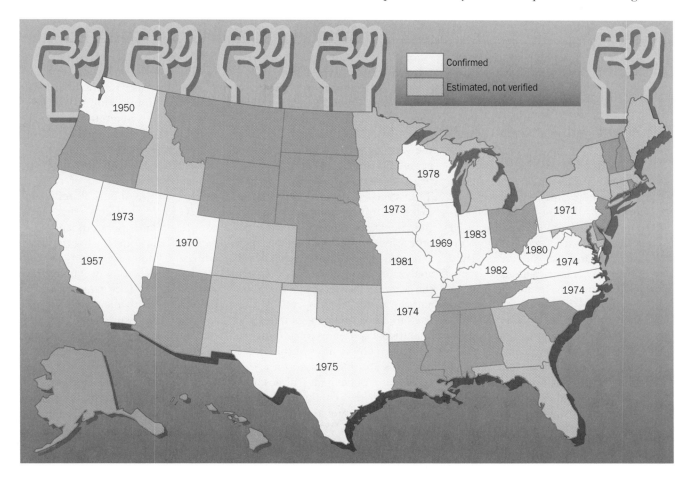

Figure 12.1   *Development of Prison Groups Between 1950 and the Early 1980s*

Source: Adapted from G. M. Camp & C. G. Camp (1985). *Prison Gangs: Their Extent, Nature, and Impact on Prisons.* Washington, DC: U.S. Department of Justice.

They have made prison life more unpredictable and in some cases have disrupted traditional loyalties between established gangs (Buentello, 1999; Hunt, Reigel, Morales, & Waldorf, 1996). The Close-Up feature, "Prison Gangs vs. Incarcerated Street Gangs," demonstrates some of the conflicts between these newer and older generations of gangs.

With youth gang involvement on the rise and with more gang-affiliated youths entering prison, there is little doubt that conflicts between youth gangs and more established gangs will become a greater problem. Further, Stevens (1997) found a link between prior commitment to a juvenile facility and membership in prison drug trafficking gangs.

4. Prison gang members transferred to new institutions formed gangs. This occurred in both the California and the Illinois systems where gang members attempted to duplicate the groups that had provided them with support and an identity in their prior institution.[8] The development of the **Texas Syndicate** (TS) in Texas also illustrates this pattern. This group

was started at San Quentin Prison in 1975 by Texas-born Mexican-American inmates for protection against other California prison gangs. By 1976, it had 500 members and it had spread to other California prisons, expanding its operations to illegal activities, such as drug trafficking, extortion, and contract murder. Its formation in Texas is traced to several inmates' previous involvement in it in California. When reunited, they formed the Texas version of this gang, which became the second largest gang in the Texas system (Buentello, 1986; Fong, 1990). Interestingly, by the mid-1990s, because the majority of its members were in Texas, this became its headquarters.

5. Copycat groups emerged in various prison systems with the same or similar names. These groups do not necessarily constitute branches of their namesakes or have any relationship between them. For example, the Mexican Mafia in California and the later formed Texas **Mexikanemi,** often called the Mexican Mafia, have no connection or relationship with each

Prison Gangs vs. Incarcerated Street Gangs

CLOSE-UP

The National Prison Gang/Street Gang Project (NPGSGP) collected responses from 32 states, and it revealed that inmate social organizations can be divided into two categories when examining the phenomenon of gangs. Inmate gang members in East Coast and Midwest correctional systems (Type I) tend primarily to be incarcerated street gangs. Their organization and activities are typically directed by leaders who have established reputations in the community. The groups' identities were established on the streets rather than in the prisons, and their original focus was external. The significant increase in incarcerated street gang members due to federal and state racketeering and enhancement statutes appears to pose common management problems of increased populations for these states.

Correctional systems in the West and Southwest (Type II) have experienced a different prison gang/STG development. Their histories include groups that were formed within the walls of the institutions. Reputations were made on associations and behavior inside the prisons rather than in the communities. Consequently, the influx of street gang members into the social organization of these systems will neces-

sitate an adjustment very different from that in the Type I systems.

In most agencies, the number of incarcerated street gang members has surpassed the number of prison gang members. The assimilation of the young gangsters into the inmate economic and social structure appears to take one of three paths. The street gang members either make their own challenges for control, negotiate alliances, or are co-opted by established prison gangs.

Phase Two of the research will analyze the interactions between the veteran prison gang members and the youth "interlopers" as it relates to adjustment for inmates and operational strategies for administrators. The complexities of these relationships are often based on a very divergent behavioral philosophy. Field interviews conducted by Pelz (unpublished) provide insight into areas of conflict. When asked how his prison gang viewed recently incarcerated street gangs, a prison gang member responded that "They don't really understand what it means to be a man. They don't know how to take care of business. Driving by a house and shooting everything that moves is cowardly. A real man walks up to you, looks you in the eye and sticks you in the gut."

Type I communities are experiencing significant growth in gang-related violence. These neighbor-

hoods are not only faced with greater numbers of gang members but a substantial increase in members who have "done time." How will these issues affect the communities?

Type II neighborhoods are faced with increases in street gang members, members who have been incarcerated and paroled or released prison gang members. Intelligence (NMGTF)* indicates that in a couple of large western and midwestern cities prison gang members who have been successfully trafficking in drugs and/or weapons have warned local street gangs that their indiscriminate violence is causing too much pressure from law enforcement. They have been warned to curtail their activity or suffer the consequences. How will the struggle for control by these entities impact crime? What strategies can be developed to counter or temper that impact?

*The National Major Gang Task Force

Source: Prepared especially for Corrections: A Comprehensive View, 2nd ed., by Beth Pelz, PhD, Associate Professor, University of Houston Downtown and Administrative/Research Coordinator, National Major Gang Task Force.

other. Also, the Aryan Brotherhood exists in various states; yet there is no central control of these gangs, and ties exist only between a few AB gangs in different systems.

Several other factors distinguish prison gangs from one another; the primary one is the motivation to join the gang (Camp & Camp, 1985). Ethnic/racial origin, based on beliefs of racial superiority (e.g., Aryan Brotherhood), was the primary basis for gang membership. Next in importance was "the homeboy orientation," which involves prior association or affiliation with others

from the same home area, such as the gangs in Illinois. Third was the sharing of strong political and/or religious beliefs (e.g., the Black Guerrilla Family). Some prison gangs have successfully brought suit in the federal courts and have obtained permission to organize as religious groups (McConville, 1985). For some of these groups, this was an impetus to obtain cover for drug trafficking operations. Another factor was a common lifestyle centering around "motorcycle machismo" as practiced by the biker gangs (e.g., Avengers). Many of these gangs are organized around and attract membership based on several of these factors, like the Mexican

Mafia, which has both an ethnic/racial and a geographical basis.

Gang Structure

Leaders of gangs are typically distinctive from their followers in several ways, including physical prowess, seniority, and the commission of violent acts. Further, members manifesting similar attributes are more likely to move up in the gang hierarchy. The leadership structure of these groups follows one of three patterns: (1) hierarchical, (2) paramilitary, or (3) control rests with a steering committee (Buentello, 1997).

The Texas-based Mexikanemi gang is structured along a **hierarchical model** (see Figure 12.2). The president is usually the founding member and is respected by all members of the group. He is responsible for making all decisions and delegating rank and authority to those under him. He generally appoints ranking officers and then allows them to designate their subordinates, which permits them to have some input in certain matters; however, his authority is absolute. Hence, he can remove someone from a position without any discussion or input from any other member. When he leaves prison, either the vice president assumes the leadership role, or there is a power struggle.

Under the **paramilitary model**—followed by the Texas Syndicate—which also follows a hierarchical structure, the organizational framework consists of a general, a captain, a lieutenant, sergeants, members, prospects, and so on. This structure differs from the hierarchical model in that when a leader is removed for whatever reason (e.g., transfer, release, victim of an assault), a vote is conducted to choose a new leader. Depending on the specific group involved, that elected member may or may not keep his position if he is transferred or released (Buentello, 1999).

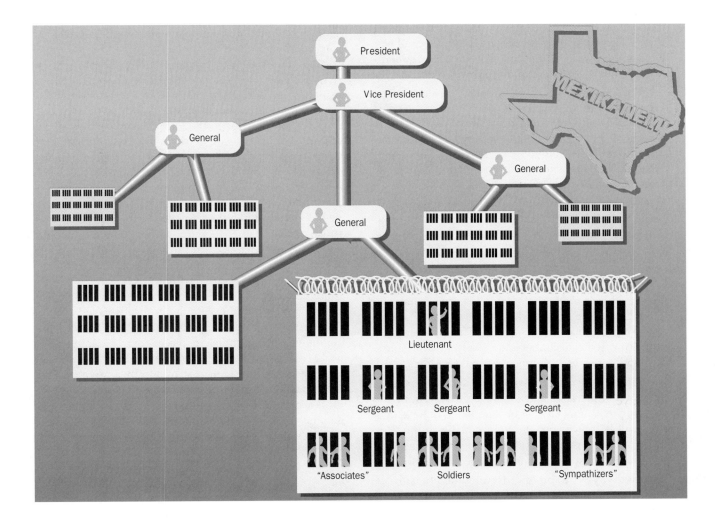

Figure 12.2 *Organizational Structure of the Texas Mexikanemi*

Source: Based on interviews. Adapted from R. S. Fong (1990). The organizational structure of prison gangs: A Texas case study. *Federal Probation, 54*(1), 40.

Under the **steering committee model,** which is preferred by the Aryan Brotherhood, a committee comprising an odd number of gang members who founded the organization governs it. When a committee member dies or is released, his vacancy is filled by anyone the council chooses. Unlike the paramilitary model, the leadership of this group is neither questioned nor voted on (Fong, Vogel, & Buentello, 1996).

It is important to note that, although, in theory, gangs demand obedience to the leadership, their ability to enforce their commands varies greatly (Fong, Vogel, & Buentello, 1995).

Types of Gang Members

There are several types of gang members. These include hard-core, general, peripheral, and associate members; wanna-be's; throwaways; and sympathizers.[9]

1. **Hard-core members** are composed of most of the "ranking" members, who wield the majority of power in the organization. They have usually demonstrated their ability to lead by various acts of violence. They expect absolute loyalty to the gang and are very committed to its goals and philosophy. Very few ever "defect."

2. **General members** are not as committed to the goals and philosophy of the organization as hard-core members. They joined because they needed protection and will generally only do what is necessary to maintain a good standing within the gang. Most defectors come from this category.

3. **Peripheral members** generally do not voice any opinions related to issues confronting the gang. They are generally very paranoid about saying or doing the wrong thing.

4. **Associate members** include inmates who associate with the gang but will never be members. For example, a black inmate who supplies drugs to an all-white gang, or an inmate who associates with the gang only for protection, are associates. Those involved in trafficking in illegal contraband usually pay the gang a fee, work for compensation, or get paid in drugs.

5. **Wanna-be's** are inmates who want to be accepted as members of the gang and will do almost anything for the gang to gain its favor. They are led to believe that they will be taken into the group in the future. Because of their desire to please the gang, these individuals are the most dangerous to correctional staff.

6. **Throwaways** are promised gang membership if they carry out assignments for the gang. The gang has no intention of making them members, and as soon as they are no longer useful, the gang will discard them. They will then be used by the gang in various ways (e.g., drug smuggling, assaults, gam-

bling). At no time will they have any knowledge of the inner workings of the gang. Depending on how much they have done or know about the internal workings of the gang, these inmates may ask for protective custody or to be transferred to another institution (Buentello, 1999; Welling, 1999).

7. **Sympathizers** are individuals with no desire to join the gang but who share the group's beliefs. They engage in certain activities that serve their own self-interest, as well as the group's, with or without payment.

Identifying Gang Members

Ralph, Hunter, Marquart, Cuvelier, and Merianos (1996) identified four variables that provided a high degree of accuracy in predicting gang membership. The most influential factor was prior adult incarceration, followed by length of sentence imposed. Third was a history of institutionalization as a juvenile, and last, a history of violent offenses. These predictions confirmed what prison managers have felt intuitively—tougher criminals become gang members.

Gang members can usually be identified by distinctive characteristics, including tattoos, clothing, jewelry, insignias, emblems, and colors (U.S. Department of Justice, 1998). For example, inmates often paint their cells in these colors. Also, graffiti, often called the newspaper of the street, marks gang territory and describes gang exploits. Inside prison, graffiti takes the form of inmate drawings. As prison systems have begun to more closely scrutinize gang activities and restrict the activities of identified members, and in some instances place identified leaders and members in administrative segregation, gangs have had to change the ways in which they operate. Some have had to resort to the use of nonmembers, associates, wanna-be's, and sympathizers to carry out gang business. Of course, this has not stopped gangs from recruiting from the general population. Whereas in the past gang members prominently displayed distinctive tattoos on their forearms, chests, and backs, some are now putting them in places that are more concealed—like on the scalp under their hair. However, in some systems, the high cost of administrative confinement has made gang placement in these high-custody units too expensive. As a result, members are kept in the general population, and they do not hide their tattoos (Fong et al., 1996). See Figure 12.3 for examples of gang tattoos and insignias.

The Recruitment and Initiation Process

Fong (1990) provides a picture of the recruitment process in the Texas system, which suggests patterns that may be operating in other gangs as well. In the Texas Syndicate, all prospective members must have a

Nuestra Familia ("Our Family")

Texas Syndicate

Aryan Brotherhood

Figure 12.3   *Prison Gang Insignias*

homeboy connection; an active member must have been a childhood friend of the prospect. Otherwise, they are placed on probation and a background investigation is conducted by the unit chairman by contacting other members who may have knowledge of the prospect. If

the prospect is "clean," all members are polled, and he is admitted if the vote is unanimous. Membership is denied if he is found to be a police informant or has a questionable sense of loyalty. Further, he may be forced by the gang to pay for protection or be used as a prostitute.

The Mexikanemi has some of the same membership requirements and procedures as the TS, but does not adhere to them as rigidly. Rather, their policies include (1) not requiring homeboy connections; (2) not doing as thorough a background investigation; and (3) only requiring a majority vote for membership. This is a major factor in their being the largest gang in the Texas system (Fong, 1990).

Gang initiation practices vary, with some groups requiring a nonviolent form of initiation and others requiring "prospects" to commit a violent act against another inmate or staff member. The "hit," while not necessarily fatal, requires that blood be drawn. The initiation appears to serve three purposes: It shows that the candidate is "really solid"; it gives gangs an opportunity to conduct their business; and it guarantees that only those who are coldhearted, violent, and loyal will be accepted as gang members (Buentello, 1986; Camp & Camp, 1985).

Gang Codes of Conduct

Gang codes emphasize secrecy and loyalty and sometimes require an outwardly cooperative attitude toward prison staff (Buentello, 1986; Camp & Camp, 1985; Fong, 1990). Fear, intimidation, threats, pressure, and violence, including murder, are used by members to achieve their objectives and by the gang to maintain loyalty, obedience, and order within the group. Actual or threatened violence is the most potent factor in gang maintenance. True gang members have little regard for human life and are not deterred by government sanctions imposed against inmates for violent behavior. They are not controlled by the rules—the laws and sanctions that guide most other people's behavior—which allows them to disregard the law and its consequences (Camp & Camp, 1985; Fong, Vogel, & Buentello, 1992).

The degree to which gangs can demand obedience to their code of conduct depends on the organization's cohesiveness and its ability to retaliate against those breaking the code (NIC, 1991). Some gangs can enforce their code even after a member has been released from prison. For example, a Texas Syndicate member was murdered execution style in Houston, Texas, for failing to abide by the oath he took when he joined the gang (Buentello, 1986). The gang hit reflects the nature of gang expectations and the rules governing member behavior. Once someone is marked for death, a volunteer may be sought to do the job, and if no one steps forward, members may be required to draw lots to decide who will do it (Fong, 1990). The rule is that if you refuse to

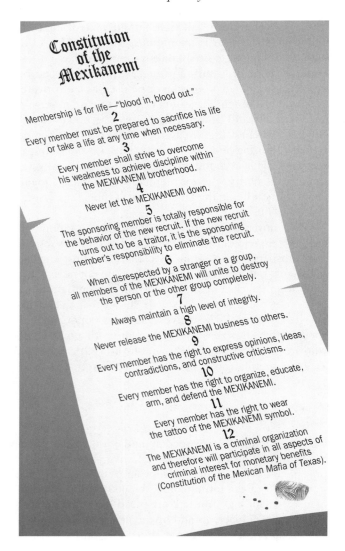

Figure 12.4 *The Mexikanemi Constitution*

Source: Adapted from R. S. Fong (1990). The organizational structure of prison gangs: A Texas case study. *Federal Probation, 54*(1), 40.

Table 12.2

Reasons for Leaving Prison Gangs[10]

Reason	Percentage*
Lost interest in the gang	20.9
Refused to carry out hit on a nongang member	18.8
Disagreed with gang direction	14.6
Refused to carry out a hit on a fellow gang member	12.5
Violated gang rule	10.4
Grew out of it	10.4
Informed prison officials about gang business	8.5
Refused to engage in gang crime	4.2

*The number of respondents in this study = 48.

Source: Adapted from R. Fong, R. E. Vogel, & S. Buentello (1995). Blood-in, blood-out: The rationale behind defecting from prison gangs. *Journal of Gang Research, 2*(4), 48.

kill someone, you will be killed. A member of the Texas Syndicate told CBS reporter Ed Bradley (1986) that this applies even if it is a friend or if "the two were raised by the same mother."

Many of the more developed groups have detailed codes of conduct, and some have written constitutions. Figure 12.4 provides an example of the rules contained in the constitution of the Mexikanemi. Fong (1990) indicates that, in this gang, the "penalty for intentionally or unintentionally violating any of the established rules is death" (p. 40). Nevertheless, some members "defect" rather than obey a gang order to kill or to abide by some other gang rule.

Whereas in the past gang membership often entailed a lifetime commitment and refusal to carry out a gang hit or abide by gang rules would result in death, there is more recent evidence that members may defect (Buentello, 1986; Fong, 1990). Preliminary research by Fong, Vogel, and Buentello (1995) provides some of the reasons for these defections (see Table 12.2). Buentello (1999) suggests some other reasons a member defects are that he (1) can no longer relate to the goals and philosophies of the gang, (2) is married and has a family to look after, or (3) feels that he can no longer perform acts of violence for no real reason. In some cases, a member may be forced to leave because (1) he was put on the hit list for committing an act against the gang, or (2) he disrespected a fellow gang member or made negative or disrespectful comments about the gang. Those forced out of the gang must seek protection from them. Some attempt to join another group or form their own gang—generally with little or no success. Release from prison enables many gang members to leave the gang without severe consequences.

Gang Methods to Perpetuate Power

Gang members with long prison sentences may not be concerned about having their sentences extended for 10 or 20 years. They present an image of being unafraid of prison administration, other inmates, or the consequences of their violence. This stance enables them to intimidate most other inmates and some staff and to kill with impunity (Camp & Camp, 1985).

Gangs typically base their power and prestige on their ability to control other inmates and certain prison activities. Drugs, money, and property are considered tangible evidence of their ability to accomplish these aims. Thus, they derive their image from the acquisition of power and from their emphasis on "ganghood," a concept that centers around the significance of belonging to the gang. For example, the Texas Syndicate constitution states that, "nothing is to be put before the [TS] and its business. Not god, religion, parole or family" (Bradley, 1986).

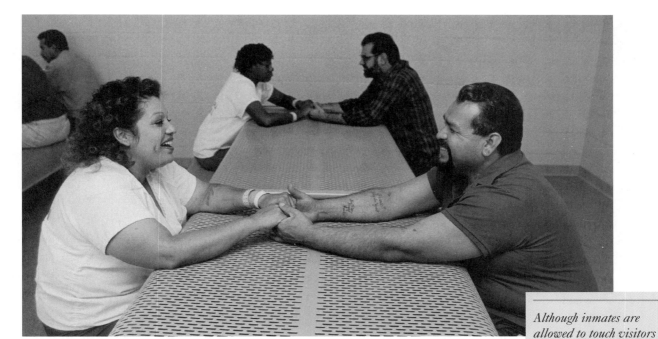

Although inmates are allowed to touch visitors only above the table, drugs are often smuggled into prison by way of the visiting room.

Gangs also maintain themselves by providing essential services (e.g., protection for members) and through their capacity to obtain and distribute contraband, particularly drugs (Camp & Camp, 1985). Many gangs bribe prison staff to bring drugs and, more recently, tobacco into prisons where it is banned. COs receive a commission on everything they bring in, and those involved can almost double their weekly salary (Crouch & Marquart, 1989). A member of the Mexikanemi describes co-opting a young, inexperienced CO:

When a young officer is assigned to a cell block, one of us would start watching him for a few days. Then, I would go up to him in order to find out where he is coming from. I would borrow a cigarette or a pen from him. If he goes for it, next thing I would do is ask him to mail a letter for me. If he goes for it I would start showing him pictures of some woman which I claimed to be my friend. I would tell him to give her a call because she would show him a real good time. If he calls her and gets some sex favors from her, I know I have him. (Fong, as cited by Crouch & Marquart, 1989, p. 211)

[At that point the officer will be asked to bring in drugs. If he refuses he will be exposed to higher ranking officers as having been involved with an inmate's wife, sister, or other close relative. This usually means termination. Moreover, once involved, the gang does not allow these officers to terminate their courier activities unless they resign from their prison jobs, because anytime an officer refuses to cooperate, he is threatened with exposure]. (Fong, 1990).

Further, street-level gang research shows that inmates recruit friends still on the streets to smuggle drugs into jail and prison visiting rooms. Young women, often former lovers with children fathered by the imprisoned gang members, are particularly vulnerable because they need money to pay rent, raise their children, and buy drugs for their own habits and for street sales. Inmates with gambling or drug debts may threaten the lives of young women who refuse to work as drug mules. As Fleisher and Rison (1999) note, because drugs sell for 5 to 10 times their street value in prison, smuggling them is worth the risk to inmates and visitors.

Other money-making endeavors include the protection rackets, thievery, and prostitution. These activities often involve intimidating and abusing weaker inmates (Buentello, 1986; Camp & Camp, 1985). For example, a gang member in Texas showed a new recruit how gang members raise money. He took two loaves of bread and made "mayonnaise sandwiches" and went down the tier and asked those guys who had money if they wanted to "buy a sandwich." A lot of guys did not want them, but whether they wanted them or not, they bought them. When asked by Ed Bradley (1986) of *60 Minutes*, "What would have happened if they refused?" the gang member replied, "They'd get their heads torn off. They are going to buy the sandwiches, there ain't no if."

Gangs have employed a number of channels to communicate with members in different units. The most common has been the U.S. mail. However, because prison officials can intercept and censor outgoing mail under certain circumstances, gangs developed codes for their letters (see the Close-Up, "How Gangs Use the Mail to Communicate"). Prison rules can prohibit inmate-to-inmate correspondence,[11] but gangs have gotten

How Gangs Use the Mail to Communicate

CLOSE-UP

Both the Texas Syndicate and the Mexican Mafia operate in secretive ways in the prison environment. On the unit level, instructions and decisions are relayed through verbal communications. For interunit communication, however, the most commonly known method is the use of the U.S. mail. Coded messages are hidden in letters. For the Texas Syndicate, the most frequently used coded method is the number code. The following coded letter is an example of this communication strategy.

Dear Bro,

Haven't heard nothing from ya for almost 4 weeks.... Remember Big Al, he just got back from the hospital after spending 3 weeks there for a major heart attack. Said it was a change. Really liked it there. The room was nice and even had a 19-inch color TV.... Said he wouldn't mind staying there for ½ a year.

Guess what, he said when he woke up in his room the first time, he almost had a second heart attack cause he couldn't believe what he saw, a real cute nurse with Dolly Parton's figure. Said she was taller, about 5 foot 8 inches in her early 20s. Big Al said they got to be real good friends. Said she even hugged him a dozen times or so a day.... Said would divorce his old lady if things get juicy with this cutie. What a two-timer. So much for Big Al.

I am getting a visit this weekend. My old man is bringing my son to see me 'cause next Monday is his B-day. Gonna be 10 years old. Wish I would be out there with him. Been away for almost 5 years since I got busted for raping that 19-year-old slut down in that Motel 6. Got 3 more years to go and I'll be a free man....

Well, such is life! Like they say, life is a bitch and you die, sometimes if ya lucky, ya marry one. Gonna put the brakes on for now. Give my best to the best and f—— the rest.

Your bro till death

In interpreting the underlying message of this letter, one must first learn the number codes. The number codes are broken down as follows:

A B C D E F G H I J K L M N
8 1 7 26 18 9 13 3 19 20 14 22 5 16
O P Q R S T U V W X Y Z
12 17 23 2 10 6 36 15 21 11 27 34

The number 4 in the beginning of the letter is a code indicator. The letter contains the following numbers:

1st paragraph: 3, 19, 6 (½ year = 6)
2nd paragraph: 5, 8, 20, 12, 2
3rd paragraph: 10, 5, 19, 6, 3

Applying these numbers to the letter designations will reveal the following message:

3 19 6 5 8 20 12 2 10 5 19 6 3
H I T M A J O R S M I T H
"Hit Major Smith."
Source: B. Fong (1990). The organization structure of prison gangs: A Texas case study, Federal Probation, *54(1), 41–42.*

---

around these rules by using wives, girlfriends, other visitors, and inmates being transferred from one unit to another to carry messages between units. Gang members have also used spiritual advisors to serve as unsuspecting messengers by persuading the advisor that the letter being sent to an inmate in another facility contains religious material. Among the most clever methods is the use of a bench warrant. This is used if one member of a gang "A" needs to convey information to three other members, "B," "C," and "D," each in different units. "A" files a lawsuit alleging brutality against a CO and petitions the court for a bench warrant identifying the other inmates as witnesses. This requires prison officials to allow witnesses to meet with the litigant, and legal visits are exempt from audio monitoring (Fong et al., 1996).

The Benefits of Gang Membership

Inmates derive many benefits from joining gangs, particularly in institutions where gangs dominate the inmate world (Irwin, 1980; Jacobs, 1974; Porter, 1982). Gangs provide their members with protection from physical and sexual assault, extortion, and theft. Independents and members of other gangs know that if a gang member is attacked or has property stolen, his comrades will retaliate. Gangs also have "private stores" and provide new inmates and those without outside resources with candy, cigarettes, pies, canned food, and other things that make prison life more tolerable. These gangs also provide a sense of belonging and opportunities for acquiring drugs, cash, and other property (Fleisher & Rison, 1999). Gang members, unlike independents, are not expected to pay back these debts at 100 percent interest.

By being assigned to strategic jobs (e.g., positions as clerks in the administration building), the gang can amass valuable information on decisions affecting their members. Gang affiliation also allows members to operate within the prison economy. Although gangs are not always in control of all illicit activities in the prisons they dominate, independents are not likely to operate without gang leadership approval. In one Texas prison, for example, an inmate who was a drug dealer on the street entered prison thinking he would continue his trafficking activity on the inside. He soon learned that the TS controlled trafficking in this prison. To deal, he had to become a member of this gang or else be killed (Bradley, 1986).

Visitors and correspondents are typically arranged for inside gang members who have no outside family or other contacts. Outside gang members also send money and arrange to have drugs and other contraband smuggled into the prison. Members of gangs with outside affiliates can expect to receive assistance when released. When asked what the gang provides for its members who are released, one Texas Syndicate member stated: "They get them an old lady. They get them dope. They get them on their feet" (Bradley, 1986).

Some gangs have education programs to teach members how to read and write. For many gang members, the group's primary functions are to provide psychological support, a feeling of belonging, a source of identification, and an air of importance. For inmates who are products of unstable families and have poor self-concepts, the gang allows them to "feel like men" and to be part of a family they never had.

Gangs as Organized Crime Groups

Close to three quarters of the 39 jurisdictions in Camp and Camp's study (1985) reported that some or all of the gangs in their prisons had counterpart gangs on the streets. The President's Commission on Organized Crime (1986) identified five prison gangs that met the criteria for organized crime groups: the Mexican Mafia, La Nuestra Familia, the Aryan Brotherhood, the Black Guerrilla Family, and the Texas Syndicate. A more recent report identified the following gangs as the six top groups: Neta, the Aryan Brotherhood, the Black Guerrilla Family, the Mexican Mafia, La Nuestra Familia, and the Texas Syndicate (Hart, 1999). These gangs are sophisticated and self-perpetuating groups. They are involved in illegal acts for power and profit, and they have operations both inside and outside of the prison. In contrast to ordinary criminal gangs, they are organized to operate beyond the lifetime of individual members and to survive leadership changes. They also have a hierarchical structure that is distinguishable and ordered by ranks based on power and authority similar to a corporation. This structure insulates gang leaders from direct involvement in criminal activity, making it difficult to use traditional law enforcement techniques to charge and prosecute them. For example, the Mexican Mafia (EME) has patterned its organizational structure after the Italian Mafia (LCN). Thus, this group consists of a chain of command with a supreme commander at the top. Generals command the different units and pass their orders down through captains, lieutenants, and sol-

For many gang members, the gang's primary function is to provide a feeling of belonging and a sense of importance.

diers. Generally, each prison is considered a separate unit and thus has its own leadership. Gruesome killings are used as a means of discipline, gaining respect, and intimidation. They also provide protection for LCN members. In turn, the LCN allows the EME to traffic in narcotics without interference and also provides loans and jobs for released gang members (Godwin, 1999).

Gangs with outside counterparts are involved in drug trafficking, extortion, robbery, prostitution, murder, and weapons trafficking (Buentello, 1986; Camp & Camp, 1985). At some point, if it has not already occurred, these gangs, particularly those designated as organized crime groups, will use the money generated from these highly profitable illegal enterprises to invest in high cash flow legitimate businesses, such as bars and restaurants.

The California-based Mexican Mafia successfully infiltrated, and eventually controlled, several federally funded projects directed toward assisting ex-convicts, parolees, youthful offenders, and addicts. In one program designed to assist ex-convicts to readjust to society, project funds were used to purchase heroin from Mexico and airline tickets for drug couriers. Program clients

Gang Profile: The Neta

CLOSE-UP

Neta was formed in 1970 by an individual attempting to stop violence between inmates in Puerto Rico. Neta developed in areas of the United States where there was a high density of Puerto Rican–American and Hispanic populations. Their factions in the United States are characteristic of traditional gangs—they are involved in the sale and distribution of CDs, extortion, strong-arming, and other such activities. In prisons, the Neta gang presents threats to staff and inmate safety, drug activity, extortion, and gang-related violence. They are known for their willingness to resort to violence.

Their structure is a clear-cut hierarchy that includes a president, vice president, recruiter, secretary, sergeant at arms, and enforcer. All members must obey the group's 24 conduct norms. Neta's colors are red, white, and blue, although some have suggested that black has replaced blue. The colors are symbolic, with red standing for blood that has been and will be shed, white standing for tranquility, and black for grief for those in Neta who have lost their lives. New Neta groups must be sanctioned by the Neta gang in Puerto Rico, which has led to the development of a faction known as "United We Stand" (UNA).

Neta perceives itself as a revolutionary group, not a criminal one. They claim that their goal is to help Hispanics help themselves by encouraging them to get an education.

They also largely believe that they have been unjustly incarcerated and victimized by the U.S. government and prison administration. Currently, Neta is involved in active recruiting within correctional facilities, and, because of their origin, may be more successful than other security threat groups (Godwin, 1999).

A court monitor's report suggested that the Neta controls a majority of Puerto Rico's 36 institutions. They exercise "a vast and frightening level of control over inmates in this system by pressuring, beating, and even killing those that violate gang norms." A 1997 internal prison study found that Neta leaders micromanage the lives of fellow inmates with near dictatorial powers. This ranges from deciding which cells inmates will inhabit to controlling access to programs such as employment, education, health care, and visiting privileges. Further, the gang has a screening committee that reviews inmates' court papers to determine if a new arrival is fit for confinement with the rest of the prison population.

In short, this study found that gangs pervade the culture of Puerto Rico's prisons to a degree which we have never known in another correctional system. The spectrum of inmates exercising power and control as openly and forcefully as they do in the commonwealth would be shocking and politically untenable in the other corrections system with which we are familiar.

While gang activities include extortion and other illicit conduct, drug trafficking is its most profitable endeavor. Internal gang documents reveal a very profitable prison drug empire that fixes prices and settles policies governing consumption.

On the outside the Neta has an "execution committee" (i.e., a gang-sponsored death squad, which when requested will do hits for crime bosses on the outside). Moreover, Neta is reported to use a front organization called the Commission to Improve the Quality of Life to exert influence that ranges across the (corrections) institution and into the senior levels of the executive and legislative branches of the commonwealth's government. For example, Senate President Charlie Rodriguez helped the head of the commission, Carlos Caceres, who is serving a 99-year sentence in the killing of a Catholic Priest, and another gang leader to obtain furloughs to attend a ceremony at the island's capital city. Further, during elections politicians visit the prison and make offers to Neta prisoners (e.g., lowering inmate sentences and parole) in exchange for their votes and support (Ross, 1997).

This indicates the extent to which gangs can dominate a prison system and even influence the political process. It is also the disastrous consequence of not taking a proactive approach to gangs or STGs.
Source: Corry Godwin (2000). Personal communication.

---

were induced to establish dealerships in East Los Angeles and give a percentage of their profits back to the gang. Project-owned vehicles were used by gang members in at least six murders (Camp & Camp, 1985).

The existence of street counterparts serves a number of purposes for the gang and individual members. For members who are released, it provides a support net-

work to assist them in settling back into the community. For TS members, this means having a place to go, financial assistance, and opportunities to join in illegal activities with other TS members. For prison gangs, this represents another source of income because outside members are often required to send a portion of the profits from their criminal activities to gang members on

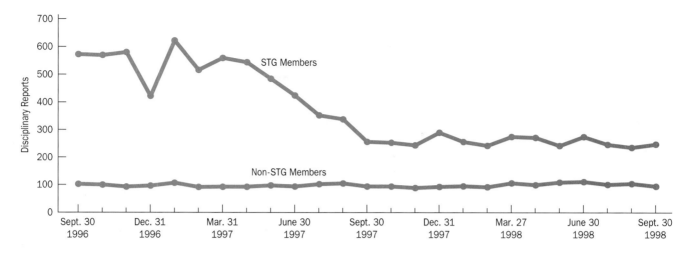

Figure 12.5 *Disciplinary Report* Chart*

*The Disciplinary Report (DR) rate is measured in number of DRs per 1,000 inmates.
Sources: S. Hart (2000); D. Ensley & K. Hensley, Bureau of Research and Data Analysis.

the inside. For example, the TS requires members to contribute 10 percent of their street income, while Mexikanemi requires 15 percent (Fong, 1990). Also, some of the money from outside activities may be used to pay attorneys to assist members with their cases and to post bond when a gang member is arrested (Buentello, 1986). Our Close-Up feature, "Gang Profile: The Neta," focuses on this gang, which views itself as a revolutionary group.

Problems Caused by Prison Gangs

The difficulties gangs can create for prison administrators vary from state to state. The major problems created by these groups include drug trafficking, intimidation of weaker inmates, and strong-arm tactics for extortion. These latter activities present problems because of the violence, which is often intensified because of the racial character of gangs, and the fact that many inmates' victims request placement in protective custody. The problems experienced by prison staff from gang activity are not usually the result of direct actions against staff but more often result from gangs pursuing their business interests. Gangs do not usually try to disrupt prison operations; yet they are determined to carry on "business" regardless of how this affects prison order (Camp & Camp, 1985). Nevertheless, some groups do actively disrupt the prison by filing frivolous litigation and falsely alleging prison mismanagement, harassment, and brutality by COs. Also, gangs have tried to disrupt prison order by instigating food and work strikes and other major disorders (Buentello, 1986; *Corrections Compendium*, 1996).

Older gang members generally recognize the value of cooperating with institutional staff to maintain a stable environment because that is "good for business." This may be lost on younger members who may challenge

prison authority to validate their tough guy image, but stronger gangs tend to control younger members to avoid these problems (NIC, 1991).

Sometimes, it appears as if some gangs and the prison administration have unofficial pacts of mutual noninterference (Camp & Camp, 1985, 1988). Moreover, some systems report fewer gang problems today than in the past. Some prison administrators do not consider gangs a problem, because (1) primarily this would mean admitting the problem and suggests they are not in control of their institutions; (2) they may not openly disrupt prison routine, which leads to the naive feeling that they cannot hurt the institution; or (3) they are viewed as part of the informal inmate structure and should only be dealt with when their actions become overt and confrontational (Hart, 1999).

Gang confrontations vary greatly, with some groups limiting them to nongang inmates (Camp & Camp, 1985). Likewise, retaliatory action among gangs differs widely, suggesting that alliances exist in some prisons, whereas in others there is competition and disagreement. From 1982 to 1985, when gangs battled for dominance in Texas, they accounted for 51 of 72 inmate homicides; they also accounted for a high proportion of nonfatal inmate stabbings. An ACA (undated) study also found that a high percentage of inmate-to-inmate violence was gang-related in both prisons (40%) and jails (42%).

Despite the fact that many gangs follow a policy of avoiding conflicts with prison staff, gang activity data from the Texas system show that between 1983 and 1988 there was a yearly average of 2,918 assaults by inmates on COs, most of which were gang-related (Fong et al., 1991). Moreover, the Florida Department of Corrections has reported that STG members present a disproportionate number of problems in prison compared with non-STG members (Hart, 1998). Figure 12.5 illustrates the specific findings of this report. The non-STG-generated disciplinary report (DR) rate was consistent every month, averaging 98. However, the DR rate generated by STGs varied greatly, averaging 334, revealing a substantially greater source of problems.

Controlling Prison Gangs

California was the first system to experience major gang problems. In the 1960s, gangs became entrenched in its institutions before administrators realized the danger these groups posed to order and security. Since this early period and with the spread of gangs to other systems, several strategies have evolved to attempt to control them. Not all tactics have been effective in all jurisdictions because of the great variation between systems:

> There are two views of how prison administrators should react to gangs. The agency policy for the management of gangs in a prison setting is determined by the length of time they have been in the system, sophistication, and problems experienced with gang activity in the past. For example, those states which have been dealing with gangs for many years have developed a formal policy to deal with them. If there has been a long history of gang disruptive behavior, agency policy generally dictates that confirmed gang members will have certain restrictions placed on them, by the fact they are members. On the other hand, many jurisdictions in the early stages of gang identification which have not experienced disruption will typically establish a policy that is focused on inmate behavior. Then, inmates are subject to disciplinary action on an incident-by-incident basis. As long as a gang member abides by the rules of the institutions, no sanctions are imposed. However, if he becomes involved in illegal gang activity, appropriate administrative action is taken. (Welling, 1997)

These views represent very different approaches to and perceptions of gangs by prison administrators. The ACA (undated) survey of gangs concluded that correctional personnel sometimes go through three stages in reacting to them, which may explain these different perceptions:

- *Denial*   This stage was found primarily on the East Coast and west to Ohio. In this stage, correctional administrators tended to deny that gangs exist.

- *Acknowledgment*   Midwest states tended to acknowledge that gangs are present; however, they had few, if any, specific procedures designed to identify, track, or control them.

- *Recognition*   "Yes we have them, now what do we do?" This tended to be the attitude of states west of Colorado. They were aware that gangs exist in their systems and were attempting to control their activities (p. 2).

Welling (1999) asserts that, at this time, approximately 90 percent of the state departments of corrections are in the recognition stage and are implementing policy and procedures to identify and deal with these groups. Historically, correctional agencies have dealt with individual behavior. With the addition of gang dynamics, correctional officials are implementing management strategies that proactively deter disruptive group behavior, as well as dealing with the individual.

To implement this new management style, agencies need assistance. During the past few years, agencies have been requesting technical assistance from security threat group management specialists to provide on-site assessment of their current management strategies, recommend policy development, and provide training for correctional staff to recognize and identify gang behavior and symbols. States are also regularly exchanging policies and management strategies, which helps create uniformity (Welling, 1999).

Strategies for Controlling Gangs

The issue of gang control focuses on how to provide a safe and constitutional environment for the general prison population in institutions with major gang problems. The general population of a prison should not have to go into protective custody to feel safe and secure. Preventing this may require a number of changes in management policies and procedures as well as structural changes in a prison's physical plant. In the remainder of this chapter, we present recommendations made by various authors, organizations, and systems who have studied the prison gang problem (see, e.g., ACA, undated; Buentello, 1986; Camp & Camp, 1985, 1988; Fong, 1990).

Developing a Prison Gang Policy   Strategic development involves recognizing the gang problem, followed by implementing an STG-specific strategy that takes a proactive approach to dealing with gangs and a management plan that can accomplish this objective (Fleisher & Rison, 1999). This requires an assessment by the best-qualified staff on the extent and nature of the problem and its effects on institutional operations, other inmates, and staff. A strategy should be broad enough to include both policies designed to deter gang activity and incentive programs to encourage nongang involvement.

Intelligence   To prevent gang activity, a better identification and information system is needed. It should include techniques for detecting early signs of gang activity and for identifying which inmates are gang members. Identifying STGs and their members is the first step in developing an intelligence system, which is the key element in recognizing the threats posed by these groups and in forging a response. "**Intelligence** in the correctional environment is selectively processed information that is of strategic value in making informed decisions regarding security management" (Trout & Meko, 1990, p. 16). Monitoring gang activities requires both a systemwide intelligence unit and an institutional intelligence officer. However, the ACA (undated) found that these units are not widely accepted within many systems and are usually underfunded and understaffed.

To monitor these groups, first, establish specific criteria to label a group as a gang. For example, it is necessary to identify the groups, gangs, or inmate organizations where there is information that they are acting together to promote violence, escape, or to conduct criminal, drug, or terrorist activity (ACA, undated).

Next, establish criteria to identity inmate gang members. According to Hart (1999), these generally may include:

- *Scars, marks, or tattoos* Subject has body marks and tattoos identified as denoting gang membership or association.

- *Symbols or paraphernalia* Subject is observed wearing colors and symbols or "throwing hand signs" identified as denoting gang membership or association.

- *Association–photographs or video* Subject is in a photograph or a video with identified gang member(s).

- *Association–observations* Subject is observed associating on a regular basis with identified gang members. This includes visitations by identified gang members.

- *Documentation–external* Information is received from outside law enforcement agencies regarding gang membership or arrests with known gang members.

- *Documentation–internal* Subject has a record of participating in, organizing, or supporting criminal gang activities within the facility.

- *Documentation–gang related* Subject's name is on a gang document or hit list or he possesses bylaws, rosters, membership card, or certificate of rank.

- *Correspondence–written* Subject corresponds with identified gang members, receives gang-related literature, or writes about gang activities.

- *Correspondence–telephonic* Subject receives or initiates telephone calls from or to known gang members.

- *Inmate information* Subject is identified as a gang member by a reliable informant.

Generally, agencies require two or more criteria to designate an inmate as a gang member. To meet constitutional standards, agencies placing restrictions on these inmates must (1) inform them of their gang member status and hold due process hearings; (2) give them an opportunity to appeal the results of this hearing; and (3) have periodic reviews of and reclassification of those who drop out of these groups. STG involvement should initially be determined during the reception process because this may be their first involvement with the state prison system. Therefore, they have not had time to establish gang contacts on the inside, and they are usually more amenable to answering questions regarding their STG affiliation. Also, new commitments are usually required to "strip down," which allows security staff to examine and photograph gang-related tattoos (Hart, 1999).

Members are officially designated as:

1. **Validated members** These are gang members who have met certain criteria established by the department of corrections that documents them as confirmed gang members.

2. **Suspected members** The correctional agency feels that these inmates are members of a gang but has not acquired sufficient documentation to classify them as members.

3. **Potential members** The correctional agency feels that although there is not enough information at this time to classify an inmate in either of the other two categories, they should review the case in 6 months.

The increasing sophistication of inmates entering our prisons requires that intelligence not be limited to STG-related activity.

> [T]his "new" type of inmate [may have] . . . advanced technological skills in illicit communications, computers, security electronics, explosives fabrication, paramilitary tactics, and automatic weaponry. . . . [of] greater concern, particularly with the drug cartels, is the specter of extraordinary levels of outside tactical and logistical support. . . . [Security planning must consider] defense against outside assault and the use of helicopters in . . . escape efforts. (Trout & Meko, 1990, p. 16)

The complexity of the information required for a prison's intelligence system varies based on the extent and nature of the problems within that facility. To be effective, an intelligence system must be raised from the level of information "kept in the heads" of a few staff to a system that uses computers to organize and store the information. Two types of intelligence, strategic or tactical, compose a good information system. **Strategic intelligence** focuses on developing a detailed information base about the characteristics of STGs, their members, and activities. More specifically, it includes:

> Identification of gang members and gangs; validation of gang membership—recognition of factors such as tattoos; and information-gathering activities (research) and data analysis that is directed toward developing a better understanding of gangs, their activities, and even measuring their numbers. (Hart, 1999)

Tactical intelligence has to do with the daily routine of gathering and processing information. Specifically, for STGs, this involves focusing on drug smuggling, escapes, planned violence, work and food stoppages, and:

> identity of [STGs] . . . membership strength, recruiting efforts, recognition features [e.g.] tattoos . . . skill levels, tactics, outside support, treaties, feuds with other groups . . . foreknowledge of emerging STGs [just entering the system or prison]. (Trout & Meko, 1990, p. 18)

Intelligence information may be acquired from a variety of other sources, including (1) responsible informants; (2) dropout inmates who are repudiating gang membership (they are usually quite willing to provide information on gang operations and members); and (3) observation of visitors' dress, colors, and home address.

Effective strategies used in Texas have included designating intelligence officers for each unit to gather information for the administration and a special prosecutor whose mandate was to aggressively prosecute in-prison violence. Two new statutes that have helped this effort include classifying weapon possession among inmates as a felony and requiring that any inmate convicted of a crime in prison serve that sentence consecutively with the initial sentence. As Buentello (1992) noted:

> [T]he intelligence officer system lets gangs know we no longer were taking a reactive stance. [The result] was an increasing number of gang members willing to provide information. Individual gang members understood that if ordered . . . by their leaders . . . they would have to commit acts of violence and [be] subject to prosecution. As a result they would give information . . . allowing staff to stop potentially violent situations. . . . [Further], as gang members began receiving additional consecutive sentences, more inmates defected from the groups. They no longer believed that being in the gang was an advantage, and they became concerned about being prosecuted and receiving additional time. (p. 60)

However, it is important to note that all staff should be part of the intelligence gathering process, assuming the same role as gang detectives on the street (Fleisher & Rison, 1999).

Finally, establishing a national central depository serving as a clearinghouse and repository for information on STGs, their members, and activities would represent a valuable intelligence resource. Consistent with constitutional requirements, state statutes, and policies, this would involve state and local jurisdictions feeding information on STGs and their members into a centralized computer system, probably under the auspice of a federal agency. This would require a system of review to remove groups as they disband and members as they drop out.[12] Part of this effort would involve centralized screening for interstate transfers of known gang leaders and members so that the inadvertent spread of STGs can be controlled. This can be done through the development of an Interstate Compact Transfer Clearinghouse (ACA, undated; Camp & Camp, 1985).

A Management Approach to Controlling STGs To control STGs and make life less comfortable for their members, jurisdictions adopting an STG-specific management approach may place some of the following restrictions on inmates identified as members of these groups (ACA, undated; NIC, 1991):

1. *Conduct Searches* Conduct strip searches and cell and living area searches at least once every 7 days to control contraband and to look for any STG-related information (e.g., notes, graffiti, lists of customers). Some systems also use canines trained in detecting drugs, metal detectors to find hidden weapons, and urinalysis to control drug use.

2. *Monitor Mail and Telephone* Open and read incoming and outgoing (except legal) mail and monitor and record telephone calls for the purpose of detecting information on STG-related activity (e.g., incoming contraband, escape attempts, assaults, and murders).

3. *Increase Custody* Reclassify STG members to maximum security or to a special administrative segregation unit to restrict or totally stop their contact with the general population. In Texas, a policy of removing gang members from the general population and placing them in administrative segregation resulted in reduced anxiety and fear among the general inmate population and in the number of inmates requesting protective custody and unit transfers (Buentello, 1992). Nevertheless, ACA (undated) cautions that "locking up gang leaders or security threat group members in segregation units creates a void for new leaders to emerge and can lead to continuing disruption within the facility" (p. 2).

4. *Monitor Inmate Accounts* Well-organized criminal groups do not usually maintain large stashes of money, because it is evidence of their involvement in illicit activities and it is contraband in many prison systems. Thus, STGs transfer money to the accounts of members or maintain outside bank accounts. Monitoring these accounts can furnish details on gang activity—customers, suppliers, extortion victims, and

The cells of inmates identified as members of security threat groups may be searched at least once a week.

outside sources of funds—and can assist staff in short-circuiting some gang endeavors. For example, a large deposit or withdrawal may indicate that a major drug deal is about to "go down," which then enables COs to intercept the drugs before they enter the prison (Camp & Camp, 1988).

5. *Set Work or Program Limitations* Restrict or prohibit STG members from certain activities or require ongoing supervision in assigned program areas. STG members may be restricted from participation in any industry programs where weapons can be made or stolen, maintenance activities, and jobs outside the prison's perimeter. Additionally, monitoring program assignments can avoid placing too many STG members in one program, enabling them to gain control of it (Camp & Camp, 1988; NIC, 1991).

6. *Restrict Visits* STG members may have "no contact visits" to restrict the flow of contraband, which, as noted, can be smuggled into the prison by visitors in body cavities. Visits may be restricted to immediate family members—parents, siblings, and spouses (including common-law wives), and children—and to attorneys and their authorized staff. This can control use of intermediaries to pass information between prisons and from outside affiliates.

7. *Set Restrictions on Sentence Credits* Restrict STG members from receiving meritorious or extra good time and from having any forfeited good time restored. This penalizes inmates for membership in STG groups and thereby discourages membership.

8. *Transfer Within and Out of State* To disrupt and fragment STG operations and communication, some systems separate and isolate gang leaders by transferring them to other out-of-state or federal facilities.

9. *Highlight the Negatives* Another method used by some systems is to provide incoming inmates with information about the consequences of joining a gang and the benefits of nongang participation in other activities (see Figure 12.6).

Reducing Idleness Institutions must also develop more programs, particularly work programs, that provide inmates with a more attractive alternative to involvement in gang activities, including jobs with pay scales relative to inmate skills and motivational levels (Fleisher & Rison, 1999). Idle inmates have nothing else to do but plot ways to subvert the prison administration. Programs should be designed to provide inmates with more benefits than they receive from the gang reward structure. One reward that gangs cannot provide is early release, which can be extremely attractive for inmates with relatively short sentences and, for long-termers, work programs with the possibility of learning and job advancement (Camp & Camp, 1988).

Making Changes in Housing Design STG members, like other inmates, spend a considerable amount of time in housing areas and transact a substantial amount of their business there. Control strategies for managing these units include making changes in their design and size. Smaller institutions and housing units make control of all inmates easier. Inasmuch as gang strength is directly related to the amount of space they control, staff must control housing units. This requires units designed to facilitate maximum staff observation and supervision. Older prisons may require renovations, such as subdividing older cell blocks to reduce their size (Camp & Camp, 1988). At new maximum security prisons, smaller housing units resulted in a reduction in the number of inmate requests for placement in protective custody. Smaller units also permit the placement of nongang inmates in units where they will not be pressured to join gangs (Camp & Camp, 1988).

The availability of sufficient space to isolate inmates, particularly STG members who have behavioral problems, plays a major role in managing violence. Although all institutions require special detention or administrative segregation units, insufficient space to segregate violent inmates reduces the ability of staff to maintain control of the prison (Camp & Camp, 1988).

You know that gang behavior can be a ticket to prison. Do you know that gang involvement inside prison can put you and your family in danger?

What is a prison gang?

It's a group of inmates with a name, colors, symbols, and bylaws. Its members share common beliefs and goals, and they engage in criminal activity, including extortion, drug trafficking, assaults, and murder.

Why do gangs recruit members?

They need you. They need self-protection and control over other inmates, other people, and other gangs. Without members, gangs become weak.

How do they recruit?

By using you. By promising you protection, support, identity, rank, and power. By offering you a false sense of "family" and "love." And, if all that fails, by pressuring, intimidating, and threatening you.

What are the signs of gang membership?

Gang members identify—"represent"—themselves by wearing similar colors, jewelry, clothing, tattoos, and hair designs and by using hand signals. They use graffiti to claim their turf. They are aggressive and hostile. And they engage in criminal behavior, such as extortion, drug activities, and group and individual violence.

What has the Department of Corrections done about prison gangs?

It has designated nine prison gangs as "security risk groups":
- Latin Kings
- Nation
- Los Solidos
- 20 Love
- Brothers of the White Strength
- Aryan Brotherhood
- Neta
- Elm City Boys
- Brotherhood of Struggle

What happens to you if you become a member of a prison gang?

You will never:
- Become eligible for parole.
- Get a furlough.
- Get an extended family visit.
- Have your lost good time restored.
- Get meritorious good time.
- Be classified lower than level 3.
- Get a 7-day job assignment.
- Get an industries job.
- Work outside a facility.

You will have:
- Your lost good time doubled and get 20 days of punitive segregation for a Class-A disciplinary offense.

The department will:
- Notify the Board of Parole of your gang membership.
- Notify your family of your gang membership.
- Put you in a "close-custody" unit if you are considered a security threat.
- Notify state and local police when you are released.

What is a "close-custody" unit?

It's highly restrictive housing, where:
- You will remain in your cell 23 hours a day.
- You will have no contact visits.
- You will earn no good time.
- Your cell will be searched three times a week.
- You will not watch television.
- Your telephone calls will be monitored and recorded.
- Your mail will be read.
- You will not recover any forfeited good time.

What will a gang do to your family if you join?

Though a gang will call itself a family and claim to be family-oriented, it will:
- Demand money from your family.
- Harm them if they fail to follow orders.
- Force them to support gang drug activities.
- Subject them to arrest for supporting gang drug activities.
- Subject them to violence from other gangs.

What can your family do to help keep you out of a gang while in prison?

They can give you the support you need while in prison: financial assistance, if necessary, and frequent visits, letters, and telephone calls. And your family can constantly remind you of the dangers to them from your gang membership.

Figure 12.6 *The Negatives of Gang Affiliation*

Source: Connecticut Department of Corrections (1995, May). Wethersfield, CT: Author.

Supervising Housing Units The physical design of the prison is of little value if the lack of adequate supervision permits gangs to control housing units. Although the amount of direct contact and interaction with gang members varies, continuous supervision is generally required to maintain tight control (Camp & Camp, 1988).

Unit management provides an effective means of increasing accountability and of obtaining information on gang plans and activities. This involves permanently assigning staff to housing units, giving them decision-making responsibility, and placing them in direct contact with inmates as opposed to supervising them from a remote location such as a control booth (Camp & Camp, 1988). Increasing staff-inmate contact by placing them in proximity for longer periods of time can also help. This, along with training in identification techniques, enables staff to be aware of leaders and those inmates likely to do their bidding. These gangs are social groups, and, as such, are likely to hang together at work, in the yard, and in the dining room. This further assists in member identification (Fleisher & Rison, 1999). Also, staff need to be trained to be sensitive to "emerging security threats" so they can develop sight recognition skills to detect and deter them (Trout & Meko, 1990, p. 16). This training enables staff to perceive subtle changes in inmates, which may be indicative of impending assaults, and other activities, such as:

> hoarding of canteen [goods] and other preparations for lockdowns; unusual huddles; extreme quiet or extreme noise; rise in weapons confiscations; increases in requests for protection or transfers; unusual disciplines; fewer inmates going to meals and programs; more sick calls and "lay-ins"; parades and chants by gangs; more classification hearing requests; and increases in requests for personal interviews. (Camp & Camp, 1988, p. 48)

Unit management also facilitates the development of trust between staff and inmates, which can result in staff receiving information useful for preventing certain gang activities. Staff can also thwart the efforts of gangs to recruit new members by orienting new inmates with no prior gang affiliation to the disadvantages of gang membership, including its problems and risks, the privileges available to nongang inmates, and ways of handling pressure to join and avoiding extortion (Camp & Camp, 1988).

A Broken-Windows Approach to Prisons This approach was developed by Wilson and Kelling (1982) for community policing. They wrote that once a window in a building is left broken and unrepaired, all of the remaining windows will soon be broken because this signals that no one cares and therefore breaking other windows costs nothing. This observation is also applicable to the quality of life in prison. Fleisher and Rison (1999) argue that:

> cell house showers that do not drain well, toilets that do not operate properly, food that is badly prepared, recreation that is boring, inmate jobs that are menial, inmates stop talking to staffers, and staffers stop talking to inmates in a congenial [an environment in which inmates fear for their safety all of the time] way are a prison's broken windows. Small repairs that are not attended to create an environment well suited for the development and expansion of inmate gangs. The responsibility of senior leadership is to control an institution's climate, oversee [gang] management and other programs, and ensure that "windows" are always repaired. (p. 236)

Creating Alternatives for Nongang Members

How do we provide the general inmate population of STG-dominated prisons with the level of security mandated by federal courts under the Eighth Amendment? Inmates need an opportunity to make a rational choice about whether to join an STG. This can be accomplished by a prison system that has a series of prisons with decreasing levels of control. At one end of the spectrum would be an "STG prison," housing no more than 500 inmates. It would have a high level of direct supervision by staff, house inmates in small units, greatly curtail opportunities for inmate contact, and have few privileges and strict regulations. Not everyone agrees that an "STG" prison is an adequate method of control. Another position is that STG inmates should be managed utilizing confinement facilities throughout the system (Hart, 1999).

At the opposite end might be a village-type, minimum security prison, providing inmates with opportunities for involvement in a wide variety of educational, vocational, industrial, and recreational programs. This range of institutions would give offenders facing terms of 10 to 25 years a choice of how they want to spend their time (McConville, 1985).

The question facing prison administrators is to what extent they are willing to recognize and exert control over STGs. As we have seen in this chapter, a number of effective responses can be employed to make prisons with STGs safer and more manageable. Finally, the likelihood is that the number of STGs, particularly gangs, will grow because there are indications that street gang members presently entering prison are more likely to form their own groups than to join established groups.

Summary

Inmate gangs became a problem in the 1970s and 1980s. Conditions that facilitated their growth included freedom of movement, remote staff supervision, inadequate protection by staff, and poor control of profitable contraband. Inmate groups that engage in criminal activity have been labeled in several ways, including gangs and the larger category, STGs.

Prison gangs have developed according to five general patterns, although gang structure and membership categories vary from gang to gang. Similarly, recruitment and initiation processes also vary from gang to gang. Given their emphasis on loyalty, gangs have employed several mechanisms through which they are able to control their members' behavior. Through the services gangs provide to their members, as well as the nature of their criminal activities, gangs are able to perpetuate their existence and power. Individual members also benefit from the exchange of services, as they are protected and they have an "in" in the underground prison economy. Some gangs in prison also have street affiliates, with a few even meeting the criteria for organized crime groups.

Prison gangs present several problems for the staff, and although they are difficult to control, some mechanisms are in place to maintain order in the institution. The reaction to gangs typically falls under one of three strategies: denial, acknowledgment, or recognition. Several factors dictate the specific strategy used to control the gang. The first priority is to establish a policy and a strategy. Good intelligence can provide the necessary information to do this. Once an STG-specific management approach is implemented, the activities of STG members are restricted. The establishment of programs and activities may also reduce time that is otherwise devoted to gang activities. Changes in housing arrangements may also help. Of utmost importance, though, is the close supervision and staffing of housing units. These strategies may control existing STG or gang activity, while providing alternatives for nongang members.

Critical Thinking Questions

1. What is the distinction between a gang and an STG? How did they develop, and what conditions facilitated their growth?

2. Discuss various gang structures and how different membership categories may fit into the gang structure. How do gangs maintain their existence in a controlled institutional environment?

3. Why would an inmate want to join a gang in prison? What possible benefits might a gang offer him? What are some of the potential drawbacks?

4. Discuss some of the problems gangs present to prison staff. What are some reactions prison staff have had to gangs in their prison? Discuss what you see as the pros and cons of these reactions. If you were the superintendent of a prison, how would you deal with the problem of gangs?

Test Your Knowledge

1. _____ are two or more inmates acting together, who pose a threat to the safety of staff and inmates or are disruptive to programs or the orderly management of the facility.
   a. Street gangs
   b. Predatory gangs
   c. Security threat groups
   d. Hog gangs

2. Which of the statements below about prison groups is one of the National Institute of Corrections (NIC) criteria for the identification of gangs?
   a. has an organized leadership with a clear-cut chain of command

   b. engages in criminal or threatening activities
   c. places emphasis on member loyalty and group unity
   d. all of the above

3. The American Correctional Association estimated that _____ of the inmate population were members of a gang.
   a. 20%
   b. 6%
   c. 50%
   d. less than 2%

4. Which of the following prison gangs meet the President's Commission on Organized Crime criteria for an organized crime group?
   a. The Texas Syndicate
   b. The Outlaw Bikers
   c. The Black Panthers
   d. The Bloods and Crips

5. Most state department of corrections are in the _____ stage with regard to dealing with gangs.
   a. denial
   b. acknowledgment
   c. recognition
   d. segregation

Endnotes

1. The ACA (undated) decided to use this concept in their research for three reasons. "[First, their] advisory group concluded that the word 'gangs' could be misleading because it had many different meanings. [Second, their] . . . advisory group further recognized that a select number of correctional administrators deny 'gangs' exist in their system. [Third, because] the term 'security threat group' would be more universally accepted and would facilitate a higher response rate to project inquiries than the term 'gangs'" (pp. 1–2). The differences between the ACA conceptualization of STGs and the narrower definition of gangs by Camp and Camp may make the data from these two studies not entirely comparable.

2. The issue of the exercise of religious freedom in prison is dealt with in Chapter 17.

3. Krajick, 1980a, 1980b; Jacobs, 1977; Porter, 1982.

4. Camp & Camp, 1985, 1988; Fong & Buentello, 1991; American Correctional Association, undated; Fong, Vogel & Buentello, 1995, 1997.

5. Using the ACA directory, all 43 megajails (1,000+ population) were polled because they resembled prisons. Additionally, 10 jails were randomly selected from jails designated by the size of their inmate population as small (0–249), medium (250–499), and large (500–1,000). Responses were received from 46 jails: 31 mega, 5 large, 5 medium, and 5 small (ACA, undated). The number of STGs in jails ranged from 0 to 261 and averaged 20.4 groups. Prisons averaged 22.4 per jurisdiction, while the

range was 0 to 491. Thus, jails and prisons averaged about the same number of STGs. Regarding inmate involvement in STGs, the range in jails was from none to one facility reporting one third of its population as participants. Jail STGs averaged 14 members, which was about one third of the average in prisons. Finally, nationwide 762 different STGs were reported to be operating in our jails and prisons, of which 50 were identified as being present in two or more systems.

6. Alaska, Georgia, Kentucky, Louisiana, Maine, Montana, New York, North Carolina, North Dakota, Vermont, and Wyoming reported no gangs. Maryland's data were not authorized for release (ACA, undated).

7. The Black Gangster Disciples, Vice Lords, Black P Stone Nation, and Latin Kings.

8. The transfer of inmate gang members in California, better known as bus therapy, resulted in the spread of both the Mexican Mafia and La Nuestra Familia throughout the system, while in Illinois the transfer of members of the Black P Stone Nation, Black Gangster Disciples, Vice Lords, and Latin Kings had similar effects (Irwin, 1980; Jacobs, 1977).

9. We should note that for official identification purposes, within a correctional setting the categories employed include validated member, suspected member, associate member, wanna-be, and throwaway. Validated member and suspected member gang defectors will be discussed later in the chapter.

10. These researchers view this as preliminary data. They feel it raises many questions, including what is the meaning of "grew out of it" and "lost interest," because on the surface these seem like "fairly insane reasons to place one's life in jeopardy." Hopefully, more detailed research using in-depth interviews will clarify these questions.

11. See Chapter 15 for a discussion of the restrictions on inmate correspondence and Chapter 14 (the *Turner v. Safley* decision) for a discussion on the Supreme Court ruling related to inmate-to-inmate correspondence.

12. Other issues involved in the establishment of this system would include determining access criteria; developing agreed-on definitions and criteria for the veracity of information; and dealing with the problems of gangs with the same name but who are not affiliated, like the Aryan Brotherhood.

Custodial Personnel

13

Introduction

Correctional officers (COs) work in an environment unfamiliar to the vast majority of Americans. Even to most people working in other parts of the criminal justice system, COs represent the backbone of the prison because they serve key social control functions and provide human services to inmates, as well as security. In the past, COs have often seen themselves—and have been viewed by others—as being on the lowest rung of the criminal justice occupational hierarchy. Until the 1970s and 1980s, little effort was made to deal objectively with COs either as people working at a difficult and demanding job or as subjects of empirical studies. They are undoubtedly the most misunderstood law enforcement officers in the criminal justice system (Drennon, 1999).

Although this chapter focuses on correctional officers, it is important to point out that custodial duties are recognized as primary responsibilities of all staff, regardless of their positions within the correctional facility. For example, within the Federal Bureau of Prisons (BOP), every employee is a federal law enforcement officer with authority to conduct searches, seizures, and arrests and to use physical force, including deadly physical force, in conjunction with their duties. They are also authorized to carry firearms outside the institution. As with other federal law enforcement agencies, like the Federal Bureau of Investigation and the Border Patrol, they are limited by federal regulations. When considering this information, we can see why there is confusion about where custodial personnel fit within the law enforcement community. Further, there is a general misunderstanding by many researchers and writers of correctional texts about the primary purpose of employees within a correctional institution (Drennon, 1999).

Because prisons are isolated and are perceived to be dangerous, some people find it difficult to understand why anyone would want to work as a CO, especially given the social, psychological, and physical factors involved in this job. Specifically, these include the closed nature of the prison itself, its physical isolation, and the supervision of individuals who can be dangerous. However, in spite of the apparently negative aspects of the job, a 1996 survey found that two thirds of the systems reported having no problem recruiting qualified individuals for CO positions (Wees, 1996). This suggests that the individuals who take and keep jobs as COs may see the work as a challenge and feel a sense of pride in being able to successfully deal with the inmate population. In the remaining one third of the jurisdictions, the recruiting problems most often noted were low wages—candidates choose higher paying local or federal jobs—and a booming economy or low unemployment. Nevertheless, there is a relatively high turnover rate (averaging about 12%) among correctional personnel (Wees, 1996). In addition to the social, psychological, and physical factors associated with working in a prison environment, there continues to be a hazing process with new recruits, particularly among those who do not conduct themselves at an acceptable level. In essence, although recruiting qualified personnel has been relatively easy in recent years, keeping them employed within a prison system is an entirely different concept (Drennon, 1999).

In 1998, there were 223,023 correctional officers employed in state and federal prisons, most of whom were white males (ACA, 1999—see Figure 13.1a). Although the proportion of black COs is greater than their percentage in the general population, this fails to reflect the percentage of blacks in the inmate population (see Figure 13.1b). This has fueled criticisms of prisons as institutions in which whites imprison blacks and which are, therefore, racist.

Recruiting of Correctional Officers

In the past the recruitment and selection of COs was difficult because of low salaries, but this changed in the 1980s and 1990s as the level of pay grew close to that of police officers (see Table 13.1). Initial requirements for COs generally include a high school diploma or GED, ages 18 to 21, no felony or domestic violence conviction, residency within the state and U.S. citizenship, and previous work experience or additional education. Recent

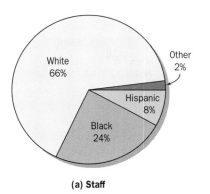

(a) Staff

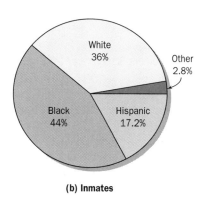

(b) Inmates

Figure 13.1 *Breakdown of Staff and Inmates by Ethnicity/Race*

Sources: ACA (1999); A. J. Beck (2000, April). *Prison and Jail Inmates at Midyear 1999*. Washington, DC: BJS, p. 10.

Table 13.1
Correctional Officers' Salaries, 1998

	Entry	Completion of Training	Completion of Probation	Maximum Salary
Highest	$32,000 (NY)	$36,000 (AK)	$36,792 (AK)	$57,648 (AK)
Median	$21,246	$22,303	$23,349	$34,648
Lowest	$15,000 (LA)	$16,296 (KY)	$16,639 (MT)	$22,381

Source: Camp & Camp (1998). *Corrections Yearbook 1998.* Middleton, CT: Criminal Justice Institute.

reductions in turnover rates and improvements in the wages and status of COs have made it easier to hire COs with good people skills (Wees, 1996). This has enhanced their ability to control inmates without resorting to force. As the time and cost of training of COs has escalated, the need to be more selective in recruiting quality COs and to retain them for longer periods has increased.

The 1980s boom in prison construction led to a large increase (37%) in the demand for new COs, which continued throughout the 1990s (Gilbert, 1999). Combined with a 12 percent annual turnover rate, the corrections field was one of the fastest growing sectors of government employment. As a result, the need for preemployment assessments increased. These assessments ensure that new CO applicants have the appropriate skills and traits to perform their jobs. Of 45 jurisdictions that conducted preemployment screening tests, all but one conducted background checks, 68 percent tested for drugs, and 39 percent conducted psychological screening[1] (*Corrections Compendium* [CC], August 1996). A later study reported that 47 jurisdictions conducted domestic violence screening (*CC*, August 1997). Table 13.2 shows New York's psychological screening rating scale. New York uses a combination of four tests[2] and one face-to-face interview to determine a candidate's psychological rating.

The CO occupation has generally appealed to individuals who are looking for job security, adequate pay, and a military type of environment (Wicks, 1980). More recently, it has attracted individuals interested in human services type of work (Gilbert, 1993, 1995). A career in corrections, because of the growth in the number of criminals being incarcerated, has been relatively easy to obtain, now pays relatively well, is secure, and has decent benefits.

The quasimilitary structure of jails and prisons appeals to a variety of potential workers. For retired military personnel looking for second careers, the prison—with its strict rules, its chain of command, and uniforms—offers a very comfortable and familiar work environment. However, some consider this an inappropriate structure for correctional work, because it does not enable correctional officers to successfully accomplish their objectives. Furthermore, there is a fundamental conflict between the paramilitary model and the reality of prison work as a human service field. Using a rigid military structure that places a premium on the ability of employees to follow orders reduces or eliminates their ability to use discretion. This is inconsistent with the actual methods used by COs to manage inmates. In reality, an officer's control over inmates depends largely on his or her verbal skills of

Table 13.2
New York State Procedures for Psychological Rating of Candidates

How the Contract Psychologists Evaluate Candidates

The candidates are evaluated by the interviewing psychologists across three major dimensions, Personal History (background), Personality Features as determined by Psychological Testing, and Key Job Performance Features:

I Personal History (background)	II Psychological Testing	III Key Job Performance Features
Education and training	Minnesota Multiphasic Personality Inventory-2 (MiN4PI-2)	Judgment
Employment history	NEO Personality Inventory (NEO PI-R)	Interpersonal skills
Driving record	The Quick Test	Level of responsibility
Legal history	Law Enforcement Screening Inventory (LESI)	Integrity
Financial history		Ability to follow regulations
Alcohol consumption		
Illicit/Controlled substances		
Aggression/Altercations		
Mental health history		

The final report integrates these three dimensions as well as how the applicant presented himself or herself during the structured interview. The report concludes with a rating of the applicant and his or her suitability for the position.

Source: State of New York, Department of Correctional Services (1998). *Psychological Screening Program for Correctional Officer Applicants.* Albany, NY: Author.

persuasion, effective use of coercive power, human relations skills, and leadership ability. (See Chapter 12 for a more thorough discussion of the differences between these models [Gilbert, 1997, 1999].)

Recent studies of CO job satisfaction (see, e.g., Cullen, Lutze, Link, & Wolfe, 1989; Hepburn & Knepper, 1993) indicate that many COs either derive more satisfaction from working in a human services capacity than a custodial one or are supportive of rehabilitation. This apparent shift in orientation may be a result of the changing nature of the CO applicant pool.

Cultural Diversity

Although it has been a long-term problem in corrections, increasing **cultural diversity** has become one of its newest concerns (Curry, 1993; Moriarty, 1991). Also known as *multiculturalism*, this view involves a

> recognition that it is neither necessary nor desirable for different ethnic groups to shed their cultural identities to participate in the larger community. [This reflects a] trend away from assimilation by way of the so-called melting pot, and toward the goal of a cooperative pluralism that enables each ethnic group to preserve its cultural identity without viewing others as a threat. (Cesarz & Madrid-Bustos, 1991)

Four trends are producing a more diverse population that will increasingly impact the American workforce, including corrections:

1. The workforce is aging significantly; by the year 2000 its median age will be 39. The correctional workforce, as well as the inmate population, will likewise become older.

2. The proportion of women entering the workforce will continue to increase. Thus, there will also likely be more female COs and inmates.

3. By the year 2000, the proportion of minorities entering the workforce will increase, for blacks by 29 percent, for Hispanics by 74 percent, and for other minorities by 70 percent. This argues for increasing numbers of these groups among correctional personnel.

4. More workers with disabilities will enter the workforce and will likely impact corrections through growth in the inmate population (Curry, 1993. Used with permission.).

Add to these trends the fact that the inmate population is also changing, and it makes sense for corrections to provide training that sensitizes staff to the cultural, sexual, and other differences of groups in their systems. "It is not enough to assume that familiarity leads to acceptance; education is essential to foster acceptance and overcome the tendency to regard others as threats" (Cesarz & Madrid-Bustos, 1991, p. 68). Further, from the standpoint of employment, it is predicted that in the early years of the 21st century there will be a shortage of skilled employees. This means that corrections departments, like other employers, will be at a competitive disadvantage if their recruitment fails to include men and women from all ages and racial or ethnic groups. Also, "staff must look like the inmates: the ideal is to have the same proportion of Caucasian, African Americans and Hispanics in staff and inmate ranks" (Carlson, 1999, p. 185). This will enable staff to better communicate with and relate to inmates and assess and predict inmate behavior (Curry, 1993).

In response to these trends correctional administrators have tried to include people of all races and both genders in the prison workforce. They have also become convinced that effectively managing correctional facilities depends upon being able to communicate with inmates, and that this requires staff who share and understand the racial or ethnic backgrounds of inmates (Carlson, 1999).

Training Correctional Officers

The need for specialized training for COs was initially recognized in 1870 at the National Prison Congress meeting in Cincinnati. However, is was not until the 1970s, with the help of federal funding through LEAA,[3] that junior colleges and universities began to offer programs that better enabled COs to meet the newer job requirements. Recognizing the need for better training, the U.S. Attorney General directed LEAA to establish a corrections academy, which resulted in the creation of the National Institute of Corrections (NIC) in 1977 (Gustafson, 1994). At the same time, judges began to order correctional agencies to implement or improve existing training programs. By the 1980s, less emphasis was placed on merely requiring training programs and more on the effectiveness of the training provided (Johnson, 1993b). Another factor that contributed to departments placing a greater emphasis on high-quality training is the legal liability jurisdictions may face if they fail to train their COs sufficiently. According to one court ruling, ". . . it is known to a 'moral certainty' that officers will be dealing with the constitutional rights of inmates (such as in using force, inmate discipline, conducting searches). And they could be held liable for failure to train" (*City of Canton v. Harris*, 1989).

To determine if supervisors are liable for inadequate training the following three-prong test was developed by the lower court in *Greason v. Kemp* (1990):

> (1) whether, in failing to train and supervise subordinates supervisors were deliberately indifferent to the plaintiffs' constitutional rights; (2) whether a reasonable person in the supervisor's position would know that his/her failure to train and supervise reflected deliberate indifference; and (3) whether his/her conduct was causally related to this constitutional infringement by his/her subordinates.

Formal training of custodial officers is provided by departments of corrections in each jurisdiction. Custodial officers also receive informal training through their everyday interactions with training officers.

Organizations such as the American Correctional Association (ACA), the American Jail Association (AJA), and the International Association of Correctional Officers (IACO) have also contributed to the professionalization of COs. By the mid-1970s, ACA was deeply involved in developing standards and accreditation programs for correctional facilities. Formal training for COs is offered by ACA at its biannual conferences and is buttressed by its journal, *Corrections Today*. AJA, which tends to focus on jail personnel, also contributes to CO training and professionalism through its journal, *American Jails*, its annual meeting, and its bimonthly training conferences for jail COs and managers. The IACO brings together correctional experts and COs for the purpose of enhancing CO professionalism. Its newsletter, *The Keepers' Voice*, provides a forum for COs. The IACO also developed a "Correctional Officer's Creed," which extols the virtues of professional CO behavior, and is presently pressing for the development of a standardized curriculum to be used in the training of COs (Hahn, 1994; Maghan, 1994). An-

other contributing group is the International Association of Correctional Training Personnel (IACTP), which developed the first standardized training certification program in the mid-1980s (Gilbert, 1999).

Correctional officers receive two types of training, formal and informal. Formal training is provided by departments of corrections in each jurisdiction, whereas informal training is furnished on the job and is accomplished in the daily interactions with special training officers as well as with inmates.

Preservice and In-Service Training

States generally require **preservice training** for new recruits before they assume their day-to-day responsibilities. This is followed by **in-service training** after employment to continue their professional development. Preservice training usually begins with classroom instruction, which averages 232 hours, but ranges from a low of 40 hours in Vermont to a high of 640 hours in Michigan (Camp & Camp, 1998). The preservice training curricula are generally uniform across jurisdictions. Many share common features, such as orientation, security procedures, first aid, weapons, offender management, communications, emergency procedures, physical training, report writing, self-defense, crisis management, substance abuse awareness, and special inmate populations (e.g., HIV/AIDS) (Vild, 1992; Wees, 1996). The median cost of CO basic training per officer was $1,500, with a range from $32 in Colorado to $10,000 in Oregon (*Corrections Compendium*, 1996).[4]

When considering the benefits and drawbacks of training for COs, it is important to recognize that academy-style training can only provide content that is generally applicable to all work locations. It cannot provide the specific information that is unique to a particular facility. On-site training at each facility is necessary to hone the general knowledge and skills developed at an academy training program. In short, recruits cannot be considered fully trained until after they complete both preservice academy training and **on-the-job training,** which provides facility-specific knowledge.

New officers also receive training in the general procedures used in each of the different duty areas within the institution. In addition, recruits are instructed in the ways inmates can place them in compromising situations or corrupt them to get them to violate institutional rules. Formal training gives new recruits the nuts-and-bolts knowledge of the day-to-day activities in which they will engage and a hint of the "realism of prison work" (Crouch, 1980). To complete training successfully, most jurisdictions require recruits to pass a test with a score of at least 70 and in some cases higher (*CC*, 1997). These higher standards along with pre-job screening and coursework provided by professional associations have facilitated the professionalization of the role of the CO.

Today, the role of all correctional staff, from new recruits to all levels of staff and administration combines the "duties of a police officer, social worker, security specialist, manager (upper, middle, and line level), teacher, and trainer" (Hill, 1997, p. 1).

Many in the field recognize the importance of continued staff development through annual in-service training within the facility, at outside workshops, seminars, and training programs and from specially developed correspondence courses. Thirty-nine jurisdictions make available some form of annual in-service training for COs (*CC*, 1997). This often includes:

> weapons, self-defense and security procedures training, racial sensitivity, social/cultural life styles of inmates and race relations, crisis management, narcotics and drug awareness, first aid, professionalism, inmate mental health and special populations, communications skills, legal issues/courtroom demeanor and supervisor/officer relationships. (*CC*, 1997)

However, it is important to note that in-service training can quickly become a joke to employees if they are continually repeating the same courses every year. The best program includes an array of core courses that requires annual refreshers and then a menu of elective courses (much like a college) from which employees can choose to satisfy their annual in-service training required hours (Gilbert, 1999).

In-service training ranges from 16 hours in Maine to 160 hours in New York; 36 out of the 51 jurisdictions reporting provide 40 hours (Camp & Camp, 1998).[5] This suggests that, despite the purported emphasis placed on training for the purpose of professional development, in reality it actually appears to have a low priority in most agencies. Johnson (1993b) notes that although "training may be high on administrators' wish lists, it is also high if not first on the list for budget reductions" (p. 16). With states worrying about finding money to house and maintain an ever-growing prison population, training often takes a backseat. Also, with many facilities already short-staffed, administrators may not want to take COs away from their assigned duties for in-service training because this might compromise prison custody and security. Nevertheless, with all the challenges and changes facing corrections, the need to place greater emphasis on career development through training and education will become more important. For agencies, this will result in greater use of employee skills, increased loyalty, better communication, and retention of valued employees (Rosazza, 1993, p. 11). Additionally, training or employee development is one of the few tangible ways agencies can motivate employees when promotions are slow and salary bonuses are not an option. This allows employees to develop a sense of professional growth, one way to motivate and retain highly competent employees (Gilbert, 1999).

A final aspect of improving the skills and capabilities of correctional officers is to encourage them to upgrade their education by taking college courses and pursuing advanced degrees. Rewards in the form of advancement and pay incentives can motivate them to do this. This can help advance professionalization and bring greater recognition and respect for the individuals engaged in this challenging task.

On-the-Job Training

On-the-job training for new recruits focuses on a "welcome to the real world" quality, which may contrast sharply with the "book learning" in the academy. Today, on-the-job training takes two forms: a structured training program and occupational socialization.

In most large agencies, structured training involves participating in some form of a Field Training Officer (FTO) Program. Although this is not classroom-based, it still requires the mastery of specific content and skills. Recruits are assigned to an institutional FTO who systematically supervises their development toward being able to operate without direct supervision. Daily reports document their progress and deficiencies.

A much less recognized form of training that is truly informal is the occupational socialization that occurs on the job outside of authorized programs. These experiences are just as much training as the highly structured "FTO" approach, but management has absolutely no control over the content, skills, or values that recruits are exposed to. In these cases, it is not unusual for recruits to be told to forget what they have learned in the formal program provided by the department and the institution (Gilbert, 1999).

When new officers enter prisons, their senses may be overwhelmed by the sights, sounds, and smells in their new work world. They may see the racial balance within their prison is heavily tilted toward minorities. They may not even be able to hear themselves think because of the cacophony of sounds (doors clanging shut, the prison's loudspeakers blaring orders). Added to this they may be bombarded by the mixed odors of urine, feces, disinfectant, sweat, and food. As they adapt to these sights, sounds, and odors they may find their attitudes toward inmates becoming more negative, a change which, depending on the CO subculture, may be reinforced by some of their coworkers. This socialization experience is largely outside the control of management.

Lombardo (1981, 1989) found that, in the 8 years between his two studies of corrections officers in a New York prison, changes had occurred in the relationships established between rookies and experienced officers. Prior to the 1980s, rookies were sometimes placed with a veteran officer only for a day or two before working on their own. The advice they received was often general and sometimes consisted only of "learn for yourself, the way I did" (Lombardo, 1981, p. 29). COs beginning their careers in the 1980s received a much more positive reception from experienced officers. This reduced the reliance of rookie officers on inmates to orient them to the prison world.

In his follow-up study of Auburn COs, Lombardo (1989) found that newer COs were more likely to maintain a greater social distance from inmates and go "by the book" in dealing with them. This increased social distance may well dampen any positive influence that COs may exert on inmates. However, Lombardo (1981, 1989) noted that because many jobs performed by COs placed them in isolated contact with inmates, they may discover that many inmates do not fit the usual stereotype applied to them. This discovery may make it easier for the new officer to accept help from inmates in dealing with unfamiliar routines and procedures.

The Roles of Correctional Officers

Today, COs must be able to balance their role as security officers and their responsibility to develop relationships with inmates to constructively change their behavior. "They routinely assume numerous essential yet sometimes contradictory roles (e.g., counselor, diplomat, caretaker, disciplinarian, supervisor, crisis manager) often under stress and dangerous conditions" (Josi & Sechrest, 1998, p. 11). COs are in the paradoxical situation of being the lowest level workers in the organization but having the greatest responsibility for managing and supervising inmates. The nature of their roles and attached responsibilities often places officers in ambiguous and conflicting situations with respect to inmates, administration, and sometimes themselves.

The development of officer work styles, or **working ideologies,** results from interactions with the other groups in the institution (Poole & Regoli, 1980). An examination of these relationships will provide a better understanding of the contemporary correctional officer. Gilbert's (1993) comparison of the work styles of police and correctional officers offers one perspective on different ways that individual officers approach their work (see Table 13.3 on pp. 308–309).

Relationships Between Correctional Officers and Inmates

Characteristically, the relationship between COs and inmates has been described as one of **structured conflict;** that is, it is a product of their organizational roles. This stems from attempts by COs to prevent disciplinary problems (Jacobs & Kraft, 1978). As a result of the need to be constantly alert to inmate violations, COs experience a great deal of tension. This, coupled with policy changes that have expanded prisoner rights, has created

a sense of frustration among COs. The policy changes, intended to protect inmates from abuses, are seen by the correctional officers as detrimental to their own interests and welfare. They feel that these changes have compromised their authority and safety (Poole & Regoli, 1980). As a result of their fears and frustrations, COs tend to deal with inmates on a more formal basis and have developed a defensive posture and a more negative attitude toward them.[6]

However, to reduce the number of inmate lawsuits, COs must develop a fundamental working knowledge of what the job entails based on law and agency policies. Further, they must not violate inmate rights and must remain within the limits of legal guidelines when interacting with inmates (Josi & Sechrest, 1998). The paramilitary model so prevalent in corrections is an inappropriate management model for prisons and jails. The discretionary power of line officers allows them to undermine most of the policies and rules unless they buy into them. Generally, this means that they must view them as consistent with their beliefs and value systems. Management cannot meaningfully direct officers to do anything—they must be persuaded that it is in their interests to cooperate and support management functions (Gilbert, 1999). See our Close-Up feature, "A Simulated Prison Experiment," for more insight into guard-inmate relationships.

Gilbert (1999),[7] on the basis of 25 years of experience working with COs, asserts that the negativism and "enforcer" (punitive) demeanor seen in COs is a public facade that they take on because it is expected of them. In reality, Gilbert feels that COs are much more likely to respect and emulate their colleagues who are able to use communication skills, human decency, and concern about inmate welfare to control their inmate charges. If the **CO subculture** is indeed characterized by these humanistic concerns, it is likely that COs will welcome and socialize into their group recruits who can emulate them. In doing so, they will reduce the danger and stress in their work environment.

Gilbert's view may be right because a certain degree of understanding exists between COs and inmates, and many COs still attempt to help inmates when problems arise, at least within the guidelines established by the institution. A CO at Auburn, New York, put it this way:

Before I'd help out with a problem I'd try to see what he's tried on his own. . . . If he's working for me and he did go through proper channels, I might tell him to wait a couple of days and then, if he doesn't hear, I'll check it out. If it's a money problem [I'll] have him bring his printout and I'll go over it with him, and if there is a problem, I'll handle it. I take the time for a good worker because they can't pay him more than $1.55 and this is a benefit. Overall, there's a lot more formal procedures now, but I've been around, and I

A Simulated Prison Experiment

The objective of this experiment was to determine whether the dehumanizing characteristics of prison result from (1) inmates who bring with them a disregard for law and order, preformed social conventions, and a propensity for impulsivity and aggression and guards who are sadistic, uneducated, and insensitive to people, or (2) if the behavior of the guards and inmates is a product of organizational roles that confer on them differential power roles.

To determine which of these premises is correct the researchers hired 22 young, mostly middle-class college students who were randomly assigned to the roles of guard and inmate. The guards were given no instructions but that they were to gain the respect of prisoners and maintain law and order. They were placed in a replica of a prison that included barred cells. Guards were given khaki uniforms and reflective sunglasses, while inmates were forced to wear stocking caps, simulating shaved heads, and prison clothing.

It soon became evident that despite their lack of experience those assigned to the CO role assumed an authoritarian stance in interacting with inmates, soon becoming aggressive and sadistic. They made inmates clean out toilets with their bare hands, they walked them into doorjambs, forced them to move boxes from one closet to another for hours, subjected them to strip searches, and placed them in solitary confinement. Further, as time went on guard aggression no longer was a reaction to perceived threats but now became "a natural consequence of being in the uniform of a guard and asserting the power inherent to the role" (p. 87).

The inmate role players immediately adopted a passive role when interacting with guards. Nevertheless, as guard abuse intensified inmates reacted with spontaneous disturbances, strikes, barricading doors, bad mouthing, and other actions directed at harassing the guards.

The researchers concluded that the relationship between guards and inmates is one of structured conflict; that is, their behaviors are a product of their organizational roles. The behavior of guards is a result of their being placed in positions of power while inmate behavior reflects their subservient positions. This type of abusive power will occur in any institution where one group of untrained individuals is given power and authority over others. Thus, the cause of this abuse is the absence of organizational norms or supervisory controls that view this behavior as unacceptable rather than the nature of the correctional institution.

Place yourself in the position of a guard or an inmate. How do you believe you would react under these circumstances?

Sources: C. Haney, C. Banks, & P. Zimbardo (1977). Internal dynamics in a simulated prison. In R. G. Leger (ed.). The Sociology of Corrections: A Book of Readings. *New York: John Wiley and Sons, pp. 65–92; W. Archambeault & B. J. Archambeault (1982).* Correctional Supervisory Management: Principles of Organization Policy and Law. *Englewood Cliffs, NJ: Prentice Hall.*

---

know where and how to get hold of people. Kind of going beyond just getting information. That's what happens when you've been here for 20 years. But I don't abuse it. It's a matter of habit, even though it's not policy. Procedures were set up because of the constant abuse, to keep people (officers) under control. (Lombardo, 1989, p. 87)[8]

Lombardo indicated that for some COs more formalized relationships have replaced more personalized, informal relationships. "Helping is now 'part of the job,' but helping is now limited by suspicion and concerns for procedure rather than being limited by more general human concerns" (Lombardo, 1989, p. 87).

A different view is espoused by Gilbert (1993) in his study of CO work style preferences. He found that a majority of COs tend to perform their jobs in a highly professional manner. This included consistently enforcing the rules but making some reasonable exceptions when necessary. As noted earlier, it also involves being genuinely concerned for the human condition of the inmates. If Gilbert's findings are correct, this would imply that the social distance between the keepers and the kept may not be as great as Lombardo has suggested. Gilbert attributes the differences between his view and Lombardo's (and others) to the fact that COs maintain the facade noted earlier (negative and punitive attitudes toward inmates) because they do not want to be perceived as "soft" on inmates.

This is supported by Demmon (1999) who indicates that the requirements of correctional personnel working for the BOP are to maintain the highest level of integrity and ethical standards and perform their duties without allowing their experiences to become personal. One way of handling inmates is in a clinical manner. COs perform their duties without allowing themselves to get caught

Table 13.3

Comparison of Muir's Typology Descriptors—Police and Corrections

Type	Police Officers	Correctional Officers
Professional Description • Is calm • Is easygoing • Is open • Is nondefensive • Makes exceptions when warranted • Is willing to use coercion and force as a last resort but prefers to gain compliance through the use of human communication skills	• Develops the beat • Takes educated risks • Provides citizens advice on law and government • Increases pressure over time to correct behavior • Uses arrest as a last resort • Tries to preserve the dignity of citizens through the use of nondemeaning behaviors and attitudes • Views offenders as not much different from self • Empathizes with the human condition of citizens and offenders • Allows for exceptions in his/her own behavior and that of others • Uses coercion and force judiciously • Is calm and easygoing • Is articulate and open • Focuses on attaining justice for individuals	• Develops the unit • Takes educated risks • Provides inmates advice on rules and regulations • Increases pressure over time to change behavior • Uses the "write-up" as a last resort • Tries to preserve the dignity of inmates through the use of nondemeaning behaviors and attitudes • Views offenders as not much different from self • Empathizes with the human condition of inmates • Allows for exceptions in his/her own behavior and that of others • Uses coercion and force judiciously • Is calm and easygoing • Is articulate and open • Focuses on ensuring due process and decency in security and control tasks
Reciprocator Description • Is calm • Is easygoing • Wants to help people • Assists persons in resolving their problems • Prefers to use clinical/social work strategies • Sometimes inconsistent in making exceptions • Prefers to "go along to get along" • Tends to reject or avoid the use of coercion or force even when it is justifiable	• Allows local "toughs" to keep citizens in line—a mutual accommodation • Uses clinical/social work strategies to help people "worthy" of assistance • Rationalizes situations • Attempts to educate, cure, or solve the citizen's problems • Has low tolerance for rejection of offered assistance • Is easily frustrated • Fails to use coercion, even when it should be used • Gives inconsistent job performance • Is stymied by irrational behavior by citizens • Displays a superior attitude toward others • Is highly articulate	• Allows inmate leaders to keep the unit quiet—a mutual accommodation • Uses clinical/social work strategies to help inmates "worthy" of assistance • Rationalizes situations • Attempts to educate, cure, or solve the inmate's problems • Has low tolerance for rejection of offered assistance • Is easily frustrated • Fails to use coercion, even when it should be used • Gives inconsistent job performance • Is stymied by irrational behavior by inmates • Displays a superior attitude toward others • Is highly articulate

(continued)

Table 13.3

Comparison of Muir's Typology Descriptors—Police and Corrections (continued)

Type	Police Officers	Correctional Officers
Enforcer Description • Is "by the book," rigid • Enforces aggressively • Seeks out violations actively • Makes exceptions only rarely • Has little empathy for others • Takes unreasonable risks to personal safety • Sees most things as good or bad • Tends to be quick to use threats, verbal coercion, and physical force (including deadly force)	• Enforces the law aggressively • Makes many arrests • Seeks out violations actively • Uses force or excessive force • Tends to view order maintenance and service functions as not part of police work • Has a strict enforcement orientation, limits service and order maintenance duties • Displays little or no empathy for the human condition of citizens/offenders • Is often the object of citizens' complaints • Is rigid, rule-bound, makes few exceptions even when appropriate • Maintains a dualistic view of human nature (good–bad; cop–criminal; strong–weak) • Dislikes management • Postures for effect • Displays Crazy Brave/"John Wayne" behaviors, takes unnecessary risks	• Enforces the law aggressively • Issues many "tickets" • Seeks out violations actively • Uses force or excessive force • Tends to view treatment functions as what others do with or for the inmates • Has a strict security and control orientation, limits service delivery duties • Displays little or no empathy for the human condition of inmates • Is often the object of inmates' filed grievances • Is rigid, rule-bound, makes few exceptions even when appropriate • Maintains a dualistic view of human nature (good–bad; officer–inmate; strong–weak) • Dislikes management • Postures for effect • Displays Crazy Brave/"John Wayne" behaviors, takes unnecessary risks
Avoider Description • Is nervous • Minimizes contact with offenders • Chooses often not to see an offense • Tends to avoid confrontation and the use of coercion • Views interpersonal aspects of the job as not "actually" part of the job • Is frequently inconsistent in work behaviors • Backs down in a confrontation • Blames others for his/her problems	• Is likely to leave situations as quickly as possible • Tends to view most functions as not being "real" police work or part of the job • Uses the patrol car to reduce contact with citizens • Is often the last to arrive in response to an emergency • Plays the "phony" tough and frequently backs down • Tends to blame others for avoidance behaviors or inadequacies • Structures the work to reduce chances of observing offenses and use of coercion • Avoids confrontations	• Is likely to leave situations as quickly as possible • Tends to view human communications with inmates as not being part of security and control • Uses the mechanical aspects of security and control to reduce contact with inmates • Is likely to be among the last to arrive at an emergency scene • Is likely to select tower duty/isolated positions away from inmates • Plays the "phony" tough and frequently backs down • Tends to blame others for avoidance behaviors or inadequacies • Structures the work to avoid observing infractions and use of coercion • Avoids confrontations

Source: M. Gilbert (1993). Discretionary Workstyle Preferences Among Correctional Officers: Implications for Correctional Training and Management. Paper presented at the Annual Meeting of the Academy of Justice Sciences. Kansas City, MO.

up in personal dialogue with inmates. This allows them to handle situations impartially without becoming emotional and allows a professional foundation to exist between the inmate and the correctional employee. Inmates tend to play a multitude of games and when COs handle a situation clinically, they are able to evaluate the situation more intensely and thoroughly before acting. One mistake commonly made by correctional personnel is that some become lonely during their shifts and talk to inmates about their personal lives. Inmates view correctional officers as the "police," and the unauthorized information received from correctional personnel can be used to compromise the position of correctional staff, including weakening the solidarity among staff in the institution.

A Role in Policy Making

The organizational structure of correctional institutions is generally based on a quasimilitary bureaucratic hierarchy in which inmates occupy the lowest position and administration the highest, with correctional officers in between.

Lombardo (1981), using measures of job satisfaction and role strain, found that the New York COs he studied saw themselves at the bottom of the hierarchy. Hepburn (1987) also found that job satisfaction for correctional officers was tied to their perception of the level of influence they had within the institution. The greater they perceived their influence to be (and that of administration) vis-à-vis inmates, the greater their job satisfaction. In his 1981 study, Lombardo suggested that any management strategy that would allow COs to assist in policy-related decisions would significantly reduce COs' dissatisfaction. By 1989 he found that these changes had occurred at Auburn. Thus, improved advancement opportunities, greater recognition for their work, and more opportunities for input resulted in much higher levels of job satisfaction. Hepburn and Knepper's (1993) findings cast additional light on the changing role of COs. They found that the COs they studied who were human services–oriented were more satisfied in their role than those who were custody-oriented. Human services–oriented officers (HSOs) "advise, support, console, refer or otherwise assist inmates with their problems and crises of adjustment produced by imprisonment" (Johnson & Price, 1981, p. 316).

They also felt that the satisfaction of HSOs derived from some of the intrinsic rewards of the work, the degree of authority they had over inmates, their autonomy, and the informality of the job. Thus, the everyday duties of HSOs involve high levels of friendliness, informality, and interpersonal skills. These COs pursue a more direct and routine contact with inmates and assist them in solving their problems. This creates a more active and self-directive job, which enables these COs to use their skills and abilities in working with inmates. Their authority is based on their relationships with inmates and on using their interpersonal skills to maintain order and help solve problems (Hepburn & Knepper, 1993). These findings support the views espoused by Gilbert (1993, 1995).

In contrast, the authority of security-oriented officers derives from the uniform they wear. Their relationships with inmates are more formal and distant. They control inmates by employing the limited rewards and sanctions at their disposal and choose to suppress rather than solve inmate problems. In this work style, COs are dependent on administrative and legal systems to provide the formal mechanism that enables them to control inmates (Gilbert, 1999).

It is not surprising that HSOs derive more satisfaction from their work; they are actively using problem-solving skills to assist and control inmates, which is more satisfying than simply policing inmates. Further, more highly educated COs are more likely to be human services–oriented (Jurik, Halemba, Musheno, & Boyle, 1987). This suggests that as corrections attracts more highly educated recruits, CO orientation will likely shift even more in the HSO direction. This also implies a greater emphasis on professionalism. This may also require a shift in orientation for administrators, because more highly educated and professionally oriented staff will want to be more involved in the organizational decision-making process. Failure to allow these COs more input in decisions may result in more disgruntled workers and affect the stability of the institution.

The Correctional Officer Subculture

The work environment of COs would appear to foster a strong, tightly knit *CO subculture,* but there is some controversy as to whether this is the case (Gilbert, 1993, 1995; Lombardo, 1989; Poole & Regoli, 1980). Obviously, the nature and strength of this subculture varies from institution to institution. Gilbert (1995) believes that beneath the tough independent exterior, the CO subculture is held together by mutual respect engendered by COs' ability to control inmates without coercion. Thus, they share the feeling that, by their behavior, they are responsible for one another's safety and for the well-being of the entire facility.

Two reasons exist for the absence of a strong CO subculture. First, interaction among officers tends to be minimal, usually occurring briefly between shifts, during staff meetings, or in the dining room. Because officers tend to work alone in their assigned areas (e.g., cell blocks, prison shops), they tend to remain isolated from one another. The second reason is the perceived expectations of administrators (and many officers), who feel that officers should be self-reliant and autonomous. Personal accountability may be stressed more than cooperation and collective responsibility. When this is the case, it leads to reduced opportunities to develop close working relationships among officers (Poole & Regoli, 1989). Although the nature of COs' work will continue to isolate them from one another, group solidarity may increase if more COs adopt a human relations orientation and prisons provide officers with more opportunities to contribute to organizational decision making (Gilbert, 1993, 1995; Hepburn & Knepper, 1993). Our Close-Up feature, "The Officer Subculture," examines the CO subculture.

Correctional Officers' Assignments

The complexity of the correctional officer's job has changed from earlier times when they were merely expected to watch the inmates, count them, lock them in, supervise them in the prison yard, or sit in a gun tower. Lombardo (1981) identified seven general categories of job assignments, based on their location in the institution, the duties required, and the type of contact with inmates. Each of these is examined briefly.

1. *Block Officers* Officers who supervise inmate living units are referred to as *block officers*, or sometimes as dormitory officers if they oversee multiple-occupancy living units. In the cell blocks, which may contain as many as 300 to 400 inmates, these COs supervise and care for inmates, lock and unlock cells, make rounds to inspect cells and other areas, and handle inmate problems as they occur. They also su-

pervise inmate cleanup crews, distribute linens and clothing, and attempt to maintain some degree of order and security. Supervising inmate living quarters, which are intensely personal for inmates because this is their "home," requires officers with highly developed interpersonal skills and an ability to calmly deal with inmate problems and confrontations without creating unnecessary enemies by being hostile, demeaning, aggressive, or quick to use force. Officers who possess such traits increase the likelihood of violence among inmates and between officers and inmates, which threatens security and control.

2. *Dormitory Officers* These officers perform similar functions except they work in a more stressful environment because they are sometimes surrounded by as many as 80 to 100 inmates and have no means of temporarily isolating inmates who become belligerent or assaultive. Their only option is to have the inmates removed to administrative segregation (i.e., a solitary confinement unit). However, in some prisons, COs who do this may be perceived as unable to control their units.

3. *Work Detail Supervisors* These officers oversee inmate work crews, act as inventory managers, order and distribute supplies for inmates, and keep account books. *Industrial shop* and *school officers* generally

A block officer monitors two adjacent cell blocks in the Suffolk County Jail from a central control area. Supervising inmate living quarters requires highly developed interpersonal skills.

Using interview data gathered from a study of two midwestern state prisons, Farkas (1997) explored the extent to which officers are expected to conform to certain informal norms of behavior. This officer code engenders solidarity among officers, providing clarification of action and a means of modifying or rejecting formally proscribed modes of action, regulating forms of behavior, and allowing officers to make supportive and meaningful helpful relationships based on a commonality of action and values. Although norms were evident in both prisons she studied, some norms were given greater weight in urban versus the town prison. She identified eight norms that officers consider to be the most salient. Vignettes from the interviews will be used to illustrate the norms.

Norm 1: Always go to the aid of an officer in real or perceived physical danger.

For most officers, helping an officer in physical danger was the most commonly mentioned norm. This was clearly demonstrated in the responses to scenario 1 in which a fellow officer appeared to be having trouble resolving a situation with an inmate. Correctional officers felt obligated to help the officer even though the situation hadn't escalated to a physical confrontation. Their main reason for this show of support was to avert an incident and to display solidarity to coworkers.

As one officer pointed out,

> We have to help each other in an emergency—that's all there is to it. We *have* to be there for one another. We're all in the same boat, so to speak. I couldn't come into work every day if I didn't know that help was there if I needed it.

Norm 2: Don't get too friendly with inmates.

"Becoming too friendly with inmates" was another key concern. At "Urban Prison" this norm appeared stronger because it was more frequently mentioned as unacceptable behavior. The possibility of manipulation by inmates or corruption of authority were the main explanations. The following is an illustration:

> One of the women I work with calls the inmates "her guys." She'll walk in and say, "How are my guys tonight?" I think that you have to keep a certain distance. This is not kindergarten, and these are not choir boys. She thinks I am too tough with them (inmates). If they want anything they ask her and she'll give it to them, too.

Maintaining social distance was also emphasized when correctional officers were asked what advice they would give to a new officer. For instance,

> [To Officer] Remember that you are not their buddy. You can be nice, but remember that you have a job to do. You've got to keep a professional distance.

Norm 3: Don't abuse your authority with inmates. Keep your cool.

Belittling inmates, playing games with inmates, or acting overly punitive toward inmates were regarded as inappropriate and as an abuse of authority. This norm was emphasized in scenarios 2 and 3, which concerned confrontations with inmates:

> Screaming or swearing at an inmate, calling him names; it's just not professional. I worked with a guy who lost his temper a number of times. He viewed inmates as scumbags and treated them accordingly. He'd get out of control and I'd make him walk away

to cool off. Nobody liked him because he was a liability; he could cause a major incident with his attitude.

Newer officers were encouraged to stay calm and "keep their cool" in altercations with inmates because this places officers and other staff in danger.

Norm 4: Back your fellow officers' decisions and actions; don't stab a coworker in the back.

Backing a coworker's decision or action in an incident with an inmate(s), *whether or not the officer agrees with it*, was also important, particularly for respondents from "Urban Prison." This was clearly apparent in results from scenario 1 in which an officer appeared to be having trouble resolving a situation with an inmate. "Fronting," which is essentially questioning or criticizing an officer *in front* of inmates, is frowned upon by most officers. There was a strong sentiment of supporting the officer while not undermining his authority. As an officer elaborated,

> You might have handled things differently, but you don't contradict your fellow officer. Someday it might be *you* on the hot seat. Training can't possibly cover all the shit that happens here. You've got to make a decision quickly and sometimes it isn't the best one.

> "Blues" are supposed to stick together, and at times that means covering for each other. We all make mistakes.

The protocol is that *if* an officer has a problem with a coworker, he should go directly to that officer and try to resolve the situation. "Squealing" to management can result in ostracizing from other COs. Just as inmates despise a snitch, so do correctional officers.

Norm 5: Cover your ass and do not admit to mistakes.

A frequently voiced concern about "covering your ass" was also identified. It was more prominent in responses by participants from "Urban Prison." Correctional officers reported "learning quickly" that they must not admit to mistakes. If an officer writes up a report admitting an error in judgment, sergeants who review the reports will be quick to point out the transgression of the normative code. The justification for this norm is that if one officer admits to a mistake it reflects on other COs. The fear is that supervisors will assume that *other* officers are implicated in the situation or that increased managerial scrutiny is necessary.

Norm 6: Carry your own weight.

Many officers complained of coworkers who did not do their job and of having to "pick up the slack." This sentiment was stronger at "Town Prison," where more experienced officers frowned on COs who left work unfinished from another shift. The general feeling was that if there is a problem on a shift, it should have been resolved before the new shift started.

Norm 7: Defer to the experience and wisdom of veteran COs.

It was very important to experienced correctional officers that new COs acknowledge their expertise. This was a stronger norm at "Town Prison." "Know-it-alls" and "gungho" types were disliked and joked about by veteran staff:

> There's nothing worse than the "know-it-alls"; they fall on their ass every time because they go off "half-cocked" thinking they know how to handle a situation. Sure we laugh at them, but they really irritate us because we're the ones who have to settle the unit down after they screw up.

It was presumed that new COs would seek advice and approval from older officers. This was an important way of socializing new officers to the way things were done at the prison or on a particular unit.

The type of prison work experience or assignment was also salient. Those officers who had experience working in a maximum security prison or segregation unit felt they were a "special breed" and should be respected for it.

Norm 8: Mind your own business.

Gossiping about other officers or "telling tales" was disfavored by many officers. This is a by-product of the "no blue against blue" sentiment. Spreading rumors about officers at work and nosing into their personal life were equally disliked:

> One male officer was spreading rumors about a female officer having an affair with a married sergeant. Nobody really listened to him; we just thought he was an idiot. We didn't invite him to go out after work anymore, because we felt that whether or not it was true, he just couldn't be trusted.

> Gossiping was also prohibited because "inmates have big ears." Inmates could use the information to obtain special favors or simply to cause trouble between two officers. This places the officers in a compromising situation.

> One big thing that an officer should never do is to badmouth or talk about another officer in the presence of inmates. This gives inmates something to hold over your head. They can "play on it" and cause all sorts of trouble.

Conclusion

Results from each prison suggested that the code was similar; however, the weight attached to certain norms varied by prison. The degree of emphasis placed on a norm is related to the threat or uncertainty perceived in relations with coworkers, inmates, or management. For respondents from "Town Prison," the norms of carrying one's weight (6) and deferring to the wisdom of veteran officers (7) were more salient. This may be attributed to the more experienced officers at the facility, many of whom had worked at other prisons. For many of them, following work norms and interactions with coworkers were the most important issues. The relatively stable administration at "Town Prison" may have ameliorated concern with managerial scrutiny. Alliances with supervisors had had time to develop in the prison's 10 years of existence.

For officers in the sample from "Urban Prison," inmates and management were alternately perceived as threats. This is evident by the emphasis placed on certain norms: "Don't get too friendly with inmates" (2); "Back your fellow officers' decisions and actions" (4); and "Cover your ass" (5). This may be due to the recent, extensive, year-long drug investigation of inmates and officers at the prison. Officers have learned to be wary of inmates and their manipulations. Backing a coworker and "covering one's ass" may also be norms that emerged in response to the atmosphere of mistrust generated by the drug probe and the administrative problems at the facility.

Source: Adapted from M. A. Farkas (1997). The normative code among correctional officers: An exploration of components and functions. Journal of Crime and Delinquency, 20(1), 23–36.

perform order maintenance and security functions. They tend to work in groups of two or three, usually in conjunction with civilian foremen, industrial supervisors, teachers, and counselors. They are in charge of groups of inmates, ranging from as few as 30 to as many as 300. Their functions include taking counts, checking the whereabouts of absentees, designing and maintaining record-keeping systems for inmate payrolls, and managing inmate interactions, problems, and complaints.

4. *Yard (compound) Officers* spend most of their time dealing with security matters and maintaining order. They are responsible for observing inmates and controlling rule breaking in the yard or recreational areas. Although this is an easy task in small groups, it can be very difficult and potentially dangerous in a yard, in which several hundred inmates may be roaming around freely. In this situation it may be hard to determine if a rule is being broken, which inmates are involved, and how to take disciplinary action without causing a disturbance. The fact that officers assigned to yard duty usually have the least seniority and experience makes this an even more dangerous situation. This is because more experienced officers have the seniority to obtain jobs that involve less or no inmate contact.

5. *Administrative Officers* These officers have little, if any, contact with inmates. They normally work in the administration building and deal with such tasks as handling finances, processing paperwork, working the switchboard, and controlling keys and weapons. They are indirectly involved with security and usually only when emergency situations arise.

6. *Perimeter Security Officers* These officers occupy the wall posts and guard towers, go on mobile outside patrols, or monitor electronic security devices. They usually spend their 8-hour shift watching the facility's perimeter to prevent escapes and the intrusion of contraband. This removes them from the ongoing activities inside the prison. A major problem with this job is boredom. Newer prisons have generally opted to use mobile patrols and electronic motion sensors to provide perimeter security, because this is more cost effective than towers both from the standpoint of construction and labor (NIC, 1987). Most institutions use two patrols during active program hours and only one when inmates are asleep. Towers are manned 24 hours a day. If electric fences become more commonly used this may reduce or totally eliminate the need for these officers (see Chapter 15).

7. *Relief Officers* These officers perform a variety of jobs in the institution, filling in for other COs who might be on sick leave, on vacation, or taking days off. Because they move throughout the institution, they are likely to have no personal identification with any one task and may find it difficult to establish personal relationships with inmates or with other officers. The exceptions are the relief officers who work in the same areas on a weekly basis. For this reason these positions are often rotational rather than permanent; these officers only work relief positions for a few months then go back to a permanent assignment (Gilbert, 1999).

Controlling Inmates

With respect to social control, prisons are like any other community in that they have rules and regulations and mechanisms for their enforcement. Rules and regulations vary from prison to prison but cover almost all aspects of inmates' daily routines from the time they arise until lights out at the end of the day. These rules are usually specified in inmate handbooks, which also contain the sanctions for those found guilty of violating these rules. The "law" (control and order) is maintained by COs through a variety of custodial and disciplinary processes. Custodial processes are daily activities and procedures designed to control and keep track of the inmates. Disciplinary actions are responses to the breaking of rules and regulations.

Custodial procedures also include the control of prisoner movement within the institution; movement in and out of the institution; counts; searches, shakedowns, and other forms of contraband control; and supervision of living quarters, work, and any other activities. Control of prisoner movement in institutions varies according to their custody level. Inmates' custody designations determine their freedom of movement within the prison and the conditions under which they can move around without supervision. More recently, inmates have been issued nonremovable wristbands with bar codes that identify them, and they are scanned as they enter and leave specific locations so that their location is always known. This is a technological innovation that has enabled prison management to better control inmates (Gilbert, 1999).

Keeping track of inmates at any given time is an important custodial function that is accomplished through counts. Counts are conducted several times during the day and night at specific hours. At maximum security prisons, counts may occur as often as every 2 hours, whereas at minimum security facilities they may occur as few as two or three times every 24 hours. During the count, inmate activities in the prison usually stop until the location of every inmate is determined. If all inmates are accounted for, the count is cleared and normal activities resume. If any inmates are unaccounted for, there is an immediate recheck, and escape proceedings are initiated if they remain unaccounted for.

Searches of individuals and their cells, often called "shakedowns," are conducted at frequent irregular intervals in most facilities. Their purpose is to discover contraband. Many things can be defined by the institution as contraband, including many innocuous items as well as those that are obviously dangerous. Because maintaining order is a paramount objective, these searches may take precedence over inmates' Fourth Amendment rights.[9]

Control of tools and keys is very important, especially in maximum and medium security prisons. The easiest way to control tools would be to ban them from the prison. However, this is not feasible because certain tools are needed to perform required maintenance, in the various industries, and in vocational training classes. Control is achieved in various ways (e.g., careful check-out/check-in procedures, searches of inmates, use of metal detectors). Inmates who are assaultive are not usually permitted to work in areas such as the kitchen and shops where knives and tools are available. Keys are also subject to rigid control. When one is lost, locks must be immediately changed to retain control of that particular area.

Contraband often enters through the visitation process, so procedures are put in place to control it. These procedures include restricting visitor lists; denying contact visitation, particularly for those inmates in maximum security facilities; searching all visitors before entering the visiting park; and searching inmates returning from the visiting park. The search of incoming materials, including mail, for contraband is also a standard practice. Nevertheless, the most common and reliable route for contraband entry is for staff to be bribed to bring it in for inmates (Gilbert, 1999).

Disciplinary Procedures

Rule violations, resulting in some formal action by correctional personnel, are quite common. A 1986 survey of state prisons found that 53 percent of the inmates had been charged at least once under their current sentences, and the proportion of violators had remained constant over a period of time (Stephan, 1989). Violators were typically younger, had more extensive criminal careers and/or drug histories, were housed in larger or maximum security prisons, were more likely to be recidivists, and slightly more likely to be male. Whites were as likely as blacks to be charged and disciplined. Research shows that about half the rule violations they studied involved administrative infractions (e.g., being in the wrong place, insolence), one fifth dealt with contraband, one fifth entailed violence without injury, while the remaining 10 percent were incidents of escape or of violence with injury (Petersilia, Honig, & Hubay, 1980).

When an inmate commits an infraction, the CO dealing with the problem has several alternatives, depending on the system in which he or she works and the nature of the violation. In general, the more serious the

violation the fewer alternatives are available to officers in dealing with the incident (Gilbert, 1999). In Florida, for example, the officer may issue a verbal warning; a corrective consultation (CC), which is a written reprimand that becomes a part of the inmate's record; or a disciplinary report (DR), which requires a formal hearing and can result in a sanction if guilt is determined. If an inmate breaks a state law, the case may be referred for prosecution to the state attorney in the jurisdiction in which the prison is located.

The courts have consistently ruled that inmates can be subject to prison disciplinary proceedings as well as subsequent criminal prosecution without incurring double jeopardy. The rationale is that the two punishments serve different purposes (i.e., to maintain prison discipline and to uphold the criminal law) (Krantz, 1988; Mushlin, 1993; *United States v. Smith*, 1972).

An inmate receiving a DR will be interviewed by one of the duty sergeants to determine the inmate's version of the offense and to get a list of witnesses to be interviewed. A formal disciplinary hearing follows, conducted either by a hearing officer or a hearing team, to "try" the case and make a determination of guilt or innocence.[10] If the inmate is found guilty, a sanction is imposed, and the DR becomes a part of the inmate's file. If found innocent, the DR is destroyed. Depending on the seriousness of the disciplinary breach, the inmate may be kept in administrative confinement while awaiting the hearing. Stephan (1989) reported that 94 percent of all inmates charged with violations of prison rules were found guilty.

The formal consequences of rule violations and criminal acts run the gamut from none to the death penalty. The more common consequences involve loss of privileges, loss of good time (in jurisdictions that award it), and confinement in a disciplinary unit. Good time is accumulated by all inmates except for those serving minimum mandatory sentences and those in disciplinary confinement. Loss of good time, or the inability to accumulate it, means that inmates will serve a longer part of their current sentence. Our Close-Up, "The Federal Disciplinary Process," provides an example of the processes associated with one jurisdiction's disciplinary actions.

Controlling Violence

Both the custody and disciplinary procedures discussed may help contribute to prison social control, but in the final analysis it is the ability of COs to put these procedures into action that dictates the extent to which they will work. As Cohen (1991) notes:

> The best video monitoring system in the world never broke up a fight in an exercise yard. The most modern construction cannot prevent a suicide. Computerized security scanning cannot prevent escapes. It is

The Federal Disciplinary Process

CLOSE-UP

The Federal Bureau of Prisons (BOP) refers to Disciplinary Reports as Incident Reports (IR). These are used by all federal correctional personnel, including physician assistants, correctional treatment specialists, and chaplains. When a violation of the regulations is observed by a federal officer, he or she is required to respond but can use discretion in handling the violation informally or formally with an IR. The greater the degree of violation, however, the more likely the event will result in an IR.

The BOP has four levels of prohibited behavior, with 400-level incidents (the lowest, least severe) to 100-level incidents (the highest, most severe). The 400-level incidents are generally handled by staff informally. They include assigning the inmate violator to additional duty. The 300-level incidents may be resolved informally, but they may also result in the loss of such privileges as commissary, telephone, and special housing. One hundred–level incidents include fighting, possession of a weapon, and assaulting an officer. These incidents can result in a transfer to a higher-security facility, or prosecution, or both.

Three and four hundred–level violations are generally handled through the Unit Disciplinary Committee (UDC). However, the UDC is unable to take away good time or hear certain categories of inmates who have committed 300-, 200-, or 100-level violations. These committees are chaired by a staff member who is trained in proper hearing procedures in order to ensure that due-process requirements are met. The 100- and 200-level IRs are generally handled by the disciplinary hearing officer (DHO). The DHO can take good time away from the inmate and impose other sanctions that are also available through the UDC. The DHO generally has responsibilities to hear cases at more than one institution.

Source: Prepared especially for Corrections: A Comprehensive View, *2nd ed. by Don Drennon, who currently works for the Federal Bureau of Prisons.*

the people who watch the video monitors, walk the pods or mods or quads, and read and interpret the computer printouts who stop fights and prevent suicides and escapes. It is the officers who spend their shifts in living units talking to and watching inmates or wards who are the real fail-safe mechanisms. (p. 88)

In dealing with violent or potentially violent situations, correctional workers must be prepared, verbally and physically, to handle the situation. Rice, Harris, Varney, and Quinsey (1989), as a function of their work in an institution for the criminally insane, developed a training program designed to help those working with violent individuals. Their program, which consists of training in violence prevention, includes several security guidelines: learning verbal "calming" techniques; dealing with individuals who are "blowing up" either by "defusing" their violence verbally or controlling them through physical intervention; and conducting a postviolence analysis, which pinpoints the causes of the incident and reestablishes a relationship with the perpetrator. They found that institutional personnel who had been trained to use their program could not only defuse these situations but also suffered fewer injuries than those who were untrained (Rice et al., 1989).

Thus, although some contend that correctional facilities are paramilitary organizations where staff maintain control by rigid enforcement of the rules, Gilbert (1999) argues that a CO's control over inmates depends mostly on his or her verbal skills of persuasion, effective use of coercive power, and human relations and leadership ability to gain voluntary cooperation in the maintenance of security and control. Use of force is a last resort and, when employed, should involve the minimum needed to achieve inmate compliance. This is further illustrated by the two scenarios presented in our In Their Own Words feature, "Controlling Violence by Defusing an Incident."

Female and Minority Correctional Officers

During the last few decades many correctional systems in this country have been required by the Equal Employment Opportunity Commission and other related affirmative efforts to hire minorities and female correctional officers. This has altered the traditional white male CO structure of many prisons. Many white male COs reacted strongly to and resisted the introduction of these minority and female officers into the prison. This hampered or retarded their assimilation into the officer workforce (Crouch, 1980; Owen, 1985).

Individuals from minority groups now constitute approximately 34 percent of the correctional officer workforce (ACA, 1999). As argued earlier, the diversification of the CO workforce will likely strengthen it and help it better deal with the demographic changes predicted for

Controlling Violence by Defusing an Incident

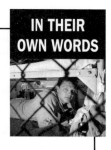

IN THEIR OWN WORDS

Scenario 1

While working as a compound officer, Officer Drennon came upon an inmate who had been recently transferred to the institution. This particular inmate had a history of assaulting federal law enforcement officers. The inmate was in an area behind UNICOR industries on a loading dock (this area was considered "out of bounds"). Officer Drennon told the inmate to get back inside the building and that he was not allowed to be out on the loading dock. The inmate responded, "If you want me inside you put me inside." This inmate's physical stature was large and had the officer engaged in a physical confrontation with the inmate there is little doubt that he would have sustained physical injury when, in fact, this was avoidable.

This was a beautiful day, with a blue sky and a few white fluffy clouds, and it was a warm day with a cool breeze coming over the mountain where the institution was located. Officer Drennon looked toward the sky, looking from left to right, and said to the inmate, "I don't know why you would like to ruin such a beautiful day. We can get into it and you'll get a couple of licks in and I'll get a couple of licks in, but you know that when assis-

tance arrives they will kick the hell out of you and drag you to seg. So, I don't know why you would want to ruin such a beautiful day." At that point, the inmate looked toward the sky, looked around for a moment, looked at the officer and said, "OK." At that point the inmate went inside the building.

The importance of this lesson is that a firm stand and a human compassionate approach can de-escalate an otherwise potentially violent situation.

Scenario 2

One afternoon during lunch period, a new officer was with Officer Drennon shaking down inmates entering the dining room. This was done within an area between two large doorways with two large doors at each doorway. A particular inmate refused to allow himself to be searched and, while screaming and yelling, was able to walk through the second set of doors into the dining hall. Although the new officer and Officer Drennon were able to restrain the inmate from getting any further into the dining hall the inmate managed to create a disturbance at a few other tables, each table containing at least four inmates. The inmates at the tables began to yell and bang their trays on

the table. Noticing the potential for a riot to ensue, Officer Drennon leaned over and whispered into the new officer's ear. Officer Drennon instructed the new officer to follow his lead and lock the doors behind them as they passed the large doors. At that moment, with one sweeping motion, Officer Drennon grabbed the inmate while going through the double doors and the new officer locked the doors behind them. The inmate was searched, put into restraints, and escorted to segregation for a 30-day commitment.

The inmate had been charged with inciting a riot, refusing an order, and assaulting an officer (which was done when getting away from the officer to go through the double doors into the dining hall). The action taken by Officer Drennon and the new officer was considered to have prevented a major disturbance within the institution.
Source: Prepared especially for Corrections: A Comprehensive View, *2nd ed. by Don Drennon (1991), who worked for the Federal Bureau of Prisons.*

---

the early 21st century. In that respect, a consideration of the following changes in the CO workforce in adult institutions between 1982 and 1999 is enlightening:

1. There was about a 968 percent increase in the number of women working as correctional officers. In 1998, they constituted almost 32% of the correctional officer workforce.

2. There was a 336 percent increase in the number of African-Americans in the CO population. However, the increase in their percentage of the CO population was very small (1.2%).

3. The number of Hispanics in the CO workforce increased by 634 percent. However, their percentage

of the CO population only increased by 5 percent (ACA, 1983, 1994, 1999).

If these trends continue, the CO workforce will indeed become diversified. The hiring of minority officers will not only diversify the CO workforce but may also have a salutary effect on the corrections field. Research by Jackson (1992) indicates that minority COs, in addition to reducing the "white keeper–minority inmate" image of corrections and providing appropriate role models, may bring a less punitive orientation toward inmates into the correctional environment.

Another factor associated with CO perceptions of the work environment is the racial composition of the inmate population and the sex and racial composition of the custody staff. "Those who work in institutions in which there are a high proportion of minority inmates and/or a high proportion of white male custody inmates, perceive the work environment more negatively in almost all respects" (Britton, 1997, pp. 99–100). This is most evident in facilities with high proportions of white COs that also have a lower proportion of white inmates. White women COs do not perceive the work more negatively than males. For them, a positive evaluation of their supervisors ultimately leads to significantly higher levels of satisfaction with their work environment (p. 100).

These results suggest that job satisfaction and job stress are produced by different factors, which depend upon racial or sex differences. Thus, for example, black male officers may feel more comfortable working in facilities in which minorities dominate the population, which translates into greater job satisfaction (Britton, 1997). This suggests that different approaches need to be tailored to different groups if we want to decrease job stress and improve satisfaction.

Female Correctional Officers in Male Prisons

Women have served as correctional workers from the time of the Walnut Street Jail, where Mary Weed was the principal keeper in the 1790s, to the present (Morton, 1992b). Their roles in corrections have, however, been limited until recently. Before the early 1970s, fe-

male COs worked almost exclusively in prisons for women or in the women's section of jails. The number of female officers employed in men's prisons began to increase when the Civil Rights Act was amended in 1972 to prohibit discrimination in the workplace. In 1993, women constituted about 17 percent of the correctional officer workforce. This increased to 31.6 percent in 1998 (ACA, 1994, 1999). In January 1998, an average of 82 percent of the female COs in 47 jurisdictions were working in male institutions. Nevertheless, resistance to female COs has been especially strong when it involves their working in higher security men's institutions.

Title VII of the Civil Rights Act of 1964 was used by women to overcome discriminatory hiring in the criminal justice field. Nevertheless, this act provides that if **bona fide occupational qualifications** (BFOQ) exist for a position, women could be excluded from a job if those BFOQs were based on gender. However, using a person's sex as a reason for denying them a job on a BFOQ basis has been very narrowly defined. Collins (1993) suggested that "a good [justified] example . . . might be . . . a single-sex post in an institution . . . where the post (specific task) involved very close scrutiny of inmates in states of undress. In this situation use of officers of the opposite sex of the inmates would be seen as an invasion of inmates' privacy rights" (p. 125). Thus, only rarely can a person's sex be legit-

Women have served as correctional officers since the 1790s. Only rarely can a person be denied a correctional job on the basis of sex.

imately used to deny them a job on a BFOQ basis. In most cases, doing so represents discrimination.

The barriers women have faced in attempting to compete with men for positions in corrections have included the Veterans' Preference System, physical requirements, sexual stereotyping, the issue of equality of assignment between the sexes, concerns regarding the safety of women in male correctional environments, and inmate rights to privacy (Bernat & Zupan, 1989; Rafter & Stanko, 1982; Walters, 1990).

The Veterans' Preference System   The underlying rationale of the **Veterans' Preference System** (VPS) has been to reward veterans for their military service and assist them in readjusting to civilian life. Civil service jobs, which include corrections officer positions, use the VPS as an inducement for veterans to apply. Because relatively few women have been in the military, they cannot receive the VPS points on hiring or promotional exams and are consequently discriminated against.

Physical Requirements   Until they were banned by the courts, physical requirements, such as minimum height, weight, and strength, were used by many corrections departments to exclude women from CO positions. Many male officers resented the intrusion of women into what they felt was a male domain, characterized by a masculine value system that promoted a macho image of those working in prison (Anderson & Richardson, 1996). They also felt women were too weak physically to protect themselves or their fellow officers in situations involving inmate violence. A male CO in Oregon reflected this view:

> I don't believe a woman should hold down a correctional officer's job that means coming in contact with prisoners. If I'm in trouble out here, particularly in the yard, and I blow my whistle and here comes some woman running up to me, this isn't a very good help at all, and I don't care whether she's a black belt or not. As you know, if somebody slapped her on the jaw it would probably bust up her face. She doesn't have the strength, number one. Number two, some of these men—and I'm sure I would feel the same way after being here so long—actually have the urge, they haven't been around women. I think it's just temptation to put a sexy looking broad working around them. (Fox, 1982, p. 68)

Some male COs fail to consider that many male officers may also not fare well in these situations by virtue of their age, weight, and lack of exercise. However, as a result of the Court's decision in *Dothard v. Rawlinson* (1977), states can no longer use height and weight as BFOQs in the hiring of COs. This means neither males nor females can be denied employment on the basis of their size.

The view by males that female COs would be unable to defend themselves or respond during a crisis does not reflect reality. Research shows quite the opposite. Two studies done several years apart suggested that female officers are actually less likely to be assaulted in male prisons than male COs. The first national study in 1992 found that, in 48 jurisdictions responding, women working in maximum security male facilities were only assaulted 27.6 percent as often as males (Rowan, 1996). Table 13.4 shows the results of a second study conducted in 1994 in which 48 states, Washington, DC, and the federal government responded to questions about male and female COs working in maximum security male institutions. The study found that 1 in 8 male officers was assaulted compared with 1 in 30 female officers. It also found that female officers were at least as firm as their male counterparts in placing inmates in segregation, with 6.7 percent of male officers using this form of punishment versus 6 percent of female officers. Various reporting officials, predominantly male administrators, have suggested that female officers listen better, seldom act macho, have a calming effect, are less confrontational, and often exercise control without using force. They also pointed out that assaulting a female officer does not enhance an inmate's reputation with other inmates (Rowan, 1996, pp. 188, 189).

These results mirror the findings on female police officers, which show (1) male police are much more likely to use force in confrontation with a suspect because of the macho factor, and (2) women consider the use of force a failure. Thus, they are more likely to use persuasion and try to talk to a suspect (Hawkins, 1999).

Further, research conducted with police found that women can train themselves to achieve a level of strength and fitness well within the normal requirements of the police profession (Holeman & Kreps-Hess, 1983). If this is the case, there is no reason to believe that female correctional officers could not do the same.

Sexual Stereotyping   Research shows that newer male correctional officers and those with more education and on-the-job knowledge are less concerned about this issue than older, less educated officers (Fox, 1982). It also

Table 13.4

Inmate Assaults on COs by Sex

Officers		% of Total	No. Assaulted	% Assaulted
Total	16,072	—	—	—
Male	14,105	87.8	1,735	12.3
Female	1,967	12.2	946	3.4

Source: R. Rowan (1996). Research perspectives: More female correctional officers mean fewer assaults overall—another myth debunked. *Corrections Today 58*(2), 186–189.

found that newly hired male COs were more likely to accept women COs as equals than "old timers" (Simon & Simon, 1993). Further, younger COs believe women perform as effectively during violent incidents and other emergencies as males (Lawrence & Mann, 1998). This was supported by data showing that women were not assaulted or injured any more than their male counterparts (Lawrence & Mahan, 1998, pp. 80–81).

The older COs may have more concerns about women working in male prisons because they subscribe to a subculture that believes that women have no business doing "men's work." In contrast, newer officers' acceptance may reflect the corrections system recruitment strategies that include a greater acceptance of diversity and more favorable attitudes toward inmates. Thus, these new officers have more positive attitudes toward rehabilitation. Changes in recruitment training and officer orientation may also have contributed to less resistance to women officers working in male facilities (Lawrence & Mann, 1998).

Equality of Assignments   Males are also threatened by female COs going after their jobs in male prisons. Women seek jobs in male facilities because they outnumber and are often larger than female facilities, thus providing greater opportunities for better work, shift assignments, and promotion.

Safety   **Sexual safety** is another sexist rationalization offered by male officers for not assigning women to direct contact positions in male prisons. Fox (1982) suggests that this perception by male COs that inmates have "uncontrollable" sexual desires that will put female COs at a risk of rape may partly reflect their own sexual appetites, which are constrained by social and organizational restraints.

Male officers may be concerned for the sexual safety of women, but Fox reported that this concern is not shared by female officers (1982). Many female COs have reported that they viewed the possibility of sexual assault as a job-related risk and were much less concerned about it than their male counterparts. A number of female officers indicated that they had accepted the threat of sexual violence in the prison in the same way as they had in the community.

Inmates have generally reacted positively to the presence of women because of the calming effect they have on male prisoners and their ability to reduce tension and hostility in the prison, providing a better living environment. Female COs tend to gain voluntary compliance from inmates by using mutual accommodations and friendly relationships with inmates. Further, with women around, inmates improve their appearance and language; also, in some instances, they are more polite to female COs (Anderson & Richardson, 1996; Lawrence & Mann, 1998).

Cross-Gender Surveillance and Searches   Although some inmates have welcomed the improved atmosphere of male

facilities that female COs bring, others resent being reminded of their sexual deprivation by the constant presence of women. Many inmates do not want to be watched by women when they are engaged in activities such as going to the toilet, showering, and sleeping. One Delaware inmate summed up the dilemma: "The issue is, should you let her (the woman CO) come down on the tier and violate my rights, or keep her off the tier and violate hers?" (Potter, 1980, p. 30).

The issues of opposite-sex observations and **cross-gender searches** of inmates have usually involved male inmates objecting to the presence of female officers on the grounds of their right to privacy. In deciding this issue, the courts have had to balance inmate privacy rights against the provision of equal employment for female COs, reasonable attempts to accommodate an institution's need to allocate responsibilities among male and female officers, and security concerns (Mushlin, 1993). The courts have tended to view female CO employment rights as more important. At the very least, they have allowed inadvertent or infrequent viewings by opposite-sex COs of inmates who are naked or using the toilet (Krantz & Branham, 1991). Some courts have gone further, approving a prison policy allowing female COs to be assigned to areas where they might see inmates partially or totally nude, showering, being strip-searched, or using toilet facilities. They ruled this did not violate male inmate rights (*Grummett v. Rushen*, 1985). Under those circumstances women could be assigned to supervise men in these areas.

Another area of concern regarding privacy involves opposite-sex searches by COs. The courts have allowed female officers to pat search male inmates, even to the extent of brief touching of the groin and anal area (e.g., *Timm v. Gunther*, 1990). It may be justifiably argued that sexism and insensitivity to women, including the rights of women to be employed in equal numbers with the same advancement opportunities, in the correctional system have historical precedent. Nevertheless, attention has been focused on the impact of discriminatory double standards on both male and female inmates. Rigid traditional notions regarding cross-gender supervision would preclude such assignments as women supervising males in a dormitory situation, while they shower and use the bathroom. At least one court (*Jordan v. Gardner*, 1992) has found it unconstitutional for male COs to frisk female inmates, although the reverse does not hold true (*Timm v. Gunther*, 1983; *Jordan v. Gardner*, 1992).[11]

Those that argue for a double standard, in which females can search males but males cannot search females, contend this is justified for several reasons (Farkas & Rand, 1999):

- Most women in prisons do not pose the same danger as men because they are more likely to be arrested for nonviolent or drug-related offenses, and violent female offenders are more likely to direct their violence against victimizers than a stranger.

- Most women in prison have suffered emotional, verbal, physical, or sexual abuse at the hands of their families, boyfriends, and strangers. Therefore cross-gender searches in prison can potentially replicate the suffering these women have experienced on the outside. Thus, these searches by male officers could cause psychological harm. For example, a clothed body search by male officers may be traumatic to abused women because it is suggestive of the control males had over them on the outside and of their powerlessness and helplessness in the face of abuse.

- Allowing men to search women would have the potential of reversing the rehabilitative effects of survivor or empowerment groups for abused women. These programs enable women to adjust to life on the outside by learning various coping skills, such as recognizing abusive patterns and ways of breaking these patterns.

- This would acknowledge the potential for sexual exploitation, which could be heightened by the opportunity that these searches provide male officers.

Based on all these reasons supporters of a double standard conclude that male searches of female inmates constitute cruel and unusual punishment.

At least at this point it would appear that the lower courts take the following stance: If the inmate is male and the search or surveillance is done by a female CO, there is no constitutional violation. This does not hold if a male officer searches a female inmate. However, the courts have failed to clarify what roles male officers can play in searching females.

COs and Unions

Unionization in the corrections field began in the 1950s but was slow to develop, particularly outside of the Northeast. This was because many states either had laws prohibiting these types of employees from organizing in this manner or prohibiting them from striking. It was not until the 1970s, when some of these restrictions began to be eased as a result of court decisions, that collective bargaining became a reality for many in the field (Fisher, O'Brien, & Austin, 1987). Correctional officers are represented by a variety of groups, including the American Federation of State, County, and Municipal Employees (AFSCME), the International Brotherhood of Teamsters (AFL-CIO), the Police Benevolent Association (PBA), and a variety of state and local employee organizations, for example, the California Correctional Peace Officers Association. In some institutions treatment and custodial staff have been represented by different unions, a condition resulting in conflicting goals

Corrections officers are increasingly joining unions and protesting low pay and dangerous working conditions. This demonstration took place in Palestine, Texas, in February 2000.

CLOSE-UP

The California Correctional Peace Officers Association (CCPOA)

Founded in 1957 by a small group of Correctional Officers at San Quentin State Prison in California, the California Correctional Peace Officers Association (CCPOA) was formed as an association to foster the increased professionalism of those engaged in the field of corrections.

Correctional law enforcement employees of the Department of Corrections (CDC) and the Department of the Youth Authority (CYA), as well as parole agents and medical technical assistants (MTAs), who have historically been aligned with the correctional officers, make up the totality of present-day membership of the association.

As of 1998, the California Correctional Peace Officers Association had a membership of over 26,000 officers in the State of California. These officers come from 33 adult correctional institutions, 11 juvenile institutions, statewide parole offices of both the Departments of Corrections and the Youth Authority, as well as the officers and supervisors of 43 conservation camps statewide (39 adult and 4 young adult).

CCPOA is structured on a chapter basis, wherein the local membership with each institution or facility elects by ballot a chapter board of directors. Within each board, the chapter president of each facility or group also sits on CCPOA's state board of directors. Currently, CCPOA's state board of directors' meetings include more than 50 chapter presidents and executive officers. The paid employees of the association are directed by and answer to the membership through their respective chapter presidents and state executive committee. The association is divided into departmental functions, which include the Labor Department, Legal Department, Legislative Department, and the Logistics section. Each of these areas reports and answers to the membership via the state board of directors. Each of these departments addresses the needs of the correctional officer in his work with the employer, the State of California, and responds accordingly through the processing of grievances, negotiations, meetings, conferences, investigations, and representation in hearings, maintaining adherence to the "Memorandum of Understanding," and in carrying out the daily fiduciary operation and responsibilities of the Association.

CCPOA has long been very active in the California legislature and has been able to build a strong and effective lobbying force in the state capitol. These efforts have been successful in obtaining the passage of major sponsored legislation, which has been designed to upgrade the working conditions of the state's correctional peace officers. Specifically, CCPOA spends a great deal of time working with the legislature on statewide issues of prison construction and public safety, in an effort to ensure that the design and operation of institutions reflects the utmost in safety for the public as well as for the officers who will work within those institutions. For example, it has recommended that California build "mega" prisons, which would cluster three or four smaller prisons at the same site as

---

and actions by the two groups. A 1993 *Corrections Compendium* survey (1994b) of the District of Columbia, the Federal Bureau of Prisons, and all states reported that in 32 of these jurisdictions correctional officers were represented by a union. Our Close-Up, "The California Correctional Peace Officers Association," provides an overview of one of the larger unions.

Reasons COs Join Unions

An important question is, "Why do correctional employees join unions?" One reason they join is because they are uncertain about their job security. Privatization of some correctional facilities will mean working for a nongovernment entity that does not provide the same benefits and has no obligation to provide job security. New technology, such as electric fences, may reduce staff. Other major issues for CO unions include the threat of HIV/AIDS exposure from a highly infected inmate population and the dangers created by understaffing.

Factors that may contribute to a successful union organizing campaign include:

- Introducing major changes in organizational structure, job content, equipment, or operating practice without providing advance notice or subsequent explanation to employees.

- Giving employees little or no information about the status of important events at the institution or about its plans, goals, or achievements.

- Making key decisions without knowing the employees' true wants, needs, and feelings.

opposed to building each at a different site. It is anticipated that this will save 10 to 15% in construction costs because this allows the consolidation of kitchen facilities, warehouses, administrative services, medical and dental facilities, libraries, and other infrastructure needed to support prison operations. This would be more cost efficient from both a construction and an operating standpoint. For example, instead of building four small kitchens a central kitchen can be built to serve all facilities. CCPOA recognizes and supports the view that intermediate sanctions can reduce prison intake. But it will only be effective as long as the community resources are available to provide the necessary supervision and support. Regarding COs, CCPOA has sponsored legislation to professionalize peace officer classes. It has even suggested pay cuts for beginning officers to fund more extended training.

CCPOA is a leader in the area of demanding quality screening, hiring, and training and maintaining retention of quality correctional officers. At present, CCPOA is working diligently, in cooperation with state officials, to develop, obtain funding for, and identify curriculum and training modules that will become CPOST—Correctional Peace Officers Standards and Training—a formalized and accredited standard for the future selection and training of correctional officers in the State of California.

Also, and equally as important, CCPOA has assisted the victim's rights movement and many responsible individuals and groups seeking to see law changes for many years. CCPOA has supported them in their dealings with the legislature and in making their issues heard in the state capitol. Being ever so knowledgeable of inmate rights, CCPOA tries to assist the victims of crime and the public of California in maintaining their personal and property rights as law-abiding citizens. The intent is to safeguard those inmate rights as are deemed appropriate by the legislature and the Courts but also to "level the playing field" with regard to the rights of the public for safety and security and to establish and maintain the rights of the victims of crime.

Some of the many voluntary efforts of CCPOA members include youth programs for at-risk children; scouting and youth organizations; city councils and community boards; the March of Dimes; safety programs, such as child fingerprinting and safety training; the Kevin Collins Foundation for Missing Children; Big Brother/Big Sister and like mentoring programs; the American Cancer Society; the Doris Tate Crime Victims Bureau; and many, many other programs and fund-raising events for the less fortunate residents within the community.

Source: Adapted from materials provided by Bob Kirchner, President, Camps Chapter of California Peace Officers Association, West Sacramento, CA.

- Using pressure (authoritarian or autocratic leadership) rather than true leadership (consultative or participative leadership) to obtain employee performance.
- Disregarding or downplaying instances of employee dissatisfaction. (Phillips & McConnell, 1997, p. 409)

Where unions exist, the contractual agreements with the jurisdictions may give employees certain rights relating to grievance procedures, seniority and job assignments, overall working conditions, and layoffs. However, unlike labor management negotiations in private industry, the subjects open to bargaining are controlled by state law. Typically, these laws allow bargaining over working conditions and personnel-related matters. Generally, both workload and safety are considered by unions to be mandatory subjects to be dealt with in the bargaining process. Issues that are viewed as managerial are not open to negotiation (e.g., applicant qualifications).

Concerns of Unionized COs

The issues that concern corrections personnel differ from those that concern union members in other areas (Potter, 1979). For example, a strike in the New York system a few years ago focused on deep, long-standing issues relating to working conditions and participation in the decision-making process rather than on economic factors. In corrections, the labor-management relationship involves an element (i.e., inmates) that is missing for other labor groups. The recent growth of prisoner rights and privileges has been seen by COs as a loss of their own rights and of a lowering of their status both in the eyes of the inmates and of the general public.

To strengthen their position vis-à-vis inmates, unions have opposed the expansion of improvement programs for inmates; established **job bidding,** which allows senior officers to bid for jobs within the institutions (they usually opt for jobs that reduce or eliminate inmate contact); and pushed for job safety. This last concern has led these unions to lobby legislators and the U.S. attorney general's office to look into the root causes of violence. The overall objectives of this effort have been to make prison work less dangerous and generate public support "on a national basis" for systemwide reforms in corrections (McEntee, 1993). Union contracts have also required mandatory training. One New York agreement, following a strike, provided for stipends for preservice and in-service training and stipulated that content and delivery of training would be subject to union review (Maghan, 1981).

Collins (1997) indicates that issues that are likely to become the subject of CO union negotiations will include employee urine testing and making the workplace smoke-free. Urine testing of employees is a highly controversial issue. The Supreme Court has ruled that, at least in some instances, urine testing can be conducted without there being any specific cause or suspicion that an employee is using drugs. Based on this case, other courts have generally ruled that random drug testing for employees involved in jobs relating to public safety can be required without violating Fourth Amendment protections. However, labor agreements may require, prior to the implementation of testing, that union consent be obtained (Collins, 1997).

Staff are also concerned about being searched. In most correctional institutions staff are not searched on a regular basis before entering the facility (Henderson, Rauch, & Philips, 1997). However, a small number of staff do bring contraband into the prison. To avoid any surprises, staff training should forewarn new recruits that their persons and anything they take into the institution are subject to search (Cripe, 1997). The prime concern of prisons is security, but staff searches should not be conducted unless "evidence exists that the employee is probably involved in the traffic of contraband or other illegal activity" (Henderson et al., 1997, p. 117). Staff members can be subject to searches of their person, lockers, cars, clothes, purses, and wallets (Cripe, 1997).

The unionization of correctional officers and the establishment of collective bargaining has had some major effects on the field (Crouch, 1980). First, it has helped to create more job security, improved training, and led to better working conditions. Second, and perhaps more important, unionization has undermined the prison's authoritarian hierarchical management system and created a tripolar structure consisting of administra-tion, officers, and inmates. As a result, officers now have more power in shaping policy, which has improved their morale.

COs and Stress

It has been recognized for some time that working in prison affects correctional officers physically, psychologically, and emotionally because they are "on the line," day in and day out, dealing with the stressors that are an inherent part of their jobs (Cheek & Miller, 1982; Connecticut Department of Corrections [CDC], 1998). For example, unlike police officers, COs experience cumulative stress from working "behind the wall"—being locked up—in a hostile and at times dangerous environment. The increases of airborne and blood-transmitted diseases, such as HIV and tuberculosis, and the growing prevalence of gang activity among the inmate population have heightened the dangers they face. Correctional officers suffer abnormally high rates of heart attacks, ulcers, hypertension, depression, alcoholism, and divorces. Woodruff (1993) points out that the average age of death for correctional personnel is 59, whereas the average life span of the population at large is 75. These serious health and social problems and the shortened life spans are commonly thought to result from the **occupational stressors** found in the correctional environment. This has resulted in an increasing emphasis on recognizing and controlling these stressors.

Occupational stressors can be divided into two categories, those associated with the characteristics of the job itself and those that are part of the organizational environment. Among the stressors associated with the corrections job are the unpredictability of inmate violence, along with their defiance and attempted manipulation of COs; having to maintain inmate discipline; having to comply with inmate rights; overcrowding; and being confined within the jail or prison environment along with the inmates. Those relating to correctional organizations include poor communication with or lack of support from supervisors or administrators; little or no input in decision making; boredom; low pay; role ambiguity (e.g., lack of sufficient information and resources to perform their jobs); role conflict (e.g., conflict between treatment and security); and low workplace support. These stressors heighten the probability of burnout, a chronic condition characterized by emotional exhaustion, depersonalization, decreased competence, and detachment from the job.[12] Burnout also increases the likelihood that mistakes will be made in the course of the workday, increasing the danger to all concerned.

Our Close-Up, "The Career Life Cycle of the Corrections Officer," provides perspective on how the events COs experience during different points in their career interact with life and family concerns and produce stress.

The Career Life Cycle of the Corrections Officer

The Connecticut Department of Corrections (1998) has developed a career/life model to better examine the events that COs experience during their career and the interrelationship between these events and life concerns. This model is designed to identify proactively the events that often provoke stress for a CO and develop a strategy to provide service to both the CO and the family. They identified six critical career life events.

Event I: Academy Graduation The academy experience provides applicants with the knowledge and skills they need to become a CO. Families and friends are introduced to the life of a CO through stories and the appropriate services that are available to help manage stress after graduation. For both the CO, and particularly for family members who are open to learning about the job, this is an excellent opportunity to review preventive measures for stress reduction.

Event II: Promotional Process New cadets are assigned to either a correctional institution or center and begin to experience the day-to-day routine of life in a prison. The stressors at this stage include disappointment when high, and perhaps unrealistic, job expectations are not met; a sense of increasing boredom with the job; the disillusionment resulting from factors such as disrespect from the public; and worrying about their competency to do the job well. For families, the "thrill" of having someone in uniform in the family has worn off, and there is little glamour to the job anymore. Stress and violence at home can erupt as the CO starts to withdraw and begin spending increasing amounts of time with workers who are more understanding of the unique demands of this job. Typically, promotional

opportunity occurs after the third year as a CO qualifies to start the process to become a lieutenant. When this is not successful, COs become at risk for a career plateau.

Event III: Plateau After the fourth or fifth year, COs can become disillusioned, as they realize that opportunities for advancement may be limited, and that they are in a risky, stressful job, where they may feel undervalued and unrespected by both inmates and the public. Career expectations may not be met, as these duties become tedious for the COs and disruptive of family life. This stage provides multiple needs for services, such as employee assistance program (EAP) services, family contact, mandated counseling, debriefings after critical incidents, and referral to help. This is a critical stage in the stress management process. But intervention at this stage is difficult. The CO's response system to stress is well established and the CO is typically well defended against outside intervention. In addition, there are few entry points for COs or their family to access services. Hence, the utility of the EAP as an entry point for stress management services becomes more important as a ready-made, credible prevention and intervention system.

Event IV: Critical Incidents For COs, *a critical incident is the most important and provides the greatest opportunity to address individual and family stress*. A *critical incident* is defined as any situation beyond the realm of usual experience in which vulnerability or a lack of control of the situation overwhelms one. This may include instances of deadly force or physical threat, the suicide of an inmate, personal losses such as the death of a colleague (killed in the line of duty or while off-duty), participation in a

community disaster, or dealing with the aftermath of inmate-on-inmate crime. At these critical points, the officers and their families are particularly open and receptive to education and intervention and are also most likely to make changes in their normal methods of coping.

Event V: Reassignment Often as a result of circumstances beyond their control, such as the closing or opening of a facility, a CO may be reassigned. Stress at this stage includes career uncertainty, a "go along to get along" mentality (e.g., "I only have five more years until retirement"), role conflict, and financial uncertainty. The key to intervention at this stage is to reach the COs and their family at the point where they are, addressing their unique needs and concerns. At this stage of their career, some COs have been promoted out of hazardous-duty jobs, away from the threats of the prison but removed from the excitement that brought them into the field. They may experience boredom, organizational stress, management/staff conflicts, confusion (e.g., "You were once 'one of the boys,' and now you represent management"), and lethargy. At this point, although COs may be cynical about the need for concrete assistance, this is the only way that caregivers can reach out to them and their families.

Event VI: Retirement Retirement and preretirement activities are the final milestone in the CO's career. The individual and/or family members often seek EAP help at this point, as they prepare for a new life. Retirement can be an exceptionally difficult experience for some, especially *(continued)*

The Career Life Cycle of the Corrections Officer

(continued)

when it means leaving the comfort and security of the "closed system" of a correctional facility. Issues at this point in the CO's career include financial concerns, loss of structure and community, diminished self-esteem, stress on existing relationships, and the possibility of beginning a second career. Although most corrections systems deal with financial concerns through a retirement system, few provide any training or education on other elements of retirement, and almost none offer help to the family. Family relationships can be especially vulnerable at this time, and it is not uncommon to see divorces between couples who have been married for 30 to 40 years.

All six of these events in the cycle represent especially stressful points for COs and their family. This increased stress creates internal motivation for change and turns these six events into prime opportunities for proactive promotion and provision of stress prevention and management services. Certainly, one way to have officers seek help for stress is to change the CO culture's negative view of seeking assistance. *Source: Connecticut Department of Corrections (1998).* Correctional Officer Maintenance Program. *Wethersfield, CT: Author.*

To combat stress and burnout in the correctional setting, Woodruff (1993) opts for a multifaceted approach. First, identify the specific stressors. He suggests giving all correctional workers the opportunity to express, in an anonymous way, their concerns and problems. Next, get feedback from all workers on the development of goals and policies that will reduce ambiguity, allow straightforward communication, and foster participation in the decision-making process. Other steps: increase training and education for the CO job, train managers thoroughly, provide stress management training, create consistent and fair evaluation practices, and institute a wellness program that encourages good health practices through prevention programs. Thus, the task of reducing stress becomes one of creating a consistent environment in which all workers are made aware of problems and can contribute to their solutions and which encourages wellness-oriented activities. In view of the expense involved in recruiting and training correctional officers, these attempts to deal with stress and burnout appear to be very necessary.

Summary

COs perform multiple functions, and thus, represent the backbone of correctional institutions. Most COs are white males. Higher salaries and better benefits have made the CO career more desirable; this has been reflected in lower turnover rates and higher standards for selection criteria. Recently, COs have been provided with formal and informal training. Preservice training often includes classroom instruction, while postemployment training may include classes, seminars, and exposure to the norms of the CO subculture. COs assume numerous, often contradictory, roles. Specifically, they must act as disciplinarians, counselors, and caretakers. Further, they must deal with inmates on a formal level, while also establishing a familiarity and humanitarian approach that facilitates a comfortable working environment. COs perform numerous functions, including overseeing living units, ordering and distributing supplies for inmates, disciplining for rule infractions, doing paperwork, and participating in mobile patrols.

Over the past few decades, the traditionally white, male-dominated CO field has been altered to include women and minorities, particularly blacks and Hispanics. The dissatisfaction with administrative treatment among COs, as well as the frustrations associated with the job, have prompted many COs to join unions. Occupational stressors exist within the CO job itself, as well as at the organizational level. The effects of job stressors on COs manifest themselves in negative ways, such as burnout, an increased number of mistakes, and higher levels of personal stress.

Still, corrections officer roles have changed significantly in the last few decades. They receive better training, more pay, and greater recognition for the work they do. They now have a greater voice in the running of the institutions in which they work and appear to stay in the career longer. They deal with inmate populations that have become progressively more difficult to handle in an environment that is highly legalistic. The future of the correctional officer profession thus appears to be heading in the direction of greater professionalization and more complicated criteria for the hiring of new recruits. These trends would appear to have significant implications for the types of individuals that will be recruited for these positions in the future.

Critical Thinking Questions

1. Discuss the structure of the training that COs undergo. Specifically, differentiate between pre- and post-employment training and formal and informal training. What do you perceive as the benefits and drawbacks of each?

2. Identify the various roles of COs. In what ways do the roles conflict? In what ways do they lead to con-

flict between COs and inmates? What factors facilitate the resolution of role conflict? What factors perpetuate it?

3. Describe the different jobs of COs and the labels associated with each.

4. What is the role of females in CO positions? How does increasing the numbers of women and minority COs change the CO subculture? What are the advantages and disadvantages associated with such changes?

5. What are the issues associated with cross-gender surveillance and searches? Discuss the pros and cons of a gender-specific standard for searches.

6. Why do COs join unions? What do unions provide?

7. Discuss the stressors associated with the CO profession. If you were a supervisor, how would you minimize the problem of burnout and its effects?

Test Your Knowledge

1. Which of the following demographic characteristics best describes correctional officers?
   a. white males
   b. black males
   c. white females
   d. black females

2. For which of the following reasons are people most likely to become correctional officers?
   a. to stop crime
   b. job security
   c. to rehabilitate criminals
   d. to have a high-status job

3. More formal relationships between correctional officers and inmates have resulted from:
   a. rising crime rates.
   b. prison overcrowding.
   c. increased inmate rights.
   d. better-educated correctional officers.

4. _____ are responsible for supervising inmates when they are in their housing units.
   a. Yard officers
   b. Wall post officers
   c. Administrative officers
   d. Block officers

Endnotes

1. Fifty states, the federal government, and the District of Columbia were surveyed. Seven jurisdictions either failed to respond to the survey or gave an N/A.

2. The State of New York, Department of Corrections (1998) uses a battery of tests that includes the Minnesota Multiphasic Personality Inventory-2, the Revised NEO Personality, The Quick Test, and Law Enforcement Screening Inventory (LESI).

3. In 1968 the U.S. Congress passed the Safe Streets and Crime Control Act, which provided funding for the Law Enforcement Assistance Administration Act.

4. Only 27 of the 52 state, federal, and other jurisdictions provided information on this question.

5. Four reported 80 to 160 hours; nine reported 16 to 24 hours.

6. Friel, 1984; Freeman & Johnson, 1982; Nacci & Kane, 1984; Lombardo, 1989.

7. Mike Gilbert, PhD, is currently an assistant professor at the University of Texas in the Division of Social and Policy Studies. His views are based on nearly 25 years of work with correctional officers both in the military and in several state systems, as well as his extensive research (Gilbert, 1993) on the role and function of correctional officers in jails and prisons.

8. L. X. Lombardo (1989). *Guards Imprisoned: Correctional Officers at Work* (2nd ed.) Cincinnati, OH: Anderson Publishing Co. Reprinted with permission.

9. Chapter 15 delves more thoroughly into inmate rights with respect to search and seizure.

10. Chapter 15 discusses in more detail the procedural aspect of the disciplinary hearing process.

11. See Chapter 15 for a thorough discussion of these issues.

12. Maslach, 1982; Maslach & Jackson, 1981; Byrd, Cochan, Silverman & Blount, 1998.

History of Prisoners' Rights, Court Access, and Remedies

14

KEY TERMS AND CONCEPTS

Civil Rights Act of 1871
Consent decree
Contempt of court
Court Deference Era
Due process clause
Habeas corpus
Hands-off doctrine
Hands-on doctrine
Injunction
Jailhouse lawyers
Legitimate correctional
   objectives
Prisoner Litigation Reform
   Act

Reasonableness test
Restrained hands-on
   doctrine
Section 1983, Civil
   Rights Act
Section 1983 actions
Selective incorporation
Slaves of the state
Special masters
Temporary restraining
   order
Tort
Totality of conditions

LEARNING OBJECTIVES

After completing this chapter, you should be able to:

1. Outline the major elements associated with the hands-off, hands-on, and restrained hands-on doctrines and the court deference approaches to inmates' rights.

2. Identify the major provisions of the Prisoner Litigation Reform Act and its impact on future inmate litigation relating to prisoner rights.

3. Outline the issues raised by the *Lewis v. Casey* decision, which restricted inmates' access to the courts.

4. Explain the circumstances under which inmates are entitled to court-appointed attorneys and the role played by "jailhouse lawyers" in assisting inmates in preparing court actions.

5. Describe the circumstances under which inmates can bring tort actions in a correctional setting and the reasons inmates prefer to bring civil rights actions rather than tort actions.

6. Explain the conditions that are required for an inmate to have a valid claim under the federal Civil Rights Act.

7. Identify the types of relief that inmates who are successful in civil rights actions can expect.

8. Recount the types of legal challenges that are typically brought by inmates using a habeas corpus petition and the new restrictions on their use in death penalty cases.

9. Describe some problems that the courts face in enforcing judicial decisions to improve prison conditions.

10. Provide an explanation of the roles and functions of *special masters* in institutional reform cases.

Introduction

Many people believe that inmates should have no rights because the crimes these offenders committed violated the rights of others. However, the framers of the Constitution decided prisoners do have rights, reflected in the First, Fifth, Sixth, and Eighth Amendments to the Constitution. Through the due process clause of the Fourteenth Amendment, these rights also apply to state inmates. Inmates' rights are further protected in federal statutes, such as Section 1983 of the Civil Rights Act of 1964 and some state statutes as well.

Legal concerns in corrections take on two perspectives: that of inmates and that of the correctional staff. For example, inmates want to know if their mail will be censored or what actions will result in their being placed in solitary confinement. Correctional staff and administrators want to know the circumstances under which they can be held liable (e.g., for confining an inmate to administrative segregation or searching a cell). These concerns lead to the question, "Which rights must inmates be allowed in a correctional facility?" If this chapter had been written 30 years ago, the answer would have been "Only those the prison chooses to allow them." However, as a result of changing judicial interpretations of what the Constitution means, the civil rights movement of the 1960s, and recognition by the courts of mistreatment of inmates at the hands of correctional officials inmates now have recognized rights (Collins, 2000).

Overview of Inmates' Constitutional Rights

The First Amendment protects freedom of speech, religion, and the press; the right to peaceably assemble; and the right to petition the government to redress grievances. Specific First Amendment claims raised by inmates are typically related to correspondence (freedom of speech) or religion. Inmates' First Amendment rights may be restricted if the imposition is related to valid penological interests (*Turner v. Safley*, 1987; *O'Lone v. Estate of Shabazz*, 1987). This is a very loose standard, given the numerous penological interests that the courts have established, as well as the overall acceptance of the judgment of prison administrators about the justification for legitimate penological interests. However, the Court has prohibited institutions from simultaneously eliminating all forms of correspondence (phone calls, letters, and visitation), although restrictions and prohibitions are almost always found constitutional.

Fifth Amendment due process claims emerge in the context of disciplinary procedures, classification issues, and transfer decisions. In *Sandin v. Connor* (1995), the Supreme Court established the due process standard as "whether the restraints on the prisoner impose atypical and significant hardship on the inmate in relation to ordinary incidents of prison life" (Carlson & Garrett, 1999). Specifically, the issue in *Sandin* was segregated confinement, and the Court held that it did not represent a form of atypical, significant deprivation in which a state could create a liberty interest. Thus, the inmate was unable to substantiate his due process claim.

Communication between attorneys and their inmate clients involves both the right of court access and the Sixth Amendment right guaranteeing counsel for criminals. Censorship of inmates is another Sixth Amendment issue involving the inmate's right to an attorney. The current view suggests that prison officials are allowed to open incoming mail from attorneys in the presence of the inmate but cannot read the contents (Palmer, 1999).

Eighth Amendment (cruel and unusual punishment) challenges are raised by inmates who contend that the conditions of their confinement are unconstitutional. Specifically, they may take issue with medical care, housing, food, clothing, safety, exercise, or use of force. To effectively raise an Eighth Amendment claim, the conditions of confinement must present an unreasonable risk of harm to the inmates, and prison administrators must be "deliberately indifferent" to the conditions. With regard to the use of force, the Supreme Court held that inmates did not necessarily have to suffer from severe physical abuse to successfully make an Eighth Amendment claim, as long as the force involved the "wanton and unnecessary infliction of pain," or it was used "maliciously or sadistically for the very purpose of causing pain" (*Hudson v. McMillian*, 1992).

In a prison context, Fourteenth Amendment equal protection issues are raised when a particular prisoner claims unfair treatment as compared with other similarly situated inmates. In general, the inmate's claims of differential treatment will not be successful if prison officials can show it is related to government objectives, such as the needs for security, discipline, and internal order. Claims of differential treatment have not been upheld in cases involving certain types of programming (e.g., early release, pay differentials in industry programs, and even in gross discrepancies in treatment between the general inmate population and those in protective custody or on death row).

The Fourteenth Amendment also forbids discrimination against U.S. citizens. Case law is almost unanimous in rejecting racial segregation of inmates for security reasons, ruling that "prisons are under a mandate to create 'maximum feasible integration' within prison walls" (Mushlin, 1993, p. 195). Discrimination is forbidden in regard to providing services and privileges and in imposing sanctions.

Women represent a minority of the prison population. As a result there are fewer female than male prisons;

Under Florida law, ex-convicts are disqualified from voting. Former inmates like J. C. Towns, shown here, are attempting to have their voting rights reinstated.

most jurisdictions have only one (or at most two) female facility. "Differences in conditions, rules, and between prisons for males and females have been fertile ground for equal protection challenges" (p. 205). In a series of major cases in Kentucky, Michigan, and Nebraska, courts espoused the position that women have the right to "par-

ity of treatment" with men in prison programs. Programs for women do not have to duplicate those for males but must be equivalent in substance if not in form.

The Evolution of Prisoners' Rights

Until the 1960s the federal courts basically refused to intervene in matters relating to prison conditions. This had the effect of making inmates **slaves of the state.** However, in the 1960s an era began in which the courts discarded their hands-off approach and recognized that inmates did not lose all their constitutional rights upon imprisonment. By the 1970s, after restoring some basic constitutional rights, which included forbidding states to incarcerate inmates under inhumane conditions, the courts became reluctant to further expand inmates' rights. At this point they took the position that although inmates retained their basic constitutional rights, these rights had to be balanced against the legitimate operational needs of prison officials to maintain order, security, and discipline.

Hands-off Doctrine

The history of prisoners' rights in the United States has gone through several phases (see Table 14.1). From the birth of our nation until the 1900s, the prevailing view as enunciated in *Ruffin v. Commonwealth* (1871) was that prisoners had no rights and, in effect, imprisonment made them "slaves of the state":

A convicted felon . . . punished by confinement in the penitentiary instead of with death, . . . is in a state of penal servitude to the State. He has, as a consequence of his crime, not only forfeited his liberty, but all his personal rights except those which the law in

Table 14.1
Evolution of Prisoners' Rights

Period	Inmates' Rights	Court Action
Hands-off approach (1776–1961)	Slaves of the state: entitled only to those rights prisons allowed them	Dismissed most cases involving claims by inmates about prison conditions
Hands-on approach (1964–1979)	Recognition by the courts that inmates were persons and entitled to basic constitutional rights	Federal and state courts considered inmates' claims that they were denied basic constitutional rights
Restrained hands-on approach (1980–1986)	Inmates' rights not as broad as those enjoyed by nonprisoners; can be restricted by legitimate prison needs to maintain order, security, discipline	Day-to-day correctional operations left to prison officials. Court action limited to instances in which basic constitutional rights abridged (e.g., inadequate food, medical care, sanitation, or safety)
Court deference approach (1987–)	Inmates still retain their rights, but now legitimate institutional needs for order, security, and discipline are more likely to prevail	Court made it clear that lower courts should defer to the judgment of correctional administrators and meant it

its humanity accords to him. He is for the time being the slave of the State. . . . Such men have some rights it is true, such as the law in its benignity accords to them, but not the rights of free men. (*Ruffin v. Commonwealth*, 1871, pp. 795–796)

The **hands-off doctrine,** though not a legal principle, aptly described this judicial position on intervention in prisoner matters. Although stopping short of stating that inmates had no constitutional rights, the courts felt that they had neither the power nor the obligation to define what rights inmates did have. Further, they were not obliged to protect them (Krantz & Branham, 1991). The courts took this position for several reasons:

1. *Separation of powers* Considering prisoners' complaints violated the doctrine specifying distinct functions for each branch of government—executive, legislative, and judicial. Thus, the courts decided issues of law and the executive branch controlled prisons.

2. *States' rights* Inmates' claims brought to federal courts were sent back to state courts because these claims encroached on the states' sovereign domain.

3. *Insufficient knowledge* Judges felt they lacked the knowledge of the complexities of prison administration and might not recognize the need for certain prison rules and practices.

4. *Fear of being deluged* Ignoring inmates' claims simplified the job of the courts because all suits involving prison conditions could automatically be dismissed (Gobert & Cohen, 1981; Krantz & Branham, 1991).

Although these reasons appeared to justify the hands-off doctrine, each was flawed. This doctrine was sustained until the early 1960s. Even at that point, in only a few cases were the courts sufficiently troubled to abandon this position (Krantz & Branham, 1991).

Hands-on Doctrine

In the 1960s, the courts began to discard their hands-off approach and established what has been called a **hands-on doctrine,** specifically focusing on prison conditions. Beginning with *Monroe v. Pape* (1961), the Supreme Court established another legal precedent when it resurrected a Civil War statute providing legislative justification for individuals to seek redress in federal court when their state civil rights were violated. This section of the federal **Civil Rights Act of 1871,** 42 United States Code **Section 1983** (commonly referred to as §1983), allowed individuals to bring action in federal court when they believed that they were deprived of their rights by a state officer, acting under color of state law, irrespective of the official's actual authority to engage in the behavior in question. This meant that state officials who violated

an inmate's constitutional rights while performing their duties could be held liable for their actions in federal court regardless of whether these actions were approved by state law or policy (Gottlieb, 1985; University of Illinois Law Forum, 1980). Also, interestingly, claimants were not required to exhaust state remedies before seeking redress in federal courts.

Further, with *Cooper v. Pate* (1964), the Supreme Court reversed a circuit court decision dismissing a Muslim inmate's petition that he was denied access to the Koran and opportunities to worship. This action recognized the right of Muslim inmates to sue prison officials for religious discrimination under the Civil Rights Act of 1871. Passed by the federal legislature, this act attempted to protect the rights of blacks after the Civil War.

The 1960s and early 1970s were very turbulent times in American history. As noted in Chapter 7, the civil rights movement and its violent aftermath prompted most minority groups, including prisoners, to become militantly assertive in demanding that they be accorded their constitutional rights. With the support and assistance of prison reform groups and social-minded lawyers, inmates began filing petitions to bring their cases before the courts. Riots, particularly at Attica in 1971, brought the problems and injustices of our prisons to the attention of judges.

The key ingredient that caused change was the activity of the federal judiciary, particularly the Supreme Court. In 1953, the Warren Court began a period in which constitutional rights were extended to disenfranchised minority groups. Beginning with the *Brown v. Board of Education* (1954) decision that rejected the "separate but equal" doctrine and mandated school desegregation, the Court expanded its rulings to encompass the rights of accused criminals. These included landmark decisions such as *Miranda v. Arizona* (1966), *Mapp v. Ohio* (1961), and *In re Gault* (1967). The same libertarian views prompting the court to extend constitutional rights to those accused of crimes also made them more willing to recognize that "[t]here is no iron curtain drawn between the constitution and the prisons in this country" (*Wolff v. McDonnell*, 1974, p. 2974). Thus, the Court acknowledged an obligation to protect the rights of the incarcerated.

Extension of the Bill of Rights to Inmates Another significant development during this period was the extension of most provisions in the Bill of Rights, through their **selective incorporation** into the **due process clause** of the Fourteenth Amendment, making them binding on the states. Thus, rights such as freedom of speech, of religion, from unreasonable search and seizure, and from cruel and unusual punishment were extended to state inmates, not just federal inmates.

During the hands-on period, from the 1960s to the late 1970s, the courts determined that there were flagrant constitutional violations in prisons. The courts began by limiting, on a case-by-case basis, the extent to which prison authorities could restrict rights. During this time prisoners were given such rights as:

> meaningful access to the courts; freedom of religion; the right to a reasonable standard of medical care; limited rights to privacy and freedom of personal appearance; some due process rights in disciplinary hearings; the right to correspond with the courts, lawyers, and government officials; freedom from arbitrary censorship of mail and publications; and the right not to be subject to cruel and unusual punishment. (Bronstein, 1985)

The courts also recognized that many specific conditions, although offensive, might not be individually bad enough to violate constitutional rights. When taken together, however, they saw that the **totality of** these **conditions** might represent a constitutionally unacceptable state of imprisonment; for example, in *Holt v. Sarver* (1970)[1] conditions of confinement at Arkansas prisons, when taken as a whole, were considered cruel and unusual punishment.

Restrained Hands-on Approach

By the early 1980s the Supreme Court had become reluctant to further expand the rights of inmates and actually began to restrict them. This was occasioned by several factors: (1) the prison populations more than doubled between 1972 and 1982; (2) most jurisdictions had fewer financial resources to deal with this increase; (3) public attitudes had hardened and there was a movement toward more punitive treatment of offenders; (4) the character of the Supreme Court changed as liberal justices appointed during the 1950s and 1960s retired and were replaced by more conservative ones; and (5) correctional practices had improved.

In changing to a more restrictive interpretation of inmate rights, the *Bell v. Wolfish* (1979) and *Rhodes v. Chapman* (1981) decisions were major turning points. This new direction attempted to balance institutional operational requirements and the purposes of incarceration with the need to protect inmate constitutional rights from oppressive government actions (Branham & Krantz, 1997). In the *Bell* case, the Supreme Court recognized that:

> . . . maintaining institutional security and preserving internal order and discipline are essential goals that may require limitation or retractions of the retained constitutional rights of both convicted prisoners and pretrial detainees. . . . Prison officials must be free to take appropriate action to ensure safety of inmates and correctional personnel and to prevent escape or unauthorized entry. (*Bell v. Wolfish*, 1979, p. 1878)

Finally, the Court focused on the types of restrictions and conditions that would constitute punishment for pretrial detainees. This is important because these inmates were not convicted and therefore could not be subject to any practice imposed for punishment. The following practices were upheld: double-bunking, body searches, restriction of incoming publications, searches of cells in the absence of the prisoners, and regulations on incoming packages. The key consideration in determining if these conditions constituted punishment was whether they were reasonably related to institutional interests in maintaining security, order, and discipline.

In *Rhodes v. Chapman* (1981) the Supreme Court reinforced its position in the *Bell* case. This case involved an overcrowded new facility in Ohio whose population was 38 percent more than the limit imposed by the number of beds in the original facility design; over half the inmates were housed two to a cell. The inmates alleged this constituted cruel and unusual punishment. The Court found that double-bunking did not inflict pain and was not of a wanton and unnecessary nature. More important, there was no deprivation of food, medical services, or sanitation, nor was there an increase in inmate violence. The Court felt that the *totality of conditions* created by overcrowding did not constitute cruel and unusual punishment. It further noted that "the constitution does not mandate comfortable prisons [nor does it require that jurisdictions] aspire to [meet] this ideal" (p. 347). The Court concluded that although lower courts should continue to examine prison conditions, unless contemporary standards of decency are not met, the running of prisons should be left to legislatures and prison officials rather than to judges. These two decisions brought an end to the intensive court scrutiny of prison conditions and ushered in an era of judicial restraint.

From 1980 to 1986, the Court took a more balanced approach to inmates, a **restrained hands-on doctrine.** It embodied several principles: (1) inmates do not forfeit all constitutional rights; (2) inmate rights are not as broad as those enjoyed by nonprisoners because inmates are imprisoned; and (3) prison officials need to maintain order, security, and discipline in their facilities. However, this era was short-lived.

The Court Deference Era

Looking at Court decisions beginning in 1987 and continuing into 1999, Bill Collins, one of the nation's foremost experts on correctional law, asserts that a new era, the **Court Deference Era,** began with *Turner v. Safley* (1987) and *O'Lone v. Estate of Shabazz* (1987): "While the courts had been talking deference for years it was not until 1987 with these two benchmark cases that the Court made it clear that when it said 'lower courts should defer to the judgment of correctional administrators,' they really meant it" (*Correctional Law Reporter*, 1999, April/May). This was further underscored by its decisions in *Hudson v. McMillian* (1992, see Chapter 15); *Washington v. Harper* (1990, see Chapter 17); and *Lewis v. Casey* (1996, see this chapter).

In *Turner v. Safley* (1987), the Supreme Court suggested that lower courts use a **reasonableness test** to resolve conflicts between inmate rights and the legitimate interests of the prison officials to maintain control. At issue in this case was a ban on inmate-to-inmate correspondence. The Court established a four-prong test for determining the "reasonableness" of a regulation:

1. *Rational Connection*   "There must be a valid rational connection between the prison regulation and legitimate government interests put forth to justify it" (p. 2262). The rule was justified because it advanced the goals of institutional security and safety, because mail between inmates can be employed to discuss escape plans and to arrange assaults and other violent acts. Also, this could help control growing prison gang problems by restricting communication between gang members, transferring them, and limiting correspondence. Further, this facility was used to provide protective custody and allowing correspondence between facilities could compromise the safety of these inmates.

2. *Alternative Means*   There must be an alternative means of exercising this right. This ban on inmate-to-inmate correspondence "does not deprive inmates of all means of expression. . . . it only bars communication between a limited class of people with whom prison officials have particular cause to be concerned" (p. 2263). Inmates can still correspond with family members outside the prison system.

3. *Impact on Rights*   What impact will the accommodation of this asserted right have on other inmates and staff? Prison officials asserted that correspondence between prisons facilitates the formation of informal organizations, threatening staffs' ability to maintain safety and internal security. The Court viewed protecting the safety of many (versus abridging the rights of a few) as within the province and professional expertise of prison officials.

4. *Absence of Alternatives*   The absence of ready alternatives to the regulation is evidence of its reasonableness. The only option offered by inmate claimants was for prison officials to monitor inmate correspondence. That meant reading all letters, which prison authorities argued was impossible.

Thus, the Supreme Court said it would not intervene in prison operations as long as the restrictions placed on inmates are reasonably related to **legitimate correctional objectives**[2]—that is, the need to maintain order, security, and discipline.

In *Wilson v. Seiter* (1991) the Court reinforced its decision in *Turner*. The inmate contended that his Eighth Amendment rights were violated by poor conditions in the prison (e.g., overcrowding, inadequate heating and cooling, unsanitary dining facilities and food preparation, and housing with mentally and physically ill prisoners; Alexander, 1991). The Supreme Court, in reversing a lower court decision, rejected the broad concept of the *totality of conditions* (*Holt v. Sarver*, 1970) and ruled that the violations must be judged separately and not seen as a "totality" that constituted unconstitutional conditions. Further, the Court said that inmates had to prove that prison officials were "deliberately indifferent" in permitting these unconstitutional conditions to exist before they could be held liable. An opinion by Justice O'Connor[3] concluded that to demonstrate "deliberate indifference" requires showing that prison officials had knowledge of constitutional violations and then failed to act (Alexander, 1991). A case that did meet this test was one in which:

> prison officials . . . were aware that the inmate had inadequate toilet facilities, but it was two months before any significant attempt to modify toilet facilities took place and three months before the prisoner was transferred to a room with adequate facilities. (*LaFaut v. Smith*, 1987)

Courts will defer to prison officials when they can show that a restriction is related to legitimate correctional goals, particularly facility security. Inmates' suits relating to basic constitutional issues such as adequate medical care, food, sanitation, and inmate safety will continue to be considered.

Court Access

The courts provide inmates with an arena in which they can bring complaints about the abridgment of their rights. Without court access, inmates have no mechanism to appeal their convictions or to effectively force prison officials to provide them these rights. Inmates are guaranteed meaningful access to the courts by the Constitution under the Sixth and Fourteenth (due process) Amendments (Project, 1997). Prisoners' right to access was initially recognized in *ex parte Hull* (1941) when the Supreme Court held that a Michigan procedure that required inmates to submit their legal petitions to prison officials for approval amounted to an impermissible denial of the right of access to the courts. In the decades following this case, though, the courts were reluctant to interfere with prison policies that restricted access to the courts. Interestingly, this trend was reversed in *Johnson v. Avery* (1969), which upheld the use of jailhouse lawyers in assisting inmates with their legal claims. This was followed by *Bounds v. Smith* (1977), which said the state could not impose boundaries between the courts and inmates and imposed an affirmative duty to assist state inmates:

> [T]he fundamental constitutional right of access to the courts requires prison authorities to assist inmates in the preparation and filing of meaningful legal papers by providing prisoners with adequate law libraries or adequate assistance from persons trained in the law. (p. 21)

Law Libraries

What constitutes an adequate library and sufficient time and access to use it? What restrictions can be placed on individual inmates? What types of materials are inmates entitled to in preparing their briefs?

Although the Supreme Court has not provided specific guidelines, the plan it affirmed for North Carolina prisons in *Bounds v. Smith* (1977) suggests standards for adequacy. This plan included the establishment of law libraries (with relevant federal and state cases since 1970) in various prisons around the state. Also, inmates at other facilities were to be given transportation to and housing at these prisons, if necessary, to allow for a full day's research. This could mean that they would have to wait 2 to 3 weeks, depending on whether or not they

were facing court deadlines (see also *Miller v. Evans*, 1992). Although *Bounds* failed to specify the books necessary for prison law libraries to meet minimum requirements, adequate facilities must allow an inmate to learn how to and be able to do legal research and to address both criminal and civil rights issues (Collins, 1997b; *Glover v. Johnson*, 1996).

The courts have not allowed prison officials to use the high cost of law books as grounds for maintaining an inadequate law library (*Bounds v. Smith*, 1977). Jurisdictions must provide either the library or transportation to one. Further, the courts have recognized that legal research takes time. Thus, the question of adequate legal access has revolved around such issues as the length of time the library is open and its availability to different classes of inmates. A court-approved plan for Georgia prison libraries mandated that (1) they be open a minimum of 9 hours per week; (2) inmates be allowed to use the library the equivalent of 8 hours every 3 weeks; and (3) the hours be varied to accommodate inmates involved in work, education, and other programs (*Mercer v. Griffin*, 1981).

Access must also be provided to inmates confined in long-term segregated units (e.g., protective custody, death row). Also, security concerns have not been viewed as a valid basis for denying inmates access to the library, limiting them to checking out books by citation, or barring them from taking part in legal training pro-

Prisons are required to provide law libraries and allow inmates to learn how to do legal research.

grams (*DeMallory v. Cullen*, 1988). Finally, the courts have required that inmates be provided such basic resources as paper and pens to assist them in filing complaints, and some have even required the limited availability of copying facilities (Mushlin, 1993).

Inmates' Preparation of Their Own Cases

The high rate of inmate illiteracy makes it questionable whether the average inmate can use a law library without assistance. Some courts have required trained paralegals to help inmates in using libraries (*Harrington v. Holshouser*, 1984). However, the Supreme Court has ruled that the presence of a law library is sufficient to provide even death row inmates with court access except after their first appeal in states with laws that require appellate courts to accept and review cases (Smith, 2000). Thus, there is no requirement that attorneys be provided except when ordered by a court because of inadequate library resources (*Murray v. Giarratano*, 1989).

Although most jurisdictions have opted to provide law libraries, many of them do not meet court standards for adequacy because an acceptable library can cost tens of thousands of dollars and require substantial space to house the books required and for inmates to do research. Deficient libraries continue to operate because no one has filed suit challenging their adequacy (Collins, 1997). When challenges have occurred, the courts have, in the absence of other alternatives, required prisons to provide inmates with the services of an attorney (*Canterino v. Wilson*, 1989).

In 1996, in *Lewis v. Casey,* the Supreme Court "somewhat tightened the meaning and impact of *Bounds,*" making it more difficult for inmates to gain access to the courts (*CLR,* 1996, Aug./Sept.). While continuing to affirm an inmate's right to court access, the Court emphasized that (1) the inmate must "have a reasonably adequate opportunity to file a non-frivolous claim"—that is, a claim in which there is a basis in fact or law[4] alleging a violation of a constitutional issue involving either his conviction or the conditions of his confinement, and (2) this does not necessarily create a right to a freestanding law library or a person trained in the law. The Court's reasoning was that *Bounds* was not meant to give inmates the wherewithal "to transform themselves into litigating engines capable of filing all kinds of lawsuits (e.g., slip-and-fall claims) and to browse through a law library trying to discover an issue upon which they can file a claim." Further, for inmates to successfully bring a claim based on an inadequate law library or legal assistance they must show that they were caused actual injury or are facing imminent injury based on the institution's deficiencies in providing appropriate resources. The "injury" must actually hinder an inmate's ability to pursue a legal claim, such as having a case dismissed or preventing the inmate from filing a claim because of the inadequacies of the prison's law library.

Thus, in the Seventh Circuit, in *Walter v. Edgars,* the court held that "absent such injury (or perhaps the clear threat of such injury) the inmate has no standing to complain about deficiencies in an agency's access to the courts system" (*CLR,* 1999, April/May, p. 83). Although this case was filed before the *Lewis* standing requirement, the court chose to enforce the new rule and require a finding of actual injury.

The Court in *Lewis* also indicated that access to the courts is, like other rights, subject to the *Turner v. Safley* (1987) rule, which allows restrictions on inmates' rights that are reasonably related to legitimate institutional objectives such as security. Thus, the Court in *Lewis* noted that restrictions such as 16-day delays in obtaining legal materials for persons in lockdown—even where they result in injury—do not violate an inmate's constitutional rights based on the *Turner* principle.

The Court also encouraged local experimentation with different methods of providing court access, such as replacing law libraries with some minimal access to legal services and providing a system of forms like those contained in two significant inmate-initiated cases, *Sandin v. Connor* (1995) and *Hudson v. McMillian* (1992). These forms would ask inmates to provide only the facts and not attempt any legal analysis. Systems would remain in effect until an inmate could show that a nonfrivolous legal claim has been frustrated or was being impeded by this system. This creates a "catch 22" situation for inmates, because without a law library or other legal assistance an inmate may have difficulty showing his suit has legal merit; this would then result in the claim being declared frivolous.

At least one thing is clear from recent decisions: the courts are requiring inmates to demonstrate actual injury or prejudice to successfully sustain a claim of lack of court access (Boston, 1997; Mushlin, 1997).[5] Our Consider This feature, "You Be the Judge," looks at the various options that systems may consider as a result of the *Lewis* decision and potential consequences or advantages of each choice.

Access to Attorneys

In federal and most state courts there is no requirement that inmates have counsel appointed to pursue appeals of their cases beyond the mandatory first appeal (*Douglas v. California*, 1963). The appointment of counsel is totally within the discretion of the court (Mushlin, 1993, 1998b). To determine whether to appoint an attorney courts ask, "Given the difficulty of the case does the plaintiff appear competent to try it himself and if not would the presence of counsel make a difference?" (*Farmer v. Hass*, 1993; Mushlin, 1998b, p. 20). Inmates formally charged with offenses committed in prison, like

You Be the Judge

CONSIDER THIS

What is the most prudent approach for a jurisdiction to take to provide inmates court access under *Lewis v. Casey*?

1. Should the jurisdiction establish a library that meets the *Bounds* requirements? Will this be sufficient? There is no certain answer to this question because, based on *Lewis*, groups like illiterates, non-English-speaking inmates, and those in segregation must suffer "actual harm" to claim that their circumstances resulted in denial of sufficient assistance to file a nonfrivolous claim. The court leaves it to prison officials to best determine how to solve this problem; thus, agencies are still faced with providing some mix of legal materials and legal assistance. Although the actual injury requirements make it harder for inmates to challenge the adequacy of the system, this does not eliminate the possibility that the issue will haunt a correctional agency in the future. *CLR* (1996, Aug./Sept.) recommends that a proactive agency provide different services for special category inmates (e.g., the illiterate and those in segregation). The only consequence for inmates will be that it will take longer for cases claiming inadequate court access to reach the courts, which extends the grace period for agencies to continue unconstitutional practices.

2. Should a facility downsize its collection? Should it reduce it to "(1) key texts in criminal law,

supplemented loose-leaf services, treatises, and how to do it materials that explain the mechanics of filing protected types of lawsuits and (2) summarize the basic rights of inmates"?

Arizona, which was a party in *Lewis v. Casey*, hired 10 paralegals to cover 34 prisons at which it had closed the law libraries and left in its general library 16 basic law texts.[6] Additional texts can be requested from a state law library. These traveling paralegals assist inmates requesting assistance in filing forms, and those with bilingual needs can receive help through a teleconference with an interpreter. Supervised by an attorney, these paralegals are only to provide assistance in cases meeting the *Lewis* requirements, involving civil rights, conditions of conferment, appeals from convictions, or habeas corpus petitions. Inmates will no longer have free copying or access to typewriters, and they will be limited to two pencils. For other proceedings, such as divorces or custody, the inmates will have to seek help from private attorneys, the courts, or other sources (*Corrections Professional* [CP], 1997, Aug. 8).

What has been the reaction to the Arizona system?

- Brenda Vogel, state library director for Maryland's DOC, "questions the motives of Arizona in changing their legal access system." She suspects that some officials were counting on the fact that inmate lawsuits would take several years to go through the courts

and that this system will survive until then. She says, "It smacks of vindictiveness. . . ." She and others doubt it will cost less because of the funds used to hire an attorney or monitor, expand the general library, and retain law librarians to monitor the use of legal texts (*CP*, 1997, Aug. 8, p. 2; Aug. 22). Also, by eliminating indigent status as a basis for paying filing fees, Arizona inmates may have to choose between spending their meager wages (about 25 cents per hour) on hygiene items, stamps for letters, or legal claims. This may well prompt some inmates to join gangs to obtain the resources they need. Is this wise?

- Lynn Branham, author of an ABA monograph on alternatives to traditional means of legal access in prison, believes this system is meant to limit as many complaints as possible. She said, "[T]his will ensure that meritorious claims won't get to court. I thought that from a policy perspective we wanted to make sure inmates got redress. . . . With a minimal access system, inmates won't be able to file claims because they won't have the access they need to answer questions such as how to respond to a dismissal or find out what immunity means" (*CP*, Aug. 22, p. 1).

- Collins contends that Branham and other critics seem to understate the issue when they argue that the goal was to give

any accused person, are entitled to counsel. This right is not extended to disciplinary actions or to placement in administrative segregation when an inmate is suspected of criminal activity (Collins, 1997b).[7] When inmates have attorneys, prison officials may not unreasonably restrict them from meeting in private and communicating with their counsel (*Ching v. Lewis*, 1990). Also, courts have usually allowed unrestricted correspondence be-

inmates a system of redress for meritorious claims, because the overwhelming majority of inmates' lawsuits result in judgments in favor of the defendants. The answer, he argues, does not lie in better law libraries but in (1) better grievance systems and (2) providing lawyers or truly skilled paralegals. Someone with independent, trained judgment needs to be able to filter inmates' complaints. Many inmates' complaints may be legitimate, in that something happened to the inmate that should not have, but they still may not demonstrate that there has been a constitutional violation (Collins, 2000).

- The *CLR* (1997, April/May) takes the position that "a low budget [to provide legal materials/services may create] a 'pay me now or [as is likely with states adopting the Arizona approach] pay me much later risk' [i.e., when the case finally reaches the courts]" (p. 83). What will other states do? Vogel believes that other DOC agencies will recognize the potential problems with Arizona's system and won't jump on the bandwagon. "I think most will take a wait and see attitude," she said (*CP*, 1997, Aug. 8, p. 3).

3. What other options should the jurisdiction consider?

The Court in *Lewis* suggested positive experimentation.

- Maryland's DOC commissioner has taken the bold step of using modern computer technology (i.e., CD-ROMs and on-line databases) to provide a cost-effective means of meeting the court access mandate. This system is reputed to minimize the conflict between inmates and librarians found in other states (Vogel, 1996, July 22). *CLR* (1997, April/May) supports this new technological approach as long as libraries have a sufficient number of computers and provide inmates with training. Illinois is considering the use of CD-ROM stations for segregation inmates (*CP*, 1997, Aug. 22). Collins's (2000) response to this is that it will allow inmates to do poor legal research faster.

- Hire attorneys, which at first glance may seem ludicrous! Prison officials are afraid of allowing the "fox in the hen house" and that the foxes will sue (Crane, 1995). What are the advantages of using attorneys? Reductions in legal book costs, security, transportation, and funds for hiring assistant attorney generals to defend numerous—possibly thousands of—suits filed each year *pro se* or by inmate law clerks could result. Attorneys are ethically bound to try to resolve clients' legal problems informally before filing suit. Jailhouse lawyers typically can't walk into the warden's office and negotiate settlements. Also, attorney assistance provides meaningful help, including preparing and filing petitions, personal interviews with inmates, fact gathering, and legal research. The attorney's responsibility ends once the legal documents are filed; she has no responsibility to be the counsel of record or to provide courtroom representation. Many private prison management companies use attorneys because this is an effective means of meeting the court access requirement, not because they like it (Collins, 1998; Crane, 1995).

- How will inmates occupy their time if they do not have libraries? According to Mike Mahoney, executive director of the John Howard Society—a prison watchdog group—inmates behave in the library (*CP*, 1997, Aug. 22). At least while in the library their minds are challenged in a positive direction. Also, libraries give inmates hope (Vogel, 1996). However, Collins (2000) contends that some correctional administrators see libraries as places where inmates meet with little supervision to make nefarious plans.

Depending on your perspective, several questions are raised by this decision. As a proactive administrator, how would you respond to the *Lewis* decision if you were opening a new prison or one with an existing acceptable legal access system? Do you think your jurisdiction should follow Arizona? If so, what are the potential consequences?

tween inmates and their attorneys. Incoming mail from attorneys may be opened (but not read) in the inmate's presence to inspect for contraband. To enable prison officials to make this determination, the courts have required that correspondence be clearly marked as from an attorney. Outgoing mail presents no legal threat, so it cannot be censored or confiscated (Collins, 1997b; Mushlin, 1997; *Wolff v. McDonnell*, 1974).[8]

Exhausting Administrative Grievance Procedures

CLOSE-UP

In September 1995, Terry Sanders, an inmate at the Illinois Stateville Correctional Center, complained to a medical technician that he had chest pains, headaches, problems breathing and sleeping, and a foul odor coming through his nose. Sanders was seen by a nurse in the health care unit and was prescribed chlorpheniramine tablets. Sanders' condition persisted. While he repeatedly asked for a thorough examination to find the cause of his problems, the only medical attention he received was a cardiograph, blood pressure measurements, and an examination of his heart and lungs.

In October 1995, he was seen by Dr. Sood, who diagnosed "dry nose" or "rhinitis" (inflammation of the nose) and prescribed a nasal spray that Sanders was to use for 2 weeks. This also proved ineffective. In May 1996, Sanders complained to a medical technician that his condition had persisted and that he had developed pains in his stomach and a bloated abdomen. He was seen by a nurse who said there might be a problem with his liver. She said she would schedule a doctor's appointment, but it never occurred. Sanders was prescribed a laxative, which also was ineffective. He again complained to a technician who told him that because he already had been seen by the medical staff, if he had a problem, he should write the health care unit. He did so, complaining of "bloated abdomen and pains," and stated that he was still having trouble with his nose.

In June 1996, Sanders was examined by Dr. Kurian, who prescribed chlorpheniramine, even though Sanders had written the health care unit in October 1995 that it had proven ineffective. Dr. Tilden, who had not examined Sanders, prescribed pink bismuth liquid for his abdominal pain. It was also ineffective. At a grievance hearing, Sanders stated that after a 4-day hunger strike he was eventually diagnosed by a Dr. Smith as having a nasal infection and was prescribed an antibiotic, which alleviated his symptoms.

Under state law, the Illinois Department of Corrections adopted a grievance procedure, which inmates were required to follow before seeking any other remedies. Sanders pursued several of these steps. However, the Coordinator of Inmate Issues found that no grievances regarding medical treatment were received by the Administrative Review Board between September 1995 and July 1996. Sanders responded that after his grievances were rejected by the Grievance Officer, he filed them with the Administrative Review Board, but that he received a form reply dated July 11, 1996, stating, "Need to see Grievance Officer and/or send Grievance Officer's final report." Sanders then resubmitted his grievance, this time receiving a response in August 1996, which stated, "The Grievance Officer's response is inappropriate. Needs to be signed by Warden before the Administrative Review Board will address grievance."

By then Sanders already had filed a federal civil rights lawsuit. Sanders pointed out that in August 1996, after his hunger strike, he eventually obtained proper medical treatment, and that it would have made no sense for him to pursue administrative remedies thereafter. Thus, he contended, the requirement that in-

Jailhouse Lawyers

Because many inmates are functionally illiterate and cannot file claims on their own, it is not surprising that they seek assistance from other inmates. Correctional officials have not viewed **jailhouse lawyers** (JHLs) positively. A JHL is an inmate who has learned legal skills and is recognized by other inmates as a legal resource. There are two types: (1) law clerks, who are inmates assigned by the prison to litigation tasks and are paid a nominal sum (starting at $45 per month); and (2) freelancers, who use their own time to study the law and work on their own cases and those of other inmates. As a result, the quality of their work varies from those who are very proficient to those who are not much better than the inmates they are assisting (Nobel, 1997; Thomas, 1988). Although prison regulations forbid inmates to be paid for privately rendered services, it is generally recognized they are paid in cash or in other ways (e.g., commissary items). JHLs typically require clients to have cash sent to an outside contact to avoid violating prison rules (Thomas, 1988).

In *Johnson v. Avery* (1969), the precedent-setting case in this area, the Supreme Court ruled that, because of a lack of reasonable alternatives, it was unconstitutional to restrict inmates' access to the courts by forbidding inmate assistance. However, the courts approved some limitations: restricting the time and place where assistance can take place (e.g., a requirement that all legal work be done in a writ room) and not permitting compensation (Mushlin, 1999; Palmer, 1991). Nobel (1997) argues that given the dependency of inmates on JHLs there is a need for extending the attorney-client privilege, which prevents lawyers from revealing confidential information disclosed in this relationship:

> Like attorneys . . . [JHLs] often learn incriminating facts about their inmate "clients" while helping them prepare cases. . . . Revealing these facts may benefit a . . . [JHL] who can bargain for a reduced sentence

mates exhaust all administrative remedies prior to filing a lawsuit should be applied flexibly, with due regard for its underlying purpose. "If circumstances make it unreasonable to require the plaintiff to run the gauntlet of internal administrative appeals," he argued, "then the doctrine should not be applied."

Sanders alleged that in spite of his many complaints over a period of months, he kept receiving ineffective treatment. He argued, "The defendants did not bother to examine me, make what should have been an obvious diagnosis or provide me with appropriate treatment." He claimed that he had a serious medical condition that was repeatedly untreated. To support his position, he introduced a pamphlet published by the American Academy of Otolaryngology–Head and Neck Surgery, explaining that a sinus infection can cause headaches lasting for days or weeks unless treated with antibiotics, and that it potentially has serious consequences. It also recognized a sinus infection as requiring medical attention.

The defendants argued that Sanders' complaint failed to meet the standards set by the Supreme Court in *Estelle v. Gamble*, namely, that the prisoner was not in "serious" medical need and that he was not subject to "deliberate indifference" causing him needless pain or injury. The defendants stated that "essentially, plaintiff claims that his nose was dry and that his stomach hurt." The defendants asked the court to dismiss the suit and require Sanders to follow all administrative procedures before he could file suit.

In rendering its decision, the court stated that while an administrative remedy may have been sufficient in the initial stages of the grievance procedure, once the warden had rejected Sanders' grievance over denial of medical care, there was no true administrative remedy available to him. Although Sanders' emergency grievance directed the warden to render a decision within 3 days, once it was denied there was no fast-track appeal to the Administrative Review Board. The court noted that any resolution of Sanders' grievance likely would take months.

The court said it appeared that Sanders did pursue the administrative remedy available to him to the point that he reasonably concluded that relief within a reasonable period of time —reasonable in view of the risk to his health—was not available through further administrative appeals. The court stated that to require a prisoner whose health is in danger to fully exhaust the administrative grievance procedure could deny him any remedy at all. In cases of denial of medical care, the threatened harm is irreparable and "relief delayed is relief denied."

The court denied the defendants' motion to dismiss this case. It required that the parties discuss settlement before the next hearing.

If you were judging this case, what issues would you examine? Specifically, how would you define what constitutes an exception to the requirement that inmates exhaust all administrative grievance procedures before filing a federal civil rights action?
Source: Adapted from Sanders v. Elyea, *1998 WL 67615 (ND, Ill).*

---

or other institutional privileges in exchange for this betrayal. . . . prison officials may [also] coerce [JHLs] into exposing their clients' secrets. . . . In either case, inmates have no legal right to prevent these disclosures. (pp. 1572–1573)

Nevertheless, the constitutionality of *Johnson v. Avery* has been questioned by some lower court decisions, including those that

- Upheld a prison regulation that prohibits inmates from drafting pleadings for each other as not being a violation of the First Amendment. The court ruled that the purpose of this regulation was not to restrict but rather to reduce inmate indebtedness (*Schneck v. Edwards*, 1996).

- Upheld a prison rule that prohibited an inmate from providing legal assistance to another inmate without prior approval (*Dawes v. McClellan*, 1996).

- Upheld a rule that prohibited correspondence between inmates in different units regardless of the fact that one was a JHL (*Goff v. Nix*, 1997).

The stereotypical JHL is an inmate scurrying around the prison looking for unacceptable conditions and then locating precedents with which to file a lawsuit. Although this is true of some JHLs, it is not the way most work. JHLs help inmates deal with many legal problems that are external to the prison, including being the victim of unfair divorce proceedings, being deprived of child visitations, or having to deal with inheritance issues, taxes, compensation claims, property liens, and name changes (Thomas, 1988). Under the *Lewis* requirements, JHLs may be the only option inmates have to deal with these issues (see p. 335). They, like any successful professional, must also be therapists and diplomats to develop trust and ferret out the true problems of their clients. JHLs are also involved in activities requiring conflict resolution

While there is no requirement that counsel be appointed to assist inmates in pursuing appeals, inmates who do have attorneys must be permitted to meet with them in private.

and management skills, which defuse potentially violent situations and help administrators manage the tensions of prison life (Thomas, 1988).

The Prisoner Litigation Reform Act

The **Prisoner Litigation Reform Act** (PLRA),[9] effective April 1996, further restricts intrusion of the courts into prison operations and thereby affects the extent to which inmates can seek relief relating to prison conditions. The PLRA limits inmates' ability to file lawsuits by requiring them to exhaust all other administrative remedies prior to filing suit, by mandating the full payment of filing fees, by imposing harsh sanctions for filing frivolous or malicious lawsuits, and by requiring that any awarded damages be used to satisfy any pending restitution orders the inmate may have. Additionally, the Anti-Terrorism and Effective Death Penalty Act of 1996 limits the ability of inmates to file successive habeas corpus claims and speeds up these proceedings in federal court. The impact of these two pieces of legislation is underscored by the *Correctional Law Reporter* (1996, June/July): "[It] imposes the biggest setbacks for inmate legal claims" (p. 1). This legislation was passed in response to two concerns. First, the PLRA limits the remedial discretion and intervention of the federal courts in correcting abuses, particularly in state prisons. Known as

STOP—Stop Turning Out Prisoners—this portion of the legislation restricts the ability of judges to put population caps on prisons or to release inmates when prisons become so overcrowded that conditions violate constitutional safeguards. Second, it attempts to limit frivolous prisoner complaints and appeals. Table 14.2 outlines the major provisions of the PLRA.

Postconviction Actions

Because a claim must be filed in a specific way with a specific type of court, the courts will not necessarily review a claim on its merits alone. Offenders have many decisions to make to most effectively file their petitions. Gobert and Cohen (1981) note that it is difficult, even for a lawyer, to choose the most effective legal and tactical means of postconviction litigation. Thus, for the untrained inmate with no legal assistance, this task may be next to impossible. Courts and legislatures have been sensitive to these problems. They have tried to streamline and simplify this process for inmates by developing model forms and placing more emphasis on the facts in the inmate's complaint than on how it is drafted or the supporting legal theory (Gobert & Cohen, 1981).

Inmate litigation usually involves one of the following: (1) tort suits involving a claim that an inmate has been hurt as a result of the negligence of someone in the corrections system (Collins, 1997), (2) civil rights actions involving an inmate claim that an institutional practice

Table 14.2

Major Provisions of the PLRA

1. Applies to all inmate claims under §1983
2. Requirements involving valid claims for relief of unconstitutional conditions
   a. In instances in which a constitutional violation of prison conditions has been found by the courts, changes relating to this condition(s) will be limited to no more than is necessary to correct the violation.
      (1) This remedy must be the least intrusive—that is, creating the fewest problems for the prison administration—and also must "give substantial weight to any adverse effect on public safety or the operation of the criminal justice system."
      (2) Termination of efforts to correct an unconstitutional condition(s) shall occur 2 years after the court order unless, based on a new hearing, the court decides to continue the court order to correct a violation of federal rights.
      (3) These same limitations also generally apply to consent decrees and preliminary injunctive relief; however, the time limitation is 90 days.
   b. To release inmates for purposes of reducing or limiting institutional populations due to unconstitutional prison conditions requires a ruling by a three-judge panel. The ruling must be based on a conclusion that crowding is the primary cause of the violation and there is no other possible means of relieving the problem.
3. Special Masters: Places limitations on the scope of their role and compensation
4. Suits by Prisoners
   a. The PLRA requires that inmates first exhaust all administrative remedies. This necessitates the establishment of state grievance systems that effectively handle inmate complaints. Examples of when exhaustion of administrative remedies is not applicable appear in our Close-Up, "Exhausting Administrative Grievance Procedures."
   b. The PLRA limits attorneys' fees to 150 percent of the hourly rate established for court-appointed attorneys. This changes prior practices, where fees were based on hourly rates, which could exceed $300 an hour in some cases (Collins, 2000).
   c. The PLRA requires inmates to pay the $150 filing fee, which in the past was waived. If inmates are indigent, filing fees are viewed as a loan to be deducted at a rate of 20 percent per month from future earnings or other monies the inmate receives. Collins (2000) asserts that this fee change is primarily responsible for a reduction in Section 1983 filings from more than 40,000 in 1995 to less than 26,000 in 1998. He considers this element to have had the greatest impact on inmate litigation.
   d. The PLRA bars prisoners from filing civil claims alleging emotional or mental injury while in custody without a prior showing of physical injury. Some courts insist on literal physical injury, but others have broadened the concept of injury to include prejudice (Collins, 1998, Oct./Nov.). Eighth Amendment standards require that injuries be more than "de minimis"—that is, insignificant. This means that COs who limit their use of force to leaving minor bumps, bruises, and other "treat at home" injuries are immune from damages.
5. Judicial Practices
   a. The PLRA mandates screening of inmate filings and that the court dismiss cases that are frivolous or malicious, that fail to state a claim upon which relief can be granted, or that seek monetary damages from a defendant who is immune from such relief. This relates to the qualified immunity test under which individuals are not liable unless they violate clearly established rights. Therefore, a CO's action can be outside the scope of policies and procedures and still not violate clearly established constitutional law (e.g., a certain form of restraint may violate agency policy but not be considered a violation of the Eighth Amendment's cruel and unusual punishment clause). The agency can fire the CO, but he or she is still protected by the qualified immunity or good faith defense if the inmate brings a suit for damages (Collins, 2000).

Sources: Prisoner Litigation Reform Act and Habeas Reform Law may drastically curtail inmate lawsuits (*Correctional Law Reporter,* 1996, June/July). pp. 1–2, 11–15; W. C. Collins, Prisoner Litigation Reform Act: Participants outline prepared for the Large Jail Network Conference, Longmont CO, January 12–14, 1997.

or condition violates his or her constitutional rights, or (3) habeas corpus actions in which inmates challenge the legality of their control by a corrections system. We will look at each type of action and then examine some misconceptions about prisoner litigation.

Tort Actions

A **tort** is a civil wrong arising from a claim by one party that another party has negligently, maliciously, or deliberately inflicted some sort of injury on him or her. The most typical tort action results from automobile accidents where one party negligently operates a car and injures another. In a correctional setting, tort actions against corrections personnel may arise out of claims by inmates relating to failure to protect them from harm, negligent loss of property, medical maltreatment, and other breaches of reasonable care that they are entitled to expect from correctional staff (Collins, 1997b).

Typically, because a tort action seeks only damages, it is filed in a state court. Often an inmate's claim can either be pursued as a tort action or as a civil rights claim.

The nature of the proof for each action is different. For example, an inmate believing that she has received inadequate medical care could pursue a tort action by claiming that the treatment was negligent. In contrast, in a civil rights action, she would have to claim "deliberate indifference" to serious medical needs, which is harder to prove than mere negligence.

In spite of the greater difficulty, inmates often prefer to bring civil rights actions (commonly called **Section 1983 actions**) because (1) these suits are typically brought in federal courts, which have historically been more sympathetic than state courts to inmates; and (2) the relief available is much broader than in a tort action. No injunctive relief is possible in a tort action, so prison officials are not required to change the conditions that led to the lawsuit. For example, although an inmate may be paid damages for negligent medical care, the prison is not required to improve health services. Also, although state restrictions may limit the damages or prevent punitive damages, these restrictions are not applicable in federal civil rights cases (Collins, 1997b).

Section 1983 of the Civil Rights Act

During the hands-on era, inmates gained the right to challenge prison conditions in the federal courts through Section 1983 of the Civil Rights Act. A successful Section 1983 suit requires proof that a person, acting under the color of state law, deprived the claimant of a constitutional or federal statutory right. This means that suits can be brought against government employees—including those under contract—for actions they engage in while employed by the state, even if those actions are not authorized by the state. Thus, a legitimate claim can arise out of an event in which a guard beats an inmate, even though prison rules forbid this action. However, to file a claim, even indigent inmates are required to pay a $150 fee to file a case in a federal district court and $105 to have a case heard by a federal appeals court. Thus far, these fees have been deemed constitutional by the Fourth, Fifth, Sixth, Eighth, and Twelfth federal circuit courts; however, not all federal circuits have ruled on this issue (Mushlin, 1997b).

Habeas Corpus Actions

Literally translated as "you have the body," **habeas corpus** is an action enabling inmates to request a hearing before a judge to air claims of illegal incarceration due to a constitutional violation involving their conviction or conditions of confinement. Habeas actions are brought by inmates who have exhausted state remedies and feel some constitutional issue exists to challenge their conviction. These challenges really represent a form of appeal beyond the normal appeals process. Death row inmates repeatedly use this option to challenge the basis of their conviction or sentence. However, under the Anti-

Terrorism and Effective Death Penalty Act of 1996, several restrictions make this more difficult. The act:

1. Limits federal review of state convictions where the state court has given the conviction a so-called full and fair review, unless the decision was "contrary to, or involved an unreasonable" application of clearly established federal law, as established by the Supreme Court.

2. Places a 1-year time limit on the period inmates can challenge their convictions in a habeas corpus action after they have exhausted all state remedies.

3. Requires that a prisoner obtain authorization from a federal appellate court before he can file a second or successive petition in district court and bars the court of appeals from allowing such a filing unless the prisoner first establishes a prima facie case that he is entitled to relief. This requires the prisoner to prove either (a) that "the claim relies on a new rule of constitutional law, made retroactive to cases on collateral review by the Supreme Court, that was previously unavailable," or (b) that both "the factual predicate for the claim could not have been discovered through the exercise of due diligence" and "the facts underlying the claim, if proven and viewed in light of the evidence as a whole, would be sufficient to establish by clear and convincing evidence that, but for constitutional error, no reasonable fact finder would have found the applicant guilty of the underlying offense" (as cited by Sellers, 1997).

4. Does not appear to restrict inmates from filing second petitions that raise grounds not raised in previous petitions (*CLR*, 1996b, June/July).

However, these limitations are only applicable if the state establishes:

> a mechanism for the appointment, compensation, and payment of reasonable litigation expenses of competent counsel in State post conviction proceedings brought by indigent prisoners whose capital convictions and sentences have been upheld on direct appeal to the court of last resort in the State or have otherwise become final for the State law purposes. (Addition of Chapter to Title 28, United States Code, Chapter 154, Section 2261)

If the state fails to provide counsel to all indigent prisoners, then these limitations are not applicable.

What is the impact of this new legislation? It basically gives inmates two opportunities to appeal their convictions. Inmates must first exhaust all state remedies. Then they have 1 year to file a habeas petition, which must include all issues the inmate wants to raise. Furthermore, the more thorough a hearing an inmate receives in state court, the more relevance this is given by a federal court and the less likely an inmate is to be granted a federal hearing.

Typically, inmates choose Section 1983 over habeas actions to pursue claims involving prison conditions or regulations because (1) there is no requirement that all state judicial remedies be exhausted before bringing this action and (2) in habeas actions no damages are awarded. Nevertheless, the Supreme Court broadened the relief available from habeas corpus actions to include release from custody and to rectify unconstitutional regulations. Thus, in *Preiser v. Rodriguez* (1973), the Court ruled that in cases involving restriction of good time, relief should be sought through habeas rather than a Section 1983 action. Inmates seeking release from solitary confinement have also used it (*Krist v. Ricketts*, 1974; *Tasker v. Griffith*, 1977).

Misconceptions about Prisoner Litigation

Inmate litigation dramatically increased beginning in the mid-1970s, but many misconceptions remain about the nature and character of this growth.

One popular view is that lawsuits are filed for entertainment value by prisoners who have a lot of time on their hands and that these lawsuits only crowd other federal courts' busy dockets. A contrasting image is that courts deny requests by indigent prisoners for appointment of legal counsel and that prisoners never win, despite the merit in some (and perhaps many) of the cases. (Hanson & Daley, 1995)

Trends in the filing of habeas complaints can be divided into three time periods: the 1960s saw a dramatic increase, filings during the 1970s decreased, and those from 1980 to 1996 saw a steady but slow increase (Thomas et al., 1988; Scalia, 2000). However, in spite of shifting trends in the number of habeas filings their percentage of total filings declined from over 85 percent in 1966 to about 27 percent in 1996 (see Figure 14.1a). Although the number of habeas filings has generally increased with the rise in prison population, the rate declined from 50 lawsuits per 1,000 in 1970 to 24 per 1,000 in 1990 to 14 per 1,000 in 1996. Three quarters of this decrease beginning in 1980 was attributable to a decline in the rate of filings by state inmates (Scalia, 1997). These data refute the popular view that inmates spend their time in prison looking for technicalities to secure their release.

In contrast, the annual percentage of total filings that civil rights actions constituted increased from less than

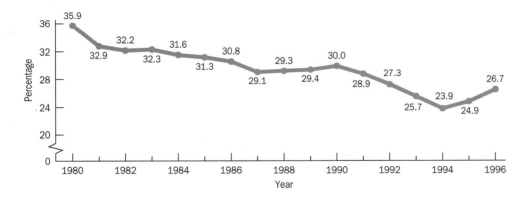

Figure 14.1a *Habeas Corpus Petitions (1980–1996)*

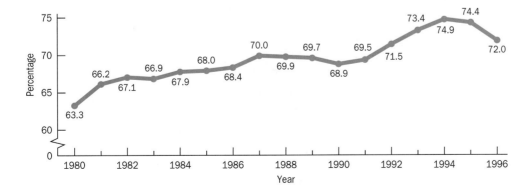

Figure 14.1b *Civil Rights Petitions (1980–1996)*

Source: J. Scalia (1997). *Prisoner Petitions in the Federal Courts, 1980–96.* Washington, DC: Bureau of Justice Statistics.

20 percent in the 1960s to more than 70 percent in 1996 (see Figure 14.1b). This suggests that state prisoners may be more concerned with correcting perceived wrongs than they are in seeking to overturn their convictions.[10] Also, although the number of civil rights filings by state prisoners increased dramatically during this period, the rate of increase has begun to slow. The number went from 218 in 1966 to 20,071 in 1986 (a 9,100 percent increase) to 40,569 in 1995 (Table 14.3). This amounted to more than an 18,600 percent increase over a 29-year period. However, between 1980 and 1996, the rate per 1,000 prisoners of filings of civil rights petitions actually decreased by 17 percent, down from 72.7 to 60.5 (U.S. Department of Justice, 1997, p. 1). Initially, the numerical increase probably occurred because this was the first opportunity inmates had to file complaints about unconstitutional prison conditions. Later increases were probably accounted for by the more than 450 percent increase in the inmate population (Beck, 1996; Bureau of Justice Statistics, 1982, 1988b). Following the enactment of the PLRA in 1996, filings dropped steadily from 1996 to 1998 (see Table 14.3). The PLRA placed restrictions on civil rights complaints filed by inmates in federal court (Litras, 2000).

Table 14.3 also provides the number of mandamus petitions filed by state prisoners. The *writ of mandamus* is a judicial remedy used to compel a lower court or government to perform a duty owed to the plaintiff. Like habeas corpus, mandamus is an extraordinary remedy, based in common law, that is only used when the plaintiff has no other adequate means to attain the desired relief. However, the courts have held that mandamus can only be used to compel a government official to perform a ministerial, or nondiscretionary, duty. Additionally, the federal courts do not have jurisdiction to issue writs compelling action by state courts and officials. Consequently, mandamus petitions are often dismissed: During 1995, more than 70 percent of mandamus petitions filed by federal and state inmates were dismissed (Scalia, 1997).

Compared with other prisoner petitions, mandamus petitions are infrequent; they also tend to be varied in nature and specific to individual circumstances. The courts have granted mandamus for limited uses such as to direct lower courts to hear and decide pending cases in a timely manner; to permit inmates to file petitions in *forma pauperis pro se*; to compel the correction of a sentence computation; to compel a state to prosecute an inmate while the inmate is in the custody of another jurisdiction; to allow inmates to vote absentee, where permitted by law; and to compel the payment of federal witness fees to inmates (p. 15).

Under Section 1983 rules, to meet basic thresholds, inmates must sue individuals acting under color of state law and must satisfy procedural requirements, such as responding in time. Nearly half of the lawsuits filed by inmates fail to meet these basic thresholds and are dismissed within 6 months (Hanson & Daley, 1995, p. 10).

Table 14.3

Prisoner Petitions Filed in U.S. District Courts by State Inmates (1980–1998)*

		State		
Year	Total	Habeas Corpus	Mandamus	Civil Rights[†]
1980	19,569	7,029	145	12,395
1981	23,602	7,786	177	15,639
1982	24,947	8,036	172	16,739
1983	26,411	8,523	202	17,686
1984	26,567	8,335	198	18,034
1985	27,190	8,520	180	18,490
1986	29,326	9,040	215	20,071
1987	32,772	9,524	276	22,972
1988	33,695	9,867	270	23,558
1989	35,895	10,545	311	25,039
1990	36,012	10,817	352	24,843
1991	35,635	10,325	267	25,043
1992	41,420	11,296	479	29,645
1993	44,980	11,574	388	33,018
1994	50,228	11,908	395	37,925
1995	54,593	13,627	397	40,569
1996	55,166	14,726	444	39,996
1997				27,658
1998				25,478

*Includes transfers, remands, and statistical closures.
[†]For 1997 and 1998, only data on civil rights were available.
Source: M. F. X. Litras (2000). *Civil Rights Complaints in U.S. District Courts, 1990–1998*. Washington, DC: Bureau of Justice Statistics; Administrative Office of the U.S. Courts, *Report of the Proceedings of the Judicial Conference of the United States* (table C-2).

Table 14.4

Areas of Prisoner Litigation

Reasons	Percent
Lack of physical security	21
Inadequate medical treatment	17
Due process	13
Invalid conviction or sentence	12
Physical conditions	9
Denial of courts, law libraries, lawyers, and interference with mail or telephone calls	7
Living conditions	4
Denial of religious expression, assembly, visitation, and racial discrimination	4

Source: R. A. Hanson & H. W. K. Daley (1995). *Challenging the Conditions of Prisons and Jails*. Washington, DC: Bureau of Justice Statistics, p. 17.

Table 14.4 shows the types of issues raised by inmates on Section 1983 cases.

Most (73%) state inmates' petitions allege civil rights violations; however, on the federal level, most inmates' petitions (74%) challenge the constitutionality of their sentences (Scalia, 1997, p. iii). These statistics represent a 96 percent increase, which can be traced to major federal sentencing reforms that took effect between 1986 and 1990. These include the establishment of federal sentencing guidelines, the abolishment of parole, the reduction of good-time conduct, the requirement of increased terms for recidivists, and the mandatory or minimum sentencing of prison terms for drug trafficking and the use of a firearm in the commission of a criminal offense (Scalia, 1997).

Table 14.5 shows that about 80 percent of inmate lawsuits are dismissed by the courts. About 20 percent are disposed of by the court's granting the defendant's motion for dismissal (Hanson & Daley, 1995).[11] In these proceedings, almost all inmates (96%) represent themselves. This is known as *pro se*. Fewer than 2 percent of the petitions filed by inmates are adjudicated in their favor (Scalia, 1997). Nevertheless, based on a study of more than 2,700 cases disposed of in 1992, Hanson and Daley (1995) concluded:

Table 14.5

Reasons for Court Dismissals of Section 1983 Lawsuits

Reasons	Percent
Plaintiff failed to comply with court rules[12]	38
No evidence found	19
Frivolous	9
Issue nonrecognizable under Section 1983	7
Defendant has immunity	4
Defendant is not acting under color of state law	3

Source: R. G. Hanson & H. W. K. Daley (1995). *Challenging the Conditions of Prisons and Jails.* Washington, DC: Bureau of Justice Statistics, p. 20.

Prisoners do win Section 1983 lawsuits, though this is statistically rare. Successful lawsuits demonstrate that some plaintiffs are not only credible but correct in their allegations of civil rights' violations. (p. 39)

Finally, Figure 14.2 tracks all federal petitions by state and federal prisoners through the federal courts.

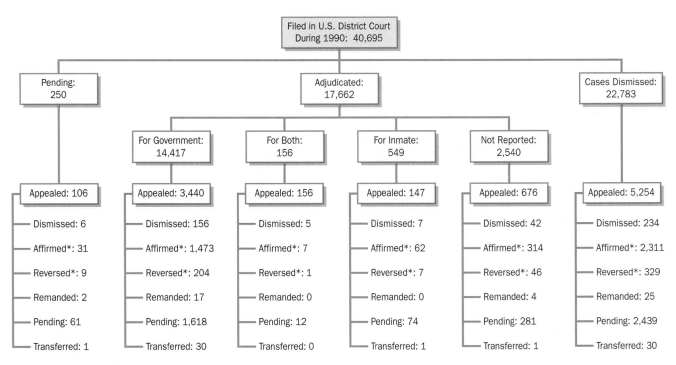

*Includes cases partially affirmed and partially reversed.

Figure 14.2 *Tracking Prisoner Petitions Through the Federal Courts, 1990–1995*

Source: J. Scalia (1997). *Prisoner Petitions in the Federal Courts, 1980–96.* Washington, DC: Bureau of Justice Statistics.

Enforcement of Judicial Orders

Potential remedies to Section 1983 actions can vary extensively; they include injunctions, consent decrees, damage awards, and attorneys' fees.

Injunctions

In civil rights actions, court orders for relief generally take the form of an **injunction,** which is a court order requiring defendants to perform or stop a specific act. Because the courts recognize that this litigation can take time to resolve, it is possible to obtain a preliminary injunction, or a **temporary restraining order.** This prevents institutional officials from continuing to engage in certain conduct or keeping an inmate in a designated status (e.g., solitary confinement). Because this is viewed by the courts as an extraordinary remedy, it is usually issued only when inmate plaintiffs can show their case is likely to succeed or that there will be possible irreparable injury. However, when the victims are suffering substantial hardship, a temporary order may be obtained by showing a "substantial chance of success" (Branham & Krantz, 1997). For example, in *Smoak v. Fritz* (1970), the judge considered the following in issuing a temporary order:

> [f]or over five weeks . . . [these inmates have] been held in solitary confinement. No charges have been lodged against them, nor have they been found guilty of any wrongdoing other than for which they were originally sentenced. Yet the duration of their solitary confinement now threatens to extend for an indefinite time, with possible physical and psychological harm. . . . (p. 612)

After a trial in which inmate plaintiffs are successful, judges may issue an injunction ordering correction of the problem. However, prison officials must be given time to develop a plan that corrects these unconstitutional conditions (Branham & Krantz, 1997). For inmates, this remedy is very important because they typically remain in custody after the lawsuit has been resolved, and this provides them with protection from further deprivations of rights of this kind.

In the past, injunctions or court orders have required a variety of changes. First, they have mandated the abolition of certain prison regulations and state statutes relating to discipline, censorship, and court access. Second, these orders required improvements in institutions or in the services provided, including medical care, sanitation conditions, the quality of food, and increases in correctional staff and better training for them (Krantz, 1988). Third, jails or prisons or sections of them have been ordered closed when found to confine inmates under conditions that violated protections against cruel and unusual punishment (e.g., *Inmates of Allegheny County*

Jail v. Wecht, 1989). Fourth, the courts have also ordered institutions to reduce their populations.

The PLRA has changed the circumstances under which courts can provide relief. First, preliminary injunctive relief must similarly "be narrowly drawn [and] extend no further than necessary to correct the harm." This must be done by the least intrusive means necessary to correct that harm. Further, substantial weight must be given to any adverse effect on public safety or the operation of the criminal justice system. When preliminary relief is granted, it automatically terminates 90 days after its entry unless the court issues a final order requiring that the conditions of the injunction be met.

One of the major intents of this provision is directed at the issue of overcrowded prisons and the granting of relief in the form of population caps or release orders in these cases (*CLR*, 1996a, June/July). The PLRA has established special procedures that include giving the institution or system a reasonable time to comply with previous court orders. Then, a three-judge panel is convened to decide if a release is justified. This court must find by "clear and convincing evidence that (i) crowding is the primary cause of the violation of the federal right; and (ii) no other relief will remedy the violation of the federal right" (Collins, 1997a, p. 3). Nevertheless *CLR* (1996, Feb./March) believes that "the courts will be able to find institutions unconstitutional and order various forms of orders, including imposing population caps. Courts that wish to flex their relief power muscles may have to do a better job of documenting the reasons for their actions" (p. 74).

Burns (1997) argues that this may well encourage judicial creativity because a court may find when examining allegations of unconstitutional prison conditions that while crowding has reached levels that constitute a federal violation, this may be secondary relative to other conditions in the prison, including sanitation, medical care, sewage, and pest control. While not ordering release, the court may order new medical facilities or judicial management of certain prison operations to rectify these or other conditions. In the long run, this may be more expensive. Only time will tell the impact of this new legislation.

Consent Decrees

Instead of going to trial, an inmate plaintiff may have constitutionally unacceptable conditions rectified relatively quickly and easily by working out a **consent decree**—which is, essentially, an injunction—with the defendant. This involves both parties agreeing to work out the terms of the settlement subject to court approval. This spares both parties the expense and uncertainty of a trial. It also gives them the opportunity to work out a mutually acceptable solution rather than have one imposed on them by the courts. There is no assurance that prison authorities will make the changes, but if they fail to do so, the court can impose fines or other sanctions.

The PLRA places similar limitations on consent and court orders, so we will discuss them together. Basically, the PLRA requires that both types of relief orders

1. be as limited as possible: (a) This requires a narrowly drawn remedy, (b) which extends no further than necessary to correct the violation; and (c) uses the least intrusive means necessary and gives substantial weight to its effect on the public safety and its impact on the criminal justice system.

2. must end in 2 years unless a court finds, based on a showing by the plaintiffs in a new hearing, current violations. If new relief is ordered it must be retailored to current violations, which will probably involve a reduction of the scope of the order (Collins, 1997a). Initially it was thought to mean that the 2-year-or-older consent decrees would be automatically terminated, but recent court decisions suggest this may not necessarily be the case. Currently, it is an open question because of the way some circuits are interpreting these decrees as contracts (Collins, 1997a, 1998).

Also, it will be more difficult to get prison officials to enter into voluntary consent decrees because of the requirement under the PLRA that they admit the violation of the rights of inmates, or the agreement is unenforceable; however, a motion before a judge can end this agreement without this admission. Nonadmission prevents individual damage suits by both former and current inmates, claiming "I am/was an inmate in your facility and you just admitted there was an unconstitutional violation. Pay me damages" (*CLR*, 1996a, June/July, p. 12). Prison officials may go to court to avoid damages, because the state may believe that the court will develop a remedial plan that is more advantageous than can be negotiated with defendants. The downside of this is that it prevents inmates and even prison officials, who may want to make improvements but lack funding, from negotiating an agreement that improves programs, making them more humane, fair, and reasonable and the prison environment safer and more liveable for staff and inmates (Breed, 1996).

Damage Awards to Inmates

Inmate plaintiffs can receive damages in tort and civil rights suits. Inmates can be awarded three types of monetary damages in civil rights actions (Collins, 1997). *Nominal damages* are awarded when inmates have sustained no actual damages, but there is clear evidence that their rights have been violated. This token payment is usually only one dollar. *Compensatory damages* relate to actual loss and can include payments for out-of-pocket

expenses the inmate incurred or for pain and suffering and mental anguish. *Punitive damages* are awarded when the wrongful act was done intentionally and maliciously or with reckless disregard for the rights of the inmate. For example, in *Smith v. Wade* (1983), a corrections officer placed an inmate (who was in protective custody because he was vulnerable to attack) in a cell with two other inmates—one of whom had been put in segregation for fighting. They went on to harass, beat, and sexually assault him. In this case, the jury awarded the inmate $25,000 in compensatory damages and $5,000 in punitive damages.

How will inmates who file lawsuits succeed under the new PLRA requirement that no federal civil action may be brought for mental or emotional injury suffered while in custody without prior showing of physical injury? The question is open as to whether this provision:

1. means that inmates cannot recover for a constitutional violation that **does not inherently involve physical injury,** such as the right to be free from racial segregation or disclosure of HIV status, the right to procedural due process, or to be free from intentional violations of the right to bodily privacy or being subjected to verbal or sexual harassment. If this is the case, rather than this provision being a useful device for screening out frivolous or merely weak cases, it becomes a requirement that "jeopardizes the enforcement of a substantial number of prisoners' rights, robbing them of vital constitutional rights" (O'Bryan, 1997, p. 1124).[13]

2. limits recovery for a constitutional violation only when a prisoner without a physical injury brings a lawsuit alleging a constitutional violation generally requiring such an injury—for example, an Eighth Amendment claim involving cruel and unusual punishment (Mushlin, 1997). Several lawsuits have applied this limitation, including two claiming an Eighth Amendment violation, one involving a sore ear an inmate claimed as a result of suffering an injury from a guard, and another involving deliberate exposure to asbestos. Both claims were denied. In the former, it was held there was insufficient injury to meet the threshold of the PLRA, while in the latter there was no evidence that contact with the asbestos had resulted in physical injury (Ashan, 1998; *Siglar v. Hightower*, 1997; *Zehner v. Trigg*, 1997).

Attorneys' Fees and Inmates' Awards

The prevailing party in a federal civil rights action may be awarded attorneys' fees. However, under the PLRA there is a 150 percent of the hourly rate cap for court-appointed criminal defense attorneys. This will cap fees at around $120 per hour or less (Collins, 1997b). Inmates winning damage awards are required to pay up to

25 percent toward attorneys' fees. This will result in fewer lawyers representing inmates in small civil rights cases because they will be unable to recoup their expenses. Moreover, this will reduce the number of cases prisoner rights groups like the ACLU National Prisoner Project can take because they are dependent upon awards from the cases they win to pay the costs of taking on new cases.

If a judgment is awarded against an inmate that includes the payment of court costs, the prisoner will be required to pay the full amount. For indigent inmates, this will be collected in the same way as filing fees—by installment at 20 percent of the preceding month's income each time the inmate's account exceeds $10 (Collins, 1997a).

Court-Imposed Remedies

Almost 3 out of 10 (27%) state facilities in 1995 were under court order or consent decree to limit the number of inmates and improve conditions relating to confinement (Stephan, 1997). This underscores the importance of the enforcement issue, but it also creates potential problems involving the separation of powers between the executive, legislative, and judicial branches of government and states' rights (Krantz, 1988).

To avoid extensive involvement in carrying out large-scale institutional changes, early court decisions generally involved injunctions prohibiting or compelling the performance of specific, easily defined acts. However, this failed to rectify the very poor conditions plaguing some institutions and prison systems. Thus, in the early 1970s, an increasing number of judges became so outraged that they ordered prison officials to make basic improvements to rectify these conditions. These judges learned that merely requiring substantial improvements in prison conditions rarely resulted in major changes. The courts could forcefully threaten jurisdictions that failed to make ordered improvements, but their bark was worse than their bite; they usually did no more than threaten. This issue was complicated by the fact that if federal courts insisted on enforcing their orders, and these facilities claimed there was no money to make the improvements, the courts had to be ready to force counties or states to provide it. This affected issues relating to the setting of priorities for use of public funds and even of raising taxes and raised further questions about the separation of powers and federal intervention in state functions. Of course, with the PLRA's least restrictive provision and criminal justice impact statement it is now easier for jurisdictions to meet court-ordered changes.

Dealing with Resistant Defendants In a number of instances, jurisdictions fail to respond to court orders requiring that certain conditions be corrected. In these instances the courts can respond by issuing a **contempt of court** citation, or they can supervise compliance with their orders or appoint an agent to do so.

The aim of a contempt of court citation, in prison cases, is to pressure defendants to provide the court-ordered relief. To achieve compliance, courts can imprison defendants or impose a fine. They can also fine for purposes of compensating inmate plaintiffs for losses or damages they sustained due to noncompliance (see Branham & Krantz, 1997; *Hutto v. Finney*, 1978; *Newman v. State of Alabama*, 1982). The courts generally use their contempt power when a community or institution makes no effort to correct conditions as agreed to in a consent decree or that were mandated by the court. However, judges are reluctant to issue contempt orders when defendants have made diligent efforts to do what is ordered. Thus, in only a few cases have the courts done more than threaten to use their contempt power (Krantz, 1988).

Enforcement of Consent Decrees In the past, when judges prepared and issued orders or accepted consent decrees, they had four options (Levinson, 1982). First, they could do all the work themselves. They could evaluate the situation, prepare the order, and administer its implementation. For example, in a case involving the Mississippi State Penitentiary, Judge William Keady issued the order and regularly visited the prison to make certain the standards he established were being met. When units did not conform to these standards, he used his power to close them. Second, a judge could place a prison system under the receivership of the state's governor. In 1979, when the Alabama State Correctional Board failed to carry out previous court orders, the judge appointed the governor as receiver for the Alabama State Correctional System (*Newman v. Alabama*, 1979). This made the governor directly responsible for making changes in the system. Third, parties to a legal action could hire a consultant to monitor changes within the institution. In 1979, the New Mexico Department of Corrections did that after signing a consent decree (Levinson, 1982). Fourth, judges could appoint a *master* to assist in executing the court's responsibilities. Many of these options may be limited by some of the provisions of the PLRA, including the ability of a master to monitor compliance unless both parties agree.

Special Masters **Special masters** are persons "appointed to act as representatives of the court in some particular action or transaction" (Black, Nolan, & Nolan-Haley, 1991, p. 673). The use of special masters is not a new idea; federal courts have frequently used them. However, more recently, they have been used in institutional reform litigation (e.g., public school segregation cases and local jail and prison reform cases). In these cases, masters have functioned in at least three different roles (Nathan, 1978).

First, judges appointed them to collect information to aid the court in making decisions about the occurrence of a constitutional violation in a complex case. In this fact-finding capacity, masters were responsible for preparing a report providing an independent statement of the nature and extent of the alleged constitutional violations. For example, a federal court in Florida appointed a medical administrator and physician to survey the medical care in the state's prisons and to determine whether these services met constitutional standards (National Institute of Corrections [NIC], 1983).

Second, courts have employed masters after ruling that a jurisdiction was operating an institution(s) with constitutionally unacceptable conditions but before ordering improvements. Here judges relied on the master's expertise to assist in developing an acceptable and effective remedial decree. Masters also function as mediators between the two parties to work out an acceptable agreement. Thus, in a Tennessee case a state court judge used a master as a court consultant to help fashion an order that rectified proven violations (NIC, 1983).

Third, masters were employed to monitor and enforce a court-ordered remedial decree requiring a correctional facility or an entire system to make certain improvements. Also, some judges have appointed masters after defendants have refused to make the ordered improvements or showed themselves incapable of doing so. In both instances the master may have done one or more of the following: fact-finding, interpreting the decree, negotiating, mediating, or assisting the defendants in planning the court-ordered changes or improvements. By the middle of 1988, court-appointed masters or monitors were supervising as many as 14 adult state correctional systems or institutions and 4 state juvenile systems or institutions, and a number were functioning in jail systems around the country (Keating, 1990).

The PLRA limits fees that can be paid to special masters to $75 per hour and requires that these payments be made by the court. The PLRA also restricts the role of the master, limiting it to:

1. acting as quasijudges; they can hold hearings and compile a report about the nature and extent of the alleged constitutional violations.

2. assisting in the development of a relief order that remediates the constitutionally unacceptable conditions.

What they cannot do is "discuss issues informally with either side or talk with one party outside of the presence of the other (known as ex parte communication) or work informally in an attempt to facilitate compliance with the relief order" (Collins, 1997a, p. 6). Thus, the master can no longer visit the prison and talk informally with inmates to get a better sense of what the problems are. Further, he cannot call a prison official and say "an inmate's attorney has complained about a poten-

tial violation in mandated hospital procedures. I checked it out and you might want to look into it as well. Tell me if you decide to do anything." Now defendants will be faced with a formal compliance hearing, which includes lawyers, witnesses, subpoenas, and the full adversary process (*CLR*, 1996, June/July).

However, preliminary reports indicate that some jurisdictions have recognized the value of a fully functioning special master who can tour prisons and converse informally with both sides. These arrangements are permissible under the PLRA, but any agreements of this type are not enforceable. Despite the low hourly rate, even California has retained the services of a special master to assist the courts in certain instances (Bien, 1997). However, Vincent Nathan (2000), one of the nation's most respected masters, feels that the PLRA has been the death knell for the future use of masters.

Summary

Prior to the 1960s, the courts had taken a hands-off approach, under which they refused to consider inmate claims of unconstitutional prison conditions. The hands-off doctrine was discarded in the 1960s for a hands-on approach, primarily because of the Supreme Court. The Warren Court extended constitutional rights to minority groups, and provisions of the Bill of Rights were selectively incorporated into the due process clause, making them binding on the states. From the 1960s through the 1970s, the courts found numerous constitutional violations, and appropriately limited the extent to which prison authorities could restrict rights by defining inmates' constitutional rights.

From 1980 through 1986 the Supreme Court took a more restrained approach to inmate rights. Two pivotal decisions, *Bell v. Wolfish* and *Rhodes v. Chapman*, reflected the Court's changing attitude. Their approach was more restrained, but inmates' rights were not completely ignored. However, this era was short-lived, because since 1987 the Court has taken a more rigid approach. Known as "the Court Deference Era," it began with *Turner v. Safley* (1987) and *O'Lone v. Estate of Shabazz* (1987). With these two benchmark cases, the Court made it clear that when it said lower courts should defer to the judgment of correctional administrators, they really meant it. This was further underscored with congressional passage of the PLRA.

Court access provides the only effective mechanism through which inmates can secure their rights. Prison officials are required to assist inmates in preparing and filing legal papers by providing either a law library or individuals who are trained in the law. Various issues, including cost, transportation, hours of operation, and available resources, surround the adequacy of and access to law libraries. The high rate of inmate illiteracy brings into question whether the average inmate can use a law library without assistance. Although there is generally no requirement that inmates have counsel appointed to pursue their cases, some choose to employ them, as attorneys provide an additional means to acquire access to the courts. When inmates have attorneys, prison officials may not unreasonably restrict access to them. Some inmates may also seek assistance from other inmates, who are called jailhouse lawyers.

However, the Court in *Lewis v. Casey* (1996) placed limitations on court access by no longer requiring that inmates have access to a freestanding law library or a person trained in the law. Further, for inmates to successfully bring a claim based on an inadequate law library or legal assistance they must show that they were caused actual injury or are facing imminent injury based on the institution's deficiencies in providing appropriate resources. The "injury" must actually hinder an inmate's ability to pursue a legal claim, such as having a case dismissed or preventing the inmate from filing a claim because of the inadequacies of the prison's law library.

Postconviction actions require specific conditions in order to be reviewed. Tort actions are one form of legal relief, which arise from a claim by one party that another has negligently, maliciously, or deliberately inflicted injury on him or her. Inmates can also bring cases to the federal courts under Section 1983 of the Civil Rights Act, which requires proof that a person, acting under the color of state law, deprived the claimant of a constitutional or federal statutory right.

In civil rights actions, court orders generally take the form of an injunction, which requires that acts either be performed or terminated. Inmates can be awarded damages in some legal actions, including torts and civil rights suits. Inmates who win damages may also be awarded attorneys' fees. Instead of going to trial, inmates may choose to work out a consent decree with the defendant. This involves both parties agreeing to work out a settlement to spare themselves the time, expense, and uncertainty of a trial.

Habeas corpus actions are used to challenge convictions and confinement conditions, although inmates typically choose to file under Section 1983 instead. There are many misconceptions about prisoner litigation; for example, many falsely believe that most inmate claims are frivolous and tie up the justice system.

Judges can mandate a variety of changes as a result of consent decrees or Section 1983 actions; however, the enforcement of judicial orders is not easy. Court orders against resistant defendants are enforced by two methods: resistant defendants can be held in contempt, or judges can supervise compliance or appoint agents to do so. Special masters may also assist the courts in certain legal actions, including making a decision about whether a constitutional right was violated, developing an acceptable and remedial decree prior to ordering a specific improvement, and monitoring and enforcing a remedial decree.

Critical Thinking Questions

1. Profile the different eras in the evolution of prisoners' rights.

2. Outline the major provisions of the Prisoner Litigation Reform Act.

3. How will the Supreme Court's decision in *Casey v. Lewis* affect your ability to do legal research in preparation for filing petitions if you are an inmate?

4. Put yourself in the position of a jailhouse lawyer. Describe the types of assistance you could provide other inmates and the compensation you might receive.

5. You are an inmate considering legal action. Under what circumstances would you file a habeas corpus petition? a civil rights petition?

6. What restrictions have been placed on inmates filing these petitions in death penalty cases?

Test Your Knowledge

1. At the present time the general consensus is that the courts have taken which of the following positions on prisoners' rights?
   a. a hands-off approach
   b. inmates are considered slaves of the state
   c. a radical hands-on approach
   d. a restrained hands-on approach
   e. court deference approach

2. Which of the following postconviction actions is most likely to be used by inmates to pursue claims of unconstitutional prison conditions?
   a. torts
   b. Section 1983
   c. injunctions
   d. habeas corpus
   e. all of the above

3. In *Bounds v. Smith*, the Court established the conditions under which special masters can be appointed.
   a. true
   b. false

4. Most recently inmates have been more likely to file civil rights petitions than habeas actions to rectify unconstitutional prison conditions.
   a. true
   b. false

Endnotes

1. See Chapter 6 for a more thorough discussion of these conditions and this case.

2. Courts use the terms *legitimate government, correctional,* or *penological interests/objectives* in corrections cases to refer to what is construed as necessary requirements for institutional operations (i.e., security, custody, and maintenance of discipline).

3. *Patzner v. Burkett,* 779 F.2d 1363, 1367 (8th Cir. 1985); *Fiacco v. City of Rensselaer, N.Y.,* 783 F.2d 319 (2d Cir. 1986); *Languirand v. Hayden,* 717 F.2d 220, 226-227 n. (5th Cir. 1983); *Wellington v. Daniels,* 717 F. 2d 932, 936 (5th Cir. 1983).

4. A frivolous claim is one in which there is no arguable basis in fact. That includes instances in which the facts are irrational or wholly incredible. For example, an inmate claims that he has been denied the right to practice his religion, but a tenet of his religion is that all practices are so secret he cannot tell what they are (*CLR,* 1996, June/July). Also, claims that have no basis in law are frivolous. For example, an inmate claims that his rights were violated because he was given paper napkins while the guards were given cloth napkins (*CLR,* 1996, June/July).

5. For example, a class of female inmates failed to demonstrate that they were denied meaningful court access despite showing systemwide shortcomings in the library law system. The court reversed a lower court, ruling that there was no violation based on the fact that these plaintiffs had failed to show that they sustained any actual injury or prejudice to existing legal claims (*Klinger v. Department of Corrections,* 1997).

6. These include non-annotated Arizona statutes, Arizona rules of court, federal district court rules, the *Classification Manual, Black's Law Dictionary,* the text of *Lewis v. Casey, Prisoners Self-Litigation Manual,* selected federal district court forms, and other basic materials.

7. In certain parole revocation proceedings, fundamental fairness requires that an attorney be provided (Project, 1994).

8. Prison officials opened an inmate's legal mail on four separate occasions outside of his presence; the court ruled this violated the inmate's right to court access. The court further noted that there were multiple violations, which made it unnecessary to demonstrate prejudice (*Biergo v. Reno,* 1995).

9. This officially took effect as Title VIII of HR 3019, Omnibus Appropriations Bill.

10. Inmates can use this as a vehicle to challenge their conviction, but this occurs only rarely. Under Section 1983 inmates can bring complaints of due process violations that relate to their original conviction. Typically, claims allege violations that occurred prior to or during the original trial and include allegations involving improper arrest or seizure of evidence or other police misconduct, perjury of witnesses, or conspiracy involving the judge and defense counsel or prosecuting attorneys (Thomas, 1988; Turner, 1979).

11. Four percent of the issues resulted in stipulated dismissals and 2 percent went to trial.

12. A failure to comply with a court rule might include, for example, the correctional facility prepared a report responding to the inmate's allegations, and the court notifies the inmate that the report will be treated as a motion for summary judgment and that the motion will be granted, unless the prisoner files an objection [this requires the inmate to refute the report's contents]. Other reasons might include a nonindigent inmate failing to pay filing fees.

13. In at least one case a court found that the injury provision of this act was inapplicable to claims relating to prison disciplinary proceedings because procedural due process does not require emotional or physical harm (*Barnes v. Ramos,* 1997).

Prisoners' Constitutional, Substantive, and Procedural Rights

15

LEARNING OBJECTIVES

After completing this chapter, you should be able to:

1. Recount how the courts have tried to balance inmates' First Amendment rights with the need of correctional institutions to limit inmates' use of mail and the receipt of publications.

2. Explain how the courts have tried to balance inmates' Eighth Amendment rights with the need of correctional institutions to use isolated confinement as a tool for maintaining discipline and control and segregating some inmates.

3. Discuss the broad issues associated with the use of force by correctional officers in the prison environment.

4. Describe the levels of control correctional staff may employ on inmates and the circumstances under which they can be used.

5. Specify the circumstances under which correctional institutions and their staff can be held liable for inmate-on-inmate assaults.

6. Explain how prison rules can violate substantive due process requirements.

7. Explain the basic considerations in determining whether inmates are required to be afforded due process in disciplinary procedures.

8. Outline the Fourth Amendment safeguards that govern urine tests and cell, pat-down, strip, and body cavity searches.

KEY TERMS AND CONCEPTS

Administrative
  segregation
Censorship
Clear and present danger
Conditions of confinement
Control
Cruel and unusual
  punishment
Deadly force
Deliberate indifference
Disciplinary detention
Electronic shocking
  devices
Empty hand control
  techniques

Excessive force
Keistering
Less than lethal force
Liberty interests
Procedural due
  process
Publisher-only rule
Reasonable force
Resistance
Restraints
Substantive due
  process
Tactical response
  teams
Verbal direction

Introduction

This chapter focuses on the extent to which inmates and pretrial detainees are afforded basic constitutional rights.[1] As noted in Chapter 14, although inmates are entitled to basic constitutional rights, legitimate prison operational needs—such as requirements for maintaining order, security, and safety—may justify the restriction of these rights. This chapter examines how the courts have balanced these legitimate institutional operational concerns against inmates' attempts to exercise their constitutional rights.

First Amendment Rights

The First Amendment to the U.S. Constitution guarantees that no laws will be enacted that restrict or abridge our freedom of religion, speech, and the press. However, under certain circumstances, courts have restricted these rights when they unduly interfere with competing and important government interests (Dormer, 1997). Because these rights are viewed as fundamental, the Court has required very compelling reasons for their restriction. The operational objectives of prisons have been among those compelling reasons. This chapter focuses on inmates' rights regarding the use of mail and the right to receive publications. Chapter 17 examines the exercise of freedom of religion and the right to medical and mental health care in prison, and Chapter 21 examines such related issues as the right to use the telephone and visitation rights.

Use of Mail

Books and letters offer inmates the opportunity to psychologically escape the rigors of the prison environment, but until the 1970s this right was severely restricted. Neither the Pennsylvania nor Auburn systems allowed inmates to receive or send letters. By the end of the 19th century, more liberal letter writing privileges were instituted (McKelvey, 1977). However, heavy **censorship** of both incoming and outgoing letters, which allowed prison staff to open inmate mail, read it, delete objectionable material, and confiscate disapproved items, was practiced and continued into the 1950s (Fox, 1983). Limitations were placed on persons with whom inmates could correspond, the number of letters received and sent, and the types of items inmates could receive in letters and packages. Inspection of incoming inmate mail was justified because it enabled prison officials to confiscate instruments of escape, any material that might incite inmates (e.g., pornography), and drugs. It also provided prior knowledge of upsetting news so staff could prepare the prisoner. Reasons given for inspecting out-

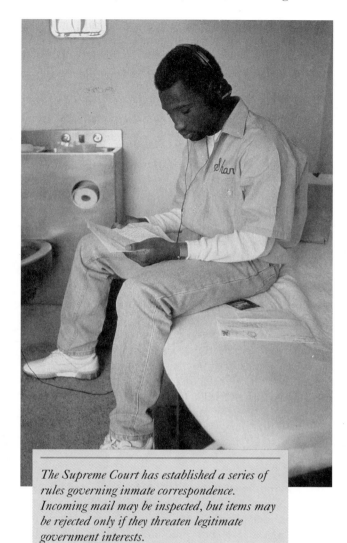

The Supreme Court has established a series of rules governing inmate correspondence. Incoming mail may be inspected, but items may be rejected only if they threaten legitimate government interests.

going mail included protecting the public from inmate scams, threats, insults, or obscene letters; preventing letters casting an unfavorable or inaccurate light on the prison; and obtaining information on possible escapes, riots, and inmate dissatisfactions (Palmer, 1999; *Palmigiano v. Travisono*, 1970).

By the mid-1970s, the courts had abandoned support for unregulated censorship of prison mail. In a series of cases, the Supreme Court established rules regulating the official inspection of inmate mail.[2] In *Procunier v. Martinez* (1974), the Court held that institutional restrictions on correspondence abridged the rights of inmates and also those of nonprisoners who wanted to correspond with inmates. Although prison staff could still inspect mail, their actions with respect to enclosed materials were to be controlled by how strongly these materials threatened legitimate government interests [e.g., in *Herrera v. Scully* (1993), the court upheld a mail search resulting in the discovery of forged motor vehicle documents].

The general rule on incoming correspondence, whether from inmates or noninmates, is that it may be rejected if found to be detrimental to the security, good order, or discipline within the institution, or if it might facilitate criminal activity (*Thornburgh v. Abbott,* 1989). The Court upheld a complete ban on inmate-to-inmate correspondence on the same basis (*Turner v. Safley,* 1987).[3]

Because outgoing correspondence usually poses no threat to prison security or other legitimate penal objectives, it can only be opened and read or censored if evidence of some valid penological interest exists. However, prisons have argued successfully that the only way to know if a letter contains this forbidden material is to open and read it (Zimmerman, 1999). Thus, in *Washington v. Meachum* (1996) the court supported the right of prison officials to read outgoing correspondence on the grounds there is no way to determine whether escape plans or other forbidden materials—such as threats of blackmail or extortion, encoded messages, or requests to nonfamily members for goods or money—are being sent except by looking at the correspondence. Further, in this case there was no evidence that the department employee who censored the mail revealed any personal information contained in the letters. The court felt that this policy was the least restrictive means available to further the interest of maintaining prison security, order, and rehabilitation.

Publications

First Amendment protections include the right to receive information and ideas, but these rights are restricted under certain conditions; for example, pornographic material is not protected. Any material that constitutes a **clear and present danger** of inciting or producing lawless actions (e.g., books about making weapons, explosives, alcoholic beverages, drugs, or escape methods) can be prohibited. This view was upheld in *Thornburg v. Abbott* (1989) and, more recently, in *Packett v. Clark* (1996).

Although staff members can screen publications, only wardens can reject them. Further, no "hit lists" of publications absolutely barred from distribution in the prison are permitted; for example, a magazine cannot be banned because it provides information on illicit drugs, but a particular issue can be if it advocates drug usage (Collins, 1997b; Mushlin, 1993). With regard to sexually explicit material, a recent Ninth Circuit decision (*Mauro v. Arpaio,* 1999) suggests that all material that simply displays frontal nudity, like *Playboy,* will now be prohibited (see also *Amatel v. Reno,* 1998). The court found that there was a rational connection between the ban and legitimate jail concerns such as security, sexual harassment, and rehabilitation. Not allowing inmates to receive these types of publications addresses two security issues: (1) magazines containing sexually explicit material have resulted in disputes between inmates, and (2) inmates have used nude pictures to sexually harass female COs (*CLR,* 1999, Oct./Nov.).

Recognizing that publications can also be used to smuggle contraband into the prison (e.g., it can be hidden in bindings), the Court upheld a **publisher-only rule,** mandating that inmates may only receive hardback books if they are mailed directly by publishers, book clubs, or bookstores (*Bell v. Wolfish,* 1979). However, a court found a book policy unconstitutional that denied inmates the right to receive gifts of books sent by friends and family from a publisher (*CLR,* 1999, Aug./Sept.; *Crofton v. Roe,* 1999).

Inmate compensation for publishing is another aspect of First Amendment rights that has been addressed by the courts. Should inmates be allowed to receive compensation for their biographies? This issue arose in response to New York's passage of its Son of Sam law. The Son of Sam law was created after the notorious serial killer David Berkowitz, who signed all his correspondence "Son of Sam," was offered money for his biography. The original law was struck down by the Supreme Court, but a revised law was upheld in 1992. The law provides victims with the opportunity to receive compensation from the inmate for any monetary gain that results from the crime. Some states, such as Florida, have taken the Son of Sam law one step further by prohibiting inmates from receiving any compensation for their biographies.

Eighth Amendment Rights

The Eighth Amendment protects us from **cruel and unusual punishment.** This clause was initially written to ban the inhumane and barbarous punishments that existed when it was adopted (e.g., breaking at the wheel, burning at the stake). Today, it is interpreted to include physical punishment and various prison practices and conditions (Luise, 1989). Typically, Eighth Amendment cases have focused on conditions and practices, such as solitary confinement, corporal punishment, use of force by guards, **conditions of confinement** (e.g., medical care, food service, and personal safety), overcrowding, and escapes.

In defining or clarifying the meaning of cruel and unusual punishment, the courts have applied a variety of "tests," which focus on:

1. punishment that is incompatible with the "evolving standards of decency that mark the progress of a maturing society" (*Trop v. Dulles,* 1958).

2. punishment that involves the infliction of "unnecessary and wanton pain" (*Gregg v. Georgia,* 1976).

3. punishment that is excessive or disproportionate to the offense (*Trop v. Dulles,* 1958).

4. punishment that is incompatible with "broad and idealistic concepts of dignity, civilized standards, humanity, and decency" (*Estelle v. Gamble*, 1976).

5. deliberate indifference to the needs of inmates—refers to prison services: medical, food, and personal safety (*Estelle v. Gamble*, 1976).

6. conditions that deny inmates the minimal civilized measures of life's necessities (*Wilson v. Seiter*, 1991).

All these rather vague tests have evolved into two basic tests: conditions of confinement and the use of excessive force (Collins, 2000).

Conditions of Confinement

Conditions of confinement cases often focus on overcrowding. In 1998, state prisons were estimated to be operating between 13 and 22 percent above capacity; California was at 23 percent above capacity, while the federal system was at 27 percent (Mumola & Beck, 1999). In 1995, the Florida legislature passed a statute allowing its state prisons to increase their capacity to 150 percent.

In deciding conditions of confinement cases the court first established the totality to conditions test, which focused on a series of conditions that when taken together represented a constitutional violation. This led to a heavy focus on overcrowding, which led some courts to rule that if there were more inmates than a facility was designed to hold, this was an unconstitutional condition. This was followed by the *Bell v. Wolfish* case, in which the Court said that there was no one-man one-cell rule and that the effects of overcrowding rather than overcrowding per se should be what the courts focus on in these cases (Collins, 1997). This was further reinforced in *Rhodes v. Chapman* (1981) and *Wilson v. Seiter* (1991), where the Court made it clear that overcrowding per se does not constitute cruel and unusual punishment in violation of the Eighth Amendment; however, the deprivation of basic needs (e.g., food, warmth, or exercise) that may result from overcrowding can be unconstitutional. The Court held that uncomfortable conditions are part of the penalty inmates pay for their criminality.

Under the PLRA, the courts are obligated to employ the least restrictive alternative to rectify this situation. Restricting a facility's population or releasing inmates is a last resort and requires extraordinary situations. Thus, the courts typically focus on rectifying these conditions in other ways (Collins, 1997b):

1. *Food* Providing nutritionally balanced meals prepared and served under sanitary conditions
2. *Shelter* Correcting the overall prison or jail environment, taking into consideration noise levels, lighting, ventilation, plumbing, building conditions, cell size, and so on
3. *Sanitation* Avoiding possible health hazards, including vermin infestation; improper food preparation and handling practices; functioning plumbing; and overall sanitary conditions
4. *Health Care* Providing appropriate medical, dental, and mental health services
5. *Personal Safety* Providing reasonable safety from serious risk of assault, rape, or other serious injury from other inmates

Perhaps the most common example of how the effects of overcrowding can create a potential constitutional violation is that of inmate safety. When overcrowding overwhelms the classification system, placement decisions are not made on the basis of a sophisticated classification instrument, but rather on where space can be found. Officials may know that a particular inmate does not belong with certain other inmates, but the availability of a bed in that unit trumps their professional knowledge and drives the decision to put the inmate in the wrong place. The result often is an increase in violence. If serious enough, this "failure to protect" can violate the Eighth Amendment's cruel and unusual punishment clause.

Similarly, sheer numbers of inmates can outstrip the ability of the medical department to provide adequate medical care. Or, an overcrowded facility may wear out much faster, creating problems with plumbing or sanitation. Other examples can be readily found.

What about relief? Assume the court finds a constitutional violation based on excessively high levels of violence. The questions for the court then become, What are its causes? and Can they be corrected? If the problem stems clearly from overcrowding, then the obvious solution is to impose some sort of population cap. However, the Prisoner Litigation Reform Act limits the court's power to take this step until other possible forms of relief have been tried and have failed. The idea of a population cap is to reduce the population of the institution back to a level where the existing staffing and physical plant can handle the population properly. If a court can't initially reduce the supply of inmates, perhaps it will be forced to order increases in the supply of staff or beds. So, instead of having one officer, the overcrowded cell block may have to have three. A cop on every corner may address a failure-to-protect problem, but it will still leave a prison staggering under the load of too many inmates (Collins, 2000).

In our In Their Own Words feature, "Dealing with Overcrowding Issues," Bill Collins (2000) presents his own perspective on how to deal with the consequences of this condition.

Isolated Confinement Isolation of inmates has long been used by prison officials as a form of discipline. Today, inmates can be isolated in **administrative segregation**

Dealing with Overcrowding Issues

Overcrowding can no longer be the basis of a claim of constitutional violations; so, it must be approached by looking at the unconstitutional conditions that result from it. If prisons are overcrowded, you will probably find that one or more of the following constitutional violations exist: an inadequate level of safety, inadequate levels of medical care, or a physical plant that has deteriorated to the point that it is creating a serious threat to the health and safety of the inmates. For example, if there are violations of public safety, one possibility is that the classification system has broken down and inmates are now assaulting one another. Thus, the prison is doing a poor job of protecting inmates, and this is a violation of the Eighth Amendment's cruel and un-usual punishment clause. Thus, you would back into the issue of over-crowding in the context of seeking relief from these conditions(s); that is, you can then begin by questioning whether the cause of a violation(s) is overcrowding. However, you do not say to the court that this facility has too many inmates be-cause it will respond, "So what?" What the courts want to know is the effect on these key human needs of having twice as many inmates. How has the institution's ability to deliver in these areas been compromised by the overcrowding?

So you have multiple conditions that the court has found to be un-constitutional, and the reason for this is that you have too many in-mates. Now you run into the PLRA limitation on when the court can impose population caps. In the pre-PLRA days the court would impose a population cap, which meant you might have to release inmates or not admit any new inmates. Now the court says you have to try something else first. I have not as yet seen what alternative the courts have or even if any overcrowding cases have come before the courts in the last 4 years.

My first thought was, well, if the court cannot reduce the population to meet what the institution can de-liver, it will then order the institu-tion to deliver more. A case in point. If the court cannot reduce the level of inmates to meet the level of staffing, I would order the institu-tion to increase staffing to meet the level of inmates. By doing this you may be able to address the failure-to-protect issue.

Source: Bill Collins (2000). Attorney at law and co-editor of the Corrections Law Reporter. *Personal communi-cation.*

---

while awaiting a disciplinary hearing, or because they are dangerous to other inmates or staff; they can also be placed in **disciplinary detention** for rule violations.

The use of a dark or isolated cell, known as the *hole*, for punishing those who violate prison rules dates to the use of the medieval dungeon. For a long time, this meant that the individual was put in a bare, unlit, and unventilated cell and given a diet of bread and water, sometimes a blanket, and a bucket for bodily needs (Barnes & Teeters, 1951; Rothman, 1980). Confinement was supposed to be for short periods—from a few days to 2 weeks. Wardens easily got around these rules by keeping inmates in the hole for the allowable limit (e.g., 6 days), removing them, and then putting them back in again. This routine could go on for months.

The practice of isolating inmates for disciplinary pur-poses has been legally challenged. However, the federal courts have refused to label this practice unconstitu-tional because it represents a valid means of protecting the general prison population, staff, and specific inmates and may also prevent disobedience and escapes (Mush-lin, 1998a; Zimmerman, 1999).

The courts have intervened in cases in which they believed the duration or conditions of confinement con-stituted cruel and unusual punishment. Some combina-tions of the following have been found to be violations (Mushlin, 1998a; Zimmerman, 1999):

1. *Diet* bread and water and certain restrictive diets not meeting basic daily nutritional requirements

2. *Personal hygiene* lack of soap, water, towel, toilet paper, toothbrush, and clothing

3. *Physical state of the cell* lack of lights, windows, mat-tresses, and general lack of cleanliness

4. *Exercise* limited opportunity for exercise

5. *Exposure* lack of heat and keeping inmates nude

6. *Pests* the presence of mice, rats, roaches, and other vermin

There are no strict rules about which combination of these factors are considered cruel and unusual punish-ment. In fact, the Supreme Court has held that harsh conditions and rough disciplinary treatment are part of the price convicted criminals pay for their offenses against society (*Rhodes v. Chapman*, 1981; *Whitley v. Al-bers*, 1986). In *Beverati v. Smith* (1997), two inmates maintained that their 6-month confinement in adminis-trative segregation was a grossly excessive punishment. However, an appeals court reaffirmed the district court decision that rejected the inmates' claims that their Eighth and Fourteenth Amendment rights were violated when they were confined to administrative segregation for 6 months following the confiscation of materials considered by the prison officials to be escape paraphernalia from the cell the inmates shared.

Not every hardship or harsh act is considered unconstitutional (Zimmerman, 1999). Indeed, a federal appeals court failed to find objectionable the placement of an inmate in administrative segregation for 4 days without clothes, water, or a mattress, with only milk (which the inmate did not like) to drink (*Williams v. Delo*, 1995). If confinement is short, the courts are more willing to allow much harsher conditions. The overriding standard for conditions to be deemed cruel and unusual punishment appears to be based on whether they jeopardize the mental and physical health of the inmate. To reach this level, they must deprive an inmate of "a single identifiable human need such as food, warmth, or exercise" (*Young v. Quinlan*, 1992, p. 365). This was determined to be the case when an inmate was denied outdoor exercise; provided personal hygiene items only if he could pay for them; and subjected to noise, constant lighting, poor ventilation, and improper food preparation (*Keenan v. Hall*, 1996). Nevertheless, for prison officials to be held liable for unconstitutional conditions they must know of and disregard an excessive risk to inmates' health or safety (*Vance v. Peters*, 1996; Zimmerman, 1999). This issue arose in *Bracewell v. Lobmiller* (1996), where an inmate was placed in disciplinary segregation and subjected to the presence of a mentally ill inmate who would throw her feces and urine, while constantly making noise. Prison officials were not liable because they did not have actual knowledge that the activities in the segregation unit were serious enough to injure the inmate.

Generally, there are no agreed-upon limits for the length of detention as long as the conditions do not constitute cruel and unusual punishment. One New Hampshire district court imposed a limit of 14 consecutive days in isolation, but other courts have upheld periods of 12 months, 2 years, 5 years, and even indefinite confinement (Gobert & Cohen, 1981; Mushlin, 1993). However, the longer an inmate is confined, the more likely it is that the court will examine the reason for confinement to see if it justifies the circumstances (Mushlin, 1993). The key is whether the punishment is disproportionate to the inmate's offense or constitutes repression of some basic right (Gobert & Cohen, 1981, 1992). Finally, the courts will generally uphold long or indefinite confinement when an inmate's status is regularly reviewed and the prisoner can work his or her way out of these units (*CLR*, 1995, April).[4]

Despite a long history that has shown the potential emotional damage and deterioration in mental functioning that can result from extended isolation under certain conditions, the courts have been reluctant to consider the psychological effects of isolation as constituting cruel and unusual punishment, as long as an inmate's basic needs are met (Luise, 1989). Long periods of isolation also tend to increase resentment and rage, resulting in more numerous and severe breaches of prison discipline upon release. This suggests the need to consider the psychological impact on the prison and to explore alternative arrangements.

Inmates' Rights to Protection Against Assault Correctional facilities are dangerous places, because they hold people either accused or convicted of crimes against other members of society. People are in prison to protect the public from their behaviors. But, who protects an inmate from being victimized by other inmates? COs may find this to be a no-win situation: When they intervene in fights, their actions may be challenged as cruel and unusual punishment; however, if they take no action, they may be accused of indifference, which may also be construed as cruel and unusual punishment. Our Consider This feature, "Do Inmates Have the Right to Self-Defense?" deals with this charged issue.

Some staff may feel the risk of assault is part of the cost of being convicted of a crime (Gobert & Cohen, 1981), but the responsibility of prison officials to protect inmates from assaults is supported by court decisions and, in some jurisdictions, it is mandated by statute or codes of regulation. A 1994 Supreme Court decision clearly states its view that inmates are entitled to protection from assaults by other inmates:

> [H]aving stripped [inmates] of virtually every means of self-protection and foreclosed their access to outside aid, government officials are not free to let the state of nature take its course.... [G]ratuitously allowing the beating or rape of one prisoner by another serves no "legitimate penological objective[s] any more than it squares with evolving standards of decency ... [nor is it] part of the penalty criminals pay for their offense against society." (*Farmer v. Brennan*, 1994, p. 4447)

Farmer v. Brennan (1994) involved a transsexual inmate, who had feminine characteristics (including having silicone breast implants and wearing "his" shirt off one shoulder). He was placed in the general population of the federal prison at Terre Haute where he was beaten and raped. Although not objecting to this placement, the inmate alleged that it was made despite knowledge on the part of prison officials that this facility had a violent environment and a history of assaults, and that he would be particularly vulnerable to attack because of his female characteristics. The issue before the Court was whether it was safe for prison officials to place anyone with this inmate's appearance in the prison's general population (*CLR*, 1994a). To be held liable under the Eighth Amendment requires a showing of **deliberate indifference,**

CONSIDER THIS

Do Inmates Have the Right to Self-Defense?

After days of threatening sexual innuendo, Indiana Reformatory prisoner Michael Evans attempted to rape cell block neighbor John Rowe. Rowe responded by hitting Evans with a hot pot and calling for help. Prison officials found that Rowe had violated prison rules by committing battery, . . . and imposed as a punishment one year in disciplinary segregation. Rowe was not allowed to plead self-defense. In *Rowe v. De-Bruyn,* the Seventh Circuit Court upheld the outcome of the prison hearing, concluding that prisoners may be denied the right to defend themselves against the violent attacks by other prisoners. The appeal to the Supreme Court was denied on the basis that the right of self-defense is not a constitutional right (*Rowe v. DeBruyn,* 1994). As a result, prisoners in the Indiana penal system face submitting to violence, even rape, or suffering potentially severe and recurrent punishment for their acts of self-defense (Kaye, 1996).

Kaye (1996, Spring) provides the constitutional basis for the right of prisoners to defend themselves:

A manual for jailhouse lawyers informs prisoners: "It is virtually certain that you retain your right of self-defense if attacked by a fellow inmate. Contrary to the arguments in *Rowe,* the due process clause supports a right to self-defense. First, it has long been held that due process protects those rights essential to the Anglo-American conception of criminal justice, and self-defense is such a right. Second, . . . an emerging strand of due process doctrine supports the argument that the state must either protect institutionalized individuals, or allow them to protect themselves. . . .

[Thus, the] courts should recognize the prisoner's constitutional right to self-defense has been an indispensable element of Anglo-American criminal justice, and it is therefore a fundamental right within the doctrine of due process. Furthermore, the ideals of the law governing the due process rights of the institutionalized can best be realized by recognizing a necessity defense in the institutional context—and this necessity defense likewise provides a sound basis for a prisoner's right to self-defense.

Necessity is a long-standing defense to criminal liability. It is properly invoked by one who has broken a law, but did so because lawbreaking was necessary to avoid a greater evil. Most commonly, necessity is claimed where the lawbreaker's life depended on the lawbreaking. While there is no universally accepted definition of necessity, its basic elements are widely agreed upon: "conduct that the actor believes to be necessary to avoid a harm or evil . . . is justifiable, provided that . . . the harm or evil sought to be avoided by such conduct is greater than that sought to be prevented by the law broken."

Examine the arguments presented by Kaye for allowing inmates the right to defend themselves. Do you believe these should be supported? *Source: Adapted from Anders Kaye (1996). Comment: Dangerous Places: The Right to Self-Defense in Prison and Prison Conditions Jurisprudence.* University of Chicago Law Review, 63, 693.

---

which is a standard of recklessness the Court defined in the following manner:

To find prison officials had den[ied] an inmate humane conditions requires [that they] . . . know . . . of and disregard . . . an excessive risk to inmate health and safety. [Thus, inmates can] prevail in these cases even without warning prison officials if the risk is obvious; actual knowledge can be implied from the circumstances of a situation. This puts prison officials on notice that willful ignorance will not suffice as a defense in these cases. Thus if an inmate presents evidence showing that a substantial risk of inmate attacks was "long-standing, pervasive, well-documented, or expressly noted" by prison officials in the past, these circumstances suggest that the

defendant-official being sued had been exposed to information concerning the risk and thus "must have known" about it. [An inmate then] can establish exposure to a sufficiently serious risk of harm "by showing that he belongs to an identifiable group of prisoners who are frequently singled out for violent attack by other inmates." (*Farmer v. Brennan,* 1994, pp. 837, 842)

In the *Farmer* case, the inmate alleged that his feminine appearance and the violent atmosphere of the prison were "circumstances" that should have alerted prison officials to the substantial risk he faced of rape and violence by placement in the general prison population (Rifkin, 1995). However, these circumstances fail to meet the new standard the Court set forth in this case.[5]

The test established in *Farmer* was used by the Eighth Circuit Court as the basis for its decision in *Webb v. Lawrence County* (1998). In this case, the court held that a young 19-year-old inmate in a cell with an older sexual offender failed to prove that prison officials were aware of the risk of harm to him (*CLR*, 1998, June/July, p. 39).

Boston (1994) also asserts that the *Farmer* ruling "ratifies a broad body of case law . . . [holding] . . . prison officials liable for violence resulting from generalized failures of prison administration" (p. 7), which would include deficiencies, such as the following (Boston & Manville, 1995):

1. Failure to appropriately classify, or segregate, particularly violent or vulnerable inmates (e.g., inmates likely to be sexually victimized) when assigning cells

2. Not providing for the adequate supervision of inmates, including the monitoring of inmates in high-risk areas—such as shower areas or certain housing areas—or keeping two COs in open dormitories to better control homosexuality

3. Failure to develop policies to deal with high rates of known patterns of assault

The Court's decision implied that administrative responsibility may be expanded to include knowledge of conditions inside their facilities and prison officials' broad knowledge of the dynamics of prison life. Thus, prison staff would be expected to know that they are acting with deliberate indifference by creating a situation with a high potential for violence (e.g., by placing a white biker with a swastika tattoo in a cell with a black inmate) (*CLR*, 1994); or by ignoring the rise of HIV and AIDS (i.e., acting with deliberate indifference requires closer scrutiny of cases involving a high potential for sexual assault, given that victimization can mean a death sentence) (Rifkin, 1995).

Finally, there is the related issue of officials or staff actively permitting, or encouraging, an inmate assault, or standing by while one occurs (Boston & Manville, 1995). For example, a court ruled an inmate's claim valid when a correctional officer instigated and directed other inmates to beat him (*Durre v. Dempsey*, 1989). Nevertheless, the courts recognize prison staff may not always be able, nor may it be wise for them, to intervene in all situations. Indeed, no Eighth Amendment violation was found when several COs, surrounded by dozens of inmates, failed to break up a fight, because they felt this would have increased their risk of injury and that of other inmates (*Williams v. Willits*, 1988).

Use of Force

The use of force in a correctional setting is affected by a variety of factors, including an inmate population with a propensity for violence; court decisions limiting the circumstances in which force can be employed; and correctional standards and training that provide more concrete guidelines on the types of force that can be employed to control inmate violence and to ensure compliance with staff directives. In this section, we examine policies and training, excessive force, reasonable force, control versus

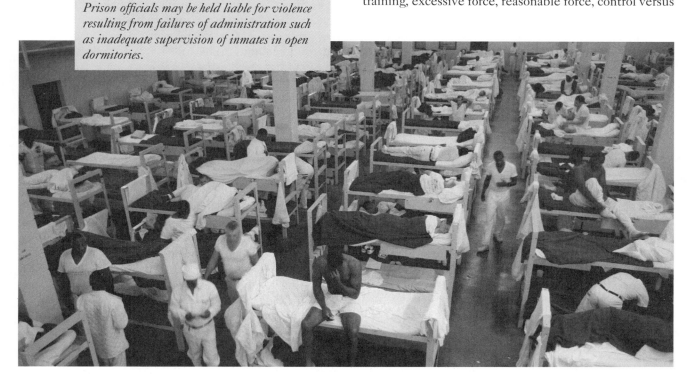

Prison officials may be held liable for violence resulting from failures of administration such as inadequate supervision of inmates in open dormitories.

resistance, restraints, deadly force, and tactical response teams.

Policies and Training In examining use of force issues it is important to focus on an agency's policies and training because they can prevent officer and inmate injury and can also enable an agency and its staff to avoid liability for excessive use of force claims. To avoid civil liability and to protect staff from facing possible criminal charges, correctional agencies must have in place policies that:

> set forth general guidelines for employees which provide clear and distinct boundaries to guide discretionary authority. Policies should not eliminate the use of discretion by correcting officers, but rather [should] structure and guide discretionary actions. [In fact] the first line of defense against potential litigation and proper employee conduct is well-written policies. In the area of use of force, policy can assist in reducing allegations of excessive force or brutality, reducing [future] civil lawsuits, improving employee decision making, and reducing the liability on the part of the organization's administrators. To avoid liability policies [they] should be attentive to the three Cs: current, comprehensive, and constitutional. (Ross, 1999, pp. 81–82)

Additionally, staff should receive training related to use of force policies and the requisite physical requirements for their use. Training should focus on how to make appropriate decisions in use of force incidents; properly using physical control skills; competency in using equipment restraints, impact weapons, and aerosols; and the importance of documenting and reporting use of force incidents. Also, COs should be trained to recognize the signs and medical symptoms of alcohol use; illicit and prescription drug use; and mental illness, heat conditions, and asphyxia so that they will avoid using certain types of force or restraint methods on individuals with these problems. For example, in the case we describe on page 368 the subject might still be alive if the arresting police officers had recognized that he was schizophrenic and taken him to a mental hospital as opposed to jail, or the detention staff had been familiar with the signs of positional asphyxia.

Excessive Force Correctional officers (COs) are responsible for large numbers of inmates, many with a known propensity for violence. It is no surprise that they are confronted with situations requiring the use of force. To understand both the appropriate and the excessive or punitive use of force requires that we examine both the legally relevant factors and the informal CO subculture.

Although the dynamics of the use of force in correctional settings have not been well-explored, available information suggests that its use is governed by a combination of subcultural norms and bureaucratic factors that broadly define expected or acceptable behavior. Before being given control of a unit, new officers are usually teamed with an experienced officer who "shows them the ropes." New officers learn as much by observing how their trainers handle situations as by what they are told. Toch (1977b) asserts that, as in a police setting, the excessive use of force by COs is based on norms in the officer subculture; these norms may justify its use by arguing that it is necessary to manage inmates.

Like police officers, COs are permitted and expected to use force under certain circumstances and in self-defense. The issue is not the use of force per se, but its use in excessive or brutal ways. Most instances of the use of **excessive force**—unnecessary force used to inflict punishment—occur in unusual circumstances, such as in riots, protests, or punitive transfers, in which inmates challenge the staff's authority. When unjustified force is employed in these circumstances, it may represent the staff's way of reestablishing administrative authority. A more serious problem involves circumstances in which inmates are brutalized for extended periods for punishment or control (Bowker, 1980); for example, as long as 5 months after the Attica riot, inmates were still being punished for their participation. Reprisals of this kind have also occurred following other riots.

The issue of misuse of force has always been a problem; but, today it is generally more under control than in previous years (Collins, 2000). Nevertheless, cases still continue to surface as our Close-Up, "Excessive Use of Force: *Madrid v. Gomez* (1995, 1998)," indicates.

In another case, eight COs at Corcoran State Prison in California were accused of violating inmates' rights. It has been speculated that the officers were using the inmates as gladiators, pitting them against one another for their own entertainment. Since 1994, at least 12 deaths have resulted from these fistfights. Twice as high as the rest of the nation, the number of deaths prompted the investigation. Indictments charged the officers with violating the civil rights of inmates by engaging in a blood sport of pitting rival gangs against one another (*CLR*, 1998, June/July, p. 7). To date, one case has been settled. The victim was paralyzed after a corrections officer shot him during a fight that was set up by the officer (*Corrections Professional*, 1999). Neither of the inmates possessed any type of weapon, nor did they pose a serious threat to the safety of other inmates. Although the California DOC refused to admit any wrongdoing, they did choose to settle the case by awarding the inmate with $2.2 million (*Corrections Professional*, 1999). Our Consider This feature, "The Trial of the Corcoran 8," on page 362 takes a more in-depth look at this case.

California is not alone in the misuse of force; three New Jersey correctional officers were accused of assaulting several INS detainees. "Prosecutors showed that officers at the jail beat and kicked the detainees and used pliers to pull hairs out of their genitals" (*CLR*, 1998,

Excessive Use of Force:
Madrid v. Gomez (1995, 1998)

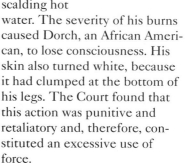

Pelican Bay is a California facility that comprises a maximum security prison and a security housing unit (SHU). Assignment to the SHU is reserved for those inmates who become affiliated with a prison gang or commit a serious disciplinary infraction once in prison (*Madrid v. Gomez*, 1995, p. 1154). Inmates filed a class action suit claiming that there was excessive use of force by the prison guards. The court found a number of incidents of excessive use of force, including the following:

- One inmate protested a correctional officer's calling him derogatory names by refusing to give back his food tray. The inmate prepared himself for a cell extraction as he continued to refuse to return the tray, but he did not threaten the correctional officer nor did he have a weapon. The cell extraction began with two shots from a Taser gun, which hit the inmate in the chest.

    Castillo testified that one of the officers then hit him on the top of his head with the butt of the gas gun, knocking him unconscious. When he regained consciousness, he was on the floor with his face down. An officer was stepping on his hands and hitting him on his calves with a baton, at which point

Castillo passed out a second time. (*Madrid v. Gomez*, 1995, p. 1159)

The incident report, however, stated that Castillo hit his head on the toilet. Both the testimony of a guard who chose to break the code of silence, as well as medical evidence, provided credibility to this incident of excessive use of force.

- Martinez spit on a guard and struck him with his food tray. The inmate was then placed in restraints against his will. Unconscious, he was removed from his cell as another inmate witnessed additional use of force. The witness testified that officers were kicking the unconscious Martinez in the head, the back, and the chest. The court found that this level of force used against Martinez was not motivated by a good faith effort to restore order or maintain the security of the prison (*Madrid v. Gomez*, 1998, p. 1160).

- Dorch, a mentally ill inmate, who had previously bitten a guard, was causing additional problems by covering himself in his own feces and urine. He was forced to take a bath so that he could be cleaned despite the fact that a shower was close by. Dorch

received second- and third-degree burns as a result of the guards' placing him in scalding hot water. The severity of his burns caused Dorch, an African American, to lose consciousness. His skin also turned white, because it had clumped at the bottom of his legs. The Court found that this action was punitive and retaliatory and, therefore, constituted an excessive use of force.

Due to the significantly high number of incidents of excessive use of force, the court "held that beating unarmed prisoners after disciplinary incidents were over, a bath of scalding water administered to a mentally ill prisoner, and the use of a Taser gun to extract a prisoner from a cell after he did not return his meal tray are examples of excessive use of force" (Mushlin, 1998, p. 52).

Although Pelican Bay has had problems, the special master appointed to supervise the institution's compliance with the court order indicates that this facility has made substantial progress in controlling improper use of force (Collins, 2000).

June/July, p. 7). The officers were found guilty of assault and misconduct.

Acceptable Levels of Force   Whether force used by staff in an institutional setting is considered to be **reasonable force** is governed by two factors: (1) the circumstances under which the force is used and (2) the amount of force employed. Thus, reasonable force involves the amount of force necessary to regain control of the situation—that is, the amount of force that would be used by a reasonable correctional officer to deal with inmate resistance in a given situation (Hemmens & Atherton, 1999).

Although stressful conditions may make it tempting for officers to personalize insults and failures, personal reprisals must never affect the decision to apply force. Also, COs must never let their egos interfere with their use of force decision. "[D]e-escalating the situation, and reducing the possibility for conflict, is the goal of the officer and must not be regarded as 'losing face'" (Atherton, 1999, p. 66).

Generally, when COs use excessive force inmates may (1) bring a tort suit in state court under state law (rarely done), or (2) bring a civil rights suit under Section 1983, claiming the excessive force violated either their

CONSIDER THIS

The problems at Corcoran can be tied to:

1. California's unique shooting policy at that time, which allowed officers to use firearms to stop physically assaultive behavior and other disturbances that presented an immediate danger of escape, loss of life, great bodily harm, or damage to a substantial amount of valuable property (Cal Penal Code SOS 3276, 1991).
2. A DOC policy that tried to integrate inmates from different ethnic and geographic groups on the exercise yard of this high-security prison, which caused fights and deadly shootings by guards (Arax, 2000, June 10, p. 1).
3. Staff and agency culture, which "tacitly embraced the physical abuse of inmates as an acceptable correctional tool and a use of firearms which was unparalleled in American experience" (CLR, 1999, Feb./March).

The Allegations

The incidents at Corcoran were brought to public attention by a series of *Los Angeles Times* news articles. These articles alleged that officers used the inmates as gladiators, pitting them against one another for their own entertainment. At least 12 deaths had resulted from these fistfights since 1994. The resulting state legislative investigation found a pattern of brutality at Corcoran, and an independent panel of experts found that almost 8 out of 10 guard shootings were not only unjustified but that the state also had failed to fully investigate these incidents (Arax, 2000). An FBI investigation yielded sufficient evidence for the prosecutors to charge eight officers with violating the civil rights of inmates by

setting up these fights (*CLR*, 1998, June/July, p. 7). In none of the shootings was deadly force required to bring these inmates under control. Examples of the alleged behavior of these officers include the following:

A sergeant held meetings with gunpost officers before the yards opened to review which inmates were going to fight (Arax, 2000, p. 3). . . .

Officer Farquhar testified that Tate [an inmate] appeared nervous as he was led out to the yard. Prosecutors say he had reason to be. He and his cellmate, Anthony James, also a Crip, had been moved to a cell block stacked with rival Mexican gang members from Southern California. Fights [between these groups were quite common]. . . . Just fifteen minutes before Tate and James were led out to the yard, Farquhar witnessed a fight between another black and a Mexican gang member. If policy had been followed, federal prosecutors argue, the fight should have dictated that the yard be shut down until that afternoon. Instead, Tate and James were released to [a yard full of Mexican gang members] as one of the accused officers allegedly blurted out, "It's going to be duck hunting season."

. . . Tate was shot and killed [by a guard] during a two-on-two fight in which neither he nor his cellmate was the aggressor. The bullet, intended for a rival Mexican gang member attacking Tate, struck Tate in the head by mistake and killed him instantly.

The Venue and the Jury

The trial was held in the conservative farm and prison belt, where half a dozen sprawling state prisons light

up the night sky and where guards double as Little League coaches and are involved in other community activities. At the outset federal prosecutors recognized that persuading a jury that COs were guilty of the use of excessive force would be difficult. The prosecution's possibility of success was reduced by the fact that the judge seated several jurors who had reason to lean toward the guard's side—one juror was a detention deputy and another had applied to the state to become a CO (Arax, 2000, June 10 & 11).

The Defense

The defense argued there was no evidence that any of the accused officers orchestrated or encouraged inmates to fight. Instead they contended:

1. The guards were the victims of flawed correctional policy—supported by top correctional officials—that required a policy of mixing rival inmates in the same small exercise yards, even though this was causing fights and deadly shootings (Arax, 2000, April 10e).
2. The Corcoran inmates were so "vile, violent, and predatory" that it was nearly impossible for even the most vigilant guards to "keep them from fighting" (Arax, 2000, April 24).

The Verdict

The eight Corcoran prison guards accused of setting up inmate gladiator fights were acquitted after 9 weeks of testimony and just 6 hours of jury deliberations.

The *Hudson v. McMillian* (1992) Case

Keith Hudson was an inmate at Angola, a Louisiana state prison, when he began arguing with a guard, Jack McMillian, who with assistance from Officer Woods, placed Hudson in handcuffs and shackles. On the way to the confinement area, Hudson claimed that McMillian punched him repeatedly while Woods held him in place and kicked and punched him from behind. The beating was watched by a supervisor who told these officers "not to have too much fun." Hudson's injuries from the beating included minor bruises; swelling of his face, mouth, and lip; loosened teeth, and the cracking of his partial dental plate, making it unusable for several months.

In deciding this case, the Supreme Court indicated there is no requirement that injuries be serious to be constitutionally unacceptable. Their decision was prompted by several factors. First, there was no reason for the force to be used, meaning it must have been for punishment. Second, it was observed and condoned by a supervisor. A third reason, not directly related to the case but important because it shows a continuing problem, was that officers Wood and McMillian beat another inmate shortly after they beat Hudson.

Hudson won $800 at the trial court level, but the court of appeals reversed this decision on the grounds that because his injuries were not serious, they could not, as a matter of law, amount to an Eighth Amendment violation. However, after a trip to the Supreme Court, a reversal of the court of appeals, and a remand for a new trial, Hudson again won $800.

Eighth Amendment protection against cruel and unusual punishment or a liberty interest under the Fourteenth Amendment (Collins, 1986).[6]

Correctional officers can justifiably use force:

1. in self-defense and in defense of other COs or prison personnel, inmates, or visitors.
2. to prevent a crime.
3. to detain or arrest inmates.
4. to enforce prison rules and discipline.
5. to protect property and prevent inmates from harming themselves.[7]

Correctional officers have to walk a tightrope, however, because inmates have the constitutional right not to be subjected to force that is excessive, inhumane, malicious or sadistic, or employed solely for the purpose of harming them. Because no distinct line exists showing how much force is constitutionally acceptable, the amount depends on the circumstances in each incident. Even a push or a shove may be unconstitutional if done completely without any basis and causes even minimal injury.

Hudson v. McMillian (1992) sets the standards for the use of force issue. In this case, the Supreme Court stated that "for purposes of establishing whether prison officials have inflicted unnecessary and wanton pain and suffering on a prisoner so as to violate the prisoner's rights under the cruel and unusual punishment clause, the core judicial inquiry is whether force was applied (a) in a good-faith effort to maintain or restore discipline, or (b) maliciously and sadistically to cause harm" (p. 2). The Supreme Court also established five factors to be examined in determining whether or not the use of force was excessive: "(1) the extent of injury; (2) the need for use of force; (3) the amount of force used in relation to need for force; (4) the threat perceived by the reasonable official; [and] (5) efforts made to temper forceful response" (*CLR*, 1995, June/July, p. 12). These five factors give courts the opportunity to examine the situation at hand to determine if there has been an excessive use of force.

Nevertheless, the *Hudson v. McMillian* standard for the use of force is a pretty forgiving one, because it is difficult to meet its requirements for viewing CO behavior as cruel and unusual punishment. Consequently, it gives maximum discretion to institutional officials in use of force situations and minimizes the degree to which courts can review these incidents. Thus, a use of force incident may violate prison policy, ignore contemporary correctional practice, be excessive, and yet still not sink to the level of being malicious and sadistic—that is, employed for the purpose of causing harm (Collins, 1997, 2000). Serious and even deadly force has been viewed by the courts as acceptable if it was necessary and not employed with the intent to cause needless harm. A clear example of excessive force occurred when a CO struck an inmate in the head and face 20 to 25 times while four COs were restraining him. This was despite the fact that he had already complied with an order to lie face down and did not resist efforts to restrain him. There was also evidence that the inmate was injured (*Estate of Davis by Ostenfeld v. Delo*, 1997).

The Court also noted that "not every push or shove . . . violates a prisoner's constitutional rights (pp. 1028, 1033), but [for force to be unacceptable, the injury does not have to be serious or significant"].[8] Our Close-Up, "The *Hudson v. McMillian* (1992) Case," clarifies this injury issue.

At this training center, corrections officers learn methods for dealing with inmate resistance to control. They are taught to use force only as a last resort.

Control Versus Resistance   Although it is important for staff to be aware of the relevant court decisions and state statutes, these legal findings fail to provide concrete guidelines about what levels of force are appropriate when confronted with various levels of resistance from inmates. To assist in making these decisions, CO training typically focuses on the parameters of *resistance* and *control* that enter into any situation in which requirements are made of inmates (Hemmens & Atherton, 1999; Ross, 1989).

Resistance refers to the actions manifested by a prisoner who is attempting to evade an officer's efforts to control him or her. The amount and type of resistance will vary based on such factors as the inmate's state of agitation; propensity to commit violence; mental stability; state of intoxication; and view of the consequences and rewards of following a staff member's request. Also important is the way in which a staff member approaches inmates. If the staff member is hostile and antagonistic, this may alter the situation from one of compliance to one requiring the use of force. Resistance may range from verbal refusal to comply to nondeadly or even deadly force.

Control is the action taken by a staff member to influence or neutralize the verbal and physical actions of the prisoner. The extent of the resistance displayed directly affects the level of reasonable (legally justifiable) control, which may range from verbal direction to physi-

cal force, including the use of chemical agents, mechanical restraints, intermediate weapons, and deadly force.

The decision to use force is a last resort. Thus, how much force to use is severely restricted and is based on the staff member's interpretation of the situation and the danger it presents. However, a rule of thumb is that a CO should use a level necessary to overcome the resistance and bring the inmate under control. This may mean that sometimes the circumstances demand that the officers skip several steps and go directly to the use of impact weapons. However, the use of force is only justified when resistance is evident. The Federal Bureau of Prisons' policy on use of force employs six levels (see Figure 15.1):

1. The first response is the arrival of an officer at the scene—officer presence. "The continuous appearance of properly uniformed officers or competent staff is always an influence on an inmate's decision to resist a direction or act inappropriately" (Atherton, 1999, p. 55). In addition to having enough staff to carry out the concrete tasks in an area, additional staff presence is needed to regularly direct attention to inmate conduct. One of the factors contributing to many correctional disasters has been the absence of officers in critical areas.

2. There is a confrontation between a correctional officer and an inmate during which **verbal direction** is the initial step to obtain inmate compliance. Sometimes an officer can enter a crowd and, using an ag-

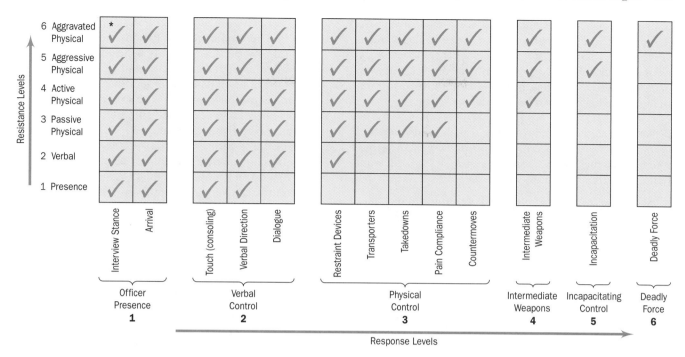

Figure 15.1 *Use of Force/Levels of Resistance Matrix*

*Checked areas represent suggested, acceptable, beginning response levels. Any response in an unchecked area requires explanation.
Source: Florida Department of Criminal Justice Standards and Training Commission (1999). *Use of Force/Levels of Resistance Matrix, Basic Recruit Training Program.* Tallahassee, FL: Author.

gressive tone without offending inmates, bring the situation under control (Atherton, 1999).

3. Force may be used when the confrontation escalates to a passive level where the inmate refuses to respond to the correctional officer's requests. This confrontation then escalates to active restraint, which can include some physical resistance.

4. The next level occurs when the active resistance involves physical attacks on the officer. At this level some forms of force may be used, including firearms, delivering both lethal and nonlethal gas, and nonlethal ammunition—gas and smoke delivery rounds and rubberized projectiles (Atherton, 1999).

5. At the fifth level, the objective is complete incapacitation, using electronic shocking devices.

6. The highest level occurs when there is a lethal attack on the correctional officer or if the escape of the inmate is an imminent possibility. At this level, lethal weapons such as firearms may be used (Correctional Training Program, 1993).

Resistance may skip the early steps, escalating rapidly and starting high up on the continuum. For example, if an inmate is coming at an officer with a knife the CO does not respond to the inmate with verbal direction.

This "use of force continuum," or matrix, is used by prisons, jails, and law enforcement agencies.

The force continuum is a guide for what is an acceptable level of control given the inmate's level of resistance. In *Williams v. Luna* (1990), the court ruled that because an inmate was following orders during a shakedown, it was cruel and unusual punishment for him to be grabbed and thrown down by guards, causing him to suffer permanent nerve damage. In *Culver by and Through Bell v. Fowler* (1994), kneeing an inmate in the groin was considered an excessive use of force that violated the Eighth Amendment. The court noted that "Although a variety of approved prisoner control techniques were available to the defendant . . . he chose to use a method of control that maximized pain and subjected the prisoner to a high risk of serious injury" (*CLR*, 1995, June/July, p. 12). In contrast, if the situation is one in which the staff member perceives the threat of danger, then force may be used. For example, in *Parkus v. Delo* (1998), an inmate brought suit "alleging that in retaliation for his assault on the psychologist the officers beat him as they subdued him and removed him to secure quarters" (*CLR*, 1998, Aug./Sept., p. 21). The Eighth Circuit Court upheld the jury's decision that there was no violation of the inmate's rights.

Whether inmate resistance is verbal or physical plays a major role in deciding the permissible control strategy in overcoming the resistance. Also, the use of force must decrease as inmates are brought under control and must cease when resistance stops or control is achieved. It is not constitutionally acceptable to beat or kick inmates once they cease resisting or are unable to resist due to being restrained by correctional officers.

Control Techniques   Effective control techniques include verbal direction; empty hand control; less than lethal force; shocking devices, such as stun guns and stun belts; and nonlethal gases, such as pepper spray.

- *Verbal direction*, or effective communication skills, is emphasized in handling most inmate resistance. Staff can generally persuade inmates to comply with their instructions using proper verbal direction (Ross, 1989). Indeed, patience and good communication skills are considered the primary methods of preventing potentially volatile situations from escalating into a violent confrontation. COs with good people-handling skills can often calm down confused and angry inmates, so that they stop their violent behavior and comply with the CO's orders. One of the keys to defusing resistance is to learn to be assertive rather than aggressive (Ross, 1989).

- There are several levels of physical force. **Empty hand control techniques** are the lowest level of physical control. These range from gently guiding inmates or temporarily immobilizing aggressive inmates by the use of force such as kicks or strikes. The courts have found this type of force acceptable if it is proportional to the circumstances. Thus, even an inmate's accidental death might not be viewed as constitutionally unacceptable (*Williams v. Kelley*, 1980), whereas abrasions, small lacerations, and loss of consciousness inflicted on a handcuffed inmate who refused to sit down might be (*Brown v. Triche*, 1987).

- When empty hand control techniques are insufficient to overcome inmate resistance, COs move to the next level of force—**less than lethal force**—which has included the use of impact weapons such as batons, stun guns, and chemical agents, such as tear gas or Mace. These weapons are to be used to temporarily disable the inmate but not to inflict permanent injury. Their use is more restricted because of the greater potential for serious injury or death (Ross, 1989).

- Currently, two new nonlethal alternatives are being employed by some systems. One alternative involves the use of **electronic shocking devices,** like Taser guns, stun guns, and

stun belts, which deliver nonlethal shocks. The Federal Bureau of Prisons' policy requires that stun guns only be used when no other lesser alternative is feasible. Another popular nonlethal instrument that is effective in controlling inmates is the stun belt. The use of remote-controlled stun belts has been approved by the BOP to control dangerous prisoners during their transport to and from court appearances. The most common stun belt is the REACT (Remotely Electronically Activated Control Technology). REACT is worn by the prisoner and can be activated at the push of a button by a corrections officer. REACT then delivers a 50,000-volt shock to the prisoner. According to its manufacturers, no physical injury has resulted from the activation of REACT and its effects are short term. Additionally, these stun belts "may remove the need for officers to become involved in a violent hand struggle, or in the worst of situations, to shoot an inmate" (*CLR*, 1999, Dec./Jan., p. 50). However, Amnesty International and various other groups are opposed to them. These groups believe that the ability of the officer to push the button at a whim causes psychological problems and can result in humiliation for the prisoner because he loses control of bodily functions.

Another concern is that some medical conditions can be aggravated by the stun belt. For example, "Los Angeles County policy says their 'Remote Electronically Activated Control Technology' should not be used with pregnant inmates or persons known to have heart disease, multiple sclerosis, or muscular dystrophy" (*CLR*, 1999, Dec./Jan., p. 51). To avoid these problems in prisons, administrators must keep guards informed about inmates' medical conditions. The BOP's response to this argument is a requirement that the medical staff review each inmate's case to determine whether any condition exists that would be aggravated by the use of a stun belt.

Other problems associated with stun belt use include:

1. Once the REACT belt goes off, there is no stopping it. Although a blast of from 1 and 3 seconds is enough to paralyze almost anyone temporarily, the manufacturer set the timer at 8 seconds to account for differences in bodily resistance to the belt.

2. A 1990 study by the British Forensic Science Service concluded that high-voltage, high-peak, short-duration pulses, such as those the stun belt inflicts, are dangerous.

The study describes stun devices as "capable of causing temporary incapacitation of the whole body: a body-widespread immobilizing effect" for up to 15 minutes. Finally, these researchers say that a stun device could potentially kill someone (Cusac, 1996, pp. 4, 6).

Another issue is whether this device is painful:

Describing his experience with the stun belt, when asked if it hurts, a training officer responded: "Yes. It does a number on you. It feels like two needles. And it will leave some pretty severe marks."

He described the time when he allowed himself to be shocked with the belt. He had built up a tolerance to electricity by taking "hits" with the electronic restraining device. He prepared himself psychologically to withstand the belt. "I had it all planned out. I was going to count 'one thousand one, one thousand two.' I never heard the beep. I was down on my back, spinning around. It was devastating. It hurt tremendously." He tells me the welts on his back took two months to heal. (Adapted from Cusac, 1996)

The first major case involving the use of a stun belt occurred in a Los Angeles courtroom. Ron Hawkins, appearing in court at his three strikes hearing and acting as his own attorney, kept interrupting the judge. The judge, agitated by the constant interruptions, finally gave the order to activate the stun belt. A federal district court issued an injunction against the stun belts' continued use in Los Angeles County, because the court felt that wearing the belt could unfairly silence defendants who might be afraid to raise an objection for fear of being shocked. The court ruled that, because Hawkins did not try to attack anyone, there were other less painful alternatives to deal with him (e.g., binding or gagging) (*CLR*, 1999, Oct./Nov.). Some states and counties have stopped or never used these belts in a correctional setting because of their potential misuse as punitive devices. However, Amnesty International reports that about 130 federal, state, and local jurisdictions now use the belts to control troublesome inmates by threatening to temporarily immobilize them with a 50,000-volt jolt of electricity (Lichtblau & Leonard, 1999, June 9).

■ Another alternative, pepper spray, is a more recent nonlethal gas that "produces involuntary eye closure due to dilating capillaries; nasal and sinus drainage; constricted airways; and temporary paralysis of the larynx causing gagging, coughing, and shortness of breath" (Edwards, Granfield, & Onnen, 1997, p. 2). Oleoresin capsicum (OC), one of the more popular pepper sprays among law enforcement and correctional agencies, is used because it is more effective on the extremely agitated, the mentally ill, or inmates under the influence of drugs (Edwards, Granfield, & Onnen, 1997)[9]. OC is a naturally occurring inflammatory agent that is found in cayenne pepper. Prior to the use of OC, most law enforcement and correctional agencies used CN or CS, forms of tear gas.[10] "The primary difference between CN and CS gases and OC is that the former are irritants, while capsicum is an inflammatory agent" (Morgan, 1992, p. 22). CN and CS were ineffective on individuals who were under the influence of drugs or alcohol. Another advantage of OC is that "OC sprays seem to leave few if any residual effects, allowing suspects to be transported without affecting transporting officers" (NIJ, 1994, p. 3).

OC also seems to have reduced the number of excessive use of force claims (NIJ, 1994). Those against the use of pepper spray claim that it can result in death. A study revealed 30 incidents of death that had occurred after the use of OC between 1990 and 1993 (Granfield, Onnen, & Petty, 1994). Of these 30 cases, 22 contained enough information to allow for a determination of the cause of death. The researchers concluded that "OC was not the cause of death in any of these cases" (Granfield, Onnen, & Petty, 1994, p. 2). Instead, these deaths occurred due to positional asphyxia—that is, the inability to breathe when the body is placed in a particular position. This asphyxia can also be aggravated by drugs, alcohol, or obesity. The researchers concluded that the use of pepper spray did not lead to any deaths and can be used as an effective nonlethal alternative.

Restraints **Restraints,** such as handcuffs, belly chains, leg irons, straitjackets, leather restraints, flex cuffs, and restraint chairs, are devices that temporarily bridle inmates. They are used to prevent escapes when transporting or escorting high-security inmates, to prevent injury to inmates or others, and to prevent serious damage to property. They are also used to control unruly or dangerous behavior, but if they are used to discipline or punish inmates, they can represent an Eighth Amendment or statutory violation (see, e.g., California Code of Regulations, 1991).

The Kick Restraint: A Hog-Tying Device

CONSIDER THIS

Currently, there is a commercially produced device called a "kick-stop restraint," which produces the same results as hog tying. This device restrains prisoners by tying their legs and arms behind their back to a strap on the prisoner's waist. The objections to this device are the same as those for hog tying. Just as inmates have died while being hog tied, inmates have also died when this device was used. A case in point was Edward Swans, a paranoid schizophrenic. When arrested by police, who neglected to check their computer files in which Swans' mental illness was recorded, he was taken to jail rather than to a mental hospital. A psychiatrist expressed the opinion that because of his schizophrenia Swans did not understand his situation and was functioning at the mental and emotional level of a 3-year-old. His behavior led to the use of the kick-stop restraint, in which six detention officers applied extreme restraints, placing their weight on Swans while he was handcuffed, tied, and lying on his stomach. Another psychiatrist testified that the behavior of the officers in restraining Swans was group-oriented torture—conduct intended for the infliction of pain. An autopsy revealed that the inmate's death was as a result of asphyxiation. The court found that not only did the deputies use excessive force, but they were also deliberately indifferent to the inmate's serious medical needs.

Source: Smith v. City of Lansing, *65 F. Supp. 2d 625 (WD Mich 1998).*

There are certain dangers associated with the use of these devices:

> Any restraint procedure which limits the normal process of expansion and contraction of the chest during the breathing process can pose a risk of asphyxia (death by suffocation) especially in an excited and "air hungry" person. Such procedures as sitting on or applying weight to a person's chest or back while they are lying down . . . can pose significant risk of [what is called positional asphyxia]. Procedures such as handcuffing a person with arms behind the back and forcing them to lie face down [may limit the breathing process]. This problem may be compounded if the person is overweight, has a [pre-existing heart condition], or has been using drugs—both certain prescription and illicit drugs (e.g., cocaine and/or alcohol). (Evans, 1999, p. 5)

Hog tying, which involves restraining a prisoner's hands behind his back, restraining his feet, and then coupling the hands and feet restraints from the back presents an even greater risk of positional asphyxia (Rosazza, 1996). This method is often used to restrain prisoners who are uncooperative. The dangers it poses require that correctional and jail personnel should examine alternative ways to restrain unruly prisoners (Rosazza, 1996); alternatives do exist. Our Consider This feature, "The Kick Restraint," describes a case in which the use of this device resulted in an inmate's death.

Courts have permitted inmates to be placed in flex cuffs to restore order after a disturbance, and for one inmate to be placed in four-point restraints with gauze padding in his mouth to stop the spread of a prison riot he had incited (*Price v. Dixon*, 1997; *Stewart v. McManus*, 1991). As a rule, however, when restraints are used for extended periods of time, clinical restraints (canvas, rubber or leather strapping) should be used as opposed to security restraints (handcuffs, leg irons, belly chains) (Atherton, 1999). Four-point restraints involve securing the inmate's arms to the bed frame above his head and securing his legs to the bed frame usually with iron restraints. The inmate is also secured across two additional body parts. According to the Federal Bureau of Prisons and the American Correctional Association, four-point restraints can only be used when all other alternatives have failed. Also, they may not be used as punishment. In *Madrid v. Gomez* (1995), the court found that fetal restraints, similar to four-point restraints except that they place the inmate in the fetal position, cause considerable pain and are ineffective in preventing inmates from kicking their cell doors. Further, it was determined that Pelican Bay, where these incidents occurred, utilized fetal restraints in numerous incidents for punitive purposes. The court held that this practice was an example of excessive use of force. However, another court found that confining an inmate with a history of being disruptive in four-point metal restraints for 28 hours was not an Eighth Amendment violation (*Price v. Dixon*, 1997).

Courts seem more lenient when lower levels of force are used that do not result in serious injury.[11] Finally, the courts have approved the forced use of antipsychotic drugs on inmates dangerous to themselves or others in emergency situations without consent (*Wilson v. Change,* 1997) and with appropriate administrative permission under other conditions (*Washington v. Harper,* 1990).

Of greater concern is the use of restraints such as straitjackets, leather straps, or chains to confine inmates to their beds and keep them in their cells and the restraint chair. In examining their use, the courts consider the reasons they are employed, the availability of other control methods, the mental state of the inmate (e.g., the likelihood of suicide or self-injury; risk of injury to others), the inmate's security status, length of time restrained, the monitoring by doctors or supervisory staff, and regular observations by COs.[12]

The restraint chair is generally used when an inmate exhibits uncontrollable violent behavior or presents a danger to himself or others. The chair allows correctional staff to place the inmate in a seated position in restraints until he no longer exhibits violent uncontrollable behavior. Many departments require that (1) a report be written justifying the circumstances of its use, (2) the inmate be checked at regular intervals ranging from every 15 to 30 minutes, (3) medical personnel also check the inmate regularly (every hour) and when she is removed from the chair, and (4) the inmate not be held in the chair for long periods of time—for example, 4 hours—without the approval of the shift commander (NIC Information Center, 1998).

The need for continued oversight by courts and other government agencies of restraint procedures is suggested by the following barbaric practices present at the Indiana Reformatory at Pendleton prior to court intervention in the early 1980s:

> At this facility, inmates who threatened suicide or who were physically disruptive were placed in restraints (*French v. Owens*, 1985). These inmates were often stripped and chained spread-eagle to their bed from 12 to 30 hours. Some inmates were forced to lie on bed frames without mattresses and were not allowed to use a toilet, which meant that they lay in their own feces and urine.

Deadly Force **Deadly force** is intended to cause death or great bodily harm. Any of the control methods thus far discussed can result in serious injury or death, but when guns are fired at inmates, the probability of causing death or serious injury is high. Although state and local regulations differ somewhat as to when deadly force is authorized, its use is generally limited to preventing an inmate from seriously injuring or killing another inmate or staff member or from committing a felony, which includes escaping. Moreover, the lethal result of the use of guns dictates that they only be used as a last resort. For example, if a fight breaks out involving two inmates representing rival gangs, raising the possibility of escalating from a fight to a riot if rival gang members join their comrades, deadly force might be necessary if the circumstances reach a point of imminent death or if serious bodily injury might occur (Atherton, 1999). However, many states may well follow the lead of California, which revoked the use of deadly force to stop inmate fights—the result of a $2.3 million award to an inmate's family after the inmate was shot by a CO attempting to break up a fight (Hemmens & Atherton, 1999).

In a correctional setting, officers do not carry guns (except for those few facilities that have enclosed gun walks) because of the danger of being overpowered by inmates. As a rule, firearms are only available to COs who patrol the institution's perimeter, have guard tower duty, or are transporting inmates outside the facility. These officers are issued weapons primarily to stop escaping inmates. On the inside, COs are given weapons in rare instances, such as during riots, disturbances, or hostage situations, where control of the facility is threatened or actually lost.

In 1986, in *Whitley v. Albers*, the Supreme Court clarified the issues surrounding the use of force in riots and disturbances in a prison disturbance in which a guard was taken hostage by several inmates. In retaking the unit, Albers, an inmate not involved in the riot and one who even helped authorities, was shot by a CO. He brought a lawsuit claiming excessive force was used and no warning shot was fired and that this action constituted cruel and unusual punishment. The Court rejected Albers' claim. Recognizing that prison officials have to make on-the-spot determinations in emergency situations, it indicated that they must be given substantial latitude in the choices made at the time of the incident. It also noted that after-the-fact analysis may well show that the degree of force used or authorized was unnecessary. However, the test is "whether the force was applied in a good faith effort to maintain or restore discipline or maliciously and sadistically (i.e., with deliberate indifference) for the purpose of causing harm" (p. 1085). With the "unnecessary and wanton" standard, the Court required proof of maliciousness and sadism. There was no indication that the shooting was motivated by either of these factors, so Albers' claim of an Eighth Amendment violation was rejected.

Deadly force can be used to stop escapes, but the courts have failed to provide COs with clear guidelines on this issue. Mushlin (1993) argues that the central consideration in approaches to the use of deadly force in correctional settings is that "it is not permissible when lesser force would be effective." Thus, deadly force is unwarranted except where essential to protect life and also possibly to prevent the escape of a dangerous felon from prison (Mushlin, 1993). However, who is a dangerous felon in prison? Are they all? Collins (2000) describes the dilemma facing COs in this situation:

> Trying to deal with the use of deadly force in an escape situation is far from easy because there are very few court decisions in this area, and they are not necessarily consistent in their approach. Likewise, jurisdictions may differ in their approach to this issue. Thus, it is really impossible to generalize about when deadly force can be used, particularly to thwart an escape. It is clear that deadly force may be used in response to some escape situations, but it is not clear

that it could be used in response to all escape situations. Correctional employees are best advised here to look to their agency policies for guidance, and agency policy setters need to closely examine their policies in light of applicable case law in statutes in their jurisdiction.

There is some agreement that one of the determining factors in using deadly force in escape situations is whether the inmate is dangerous. But the question is who in prison is considered a dangerous felon, who in jail is considered dangerous, and how do you translate that into something that an officer in a tower, for instance, can be able to know instantly, I can shoot or I can't shoot at this person. It's hard enough for the officer to decide, in sort of graphic terms, is the escapee far enough up the wall that I can shoot him now or if I miss him am I going to be shooting into a crowd of other people? What makes this more difficult is the fact the officer also has to decide, let's see now, who is that guy and what is he convicted of, and is that a dangerous felon or is that a non-dangerous felon? If so, do I shoot the rubber bullets, or do I shoot him with bullets? (Collins, 2000)

The American Correctional Association (1989) indicates that most jurisdictions have adopted some variation of the following procedures. For example, the BOP's rules dictate:

> At institution perimeter walls, prior to using firearms, staff must reasonably believe that an inmate has the capability to escape. For example, the inmate may be carrying items that could be used to escape, such as . . . ladder, blankets, grappling hooks [etc]. An employee [determining an escape is in progress] shall issue a verbal warning, then fire a warning shot prior to shooting the subject. (PS5558.12, 1996, p. 4)

This rule suggests another variable, the security level of the facility, should be considered in deadly force circumstances:

> Ordinarily, firearms are not to be used to prevent escapes from minimum security level institutions; however, they may be used when the escaping inmate has used or threatened to use force likely to cause serious physical injury to, or has manifested an imminent threat of death or serious physical injury to, staff, other inmates, or the community. Verbal warnings and warning shots should be used when feasible. (PS5558.12, 1996, p. 5)

As a major criterion for placing inmates at minimum security facilities is that they are nondangerous, this would seem to rule out the use of deadly force within them (Walker, 1994).

California's recent addition of electrified fences to 25 maximum and 23 medium security institutions adds another dimension to the use of deadly force in escapes. The 13-foot-high fence is located between two 12-foot-high fences topped with razor wire and carries 4,000 volts and 650 milliamperes—only 70 milliamperes are required to kill someone. Signs warning inmates that this fence is dangerous "show a man hit by a bolt of electricity falling backwards [and say] 'Danger, Peligro, Keep Out. Alto Voltaje, No Entre'" (Buzbee, 1993, p. A-18). California estimated that it has saved $40 million per year by reassigning all 173 perimeter COs except those responsible for supervising the vehicle and sally ports (Hancock, 1997). Other states like Arkansas, Missouri, and New York have begun to follow California's lead (*AP*, 1997, January 12; *Corrections Digest*, 1997, March 14, p. 10; Metzgar, 1996).

The question arises as to whether the courts will find the use of deadly force without human decision making constitutional, or will the fact that prisons hold dangerous people be sufficient to apply current case precedents to escapees?

Tactical Response Teams In response to the increasing number of incidents involving the excessive use of force, many departments of corrections (DOCs) have developed **tactical response teams** (Atherton, 1999). "These teams may be called in for many reasons, from planned forced cell moves and searches to unexpected life-threatening hostage situations" (*Corrections Compendium*, 1995, p. 4). Although the team structure may vary among the states, 43 (94%) DOCs have their own tactical response team (*Corrections Compendium*, 1995, p. 4). Most of the teams comprise snipers, hostage negotiators, and rescuers (*Corrections Compendium*, 1995). They receive extensive training covering topics such as riots, the latest nonlethal weapons, the use of chemical agents, hostage negotiation, and the proper procedure for cell extraction. In addition to the initial training provided, tactical response teams also undergo yearly training to ensure that they are up-to-date on the latest information. Tactical response teams are referred to by many names: Special Weapons and Tactics (SWAT); Special Emergency Response Team (SERT); Correctional Emergency Response Team (CERT); Tactical Response Team (TRT); Special Reaction Team (SRT); and Special Operations Response Team (SORT). No matter what you call them, it all comes down to these variables: (1) they are all prepared to do essentially the same job; (2) they are made up of highly trained professional individuals; (3) they have an uncommon dedication, which sometimes means placing their lives in extreme jeopardy; and (4) they must display total discipline (*Corrections Compendium*, 1992, p. 3).

Tactical teams are generally used to control crowds when an upcoming execution is scheduled, to handle riots and cell block extractions, to rescue hostages, and to handle escape attempts. Many departments require that a videotape be made of each incident to dispel any subsequent inmate complaints of excessive force. Cell extractions generally are necessary

> when inmates are being self-destructive, to prevent property damage, to move inmates according to administrative or court orders, to vacate a cell for operations purpose (sanitation, searches, etc.), and to attend to ill inmates. Normally, most forced cell entry experiences occur in high security environments [containing] the most disruptive, high risk inmates. (Atherton, 1999, p. 62)

CERT teams follow a standard procedure during which they enter the cell, handcuff the inmate's arms and legs, and carry the inmate to the new cell. Most cell extractions are performed routinely without any problems. However, sometimes, an inmate will file a complaint alleging excessive use of force. In *Stenzel v. Ellis* (1990), an inmate claimed that during a cell extraction officers used excessive force by pushing his head and face into a wall. The standard for excessive use of force requires the inmate to demonstrate that there was an unnecessary infliction of pain. The court found that there was no violation constituting cruel and unusual punishment during this forcible cell extraction.

Another similar finding occurred in *Stanley v. Hejirika* (1998); the court, again, held that the inmate failed to show there was an unnecessary use of force. In the majority of the lawsuits filed against tactical teams, the departments of corrections usually prevail.

Despite the relatively small number of lawsuits that have been filed, response teams seem to be quite successful in achieving their goals. California's tactical teams have effectively handled a number of minor incidents, while serving as a deterrent to larger disturbances. Other states have seen similar results from their response teams. It seems that these new teams have proved to be an effective and essential tool to combat violence and other disturbances in contemporary prisons.

Due Process Procedures in Institutions

Institutions are required to afford inmates certain due process rights. The rules that govern inmate behavior, the procedures that are employed to determine guilt or innocence when rules are violated, and the imposed punishment may be subject to due process protections. This section discusses those due process safeguards.

Rules and Regulations

Prisons are closed communities whose populations include a disproportionate number of society's most dangerous members. By their behavior, most inmates have shown a disregard for normal legal constraints. Thus, de-

veloping rules that effectively control conduct, ensure staff and inmate safety, promote orderly and efficient prison operations, and prevent escapes is not an easy task. Also, the inmate population's tendency toward violent and predatory behavior requires a different set of rules not normally regulated on the outside (e.g., removing pepper from dining rooms because it can be used to blind someone). Because many rules are written in ambiguous or vague language, interpreting them may cause problems when attempting to enforce them and determine guilt. Examples of ambiguous regulations include rules forbidding inmates to engage in "vicious eyeballing," "insolence," "ill language" toward any officer, or in conversation with another inmate (American Bar Association, 1977).

Prison rules bearing no rational relationship to legitimate penal objectives would appear to violate requirements of **substantive due process**—or basic rights to life, liberty, and property—because to be constitutional, legislation must be fair and reasonable in content and application (Garner, 1999; Mushlin, 1993). Thus, if rules do not directly affect institutional order, they may violate an inmate's right to be free from arbitrary and unreasonable actions. For example, in one prison there was a 10-year-old rule forbidding inmates from sitting on a bench in the prison yard. This rule, intended to keep inmates from sitting on a freshly painted bench, remained in effect long after the paint dried, and an inmate was given 5 days in solitary confinement for violating this rule. However, courts rarely entertain cases about prison regulations, because they do not want to become involved in the daily management of prisons. To be fair, prison rules should be clear, intelligible, available to inmates, and only prohibit behavior that threatens important institutional interests such as order, security, and safety (*Arey v. Robinson*, 1992; *Ross v. Delaware*, 1997).

Some courts have considered the failure to provide inmates with copies of the rules and to read them to illiterate inmates as a violation of due process (Mushlin, 1993). Further, most jurisdictions provide inmates handbooks delineating the disciplinary rules, but few handbooks provide the sanctions for these violations. This raises questions of how penalties for violations are decided and undermines the deterrence effects of these rules. Consequently, it "has been held that inmates have the right to know the scope of punishment possible for infractions" (Mushlin, 1993, p. 428).

The Right to Procedural Due Process

Most cases dealing with due process involve issues relating to **procedural due process,** which focuses on the procedures used to deprive an inmate of life, liberty, or property. In these instances the courts are more concerned with the steps the state takes to make its decision rather than on the final decision ("It is not what you do, it is how you do it") (Collins, 1997, p. 106).

Prior to 1995, states were required to provide inmates with due process procedures before depriving them of a constitutionally protected right—a **liberty interest.** A liberty interest is also created by state statutes or prison regulations that limit an agency's discretionary decision making by saying it can only act if certain facts or conditions exist. In *Hewitt v. Helms* (1983), the Court found that Pennsylvania had statutes and regulations whose language created an inmate's right to remain in the general population. Therefore, before being placed in segregation an inmate was required to receive certain minimal due process protections, including notice of the decision and an opportunity to respond (Collins, 1997; Mushlin, 1993).

However, in 1995, the Supreme Court, in *Sandin v. Conner,* gutted most of *Wolff v. McDonnell* (1974), which had "more effect than any other [decision] . . . in introducing the idea of legality into prison life" (*CLR,* 1995, Aug./Sept., p. 17).[13] The Court held that state inmates were no longer entitled to due process procedures simply because state, federal, and prison rules and statutes identified and mandated certain procedures before an inmate could be deprived of certain privileges and conditions. The Court stated that this ruling was in response to the tendency of inmates to comb through regulations looking for "mandatory" language upon which to base entitlements to certain state-conferred privileges. Some of the cases cited by the Court included inmates filing liberty interests in "[not] receiving a tray lunch rather than a snack lunch; being transferred to a smaller cell without electrical outlets for television and . . . [not receiving] . . . a prison job; not receiving a paperback dictionary; . . . not being placed on a food loaf diet" (*Sandin v. Conner,* 1995, p. 2300). Nevertheless, *Sandin* recognized that if a disciplinary hearing could result in changing an inmate's release date—by, for instance, taking away good time previously granted—due process protections as defined by *Wolff* still applied (Collins, 2000). The Court also overturned its previous ruling in *Hewitt.*

The Court further noted that existing due process procedures not only involved courts in the day-to-day management and associated financial expense of a volatile prison environment but had also created a situation where states were reluctant to codify prison policies, to avoid creating liberty interests (which form the basis of inmate litigation). Instead, they had allowed correctional officers to use their discretion in making decisions. To avoid this, the Court narrowly defined the two factors under which inmates were entitled to due process protections: the Court required an inmate to show that the discipline imposed was atypical and represented a significant hardship on the inmate in relation to the ordinary incidents of prison life and that it affected the duration of the inmate's sentence.

Ordinary Incidents of Prison Life In explaining its ruling in *Sandin* on the more restrictive nature of prison life, the Court stated that "[l]awful incarceration brings about the necessary withdrawal or limitation of many privileges . . . [also] discipline by prison officials in response to a wide range of misconduct falls within the expected parameters of the sentence imposed by a court of law" (p. 2301). Thus, Conner's placement in disciplinary segregation for 30 days was ruled by the Court not to be atypical, because the conditions he endured mirrored those imposed on inmates placed in administrative segregation and protective custody. The Court stated that atypical events include involuntary commitment to a mental hospital, unwanted administration of drugs, and nutritionally inadequate meals (*Sandin v. Conner,* 1995). Also, based on a comparison of inmates inside disciplinary segregation and those in the general population, the state action in placing the inmate was not a major disruption to his environment (*Sandin v. Conner,* 1995). Other ordinary incidents now falling within this standard include (1) routine interstate transfer to another facility; (2) transfer to a higher security facility; (3) confinement in a special housing unit (Keeplock); and (4) transfer to less amenable and more restrictive quarters.

The Court has also examined the use of more restrictive types of confinement. Both Keeplock and supermax (SHU) confinement have been upheld under this rule. In *Husbands v. McClean* (1998), the court examined several issues before finding Husbands' confinement for 6 months justifiable under *Sandin.* First, the Court noted that lengthy confinement in New York state prisons was prevalent. New York state law imposed no limit on the amount of SHU time an inmate with Husbands' level of violation could receive. As of March 1997, 1,626 inmates had SHU sentences ranging from 59 days or less to 365 days or more (Table 15.1).

The Court also noted that inmates in SHU confinement experience the same basic conditions of confinement as inmates in special housing units. In other special housing units (e.g., protective custody, administrative confinement, disciplinary confinement), SHU confinement is the same as supermax confinement. It is reserved for those inmates who have demonstrated an inability to follow the rules in other confinement settings (see Chapter 8). The confinement includes place-

Table 15.1

Number of Days in Confinement

	59 or less	60–119	120–179	180–364	365+
Number of inmates	28	129	127	545	797

Source: *Husbands v. McClean,* 1998.

ment in single occupancy cells to provide separation from the general population. Inmates also receive:

> two showers per week vs. three for the general population inmates . . . one hour per day of outdoor exercise, unlimited legal . . . and one non-legal visit per week. Inmates are allowed to receive and send privileged or personal correspondence, have access to counseling services daily, have an opportunity to participate in a cell study program (to the extent possible based on overall behavioral adjustment). Counselors, teachers, or other appropriate staff members may visit SHU inmates to provide assistance. All inmates in SHU have daily access to sick calls and are permitted to receive books and periodicals from both the law library and the general library. (*Husbands v. McClean*, 1998, p. 9)

The judge noted only insignificant exceptions that distinguished SHU inmates from the general population. First, general population inmates usually spend their out-of-cell time at programs or at meals. Although the inmates in SHU are unable to attend programs and meals, they do have an opportunity to participate in a cell study program and are provided with all of their meals in the SHU setting. However, the judge noted that general population inmates may also be subject to restrictive confinement conditions. For example, the superintendent may detain inmates from the general prison population in their cells and suspend shower and exercise privileges at any time for the safety and security of the facility. General population inmates' out-of-cell time also may be temporarily curtailed for nondisciplinary reasons, such as when (1) inmates are in idle status because of the unavailability of programming or their refusal to program; (2) inmates are in the reception company at a new facility awaiting evaluation and assessment; and (3) inmates are unable to participate in programs for medical or mental health reasons. Therefore, based on a comparison between inmates housed in SHU and those in the general population, the state's action in placing Husbands in SHU for 180 days did not cause a major disruption in his environment.

The effects of conditions and duration of confinement have been used by the courts to determine what constitutes an atypical and significant hardship. In one case, a federal appeals court set forth a four-point test to make this assessment:

1. The discipline subjects the inmate to a grievous loss of liberty.

2. The discipline is grossly disproportionate to either the offense charges or the inmate's total sentence.

3. Highly unusual or unique circumstances exist with regard to confinement.

4. The discipline shocks the conscience (*Cespedes v. Coughlin*, 1997).

Following *Sandin* "other courts have been very reluctant to find that any length of stay in segregation meets the requirements of being atypical and significant hardship" (*CLR*, 1998, June/July, p. 13). Consider the following circumstances:

■ Inmates were forced to live in a rat-infested cell with a lack of proper food and bedding and no recreational time. Court ruling: conditions were not so bad that exposure to them for 6 months imposed an atypical hardship in relation to ordinary incidents of prison life (*Beverati v. Smith*, 1997).

■ A sentence of 15 months in administrative segregation did not meet the requirements of atypical and significant deprivation (*Griffin v. Vaughn*, 1997).

■ Neither a prisoner's transfer to a more restrictive prison nor placement in segregation falls outside the expected scope of the sentence (*Whitford v. Boglino*, 1995; *Penrod v. Zavaras*, 1996).

Additionally, most courts have found that administrative segregation sentences do not impose atypical and significant hardships as long as the sentence is 1 year or less. However, it should be noted that the actual sanctions imposed by the administrative segregation are to be considered for each case. For example, in *Brooks v. DiFasi* (1997), the court held that *Sandin* did not create a universal rule that disciplinary confinement may never entail a liberty interest. Thus, courts must first make factual determinations of actual conditions of challenged punishment and compare them to ordinary prison conditions. Therefore, although it is a difficult task, inmates can show that they have been deprived of due process by administrative segregation that has imposed an atypical and significant hardship upon them. Thus, the Ninth Circuit Court found a prisoner's transfer to a prison where conditions violate the Eighth Amendment would impose atypical and significant hardship (*Keenan v. Hall*, 1996).

Searches

The Fourth Amendment was designed to protect people from unreasonable searches and seizures of property by government officials. Although the courts have required warrants prior to most searches, they have recognized the need for warrantless searches under limited conditions—for example, stop and frisk or during an arrest (Inbau, Thompson, Zagel, & Manak, 1984).

The courts have considered jail and prison settings, by their nature, to justify warrantless searches under some conditions—for instance, to control contraband (*Hudson v. Palmer*, 1984). Thus, anyone entering or moving about in prison (e.g., staff, inmates, and visitors) should expect some intrusion into their privacy. The courts have recognized the need to balance requirements for maintaining order and security against the intrusiveness of searches (e.g., a pat-down search is less intrusive than a strip search). The circumstances of the search and the manner in which it is conducted are also relevant (Collins, 1997). Thus, even though strip searches of visitors suspected of bringing in contraband may be justified, there is no justification for making rude comments during this process.

Cell Searches

The Supreme Court has ruled pretrial detainees and convicted offenders have no expectation of privacy or Fourth Amendment protection in their cells (*Bell v. Wolfish*, 1979; *Hudson v. Palmer*, 1984). Thus, cell searches, or "shakedowns," can be conducted by prison officials on a random and routine basis outside the presence of the inmate. No specific justification for these searches is required. However, the Court has cautioned prison officials not to "trash"—leave in shambles—an inmate's cell while searching it or conduct searches to harass inmates. If this occurs, inmates can file claims under the Eighth Amendment's cruel and unusual punishment clause and sue to have destroyed property replaced under state tort law (*Hudson v. Palmer*, 1984; Zimmerman, 1999).

Pat-Down or Frisk Searches

As a rule, the courts have allowed COs to randomly or routinely conduct frisk searches for contraband. The

question of whether COs can search inmates of the opposite sex raises legal as well as social issues. Generally, it is preferable that these searches be conducted by staff of the same sex (Henderson, Rauch, Phillips, 1997). Chapter 13 examined the issue of cross-gender pat-down searches.

For some time institutions have been randomly requiring inmates to "drop urine" (provide a urine specimen) to screen for drug use. The courts have upheld these practices because of their importance in maintaining order and security and the reliability of these tests. However, they have required that samples be obtained in ways that do not humiliate inmates or subject them to harassment (Collins, 1997; Mushlin, 1993). Both random and nonrandom testing has been approved. In nonrandom testing, there is some basis for choosing a particular inmate—for example, information that an inmate is using or has had a history of drug use or an inmate exhibiting suspicious behavior (*McDiffett v. Stotts*, 1995; *Riveria v. Coombe*, 1995).

Strip Searches

Strip searches involve visual examination of the inmate's naked body and, in the case of males, require that they lift their genitals and bend over and spread their buttocks as well. With females, the vaginal and anal cavities are inspected, and they may be required to lift their breasts. The courts have reluctantly allowed strip searches when there is reasonable suspicion that inmates are concealing contraband and when conducted in a reasonable manner. The Supreme Court approved these searches in circum-

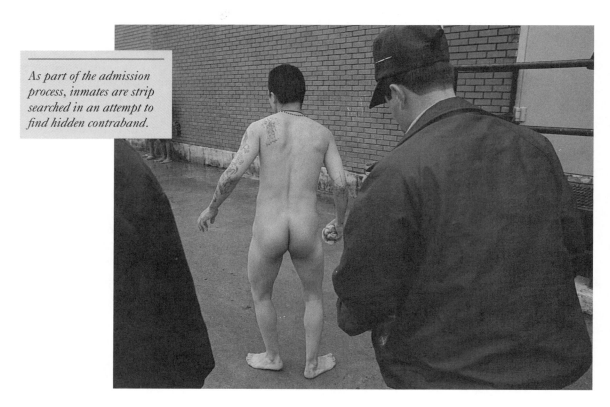

As part of the admission process, inmates are strip searched in an attempt to find hidden contraband.

stances in which inmates or pretrial detainees have opportunities to obtain contraband (e.g., during contact visits or trips to court or the hospital) (*Bell v. Wolfish*, 1979). Because inmates in segregation units and maximum security are more dangerous, searching them upon entering or leaving their cells has been justified. Strip searches have also been upheld when they have continued to uncover contraband. Thus, a prison policy of searching all inmates returning to their cells was considered justified when large quantities of dangerous contraband (knives and hacksaw blades) continued to be found, and there was evidence these searches reduced violence (*Bruscino v. Carlson*, 1988).

The more sensitive nature of these searches by opposite-sex officers raises more compelling privacy concerns than pat-down searches. The courts have recognized that the rights of female officers to equal opportunity in employment may require that they view inmates who are in a state of undress, such as during body cavity searches. However, a reading of several decisions suggests most courts draw the line at cross-gender strip searches and view inmate's privacy rights as generally outweighing other considerations (*Grummett v. Rushen*, 1985; *Michenfelder v. Summer*, 1988). Nevertheless, a Seventh Circuit Court decision eliminated the right to privacy in searches. The court based its decision on institution objectives, noting that the importance of being able to use female officers throughout the institution both makes good use of staff and avoids questions of violating female COs' rights (*Johnson v. Phelan*, 1995). *CLR* (1998, Feb./Mar.) contends that most courts will not follow the Seventh Circuit's lead because:

> maintaining practices which continue to show respect for inmates' privacy rights, especially around the cross-gender issue and in the manner more intrusive searches (strip, cavity probes) are conducted remains prudent, if not constitutional. (p. 76)

In emergency situations, such as following a riot or a disturbance, the need for quick action and for all officers to be employed in the most efficient manner justifies cross-sex searches. Further, recognizing that this type of search is humiliating enough, the courts have admonished prison officials that inmates may have cause for legal action if they are conducted in a cruel or malicious manner or with intent to harass, humiliate, or intimidate the inmate (Gobert & Cohen, 1981; Mushlin, 1993).

Body Cavity Searches

There is ample evidence that inmates occasionally use body cavities to hide contraband. In *Bruscino v. Carlson* (1988) inmates testified to what they called **keistering**—concealing such items as hacksaw blades, handcuff keys, and drugs in their rectums to bring them into the prison. There must be reasonable cause or a clear indication that the inmate is hiding contraband in a body cavity to

conduct a body cavity search. In high security control units—those housing a system's most difficult inmates—the Supreme Court approved routine searches of this kind whenever inmates return from trips outside of the prison (*Bruscino v. Carlson*, 1988).

Although not mandating that these examinations be conducted by physicians, the courts require that they be done by trained medical staff, under sanitary conditions, and in a manner that respects the inmate's dignity and privacy (Mushlin, 1993). In *Tribble v. Gardner* (1988), a court viewed as unconstitutional the use of these searches as a threat to influence inmate behavior (e.g., a guard's remark to an inmate who was to be searched that "Today you meet Mr. Big Finger"). Finally, while these searches should not generally be conducted with the assistance of opposite-sex officers, emergency situations can override inmate rights to privacy.

Restricted Items

The courts have found that the seizure by prison officials of an inmate's property is not a Fourth Amendment violation if the seizure serves legitimate institutional interests. Only prohibited items can be confiscated and inmates must be provided with a list of seized items. Although many things can be viewed as threatening institutional security, the courts will generally view as unreasonable the seizure of religious and legal materials, such as trial transcripts and legal papers (Gobert & Cohen, 1992; Palmer, 1992).

Summary

This chapter examined how the courts have balanced legitimate institutional operational needs, such as requirements for maintaining order, security, and safety, against inmates' constitutional rights.

The First Amendment guarantees that no laws will be enacted that restrict or abridge our freedom of religion, speech, and the press. However, under certain circumstances, courts have restricted these rights when they unduly interfere with competing and important government interests. Prison officials can inspect inmates' mail, but only to control contraband, prevent escapes and blackmail schemes, and bar material that might incite inmate disturbances. Inmates can only receive books if they come directly from the publisher because this enables the control of contraband that can be smuggled in book bindings and other places. To prevent inmates from receiving benefits from their crime, the courts have allowed victims to receive any compensation that results from the sale of inmates' biographies and other related materials.

The Eighth Amendment protects us from cruel and unusual punishment. Typically, Eighth Amendment cases have focused on conditions and practices, such as solitary confinement, corporal punishment, use of force by guards, and conditions of confinement. The Court uses two basic tests to determine whether violations exist: conditions of confinement and the excessive use of force. In conditions of confinement cases, the Court examines whether the effects of institutional practices (e.g., overcrowding) have led to the deprivation of basic human needs (e.g., food, warmth, exercise, shelter, health care, personal safety). To rectify these conditions the courts are required to use the least restrictive alternative.

Cases in this area have focused on the isolating of inmates for disciplinary purposes, which is not per se unconstitutional. Court intervention has occurred when the duration or conditions of confinement were seen as cruel and unusual punishment. To be held liable for unconstitutional conditions, staff must know of and disregard an excessive risk to inmates' health or safety. However, the longer an inmate is confined, the more likely it is that the court will examine the reason for confinement to see if it justifies the circumstances.

Recognizing that correctional facilities are dangerous places and that inmates have been denied virtually every means of self-protection, the courts have held prison officials responsible for the protection of inmates. However, a showing of deliberate indifference—which involves knowing of and disregarding an excessive risk to inmates' health and safety—is required to hold prison officials liable. However, if the risk is obvious and actual knowledge can be implied from the circumstances of a situation inmates can also prevail.

Correctional officers (COs) are confronted with situations requiring the use of force. Reasonable force involves the amount of force necessary to regain control of the situation.

Training and agency policies are the key to preventing officer and inmate injuries and also can enable an agency and its staff to avoid liability.

Decisions to use force in correctional settings are governed by two factors: the extent of an inmate's resistance and what force is required to bring the inmate under control. Control options range from verbal commands to the use of deadly force. The rule of thumb is that an officer should use one level of force above the type of resistance that inmates are displaying. Communication skills are emphasized in handling most inmate resistance.

In response to the increasing number of incidents involving the excessive use of force, many departments of corrections (DOCs) have developed specialized response units. Tactical response teams are generally used to control crowds when an upcoming execution is scheduled, to handle riots and cell block extractions, to rescue hostages, and to handle escape attempts. Cell extraction teams are used to remove an inmate from a cell when he or she is being self-destructive, to prevent property damage, and to move inmates to other locations.

Due process issues in an institutional setting are generally related to procedural due process, which focuses on the procedures used to deprive an inmate of life, liberty, or property. *Sandin v. Conner* greatly restricted an inmate's right to procedural due process by holding that state inmates were no longer entitled to due process procedures simply because state, federal, and prison rules and statutes have mandated certain procedures before an inmate could be deprived of certain privileges and conditions. To sustain a claim inmates are required to show (1) that the discipline imposed was atypical and represented a significant hardship on the inmate in relation to the ordinary incidents of prison life and (2) that it affected the duration of the inmate's sentence.

The Fourth Amendment was designed to protect people from unreasonable searches and seizures of property by government. However, the courts have recognized the need to balance requirements for maintaining order and security against the instructiveness of searches (e.g., a pat-down search is less intrusive than a strip search). As a rule, the courts have also allowed COs to randomly or routinely conduct frisk searches for contraband. It is recommended that, where possible, these searches be conducted by a same-sex staff member.

Critical Thinking Questions

1. As a prison warden, what types of policies and procedures would you establish to guide COs in the handling of incoming and outgoing inmate mail? Justify the policies you develop.

2. If you were an inmate developing a conditions of confinement lawsuit, what factors would you consider? What restrictions have the courts imposed on the use of isolated confinement by correctional institutions?

3. As an attorney for a group of inmates suffering deprivations because of overcrowding, how would you approach this case?

4. As an inmate in a high-security facility, what constitutional arguments would you raise if you were assaulted by a group of inmates?

5. If you were the chief training officer at a corrections academy, how would you prepare your new recruits for handling situations that require the use of force?

6. The use of certain control and restraint devices has been very controversial. Identify these devices and discuss the potential hazards of employing them.

7. As a CO in a correctional facility, how would you bring a disruptive inmate under control?

8. Under what circumstances would an inmate be accorded due process procedures when his or her conditions of confinement have been changed for disciplinary reasons?

9. As a CO, what rules are you required to follow when conducting urine tests and cell, pat-down, strip, and body cavity searches?

Test Your Knowledge

1. Which of the following is false? Prisons can prevent inmates from receiving publications that:

   a. are published by a revolutionary organization.

   b. are a clear and present danger to institutional order or security.

   c. contain information about narcotic and hallucinogenic drugs.

   d. are not sent directly from the outside publishers.

2. Choose the false statement. Correctional officers can use force:

   a. in self-defense.

   b. to enforce prison rules.

   c. to prevent prisoners from harming themselves.

   d. to punish disruptive inmates.

3. The _____ Amendment protects inmates from being subjected to cruel and unusual punishment.

   a. First

   b. Fourth

   c. Fifth

   d. Eighth

4. The discussion of the use of force in corrections indicated that:

   a. deadly force can never be used inside a prison.

   b. for force to be used, resistance must be evident.

   c. tear gas is regularly used as a means of controlling disruptive inmates.

   d. restraints are regularly used as a means of punishing disruptive inmates.

5. In inmate-on-inmate assaults, staff can be held liable:

   a. for mere negligence.

   b. in all instances in which inmates are seriously injured.

   c. when evidence is presented of deliberate indifference.

   d. in no cases because of state immunity statutes.

Endnotes

1. I would like to thank Bill Collins, attorney at law and co-editor of the *Corrections Law Reporter,* for reviewing this chapter, providing information and suggestions for its improvement, and helping me wade through some more complex legal concepts. Also thanks go to Jennifer Walgen for updating the first draft of this chapter.

2. *Procunier v. Martinez,* 1974; *Turner v. Safley,* 1987; *Thornburg v. Abbott,* 1989; Project, 1994.

3. See Chapter 14 for a complete discussion of the basis for the decision.

4. Our discussion of the federal prison at Florence in Chapter 8 describes how inmates work their way out of this supermax prison. Also, see *CLR* (1995), which discusses *Giano v. Kelly.* In this case, the court indicated that continued confinement was justified as long as there were meaningful periodic reviews, with the burden resting on officials to prove the quality of the review.

5. When the *Farmer* case finally got to trial, the jury verdict was based on the finding that Farmer had not been sexually assaulted at all. Thus, it never addressed the question of whether the officials had actual knowledge of a risk to him (Collins, 2000).

6. Convicted offenders can bring action under the Eighth or the Fourteenth Amendment. However, pretrial detainees are not protected by the Eighth Amendment, so their claims are limited to the Fourteenth Amendment. However, in *Whitley v. Albers* (1986) the Supreme Court stated that, at least with respect to prison inmates, there is no difference in the level of force that would constitute an Eighth versus a Fourteenth Amendment violation. Thus, given that prison inmates are afforded no greater protection under the due process clause than under the cruel and unusual punishment clause, there is no advantage to bringing a dual action. Therefore, inmates will typically bring action under the Eighth Amendment.

7. American Correctional Association, 1994; Collins, 1997b; Hemmens & Atherton, 1999.

8. *Johnson v. Glick,* 1973; *Whitley v. Albers,* 1986; *Hudson v. McMillian,* 1992.

9. No research is currently available from corrections, but data from the Baltimore County Police Department following the implementation of policies for the use and training of police officers found that 156 out of 174 confrontations involving the use of OC (pepper spray) successfully incapacitated humans.

10. CN stands for chloroacetophenone and CS is short for o-cthlorobenzylidene malononitrile. CN was the first of the chemical sprays widely used by law enforcement and corrections as a less-than-lethal method of bringing suspects and inmates under control. Its major drawback is that those using it may also become contaminated, and this resulted in a reluctance by officers to use it. CN was replaced by CS (sometimes called super tear gas) because it was less toxic, safer, and more effective (e.g., having more immediate effects than CN). OC (oleoresin capsicum) has replaced CS because of its inflammatory properties, which make it more effective. Also, it is more effective on violent, intoxicated, drugged, and mentally ill subjects and requires no special decontaminating procedures (Edwards et al., 1997).

11. *Whitley v. Albers,* 1986; Boston & Manville, 1995; *Bodie v. Schneider,* 1997; *Norman v. Taylor,* 1994.

12. See, for example, state regulations in Florida and California (California Code of Regulations, 1991; Florida Department of Corrections, 1991).

13. Collins asserts that "there is some potential limitation to *Sandin*'s reach. State law or courts interpreting state constitutions may continue to mandate *Wolff*-type procedures"

(Collins, 1997). In *Wolff v. McDonnell* (1974), the Supreme Court dealt with the procedures to be employed when inmates are deprived of good time or placed in disciplinary confinement. Inmates must:

a. receive at least 24-hour advance written notice of the charges.

b. have the right to a hearing at which the truth of the allegations is investigated.

c. have an opportunity to call witnesses, including inmates if institutional security is not compromised, present evidence, and confront and cross-examine accusers.

d. have access to assistance. In complex cases or those involving illiterate inmates, assistance can come from fellow inmates or staff.

e. have an impartial hearing officer or a committee that excludes victims, witnesses, or those who have a strong personal animosity toward the inmate.

f. be found guilty on the basis of evidence (e.g., the eyewitness testimony of a guard).

g. have the right to appeal an adverse disciplinary finding.

h. have a written record. (Collins, 1997b; Gobert & Cohen, 1981, 1992).

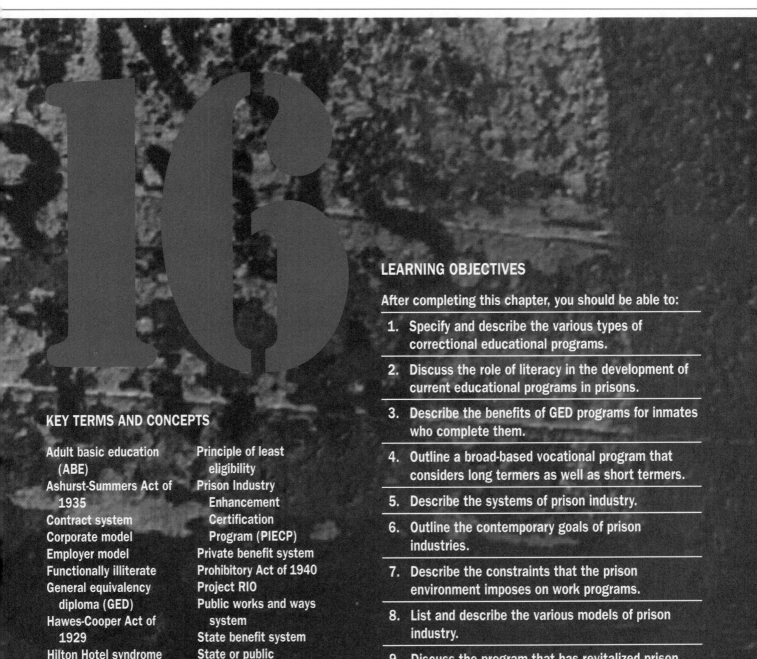

Basic Prison Programs: Educational, Work, and Recreational

16

KEY TERMS AND CONCEPTS

Adult basic education (ABE)

Ashurst-Summers Act of 1935

Contract system

Corporate model

Employer model

Functionally illiterate

General equivalency diploma (GED)

Hawes-Cooper Act of 1929

Hilton Hotel syndrome

Lease system

Leisure education model

Life skills programs

Main customer model

Manpower model

Peer tutoring

Piece-price system

Principle of least eligibility

Prison Industry Enhancement Certification Program (PIECP)

Private benefit system

Prohibitory Act of 1940

Project RIO

Public works and ways system

State benefit system

State or public account system

State-use system

Therapeutic recreation (TR)

Value clarification

Walsh-Healy Act of 1936

LEARNING OBJECTIVES

After completing this chapter, you should be able to:

1. Specify and describe the various types of correctional educational programs.

2. Discuss the role of literacy in the development of current educational programs in prisons.

3. Describe the benefits of GED programs for inmates who complete them.

4. Outline a broad-based vocational program that considers long termers as well as short termers.

5. Describe the systems of prison industry.

6. Outline the contemporary goals of prison industries.

7. Describe the constraints that the prison environment imposes on work programs.

8. List and describe the various models of prison industry.

9. Discuss the program that has revitalized prison industries.

10. Discuss the benefits of recreational programs.

Introduction

Major correctional institutions are like islands, distanced from the mainland but still required to provide the same basic services for their residents (Benestante, 1999). Although separation is a factor, requirements for prison self-sufficiency are dictated largely by the need for security and the size of the inmate population. Because it is impractical, dangerous, and costly to transport inmates to services and programs in the community, prisons must provide for nearly all inmate needs on the premises. Inmates must be fed, housed, clothed, and provided with medical care, psychiatric care and counseling, religious services and activities, education, vocational training, work, recreation, and contact with people outside of the prison.

One of the most potent beliefs affecting prison programming, services, and conditions is the **principle of least eligibility,** which states that "the condition of the prisoner should be inferior, or at least not superior, to that of the lowest classes of the noncriminal population in a state of liberty" (Hawkins, 1976, p. 41). Thus, few politicians, correctional administrators, or members of the public have humanitarian concerns for the repressive conditions of inmate confinement. Many feel that inmates have been treated too well—the **Hilton Hotel syndrome.** This belief holds that inmate living conditions are better than those enjoyed by the majority of free-world Americans (e.g., being fed too well, provided with color televisions, given the opportunity to lift weights, and provided with free college education). Still, there are at least three reasons for providing programs and services for inmates: (1) they can help some inmates desist from crime, (2) the courts have mandated that they be provided, and (3) they enhance control of inmates.

Two contrasting views impact programs and services for inmates: One favors providing inmates with at least adequate resources, and the other favors providing them with the barest minimum needed to subsist. Some may argue that the latter is all they deserve, but it is important to remember that most inmates will be released at some point, and for some, their terms of imprisonment will not be very long. If they are to be no worse on release than when they were first incarcerated, they must be provided with basic services and programs. Humane conditions can also provide inmates who are receptive to change with the opportunity to turn their lives around. The consequences of not providing these services were noted by former Chief Justice Warren Burger in his famous "Prisons Without Fences" address:

> It is predictable that a person confined in a penal institution for two, five or ten years, and then released, yet still unable to read, write, spell or do simple arithmetic and not trained in any marketable vocational skill, will be vulnerable to returning to a life of crime. And very often the return to crime begins within weeks after release. What job opportunities are there for an unskilled, functional illiterate who has a criminal record?
>
> The recidivists who return to our prisons are like automobiles that are called back to Detroit. What business enterprise, whether building automobiles in Detroit or ships in Norfolk, Virginia, or airplanes in Seattle, could continue with the same rate of "recall" of its "products" as our prisons? (Burger, 1983, p. 5)

The costs associated with these programs are outweighed by the savings to society (e.g., police services, court costs, losses from thefts) when a released offender does not return to a life of crime. In this chapter, we will examine three types of programs for inmates: educational, work, and recreational.

Educational Programs[1]

Of the prison programs available for inmates, education is probably the most important. The reasons for this include (1) academic skills (reading, writing, and math) are fundamental to achieving success in the labor force, and (2) a large proportion of the inmate population is deficient in these skills. This section reviews the history and development of correctional education and the range of current programs.

History of Prison Educational Programs

The recognition of education as important in reforming offenders in the United States can be traced to the Walnut Street Jail. There, religious and secular education were intertwined, because if the clergy expected inmates to study the Bible, they had to first teach them to read.

The Quakers were the first to advocate secular education of offenders, but they were met with opposition by many who feared that education would make criminals more dangerous (Barnes & Teeters, 1951; Chenault, 1951). Before the Civil War, inmates were almost exclusively taught by prison chaplains, typically, because prisoners were not permitted to meet in groups, and instruction was restricted to night hours. Lewis (1922/1996) provides a vivid picture of the resulting learning environment:

> [T]he chaplain standing in the semi-dark corridor, before the cell door, with a dingy lantern hanging to the grated bars, [teaches] the wretched convicts in the darkness beyond the grated door the rudiments of reading or numbers. (p. 341)

Post–Civil War Correctional Education   After the Civil War, new methods for reforming offenders were sought, and education came to be a key element in the development of the reformatory model. The origin of contemporary correctional education is usually traced to the establishment of academic and vocational training by Zebulon Brockway at the Elmira Reformatory. However, few institutions copied its programs, primarily because of the heavy emphasis placed on work at most prisons. When restrictions were placed on prison industries during the early 20th century, education became an acceptable substitute to keep offenders busy (Cavan, 1962). Typically, these programs were of low quality because they were not well-financed, which led to the use of a few civilian teachers on a part-time basis; however, the instruction was primarily provided by nonprofessionals (e.g., inmates, chaplains, or guards).

A nationwide study by MacCormick (1927–1928) concluded that there were no complete, adequately financed and staffed correctional education programs in the entire country. By 1950, in both the federal and New York systems most inmates who needed and wanted to acquire more education had the opportunity to do so. Important gains were also made in New Jersey, California, Illinois, Michigan, Wisconsin, and Minnesota (Chenault, 1951). However, programming in most states was confined to the elementary level, and instructional time was limited to between 5 and 10 hours a week because of the continuing emphasis on work and maintenance activities (Caldwell, 1965).

The 1960s Through the Early 1980s Era In the 1960s, correctional education began to see a greater emphasis on both academic and vocational programs (Simms, Farley, & Littlefield, 1987). Correctional education received a major boost when Congress passed the Adult Education Act in 1964. This provided funding for programs that targeted adults who had deficiencies in communication, computation, or social relations that substantially impaired their ability to get or retain employment commensurate with their abilities (Pollack, 1979). By the late 1970s, this act was credited with providing funding for the recruitment of more professional staff, the development of better teaching materials, and new methods of presentation.

From 1973 to 1983, the pattern of enrollment in educational programs was relatively constant, with the highest number of inmates participating in vocational training, followed by GED, adult basic education, and postsecondary education. The average amount spent per student per year rose from $906 in 1977 to $1,579 in 1983.[2]

A Priority in the 1980s Several factors brought correctional education to the nation's attention in the 1980s (Wolford, 1987). First, the prison population more than doubled over a 15-year period. Second, the de-emphasis on rehabilitation, coupled with a more punitive response to crime, left education as one of the few programs offering inmates the opportunity for change. Third, intervention by the courts in correctional facilities regularly called for improvement in education programs. Finally, the staggering levels of inmate illiteracy and related educational problems focused attention on prison education programs. The truly grim state of the educational attainment of offenders is reflected by the fact that, in the late 1970s, only 28 percent of the inmate population had completed high school, compared with 85 percent of comparably aged males in the general U.S. population (Flanagan, Hindelang, & Gottfredson, 1980; U.S. Department of Justice, 1988). More recently, an Ohio study found that 15 percent of its inmate population had a college degree. Nationally, the figure is about 25 percent (McClone, 1998). Our Close-Up, "Literacy in Prison," provides a more current perspective on inmate literacy.

Several other factors also helped shape correctional educational programs (Wolford, 1987). First, restricted resources, staff, and expertise limited their availability. Second, relatively few inmates sought to participate in these programs. The last factor prompted mandatory literacy requirements.

Types of Correctional Educational Programs

Almost all correctional institutions offer some type of educational programming. The range of programs available is usually related to the institution's size, security level, location, and the characteristics of its inmates. A *Corrections Compendium* (1997)[3] study found that 304,727 inmates, constituting about 26 percent of the prison population, participated in education programs in 1996. According to Steve Steurer, director of the Correctional Educational Association, "If the number of eligible inmates enrolled in these programs seems small, it may be because the correctional budget has been cut dramatically in the last few years" (Lillis, 1994e, p. 5). Steurer contends that most inmates would enroll in correctional educational programs if they were available. Twenty-six out of 43 jurisdictions reported that they had waiting lists for inmates wanting to enroll in classes (*CC*, 1997, Sept.).[4] Nearly half of all inmates participate in academic education during their prison stay, and about one third are involved in vocational training.[5]

At the urging of Warren Burger, former Chief Justice of the Supreme Court, the Federal Bureau of Prisons created an education task force, which established a mandatory adult basic education policy. Initially, all inmates testing below the sixth-grade level were required to enroll in the literacy program for 90 days. At that time, they could disenroll, but would not be promoted above entry-level jobs in prison industry programs or work assignments unless they had achieved a sixth-grade performance level. This requirement was later raised to an eighth-grade level because of increasing performance expectations by employers. In 1991, the minimum time

Literacy in Prison

In 1991 the U.S. Congress passed the National Literacy Act to enhance the literacy and basic skills of adults, to enable them to function effectively in their work and lives, and to strengthen and coordinate adult literacy programs. In 1992, because national information on literacy levels was lacking, a study was conducted that surveyed 25,000 persons from the general population who were 16 and over and 1,100 prison inmates in 80 state and federal prisons. In this study, literacy was defined as "Using printed and written information to function in society, to achieve one's goals, and to develop one's knowledge and potential (p. 3)." Literacy was measured in terms of three scales: proficiency in prose, document, and quantitative literacy. Scores on each of the three scales were divided into five levels. Key findings included:

• About 70 percent of the inmate sample scored in the lowest two levels on all three scales, whereas about 50 percent of the general population performed at these levels.

• Almost 65 percent of the prison population belonged to minority groups (42% black, 18% Hispanic, and 3% other) versus 24 percent of the general population (11% black, 10% Hispanic, and 3% other). Fifty-one percent of the inmates had a high school diploma or GED compared with 76 percent of the general population. However, minority adults both in and out of prisons have less education on the average than whites. Given that performance is to some extent tied to

educational attainment, it is not surprising that this study found that (1) inmates without high school diplomas or GEDs had lower levels of proficiency than those with GEDs, high school diplomas, or some postsecondary education; and (2) when the inmate and general populations were compared by educational attainment, prisoners performed as well as or better than their counterparts in the general population.

• Although male and female inmates performed equally on the literacy scales, they both had lower proficiencies than their counterparts in the household sample.

• More inmates (36%), when compared with the general population (26%), had at least one disability. For prisoners, this disability significantly more often involved a learning disability or mental or emotional conditions. The proficiencies of inmates with a learning disability were lower than most other inmates with disabilities and those in the general population with a learning disability.

• Holding race/ethnicity, sex, age, and level of education constant, prisons and household populations had similar proficiency levels on all scales. "Thus differences in overall performance between the prison and [general] populations may be attributed to differences in [race/ethnic] . . . composition and educational attainment." (p. xix)

This study concluded that even inmates with high school diplomas do not necessarily possess the literacy skills needed to function in society. Also of concern was the fact that almost four times as many inmates

had a learning disability as the general population. These inmates scored at the low end of the literacy scale, which meant they were only able to perform the most basic literacy tasks and suggests the need for developing programs tailored for this group. Further, this study found that one third to one half of the general population performing at literacy levels 1 and 2 were out of work. Because more than two thirds of the inmates performed at these levels, unless their skill levels are improved substantially, their prospects for employment are dismal. Finally, even though this study demonstrates the need for improvement in correctional education, these researchers believe that:

> Prisons should not be expected to shoulder all the responsibility: individuals, groups, organizations, schools and colleges and businesses need to reach behind prison walls with efforts aimed at improving the literacy skills. [To accomplish this] will take a comprehensive strategy, the purpose of which should be to prepare the whole person for succeeding in the world beyond prison walls. (p. xxiii)

Given the current emphasis on making the prison experience more punitive and on cutting programs to use these funds to build more prisons to house inmates, do you think legislatures will take these recommendations seriously?

Adapted from K. Haigler, C. W. Harlow, P. E. O'Connor, & A. Campbell (1994, Oct.). Literacy Behind Bars: Profiles of the Prison Population from the National Adult Literacy Survey. Washington, DC: U.S. Department of Education, Office of Education Research and Improvement.

Educational programs for inmates include tutoring in basic skills like reading and writing. Tutors may be other inmates or volunteers from outside the prison.

inmates were required to stay in the program was raised to 120 days, and a **GED (general equivalency diploma)** or high school diploma was required for inmates to qualify for top-level prison jobs (McCollum, 1992).

By 1989, 16 states and the District of Columbia had legislatively mandated literacy programs (Hills & Karcz, 1990). The programs ranged from adult basic education and literacy training to high school completion. The critical need for these programs in prison is evidenced by the fact that between 40 and 75 percent of the U.S. prison population is **functionally illiterate** compared with about 25 percent of the free adult population (Ryan, 1990; Tracey, 1993). The functionally illiterate generally lack the reading skills to gain or maintain employment at wages sufficient to support their dependents.

Adult Basic Education and Literacy Programs **Adult basic education** (ABE) programs for inmates have been the mainstays of correctional education. They stress literacy and mathematical skills, science, and social science as a foundation for further education and training. In 1996, 43 jurisdictions provided ABE programming for 48,871 inmates (*CC*, 1997, Sept.).

Literacy programs are not always distinguishable from ABE efforts because they sometimes have similar components. Basic literacy programs focus on providing basic skills to low-level readers and nonreaders. These programs vary, but they are usually personalized in their approach to learning. For example, many teachers help

inmates to write letters home to serve as an impetus for future learning:

> I wanted to write my girlfriend but I didn't know how to, couldn't spell or nothing but Mrs. Smith helped me and I got to writing. I saw my success and then I wanted to keep going [in school]. (as cited by Bellorado, 1986, p. 78)

One-on-one **peer tutoring,** in which inmates tutor other inmates, and volunteer tutoring often supplement classroom work when funds are scarce or to reach inmates who will not attend school (*CC*, 1997, Sept.). In the 1980s, the number of both inmate and volunteer teachers and tutors began to increase because of the development of training programs for volunteer tutors (Wolford, 1987). Most volunteers are inmates, who are often successful because they understand the frustrations and goals of their fellow prisoners. Our Program Focus, "Inmates Teaching Inmates," profiles the Maryland Peer Tutoring Program, which has served as a model for other jurisdictions.

Community volunteers have also assisted in inmate basic literacy programs. They have the added advantage of providing inmates with free-world contacts. An estimated 2,000 volunteers from national organizations, including Literacy Volunteers of America, currently provide tutoring in local and state adult and juvenile

Inmates Teaching Inmates

PROGRAM FOCUS

Since 1984, education has been mandatory for those inmates who score below an eighth-grade equivalency on a reading achievement test. . . . Any inmate with a high school diploma or a GED is encouraged to apply to become a peer tutor in this program. . . . [Thus,] the peer tutoring program seeks not only to serve low-level students but to allow tutors to experience the joy and satisfaction of helping a peer achieve in school—an opportunity lacking in the lives of most offenders. The Division of Corrections reward[s] them with an extra five days of good time for each month of sentence served. . . .

The Peer Tutoring Reading Academy trains inmates to tutor peers who function below the third-grade level in reading. The program is designed to develop basic skills and self-esteem by using real-life materials, such as newspapers, sports magazines, driver's license booklets, mail-order applications, legal documents or whatever a student chooses as the basis for initial instruction. The program [uses several professionally developed programs to help learners]. . . .

Under the direct supervision of a certified reading teacher, the inmate-tutor and inmate-learner diagnose learning needs and then formulate a written education plan that includes realistic personal goals with measurable reading, writing, and, often, math objectives. Tutor-training sessions are conducted weekly and sometimes daily as the situation dictates. Tutor applicants are carefully screened and work through a probationary period. . . . The program boosts both tutor and student confidence and self-esteem, confers a sense of ownership of the educational program, and enhances tutor skills and status with other inmates. . . .

At the present time there are nine peer tutoring sites. At each site there are at least ten tutors who instruct at least two, and sometimes three, students per day. Most sites have about fifteen trained tutors. This translates into about three hundred students instructed per day in the literacy laboratory setting. The peer tutoring program is very cost-effective, as it utilizes inmate-tutors who are paid a small daily stipend (and time off their sentences) for their work. This amounts to a kind of community service behind bars. Since tutoring is a full-time job, tutors work many more hours than tra-

ditional community-based literacy volunteers. . . .

The central measure of the effectiveness of any educational program is the educational advancement of students. Data collected by the Maryland State Department of Education show that, on average, literacy laboratory students gain about three months in reading skills level for every month of instruction. . . . The quality of the program has not escaped the notice of national studies. In 1986, the National Institute of Corrections (NIC) of the United States Department of Justice cited the peer tutoring literacy laboratories in the Maryland Correctional Training Center and the Maryland Correctional Institution-Jessup as two of the nine best literacy programs in adult prisons in the United States. . . . The U.S. Secretary of Education chose the peer tutoring program as a runner-up in a 1990 competition for the most effective adult education programs. . . .

Source: S. J. Steurer (1991). Inmates Helping Inmates: Maryland's Peer Tutoring Reading Academies. Yearbook of Correctional Education, pp. 135–139. Used with permission.

---

facilities. Many local organizations, such as religious groups, also furnish tutors to assist inmates (Tracey, 1993). In Pennsylvania some correctional officers (COs) are trained as tutors by the State Department of Education. They not only supplement inmate tutors but also serve as advocates for correctional education programs (Wolford, 1987).

GED Programs Although programs vary from state to state, most general equivalency diploma (GED) programs focus on the further development of reading, language arts, composition, and mathematical skills. This provides an opportunity for inmates to utilize their time in prison for remediating their educational deficits or be-

coming more employable upon release (*CC*, 1997, Sept.). Teachers use a variety of approaches, including direct instruction, independent study, and computer-assisted instruction. Although some programs focus exclusively on preparing inmates to pass the GED test battery, others choose to emphasize lifelong learning skills and to promote problem-solving and "learning to learn" skills. For many uneducated inmates, receiving the GED is their first successful experience in education and represents a milestone in their lives (Hold, 1998). In 1996, 37,520 U.S. inmates earned a GED or high school equivalency degree (*CC*, 1997, Sept.). Beyond the educational value of the GED, other gains include improved self-esteem and better parenting skills and practices (BCEL,

1992; Hold, 1998). There is certainly reason to believe inmates obtaining their GEDs can benefit in the same way. In 1996 more than 366,433 inmates were enrolled in GED programs (*CC*, 1997, Sept.).

Life Skills Programs A major factor in the incarceration of most offenders is their inability to function effectively in society (Shelton, 1985). For many, this may be due to deficiencies in basic academic skills; for others, however, a lack of basic "life skills" may also be a major contributing factor. Some individual prisons and state systems have developed their own **life skills programs** (e.g., California and Florida), and others have adopted "packaged" programs (e.g., Reasoning and Rehabilitation, by Ross and Associates; and Adult Crossroads, by the National Corrective Institute) (Bellorado, 1986; Johnson, 1994). These programs provide inmates with practical knowledge in many areas, including:

- *Employability/job search skills,* such as career/job awareness, the use of classified ads, writing business letters and resumes, filling out applications, interview techniques, and appropriate behaviors on the job.

- *Consumer skills,* such as money management, comparative shopping, understanding labels and bills, using credit, and shopping for food, housing, clothing, and transportation.

- *The use of community resources,* such as using the telephone, obtaining help from social service agencies, interpreting postal forms, using the library, and finding child care.

- *Health and safety skills,* such as reading warnings, using prescription drugs, practicing first aid, and maintaining a balanced diet.

- *Parenting and family skills* (sometimes included under health skills), such as child-rearing practices, understanding [the things that lead to] child and wife abuse, and finding alternative ways to settle conflicts.

- *Civic skills,* such as passing a driver's test, registering to vote, interpreting legal forms, filling out tax forms, and understanding the Bill of Rights. (Bellorado, 1986, p. 96)

A 1996 *Corrections Compendium* study focused on two types of programs that encompass components of the life skills area. They found that 33 states offered job readiness training, and prerelease programs were offered by 27 systems (*CC*, 1997, Sept.).

Developing "Thinking Skills" Offenders not only have significant academic deficits but they also have thinking deficits and attitudinal problems that are directly responsible for their being in prison. To address these deficits, a new field of cognitive/behavioral approaches

to changing offender behavior, *cognitive intervention*, has become an effective means to improve prosocial thinking and behavior. The theory is that many offenders fail to learn the cognitive skills necessary for developing the problem-solving and moral-reasoning abilities required for effective social adaptation. To correct these deficits, offenders have to be taught how to think so they can learn how to come to prosocial conclusions. Figure 16.1 diagrams a program in which a living skills component, involving cognitive skills training, precedes all of the other training and is intended to facilitate the development of prosocial reasoning, evaluation, and problem solving in the other social skills areas.[6] Unlike most correctional programs in the past, cognitive intervention programs are based on the results of meta-analyses of successful rehabilitation programs. Leading researchers in this field have demonstrated the efficacy of the cognitive/behavioral approach in reducing the recidivism of offenders (Andrews, Bonta, & Gendreau, 1993,

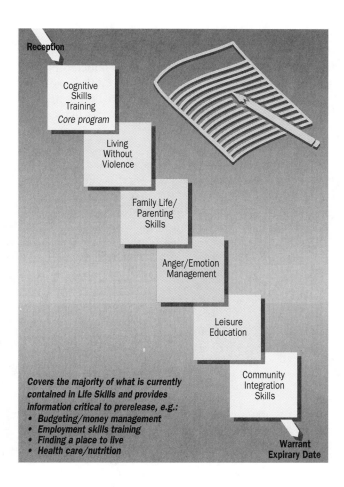

Figure 16.1 *Living Skills Programming within the Correctional Service of Canada*

Source: E. A. Fabiano (1991, June). How Education Can Be Correctional and How Corrections Can Be Educational. *Journal of Correctional Education, 42*(2). Adapted with permission of publisher.

1996). Gendreau (1993, 1996) outlines the characteristics of both effective and ineffective correctional programs based on these meta-analyses. The National Institute of Corrections (NIC) has funded this approach based on the scientific literature of "what works" in corrections. As a result, cognitive intervention programs have proliferated in corrections.

One such successful cognitive intervention program developed with the assistance of the NIC is the Windham School District's (WSD) Turning Point program. This program, developed in 1996, is resulting in fewer disciplinary infractions among completers and a reduction in criminal thinking, as measured by the Criminal Sentiments Scale (Andrews & Bonta, 1998). Turning Point addresses essential thinking skills, such as critical reasoning, anger management, impulse control, and the development of noncriminal thinking patterns. Like other programs of its type WSD's Turning Point targets offenders with a history of disciplinary incidents and others who are at high risk of recidivating. No longer are all offenders cycled through identical programs and services; rather, they are placed in programs that match their specific needs.

According to Cox (2000), the developer and coordinator of this program, internal research conducted in 1999 by the WSD showed a decrease in overall disciplinary infractions and improvements in prosocial thinking. The sample group (649) showed a 38.3 percent decrease in overall disciplinary infractions, and 60.5 percent of the completers showed reduced disciplinary infractions. Estimated annual cost savings in reduced disciplinary incidents was over $200,000 with this sample group. Further research relating to changes in criminal thinking found that 21.5 percent of the 1,020 students who had completed the course had improvement in prosocial thinking.

Other research found that the changes seen in attitudes and behaviors were the result of the treatment effects of the program and were not likely due to any other variable. Another interesting finding from the disciplinary study showed that significant differences in disciplinary reports between the treatment and nontreatment groups ceased within 3 months of their completing treatment, but then the disciplinary incidents for the treatment group dropped for over a year afterward. Withrow and Cox (2000) speculate that as offenders complete the treatment, thinking they are "cured," they stop using their newly learned thinking and behavior skills. After slipping back into their old ways and suffering the consequences, a majority of the offenders begin to practice their new skills and the disciplinary incidents again drop off for more than a year after treatment.

Vocational Educational Programs The work histories of most inmates show that they have usually been employed at low-paying, low-status jobs with high and fast turnover rates or have never been employed. Correctional vocational educational programs are thought to be the best vehicles for breaking the cycle of recidivism (Simms, Farley, & Littlefield, 1987). These programs

Successful cognitive intervention programs reduce the rate of disciplinary infractions and produce improvements in prosocial thinking. This inmate has just completed the STEP program at Rikers Island Prison in New York City.

Project RIO

PROGRAM FOCUS

Statistics from the Texas Department of Criminal Justice (TDCJ), Pardons and Parole Division, indicate that ex-offenders who secure work return to prison at a rate of one third of those who do not secure work. **Project RIO** (Re-Integration for Offenders) is a multiagency employment initiative that matches ex-offenders with employers and was developed to increase employability. Its plan is to reduce recidivism and unemployment of ex-offenders by providing a link between education, vocational training, and services in TDCJ and job placement and training in the community. The program involves several steps:

1. Prospective inmates are assessed to determine eligibility. If selected, a specialist does a complete assessment that includes aptitudes, skills, interests, education, and work histories.
2. An Employability Development Plan (EDP) is then developed based on the assessment results and availability of jobs in the community where the participant will be released.
3. Based on the findings of the assessment, the participants are referred to appropriate academic and/or vocational programs.
4. Upon inmate release, referrals are made to the Texas Workforce Commission to continue training or for job placement.

Another important component of this program is its postprison services. As one releasee put it:

I got out of prison April 22 [1996] after being locked up for 10 years for robbing a bank at gunpoint. For 3 weeks, I just hung out, reacclimating to society. But I got restless the fourth week and tried to get a job. But nobody called me back. At the same time, my parole officer kept asking me "Have you gone to RIO yet?" I thought the program would give me only menial jobs like heavy cleaning work, but finally I went just to appease [him]. [After I completed RIO's 5 day job payment preparation course] I got the first job I interviewed at, a sales agent. (Finn, 1998, p. 8)

Another RIO participant had this to say:

As I walked in the front door, I was guided through a clear process. First, I took RIO's week-long job preparation course, where I knew some of the information but learned some new things, especially how to handle being an ex-offender during the job interview. I landed a job at a rehabilitation center because I learned from RIO that I should look the interviewer in the eye, how to answer the question "Why should we hire you?" and how to explain my past. . . . (p. 9)

After examining the records of 6,500 RIO participants they found that nearly one fifth avoided reincarceration. This means after deducting the cost of the RIO ($4,000) the state saved over $16,000 per inmate, which totaled more than $15 million (Finn, 1998).

Source: P. Finn (1998, June). Texas Project RIO. *Washington, DC: U.S. Department of Justice.*

---

are aimed at providing inmates with contemporary marketable skills relating to specific jobs on the outside. In contrast to academic instruction, which can use a variety of facilities for instruction, vocational programs require shops that simulate, as much as possible, real work situations. Better vocational programs are typically located in buildings separated from cell blocks (Simms, Farley, & Littlefield, 1987). Educators working in these programs feel that this separation facilitates a more authentic free-world worksite, which has positive effects on inmate work attitudes and habits. However, Johnson (1993c) suggested that there are advantages to having these programs in proximity to and integrated with academic programs. Specifically, physical proximity enables academic and vocational instructors to work more closely to coordinate programming and to communicate about specific inmate problems. Good vocational training programs require materials and equipment that are similar to those currently being used in business and industry. It does not benefit inmates to learn to repair typewriters when most businesses are using computers.

The "acid test" for vocational educational programs is whether they lead to jobs on release. Florida tracked 1,572 released inmates who received a certificate of achievement in a vocational training program. Forty-eight percent found jobs; however, only 14 percent were working in occupations directly or indirectly related to their vocational training. No employment information was found on the remaining 52 percent. The crucial question raised by these data was why so few inmates were employed in occupations directly related to their training. Our Program Focus, "Project RIO" (Re-Integration for Offenders), is an example of a successful vocational program designed to deal with recidivism and unemployment.

The types of vocational training provided by the Windham School District illustrate the possibilities for varied training that correctional systems can furnish. During the 1997–98 school year, 15,577 of the 75,000 inmates who participated in educational programs were enrolled in six basic program areas involving 40 trade areas (Benestante, 1999). The basic program areas included manufacturing trades, business/marketing, agriculture, health and human relations, construction, and automotive technology (Benestante, 1999). Instruction was given in traditional shop facilities and on-the-job work areas such as industrial, construction, and farm shops (Texas Department of Criminal Justice, 1993). Programs were offered based on their appearance on the Texas Education Agency's list of approved courses and their identification as having high employment possibilities. All courses focus on the knowledge and skills needed to meet entry-level industry standards (Benestante, 1999).

To meet the needs of the prison population, vocational training programs are organized into four different delivery systems (Benestante, 1999):

- *Regular vocational programs* are 600-hour courses.
- *Short courses* are to teach a specific number of skills and related knowledge in a time frame ranging from 45 to 200 hours. This provides those who are serving short sentences, or who are about to be released, with an opportunity to acquire some skill training. These courses can also serve as a refresher or as skill enhancement for inmates with existing skills in the area. Thirty-eight short courses are offered, including keyboarding, short-order cook, brake repair, and institutional maintenance. The Windham School District has a partnership with Texas Correctional Industries (TCI) to provide diversified career preparation courses. These courses integrate classroom instruction with skill training in prison industries rather than vocational shops.
- *On-the-Job Training* (OJT) provides specialized training or knowledge in recognized occupations where employment exists in business or industries. Offenders who are assigned to specific jobs receive training in employable skills.
- *Apprenticeship programs* provide training in labor areas registered under the auspices of the Bureau of Apprenticeship and Training of the U.S. Department of Labor. To assure that standards are maintained, craft committees consisting of labor, management, and department representatives regularly monitor these programs. The programs require inmates to complete up to 8,000 hours of work and 44 classroom-related instructions. This training is provided after work hours.

Postsecondary Programs Lectures given at Elmira between 1876 and 1900 by professors from a nearby college were the first exposure inmates had to postsecondary education (Pisciotta, 1983). In 1925 extension courses were offered at San Quentin, California. The first real college program was a joint venture between Menard Correctional Center and Southern Illinois University that began in the 1952–53 school year (Morris, 1974). During the 1960s, the number of college courses offered in prisons increased rapidly. A 1973 survey found that 218 prisons offered college programs, more than three fourths of which involved actual in-house classes by college and university instructors (Davis, 1978).

A major contributor to expanded college offerings in prison was Project New Gate. Funded by the Office of Economic Opportunity, it was first introduced in 1967 at Oregon State Prison. By 1972 programs were operating in state prisons in Minnesota, New Mexico, and Pennsylvania and at two federal youth centers. The goal of New Gate was to establish self-contained programs to prepare a sizable number of inmates for college by offering quality courses, academic and therapeutic counseling, and individual attention from staff members. Unique to this program was a postrelease component that assisted inmates in the transition from prison to life outside. It furnished financial and other assistance to releasees, including the initial provision of housing at release centers on or adjacent to campus while they completed their course work (Seashore, Haberfield, Irwin, & Baker, 1976). By the 1990s, the number of inmates involved in college programs had increased substantially.

There has been little hostility toward furnishing adult basic education, GED, or related high school programs to inmates because they are available at no cost to everyone on the outside. However, college programs are not seen as so remedial; some believe that inmates should not be afforded an opportunity that is outside of the financial grasp of many in the general public. This is another point at which the principle of less eligibility becomes an issue. Perhaps people would be less critical if they recognized the benefits to society of allowing inmates to pursue postsecondary degrees. Indeed, a follow-up study of inmate participants from New York State correctional facilities who had been in college programs in 1986–87 and had been released for at least 12 months found a significant difference between the return rates of those earning their degrees (26.4%) and those who had withdrawn or were administratively terminated (44.6%). Further, successful degree recipients returned at much lower rates than would be expected when compared with the overall male return rate (41.1%) (Clark, 1991).

Prior to 1994, Pell Grants generally provided $1,500 per year per inmate, providing about 26,000 inmates with the opportunity to take college courses. Congress eliminated inmate eligibility for these grants in the program

Table 16.1

Educational Programs Offered and Student Enrollment

	Number of Systems Offering							
	2-Year Degree		4-Year Degree		Graduate Courses		Correspondence Courses	
	1993	1996	1993	1996	1993	1996	1993	1996
Number of	37*	14†	21‡	6	7	0	36	39
Students Enrolled	33,219	7,693	3,656	2,259	202	N/A	115,270	1,274

*Only 36 reported enrollment figures.

†Two systems reported combined enrollment for 2- and 4-year degrees [Indiana (801) and North Dakota (17)].

‡Only 18 programs reported enrollment figures.

Source: J. Lillis (1994f). Education in U.S. Prisons: Part One. *Corrections Compendium, 29*(3): 10–16; (1997, Sept.). Educational Opportunities in Correctional Settings. *Corrections Compendium.*

year 1994–1995. This has had a continual impact on those inmates wishing to take college classes or earn a degree. Since 1994, most systems have terminated college education programs, and the remaining few have substantially reduced their scope. A 1997 study found that 27 (or 66 percent) of those responding to the survey indicated that the loss of Pell Grants eliminated most, if not all, inmate opportunities for taking college courses (*CC*, 1997, Sept.). Table 16.1 shows the changes between 1993 and 1996 in the number of jurisdictions offering different levels of education (*CC*, 1997, Sept.; Lillis, 1994f).

The loss of grants makes other educational options important. Our Program Focus, "Alternatives to Classroom Instruction," examines other options.

Mandatory Participation and Incentives

This section focuses on issues related to the difficult problem of motivating inmates who have generally had very negative experiences and failed in school. An important question to ask is whether to make schooling mandatory for those who need it. Another consideration is the use of monetary rewards for attending school. Getting those who need the skills to attend is important because success in this endeavor may turn their lives around.

Voluntary or Coerced Entry   Typically, inmates who voluntarily participate in educational programming are more motivated than those who are required to enroll. However, there are inmates, usually dropouts, who need basic literacy skills and would not go to school if they were not required. Thus, despite test results indicating the need for basic education, inmates do not always see the urgency of participating in education programs because they may fear ridicule or believe they are doing well enough with their limited education (Conrad, 1981). Inmates' views that schooling either is not manly or represents conformity to the straight world may also reduce participation.

For many inmates, forced attendance may be a face-saving device that gives them the push they need to start. Many teachers in correctional settings report even a small taste of success can "hook" even the initially unmotivated inmate (Bellorado, 1986). Similarly as Dana Hold (1998), a teacher in TDCJ's Windham School District, notes: "The face of a man who has earned his first certificate for basic reading makes all the work worthwhile." Thus, there is ample justification for systems to continue requiring inmates who fall below certain basic achievement levels to attend school for at least a minimum period. The success of these efforts can be seen in the fact that between 1981 and 1990, literacy program completions in the federal system rose 700 percent (McCollum, 1992).

Incentives for Participation   Ideally, education should be pursued for the sake of learning and the help that the knowledge can provide the individual in many endeavors. For inmates who are more concretely and materially oriented, this may be too elusive as a goal. Moreover, in some systems, inmates may have to choose between earning a wage, small as it often is, or attending school. For inmates without personal resources or relatives or friends who send them money or goods, this may be too great a sacrifice. However, if wages are paid to inmates who attend school, work holds no monetary advantage over education. Other ways of resolving this problem have been to schedule educational programming in the evenings or, as in Texas, to give inmates 3 hours per day (15 hours per week) off work to attend classes. Positive rewards (e.g., pay raises) for completing educational programs also serve to motivate students to participate in and complete them (Bellorado, 1986). As Jenkins (1999) points out:

incentives are a reasonable way to encourage participation, especially when other prison assignments provide incentives as well. It is important to treat school participation as a regular "job" with the benefits of other institutional assignments. (p. 91)

Alternatives to Classroom Instruction

PROGRAM FOCUS

As we move into the new millennium, it is important to explore different alternatives to traditional classroom education because public opinion and a growing correctional population may make old methods less feasible. There are many options available. One of the relatively untapped sources of assistance is the use of volunteers. This includes colleges and universities, who can provide volunteers and interns; religious groups; and the growing number of senior citizens who are looking for a productive way to spend some of their time during retirement. Of course, to obtain volunteers from these segments of our society it is necessary to allay the initial fears these people have of working in a prison setting. Volunteers must also receive training that familiarizes them with the prison environment and its rules.

Technologies are also available that can be used to deliver education and training to incarcerated inmates. These include network-based computer-assisted instruction, CD-ROM reference systems, interactive video classrooms, satellite broadcasting, and Internet services (Jenkins, 1999). Research shows that computer-assisted learning can produce gains in a matter of weeks (Jenkins, 1999). However, the only problem with using technology is that it can be quite expensive to install and maintain. Some forms of technology—like teaching inmates enrolled in GED programs by using prepared videos offered by such organizations as the Kentucky Educational Television—are less expensive. These are used in conjunction with an inexpensive workbook (Jenkins, 1999). Distance learning links students and instructors who may be in different states. Its use is limited by (1) the tuition and fees charged postsecondary inmate students and (2) the cost of buying and installing the equipment necessary for using this type of learning (Jenkins, 1999). This is also another way for isolated institutions to take advantage of some of the benefits available in urban settings. Not only can inmates benefit from distance learning but staff can also take advantage of the postsecondary and other courses offered. When jurisdictions recognize that this type of investment can benefit a large number of students over time the initial startup cost may not seem so overwhelming.

Next, we examine a study of distance learning by a professor who both taught the classes and did the research. It compares the performance of on-campus students, foreign and American, with prison inmate students in two undergraduate management classes. The on-campus students were at a state-supported regional university with almost 16,000 students. It accepts almost all of our applicants, and as a result received the second-lowest rating for exclusivity given by guides to colleges and universities. Thus, these on-campus students' skills are probably comparable to those of prison inmate students.

Remote Teaching

I discovered that I would be teaching remote students the first day of the Personnel Management class when I noticed a television monitor on the desk of the classroom and realized that my own face was on the monitor that was being viewed by 13 remote inmate students, at three different correctional facilities. . . .

I encourage class participation, however, and I found that the prisoners were much more willing than my on-campus students to ask and to answer questions. For example, when I asked for suggestions of nontraditional recruitment sources, one incarcerated student suggested that ex-convicts could be a useful source of qualified employees. This is certainly true, although it was not mentioned in the textbook.

I was worried about the possibility that the prisoners would cheat on the tests. Unlike on-campus students, I could not watch them as they took the tests. I also assumed

Educational programs may sometimes be subverted by some custodial staff and administration because they view the goals of the prison to be mainly security, order, and discipline. This punitive view of the prison, coupled with negative attitudes toward inmates, conflicts with educational goals aimed at helping inmates to realize their potential and may reduce the effectiveness of these programs (Bellorado, 1986). Another obstacle is that many programs operate with limited budgets, which are likely to be the first cut in times of budget shortfalls. Thus, even though inmates have the right to receive certain services, education is not seen as a protected right for inmates (Rinehart, 1990).

In the final analysis, even though correctional educational programs are not panaceas for all of the problems faced by inmates released from prison, they can help those who are interested in leading conventional lives. They do this by providing opportunities to develop basic academic skills and to learn a trade that gives them a better chance of getting and keeping a job upon re-

that the prisoners might have questionable moral character. I discovered no evidence of cheating. I never received identical answers to a test question from two incarcerated students in the same prison.

The qualitative evidence indicates that, for the Personnel Management class, the incarcerated students were more enthusiastic and motivated than the on-campus students. My explanation for this is that the class was the highlight of the incarcerated students' day. Whereas on-campus students could look forward to dates, drinking, and dancing after class, incarcerated students had little to anticipate except another night of confinement.

The next semester, in International Management, I had 7 prisoner-students, at four different correctional facilities. Six of the seven had been in my previous class. (Two remote students were at a community center about 75 miles away.) Among the on-campus students, I was expecting the nine American-born students to outperform the 40 international students, on average. Although the course material would be more relevant to international students, who would be more likely to work in other countries, I believed that the international students would generally do a poor job of writing the required essay, due to their limited English communication skills.

In the International Management class, the incarcerated students did not participate as much as in the Personnel Management class, and the on-campus students participated more.

Qualitative observations suggested that the remote students would be less satisfied with their educational experience than the on-campus students. In particular, they should have been frustrated with the technical difficulties of the Talkback Television instruction system, with the delay in receiving their graded work, and with their inability to consult with me after class hours. If they felt any dissatisfaction, it was not reflected in the quantitative results. They significantly outperformed the on-campus students in the Personnel Management class (although the magnitude of between-group differences was rather small), and they held their own in the International Management class. There was no evidence that the quality of education received by the remote students was inferior to the quality of education received by the on-campus students. These results also indirectly shed some light on the controversy over the efficacy of higher education for prisoners. Studies conducted prior to 1994, when Pell Grants were still available for incarcerated students, suggested that higher education had a positive impact on prisoners and that the academic performance of

prisoners and on-campus students was roughly equal. If higher education really does reduce recidivism rates for prisoners, then Congress' decision to cancel Pell Grants for incarcerated students was shortsighted and should be reversed.

Live lectures are not about to become extinct, but technology will make it increasingly feasible to simultaneously instruct on-campus and remote students. This will make it possible for inaccessible students, such as incarcerated students, to received education that is of the same quality as that which on-campus students receive. Remote students may always be less satisfied than on-campus students, because on-campus students will always have greater ease of interaction and access with their professors, and these complaints must be taken seriously. But as long as remote students receive an education of equivalent quality to that of live students, they will have been well-served by an educational system that reaches out beyond the physical boundaries of the traditional university to include them.

Sources: H. D. Jenkins (1999). In P. M. Carlson and J. S. Garrett, Education and Vocational Training. *Gaithsburg, MD: Aspen Publications. Adapted from J. P. Rudin (1998). Teaching Undergraduate Business Management Courses on Campus and in Prison.* Journal of Correctional Education, 49(3): 100–105.

lease. Moreover, estimates indicate that it costs about $2,500 to educate an inmate versus $15,000 to keep one incarcerated (Lillis, 1994f).

Finally, it should be noted that not only are correctional educational programs cost effective, but they also have an impact on inmate behavior in the institution:

> Educated inmates are better behaved, less likely to engage in violence, more likely to have a positive effect on the general population. Thus, these inmates

can be a stabilizing influence in an often chaotic environment, enhancing the safety and security of all who live and work in correctional facilities. (Center on Crime Communities and Culture, 1997, p. 8)

How do inmate students feel about correctional education? This question is answered by our In Their Own Words feature, in which students from a class in TDCJ's Windham School District[7] talk about the value of educational programming.

IN THEIR OWN WORDS

Students Talk about the Value of Educational Programming

Dana Hold, a teacher in TDCJ's Windham School District, asked one of her classes to share some of their thoughts and feelings about their opportunities to attend academic and vocational classes.*

Offender 1: I chose to attend school because I realize the important of education. I will need a education to become successful in the fiature. Also due to my position it help me to communicate with people and get readly for society. The important of school is for me to improve in all aspect. Also to achieve knowledge about reading. writting math. That I didn't know cause of the kinds of knowledge being out of my *life*. I knew that I had to make a effort. The decision was for me to attend school. Seeking for help. I have receive that from my teacher, Mrs. Hold; whose I give most respect for the encouragement.

Offender 2: School to me, Mrs. Hold is a place where, I as an individual can achieve my goals in success for the free world, when I am released from prison. Your computer class helps me with my accomplishments in higher educational courses that I'arn enrolled in through Lee College

and Sam Houston. As a teacher, Mrs. Hold you have been one of the best, who have motivated me in any level of academie. My motivation concerning education was very low. However, you took me to the next step in having high self-esteem. Lastly, Mrs. Hold this computer class is the best class in my opinion, throughout the Windham School System.

Offender 3: I come to school so I can get an education that I wasn't able to get when I was growning up as a kid. I also have grandchildren that I want to see with a good education. My mother and father didn't have any education. Children learn from their parents this is why I come to school. Most importantly I don't want my grandchildren to ask me something and I can't help them.

Offender 4: I feel that school is a essential tool that every person should be involved with. The opportunity to learn is most important. The individual who aspire to attain knowledge is one who wishes to expand his or her world. School is a unique institute. It exist on all levels, constantly offering the knowledge seeker variety.

Offender 5: Windham school district is very important to me. It is not only a place for me to get an education, but it also is a place

for me to get away from the hostility in prison.

Offender 6: Having the ability to come to school gives me a chance to broaden my skills, and to have the knowledge to be able to improve different areas that I'm not accustom to knowing. I'm really thankful to be able to attend Windham to further my education. By being a student, I realize theres a lot I've forgotten.

Offender 7: Coming to school is very important to me for many reasons. I come to school because I enjoy the teaching and the learning that is preparing me for society. And since it's beneficial to my future, I want everything to do with it. Besides, you've got to have an education for almost every job opportunity today. And most importantly I come to school to educate myself even better than I've already have to prevent myself from returning to prison.

Offender 8: School is the opportunity to better yourself. One of the main factors for adults or even children to commit crimes is the lack of money or the means in order to "legally" obtain money. One of the reasons they cannot obtain money is the lack of skills to obtain employment. School offers the individual to better his or her education so

Prison Work Programs[8]

Prison work for inmates consists of two general types of jobs: those that maintain the institution (preparing meals, cleaning the dormitories) and those that are industrial or productive in nature. Work in prison serves several functions: it keeps the prison running, keeps inmates busy, saves the state money, produces goods and services used by other institutions and governmental

agencies, and teaches a useful skill. These purposes make work a necessary and important part of any prison's program.

The recent limited revival of chain gangs, which are work programs for punitive purposes, gives the impression that other work programs are also coercive. For those who work hard for the rights of workers (organized labor) this provides a negative view of correctional industries and hampers their ability to get cooperation

that once released, he or she will have the skills to find and obtain employment. School is the "hallway" to success if one take's it seriously and applies it to his or her's best use.

Offender 9: Windham School is the most important thing in my life right now. One reason is because I don't have my G.E.D., and it's a fact that no one would give me a job without it. Now that I'm getting the education I need I feel much better about myself. Getting my G.E.D. means a new life for me that's why I do whatever it takes to get it. Thanks Windham!

Offender 10: This class is teaching me to use my brain again. It has gotten lazy over the last 30 years. Age 51.

Offender 11: School is important to me because I want to better my education. Also it helps me to stay busy and I use my time wisely—it also helps me out of mischief.

Offender 12: This class (Ms. Holds) has a very significant value to me. I'm a high school dropout trying to obtain a college degree. Math is my weakest subject (and though I TASP exempt) I have a personal goal to improve my math level to be able to comprehend more. If math improves the ability to

think, and thinking is a must in all things, I need math. I hope to one day be able to help my grandkids have a better education than I have. Homework can be difficult and I truly want to be a positive contributor to my grandkids. Education is the basic foundation of success and education is the prime candidate for recidivism.

Offender 13: To me, school is very important! My education is what I come to school for. If I would of stayed in school. I don't think that I've of been here. However, since my confinnient in here school is what keeps me going. Knowledge is power. A few years ago I couldnt write these few lines. Now I can! Being here is an opportunity that not to many people have.

Offender 14: School is very important to me because I don't get my G.E.D. when I was in the Free world, and now I hope the chance to get my G.E.D. and learn more about math and writing, so school here on the unit is very very much enportent to me.

Offender 15: I think school is the greates thing a person can go to. Cause you learn as much as possible and that gives you lots of pride and drive to continue to more things in life. Plus now days everywhere you go to aply

for ajob they want an G.E.D. and for sure, the more you learn the more you earn and the more you can help your family our love ones.

Offender 16: As I do my time here on the Unit I have come to look forward to my Windham classes. In a funny kind of way. it gaves me a peace of mind. Time to think. A time in which I find myself at ease and relax the most. Beside all this I'm also, learning something that I can walk out of here with. Why would on spend time here and not get something out of it. As I see it . . . time to go.

Offender 17: The Windham School System is important to others as well as for me. Because. It gives those of us behind bars in the Texas Penial System the chance to better ourselves throu Education. So, that when the time comes for us to be released we will be prepared to meet the challenges of society. In other words we will not be ignorate of the opportunities available to us to expand our livelyhood.

These unedited inmate student accounts are presented as they were written. Hold, D. (1998).

---

from organized labor to support expanding these programs. Recently, California started a chain gang program for parolees returning to prison; it is based on the deterrence idea that if a prison is sufficiently uncomfortable inmates will not return. This program (Structured Punishment Work Detail) involves inmates performing intense manual labor with primitive hand tools. One task involves inmates' cleaning up a sewer site, which requires breaking up granite and concrete and hauling it

away. Inmates also have less recreation; fewer opportunities to shop at the commissary; no family (conjugal) visits; no packages from home; and phone calls limited to family emergencies (*Corrections Alert*, 1998).

The History of Inmate Labor

The roots of prison labor in the United States can be traced to the English jails of the 11th through the 13th centuries where inmate work actually paid for the costs of imprisonment as well as the sheriff's salary (American Correctional Association, 1986b). With the establishment of the Bridewell and other workhouses in the 14th century, hard labor was seen to provide payment for one's keep as well as a means of reformation. Work was also an important element in programs at the Hospice of San Michele (1704) and Maison de Force (1775), which were antecedents of later juvenile and adult institutions. The types of work selected were highly diversified and attempts were made to minimize competition with free labor even though no organized labor movement existed at that time. During the mid-1700s prison reformers such as John Howard and Cesare Beccaria viewed inmate labor as a primary method of reformation and a key factor in using imprisonment to replace capital punishment.

The Nature of Prison Work

In the United States inmates have traditionally been occupied in work either related to the maintenance or sustenance of the institution or in item-producing industries. The rest of this section discusses prison maintenance work programs and those that help the community.

Prison Maintenance Programs Correctional facilities require a variety of maintenance tasks and services to function. While civilians could be employed to do this work, inmates have traditionally done it because they are an available and less costly source of labor. It also occupies their time, which reduces problems associated with idleness. These jobs include janitorial work; maintenance and repair of the physical plant and equipment; food preparation and service; nonconfidential clerical and stenographic work; repair, laundering, and cleaning of clothing; medical and dental assistants; landscaping; power plant operation; teaching; and serving as orderlies. Inmates may also perform domestic, maintenance, and other functions at the warden's house, assistant warden's house, and COs' quarters.

The scarcity of prison industry jobs and other work and programming tends to result in the overassignment of inmates to these activities. The result is that two, three, or even more persons may be working at a job that would normally only need one person. Conrad (1986) provides an excellent illustration:

> [In] my observations of the mess hall at the Indiana Prison at Michigan City, I had a depressing but significant dialogue with the chief steward. He told me that over-assignment to the mess hall was so serious that he had several times as many men as he could keep occupied. His solution was to assign one four-man table to each man and require him to clean it up after each meal—a task that might occupy him for five whole minutes out of the day. Yet the Captain's

assignment board would show that all these men were on full-time assignments. Was such a job meaningful, I asked? (p. 75)

The response of a correctional veteran to this description suggests how this set of circumstances has been rationalized within the correctional setting:

> If the prisoner working his table does a good job, is encouraged to do so, and is praised when he does, then he is getting a job experience that he may never have had before. After all, it's the quality of the work that counts, not the mere number of hours that the prisoner puts in. A man who has learned to take pride in his work has learned something that will keep him a regular job when he gets out, right? (pp. 75–76)

Obviously this view is questionable, but it serves as a good rationale for continuing these practices. However, it does little to foster good work habits and may lead to job failure on the outside. Nevertheless, from a prison administrator's viewpoint, it helps spread the work available "inside the fence" to the largest number of inmates (Grieser, 1997).

The problems of prison work are compounded by at least three conditions (Flanagan, 1989). First, for a variety of reasons, many inmates simply have no desire to work, and prisons are limited in their capacity to provide incentives for productive and conventional work. Second, in contrast to life on the outside where time is valued, inmates live in an environment where time is an enemy, and there are few productive or legal activities to occupy them. Third, work opportunities that come close to real-world employment are rare.

Agricultural, Forestry, and Road Work Activities The employment of inmates in agricultural, forestry, and road work activities has long been a part of the prison system. As noted in Chapter 6, these were the principal activities in southern institutions. This work included picking cotton, cutting lumber, harvesting crops, building roads, fighting fires, raising livestock, and maintaining parks and state buildings.

This category of work assignments has both benefits and drawbacks for inmates and the corrections system. On the one hand, it has been argued that these activities help defray the cost of incarceration. The Texas prison system operates under a legislative mandate to be as self-sufficient as possible. As a result, its agricultural division grows most of the food that is consumed by the staff and inmates. This division includes farms that produce millions of pounds of fresh and cannery vegetables, dairy farms, poultry farms that produce 5 million dozen eggs, and 3,000 swine. These operations are so successful that they have produced substantial surpluses (in 1999 total outside sales were $5 million) and kept food costs down to only $2.00 per inmate per day (Benestante, 2000b).

Prisoners in the California conservation camp program assist in a controlled burn to reduce the risk of forest fires.

This type of work has been one reason for the development of camp-type institutions that are typically minimum security. Their existence allows the assignment of inmates who are least dangerous to these less costly facilities and makes it possible to separate offenders who are young and unsophisticated from those who are seasoned and more likely to be committed to a career of crime. Our Program Focus, "Prisons Without Walls," describes the California camp system.

With the public mood intent on imprisoning more and more offenders, there is little doubt that these types of work assignments will continue. It would not be surprising to see correctional systems employing more inmates in these types of activities as the costs of incarcerating them continue to escalate. The Federal Bureau of Prisons is developing interagency agreements with the National Parks and Forest Services and other interested agencies in which inmates can work (Pospichal, 1991). This has even filtered down to some local corrections; for example, the sheriff of Manatee County, Florida, created a farm operation in which inmates work to raise vegetables and other foodstuffs for consumption in the county jail.

Changing Attitudes Toward Prison Industries

In the United States work was an integral part of both the Pennsylvania and Auburn systems. Individual labor char- acterized the Pennsylvania system, and congregate work was a key factor in the Auburn regimen. This latter feature enabled the establishment of factories in prisons with the potential for making them self-supporting and was a major reason this model became dominant in this country. These factories within the prisons evolved to become the modern correctional industries that exist today.

Two Historical Types of Prison Industry Systems The period after the Civil War lasting until the end of the 1800s represents the heyday of prison industries in this country. Auburn-type (industrial) prisons were most numerous in the Midwest and Northeast. Two basic types of prison industry systems operated during this era and were primarily distinguished by the degree of private involvement.

The **private benefit system** included:

- The **lease system** Under this system the state gave up the care and custody of inmates.

- The **contract system** (Auburn model) Under this system the state retained control of prisoners. Work was done in the prison under contract to private companies who paid the state a per diem charge per worker and furnished the necessary instructors, machinery, and raw material. The state furnished the facilities for work (housing, utilities, and guards for the supervision of the inmates), but it had no responsibility for the sale of the finished product.

PROGRAM FOCUS

Prisons Without Walls

The conservation camp programs has evolved from the system of road camps inaugurated in 1915 to 38 camps, of which 3 are female. These inmates are used for fire protection and suppression, resource conservation, and other public works projects. Camp tasks include the reduction of fire hazards, construction of fire and truck trails, reforestation, CalTrans road work projects, and jobs related to the maintenance and operation of the camps. In-camp projects range from sign making, to working in sawmills, welding, cabinetry, vehicle repair, and auto body work. Another major function of the camps is to alleviate overcrowding in prisons. Over 4,000 men and women inmates live and work in conservation camps located in some of the state's most secluded wilderness areas. Additionally, the camps are intended to have desirable impacts on participants—to help build positive self-images and good work habits.

The inmates are selected for the camp by using a sophisticated classification system and trained by the California Department of Forestry and Fire Protection. On average, inmates in camps are serving the remaining 9 months of a 2-year sentence. Inmates selected cannot have any sex-related offenses, escapes, arson, or any history of violent crimes. Most of the inmates are serving time for alcohol, drug, or property-related crimes.

Doin' Time

Inmates and wards (young adults) in the Conservation Camp Program receive increased time reductions through their successful participation in camp programs. Wards from the California Youth Authority will receive 1 day off of their sentence for every 3 days of incarceration, and felons incarcerated in the camps have the ability to receive "day for day." In addition, the schedule is more relaxed, greater freedoms can be earned, and the participants develop a sense of pride and accomplishment in their work at the camps. Often, these intangible rewards of pride, work ethic, teamwork, and appreciation are the first experience some of these individuals have ever had. Active participation in the camp program also leads to the development of a greater understanding of their "social responsibility."

Further, participation in the camp program resulted in lower recidivism rates for camp populations compared with those in institutions. Camps range in size from 80+ to 160+ inmates who must learn to function with minimal custodial supervision (i.e., 3 officers). The operation of each camp relies heavily upon the work of the inmates—clerks, cooks and dining room crew, maintenance persons, janitors, and those assigned to the outside project crews. Each CO maintains counts, completes assorted paperwork, and supervises the inmates' work, but his or her primary duty is to monitor the "tone and temperament" of the population. The inmates respond accordingly to this environment of increased freedoms and responsibilities. Although they may have been heavily "gang-related" on the streets, respect for one another and the requirement to "get along" is fostered by inmates and staff alike. There is an age-old saying at camp, "This is camp, we don't play the same games as you would in the institution!" Racial and gang-related differences are predominantly put aside.

Those in the camps who are assigned to the outside crews work 5 days a week, 8 hours per day with a captain from CDF. At 8:00 in the morning, the crews line up in the parking lot for release to their respective captains. Inmates who can accept responsibility can rise to higher positions on each crew. Before returning to camp, the crews will work on an assorted number of projects. They will do trash pickup on the sides of streets, trim trees along highways, clean out rivers and waterways, work at building county and state parks, and repair museums or public buildings. Inmates and wards are usually paid $1 to $2 per day for their work, depending upon their job classification and responsibilities.

After work, the evenings are considered free time, with the inmates enjoying outdoor recreation, watching TV, reading or writing letters, or working on hobbycraft projects in an organized hobbycraft program at each of the camps.

- The **piece-price system** Although similar to the contract system, it differed in several ways: (1) state officials had full control of the production process; (2) the contractor furnished the raw materials; (3) prison authorities were responsible for manufacturing the product; (4) the contractor paid the state an agreed amount for each finished article it accepted. (Byers, 1910; Gillin, 1935)

The **state benefit system** employed inmates for the benefit of the state or its political subdivisions.

- In the **state or public account system,** the state or municipality became a manufacturer

Emergency Preparedness and Response

Inmates and wards along with their custodial officers and work captains respond to social and natural disasters with dynamic speed. Most camps work toward a response time of "30 minutes out the gate" after the call is received. Inmates and wards will be paid $1 per hour for their work during these emergency situations. Every conceivable disaster has been encountered by the camp workers, including fire, flood, riot, search and rescue, hazard materials clean-up, and vehicle accident clean-up.

Restitution, Restorative Justice, and Reduced Costs

The cost of incarcerating camp inmates is between $13,000 and $18,000 for a year, whereas institutional costs per inmate are upward of $35,000 per year. Although inappropriate for those felons who display complete disregard for society's mores and laws, a majority of convicted felons can be responsibly placed in a Conservation Camp program.

Along with the reduced costs of incarceration, the camp inmates learn work skills, develop greater interpersonal skills, understand the value of giving of self, and in a way, are a living example of restorative justice. They gain skills for themselves and empathy for victims, and in addition, the public reaps the rewards of their reduced labor cost and their public projects. In addition, by law in California, most camp inmates pay victim restitution and court fines related to their incarceration, with a percentage taken out of their weekly paycheck.

The Conservation Camp program is often talked about as a "win-win" program in California Corrections.

Inmate and Ward Reflections

A ward at a camp shared his experiences:

> When I got to camp, it was like Beverly Hills compared to the institutions I'd been in. We worked in the public and the people always thanked us. . . . We went to fires and I learned a lot about myself. . . . At camp I felt human again (vs. institutional placement). . . . We are always praised by the community we work in and it helped me realize that it is better to give than to receive. . . . I came to realize how selfish I was on the streets. . . .

Another camp inmate offered the following view:

> I had a problem on the streets with wanting big money and doing drugs. . . . I knew that I wanted to come to camp but the line for camp is long in the institution. . . . I don't take this chance lightly . . . , yea, sometimes the cops expect too much from us, and the guys here get on my nerves and I get tired of working, but I've learned a lot about myself in the last 18 months. . . . I take pride in what I do at the camp and try to help the younger "hardheads" out. . . . I only hope that I can reach the goals that I set for myself and do as well on parole as I am here.

Thus, camp life is difficult because it is reality based (i.e., includes levels of responsibility matched with levels of freedom). They do not follow a "boot-camp" or a "chain-gang" model. On average, 100 individuals from diverse backgrounds are put into a program to accomplish common objectives, which include betterment of self, the betterment of and co-existence with others, and giving back to the community what was taken. It is a program, that although not often publicized, has worked well for over 50 years and continues to prove itself as a model of incarceration for the inmates in the camps as well as for the public of the State of California.

What is the future of the conservation camps? With populations growing in California, and with the prison population mirroring that of the state, it is anticipated that additional conservation camps will be developed. When one considers the costs of incarceration for the camps versus the "return derived" from the camps, it is easy to justify expansion and new camps.

What are your views about camp programs? Do you believe that benefits to inmates, the prison system, and society are sufficient to justify giving inmates this type of freedom? *Source: Drawn from materials supplied by Mack Reynolds, public information officer, Camps Program Unit, California Department of Corrections.*

and the prison became an industrial establishment operating in the same manner as any outside free industry. The institution purchased raw materials, supervised production, set prices, and sold the product on the open market. This put prisons in direct competition with private enterprise.

- The **state-use system** differed from the public account system in that sales were limited to public institutions, municipalities, and political divisions of the state. The state did not compete directly with private sector industries, which were only indirectly affected by curtailment of sales to government agencies.

- The **public works and ways system** was quite similar to the state-use system in that prison labor was used to benefit the government entity. However, instead of being employed in manufacturing products, inmates were used for construction, repair, and maintenance of prisons or other public structures, roads, and parks. This system was used extensively in the South.

Legislation and Prison Industries   Prison industries began to decline at the beginning of the 20th century. Strong opposition from the private sector business community and organized labor, combined with several major scandals involving abuse of inmate laborers, led to significant congressional action that severely curtailed correctional industry programs. During the next 40 years, increasing pressure from unions and business culminated in four key pieces of restrictive federal legislation:

1. The **Hawes-Cooper Act of 1929** allowed states to block the importation of prison-made goods.

2. The **Ashurst-Summers Act of 1935** prohibited the interstate transportation of convict-made goods, except for certain agricultural commodities, to states where such products were prohibited.

3. The **Walsh-Healy Act of 1936** prohibited the use of prison labor to fulfill general government contracts that exceeded $10,000.

4. The **Prohibitory Act of 1940** prohibited the interstate transport of all prison-made products except agricultural commodities and goods produced for states and their political subdivisions. (Flynn, 1951)

By 1940, restrictive legislation limiting the open-market sale of prison-made goods also existed in most states.

All of this legislation nearly sounded the death knell for prison industries. At the beginning of the 20th century, 85 percent of all inmates worked in prison industries. However, by 1940, this had dropped to 44 percent; and by 1997, only 6.2 percent of the inmate population worked in prison industries (Garvey, 1998, cited in Marshall, 1999). However, new prison jobs are being created steadily. Thus, the actual number of inmates employed has been increasing, but the steady growth of the prison population resulted in the percentages employed remaining flat or even decreasing (Ingley, 2000). Only during World War II was there a brief resurgence of prison industries because of an executive order lifting restrictions on inmate-produced goods needed for the war effort. This order was revoked at the end of the war and prisons returned to their prewar state of idleness (Flynn, 1951). However, during the wars in Korea, Vietnam, and the recent Persian Gulf War, federal prisons produced materials for those war efforts.

Prison industries further stagnated until the 1970s because of the emergence of correctional rehabilitation, which viewed education and treatment as the primary methods for reforming offenders. Work was considered of minimal rehabilitative value and was relegated to a position of insignificance (Hawkins, 1983).

Contemporary Prison Industries

The recent resurgence of prison industries was influenced by several developments. In 1967 the President's Commission Task Force on Corrections issued a report at a time when the medical model of rehabilitation was coming under attack and losing credibility. This report stressed reintegration as the key to reforming offenders, and it emphasized the development of skills that enable inmates to be self-supporting on release. For this to occur, programs paralleling those in the private sector that would provide inmates with the knowledge, skills, practice, and experience to "make it" in the community after release were needed. The cycle of prison reform had come full circle, and work replaced treatment programs as the means to reform offenders. Cullen and Travis (1984) found that this coincided with public views that work had the greatest potential for rehabilitating offenders. A study of inmates during this period showed that they shared a similar view (Dinitz & Huff, 1988).

Also, during the 1970s, more punitive public attitudes resulted in the harsher treatment of inmates. This involved not only more offenders being sentenced to prison but also receiving longer terms. This increased the prison population substantially at a time when resources for adding more beds were not available. The resulting overcrowding caused prisons to focus attention on inmate work as a means of partially offsetting the increasing need for greater state funding for corrections and to reduce idleness.

Finally, an increasing emphasis on the use of the private sector to solve public problems led to private enterprise again becoming involved in prison industries and in other aspects of corrections. First, a broadened national economy dominated by large manufacturers was not threatened by competition from relatively small prison production operations. Second, American industry had shifted its labor-intensive production operations, for which prisons are best suited, to foreign countries. This offered U.S. companies an opportunity to recapture enterprises that had gone overseas by using prison labor, which could produce many of these products at competitive prices (Dwyer & McNally, 1993). Third, and most important, was the passage of the **Prison Industry Enhancement Certification Program** (PIECP) provision to the Justice System Improvement Act of 1979. The PIECP established partnerships between state or local prison industries and the private sector. It further set forth minimum conditions under which interstate shipment of prisoner-made goods could take place. It also was an essential step in promoting private

Prisoners at Liberty Correctional Institution in Florida work at digitally mapping utility company records as part of PRIDE Enterprise's workforce within the state's prison system.

sector involvement in correctional industries because most markets today cross state lines (Auerbach, Sexton, Farrow, & Lawson, 1988). Together, these factors enabled the rejuvenation of prison industries that had stagnated since the 1930s (Auerbach, Sexton, Farrow, & Lawson, 1988; Miller & Grieser, 1986).

Support for Prison Industries   Inmate labor is currently receiving support from widely divergent groups of people who view it as serving a variety of goals (Flanagan, 1989; Guynes & Grieser, 1986). These goals can be consolidated into three categories:

■ *Inmate Related*   Most offenders have been unsuccessful in the work world, in part because they lack exposure to the norms and practices of work. Prison jobs can enable inmates to learn these responsibilities and job skills.

Prison jobs based on real-world work truly provide inmates with the experiences needed to be successful on release. On these jobs inmates are supervised by free-world managers who emphasize promptness, attendance, and quality and quantity of output. A broader objective is life management experience, which gives offenders the opportunity to legitimately provide for themselves. It does this by paying them wages and requiring them to manage their income to pay for room, board, and other life needs and save some for release (gate money).

Jobs that pay inmates a reasonable wage enable them to save their gate money. Because inmates coming out of prison often have trouble getting jobs, this money can help them secure a residence, eat, and pay for transportation, clothes, and other necessities. Ex-offenders who leave prison with sufficient gate money have a lower recidivism rate than those who do not. Thus, providing them with opportunities to earn release money makes good correctional sense (Guynes & Grieser, 1986).

■ *Institution Related*   Reducing idleness has become an even greater concern today because of overcrowding. Involving inmates in prison industries gets them out of their cells and dormitories, provides a meaningful daily activity that can reduce their tensions, and structures their time, which adds an element of order to institutional life. When large numbers of inmates are idle, they have time for illicit pursuits, which can result in institutional violence or other rule violations. Studies have shown that prison industry programs appear to reduce the level of misbehavior in prisons (Flanagan, Thornberry, Maguire, & McGarrell, 1988). This was demonstrated by a federal study that found that participants in vocational and industry programs were significantly less likely to be the subject of incident violations while incarcerated (Saylor & Gaes, 1992). Finally, prison industries can reduce net operating costs by providing the correctional system with a variety of products, reduced costs for alternative programming when inmates are employed rather than idle, and profits from the sale of industrial products and services.

■ *Societal Benefits* Society benefits from the savings achieved when prison industry programs provide goods and services to governmental agencies or meet other societal needs. Road crews work on highways, parks, and other public or government areas and assist the community by making repairs and cleaning up after disasters strike. In North Carolina after Hurricane Floyd hit in 1997 inmate workers not only assisted in the general cleanup but also helped some senior citizens repair their homes and property. Whereas citizens may complain about inmates working in the community in normal times, during emergencies not only are there no complaints but inmate help is well received (Soonachan, 2000). However, only a few states use inmates for this type of work.

A more recent effort to make convicted offenders pay for the criminal justice costs associated with their crime is to charge them for court costs. Wages inmates earn for prison work can be used to make these payments. Another goal in states that pay inmate workers wages is for them to use part of their income to help support their outside dependents and thereby reduce the burden on the welfare system. In private sector industry programs, they may also pay income taxes and social security (Grieser, 1997). Inmates often have restitution payments deducted from their wages to compensate their victims. As of 1996, inmates employed in the PIECP had returned over $23 million of their pay over a 17-year period for victim restitution, family support, room and board, and taxes (Grieser, 1997).

Conflicting Goals of Prison Work Programs The fact that prison work programs have multiple goals that can con-

flict with one another raises questions about the extent to which these goals can be achieved simultaneously (Guynes & Grieser, 1986). For example, the need to reduce idleness may result in the overassignment of inmates to prison jobs, compromising goals such as providing real-world job experiences or teaching job skills. Likewise, requiring that inmate compensation include provisions for both victim restitution and dependent assistance may increase expenses, adding to the cost of services and products. This may reduce their competitiveness with the private sector (Flanagan, 1989; Grieser, 1997).

Constraints on Prison Work Programs Operating industries in the prison environment involves factors not at issue in outside businesses, such as using inmate workers and security concerns (Guynes & Grieser, 1986).

■ *Inmate Workers* Prison industries are limited to selecting workers from the institutional population. Although every system has some qualified inmates, the vast majority are underqualified. Some states have developed vocational programs that provide inmates with the training or skill development required to work in their prison industrial programs. For example, the federal prison system has linked these components by establishing an Industrial Education and Vocational Training Division (IEVT), which manages and coordinates these programs (Pospichal, 1991). IEVT conducts preindustrial programs that give inmates hands-on skill training at actual production sites before assuming their positions in a prison industrial setting. It also provides refresher, continuing, and advanced training as needed during production in addition to requiring educational achievement for promotion or other advancements.

Another problem is that many inmates have little or no motivation to work so they require more supervision. This low motivation often results from inmates seeing no direct relationship between productivity and rewards for themselves.

■ *Security Requirements* Security concerns, ranging from dealing with one disruptive inmate to controlling the entire population through a lockdown, often impede production goals. Budgetary constraints may add to this problem by curtailing the number of available COs to supervise inmates. One solution to this problem, used by several states and by the BOP, is to hire personnel with prior experience in private industry into production positions (e.g., assistant shop foremen) and train them in the unique demands of operating manufacturing shops in a correctional environment while they supervise inmate workers. They are then eligible for promotion to shop foremen and higher level central office positions (Grieser, 1997).

Another problem is tool regulation, which although critical in a correctional facility can obstruct production. There are two approaches to this issue: (1) Adopt a strict tool control policy that reduces production time by an hour a day; and (2) focus on maximizing production and live with the risks of less strict control (Agresti, 1991).

Lockdowns, which are used to control serious disruptive prison situations, can be managed to minimize the disruption of industry schedules by giving prison industry inmates priority to return to their jobs when conditions permit. Callouts, where inmates are removed from work for a special purpose (e.g., dental appointment), counts, and mealtimes also make it difficult for prison industries to maintain an 8-hour work schedule. Counts can be scheduled before and after work hours and, if necessary, during the lunch hour. Several states have developed successful approaches to deal with inmate-caused callouts, including pay reductions if inmates leave work for other than a parole or classification hearing or drug counseling and evening counseling schedules. Solutions to problems caused by meals have included earlier meal schedules, having inmates "brown bag it," and creating an on-site dining area and using carts to deliver the food.[9]

A final problem for industry is the competition for inmates to work in institutional support services (e.g., kitchen and maintenance). The Washington State correctional system attacked this issue by establishing a three-step system under which all inmates initially worked in institutional maintenance. They could then graduate to state-run tax reduction workshops and then to private sector plants (Miller & Grieser, 1986).

Providing Reasonable Pay and Incentives   A requisite for industry success is reasonable compensation for inmates, which is difficult because of the court-supported view that the state owns the inmates' labor and is not obligated to pay them for work done (Grieser, Miller, & Funke, 1984; Mushlin, 1993). In many states this has resulted in inmates receiving low wages (10 to 65 cents daily) or no pay and/or good-time credits (Burns, 1975). The recent emerging view of prison industries as busi-

ness operations has placed greater emphasis on giving inmate workers sufficient incentives to produce quality products. Average daily inmate salary rates for 1998 were:

Prison-Operated Industry	Private-Operated Industry	Nonindustry Jobs
$1.60 to $7.06	$24.27 to $38.23	$.99 to $3.13

It should also be noted that some states like Texas pay nothing and others pay almost nothing—$.10 to $.15 (Camp & Camp, 1998).

More states appear to be providing some form of bonus or incentive pay for performance. For example, Michigan and Montana as part of the PIECP programs have wage plans that include increased pay for longevity and seniority. Reportedly, this has reduced inmate turnover. They also pay quarterly bonuses based on profitability. Correctional industries operating under PIECP guidelines are required to pay their inmate workers prevailing wages for the job functions they perform. Generally, workers with little or no experience will start at the federal minimum wage and then progress up the scale according to their ability and job performance. Deductions are made for taxes, room and board, victim restitution, and dependent support. This is designed to reinforce the real-world aspects of work that these programs are attempting to create. Other state-provided incentives have included additional good-time credits and privileges such as special housing, added recreation time, extra telephone time and visits, and special meals (Mann, 2000). The federal system's industry program, UNICOR, deals with motivation through promotion or demotion, incentive pay, premium pay, and other benefits, including a scholarship and incentive awards program (Pospichal, 1991).

The Quality of Prison Goods and Services   In the past, prison industries have been plagued with complaints of poor-quality products. State agencies have used this as a basis for not purchasing prison-made products. The recent emphasis on operating these industries like private business has resulted in better quality control through inspections and inmate incentive programs. For example, in Oklahoma inmate incentives are tied directly to product quality. Here a certain amount of money is placed in a fund based on the production of satisfactory merchandise. However, double the amount is taken from it when faulty products are returned (Miller & Grieser, 1986). These and other similar procedures that emulate private sector practices have increased the salability and desirability of inmate-produced items (Grieser, 1997).

The Corporate Model   For three quarters of a century federal legislation (cited earlier in this section) has virtually eliminated private sector involvement in correctional industries. Throughout this period the *state-use system* has been the mainstay of correctional industries, in which operations are overseen entirely by a public agency and the market is primarily governmental agencies. Variations to the state-use model include the **corporate model,** which employs an entity to act in place of the government in the same capacity (Ingley & Cochran, 1999). The corporate model involves establishing a quasi-independent or wholly owned government corporation that operates and manages prison industries yet is connected to the corrections department for security purposes. It is structured similarly to a private corporation, with a chief executive or operating officer that reports to a policy board or board of directors. While their markets are still governmental agencies, the corporate structure provides more flexible financial management and borrowing arrangements (Grieser, 1997). UNICOR, the federal program established in 1934, is the grandfather of this approach. Florida, California, and Georgia have also employed other variants of this model. Our Program Focus, "PRIDE," discusses Florida's program.

The Resurgence of Prison Industries

The unprecedented growth of the U.S. economy during the 1990s and into the new millennium combined with the shortage of qualified workers has renewed interest in prison labor as a new "alternative" source of labor. Also record sales and profits during this period make it difficult to sustain an argument that prison industries are affecting industry income. This has generated a new interest in the relatively obscure Prison Industry Enhancement Certification Program (PIECP), which was established in 1979 as an exception to the Ashurst-Summers and Walsh-Healy Act restrictions. A major Illinois prison riot and the characterization of prisons as schools for crime caused Congress to take measures to encourage prison industries, provided that "they not engage in unfair competition with private sector businesses and labor" (Federal Register, 1998). Ingley and Cochran (1999) describe PIECP as an effort to create a "level playing field" for all stakeholders in the public and private sectors and a common purpose for both groups to pursue together. PIECP

> is designed to place inmates in a realistic working environment with compensation that equals the local comparable wage for similar work. These wages allow offenders to offset the cost of their incarceration, compensate crime victims, provide family support and pay taxes. During this time, inmates learn marketable skills that increase their potential for meaningful employment and successful transition to the community upon release. (p. 82)

The PIECP offers correctional industry programs an opportunity to participate in the interstate market pro-

vided they conform to safeguards for free-world labor and industry and for the inmate workers.

Private Sector Models Three models represent the roles that the private sector plays in correctional industry programs (Mann, 2000).

1. Under the **main customer model** the public agency supervises and administers all aspects of the program. The private sector is engaged in a PIECP enterprise only to the extent that it purchase all or a significant portion of the output of a correctional industry business. A customer model private sector partner assumes no major role in industry operations, does not direct production, and has no control over inmate labor.

2. Under the **employer model** the private sector owns and manages the business and employs inmates to produce its goods or services. The department of corrections assumes no major role in industry operations, does not direct production, and exercises minimum control over inmate labor performance (Federal Register, 1998).

3. Under the **manpower model** the private sector partner manages the industry shops and supervises the inmate workers; however, the public agency administers the programs and pays the inmates (Ingley & Cochran, 1999).

The Future of Prison Work and Industry Programs

Private sector involvement in prison work programs cannot solve all the problems that plague corrections. Although the goal is to achieve productive, cost-effective, and meaningful work programs, the corrections environment and inmate population place limitations on the achievement of these objectives. However, at a time when correctional budgets are stretched to the limit, private sector work programs offer opportunities to experiment with programs that might otherwise be impossible. They also represent a commitment by the business community to use its expertise "to open a pathway for those at the very bottom of the social order who might otherwise continue to fail at their own and society's expense" (Auerbach et al., 1988, p. 65). A Texas program, called Project Re-Enterprise (PRE) (Moses, 1996), is an example of private sector businesses, corrections, and other interested groups collaborating on an initiative to hone the job-seeking skills of inmates. Employing *mock* job fairs to instruct inmates on interviewing skills and how to complete job applications, PRE has grown from a pilot project to a program that involves more than 300 businesses in several correctional institutions.

Expansion of work programs is limited by the deficiencies of the inmate labor force that require costly and

PRIDE: A Variation of the Corporate Model

PRIDE Enterprises, a not-for-profit 501(c)(3) corporation, was formed in 1981 and authorized by the Florida legislature to manage and operate the state's correctional industries. It is an example of a public/private partnership with the State of Florida and the business community. PRIDE is a multifaceted organization that intertwines business and social mission objectives. The company operates 50 industries in 21 of Florida's state prisons and one county jail. It produces over 3,000 products and services. In 1999, it employed and trained over 4,700 inmates in formal, externally certified on-the-job training programs (PRIDE Enterprises Annual Report, 1999). PRIDE operates under legislatively mandated business and social mission goals.

Training and Postrelease Job Placement

PRIDE operates a comprehensive industry training program that includes certified job skills training, orientation and prerelease workshops, employability skills training, and optional education through distance learning. Through 1999, 85 percent of PRIDE's industry on-the-job training programs were certified by business and educational organizations. This ensures that PRIDE's training processes, which include over 350 occupational skills, meet private sector businesses' and industry standards so upon release inmates will have marketable skills.

PRIDE is one of the few correctional programs that provide postrelease job placement and other support services to workers upon release to the community. In 1999, PRIDE Job Developers found jobs for nearly three fourths of its workers released and available for employment. While participating in the program, the ex-offenders receive job placement counseling, referrals to community social service agencies, and assistance with transportation and shelter as required. This has been expanded to form an affiliate company to serve more ex-offenders and others with barriers to employment (Mann, 1999).

The success of PRIDE's on-the-job training and postrelease job placement programs is demonstrated by the fact that through 1998, approximately 84 percent of PRIDE's former workers had not returned to crime (PRIDE Enterprises Annual Report, 1999).

Reduces Inmate Idleness

One of PRIDE's primary goals is to serve the security goals of the state through the reduction of inmate idleness and to provide an incentive for good behavior. While the dramatic growth in Florida's prison population has reduced the percentage of PRIDE inmates working in correctional industries, PRIDE continues to support over 2,600 workstations and provide meaningful work and training to thousands of inmates. Restricted by law from unreasonably competing with the private sector and from selling the goods to nongovernmental entities, PRIDE has taken steps to develop new industries and increase sales that should serve to increase the demand for inmates and have positive effects on reducing idleness (Florida Auditor General, 1996).

Reduced Costs to State Government

PRIDE employs male and female inmates from 6 to 8 hours a day at wages from \$0.20 to \$0.55 per hour, depending on industry longevity and job skill classification. In its PIE programs, PRIDE pays its workers at rates ranging from the federal minimum wage upward to the prevailing wage established for their job function. Fifteen percent of an inmate's wages are contributed to court-ordered victim restitution and court costs. Another portion of its annual net sales is returned to the state general fund, which helps offset inmate incarceration costs. In 1999, for example, PRIDE contributed approximately \$265,000 to the Department of Corrections for victim restitution and nearly \$1 million to the department's general fund to offset the state's cost of inmate incarceration (PRIDE Enterprises Annual Report, 1999). In addition, PRIDE provides its own staff for supervising the inmate workers, thereby reducing the need for correctional officers and their associated costs.

PRIDE is totally self-supporting and employs modern business principles, strategies, and quality measurements to operate independently of government. In its efforts to expand its operations and to employ and train more inmates, PRIDE, in the late 1990s, began an ambitious growth plan that included the addition of new PIE programs and other private sector partnerships.

Source: Prepared especially for the second edition of this text by Tim Mann (2000), general manager, Labor Line, an affiliate of PRIDE.

unprofitable academic and vocational training prior to employment in these programs. Added to this is the overriding concern with security in correctional facilities. When security is threatened, production will be sacrificed. Recently, the renewed involvement of business in prison industries has begun to raise some objections from labor and business groups. However, the cries of unfair competition by labor and business must be counterbalanced against support for prison programs expressed by many partners, vendors, and suppliers that have been an integral part of the prison industries over the last few years. Moreover, the many benefits of industry programs for prison administrators, the inmates, and society as a whole must not be underestimated (Grieser, 1997).

Yet for all of the preceding reasons, the goal of full and meaningful employment in the prison setting is not likely to be realized (Flanagan, 1989). Still, it should be pursued because this approach holds the promise of eliminating some of the debilitating effects of idleness by providing meaningful ways of "doing time" and other potential benefits for inmates. For society the benefits outweigh the costs. Further, there is the potential for reducing recidivism. The results of a federal study support this view. This research focused on:

> inmates who participated in UNICOR work and other vocational training [while] in prison. This study found that these inmates [as compared with those not participating in these activities] showed better institutional adjustment, were less likely to be revoked at the end of their first year back in the community, were more likely to be employed in the halfway house and community, and earned slightly more money in the community. (Saylor & Gaes, 1992, p. 25)

Finally, one should judge prison work programs both in terms of these objectives and in the improvements made over the abysmal conditions of the recent past.

Recreational Programs[10]

Recreational activities form an important part of prison programming and have a number of benefits essential to successful prison management. As five federal prison wardens stated in 1979 at the second revision of the Adult Correctional Facilities Accreditation Standards, "Give me an institution with a good chaplain program and a good recreation program and I will show you an institution that will not have a riot" (McCall, 2000). Recreational and leisure-time programs encourage inmates to make constructive use of their free time, offering movies, games, sports, social activities, arts and hobby crafts, wellness, and other group and individual activities. They address an inmate's interest from the youngest to the oldest, and they reflect gender differences. The expected objectives of a complete recreational program are to (1) keep inmates constructively occupied and reduce idleness; (2) provide for the physical, emotional, and social well-being of inmates; (3) encourage and assist inmates in adopting healthy daily lifestyle traits through participation in physical fitness and health education programs; and (4) reduce the need for inmate medical treatment (PS5070.10, 2000, Feb. 23).

Tougher sentencing laws have resulted in inmates serving longer sentences, which has led to a reexamination of prison recreation. With a growing population serving determinate sentences, programs must be designed to meet the needs of male and female inmates. Further, the graying of the inmate population has resulted in the need for leisure programs specifically aimed at chronic care, nonambulatory inmates with a variety of medical restrictions. Females and males are different, and recreational programs must reflect these differences. A general model for today's inmate leisure activities is built around four dimensions: social, physical, psychological, and health promotion and disease prevention (Rison, 2000). These programs provide a means for developing social and interpersonal skills. Our Program Focus, "Therapeutic Recreation," looks at a broader concept of recreation that is increasingly being used in corrections settings.

The challenge for prison staff is to offer leisure activities designed to attract inmate participation regardless of ethnic, racial, age, physical capabilities, or sex differences.

History

For as long as offenders have been imprisoned, they have probably engaged in recreational activity, either organized on their own or by the prison staff. For example, in the early 1600s, Miguel de Cervantes, who wrote *Don Quijote de la Mancha*, reportedly organized his fellow captives into a theater company while awaiting trial during the Spanish Inquisition. In early colonial jails, and later in both Pennsylvania and Auburn-type prisons, provision was made for exercise.

The Elmira Reformatory, which opened in 1876, was the first institution to offer a diversified recreational and leisure program that included organized sports, an indoor gymnasium, social clubs (e.g., debating), an inmate newspaper, and drama and arts programs (Burns, 1975; Nicolai, 1981). These programs were atypical and only a few prisons had them until well into the 20th century. More typically, recreation in prisons was limited to three areas: (1) the yard, described in Chapter 7, "The Big House," where inmates could walk around, sit down, or congregate in small groups, and where, on weekends and holidays, outdoor sports were allowed; (2) the library, offering a limited selection of reading matter that was usually of little interest to most inmates; and (3) the auditorium, where movies were shown on Saturday evening and church services were offered on Sunday.

Following World War II, there was a belated recognition of the significance of recreational programs in prisons by both the American Correctional and National Correctional Recreation Associations. However, it was not until 20 years later that a sustained effort to develop

Therapeutic Recreation

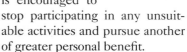

Therapeutic recreation (TR) represents a broader focus on standard recreational programs. What makes TR unique is its concentration on "the knowledge of leisure and recreation as these phenomena relate to achieving optimal health care" (Austin, 1996, p. 1). In corrections, the objective of TR is to "help inmates develop new leisure skills that will assist them in reentering the community upon release" (McCall, 1996, p. 85). In this regard, it helps inmates to develop an awareness of how recreational activities can better assist them in dealing with difficult situations through anger management and aggression control. Participation in leisure activities is therapeutic to the degree that it enables an inmate to attribute leisure behavior to personal abilities and improve self-perception of personal capabilities. The therapeutic recreation model in correctional settings today is the **leisure education model** (see Figure 16.2), which encompasses the following:

1. Leisure Education
   a. The individual is exposed to the role that recreation has played and will continue to play in his life. He learns how leisure experiences can enhance the quality and increase the number of options available to him.
   b. **Value clarification** enables each inmate to identify his need for praise, belonging, and acceptance. Self-esteem, self-concept, self-control, self-image, and self-worth are also identified as necessities. Next, methods for achieving and satisfying these values are examined at length.
      • Inmates are taught to understand that all people have a need for praise and the importance of engaging in leisure activities that

have the potential to satisfy this need.
      • Inmates also are taught to recognize where they have uncontrolled tempers and to learn activities that use hostile energy positively and divert attention from further negative action.

2. Needs Assessment
   The next step involves compiling a "needs assessment inventory," including both a history of their leisure pursuits and future desires for leisure activity. This assessment should reveal (1) the recreational pursuits, activities, and frequency of participation prior to incarceration, and (2) the leisure activities the individual would enjoy but for various reasons has not participated in.

3. Leisure Counseling
   The final step is to provide leisure counseling and opportunities for skill acquisition. As the individual becomes involved in the leisure service program, a TR specialist

helps the inmate discuss his satisfactions or dissatisfactions with the current activities. The inmate is encouraged to stop participating in any unsuitable activities and pursue another of greater personal benefit.

One of the reasons for changing the basis of leisure education programs in correctional settings to TR is that it refocuses their emphasis from just being recreational in nature to being part of the treatment program offered for inmates. This is more palatable to the public and lawmakers who are insistent on making prisons tougher by eliminating the notion held by some people that prison recreation resembles a country club.

Source: Unless otherwise noted, this material is adapted from G. McCall (1996). Corrections and Social Deviance. In D. Austin & M. E. Crawford (Eds.), Therapeutic Recreation: An Introduction (2nd ed.). Boston: Allyn and Bacon.

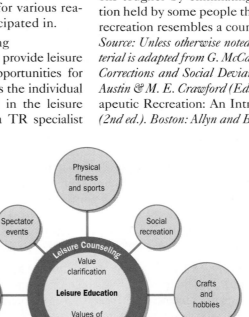

Figure 16.2 *Leisure Education Model*

Source: G. McCall (1996). Corrections and Social Deviance. In D. Austin & M. E. Crawford (Eds.), *Therapeutic Recreation: An Introduction* (2nd ed.). Boston: Allyn and Bacon. Reprinted by permission.

diversified prison recreational and leisure programs began. The Attica riot (which focused attention on many prison problems) and court mandates regarding prison conditions forced institutions to establish new programs. During the 1970s, the membership of the National Correctional Recreation Association began to change from COs interested in recreation to full-time professional personnel with degrees in recreation or physical education (McCall, 1981).

Benefits for Inmates and Institutions

The Federal Bureau of Prisons (BOP) has the most complete facilities for recreational programs and the best educated and trained staffs (McCall, 1993). These programs have several important functions. First, they play a major part in alleviating the dull monotony of prison life. Recreation provides a constructive means for inmates to use much of their unstructured prison time. If not available, many inmates are likely to pursue activities threatening prison safety and security. Second, good recreational programs function as safety valves for dissipating the tensions created by the prison's unnatural environment (Crutchfield, Garrette & Worral, 1981; McCall, 1981); they enable inmates to release pent-up energy, anger, and frustration in healthy and productive ways. Hopefully, these lessons in self-control will carry over to the outside once inmates are released (McCall, 1993).

Activities especially directed toward dealing with stress and anxiety in prison may include softball, basketball, football, and other physical activities. A number of activities also provide opportunities to escape the harsh prison environment. Movies and reading can reduce tension by allowing inmates to become involved with something other than their current circumstances so that, at least temporarily, they can forget the oppressiveness of the prison (McCall, 1981). Concerts given by outside or inmate groups serve similar functions:

> After a concert given by the Baltimore Symphony at the Maryland Penitentiary, Glenn Grainger, a trumpet playing inmate, remarked, "Music is a very good thing here, a chance to get away from the frustrations and let off tensions. . . ." (Nicolai, 1981, p. 33)

Both inmates and staff agree that recreation makes prisons safer places. Ron Speckman (1981), a former prison inmate, writes that physical exertion in recreational programs reduces prison violence and disciplinary problems and results in fewer "write-ups." McCall (1981) found that in all the riots spanning the period from Attica to New Mexico (1971–1980) better recreation was an inmate demand, and in half it was among the top three demands (Gould, 1981). In a 40-state survey of 66 facilities, including some for females, more than three quarters of the administrators felt having in-

mates active in recreation resulted in fewer security problems (Jewell, 1981). A study of arts-related recreational programs found decreases of from 54 to 100 percent in the monthly incident reports of program participants. Theater programs led to the greatest decreases (Nicolai, 1981). This type of program may even provide a means of reaching extremely alienated inmates:

> A mentally troubled inmate at Joseph Harp Correctional Center in Lexington, OK, had not talked to anyone for years and was physically filthy. [Soon after] arts and crafts programs were introduced the inmate made a rug—then started cleaning himself up, started talking, and soon the staff could not shut him up. (Welch, 1990, pp. 1, 5)

Staff who participated in this programming learned to appreciate the benefits of constructive leisure for inmates and the institution.

A third benefit of good recreational programs is they can have effects beyond the individual's prison stay. Constructive use of leisure time as a factor in preventing crime participation has received little attention. McCall, in an Indiana study, found that little crime is committed during either work or personal maintenance time and most is committed during leisure time. Leisure time exceeds the other two time periods on the outside and even more so in prison, so learning to use it appropriately is important (Gould, 1981). This, coupled with our previous discussion of inmate idleness, suggests that failure to provide for constructive leisure activities both in prison and on the street creates a high-risk situation for criminal and other deviant behavior.

An experiment with probationers conducted by McCall and summarized by Gould (1981) provides additional justification for this thesis:

> [I]ndividuals who satisfied a personal value or gained self-esteem through some sort of leisure activity had less of a tendency to commit crimes. . . . [She notes that] if you don't just go to a bar after work, but have something productive to look forward to that meets your needs, it can have an effect. (pp. 22–23)

In another experiment using institutionalized offenders, McCall compared 125 offenders who chose to participate in an enhanced recreational program with 125 offenders who did not. She found that, on release, there was a significant difference in the types of activities chosen by the two groups (Gould, 1981).

Recreational and arts programs can also help build an inmate's self-image and teach social skills, self-expression, how to think creatively, aggression control, self-discipline, and respect for authority (Welch, 1990). The voluntary nature of recreational programs enables inmates to set their own "standard for success." As a result, there is a high probability that inmates who participate will experience feelings of success. For example, in sports like jogging, the individual is competing against himself and improvement is assured as long as the individual continues to participate. Team sports provide an excellent way to teach getting along with others, anger control, and how to deal with authority. Other activities, such as involvement in theater productions, can teach delayed gratification and cooperation. McCall (1993) asserts that recreational programs encourage decision making, which is critical to an inmate's "making it" on the outside.

Finally, involvement in arts and crafts programs teaches inmates hobbies and can also provide income. Inmates can sell their work through shows and gift shops and can compete in outside shows for monetary prizes. Recreation is neither a panacea for the ills of imprisonment nor a solution to the crime problem, but it certainly can make prison life safer and more bearable and provide releasees with constructive leisure options to be used in the outside world. Thus, the benefits of a good recreational program far outweigh its costs.

Recreational Programming

An effective recreational program requires well-trained professional staff, adequate funds for equipment and supplies, and areas and facilities for a year-round program of diversified outdoor and indoor activities.

One public and political view of recreational facilities is that they are luxuries—the first step toward turning the prison into a "resort hotel"—the principle of least eligibility viewpoint. For example, one warden justified the lack of a gymnasium in his institution by commenting that "some high schools in this state . . . do not have gymnasiums" (Nagel, 1973, p. 98). Although it is regrettable that some schools lack gymnasiums or other recreational facilities, this is hardly a basis for not providing them in correctional institutions. Inmates are confined there for months and even years on end. Their options for recreation are limited to those available in the institution, whereas those outside have available to them not only schools, but also parks, boys' clubs, playgrounds, pools, lakes, theaters, mountains, seashores, and sporting events. Although many prisons lack adequate recreational facilities, it is encouraging that planners of newer correctional facilities are including recreational programs (Rison, 2000).

Community Group Participation Prison chapters of Jaycees and Toastmasters[11] receive assistance, funds, and active participation from local outside chapters. This gives inmates additional contact with the outside world, which can reduce feelings of isolation and alienation and provide helpful community contacts (Speckman, 1981). Volunteers are a vital part of any prison recreational program; they augment program staff and may have talents not possessed by staff (McCall, 1993). With shrinking program dollars, their contribution is of even greater significance.

Competition is the essence of athletics, but security considerations limit the extent to which inmate teams and athletes can compete with their community counterparts. Nevertheless, in some state and federal prisons, community teams regularly play football and softball and lift weights against inmate teams (Telander, 1987). For example, Murphy and Von Minden (1981) described an invitational softball tournament at the Correctional Center in Lincoln, Nebraska, nicknamed "cops and robbers," because it included teams from various law enforcement agencies. Some prisons also allow inmate teams to participate in outside recreational activities. Although there is the risk of an inmate deciding to go deep for a football pass or a high fly in baseball and not coming back, good screening can go a long way toward avoiding this problem. In selecting inmates to compete outside the prison, ability is not the major concern but rather whether they will behave appropriately and benefit from the experience (Murphy & Von Minden, 1981). Further, inmate teams and athletes are often able to win against opponents because they have ample time to practice and may have been together longer than most outside teams. Sportswriter Rick Telander (1987) notes that a team of guys doing time can develop closer ties than the Lakers.

Many correctional institutions are able to bring outside individuals and groups to the prison to entertain offenders. This has included such show business personalities as Johnny Cash and B. B. King and community and regional traveling groups including rock bands, theater groups, and bands and choral groups from local schools and colleges.

Overcrowding and Budget Constraints Prison population projections indicate a continuing rise, so the need for recreation that constructively occupies inmates and provides creative outlets for their energies is more important than ever. However, despite a well-substantiated need for these programs, overcrowding, funding concerns, and the "get tough" attitude that views recreational programs as a frill threaten their survival. Spaces once available for recreation have been used to build temporary or permanent structures to house inmates. The paradox is that the more inmates there are, the more programs that will be needed to teach them new skills and to relieve the tension of overcrowding. A sad commentary on this scenario is that as resources become scarcer, we find that almost all monies are going into inmate maintenance (e.g., food, health care, bed space). With funding such a critical issue in corrections today, money for recreational programs must be generated from the institution. Currently, canteen profits, telephone revenues, inmate art sales, and many other creative activities augment these meager recreational budgets (McCall, 1993).

Weightlifting

PROGRAM FOCUS

States first began to examine their weightlifting policies in the early 1990s, when media reports suggested that inmates coming out of prison were stronger and allegedly more dangerous than when they went in. Additionally, legislators viewed weights as a luxury that states could no longer afford (Clayton, 1997). For this and other reasons, 3 states have banned weights completely and 10 others have banned freestanding weights (Clayton, 1999).

The arguments in support of weightlifting are many. The National Correctional Recreation Association (NCRA) takes the position that "weight-lifting programs are an integral part of rehabilitation services within the spectrum of corrections" and that properly administered, weightlifting programs are a vital tool in the daily management of a volatile environment as well as a potentially cost-effective measure (Clayton, 1998).

Clark (1998) argues that the pursuit of physical conditioning leads to a greater sense of confidence, integrity, and self-respect. Weight training teaches the participant to set and achieve worthwhile and constructive goals. Setting and achieving these goals leads to a sense of direction and the ambition to succeed in other areas of one's life. In response to citizen and correctional officers' fears that weightlifting makes inmates dangerous, Clark asks, "Does getting a great workout increase the average citizen's desire to commit a crime or his or her propensity toward violence? Of course not, so why assume that a great workout encourages inmates to commit crimes?"

One compromise used in both California and Texas requires that weightlifting be part of a formal recreational program and places limitations on inmate participants. For example, in the Texas correctional system the use of free weights for weightlifting is considered a privilege—one available only in organized and supervised weightlifting programs. To enter these programs inmates have to demonstrate exemplary behavior while being incarcerated and be medically approved.

Properly trained recreation program specialists, or recreation officers, supervise all free weight programs. The recreation program specialist is required to maintain a record of those participating in each session. Free weight programs have become important to both the offender and the agency for relieving tension, for long-term participation in structured programming, and as a management tool (Porter, 2000).

Considering both the pros and cons of weights in correctional settings, should they be totally removed, available to all inmates, or part of a structured weightlifting program? *Source: Adapted from S. L. Clayton (1997, Nov.) Weight Lifting in Corrections: Luxury or Necessity? On the Line, 20(5): 1, 3; R. J. Clark (1998). Weight Training in Prison: Pros and Cons. Corrections Today, 59(2): 16; C. Porter (2000). Recreation program administrator, Windham District, Texas Department of Criminal Justice. Personal communication.*

As the get tough movement has gathered steam there are increased calls for the removal of recreational programs (specifically TVs, weight rooms, etc.). If this sentiment results in termination of these programs, their positive influences will be lost and inmates will likely become more difficult to manage (Nossiter, 1994). The consequence for prison and jail staff is that corrections work will become more difficult and dangerous. Our Program Focus, "Weightlifting," examines the controversy over whether this form of recreation should be continued in correctional settings.

Summary

This chapter has examined three types of programs for inmates: educational, work, and recreational. One of the most potent beliefs affecting prison programming, services, and conditions is the principle of least eligibility, which states that "the condition of the prisoner should be inferior, or at least not superior, to that of the lowest classes of the noncriminal population in a state of liberty." However, if inmates are not to be worse on release than when they were first incarcerated, they must be provided with basic services and programs.

Educational programs are probably the most important prison programs available for inmates because (1) academic skills (reading, writing, and math) are fundamental to achieving success in the labor force, and (2) a large proportion of the inmate population is deficient in these skills. Between 40 and 75 percent of the U.S. prison population is functionally illiterate, compared with about 25 percent of the free adult population.

Adult basic education programs for inmates have been the mainstays of correctional education. They stress literacy and mathematical skills, science, and social science as a foundation for further education and training. General equivalency diploma (GED) programs focus on the further development of reading, language arts, composition, and mathematical skills. This provides a opportunity for inmates to utilize their time in prison for remediating their educational deficits or becoming more employable. Beyond the educational value of the GED, other gains include improved self-esteem and better parenting skills and practices. Life skills programs focus on developing employability and job search skills and consumer, safety, parenting and family, and civic skills. They also teach inmates how to use community resources. A new field, cognitive intervention, has become an effective means to improve prosocial thinking and behavior.

Vocational programs are thought to be the best vehicles for breaking the cycle of recidivism. These programs are aimed at providing inmates with contemporary marketable skills relating to specific jobs on the outside.

There is little hostility toward furnishing adult basic education, GED, or related high school programs to inmates because they are available at no cost on the outside. However, this is not the case for college programs. With the end of Pell Grant funding for inmates in 1994 most systems terminated their college education programs, and the remaining few have substantially reduced their scope. This is despite the positive impact of these programs on recidivism rates. Recognizing this had led some states to develop alternative means of funding for inmates who want to take college courses.

Prison work for inmates consists of two general types of jobs: those that maintain the institution (preparing meals, cleaning the dormitories) and those that are industrial or productive in nature. Work in prison serves several functions; it (1) keeps the prison running, (2) keeps inmates busy, (3) saves the state money, (4) produces goods and services used by other institutions and governmental agencies, and (5) teaches a useful skill.

Up until the 1930s, prisons employed most of their inmates. However, pressure from organized labor and manufacturers led to legislation that allowed states to block the importation of prison-made goods, prohibit the interstate transportation of convict-made goods to states where they were prohibited, and ban the use of prison labor to fulfill major government contracts.

The most important factor in the resurgence of prison industries was the passage of the Prison Industry Enhancement Certification Program (PIECP). This created a partnership between state or local prison industries and the private sector and set forth minimum conditions under which interstate shipment of prisoner-made goods could take place.

The corporate model is used by some jurisdictions to manage their prison industries. This involves establishing a quasi-independent, or wholly owned, government corporation that operates and manages prison industries yet is connected to the corrections department for security purposes. It is structured similar to a private corporation, with the chief executive or operating officer reporting to a policy board or board of directors. Although their markets are still government agencies, the corporate structure provides more flexible financial management and borrowing arrangements.

Three models represent the roles that the private sector plays in correctional industry programs associated with PIECP: (1) the customer model, under which the public agency supervises and administers all aspects of the program while the private sector purchases all or a significant portion of the output; (2) the employer model, under which the private sector owns and manages the business and employs inmates to produce its goods or services; and (3) the manpower model, under which the private sector partner manages the shops and supervises the inmate workers and the public agency administers the programs and pays the inmates.

Recreational programs are intended to encourage inmates to make constructive use of leisure time; help alleviate the dull monotony of prison life; and function as safety valves for dissipating the tensions created by the prison's unnatural environment. It is interesting that research shows that both inmates and staff are in agreement that recreation makes prisons safer places.

Recreational activities form an important part of prison programming and have a number of benefits essential to successful prison management. Therapeutic recreation (TR) represents a new broader focus; it is unique because it concentrates on the knowledge of leisure and recreation as these phenomena relate to achieving optimal health care. In corrections, the objective of TR is to help inmates develop new leisure skills that will assist them in reentering the community upon release.

Recreational and arts programs can also help build an inmate's self-image and teach social skills, self-expression, how to think creatively, aggression control, self-discipline, and respect for authority. The voluntary nature of recreational programs enables inmates to set their own standard for success. As a result, there is a high probability that inmates who participate will experience feelings of success.

The most controversial component of prison recreational programs is weightlifting. Those who support the removal of weights from correctional settings argue that inmates are going into prison bad, and they are coming out bigger, badder, and more dangerous. Supporters argue that the pursuit of physical conditioning leads to a greater sense of confidence, integrity, and self-respect. Also, the training teaches participants to set and achieve constructive goals.

Critical Thinking Questions

1. Do you think inmates should be allowed to participate in college programs? Why or why not?

2. Should inmates who lack basic skills be required to participate in literacy and life skills programs as a condition of their release?

3. Some argue that prison industries hurt nonprison businesses, especially small businesses. Do you agree?

4. Do you support the availability of life skills programs in prisons?

5. Discuss the controversy surrounding recreational programs in prisons. What is your opinion?

Test Your Knowledge

1. The Peer Tutoring Academy teaches
   a. correctional officers to assist in educational programs.
   b. citizen volunteers to tutor inmates.
   c. qualified inmates to tutor other inmates.
   d. inmates to assist instructors in vocational programs.

2. Enrollment in which of the following programs is required of inmates whose achievement falls below a certain level?
   a. Basic literacy programs
   b. Vocational training programs
   c. GED programs
   d. High school diploma programs

3. Which of the following is not a reason why the prison environment is not conducive to a meaningful work experience?
   a. There are not enough inmates available for labor.
   b. Many inmates have no desire or incentive to work.
   c. Time is valued less in prison.
   d. There are few opportunities for real-world employment experiences.

4. The system of prison industry in which a company agrees to pay a specific price for each specific article manufactured by prison labor is known as the
   a. lease system.
   b. piece-price system.
   c. public works system.
   d. state-use system.

5. Under the PIECP Program:
   a. States are required to sell their product to state agencies.
   b. Products by the prison system can only be used in this system.
   c. Correctional industries can sell products across state lines.
   d. Inmates are prohibited from producing any goods that compete against private industry.

Endnotes

1. Dr. Silverman would like to thank Dr. Judi Jones Benestante, educational specialist; Brian Cox, licensed specialist in school psychology; Dana Hold, teacher, Windham School District, Texas Department of Criminal Justice; Steve Steurer, executive director, Correctional Educational Association; and Alice Tracy, assistant director, Correctional Educational Association for providing information and reviewing this manuscript for the second edition of this text and offering useful suggestions to improve its authenticity.

2. Dell'Apa, 1973; Bell, Conard, Laffey, Lutz, Simon, Stakelon, & Wilson, 1979; Ryan & Woodard, 1987.

3. Forty-one states and the federal system provided data. The states that either did not provide information on the number of inmate participants or failed to provide any data for this survey were Alabama, Alaska, Arizona, Georgia, Maine, Massachusetts, Montana, Oklahoma, and Utah (*Corrections Compendium*, 1997, Sept.).

4. Fourteen states either failed to respond to the survey or to this question (*CC*, 1997, Sept.).

5. Beck, Gilliard, Greenfeld, Harlow, Hester, Jankowski, Snell, & Stephan, 1993.

6. Ross, 1980; Ross & Fabiano, 1982, 1986; Ross, Fabiano, & Eweles, 1988; Fabiano, 1991.

7. The Windham School District was established by the state legislature in 1969 to provide educational programs within the Texas Department of Criminal Justice (TDCJ) facilities. Currently, it provides literacy, career, and technology education to inmates in both the TDCJ correctional facilities and to a number of state jails throughout Texas. It is unique because it is an independent school district operating within a corrections system. Thus, students receive certificates of completion and diplomas from an independent school district, which does not indicate that it is associated with the prison system. This at least removes some of the stigma associated with incarceration.

8. Dr. Silverman would like to thank Tim Mann, general manager, Labor Line, an affiliate of PRIDE, for writing the initial update of this section. He also thanks Gwyn Ingley, executive director, Correctional Industries Association, and Robert Grieser, manager, Research and Activation Branch, Federal Prison Industries, for providing information and reviewing this manuscript. Thanks also go to John Benestante, assistant director for industries, TDCJ, and Tony D'Cuna, chief of operations, Texas Correctional Industries, TDCJ, for offering useful suggestions to improve this section. Finally, as a result of the time and effort all these colleagues spent on this section its authenticity was greatly improved.

9. Agresti, 1991; Miller & Grieser, 1986; Grieser, Miller, & Funke, 1984.

10. The author would like to thank Gail McCall, Ph.D., associate professor, Department of Recreation, University of Florida, for providing information and reviewing this manuscript. Thanks also goes to Richard Rison, retired warden from the BOP.

11. See Chapter 10 for discussions of these programs.

Basic Prison Services: Health, Treatment, Food, and Religion

KEY TERMS AND CONCEPTS

Acquired immune
  deficiency syndrome
  (AIDS)
Behavioral contracting
Behavior modification
Bona fide religious belief
Clinical Pastoral
  Educational Movement
Cognitive approach
Cognitive therapy
Co-occurring disorders
Cook/chill method
Cycle menu
Daily sick call
Decentralized dining
Deliberate indifference
Hepatitis C (HVC)
Hospice care
Human immunodeficiency
  virus (HIV)
Imams
Kairos Prison Ministry
  (KPM)

Managed care
Multiple drug-resistant
  TB strains
Muslim community
Nation of Islam
National Commission
  on Correctional
  Health Care
  (NCCHC)
Order of Misericordia
Prison Fellowship (PF)
Reasonableness test
Shadow board
Special diets
Telemedicine
Therapeutic
  community
  treatment model
Token economies
Tuberculosis (TB)

LEARNING OBJECTIVES

After completing this chapter, you should be able to:

1. Describe the basis for inmate rights to adequate health care.

2. Discuss correctional treatment programs, including mental health, behavior modification, and cognitive approaches.

3. List and describe the issues in providing inmate health care.

4. Discuss the use of private care providers for inmate health care.

5. Describe drug abuse problems among inmates and the use of therapeutic communities in their treatment.

6. Specify the characteristics of inmates with co-occurring disorders and the type of prescribed treatment for them.

7. Discuss the incidence of infectious diseases and the severe problems they pose for corrections.

8. Describe the AIDS and tuberculosis problems in corrections, and discuss the problems in dealing with HIV-infected inmates.

9. Explain the significance that food has for inmates.

10. Discuss the factors associated with food preparation in an institutional setting.

11. Identify the characteristics and functions of the contemporary prison chaplain.

12. Discuss the legal issues associated with religious restrictions in a correctional setting.

13. Specify the personality characteristics that are necessary for a prison chaplain to be effective.

Introduction

This chapter focuses on certain basic prison services. We begin with a focus on health services, examining legal issues surrounding the provision of these services and the delivery systems used to provide them. We also focus on infectious diseases, such as AIDS, tuberculosis, and hepatitis, which are easily spread in an institutional environment. We end the section with a discussion of treatment, including both mental health and drug programs. Next, we address the issues and methods associated with the provision of food services. Finally, we examine religion, including discussions of legal and other issues surrounding the provision of religious services in correctional settings. Further, we discuss the role of the chaplain and the means by which inmates can practice their religions.

Health Services[1]

Outside of prison, people are responsible for their own health care and usually have at least some choice of their practitioner. Inmates, on the other hand, are dependent on an institution's health services, which are often unsatisfactory. Inadequate medical services are one basis for inmate court challenges. The importance of medical service can be seen in the frequency with which complaints about it head the list of riot demands or are the target of inmate court petitions (Anno, 1991a).

History of Prison Health Care

Like most prison activities, health care received little public scrutiny prior to the 1970s, which meant that "almost anything could go" (Prout & Ross, 1988, p. 228). The Attica rebellion, often cited as a key event in prison medical reform because of the prominence given by inmates to medical grievances, prompted investigations and surveys of the health care delivery system in prisons and jails (Anno, 1989). Numerous deficiencies were found, including unsanitary conditions; correctional staff impeding access to medical services; institutional physicians who were either unqualified to take or could not pass state licensing exams; and use of inmates as caregivers (Anno, 1989). These conditions were aggravated by the fact that 95 percent of the prison inmates required some type of medical attention, and two thirds had not had medical examinations prior to their imprisonment (Prout & Ross, 1988).

By the 1970s, inmate medical care had improved as a result of the growing recognition that everyone was entitled to adequate medical care. Also, the courts began to intervene in prison matters and established an inmate's right to health care (*Estelle v. Gamble*, 1976; *Newman v. Alabama*, 1972). Key medical, correctional, and legal professional organizations also affirmed an inmate's right to adequate medical care and established commissions to develop standards and regulations for jails and prisons on the essentials of health care.

Deliberate Indifference

In *Estelle v. Gamble* (1976), the Supreme Court firmly supported the constitutional obligation of government to provide inmates with adequate medical care. This decision established a test to determine if the manner in which treatment was given constitutes "cruel and unusual punishment." This test required evidence of **deliberate indifference** to serious medical need. Examples of deliberate indifference include a denial of or a delay in providing treatment, providing inadequate treatment, and failure to have qualified medical staff.[2]

In general, constitutional prohibitions against cruel and unusual punishment do not require that an inmate be free from or cured of all real or imagined medical conditions while in custody nor have "unqualified access" to health care (Vaughn & Carroll, 1998). What is essential is that an inmate be provided with medical care (i.e., diagnosis and treatment) that is comparable in quality and availability to that obtainable by the general public (Anno, 1993). Nevertheless, prison officials have considerable discretion when determining the kind of medical care inmates receive (Vaughn & Carroll, 1998). For example, one lower court held that inmates are only entitled to medical care for "serious medical needs" (*Snipes v. DeTella*, 1996; Vaughn & Carroll, 1998). The Supreme Court in *Farmer v. Brennan* (1994) made it clear that prison officials cannot be held liable unless they "recklessly disregard a known substantial risk of harm."

Some of the following court decisions provide a more concrete picture of what is and is not deliberate indifference:

- Eight untreated heat strokes are a serious medical need and sufficient to establish deliberate indifference (*Kost v. Kozakiewicz*, 1993).

- A delay of 9 days before setting an inmate's broken hand was considered deliberate indifference (*Senisais v. Fitzgerald*, 1996).

- A month delay in treating a serious gynecological problem rose to the level of deliberate indifference (*Casey v. Lewis*, 1993).

- An inmate had to wait close to 3 years to have a salivary gallstone removed. The court held that this constituted deliberate indifference to a serious medical need (*Abdush-Shahid v. Coughlin*, 1996).

- An 11-day delay in elective heart surgery was considered acceptable by the courts because the inmate's chest pains were treated effectively (*Olson v. Stottsdefnads*, 1993).

A jurisdiction cannot refuse to provide inmates with needed or essential care because funds are unavailable

(Isele, 1979). With rising health costs and new developments in medical care, it is necessary to provide a formula to assist prison health care administrators in making decisions in gray areas between "urgent and clearly elective procedures" and those that are experimental. This will help defuse public antagonism toward providing expensive services to those seen as "less deserving" (Anno, 1989).

Providing Inmate Health Care

Although the vast majority of inmates are young, they tend to have more medical problems than comparably aged persons in the general population. "Contributing to their greater need of health services are higher rates of HIV/AIDS, other sexually transmitted diseases (STDs), tuberculosis, and other infectious diseases among prisoners, as well as their lifestyle choices (e.g., tobacco use, drug and alcohol abuse, sexual activity)" (Anno, 1997). Adequate medical care in prison requires appropriate assessment and follow-up care. These services can be provided by in-house medical staff, on-call private practitioners, or health care companies.

Health services delivery within prisons has been increasingly strained over the last decade primarily as a result of (1) more inmates coming into the prisons, (2) new inmates being less healthy than their counterparts of just a decade ago, (3) added costs for HIV/AIDS treatment, and (4) increasing medication costs (Anno, 1991a; *Corrections Compendium*, 1999a). Additionally, longer sentences, combined with minimum mandatory conditions and the increased incarceration of drug offenders, many of whom are over 40, has contributed to the aging of the prison population (Austin & McVey, 1989). These factors have placed increased demands on prison health services for both general care and specialty services (Anno, 1991a; *Corrections Compendium*, 1999a).

Prison health services must also provide for the special needs of handicapped inmates, women with obstetrical and gynecological problems, and those with mental health problems (e.g., suicidal inmates, self-mutilators, substance abusers, the mentally ill, the retarded, and sex offenders). Providing care for inmates with special health needs increases the cost of furnishing these services because of the need for more staff, specialized housing, equipment, and expanded medications (Anno, 1991a; National Institute of Corrections, 1997). The cost of correctional health care is about $2 billion a year, or about 10 percent of total departmental budgets. The average cost per inmate for health care through June 30, 1999 was $2,248, which was a 10 percent increase from the previous year (*Corrections Compendium*, 1999a).

Prison Medical Facilities   Institutions with under 100 inmates often have "clinics," staffed by nurses or paramedics who are on-site or on short call during the day and on call at night.[3] They are typically used for physical examinations and simple medical procedures. "Infirmaries," the most common type of medical facility, are generally found in jails and prisons with populations of 500 or more. They provide bed care and typically have around-the-clock nursing care.

Infirmaries and, to a lesser extent, clinics can deal with minor conditions, but they typically send inmates to outside hospitals for more complicated treatment. For both security and financial reasons, prison administrators are reluctant to send inmates to outside facilities that do not have a secure ward (Anno, 1991a). As a result, prisons of all sizes have expanded their medical facilities to reduce, where possible, the use of outside facilities.

Daily sick call is the process by which inmates who perceive themselves to have a health problem get permission to go to morning clinic sessions. This daily ritual has drawn up to 10 percent of a prison's population (Anno, 1991a). This relatively high proportion of use is believed by most correctional staff to be an excessive use of health services by inmates. It also may be seen as malingering.

Overuse of health care services also has been attributed to extremely conservative prison policies that require inmates come to the health unit to receive services and products available over the counter in the free society (Anno, 1997). By making basic over-the-counter medications for problems such as colds, heartburn, and constipation available in housing units, some states have reduced the number of inmates at sick call. Having lotions, soaps, and shampoo in commissaries further reduces the need to get these items at sick call.

Controlling Correctional Health Care Costs   Overuse of prison health care and rising health care costs have resulted in new correctional practices to control inmate medical care costs.

- *Medical Co-payments*   Almost all jurisdictions charge fees for health care services, which range from $.50 to $5 per encounter. Where medications are charged, the average cost is $2 (*Corrections Compendium*, 1999a). By charging a fee for medical care, inmates with marginal or nonexistent conditions are less likely to overuse or abuse correctional medical systems. Inmates are forced to think twice about using their limited funds for medical co-payments rather than discretionary items in the commissary.

- *Telemedicine*   Correctional departments increasingly are using **telemedicine,** which uses advanced video technology to link an inmate in a correctional institution with a physician who could be hundreds of miles away (Engleman, 1995). Telemedicine involves the use of cameras at each site, and hookups to equipment, such as electronic stethoscopes and

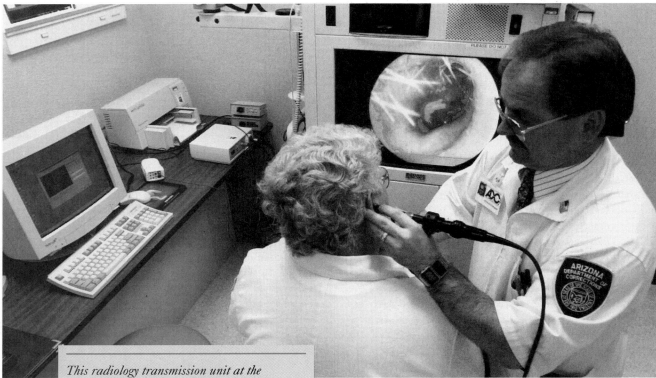

This radiology transmission unit at the University of Arizona medical center helps control correctional health care costs by allowing inmates at the Arizona State Prison to be evaluated for medical problems without being transported to a doctor.

X-ray and EKG machines (Gailiun, 1997). Physicians can diagnose and prescribe treatment from remote locations. Through telemedicine, inmates can receive care from cardiologists, neurologists, and even psychiatrists.

Whereas only six states were using telemedicine in 1995, only two years later almost every state was using or planning to use telemedicine (National Institute of Corrections, 1997). Because many prisons are located in rural areas and have difficulty recruiting qualified medical personnel and accessing specialists, telemedicine is being widely adopted by prison administrators (McDonald, Hassol, & Carlson, 1999). Telemedicine not only can reduce health care costs but also can reduce waiting time for specialists, increase new services, and improve care (McDonald, Hassol, & Carlson, 1999; National Institute of Justice, 1999).

■ *Managed Care* Almost all correctional systems use some form of **managed care** to control costs (Prison Health Care, 1997). Managed care methods are one of the most effective means of controlling medical costs. In managed care, treatment is matched to the type of condition, with costs controlled through the type of care, who delivers the care, and medications administered. Treatment criteria, or levels of care, are established in advance with the medical provider being required to follow the established criteria.

■ *Use of Computers* In 1997, 40 correctional departments were using computers to administer and manage inmate health care. Computers are used to track medication costs, chronic diseases, inmate fees, and medical services, as well as monitor contracted medical care (National Institute of Corrections, 1997). Computers enhance administrative efficiency and thus costs.

■ *Other Cost Control Approaches* Many correctional systems are using additional means to control costs: bulk purchasing of medications and pharmacy supplies, preauthorization of elective or nonessential surgery, negotiating fixed rates for hospital care, and consolidating sites for elderly and terminally ill inmates.

Responding to the Terminally Ill Inmate Correctional systems and states are responding to the increasing numbers of terminally ill inmates due particularly to the increase in HIV/AIDS and longer prison sentences (National Institute of Corrections, 1998). In 1997, 24 correctional systems were providing **hospice care** to terminally ill inmates, and another 20 were considering initiating some form of this program (National Institute of Corrections, 1998). According to the National Prison Hospice Association (2000), *hospice* is

> an interdisciplinary comfort-oriented care that allows seriously ill and dying patients to die with dignity and humanity with as little pain as possible in an environment where they have mental and spiritual preparation for the natural process of dying.

Hospice teams are made up of medical staff, chaplains, mental health staff, social workers, and hospice volunteers. Most prison hospice programs make use of trained inmate volunteers. Terminally ill inmates usually are granted special privileges to make them more comfortable, provide emotional support, and offer increased family visitation (National Institute of Corrections, 1998). These programs usually offer counseling in death and dying to family members.

Hospice-type programs for inmates seem to have the benefits of improved quality of life and medical care, improved inmate and staff morale, and reduced medical costs (National Institute of Corrections, 1998). Institutions also have encountered difficulty with hospice programs, including inmates not trusting staff, staff not believing inmates are deserving of dignified death, and difficulty establishing a hospice team.

National Accreditation One way for states to upgrade care and move toward correcting the often abysmal state of prison medical care is to go through voluntary accreditation. This is offered by the **National Commission on Correctional Health Care** (NCCHC), which is composed of representatives from 37 organizations that have an interest in correctional health care. Accreditation involves site visits by an independent team from NCCHC to determine whether the facility is meeting standards established by this commission. To become accredited, prisons must meet all of the 37 "essential standards" and 85 percent of applicable "important standards." Facilities that initially fail to be accredited are provided with technical assistance to aid them in becoming accredited (Anno, 2000). Accredited institutions acquire the status and benefits that go with this certification, while also reducing their liability. Anno (1993) noted that no system that was accredited by NCCHC had been successfully sued by inmates in class action suits that have challenged the adequacy or availability of their health care.

Increase in Infectious Diseases

A rising tide of infectious diseases in the nation has impacted jails and prisons as infected inmates enter correctional systems. Administrators are concerned about the potential spread of infectious diseases in their facilities because of close living (and often overcrowded) conditions, the cost of medical care, and the potential spread of diseases in the communities to which inmates will return.

AIDS The AIDS epidemic is one of the most pressing social and public health issues facing our nation. Drug-using offenders represent one group at high risk of contracting AIDS. **Acquired immune deficiency syndrome** (AIDS) is a condition in which the body's immune system is unable to fight illness and disease, making individuals susceptible to a host of infections that otherwise do not affect healthy people. In essence, the **human immunodeficiency virus** (HIV), which causes AIDS, infects and destroys the body's ability to fight disease. As a result, people die from cancer, pneumonia, and other diseases. There presently is no cure for AIDS.

A blood test is the only way to determine if a person has the AIDS virus. Individuals testing HIV-positive may not show any signs of being ill, because it can take up to 10 years for a person to manifest symptoms of the disease. However, some become sick and die after just a few years, or sooner. Once a person has the disease, she or he will remain infected for life.

Infected individuals who do not show any signs or symptoms of AIDS are considered to be asymptomatic. When symptoms are severe and persist, the individual is considered to have AIDS. Early in the disease, the symptoms are usually not life threatening; however, they can affect the HIV person's lifestyle and overall health. A variety of medications are available that can reduce AIDS-related symptoms and delay their onset. Recently developed medications, called protease inhibitors, can restore an individual to near normal health for an extended period of time. These medications are very expensive, though. As the disease progresses, infected individuals are likely to develop opportunistic infections, such as certain cancers and pneumonia, which are very rare in the general population.

As of 1999, a total of 26,653 cumulative AIDS cases were reported among state and federal correctional inmates, of whom 57 percent showed no symptoms (*Corrections Compendium*, 1999b; Maruschak, 1999). The AIDS incidence rate among correctional inmates was more than five times the rate in the U.S. population as a whole. HIV-infected inmates constitute 2.1 percent of the population in prison and range from less than 1 percent in some systems to a high of about 11 percent. As of 1997, AIDS-related deaths among prison inmates accounted for 19 percent of all reported inmate deaths, down by one third since 1995 (Maruschak, 1999).

Between 1991 and 1997, the number of HIV-positive inmates grew at a slower rate than the general population. Overall, 2.8 percent of black inmates and 2.5 percent of Hispanic inmates reported being HIV-positive, compared with 1.4 percent of white inmates (Maruschak, 1999). More than 90 percent of those infected are males (*Corrections Compendium*, 1999b).

HIV-Testing and Housing Policies Although policies vary widely, all correctional systems have policies for testing inmates for HIV. Twenty systems test all inmates upon entry, 12 test high-risk groups, 36 test if requested by the inmate, and 29 will do so if requested by a physician (*Corrections Compendium*, 1999b). Almost all systems test inmates who manifest clinical symptoms of the disease.

Until 1988, virtually every correctional institution segregated HIV-positive inmates. By 1993, however, there was an almost universal move away from such blanket policies. By 1997, only two correctional systems segregated inmates with HIV (Hammett, Harmon & Maruschak, 1999; Hammett, Harrold, Gross, & Epstein, 1994). In some correctional systems, AIDS inmates live separately but otherwise mix with the general inmate population. This allows AIDS inmates full access to work assignments and other programs. Although most correctional systems have some form of compassionate release or furlough policies on the books, few HIV/AIDS inmates have ever been released under such programs.

HIV-Prevention and Treatment Programs Although HIV-prevention programs are becoming more widespread in correctional facilities, few correctional systems have implemented comprehensive and intensive HIV-prevention programs in their facilities. Nearly two thirds of state and federal correctional facilities provide instructor-led HIV-prevention counseling, and 13 percent have peer-led programs. Only one third of facilities have multisession counseling (Hammett et al., 1999).

Reasonable precautions must be taken to protect inmates and especially staff. The Center for Disease Control and Prevention (CDC) has issued a series of guidelines for health care and public safety workers, including correctional officers, concerning steps that should be taken as precautions when working with individuals who may potentially be HIV-positive or who may have other communicable diseases, such as hepatitis B. The CDC recommends that all personnel treat all prisoners as though they were HIV-infected to protect staff and inmates from the possibility of becoming exposed to the HIV virus from an infected inmate.

Because inmates are not eligible for Medicaid, which is the prime public health care method of financing AIDS-related treatment, the costs of health care for AIDS inmates must be covered entirely by the systems in which they are incarcerated. With the introduction in 1996 of protease inhibitors and combination antiretroviral therapies, the possibility of delaying the progression of HIV has resulted in a dramatic increase in the survival time of infected individuals (Hammett et al., 1999). However, at a cost of about $12,000 per patient per year, there has been an escalation in medical costs as a budget item for institutions.

The use of these new drugs has presented challenges for prison administrators. Inmate failure to regularly take the medications, which sometimes have unpleasant side effects, can bring on opportunistic infections, further harm immune system functioning, and produce cross-resistance to other drugs. The strategy for administering medications must be made between the inmate and the physician. This often requires an open and trusting relationship, which may be difficult to achieve in a correctional facility (Hammett et al., 1999).

Disclosure of an Inmate's HIV Status Issues surrounding disclosure of inmates' HIV test results are difficult and legally complex. In general, courts have limited inmates' privacy and confidentiality rights regarding their HIV status (Hammett et al., 1999). Decisions concerning whether to release such test results are governed by legal and policy standards and mandates. Current correctional practices permit AIDS-related medical information to be provided to those who need to know. These include correctional administrators, physicians, other medical staff, and probation officers as well as the inmate (Hammett et al., 1994; Takas & Hammett, 1989).

Two Supreme Court cases may have an impact on the services HIV-infected inmates might receive in prison. In *Bragson v. Abbott* (1998), the Supreme Court held that HIV-related discrimination is prohibited under the Americans with Disabilities Act. In *Pennsylvania Department of Corrections v. Yeskey* (1998), the Court held that reasonable accommodations must be made for HIV-positive inmates under the Americans with Disabilities Act (Hammett et al., 1999). These court rulings seem to imply that inmates cannot be discriminated against in work assignments based on their HIV status, unless the job could involve a direct threat to health. Interestingly, though, the Supreme Court (*Hopper v. Davis*, 2000) left intact a lower court's ruling (*Onishea v. Hopper*, 1999) permitting Alabama prisons to segregate hundreds of HIV-positive inmates and keep them from educational programs and religious services where they might mix with other prisoners. Indeed, in practice, it seems that inmates who have contracted AIDS are victims of discriminatory administrative practices.

Tuberculosis **Tuberculosis** (TB) is an infectious disease that is spread by bacteria in the air resulting from the coughs or sneezes of infected individuals. It is the leading infectious disease killer worldwide. With the creation of anti-TB drugs in the early 1950s it became a treatable disease. In the United States, TB steadily declined in incidence for more than 30 years until the mid-1980s when the trend started to reverse. By 1992, over 26,000 new cases were reported nationwide, representing an increase of more than 20 percent since 1984

(Hammett & Harrold, 1994; Nadel, 1993). Although TB has always been a problem in prisons and jails, correctional systems such as New York and California saw a fivefold to tenfold increase in cases during the late 1980s and early 1990s. Since 1992 the incidence of TB has dropped off again both in correctional facilities and in the general population due mainly to increased public funding for TB control and aggressive screening and treatment within correctional institutions (Hammett et al., 1999; Kendig, 1998).

High TB infection among inmates is due to a number of factors, the most significant being HIV/AIDS. AIDS-infected individuals have weakened immune systems, making them more susceptible to TB. Other factors contributing to the TB increase include drug abuse, prison overcrowding, homelessness, and an increase in immigrants from parts of the world with higher levels of TB infection (Hammett & Harrold, 1994). Failure to comply with medical treatment increases the possibility of transmission of the disease.

The emergence of **multiple drug-resistant TB strains,** which are resistant to normal drug treatments, further resulted in the reactivation of the disease. A 1997 survey of state correctional systems found more than 15,000 TB-infected inmates, with more than half of the systems not reporting test results. Based on such data, it appears that as many as 10 percent of all prison inmates may be TB-infected (Hammett et al., 1999; Hammett & Harrold, 1994). Eighteen correctional staff were diagnosed with TB in 1997, and one died as a result of a multiple drug-resistant outbreak in New York State (Hammett et al., 1999).

Jails face a particularly difficult problem in responding to TB because of the rapid turnover and short stays of its inmates. Due to their longer stay, virtually every state prison system screens inmates for TB. Thus, prison inmates are more likely than jail inmates to receive treatment for active TB. Inmates with TB who also have HIV/AIDS are more difficult to diagnose.

Guidelines from the CDC call for the immediate isolation of inmates suspected of or confirmed to have contagious TB (Hammett et al., 1999; Hammett & Harrold, 1994). Masks must be worn and adjacent areas must be protected to prevent contamination when doors are opened. Such arrangements have forced correctional systems to retrofit, or design and build, special facilities to care for inmates with active TB. Completion of drug therapy is important to prevent relapse or the development of multiple drug-resistant strains.

Hepatitis C   According to the CDC, deaths from chronic **hepatitis C** (HCV) are expected to triple in the next 10 to 20 years (Reindollar, 1999). Four million Americans probably have this liver disease, which is the most common serious blood-borne infection in the United States with 8,000 to 10,000 people a year dying from it (*New York Times*, 1999; Reindollar, 1999). HCV is a silent killer that may not show any symptoms for years while seriously damaging the liver, leading to cirrhosis (scarring of the liver) and liver failure (Reindollar, 1999).

Inmates are about 20 times more likely than the general public to acquire HCV, which is spread primarily through shared needles (Reindollar, 1999). Reports of studies done in various prisons indicated that 41 percent of California inmates were infected with HCV, 30 percent in Maryland, and 29 percent in Texas (*New York Times*, 1999). Prison administrators are aware of the problem but have been slow to respond; only one state, Colorado, conducts routine HCV testing among inmates (Reindollar, 1999). As liver expert Robert Reindollar, M.D., states, "Correctional administrators and physicians recognize that a wave of advanced liver disease is on the way, but how best to stop it is a difficult question" (1999).

Correctional staff, including prison medical workers, are at risk of contracting HCV from exposure to infected blood. Universal precautions that apply to HIV/AIDS also apply to HCV, and should be used by all correctional staff.

The first treatment for HCV was alpha interferon, which prevents the virus from replicating. The most effective treatment for HCV is through a combination of the drugs interferon and ribavirin, which has been shown to be nearly three times as effective as interferon alone in reducing HCV virus levels. However, this drug combination therapy can cost upward of $10,000 a year, further straining correctional system medical budgets (Johns Hopkins, 1999; *New York Times*, 1999; Reindollar, 1999). Interferon only, which is much cheaper than drug combination therapy, is the treatment of choice in most institutions. As awareness about HCV grows, correctional administrators will have to grapple with how to pay for HCV inmate treatment.

Treatment Programs

Mental health, cognitive and behavioral modification, and drug treatment programs represent the major forms of treatment available to inmates.

Mental Health Programs

Although the *Estelle* decision related only to medical care, lower court decisions quickly extended the deliberate indifference standard to psychiatric care for serious mental or emotional illness.[4] The courts have made no distinction between the right to health care and the right to mental care for psychiatric or psychological impairments (Branham & Krantz, 1997). Thus, courts see deliberate indifference to serious psychological needs of inmates as unconstitutional. Court rulings have provided some guidance on how this standard is to be defined. Conditions such as

Florida's Correctional Mental Health Facilities

PROGRAM FOCUS

During the 1980s, the Florida Department of Corrections (DC) developed a comprehensive approach to serving inmates with severe mental illnesses. This involved six in-patient Crisis Stabilization Units (designed for short-term stabilization), and five Transitional Care Units for those inmates returning from the Corrections Mental Health Institution (CMHI)—the deep-end acute care, close custody prison located in Chattahoochee, Florida. It is estimated that 5 percent of the approximately 66,000 Florida inmates have been diagnosed as severely disturbed.

CMHI, enacted by the Florida legislature in the mid-1980s, was operated by DC with the clinical services required to be provided by the Florida State Hospital. An aggressive comprehensive acute care treatment regime was developed in the early 1990s. This included a Total Quality Management (TQM) system, a case management model, and enhanced use of the multidisciplinary treatment teams—which included psychiatry, psychology, nursing, direct care, rehabilitation therapy, social work, and a very important component, the security staff.

Mixing two totally different organizational cultures like correctional officers and mental health professionals can be like oil and water. As described in Chapter 11, the culture of an organization attracts and retains staff who ascribe to the assumptions, values, and expected behavior of the organization. Correctional staff, by the nature of their job, have the responsibility of the security and safety of the community, staff, and inmates, many of whom are difficult and dangerous individuals. Many correctional facilities are located in rural areas; therefore, the job market in economically suppressed areas often draws employees to corrections. On the other hand, people who become nurses, psychologists, psychiatrists, and other people who are in the helping profession are drawn to their profession to improve humanity.

It is easy to see that there is a natural potential clash of basic assumptions and values of these two employee groups. It is also difficult for people in the helping profession to really care and help individuals who have done despicable acts. At CMHI, there were two death row beds (for inmates on death row that were acutely mentally ill), and approximately one third of the 110 inmates were there for some form of brutal homicide. Also, acute psychiatric units have inmates who exhibit bizarre and aggressive behavior, such as explosive episodes, feces smearing, self-mutilation and hallucinations. This impacts the therapeutic attitudes of the clinical staff and increases the attitudes of security staff that the inmates have no worth.

One example of conflict for the clinical staff is treating death row inmates who are suffering from acute mental health issues. The clinical staff's job is to stabilize the inmate patient and return him to death row. This exceeds the notion of normalization. Security staff face another

---

acute depression, nervous collapse, and paranoia are considered sufficiently dramatic to represent serious medical needs. Nevertheless, the "courts continue to rely heavily on [the] . . . judgment [of mental health professionals] to determine whether care is adequate and defer to those judgments except in the most gross circumstances"—that is, when failure to respond to special needs produces unnecessary suffering (Mayer, 1989, p. 275).

The basic components of a correctional mental health treatment system grew out of *Ruiz v. Estelle*. These include:

1. a systematic program for screening and evaluating inmates to identify those needing treatment

2. treatment programs that entail more than segregation and close supervision of inmate clients

3. sufficient numbers of appropriately trained mental health professionals

4. maintenance of accurate, complete, and confidential records of the treatment process

5. avoidance of medication in dangerous amounts, by dangerous methods, or without appropriate supervision and evaluation

6. a separate program for identifying, treating, and supervising inmates with suicidal tendencies (Cohen, 1988)

The issue of enforced psychiatric and mental health treatment in a correctional setting also has been addressed by the Supreme Court. Psychiatric drugs can be administered for treatment against an inmate's will "if the inmate is dangerous to himself or others, and the treatment is in the inmate's medical interest" (*Washington v. Harper*, 1990, p. 1033, n. 3). Treatment must be for a medical reason, however, not merely for control of inmate behavior.

Further, the Court rejected an inmate's right to a judicial hearing in this matter. Recognizing that the real question in this case involved the benefits versus the risks of antipsychotic medication, it felt that this issue could be best resolved by an administrative hearing conducted by

kind of conflict. Many behaviors by inmates are seen as requiring disciplinary action or Disciplinary Reports (DRs). DRs affect the inmate's work assignments, custody levels, and early release (gain time). However, in a mental health facility, behavior by inmates must first be reviewed by the clinical staff to determine if the behavior is a symptom of the mental illness or just bad behavior. This leads to a natural conflict between treatment staff and correctional staff. If you are a corrections officer and are struck and hurt by an inmate, the "why" doesn't mean much to you. If you are a mental health professional, the symptoms and competencies are the major concern. When correctional officers cannot issue DRs without clinical approval a natural friction arises between these staffs.

Recruiting security staff can be difficult, but many prisons are in rural areas where work is scarce; thus, this is the "job" to have. On the other hand, health-care staff require special training, and unless they wish to live in a particular area, working at a prison is not considered the ideal job. Also, health professionals have more economic opportunities, both public and private, than security staff because of their training and licenses.

It is a real tribute to the professionalism in the field of corrections when wardens and chief health officers set a culture where both staffs have to work together to achieve the mission of the institution. This culture is determined by how we manage, who we hire, what their values are, and how they behave. This is a major issue when roles and responsibilities of staff are in natural conflict. However, it can be done—and effectively. A major problem in this area is turnover of superintendents, chief health officers, and program directors. In a 4-year period at CMHI, there were four different superintendents. With each change, the relationship between security and health-care staff had to be reestablished.

Private sector corporations change, evolve, and cease to exist just like public organizations. In 1999, CMHI was closed because of a decision to use the facility for a different type of offender. The responsibility for CMHI was moved to the Zephyrhills Correctional Institution, which also had a CSU (Crisis Stabilization Unit). Mental health services to inmates in the Florida prison system continue to change and evolve. In controversial issues like health care in prisons, change and controversy are constants. There is no doubt that giving inmates their constitutional level of mental health care, in a secure prison environment, with two sets of employees with different missions, is a unique challenge.

Source: Prepared especially for the second edition of this text by Joel De Volentine, former director of clinical services at CMHI from 1993 to 1997. He currently serves as a district manager for the Florida Department of Juvenile Justice.

an independent mental health professional not involved in the diagnosis or treatment of the inmate in question. The Court upheld Washington State procedures requiring that inmates be given notice of this adversary hearing and a tentative diagnosis, be present and be allowed to cross-examine witnesses, and be allowed the assistance of a lay advisor (Burlington, 1991; Cohen, 1993).

Our Program Focus examines Florida's correctional mental health facilities, highlighting an example of how one correctional system provides mental health treatment.

It has been estimated that from 7 to 15 percent of jail and prison inmates have current symptoms of serious mental disorders and are in need of psychiatric care (*Corrections Compendium*, 1998; Morris, Steadman, & Veysey, 1997). For some inmates, the sheltered and structured environment of an institution can be less stressful than living on the outside, but for many with mental illness confinement intensifies the ability to cope. As psychiatrist Dr. E. Fuller Torrey notes, "Being in jail or prison when your brain is working normally is, at best, an unpleasant experience. Being in jail or prison when your brain is playing tricks on you is often brutal" (*Corrections Compendium*, 1998). For the mentally ill, the nature of one's environment will have a major influence over how well an inmate will stabilize, decompensate, or how severe an episode will be (*Corrections Compendium*, 1998, p. 2).

Treatment for the Seriously Mentally Ill Major mental illnesses, which can include schizophrenia, major depression, bipolar disorder, and other psychoses, are seriously disabling and chronic in nature. These brain disorders often have their origin in biochemical or neurological abnormalities. Sometimes mental illness also is caused by head injury. The brains of mentally ill individuals function differently from others (*Corrections Compendium*, 1998).

The two main treatment methods for serious mental illness are medications and placement in a therapeutic environment. Through the classification process, mentally ill inmates can be identified and recommended for medication treatment, counseling, or placement in

The Lifestyle Approach to Correctional Intervention

Tim rises early from his bunk at the Federal Correctional Institution in Schuylkill, Pennsylvania, more excited than usual and with expectations different from those he has grown accustomed to after many years behind bars. Several months ago Tim's cellmate, John, had shared with him the contents of a handbook for a class he was attending entitled "Lifestyle Issues." The information piqued Tim's interest and he requested admittance into the program. Tim had been in other prison programs, but this seemed different. Instead of focusing on past problems or current difficulties, the Lifestyle program seemed to emphasize a person's innate ability to change and learn from others by discussing shared experiences. The cause of Tim's excitement is that today, after spending nearly 6 months on a waiting list, he is scheduled to attend the first session of the Lifestyle Issues group.

The class in Lifestyle Issues provides participants with an introduction to the lifestyle model and the concept of lifestyle change. As Tim will soon discover, the goal of this 10-week class is to help participants identify the behaviors associated with a drug, criminal, or gambling lifestyle and the thinking styles that serve to protect these lifestyles. John informs Tim that this entry-level class "made me realize and understand the different lifestyles that exist in the world and helped me identify the thinking errors I was making." A recent graduate of the Lifestyle Change Program who had completed all three levels of the program advises that "in the first level (Lifestyle Issues) I began to recognize my weak spots, understand that my thinking was different from other people, and realize that I had a choice; it was all downhill from there." Tim can make good use of this information as he prepares for his first session of the Lifestyle Issues class.

The next level of the Lifestyle Change Program is designed to provide participants with insight into the drug, criminal, and gambling lifestyles, the three lifestyles that may be most problematic for offender populations. Three 20-week classes are offered: an Advanced Drug Lifestyle group, an Advanced Criminal Lifestyle group, and an Advanced Gambling group. Tim is free to enroll in all three groups or select the one he believes is most relevant to him. Because Tim has a history of both drug abuse and habitual criminality but apparently has never had a problem with gambling he may eventually decide to take the Advanced Drug and Criminal Lifestyles groups but pass on the Advanced Gambling Lifestyles group. The goal of these groups is to stimulate self-reflection and encourage participants to identify how the lifestyle manifests itself in their own lives. In the words of one former participant, "The second level was more intense than the first; this is where I started to believe that I could change." A longtime participant explains to Tim the changes he experienced over the course of his involvement with all three advanced groups: "First you see the lifestyle issues in everyone around you, then after a while you see it in yourself, and that is when you really start to change."

The third level of the Lifestyle Change Program consists of Re-

---

special mental health units. Often, mentally ill inmates receive treatment in separate units or a hospital. Because of the often disruptive behaviors caused by mental illness, separate mental health units are desirable. Although most prison systems have established specialized programs and units for mentally ill inmates who exhibit severe systems, lack of space often results in inmates with less severe symptoms being returned too quickly to the general population (*Corrections Compendium*, 1998).

Standard correctional discipline practices seldom work when applied to seriously mentally ill inmates with behavior problems. Training of correctional officers and the establishment of a continuum of care for mentally ill inmates will result in less institutional disruption and more humane treatment for individuals with serious brain disorders (*Corrections Compendium*, 1998).

Methods Used to Modify Behavior Other types of mental health treatment in prison usually consist of some form of counseling or behavioral therapy. The goals of treatment are to relieve psychological problems that may help inmates to adjust better to the institution and reduce their future criminality. The efficacy of treatment in reducing criminal behavior and the role of psychological disturbance as a broad cause of criminal behavior has been questioned by criminologists and psychiatrists (see, e.g., Conklin, 1992; Szasz, 1970). This type of criticism had a hand in the demise of rehabilitation as a way to deal with criminals.

Some of the commonly used treatments in corrections (see, e.g., Lester & van Voorhis, 1997) include behavior modification and cognitive approaches. **Behavior modification** is based on a variety of learning principles that can change inmate behavior, altering it through a care-

lapse Prevention. Although this is a 40-week class, most participants continue cycling through the group until they are released or transferred. What they discover is that with the introduction of new group members discussions on topics like problem solving, stress management, and goal setting take on a different meaning each time they are introduced. As one current participant relates, "learning what makes us relapse before it actually happens" is what the Relapse Prevention group is all about. Another current participant remarks, "I cannot explain what I've learned from participating in this program, I just know that it makes sense to me—something might happen to me in the course of a day and bam, something in my head will remember 'what that is' or how to deal with 'it.'" He adds that "for me, attending classes every week reminds me what I have to look forward to if I choose to remain in a drug and criminal lifestyle."

The philosophy behind the Lifestyle Change Program is that group interactions are capable of facilitating the natural change process

that exists in all people just as surely as we learn a lifestyle from one another. These group meetings are not viewed as treatment but as an opportunity to develop one's personal resources through education and skills training. There are four overarching goals pursued in the Lifestyle Change Program. First, participants are encouraged to take responsibility for their actions instead of blaming them on outside influences. Second, the Lifestyle Change Program seeks to promote participant self-confidence. A third overarching goal of the Lifestyle Change Program is to help participants challenge their drug and criminally oriented belief systems and construct new self- and worldviews. Finally, sources of social support are identified and cultivated because research and experience suggest that social support is one of the best predictors of future success for those released from prison and drug rehabilitation programs.

In 1997 a 5-year follow-up was conducted on 291 inmates who had completed one or more levels of the Lifestyle Change Program. Eighty-two inmates who had signed up for

the program but had been transferred or released prior to participating in the first session of the Lifestyle Issues class served as control subjects. The follow-up revealed that the control group had accumulated three times as many disciplinary reports as program participants from initial program participation (or planned participation in the case of control subjects) to follow-up. A comparison of participants and controls released from custody 3 or more months before the end of the follow-up disclosed a nonsignificant trend in which participants were less likely to have been rearrested than controls. Because of the relatively small number of inmates included in the community follow-up a second follow-up is planned in the near future.

Source: Updated especially for the second edition of Corrections: A Comprehensive View *by Glen Walters (1998), Psychology Services, Federal Correctional Institution-Schuylkill.*

fully designed system of external rewards and punishments. In **cognitive approaches,** an inmate's thoughts and beliefs are changed, leading to behavioral change.

Token economies, a form of behavior modification, involve tangible payoffs (points, tokens, etc.) to inmates who manifest certain behaviors. These tokens are accumulated over a period of time and can be spent on a variety of goods and privileges (e.g., goodies from the commissary, living in a special unit with more privacy). In this way, the desirable behavior can become part of the inmate's behavior repertoire in prison and may even be generalized to behavior on the outside.

Behavioral contracting, also a form of behavior modification, is the negotiation of a written agreement between inmates and corrections personnel. This contract may specify that if inmates in correctional programs behave in certain ways they will be rewarded. If negoti-

ated and executed in good faith, this contract can induce the motivation needed by the inmate to achieve desired behavioral changes.

In **cognitive therapy** the underlying notion is that much of our behavior is driven by faulty thoughts and beliefs. To change a person's behavior successfully, changes in the thoughts and beliefs supporting it are required (Ellis, 1980). Our Program Focus, "The Lifestyle Approach to Correctional Intervention," profiles a program developed by Glen Walters (1998) to teach inmates to recognize and modify various thinking patterns associated with criminals.

Drug Treatment

Another aspect of prison medical care is treatment for substance abusers, especially drug offenders. Inmates sentenced for a drug offense accounted for 31 percent of the growth in total admissions to state prisons from 1986 to 1993 (Beck & Gilliard, 1995). Drug offenders accounted for 21 percent of state and over 60 percent of federal prisoners in 1997 (Mumola, 1999). In a 1997 survey of more than one million state and federal inmates, over 80 percent reported having used illegal substances, 57 percent had used drugs within one month prior to their incarceration, and 33 percent reported being under the influence of drugs at the time of their crime (with 52 percent reporting being under the influence of alcohol or drugs while committing their offense) (Mumola, 1999). About 19 percent of inmates reported committing their offense for drug money.

Although it has been estimated that upward of 80 percent of all inmates have serious substance abuse problems, only 1 in 10 had received treatment for their drug abuse since admission to prison (Belenko, Peugh, & Califano, 1998; Mumola, 1999). This is a *decrease* from the 1 in 4 inmates reporting such treatment in 1991 (Mumola, 1999). The likelihood of an inmate receiving substance abuse treatment increases the longer he or she remains in prison, and thus the proportion of inmates who will receive treatment prior to release will undoubtedly increase. Also, 16 percent of inmates in 1997 reported being involved in self-help or peer counseling programs. Over half (56 percent) of all inmates have, at one time or another, been in a substance abuse treatment program (Mumola, 1999).

Programs   Responding to the problem of drug-involved offenders, all states and the federal system have developed some form of substance abuse program for convicted offenders (*Corrections Compendium*, 1999b; Office of Justice Program, 1998). In 1997, 9.2 percent (109,800) of all prison inmates were enrolled or had participated in formal drug treatment services since entering prison (Mumola, 1999). In mid-1999, 45 correctional systems reported a total of 279,090 inmates were participating in some form of substance abuse treatment, including Alcoholics Anonymous, Narcotics Anonymous, and peer support groups (*Corrections Compendium*, 1999b).

Entering Treatment   Offenders enter correctional treatment programs in several ways. First, judges can mandate that an incarcerated offender participate in a prison treatment program. Second, inmates may be identified as having a drug problem during the classification process and be assigned to a treatment program. Third, inmates can enter a treatment program at their own request.

In-prison treatment encompasses a wide range of services and modalities. The most frequent treatment offered is group counseling conducted by professionals or by peers in a self-help program. Other treatment elements include drug education, individual counseling, and residential programs (Beck et al., 1993; Mumola,

1999). Almost every institution in the nation has peer support groups, usually in the form of Alcoholics Anonymous (AA), Narcotics Anonymous (NA), or Cocaine Anonymous (CA) programs (Marlette, 1990a).

Treatment for addiction consists of a broad range of formal organized services that have a variety of different goals, including reducing or ending drug and alcohol use, substantially reducing violent behavior, reducing educational or vocational deficiencies, obtaining legal employment, and changing the individual's values to be more conventional toward work, family, and the law (Institute of Medicine, 1990). All treatment programs encompass at least some of these goals. Most focus on restoring individuals to a drug-free lifestyle and helping them to improve their capacity to function effectively in society, including reducing or eliminating criminal behavior.

Technically, virtually every formal treatment program in the nation is voluntary; inmates do not have to participate in treatment if they do not want to. However, there are strong pressures on an inmate to "voluntarily" participate in treatment, especially if one has been court-ordered or assigned through the classification process. The available literature provides evidence that court and other legal treatment mandates have a positive effect on increasing retention in treatment.[5] Length of time in treatment is the single most important factor related to successful treatment outcome.[6]

The Therapeutic Community Model   Available research has shown that the long-term **therapeutic community** (TC) **treatment model** has the best chance of success in working with hard-core drug abusers with criminal justice involvement. Best results appear to be achieved with residency of at least 9 to 12 months followed by some form of aftercare.[7] Multiyear studies of a variety of in-prison TC treatment programs show that program graduates have a significantly reduced rate of parole violations in comparison to nongraduates and those not in treatment, and they have fewer rearrests, convictions, and reincarcerations.[8] TC programs have shown that 3 out of 4 inmate graduates do not return to crime 3 years after release, while 9 out of 10 who are not treated do return to crime (Lipton, 1995). Our Program Focus, "The Stay'n Out and Serendipity Programs," on pages 424–425 highlights two successful programs: a prison-based therapeutic community drug program and a community-based aftercare program for its graduates and for those mandated by the criminal justice system to receive treatment.

Co-Occurring Disorders   Individuals with either a mental health or substance abuse problem are more likely to have a **co-occurring,** or dual, **disorder** (Peters & Bartoi, 1997; Sciacca, 1991). Individuals who use drugs or alcohol and also have a mental disorder are considered to have a co-occurring, or dual, disorder. Research has shown that

about half of individuals with serious mental illness also have a co-existing alcohol or drug disorder, and they seek substance abuse treatment at rates of two to four times higher than found in the general populations (Pepper & Hendrickson, 1996; Peters & Bartoi, 1997). Rates of mental disorders found among prisoners are four times higher than the general population, and substance abuse is four to seven times higher. It is estimated that 3 to 11 percent of inmates have co-occurring mental health and substance abuse disorders (Peters & Bartoi, 1997).

Traditional prison-based drug-treatment programs have not focused on treating the mentally ill, or the interaction between drug and alcohol use and mental illness. Likewise, prison mental health programs have focused on stabilizing inmates through medications while not treating the substance abuse problem. Dual diagnosis programs constitute an effort by corrections to recognize the need to treat both mental illness and a co-occurring substance abuse disorder.

Our Program Focus, "Dual Diagnosis Case Study: Inmate Bill Smith," on pages 426–427 considers the history of an inmate with co-occurring disorders.

Prison Food Service[9]

Although all programs affect inmate life, food service may have the greatest immediate significance. Three times every day inmates are affected by the food that is served (Ayres, 1988; Boss, Schechter, & King, 1986). Bad food is the primary target of inmate complaints and lawsuits; in fact, it has been a factor in most inmate riots and disturbances (Barnes & Teeters, 1951; McKelvey, 1977).

Food is a basic necessity of life, and in prison it becomes more important because meals are one of the few things to which inmates look forward. Unlike free citizens who can choose what and where they eat, inmate choices are limited to what is served and to eating in the same place every day (Stokes, 1993). Prison food services are faced with several major challenges:

1. attempting to satisfy the diverse tastes and special dietary needs of inmates.

2. providing a sufficient amount of food within budgetary constraints.

3. minimizing disruptive behavior in food service areas.

4. avoiding the sabotage of equipment.

5. minimizing inmate lawsuits.

6. working in a dangerous environment with many potential hazards, such as knives, equipment, heat, and hot water. (Johnson, 1998; Stokes & Associates, Inc., 1985)

To meet these growing challenges, prisons and jails have modified their food service operations. Early on, a correctional officer who enjoyed cooking generally ran the kitchen. Today, most institutions employ qualified food service administrators to manage these operations. As with other services, the laissez-faire attitude toward food preparation has been replaced by a set of minimum

The Stay'n Out and Serendipity Programs

PROGRAM FOCUS

Stay'n Out

The Stay'n Out program in New York is one widely known example of a prison-based therapeutic community (Wexler & Williams, 1986). Replicated in other correctional systems, the New York program currently provides 180 beds for men at the Arthur Kill Correctional Facility on Staten Island and 40 beds for women at the Bayview Correctional Facility in Manhattan. Originally modeled after Phoenix House, a well-known TC, inmates are recruited from various state correctional facilities. Treatment lasts an average of 9 to 12 months. Most program staff are graduates of TCs and ex-offenders and ex-substance abusers—a common characteristic of most TCs. These staff provide successful role models, showing that successful rehabilitation is possible.

Treatment is viewed as a developmental growth process with clients taking on increasing responsibility as they advance through the program. First, clients are in an orientation or adjustment phase designed to familiarize them with program rules and expectations and build mutual trust. This is accomplished through individual and group counseling, encounter sessions, and seminars. New clients are assigned low-level jobs with little status. As inmate-clients progress through treatment, they take on increasing responsibility for program activities and in turn receive increased status and privileges.

Clients attend daily morning and evening meetings, which function to increase communication and cohesion as well as focus on the day's activities. Daily afternoon seminars help unite the group, encourage the development of individual viewpoints, and help reduce the fear of speaking before others. These seminars include such life skills issues as how to set goals, seek employment, and manage a household.

Counseling groups include about 10 clients and focus on attitude, behavior, and work performance. Meeting twice a week for an hour each, these groups are less intense than the encounter groups, which are held two or more times each week. Encounter groups are confrontational and are designed to reduce individual defenses and influence meaningful behavioral change. These groups focus on in-depth issues such as impulse management, self-discipline, respect for authority and others, and interpersonal relationships.

In the final period of treatment, transitional issues related to "making it" on the outside are addressed. Clients are involved with other self-help networks, such as Alcoholics Anonymous and Narcotics Anonymous, and serve as role models to "newer" program participants. Once released from prison, usually on parole, there are a variety of support systems available, including residential halfway houses, support groups, and outpatient counseling. Clients usually maintain close contact with program staff and become members of a "community" of recovered addicts organized by the program (Reform, 1988; Wexler & Williams, 1986).

In 1994, a Relapse Services Unit was added to the complement of services provided at the Arthur Kill Correctional Facility. This 60-day program provides short-term intensive residential services to inmates who have been returned to custody from Department of Corrections work release facilities after testing positive for alcohol or controlled substances. After satisfactory completion of the program, participants are returned to their prior work release status.

Serendipity

Serendipity, located in the Bedford Stuyvesant section of Brooklyn, New York, is a 50-bed co-ed community-based residential treat-

---

standards. These have been either voluntarily imposed by state corrections departments or mandated by court decisions, often guided by American Correctional Association (ACA) Standards for Adult Correctional Institutions (ACA, 1981b, 1990). The expertise required to deal with the complexities of prison food preparation has resulted in the development of specialists in this area (Ayres, 1988; Boss et al., 1986; Stokes et al., 1985).

Menu Planning

Today, planning prison menus includes the need to meet basic nutritional requirements, to provide varied and appealing meals, and to do all of this within strict cost constraints. Most correctional systems use some type of **cycle menu** covering a certain time period, at the end of which the menu is repeated (Stokes, 1991).[10] Twenty-nine of the 40 jurisdictions that responded to the *Corrections Compendium* (1999) survey used master menus developed within central offices, and 13 have them prepared at the institutional level. These menus provide a nutritionally adequate diet according to the recommended dietary allowances established by the Food and Nutrition Board of the U.S. Department of Agriculture (Johnson, 1998). They may also include popular menu items and avoid undue repetition and a

ment facility. Originally instituted as an aftercare program for graduates of Stay'n Out, the program has since been expanded to serve men and women mandated to treatment by the criminal justice system in lieu of incarceration. Average length of stay in the program is 9 to 12 months. The primary focus of the program is to prepare participants for successful return to the community. Central to the program is a continuity of care, utilizing an extensive network of community resources. Residents are restricted to the center for an initial orientation period and are escorted to community agencies for assessments conducted outside of the center. In addition to individual, group, and family counseling, residents receive extensive vocational and employment counseling and use the community resource network to help secure health care, housing, vocational training, and job placement. Stipends are provided for lunch and travel to and from work. Residents also receive remedial education as needed, continued drug and alcohol counseling, life skills classes in areas such as money management and installment buying, and medical care. They are also encouraged to do volunteer work in the community, an activity that contributes to the resident's recovery while build-

ing support for the program among local residents and elected officials.

Participation in the aftercare program at this facility for a period of 6 months to a year is recommended upon completion of the residential phase. For the first 3 months after leaving the center, the former residents are expected to attend a once-a-week evening group to discuss their adjustment and assist them in problem solving. During the second 3-month period, residents attend group every other week, while for the last 6 months, attendance is on a monthly basis (Callender, 1993).

Serendipity is an example of an aftercare program that gradually reintegrates an offender back into the community prepared to successfully face the challenges of living a life free from drugs and crime.

Here's what some graduates say:

The Serendipity program helped me a lot. I didn't know where I was going. I had a lot of issues that I didn't want to deal with. Being in Serendipity helped me deal with a lot. I went to school. I learned how to be a responsible parent again. I have gained a lot for myself and the program helps. I'm very grateful for what I have gained for myself today. The Serendipity program helped me a lot and others too. I have a

lot to live for today. (Joanne Murray, Serendipity graduate, November 2, 1998)

I'm not that bad person I thought I was. I was just a sick person who didn't know how to get help—'till I came here, and I learned what life is really about. And life is fun. I didn't think I would be able to live without the drugs. I had no direction in life. Here in Serendipity, with the help of the counselors and my peers, I've learned what it is to have direction in life. My whole life is changed. My attitude. My behaviors. I have no desire of getting high today. I have a good network, a good foundation behind me. I have my children back in my life. I have a job today. I go to school. I'm trying to get my GED. I feel that I am ready for society once again. (Carlos Pagan, former resident, now part owner of a successful small business, 1997)

Source: Prepared especially for the second edition of this text by Blossom Regan (1999), director of Program Development, New York Therapeutic Communities, Inc., Stay'n Out and Serendipity Programs.

monotonous diet while maintaining average daily food costs at allotted amounts (see Table 17.1).

To add variety, some systems include ethnic meals such as Mexican, Italian, Irish, Asian, and African-American foods and plan special meals for holidays, for example, Cinco de Mayo and St. Patrick's Day (Ayres, 1988; Stokes et al., 1985).

Health trends on the outside have influenced prison menus by prompting many facilities to begin following "Heart Healthy" menus that emphasize grains, fruits, and less red meat. Methods of preparation are also changing, from less frying in grease to more baking, broiling, and stewing. Inmates should also be educated about the

Table 17.1
Daily Food Service Costs

	Highest Cost	Lowest Cost	Median Cost
Total Cost for All Food-Related Expenses*	$5.30 (MT)	$2.05 (FL/MS)	$3.66
Cost for Raw Food†	$0.80 (OH)	$3.70 (RI)	$2.45

*Twenty-four jurisdictions provided data.
†Thirty-six jurisdictions provided data.
Source: *Corrections Compendium* (1999, July).

PROGRAM FOCUS

The following narrative case study is written about a fictional inmate's experience in an actual dual diagnosis program developed by the Bureau of Prisons and located at the Federal Medical Center in Lexington, Kentucky. Bill Smith is a 32-year-old, divorced, Caucasian male. An overview of the Dual Diagnosis Drug Abuse Program is provided, and an effort has been made to simulate actual experiences an inmate might have while participating in this program.

At the age of 10, Bill began to experience mental health problems that were evident both at school and home: loud verbal outbursts, difficulty paying attention and following instructions, poor interaction with others, inability to sit still and remain quiet, and an inability to sleep. A physician diagnosed him with attention-deficit hyperactivity disorder and prescribed Ritalin. At the age of 15, Bill began experimenting with marijuana and alcohol, which he found helped him feel calm and "normal." At school he was attention-seeking, impulsive, and an underachiever. By the time he reached high school, Bill was engaging in high-risk behaviors, including high-speed car chases, cliff diving, increased drug use, and sex with multiple partners.

After graduating from high school, Bill served 4 years in the Army where he experimented with speed (methamphetamine), used marijuana and alcohol on weekends, and also received a DUI. After leaving the Army, Bill found a job. At a party Bill was introduced to 19-year-old Sheila. Two months later they got married.

Sheila introduced him to cocaine, and they continued to party frequently until she became pregnant.

Bill and Sheila's marriage began to deteriorate following the birth of their daughter. After becoming a mother, Sheila stopped partying, but Bill continued partying and staying out all night. As tensions in the marriage increased, Bill began using alcohol and marijuana daily and speed on weekends as a way to cope with the increasing stress. Bill also found the drugs useful in dealing with his manic symptoms, including racing thoughts and an irritable mood. Bill also had affairs with multiple women.

At the age of 27, Bill's problems escalated. He received a second DUI, and his daily use of drugs caused his work performance to deteriorate; eventually he was fired. Because of his drug use, numerous affairs, and inability to keep a job, Sheila filed for divorce. To cope with these problems, Bill continued using drugs and started taking speed daily.

Soon after his divorce, Bill experienced symptoms of severe depression, including intense feelings of sadness, staying in bed and sleeping for days at a time, loss of appetite, a loss of hope regarding the future, and thoughts of suicide. Eventually, Bill attempted suicide by taking an entire bottle of Valium with a pint of whiskey. He was hospitalized for 30 days, where he was diagnosed with "Bipolar I Disorder, Most Recent Episode Depressed." Following discharge, Bill immediately stopped at the local bar to have a few drinks with his friends. He stopped taking his prescribed medication and again continued his daily drug and alcohol use.

Eventually, Bill began transporting drugs into his community, making what he thought was "fast, easy

money." He would go on excessive spending sprees, drive expensive cars, take exotic vacations, and wear expensive clothes and jewelry. Bill also experienced the return of manic symptoms, including racing thoughts, irritability, paranoia, and nervous energy. Bill found that speed and marijuana helped him to cope with these experiences.

At the age of 30, Bill was arrested and charged with possession with intent to distribute methamphetamine. He was found guilty in federal court and sentenced to serve 70 months in a federal prison, with three years of supervised release. The judge also recommended Bill receive drug treatment in prison.

During the last 36 months of his sentence, Bill volunteered for the residential drug abuse program. During his interview for admission to the program, Bill exhibited fast speech, flight of ideas, and an inability to keep his hands and legs still. He reported feeling agitated and having a decreased need for sleep. Bill was diagnosed with Bipolar I Disorder, Most Recent Episode Manic; Alcohol and Cannabis Dependence; and Amphetamine Abuse. Because of his co-occurring substance abuse problem and mental health issues, Bill was accepted into the Dual Diagnosis Program and placed on the waiting list.

Several months later, Bill began participating in the Residential Drug Abuse Program. He moved from his housing unit to a unit set aside for 117 other men participating in the drug treatment program, of whom 15 were in the Dual Diagnosis Program with Bill. Inmates in the drug program were expected to maintain clear conduct, display a receptive and positive attitude, be open to feedback, and perform to the best of their ability.

Bill learned the drug program lasted for 9 months and was divided into three phases. During this time, he would continue working at his current prison job in the morning and participate in the drug program during the afternoon. He would be involved in groups focusing on denial, the harmful effects of drug use, rational thinking, criminal thinking errors, wellness, and relapse prevention. In addition, Bill would participate in a group with the other dually diagnosed inmates learning about mental illness and his specific diagnosis, the importance of psychotropic medication, how to self-monitor for warning signs of decompensation, and a variety of problem-solving skills, including accessing community mental health resources, time and stress management, establishing a sleep routine, and how to talk with friends and family about having a mental illness. He also would participate in other treatment groups and would attend individual therapy where he would develop a treatment plan and receive assistance in attaining his treatment goals. A psychiatrist would evaluate Bill for medication and monitor him on a monthly basis. He also would be actively involved in AA and NA meetings.

During his first month in the drug program, Bill met with his therapist to develop his treatment plan. They identified three main problem areas: drug addiction, mental illness, and criminal activity. General goals and specific treatment activities were developed for each problem. For example, for his drug addiction, Bill's general goal included abstaining from the use of all illicit drugs. Specific treatment activities included attending and participating in all mandatory meetings of the residential program, ex-

ploring consequences of his chemical dependency through writing a weekly journal, and sharing the intensity of his drug and alcohol addiction with members of his process-oriented therapy group. Bill's mental health goal was to gain an understanding of his diagnosis and how it had impacted his life, with specific treatment activities outlined. Bill's final treatment goal was to maintain a pro-social, crime-free lifestyle.

At the end of phase 1 of treatment, Bill completed a detailed 20-page autobiography (five-page minimum required) and discussed his commitment to participate in the remainder of the program in front of his peers. He had an enthusiastic attitude, eagerly participated in classes and groups, and willingly took his psychotropic medication. His therapist cautioned him about his impulsive behavior, including inappropriate sexual comments in group, interrupting others while they were speaking, and monopolizing group time. She gave him specific advice about how to deal with these issues. By the end of phase 2, Bill had learned about the connection between his thoughts, feelings, and behaviors; anger management; and thinking patterns that contributed to his criminal activity. In his dual diagnosis group he participated in role-plays designed to assist him in dealing with stigmas associated with mental illness, pressures to stop taking medication, and telling friends and family about having a mental illness.

During Bill's final treatment phase, he learned about relapse prevention. He wrote a relapse prevention plan outlining goals for continuing his recovery upon release. He also designed an "emergency sobriety card," which listed the steps he

would take when tempted to use drugs. He wrote a plan detailing the steps he would take if he experienced manic or depressive symptoms. He focused on release issues, including finding mental health self-help support groups in the community, accessing community mental health resources, and obtaining psychotropic medications.

In her treatment summary, Bill's therapist recommended that following release he attend weekly mental health self-support groups, join a substance abuse support group, have regular psychiatric appointments, take his medications, attend vocational counseling, and obtain a sponsor in the community to provide him with support and guidance in his continued recovery.

After graduating from the Residential Drug Abuse Program, Bill was placed into a halfway house to help him adjust to reintegrating back into his society. Bill will need extra support and guidance to help address his dual disordered needs. Bill is at an increased risk of relapse based upon having a dual disorder. Not only does he have to focus on his sobriety, he also must take the necessary steps to maintain his mental health. In the Dual Diagnosis Drug Abuse Program, he was given the necessary tools to sustain a life of sobriety and mental stability. However, the choice to stay in recovery is his.

Source: Prepared especially for the second edition of Corrections: A Comprehensive View *by Redonna K. Chandler, Kellye H. Allen, & Daniel A. Lee of the Federal Medical Center, Lexington, KY.*

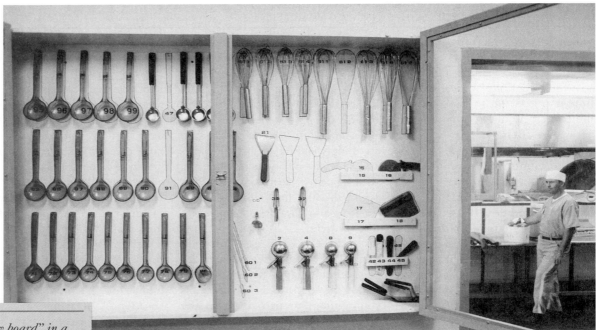

A *"shadow board"* in a prison kitchen has outlines of kitchen implements so that any missing items can be noted immediately.

benefits of good eating habits, as this will help them understand what is good for them versus their preferences and poor eating habits (Johnson, 1998).

Court rulings have required jails and prisons to provide inmates with **special diets** to fulfill therapeutic and medical requirements and to accommodate, where possible, the special dietary restrictions of legitimate religious groups. To protect themselves from lawsuits alleging an inmate has become ill because of not receiving a prescribed diet, many institutions require that inmates sign when receiving these meals. To educate inmates who have health problems (e.g., diabetics) that require a special diet, some facilities conduct therapeutic clinics or provide individual instruction on the proper foods to eat and the need to restrict their diet (Stokes, 1991).

The issue of whether correctional facilities are required to provide religious diets and special meals for religious celebrations relates to the First Amendment right to free exercise of religion. The federal courts have allowed religious exercises to be regulated based on legitimate institutional needs (e.g., security expense; see *Abdullah v. Fard*, 1997; *Jenkins v. Angelone*, 1996). They have also been divided over the extent to which prison authorities can impose restrictions and the degree to which they need to substantiate their justifications (Boston, 1990). Indeed, one federal court upheld a New York prison official's refusal to provide a Rastafarian diet on the grounds that its requirements were too complex (*Benjamin v. Coughlin*, 1989). On the other hand, this prison had also been ordered to provide observant Jews with a nutritionally adequate kosher diet (*Kahane v.*

Carlson, 1975; *Bass v. Coughlin*, 1992). It should not be surprising that the manner in which prisons have met inmate requests for religious diets has varied considerably. The two types of diets most frequently requested are vegetarian and nonpork. By providing extra portions of protein-rich foods, vegetables, and salads, the nutritional needs of vegetarians can be met.

Feeding of Inmates

Jennings asserts:

> There's an old saying in . . . corrections [that] . . . any time there's a disturbance it's going to be in a cafeteria. . . . [B]ecause of the large number of inmates that are there the stress level has gotten to such a point that if the soup is cold, that's going to set inmates off. . . . (as cited by Boss et al., 1986, p. 114)

This quotation highlights the highly volatile nature of the dining area environment. Controlling this area requires an understanding of the factors that can ignite inmate populations, including both the manner in which food is prepared and serving issues.

The emphasis placed on food by inmates makes variation, flavor, texture, appearance, palatability, and temperature vital. No one likes to eat food that is under- or overcooked, dry, or unappetizing. Stokes (1998) asserts that one major problem correctional facilities have is maintaining appropriate food temperatures.[11]

Except for those restricted to their cells, most prisoners are fed in large dining areas. In newer prisons, these areas generally accommodate about half the prison population (i.e., about 250 to 500 inmates). They provide an informal setting where inmates eat at four-to-six-person tables in two sittings. To minimize the potential for a riot or disturbance, no more than 125 inmates should be fed at one time (Stokes, 1993). To prevent disturbances, rules on appropriate behavior are clearly established, often posted, and enforced through adequate and firm supervision. For example, many institutions prohibit passing food from table to table to keep some inmates from pressuring others to give them their food (Ayres, 1988).

Another trend in newer facilities is **decentralized dining** under which inmates are fed in dayrooms, cell blocks, small satellite areas, or in the pods in the more contemporary jails (Stokes, 1993). This reduces the number of inmates congregated in one location at a given time and enhances security by reducing inmate movement within the prison or jail (Stokes, 1991). Under this arrangement, food can be delivered to areas in any one of the following ways: insulated trays, heated carts, hot or cold carts in bulk, or by retherm systems.[12]

The serving line is an area where inmate behavior problems often occur (e.g., inmates skipping ahead of others). Inmate workers also normally do the serving, which can result in inequitable food distribution either due to friendship or intimidation. Both instances can spark fights and demands for extra servings by other inmates (Ayres, 1988). Stationing a correctional officer behind the serving line to pay strict attention and immediately intervene when problems arise can help (Stokes et al., 1985).

A prison food service department can be a potential source of contraband items, including knives, tools, caustic substances, and particular food items that can be used in making alcoholic beverages. Civilian personnel supervising inmates in food preparation need to be trained in security techniques and practices. To control tools and implements such as knives, inmates are required to check these items out. When they are returned, many facilities require they be placed back on a **shadow board,** which has an outline of each item so staff can tell if an item is missing and what type of item it is (Ayres, 1988).

Also, a secure storage area is needed for food items that can be used in making alcohol (e.g., yeast, sugar) or that are highly sellable in the black market (Stokes et al., 1985). Shakedowns and searches of inmates, trash, and other items leaving the kitchen area can prevent the removal of items. Close scrutiny of inmates as they unload incoming supply trucks is important, because contraband can be hidden in numerous places on these vehicles. Inexperienced staff may not see the hazards of inmates taking certain foods from the kitchen. For example, a handful of salt and pepper can be used to cause temporary blindness and animal bones can be made into weapons. Prevention requires close monitoring of all inmates in the dining area and perhaps searches to prevent removal of food or utensils.

Overcrowding and Prison Emergencies

At some overcrowded prisons, cooking may start early in the morning, and food may be served all day long, which means there is no break from one meal to the next. This places tremendous stress on food service operations. Furthermore, some institutions have had to establish satellite serving areas in other parts of the facility because existing dining rooms cannot accommodate a larger population within allotted meal hours (Boss et al., 1986). A more efficient solution is to adopt the **cook/ chill method**[13] of food production, which allows large quantities of food to be precooked and stored in advanced. This takes the pressure off the need to prepare food for each meal. For example, the staff can prepare enough chili to meet menu needs for an entire month at one time. Thus, as long as institutions have sufficient freezer space, existing kitchen facilities can meet food service needs (Stokes, 1993). Finally, institutions must have contingency plans to feed inmates if the food service department is temporarily incapacitated because of a prison disturbance or another emergency.

What can we expect in the future? According to Johnson (1998), (1) more emphasis will be placed on having one centralized kitchen made necessary by the trend in building more than one prison at a given site, and (2) private contractors will be used to provide food service. One potential problem with using private companies is that they adhere to a rigid diet of 3,500 calories with less meat than is provided when the prison runs the kitchen. This may be insufficient to satisfy inmates' appetite for fat, which could lead to inmates walking around hungry and creating tension that results in fights or disturbances. Also, inmates may buy less healthy food from the commissary. Second, private contractors may serve food that is cold and unappealing. Third, private contractors may charge inmates for their meals, forcing them to choose between eating and buying basic things from the commissary (e.g., deodorant). At this time, 28 states report using a private contractor in at least some of their facilities for food service (*Corrections Compendium*, 1999, July).

Religious Programs[14]

Although churches have historically provided asylum for accused individuals and religion has often tempered the treatment of criminals, the most direct influence of religion has been through the work of chaplains. As far back as 539 A.D., church members considered it an obligation to visit those in prison despite their offenses (Wines, 1895). The **Order of Misericordia** was founded in 1488 to provide assistance and consolation to offenders condemned to death, accompany them to the gallows, furnish religious services, and provide a Christian burial

(Kuether, 1951). In the United States, as prisons developed, chaplains visited offenders or became regular members of the prison staff. They were the earliest paid noncustodial staff and provided education and counseling in addition to religious programs (Johnson, 1968; Tappan, 1960).

The early prison chaplains worked under poor circumstances and were often thwarted in their efforts by prison administrators who considered them a hindrance to prison operations. Thus, early prisons usually failed to attract a high caliber of chaplain.

The beginning of the 20th century ushered in a progressive era that brought about changes in attitudes and practices regarding the treatment of offenders (Rothman, 1980). As other professionals (e.g., teachers) began to work in corrections, the chaplain's role became limited to ministering to the spiritual needs of inmates (Kuether, 1951). Many chaplains responded by becoming part of the new treatment team or program component that developed in prisons to rehabilitate offenders. During the 1920s and 1930s, the **Clinical Pastoral Educational Movement** emerged, resulting in clinical training for clergy and the viewing of prison chaplaincy as a specialty subgroup of the clergy (Kuether, 1951). Young clergy began to see chaplaincy as a lifelong calling, and subsequently a professional identity developed around this specialty. This made it possible for prison systems to employ young, well-trained clergy rather than the discouraged and spent clergy previously available. More than any other development in the 20th century, this changed the standing of chaplains in penal facilities (Solomon, 1991).

Legal Issues and Religious Practices

Outside of prisons, individuals do not have to ask permission to practice their religion, which might involve special diets, the wearing of medals, and attendance at religious services. In prison, uninhibited religious expression may not only conflict with concerns relating to security and safety, but may also strain limited budgets (Mushlin, 1993). The courts have been uncomfortable in deciding whether a particular faith constitutes a religion and have hesitated to withhold recognition of any religion because this would be inconsistent with the protection of free religious expression (Cohen, 1981).

Not all groups claiming to be religions have been recognized by the courts. Although the courts do not agree about how to determine when an inmate's religious beliefs deserve First Amendment protection, two requirements seem to emanate from the salient cases: (1) that the beliefs be sincerely held, which is difficult to determine because there are no objective criteria (Van Baalan, 1998), and (2) that the beliefs be religious in nature (Mushlin, 1993; see *Africa v. Pennsylvania*, 1982). For example, the Supreme Court found that a group calling itself MOVE lacked certain traditional religious characteristics [e.g., failure to address fundamental and ultimate religious questions (*Africa v. Pennsylvania*, 1982)]. A **bona fide religious belief** is found in a religion's published theology and is associated with a particular religion.

With respect to providing facilities and clergy to inmates of all recognized faiths, the Supreme Court indicated that it was not necessary for prisons to do so. They were only required to afford all inmates a reasonable opportunity to be able to practice their religion (*Cruz v. Beto*, 1972). In coming to this conclusion, the Court was influenced by the fact that in many prisons there might be 120 or more distinct sects, which would require an extraordinary number of clergy and facilities if prison officials had to provide them equally to each religion (*Gittlemacker v. Prasse*, 1970). Allowing groups to share facilities is one option used by prisons and approved by the courts to accommodate different faiths (*Blair-Bey v. Nix*, 1992).

In determining the legitimacy of these restrictions, the Supreme Court has enunciated the **reasonableness test** first set forth in *Turner v. Safley*[15] and applied specifically to restrictions on religious practices in *O'Lone v. Estate of Shabazz* (1987). To justify a restriction on religious practices prison officials must show that it is reasonably related to legitimate government interests (usually involving security, safety, conserving resources, and rehabilitation). In the *O'Lone* case, prison officials prohibited inmates working on details outside the prison from returning to the institution to attend a Muslim religious service held every Friday afternoon. Prison administration was able to demonstrate that this practice would create security problems and impede rehabilitation. These rationales were viewed as legitimate penological concerns or objectives by the Court. In contrast, in *Hamilton v. Schiriro* (1994), prison officials were ordered by a court to make provisions for an inmate to engage in practices associated with her religion. This included letting her hair grow, using a sweat lodge, and using herbs and medical plants, feathers, beads, and musical instruments for dancing. "Although Native American religion and its practices are not familiar to many it is a bonafide religion" (p. 1022). A second factor involves the prohibition of a religious activity or practice. This requires that prison administrators show that there are readily available alternative means of accommodating an inmate's (or groups of inmates') constitutional rights to practice their religion (e.g., inmates could congregate for prayer or discussion at other times; inmates were given different food when pork was served). A third factor involves the cost both in dollars and effects on the rest of the inmate population that an accommodation to one group's right to practice their religion might entail. The issue here is whether making special arrangements for one group would upset others enough to lead to violence.

Chaplain Functions

Two studies of chaplains (Shaw, 1990[16]; Stout & Clear, 1992[17]) provide a contemporary look at prison chaplains. The majority of chaplains in both studies were white, male, and between the ages of 30 and 59. Whereas half of the chaplains in the federal prison survey were married, only one third of those in the New York system were. Seventy-nine percent of those in the federal system had attended seminary, and nearly all reported some form of graduate education.

The chaplain's main "mission" is to minister to inmates (Holt, 1998). Shaw's research (1990) indicates that chaplains consider themselves advocates for inmates. Because chaplains have historically been concerned with the injustices of the criminal justice system and the living conditions of inmates, it has sometimes placed them at odds with prison administrators. Chaplains regularly walk the tiers and interact with inmates where they live. This can lead them to empathize with inmates and for inmates to expect them to be sympathetic. Thus, chaplains may serve as a "wailing wall" or become a "court of constant complaint" for perceived injustices. These injustices are noted and responded to by chaplains. Shaw also found that chaplains express distress about simplistic public views of all offenders being "bad" and the fact that these views are not likely to change. They also see themselves as inmate advocates.

> The Church is in the prison not just for the "service and maintenance" of inmates, but also to watch the government lest it sin worse than the inmates. (p. VIII-10)

> [There is a] near total dependance on the chaplain to stand up for these men—and when you win them a right denied, there is a personal satisfaction of David defeating Goliath again. (p. VI-4)

In their unofficial capacity as inmate ombudsmen, chaplains encounter situations (e.g., guard abuse) that can strain relations with staff. Shaw recounted an incident in which he witnessed and reported a guard beating an inmate. Intense pressure was used to try to get the inmate to retract his statement. He was threatened by one officer, kept locked on various tiers for hours, and locked off others.

Chaplains' Responsibilities From an administrative standpoint, the prison chaplain is responsible for coordinating and supervising all religious activities and services. It should be noted that in private prisons these functions are supervised by a program director (Holt, 1998). During inmate orientation, the chaplains identify the inmates' religious needs and make them aware of available services.

Part of determining an inmate's religious needs involves ascertaining whether their faith group is an offi-cially recognized religious group. To attempt to deter the formation of sham religious groups, corrections systems have established guidelines about what is recognized as a legitimate faith group. Such guidelines include belief in a divine or superior being, worship practices, identifiable leaders in the free world, and an ongoing history.

All chaplains lead worship services for those of their own faith and may also be present at or even lead those of other denominations (Van Baalan, 1998). In some institutions, they may resemble a "large unruly high school study hall" (Shaw, 1990, p. IV-22). This situation is aggravated by the fact that, in many prisons, chapel services are among the few times when inmates from different units (who normally have no contact with each other) get together. Thus, if inmates want to create a disturbance, attack another inmate, or plan an escape, religious services could present an opportunity to do so.

Some chaplains measure the success of their services not by their impact on inmates but on whether they can "get from start to finish without any incidents" (Shaw, 1990, p. IV-22). It is not surprising that some inmates who are genuinely religious do not attend chapel because they find the rowdy atmosphere offensive.

Outside Clergy and Volunteers Prisons range from having no full-time chaplains to one or two full-time clergy. To minister to inmates of faiths other than their own, chaplains attempt to recruit outside clergy or volunteers to serve these inmates (Van Baalan, 1998). Stout and Clear (1992) found that almost all BOP chaplains felt both comfortable and effective in ministering to inmates of other faiths. Historically, it was not easy to get mainstream church groups to provide clergy to lead religious services and volunteers to assist in other religious activities. Mainstream churches also tended to be disdainful of prison chaplains. This sometimes isolated these clergy from their faith groups, thereby reducing their support network (Shaw, 1990; Stout & Clear, 1992). However, in some jurisdictions this is changing (Holt, 1998).

In some prisons, religious volunteers may range from 80 to 90 percent of all volunteers in prison (Van Baalan, 1998). Chaplain Solomon (1991) notes, however, that religious volunteers today are more sophisticated than in the past largely because of the recruitment and training done by groups such as **Prison Fellowship** (PF). Many chaplains rely on these organizations to recruit and train volunteers and to provide teaching, mentoring, and aftercare programs for released inmates. Their participation in religious activities helps inmates involved in these programs to make contact with prominent members of the community and has served to elevate the standing of chaplains among both staff and inmates (Solomon, 1991). For the volunteers, it has served to

The Horizon Program

PROGRAM FOCUS

Residents in this program live in separate housing, which is divided into eight-person pods consisting of six new inmates and two experienced residents. This setting is designed to be conducive to individual and small group work. During this period inmates maintain their normal 40-hour-a-week schedule but also participate in nightly faith-based therapeutic, outreach, and recovery programs (e.g., anger management,

parenting skills, victim awareness, addiction issues, and religious-based programs). This "community" is self-governing; residents establish the rules and deal with all problems. Kairos Outside also offers a weekend program for participants' wives and families. At the end of 6 months, they have a "Family Day," which takes place in the prison's visiting area and is supported by local churches. Transportation assistance is extended, where possible, to families not living nearby the prison. Additionally, with the cooperation of state departments of cor-

rections, some prerelease programs have been established. They are housed at minimum security units and involve participants in community re-entry preparation prior to their release.

What are your views of this program? Does this change your views on religious programs in prison?
Sources: Kairos, Inc. (1999b). The Kairos Horizon Program Project. *Orlando, FL: Author; Kairos (2000, Jan.).* God's Speed: Special Time. The Newsletter of Kairos Prison Ministry. *Orlando, FL: Author.*

---

help educate them about prisons and provide a new perspective on inmates. Hands-on volunteer ministry helps citizens to understand that most inmates are not the animal-like monsters portrayed in the media but are indeed real people with hopes and dreams very often like their own.

Prison Fellowship (PF) represents an outstanding example of a national religious group with a prison focus. PF is composed of churches and volunteers involved in prison evangelism and a variety of inmate support activities both in and out of prison. It is active in more than two thirds of our nation's prisons.

Another program, the **Kairos Prison Ministry** (KPM), is an interdenominational Christian ministry. Its purpose is to bring Christ's love and forgiveness to all incarcerated individuals, as well as those who work with them (Kairos, 1999). Additionally, it establishes Christian communities on the inside, among the population of correctional institutions and, on the outside, among those who were incarcerated and their families. This begins with a 3-day seminar in which inmates are taught Christian principles and are encouraged to remove their masks so that the team can pour Christian love on the real person rather than on the person they pretend to be. This is accomplished by creating a safe environment to enable inmates to begin to show themselves and thereby realize what life can be like in a loving community. The basic component of these programs is to develop weekly share groups, during which inmates may share their experiences and feelings over the previous week. Outside groups are developed in a similar fashion. This recognizes that the spouses, parents, and other relatives of the incarcerated "do time" along with their loved ones. It is also important to note that the public associates families, particularly the inmates' wives, with the offense.

Active in 27 states (Campbell, 1999), KPM also provides significant transitional services to inmates (Solomon, 1991). Research shows that involvement in KPM has had a positive effect on recidivism. Indeed, a group of 500 inmate program participants were followed for a period of 2 years after their release. Compared with a control group, which had a recidivism rate of 28 percent, those who attended and remained active in Kairos had a rate of 9 percent (Kairos, 1997). Our Program Focus, "The Horizon Program," describes a therapeutic community environment program that Kairos has begun in several institutions.

Fundamentalist religious groups have been very active in the volunteer movement. The nature of their literature, emotionally charged services, and the experience of declaring oneself "born again" makes them extremely popular with inmates (Shaw, 1990). This is further enhanced by their willingness to provide secular and religious assistance. For example, Living Witnesses for Christ volunteers minister to inmates' religious needs and assist them in legal efforts to win their freedom and, upon release, help them get jobs and housing. They also visit inmates' families prior to release to explain their role in the inmate's reintegration into society (Angolite, 1981). Finally, the Olive Institute, in Miami, Florida, provides in-house seminars for Jewish inmates that deal with the high holidays (Van Baalan, 1998).

Inmate-Led Religious Groups One area causing problems and controversy involves inmate-led religious groups. The extent to which prison systems allow inmates to lead religious activities varies. In the federal system, in-

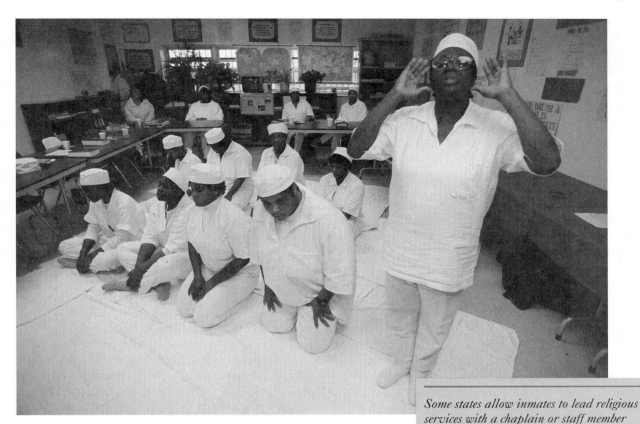

Some states allow inmates to lead religious services with a chaplain or staff member present. Here Muslim inmates at Ferguson Prison in Texas celebrate Ramadan.

mates are not permitted to do this unless the prison's chaplain is of a different faith and no assistance is available from local community religious groups. No professional (e.g., a dentist) is allowed to practice his or her profession while incarcerated in a federal prison (Schulze, 1991). Some states allow inmates to lead religious services with a chaplain or a staff member present, but there is a tendency to require the presence of an outside clergy person or religious representative of that faith (Mushlin, 1993). In considering the constitutionality of the sponsor requirement, the courts have been heavily influenced by the security problems posed by inmate-led services.

Muslim Clergy As we noted in Chapter 7, some Muslim clergy began seeking religious converts among inmates in the prisons in the 1960s and 1970s. One group represents a hybrid religion and should be regarded as an organization begun in the United States in the 1930s by blacks that combined the tenets of Islam and Christianity. It was called the **Nation of Islam** by its founder, Elijah Muhammad. The name was later changed to "American Muslim Mission" by his son, Imam W. D. Muhammud, who removed all racial restrictions on membership. It later became assimilated with the Sunni Muslim community and is now known simply as the **Muslim Community** (Van Baalan, 1999). This group, which now consists of Middle Eastern immigrants and

converted African Americans, represents the largest group of Muslims in the United States identifying with one Islamic leader. In 1979, Minister Louis Farrakhan left this group and started his own Muslim sect using the resurrected name, Nation of Islam. This group is viewed as outside traditional Islamic practice because it does not follow the Qur'an (the holy book of the Muslims) but instead has its own books (Hafiz, 1993). Farrakhan's policies have been described as reactionary; they are based on beliefs that include black superiority, scapegoating of Jews, and economic self-sufficiency (Holmes, 1994; Marriott, 1994; Terry, 1994). According to Hafiz (1993), Nation of Islam ministers have not been employed in state or federal prisons. Nevertheless, there are Nation of Islam groups functioning within our prisons and also those associated with the Moorish Science Temple of America, another hybrid offshoot. Hafiz cautions that chaplains need to attend meetings of religious groups to ensure that the activities are of a religious nature.

The increasing institutional presence in prison of Muslim **Imams** (qualified clergy) who are hired as chaplains has added a new dimension to the prison religious scene (Shaw, 1990). Initially, Imams were not given a warm welcome because they had to deal with correctional personnel (including chaplains) who had negative experiences with some Islamic inmates (e.g., being called "white

CLOSE-UP

Imams: Providing Religious Leadership for Muslim Inmates

The growing number of inmate adherents to the Islamic religion created a need for qualified clergy (Imams) to conduct worship and other activities for these inmates. According to Abu Ishaq Abdul-Hafiz—one of eight full-time Muslim Imam chaplains now in the federal prison system—the lack of Imams in prisons had led to the development of practices by inmate Muslim groups that were not accepted in the faith. Abdul-Hafiz, who serves as a chaplain at the Terminal Island Federal Correctional Institution, provides spiritual guidance to inmates of all faiths at the prison. However, he considers his main mission to be exposing the Muslim religion for what it really is—peace and harmony for all people. He feels that all religions

actually are from one source, are the same, and that we're all talking about the same God.

He has touched the lives of a number of inmates both Muslim and non-Muslim. A 44-year-old heroin addict indicated that Hafiz had inspired him to find another life path and in effect had saved his life. Buddhist inmates credited him with reviving their interest in practicing their faith, while Jewish inmates appreciated his help in securing literature for them. Hafiz has also created a strong bond between the prison and the external Islamic community, which has helped to expose inmates to a wider view of the faith.

An estimated 5 to 7 percent of male black inmates claim Islam as their religious preference. Like the Christian faith, the Islamic religion has several "sects." This complicates the job of non-Muslim chap-

lains and reinforces the need for Imams as chaplains in prison systems with substantial black inmate populations (Hafiz & Hamidullah, undated; Rae-Dupree, 1991; *Volunteer Today*, 1993).

Finally, since the late 1990s, for the first time we have seen new pre-Christian European groups meeting at certain prisons (e.g., Wiccan, Odinoist). Some of the Aryan Nation's followers identify with these groups while in prison. At this time, the Church of Jesus Christ Christian has not been allowed to meet but Hafiz (1998) feels that they will be allowed to assemble very soon. This is the main faith of the Aryan Nation. Their extreme racist views and violent activity in and out of prison will make this a security concern when they are allowed to meet.

---

devils" or taunted and threatened by them). However, since the 1990s, Muslim chaplains have not only been accepted but are considered assets in those facilities that employ them full time. They have been able to educate staff on Muslim religious matters so that requests concerning religious practices can be evaluated. This has reduced litigation by inmates based on denial of opportunities to engage in legitimate religious practices (Hafiz, 1993).

Without Imams, the Muslim religion in prison has tended to develop extremist ideas and practices that are not accepted by the faith. In some cases, its members have been seen by staff as a gang using religion as a pretext to meet and run gang business. Other inmates have seen it as an exclusively black religion. The role of the Imam chaplain has been to eliminate stereotypes and to ensure that these religious groups are operating in accordance with the tenets of the religion and prison rules. He can also encourage members of Muslim communities to do volunteer work in the prisons so inmates can have contact with blacks who are successful and will provide them with assistance when they are released (Hafiz, 1993). However, as prison chaplains, Imams do not minister exclusively to Muslims but to inmates of all faiths (Van Baalan, 1998). The Close-Up on Imams describes their role as chaplains in prisons.

Regulating Religious Items Chaplains also function to assist inmates in obtaining literature and other materials necessary for the practice of their faith. Despite their recognition of an inmate's First Amendment right to religious expression, the courts have recognized that restricting personal possession of items and their use in religious services may be necessary (e.g., wine). Thus, only chaplains can keep or use wine during religious services over which they preside. Inmates have been allowed to keep items such as beards, prayer rugs, medals and chains, rosaries, yarmulkes, and turbans.

Responding to Inmate Needs Chaplains counsel inmates either individually or in a group setting, and these sessions may focus on religious as well as secular concerns. Inmates who seek help in dealing with their problems from prison counselors, particularly mental health professionals, are more likely to be seen as "crazy" by their fellow inmates because of the common view that anyone seeking this kind of help must be severely disturbed. In contrast, going to a counseling session with a chaplain is not seen as visiting the "shrink" because of the religious context in which these sessions are held. Also, chaplains may refer inmates to receive other types of treatment. The important role played by chaplains in inmate treatment has led some states to recognize them as integral members of prison treatment teams.

In the course of counseling and moving about the institution, chaplains invariably acquire information on an inmate's criminal history and violations of prison rules. Most state statutes view communication between minister and penitent as privileged. Thus, the minister receiving the information cannot be compelled to divulge it unless the individual giving it waives the legal right to secrecy (Kaplan & Waltz, 1987). However, although chaplains are employees of the institution and the policies and procedures governing their role consider communication with inmates confidential, this policy is not absolute. They are generally required to divulge information that threatens the safety or security of the institution, its staff, or other inmates (Federal Bureau of Prisons, undated; Florida Department of Corrections, 1982; Texas Department of Corrections, 1986). This places chaplains in a catch-22 situation—their effectiveness with inmates is reduced if they are seen as "snitches," but they will be seen as "traitors" by staff if they fail to divulge critical information.

Chaplains play an important role in helping inmates to deal with family-related issues. They counsel inmate families, meet with them during visits, and assist inmates in reestablishing family ties. Chaplains also help inmates with things such as requests for visits, clothes and commissary money, and guidance for inmates' families in obtaining financial or social service assistance (Texas Department of Corrections, 1986). Chaplains may also receive calls reporting family problems and are usually responsible for notifying the inmate or the family of emergencies, including death and serious illness. This latter aspect is one of the more stressful aspects of the chaplain's job.

Inmates' marriages also fall within the chaplain's province. Some jurisdictions allow the chaplain to perform the ceremony; in others they instruct the inmate about proxy marriages (Holt, 1998). Although the Supreme Court, in *Turner v. Safely* (1987), upheld an inmate's fundamental right to marry, it acknowledged the right of prison officials to regulate the time and circumstances under which the marriage may take place. The Court further noted that despite the limitations imposed by imprisonment there may be significant beneficial elements of marriage sufficient to form a constitutionally protected marital relationship in the prison context. They include:

1. expressions of emotional support and public commitment.

2. the recognition that certain religious groups view this as an expression of both spiritual faith and personal dedication.

3. the recognition that most inmates will eventually be released, and thus they are formed with the idea that they will be consummated.

4. marital status is often a precondition for the receipt of government benefits (e.g., social security).

Although not noted by the Court it would be fair to assume that inmates who are married and have a home to come to will have a better chance of being successful on release. Since *Turner*, the courts have been unwilling to deny an inmate the right to marry unless the prison can offer powerful reasons for forbidding the inmate to do so (Mushlin, 1993). For example, forbidding a prison's employee from marrying an inmate did not violate the equal protection clause of the Fourteenth Amendment. The Supreme Court indicated that the regulation was rationally related to a legitimate security concern and was established to prevent inmates from romantic involvement with COs to obtain preferential treatment (*Keeney v. Health*, 1995). Do you think inmates should have the right to marry, and if so, what restrictions would you impose?

Finally, chaplains are responsible for visiting inmates in special housing units, including protective or disciplinary segregation and in the prison hospital. Recently, this has included ministering to the needs of AIDS patients. The incidence of AIDS and the aging of the prison population will result in a larger number of inmates dying in prison (U.S. Department of Justice, 1989). The BOP and some state systems (e.g., Texas) have developed hospices to ease the tension involved in the dying process (Holt, 1998).

Why Inmates Join Religious Groups

Inmates join religious groups for a variety of reasons, including the following (Dammer, 1996):

1. In some cases inmates gain direction, meaning, and hope to reform from a life of crime.

2. Religion promotes a personal behavioral change. The rules and discipline that the serious practice of religion requires help inmates develop better self-control and, thus, avoid both staff and inmate confrontations.

3. To feel safe in prison inmates need a group to protect them from other individuals or groups. Without this protection, inmates believe they may be subject to physical confrontations.

4. Inmates incarcerated for certain sex offenses (child molestation or sexual assault of an older woman) know they will be stigmatized as a deviant, which places them among those least respected of all the inmates. This also means they will be subjected to verbal and physical abuse. Involvement in a religious group while in prison gives these inmates a respite from the fear of being attacked by other inmates, and participation in services provides a safe haven.

5. For inmates with HIV, who are despised and subjected to cruelty by others, religious services can provide psychological assistance from fellow worshipers

How to Supervise Private Correctional Facilities

Holt asserts that privately operated prisons need to provide the same programming (i.e., the same response to offender needs, spiritual growth and development, male/female issues) as the state system (TDCJ). The one limitation is whether the warden and the corporation will abide by the rules. Further, if some details are not very carefully spelled out in the contract, especially if it is a cost factor, some of the private corporations may say, "Well since it's not spelled out in the contract, we're not required to provide that." Technically, this is cor-rect. Unless an offender files a grievance or a lawsuit sometimes some issues are not addressed. In his capacity as regional coordinator, Holt is responsible for supervising private facilities. He states, "As I visit on the units, I certainly inquire about what's taking place and then also give guidance about our expectations on those units. One of my concerns is that units provide inmates with work and other opportunities that can lead to work on the outside. This would require the state to develop contracts with privately operated prisons that more specifically spell out the programming needs, whether it's religious, educational, or substance abuse or prerelease preparation. We've been very good in spelling out security things, but we've not been too good in spelling out our expectations in rehabilitation.

"There is also a need to do a lot more with immediate family reconciliation, anger management and communication skills, and job awareness—those types of things that are geared toward the release of inmates. Also doing a lot more with immediate family reconciliation would also facilitate release success."
Source: W. Holt (1998). Chaplaincy regional coordinator, Texas Department of Criminal Justice Institutions Division.

and faith representatives (e.g., chaplains). This also may be the only place where these inmates can interact with other inmates in a positive manner.

6. Religious services provide inmates with one of the few opportunities to meet other inmates for purposes of (a) enjoying regular social interaction with friends and groups of individuals with similar interests and feeling accepted by those in the group and (b) passing contraband.

7. For inmates, religion provides an opportunity to meet with civilian volunteers, some of whom are of the opposite sex.

8. Involvement in religion provides inmates with free access to special resources, including goods such as food and coffee, holiday greeting cards and books, musical instruments, and food privileges during certain religious holidays. Inmates may also gain opportunities for individual favors from faith representatives (e.g., phone access and letters of recommendation for parole hearings or transfer to another institution).

The reality of inmate manipulation causes chaplains to be on guard and constantly question inmate motives. There can be danger involved in putting trust in some inmates. Chaplain Shaw (1990) reports a case of an inmate who was imprisoned for brutally killing a store owner and his female clerk, whom he mutilated. Not long after being sent to prison, this inmate secured a job as a trusted clerk in the prison chapel. He later brutally murdered a female corrections officer. Shaw, who had contact with the offender, said he was stunned at how an inmate with his record and demeanor was able to gain the confidence of the chaplain in such a short period of time. Finally, a *Corrections Compendium* study (1998, April) reports that less than 50 percent of the inmate population participates in religious activities.

Chaplains in Private Facilities With many states and the federal government using private correctional facilities, the question arises, What standards must they meet to provide an acceptable religious program? In our In Their Own Words feature, Chaplain Holt (1998), regional coordinator of chaplains for Texas prisons, addresses the issue of how to supervise private facilities so that they provide acceptable religious programs.

Other Chaplain-Related Issues

As paid members of the prison staff, chaplains come under the direct control of the prison warden or jail commander and in the state and federal systems are also supervised by the department supervisor of chaplains. Unlike other staff, chaplains owe their primary allegiance to their religious group and must be responsive to its theology or belief system. This may create conflict with prison administrators when religious values and institutional or custodial goals are at odds (Stoltz, 1978, as cited by Shaw, 1990). Thus, in some systems or institutions, COs do not view chaplains any more favorably than do prison administrators because they feel that they are "do-gooders" who interfere with their routines. Further, this lack of unity among staff can lead to a lack of communication between chaplains, administrators, and staff. However, in systems like the Federal Bureau of Prisons, there is a concerted effort to integrate chaplains with staff and administrators (Van Baalan, 1998).

Finally, chaplains also minister to staff and their families during occasions such as marriages, funerals, and baptisms (Federal Bureau of Prisons, undated; Florida Department of Corrections, 1982; Texas Department of Corrections, 1986). Being able to feel welcome in the prison chapel and comfortable in looking to the chaplain for spiritual direction and support can be of major assistance to staff. Despite occasional resentment between chaplains and staff, 88 percent of BOP chaplains felt that their ministry was successful with staff (Stout & Clear, 1992). Chaplains also play an important role in helping staff gain an understanding of inmate religious practices.

Characteristics of Effective Chaplains

Prison chaplains have a difficult and demanding job. The essence of this is captured by Emmett Solomon (1990), former administrator of the chaplaincy programs for the Texas Department of Criminal Justice, who notes:

> Since the prison is a "cold war" the chaplain has to continually be alert to his/her being used as a pawn in that conflict. This factor requires him/her always to evaluate every situation and the motivation of every request. It requires the development of "tough love" in order to function effectively in the adversarial setting [of the prison]. In this age of specialization the chaplain is still a generalist, interested in the client's overall welfare. (p. 1)

Solomon's view parallels the perceptions that Shaw's chaplain respondents have of themselves. They reported themselves to be tough and resilient individuals with strong shoulders to bear the burdens of others. Their self-defined toughness is not a traditional macho approach to their work but instead recognizes "their own vulnerability and [the] dangers associated with giving in to situations [that] could cause undue stress" (Shaw, 1990, p. IX-9). Also, like other professionals, experienced chaplains realize the need to separate themselves emotionally from inmate problems when they leave the facility and to maintain a degree of emotional distance from inmates and their problems. One quality that appeared to be essential in dealing with the stresses of working in a prison or jail environment was a "sense of humor" (Shaw, 1990). Given these positive feelings, it is not surprising that Stout and Clear (1992) found that almost all BOP chaplains felt the job they did was important. In fact, 8 of 10 chaplains indicated that they would rather work as chaplains than any other job. This is in spite of the fact that their salaries are not commensurate with the education and training required for the job (Holt, 1998).

Research and New Directions

One of the new models being used for prison ministries allows for both a more therapeutic relationship and greater interaction between inmates and chaplains. This involves a team ministry that includes chaplains and health care. Ahrens (1998) states that

> those of us in prison ministry can't help but wonder whether there might be a connection between spirituality and health care and whether the spiritual well-being of inmates impacts on their health. (p. 6)

Wisconsin is currently experimenting with a spiritual health care program involving HIV/AIDS inmates. This seeks to develop cooperative relationships between spiritual leaders and health care workers so that they can counsel inmates who have concerns about their HIV status (Ahrens, 1998, April).

Finally, with respect to chaplain effectiveness, at least one study found that "of the successful releasees who credited a specific staff member with being a major influence in their reformation, one sixth cited the prison chaplains and religious workers." This is true despite the fact that these employees represent less than one percent of the prison staff (Glaser, 1969, pp. 93–94).

Summary

This chapter focuses on healthy treatment, food, and religious services for inmates.

Inadequate medical services are one basis for inmate court challenges. The history of prison health service was pretty bad until the 1970s, when there began a growing recognition that everyone was entitled to adequate medical care. The Supreme Court added a further push when it ruled that inmates must be provided with medical care (i.e., diagnosis and treatment) that is comparable in quality and availability to that obtainable by the general public. Also, it stated that jurisdictions cannot refuse to provide inmates with needed or essential care because funds are unavailable. To determine that institutions or their employees are not providing adequate care there must be a showing of deliberate indifference to inmate medical care. However, prison officials cannot be held liable unless they "recklessly disregard a known substantial risk of harm."

Although the vast majority of inmates are young, they tend to have more medical problems than comparably aged persons in the general population. This is because of their lifestyles, which often involve risk taking, poor diets, and drugs. The result is higher rates of HIV/AIDS, other sexually transmitted diseases, tuberculosis, and other infectious diseases.

Providing health care to inmates has been increasingly difficult because of an increasing prison population that is less healthy than inmates in the past, added cost for medications, and the treatment of inmates with HIV/AIDS. Some of the methods that have been employed to control health care for inmates include medical co-payments, telemedicine, managed care, use of computers, and other cost-control approaches (e.g., negotiating fixed rates for hospital care). Correctional systems and states are responding to the increasing numbers of terminally ill inmates by establishing hospice care facilities.

The courts make no distinction between the rights of inmates to health care and their rights to mental care for psychiatric or psychological impairments. Thus, courts see deliberate indifference to psychological needs of inmates as unconstitutional. The Supreme Court ruled that forced administration of drugs to inmates can be done if the inmate is dangerous to himself or others, and the treatment is in the inmate's medical interest. For some inmates, the sheltered and structured environment of an institution can be less stressful than living on the outside, but for many with mental illness, confinement hinders their ability to cope.

The two main treatment methods for serious mental illness are medications and placement in a therapeutic environment. Often, mentally ill inmates receive treatment in separate units or a hospital. Other types of mental health treatment in prison usually consist of some form of counseling or behavioral therapy, such as behavior modification, token economies, behavioral contracting, and cognitive therapy.

It has been estimated that upward of 80 percent of all inmates have serious substance abuse problems. Responding to the problem of drug-involved offenders, all states and the federal system have developed some form of substance abuse program for convicted offenders. Available research has shown that the long-term therapeutic community (TC) treatment model has the best chance of success in working with hard-core drug abusers with criminal justice involvement. Best results appear to be achieved with residency of at least 9 to 12 months followed by some form of aftercare.

Individuals with either a mental health or substance abuse problem are more likely to have a co-occurring or dual disorder. Dual diagnosis programs constitute an effort by corrections to recognize the need to treat both mental illness and a co-occurring substance abuse disorder.

Food is a basic necessity of life, and in prison it becomes more important because meals are one of the few things to which inmates look forward. Today, planning prison menus includes the need to meet basic nutritional requirements, to provide varied and appealing meals, and to do all of this within strict cost constraints. To accomplish this most correctional systems use some type of cycle menu.

In prisons a centralized dining area is highly volatile because it serves large numbers of inmates at any given time. Controlling this area requires an understanding of the factors that can ignite inmate populations, including both the manner in which food is prepared and serving issues. Another trend in newer facilities is decentralized dining, under which inmates are fed in dayrooms, cell blocks, small satellite areas, or in the pods in the more contemporary jails. Prison food service departments can be a potential source of contraband items, including knives, tools, caustic substances, and particular food items that can be used in making alcoholic beverages.

At some overcrowded prisons, cooking may start early in the morning, and food may be served all day long, which means there is no break from one meal to the next. A more efficient solution is to adopt the cook/chill method of food production, which allows large quantities of food to be precooked and stored in advance.

In prison, uninhibited religious expression may not only conflict with concerns relating to security and safety but may also strain limited budgets. Although the courts do not agree on how to determine when an inmate's religious beliefs deserve First Amendment protection, two requirements seem to emanate from the salient cases: (1) that the beliefs be sincerely held, which is difficult to determine because there are no objective criteria, and (2) that the beliefs be religious in nature. Prisons are not required to provide facilities and clergy to inmates of all recognized faiths, only to afford all inmates a reasonable opportunity to practice their religion.

The Supreme Court has used the "reasonableness test" to determine the legitimacy of restrictions on religious practice. To justify a restriction prison officials must show that it is reasonably related to legitimate government interests (usually involving security, safety, conserving resources, or rehabilitation). To prohibit a religious activity or practice, prison administrators must show that there are readily available alternative means of accommodating inmates' constitutional right to practice their religion. Officials may also prohibit religious practices on the basis of cost or disruptive effects on the rest of the inmate population that an accommodation to one group's right to practice their religion might entail.

Chaplains' main mission is to minister to inmates. Thus, they regularly walk the tiers and interact with inmates where they live. From an administrative standpoint, the prison chaplain is responsible for coordinating and supervising all religious activities and services. They also attempt to deter the formation of sham religious groups. To be recognized as a religion, practitioners must show that the faith believes in a divine or superior being and has worship practices, identifiable leaders in the free world, and an ongoing history.

The increasing institutional presence in prison of Muslim Imams (qualified clergy) hired as chaplains has added a new dimension to the prison religious scene. They have been able to educate staff on Muslim religious matters, providing a basis for evaluating requests for religious practices and potentially reducing inmate litigation. Without Imams, the Muslim religion in prison has tended to develop extremist ideas and practices that are not accepted by the faith.

Critical Thinking Questions

1. You are planning to open a new correctional health care unit. What inmate health issues do you need to consider?

2. As a prison administrator, what inmate health care issues should you be familiar with?

3. As a fiscal officer for a department of corrections, what factors must you consider in developing an annual budget for the inmate health care system?

4. Discuss the impact of HIV, tuberculosis, and hepatitis C on a corrections system.

5. As the head of a prison health service unit, what would you face in dealing with the mentally ill?

6. Describe the drug abuse problem among inmates and the TC approach to treating them.

7. Discuss the problem of infectious disease, including TB and AIDS, within prisons.

8. In planning for the treatment of inmates with substance abuse, what types of programs would you include in a comprehensive substance abuse program that will meet the needs of the inmate population?

9. What are the special challenges that prison food services face?

10. In planning for a food service unit in a new prison, what factors would you consider in designing this new unit?

11. Assume you are appointed to head a food service department in prison. What are some of the issues that you will have to deal with?

12. As a newly appointed chaplain in a prison setting, what religious issues would you face?

13. As the legal officer for a department of corrections, what issues will you have to confront in dealing with inmate religious groups?

Test Your Knowledge

1. An inmate's right to adequate medical care is derived from:
   a. state laws.
   b. constitutional guarantees.
   c. institutional rules.
   d. public opinion polls.

2. Deliberate indifference to a serious medical need has been ruled by the courts to be in violation of constitutional guarantees:
   a. for equal protection.
   b. to due process.
   c. against cruel and unusual punishment.
   d. for separation of powers.

3. Research concerning the effectiveness of therapeutic community–type programs has shown that:
   a. prison-based therapeutic communities are more effective than community-based.
   b. effective results can be achieved with 6 months of residential treatment.
   c. TC prison program graduates have reduced rearrest and recidivism rates when compared with nonprogram participants.
   d. male offenders typically have better outcomes than female offenders.

Endnotes

1. Dr. Silverman would like to thank Harvey Landress for updating the sections on medical care, mental health, substance abuse, and infectious diseases. Thanks also to B. Jaye Anno, Ph.D., past chair, National Commission on Correctional Health Care, for providing information, reviewing the manuscript, and offering useful suggestions to improve the accuracy of the material on medical services.

2. Isele, 1977; Knight, 1986; *Grubbs v. Bradley*, 1982; *Hughes v. Joliet Correctional Center*, 1991; *Warren v. Fanning*, 1991.

3. Although many prisons call their medical units "hospitals," in most cases, these facilities are really only clinics or infirmaries because they are only equipped to provide ambulatory care (e.g., intake, medication distribution, chronic condition clinics, and in-patient and emergency care). They are not equipped to do full-scale surgical procedures, many diagnostic procedures, or provide most specialized types of treatments (Anno, 1991a).

4. Lopez & Cheney, 1992; *Inmates of Allegheny County Jail v. Pierce*, 1979.

5. Lipton, 1995; Chaiken, 1989; DeLeon, 1988; Hubbard et al., 1989; Pompi & Resnick, 1987.

6. DeLeon, 1984; Inciardi et al., 1997; Anglin & Hser, 1990.

7. Lipton, 1994, 1995; Inciardi et al., 1997.

8. Inciardi et al., 1997; Lipton, 1995; Wexler & Lipton, 1993.

9. Dr. Silverman would like to thank Judy Ford Stokes, president of Judy Ford Stokes & Associates, Inc., Atlanta, Georgia, food management and design consultants, and Lavinia Johnson, CEP training development coordinator, Food Service Specialty, Virginia Department of Corrections, for providing information, reviewing the section on food services, and offering useful suggestions to improve this section's authenticity for the second edition of this text.

10. It is preferable for a system or facility to have a computerized nutrient analysis of its cycle menu done by a university or some other creditable organization because this can be used to refute inmate court challenges to the nutritional value of the food served (Stokes, 1991). Also, in this respect

Stokes (1991) notes that it is advisable to use a nutrient analysis database of recipes like those of the military service.

11. By complying with new U.S. Department of Agriculture temperature standards this may become less of an issue. As of January 1994, a new standard (Hazard Analysis Critical Control Point, HACCP) requires constant temperatures to be maintained for food, from the point of receiving through storage, through the entire food production process, and in serving. Cold food must be maintained at temperatures no higher than 41°F and hot food must be served at temperatures of at least 160°F. To meet these new standards and document compliance, refrigerated work counters must be installed and used in some production areas (e.g., salad bars). In addition, rethermalization systems will need to be used in many facilities to ensure proper temperatures.

12. Rethermalization units are mobile and can be used to retherm bulk food or individual food serving trays. Hot food items are placed in the retherm units and cold food in separate carts and rolled to cell areas or decentralized dining rooms. The retherm units are plugged in, and 15 to 30 minutes later hot food is ready to be assembled with cold food and beverages for delivery to the inmate. This system can also be used in kitchens with adjacent dining areas (Stokes, 1993; Stokes & Associates, undated).

13. The cook/chill production method, a type of cook-to-inventory system, prepares food according to inventory levels using standardized recipes. It is based on maintaining predetermined amounts (par levels) of menu items on hand at all times. For example, if the par level for chili is 400 gallons and only 150 gallons exist in storage, then 250 additional gallons would need to be prepared. Food prepared today may be served next week (Stokes, 1993). For a more complete discussion of this method consult "Your Kitchen Can Pay for Itself" prepared by Judy Ford Stokes & Associates, Atlanta, Georgia (undated).

14. Dr. Silverman would like to thank Richard Shaw, chaplain at the New York State Summit Shock Incarceration Facility and Albany County Jail; Susan Van Baalan, chaplaincy administrator, Federal Bureau of Prisons; Jerry Groom, retired administrator of chaplaincy programs, and Winston Holt, chaplaincy regional coordinator, Texas Department of Criminal Justice; and Imam Abdul Hafiz, chaplain, Federal Correctional Institution–Terminal Island, for providing information, reviewing this manuscript, and offering useful suggestions to improve its authenticity.

15. Note that the rules established in the *Turner* decision will continue to be the standard for evaluating inmates' versus institutional concerns in cases other than those involving religious issues.

16. Shaw (1990) surveyed all Catholic, Jewish, and Islamic chaplains listed as official chaplains in the federal and state prisons in New York State and in county and city jails. In comparing the characteristics of his sample with data on chaplains provided by the New York Department of Corrections, Shaw found that in terms of age and sex his sample closely paralleled chaplains in the state; however, in terms of years of service, his respondents were more seasoned (9.4 average years of service versus 4.04). Out of 270 questionnaires sent out, 70 responses were received.

17. The Stout and Clear (1992) survey was based on 113 responses from chaplains attending a BOP chaplains' meeting in June 1990—not all chaplains completed the survey.

The American Jail

18

LEARNING OBJECTIVES

After completing this chapter, you should be able to:

1. Specify the functions of jails, and describe the types of people who tend to populate them.

2. Trace the history of the modern jail.

3. Identify the types of special category inmates that jails have to deal with and the problems presented by each.

4. Contrast the three types of jail design, and explain how each affects the supervision of inmates.

5. Describe the processes and problems that occur when offenders are first brought to jail.

6. Discuss the essential issues involved in creating an effective jail staff.

7. Outline major jail trends and management issues.

Introduction[1]

Once police arrest lawbreakers, they are taken to either a holding facility or a jail. Holding facilities generally keep people up to 72 hours and are often located in police stations for the convenience of arresting officers. Individuals held for extended investigations or charged with a criminal offense are transported to one of the more than 3,300 jails in the country (Harlow, 1998). At midyear 1998, local authorities supervised an estimated 687,973 inmates, 12 percent of whom were in alternative community programs outside of the jail. Admissions and releases on a given day averaged over 50,000 (Perkins, Stephan, & Beck, 1995; Beck, 2000).

About 10 percent of the jails house about 90 percent of the jail inmate population, with seven states holding more than half of the jail population (Beck, 2000). Thus, jails are complex institutions that hold dangerous pretrial detainees, short-term-sentenced inmates, work releasees, and those awaiting transportation to state or federal prison. They also hold the drunk, substance abuser, disorderly, and mentally ill. Their detention population includes both pretrial detainees (who constitute about 57 percent of the inmates) and sentenced inmates (Gilliard, 1999). Characteristically, this population includes juveniles and adults, males and females, and the elderly, sick, and mentally ill. These jails are administered by local officials and are designed to hold persons from a few hours to 1 year in most states. However, at least 12 states permit jails to hold people for more than a year (Kerle, 2000). Prisons are state or federal facilities that hold persons serving felony sentences of generally longer than a year. Because most states and the federal government operate more than one facility, the population of prisons is typically more homogeneous than a jail with respect to the level of dangerousness of the inmates' security or custody level, age, and sex. Thus, the diversity of jail populations poses unique challenges (Miller, 2000).

Typically, after booking inmates who can post bail can be released. Within 24 hours, the inmates that remain make their first appearance in court and may be able to obtain release on their own recognizance (ROR) upon a promise to appear in court. Those who are not released remain in a pretrial status until their trial.

Characteristics of the Jail Population

The jail population rose 307 percent between 1983 and 1999, and there were also significant changes in its characteristics (Beck, 2000; Gilliard, 1999; Perkins et al., 1995):

- The population of females increased from 7.1 to 11.2 percent.

- The proportion of white inmates dropped from 46 to 41.3 percent.

- The proportion of blacks rose from 37.5 to 41.5 percent.

- The Hispanic population rose from 14.3 to 15.5 percent.

Table 18.1 presents a profile of the jail population over different time periods.

In addition to their alleged criminality, many jail inmates are affected by such problems as illiteracy, substance abuse, and varying degrees of mental instability. These problems tend to go untreated in the outside world. Consequently, the jail—a community agency—becomes a catchall for society's problems. Thus, when nobody else can take care of the problem, the person ends up in jail. This includes both the mentally ill for whom there are insufficient local facilities and hard-core welfare recipients who are no longer eligible for participation in this program (Parrish, 2000).

Finally, another reason the jail population rose considerably between 1983 and 1996 is because of overcrowding in state and federal prisons and local programs. Whereas in 1983 only 9.1 percent of the jail population (20,253) was being held for other authorities, this figure had risen to 12.2 percent (61,200) in 1996 (Harlow, 1996; Perkins et al., 1995). Unless prison construction keeps up with changes in sentencing policies (e.g., three strikes and truth-in-sentencing laws), this situation is not likely to improve.

Certain categories of inmates require special attention because of the potential risks they pose to themselves and other inmates and staff. These include drug and alcohol abusers, the mentally ill, those who are potentially suicidal, and juvenile inmates. Women are also a special category because their relatively small numbers have made it difficult for jails to meet their program and service needs.

Substance Abusers

A majority of jail inmates are physically and/or psychologically dependent on one or more legal or illegal substances. A 1998 study of 30,000 arrestees entering 35 metropolitan jails found that about two thirds of the adult arrestees and more than half of the juvenile arrestees tested positive for at least one drug. Among adult males, marijuana was the drug most frequently detected in 23 of the 35 sites. Cocaine was the drug most likely to be detected in the remaining 12 sites. Among females, cocaine was the drug most frequently detected in 29 of 32 sites, with methamphetamines the most frequently detected drug among females at the remaining 3 sites (ADAM, 1999). Thus, an important task of jail personnel is to identify those under the influence and provide appropriate medical care (Peters, Kearns, Murin, & Dolante, 1992).

Addicted inmates and those selling drugs are the most likely of all inmates to introduce illegal drugs into a

Table 18.1

Selected Characteristics of Jail Inmates, by Conviction Status (1996, 1989, and 1983)

	Percent of Jail Inmates				
	1996			1989	1983
	Total*	Convicted	Unconvicted		
Sex					
Male	89.8%	89.8%	90.3%	90.5%	92.9%
Female	10.2	10.2	9.7	9.5	7.1
Race/Hispanic Origin					
White non-Hispanic	37.3%	39.7%	32.4%	38.6%	46.4%
Black non-Hispanic	40.8	38.9	44.7	41.7	37.5
Hispanic	18.5	18.3	19.1	17.4	14.3
Other†	3.5	3.2	3.8	2.3	1.8
Age					
17 or younger	2.3%	1.4%	4.1%	1.5%	1.3%
18–24	28.5	27.9	30.2	32.6	40.4
25–34	37.4	38.9	34.7	42.9	38.6
35–44	23.9	24.4	22.6	16.7	12.4
45–54	6.3	6.0	6.9	4.6	4.9
55 or older	1.5	1.5	1.4	1.7	2.4
Marital Status					
Married	15.7%	16.0%	14.4%	19.0%	21.0%
Widowed	1.4	1.3	1.8	1.0	1.4
Divorced	15.6	16.3	14.2	15.1	15.7
Separated	8.7	8.4	9.1	8.2	7.9
Never married	58.6	58.0	60.5	56.7	54.1
Education					
8th grade or less	13.1%	12.7%	14.2%	15.6%	17.7%
Some high school	33.4	31.7	36.6	38.2	41.3
High school graduate	40.0	42.5	35.3	33.1	29.2
Some college or more	13.5	13.1	14.0	13.1	11.8
Military Service					
Veteran	11.7%	11.9%	11.1%	15.5%	21.2%
Nonveteran	88.3	88.1	88.9	84.5	78.8
U.S. Citizenship					
Citizen	91.8%	93.2%	89.1%	–	–
Noncitizen	8.2	6.8	10.9	–	–
Number of jail inmates	507,026	318,068	169,377	395,554	223,552

Data were missing for marital status on 0.1% of the inmates; for education, 0.7%; for military service, 0.1%; and for citizenship, 0.1%.

*Total includes inmates with an unknown conviction or no offense.

†This includes Asians, Pacific Islanders, American Indians, Alaska Natives, and other racial groups.

– Not available.

Source: C. W. Harlow (1998, April). *Profile of Jail Inmates, 1996.* Washington, DC: Bureau of Justice Statistics.

jail. Because the use of drugs in jail can result in serious overdoses or even death, inmates manifesting the signs of drug use require immediate attention. Drug trafficking in a facility can also cause other problems, including intimidation, coercion, and possible injury to inmates who find themselves in debt to those supplying the drugs. Thus, dealing with the problem and treatment are essential (Hecht, 1992).

Alcohol abusers arrested for driving a vehicle while under the influence (DUI) form another portion of the jail inmate population—about 7 percent in 1997 (Maruschak, 1999). Convicted DUI offenders served an average of 11 months in jail, and 43 percent had prior DUIs or had been sentenced for other crimes.

Processing alcoholics into jails can pose difficult and potentially dangerous problems for both staff and inmates. If the arrestee's addiction is severe, sudden withdrawal often results in episodes that require prompt medical treatment. In addition, some inmates who look to be heavily under the influence may not have been drinking at all but instead are suffering from a chemical imbalance resulting from diabetes.

The loss of self-control due to alcohol intoxication makes many drunks very uncooperative during the intake and detoxification process and may even lead to violent behavior. This is not surprising considering the National Institute on Alcohol Abuse and Alcoholism indicates that 25 percent of alcoholics have antisocial personality characteristics (Samuels, 1991). Thus, the training of jail staff in the nonviolent management and control of the intoxicated is important. Given the high incidence of alcohol abusers entering our jails, mandatory drug and alcohol screening standards need to be developed (Mays, Fields, & Thompson, 1991). These regulations must make allowances for jail size, different populations, and availability of resources. For this to become a reality, states must share in funding for treatment programs because local governments lack sufficient resources to effectively screen, house, and treat drug- and alcohol-dependent inmates (Mays et al., 1991).

Many treatment clinics refuse to deal with violent drinkers, making a good detoxification treatment program in every jail even more important. Most megajail systems (over 1,000 inmates) have detox treatment programs of some kind, but small jails (under 50 inmates) lack sufficient resources for adequate detox programs. As a result, detoxification is often done without appropriate counseling or treatment.

In larger cities and counties, "common drunk" arrestees have begun to be diverted from jails into residential **detoxification centers,** which specialize in treating alcoholics. This is best done if the jail works in tandem with an outside community agency; for example, the Elmwood Deuce Alcohol Treatment Program in Santa Clara County, California, combined the efforts of the Santa Clara County Bureau of Alcohol Services with the Santa Clara County Department of Correction and the Santa Clara Adult Probation Program to provide services for alcoholic arrestees (Samuels, 1991).

Mentally Ill Inmates

A substantial number of inmates entering jail suffer from mental illness. **Deinstitutionalization**—the closing of centers that housed and treated the mentally ill in favor of community-level treatment—during the last 30 years has resulted in relatively large numbers of mentally ill persons reentering the community without support, with many becoming homeless. In most counties, the jail is the largest repository for this population (Zupan, 1991). The impairments these inmates have can lead to behavior that causes conflicts with other inmates, an inability to understand or follow instructions, and self-destructive behavior. Obviously, this category of inmate can be best served in mental health facilities and institutions geared to meet their needs.

A 1992 survey of 1,391 city and county jails found that more than 1 in 14 people in these jails were seriously mentally ill (Torrey et al., 1992). This represented 7.2 percent of the inmate population—a tenfold increase in their proportion since 1980. Thus, on any given day in 1991 jails held more than 30,700 people with serious mental conditions. More recent data show that in 1996, 10 percent of the jail inmates reported a mental or emotional problem (Harlow, 1998). Torrey et al. also found that 29 percent of the jails confined seriously mentally ill persons with no criminal charges against them, often because communities lacked facilities for psychiatric emergencies. Even though most were arrested on criminal charges, the vast majority of their offenses were trivial misdemeanors (e.g., disorderly conduct) that were manifestations of their disorders. About one third of these individuals were homeless, and jail represented one part of a continuous cycle that includes the street as well as stays in jails and mental hospitals. Moreover, despite the best efforts of jail staff, many of these inmates were cruelly abused, suffering torment, rape, and beatings by other inmates. The net result is that jails are being used as dumping grounds for this group.

Torrey et al. (1992) made the following recommendations to alleviate the problem:

1. States that fail to amend their laws to eliminate the jailing of mentally ill people not charged with a crime should lose eligibility for mental health block grants.

2. More jail diversion programs for the mentally ill are needed.

3. Evaluation of the seriously mentally ill should occur within 24 hours after booking.

4. There should be a transfer of state mental health funds to jails in states where mental health authorities have failed to set up **jail diversion programs** (programs to remove the mentally ill from jails).

5. Follow-up of the mentally ill when released from jails should be required.

6. Training should be provided for jail officers who deal with the mentally ill.

7. Mental health trainees should be required to spend a minimum of 6 hours in on-site training in jails.

8. Mental health professionals should be required to provide mental health services to the jail 2 hours each week.

9. There needs to be greatly improved federal and state statistical reporting to reflect the existence of the seriously mentally ill in jails.

10. Each jurisdiction with a jail should have a standing mental illness committee that includes representatives from the jail, local mental health department,

The Mentally Ill in Jails

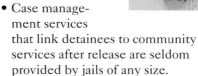

CLOSE-UP

Key Issues

In today's overcrowded jails, an alarmingly high number of inmates are affected with acute serious mental disorders requiring mental health treatment and service. Few jails are equipped to provide comprehensive services, yet they are legally and morally bound to meet at least a minimum standard of care.

Key Findings

Most have no policies or procedures for managing and supervising mentally disordered detainees. Numerous challenges to providing treatment are indicated in the following:

- Approximately 84 percent of survey participants reported that mental health services are received by one tenth or fewer of their inmates.

- Smaller jails (those with capacities of up to 90) tend to provide screening and suicide prevention services but little else, whereas jails with capacities of more than 1,000 can offer comprehensive programs with multiple service components.

- Case management services that link detainees to community services after release are seldom provided by jails of any size.

Source: H. Steadman & B. M. Veysey (1997). Providing Services for Jail Inmates with Mental Disorders. American Jails, 11*(2): 23.*

---

local public psychiatric inpatient unit, and the local chapter of the National Alliance for the Mentally Ill.

Our Close-Up details the results of an NIJ study to identify innovative policies and practices to address the needs of mentally disordered offenders in the nation's jails, while our Program Focus provides an example of an interface between jail mental health staff and programs in the community.

Five principles developed by researchers suggest how jails should approach this issue:

- The jail is, and should remain, primarily a correctional facility.

- Minimum professionally acceptable mental health services are required in every jail and lockup.

- Jail mental health services should focus on screening and identification of need, crisis intervention, short-term treatment or stabilization, and case management or referral.

- There is no single best way to organize services (Steadman & Veysey, 1997, p. 23).

- As with prisons, the more progressive thinkers favor treating many of those with substance abuse and mental health problems as inmates with co-occurring disorders (Kerle, 1998).

Suicidal Inmates

Suicide has been the leading nonnatural cause of death within jails. In 1991, there were 131 suicides; 124 occurred in 1992; and 234 occurred in 1993. Suicides represented a large majority of all nonnatural deaths in jails during these years (Beck, Bonczar, & Gilliard, 1993;

Perkins et al., 1995). Depression, anxiety, embarrassment over their arrest, and the fear that incarceration may devastate their lives lead some to decide that suicide is a preferable alternative. An in-depth survey of jails in which 339 suicides occurred found that 30 percent occurred in holding facilities, with the remainder occurring in detention facilities (Hayes & Rowan, 1988). An analysis of those who committed suicide in jail follows.

Characteristics of Suicidal Inmates

- 72% were white
- 94% were male
- Mean age was 30
- 52% were single
- 75% were detained on nonviolent charges
- 27% were detained on alcohol- or drug-related charges
- 89% were confined as detainees
- 78% had prior charges, yet only 10% were previously held on personal or violent offenses
- 60% were intoxicated at the time of incarceration
- 30% of suicides occurred between midnight and 6:00 A.M.
- 94% of suicides were by hanging; 48% used their bedding
- Two out of three victims were in isolation
- 51% of suicides occurred within the first 24 hours of incarceration
- 29% occurred within the first 3 hours (pp. X–XI)

CTAP for the Chronically Mentally Ill

PROGRAM FOCUS

Community Treatment Alternatives Program (CTAP) in the Jefferson County (Kentucky) Jail is a program implemented, run, and staffed by Seven Counties Mental Health Center in Louisville, Kentucky. Its purpose is to provide community-based mental health services as an alternative to incarceration for adjudicated offenders with chronic mental illness. Chronic offender status (usually misdemeanants) and severe mental illness (e.g., bipolar disorders) are the criteria for admission.

Clients are referred to the program by other mental health professionals, judges, an attorney, the court liaison, or a jail mental health worker. Caseworkers from seven counties visit the jail each morning to assess potential clients. Based on a review of this assessment, the caseworker decides whether the detainee is appropriate for the program.

If the decision is affirmative, correctional services, community men-

tal health services, and the courts work together to develop a coordinated plan for securing the detainee's release from jail and assist in meeting the detainee's mental health needs. CTAP detainees are released from jail directly into the community; approximately half live in their homes; others reside in boarding facilities or other programs providing housing, such as the Volunteers of America's Mentally Ill Men at Risk for Homelessness Program.

The CTAP caseworker places a high priority on helping to set up appropriate housing before an inmate's release date. At times, judges cooperate in this effort by, for example, delaying release for a week or so until housing is found.

Detainees in the community are supervised closely. In the first month after release, the detainee's contact is mainly with the CTAP caseworker. After that, the case is turned over to Seven Counties staff. Detainees usually come into the center for appointments and, in addition, Seven Counties staff do home visits to check life

management skills. Medications are monitored closely; some detainees must come to the center each day to receive their medications, whereas others are given injections.

The monthly meetings among jail mental health staff, CTAP caseworkers, and the court liaison provide an opportunity to strategize and decide who in the jail should be targeted for the program's services. CTAP detainees must sign a contract that commits them to the program for a 2-year period and sets out the jail term in case of revocation for such actions as failure to participate in the treatment plan. When a contract is violated, the detainee appears before the judge, who can change the sentence from treatment to the contract-specified jail term or to a new 2-year contract with additional prospective jail time added.

Source: Adapted from H. Steadman & B. M. Veysey (1997). Providing Services for Jail Inmates with Mental Disorders. American Jails, 11(2): p. 23.

Jail staff can be taught to recognize and successfully intervene in situations involving potentially suicidal inmates. Staff need to watch for physical signs of depression, including:

- sadness and crying
- withdrawal or silence
- sudden loss or gain in appetite
- insomnia
- mood variations
- lethargy

At-risk inmates may exhibit other warning signs and symptoms that include:

- Intoxication/withdrawal
- Talking about or threatening suicide
- Previous suicide attempts
- History of mental illness

- Projecting hopelessness or helplessness
- Speaking unrealistically about the future and getting out of jail
- Increasing difficulty relating to others
- Dealing ineffectively with the present; preoccupied with past
- Giving away possessions; packing belongings
- Severe aggressiveness
- Paranoid delusions or hallucinations (Hayes & Rowan, 1988, p. 41)

Professional standards and practices require that staff interview new inmates and complete a comprehensive medical and mental health screening on each within 14 days of entering the jail (Parrish, 2000). If this indicates a suicide potential, further processing must be stopped and a mental health evaluation must be conducted. If mental health resources are not readily available, a suicide watch must be instituted so that the detainee is continually observed by staff to prevent self-injury. Individuals will not always answer the initial questions truthfully (Kennedy, 1994); therefore, it is important that all inmates be closely observed and supervised during the first 72 hours of incarceration. Failure to supervise this vulnerable population will allow them the time and certainly the opportunity to kill or seriously injure themselves (Rowan, 1991).

Juveniles in Adult Jails

The placement of juveniles, usually between the ages of 14 and 17, within adult jails has been a continuing problem. Between 1990 (2,301) and 1998 (8,090), the number of juveniles held in adult jails increased 3½ times. In 1998, of the more than 8,000 juveniles housed in our jails, 6,542 were held as adults (Gilliard, 1999). Juveniles constitute about 1.33 percent of the jail population. Some critics argue that no juveniles should be housed in adult jails (Gilliard, 1998; Zupan, 1991). Schwartz (1991) has proposed legislation prohibiting the placement of juveniles in jails under any circumstances. However, in many counties with small populations, juvenile institutions do not exist and the only alternative is the county jail. In larger jurisdictions, juveniles may be transferred to the jail by the order of a court due to the seriousness of their crimes.

Throughout our history, many instances of abuse of juveniles within adult institutions have occurred. Juveniles have been victims of sexual assaults, physical and emotional violence, and intimidation. Special conditions, standards, and laws protect juveniles when they are placed in jails, including

1. *Separation:* Strict separation by sight and sound of juveniles from the adult population. This requires jails to have separate living units, recreation, and educational facilities for juveniles that totally isolate them from adults.

2. *Judicial Review and Authorization:* Juveniles cannot be incarcerated in a jail unless this confinement is reviewed and ordered by a court. Arbitrary placement in jails without judicial review and approval is almost universally prohibited.

3. *Nutrition:* Juveniles require different nutritional standards and, therefore, two different menus and food service policies are required to ensure proper nutrition for both populations.

Recognizing the dangers of keeping juveniles in jails, Congress passed the **Juvenile Justice and Delinquency Prevention Act** (JJDP) in 1974. It mandated that juveniles detained in adult jails be out of the sight and sound of adult inmates. To obtain federal funds, states were required to comply with the JJDP Act. That threat did not work, because in 1980, most states were still out of compliance; so Congress amended the JJDP Act to end the practice of juvenile jailings. However, by 1988, 13 states and territories still were not in compliance with these laws (Sweet, 1991); some still had not complied by 2000. Unfortunately, the separation requirement for juveniles in jails has been relaxed, and, depending on the circumstances, jails can now hold juveniles for longer periods of time without violating the requirements to receive federal grants (Kerle, 2000).

Juvenile inmates are typically charged with more serious offenses, including multiple drug-trafficking offenses, sex offenses, aggravated robberies, felonious assaults, murder, and weapons charges. This population is characteristically young, streetwise, and gang-affiliated. These are individuals who are serving long sentences and are predisposed to defiant, aggressive, and violent behavior. However, some do not have the juvenile delinquency careers that their counterparts have. Some of these youths are serious first-time offenders with minimal correctional instructional history and minimal institutional adaptability skills.

From a mental health standpoint, the majority are diagnosed with conduct disorders, a forerunner of the adult diagnoses of antisocial personality. In conjunction with their mental health problems, these youths often are also substance abusers and suffer from other major psychological disorders. Moreover, they often face long sentences that give them little to look forward to. When you combine these factors, it is not difficult to understand why they are management problems. Specifically, they're prone to be aggressive and violent, often without provocation, which places them in situations where COs must use correctional behavioral techniques to manage their behavior. According to Dugan (1998), "Gang-related activity will be much more significant in a setting that might be less structured and supervised than what they might have experienced in a juvenile setting. Unsupervised activity on a unit housing a juvenile population is a security and behavior management nightmare waiting to happen" (p. 83).

A high staff-to-resident ratio, direct increased visual supervision, and heavy structured programming, that is staff-led and managed, can reduce this activity. Unfortunately, few jails can afford to provide the types of resources necessary for this type of supervision and programming (Dugan, 1998). Other factors that require attention include:

- protection of vulnerable youths from (1) the sexual advances of older adult inmates or (2) from being forced to give up property, conceal drugs or weapons, or perform other favors.

- their legal right to education. Although most jails provide GED programs these largely self-taught programs will not meet mandatory

Can Jails Handle Juveniles?

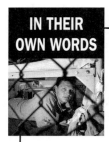
IN THEIR OWN WORDS

I think that the incredible overreaction that prompted advocates to demand that juveniles be completely removed from adult-serving facilities represented a profound lack of trust for the jail profession. Some of that distrust was surely earned, but there was an overreaction. I believe that jails can properly separate juveniles from adults, by sight and sound, in well-designed and well-managed facilities, and that in many instances such a solution is much better for the juveniles who otherwise suffer displacement from their communities (often by hundreds of miles) and end up with less adequate facilities. All of this leads to my belief that jails are much more capable than they are given credit for. The field has come such a long way in the past 20 years and continues to rocket forward toward professionalism and excellence. I am therefore sensitive to the attitudes espoused by the juvenile advocates and others who want to write jails off.
Source: R. Miller (2000), president of CRS, Inc.—which does consulting on jails and publishes several national jail reports. Personal communication.

requirements for the education of those who are of school age. (Collins, 1996)

Finally, some say that jails can handle juveniles. See our In Their Own Words feature, "Can Jails Handle Juveniles?" in which Miller (2000) states his views on this issue.

Women

In 1998, females constituted about 11 percent of the total jail population (Gilliard, 1999). Although women represent a small proportion of the inmate population, state laws require that programs and services be equally available to them (Dale, 1991). This creates special and unique problems not usually found in managing the male population. Similar to men, women fall into many different categories requiring different levels of security. There are female inmates who are mentally and physically ill, suicidal, assaultive, or in need of protective custody or of otherwise being separated from other inmates. They must be segregated according to standards established by law. Except for a few large jurisdictions, most jails do not have the physical plant or financial resources to provide adequate separate living accommodations. In most small- and medium-sized facilities, all female inmates are either housed together or their living unit is subdivided into smaller clusters to handle the many different classifications of inmates (Schafer & Dellinger, 1993a, 1993b).

To protect women from verbal and physical harassment and potential assault, state laws and professional standards mandate that male and female inmates be housed in units separated by sight and sound. However, some jurisdictions find it advantageous to mix male and female inmates during periods of educational, substance abuse treatment, and other programs. This is also the case during the booking process (Lucas, 1999).

The History of Jails

The English jail was the model on which American jails were developed. The colonial version of English jail facilities was very informal and used only to detain those awaiting trial. Later, these facilities began to be used to house convicted minor offenders. We look at jails in England and in the United States.

Jails in England

The **gaol,** as the jail was referred to in England, was an institution developed in medieval England. One of the first confinement facilities in the City of London (although not a gaol in the strict sense) was the Tower of London. Construction began after William I arrived following the Battle of Hastings in 1066. Various small gaols were constructed and used as the city developed under the different Norman kings (Moynahan, 1992). In 1166, Henry II ordered jails to be constructed in every shire (local government entities similar to our counties) (Pugh, 1968). As towns and cities grew, and the number of displaced persons and crime increased, more laws were passed to deal with this problem. The vagrancy laws passed between 1349 and 1743 were intended to further control the problem of displaced persons (Chambliss, 1964).

As noted in Chapter 4, during the 17th century, the house of corrections was developed in England. These institutions, which were closely related to jails, served as facilities for both punishment and reform. During the 18th century, they merged with gaols and were housed under one roof, where they served as places for both the detention of suspects and penal facilities for convicted petty offenders (Barnes & Teeters, 1951). By the 19th century, these houses of corrections had been completely amalgamated with jails (Goldfarb, 1973).

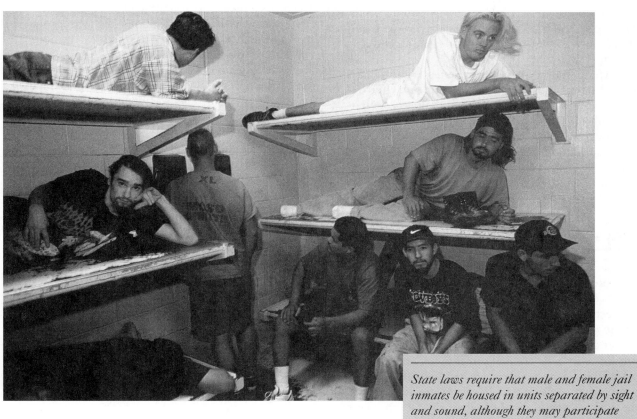

State laws require that male and female jail inmates be housed in units separated by sight and sound, although they may participate together in educational and other programs.

Jails in the United States

The first jail built in America was constructed in Virginia, during the establishment of the Jamestown settlement, and began housing inmates in 1608. Colonial jails were rarely used as places of imprisonment or punishment but were instead employed for pretrial confinement (Rothman, 1971). Early jails had no distinctive architecture or special procedures and were located close to the stocks and pillory or whipping post. They had no cells; instead, inmates were housed in small rooms holding up to 30 people.

Consistent with the household model, the keeper and his family lived in one of the rooms, while prisoners lived in the others. Inmates were required to supply their own amenities, either by purchasing them from the jailer or getting them from their families. This practice of collecting money from inmates for services was known as the "fee system." Although this system was modified, it saw a resurgence in the 1990s when jails began charging fees for medical service, room and board, educational service, and hygiene supplies. This reflects the least eligibility principle described in Chapter 16.

Houses of correction and workhouses were often established near the public jail. Their functions included the punishment of rogues, vagabonds, and strangers and putting the idle poor to work (Rothman, 1971). As in England, jails and workhouses gradually merged, and jails have since served both pretrial detention and correctional functions.

After World War II, the United States spent billions on interstate highways and roads, undertook a large expansion of schools and universities, and initiated a monetary assault on the increasingly polluted environment. Also during this period, the jail-building industry experienced a multibillion dollar construction bonanza. From the 1970s through 1993, more than 1,500 jails were built—most to replace older facilities (Kerle, 1993).

Security and Jail Designs

Specific architectural features of jails greatly influence how inmates are supervised, protected, and managed. Like other community agencies (e.g., schools), jails must effectively manage groups of individuals. The architecture of jails and the manner of their construction can either strictly limit management options or expand opportunities for efficient and effective services. Jail architecture began to evolve dramatically in the 1970s. This evolution coincided with the intervention of the federal courts, which brought to light the fact that past design, construction, and management techniques were flawed. Today, three principal jail designs are used in the United States: linear intermittent surveillance, podular remote surveillance, and podular direct supervision (Parrish, 2000).

Linear Intermittent Surveillance

The **linear design** is the older, more traditional design for jails. In linear facilities, cells are constructed in long straight rows aligned with corridors where correctional staff walk from cell to cell to supervise inmate activities (Figure 18.1). This inhibits the ability of staff to supervise inmates because they can only see those cells directly in their view, which may represent only a fraction of those within an assigned area. It is impossible, in a linear design, to observe all cells from a single location. Therefore, inmate misbehavior, vandalism, and violence can occur when the staff are not directly in front of a given location or cell.

The traditional linear design usually lacks sufficient space for recreation, leisure, and program activities, which are vital for maintaining a calm and safe environment. Also, the lack of continuous supervision means these facilities require maximum security construction, equipment, and furnishings. However, in spite of this, graffiti and vandalism remain significant problems.

Podular Remote Surveillance

To enhance the ability of staff to observe the activities of all inmates within their living units, the architectural designs of the 1970s introduced the **podular remote surveillance** style of inmate management (Figure 18.2). These facilities resolved many problems of linear intermittent design by changing the basic configuration of the inmate living areas. This was done by situating inmate cells on the exterior perimeter and providing open interior space for inmate activities. Secure control rooms allow staff to observe inmate areas and activities from a central and protected location, rather than patrolling corridors.

Although this improved surveillance of inmate activities, secure control rooms effectively isolated staff from the inmate environment. Even though there was greater observation capability, this design did not improve, and perhaps even reduced, the ability of staff to supervise inmates actively and effectively. Podular remote facilities also use "secure" construction, equipment, and furnishings. However, they still experience graffiti and vandalism as well as other problems. One administrator reported that inmates considered the officers weak because they stayed out of the pod when problems arose. Also, when they called for assistance, responding staff did not know what they were walking into because of their limited contact with inmates (Heuer, 1993).

Podular Direct Supervision

In the 1970's, the federal government designed and constructed three pretrial federal detention centers (jails) in

Typical Housing Unit

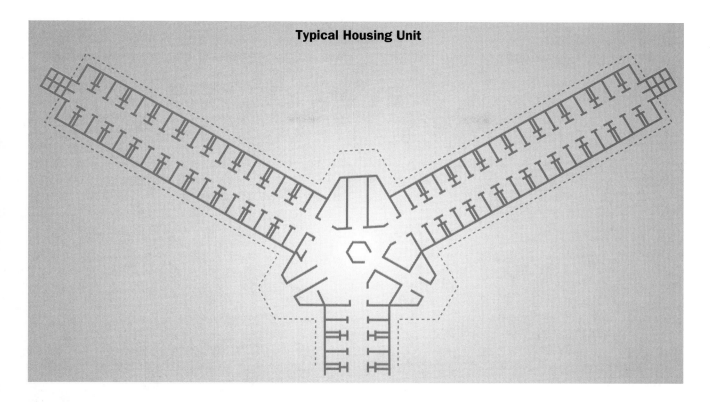

Figure 18.1 *Linear Intermittent Surveillance*

Source: U.S. Department of Justice, National Institute of Corrections (1993). *Podular, Direct Supervision Jails Information Packet.* Washington, DC: U.S. Department of Justice.

Typical Housing Unit

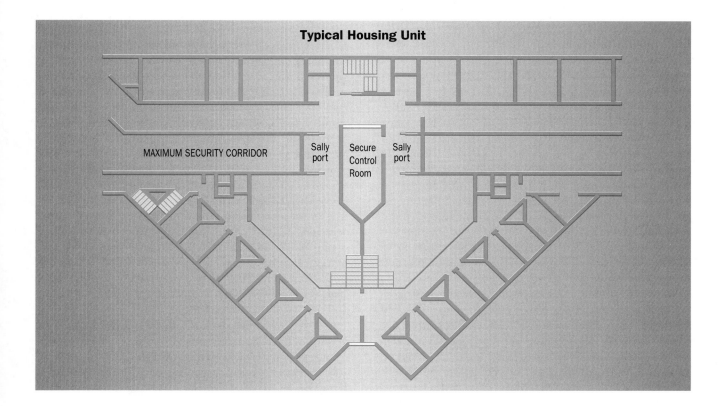

MAXIMUM SECURITY CORRIDOR

Sally port

Secure Control Room

Sally port

Figure 18.2 *Podular Remote Surveillance*

Source: U.S. Department of Justice, National Institute of Corrections (1993). *Podular, Direct Supervision Jails Information Packet.* Washington, DC: U.S. Department of Justice.

This direct supervision facility in California houses a daily average of 2,600 prisoners. Inmates are locked in groups of about thirty in living pods separated from other inmates by numerous locked doors and inaccessible corridors; they are guarded from above by sheriff's deputies in control booths.

New York City, San Diego, and Chicago. They incorporated **podular direct supervision** designs that permanently situated staff among the inmates within each housing unit and used "soft" furnishings, such as wood doors, regular beds, and tables, along with other furnishings that tended to normalize the living environment (Figure 18.3). In these facilities, inmates were confined fewer hours in their rooms; so, they had more recreation, leisure, and program activities and received intensive personal supervision. This design changed the traditional character of a jail and required that inmates take more responsibility for their behavior (Nelson, 1988; Zupan, 1991). The movement of staff about the pod and their constant interaction with inmates enabled them to control these units. A survey found that administrators of these facilities reported that staff felt safer and had fewer incidents of violence than their counterparts in indirect facilities. This research also suggested that it cost an average of 45 percent less to build and 33 percent less to staff and maintain than indirect supervision jails (Farbstein & Wiener, 1989).

Several factors slowed local adoption of the direct supervision jail concept. These included beliefs that county inmates were more violent than federal inmates,

these facilities were prohibitively expensive to build and operate, and because of their normalized furnishings the public would not consider them to be punitive enough to punish offenders sufficiently. Many believed inmates would wreck the furnishings and violence would escalate. These questions were answered in 1981, when Contra Costa County, California, opened the first county-managed direct supervision facility. Since then, this style has rapidly been accepted throughout the country. Nevertheless, there is still some resistance to the adoption of these models, primarily based on the fact that these facilities provide a more normalized environment and also require COs to communicate, manage, and interact with inmates (Farbstein & Wiener, 1989). Nevertheless from an economic perspective, these facilities are actually cheaper to build and operate. The reason people think direct supervision facilities are more expensive is because they do not look traditional (Parrish, 2000). Another factor is that this model does not offer the same efficiencies of jails with less than 100 beds—which includes two thirds of all jails (Miller, 2000).

Further research over a 10-year period, beginning when one jail opened a new direct supervision facility, found that of 70 categories of negative behavior there was a reduction in 51, particularly in aggressive behavior. However, as the daily population of this facility exceeded its rated capacity by 12 percent the number of reported infractions "skyrocketed to 116 percent over the previous two years" (Bayens, Williams, & Smykla, 1997). This

Typical Housing Unit

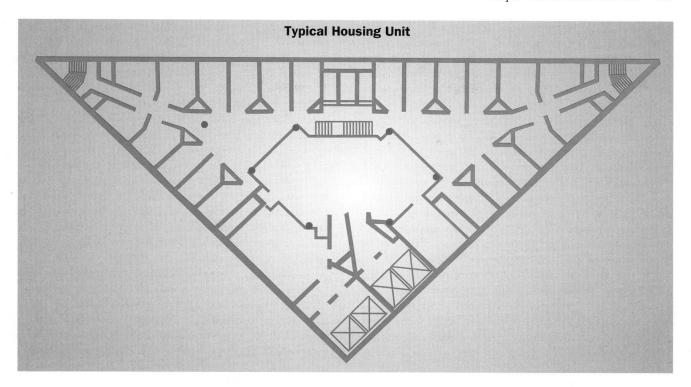

Figure 18.3 *Podular Direct Supervision*

Source: U.S. Department of Justice, National Institute of Corrections (1993). *Podular, Direct Supervision Jails Information Packet.* Washington, DC: U.S. Department of Justice.

shows that even the best of facilities and supervision styles will be adversely affected by overcrowding.

Security and Control

The primary goal and responsibility of jails is to provide and maintain a controlled environment that ensures the safety and security of the public, staff, and inmates. Control of inmates can be achieved in a variety of ways (e.g., the style and quality of the facility; the presence of solid walls, bars, and locks). However, as is the case in a variety of institutions, architecture alone is a short-sighted approach to control because it fails to consider the human factor.

The outer perimeter of the institution forms the first line of control. This consists of secure walls, protected windows, and controlled access to the points of entrance and exit. If it is poorly designed, not routinely inspected, or otherwise ignored, the facility will soon be unable to perform its primary function—to maintain inmates in a controlled environment. A sound and well-maintained perimeter allows maximum flexibility in the interior design and normal operations of the facility. This is particularly important for jails because many of them are located in the downtown area of a city or in proximity to populated areas.

Recently, **campus-style facilities** have begun replacing older, more traditional stone-walled jails. These jails, which house inmates of all levels of security, are usually double-fenced, with alarms; are surrounded with barbed or "razor" wire; and have external mobile patrols. These closely grouped, freestanding structures allow for more effective classification (Parrish, 2000). Inside the perimeter the buildings are arranged in a circular fashion with the inside green space often used for outside recreation. Many new jails, especially in urban downtown justice centers, are designed to blend with the surrounding court and civic architecture. These rely only on the building exterior to provide adequate security against escape.

Supervision and Jail Design

Facility design enables staff to supervise and be in contact with inmates, which enhances control. Indefensible space (e.g., concealed alcoves and dark corridors) has the opposite effect. Inmate spaces require continual inspection so that predatory inmates cannot use them to carry out their own agendas. The modern podular jail enables staff, at a quick glance or a short walk, to see and hear the activities within the entire living unit.

The staffing and operational costs of a facility are directly proportional to the number of inmates a single staff member can supervise in a unit. As modern jails have adopted professional standards, classification, and greater staff training, the number of inmates that can be supervised has increased.

Smaller groups of inmates are easier to control, but the cost of doing so is high. Classification of inmates into groupings based on their anticipated need for supervision allows the best allocation of resources. For the less violent and compliant, larger groupings are appropriate. For those posing a definable risk, small groupings with additional security controls and staff supervision may be necessary. In the 1970s, most jail professionals believed that 50 inmates was the maximum number that could be safely supervised in jail living units by one CO. Today, staff in direct supervision facilities are routinely supervising 60 to 70 low-security inmates. Sometimes, however, a second officer is assigned to units with more than 70 inmates (Parrish, 2000). Other variables include the housing configuration and the way services are handled. If inmates go out of the pod for services (e.g., educational programming or medical attention), then officers have a higher level of supervision because they are not all in the pod at once.

In small jails (50 beds or under), "proper staffing . . . has proved to be a thorn in the side of many localities" (Kerle, 1998). Ideally, these jails should have at least two officers per shift, one to interact with inmates and another to operate the control center—and when possible, a third officer for backup (Miller, 2000). One problem is that "from a practical political standpoint most county boards will never appropriate the necessary funds for two officers, particularly on the midnight shift. A survey of these facilities found that:

> Twelve percent of the newer facilities failed to provide any staff, relying instead on radio dispatchers (who by definition cannot leave their post to check inmates), electronic or other unspecified means considered equally unsatisfactory by jail experts. Thirty nine percent failed to provide female staff at all times while female inmates were in jail. (Kimme, 1988)

The Jail Admissions Process

Intake, booking, receiving, classification, and orientation are terms that refer to the procedures used to introduce newly arrested individuals into local corrections. During the **intake process,** a term that describes the overall admissions process, certain types of information must be acquired from those being admitted to ensure the health and safety of other inmates while protecting and maintaining the institution's security. This information includes who they are and whether they are who they claim to be; whether they have consumed a dangerous drug and/or alcohol; if they are injured or in some form of distress; and if they are violent or potentially suicidal. Knowledge of these factors and others will help determine an appropriate housing assignment.

In older and more traditional linear jails, the intake space was purposely designed with stark cells and "drunk tanks" to temporarily house new intakes. In these facilities, violent offenders are admitted with the nonviolent, the sophisticated with the unsophisticated, the predators with the prey; and many are intoxicated. Thus, the intake unit can be the most violent and disruptive one in the entire jail. Another factor that can make the intake process more dangerous is the influx of a large number of arrestees at one time (Lucas, 1999).

In direct supervision facilities, the intake unit encourages and promotes normalized behavior. This includes an open environment, reduced levels of sound, normalized furnishings, and immediate and thorough screening and supervision by professional staff. These factors have helped to reduce levels of suicide, violence, vandalism, and disruptive behavior in these facilities (Wallerstein, 1989).

Drunk drivers, misdemeanants, traffic offenders, shoplifters, and others arrested on minor felony charges will often post bail or be released to a variety of programs serving as alternatives to incarceration. Even those arrested on more serious felony charges may soon be free either on bail or through a reduction or dismissal of charges. For many, then, jail is a short-term confinement experience that never goes further than the initial booking and release process. At some time during the intake process, each inmate will have the opportunity to do several things. Depending on state law and agency policy, this includes making two or more telephone calls to family, friends, or attorneys, and/or arranging either a cash, property, or bail bond within the first few hours of confinement. These calls are important because they notify family and friends of an arrestee's custody status and, for many, begin the process of obtaining the means of release. For those remaining, it can be the start of an extended incarceration experience.

Medical and Mental Health Screening

One of the first steps in the intake process is screening inmates for medical and mental health problems. Jails have a legal obligation to identify and treat arrested individuals who are sick, injured, overdosed, or subject to emotional distress (Dale, 1989). Each year in the United States, many individuals who appear merely intoxicated die of a variety of causes, including diabetic comas, drug overdoses, or alcohol poisoning. Many minor first offenders attempt or commit suicide when they find

The booking process includes obtaining the new inmate's fingerprints, which are compared with those in existing fingerprint files.

themselves alone, embarrassed, and depressed because of their incarceration.

In large jail systems, medical examinations and mental health interviews are part of the intake process. Many small jails cannot afford to have specially trained personnel continually available to identify and treat the variety of problems experienced by many of those arrested. (See Chapter 17 for a discussion of prison health services.)

Are you a diabetic? Are you presently taking any prescription medication? Have you ever used drugs? If so which ones, and when was the last time you used them? Are you now thinking about or have you ever thought about injuring or harming yourself or others? These are some examples of questions that must be answered to protect the jail against potential liability, while assisting those in distress. However, many inmates fail to answer these questions honestly, so staff must be aware of the various symptoms that may suggest an inmate has a particular problem. Once a problem is identified, prompt action by jail personnel is required to ensure against any future or further injury. Whether the problem is medical, one of drug ingestion, or psychological, a trained professional should examine and evaluate the situation (Jones, 1989).

Jails differ from prisons in some ways. In comparing a 1,000-bed jail with a 1,000-bed prison over 1 year, the population turnover in the prison is around 1,500, whereas jail turnover exceeds 24,000! This has profound implications for medical treatment in the jail setting. A 1,000-bed jail has about 450 new admissions each week—spread unevenly throughout the week with peak times usually during the late night and early morning hours on weekends. Most are under the influence of drugs and/or alcohol, and 8 percent suffer from mental illness. More than 50 percent of the jail population will leave the jail within 24 to 48 hours of being booked. A medical model set up to provide physical exams and diagnostic services quickly could provide these arrestees with invaluable medical information (O'Toole, 1997). For example, if a person booked into the jail was given a tuberculin (TB) test, which takes at least 72 hours to read, and he or she left jail before the results were available, the person would not know if he or she had TB. A much better interface between jail medical programs and county public health agencies would help. Most inmates do not have a medical plan or a regular doctor, which makes it imperative that more attention be paid to their health from the standpoint of protection for the public at large (Kerle, 2000).

Inmate Identification

Once cleared medically, the inmate must be accurately identified through a **booking process** that obtains personal information such as age, height, weight, date and location of birth, address, next of kin, social security number, and driver's license number. For positive identification, fingerprints are taken, classified, and compared with those in local, state, and national automated fingerprint files. If a fingerprint match is confirmed, identification is complete. For first-time arrestees, a new file will be started for future reference.

A photograph, or "mug shot," is taken of each person booked. Today, the integration of computer graphics and video allow **video mug shots** to be stored in an automated system and transferred for viewing to any desired location. Once identification and assessment are completed, inmates are either released on bail, on their own recognizance, or on a promise-to-appear citation. Those not released will be thoroughly searched, all their clothing and property will be removed and stored, and they will be issued jail clothing and personal hygiene items. They are then transferred to an intake housing unit to await classification, orientation, and further housing assignment.

Classification and Orientation

As we discussed in Chapter 8, **classification** is a management process that separates inmates according to preestablished security and custody levels and other characteristics (e.g., the need for protective custody or special medical problems). It allows assignment to compatible groups, which reduces violence and conflict while enhancing facility programming. Jails that do not adequately classify inmates can expect continual violence and disruptive conduct. The nationally recognized NIC objective classification system is generally considered the standard classification model. However, in smaller jails, the classification process is usually subjective (i.e., it rests on the officers' feelings about the inmate) (Parrish, 2000). Subjective systems take many of the same factors into consideration but are based on the limited resources available (Brennan & Wells, 1992).

During the **orientation process,** inmates are acquainted with the rules and regulations applying to conduct while in custody and the requirements for and availability of work, education, religious, and substance abuse programs. Institutions that have formal orientation programs may wait 24 to 72 hours before holding these sessions because many detainees will make bail during this period. Orientation information is usually presented in small groups using videotapes, pamphlets, or classroom instruction. Institutions without formal orientation programs may just pass out booklets or other printed materials to inform inmates about facility rules and procedures. Once inmates have been completely processed, they can be assigned to appropriate living quarters.

Jail Management

Irrespective of jail size, effective management requires that jail administrators establish and enforce policies requiring all command and supervisory jail staff to make frequent visits, each day and each shift, to inmate living areas. This proactive posture, which has been labeled "management by walking around" (see Chapter 11), can prevent lazy or weak staff from retreating from inmate contact. Lack of contact by management with line staff, insufficient interaction with inmates, and failure to conduct routine inspections are management deficiencies that allow small incidents and problems to fester into major problems such as disturbances or riots. Proper jail management requires jail administrators to be highly visible and accessible to the public, staff, and inmates. Our In Their Own Words feature, "A Jail Administrator Speaks Out," on page 458 provides a perspective on the management of a jail.

Legal Issues

Jails that properly classify and supervise inmates reduce tension and stress while increasing the feeling of safety among staff and inmates. A jail that fails to provide a safe environment for staff and inmates is not functioning according to constitutional standards (Catanese & Hennessey, 1989; Peed, 1989). A constitutionally acceptable environment requires adherence to standard safety codes, provides levels of supervision that adequately control violence, and corrects situations that violate basic inmate rights (Marchese, 1990). Failure to comply can often result in court-imposed judgments requiring jurisdictions to make changes far exceeding the cost of correcting and monitoring the initial problem. Tax dollars are much more effectively used when they provide safety in comparison to being paid out as damages and attorneys' fees. For example, in 1982, the federal court in San Francisco, California, fined the county $2.6 million and $300 per day for every inmate over the court-imposed population capacity. Even though inmates only win a few of the thousands of lawsuits filed each year against jail overcrowding and other correctional problems, the time and expense to the governments involved in these suits can be substantial (Dale, 1987; Hager, 1992).

Accreditation

The best method that jails can use to determine whether they are providing a safe environment is to go through the accreditation process. To be accredited jails must develop policies and procedures that can reduce the likelihood of successful inmate lawsuits (Henn, 1996). These also improve working conditions. Although accreditation is not required to operate a safe and effective jail, this process does "ensure that all areas are analyzed and none are overlooked because they require significant changes to meet standards. This provides an excellent incentive for jails to meet national standards" (Ryan & Plummer, 1999, p. 157). Further, this is an excellent way for small jails to acquire the funding necessary to meet constitutional standards for inmate life and health and safety standards (Todd, 1993). To meet accreditation standards, jail staff may engage in a variety of activities, including, but not limited to, rewriting potentially problematic policies, conducting mock audits, changing sanitation and security procedures, and obtaining feedback from several staff members.

Aside from the honor of being an accredited jail, other benefits can include:

- Improved staff morale and unification.

- Making staff aware of being one of the best in the country (only 100 jails out of 3,300 have been granted accreditation). It also allows department bragging rights in some states for being the only accredited facility or among an elite few (Wagner, 1999; Parrish, 2000).

- Transforming a department into a nationally recognized leader in corrections (Wagner, 1999).

- "[Setting] a pattern for consistent management throughout the facility by communicating to employees what is expected" (McCarthy, 1988, p. 88).

- Providing a basis for seeking funding from a county commission by showing objectively where the jail fails to meet national standards

with respect to programming and staffing. Following accreditation one small jail was able to convince the county board that their staffing levels were low considering the jail layout. This resulted in funding for four staff members (Todd, 1993).

Finally, for jails to overcome the belief that

what goes on behind the walls is a mystery and therefore bad, they must follow ACA accreditation standards that set professional levels of achievement and remove the mystery of what goes on in jails and maintain a community level of accountability that sets an agency among the elite of the correctional world. (Ryan & Plummer, 1999)

However, deficiencies uncovered during the accreditation process have no legal basis to require jails to make these changes. In contrast, problems discovered during state jail inspections can be required to be fixed under state law. Although jail inspections may not be popular with jail administrators, some local and state-elected officials believe they can serve as a much-needed push to require jails to clean and shape up substandard procedures and operations (Kerle, 1998).

Jail Capacity

Each jail has a rated, or a **design, capacity,** a figure that specifies the number of beds built (or remodeled) to accommodate more inmates. Thus, jails contain finite amounts of housing space

Severe overcrowding has created a boom in the construction of new jails like the "Twin Towers" jail in Los Angeles.

A Jail Administrator Speaks Out

IN THEIR OWN WORDS

As the administrator of a 3,400-bed jail system, I deal with a broad range of issues: 1,300 employees, a $75 million operating budget, 60,000 bookings per year, and an average daily census that routinely exceeds the capacity by 300 to 400 inmates. Based on more than 18 years of experience in managing this system, it is my belief that there are three areas of concern that must be addressed by a successful commander. They include (1) personnel, (2) facilities, and (3) sound management practices.

Personnel

Noted criminologist Austin McCormick once stated: "If only I had the right staff, I could run a good prison in an old red barn." I always paraphrase his statement to reflect that I could run a good "jail" under such circumstances, but the importance of his words cannot be overemphasized.

Routinely, when I speak to civic groups or give tours of our facilities, people indicate that the crowded conditions must be the most significant problem that I face. In fact, however, the need to recruit, employ, and retain qualified personnel is the critical issue before me; for without "the right staff" I cannot deal with the overcrowding.

Consequently, I spend a great deal of time with our Recruitment and Screening Section. It is an important function of an effective administrator, not one that should be delegated to subordinates. Finally, working conditions are of extreme importance to staff. Those individuals are the completely innocent, and often unappreciated, long-term residents in our facilities. Ideally, they are in jail for 10 to 35 years; they simply go home at the end of each shift. It will never be possible to adequately compensate them for that service, so it is important to make their daily tour of duty meaningful and satisfying. Toward that end, the proper design and operation of jail

facilities can have a significant impact.

Facilities

Progressive jail design has evolved over the past 20 years from the linear and podular remote surveillance models to direct supervision. Unfortunately, some jurisdictions pay only nominal lip service to the concept of total control, cost-effective, design and staff efficient operations that are the hallmarks of direct supervision facilities. What they opt for instead is often referred to as a "new generation" jail—a nebulous term that connotes innovation but cannot be defined.

It is imperative that a jail administrator commit to an operational philosophy and then live by it on a daily basis. To my mind, direct supervision is the practical innovation in jail design and operation, but it requires commitment from the very top of the administration to be successful. Without that, staff will tend to retrench over time, and bit by bit give up operation of the facility, be-

(cells/rooms/dormitories) and support facilities to manage specified inmate populations (Parrish, 2000). Furthermore, a facility needs to set aside about 10 percent of its beds so that inmates can be properly classified and separated. Thus, in a 1,000-bed facility, the operating capacity is 900. This can be better understood by comparing the facility with a hospital setting. If the facility has 1,000 beds, it cannot house 1,000 patients because of patient medical conditions. Similarly, inmates cannot be housed together if one has an infectious disease and the other is having a baby.

A crowded jail creates significant management problems. As the number of inmates in living units rises beyond design capacity, the many required support systems (e.g., visiting, recreation, food service, medical care) begin to deteriorate. To relieve jail overcrowding, federal and state courts have forced local governments to release more pretrial detainees or require a new building program among other things (Wilkinson & Brehm, 1992). All too often, jails are constructed without consid-

ering the impact of future community population growth or changing attitudes about crime and punishment. As a result, jails can become overcrowded and the staff's ability to supervise and manage inmates diminishes proportionally.

Jail Regionalization

State jail standards, crowding, and a landslide of inmate lawsuits have given continued impetus to questions about which agency should administer county jails. Although most jails (more than 75%) now come under an elected sheriff's command, there has been a considerable movement to separate law enforcement from correctional functions (*Who's Who in Jail Management*, 1999). Three of California's 58 counties, New Hampshire's 10 counties, 6 of Florida's 67 counties, 4 of Maryland's 23 counties, 55 of Pennsylvania's 67 counties, and 15 of New Jersey's 21 counties now oper-

cause it is easiest to allow inmates to run their own space and retreat to the hallways and control rooms.

It should be apparent that a properly designed facility makes an administrator's job more manageable; equally as important are his or her ability and attitude.

Sound Management Practices

The administrator wields a certain amount of power and thus control over the operation of a jail, but specific personal attributes are often exhibited by the most successful.

- *Leadership* This involves more than giving orders. It includes setting a personal example both on and off duty. The sheriff who hired me said, "community service is part of your job." One's commitment to the job must be complemented by a similar dedication to the public and taxpayers in nontraditional settings.

- *Hands-on Management* A great administrator is one who pays attention to details but does not get bogged down in them. There is no substitute for personal observation. He or she does not assume that information and directives will be passed on accurately (or at all) through the chain of command.

- *Consistency* Continuity is good for staff and system development, so good administrators remain in place for a few years (or more). A change-agent administrator often does little more than put a new table of organization in place. A competent administrator watches for spontaneous policy changes. A jail is somewhat like a large ship: although it is difficult to change its direction, on occasion it shifts direction without a turn at the helm.

- *Perseverance* Be prepared to resolve an issue more than once. Some problems tend to recur periodically.

- *Patience* Be willing to solve problems in a piecemeal fashion over time.

Jails and the people who work in them are generally not front-page news unless there has been an escape or there are plans to build a new facility. However, the local jail represents a significant portion of a community's criminal justice expenditures. It makes sense, therefore, that the investment should result in the recruitment and retention of well-qualified employees, that the facility should be of practical design and provide a good work environment for staff, and that the administrator should employ sound management practices. His or her success on the job can serve as validation of my personal belief that *one person can make a difference.*
Source: D. Parrish (2000). Colonel/ commander, Hillsborough County Florida Sheriffs Jail System.

---

ate separate departments of corrections. Six states (Vermont, Connecticut, Rhode Island, Delaware, Hawaii, and Alaska) run state-operated jail systems. By the year 2003, West Virginia's 55 counties will be amalgamated into a series of state-operated **regional jails**—centralized facilities that serve two or more jurisdictions. Today, Kentucky has only 84 jails in 120 counties and although the elected jailer remains a fixture in Kentucky politics, many of these jails have been downgraded to a holding facility status (*Who's Who in Jail Management*, 1999).

Much of the discussion about regional jails stems from the large number of small jails that still dot this country's landscape. In states like North and South Dakota, regional jails have been established for a number of years. North Dakota, with 53 counties, has only 22 jail facilities; South Dakota, with 66 counties, has only 29 jail facilities; and Nebraska has only 67 jails in 93 counties (*Who's Who in Jail Management*, 1999).

The economic arguments in favor of regionalizing many of the small jails are strong. In Iowa, 95 of the 99 counties operate jails. The rated capacities of these jails include 71 holding under 20, with 21 of these holding fewer than 10 inmates and 1 that holds 30 inmates. Thirty-one of these jails have an average daily population of less than 5. Regardless of size, each jail is required to meet state jail standards, including full 24-hour staffing, initial and continuing education, and medical services (Gardner, 1992). Thus, larger jails can reduce the per-inmate cost of providing these services compared with smaller facilities. Contrast this with Virginia, which has 19 regional jails representing a total of 24 counties and 11 cities. Virginia law permits any two or more counties or cities to establish and operate a regional jail. However, to receive maximum state reimbursement for construction of new facilities or renovation of old ones, three or more jurisdictions must participate (Leibowitz, 1991; *Who's Who in Jail Management*, 1999).

In some localities, regional jail arrangements are informal rather than formal; that is, a handshake between county officials cements an agreement by one county to hold another's prisoners for a fee. In some states, like Nebraska, South Dakota, Kansas, and Iowa, the de facto regional jail constitutes a way of life. Some jails find it impossible to separate women by sight and sound from males and so they instead arrange to ship them to other jurisdictions; in others, crowding forces jail staff to search for additional space (Crabtree, 1993).

Jail Staff

In 1993 jails employed 165,500 people, of whom 117,000 were COs. An estimated 69 percent of the COs were non-Hispanic whites, 23.2 percent were non-Hispanic blacks, 6.7 percent were Hispanic, and other groups constituted less than 1 percent. Male officers outnumbered females by about three to one (Perkins et al., 1995).

In many communities, the public considers the jail as an agency that is "out of sight and out of mind" and, therefore, does not consider the human dynamics involved in jail operations. Many believe that COs are undereducated, poorly trained, and unsophisticated. This may have been the case in the past, but there has been considerable improvement due largely to court action. Most states today require at least a high school diploma to work in a jail. The people who have the potential to be the best officers cannot be attracted by paying substandard wages. One very important step in attracting them is to begin paying jail officers the same as police officers. In 1998, salaries in 116 reporting jurisdictions for starting deputies and jail officers averaged $24,524—ranging from $16,640 in Bernalillo County, New Mexico, to $36,339 in Los Angeles County, California. Maximum salaries averaged $37,960—ranging from a low of $24,814 in Bernalillo County, New Mexico, to a high of $56,711 in Los Angeles County, California (Camp & Camp, 1998).

Most jails are under the control of county sheriffs and in many, jail duty is required of road deputies as the first step in their law enforcement career ladder. An advantage to this approach is that officers quickly learn the behaviors and characteristics of those with whom they will be dealing when they transfer to patrol duty. Its disadvantage is that the deputy sheriff does not see corrections as a desirable career path. The jail is only an entry assignment to be followed by a full career in law enforcement. High turnover, loss of valuable experience, lower pay than law enforcement officers, and the absence of commitment to corrections are all major disadvantages of combining corrections and law enforcement into a deputy sheriff's career path (Reed, 1993). Some sheriff's departments no longer have this entry require-

ment; instead, they have created two separate career tracks—one for law enforcement and the other for corrections—with equal pay. This also recognizes that more training is required in jails that use a direct supervision model, so it is not cost effective to use corrections as an entry-level position (Kerle, 2000).

Professionalization of COs

As our jails become increasingly professionalized, the requirement for trained, quality staff becomes more important. Some states now mandate that jail correctional personnel be certified through academy training. In 1998, 115 systems reported an average of 274 preservice training hours—ranging from 1,056 hours in Alemdage County, California, to no hours in several jurisdictions (e.g., Harris, Texas) (Camp & Camp, 1998). Even in states that require training, it still generally falls below the number of hours required for entrance into law enforcement. The reluctance of government to meet its training obligations has served as a stimulus to the American Jail Association (AJA) to fill this void by issuing monthly training bulletins. AJA also conducts two training sessions a month in different sections of the country. Refresher training is vital and offered in many areas (e.g., CPR, fire safety, riot techniques, interpersonal relations skills). In 1998, 115 systems required an average of 33 hours of in-service training—the range was from 0 to 120 (Camp & Camp, 1998).

Staff-Inmate Communication

The safety and security of the jail demands that staff control the inmate population. If staff are hesitant or actually do not enter certain sections of the jail, then control of those areas is, in effect, relinquished to the inmates. A jail with adequate control rarely has escapes, maintains effective supervision, and has few serious injuries; staff are in charge of all functional inmate space.

Effective supervision of inmates requires that trained staff be in frequent, interpersonal contact and communication with inmates because, left to their own devices, predatory inmates will assume control of their units to further their own agendas. Merely observing inmate behavior from a remote location or walking by a cell block every half hour does not constitute effective supervision (Heuer, 1993). Staff-inmate communication is nurtured by close personal and professional contact. Supervising behavior, answering questions, scheduling events, inspecting cells, assembling work details, and conversing informally are methods staff can use to open lines of communication. Uncommunicative staff tend to become isolated, making it more difficult for them to obtain full cooperation from inmates.

Inmates know the difference between "easy time" (having certain privileges) and "hard time" (being locked up in disciplinary confinement). Ideally, inmates should be given the opportunity to decide which type of "time" they want to do. Compliance with facility rules and regulations ensures reasonably comfortable living conditions with increased access to such things as additional freedom of movement, recreation, library, programs, television, telephones, and visiting. In contrast, noncompliance results in increasing restrictions on personal freedom and reduction of privileges.

Jail Programs

An increased emphasis on jail programming has resulted from a growing recognition that occupying inmates through recreational and established programs will reduce their involvement in violence and other illegal activities, may reduce their rate of return to criminal pursuits, and can even result in revenue for the jail. Today, jail programs include recreation, some education, alcohol and drug abuse counseling, and in a few instances work and industry programs.

Recreational Programs

Access to recreation and physical exercise, within security constraints, is a constitutional right of inmates. Sufficient indoor and outdoor space and adequate time must be provided to all inmates in custody. Many jails, particularly those in downtown areas of a city, have very limited space for recreational and exercise programs and may use the jail roof for this purpose. Newer direct supervision jails often have both indoor recreational areas and outside areas with basketball hoops.

Educational and Substance Abuse Programs

A substantial number of inmates who come to jail have significant educational deficiencies. Some jails have educational programs that include parenting classes, gardening, anger management, computer instruction, health clinics, and life skills classes. Some of the most innovative correctional education programs today are found in jails. For example, the Hillsborough County Florida Detention Department uses computer-assisted instruction in addition to traditional adult basic education (ABE) programs. With 60 computers in seven labs located throughout two facilities, they engage a significant number of inmates in this integrated learning approach. As with all of their programs, the computer labs provide an open entry/open exit format (inmates are allowed to enter and exit any time during their confinement in-

stead of the traditional semester program concept). The program serves both male and female inmates, including juveniles awaiting trial in adult court. Preliminary research shows the program is well received by both staff and inmates. Inmates have been increasing their average grade levels between 1.5 and 2.0 years in 60 hours of instruction (Smith, 1994). Recognizing the success of these programs, small jails (under 50 beds) have also begun using computers in their educational programs (Miller, 2000).

Given the large proportion of jail inmates with a substance abuse history, drug education classes and even short-term treatment programs can help addicts to deal with their problems. For example, the DEUCE Program operated in Contra Costa County, California, is an intensive three-phase, 90-day effort at reducing substance-abuse-related recidivism through the use of a therapeutic community in a jail setting. DEUCE was developed for multiple-offending drunk drivers and dual- or poly-addicted individuals. The program focuses on substance abuse education, intervention, prevention, and employability. Traditional educational instruction is paired with individual and small group treatment and 12-step sessions similar to those used by Alcoholics Anonymous. Each hour of the day and evening is oriented to the program. Individuals must apply for admission and are prescreened by program staff (Blount, 1994).

Jail Industry Programs

Since the mid-1980s, an increasing number of the nation's jails have been creating productive industry programs. According to the National Institute of Justice, the concept is simple: Use inmate labor to produce a product or service of value that benefits inmates, jails, and communities. A 1993 national jail survey indicated that, in the jails reporting (11 percent of all jails), 18 percent of their inmates worked at least a 6-hour day (*American Jails*, 1994).

Hennepin County, Minnesota, houses the earliest private sector jail industries program in the nation. It conducts training seminars and provides technical assistance to jails interested in developing these programs. Several exemplary programs are now in existence. In the Philadelphia Jail, the Prison Industries Program turns out furniture, mattresses, clothing, and other items. Another program, in Strafford, New Hampshire, was the first to gain federal certification to ship goods over state lines. Nearly 20 percent of the 100 inmates in this jail work for local private companies and are paid full wages. The largest employer is an electronics firm that hires their inmate-workers after their release. Finally, according to an NIJ survey, 17 percent of jail inmates work 6 or more hours daily (Miller, 2000).

The Problems of Instituting Jail Programs A number of factors impede the development of effective jail programs for all categories of inmates. Those awaiting trial cannot be required to participate in any ongoing work programs except to maintain their housing areas. Many inmates only spend a few days in jail and will not benefit from education and substance abuse programs. Any programs for short-term inmates must be designed to provide motivation, orientation, and referral to community resources to facilitate further progress on release. Another consideration is the size of the jail. Small jails, which constitute the majority of jail facilities, often lack the resources necessary to conduct such programs (Mays et al., 1991).

Although jail programming can benefit many inmates, even in 503 of the largest jails only a small proportion of the inmates in each system is involved in jail programs (Beck, Bonczar, & Gilliard, 1993). Some 420 of these systems offered at least one of four programs (drug treatment, alcohol treatment, psychological counseling, or educational programming), but only 127 offered all of them. There is no indication whether the low participation rate is due to limitations on program space or lack of inmate interest. A better idea of how inmates spend their time can be seen in Table 18.2.

The Future of the American Jail

The American public and its leadership have sent mixed signals about the proper role of jails. Are jails established to administer punishment, to simply warehouse offenders, or to attempt to correct past behaviors? The answers to these important questions have changed from time to time and, as indicated in our discussion of the history of corrections, will likely continue to change. There is no solid evidence that punishment or incarceration helps to reduce future jail populations or crime in the community. Thus, the current policy of building more jails and prisons as a way of dealing with the crime problem is not likely to reduce significantly the level of crime. Nor will it deal with overcrowding on a long-term basis because it does not reduce the reasons people commit crimes nor will it assist them in adopting a noncriminal lifestyle. The jail of the future must strive to use the limited available community resources in its capacity as a community agency and work in tandem with other government agencies at all levels to direct the incarcerated person into a noncriminal lifestyle (Powell, 1993; Sluder & Sapp, 1994).

People who manage our future jails must recognize the role played by politicians in shaping these facilities. Current laws like three strikes and truth in sentencing will all have an impact on jails because they increase the number of offenders coming into the system. If states do

Table 18.2
Activities of Jail Inmates (1996)

Activity in Jail	Percent of Jail Inmates
In the 24 hours before the interview	
Watching television	
Watched	73.8%
Did not watch available television	17.7
Television not available to watch	8.5
Reading	
Read	68.0%
Did not read available material	17.4
Reading material not available	14.7
Physical exercise	
Participated	43.5%
Games, arts and crafts, and other recreation	
Participated	55.4%
In the previous week	
Work assignment*	
Any	26.4%
General janitorial	9.4
Food preparation	9.4
Maintenance, repair, or construction	3.5
Grounds and road maintenance	2.8
Laundry	2.1
Library, barbershop, office, or other services	2.7
Goods production	0.7
Other	1.1
Visits from family/friends	
Visits in past week	42.1%
None	21.9
None since admission	35.9
Telephone calls with family/friends	
Calls in past week	76.9%
None	19.7
Not allowed	3.4
Religious activities†	
Participated	54.9%

*The detail adds up to more than total because inmates may have more than one work assignment.
†This includes religious services, private prayer, and meditation.
Source: C. W. Harlow (1998, April). *Profile of Jail Inmates, 1996.* Washington, DC: Bureau of Justice Statistics.

not plan ahead for future population increases, the number of inmates awaiting transportation to state and federal facilities will increase; new jails will have to be planned with this in mind. Those that build and operate jails in the future must consider what local political bodies, such as county commissions, expect an inmate's stay in jail to be like. Because they fund new construction and operating budgets, their wishes must be considered. The problem is that these groups inject themselves into the day-to-day operations of jails, which, in essence, takes control of the jail away from the people who manage the facility. We already see this in several areas, such as the removal of weights and tobacco products and pressure to eliminate programming (e.g., education) (Parrish, 2000).

Finally, we must recognize the importance of having qualified jail administrators to manage our jail facilities, which are complex in nature. They have to handle populations with different needs (juvenile, the mentally ill, the violent). One solution lies in the Certified Jail Manager (CJM) program developed by the American Jail Association. AJA promotes the concept of voluntary certification for all jail managers. Certification is one part of a process called *credentialing,* which attests to current competency in a specialized field. Those who have the requirements to take the certification examination and pass it will be viewed as reaching one of the highest levels of achievement in their field. This

- provides evidence to the public that CJMs have been examined by an independent professional organization and found to possess current competency in the field of jail management.
- encourages continuing education and professional growth.
- indicates to one's peers that the individual has taken the time and effort, beyond job experience, to learn the body of correctional knowledge, thus exhibiting a significant commitment to working in the profession of jail management.
- elevates professional standards of jail operations by providing better educated professionals in the field.
- provides an incentive for jail managers to pursue continuing education because every 4 years they are required to become recertified to hold this status. (AJA, undated)

Summary

Jails are short-term complex institutions that hold pretrial detainees, short-term-sentenced inmates, work releasees, and those awaiting transportation to state or federal prison. Characteristically, this population includes juveniles and adults, males and females, and the elderly, sick, and mentally ill. Jails are administered by local officials and are designed to hold persons from a few hours to 1 year in most states. In addition to their alleged criminality, many jail inmates are affected by such problems as illiteracy, drug and/or alcohol abuse, and varying degrees of mental instability. These problems tend to go untreated in the outside world. Consequently, the jail—a community agency—becomes a catchall for society's problems.

The English jail was the model on which American jails were developed. The colonial version of English jail facilities was very informal and used only to detain those awaiting trial. Later, these facilities began to be used to house convicted minor offenders.

Specific architectural features of jails greatly influence how inmates are supervised, protected, and managed. The linear design is the older, more traditional design for jails. In these facilities, the cells are constructed in long straight rows aligned with corridors where correctional staff walk from cell to cell to supervise inmate activities. This inhibits the ability of staff to supervise inmates, because they can only see inmates in one cell at a time. In the 1970s, the podular remote surveillance model was developed to enhance the ability of staff to see the activities of all inmates within their living units. This design situates inmate cells on the exterior perimeter and provides open interior space for inmate activities. A centrally located control room allows staff to observe inmate areas and activities. The latest design, the podular direct supervision model, permanently situates staff among the inmates within each housing unit and uses "soft" furnishings to normalize the living environment. The modern podular jail enables staff, at a quick glance or a short walk, to see and hear the activities within the entire living unit.

During the intake process certain types of information must be acquired from those being admitted to ensure the health and safety of other inmates and to protect the institution's security. This includes whether new arrivals have consumed a dangerous drug and/or alcohol, are injured, and if they are violent or potentially suicidal. It also is critical to monitor minor first offenders because many attempt or commit suicide when they find themselves alone, embarrassed, and depressed because of their incarceration. Also, a majority of jail inmates are physically and/or psychologically dependent on one or more legal or illegal substances that require that they be identified for safety and treatment reasons.

Classification is a management process that separates inmates according to preestablished security and custody levels. It allows assignment to compatible groups, which reduces violence and conflict while enhancing facility programming.

A substantial number of inmates entering jail suffer from mental illness. This causes problems for jail staff because these facilities are neither designed nor staffed to handle these individuals. Mental illness can lead to conflicts with other inmates, an inability to understand or follow instructions, and self-destructive behavior. Obviously, mentally ill inmates can be served best in mental health facilities, but insufficient space in these hospitals means many end up in jail.

Another area of continuing concern is the placement of juveniles (14 to 17) in adult jails. This youthful population are characteristically young, streetwise, substance abusing, gang-affiliated individuals who are serving long sentences and are predisposed to defiant, aggressive, and violent behavior.

Although women represent a small proportion of the inmate population, state laws require that programs and services be equally available to them.

Irrespective of jail size, effective management requires that jail administrators establish and enforce policies requiring all command and supervisory jail staff to make frequent visits, each day and each shift, to inmate living areas. This proactive approach has been labeled "management by walking around." Operating in this manner can prevent lazy or weak staff from retreating from inmate contact. The primary role of jail staff is to maintain control of inmates so the safety and security of the jail is not compromised. If staff are hesitant or actually do not enter certain sections of the jail, then control of those areas is, in effect, relinquished to the inmates. A jail with adequate control rarely has escapes, maintains effective supervision, has few serious injuries, and has its staff in charge of all functional inmate space.

The best method that jails can use to determine whether they are providing a safe environment is to go through the accreditation process. This uncovers jails' deficiencies; however, it has no legal basis to require that these changes be made. In contrast, problems discovered during state jail inspections can be required to be fixed under state law.

An increased emphasis on jail programming has resulted from a growing recognition that occupying inmates through recreational and established programs will reduce their involvement in violence and other illegal activities; may reduce their rate of return to criminal pursuits; and can even result in revenue for the jail. Access to recreation and physical exercise, within security constraints, is a constitutional right of inmates and provides a means for inmates to reduce tensions. Educational programming is important because a substantial number of jail inmates have significant educational deficiencies. Given the large proportion of jail inmates with a substance abuse history, drug education classes and even short-term treatment programs in jails can help addicts to deal with their problems. Since the mid-1980s, an increasing number of the nation's jails have been creating productive industry programs. This not only provides inmates at least limited skill development but reduces inmate idleness and provides income for the jail.

Critical Thinking Questions

1. As a jail planner, which one of the three types of jail designs would you use as a model to build a new jail?

2. Develop a presentation on jails' functions and inmate characteristics that would be suitable for a corrections class.

3. Provide profiles of each special category inmate in a jail setting.

4. Assume you are writing a paper on the differences between jail and prison. What types of comparisons would you make?

5. As sergeant in charge of a booking area, what methods would you use to accurately identify a new inmate, and what types of screening would occur before an inmate enters the jail population?

6. Present arguments for and against the housing of juveniles in adult jails. Also, identify the policies and procedures that should be followed when housing juveniles in adult jail facilities.

7. As a newly appointed jail administrator, what policies would you develop and what practices would you adopt to effectively manage your jail?

8. As county commissioner of a sparsely populated area, why would you consider joining with other nearby counties to develop a regional jail?

Test Your Knowledge

1. Early colonial jails were used primarily for:
   a. pretrial detention.
   b. rehabilitation.
   c. punishment.
   d. deterrence.

2. Which of the following jail designs appears to provide the most effective form of inmate supervision?
   a. linear intermittent
   b. podular direct
   c. podular remote
   d. all of the above

3. The most common crime for which alcohol abusers are jailed is:
   a. homicide.
   b. assault.

   c. disorderly conduct.

   d. driving under the influence.

4. Which of the following programs can be found in contemporary jails?

   a. education

   b. substance abuse

   c. industry programs

   d. all of the above

   e. only a and b

Endnote

1. The author would like to thank the following individuals for reviewing this chapter and providing recommendations to improve its content: David Parrish, colonel/commander of the Hillsborough County Florida Sheriffs Jail System; Ken Kerle, managing editor, *American Jails;* and Rod Miller, president, CRS, Inc., which publishes monographs dealing with legal issues in corrections.

Probation

19

LEARNING OBJECTIVES

After completing this chapter, you should be able to:

1. Describe the history of probation, including the role played by John Augustus in its development in the United States.

2. Discuss the use of risk prediction scales in deciding which offenders should be placed on probation.

3. Differentiate between control and treatment conditions.

4. Outline the basic organizational arrangements under which probation services are administered in different states.

5. Identify the methods that are employed in assigning cases to probation officers.

6. Describe the way in which probation officers are hired.

7. Describe the five basic uses of the PSI and the nature of the information that should be included in these reports.

8. Describe some of the factors that cause POs to "burn out."

9. Summarize the general results of studies on the effectiveness of probation and specific types of treatments applied to clients.

Introduction

One of the most critical problems currently affecting corrections is the escalating number of convicted offenders combined with demands to incarcerate more of them. Although prison overcrowding has become a chronic problem, the "drug wars" of the 1980s and 1990s and hardening public attitudes toward criminals have heightened the problem. In spite of two decades of massive prison construction, current incarceration policies have led to a growing prison space shortage.

Another contributing factor to overcrowding has been the number of offenders receiving minimum mandatory sentences. These sentences require offenders to serve a specific number of years before being eligible for release. However, lack of space in the early 1990s led to inmates not encumbered with minimum mandatory sentences being released well before their sentences expired to make room for the more recently convicted ones. This game of "musical cells" has led to public dissatisfaction with corrections, renewed calls for "truth in sentencing," and pressure to resolve the problem by building more and more prisons. This has escalated the cost of corrections to a point where it may soon become unaffordable.

Probation and parole (or some type of postprison supervision) have the potential to control the soaring costs of corrections. In this chapter, we will explore probation and in Chapter 21 we will examine parole. As we will see, probation is a sentence that keeps the offender from the stigmatizing effects of prison.

Probation As an Alternative to Prison

Probation is the most frequently imposed sanction available to sentencing judges. Recently, nearly three million adults, or approximately 60 percent of offenders under correctional supervision, were on probation (Bureau of Justice Statistics, 1996b). **Probation** is a sentence in which the offender remains in the community under the supervision of a corrections agent and is subject to court-imposed conditions. According to Champion (1990, p. 16), the correctional philosophy underlying probation gives "offenders . . . the opportunity [to] prov[e] themselves capable of refraining from further criminal activity." This philosophy is in keeping with the meaning of the Latin word *probare*—to prove—from which the term *probation* is derived.

While serving their sentences, probationers are under intermittent supervision and have access to the resources and services available in the community. Probation may also provide an economical alternative to prison. One of the major criticisms of probation is that keeping offenders in the community could result in additional criminality. Another criticism is that it is too lenient and may not be a deterrent or even serve a retributive purpose.

Before proceeding, it is important to note that our consideration of probation in this chapter is limited to

Offenders on probation are supervised by probation officers while serving their sentences. The purpose of probation is to give offenders a chance to prove that they can refrain from committing additional crimes.

standard probation. Chapter 20 addresses the intermediate sanctions that have been developed to fill the gap between regular probation and imprisonment, and that discussion will include intensive supervision programs.

The History of Probation

The practices preceding probation, which emerged in England over several centuries, helped mitigate the harsh punishments in effect then. These practices, which were imported to the United States by the English settlers, included benefit of clergy, judicial reprieve, and recognizance.

Benefit of clergy allowed individuals accused of serious crimes to appeal for leniency by reading the 51st Psalm in court. Benefit of clergy came into widespread use, but abuses eventually led to reduction in its use and to its abolition in 1827. It was briefly practiced in the states but quickly fell into disrepute because of its arbitrary nature (Hussey & Duffee, 1980).

Judicial reprieve was another way judges exercised discretion. Under this 19th-century practice, convicted offenders could apply for a temporary suspension of their sentence. Its purpose was to allow a defendant to apply to the Crown for a pardon while at liberty (United Nations, 1970). In the United States, judicial reprieve was transformed so that in many cases the sentence was suspended indefinitely and the court controlled the defendant over long periods of time. In 1916 the U.S. Supreme Court declared this process unconstitutional because it interfered with legislative and executive powers to enact and enforce laws (*Ex parte United States*, 1916). This ruling had the effect of bringing probation practices under the provisions of state penal codes.

Recognizance allowed an offender to be released from custody during court proceedings. This type of release, which is still in use today, releases accused individuals from jail who are awaiting trial.

Probation, as an alternative to incarceration, was impelled by the effort to give judges flexibility and the ability to personalize the punishment process. Massachusetts led the way in this regard through the work of a well-to-do Boston shoemaker and philanthropist who had a strong interest in the court process.

The Father of Modern Probation John Augustus (1785–1859) was influenced by the temperance movement, a group dedicated to reforming drunks. He often attended sessions in the Boston Municipal Court trying to influence public drunks appearing before the court to change. In 1841 he became the first unofficial probation officer (PO) when he intervened in the case of a common drunk who had been convicted and was about to be sentenced to a 6-month term in the Boston House of Corrections. Augustus asked the judge to let him super-

vise the man for 3 weeks, guaranteeing his later court appearance and pledging to pay all court costs. The judge agreed and 3 weeks later Augustus and his charge returned to the courtroom. The judge, impressed with the changes the "probationer" had made, suspended the jail sentence and substituted a small fine (United Nations, 1951).

From this modest beginning Augustus began to regularly stand bail for and assist a variety of minor offenders in the Boston Municipal Court. He continued this work until 1858, a year before his death. During this time he supervised about 2,000 men and women (Champion, 1990; Lindner & Savarese, 1984). Although his work was not formally evaluated, Augustus indicated that most of his "probationers" eventually led law-abiding lives. His work led to the statutory creation of probation services in Massachusetts. He devised the initial investigative and screening procedures, supervisory practices, and delivery of services to offenders that form the basis of probation today. After his death and until Massachusetts passed probation legislation, the practice of having only volunteers work with the offenders continued (Lindner & Savarese, 1984; United Nations, 1951).

The Early 20th Century The probation movement gained momentum during the early part of the 20th century. By 1920 every state had passed legislation that permitted juvenile probation, and 33 states allowed adult probation. However, not until 1954 was probation available to adult offenders in all states (Rothman, 1980; Task Force on Corrections, 1967).

Following World War II, POs began to use psychological concepts and rehabilitation was emphasized for the next 25 years. As noted earlier, this approach had limited success, and in the late 1960s it was supplanted by the reintegration model; in the 1970s treatment in prison began to be de-emphasized. The reintegration model stressed community placement for offenders because the resources to help them were available there. It fit well with probation because it had long been dealing with offenders in the community. However, by the late 1970s reintegration was overtaken by a new emphasis on law and order, which stressed punishment for criminals.

Probation and Just Deserts As the purpose of criminal sanctions in the 1980s and 1990s shifted to retribution and just deserts, so did probation's focus. This was reflected in the development of the intermediate sanctions described in Chapter 20. It involved a shift from the brokering of treatment services to a primary emphasis on risk management strategies, which were to be accomplished through more intensive supervision and stricter conditions. Prison overcrowding during this time led to a greater proportion of felony offenders being placed on probation. In 1995, 1.5 million people on probation (58% of all probationers) had been convicted of a felony (Bonczar, 1997). This has raised questions about community safety and the extent to which these sanctions subject convicted offenders to retribution when they remain at relative liberty in the community. Thus, the idea of leaving convicted offenders in the community is not viewed favorably by those taking a just deserts approach to corrections.

In spite of the criticisms of probation, however, it has continued to prosper for several reasons. These reasons include its popularity among corrections people, its low cost compared with incarceration, and the need for alternatives to prison. One problem that has resulted from its growing use is that funding has not kept up with the large number of cases sentenced to probation. Over the period from 1980 to 1994 the probation population in the United States grew by an average of 7.2 percent annually (faster than general population growth), or more than 1.8 million people (Bureau of Justice Statistics, 1996). Unfortunately, states have failed to provide appropriate resources for probation services to keep up with increased caseloads, and this has resulted in a level of "probation overcrowding" comparable to that found in prisons (McCarthy & McCarthy, 1991).

Probation Caseloads Today   At the beginning of the 1990s a record number of adults were on probation. According to the Bureau of Justice Statistics (1996), nearly 3 million adult offenders were on probation in 1994, representing 1 out of every 62 people 18 years of age or older. There were more than 1.72 million admissions to probation during 1997 (Bonczar, 1997).

Table 19.1 shows a probation population increase of 3.9 percent during 1995. Of 52 jurisdictions (50 states, the District of Columbia, and the federal system), 44 showed increases and 6 decreased. The 1997 national rate (not shown) was 1,647 per 100,000 adults, with the South having the highest rate at 1,850. Twelve states had rates that were over 2,000 per 100,000 adult residents, and 3 of these states (Delaware, Texas, and Washington) had rates over 3,000 per 100,000 population. Although not shown in the table, the number of probationers more than doubled from 1980 to the end of 1994. According to the Bureau of Justice Statistics (Bonczar, 1997) as of 1995 58.3 percent of the probationers were non-Hispanic whites and 20.9 percent were females.

Determinants of Probation

When offenders are sentenced to probation a decision has to be made about the structure of the sentence. This decision will involve several variables: the sentence length, the supervision level required by the offender, and the number and nature of the conditions to be imposed. Sentence lengths, for both probation and prison,

tend to vary directly with the seriousness of the crime (Cunniff, 1987). Before conditions are imposed, a risk assessment is completed.

Risk Assessment   **Risk prediction scales** may be employed to determine the supervision level required by an offender. These scales attempt to predict offenders' future behavior and the outcome of probation (Gottfredson & Tonry, 1987). Although these scales can select some individuals who will act in the manner predicted, they are never perfect. Thus, some individuals predicted to be successes will not be (false positives), and some who are predicted to be failures will succeed (false negatives). It is not possible to send all individuals who are convicted to prison, so any improvement in the predictive process that can reduce the number of both false positives and negatives will result in a more effective placement of offenders.

Risk assessment scales are used almost universally in the United States. Wisconsin pioneered the use of risk/needs assessment scales to assign probationers to various supervision levels. The Wisconsin model included five components: a risk assessment scale, a needs assessment scale, a workload budgeting and deployment system, a management information system, and a standard reclassification process. When implemented in Wisconsin, this model had an impact on:

1. *How often cases were seen*   Based on both risk and needs assessment scale scores, three levels of contact were developed (every 14 days, every 30 days, every 90 days).

2. *Planning and evaluation capabilities*   Information generated during the entire assessment and supervision process was used for future planning.

3. *The Bureau of Community Corrections budgeting process*   The model provided data on statewide PO workloads.

4. *Accountability measures*   This was accomplished by identifying client needs and providing information about how well these needs were met (National Institute of Corrections, 1981b).

The scale's risk assessment component generally was found to separate low-, medium-, and high-risk offenders moderately well in terms of predicting recidivism. It also did significantly better when compared with POs' intuitive judgments (Baird, Heinz, & Bemus, 1982; Brown, 1984). However, the scale's needs assessment element was found to have little predictive value (Program Services Office, 1983).

Conditions of Probation   **Probation conditions** are imposed on all probationers as part of their sentences.

Table 19.1

Adults on Probation (1995)

Region and Jurisdiction	Probation Population 1/1/95	1995		Probation Population 12/31/95	Percent Change in Probation Population During 1995	Number on Probation on 12/31/95 per 100,000 Adult Residents
		Entries	Exits			
U.S. total	2,981,022	1,578,182	1,451,948	3,096,529	3.9%	1,596
Federal	42,309	18,601	22,404	38,506	—	20
State	2,938,713	1,559,581	1,429,544	3,058,023	4.1	1,576
Northeast	526,375	232,686	214,444	544,620	3.5%	1,402
Connecticut	53,453	37,135	36,081	54,507	2.0	2,201
Maine	8,638	:	:	8,641	—	923
Massachusetts	46,670	34,611	37,601	43,680	−6.4	941
New Hampshire	4,323	3,432	3,408	4,347	.6	509
New Jersey	125,299	59,376	57,552	127,123	1.5	2,125
New York	163,613	45,061	35,175	173,499	6.0	1,276
Pennsylvania	99,524	39,764	32,465	106,823	7.3	1,166
Rhode Island	18,179	9,813	9,314	18,678	2.7	2,483
Vermont	6,676	3,494	2,848	7,322	9.7	1,672
Midwest	642,546	418,160	387,163	676,997	5.4%	1,485
Illinois	104,664	63,862	61,723	109,489	4.6	1,258
Indiana	83,177	76,593	70,312	89,458	7.6	2,073
Iowa	15,902	10,456	9,779	16,579	4.3	783
Kansas	17,256	11,831	7,726	16,547	−4.1	884
Michigan	142,640	68,000	62,338	148,337	4.0	2,110
Minnesota	81,972	55,911	57,131	83,778	2.2	2,490
Missouri	36,295	21,887	18,453	40,595	11.8	1,030
Nebraska	18,639	15,485	14,697	19,427	4.2	1,627
North Dakota	2,036	1,474	1,219	2,291	12.5	486
Ohio	90,190	68,077	59,558	99,603	10.4	1,201
South Dakota	3,874	4,393	4,643	3,624	−6.5	693
Wisconsin	45,901	20,191	19,584	47,269	3.0	1,254
South	1,214,375	618,343	573,402	1,254,817	3.3%	1,846
Alabama	31,284	4,696	4,498	31,416	.4	990
Arkansas	19,606	8,431	5,656	22,381	14.2	1,220
Delaware	15,507	7,395	6,555	16,347	5.4	3,036

(continued)

Normally, there are two types of conditions imposed: control and treatment. **Control,** or general, **conditions** are imposed on all probationers and include:

> obeying laws, not associating with known criminals, reporting regularly to the probation officer, submitting to searches, not possessing firearms, not using alcohol excessively, not leaving the jurisdiction without permission, and otherwise reporting any significant changes in status (e.g., residence, employment) to the probation officer.

Treatment, or specific, **conditions** are made to fit the offender's particular problems and needs. These may include:

> psychiatric treatment, payment of restitution, participation in a community work program, maintenance of employment, involvement in drug and alcohol treatment, curfew observation, participation in a training or educational program, and any other specific prohibitions or requirements imposed by the court.

Table 19.1

Adults on Probation (1995) *(continued)*

Region and Jurisdiction	Probation Population 1/1/95	1995 Entries	1995 Exits	Probation Population 12/31/95	Percent Change in Probation Population During 1995	Number on Probation on 12/31/95 per 100,000 Adult Residents
South *(continued)*						
District of Col.	11,306	4,733	5,777	10,262	–9.2	2,334
Florida	247,014	146,989	133,585	255,550	3.5	2,367
Georgia	140,694	69,102	67,228	142,453	1.3	2,699
Kentucky	11,417	5,582	5,500	11,499	.7	398
Louisiana	33,604	11,431	11,282	33,753	.4	1,088
Maryland	76,940	35,530	41,441	71,029	–7.7	1,884
Mississippi	9,042	3,511	2,958	9,595	6.1	496
North Carolina	90,418	49,804	42,301	97,921	8.3	1,815
Oklahoma	26,285	14,195	13,029	27,866	6.0	1,161
South Carolina	40,005	16,643	14,482	42,166	5.4	1,545
Tennessee	34,896	20,431	18,594	36,733	5.3	931
Texas	396,276	200,365	181,144	415,497	4.9	3,119
Virginia	24,089	19,394	19,219	24,264	.7	485
West Virginia	5,992	111	153	6,085	1.6	433
West	555,417	290,392	254,535	581,589	4.7%	1,397
Alaska	2,899	960	1,296	2,563	–12.0	619
Arizona	34,365	15,514	10,728	32,532	–5.3	1,076
California	277,655	142,560	133,229	286,986	3.4	1,259
Colorado	39,065	25,042	21,840	42,010	7.5	1,519
Hawaii	13,088	6,620	6,385	13,323	1.8	1,518
Idaho	5,770	6,110	5,711	6,169	6.9	757
Montana	5,656	2,022	1,833	5,845	3.3	922
Nevada	9,410	6,043	5,377	10,076	7.1	890
New Mexico	8,063	7,727	7,514	8,276	2.6	698
Oregon	38,086	13,397	11,758	39,725	4.3	1,695
Utah	7,714	4,136	3,372	8,478	9.9	664
Washington	110,279	58,476	43,640	122,306	10.9	3,048
Wyoming	3,367	1,785	1,852	3,300	–2.0	960

— Not calculated

: Not known.

Source: Bureau of Justice Statistics (1997). *Correctional Populations in the United States, 1995.* Washington, DC: U.S. Department of Justice, p. 33.

The conditions imposed on offenders are supposed to help them successfully complete the probation sentence.

Financial penalties are another distinctive category of probation conditions. These include court costs, probation supervision fees, restitution, and other fees. With correctional costs soaring, making convicted offenders contribute to their supervision costs has gained widespread political support (Parent, 1990a). In 1991, probation agencies in 28 states had statutory authority to collect fees from probationers, with another 7 states considering implementing them (Davis, 1991). Parent (1990a) found that these fees averaged between $20 to $25 per month and ranged from $10 to $50. In looking at the impact of fee collection on agency budgets, Parent (1990a) found that in 10 jurisdictions probation agencies retained the money collected. The amounts collected made up from about 3 percent to 50 percent of their budgets.

A very important function of the PO is to make sure that probationers understand and adhere to the conditions placed on them. Thus, they must explain each of the conditions to their clients and inform them of the consequences—such as revocation—for failing to follow them.

Offenders on probation are subject to treatment conditions that fit the offender's particular problems and needs. Those conditions may include participation in a community work program.

Organization and Administration of Probation Services

Originally, probation services were administered by county courts. This arrangement was carried forward into the early part of the 20th century during the development of juvenile courts. As the adult probation system expanded, different organizational arrangements were tried. Today, there are five organizational variations of probation services across the United States:

1. within the state executive branch
2. within local (county or municipal government) executive departments
3. under the state judiciary
4. under local courts
5. under various combinations of the first four

Thus, probation services are either centralized (i.e., under the administration of a state agency) or decentralized (i.e., under the administration of a county or municipal agency); in the judicial arena or in the executive arena; under the correctional system's umbrella or separate from it; and combined with the parole function or separate from it.

The most common form is a centralized arrangement within the executive branch under the supervision of the state corrections department (Bonczar, 1997). The major argument for centralization is that a uniform stan-

dard of services is available in a state compared with local programs. When probation services are combined with other state correctional services, consistency and continuity in the policies affecting all correctional services can be achieved.

Arguments for judicial and local placement of probation contend that it is a judicial disposition that should be overseen by the court. Another justification is that support for programs will be stronger when they are responsive to community input, which is obviously more likely if decisions are made locally. Flexibility will be enhanced because there is no large, rigid bureaucratic structure with which to deal (Nelson, Ohmart, & Harlow, 1978).

Caseload Management

As early as 1917, the caseload issue surfaced and an optimum figure of 50 cases per officer first appeared in the literature. This figure was not based on research but on the opinion of probation directors at this time. Better service and lower recidivism rates would seem to result from lower caseloads, but this was too simple an answer for a fairly complex problem.

More than three decades ago, the San Francisco Project dispelled the myth that smaller caseloads improved probation effectiveness (Robinson, Wilkins, Carter, & Wahl, 1969). This study found almost identical violation rates in caseloads ranging from 50 to 250. The conclusion was that the caseload concept was meaningless without some type of classification and matching of offender type, service to be offered, and staff (Task Force on Corrections, 1973). In 1993 the average regular caseload in 46 jurisdictions responding to a survey was 118, ranging from a high of 400 in California to a low of 13 in South Dakota (Camp & Camp, 1994c).

Recently, the American Probation and Parole Association (1999) published an "issue paper" on caseload standards. The conclusion of this influential organization was that this is a very complex issue and that workload is a more useful concept than caseload. Therefore, POs might be assigned different caseloads in relation to the difficulty of managing their cases. The APPA suggested that cases be classified as high, medium, and low priority, and officer assignments then should be determined by equal workloads.

Probation departments employ various methods of assigning cases to their officers. In some offices cases may be assigned on a random basis; that is, as cases come into the office they are assigned to the next officer in the staff rotation. This is the most inefficient and least effective assignment method. In some offices cases are assigned by geographic area. A PO supervises all probationers who live within a defined area. This arrangement may yield a more efficiently served caseload for probation officers in that they will travel less and get to know the area in which their clients live better. A third method of assigning clients is to attempt to match clients who have particular problems (e.g., drug abuse or sex offenders) with officers who may have special skills in dealing with them. A final way of assigning cases is based on a classification scheme such as the one suggested by the APPA. Here, each case is assigned based on the level of supervision predicted, and PO workloads are balanced on this basis. Although this approach is rational, it is difficult to maintain (Abadinsky, 1997; McCarthy & McCarthy, 1991).

Probation Officers

Probation officers are the workhorses of much of the probation system. In this section, we look at how they are selected, their main duties, and problems with stress.

Selection of POs

At the beginning of 1994 there were about 57,200 probation workers in 52 jurisdictions (Camp & Camp, 1994c). Available information on the characteristics of these officers revealed that approximately half were women, and 22 percent were nonwhite. The average probationer caseload was 118. The average annual entry salary reported was approximately $24,000 (ranging from $16,000 to $44,000); the average maximum salary was $40,000 (ranging from $29,000 to $109,000).

Probation officers are selected either through a civil service merit system, an appointment system, or some combination of the two (Abadinsky, 1997). The **merit system** requires applicants to qualify by meeting certain minimum requirements and scoring above a certain level on a written exam. Some systems also evaluate and rate applicants on the basis of education and experience. This method is also used by some agencies in determining promotions.

Under the **appointment system,** a pool of applicants meeting certain minimum requirements is developed (e.g., have a BA degree) but no examination is mandated. Agency administrators interview "qualified" candidates and select whomever they please from this group.

In the combined system the written exam initially screens candidates. Those who have qualifying scores are placed on a list from which candidates are interviewed and selected. Today, the vast majority of agencies in the United States require POs to hold a bachelor's degree, usually in a specified area, such as criminology or one of the social sciences (Champion, 1998). In addition to educational requirements, most of the agencies around the country require both preservice and in-service training.

The requirement that newly hired POs participate in preservice training programs has grown recently. A substantial majority of the states have instituted training programs, which range from a minimum of 24 hours in South Dakota to 540 hours in Oklahoma (Camp & Camp, 1994c). In some states successful completion of training leads to certification, which is required before the individual can begin to work as a PO. Most states also require a minimum number of in-service training hours (usually 40) each year. The in-service training is intended to keep officers current with new developments.

Probation Officers' Duties

In most jurisdictions, the two major services provided by probation officers are investigation and supervision. Depending on state statutes or on the sentencing judge's discretion, an investigation of the defendant may be conducted after conviction but before sentencing. The fruits of this investigation are embodied in the *presentence investigation report (PSI).* Supervision entails surveillance and providing social services.

The Presentence Investigation Report   The **presentence investigation report** has five basic purposes, each of which may serve a different set of constituents (Abadinsky, 1997; Champion, 1990; McCarthy & McCarthy, 1991):

1. to help the sentencing judge impose the most appropriate sentence.

2. to establish a probation or parole supervision and treatment plan for the offender regardless of the sentencing disposition.

3. to help jail and prison personnel classify the offender.

4. to provide parole authorities with information that eventually can be used in release planning, including

special conditions needed to ensure parolees greater success.

5. to serve as a rich information source to criminal justice and correctional researchers.

The information for the PSI comes from interviews with the offender; his or her family, teachers, police, and employers; and an examination of various offender records and reports. The records include the individual's arrest record, the police offense report, previous PSI reports, previous institutionalization records, educational records, reports of psychological or psychiatric evaluations, and any treatment records. From these sources the PO should develop a report that contains:

- a complete account of the offense and the attendant circumstances.

- a description of the victim's status (impact of the crime, losses suffered, restitution due) and the victim's statement.

- the offender's criminal history, including juvenile training school reports.

- the offender's educational history and employment, including present levels of functioning.

- family background, social history, marital status, dependents, religious affiliation, interests and activities, and medical and psychiatric history.

- special resources that might be available to assist the offender (e.g., treatment centers, special educational or vocational programs).

- a summary of the significant information and the specific recommendations for sentencing and service needs.

The value of the PO's work lies in the significant weight the recommendations are likely to carry with the judge. This is as it should be because the PO has had the opportunity to see the offender in the community and develop a perspective on his or her "general lifestyle" (Carter, 1966). From this the PO has to evaluate the risks posed by the offender to the community and make decisions about (1) the nature of the recommended sentence (probation or prison); (2) the security level required with a prison sentence; (3) the offender's rehabilitative potential; and (4) any negative public reaction to a probation sentence.

Should the PSI's contents be disclosed to defendants and their attorneys to contest damaging information? In the juvenile case of *Kent v. United States* (1966), the Supreme Court said that all social service records that affected a defendant's disposition should be disclosed to defense counsel. Presumably, this would include the PSI in the case of adults. Therefore, the present trend is to make the PSI available to the defendant, omitting the

following: the PO's recommendations, diagnostic information that might seriously disrupt a rehabilitation program, information collected under the promise of confidentiality, and other information that could be deemed "harmful" to the offender or others (Adair & Slawsk, 1991).

Several criticisms have been leveled at PSI reports. Among these are that many POs are so overloaded with cases and investigations that they may not have time to produce adequate reports. However, judges typically follow PSIs even though they may feel the information is based on hearsay and may not completely trust it. Misinformation and incomplete information may make a number of PSIs misleading (Blumberg, 1970; Dickey, 1979; Rosecrance, 1988).

Another criticism leveled at the PSI concerns the accuracy of the report's diagnostic information. These reports may contain clinical "impressions" about the subject that could be taken as fact. These impressions tend to be relatively unreliable in that another clinician interviewing the same subject may come to very different conclusions (Robitscher, 1980).

Additionally, there are for-profit agencies in some areas that prepare PSI studies for a fee. This can produce a problem with respect to equal justice in that only the well-to-do can afford the required fee to obtain private PSIs (Abadinsky, 1994; McShane & Krause, 1993).

Perhaps the most stinging criticism of PSIs came from John Rosecrance, a long-time probation officer. Rosecrance said that above all else probation officers focus on the current offense and prior record in making sentencing recommendations. Further, he noted that "the efficacy of current presentence investigation practices is doubtful" (Rosecrance, 1988, p. 253). In the end, Rosecrance saw the PSI as performing the largely symbolic function of maintaining the "myth of individualized sentences . . . without influencing sentences significantly" (Rosecrance, 1988, p. 253).

Supervision and Service Delivery to Probationers The second major function of probation officers is the supervision of offenders placed on probation. There are two major duties required in client supervision: (1) surveillance, or controlling the offender, and (2) providing social services. The first duty is similar to that of a police officer, whereas the second is akin to that of a social worker. These two duties can conflict and create a dilemma for POs in dealing with their clients. If law enforcement is emphasized, clients may develop a distrust of POs and reject their efforts to provide help. By contrast, emphasizing helping may cause POs to overlook the risks clients represent to themselves or the community. Most POs probably develop a supervision approach that lies between these two extremes.

There are at least three models under which POs deliver supervisory services to their clients: the law enforcement model, the caseworker model, and the resource broker/advocate model (Abadinsky, 1997; McCarthy & McCarthy, 1991).

- *The Law Enforcement Model*   Under the **law enforcement model,** law enforcement–oriented POs operate under the control model of supervision (Abadinsky, 1997). This approach to supervision has become more popular and heavily used since the advent of retribution and the implementation of risk control strategies. Its emphasis, tilted toward surveillance and arrest activities, is controversial. Many jurisdictions in which POs are expected to be law enforcers or peace officers discourage the use of firearms in carrying out their duties. This places POs in dangerous situations. According to Parsonage (1990), however, the practice of allowing POs to carry a weapon is becoming more common.

- *The Caseworker Model*   The **caseworker model** centers on providing treatment or counseling and developing a one-on-one relationship between the PO and the client. When clients develop trust in their POs, they may be positively influenced by them. This harkens back to John Augustus, whose work with offenders was based on the positive helping role. Allen, Eskridge, Latessa, and Vito (1985, p. 175) describe this approach in the following way:

  > Casework is a way of working with individuals. It is consciously chosen to help the offender become better adjusted to the demands of social living. Casework in probation and parole follows the traditional medical model and remains intact in most probation and parole agencies. In reality, however, the supervising officer does not have the time or energy to devote to individual cases. Perhaps the most basic criticisms of the casework approach are that the probation or parole officer tries to be all things to all people, and does not adequately mobilize the community and its support systems. In addition, large caseloads, staff shortages, and endless report writing leave the supervising officer unable to perform all the tasks called for by casework. Coupled with the trend away from the medical model, probation and parole administrators have initiated—the brokerage approach.

- *The Resource Broker/Advocate Model*   Under the **resource broker/advocate model,** POs are not required to have the time or skills to treat their clients, instead, they act as referral agents. Thus, they must identify client needs and problems and find the community agencies that can help meet them. One motivational tool often used in this approach is to have clients participate in the development of the plan to deal with their needs and problems. Beyond referring their clients to community resources POs also act as advocates for them, supervise them, and monitor their progress. In this approach a PO's relationship with community service agencies is more important than the relationship with clients (Culbertson & Ellsworth, 1985; McShane & Krause, 1993).

The brokerage approach assumes that the community is the most logical place for clients to receive the services necessary to complete probation (or parole) successfully. It emphasizes rehabilitation but removes the PO from having to provide the services personally. It also has the potential to reduce the conflict inherent in the PO role. However, it also has drawbacks. The PO–client relationship is not very strong, and this may reduce the PO's ability to influence clients. Additionally, needed services may not be available within the community or agencies may refuse to take criminal clients. Where these conditions exist, the effectiveness of this approach will be reduced.

Stress and Burnout Problems

The effects of stress on police and correctional officers are well documented (see, for example, Lombardo, 1989; Malloy & Mays, 1984; Terry, 1981). Because they face many of the same work-related conditions as both police and correctional officers, POs are also exposed to high levels of stress. According to Simmons, Cochran, and Blount (1997), stress among probation officers results from several sources, including job dissatisfaction, role conflict, role ambiguity, client-officer interactions, excessive paperwork and performance pressures, low self-esteem and public image, job risks, and liabilities (see also Sigler, 1988; Whitehead, 1985, 1987).

Some of the specific reasons that cause the most job dissatisfaction among POs derive from the organizational environment. These include low pay, excessive caseloads, poor supervision, lack of control over one's job, and lack of input into agency policy (Simmons et al., 1997). Role conflict results from being faced with job and performance expectations on the part of supervisors that conflict with those of the PO. Role ambiguity, which is related to role conflict, results from poorly defined program goals, which make it difficult for POs to remain focused. A recent research project involving 186 randomly selected probation officers in Florida found that many of these POs perceive "major stressors that derive primarily from the organization and only marginally from the tasks they are asked to perform (Simmons et al., 1997, p. 226).

The recent shift toward a control or law enforcement orientation in dealing with probation and parole clients is likely to make the interaction between the PO and client more antagonistic. Brown (1993) indicates that mental preparation for the crises involved in this more antagonistic setting is likely to reduce stress. Although the antagonism may reduce the role conflict and ambiguity for the PO, it may also reduce greatly the positive influence that the PO can have on his or her clients.

In spite of the negative factors associated with probation work, many POs stay with their agencies. Simmons et al. (1997, p. 227) conclude that other factors must be at work in the personal and professional lives of probation officers, and these factors might include "loyalty, commitment, and attachment to the job."

Revocation of Probation

When probationers fail to live up to the conditions imposed by the court they can be subjected to **revocation** proceedings. For probationers, POs have the authority to recommend and begin the process, but the actual power to revoke an offender's probation is in the hands of the sentencing judge. Normally, revocation can result from two types of violations, those that deal with law-breaking and those that are technical. Technical violations include one or more of the conditions of the probation or parole contract (such as periodically reporting in) that are not spelled out in the law. The parties involved in revocation (the PO and the judge) have considerable discretion. Clients are not automatically revoked when they fail to abide by some of the conditions of their contracts. If an offender violates conditions the PO can ignore it, take informal action (e.g., reprimand the offender), order the client jailed for a short time, or report it to the sentencing judge. If a decision is made to revoke, a formal process controlled by guidelines set by the Supreme Court must be followed.

Court Decisions on Revocation

In *Mempa v. Rhay* (1967) the U.S. Supreme Court decided that probationers are entitled to counsel at revocation hearings. This decision was important because it was the first time the Court recognized the due process rights of probationers. Two Court decisions in the early 1970s provided the present guidelines used in revocation hearings. The first of these decisions was *Morrissey v. Brewer* (1972), which applied to parole revocation proceedings (to be discussed in Chapter 21). The due process protections that were established for parolees were extended to probationers a year later in *Gagnon v.*

Scarpelli (1973). These two cases mandated that probationers and parolees be provided with the right to a two-stage hearing, including due process protections, during revocation proceedings. In the first hearing a determination is made about whether probable cause exists that the probationer violated any specific conditions of his or her contract. The second hearing consists of the general revocation proceeding. During both hearings the offender is guaranteed basic due process rights.

Reasons for Revocation

Probationers face revocation for a variety of reasons. Research reviewed by Champion (1990) suggests that the most frequent reasons include arrest for a new crime, alcohol or drug abuse, escape, weapons possession, traffic violations, and difficulties with probation or parole officers or halfway house staff.

The Bureau of Justice Statistics (Bonczar, 1997, p. 10) reports that in 1995 41.1 percent of adult probationers facing a disciplinary hearing did so for absconding or failing to maintain appropriate contact. Of the remainder, the most common reasons were committing a new offense (38.4%), failure to pay fines or restitution (37.9%), and failure to attend or complete drug or alcohol treatment (22.5%).

Of the probationers facing a disciplinary hearing, 42 percent were allowed to remain on probation with the stipulation of additional conditions. Another 29 percent were sent to jail or prison, and 29 percent had probation supervision reinstated with no additional conditions (Bonczar, 1997).

Revocations of probationers rose sharply between 1980 and 1990. According to a survey conducted by Parent, Wentworth, Burke, and Ney (1994), in many

A frequent reason for revocation of probation is drug abuse.

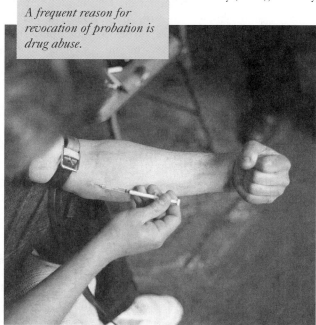

states more persons are admitted to prison after revocation than are sentenced directly for a crime. Parent et al. (1994) feel that two factors account for this: the very large number of offenders on probation, and increased emphasis on surveillance with better ways to detect violators. The large rise in revocations has contributed to the prison overcrowding problem, which, in turn, has led to early releases for many of those revoked. An additional problem has been the trend to disregard some of those supervisees who abscond. The discretionary manner in which these problems were handled within and across jurisdictions led to discrepancies in the way in which these cases were disposed.

Several reforms have begun to be implemented to restructure the process:

- Development of written policies on revocations. In states where this has been done (e.g., South Carolina), the policies generally covered the agency's goals, had clear definitions of the different violation categories, and set guidelines that matched violation categories with sanctions (e.g., which violations deserve revocation, which deserve imprisonment, which deserve to remain in the community under increased supervision, etc.).

- Refining procedures by which agency goals are to be accomplished. This included such things as spelling out in greater detail the enforcement actions POs may take on their own and those that require approval.

- Expanding the sanction choices available to the agency. Thus, instead of having the option of continuing supervision or imprisonment, which might be too lenient or too harsh, the whole range of community sanctions might be used.

- Taking a more active approach to apprehending absconders. This new approach includes an expansion of POs' responsibility in trying to contact them; a greater use of existing information sources (e.g., driver's license bureau); the development of enhanced fugitive units, which target specific absconders for apprehension; and finally, the development of sanctions to match absconder risk, rather than just placing all apprehended absconders in prison. (Parent et al., 1994)

Finally, one means of reducing the number of revocations is for POs to develop reasonable and understandable rules for clients to follow. Success can be further enhanced by specifying client objectives, defining their importance, and identifying appropriate resources to assist in their achievement. Revocation can be greatly reduced if court or parole board objectives are translated into concrete behavioral expectations that clients can understand and meet. For example, if the court orders a client to pay restitution to the victim, this can be translated into the following requirement: The client will pay the victim at least $15 per week until the amount of $575 is paid (Cohn, 1987).

Measuring the Effectiveness of Probation

The effectiveness of correctional strategies, including probation, should be measured in terms of their goals. Generally, probation agencies measure effectiveness in terms of revocation or recidivism rates. Both measures have been criticized because they have shortcomings.

Revocation and recidivism tend to be defined differently in different agencies (Albanese, Fiore, Powell, & Storti, 1981; Maltz, 1984). Generally, *revocation* of probation involves a termination of that status for cause and is likely to result either in the imposition of more stringent conditions and supervision or imprisonment. *Recidivism* is variously defined in terms of a rearrest, a reconviction, or a reincarceration. The disparities in these definitions make cross-agency comparisons difficult at best and meaningless at worst. Waldo and Griswold (1979) consider that arrest and conviction for any crime is not a sufficient condition for the strict definition of recidivism. This is because the client's rearrest may result from a variety of situations that are more or less serious, such as a technical violation of probation conditions. Additionally, the arrested client may not even be guilty. For example, if revocation occurs because the client is unable or refuses to maintain employment, this will have a significantly different meaning from if it is due to an arrest for armed robbery. Yet, in the gross measure of agency success both arrestees may be counted as recidivists.

Additionally, POs' discretion in their responses to the violation of conditions will affect revocation (McCarthy & McCarthy, 1991). Thus, service-oriented POs may overlook relatively minor violations because they feel that the beneficial effects of remaining in the community outweigh those of imprisonment. Law enforcement–oriented officers may hold a different perspective and revoke offenders for the same violation. These considerations can also apply at the agency level, depending on its policy.

Studies of Effectiveness

Reviews of probation effectiveness studies (e.g., Allen, Carlson, & Parks, 1979; Geerken & Hayes, 1993) have reported inconsistent findings. This inconsistency holds true whether probation was compared with other sanctions, whether the recidivism rates were only for probation, or whether factors that might enhance probation success were being evaluated. A number of writers (see, for example, Maltz, 1984; McCarthy & McCarthy, 1991) have concluded that because of the methodological problems (noncomparable subject groups, varying defini-tions of recidivism), little can be generalized from re-search findings. However, they infer that, except for indi-viduals with several prior felony convictions, probation seemed as effective as other sanctions in terms of recidi-vism. The reviewers indicated that agency rates of 30 percent or below were seen as representing effective pro-grams. Nevertheless, McCarthy and McCarthy (1991) note that in over half the studies reviewed, significant correlations were found between higher recidivism levels and the offender's previous criminal history, youthful age, status other than married, unemployment, educa-tion below fourth grade, drug or alcohol abuse, and com-mission of property offenses. Of these the most signifi-cant was having a history of several felony convictions.

In reviewing the effects of specific treatments ap-plied to probationers, Allen and his colleagues (1979) grouped the treatments into three categories. These in-cluded those that emphasized vocational counseling or employment, counseling, and drug treatment. Study findings only weakly supported the effectiveness of pro-grams (e.g., vocational evaluation, job coaching, and job referral) that only concentrated on enhancing employ-ment. The same appears to be true for psychological counseling programs. Some sex offender and other types of counseling programs reported successful results, but many programs found no differences between individu-als who received counseling and those who did not. The findings in the counseling studies were complicated by the poor definition and description of the treatment methodologies used. With respect to outpatient drug treatment there also were mixed findings. Whereas suc-cess has been reported in some studies using intensive supervision along with education and treatment, meth-adone maintenance, or behavior modification, other stud-ies did not report such findings.

The Rand Study and Subsequent Research A study con-ducted by the Rand Corporation (Petersilia, Turner, Kahan, & Peterson, 1985) examined probation effective-ness for more than 16,000 California offenders. Some of the major results of this study, which followed the sam-ple for 3½ years, were as follows:

1. During the follow-up period, two thirds of the proba-tioners were rearrested, over half were reconvicted, and over one third were incarcerated. Those proba-tioners with criminal histories similar to those of prison inmates were 50 percent more likely to get re-arrested as compared with other probationers.

2. Knowing the type of conviction, prior criminal record, and use of alcohol and drugs resulted in accu-rate prediction of reconviction in two out of three cases for the probation sample.

3. Once information on the offender's background and criminal history was considered, the PO's sentencing

recommendation contributed little to enhancing the prediction of recidivism. About two thirds of those in each group recommended for either probation or im-prisonment were rearrested.

4. When using factors associated with actual probation success, this study concluded that only 3 percent of the sample could have been placed on probation with at least a 75 percent chance of succeeding.

Based on their findings, the Rand researchers concluded that more use should be made of risk assessment scales along with improved case management procedures. They also found that there was a need for the develop-ment of different strategies to control offenders in the community.

Studies in other states achieved dramatically differ-ent results. A study of Missouri and Kentucky felony probationers found rearrest and reconviction rates that were about one third as high as those found in Califor-nia (McGaha, Fichter, & Hirschburg, 1987). A similar study in New Jersey (Whitehead, 1989) indicated that rearrest and reconviction rates there were two thirds as high as in California. Whitehead (1991) also found that when incarceration was used as a measure of re-cidivism, rates were only 17 percent after a 4-year follow-up.

The Langan-Cunniff Study We conclude our discussion of probation effectiveness with a review of research re-ported by Langan and Cunniff (1992) because this is the largest follow-up study to date. Their results were based on a sample of 79,000 felons from 17 states, sentenced to probation in 1986 and followed through 1989. Figure 19.1 provides a graphic picture of what happened to these offenders over a 3-year period. Nearly two thirds of these felony probationers were arrested for a new felony or were charged with technical violations.

As a rule, violators who were sent to prison did more than just fail to meet some technical probation condi-tion. Two thirds of those sent to jail or prison had at least one felony arrest. The types and numbers of offenses for which these offenders were arrested raises some serious concerns about placing them on probation. Close to half (34,000) of these probationers accounted for 64,000 felony arrests during the 3-year follow-up period. About 20 percent of the group was arrested three or more times. The offenders most likely to commit subsequent crimes were those on probation for robbery, drug posses-sion, and burglary.

What happened to those committing subsequent of-fenses is quite telling. Three quarters of those arrested after the first felony were convicted (64% for a felony and 11% for a misdemeanor), and 88 percent of this group was sentenced either to prison (42%) or jail (46%). Judges sentenced 49 percent of them to prison after their second convictions, and by their third convictions 70 percent were sent to prison.

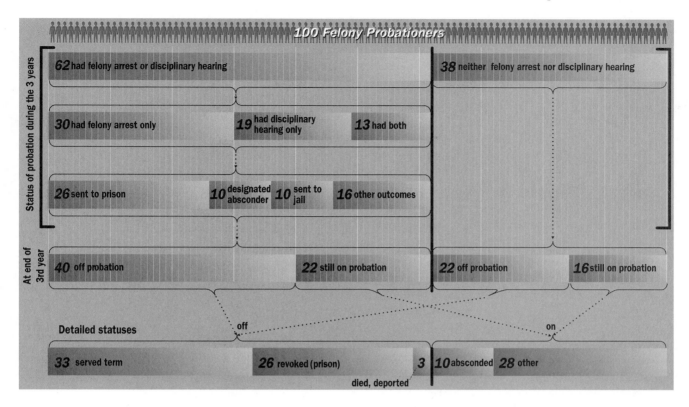

Figure 19.1 *100 Felons Tracked Through Their First 3 Years of Probation*
Source: P. A. Langan & M. A. Cunniff (1992). *Recidivism of Felons on Probation, 1986–89*. Washington, DC: U.S. Department of Justice, Bureau of Justice Statistics.

At the end of the 3-year follow-up period, only 33 percent had completed their probation sentences. Looking at those who completed their probation terms is far from comforting; this group was not trouble free (Langan & Cunniff, 1992, p. 8; see also Bonczar, 1997):

- 41% had at least one felony arrest while on probation, and one third of these also had a disciplinary hearing
- 24% had at least one disciplinary hearing
- 16% had at least one sentence to jail
- 31% of those with a special condition had not fully satisfied the condition
- 53% of those with a financial penalty had not fully paid the penalty

It appears, however, that regardless of the recidivism level, the most recent probation trend has been to expand the level, intensity, and types of supervision available in the community. These newer forms of supervision, often referred to as intermediate sanctions, are discussed in Chapter 20.

Summary

The supervision of offenders in the community has grown tremendously in the more than 150 years since John Augustus began his work in Boston. There is no question about its importance to both corrections and the community given that about three fourths of the offenders under correctional supervision are in the community. This fact has at least one important ramification: It provides an alternative sanction that avoids the potentially debilitating effects of imprisonment while saving taxpayers a significant amount of money. In spite of the importance of community supervision, there are nagging concerns among much of the public about its effectiveness, whether it is punitive enough, and whether society can be protected from victimization at the hands of those convicted offenders who remain in the community. To deal with these concerns and keep some of the advantages of community programs, there has been a proliferation of programs attempting to provide more supervision and impose tougher conditions. Thus, these more rigorous programs could be construed by the public as more punitive. It is these programs, referred to as intermediate sanctions, that we describe in Chapter 20.

Critical Thinking Questions

1. Briefly summarize the history of probation. What role did John Augustus play in its development?

2. How are risk prediction scales used in deciding which offenders should be placed on probation?

3. Identify the basic organizational arrangements under which probation services are administered in this country and the methods employed in assigning cases to probation officers.

4. List the five basic uses of the presentence investigation and the basic types of information that should be included in each report.

5. Discuss the supervisory styles and service delivery strategies characteristic of different probation officers.

6. Summarize the general results of studies on the effectiveness of probation.

7. What due process rights are probationers entitled to during the revocation process?

8. What different types of procedures are employed in the hiring of probation officers?

9. Discuss some of the factors that cause probation officers stress.

Test Your Knowledge

1. _____ is an early antecedent of probation that allowed individuals accused of serious crimes to appeal for leniency by reading the 51st Psalm in court.
   a. Benefit of clergy
   b. Judicial reprieve
   c. Recognizance
   d. Executive clemency

2. Today, probation officers are more likely to operate under the _____ orientation.
   a. counseling
   b. law enforcement
   c. caseworker
   d. broker/advocate

3. The most common form of organizing probation services in the United States is:
   a. within local county executive departments.
   b. within the state executive branch.
   c. under the state judiciary.
   d. under the local courts.

4. Probationers are entitled to certain procedural due process rights at revocation hearings. Which of the following is *not* one of them?
   a. right to a jury trial
   b. right to present evidence
   c. right to cross-examine witnesses
   d. right to have a fair hearing

Intermediate Sanctions: Getting Tough in the Community

KEY TERMS AND CONCEPTS

Boot camps

Community service orders

Continuous signaling devices

Day fines

Day reporting centers

Electronic monitoring

Halfway house

House arrest/home confinement

Huber Act

Intensive probation supervision (IPS)

Intermediate sanctions

Net widening

Programmed contact devices

Shock incarceration

Study release

Tracking devices

Work release

LEARNING OBJECTIVES

After completing this chapter, you should be able to:

1. Discuss the reasons for the increase in intermediate sanction programs.

2. Define the term *intermediate sanction*, discuss its historical antecedents, and identify the types of programs that compose it.

3. Describe and discuss the goals of these programs and their philosophical underpinnings.

4. Delineate the factors that must be considered to successfully establish a halfway house.

5. Explain the goals and positive effects of work and study release programs and their development in the United States.

6. Explain how intensive supervision programs work and the purposes for which they were established.

7. Describe home confinement, the role that surveillance plays in it, and its advantages and disadvantages.

8. Describe the various forms of electronic monitoring, explain how they work, and discuss the ethical issues involved.

9. Describe shock incarceration and boot camps, and differentiate between them.

10. Explain the functions and goals of day reporting centers.

Introduction

One of the most important correctional developments in recent years has been the use and expansion of **intermediate sanctions,** punishment that falls somewhere between probation and incarceration. These programs carry names such as intensive probation supervision, house arrest/home confinement, electronic monitoring, community service orders, shock incarceration/boot camp, day fines, and day reporting centers. This development is attributed to three primary concerns: the prison overcrowding crisis facing many correctional systems; the growing dissatisfaction with regular probation that is viewed as too lenient on felony offenders; and fiscal conservatism and budget constraints that have forced correctional administrators and policy makers to search for less costly alternatives to incarceration without appearing to be too "soft" on crime.

Intermediate sanctions appear to be an ideal answer to these concerns because they seem to be less costly than prison, yet are more punitive than standard probation. Many would agree that economics has fueled the rapid growth of these programs (Petersilia, 1987). They have received highly visible and favorable media attention at the local, state, and federal levels as innovative sentencing options designed to fill the gap between regular probation and incarceration on the continuum of sanctions.

Despite the rapid growth of intermediate sanction programs, we are only beginning to evaluate systematically their efficacy. The following questions have been raised about these programs: (1) Are they cost effective? (2) Do they help reduce prison overcrowding, or do they just widen the net? and (3) Do they maintain enough control over offenders so that the safety of the community is not compromised (Clear & Hardyman, 1990; General Accounting Office, 1990b; Tonry, 1990; Tonry & Will 1988; Wagner & Baird, 1993)? These are some of the issues addressed in this chapter, along with a description of several types of intermediate sanction programs.

Historical Development of Intermediate Sanctions

Intermediate sanctions are not a new idea. Programs with similarities to intermediate sanctions can be traced to sixth-century France when St. Leonard obtained the release of prisoners from the king (James, 1975). These individuals were given temporary food and shelter in St. Leonard's monastery at Limoges until they could return to their communities. During this period and throughout the Middle Ages, it was not uncommon for religious orders to assist prisoners in such a humanitarian fashion.

As early as the 1820s a need was recognized for halfway houses to assist those released from prison. However, because public opposition to this concept was too strong, it was not implemented until about 20 years later (McCarthy & McCarthy, 1991). Later, in 1914, the first formal work release program was implemented in Wisconsin. In the 1960s, a growing emphasis on community-based corrections led to the establishment of a variety of residential treatment programs (Public Health Service, 1976). From the 1950s through the early 1970s, the first modern intensive supervision programs emerged (Clear & Hardyman, 1990). Other intensive supervision programs were developed in the mid-1980s and included house arrest/home confinement programs, boot camps, electronic monitoring, and day reporting centers (Gowdy, 1993; Parent, Dunworth, McDonald, & Rhodes, 1997).

Initially, the programs started in the 1980s were described as intermediate *punishments*, not intermediate *sanctions*, because this terminology seemed "tougher." Legislators, pushed by public opinion, wanted these programs to appear more punitive than standard probation because the emphasis was being placed on the correctional goal of "just deserts." A complicating factor was that as these programs were being developed, rehabilitation was being rejected as a primary objective for corrections. Rehabilitation did not fit in with the just deserts philosophy underlying these programs. This emphasis on punishment was in direct contrast to the philosophical ideals that had characterized the community-based programs implemented earlier. A review of the philosophical underpinnings of intermediate sanctions may provide the reader with a better understanding of how earlier programs differed from later ones in concept and impact.

Changing Correctional Philosophies

The earliest community programs established between incarceration and release in the United States were based on humanitarian concerns. Halfway houses were created to provide temporary shelter and food for offenders who were often too destitute to resume normal (noncriminal) residence in the community. Work release programs focused on helping offenders find employment, reestablishing family ties, and easing the transition into the community. Later, these programs served offenders not only as postincarceration alternatives but also as preincarceration dispositions. This provided them with the opportunity to change their criminal lifestyle *before* it led to incarceration.

In the 1960s, dissatisfaction with correctional practices led to a new movement among practitioners and academics to decrease the use of incarceration as punishment. These professionals agreed that incarceration was debilitating and ineffective. Some states even called for abolishing imprisonment for some classes of offenders (Task Force on Corrections, 1973). Rather than incarceration, emphasis was placed on the humanitarian, reintegrative, and managerial aspects of community-based corrections.

In the late 1970s, the philosophy of community-based programs began to shift from a humanitarian or rehabilitative perspective to one guided by economics and a need to be more punitive (Byrne, 1986). Thus, it is now more appropriate to call these programs "corrections in the community" because their emphasis now includes more traditional correctional objectives such as control and just deserts. Although attempts continue to move intermediate sanctions back to a philosophy based on humanitarianism and rehabilitation, current public attitudes toward correctional programming make it unlikely that this will occur.

Purposes of Intermediate Sanctions

It has been difficult to determine exactly what intermediate sanctions programs are supposed to accomplish. Remember that recent programs developed and expanded largely in response to the overcrowding crisis. Thus, the policies behind these programs were rarely based on logical and consistent theoretical principles. Instead, most developed without any explicit theoretical rationale of what program outcomes should be.

Because interest in intermediate sanctions grew out of practical and expedient concerns, it is no surprise that their theoretical underpinnings are weak. This has caused confusion in defining them. What has resulted is perplexing and redundant terminology in describing these sentencing options, including terms such as *intermediate punishments, intermediate sanctions, alternatives to incarceration,* and *sentencing alternatives* (Morris & Tonry, 1990; U.S. Department of Justice, 1990). To provide some consistency and clarity, the U.S. Department of Justice (1990, p. 3) labeled these programs *intermediate sanctions* and provided the following definition: "... a punishment option that is considered on a continuum to fall between traditional probation and traditional incarceration." Defined in this way, these programs provide multipurpose sentencing options for dealing with high-risk offenders who require more surveillance and control and whose crimes demand more punishment than can be provided by traditional probation but less than is required by imprisonment. They also include elements from all the traditional correctional goals. The punitive aspect of intermediate sanctions reflects the goals of retribution and just deserts. Other traditional goals such as deterrence (both general and specific), incapacitation, and rehabilitation also are found in the various program rationales. Therefore, as we examine programs in this category, we must keep in mind their multipurpose functions.

Types of Intermediate Sanction Programs

Intermediate sanction programs today meet the need for a graduated sentencing system. Whereas some programs are new—such as community service orders, day reporting centers, and day fines—others have been part of the correctional process from its earliest beginnings and had a much different focus (Parent et al., 1997). The older programs, residential community correctional facilities such as halfway houses and work release centers, filled the gap between probation and jail or prison sentences long before *intermediate sanctions* became a corrections buzzword. These latter programs are discussed first so that some historical continuity is provided.

Treatment-Oriented Halfway Houses

Halfway houses were the earliest form of what are now called intermediate sanctions. Initially, halfway houses served as an intermediate step between prison and release into the community, thus the designation *halfway-out programs.* Today, they also are used as an alternative to prison commitment, and when used in this manner, they are called *halfway-in programs.* Whether halfway houses function as post- or preincarceration programs, they are clearly transitional residential facilities that operate in community settings. The following provides a good definition of halfway houses:

Halfway houses are transitional residential facilities in the community that help released offenders adjust to life outside prison. Many offer services such as job training programs.

The very name halfway house suggests its position in the corrections world: halfway-in, a more structured environment than probation and parole; halfway-out, a less structured environment than institutions. As halfway-in houses they represent a last step before incarceration for probationers and parolees facing . . . revocation; as halfway-out houses, they provide services to prereleasees and parolees leaving institutions. Halfway houses also provide a residential alternative to jail or outright release for accused offenders awaiting trial or convicted offenders awaiting sentencing. (Thalheimer, 1975, p. 1)

Although most halfway houses function according to this basic definition, there is great diversity in their actual operation and the services they provide to offenders.

The appeal of halfway houses can be traced to three goals or ideals that are encompassed by these programs. The *humanitarian ideal* of halfway houses was based on the perception that removing offenders from the harsh prison environment was more beneficial than continued exposure to the criminogenic effects of incarceration. The *reintegrative ideal* held that temporary assistance for offenders made the transition back to the community much easier. This included assisting offenders to (1) find employment, (2) reestablish family and community ties, and (3) access rehabilitative services in the community. All these factors would facilitate the third ideal, the successful *rehabilitation* of the offender. Maintaining offenders in halfway houses also resulted in reduced costs when compared with imprisonment (Latessa & Allen, 1999). This created positive managerial practices that were embraced by practitioners and policy makers.

History of Halfway Houses Public indifference, opposition by progressive organizations like the American Prison Association, and concerns about allowing ex-offenders to associate with one another had a contaminating effect on the creation of halfway houses. The result was that only a few halfway houses developed during the latter part of the 19th and first half of the 20th centuries.

The first halfway house in the United States (Isaac T. Hopper House) opened in New York in 1845, followed by one in Boston in 1864 and another in Philadelphia in 1889. In 1896 the first of the Hope Houses was opened in New York, followed by others in seven states (Keller & Alper, 1970; McCarthy & McCarthy, 1991; McCartt & Mangogna, 1973). However, it was not until the 1950s with the opening of the Dismas House, St. Leonard's House, and 308 West Residence that there was a real beginning of a national halfway house movement (Keller & Alper, 1970). Major boosts to this movement resulted from the endorsement of the halfway house concept in 1961 by Attorney General Robert F. Kennedy and the formation of the International Halfway House Association in 1964 (McCartt & Mangogna, 1976). Additional impetus for these programs was provided by the President's Crime Commission (Task Force on Corrections, 1967) and the National Advisory Commission on Criminal Justice Standards and Goals (Task Force on Corrections, 1973). These groups supported the humanitarian, rehabilitative, and reintegrative ideals that community-based corrections provided. In addition, halfway houses were thought to provide a positive managerial approach because they seemed more cost effective than incarceration. This level of support and positive view of these programs led to the presence of halfway houses in almost all states by the mid-1970s as well as an expansion of the programs offered in them and the types of clients served (Latessa & Allen, 1982). Also, during this period private agencies began operating many of these programs. As a result, many standard procedures required in government programs no longer applied. General guidelines for the implementation and operation of halfway houses were developed during this time to provide consistency in program characteristics.

An important question about halfway houses is whether they realize their rehabilitative goals and other objectives. The most comprehensive review aimed at answering this question was initially done by Seiter, Carlson, Bowman, Granfield, and Beran (1977) and later updated by Latessa and Allen (1982). Based on an examination of 44 studies, Latessa and Allen concluded that halfway houses may be as effective as any other parole strategy. Also, for that period of time (the late 1970s), they probably were more cost effective than incarceration in a state prison. Donnelly and Forcshner (1992, p. 349) assert that "given that halfway house clients are probably a higher risk group than parolees and that recidivism rates are similar for the two groups, halfway houses may be doing a better job than the evaluations can measure."

Halfway House Guidelines Rachin (1972) established guidelines for opening and operating halfway houses that focused on size, site selection, community relations, and space requirements. Programs housing 20 to 25 clients are considered the optimum size for halfway houses. This number is based on costs, retaining small group interactions, and keeping the number of offenders down for community acceptance. Site selection is very important in successfully implementing halfway houses. Zoning, public transportation availability, community resistance, the type of physical facility, the neighborhood environment, and commercial service availability are important factors to be considered.

Delancey Street Foundation

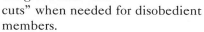

Background

The Delancey Street Foundation was started in 1971 by Dr. Mimi Silbert and John Maher, a former addict and member of Synanon (a program from which Maher developed the Delancey Street concept). Although Delancey Street is primarily for addicts, the program accepts all types of individuals—many of whom have been serious criminal offenders. Whereas some residents enter the program by self-referral, others are interviewed in jail or prison by current residents as prospective residents.

The Delancey Street complex is not the usual halfway house operation. The beautiful buildings, located in the Embarcadero area of San Francisco, were built in large part by Delancey Street residents. The complex can house approximately 500 residents. Besides the residences, there are training school businesses that provide vocational skills to all residents and produce income for program operations. (Delancey Street is totally self-sufficient and does not solicit donations or receive tax money.) Satellite programs have been established in Los Angeles, New Mexico, North Carolina, and upstate New York.

A Therapeutic Community

Delancey Street operates as a therapeutic community and all programs are run by the residents themselves. Residents generally start by working at menial jobs, such as building maintenance. As they progress, residents work on achieving their high-school equivalency certificate and move on to greater responsibilities in the program's training businesses, which include a moving and trucking school, a restaurant and catering service, a print and copy shop, and an automotive service center. Many residents are rewarded with social outings and enriching experiences to facilitate their socialization process.

There are three simple and universal rules that every resident must understand and follow: no violence, no threats of violence, and no drugs and/or alcohol. In addition, everyone must work and make a commitment to the program of at least 2 years (though they are free to leave the program at any time). Most stay in the program 3 to 4 years. Discipline is handled by 12 "barbers," who are generally veteran residents. The barbers divide the disciplinary responsibilities and give verbal "haircuts" when needed for disobedient members.

Impact on Participants

The program has received enthusiastic support from the public and the media because of the positive impact program supporters claim it has had on the lives of the residents (some of whom were viewed as hopeless, drug-addicted criminal offenders). However, empirical evidence to support these claims is not available. The criticisms of the program have centered on claims that the program cultivates a dependence on the program that is not healthy. Indeed, some refer to it as a cult experience.

Halfway houses should make maximum use of community resources, including educational, religious, vocational, recreational, and medical services. Thus, they need to become fully integrated into the community. Community relations are also enhanced by establishing boards consisting of representatives from key areas, including political entities, criminal justice agencies, religious organizations, and representatives from businesses and citizens in the community. Space requirements should meet the needs for the maximum number of offenders to be housed in the facility. Standards set by the American Correctional Association (ACA) for matters such as bathroom facilities, sleeping areas, and day rooms must be met to gain ACA accreditation. Space requirements must also conform to the standards set by local boards as well as to legislatively enacted statutes.

Private Operation of Halfway Houses Halfway house numbers generally have declined in the 1980s and 1990s. Issues of costs (which are higher for halfway houses than for other intermediate sanction programs), recidivism, and public resistance have plagued these programs. Most of these programs today are privately run: A recent survey revealed that over 85 percent of halfway house programs presently operating are privately administered (Camp & Camp, 1994a). As a result, we can expect to see an even greater diversity in the goals, planning, implementation, programming, and operation of these programs in the future (McCarthy & McCarthy, 1991). The Program Focus, "Delancey Street Foundation," describes a private halfway house program in California. It is different from most halfway houses in that it houses several hundred residents.

Work and Study Release Programs

Prisons in the United States release over 400,000 offenders each year. Unfortunately, within 3 years as many as 40 percent of these individuals will be incarcerated again. Often one of the major factors associated with recidivism is a lack of job training and work opportunities (Turner & Petersilia, 1996, p. 1). **Work release** programs provide offenders the opportunity to learn and apply job skills.

Work release, also known as *work furlough* or *day parole*, is a program that allows specially selected inmates to work in the community while still incarcerated. These programs provide a controlled environment in which inmates can make a transition back to residence in the community. Inmates participating in work release programs must meet the same job eligibility criteria as other employees. They must work under the same conditions required of their civilian counterparts and, ideally, receive the same wages. **Study release** allows inmates to go into the community to pursue educational opportunities such as vocational training and college courses not available inside the prison. Study release functions the same as work release, and the program is often conducted out of the same facility as work release. We will focus on work release only, but keep in mind that the same principles guiding work release also apply to study release programs.

During nonworking hours, inmates are confined to either a correctional institution for institutionally based programs, or to a specially designated residential facility. During confinement hours, inmates must follow all of the same rules normally required of an incarcerated population as well as adhere to the rules and regulations established for work release participants.

Early Work Release Programs

Work release programs really did not develop in the United States until the 1960s, but a form of work release operated in a few states in the early 1900s. The first work release program was established in Wisconsin in 1914 under the **Huber Act.** This law authorized counties to set up a program for misdemeanants, serving one year or less, to be released during certain hours to work in the community (McCarthy & McCarthy, 1991). These inmates were supposed to be paid wages comparable to those for civilian employees.

Although the Wisconsin program generally was considered successful, during the next 40 years only Nebraska, West Virginia, and Hawaii (then a territory) established work release programs. Until North Carolina began an extensive work release program in 1957 for misdemeanants (later extended to felony offenders), interest in work release largely was dormant (Doeran & Hageman, 1982). By the 1960s, work release programs were used fairly extensively. With the passage of the Prisoner Rehabilitation Act of 1965, work release was es-

tablished for federal inmates. By 1975, all 50 states and the federal system had some form of work release operating. In the early 1990s, approximately 21,000 inmates were participating in work release and 750 in educational release throughout the United States annually (Davis, 1993a).

Goals and Objectives of Work Release

Work release initially was instituted as a postincarceration community correctional program. Although many work release programs have been established with humanitarian, rehabilitative, and reintegrative goals, early work release programs were meant to be punitive or retributive (Doeran & Hageman, 1982). Early program advocates questioned why criminal offenders were allowed to remain idle while law-abiding citizens labored. At the time there was a labor shortage and inmate workers were needed in the workforce. Today, the reverse argument is used by those who oppose inmate work programs; that is, why should inmates work at paying jobs when law-abiding citizens are unable to find employment? Whatever the answer, work release still serves multiple goals whether the program is institutionally based or community-centered. Thus, providing inmates with work can be viewed as both punitive and rehabilitative.

Operation of Work Release Programs

Work release programs are operated by local, state, and federal authorities. Currently, 43 states authorize work release for inmates. However, only about one third of the prisons actually operate work release programs, and fewer than 3 percent of prison inmates are involved in these programs (Turner & Petersilia, 1996).

Misdemeanant programs are usually operated by local authorities and generally administered by the county sheriff's office as part of the jail program. State-run programs typically are operated either out of prisons or out of specially designated residential facilities like community correctional centers or prerelease centers. These programs target felony offenders who are nearing the end of their sentences. Federal programs, administered by the Federal Bureau of Prisons, may contain misdemeanant and felony offenders. Both state and federal agencies sometimes contract with local agencies to house their inmates if they meet program eligibility criteria. This is done because many state and federal prisons are located in rural areas where there may be a shortage of employment opportunities. The current trend, however, is for local, state, and federal agencies to contract with private organizations to administer community correctional programs such as work release. These agencies may be nonprofit groups, such as the Salvation Army or Goodwill, or they may be for-profit companies.

The most important factor in the success of work release programs is the selection and screening of inmates who can safely and securely work in the community.

State-run work release programs screen offenders who are nearing the end of their sentences to identify those who can work safely and securely in the community.

Having specific guidelines and procedures for the selection of program participants in place is critical for program operation. Although potentially dangerous and violent offenders must be eliminated from program eligibility, no foolproof system is available for selecting "safe" inmates.

Program participant selection is based on a variety of factors that must meet statutory and administrative requirements. These factors may include voluntary application, current offense, institutional behavior, classification level, length of time remaining to be served, escape history, criminal history, judicial approval, employment availability, compliance with all vehicle and insurance laws and regulations if necessary, and voluntary contractual compliance with program requirements (e.g., consent to search, drug testing).

When inmates apply for program admission, work release staff investigate and evaluate them for eligibility. The decision to place an inmate on work release normally is made by a committee of institutional and program personnel. If admission is denied or delayed for any reason, candidates are notified promptly. Most programs have an appeal process for those who are denied or delayed. Inmates approved for these programs usually are required to complete a thorough orientation to ensure they fully understand all the program rules and regulations. In addition, an employability assessment is made and, if necessary, program staff assist them in obtaining employment. Staff see to it that appropriate allocations of the inmate's wages are made to allow for room and board, victim restitution, family support, fines, court costs, spending money, and any other financial obligations. Any funds remaining generally are placed in savings until release.

Effectiveness of Work Release

Does work release reduce recidivism? Early research did not show that work release significantly reduced recidivism of program participants when compared with inmates released outright (Waldo & Chiricos, 1974). In recent years, there have been few studies examining the effectiveness of work release in reducing recidivism. Some programs report that offenders in work release have fewer disciplinary reports than those in prison (Houston & Koch, 1993). Evaluation of the work release program operated by Washington State found that of 965 inmates participating, 544 (or 56%) were deemed successful. Another 131 (13.5%) were "moderately successful" (Turner & Petersilia, 1996, p. 5). This would indicate that work release is a positive behavioral management tool during the transition period from incarceration to release into the community.

In the future, we may see a decline in the use of work release and halfway house programs for low-risk offenders as the development and implementation of day reporting centers increases. From an economic perspective, day reporting centers (to be discussed later in this chapter) are less costly to operate than halfway houses because they eliminate offender housing costs. However, there are good reasons for retaining halfway house and work release programs because they fill an important gap in correctional programming. While recognizing that residential community corrections programs such as halfway houses and work release are not as secure as prison, Parent (1990a, p. 10) feels that these programs can play a significant role in risk management. He argues that if community residential placement is to be used in this manner:

> it should be reserved for the higher risk . . . offenders . . . deemed suitable for community supervision. . . . In order to use [this placement] as part of a risk management strategy . . . jurisdictions need precise tools for measuring the relative risks posed by different categories of offenders. . . . [These programs] can be used in several ways to enhance . . . risk management. . . . They can incapacitate higher-risk offenders by imposing stringent limits and controls on their movement or behavior during the initial weeks or months of community supervision. They can provide treatment to offenders selected on the basis of objective needs screening. They can deter technical violations of probation or parole or, failing that, provide an alternative to imprisonment for offenders who commit repeated technical violations but present little risk of committing new crimes.

Intensive Probation Supervision Programs

It is not unusual today to find probation caseloads that number in the hundreds. The result has been that probation officers are handling increasingly more serious offenders, and they are able to spend less time with them. As a result, many jurisdictions are targeting the most serious probationers for caseloads of 20 to 25 offenders per officer in new supervision programs. Although occasionally known as intensive supervision programs (ISP), today these programs are most often referred to as **intensive probation supervision** (IPS), and that is the designation we will use. These programs, which are meant to be more punitive and controlling than regular probation, have been implemented in some form in every state as well as in the federal system (Clear, Flynn, & Shapiro, 1987; Morris & Tonry, 1990). IPS programs increase the supervision and surveillance levels of high-risk felony offenders (Smith & Akers, 1993). By reducing officer caseload, more time can be spent supervising each offender. Increasing the frequency of contacts between officers and offenders allows for more intensive surveillance. Widely recognized as one of the most popular new intermediate sanctions, these programs are designed specifically to serve prison-bound offenders (Lurgio, 1990). Additionally, they are expanding in response to the serious overcrowding problem and system overload faced by most correctional agencies (Byrne, Lurgio, & Baird, 1989; Clear, Flynn, & Shapiro, 1987). These programs generally are viewed as reducing the costs of punishing offenders by not incarcerating them and instead keeping them in the community under strict supervision (Petersilia, 1990). Although there are differences in how these programs operate, most have similar requirements (Byrne & Pattavina, 1992; Erwin, 1990;

Table 20.1

Key Features of IPS Programs in 34 States*

Program Feature	Number	Percent (%)
Curfew/house arrest	28	82
Electronic monitoring	19	56
Mandatory referrals for treatment/ special conditions	10	29
Team supervision	12	35
Drug monitoring	26	76
Alcohol monitoring	25	74
Community service	23	68
Probation fees	9	26
Split sentence/shock incarceration	12	35
Community sponsors	2	6
Restitution	17	50
Objective risk assessment	19	56
Objective needs assessment	19	56
Other court costs/fees	11	32

*A total of 41 states have IPS programs according to the GAO nationwide survey, conducted in Spring 1989. Detailed program description data were unavailable for 8 states. Although there is currently no IPS program operating in Massachusetts, the table includes descriptive data from the previously evaluated Massachusetts program. Thus, 34 states provided GAO with the information summarized in the table.

Source: J. M. Byrne & A. Pattavina (1992). The Effectiveness Issue: Assessing What Works in the Adult Community Corrections System. In J. M. Byrne, A. J. Lurgio, & J. Petersilia (Eds.), *Smart Sentencing: The Emergence of Intermediate Sanctions.* Thousand Oaks, CA: Sage Publications, p. 289. Reprinted by permission of Sage Publications, Inc.

Morris & Tonry, 1990; Pearson & Harper, 1990; Petersilia, 1987). Table 20.1 shows various features of IPS programs in 34 states.

These programs have been employed as front-door programs, in which the offender is placed under increased control generally through some type of intensive probation. They also have been used as back-door programs, in which the program functions as an early release mechanism for high-risk offenders who may not meet the criteria for regular parole (Byrne, 1990).

Early IPS Programs   In the 1980s IPS programs were embraced as a correctional breakthrough and expanded rapidly across the country. However, they can be traced to the early 1950s when the California Department of Corrections began to experiment with different size probation caseloads (Carter & Wilkins, 1976). Clear and Hardyman (1990, pp. 42–43) write: "The way many people today present the [IPS] concept is almost as though the idea was just discovered in the last few years. Of course, the idea of the [IPS] is not only an old one, but it is also well-studied." When the idea was revitalized in the 1980s, many facets of the earlier programs were incorporated into the new ones, but program objectives were different. Their revival is somewhat surprising, because the research results revealed that early program objectives were not achieved and most of them were later abandoned. We will compare earlier programs with the newer ones to study their similarities and differences.

Several projects, called intensive interventions, began in 1953 and continued until the early 1970s in California. These projects evaluated the effectiveness of various levels of probation supervision. The Public Health Service (1976, p. 520) characterizes these earlier programs as "alternatives to institutionalization . . . which [could] be . . . clearly distinguished from regular probation supervision. [They were] called intensive intervention in lieu of institutionalization."

These early programs were seen as alternatives to incarceration for those offenders who required greater control and supervision than was provided in regular probation (Empey, 1967; Public Health Service, 1976). Although this idea is much the same for the programs most recently implemented (i.e., alternative sentencing for prison-bound offenders), there are major philosophical differences between today's programs and those of the 1950s.

During the late 1950s and throughout the 1960s, public and professional support for incarceration declined. There was greater acceptance of community-based programs and alternative measures for prison-bound offenders. These earlier programs also were intended to be rehabilitative. They were considered improvements

over imprisonment and were instituted "to avoid the negative effects of isolation from the community, the severing of family ties and noncriminal associations, and the institutional culture" (Public Health Service, 1976, p. 520).

The belief was that increased officer contact with the offender enhances the officer's helping role and assists in promoting positive behavioral changes. In general, these experiments attempted to determine the optimal caseload (Clear & Hardyman, 1990).

The various studies in California, including the study of the Special Intensive Parole Unit (SIPU) from 1953 until 1964, the Alameda County parole experiment in Oakland in 1959, and the study of federal probation and parole conducted at Berkeley in the 1960s, showed that reducing the caseload did not increase offenders' success. It also did not substantially increase the amount of officer contact with offenders in most instances (Banks, Porter, Tardin, Siler, & Unger, 1977; Carter & Wilkins, 1976; Clear & Hardyman, 1990).

Program Developments in the 1980s Even though these programs appeared to fail (as evidenced by their abandonment in the 1970s), when they were revived in the 1980s, their objective was to increase offender control. This was done by restricting offenders' freedom in the community. The important issue was enhancing public safety by increasing offender surveillance and supervision.

Tracking devices enable parole officers to pinpoint an offender's exact location at any given time. This enhances officers abilities to restrict an offender's freedom in the community.

Does IPS Work?

CLOSE-UP

A study was conducted by the Rand Corporation of 14 programs in nine states to answer the question of whether participation in this type of program affected an offender's subsequent criminal behavior versus involvement in more traditional sanctions (i.e., prison and routine probation) (Petersilia & Turner, 1993). The study involved 2,000 nonviolent offenders assigned randomly to an experimental group (i.e., an IPS program) or a control group who were either given routine probation, parole, or prison.

- *IPS was found to be effective in providing surveillance.* It was designed to be much more stringent than routine supervision and in every site it delivered more contact and monitoring than routine supervision. There was no clear indication whether these increased surveillance levels reduced an offender's subsequent involve-ment in crime. Thus, while in Seattle face-to-face contacts averaged 3.4 per month and in Macon they numbered 16.1, at both sites almost the same percentage of IPS offenders were arrested—46 versus 42 percent.

- *The programs were effective as inter-mediate sanctions.* Most IPSs had significantly higher levels of features curtailing freedom, which can be construed as punishment. This examines the same factors we previously cited: frequent contacts and drug testing. Did these more stringent control and surveillance methods subject IPSs to more punitive action by finding and punishing those who violated their conditions? In fact, IPS did have higher rates of technical violation than controls, which meant that it did achieve its objective of being more coercive and punitive. However, these results should be interpreted with caution because their closer surveillance may increase the probability that they were caught for a larger percentage of their violations. This was substantiated by interviews with IPS participants, which found that they believed there was a higher likelihood they would be caught and treated more harshly for violation than their counterparts on routine probation.

- *The effect on recidivism was not as successful.* IPS participants were subsequently arrested more often, did not have a longer time until they committed a crime, and their offenses were not less serious than control group members. Thus, 37 percent of IPSs were arrested as compared with 33 percent of the controls. However, remember that IPS offenders are more closely monitored and thus may be more likely to be caught in the enforcement net, while those on routine probation and parole may escape it. Thus, IPS offenders may well be committing the same or fewer of-

---

Although the public is skeptical about the correctional system's ability to effectively supervise offenders in the community, it is also aware of the limited resources and funding available to imprison all of them. The public, legislators, and policy makers were ready to support any sanction that increased the severity of punishment for the offender while being cost effective and providing greater community safety.

To summarize, the philosophy of the programs implemented in the 1980s embodies "two overriding and ambitious goals" (Byrne, 1990). The first goal is the alleviation of prison overcrowding and its negative effects and costs. The second is the protection of the public by using surveillance and techniques that reduce opportunities for recidivism. Although Byrne says that IPS can achieve a rehabilitative end, that is not a priority with most of these programs. The questions that should be addressed in IPS programs are similar to the ones addressed in the early California programs: Do smaller caseloads increase contact with offenders? Does this increased contact work to reduce recidivism? We may find that too much is expected from current programs, and they will experience the same shortcomings that occurred earlier.

Successes of New IPS Programs   Research on the new programs shows most have not significantly reduced recidivism of participants when they were compared with true prison-bound offenders. This is in contrast to initial program evaluations, which reported success in this area (Erwin, 1987; Pearson, 1987). Researchers conducting the recent studies on IPS have questioned both the methodologies used and the target population selected to participate in these programs (Byrne, 1990; Clear, Flynn, & Shapiro, 1987; Petersilia, 1987; Petersilia & Turner, 1993; Tonry, 1990).

One concern is that these programs may be widening the corrections net. **Net widening** occurs when a sanction extends the control "net" over offenders who could be effectively supervised with less intrusive methods (i.e., under regular probation, which involves less surveillance and control) than those employed in IPS. This

fenses than those under routine supervision.

- *Whether IPS is more cost effective depends on with what it is being compared.* When compared with routine probation, it is more expensive because caseloads are much smaller—generally about 25 offenders per PO or team. Comparing all the costs, including those associated with handling the higher rates of technical violations and rates of imprisonment (court costs), IPS costs per year averaged $7,200 per offender versus $4,700 for the controls on routine supervision. However, the costs per day for imprisonment are much more per offender than for IPS, especially when the cost of building new prisons is considered.

- *IPSs were more involved in treatment, and this was found to be related to a reduction in recidivism at some sites.* Comparing IPS offender involvement in programming with that of controls found IPSs had higher rates of involvement in some counseling (45% versus 22%); paid employment (56% versus 43%); and restitution (12% versus 3%). Only in the area of community service was there no difference.

- *This research suggests that IPS is better at achieving some goals than others.* For jurisdictions primarily interested in reducing recidivism, prison overcrowding, and system costs, IPS may not meet all these objectives. On the other hand, if the objective is to develop a more comprehensive and graduated sentencing structure, IPS can assist in achieving this goal. It can take its place as one of the intermediate sanctions between prisons and probation. Like other intermediate sanctions, it may impose more stringent controls on offenders than routine probation. It may also achieve greater flexibility in sentencing decisions by providing punishments that more closely fit the crimes. However, Petersilia and Turner (1993) cau-

tion that the public must be made aware that if jurisdictions plan to use IPS programs as a means of reducing recidivism they may not accomplish that goal.

Finally, IPS programs are still in the testing stage and need to be further refined. One way it might be more effective is to select offenders for IPS earlier in their careers. These offenders may better benefit from both the deterrent and rehabilitative aspects of IPS because they are not as committed to the criminal lifestyle.

What do you think? Also, do you think these programs should be eliminated if they do not reduce recidivism, or is the fact that they provide more diversified sentencing options and more punishment than routine probation sufficient to justify their continued funding?

Source: Adapted from J. Petersilia & S. Turner (1993). Evaluating Intensive Probation/Parole: Results of a Nationwide Experiment. *Washington, DC: National Institute of Justice.*

view is supported by data showing that many of these offenders have criminal characteristics more like offenders who should have been placed on "regular" probation than like those of the prison-bound population. The fact that these less serious offenders are included in IPS effectively counters claims that these programs reduce prison overcrowding. Net widening also raises questions about the cost savings associated with placing offenders in IPS if they could have been supervised in less costly regular probation. Our Close-Up, "Does IPS Work?" focuses on a Rand study that was designed to answer these and other questions.

House Arrest/Home Confinement Programs

House arrest/home confinement programs have been very popular with both the public and legislatures. In these programs, offenders are confined to their homes or designated residences at all times unless officially permitted to leave for employment, community service, medical needs, or other reasons. Presently, the largest in-

termediate sanction program of this type in the nation is Florida's Community Control Program, known more popularly as "house arrest." Similar programs are being implemented across the United States, and although house arrest has many of the same characteristics as IPS programs, there are significant differences.

In many instances, house arrest/home confinement programs are stand-alone programs. They generally operate under statutes separate from those that guide and define probation programs. The differences between intensive supervision programs and house arrest programs include the following:

1. House arrest is nearly always designed to ease prison overcrowding and serve a prison-bound population.

2. House arrest is usually a sentence imposed by the court; it is virtually never an administrative tool used by program administrators to manage existing caseloads.

3. Most house arrest programs are designed to be much more punitive than IPS programs.

CLOSE-UP

Florida's Community Control Program

In 1982, the Florida Department of Corrections was forced by federal court orders to set a maximum capacity figure not only for each individual facility but also for the prison system as a whole. Florida lawmakers, realizing that prison construction would not keep up with prison population growth, passed the Correctional Reform Act of 1983. Included within the act was a mandate for the establishment of a community control program.

The Correctional Reform Act defined community control as:

[A] form of intensive supervised custody in the community, including surveillance on weekends and holidays, administered by officers with restricted caseloads. Community Control is an individualized program in which

the freedom of the offender is restricted within the community, home, or noninstitutional residential placement, and specific sanctions are imposed and enforced. (Joint Legislative Committee, 1983, p. 446)

The act emphasizes punishment and confinement for its target population of felony offenders, not rehabilitation. The goals of the program are (1) to help reduce prison overcrowding, (2) to reduce commitments to prison, and (3) to provide a safe diversionary alternative to incarceration (Florida Department of Corrections, 1988, p. 3).

A major study conducted by the National Council on Crime and Delinquency focused on the issue of net widening. This study found that 54 percent of the program participants were true diversions from incarceration (high-risk offenders), whereas 46 percent resembled reg-

ular probationers (Wagner & Baird, 1993). Finally, a 5-year recidivism study conducted by Smith and Akers (1993) reported high levels of recidivism (78%). When these rates were compared with the recidivism rates of a matched group of prisoners, the researchers found that there was no significant difference between the two groups. The recidivism rates of community control participants exceeded the rates reported by comparable intermediate sanction programs in other states.

During the first 8 years of Florida's Community Control Program operation, more than 60,000 participants were admitted to the program. The size, longevity, and continued political endorsement of the program suggest that it is the largest and most important program of its type in the country (Morris & Tonry, 1990; Tonry & Will, 1988).

---

4. House arrest represents a greater departure than IPS from the traditional probation model.

5. House arrest is the "last chance" before imprisonment, and revocation should lead to prison. (Petersilia, 1987)

The surveillance and supervision functions in home confinement programs are extremely important for their successful operation. Although other features such as offender counseling and substance abuse treatment may be provided to offenders in these programs, the services are secondary to enforcing restriction of offenders to their homes or designated residences. The Close-Up, "Florida's Community Control Program," provides an illustration of how house arrest/home confinement programs function.

Electronic Monitoring Surveillance

Electronic monitoring also has gained widespread acceptance both as a cost-effective alternative to incarceration (Lilly, Ball, & Wright, 1987) and as an enhancement to supervising offenders in the community (Morris & Tonry, 1990). Sometimes it is used to increase control

over offenders who have violated the conditions of their intensive probation or parole, house arrest, or another form of community supervision. Although it is primarily employed to monitor offenders who have already been sentenced, in some jurisdictions it is also used for offenders awaiting trial (Schmidt, 1989a). There are several key decision points at which electronic monitoring can be chosen as a sanction ranging from pretrial to postincarceration.

A 1988 survey revealed that almost 90 percent of the offenders supervised by electronic monitoring were male, which is consistent with their proportion in our nation's prisons and jails (Schmidt, 1989). It also found that offenders in these programs had been convicted of a wide range of criminal offenses, with major traffic violations (i.e., DWI/DUI) composing the largest category. The proportion of traffic offenders in electronic monitoring programs may be accounted for by the fact that these programs started at local rather than state levels.

History of Electronic Monitoring The use of electronic monitors for offender surveillance can be traced to the 1960s when Schwitzgebel, Pahnke, and Hurd (1964) suggested using them to track the mentally ill, probationers, and parolees. They were later tested on 100 volunteers to assess their social and psychological effects (Schmidt & Curtis, 1987). Despite Schwitzgebel's interesting results, it took almost 20 years for his idea to take hold in corrections.

The first formal electronic monitoring program was implemented in 1983 when Albuquerque, New Mexico, District Court Judge Jack Love, reputedly inspired by a "Spiderman" comic strip, placed a probation violator on electronic monitoring for one month. This was followed by a pilot project implemented in 1984 in Palm Beach County, Florida, initially targeting drunk drivers (Palm Beach County Sheriff's Office, 1987). Since its implementation in 1983, electronic monitoring has expanded rapidly across the United States. By 1990, it had been adopted in all 50 states by local, state, and federal correctional agencies (Renzema & Skelton, 1990).

Types of Electronic Monitors Electronic monitors are best described as telemetry devices designed to verify that an offender is at a given location, or not in a prohibited location, during specified times. Generally, a host computer is programmed to verify electronically the offender's presence at home during nonworking hours but does not operate while the offender is away from home. These systems can only alert community supervision officers to the presence or absence of monitored offenders at certain locations. They cannot report where the offenders are if they are not where they are supposed to be. However, new technology using global positioning systems (GPS) now can continuously monitor location at all times (Apgar, 1998). This technology may prove especially effective for tracking some probationers and parolees such as sex offenders.

A review of the current technology will help clarify just what electronic monitoring devices can and cannot do. These devices fall into one of three categories: continuously signaling with and without telephones, programmed contact, and tracking devices.

Continuous signaling devices with telephone service consist of three components:

1. A cigarette pack–sized transmitter, which may or may not be tamper-proof, is strapped to the offender's ankle or wrist; it sends an encoded signal at regular intervals.
2. A receiver-dialer, which receives the signal, is located in the offender's home; it reports the information automatically by telephone.
3. The central computer, which can be in any of various locations, accepts reports from the receiver-dialer.

When any interruption in the signal occurs, it compares the report with the offender's curfews or work schedule. If the information indicates that the offender is on an unauthorized absence, the computer either records the

information for review later, or alerts community supervision staff immediately, depending on program policies and procedures (Schmidt & Curtis, 1987). Some continuous signaling monitors have extended options, including visual telephones and alcohol detection devices. The alcohol detection devices are designed to verify both the alcohol level *and* the person's identity at the same time (Mitsubishi Electronics Inc., 1990).

A continuous signaling device without a telephone has only two components: a transmitter strapped to the offender, which sends out a continuous signal, and a portable-receiver located in the monitoring officer's car, which picks up the signal. The portable-receiver can detect the signal within a one-block range of the offender's location allowing the officer to check on the offender both at home and in other places (Schmidt, 1989). This device allows flexibility in checking the offender's whereabouts, but it is more expensive because it requires direct monitoring by a community control officer.

The second category of electronic monitoring equipment is the **programmed contact device,** which consists of either a wristlet or a voice verification unit and a central computer. The computer, located in a designated office, is programmed to call the offender during the hours the offender is scheduled to be monitored. The calls may be random to keep the offender off guard, or programmed for a specific time. If a wristlet is used, a telephone with a verifier box is utilized so that when the computer calls, the wristlet can be inserted into the verifier box to confirm that the offender being monitored answered the call. The voice verification unit is in a tamper-proof box attached to a handset, which can connect to any telephone in the offender's home. When the computer calls for a voice check, the offender must repeat the words the unit requests. The unit analyzes the voice pattern and compares it with words previously recorded by the offender to see if they match. If they do not match, usually a second test is made and if there is a second failure, the correctional agency is notified.

The third type of electronic monitoring system, the **tracking device,** is in the earliest stages of development (Arnold, 1991). The design of these devices is similar to those used to track endangered, wild animals. Using a geographic grid system, they can pinpoint the offender's exact location at any given time. The range of these devices will most likely encompass a city or county, greatly expanding their useful range.

The tracking device will no doubt increase correctional officials' ability to exercise greater control and to satisfy the "get tough" demands of the public and legislators, but it raises ethical issues. These issues include questions about net widening as well as concerns over intrusiveness and invasions of privacy.

Financial costs also must be considered. In Florida, for example, offenders are required to have telephones and are expected to pay an additional $30 per month in supervision fees. Does this exempt those who cannot meet these financial obligations from participating in the program and subject them to imprisonment in the place of electronic monitoring? Again, these issues have not been satisfactorily investigated.

Effectiveness Do these programs achieve their desired goals? Electronic monitoring programs have been proposed as a major cost-saving device for overcrowded jail and prison systems. The popularity of electronic monitoring in recent years can be attributed to both its claimed punitiveness and economic benefits. However, although electronic monitoring of offenders does seem to add an additional punitive measure to the sanctions continuum, recent research calls into question the programs' cost/benefit claims (Morris & Tonry, 1990; Tonry & Will, 1988). Beyond these justifications, however, Clear (1988, p. 671) says that electronic monitoring is "a method in search of a theory"; we use the technology because it is available, not because it achieves some desired end.

Bonta, Wallace-Capretta, and Rooney (2000, p. 61) examined three Canadian programs that employed electronic monitoring. They found that use of these devices was associated with net widening and that it did not appreciably add to "traditional forms of community control." Their major findings were that electronic monitoring aided offenders in completing their sentences, but that reduced rates of recidivism were not evident.

Does this mean that electronic monitoring has no beneficial effects? Hardly. An examination of 49 offenders on electronic monitoring by Gainey and Payne (2000) found that although many of these offenders did not feel especially punished, their point of reference was jail. Therefore, for some offenders the restrictions, shame, and stigma associated with electronic monitoring may provide real punishment.

Community Service Orders

Community service orders originally were touted as an alternative to incarceration. These programs were designed to require offenders to complete a specified number of community service hours in lieu of secure confinement. Recent research has established two very clear conclusions. First, many of these orders are probation add-ons and, thus, they are not alternatives for truly prison-bound offenders (see, for example, Mays & Winfree, 1998, pp. 292–294). Second, to date there is virtually no evidence that community service orders provide either rehabilitation or deterrence (Parent et al., 1997, p. 2).

Shock Incarceration and Boot Camps

The terms *shock incarceration* and *boot camp* are often used interchangeably, but there are differences in the two programs. **Shock incarceration,** sometimes called shock probation or parole, consists of a short incarceration period in a state prison followed by a return to community supervision (e.g., intensive probation supervision). **Boot camps** provide a very structured and regimented environment similar to that found in military basic training. Inmates sentenced to boot camps usually are separated from the general prison population either by assignment to special dormitories or to special facilities.

Shock Incarceration Shock incarceration grew out of the European tradition of *sursis*, the legal suspension of an offender's sentence. With sursis, the sentence is fulfilled if, after release, no further offenses are committed during a designated period. Shock incarceration's advantage over sursis is that it provides for supervision of offenders once they are released from incarceration. With sursis, authorities have little or no control or supervision over the offender once the sentence is suspended.

The first shock incarceration law was passed in Ohio in 1965. In 1974, Ohio enacted a shock parole program. Shock probation and parole supporters contend that these programs:

- impress offenders with the seriousness of their crimes without imposing a long prison term.

- give courts a way to release offenders deemed amenable to community-based treatment, based on more extensive assessments than were available at the original sentencing.

- let courts appropriately achieve a just compromise between punishment and leniency.

- let courts combine treatment and deterrence purposes when sentencing offenders.

- allow young offenders serving their first prison terms to be released before they have been socialized into the prison culture. (Parent, 1989, p. 51)

Correctional Boot Camps Boot camps, which emphasize military style discipline, have caught the attention of the public, legislators, and policy makers. The first boot camp programs began operating in Oklahoma in November 1983 and in Georgia one month later (Parent, 1989; Wright & Mays, 1998). By 1992, 25 states and the federal government were running these programs (MacKenzie & Souryal, 1994). Boot camps, like other intermediate sanctions, are designed to alleviate overcrowding, reduce recidivism, and cost less than incarceration. Additionally, in an era when the public increasingly wanted criminals to be punished, the strict military regimentation and discipline of these programs resulted in their being perceived as "tough on crime." Their growth can be attributed to the fact that politicians and

Most boot camp programs are designed for young male offenders convicted of nonviolent crimes. They employ a strict military regimen that emphasizes constant supervision and discipline.

the public were impressed with both their punitiveness and their cost effectiveness.

Most boot camp programs are designed for young (16- to 25-year-old) male offenders convicted of nonviolent crimes. About half of the states allow female participation, yet the number of beds available for women is limited. In 1992, in close to two thirds of the programs, participation was voluntary, while in 7 out of 10 dropping out was voluntary. Initially, these programs emphasized a strict military regimen centering around drill, strictly controlled unquestioning behavior, physical conditioning, and hard work. This is generally accomplished by the drill sergeants who constantly supervise and discipline the inmates and keep them busy during their waking hours. Later programs have placed more emphasis on rehabilitation (e.g., education, substance abuse counseling, life skills training) (MacKenzie & Souryal, 1994).

At a typical boot camp prison for adults:

male inmates have their heads shaved (females may be permitted short haircuts). At all times they are required to address staff as "Sir" or "Ma'am," must request permission to speak, and must refer to themselves as "this inmate." Punishments for even minor rule violations are summary and certain, frequently involving physical exercise such as push-ups or running in place. A major rule violation can result in dismissal from the program.

[The] day begins with pre-dawn reveille followed by one to two hours of physical training and drill. . . . [From there] they march . . . to breakfast where they must stand at attention while waiting in line, [moving] in a military manner as the line advances . . . stand at attention behind their chairs until commanded to sit, and eat in silence. After breakfast they march to work sites where they participate in hard physical labor. . . . When the 6 to 8 hour work day is over the inmates return to their compound where they participate in more exercise and drill. Dinner is followed by evening programs that include counseling, life skills training, academic education or drug education and treatment. There is little or no free time.

As their performance and time in the program warrants, [boot camp] . . . inmates gradually earn more privileges and responsibility. A special hat or uniform may be the outward display of their new status. Those who successfully finish the program usually attend an elaborate graduation ceremony with visitors and family invited to attend. Awards are often presented to acknowledge progress made during the program, and the inmates may perform the drill routines they have practiced throughout their time in the boot camp. (MacKenzie, 1993, pp. 22–23)

The nagging question was whether these programs, which were touted as being tough, could realize their objectives. A multisite evaluation of eight state-level boot camp programs by MacKenzie and Souryal (1994) addressed these questions. Their study found that "the recidivism rate of boot camp graduates did not differ from . . . similarly situated inmates who had served longer terms of incarceration" (p. 41). The critical factor in whether these programs successfully reduced over-crowding was related to program design. Where the department of corrections was allowed to select boot camp participants, overcrowding was most likely to be alleviated. This was because they generally maximized the selection of offenders who otherwise would have been sent to prison.

Two recent evaluations of boot camp programs found that the boot camp experience actually may increase the recidivism rates of participants. An examination of Oklahoma's Regimented Inmate Discipline (RID) Program found that "boot camp graduates recidivated more frequently than either traditionally incarcerated inmates or probationers" (Wright & Mays, 1998, p. 71). This finding was supported by research on North Carolina boot camp participants. Jones and Ross (1997, p. 147) examined 331 boot camp participants and found that this experience was more likely to result in "rearrest for drug offenses, offenses categorized as 'other,' and all types of offenses combined."

This research suggests that states should be cautious in implementing boot camp programs, clear in their program goals, and consistent in defining concepts like recidivism. Additional research is needed to determine if these outcomes are universal or unique to the states examined.

The military aspects of these programs had little deterrent effect. Moreover, the authoritarian atmosphere was felt to be less conducive to allowing other treatment programming to achieve its desired results. Some boot camp participants responded negatively to the confrontational environment of boot camps, and for some, jail or prison time seemed desirable to the rigorous, heavily regimented routine of the boot camp (see, e.g., Gowdy, 1993).

Longer program length—6 months versus 3 months—was felt to be related to the effectiveness of the rehabilitative programming because offenders had more time to benefit from programs such as substance abuse treatment and education. This, coupled with intensive supervision on release and continued work, education, and treatment programming, was believed more effective in reducing recidivism. Voluntary participation was also considered related to the effectiveness of rehabilitative programming. Offenders who volunteered were seen as possessing a greater sense of self-control, which was believed to result in higher levels of commitment to the program.

In examining inmate attitudes toward incarceration, boot camp inmates developed more positive attitudes toward their prison experience over time, which was not the case for conventional prison inmates. Interviews with boot camp inmates revealed that:

> they believed that the experience had been positive and that they had changed for the better. Although . . . initially [they] entered because they would spend less time incarcerated near the end of their time in boot camp they said that the experience had changed them for the better . . . and that they were proud of themselves for being able to complete such a program. (p. 41)

These findings also were supported in an examination of 560 participants of Oklahoma's RID Program (Wright & Mays, 1998).

Before we leave the discussion of the objectives of correctional boot camps, it is important to address the question of cost savings. As with other intermediate sanctions, we must approach cost-saving claims somewhat cautiously. If boot camps add bed spaces to a state correctional system, no cost savings will be realized. Furthermore, although boot camp participants are confined for shorter time periods than prison inmates (120–180 days versus 3 years, for example), the per diem costs for boot camps actually may be higher than those for prisons. The result, as Parent and his associates (1997, p. 4) found, was that in "a multijurisdictional study . . . only two of the five boot camps examined saved jurisdictions a substantial number of prison beds by their use of boot camps." Further, they found that "a sensible cost analysis would include the costs of aftercare programs, which may be substantial" (Parent et al., 1997, p. 4).

The Future of Boot Camps   First-generation boot camps tended to follow a strict military regimen in response to public and political demands for programs that were tough on offenders. However, evaluators found that these programs centering around "scaring youths straight" through a tough military style boot camp program have not been effective. It is unrealistic to believe that you can take a group of 16- to 25-year-old, out-of-control youths, most of whom had been part of antisocial groups or gangs for years, and in the space of 3 to 6 months alter their criminal lifestyle by subjecting them to an authoritarian regimen. Years ago many juvenile delinquents were coerced to join the military and did straighten up, but current boot camps leave out an important element of this process: Following their boot camp experience, military recruits went on to spend some time in a highly structured military environment, which provided jobs, housing, and the like. By contrast, correctional boot camp graduates simply are sent back home (Jones & Ross, 1997).

Second-generation boot camp programs have capitalized on the idea of special programs, but their emphasis has changed. The time spent in military-oriented activities has been reduced to about one quarter of a typical 16-hour day with the remainder of the time occupied with programming that includes education, the teaching of problem-solving skills, anticriminal role modeling, anger control, and programs dealing with substance abuse (Sharp, 1995). If they are to avoid being just another correctional fad they to have to do more than just appear to be tough. Future boot camps will have to de-emphasize the idea that they are a quick fix and strengthen their treatment and aftercare programs so that they better meet the needs of boot camp inmates (Cowles, Castellano, & Gransky, 1995). Additionally, if they are used for females, they will have to be modified to meet this population's special needs (e.g., women abused by men being placed in a situation in which a male instructor is verbally "abusing" them) (Sharp, 1995). The Close-Up, "New York's Shock Incarceration Program," on pages 498–499 suggests the direction this kind of program will take.

Day Fines

One of the most promising intermediate sanctions seems to be **day fines.** Day fines, or structured fines as they sometimes are called, "are a monetary sanction adjusted according to the seriousness of the offense and the financial status of the offender, to guarantee that every sentence imposes a negative impact" (Bureau of Justice Assistance, 1996, p. iii). This sanction has been used in Europe for some time and it takes the notion of fining beyond minor crimes like traffic offenses and applies it to a broader range of crimes (Morris & Tonry, 1990; Winterfield & Hillsman, 1993).

The Bureau of Justice Assistance (1996, p. 2), in promoting the use of day fines, says that this intermediate sanction can provide greater offender accountability, deterrence, fairness, effective and efficient use of limited resources, revenue, and credibility for the courts. As an illustration of fairness, an offense might warrant a 3-day penalty. For a college student working a part-time job the fine might end up being $60 (3 days × $20 per day). For a university professor the fine for the same offense could be $300 (3 days × $100). Therefore, day fines promote the principle of individualized justice (an equal burden) over equity (the same fine for similar offenders).

Day Reporting Centers

Day reporting centers (DRCs) are one of the newest innovations in the wide array of intermediate sanctions. However, they have been slow to catch the attention of correctional administrators and policy makers. In 1990, a national study by Parent (1990b) found that only 14 day reporting centers were operating in the United States.

Origins of DRCs Although DRCs did not emerge in the United States until 1986, they have been widely used in other countries since the early 1970s, most notably in Great Britain. These programs were created by correctional reformers who sought alternatives for chronic minor offenders. Generally, these offenders were not dangerous and many became incarcerated primarily because judges had exhausted their sentencing options. Reformers argued that incarcerating these offenders would intensify their propensity to commit criminal acts.

In 1972 Parliament created four day treatment centers (DTCs), and several similar programs were established by probation officers around England and Wales (Parent, 1990b). Although most of these centers developed without central planning and standards and were diverse, collectively, their program content focused on four primary areas: social/life skills, health/welfare activities, arts and crafts, and sports (Mair, 1988). In the 1980s the British DTCs caught the attention of correctional leaders in Massachusetts and Connecticut who were searching for alternatives to ease jail and prison overcrowding. Legislators in those two states, impressed with these DTCs, appropriated funds to develop, implement, and operate DRCs (Parent, 1990b). These programs were adaptations of the British DTCs. However, although program goals and objectives were clearly defined and systematically applied, programs developed in the United States were still diverse. The Program Focus, "The Metropolitan Day Reporting Center, Boston," on page 500 focuses on one DRC program in Massachusetts.

Goals and Purposes of DRCs In British DTCs, the overriding goal was to provide an alternative to imprisonment for a targeted group of offenders. DTCs also reported goals that included reducing recidivism and developing offenders' skills (Mair, 1988). These goals are similar to those outlined in the study of DRCs in the United States (Parent, 1990b). The major functions of DRCs in the United States have been (1) to reduce jail and prison overcrowding, (2) to enhance probation and parole supervision, and (3) to treat offenders' problems.

DRCs are similar to work release programs but are more cost effective because they are nonresidential. DRCs also are likely to be more program intensive than work release and generally offer a variety of programs. An evaluation of a day reporting center in Cook County, Illinois, provides an indication of the treatment potential of DRCs. When the Cook County program began in 1993 it served between 30 and 50 clients weekly. By 1996 this program involved 400 participants daily. In their analysis of program outcomes, McBride and

New York's Shock Incarceration Program

CLOSE-UP

To qualify for admission offenders must be under 35, eligible for parole within 3 years, have not committed violent or sex offenses, nor have been sentenced to an indeterminate prison term. At screening inmates are informed about the program and must decide whether they want to serve their full prison term or volunteer for the program. Volunteers go through a program divided into two 6-month phases.

Phase 1 involves an intensive incarceration program. All staff in these programs receive special training in military and treatment curriculum. Group teamwork and unity are emphasized to facilitate staff from different disciplines in working together as a team because this program follows a therapeutic community model.

Although inmate programming includes physical training, drills, and ceremonial formations, this component only composes 26 percent of a 16-hour day. For 6 hours each day,

inmates perform hard labor on facility and community projects. In 1994, inmates performed 1.2 million hours of work on projects that would have cost municipalities $6.3 million to complete.

The network program, which forms the basis for the therapeutic community structure of these programs, focuses on fostering responsibility for self, to others, and for the quality of one's life. Inmates are formed into platoons, and they live together as a unit. They hold daily network community meetings to resolve problems and reflect on their progress. Networks help inmates adjust to community living and develop socialization, employment, communication, and decision-making and critical thinking skills. Part of this involves teaching inmates that responsible behavior results from recognizing the difference between wants and needs and appropriate versus dysfunctional ways (e.g., crime and substance abuse) of getting needs met.

As distinguished from other boot camps, substance abuse treatment

takes place in a therapeutic community context. All inmates participate in Alcohol and Substance Abuse Treatment (ASAT), which includes drug education and group counseling for a minimum of two 3-hour sessions per week. ASAT is modeled after the 12-step recovery program of Alcoholics and Narcotics Anonymous and is staffed by trained substance abuse counselors.

Educational achievement is a central objective of these programs. A minimum of 12 hours per week is spent on academic work, which amounts to at least 260 hours at the end of 6 months. The success of this component is exemplified by a 68 percent passing rate on the GED tests as compared with 52 and 59 percent rates for minimum and medium custody inmates, respectively. This occurred despite the fact that boot camp inmates were in prison for shorter periods of time than the other two groups. Finally, inmates who have been removed for disciplinary reasons or are in danger of removal for unsatisfactory program adjustment can opt to be

---

VanderWaal (1997) found that this largely African American client population:

- reduced their drug use while in the program (average length of stay was 54.3 days)
- improved their court appearance record
- reduced their rearrest rate on new charges
- increased their willingness to participate in other treatment programs

Such positive results are not universal. Marciniak (1999) evaluated 204 offenders sentenced to a DRC in North Carolina and found that net widening occurred, and there were high rates of termination from the program. Two of her conclusions seem especially important not only for DRCs but also for other intermediate sanctions. First, selection of program participants—who gets chosen, how, and by whom—is critical to success. Second, the intermediate sanctions programs that accept

long-term commitments are likely to see higher failure rates than those with short-term commitments. Again, we are just beginning to accumulate research data on DRCs and additional research efforts are critical to fully assess their effectiveness.

Future of Intermediate Sanctions

As we begin the 21st century, we can expect intermediate sanctions to continue being an integral part of corrections. Although studies show recidivism rates in halfway house and work release programs are not significantly lower than for offenders given harsher or more lenient sentences, these programs continue to be widely used. We can expect the same pattern for IPS programs, house arrest/home confinement, electronic monitoring, community service orders, correctional boot camps, day fines, day reporting centers, and resi-

placed in the "reevaluation program." These inmates receive refresher training, which focuses on reviewing program concepts and expectations. Satisfactory completion of this refresher course results in readmission to the program.

Phase 2 of this program is called "AfterShock" and is operated by the division of parole. Prior to an inmate's release POs work closely with him, his family, and community service agencies to develop sound residence and employment programs to ensure a smooth transition from the facility to the community. Further, suitable housing is provided by the division's Community-Based Residential Program for shock incarceration (SI) inmates without a suitable home environment to which they can return. POs supervising SI graduates have reduced caseloads, with two officers responsible for 38 SI graduates for a 6-month period. This allows increased contacts between officers and parolees for employment, curfew checks, and drug testing. Within 1 week of SI release, program objectives call for SI parolees to have a job, and within 2 weeks they are to be enrolled in an educational or vocational training program. SI graduates are also required to participate in network meetings, which are designed to reinforce the principles of positive decision making learned at institutional meetings. They must also attend relapse counseling meetings, which focus on factors that may lead to relapse, reinforce principles of sobriety learned in shock facilities, and discuss common problems and solutions to adjustment to community life.

A major goal is cost containment. New York estimates that it saves $2.11 million per 100 inmates completing this program. With 10,927 program graduates as of September 1994, the state estimates savings of $225 million. As to the rates of return to prison, SI graduates when compared with control groups—program dropouts, inmates eligible but not entering the program, and those paroled before shock incarceration was established—had higher success rates after 3 years and had rates that were equal to or better than comparison groups after 4 and 5 years.

Given that this program saved the state money, provided municipalities with free labor to complete needed projects, and had recidivism equal to or better than sending inmates to prison, it would seem that programs of this kind have a place in the spectrum of correctional programming. What do you think of this program? Do you believe these programs are a fad, or will they become a regular part of correctional programming?

Source: Adapted from C. L. Clark, D. W. Aziz, & D. L. MacKenzie (1994). Shock Incarceration in New York: Focus on Treatment. Washington, DC: National Institute of Justice; New York State Department of Correctional Services & the New York Division of Parole (1995). Seventh Annual Shock Legislative Report. Albany, New York: Author.

---

dential community programs even though they too have not led to significant reductions in recidivism. Recidivism may be an issue for these programs, but the driving force behind the new programs centers more on economic issues.

These programs seem more cost effective than incarceration. Indeed, advocates suggest that placing offenders in these programs has saved millions of dollars by eliminating the need to build new prisons. However, before we jump to the conclusion that millions of dollars can be saved, we need to consider three points. First, as Morris and Tonry (1990, p. 234) point out, "cost comparisons are complicated [and] glib claims about cost savings associated with intermediate punishments often do not stand up to careful scrutiny." Second, Parent et al. (1997, p. 4) support this contention by adding that "The few studies that have attempted rigorous cost-benefit analyses of intermediate sanctions found their financial payoff was smaller than expected." Finally, given that intermediate sanctions are labor intensive and if they do not totally replace the most costly programs of incarceration, alternative forms of incarceration (halfway houses, reintegration centers, and correctional boot camps) actually will contribute to an overall increase in corrections budgets (Morris & Tonry, 1990; Souryal, 1997).

As noted earlier, we may be approaching these sanctions unrealistically. Their real focus is neither recidivism reduction nor cost savings. What intermediate sanctions are, and will continue to be, is a component of a complex sentencing system, allowing for a wider range of sentencing alternatives. This reflects a more advanced, comprehensive approach to sanctioning offenders that is commensurate with the severity of their crimes. Our laws distinguish gradations in the severity of criminal behavior, so our punishments also need to reflect those gradations (Thornberg, 1990). Thus, by adding intermediate sanctions to our arsenal of sentencing alternatives, we are better able to impose the least

The Metropolitan Day Reporting Center, Boston

PROGRAM FOCUS

At age 22, Bill is serving his second prison term, this time, two years in the Billerica House of Correction for an assault conviction. The Billerica House of Correction is run by the Middlesex County Sheriff and serves a large urban county west of Boston. The facility houses felons with prison terms of up to 30 months. Officials must keep Billerica's population below a court-ordered limit.

Ninety days before his minimum parole eligibility date, Bill was offered the chance to serve the rest of his prison term under the supervision of the Metropolitan Day Reporting Center (DRC), a program operated by the Crime and Justice Foundation. It is one of four similar programs funded by the Commonwealth of Massachusetts to reduce crowding in county houses of correction.

Bill lives with his mother in Framingham, about 30 miles southwest of Billerica. Today, it takes him 45 minutes to drive to Billerica, where he reports to the Metropolitan Day Reporting Center office located in the work release unit, a residential facility outside the prison's security perimeter. After checking in with center staff, he fills out an itinerary, showing where he will be each moment of the next day and giving phone numbers where he can be reached at each location.

After Bill gives a urine specimen for drug testing, he and his counselor spend 15 minutes planning Bill's budget for the coming month. He then goes to work at a metal fabrication plant, a job he got through Comprehensive Offender Employment Resources, a community program. He calls center staff at noon and gets two additional phone calls at random times during the day from center staff. After work, Bill returns to Metro DRC offices to at-

tend a group drug use counseling session. He then goes home. During the evening and early morning hours, he gets two random phone calls to assure he is complying with curfew requirements. Last week Bill had 42 in-person and telephone contacts with DRC staff.

If he continues to obey all DRC rules, Bill will be paroled in 6 weeks when he reaches his minimum eligibility date. But, if he violates even one major rule—for example, if he has a single positive drug test or is out of contact with center staff for more than 2 hours—he will be returned to the House of Correction. He will also lose his minimum parole date and probably serve until the expiration of his sentence (Parent, 1990b, p. 6).

---

restrictive sentencing alternative commensurate with an offender's crime.

We can expect to see intermediate sanctions expand across the country through the continued implementation of a wide variety of the programs discussed here. The enthusiastic support these programs have received from academics, correctional reformers, policy makers, legislators, the judiciary, prosecutors, and correctional administrators is a good indication that a wide range of people have a vested interest in seeing intermediate sanctions "work." With this kind of support, we can expect to see impediments removed and reforms made when necessary to see that these programs continue to function properly. No longer are we prone to "throw the baby out with the bath water" as we did in the past when programs failed to reach our expectations. After all, the business of "correcting" should apply to programs as well as people.

Summary

Intermediate sanctions have been created or expanded for a variety of reasons. An expanded range of sanctions allows the criminal justice system to more closely tailor

the punishment to fit the severity of the crime for which the offender has been convicted. This eliminates the probation, prison, or nothing choices that traditionally have existed.

Additionally, intermediate sanctions may provide less costly, more effective treatment alternatives and relieve some of the population pressures on correctional facilities. Unfortunately, many of these programs have not been able to deliver on some of the extravagant promises made on their behalf early on. Better funding, more realistic expectations, and careful evaluation may establish intermediate sanctions as viable alternatives to traditional probation and incarceration.

Critical Thinking Questions

1. How is the term *intermediate sanctions* defined? What types of programs are included in this set of sanctions?

2. What factors contributed to the development of intermediate sanctions in the 1980s and 1990s?

3. Describe and discuss halfway houses, their development, organization, and present status.

4. Compare halfway houses with work release programs.

5. Compare intensive probation supervision with house arrest in terms of procedure and goals.

6. Discuss the various types of electronic monitoring devices and the legal and ethical issues associated with their use.

7. Describe first- and second-generation boot camps.

8. What are day reporting centers, and what are their objectives?

Test Your Knowledge

1. Intermediate sanctions:
   a. are not intended to be punitive.
   b. fall between traditional probation and imprisonment.
   c. are designed exclusively for rehabilitative purposes.
   d. are only for convicted misdemeanants.

2. Halfway houses:
   a. are rarely operated by private agencies.
   b. were only developed in the 1980s.
   c. should be designed to house between 20 to 35 residents.
   d. are not used as an alternative to sending offenders to prison.

3. Work release programs:
   a. are generally unsuccessful because they admit too many problem inmates.
   b. have been discontinued because they are not cost effective.
   c. are sometimes operated by private agencies.
   d. are only used as an alternative to imprisoning felons.

4. Research shows that offenders in IPS programs:
   a. have lower arrest rates than those on routine probation.
   b. are subject to more surveillance and control than those on routine probation.
   c. do not participate in treatment programs as frequently as those on routine probation.
   d. have fewer technical violations than those on routine probation.

5. The discussion of electronic monitoring indicated that:
   a. with the technology available today, correctional officials can track offenders' specific whereabouts.
   b. legal concerns have caused some jurisdictions to discontinue these programs.
   c. these programs have been used to increase control over offenders who violated IPS conditions.
   d. these programs have replaced ordinary IPS programs in some states.

Visitation, Parole, and Sex Offenders

21

KEY TERMS AND CONCEPTS

Broad community notification
Civil commitment laws
Conjugal visits
Consolidated model
Contact visits
Demoralization
Discretionary parole
Dismemberment
Furloughs
Independent model
Mandatory release
Parenting programs
Parole
Strip searches
Visitation

Introduction

The gulf between prison and the free world is bridged by outside contacts inmates have with people important to them. If maintained throughout the inmate's prison stay, these relationships can help keep inmates bonded to conventional, prosocial activities inside and outside of the prison. This chapter focuses on the conditions under which inmates have contacts with loved ones and friends, the problems associated with transitioning back to freedom through parole, and new laws affecting sex offenders on parole.

Recently both institutional and community corrections officials have recognized the importance of allowing incarcerated individuals to maintain ties to their families and friends in the free world. Therefore, most corrections systems around the United States have developed or expanded visitation programs to help inmates maintain those ties. The presumption is that the more connected inmates are to community contacts the more likely they are to make a successful transition from behind bars to the outside world.

Visitation

The origin of **visitation,** the practice of allowing friends or relatives to visit inmates, is obscure. In the Walnut Street Jail and its predecessors, dating back to 1718, visitors were permitted to call on inmates (Barnes & Teeters, 1951). However, the principle of separation, central to both the Pennsylvania and Auburn prison systems, dictated that inmates be isolated from the outside world and their families and friends. This policy gradually was modified to allow well-behaved inmates visits from friends and relatives in most prisons (Pettigrove, 1910). Early on there was wide variation in visitation policies, with progressive wardens recognizing its importance, others merely tolerating it, and some sabotaging it.

Visitation Rules

Opening prisons to visitors creates security problems and requires some regulation. Each facility has rules relating to visiting and processing of visitors that vary according to the prison's security level and, sometimes, the inmate's custody level. Generally, the higher the security level the more restrictive the visiting conditions. These procedures are designed to maintain security and control. Remote prison locations impede visitation, as do institutional conditions that sometimes may be inhospitable. Visitation conditions range from noncontact situations in some maximum security prisons to totally private conjugal visits, which are allowed in several states.

Visits by family members contribute to rehabilitation and the orderly nature of prison life. However, visits may be suspended to punish violations of prison rules.

Until the 1950s visits were viewed as rewards for good behavior. Since then, prison officials have begun to see the visits as contributing to the rehabilitative process, to postrelease success, and to the orderly nature of prison life (Knight, 1986; Schafer, 1989). Nevertheless, prison regulations and practices continue to control visitation by restricting the who, what, when, how long, and where of it.

The courts have held that prison authorities can regulate visiting for security and other purposes (Project, 1994). They have upheld types (contact or noncontact), number, and duration of visits; who may visit; the suspension of visiting to punish prison rule violators; and inmates' transfers to other prisons despite being less convenient locations. Nevertheless, the courts will not permit restrictions that are arbitrary, vague, or discriminatory such as restricting "objectionable" visitors (Knight, 1986; Mushlin, 1993; Palmer, 1991).

Impact on Postrelease Behavior

With severe prison overcrowding and current antitax sentiments, programs that reduce recidivism are very attractive. Several studies have found positive relationships between the maintenance of strong family ties during imprisonment and postrelease success (Flanagan, 1996). Holt and Miller (1972) conducted an extensive study on California parolees. They found that those who received visits while in prison experienced significantly fewer and less serious difficulties on release.

Every person who wants to visit—family member or not—must complete an application to be placed on the inmate's approved visitor list. Most visitors are family members, and they may include an inmate's children. Hairston and Hess (1989) found that 30 states place some restrictions on visits by unaccompanied children. A study of visits in three California prisons found that the typical visitor was female (wife, 42%; mother, 14%; or girlfriend, 11%), had an average age of 35, lived in the general area, and visited the prison a couple times per week. These women revealed "a strong sense of mission and purpose . . . that of being with their loved ones, no matter what their hardships" (Neto, 1989, p. 34).

Most research supports use of visitation programs but fails to explain why family contacts during imprisonment reduce antisocial behavior after release. Hairston (1988) provides a perspective on this process. Drawing from the social support literature, she notes that the social network families provide protects inmates from a variety of stressful stimuli. Abandonment by family can make the prison experience more demoralizing. Therefore, on release the offender has fewer positive feelings of self-worth and resources to resist recidivating. Families also may motivate inmates to take advantage of prison programs and services that can lead to better jobs on release, improved interpersonal relations with family members, and the elimination of substance abuse.

The interactionist perspective provides another explanation of the impact of family ties on inmates by examining primary versus secondary group involvement. Primary groups, such as families, are small. Members have intimate personal ties by which they can meet basic needs for companionship, love, security, and an overall sense of well-being. These close ties lead members to be more concerned with one another's welfare and to terminate certain behavior patterns at their request. Also, individuals are accepted based more on the kind of person they are rather than on their accomplishments. Secondary groups involve more formal relationships, fewer emotional ties, limited interaction, and a greater emphasis on economic and social accomplishment. Without strong primary group contacts a person is more likely to feel forsaken and drift into an anomic state in which he or she is not controlled by conventional rules and customs. By maintaining family contacts, inmates can retain socially acceptable roles as siblings, parents, or children. This reinforces their sense of individual worth and can offset the stigma of the inmate role and the negative evaluations inmates get from prison staff and society. If family ties are broken, releasees may be left only with the ex-convict role with its negative connotations.

Impact of Incarceration on Prisoners' Wives

Inmates' families are sometimes viewed as "the second victims of their crimes." Wives compose a primary group left behind when husbands are imprisoned. Wives first must cope with the crises of arrest and sentencing. Fishman's (1990) in-depth study of 30 prisoners' wives provides a rare look at this group. Initially, imprisonment produces a double crisis (dismemberment and demoralization) for wives and other family members. **Dismemberment** refers to the adjustment made to the loss of a husband or other family member. For many it is like the death of a loved one. The obvious difference is that imprisoned husbands are alive and one day may rejoin the family. Families also must deal with the **demoralization** caused by the shame and stigma of a family member in prison. They now must establish new relationships with a person who is "living while dead" (Schwartz & Weintraub, 1974).

Inmates' wives also have to deal with the economic issues related to their husbands' imprisonment. They have to decide whether to get a job, remain at home, and/or apply for welfare. Most wives experience severe financial problems following their spouses' imprisonment, including being on the edge of subsistence, being inundated with household and child-related expenses, and having to obtain money for their incarcerated husbands and for travel costs to the prison. Some also have to decide whether to move close to where their husbands' prison is located (Fishman, 1990).

On a personal level, most inmates' wives have physical deprivation feelings, which include not having their husband's companionship and the hardships of not having them available to pay bills, provide income, or make home repairs. This often is compounded by sexual frustration. Wives with children experience child management problems similar to those of single mothers. They also have to decide how to explain the father's absence, which tends to upset the children and make them fearful and insecure. In Fishman's (1990) study, wives with school-age children did not try to conceal the arrest or incarceration because these youngsters learned about it from others.

Children and Visitation

Neto (1989) further found that more than 50 percent of her subjects "usually" or "sometimes" brought their children, half of whom were 6 or younger. Those who did not cited added expenses, avoiding exposure of children to the prison environment, and difficulty in handling the children on the bus or in the visiting area.

Research has demonstrated the importance of frequent visits between inmates and their children for the well-being of all concerned. However, prison regulations and facilities often neglect children's special needs, and instead focus on parental responsibility for controlling children's behavior (Hairston & Hess, 1989; Schafer, 1991). Special play areas are required for children and newer prisons often include these areas, but only three states (New York, Missouri, and South Carolina) require them. At New York's Arthur Kill Correctional Center, the children's area was transformed into "Kiddie Land" through the cooperative efforts of staff and inmates. Inmate funds from vending machine profits were used to purchase toys and furniture, while prison art classes painted murals, and a floor covering class installed the carpeting. The children are supervised by volunteer "grandparents" recruited through New York City's Foster Grandparent program. President James Thorpe of the inmate Jaycees attributes the center's success to these volunteers. During the first year the center served 1,200 children (New York State Department of Correctional Services, 1988).

Visiting Schedules and Visiting Spaces

In a 45-state survey, Schafer (1991) found that between 1976 and 1987 prison visiting policies became less restrictive. The number of total available visiting hours during that period increased.

Visiting hours vary: two states (Florida and Texas) restrict hours to Saturday and Sunday; in others the range is from 3 to 89 hours and up to 7 days per week. Twenty-three states allow visits on 5 or more days per week. In prisons built before 1950 visiting areas had space for less than 20 percent of their prison populations, whereas those built later could accommodate up to 30 percent. If a visiting area has space for only 20 percent of the population, this means that only about 10 percent of the inmates can receive visitors, assuming one visitor per inmate. The American Correctional Association (1983) recommends that an institution with 500 inmates should have a visiting area that will accommodate at least 150 people.

Impact of External Conditions on Visitors

The economically disadvantaged status of many inmates' families makes it difficult for them to visit frequently. Transportation assistance and visitor centers sometimes help these families to overcome this problem.

Transportation Assistance Prisons often are not built close to the population centers from which most offenders come. This makes visiting difficult for relatives who are likely to be poor. Neto (1989) found that 70 percent of the visitors traveled by car; often their cars were undependable. The rest typically traveled by buses, which might drop them off a few miles or more from the prison. Neto found that both distance and the lack of a car reduced visitation frequency.

Public and private agencies in some states offer assistance to inmate families by providing transportation from population centers or from public transportation drop-off points. A survey of 56 U.S. state and federal systems found that in close to half, government or private organizations made arrangements for free or low-cost transportation for inmate families. As an example, New York State provides free transportation to 37 institutions on buses with escorts trained to answer questions on visiting procedures and provide referral assistance for visitors with problems (New York State Department of Correctional Services, 1988). In California, Centerforce operates 34 centers that provide transportation from local drop-off points to institutions.

A few organizations, like Centerforce, also provide inmate families financial assistance to help defray the costs of overnight stays when they visit. Others, like Harvest House, Inc., in Boonville, Missouri, operate hospitality centers located close to prisons, which provide lodging and sometimes meals (Coombs, 1991; Mustin and Bee, 1992).

Visitor Centers and Hospitality Houses
A woman walks slowly up the hill toward the Washington State Reformatory in Monroe. Her husband, a new inmate, has asked her to come visit. On the phone it seemed such a small request, but the closer she gets to the prison's towering brick wall, the more forbidding it looks. As she pauses to gather her courage, her eye catches a slate blue house with a red door across the street. "The Matthew 25:36 House," a sign reads. . . . The woman knocks on the door and is greeted by the Hospitality House's director, Mary Parker Cosby. "I was on my way to visit my husband

at the Reformatory," the woman stammers, "but now I'm too scared to go there."

"It's really not so bad," Cosby says, as she invites her inside. "Let me tell you what to expect . . . ." In a few minutes, Cosby sees the woman off with a smile and a hug and tells her, "Please stop by afterward and tell me how it went." When the woman returns to report a successful visit she learns [about all the services Matthew 25:36 provides]. (Coombs, 1991)

Located adjacent to or near prisons in only a few jurisdictions, facilities like this serve as way stations providing services for relatives and friends visiting inmates. The largest program is operated by Centerforce in California. It operates 34 hospitality centers, which serviced 255,489 adults and 109,855 children in 1997. The services included transportation, child care, emergency clothing, information on visiting regulations and processes, referrals to other agencies and services, emergency food, crisis intervention, and a sheltered area (Centerforce, 1998).

Visiting Conditions

All institutions require visitors to present acceptable identification. Almost all require appropriate attire for visitors (Schafer, 1989). Furthermore, many institutions limit the items that can be taken into the prison. Some provide lockers; others require that handbags and other items be locked in cars. This underscores the value of visitor centers that inform visitors about what items are forbidden and provide lockers for storing them.

To prevent visitors from bringing contraband (drugs, weapons, money, tape recorders, cameras, etc.) into the prison, all closed facilities typically require searches of persons and belongings. Most facilities employ metal detectors to search for weapons (Neto, 1989). COs typically search belongings and may do external pat-down searches of visitors. Although rarely done, the courts have upheld **strip searches,** in which the person is forced to remove all clothing and submit to a complete body search, when there is "reasonable cause" based on "specific objective facts" indicating a visitor will attempt to smuggle contraband into the prison (Palmer, 1991).

During the Big House prison era, visitation typically was of a noncontact nature, with visitors and inmates either separated by glass partitions and communicating through telephones or separated by mesh screens. Today, most systems allow **contact visits** for most inmates. Schafer (1991) found that 90 percent of the prisons she surveyed permitted contact visits for all inmates, and most others had facilities for both contact and noncontact visits. Maximum security inmates are likely to be denied contact visits (National Institute of Corrections, 1987). Although the courts recognize contact visits as desirable, no decision has supported entitlement of convicted inmates to them (Mushlin, 1993). In *Block v. Rutherford* (1984), the U.S. Supreme Court upheld a blanket ban on jail contact visits as long as it was reasonably related to the facility's security. The security issues raised in this case included preventing the introduction of contraband and keeping detainees and their visitors from exposure to violent offenders awaiting trial.

The Task Force on Corrections (1973) of the National Advisory Commission on Criminal Justice Standards and Goals recommended that visiting facilities provide a natural environment that encourages ease and informality of communication. Required supervision should be done in an unobtrusive manner that does not eavesdrop on conversations or otherwise interfere with the participants' privacy.

Visiting area rules usually center around the following:

- *General behavior* typically involves the control or management of children; movement around the visiting room (changing seats, moving chairs); chatting with other prisoners and visitors; and control of loud voices, abusive behavior, and profanity.

- *Physical contact* usually forbids behavior such as petting, sitting on laps, prolonged kissing, sexually stimulating activity, necking, hands under clothing, or touching or stroking breasts, genitalia, or thighs (Schafer, 1989).

Fishman examined the ambience and rules of visiting programs at five Vermont institutions. At one facility the ambience was pleasant, but the rules prohibited movement around the room. At three other institutions the rules were restrictive, and the ambience was uninviting and dismal. Wives reported they could not help overhearing other conversations and arguments. This, along with surveillance by the COs, undermined privacy and inhibited spontaneous and authentic emotional communication.

At only one of the five facilities did the ambience and rules encourage normal interaction between inmates and their families. Like other community facilities it provided inmates with more freedom. Thus, it enforced system visiting rules less stringently but still emphasized security and allowed visiting under the "watchful eyes of at least one guard." Visiting took place in a less structured environment. During the warmer months inmates could take their families outdoors to play with the children and have picnics. Also, there were places where they were allowed to be somewhat alone, facilitating greater physical and verbal intimacy.

Private Family/Conjugal Visiting

Conjugal visits typically have been limited to private visits between inmates and their spouses, but some programs now include other family members, usually children, parents, and, in a few cases grandparents and siblings. The comments of wives in Fishman's (1990) study suggest the need for more natural and intimate visiting arrangements, but there has been resistance to establishing these programs based on several issues. These include morality, misconceptions of its impact on the correctional environment, and punitive views about the purpose of incarceration (Johns, 1971; Task Force on Corrections, 1973).

Few studies in the past have focused on attitudes toward conjugal visits. Bennett (1987, 1989) surveyed most institutions in eight states (California, Connecticut, Minnesota, Mississippi, New Mexico, New York, Washington, and Wyoming) with conjugal visitation programs and compared them with a random sample of prisons without programs. Almost half of the sample (including 34% without programs) endorsed the idea of private family visiting with suitable security safeguards and proper administration.

Although critics consider the major purpose of conjugal visits to be sexual satisfaction, participants consider emotional closeness and a better understanding of each other to be equally important (Burstein, 1977). The major benefits are viewed as the stabilization and enhancement of marital and family relationships and the provision of a support group when inmates are released (Bennett, 1987, 1989; Burstein, 1977; Hopper, 1989; Lillis, 1993b).

Benefit to Inmates   The fact that all but one of Burstein's sample asked their wives to bring the children means that inmates do not just see the visits exclusively as opportunities for sexual intimacy. Evidence also shows these visits have an impact on marital stability after release. Burstein found that combined divorce and separation rates for nonparticipants were four times higher than for participants. Furthermore, almost half of superintendents in Bennett's study felt conjugal visits would reduce disciplinary problems and improve parole planning.

Both inmate participants (90%) and nonparticipants (85%) agree it is an important behavioral control method. This is further confirmed by New York studies that found inmates not approved for family visits had a larger number of, and more serious, disciplinary infractions than those in the program. More than one third of the inmates with poor disciplinary records who were not initially approved improved their behavior sufficiently to be approved later (Howser, Grossman, & MacDonald, 1984).

Evidence supports a positive relationship between program participation and community adjustment. In New York the actual return rate of program participants was lower than projected, based on the rate of return of all releasees from custody (MacDonald & Bala, 1986). In 1980, 11.7 percent of releasees were projected to return, but the actual return rate for program participants was 3.9 percent. In 1986, 26.5 percent were projected to return, and 19.6 percent of program participants actually did.

In the past, it has been argued that conjugal visit programs would reduce homosexuality, violence, and sexual assaults. Although administrators did not agree (Bennett, 1989), inmates—particularly those participating in the program—felt that it did reduce homosexuality (Burstein, 1977; Hopper, 1989). If involvement in consensual homosexual relationships in prison is motivated by the need for sexual release, loneliness, and other emotional needs, private family visits are likely to reduce homosexual relationships. However, when prison rape and violence are motivated by the need to dominate and to dissipate anger and aggression, conjugal visits may not substantially reduce these behaviors except for program participants, who may refrain to keep their visiting privileges.

Objections to Conjugal Visits   Conjugal visiting is opposed on several grounds. First, critics claim that it will generate negative attitudes by inmates who are unable to participate. In Mississippi in 1963 and 1984, Hopper (1989) found fewer than 15 percent of the unmarried inmates objected to married inmates having conjugal visits. Second, concerns are raised about the problems of controlling the introduction of drugs and other contraband. Bennett found that administrators saw drug smuggling as a danger but not a problem requiring anything more than constant vigilance and the use of standard precautionary measures. A third set of concerns involves negative public and political reaction arising from anxiety about escapes, questions about program morality, feelings that inmates are not entitled to this privilege, and the added costs resulting from pregnancies. However, three quarters of the facilities using public education to portray program goals as reuniting the family and improving postrelease success encountered no public resistance (Bennett, undated).

Finally, although most of these programs are state funded, several started with donations and were organized by staff and inmate volunteers (Bennett, undated). Financing also came from inmate welfare funds and payments made by inmates when their families used these facilities. There even have been efforts at privately created and funded conjugal visitation programs (Leone & Kinkade, 1996).

Bennett estimated yearly costs at $100,000 to operate a program with three visiting units, including supervision and security, repair, upkeep, replacement of damaged furnishings, and utilities. This may seem high, but inmate welfare funds and maintenance by volunteers can help reduce the costs. This seems like a small price for a program that has a positive impact on prison discipline and increases postrelease success.

Visitation Program Characteristics   Although the programs vary considerably, it is possible to develop a basic picture of them (Bennett, undated). Most are located in a prison but are separated from the general population. They are composed of one- or two-bedroom units with bathrooms and linens, fully equipped kitchens, and outside activity areas; some have barbecue grills. In most cases inmate eligibility is tied to disciplinary records and participation in prison programs. Condemned prisoners, chronic disciplinary problems, those convicted of heinous crimes and those with histories of family violence, sex offenses, or serious psychiatric problems may be excluded or may require special screening to participate. Depending on the space available and institutional policy, visits can occur from every 2 weeks to every 6 months (Bennett, undated).

Family Counseling and Parenting Programs

What happens during visitation affects the frequency and length of visits. The way inmates interact with family members will strongly impact the continuation of these visits and maintenance or enhancement of family ties. Inmates frequently are not skilled in sustaining and enriching family relations, may lack good communication skills, and may bring anger and frustration from the prison environment to the visiting situation. Family members may harbor feelings of guilt, alienation, frustration, and anger resulting from their loved ones' imprisonment. Research shows that female inmates feel strongly about the importance of loving their children and guiding their appropriate social, behavioral, and attitudinal development (Leflore & Holston, 1990). Even male inmates serving very long sentences, most of whom were unmarried fathers with little or no contact or knowledge of their children's whereabouts, still perceived themselves as fathers and wanted to improve their parenting skills (Hairston, 1990). These factors point to the need for programs to enhance both interpersonal and parenting skills.

Several jurisdictions have established programs addressing living in a home where addiction problems exist, alternatives to violence, spouse abuse and being the victim of abuse, and written and verbal communication with wives and children. These **parenting programs** are important because few inmates had positive relationships with their parents and they carry with them a disastrous legacy likely to be passed on to their children if they fail to get help (New York State Department of Correctional Services, 1988). However, despite the potential benefits of these programs only a few are currently operating (Hairston & Lockett, 1987; Jorgenson, Hernandez, & Warren, 1986). The focus of New York's program, "the road back from crime is a family affair," captures the essence that family breakdown is at the root of crime.

The Telephone: Augmenting Visitation

Beginning in the late 1960s and early 1970s, inmates were allowed to use telephones to contact family and friends. By 1979, all states but Ohio permitted inmates to make nonemergency phone calls, and today all correctional systems in the United States and Canada permit inmates telephone access. According to Fishman (1990), telephone contacts with family members, whether frequent or not, reinforced marital ties and mitigated the pain of separation for both wives and their incarcerated husbands. Irrespective of the type of prison their husbands were in, wives felt there was never enough time during visiting to interact with their spouses in a realistic way (Fishman, 1990). Thus, telephone calls added an opportunity for more frequent communication and were seen as visits by most of these wives.

Finally, the telephone allows inmates to participate more frequently in the day-to-day functioning of their homes and to maintain their positions within the family. Wives had the opportunity to place their husbands in the role of an understanding but distant observer in their lives. This made it easier to believe their relationship was worthwhile and worth waiting for until their spouses were released. Not all communication was positive and reinforced marital ties. Some couples who communicated regularly argued over a variety of things. Disagreements erupted over the wives' resisting their husbands' attempts to dominate their lives. Overall, however, the telephone had more positive than negative effects on these relationships (Fishman, 1990).

Restrictions on Phone Calls   A *Corrections Compendium* survey (Davis, 1990) found that more than half of the systems allowed either unlimited or daily telephone usage. In most remaining jurisdictions, calls were limited either by institutional policies, inmate custody or security classification, or privilege level. Most systems restricted calls to from 5 to 20 minutes. Half the jurisdictions required inmates to pay for local calls, and in most of the others calls had to be made on a collect basis. All jurisdictions required long-distance calls to be made collect.

Most states report few or no problems with inmate phone usage. The few problems that did occur included threats to relatives, girlfriends, or others; drug deals; using the phone to buy merchandise with stolen credit card numbers; and obscene phone calls. Despite some misuse, corrections systems overwhelmingly consider inmate phone use to be beneficial (Davis, 1990).

A 1995 update of the 1990 phone use survey found that the 1990 figures on access, use, and monitoring remained essentially the same. However, the major change was that litigation was no longer centered on phone access but on the "rates charged to inmates and the people who accept collect calls from prisoners" (Wunder, 1995a, p. 6). This is because inmate phone use has become profitable for both phone companies and for most state corrections departments. "The average DOC commission rate from the phone companies is 28.08% [and] . . . 31 responding departments of corrections received approximately $96.4 million . . . in revenues from phone companies in 1994" (Wunder, 1995a, p. 6). Critics contend that these exorbitant profits make rates higher and discourage inmates from maintaining ties to the outside world to which they eventually will return. However, supporters argue that the profits received by correctional facilities for phone calls are channeled into inmate welfare funds to be used for programming and rehabilitation (Wunder, 1995a). Only time will tell if and how the courts will settle this controversy.

Furloughs: Visitations in the Community

Prison **furloughs** are short-term escorted or unescorted trips away from the prison, granted so that inmates can find jobs or housing prior to release; participate in treatment or religious programs, recreation, or shopping; or strengthen family ties. They are different from releases for emergency purposes, which are only granted to inmates for serious family illnesses or death. Although common in Europe, in the United States they are a recent development (Burns, 1975). In the mid-1960s only two states had programs, but by 1987 all states, the District of Columbia, and the Federal Bureau of Prisons had some form of furlough or temporary release (Contact, 1988; Smith, undated).

Furloughs serve several functions. First, they foster inmate self-esteem because of the trust they imply. This can reduce feelings of dependency and allow inmates (particularly long-term inmates) to recognize they still can make decisions about their actions. Second, they reinforce family ties and enable inmates with children opportunities to reassert their presence and reinforce their roles as parents. Families also can begin to accept the inmate as part of the household. Third, they facilitate release planning by gradually reintegrating offenders back into the community and by exposing them to the community programs and experiences that are unavailable in prison. Finally, they also promote rehabilitation and enhance crime prevention (Markley, 1973; Smith, undated). The 1988 Bush-Dukakis presidential campaign turned *furlough* into a dirty word. Studies conducted between 1987 and 1989 showed the bad press generated by the Willie Horton incident negatively affected furlough policies (Contact, 1988; Marlette, 1990b; Smith, undated). The number of states granting furloughs dropped from 39 to 34, and the number of furloughs granted went from 200,000 to 170,000, while the number of inmates participating increased from 53,000 to 55,000.

Furlough eligibility requirements vary by state. Approval is usually dependent on an inmate's security classification, the amount of time served, proximity of parole, type of crime committed, behavior in prison, and reviews by a facility committee and the head of the corrections department (Contact, 1988; Marlette, 1990b; Smith, undated). Some states also consider input from victims and local law enforcement. Most systems require a sponsor (a relative or other approved person) for the inmate. Furloughs range from the 4 to 12 daylight hours allowed by Florida to the 210 days allowed in Oregon, which uses them to ease overcrowding.

More than 80 percent of the systems report a 98 percent or higher success rate, and only two had rates below 90 percent. Twenty-seven jurisdictions provided information on rule infractions: There were 971 revocations of furloughs reported, or about 2 percent of all furloughs granted. Most infractions were for late returns, alcohol or drug use, or failure to arrive at an agreed-on location. Less than 1 percent of the revocations were for "new crimes," most involving escapes, some property crimes, and a few assaults (Marlette, 1990b). In the thousands of furloughs studied there were two reported homicides: one involved a wife and another a girlfriend (Marlette, 1990b).

In 1988, 38 jurisdictions allowed furloughs for inmates serving life terms, and none were revoked (Contact, 1988). Virtually all systems found furloughs to be helpful in preparing inmates for release and promoting institutional morale.

Now that we have considered family and conjugal visitation programs, phone contacts, and furloughs, it is time to turn our attention to the actual point of release. In some states parole has been eliminated outright and in others it has been severely curtailed through the use of determinate and other guided sentences. Nevertheless, a number of states still utilize indeterminate sentencing schemes and even those states with determinate sentencing (and mandatory releases) still may consider an inmate's early release a form of parole. Therefore, in the next section we will turn our attention to release from prison and supervision in the community. Parole remains the smallest part of the corrections component. However, as we will see it is vitally important and faced with a number of extremely serious challenges.

Parole: Serving Time in the Community

Parole involves the conditional release of inmates from prison to serve the remainder of their sentences under community correctional supervision. In effect parole is a shift in the place and type of supervision for an incarcerated offender. Normally, parole is associated with indeterminate sentences and is granted to inmates by a legally constituted parole authority (such as a parole board) when they have served a prescribed minimum portion of their sentences and met certain behavioral criteria within the prison. Technically, parole is not a sentence: it is a legal status.

Parole can fit well in either the rehabilitation or reintegration models of corrections. Because successful program participation and good behavior within the prison are prerequisites for parole consideration, it has a natural relationship to rehabilitation. The fact that inmates serve part of their sentence in the community adheres to the reintegration model's tenets. Whatever the model under which it operates, parole has played an important part in the American correctional process for more than 100 years. In this section, we discuss parole's development in the United States and its organization and administration.

The term *parole* comes from the French phrase *parole d'honneur,* which means "word of honor." The French used the term to denote an inmate's release for good behavior and, based on his word of honor, that he would obey the law upon release. Parole's roots can be traced to the practices of clemency, indenture, and transportation. These practices often included a conditional form of release from a penal sanction. Parole as we know it today in the United States evolved largely from practices initiated during the middle of the 19th century by Alexander Maconochie and Walter Crofton, whose work was described in detail in Chapter 5. The mark system developed by Maconochie was similar to the indeterminate sentences that were developed to accompany parole in the United States. It assumed that an inmate would be released from incarceration on the basis of his behavior rather than as a mere function of serving time. However, Maconochie felt that release should be unsupervised, so his system was not a direct forerunner of parole. That distinction fell to Walter Crofton's adaptation of Maconochie's mark system for the Irish prisons. It was in this context that conditional postrelease supervision was developed.

Developments in U.S. Punishment Philosophy

In the United States, prior to the use of parole, early release often involved a governor's power to commute sentences and pardon inmates. Commutation was first used in 1817, when New York enacted a law permitting a 25 percent sentence reduction for first-time offenders serving 5 years or less (Burns, 1975).

In the 1870s, New York began planning the Elmira Reformatory and introduced indeterminate sentences. This resulted from the work of Maconochie and Crofton as well as the reforms suggested at the Cincinnati National Congress on Penitentiary and Reformatory Discipline of the National Prison Association. The Elmira Reformatory opened in 1876 as a separate institution for youthful offenders. To be eligible for release, inmates there had to have jobs waiting for them. Releasees were supervised by volunteers, because there were no paid parole officers at that time (Pisciotta, 1983).

By 1900, approximately 20 states had enacted parole statutes. However, it was not until 1944 that every state had a parole system. Parole's development was aided by several factors. First, the parole concept was strongly supported by the correctional community. Second, discretionary release of inmates allowed prison authorities

to better control disciplinary problems, stimulate inmate reform, and relieve overcrowding. Finally, the wide use of pardons in many states made it easy to shift to granting releases based on inmates' progress in prison.

As rehabilitation declined and was replaced by retribution, determinate sentencing statutes in many states led to a significant decline in the use of **discretionary parole,** release of an inmate at the parole board's discretion. Many states that abolished discretionary parole adopted a procedure called supervised **mandatory release.** In this form of release inmates are placed under a parole officer's supervision after they have served their original sentences minus good-time credits. The difference between parole and supervised mandatory release is that in the former a parole board makes the release decision, whereas the latter is made by a corrections official or committee. Both types of releasees are treated similarly in that they must adhere to specified conditions and are supervised by a parole officer in the community after release (McCarthy & McCarthy, 1991; McShane & Krause, 1993).

Types of Release from Prison   Release from prison can be either conditional or unconditional. Conditional releases typically include parole, supervised mandatory release, and supervised work furloughs. The vast majority of unconditional releases occur at the expiration of inmates' sentences and most of the rest are a result of commutation. Since the late 1970s the proportion of inmates given conditional releases from prison has remained relatively stable (between 80% and 85% of all releases). However, the proportion of those released on discretionary parole has declined steadily since 1977 (from 71.9% to 50% in 1995), while supervised mandatory releases have increased commensurately (Bureau of Justice Statistics, 1997; Jankowski, 1991; Snell 1995).

At the end of 1995, there were 700,174 adult offenders on some form of parole supervision in the United States (Bureau of Justice Statistics, 1997). This figure, a record high number, represents a 1.4 percent increase over 1994 and a 133.2 percent increase over the 1985 figure. According to the Bureau of Justice Statistics (1997, p. 126), at the end of 1995 47 percent of the parolees were nonwhite and 10 percent were female. Table 21.1 shows the probation, jail, prison, and parole populations in the United States from 1985 to 1995. Table 21.2 gives a state-by-state breakdown of parole populations in 1995.

Organization and Administration of Parole Services

Three basic services can be offered to inmates by a parole agency: release, supervision, and consideration of executive clemency. Compared with probation services, parole services are more uniformly organized in that

Table 21.1

Number of Adults on Probation, in Jail or Prison, or on Parole (1985–1995)*

Year	Total Estimated Correctional Population	Probation	Jail	Prison	Parole
1985	3,011,500	1,968,712	254,986	487,593	300,203
1986	3,239,400	2,114,621	272,735	526,436	325,638
1987	3,459,600	2,247,158	294,092	562,814	355,505
1988	3,714,100	2,356,483	341,893	607,766	407,977
1989	4,055,600	2,522,125	393,303	683,367	456,803
1990	4,348,000	2,670,234	403,019	743,382	531,407
1991	4,535,600	2,728,472	424,129	792,535	590,442
1992	4,762,600	2,811,611	441,781	850,566	658,601
1993	4,944,000	2,903,061	455,500	909,381	676,100
1994	5,141,300	2,981,022	479,800	990,147	690,371
1995	5,374,500	3,096,529	499,300	1,078,545	700,174
Percent change					
1994–95	4.5%	3.9%	4.1%	8.9%	1.4%
1985–95	78.5	57.3	95.8	121.2	133.2
Average annual percent change					
1990–95	4.3%	3.0%	4.4%	7.7%	5.7%
1985–95	6.0	4.6	7.0	8.3	8.8

*Counts for probation, prison, and parole populations are for December 31 of each year and have been revised based on the most recently reported counts. Jail population counts are for June 30 of each year. Prisoner counts are for inmates in custody only.
Source: Bureau of Justice Statistics (1997). *Correctional Populations in the United States, 1995.* Washington, DC: U.S. Department of Justice, p. 5.

they are centrally administered at the state level by the executive branch of government.

Parole services are administered based on one of two models: the *independent model* or the *consolidated model.* Those that operate under the **independent model** may have different names such as parole board, parole commission, or board of pardons in the various states. These autonomous units have the power to make parole release decisions and to supervise all conditionally released inmates (Task Force on Corrections, 1967). In states with parole boards, the governor usually appoints members. Board size varies from 3 to 15 members, and only a few states require any special qualifications (e.g., a bachelor's degree) for parole board members (Parker, 1975).

Under the **consolidated model,** parole services are in the state corrections department and responsibility is shared by the paroling authority and the corrections department. Thus, the parole authority makes release decisions and the corrections department supervises all conditionally released inmates. Parole and probation supervisory

California prisons use real-time video conferencing to allow victims to take part in parole hearings held at locations far from the place where the crime was committed.

Table 21.2

Adults on Parole (1995)

Region and Jurisdiction	Parole Population (1/1/95)	1995		Parole Population (12/31/95)	Percent Change	Number on Parole*
		Entries	Exits			
U.S. total	690,371	411,369	391,298	700,174	1.4%	361
Federal	61,430	29,491	22,552	59,136	—	30
State	628,941	381,878	368,746	641,038	1.9	330
Northeast	173,882	77,451	67,082	184,122	5.9%	474
Connecticut	1,146	1,934	1,847	1,233	7.6	50
Maine	40	1	2	41	2.5	4
Massachusetts	4,755	3,727	3,702	4,639	−2.4	100
New Hampshire	835	702	762	785	−6.0	92
New Jersey	41,802	17,198	11,589	47,411	13.4	793
New York	53,832	27,158	25,422	55,568	3.2	409
Pennsylvania	70,355	25,814	22,935	73,234	4.1	799
Rhode Island	525	597	529	593	13.0	79
Vermont	592	320	294	618	4.4	141
Midwest	82,478	62,155	56,698	87,364	5.9%	192
Illinois	26,695	22,706	19,860	29,541	10.7	339
Indiana	3,409	5,310	5,120	3,599	5.6	83
Iowa	3,696	1,665	1,826	3,535	−4.4	167
Kansas	6,291	3,741	3,938	6,094	−3.1	325
Michigan	12,846	9,078	8,062	13,862	7.9	197
Minnesota	1,904	2,581	2,368	2,117	11.2	63
Missouri	12,592	5,352	5,278	13,023	3.4	330
Nebraska	771	718	828	661	−14.3	55
North Dakota	94	209	189	114	21.3	24
Ohio	6,453	5,332	5,203	6,582	2.0	79
South Dakota	662	590	564	688	3.9	132
Wisconsin	7,065	4,873	3,462	7,548	6.8	200
South	253,731	101,722	111,741	243,309	−4.1%	358
Alabama	7,235	1,525	1,525	7,235	.0	228
Arkansas	5,224	4,108	4,477	4,855	−7.1	265
Delaware	1,029	40	259	810	−21.3	150

(continued)

services are combined under this model in states that have centralized probation services.

In deciding whether to release an inmate, parole authorities often consider the protection of society from predatory criminals as their first responsibility. This raises the question of the predictive power of risk assessment scales, a topic discussed in Chapter 19. Release is granted or denied based on evaluating information that is obtained through hearings and interviews, usually within the institutions served by the board, or through reviews of institutional reports. In most states the potential parolee is briefly interviewed by board members or by hearing examiners who report their recommendations back to the board.

The development of guidelines has been of great assistance to parole boards in making release decisions.

Parole boards have used the following criteria in the past: the nature of the inmate's crime, time served with respect to the sentence received, the inmate's age, substance abuse history, criminal history including previous sanctions received, and adjustment and program participation. In creating guidelines to be used in making parole decisions, a process similar to that used for constructing sentencing guidelines has been employed. These guidelines attempt to more accurately gauge the risk the parolee poses for the community (Clear, 1988).

Supervision of Parolees

Like probation officers, parole officers (called parole agents in some states) are responsible for supervising clients in the community. However, unlike probation of-

Table 21.2

Adults on Parole (1995) *(continued)*

Region and Jurisdiction	Parole Population (1/1/95)	1995		Parole Population (12/31/95)	Percent Change	Number on Parole*
		Entries	Exits			
South *(continued)*						
District of Columbia	6,574	2,702	2,580	6,696	1.9	1,523
Florida	20,573	3,769	9,649	13,746	−33.2	127
Georgia	17,505	10,862	9,479	19,434	11.0	368
Kentucky	4,380	3,256	3,379	4,257	−2.8	147
Louisiana	17,112	9,793	7,877	19,028	11.2	613
Maryland	14,795	11,921	10,968	15,748	6.4	418
Mississippi	1,519	840	847	1,510	−0.6	78
North Carolina	20,159	11,530	13,188	18,501	−8.2	343
Oklahoma	2,604	661	909	2,356	−9.5	98
South Carolina	6,077	1,522	1,702	5,897	−3.0	216
Tennessee	9,353	3,357	3,859	8,851	−5.4	224
Texas	108,563	24,425	29,899	103,089	−5.0	774
Virginia	9,649	10,766	10,227	10,188	5.6	204
West Virginia	1,380	645	917	1,108	−19.7	79
West	118,850	140,550	133,225	126,243	6.2%	303
Alaska	412	439	392	459	11.4	111
Arizona	4,351	5,693	5,935	4,109	−5.6	136
California	85,082	118,948	112,223	91,807	7.9	403
Colorado	2,463	3,021	2,460	3,024	22.8	109
Hawaii	1,650	668	629	1,689	2.4	192
Idaho	931	539	676	862	−7.4	106
Montana	710	431	386	755	6.3	119
Nevada	3,529	1,787	1,856	3,460	−2.0	306
New Mexico	1,078	815	775	1,118	3.7	94
Oregon	14,264	6,160	5,405	15,019	5.3	641
Utah	2,417	1,818	1,504	2,731	13.0	214
Washington	1,650	75	850	875	−47.0	22
Wyoming	313	156	134	335	7.0	97

*on 12/31/95 per 100,000 adult residents

— Not calculated

Source: Bureau of Justice Statistics (1997). *Correctional Populations in the United States, 1995.* Washington, DC: U.S. Department of Justice, p. 127.

ficers, parole officers devote a major portion of their time to client supervision.

POs can require clients to make periodic visits to their offices. On some occasions the clients may be ordered to submit to urinalysis. This allows the PO to determine the drug use patterns of clients who may have had substance abuse problems. POs also visit parolees in their homes and at their job sites. These field visits help officers verify employment and identify problems that might be occurring. They also reinforce to clients that they are under surveillance while they are serving the remainder of their sentences in the community.

Increasingly, parole officers, like their probation counterparts, are relying on technology to monitor the locations of their clients. This could involve the use of active or passive tracking systems (see Renzema &

Skelton, 1990). Recent technological advances allow parole officers to place clients under 24-hour surveillance. Such monitoring will improve detection of parole violations and "This may deter illegal behavior, and provide the opportunity to target and incapacitate those who are violating their conditions of parole" (Montes, 1996, p. 91).

Close surveillance of offenders, especially those who continue to violate the law, is not without its risks. As a result, some states now regularly arm parole (and probation) officers. Abadinsky (1994) is a strong advocate of both the law enforcement approach and the need for POs to carry firearms. His notions, described in the Close-Up "Should POs Be Armed?" are not only based on years of studying this area but are also drawn from his experiences as a parole officer in New York City.

Should POs Be Armed?

CLOSE-UP

As a private citizen with a working knowledge of probation and parole, I have certain concerns about personal safety—that of my family, friends, and neighbors. It is from this (I believe typical) layperson's perspective that I evaluate a p/p [parole/probation] agency. Let me provide some typical examples. It is not unusual during the course of an office or home visit for a p/p officer to discover that a client is using heroin or cocaine. If the offender is unemployed, the drug habit is probably financed by criminal activities—the client is a clear and present danger to himself (herself) and to the community. A p/p agency whose officers cannot

immediately (and safely) arrest such an individual is not providing an adequate level of client service or community protection. P/p agencies also supervise offenders who have been involved in (1) sex offenses against children, (2) vehicular homicide as a result of intoxication, (3) burglary, and (4) armed robbery. A p/p agency whose officers have no responsibility to enforce prohibitions, through investigation and arrest, against (1) frequenting play areas, (2) drinking and driving, or (3) carrying tools for forced entry or who cannot (4) investigate money or a lifestyle that cannot be supported by the offender's employment status is not providing the minimum acceptable level of community safety. Furthermore, the adult p/p client is a serious law vio-

lator who has proved to be a potential danger to the community. Many have been involved in crimes of violence, and the public and elected officials expect that probationers and parolees, if they are to remain in the community, will be under the scrutiny of p/p authorities. This is why the law of most jurisdictions empowers p/p agencies with law enforcement responsibilities (Abadinsky, 1994, pp. 341–342).

Given Abadinsky's concerns do you think POs should be armed? What are the positive and negative aspects of arming POs?
Source: H. Abadinsky (1994). Probation and Parole—Theory and Practice, *5th ed. Englewood Cliffs, NJ: Prentice Hall, pp. 341–342.*

Revocation When probationers or parolees fail to live up to the conditions in their contracts they can be subjected to revocation proceedings. For both probationers and parolees POs have the authority to recommend and begin the process, but the actual power to revoke an offender's probation is in the hands of the sentencing judge. For parolees it is done by either the parole board or hearing officers. Normally, revocation can result from two types of violations, those that deal with lawbreaking and those that are technical (i.e., a violation of one or more of the conditions of the probation/parole contract). The parties involved in revocation (the PO, the hearing body, the judge) have considerable discretion. Clients are not automatically revoked when they fail to abide by some of the conditions of their contracts. If an offender violates conditions the PO can ignore it, informally reprimand the offender, or report it to the sentencing judge or parole authority. If a decision is made to revoke, a formal process controlled by guidelines set by the Supreme Court must be followed.

Two Court decisions in the early 1970s provided the present guidelines used in revocation hearings. The first of these decisions was *Morrissey v. Brewer* (1972), which applied to parole revocation proceedings. The due process protections that were established for parolees were extended to probationers a year later in *Gagnon v. Scarpelli* (1973). These two cases mandated that parolees (and probationers) be provided with the right to a two-stage hearing, including due process protections, during

revocation proceedings. In the first hearing a determination is made as to whether probable cause exists that the parolee violated any specific conditions of his or her contract. The second hearing consists of the general revocation proceeding. During both hearings the offender is guaranteed basic due process rights.

In parole hearings, counsel is not guaranteed but rather this is decided on a case-by-case basis by the hearing body. Consideration must be given to the fact that uneducated clients might have difficulty presenting their version of disputed facts, particularly if the issues involved are complex. The same is true in cases in which the violation is not disputed but there are substantial reasons to justify or mitigate it. Table 21.3 provides a list of procedural protections accorded parolees drawn from a national survey conducted by the ACA of parole boards in 1988. Although these data are not complete, they indicate parolees pose a greater threat proportionally; more are revoked for committing new crimes.

The Effectiveness of Parole Supervision The effectiveness of correctional strategies, including parole, should be measured in terms of their goals. Generally, parole agencies measure effectiveness in terms of revocation and/or recidivism. Both measures have been criticized because they have shortcomings.

A Rand Corporation study (Petersilia, Turner, & Peterson, 1986) compared the recidivism of probationers with parolees. Because of the differences between of-

Table 21.3

Procedural Due Process at Parole Revocation Hearings

Due Process Protection	Preliminary Hearing		Final Hearing	
	Number*	%	Number*	%
Written notice of alleged violation	45	88.2	51	100.0
Disclosure of evidence of violations	42	82.4	51	100.0
Opportunity to confront and cross-examine adverse witnesses	44	86.3	47	92.2
Representation by counsel	31	60.8	40	78.4
Opportunity to be heard in person and to present evidence and witnesses	43	84.3	51	100.0
Written statement of reasons for the decision	45	88.2	48	94.1

*This refers to the number of states or paroling authorities (includes the federal government) with the specified procedure.
Adapted with permission from E. E. Rhine, W. R. Smith, & R. W. Jackson (1991). *Paroling Authorities: Recent History and Current Practice.* Laurel, MD: American Correctional Association.

fenders placed on probation and those incarcerated, the samples were matched with regard to several offense criteria. This study determined that parolees recidivated more quickly and had higher recidivism rates than probationers. However, the crimes for which they were revoked were no more serious than those committed by the probationers.

A study by Beck and Shipley (1987) shed some important light on parole effectiveness. This research, conducted in 22 states, was based on a sample of 3,995 parolees, aged 17 to 22, who were followed for 6 years. Figure 21.1 shows the cumulative percentage of offenders rearrested, reconvicted, and reincarcerated by 12-month intervals. The major results of this study include the following:

■ *Rearrests*   Over two thirds of the parolees were arrested within 6 years. One third of the group was rearrested in each of the first 2 years.

■ *Reconviction and Reincarceration*   Slightly over half were reconvicted within 6 years, and 49 percent of these were reincarcerated within this period.

■ *Volume and Type of New Offenses*   These parolees averaged two new arrests; over half were for property offenses, about one third for drug offenses, and almost one sixth for violent offenses.

■ *Recidivism and Prior Violent Crime*   Offenders with prior arrests for violent crime had a greater likelihood of arrests for another violent crime. Offenders on parole for property offenses with a record of one violent crime had the highest rearrest rates.

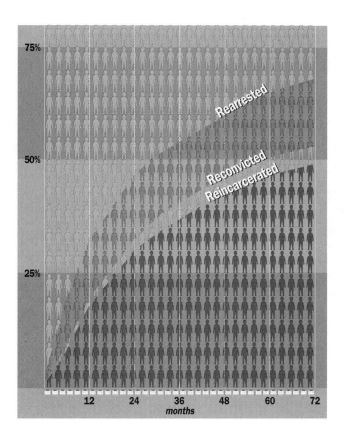

Figure 21.1   *Cumulative Percentage of Young Adults Paroled in 1978 Who Were Rearrested, Reconvicted, and Reincarcerated (by 12-Month Intervals)*

Source: A. Beck & B. E. Shipley (1987). *Recidivism of Young Parolees.* Washington, DC: U.S. Department of Justice, Bureau of Justice Statistics.

Several later studies have resulted in somewhat similar findings. A parole study in Hawaii (Attorney General's Office, 1989) found that of the 366 parolees studied, 46 percent were arrested before their terms expired. Gould, MacKenzie, and Bankston (1991) followed 102 nonviolent offenders for 12 months after release from Louisiana prisons. They found that 25 percent of this sample had their parole status revoked during that period. Another Louisiana study (Geerken, Miranne, & Kennedy, 1993) followed 327 offenders convicted of burglary and armed robbery who were paroled between 1974 and 1981 for the term of their supervision. They found that 46 percent of them were arrested for an index offense during that period.

To summarize, studies of parole effectiveness tend to show an inconsistent but relatively poor outcome; that is, the proportion of parolees arrested for both technical and criminal violations is unacceptably high. As a general rule there appears to be a relationship between parole failure and seriousness of criminal histories.

Sexual Offenders in the Community

One of the emerging problems facing parole officers is supervision of what may be labeled *special needs* offenders. Particularly troublesome among the special needs offenders are convicted sex offenders who will be released back into the communities from which they came. In this section, we will examine the issue of public safety and sex offenders. Evidence of treatment programs related to sex offenders is not particularly promising, and news coverage of several high-profile cases has made the reintegration of paroled sex offenders back into communities a cause for concern among the public and politicians.

Sex Offenders and Registration Laws

The presence in the community of violent sexual offenders stirs up strong public concerns that impact lawmakers. The Jacob Wetterling Crimes Against Children and Sexually Violent Offender Registration Act "was named for an 11-year-old boy who was abducted in October 1989 near his home in St. Joseph, Minn., by an armed, masked man" (National Criminal Justice Association, 1997, p. 5). To date, Jacob Wetterling is still missing. This act which was passed in 1994, "requires states to create registries of offenders convicted of sexually violent offenses or crimes against children and to establish more rigorous registration requirements for highly dangerous sex offenders" (Matson with Lieb, 1997, p. 3). Also, states must provide law enforcement agencies with registry in one location that is easily accessible (Sorkin, 1998, p. 16). At the time the Jacob Wetterling Act was passed in 1994, states were not forced to inform the public of sex offenders' whereabouts. However, the act was

A demonstrator in Placentia, California, demands the removal of a repeat child molester from a residence in the community. Many states have passed laws requiring that the names and addresses of sex offenders be registered with a central agency.

taken very seriously and those states that did not comply received a 10 percent reduction in their grant funding (Matson with Lieb, 1997). Most states have chosen to comply with the act.

In addition, many states have passed their own registration laws. Several key features of the registration laws are common among the states. The states require offenders to register with either a central agency or a law enforcement agency in the community within which they will reside (Finn, 1997). In most states, law enforcement agencies maintain the central sex offender registry (Walsh, 1997, p. 24-3). In all states, the offender must at least register his name and address. Additional requirements may include providing date of birth, fingerprints, social security number, photograph, criminal history, place of employment, and a blood sample (Walsh, 1997). The length of time for registration varies from state to state. The most common time frame requires the offender to register prior to release from the institution. However, the periods range from 'immediately' upon conviction or release from incarceration to 48 hours from entering the county, to 30 days from the date of conviction or release, entering the county, or establishing residence, to 60 days from entering into the jurisdiction if convicted in another state. (Walsh, 1997, p. 24-4)

The duration of the registration requirement also varies by states. States may require offenders to register anywhere from 5 years to life. Failure to comply with registration laws can result in penalties anywhere from mere violations to felonies and can even result in probation or parole revocation (Walsh, 1997).

Registration laws have both proponents and opponents. The proponents often cite public safety as one of the main arguments for registration laws. They argue that registries are tools that help law enforcement prevent or solve crimes (Matson with Lieb, 1996, July, p. 2). The registry's purpose is to provide law enforcement officials with useful information that will facilitate their investigations. Another benefit cited by proponents is that "registration laws also create legal grounds to hold sex offenders who do not comply with registration and are later found in suspicious circumstances" (p. 2). This allows the police to question offenders who are found near a schoolyard, and if the offender is not registered the individual can be charged with failure to comply with the registration law (Matson with Lieb, 1996, July).

Proponents of registration laws contend that the laws provide a deterrent against future crimes. "Another intended effect of registration is psychological. Once registered, offenders know they are being monitored" (Matson with Lieb, 1996, July, p. 3). Therefore, they are less likely to commit new crimes because they know they easily can be detected. Deterrence increases public safety. Finally, proponents maintain that "access to the registry, or the active release of information by law enforcement or school districts, is intended as a means of citizen protection, particularly for parents to protect their children" (p. 3).

Opponents of registration laws cite numerous reasons why these laws should not be enacted: "Registration programs are inconsistent with the goals of a society committed to protecting individual liberties" (Matson with Lieb, 1996, July, p. 3). Registration laws can violate individual rights by subjecting offenders to continued punishment and possibly harassment. Opponents also argue that "by forcing sex offenders to register, society sends a message to these individuals that they are not to be trusted, that they are bad and dangerous people" (p. 3). This message hinders rehabilitation and instead leads the offender to believe that there is no way out of the criminal lifestyle, further alienating the offender from society (Matson with Lieb, 1996, July).

Opponents further argue that "registration laws encourage sex offenders to evade the attention of the law" (p. 3), making future criminal investigations difficult (Matson with Lieb, 1996, July). Therefore, instead of increasing public safety, registration laws may have the opposite effect. Another aspect of registration laws that opponents often cite is that "registration creates a false sense of security" (p. 4). The public may not realize that the registry contains only a small portion of sex offenders:

only a small proportion of sex crimes are reported, and an even smaller number results in convictions; many offenders plea-bargain to nonsexual offenses; sex offender registration laws can apply to limited categories of offenders; and many offenders were convicted prior to passage of the law. (p. 4)

Finally, opponents fear that registration will encourage citizens to become vigilantes (Matson with Lieb, 1996, July, p. 4). Some states allow for public disclosure of the registry, which can lead to harassment of the offender within the community (Matson with Lieb, 1996, July). Offenders become victims of community ostracism and harassment and may be forced to move frequently.

Community Notification Laws

In addition to registration requirements, Washington became the first state to enact a community notification law, the Community Protection Act. Passed in 1990, this act "included a community notification law authorizing public officials to notify the public when dangerous sex offenders are released into the community" (Matson with Lieb, 1996, November, p. 1). The main objectives of community notification were increasing public safety and providing public protection. Other objectives of the act included providing assistance to law enforcement in the hopes of preventing future crimes by utilizing the registry as a tool in criminal investigations (November).

In 1996, as a result of the rape and strangulation of 7-year-old Megan Kanka by a released child molester, the federal government passed Megan's Law (Sorkin, 1998, p. 17). This law amended the Jacob Wetterling Act: "Megan's Law requires States to release registration information to the public when it is necessary for public safety" (p. 17). States were no longer given the option about releasing the information. However,

Megan's Law allows states discretion to make judgments in determining if disclosure of information is necessary for public protection and in specifying standards and procedures for making these determinations. (Matson with Lieb, 1997, p. 3)

The government also enacted the Pam Lyncher Sexual Offender Tracking and Identification Act of 1996. There are three general requirements of this act. "First, it obligates the Attorney General to establish a national database at the FBI to track the whereabouts and movements of convicted sex offenders" (Sorkin, 1998, p. 17). By allowing the FBI to create this database, the act provides law enforcement agencies with improved and updated information on the location of sex offenders who move from state to state. "Second, the Act requires the FBI to handle sex offender registration in States lacking a minimally sufficient sex offender registration program" (p. 17). Finally, "the Lyncher Act amends the Wetterling Act to prescribe more stringent registration requirements" (p. 17). The purpose of the stricter requirements is to protect the public, by requiring "lifetime registration for violent and habitual sex offenders, and requiring submission of offenders' fingerprints and photographs with other registry information" (p. 17). Therefore, this act is aimed at reinforcing compliance with the Jacob Wetterling Act by improving registration programs as well as establishing a national database.

As a result of Megan's Law, many states enacted their own statutes. Although the laws vary among the states, three notification categories exist. The first category is known as **broad community notification**: "These states authorize broad dissemination of relevant information to the public regarding designated sex offenders" (Matson with Lieb, 1997, p. 5). The 18 states currently using this method "use numerous methods for releasing information, including the telephone, CD-ROM, the Internet, and notices in newspapers" (p. 5).

California was the first state to allow "the release of a CD-ROM containing the names, physical descriptions, criminal histories, residential zip codes and often the photographs of nearly 64,000 sex offenders convicted statewide, almost all of whom must register every year for life" (Purdum, 1997, July 1). The information is publicly available at various law enforcement agencies throughout the state (July 1). California took release of this information one step further by setting up a booth at the Sacramento County Fair. California's Justice Department exhibit was just down the midway from the electronic fortune teller and virtual-reality boxing. It offered nine color computers to search a database of 64,000 convicted child molesters and rapists, with pictures, offenses, names, and addresses sorted by postal code. The "information also is available to Californians at police stations and through a 900 number as a result of Megan's Law, which requires release of information on known molesters" (*Chicago Tribune*, 1997, Sept. 14).

In Tampa, Florida, lawmakers also have implemented community notification through a program that includes the disclosure of the names, addresses, and photographs of known sex offenders on a local cable television program—with mixed responses. Critics claim that the program makes readjustment to society impossible as well as instigates vigilantism, whereas proponents claim that it is necessary for public protection and children's safety.

Delaware has expanded community notification by becoming the first state to include a sex offender designation on driver's licenses (Janofsky, 1998, April 21). Under this law, anyone convicted of any of 12 sex crimes in Delaware would be reissued a driver's license with the designation of "y" on the reverse side. If the offender moves to another state and applies for a driver's license, the designation would enable authorities in the new state to identify the person as a sex offender when the old license is turned in (April 21). The new law is targeted to alleviate the problem of offenders who fail to register when they move to a new state.

The second type of notification used in some states is notice to individuals and organizations at risk. Fourteen states use this method to provide notification only to individuals or organizations at risk: "These states provide more limited notification, with the release of information based on a need to protect an individual or vulnerable organization from a specific sex offender" (Matson with Lieb, 1997, p. 5). Most of the affected organizations are linked to child services such as schools, day care centers, or other child-related organizations.

The final type of notification used in some states is providing access to the registration information: "States in this category allow access to sex offender information by citizens or community organizations through their county sheriff or local police department" (Matson with Lieb, 1997, p. 6). Access varies and may be provided to the public, to those who are at risk, or only to organizations at risk (Matson with Lieb, 1997).

Once the state decides on the type of notification, it then must decide which offenders are subject to notification laws. "The majority of state statutes define the population of offenders that are subject to community notification as those convicted of a sexually violent offense or sexual offense against a victim who is a minor" (Matson with Lieb, 1997, p. 10). Many states allow law enforcement agencies to make the final decision on who should be subject to these laws. Most agencies rely on information provided by the offender's releasing agency such as "offense history, patterns of abuse, response to treatment (if given) while incarcerated, and a variety of other personal information" (Matson with Lieb, 1997, p. 11). Finally, some states utilize a formal risk assessment instrument: "These instruments consist of scales that assign point values to various behaviors and past offenses" (p. 11).

Next, the states must then decide the scope of the notification in terms of who should be notified of the information. "In a few states, the statute spells out the geographic vicinity for notification" (Matson with Lieb, 1997, p. 12). However, most states follow a tiered approach, which is determined at the discretion of law enforcement agencies:

law enforcement, following guidelines, release information dependent upon the tier of risk:

Tier I (low risk): Information may be shared with other law enforcement agencies and any victim or witness to the offense.

Tier II (moderate risk): Includes the activities listed above, but in addition, schools, child care centers, family day care providers, businesses, organizations, and community groups may be notified of the offender's release.

Tier III (high risk): In addition to the actions above, members of the public who are likely to encounter the offender are notified. (Matson with Lieb, 1997, p. 13)

This approach is the most common one for determining who should be notified.

Finally, some states allow criminal justice agencies to determine who should be notified. The states also vary according to who conducts the notification. In most states, law enforcement agencies are responsible for the notifications. "Typical methods of notification include press releases, flyers distributed throughout neighborhoods, ads in newspapers, and direct mailings to the offender's neighbors" (Matson with Lieb, 1997, p. 13). Another method that is utilized in Louisiana requires the offender to conduct the notification (Matson with Lieb, 1997).

To summarize, community notification laws provide several benefits. These include public safety, assistance in law enforcement investigations, public awareness of sex offenders, and improved relationships between probation and parole officers and the public (Finn, 1997).

Although there are a number of advantages to these laws, there are also disadvantages. Some of the disadvantages are a false sense of security in the community and vigilante acts against offenders. Although harassment is a serious problem that is being addressed, it appears to be occurring in only a small percentage of cases and hopefully can be solved before it gets worse.

Legal Challenges

Sex offenders have presented various legal challenges to registration and community notification laws. The most common constitutional challenge is based on protection against ex post facto laws. Offenders claim violations because the

retroactive application to offenders who had already been sentenced at the time the statute went into effect constitutes double jeopardy in that notification, and because of the purported stigma attached to it, punishes offenders who have already served their time. The ex post facto analysis turns on whether the law is punitive or regulatory in nature. (Finn, 1997, p. 15)

Challenges to the retroactive application of these laws have occurred in various states. In most states, the laws have been upheld, but some states have struck down the laws (Matson with Lieb, 1997). In Washington, the state courts based their decision on whether the registration or notification laws were punitive in nature. The laws were upheld as being regulatory in nature and aimed at protecting the public (Cohen, 1997). However, in other states, such as Louisiana, the laws were struck down because of their broad nature. In Louisiana, "the law has been challenged several times, and its retroactive application was found unconstitutional in 1994, with regard to the broadest notification provisions" (Matson with Lieb, 1997, p. 18). However, "three United States Circuit Courts of Appeals have recently upheld the retroactive provisions of New Jersey, New York, and Washington notification laws" (p. 17). Most courts also have ruled that because the laws do not violate ex post facto protections, they also do not constitute double jeopardy because they are not imposing punishment. The U.S. Supreme Court has refused to hear legal challenges to community notification laws (Greenhouse, 1998).

Another legal challenge that has been presented by sex offenders is violation of the Eighth Amendment's protection against cruel and unusual punishment resulting from the stigmatization that occurs with registration and notification. However, because the various state courts have determined that these laws do not represent punishment, there can be no violation of the Eighth Amendment:

For example, in 1991, the Illinois Supreme Court reasoned that the offender's criminal history is public information, so no additional stigmatization is attached to registration or notification, and therefore [it] is not considered punishment under the Eighth Amendment. (Matson with Lieb, 1997, p. 19)

Sex offenders also challenge these laws based on due process claims. Most states have responded to these challenges by making "provision either for offenders to petition for relief from notification or for the initial determination of notification to be reviewed by other officials" (Finn, 1997, p. 15). Offenders who claim that their privacy rights have been violated also have met with little support from the courts. Most courts have determined that the right to privacy is not violated because the offender's criminal background information is public and cannot represent additional punishment or stigmatization. "Thus, sex offender registration laws, including posting of warning signs, will likely withstand any legal challenge. They will be dealt with as a matter of public policy and gauged for effectiveness" (Cohen, 1997, p. 30-3).

Additionally, sex offenders have claimed equal protection violations. This Fourteenth Amendment clause requires states to provide equal protection to every person. Sex offenders claim that they are being targeted as a "suspect" class and are being denied equal protection. However, the courts disagreed and "held that first, sex offenders are not a suspect class, and second, no fundamental right is affected by registration or notification" (Walsh, 1997, p. 24-14). Also, the courts applied the rational basis test, which determined that the state's application of these laws for public protection is legitimate and is rationally related to the purpose of public safety (Walsh, 1997).

Most challenges by sex offenders to registration and notification laws have been unsuccessful. Therefore, these laws continue to remain in effect in the hopes of increasing public safety and providing citizens with notification and necessary information about released sex offenders within their communities.

Civil Commitment

In addition to sex offender registration and notification laws, some states have pursued the strategy of civil commitment of sex offenders once their prison terms have expired. These laws allow the state to detain an inmate beyond his release date while criminal justice personnel conduct a hearing to determine whether he should face a civil commitment proceeding.

In Washington State a judge and jury hear evidence about the offender's potential for committing further sexual acts. To be committed, the prosecution is required to prove, beyond a reasonable doubt, that the offender is "a person who has been convicted or charged with a crime of violence and who suffers from 'mental abnormality or personal disorder which makes the person likely to engage in predatory sexual violence'" (London, 1991, p. 16).

Those found to meet these criteria are committed indefinitely to a special 36-bed unit in the state prison at Monroe. Here they are separated from other inmates, do not eat their meals with them, and do not wear prison uniforms. They are not allowed to participate in work or any activities outside the prison compound. These offenders receive individual and group therapy treatment. To be released, offenders periodically can petition the court to determine if their treatment has worked. However, many sex offenders have antisocial personalities that require aversive and intensive forms of behavior therapy to be successful. The state psychiatric association has contended that as a result many of these offenders will be confined for life.

Those favoring a law like Washington's argue that it is a vehicle for both offender treatment and for community protection. However, critics view it as a means of circumventing traditional civil commitment procedures. As a result of Washington's actions, several states adopted similar civil commitment laws. Generally, there are three models of **civil commitment laws:** the sexual psychopathy model, the mental health commitment model, and the postprison commitment model.

- The *sexual psychopathy model* is utilized in Illinois and Minnesota. These laws, which have existed since the late 1930s, have been declared constitutional by the U.S. Supreme Court (Lieb, 1996). However, the Illinois

model presents a choice to the state of pursuing either criminal prosecution or a violation of the sexual psychopath law (Lieb, 1996).

In addition, Minnesota has developed a sex offender screening tool to help identify those high-risk sex offenders who require a civil commitment hearing before release from prison (Minnesota Department of Corrections, 1997). This tool can be quite effective because it can be applied uniformly to all offenders (Minnesota Department of Corrections, 1997). The screening tool incorporates several general categories, and the offender is given a score based on the number of offenses committed. Several questions are asked on the assessment instrument about the subject's current incarceration term. Once scored, high-risk offenders as well as violent offenders are "referred to the county attorney, and, if not ultimately committed, supervised more closely than other releases" (Minnesota Department of Corrections, 1997, p. 1). This tool has been quite effective in determining those offenders who pose a potential threat due to the high risk of their reoffending.

- The *mental health commitment model* is utilized solely in New Jersey. The determination of civil commitment in this model requires the state to utilize current mental health commitment definitions (Lieb, 1996). The law targets those offenders "whose conduct is identified by the sentencing court as characterized by a 'pattern of repetitive, compulsive behavior' or who are identified by the Department of Corrections or the Parole Board, [to] be evaluated at the end of their term for potential commitment" (p. 5). This model focuses on the civil commitment based on a mental health determination. However, the definition of mental illness was modified to exclude a finding of psychosis because many sex offenders do not possess this characteristic (Lieb, 1996).

- The *postprison commitment model* seems to be the most accepted and is utilized in states such as Arizona, California, Kansas, North Dakota, Washington, and Wisconsin. Washington was the first state to pass postprison commitment laws and other states quickly adopted similar statutes. For example, in May 1998, Florida Governor Lawton Chiles signed the Jimmy Ryce Involuntary Civil Commitment for Sexually Violent Predators' Treatment and Care Act in reaction to the kidnapping, rape, and death of a 9-year-old boy. "The law calls for mental health experts to evaluate repeat sexual offenders nearing the end of their prison sentences" (Samolinski, 1998).

The laws generally contain the same provisions, but there are a few differences among the states. For example, "Washington's program is located in a mental health facility within the confines of a prison, whereas the Arizona, California, Kansas, and Wisconsin programs are in a hospital setting" (Lieb, 1996, p. vi). Most of the other elements are similar. For example, the civil commitment procedures require showing that an individual has a clinically recognizable disorder and represents a danger to himself or others as a result of this illness. The success of the treatment aspect has yet to be determined.

As a result of the passage of civil commitment laws, a number of legal challenges have been brought to the courts. Many offenders claim that civil commitment violates ex post facto law prohibitions because it is retroactive and applies to those offenders in prison who committed crimes before the law existed. Offenders claim that punishment for past conduct violates ex post facto protections. Another legal challenge is that civil commitments violate double jeopardy protections; offenders claim they are being tried twice for the same crime.

Kansas v. Hendricks   The results of these legal challenges vary among the states. However, the U.S. Supreme Court addressed these challenges when it heard *Kansas v. Hendricks* (1997). Kansas passed a Sexually Violent Predator Act that allowed for the commitment of offenders who had a mental abnormality or personality disorder and who probably would commit predatory sexual offenses (*Kansas v. Hendricks*, 1997). Leroy Hendricks, who had committed numerous offenses over a long period, was the first offender to be committed under the new law. Hendricks presented legal claims such as violation of the ex post facto law prohibition and double jeopardy. The Kansas Supreme Court held that the law was unconstitutional because the mental abnormality definition does not satisfy the substantive due process requirement "that involuntary civil commitment must be predicated on a finding of mental illness" (p. 2-3).

The U.S. Supreme Court ruled that the act's definition was sufficient because it defined a sexually violent predator as "any person who has been convicted of or charged with a sexually violent offense and who suffers from a mental abnormality or personality disorder which makes the person likely to engage in predatory acts of violence" (*Kan. Stat. Ann.*, 1994). In addition, the act requires as a prerequisite that the person is dangerous either to himself (herself) or to the community and that commitment proceedings must follow proper procedures (*Kansas v. Hendricks*, 1997). The Court ruled that "the statute thus requires proof of more than a mere pre-disposition to violence; rather it requires evidence of past sexually violent behavior and a present mental condition that creates a likelihood of such conduct in the future if the person is not incapacitated" (p. 8).

The Court has upheld statutes in the past that combine dangerousness with additional factors, which in this case are present because Kansas couples dangerousness with a finding of mental abnormality or a personality disorder (*Kansas v. Hendricks*, 1997). This determination is significant in that it allows a finding of a mental abnormality. The Court held that mental illness per se is not required; a finding of a mental abnormality or personality disorder will suffice to meet the due process requirement.

The Court then addressed Hendricks's argument that the act provided no treatment for his condition based on the fact that the act stated that it was impossible to treat sexually violent offenders (*Kansas v. Hendricks*, 1997). The Court's response was that "it would be of little value to require treatment as a precondition for civil confinement of the dangerously insane when no acceptable treatment existed" (p. 15). Therefore, treatment is not required if the condition is untreatable. The Court then focused on Hendricks's argument that the act does state that treatment is possible for sexually violent offenders, but that the act fails to provide for such treatment. The Court concluded that adequate treatment was provided by the act itself as well as by a program conducted by the Kansas Department of Health and Social Rehabilitative Services (*Kansas v. Hendricks*, 1997). Although the Court determined that the act adequately provided treatment, it did not require treatment provisions as part of future sexually violent predator acts.

The Court also addressed the issue of whether there was an ex post facto law or double jeopardy violation. The Court determined that the statute was not intended to be criminal in nature, it did not meet the goals of retribution or deterrence, and it did not subject the offender to additional punishment. Instead the statute was civil in nature and was intended to protect the public welfare (*Kansas v. Hendricks*, 1997). The Court concluded "that the Act is nonpunitive thus removes an essential prerequisite for both Hendricks' double jeopardy and ex post facto claims" (p. 17). Further, the Court held that because the act is civil in nature, there can be no double jeopardy violation because there is no second prosecution (*Kansas v. Hendricks*, 1997). The Court ruled that the act was constitutional, met due process requirements, did not require the use of a mental illness definition per se, and there were no ex post facto law or double jeopardy requirement violations.

This decision's effect is quite significant. *Kansas v. Hendricks* (1997) allows for the civil commitment of sexually violent predators upon completion of their prison terms. This decision will affect numerous sexual predators throughout the country. As yet, the impact of this decision has not been determined.

Summary

One of the persistent problems in the criminal justice system is how to help inmates maintain family and friendship ties while they are incarcerated. There also is the continuing concern over how to help offenders who have been imprisoned to make the transition successfully back into family, work, and community life.

Prison programs such as family and conjugal visits help spouses to maintain some semblance or normalcy in an otherwise abnormal situation. It is difficult, even under the best of circumstances for inmates to continue to function as spouses and parents when they are imprisoned some distance from their families. However, the use of visitation and telephone privileges can help those behind bars to maintain reasonably frequent contacts with their spouses and children. It is no substitute for being there in person, but it is better than no contacts at all.

Family contacts also should help offenders reestablish connections that will assist them in parole planning. Institutional committees and parole officers want to know that released inmates have a job and a place to live when they return to the community. Any way that parole officers can help strengthen family ties is likely to contribute to overall parole success.

Parole fell into disfavor, beginning with Maine's elimination of parole in 1976, but its use in one form or another has made a substantial comeback in corrections. Today we find increasing numbers of offenders serving the remainder of their sentences in their home communities under the supervision of parole officers. This means that meager parole resources will be stretched even further in the coming years. The pressures to closely supervise parolees and to alter their behaviors may increase as the public demands safety. Safety concerns especially may become conspicuous as certain special needs offenders, such as sex offenders, are returned to live in America's neighborhoods.

Critical Thinking Questions

1. What are the effects of visits and family ties on recidivism?
2. How are wives affected by the incarceration of their husbands?
3. Discuss some of the differences between visiting conditions from prison to prison. Who generally comes to visit inmates?
4. How do security and custody concerns affect visiting?
5. Define private family/conjugal visits. What are the arguments for and against this program?
6. How do telephones serve to augment visiting?
7. What are the benefits of prison furlough programs?
8. Differentiate between the independent and consolidated models of parole services.
9. Summarize the general results of studies on the effectiveness of probation and parole.
10. What due process rights are parolees entitled to during the revocation process?
11. What events have led to additional laws regarding the release and supervision of sex offenders?
12. What kinds of special challenges do released sex offenders present for parole officers?

Test Your Knowledge

1. Which of the following statements best characterizes the effects of family ties on recidivism?
   a. Lack of family ties can increase recidivism.
   b. Inmates with strong family ties never come back to prison.
   c. Family ties have no apparent effect on recidivism.
   d. Lack of family ties can reduce recidivism.
2. Court rulings regarding restrictions on visitation do not allow prisons to:
   a. limit the number of visits.
   b. exclude "objectionable" visitors.
   c. suspend visits as punishment.
   d. limit the duration of visits.
3. Which of the following services are not provided to prison visitors?
   a. transportation
   b. child care
   c. legal counsel
   d. information on regulations
4. Which of the following best describes the official objective of conjugal visits?
   a. reduce prison rape
   b. reduce prison homosexuality
   c. improve inmate responsibility
   d. maintain inmate family ties
5. Probationers and parolees are entitled to certain procedural due process rights at revocation hearings. Which of the following is *not* one of them?
   a. right to a jury trial
   b. right to present evidence
   c. right to cross-examine witnesses

Glossary

Abolitionists: Term applied to individuals who are against capital punishment.

Abscond: In corrections, to depart without authorization from a geographical area or jurisdiction, in violation of the conditions of probation or parole.

Absolute Pardon: A pardon for British subjects banished to Australia that restored all rights including the right to return to England.

Academy of Criminal Justice Sciences: A professional organization for criminal justice professionals and academics.

Accomplished Characters: Big house inmates good at providing diversions and entertainment.

Accomplished Gamblers: Inmates whose gaming skills or luck enabled them to acquire substantial winnings, putting them in a position of power relative to the inmate economy.

Accreditation: A process by which facilities or agencies are certified by the American Correctional Association as meeting a set of standards for their physical plant, operations, performance, staffing, programs, and services. *Also see* National Commission on Correctional Health Care.

Acquired Immune Deficiency Syndrome (AIDS): A condition in which the body's immune system is unable to fight illness and disease, making sufferers susceptible to a host of infections that otherwise do not affect healthy people.

Acquittal: The verdict in a court that the defendant is not guilty of the offenses for which he or she has been tried.

Act of October 14, 1940: Prohibited the interstate transport of all prison-made products except agricultural commodities and goods produced for states and their political subdivisions.

Adjudication: The process by which a court arrives at a decision on a case; also the resulting decision.

Adjustment Centers: The euphemism applied to segregation units in California during the rehabilitation era.

Administrative Facilities: Institutions with special missions. They include Metropolitan Correctional Centers (MCCs), Metropolitan Detention Centers (MDCs), Federal Medical Centers (FMCs), and U.S. penitentiaries (USP). Administrative facilities are capable of holding inmates in all security categories.

Administrative Segregation (AS): A form of separation from the general population sometimes imposed by classification committees for inmates who pose serious threats to themselves, staff, or other inmates or to institutional security; are under investigation for serious rule violations; or are awaiting transfer.

Adult Basic Education (ABE): Educational programs that stress literacy and mathematical skills as a foundation for further education and training. Generally viewed as a feeder system for GED preparatory classes.

Adult Education Act (1964): A federal act that provided funding for programs targeting adults with deficiencies in communication, computation, or social relations substantially impairing their employment chances.

Aftercare: In the criminal justice system this term usually refers to postrelease supervision for juveniles but is sometimes used to denote other programs that provide reentry into the community from jails or prisons.

Aggravated Assault: Unlawful intentional infliction of serious bodily injury (or unlawful threat or attempt to inflict bodily injury or death) by means of a deadly or dangerous weapon with (or without) actual infliction of any injury.

Aggravating Factors: Circumstances about a crime that cause it to be considered more serious than that of the average instance of that offense.

Alcoholics Anonymous (AA): An independent organization established in the 1930s that uses a 12-step program to help members overcome addiction to alcohol.

American Correctional Association (ACA): A professional organization, founded in 1870, for correctional personnel and others interested in corrections. Heavily involved in research, accreditation, and training.

American Jail Association (AJA): An organization that focuses on jail personnel and also contributes to correctional officer training and professionalism.

American Jails: Journal published by the American Jail Association (AJA) that deals with jail issues.

American Muslim Mission: *See* Nation of Islam.

American Prison Association: Created in 1870, it was the forerunner of the American Correctional Association.

American Society of Criminology: Professional organization for academic criminologists and others. Not specifically concerned with corrections but contributes by promoting and generating research to inform practitioners in the field.

Americans with Disabilities Act of 1990: A federal act that prohibited government agencies like correctional institutions from denying qualified disabled persons access to programs and services.

Amnesty International: An organization that is concerned with human rights abuses (including opposition to capital punishment) and carries on campaigns to reduce or abolish them.

Amsterdam Workhouse: An early Dutch workhouse.

Antebellum Plantation Model: A farm organized in the manner of pre–Civil War plantations.

Antipsychotic Drugs: Any drug, such as Thorazine, used to relieve or control the symptoms of (e.g., delusions, hallucinations), but not "cure," psychotic disorders.

Antisocial Personality Disorder: A disorder characterized by callousness, impulsiveness, lack of loyalty, and a chronic indifference to and violation of the rights of others. These individuals are often in trouble with the law.

Appeal: The request (and the resulting process) that a court with appellate jurisdiction review the judgment, decision, or order of a lower court and set it aside.

Appellant: The person making an appeal.

Appointment System: As used in employee hiring, a pool of applicants meeting certain minimum requirements is developed (e.g., have a B.A. degree) but no examination is mandated. Agency administrators interview qualified candidates and select whomever they please from this group.

Arraignment: The court hearing at which a defendant is formally charged with an offense.

Arrest: The taking of a person into physical custody by authority of law for the purpose of charging him or her with a criminal offense.

Arson: The intentional damaging or destruction (or attempt to do so) by means of fire or explosion, of the property of another without the consent of the owner, or of one's own property or that of another with intent to defraud.

Aryan Brotherhood (AB): White inmate gangs that formed in reaction to the development of minority-based gangs. Their credo espouses white superiority.

Ashurst-Summers Act of 1935: Prohibited the interstate transportation of convict-made goods to states where such products were prohibited and required labels on all prison products sold in interstate commerce.

Assault: Unlawful, intentional infliction (or attempted or threatened infliction) of injury upon the person of another.

Asset Forfeiture: Government seizure of property derived from or used in criminal activity. Typically used to strip drug traffickers, racketeers, and white collar offenders of their economic power.

Assistant Superintendents: Persons within the executive management team who specialize in managing certain prison functions, such as security, treatment programs, business operations, or prison industries. Also responsible for supervising the operations of their specific area.

Associate Members: Inmates who associate with gang members but will never join the gang.

Asylums: The term used to denote early facilities used to house the mentally disturbed.

Asymptomatic: HIV-infected individuals not showing any signs or symptoms of AIDS.

Attica Revolt: A name given the riot that occurred at the Attica correctional facility in New York in 1971.

Auburn System: The approach to imprisonment, also called the congregate system, developed in New York at the Auburn penitentiary. It was designed to reform inmates through congregate labor, a strict rule of silence, harsh discipline, and isolation at night.

Augustus, John: Considered the first probation officer. Between 1841 and 1858 he took responsibility for supervising and assisting offenders who were released into his custody by Boston judges.

Authoritarian Organizational Model: In these organizations, decision-making power is in the hands of one person or a small number of high-level "bosses."

Authority Revolution: The erosion in respect for authority, tradition, and adults by young people that began during the 1960s.

Baby Boom: Refers to the demographic changes caused by the large number of males born between 1945 and 1960 who reached their most crime-prone ages during the 1960s and 1970s.

Back-Door Program: A community program that functions as an early release mechanism for high-risk offenders who may not meet the criteria for regular parole.

Bagnes: Secure stockades established at French seaports to house slaves and others. They were also used to hold crippled galley convicts while they were in port. They were eventually transformed into workhouses and served as a transition from the galleys to prisons.

Bail: To effect the release of an arrested person in return for a promise that he or she will appear at required court proceedings granted by a pledge to pay the court a specified amount of money for failure to appear. Also refers to the money pledged to the court.

Bail Bondsman: A person, usually licensed, in business to effect releases on bail for those charged with offenses and held in custody by pledging to pay a sum of money if the defendant fails to appear in court as required.

Banishment: A form of punishment by which the offender was expelled from his or her home area or country either temporarily or permanently. Could include enslavement or exile of offenders to a penal colony.

Barrio Gangs: Neighborhood gangs organized in Mexican-American areas in California for "territorial protection."

Battery: A completed assault.

Beccaria, Cesare: Italian economist/criminologist who, with Jeremy Bentham, was the founder of the classical school of criminology.

Behavioral Contracting: The negotiation of a written agreement between inmates and corrections personnel that specifies that if the inmates behave in certain ways they will be rewarded.

Behavioral Deep Freeze of Incarceration: A lifestyle adopted by long-term inmates in which they either develop guarded or no relationships with other inmates. This is to avoid facing the devastation of having relationships terminated by transfer or releases.

Behavior Modification: A technology based on the principles of learning used in the treatment of behavioral problems, as well as in teaching any adaptive forms of behavior. The assumption is that all behavior is learned and that socially acceptable behavior can be learned as a substitute for deviant behavior.

Bench Warrant: A court document directing that a law enforcement officer bring the person named therein before the court.

Benefit of Clergy: Although originally available only to religious officials in England, this privilege was later extended to laypersons by defining clerical status in terms of literacy. In practice, this meant, that if a prisoner could read a verse from the Bible he could avoid the death penalty. By the late 1600s women could use this privilege on the same basis as males.

Big House: A pre-1950s-type prison resembling a military fortress with large cell blocks. These also had a unique subculture and hierarchical inmate status systems.

Billing for Medical Care: A recent practice by which some correctional systems charge inmates with resources for the medical care they receive.

Bill of Rights: The first 10 amendments to the U.S. Constitution.

Black Codes: These were penal codes, specifically aimed at controlling black slaves in the pre–Civil War South, that inflicted more severe punishments on slaves than on whites for many offenses.

Black Guerrilla Family (BGF): A black prison gang that formed to protect and advance the position of their race. Their philosophy advocated violence to achieve their objectives.

Black Muslims: An organization begun in America in the 1930s by blacks that combined the tenets of Islam and Christianity.

Black Panthers: A group of dissident blacks who organized in Oakland, California, in 1966 in reaction to police brutality in the black community and to provide protection for blacks from the police. Their objective, with respect to inmates, was to unite all prisoner movement groups through an inclusive ideology emphasizing their similarities and minimizing their differences.

Black Rage: The deep anger and hatred that blacks have felt over being subjected to more than three and a half centuries of humiliation, prejudice, and discrimination.

Blood Feud: An ongoing conflict between two kinship groups. Acts against one individual were viewed as acts against that person's entire kinship group and required the victim's family, tribe, or community to take action against the other group, which in turn was required to retaliate.

Bloods: A California street gang, which like the Crips, is seen as part of a new, more violent influx of gangs into the prisons.

Body Cavity Searches: Searches conducted of body orifices (e.g., the anus) for contraband.

Bona Fide Occupational Qualifications (BFOQ): Job qualifications that are in and of themselves necessary for adequate performance of that job and can be used to exclude individuals not having them.

Bona Fide Religious Belief or Practice: A belief or practice that is found in a religion's published theology or expert testimony and indicates it is associated with a particular religion.

Booking Process: A law enforcement or correctional administrative process after arrest that officially identifies the person, time, reason for arrest, and arresting authority after which the arrestee may be released on bail, released on recognizance, or placed in detention.

Boot Camps: A form of split sentence used with juveniles and youthful offenders. These programs consist of a 3- to 6-month residential phase in a very structured and regimented environment similar to that found in military boot camps and, in some instances, is followed by some form of community aftercare and supervision. Newer programs de-emphasize the military regimen and put more stress on treatment programs, such as education, work, substance abuse treatment, and developing a prosocial lifestyle.

Branding: The practice of placing a mark on an individual to identify him or her as a criminal. The marking could be done on the skin by using a hot metal brand, by sewing letters onto a garment, and so on.

Bridewell: An old palace donated to the city of London by King Edward VI. It was renovated and opened about 1516 as the first workhouse.

Bridle: An iron cage that fit over the head and had a front plate that was sharpened or covered with spikes designed to fit into the mouth of the offender. This was intended to punish the individual as well as to keep him from speaking.

Broad Community Notification: A type of law that permits states to disseminate information about sex offenders in the community to the public.

Brockway, Zebulon T.: A noted prison reformer who opened the first reformatory at Elmira, New York, in 1877, which he headed for the next 20 years. He is also credited with developing the first parole system in the United States.

Brutalizing Effect: Argument that the death penalty may lead to an increase in the number of murders because it reinforces violence.

Building Tenders: Inmates who were given the authority to maintain order within the tanks at Texas prisons. Performed functions similar to trusty-shooters but did not carry firearms.

Bulls: *See* Hacks.

Bureaucratic Organizational Model: Establishes a formal organizational structure, which includes a hierarchical structure with varying levels of authority, a formal chain of command, and a vertical authority and communication structure that flows from the top of the hierarchy to the bottom.

Burglary: The unlawful entry of any fixed structure, vehicle, or vessel used as a residence, industry, or business with (or without) force with the intent to commit a felony or larceny.

Burnout: A state of emotional exhaustion and cynicism that frequently occurs among individuals who are involved in "people work." This is particularly true for those who work closely with others under conditions of chronic tension and stress. It is frequently characterized by emotional exhaustion, depersonalization, decreased competence, and detachment from the job caused by stress.

Callouts: The taking of inmates from regularly scheduled activities (e.g., work) for a special purpose (e.g., a dental appointment).

Campus-Style Facilities: Prison facilities in which the buildings are arranged in a circular fashion with an inside green space used for recreational activities. Security levels can vary, but usually they are often minimum security facilities.

Capital Offense: A criminal offense punishable by death.

Capital Punishment: The death penalty.

Career Criminals: A person having a past record of multiple arrests or convictions for serious crimes or an unusually large number of arrests for crimes of varying degrees of seriousness.

Caseload: In corrections, the total number of clients registered with a correctional agency or agent at a given point in time.

Casework: A way of working with individuals generally used by social workers. It follows the traditional medical model. Theoretically, many probation and parole agencies expect their officers to use this approach; however, large caseloads make following this approach difficult.

Caseworker Model: One of the models under which probation officers deliver supervisory services to their clients. This one centers on the PO providing treatment or counseling and developing a one-on-one relationship with the probationer.

Catch-22: A situational dilemma in which any decision made will have negative consequences. Akin to "damned if you do and damned if you don't."

Catchers: Victims of sexual assaults in prisons. Also known as punks or kids.

Cell Blocks: A building or part of a building within a prison containing an array of cells that serves as housing for a group of inmates. Usually found in Auburn-type prisons.

Censorship: The practice that allows prison staff to open inmates' mail, read it, delete objectionable material, and confiscate disapproved items.

Central Core Members: Gang members with a very strong commitment to a gang; usually includes gang leaders and close friends.

Certified Court Orders: Certified orders committing convicted offenders to the custody of the department of corrections.

Chain Gang: A group of inmates, usually chained together, used by Southern county and state correctional agencies for working at clearing highway rights-of-way, and so on.

Chain of Command: This recognizes that to maintain control of a large organization a leader must delegate oversight of its many workers and activities to executive managers who in turn delegate authority to middle managers and they give authority to first-line supervisors.

Characters: Inmates who were good at providing humorous diversions by virtue of their storytelling abilities, dress, or general behavior.

Charge: An official allegation that a specified person has committed a specific offense.

Chemical Agents: These include gases that temporarily immobilize individuals subjected to them.

Chicanos: During the rehabilitation era, a term applied specifically to Mexican-American inmates from Los Angeles.

Child Molester: An individual who sexually abuses children. This person has a preference for children as sexual objects.

Choice Theory: The modern version of classical theory. It emphasizes the rational weighing of the specific costs and gains in the decision-making process governing criminal events. *Also see* Rational Choice Theory.

Chronic Offenders: Originally defined by Wolfgang in his cohort studies to denote offenders arrested five or more times. Although small in number, they account for a disproportionate amount of serious crime.

Citation: A written order issued by a police officer directing an alleged offender to appear in a specific court at a specified time to answer a criminal charge.

Citizen Dispute Settlement Centers: *See* Neighborhood Justice Centers.

Civil Commitment: A formal nonpenal commitment to a treatment facility resulting from findings made during criminal proceedings, or civil proceedings involving the mentally ill or disturbed, the incompetent, sex offenders, or substance abusers.

Civil Rights (Section 1983) Actions: *See* Section 1983 of the Civil Rights Act.

Civil Rights Act of 1871: An act passed by the federal legislature that attempted to protect the rights of blacks following the Civil War.

Civil Rights Act of 1964: Prohibits discrimination in the workplace.

Civil Rights Movement: The fight to gain the rights of full citizenship and reduce racism against African Americans that began to strongly manifest in the late 1950s and early 1960s.

Class Action Lawsuits: Lawsuits that provide a means by which a large group of persons interested in a matter can pursue legal action by having one or more of them sue or be sued as representatives of the class.

Classical Theory: An 18th-century theory of criminal behavior that assumes that human beings have free will, are rational, and make behavioral decisions based on the consequences of their actions before engaging in them. If the consequences are positive they will engage in the behavior, and if not they will avoid it.

Classification: The sorting out procedure that results in matching a prisoner to the appropriate level of supervision (custody), institution (security), programs, and services to meet his or her needs and that periodically reviews the inmate's placement to achieve the most appropriate assignments possible.

Classification Committee: A committee composed of several correctional staff members that has the responsibility of classifying and periodically reclassifying inmates.

Clearance: For UCR purposes the closing of a case by effecting the arrest of a suspected perpetrator. Also cases can be exceptionally cleared when some element beyond law enforcement control precludes formal charges (e.g., the victim

refuses to testify, or the offender is being prosecuted for another crime).

Clear and Present Danger: Doctrine in constitutional law providing that governmental restrictions on freedoms of speech and press will be upheld if necessary to prevent grave and immediate danger to interests that the government may lawfully protect.

Clemency: An executive or legislative action whereby the punishment of a person or persons is reduced or stopped.

Clinical Pastoral Educational Movement: A movement among the clergy that led to clinical training for them and which viewed prison chaplaincy as a specialty subgroup of the clergy.

Cliques: Primary and semiprimary groups formed by prisoners, from the same tip or from several tips, who have regular contact (e.g., at work, in the yard) and share an interest in some prison activity, subcultural orientation, and/or preprison experience.

Close Custody Inmates: Reserved for inmates with past assaultive or escape histories. Constant supervision and full restraints are required when leaving the facility. During the day, they are permitted to leave their cells and go to other parts of the institution on a check-out/check-in basis under staff observation.

Close Security Facilities: Perimeter security is the same as for maximum security prisons but with single, outside cells. When not in their cells inmates are normally under direct supervision. These Level IV facilities usually have inmates of different custody categories and more programming.

Cluster-Type Vocational Training Courses: Offer 100-hour blocks of instruction in related but different subject areas of a given trade.

CN: A standard type of tear gas.

Cocaine Anonymous (CA): Similar to Narcotics Anonymous.

Co-Correctional Facilities: Facilities that house both men and women. Normally, both sexes participate in most programs and share services.

Co-Corrections: *See* Co-Correctional Facilities.

Cognitive Approaches: Treatment approaches based on the assumption that incorrect thinking underlies and drives most behavior and that if the thinking is corrected problem behaviors will be changed.

Cognitive Therapy: *See* Cognitive Approaches.

Cohort Studies: Studies that use a sample of individuals who have a characteristic such as year of birth in common.

Collective Incapacitation: A form of incapacitation that would impose the same sentence on all individuals convicted of the same offense (e.g., armed robbery).

Colonial Period: The period of English rule over its American colonies that ended with the American Revolution.

Combined Preemployment Screening System: A written exam screens candidates, and those who have qualifying scores are placed on a list from which candidates are interviewed and selected.

Commissary: The prison "store" where inmates can buy items such as cigarettes, shampoo, candy, and so on.

Commitment: A judicial action placing an individual in a particular type of confinement as authorized by law.

Common Law Marriage: Refers to the acceptance of the existence of a marital relationship between a man and woman who have never legally married. This relationship is usually based on the fact that they lived together for some period of time.

Community Control: A term used to denote various forms of community supervision and known more popularly as "house arrest." *See* House Arrest for a more detailed definition.

Community Custody: This is lowest custody level; it is ordinarily reserved for inmates who meet the qualifications for participation in community activities. These inmates may be eligible for the least secure housing (including outside the institution), may work outside with minimal supervision, and may participate in community-based programs.

Community Policing: Collaboration between the police and the community on how to identify and solve problems with crime.

Community Security Facilities: Nonsecure facilities that include prerelease centers (such as work release or educational release), halfway houses, and other nonsecure settings. Also called Level I.

Community Service Orders: Originally touted as an alternative to incarceration, these programs were designed to require offenders to complete a specified number of community service hours in lieu of secure confinement.

Commutation (of Sentence): An executive act changing a punishment from a greater to a lesser penalty. In corrections, this usually results in the immediate release or reduction of the time to be served or changes a sentence of death to a term of imprisonment.

Compelling Government Interest: For correctional facilities, this means anything representing a serious threat to a prison's security, order, or discipline.

Compensation: An early process that attempted to circumvent blood feuds by having both the perpetrator and the victim agree to some form of payment by the perpetrator to the victim or his family to compensate for the damage done. Also known as wergild.

Compensatory Damages: Used to compensate the injured party for the injury sustained and nothing more.

Concurrent Sentence: A sentence that is one of two or more sentences imposed at the same time. After conviction all or part of each term is served simultaneously.

Conditional Releases: Releases in which the correctional system maintains some supervision over the releasee for a specified period of time. Typically includes parole, supervised mandatory release, and supervised work furloughs.

Conditions of Confinement: One of the two tests courts use to determine if cruel and unusual punishment exists within a facility. It examines whether basic human needs (such as food, health care, sanitary conditions, etc.) are being met in a constitutional manner.

Conditions of Release on Probation/ Parole: Restrictions or mandates imposed on all probationers as part of their sentences or on parolees as an aspect of their release.

Confidential Communication: Similar to a privileged communication but the protection is not absolute. In a corrections context, the recipient of the information is generally required to divulge information that threatens the safety or security of the institution, its staff, or other inmates.

Confinement: In corrections, the physical restriction (by barriers or guards) of a person to a clearly defined area from which he or she is lawfully forbidden to depart.

Conjugal Visiting Program: *See* Conjugal Visits.

Conjugal Visits: A visit under which inmates and their visitors (usually wives, but in some earlier circumstances prostitutes) were allowed privacy. Emotional and sexual intimacy is presumed to occur.

Conning: In treatment, this involves inmates' attempts to fool the counselor or therapist into believing that the treatment being received was causing positive changes in the person doing the conning. Its purpose is to achieve an early release.

Consecutive Sentence: A sentence that is one of two or more sentences imposed at the same time; after conviction the sentences are served in sequence.

Consent Decree: A court judgment in which both parties agree to work out the terms of the settlement subject to court approval.

Consolidated Parole Board Model: Under this model the parole board makes the release decision, but field parole services are in the state department of corrections and authority is split between these two administrative units.

Contact Visits: Prison visitation that permits visitors and inmates to have a limited degree of nonsexual physical contact.

Contempt of Court: Intentionally obstructing a court in the administration of justice, acting in a way calculated to lessen its authority or dignity, or failing to obey its lawful orders. To achieve compliance with its orders, courts can imprison or fine defendants.

Continuous Signaling Devices: These electronic monitoring devices consist of three components: a transmitter, a receiver-dialer, and a central computer. These devices allow POs to keep track of parolees or probationers who have confinement or curfew requirements as conditions of their release.

Contraband: Items that are declared illegal or off-limits to inmates by prison authorities.

Contract System: Under this system the state retained control of prisoners. Work was done within the prison under contract to private companies who paid the state a per-diem rate per worker and furnished the necessary instructors, machinery, and raw material for the production of the products, which it then sold.

Control: Refers to the actions taken by prison staff to influence or neutralize the verbal and physical actions of a prisoner who is offering resistance. The extent of the resistance determines the appropriate level of control to be imposed by the staff.

Control Conditions: These conditions, which are imposed on all probationers and parolees, include obeying laws, not associating with known criminals, and reporting regularly to their probation officer.

Controlling Customer Prison Industries Model: Under this model, the private sector is the primary or exclusive customer of a business operating as part of a prison industries program that it owns or has helped capitalize and which it may or may not manage.

Convict: A name given to inmates, also known as hogs, wise guys, bad dudes, or outlaws. Inmates with this status are the most respected figures in contemporary prisons and dominate the inmate world in violent prisons; they emphasize their toughness and willingness to use violence to maintain their status.

Convict Code: The dominant value system in the Big House heavily influenced by the thieves code, which included the following values: do your own time; don't rat on another prisoner; maintain your dignity and respect; help other thieves; leave most other inmates alone; and manifest no weakness.

Conviction: A court finding, based on the results of a trial or on the plea of guilty by the accused, that the defendant is guilty of the crime with which he or she has been charged.

Co-Occurring Disorders: Individuals who have a substance abuse problem and a mental disorder are considered to have a co-occurring disorder.

Cook/Chill Method of Food Production: A method that allows large quantities of food to be cooked in advance and then stored for later use.

Cool Inmates: The term applied to the form of prison adaptation by female inmates who were professional criminals and viewed their incarceration as a temporary experience that was a part of being involved in crime. Their goal was to minimize their time in prison and to do easy time.

Corporal Punishment: Any form of punishment applied to the body.

Corporate Prison Industries Model: A logical extension of current efforts to operate prison industries using free-world business practices. This model establishes a quasi-independent corporation that operates and manages prison industries yet is connected to the corrections department for security purposes.

Correctional Agency: A federal, state, or local agency whose principal functions include intake screening, custody, confinement, treatment, or presentence investigation of alleged or adjudicated offenders.

Correctional Facility: An enclosed area operated by a government agency for the physical custody (and/or treatment) of persons sentenced or subject to criminal proceedings.

Correctional Funnel: A method of describing the process by which apprehended offenders may be screened out of the system at different points along the way. When viewed in this way, this screening process takes the shape of a funnel, which functions like a sieve through which most cases "leak" out before they are retained in some correctional program (such as probation or prison).

Correctional Institutions: This term came into widespread use during the rehabilitation era to connote changes in the focus of prisons from punishment to treatment. Today, it continues to be a method of referring to prisons, a state system, the federal system, and even local systems that deal with detainees and offenders.

Correctionalists: Penal specialists, many with college degrees, who began to work in or study prisons during the rehabilitation era.

Correctional Officers (COs): Custodial personnel who directly supervise inmates.

Correctional Supervision: Authorized and required guidance, treatment, and regulation of the behavior of a person who is subject to adjudication (or who has been adjudicated to be an offender) performed by a correctional agency.

Corrections: Has at least two definitions: (1) the official responses taken by criminal justice agencies to punish convicted offenders in the United States; (2) the agencies, programs, and organizations on the local, state, and federal levels that detain those accused of crimes and those convicted of them.

Corrections Today: Journal published by the American Correctional Association (ACA) that deals with correctional and other related criminal justice issues.

Corrupt Favoritism: Informal control mechanism whereby guards granted special privileges to certain key inmates in exchange for their assistance in maintaining order.

CO Subculture: The norms, behaviors, and adaptations developed by correctional officers to cope with their work environment. This is influenced by such factors as administrative concerns and the dangerous nature of the prison environment. These norms are initially transmitted as part of the socialization process sometime during training.

Cottage Industry: Any type of productive work that can be done by an individual alone or in the confines of his or her cell.

Cottage Plan: A correctional compound that consists of several small units, each housing approximately 30 inmates, surrounding a central building that has regular cells. It may also have buildings used for program activities. This type of facility has usually been used with women and juveniles.

Counts: Process for determining the whereabouts of every inmate by physically counting them. These are conducted several times each day, and all prison activities usually stop until all inmates are accounted for.

Court Deference Era: The period, beginning about 1987, in which the Supreme Court's rulings made it clear that lower courts should defer to the judgment of correctional administrators.

Court Intervention: A recognition by judges about the mid-1960s that courts needed to intervene in prison operations to end many unconstitutional conditions, which led to the hands-on era in court-prison relations.

Court Order: A mandate, command, or direction issued by a court in the exercise of its judicial authority.

Covert Sensitization: A behavior modification technique to change the effect associated with a deviant behavior by pairing an imagined stimulus with imagined dire consequences.

Crazies: Inmates who are unpredictable and considered dangerous.

Creative Sentences: Offbeat sentences imposed by some judges (usually in misdemeanor cases).

Credit Cards: *See* Inmate Credit Cards.

Crime in the Suites: A term used to describe white collar or business crime.

Criminal Career Incapacitation: A form of selective incapacitation that targets classes of criminals who, on the average, have active high rates of crime (e.g., burglars).

Criminal Homicide: The causing of the death of another person without legal justification or excuse.

Criminally Insane: This term lumped together a number of categories of individuals that had in common the fact that they were involved in some way with the criminal justice system and had some type of mental problems. These included those found incompetent to stand trial, persons acquitted by reason of insanity, and inmates who became mentally ill while serving their sentence. These individuals were confined in either state mental hospitals, special wards of these facilities, or separate institutions. Today, these individuals are generally referred to as mentally ill offenders. They may be classified according to their status in the criminal justice system, which includes incompetent to stand trial, insane or mentally ill, or mentally disordered.

Criminal Offense: An act committed or omitted in violation of a law forbidding or commanding it, which carries possible penalties (e.g., incarceration) upon conviction.

Criminogenic Social Conditions: Conditions within the society that are likely to produce criminal behavior in the people influenced by them (e.g., dysfunctional families, neighborhoods, and communities).

Crips: A California street gang, which like the Bloods, is seen as part of a new, more violent influx of street gangs into the prisons.

Crofton, Sir Walter: *See* Irish System.

Cross-Gender Searches: Bodily searches of inmates by guards of the opposite sex.

Cruel and Unusual Punishment: Conditions and practices in prisons, such as solitary confinement, corporal punishment, use of force by guards, and other conditions of confinement, that may go beyond the limits allowed by the U.S. Constitution.

CS: A super tear gas that is approximately 10 times stronger than CN gas.

Cultural Diversity: A recognition that it is neither necessary nor desirable for different ethnic groups to shed their cultural identities to participate in the larger community. It reflects a trend toward the goal of a cooperative pluralism that enables each ethnic group to preserve its cultural identity without viewing others as a threat.

Custodial Processes: Daily activities and procedures designed to control and keep track of the inmates.

Custody: Legal or physical control of or responsibility for a person or thing.

Custody Level: The degree of staff supervision required to safely confine an inmate.

Cycle Menu: A menu detailing daily meals and covering a relatively long time period (e.g., 6 weeks), at the end of which the menu is repeated. These menus provide a nutritionally adequate diet, include popular menu items, and avoid undue repetition and monotony while maintaining average daily food costs at allotted amounts.

Daddies: *See* Jockers.

Daily Sick Call: The process by which inmates who claim to have a health problem (e.g., a headache) get permission to go to morning clinic sessions.

Day Fines: A European innovation that allows judges to impose monetary sanctions that are commensurate with the seriousness of the crime while tying their amount to the offender's income and assets.

Day Reporting Centers: Community-based programs that allow the clients participating in them to attend program functions during the day but to live at home.

Deadly Force: Force that is considered likely to or is intended to cause death or great bodily harm.

Death Qualification: The process of prequalifying jurors for capital punishment cases by having them answer questions about their attitudes toward the issue.

Decentralized Dining: A system for feeding inmates, under which they are fed in dayrooms, cell blocks, small satellite areas, or in pods in the new generation jails.

Declaration of Principles: A set of principles for prison reform that were adopted at an 1870 conference. The principles advocated reform over punishment.

Deinstitutionalization: A philosophy or process of reducing or closing the number of remote state facilities that house the mentally disturbed, retarded, or delinquents and dealing with them at the community level instead.

Delegation (Managerial) Model: A form of participatory management stressing that input from all workers is critical, because line workers (officers) can be your best "idea" people for solving real problems.

Deliberate Indifference: The meaning of this concept from a legal standpoint is far from clear. However, court cases suggest deliberate indifference occurs if prison officials know or should have known, because the condition is obvious, of a risk to inmates' health and safety and take no action.

Delinquency: Juvenile actions in violation of laws, status offenses, or other juvenile misbehavior.

Demoralization: The shame and stigma suffered by a family when one of its members is convicted of a crime and imprisoned.

Department of Corrections: A government agency that is headed by a politically appointed director who develops policy and oversees the operation of mandated correctional facilities and programs.

Depo-Provera: A hormone-based drug used most effectively to treat sex offenders who are attracted to young males (pedophiles) and exhibitionists. Clinical experiments have shown it reduces the intensity of deviant sexual urges and erotic fantasies. To be effective it must be used in conjunction with a program of group counseling.

Deprivation Model: Argues that inmate culture is a collective response to the deprivations imposed by prison life (e.g., lack of heterosexual relations).

Design Capacity: A figure that specifies the number of beds intended to accommodate inmates; this is the limit the facility was designed to hold.

Detainee: Usually a person held in local, very short term confinement while awaiting consideration for pretrial release, first appearance for arraignment, trial, or sentencing.

Detainer: A warrant placed against a person incarcerated in a correctional facility, notifying the holding authority of the intention of another jurisdiction to take custody of that individual when released.

Detention: The legally authorized confinement of a person subject to criminal or juvenile court proceedings, either until commitment to a correctional facility or release.

Determinate Discretionary Sentences: Sentences provided by a legislative body for the courts in its jurisdiction that include a range of time to be served for each crime. Judges can then use their discretion to impose the exact term to be served by the convicted offender.

Determinate Presumptive Sentence: Specifies the exact length of time to be served by persons convicted of that offense. Judges must impose these sentences unless there are aggravating or mitigating circumstances, in which case they may lengthen or shorten them within narrow boundaries and with written justification.

Determinate Sentence: Imposes a specified period of time for incarceration.

Deterrence: A philosophy underlying punishment. It is based on the belief that the pain generated by the punishment will discourage future criminality.

Detoxification Center: Any community facility or program, public or private, for the short-term medical treatment of acutely intoxicated persons, or drug or alcohol abusers, often substituting for jails for persons taken into custody.

Deviance Amplification: Mislabeling a group's behavior as a consequence of certain biases or preconceptions about the group members. Thus, in some cases the conceptions and fears guards have about black inmates will result in mislabeling this group's behavior as violent (e.g., horseplay may be seen as fighting).

Devil's Island: A French penal colony off the coast of French Guiana in South America.

Diagnostic and Statistical Manual **(DSM-IV):** A manual published by the American Psychiatric Association that contains a classification of mental disorders. It is used in the process of diagnosing mentally disordered individuals. The manual is revised about every 10 years.

Dingbats: Crazy but harmless inmates.

Discharge: To release an individual from confinement, supervision, or any legal status imposing an obligation upon the subject person.

Disciplinary Detention (DD): The punishment given to some inmates found guilty of a serious rule violation. These inmates are usually placed in more secure units, and their privileges are restricted.

Disciplinary Report (DR): A written report citing an inmate's involvement in a relatively serious rule violation. An investigation and/or hearing is held to determine the validity of the complaint and to impose punishment where appropriate.

Discretionary Authority: Authority exercised by the prosecutor to decide which cases get prosecuted.

Discretionary Parole: The release of an inmate at the discretion of a parole board.

Dismemberment: (1) As a punishment, it is the practice of severing a part of the body (e.g., a hand). (2) As a social condition, it refers to the adjustment made to the loss of a husband or other family member, such as when a loved one dies or is incarcerated for a lengthy period.

Disparity: In corrections, this term refers to the failure to provide equal programming for both male and female inmates.

Disruptive Group: Organizations that may have a common name or identifying symbol whose members engage in activities that include unlawful acts that vio-

late the policies of departments of corrections. *Also see* Gang.

Diversion: The official suspension of a criminal or juvenile procedure at any point after official intake but before an official judgment has been rendered; the referral of that person to a nonjustice agency or no referral at all.

Doing Time: Adapting to imprisonment by avoiding trouble (i.e., situations that might result in one's sentence being extended) so the inmate can get out fast.

Do-Pops: Half-trusties; their duties included "popping doors" open for superiors, cleaning buildings, waiting tables, and caring for animals.

Driving Under the Influence (DUI): The Uniform Crime Report category used to record and report arrests for offenses of driving or operating any vehicle or common carrier while drunk or under the influence of liquor or drugs.

Drug Courts: Courts set up specifically to handle drug-related cases.

Drunk Tank: A section or cell within a jail in which inebriated arrestees are placed to sober up before being further processed.

Ducking Stool: A chair suspended over a body of water into which offenders were strapped and then repeatedly plunged into the water.

Due Process Clause, Fourteenth Amendment: This clause protects persons from state actions. There are two aspects: procedural, in which a person is guaranteed fair procedures, and substantive, which protects a person's property from unfair governmental interference or taking.

Due Process Protection: The protections accorded individuals being processed by the criminal justice system under the Fifth, Sixth, and Fourteenth amendments to the U.S. Constitution.

Early Release Programs: Inmate release processes that include early parole or sentence reduction for certain offenders (e.g., early release of usually nonviolent offenders within a few months of sentence completion) to cope with overcrowding in accordance with court-imposed population caps.

Eastern Penitentiary at Cherry Hill: Opened in 1829, it was the first facility to put into effect the Pennsylvania System.

Economic Marginality: Refers to individuals living at or below the poverty level.

Economic Sanctions: Any sanction imposed on convicted offenders that is economically based. These include fines, restitution, court costs, surcharges on fines, and asset forfeiture.

Eighth Amendment: Prohibits excessive bail, excessive fines, and cruel and unusual punishment.

Electrified Fences: Fences used in prison perimeter security that are topped with razor wire and carry several thousand volts and well over the 70 milliamperes required to kill someone.

Electronic Monitoring: Electronic telemetry devices designed to verify that an offender is at a given location during specified times.

Elmira Reformatory: Opened in New York in 1877, it was headed by Zebulon Brockway, who attempted to implement the Declaration of Principles there. Brockway developed a progressive basic learning program at the facility.

Employer Prison Industries Model: In this model, the private sector owns and manages the business employing inmates to produce its goods or services. It has control over firing, hiring, and the supervision of inmates.

Empty Hand Control Techniques: Control techniques that do not involve any weapons and range from gently guiding inmates, to those that temporarily immobilize them, to force such as kicks or strikes used against aggressive inmates.

Enforcer Demeanor: The negative attitude displayed by COs in public because they feel it is expected of them.

Equal Employment Opportunity Commission: Federal body that oversees the hiring of minority and female correctional officers to reduce discrimination.

Equity: The belief that like treatment should be accorded similar criminals who have committed similar crimes.

Escape: The unlawful departure of a lawfully confined person from official custody.

Ethnic/Racial Organizations: Ethnically and racially based prison organizations that focus on cultural awareness and education, largely populated by blacks, Hispanics, and Native Americans.

Excessive Force: Force used beyond the need and circumstances of the particular event, which means it was unnecessary or was used to inflict punishment.

Executive Clemency: A pardon granted for meritorious conduct such as participation in medical experiments; also general clemency on major holidays.

Executive Management Team: This team includes assistant superintendents who specialize in managing certain prison functions such as security, treatment programs, business operations, or prison industries.

Exhibitionists: Individuals (almost always male) who achieve sexual arousal by exposing their genitals to persons of the opposite sex. Usually occurs in a public place.

Exile: The expulsion of an individual from a particular area or country as a punishment for wrong done by that individual. Exile can be temporary or permanent.

Facility Security Level: The nature and number of physical design barriers available to prevent escape and control inmate behavior.

Family Visits: A program that allows private overnight visits between inmates and close family members, including wives or husbands, children, parents, grandparents, and siblings.

Farm Prisons: *See* Plantations.

Farnham, Eliza: The matron at Mount Pleasant prison in 1844, which was the first separate prison for women in the United States. She transformed this into a model facility with a homelike environment.

Federal Bureau of Prisons (BOP): Organization created by Congress in 1930 that is responsible for incarcerating individuals convicted of violating federal laws.

Federal Prison System Classification Model: An objective classification system that is based on several principles, including confinement of inmates in the least restrictive, appropriately secure facility; separation of security and custody dimensions; and standardized objective instruments. Staff judgments can override placement based on objective confinement criteria.

Fee System: The practice of collecting money from inmates for services (food, bedding, etc.) rendered to them while in custody.

Felony: A criminal offense punishable by death or by incarceration for a year or more in a state prison.

Fines: Monetary sanctions that can be imposed on convicted offenders. They can be the only sanction imposed or can be given in conjunction with others (e.g., incarceration).

First Amendment: Guarantees that no laws will be enacted that restrict or abridge our freedom of religion, speech, or the press.

First-Line Supervisors: Lowest level of administration within the prison (e.g., corporals, unit managers) who supervise line personnel.

Fish: A newcomer to prison.

Flawed Execution: Includes those where the equipment or method of execution malfunctions.

Flex Cuffs: *See* Handcuffs.

Flogging: Whipping, also known as scourging; widely employed as a means of corporal punishment.

Folsom Prison Strike: The longest of the prison demonstrations that was part of the prisoner movement. It occurred in 1968, lasted 19 days, and involved nearly all 2,400 inmates. It commenced when inmates refused to leave their cells after having smuggled out a list of 29 demands. The warden locked the prison down. Despite outside assistance, the strike ended after 2 weeks when supplies ran low and the warden offered to lift the lockdown if inmates went back to work.

Ford v. Wainwright: A 1986 decision in which the Supreme Court prohibited the execution of the insane.

Fourth Amendment: Protects people from unreasonable searches and seizures of property by government officials.

Fraud: Offenses of conversion or obtaining of money or some other item of value by false pretenses. As an offense, this category does not include forgery, counterfeiting, or embezzlement.

Freelancers: Jailhouse lawyers who seek their own inmate clients.

Front-Door Program: A community program in which the offender is placed under increased control, generally through some type of intensive probation, instead of being sent to prison.

Fry, Elizabeth: An English Quaker, who in 1813 began a movement in England to improve conditions under which women were incarcerated. She campaigned for separate facilities for women to be staffed and supervised by women.

Functionally Illiterate: An individual who may have completed middle or high school but functions at a much lower level than his or her education would indicate and does not have the skills to generally gain or maintain employment at wages sufficient to support dependents.

Furloughs: Short-term escorted or unescorted trips away from the prison, granted so that inmates can find jobs or housing prior to release; participate in treatment or religious programs, recreation, or shopping; or strengthen family ties.

Furman-**Commutee:** Death row inmate whose sentence was commuted as a result of the *Furman* decision, which ruled that the death penalty violated the equal protection clause of the Fourteenth Amendment.

Furman v. Georgia: A decision in 1972 in which the Supreme Court struck down existing capital punishment statutes, ruling that the death penalty violated the equal protection clause of the Fourteenth Amendment.

Gags: Any device used to muzzle an individual to keep him or her from speaking.

Galleys: Oar-driven ships used in commerce and warfare for hundreds of years until the 17th century by Mediterranean nations. During the Middle Ages, convicts and other undesirables were sentenced to galley servitude.

Game Families: Pseudofamilies found in female prisons. Each had a core group of 6 to 12 long termers and was a stable, well-recognized force within the prison.

Gamblers: Inmates of upper middle class status, who obtain economic power through wagering their skills.

Gang: Any organization, association, or group of persons, either formal or informal, that may have a common name or identifying sign or symbol, whose members or associates engage in or have engaged in activities that include, but are not limited to, planning, organizing, threatening, financing, soliciting, or committing unlawful acts or acts that violate the policies, rules, and regulations of the

corrections system or the state code. *Also see* Disruptive Group.

Gang Codes of Conduct: Gang norms that involve expected behavior and regulate member activity. These codes emphasize secrecy and intense loyalty.

Gang Colors: A color or pattern of colors that identifies a particular gang. The color is worn by gang members as part of their clothing.

Gang Hit: A gang "contract" to kill someone. The general rule associated with this contract is that if the person selected to do the job refuses to do the killing he will be killed.

Ganghood: A concept that emphasizes the significance of belonging to the gang. An example of this is found in the credo of the Texas Mafia: "Nothing is to be put before the Texas Mafia and its business. Not God, religion, parole, or family."

Gaol: The British term for the jail, developed in medieval England.

Gaol Fever: A set of illnesses in jails of the 17th and 18th centuries caused by the unhygienic conditions found in them. These conditions produced serious epidemics of typhus as well as malignant forms of dysentery.

Gatekeeper Function: Police discretionary actions (decision to arrest or not arrest) that allow them to determine how far some individuals are processed into the criminal justice system.

Gate Money: The money an inmate has when he or she is discharged from prison.

Gender Bias: Bias toward or discrimination against an individual on the basis of his or her gender.

General Deterrence: The belief that the punishment imposed on an offender shows others what will happen to them if they engage in similar acts, which will then discourage them from doing them.

General Equivalency Diploma (GED): Diploma given in lieu of a high school diploma. Persons who do not finish high school may instead take the general equivalency test to demonstrate they have enough knowledge to graduate.

General Members: Members who joined the gang for protection. Most are not as committed to the gang as hardcore members. Most defectors come from this group.

Gleaning: An adaptation to imprisonment adopted by a small number of in-

mates who used available prison resources to improve their minds and their postprison employment potential.

Good Time: A statutory provision for the reduction of time served on a sentence through the accumulation of credits that are either automatic (e.g., 1 day for every 2 days served) or earned (e.g., given for participation in programs, exceptional conduct).

Gregg v. Georgia: A 1976 decision in which the Supreme Court reinstated the death penalty after striking it down 4 years earlier in *Furman v. Georgia. Gregg* affected states that had rewritten their statutes to reflect the constitutional standards in *Furman.*

Group Counseling: A therapeutic program usually involving 10 to 12 inmates (and a staff member) meeting at least weekly for a 1- or 2-hour session to discuss their problems.

Guillotine: An instrument developed in France used for beheading people. It was presumed to make the beheading more humane.

Gulags: A chain of prisons, labor camps, insane asylums, and villages operated in the Siberian region of Russia to confine and exile those opposing the government.

Habeas Corpus: An action enabling inmates to request a hearing before a judge to air claims of illegal incarceration.

Habitual Offenders: In legal terms, a person sentenced under the provisions of a statute that punishes more severely anyone convicted of a given offense who has been previously convicted of other specified offenses. Sometimes also referred to as career or repeat offenders.

Hacks: Also called screws or bulls; this was another name for prison guards.

Half-Steppers: This term was used to describe certain black inmates during the prisoner movement era who leaned toward revolutionary ideas but were unwilling to adopt the regimented and spartan lifestyle of true revolutionaries. They made a show of being revolutionary, but they were more concerned with being part of a radical group that would make doing time easier.

Half-Trusties: In the Arkansas prison farms, these were the inmates who had a status between the trusties and the rank men. They had duties that allowed them to avoid working in the fields. Also called do-pops.

Halfway Houses: Transitional residential facilities that operate in community settings and provide more intensive supervision than probation or other nonresidential programs but less than incarceration. Typically, they are oriented toward providing or brokering treatment services for their residents.

Halfway-In: Halfway houses that are used as an alternative to prison commitment.

Halfway-Out: Halfway houses that serve as an intermediate step between prison and total release into the community.

Handcuffs: Temporary restraints that help control inmates in situations where they might escape, injure themselves or others, or become unruly or dangerous.

Hands-off Doctrine: The position of the courts, prior to the mid-1960s, that they had neither the power nor the obligation to define or protect what constitutional rights inmates had.

Hands-on Approach: The term applied to the approach by the courts, after it discarded its hands-off approach in the 1960s, of dealing with prison conditions, recognizing that prisoners had certain constitutional rights, and intervening to be sure they were accorded these rights.

Hard-Core Members: The ranking members of the gang; they wield the majority of its power. They demonstrate their ability to lead through violence. Few ever defect.

Hard Time: Serving a sentence under conditions that cause relatively severe discomfort.

Hawes-Cooper Act of 1929: Allowed states to block the importation of prison-made goods.

Head Building Tender: The building tender in charge of a specific cell block or tank in a Texas prison.

Hepatitis C (HVE): A liver disease, this is the most common blood-borne infection in the United States, with 8,000 to 10,000 people dying from it each year.

Hierarchical Model: An organizational structure based on one all-powerful leader. He makes all decisions and his authority is absolute. When he leaves the prison or dies, the vice president suc-

ceeds him. The Texas Mexikanemi uses this structure.

High Mask Lighting: System used as part of an institution's perimeter security system. Usually five to eight lights, each illuminating a large area, are placed on poles 100 to 120 feet to completely light the prison compound and its perimeter.

High-Security Institutions: Known as U.S. penitentiaries (USPs), they have highly secure perimeters, multiple- and single-occupant cell housing, and close staff supervision and movement controls.

Hilton Hotel Syndrome: Expresses the concern that inmates' living conditions are better than those enjoyed by the majority of free-world Americans.

Hoe Line: An assignment on the Texas prison farms that included carrying hoes and other tools and marching to work sites up to 5 miles away.

Hog: *See* Convict.

Holding Facilities: Facilities that contain arrestees up to 48 hours and are often located in police stations for the convenience of arresting officers. Also known as lockups.

Hole: An inmate term for solitary confinement.

Homeboy: The term applied to individuals who share some common experience such as coming from the same town or neighborhood, having the same ethnic-minority status, or being a member of the same youth gang.

Homeboy Connection: *See* Homeboy, Homeboy Orientation.

Homeboy Orientation: A pattern of prison gang membership based on relationships formed outside of the prison. Usually based on coming from or growing up in the same neighborhood or having been boyhood friends.

Homeboy Pattern: Illustrated by the Mexican Mafia pattern of formation, this refers to gangs formed from a nucleus that shares ethnicity, a subculture, and membership in a youth gang.

Home Confinement: *See* House Arrest.

Homicide: A generic term meaning the killing of one person by another.

Honor Blocks: A dormitory or area within a prison reserved for inmates who have maintained good behavior over relatively long periods of time. Inmates there usually have more privileges.

Hooch: An alcoholic beverage made in prison.

Hoosiers: Dull, backward, and provincial individuals with little knowledge of crime who came from rural areas.

Hospice Care: In corrections, facilities set up to care for dying inmates.

Hospice of San Michele: A multipurpose facility developed in the early 18th century in Rome, Italy. The unit that housed juveniles anticipated many features that became an integral part of early adult and juvenile systems in the United States. The cellular design of the facility represents its most lasting contribution.

House Arrest: An intermediate sanction that involves confinement to one's residence or some other designated location. The offender may only leave that location to go to work, attend school, see a doctor, or engage in some other mandated activity (e.g., community service). Supervision is typically done by POs with smaller caseloads who make more frequent personal and telephone contacts with offenders at work, at night, and on weekends and holidays. Control may be further enhanced through some form of electronic monitoring. Also called home confinement.

Huber Act: A 1914 Wisconsin law that authorized counties to set up work release programs for misdemeanants serving one year or less.

Hulks: Abandoned military vessels that were used as floating prisons by the English during the 18th and 19th centuries.

Human Immunodeficiency Virus (HIV): The virus that causes AIDS. It infects and destroys the body's ability to fight disease.

Human Services–Oriented Officers (HSOs): COs who advise, support, console, refer, or otherwise assist inmates with their problems and crises of adjustment produced by imprisonment.

Hustling: (1) In a prison context this describes ways in which inmates exploit their prison jobs to obtain salable goods or provide special services, which are in turn sold to other inmates. (2) On the outside, an activity through which individuals achieve their criminal objectives through persuasion and use of their wits rather than force.

Illiteracy: A lack of the reading, writing, and computational skills required to function adequately in society.

Imam: A Muslim clergyman.

Importation Model: Asserts that the inmate subculture is shaped by a socialization process involving the adoption of a criminal value system to which the inmate is exposed prior to confinement.

Incapacitation: A philosophy that advocates the use of punishments that prevent offenders from committing additional crimes.

Incarceration: Placement in a jail or prison. As a sanction, it is usually imposed when it is felt the community must be protected from further victimization by the offender.

Incompetency to Stand Trial: A person who lacks the capacity to understand the nature of the proceedings against him or her and to consult with and assist counsel in the preparation of the defense.

In Custody: The second highest level of custody assigned to an inmate, requiring the second highest level of security and staff supervision. These inmates are assigned to regular quarters and are eligible for all regular work assignments and activities under a normal level of supervision. They are not eligible for work detail outside the institution.

Indenture System: The system under which an individual was forced (or volunteered for compensation) into a period of servitude. Those forced into this system were typically convicted offenders but sometimes included individuals who were kidnapped. The practice was associated with English transportation of criminals to its American colonies.

Independent Parole Board Model: Autonomous units that have the power to make parole release decisions and to supervise all conditionally released inmates.

Independents: Inmates who do not affiliate with a gang or other such groups.

Indeterminate Sentence: Under strict indeterminate sentencing, judges assign custody of the offender to the department of corrections, and his release is dependent on his readiness to function prosocially in society. In most cases, it is used in a modified form, which consists of a range of time (e.g., 3 to 5 years) that is defined in terms of a minimum period to be served before release can be con-

sidered and a maximum period after which the inmate must be released. It is usually associated with rehabilitation and parole.

Index Crimes: The Part I crimes dealt with in the FBI's Uniform Crime Reports. These crimes include murder and nonnegligent manslaughter, rape, robbery, aggravated assault, burglary, larceny, motor vehicle theft, and arson.

Infirmaries: The most common type of medical facility in correctional settings; generally found in jails and prisons with populations of 500 or more inmates. They provide bed care for inmates and thus have round-the-clock nursing care.

Injunction: A court order requiring defendants to perform or stop a specific act.

Inmate Accounts: These are analogous to inmate bank accounts that are managed by prison personnel. They contain any money that has been sent to the inmate by his or her family or that the inmate has legitimately earned by working.

Inmate Credit Cards: Issued by some jurisdictions in an attempt to cut down on the illegal economy in prisons. Inmate credit cards replace money, which is declared contraband, and can be used to make commissary purchases. Some prison systems issue electronically sensitive cards that are used to scan inmates' accounts and deduct the appropriate amount when purchases are made.

Inmate Custody Category: The degree of staff supervision necessary to ensure adequate control of the inmate.

Inmate Handbook: A booklet containing information about the rules, regulations, programs, and procedures within the prison with which the inmate should become familiar.

Inmate Social World: The set of norms and behaviors that characterize inmate society.

Inmate Subculture: Provides ways of thinking, feeling, and acting about all aspects of prison life to help inmates cope with the special circumstances of prison life.

Insanity: A legal term connoting a mental disease or disorder of sufficient seriousness to absolve an individual of responsibility for the commission of a crime.

In-Service Training: Any form of specialized training to enhance the job skills

of an individual occurring after the individual has assumed the day-to-day responsibilities of that job. This includes outside workshops, seminars, and training programs and participation in specially developed correspondence courses.

Inside Cell Block Design: A design in which cells are built back to back, sometimes five tiers high, in a hollow building. These cells have doors that open onto galleries or walkways 8 to 10 feet from the outer wall of the building.

Intake Process: A term that describes the overall admissions process into jail or prison.

Intelligence: Selectively processed information that is of strategic value in making informed decisions about security management.

Intelligence Officer: The individual responsible for the collection of intelligence information or who is in charge of the intelligence unit.

Intelligence Unit: A correctional organization's unit that is responsible for the collection of strategic information that can be used to deal with potential prison security problems.

Intensive Parole Supervision: *See* Intensive Probation Supervision. The only difference is that this is used as an early release mechanism for high-risk offenders who do not meet the criteria for regular parole.

Intensive Probation Supervision (IPS): An intermediate sanction designed to serve prison-bound offenders. It is meant to be more punitive and controlling than regular probation by reducing the size of officer caseloads, thus allowing for more intensive surveillance and the imposition of stricter conditions.

Intermediate Sanctions: A punishment option that is considered on a continuum to fall between traditional probation and traditional incarceration. This provides sentencing options for those requiring more surveillance and control than can be provided by probation but less control than imprisonment.

Intermediate System: *See* Irish System.

Intermittent Sentence: A sentence to periods of confinement interrupted by periods of freedom.

International Association of Correctional Officers (IACO): An organization that brings together correctional experts and personnel from many areas around the world.

Interstate Compact: An agreement between two or more states to transfer prisoners, parolees, or probationers from the physical or supervisory custody of one state to that of another where the state with original jurisdiction retains legal authority to confine or release the prisoner.

Irish System: Sir Walter Crofton's system, which punished convicts for their past crimes and also prepared them for release. This was accomplished by giving them the opportunity to earn increased responsibility and privileges while progressing through four stages. Also called intermediate system.

Jail Diversion Programs: Programs designed to remove the mentally ill from jails.

Jailhouse Lawyers (JHL): Inmates who, without formal training, become proficient in writing writs and briefs and who help other inmates in dealing with appeals, violations of inmates' rights, and other legal matters.

Jailing: The adaptation to imprisonment generally adopted by a "state raised youth." These prisoners almost completely orient themselves to the prison, which becomes the world around which their lives revolve.

Jails: Local institutions usually run by law enforcement agencies. These institutions hold pretrial detainees, short-term (up to one year) sentenced misdemeanants, and those awaiting transportation to state or federal prison. They also hold the drunk, disorderly, and mentally ill.

Jitterbugs: The term used by adult or older inmates to describe many youthful inmates.

Job Bidding: Allows senior correctional officers to bid for specific jobs within the institution.

Jockers: Sexual aggressors who take the traditional masculine role in oral or anal intercourse during a homosexual encounter. Also known as wolves, daddies, and pitchers.

Judicial Order: A court order that involves the exercise of judicial discretion and affects the final result of litigation.

Judicial Reprieve: Under this practice, convicted offenders could apply for a temporary suspension of their sentence while they appealed to the Crown for a pardon while at liberty.

Juice: Possessing information and influence that come through a job or relationships with authority figures. This allows the inmate to circumvent rules or avoid delays to get things done.

Jurisdiction: The territory, subject matter, or persons over which lawful authority may be exercised by a court or other justice agency, as determined by statute or constitution.

Just Deserts: A term used in conjunction with retribution to indicate that offenders should be punished to repay society for the harm done by their crime.

Justice Model: Takes a just deserts or retributive approach, while emphasizing a justice-as-fairness perspective. This model appears to fit the present public mood for more punishment and the use of determinate sentencing and the shift away from rehabilitation.

Justifiable Use of Force: COs can use force in self-defense and in defense of others; to prevent a crime; to detain or arrest inmates; to enforce prison rules and discipline; to protect property; and to prevent inmates from harming themselves.

Juvenile Justice and Delinquency Prevention Act: Passed by Congress in 1974, this act mandates that juveniles detained in adult jails be kept out of sight and sound of adult inmates.

Juveniles: Individuals can be subject to juvenile court proceedings because of statutorily defined events or conditions in which these individuals were involved. The status of *juvenile* is statutorily defined by an age range, usually from 7 to 17.

Kairos Prison Ministry (KPM): Emanates from mainline churches. Puts on seminars to teach inmates religious principles. Also provides significant transitional services to inmates.

Keepers' Voice: Newsletter published by the International Association of Correctional Officers (IACO), which provides a forum for correctional officers.

Keistering: A prison term referring to the concealment of such items as hacksaw blades, handcuff keys, and drugs by inmates in their rectums to bring these items into the prison.

Kid: An individual, usually young and weak, who has been coerced or forced into being another inmate's sex slave.

King's Peace: A law by which the king extended his protection to those in his presence and in the local area in which he was staying.

Kite: An anonymous note to a guard's superior detailing his past dereliction of duty.

Knout: A Russian wooden-handled whip typically consisting of several rawhide thongs twisted together and terminating in a single strand. Sometimes the hide was plaited with wire, dipped in liquid, and then frozen before use, or the thongs had hooks or rings attached to the ends.

La Nuestra Familia (NF): A group of Northern California Mexican-Americans who formed their own gang to protect themselves from attacks by members of the Mexican Mafia. Today, this group is considered an organized crime group and has units both inside and outside California prisons.

Larceny: Unlawful taking or attempted taking of property other than a motor vehicle from the possession of another, by stealth, without force and without deceit, with the intent to permanently deprive the owner of the property.

Larceny-Theft: Uniform Crime Reports designation for larceny.

Law Clerks: In corrections, these are inmates assigned by the prison, as jailhouse lawyers, to litigation tasks.

Law Enforcement Model: One of three models under which probation officers deliver supervisory services to their clients. In this one, law enforcement–oriented POs operate under the control model of supervision, which is heavily tilted toward surveillance and arrest of probationers.

Lease System: A method of contracting with a private company or individual to control and operate prison shops or to be entirely responsible for groups of convicts or for an entire prison. Contractors paid states a fee or a portion of the profits from inmate-produced goods for this privilege.

Least Restrictive Means Test for RFRA Cases: Prison officials can only ban legitimate practices that are an important part of a religion if they show the restriction is based on a compelling government test, and there is no alternative means of allowing inmates to engage in this practice that does not compromise a compelling government interest. *Also see* Religious Freedom Restoration Act.

Leather Restraints: Used to humanely restrain agitated inmates.

Left-Wing Political Groups: Political groups espousing a socialist or communist political philosophy.

Leg Irons: Cuffs placed on inmates' legs.

Legitimate Correctional Objectives: In corrections, this refers to institutional objectives that are seen as a constitutionally acceptable basis for prisons' placing restrictions on inmates' rights because they are necessary for maintaining a safe and secure facility environment. These include maintaining institutional security and preserving internal order and discipline.

Legitimate Prison Economic Systems: Consist of inmate funds and goods obtained through approved channels. Inmates can acquire money from relatives and friends, work assignments, veterans' benefits, or their hobbies (e.g., by making items that can be sold at gift shops located outside the prison). Friends and relatives can also send them goods that can be sold or traded.

Leisure Education Model: The Therapeutic Recreation (TR) model found in corrections today. It encompasses value clarification, in which inmates learn to identify their needs for praise, belonging, and so on; needs assessment, in which they further identify their needs; and leisure counseling, in which they learn how to acquire leisure-based skills.

Less Than Lethal Force: The next level of force after empty hand control techniques. It includes the use of impact weapons, such as batons, chemical agents, and electrical shocking devices, to temporarily disable the inmate but not to inflict permanent injury.

Level I: *See* Community Security Facilities.

Level II: *See* Minimum Security Prison.

Level III: *See* Medium Security Prison.

Level IV: *See* Close Security Facilities.

Level V: *See* Maximum Security Prison.

Lex Talionis: The principle of an eye for eye. This was used as a means to regulate the extent to which victims could retaliate against those who injured them.

Liberty Interests: Interests that require due process protection and are defined by the Constitution, court orders, statutes, regulations, or standard practice policies or customs. In the case of statutes or regulations, liberty interests exist only if these rules have in them mandatory language and substantive predicates (i.e., they stipulate specific conditions or requirements).

Life Skills Programs: Educational programs that provide inmates with practical knowledge in employability/job search skills, consumer skills, the use of community resources, health and safety skills, parenting and family child skills, and civic skills.

Life Without Parole (LWOP): A sentence intended to ensure that an individual who receives it will spend the rest of his or her life in prison. It is seen by some as a feasible alternative to capital punishment.

Linear Design Supervision: Supervision in jails and prisons in which the cells are constructed in long straight rows aligned with corridors where correctional staff walk from cell to cell to intermittently supervise inmate activities.

Line Personnel: The workers who directly perform the activities that accomplish the goals and objectives of the organization (e.g., correctional officers).

Literacy: The possession of the skills required to function effectively in society.

Literacy Programs: Educational programs that focus on providing basic skills to low-level readers and nonreaders.

Local Corrections: The system of facilities and programs dealing with convicted misdemeanant offenders and pretrial detainees.

Lockdown: An action taken by prison administrators consisting of keeping inmates locked in their cells when a breakdown of order appears imminent.

Lockstep: A formation in which convicts were marched from place to place in "close-order single file," each looking over the next man's shoulder with their faces pointed to the right to prevent conversation and with their feet moving in unison. This formation began in the Auburn era and was used in American prisons well into the 1930s.

Long-Term Offender (LTO): An offender sentenced to a long term (e.g., 25 years or life in prison). This group includes younger inmates, middle-aged inmates, career criminals with long sentences, and elderly inmates who have grown old in prison.

Low-Security Institutions: A level of security that is higher than minimum security, with a higher staff-to-inmate ratio. These have strong work and program components for inmates.

M-2 Sponsors Program: A program in which community volunteers were trained to function as visitors for inmates who had no family or friends to visit them.

Mace: A type of tear gas that is the least incapacitating of the gases currently in use.

Maconochie, Alexander: *See* Mark System.

Main Customer Prison Industries Model: Here the private sector buys a substantial portion of the output of a prison-owned and –operated business but has no other connection with it.

Mainstreaming: The practice of placing individuals with special needs in the general population of a facility.

Maison de Force: Established in 1773 in Ghent, Belgium. It had a rudimentary classification system in which felons were separated from misdemeanants and there were separate sections for women and for children. Work was the primary method of reform.

Managed Care: Programs that attempt to control health-care costs.

Management by Walking Around: Management in which administrators go out into the institution(s) to obtain a first "foot" look at and a real feel for what is actually going on in the institution(s).

Management Variables: Used to temper computer scores with human decision making when determining the appropriate security level institution for an inmate. It includes judicial recommendations, the inmate's participation in programs, his or her psychiatric evaluation, the level of overcrowding in the institution, and whether the inmate is considered an escape risk.

Mandatory Release: Under this form of release inmates are placed under the supervision of a parole officer after they have served their original sentences minus earned or administratively awarded good time.

Mandatory Sentences: These sentences mandate incarceration, often for specified lengths of time, for certain categories of offenders (e.g., drug traffickers). They generally do not permit judges any discretion in the sentence to be imposed.

Manpower Prison Industries Model: Under this model, the private sector partner manages the industry shops and supervises the inmate workers; however, the public agency administers the programs and pays the inmates.

Manslaughter, Involuntary: Causing the death of another person unintentionally but with recklessness or gross negligence. Also referred to as negligent manslaughter.

Manslaughter, Vehicular: A form of involuntary manslaughter caused by grossly negligent operation of a motor vehicle.

Manslaughter, Voluntary: Intentionally causing the death of another without legal justification but under conditions of extreme provocation. Also referred to as nonnegligent manslaughter.

Marginal Members: Peripheral members of the gang who are called on when the gang needs to present a strong show of force or power.

Mark System: A system developed by Alexander Maconochie under which sentences were to consist of a specified number of marks or points based on the seriousness of the offense. Marks represented a debt, and the offender had to earn enough marks to pay off the debt before he could be released.

Marxist Position: Pertaining to the teaching of Karl Marx. It argued that current inequities in society were rooted in the system of corporate capitalism. Under capitalism, the ruling elite controlled government and the workplace by effectively setting one group of exploited people against another.

Matron: In early women's prisons, the woman who was the chief supervisor of the women's prison or unit.

Mature Offenders: Older inmates. The minimum age for this group varies according to whom is defining the group; it ranges from 45 to 65.

Maximum Custody Inmates: Pose the most serious threats to other inmates or staff or may be high escape risks. They are confined in single cells; are only removed for authorized activities when es-

corted by at least one staff member; are involved only in programs conducted in their cells; eat in their cells; and are allowed only noncontact visits.

Maximum Security Prison: A prison with the highest level of security, which is generally considered to be an end-of-the-line facility. Inmates here require secure housing in the most secure perimeter and separate management for activities such as work, exercise, and food service. Inmate housing is normally in single inside cells. Supermax facilities represent the highest security level. Also called Level V.

Maximum Sentence: The maximum penalty provided by law for a given criminal offense.

McCleskey v. Kemp: A 1987 ruling in which the Supreme Court said that only evidence of racial bias particular to a case at hand was relevant.

Medical Model: An approach to dealing with crime as an illness that views criminals as "sick." To cure them requires a diagnostic process that identifies their problems and the program of treatment that remediates these problems.

Medium Custody Inmates: These types of inmates move about the institution during the day within sight of a CO. They are eligible for all programs and activities within the main perimeter. Indoor contact visits are permitted.

Medium Security Prison: Usually has external perimeter security that is similar to levels IV and V. Housing is in single cells, rooms, or dormitories. These institutions provide a wider variety of programs and activities and allow greater freedom of movement within the facility than high-security institutions. Also called Level III.

Megajails: A term used to denote jails with populations in excess of 1,000 inmates.

Mentally Disordered: Individuals who are classified as mentally or emotionally disturbed. The term is sometimes restricted to those having a disabling mental disorder like schizophrenia or an affective disorder.

Mentally Handicapped: Those suffering from mental retardation. The mentally retarded tend to be overrepresented in the prison population.

Mental Retardation: A condition characterized by significantly subaverage general

intellectual functioning that exists concurrently with deficits in adaptive behavior.

Merchants: Inmates who obtain or manufacture scarce luxury items, both legal and illegal (e.g., cigarettes, "hooch," weapons) to be sold or traded in the inmate economy.

Merit System: As used in employee hiring, the merit system requires applicants to qualify for a specific job by meeting certain minimum requirements for that job and scoring above a certain level on a written exam.

Mexican Mafia: A California prison gang formed by a group of Mexican-American inmates from the Marvilla section of East Los Angeles. Today, it has groups throughout California prisons and is viewed as an organized crime syndicate.

Mexikanemi: A Texas gang that was an offshoot of the Mexican Mafia.

Micromanagement: A practice in which politicians try to tell correctional officials how to implement particular policies.

Middle Managers: Supervisors responsible for overseeing the delivery of specific services, such as education, in the prison.

Mildly Retarded: Individuals who have IQs ranging from 55 to 69 (based on a Wechsler Adult Intelligence Scale IQ) but who can essentially function on an independent basis.

Milieu Therapy: A form of therapeutic community.

Minimal Necessities of Civilized Life: The factors considered by the courts in making decisions about the constitutionality of the totality of prison living conditions. These include food, shelter, sanitation, health care, and personal safety.

Minimum Custody Inmates: Inmates who do not pose risks associated with higher custody levels. They can move about the facility without being directly within the view of staff, are eligible for all inside jobs and supervised assignments outside the prison's perimeter, and have access to all programs and activities.

Minimum Mandatory Sentences: Sentences that require a specific term to be served before good-time credits can be accumulated or release can be considered.

Minimum Security Prison: Uses an open design with perimeters consisting of a single fence or clearly designated un-armed "posts." It uses no detection devices but does have intermittent external mobile patrols. Housing is in open units varying from dormitory style to single- or multiple-occupancy rooms. It places a heavy emphasis on programs and activities. Also called Level II.

Minnesota Multiphasic Personality Inventory (MMPI): An objective personality test sometimes used in pre-employment screening to select job candidates.

Misdemeanor: An offense less serious than a felony and which may be punished by a fine and/or incarceration, usually in a local jail, for up to one year.

Mission Statement: A policy statement that delineates the purpose, goals, and objectives of the organization.

Mitigating Factors: Factors (e.g., no prior criminal record, juvenile) that might demonstrate that the death penalty is unwarranted in the case.

Mix: Behavior and associations that got the inmate in trouble on the outside and that can keep him or her in trouble within the institution.

Mobile Patrols: These are vehicles manned by armed correctional officers that are used to patrol the perimeter of the prison compound.

Mobility Impaired: A condition under which an individual needs assistance (e.g., a wheelchair) to get around.

Moderately Retarded: Individuals who have IQs between 40 and 54 (based on a Wechsler Adult Intelligence Scale IQ) and can learn to care for themselves but are not likely to function independently.

Monasteries: Religious facilities used to house members of religious orders.

Mood Disorders: Another name used for affective disorders (e.g., depression).

Moorish Science Temple of America: A hybrid offshoot of the Black Muslim movement.

Mortification Process: The process by which prison routines deprive individuals of key aspects important for maintaining their self-concept.

Mother-Child Programs: Programs that help maintain the bond between a female inmate and her child.

Mug Shots: The photographs taken during the booking process.

Multiculturalism: *See* Cultural Diversity.

Multiple Drug-Resistant TB Strains (MDR-TB): TB strains resistant to normal drug treatment.

Murder: Intentionally causing the death of another person without extreme provocation or legal justification or causing that death while committing or attempting to commit another crime.

Murton, Tom: A reform warden who exposed the barbaric conditions under which Arkansas prisons operated. He attempted in the late 1960s to bring these prisons up to mid-20th-century standards.

Muslim Community: The name used by the Sunni Muslim community. It consists largely of Middle Eastern immigrants and African Americans and is the largest group of Muslims in the United States identifying with one Islamic leader.

Mutilation: Any form of punishment in which the individual is mutilated, such as dismemberment.

Mutual Agreement Program: A program involving a contractual agreement between a prisoner and/or state prison and parole officials by which the prisoner attempts to complete a specific self-improvement program to receive a definite parole date.

Narcotics Anonymous (NA): A self-help organization that supports recovering addicts, which follows the 12-step program originated by AA. This is a worldwide organization with groups operating almost everywhere. Groups hold open meetings, at which anyone is welcome, and closed meetings exclusively for members, at which personal problems or interpretations of the 12 steps are discussed.

National Central STG Depository: A proposed clearinghouse and repository for information on STGs, their members, and activities that would represent a valuable intelligence resource.

National Commission on Correctional Health Care (NCCHC): Composed of representatives from 36 organizations that have an interest in correctional health care and who set standards for prison medical services. It also conducts site visits to evaluate jails and prisons for accreditation purposes, which

requires that they meet certain minimum standards.

National Correctional Recreation Association: A professional association of full-time professional correctional personnel who are committed to promoting professional programs and services that assist the inmate in eliminating barriers to leisure, in developing leisure skills and attitudes, and in optimizing leisure participation.

National Council on Crime and Delinquency: A professional organization consisting mainly of criminal justice personnel, many of whom are involved in community corrections and correctional research.

National Institute of Corrections Model: An objective classification system that incorporates elements such as custody, security, needs assessment, program monitoring and assessment, reclassification, and a management information system.

National Lawyers Guild: A communist front organization composed of left-wing lawyers that was active in the prisoner movement.

National Prison Association: An association founded at the National Prison Congress. Today, it is called the American Corrections Association.

National Prison Congress: At this conference held in 1870, the leading reform ideas of the era were discussed and incorporated into the Declaration of Principles, which advocated a philosophy of reformation as opposed to the adoption of punishment. This was the first meeting of what today is called the American Corrections Association.

Nation of Islam: The name given to the original Black Muslim movement in the United States by its founder, Elijah Muhammad. This was later changed to the American Muslim Mission by Muhammad's son. The name was resurrected by a splinter group led by Louis Farrakhan.

Needs Assessment: Assessment of an inmate's program and service requirements.

Neighborhood Justice Centers: Centers in which volunteer mediators act as hearing officers and attempt to resolve relatively minor disputes between citizens that might otherwise wind up in the courts. The solutions that are worked out are agreed to by both parties.

Net Widening: Occurs when a sanction extends the "net" of control over offenders who could be effectively supervised with less intrusive methods.

New Court Commitment: The imprisonment of a person being admitted on a new sentence and not being readmitted on any previous sentence still in effect.

New Penology Model: Model under which persistent pressures for more humane practices and programs to reform offenders were applied. This movement traced its roots to the principles enunciated in 1870 at the National Prison Congress.

New York House of Refuge: The first correctional unit in the United States developed to house juveniles apart from adults. It was opened in 1825 and had a separate building for housing women.

Nimby: Acronym for "not in my back yard," the position usually taken by citizens when an attempt is made to locate some type of correctional program in a specific area of their community.

Nolle Prosequi: A formal decision by the prosecutor not to prosecute further.

Nolo Contendere: A plea in court in answer to a charge, stating that the defendant will not contest the charges but neither admits guilt nor claims innocence. Tantamount to a guilty plea.

Nominal Damages: A token sum awarded to a plaintiff where there is no substantial loss or injury.

Noncontact Visitation: A condition of prison visitation in which visitors and inmates are denied physical contact either by being separated by glass partitions and communicating through telephones or by mesh screens.

Nondisruptive Groups: These are formal or informal groups of inmates that are not seen by prison personnel as a threat to the security of the prison.

Not Guilty by Reason of Insanity: A plea or verdict in a criminal proceeding that the defendant is not guilty of the offense(s) charged because when the crime was committed the defendant did not have the mental capacity to be held criminally responsible for his or her actions.

Objective Classification Systems: Approaches to classification that provide more accurate information on the charac-

teristics of the prison population than subjective systems. They use evaluation instruments containing explicit criteria. These systems can also be used to make projections about security, custody, and staffing needs for new institutions and the expansion of existing prisons.

Occupational Stressors: Factors associated with the job itself (e.g., negative inmate behavior, overcrowding) and those which are part of the organizational environment (e.g., lack of administrative support) that make people feel uncomfortable, overwhelmed, unhappy, fearful, or anxious. These emotional responses to stimuli may have dysfunctional psychological (e.g., depression) or physiological consequences (e.g., heart attacks and hypertension).

Offender: An adult (or juvenile tried as an adult) convicted of a criminal offense.

Officer Subculture: *See* CO Subculture.

Ombudsman: An individual who acts as an advocate for a specific group.

On-the-Job Training: Informal training of correctional officers, accomplished while working, via daily interactions with older, more experienced officers as well as with the inmates.

Operational or Tactical Intelligence: A means of obtaining information about the current activity of an individual or group. For example, with STGs this would involve acquiring knowledge of current criminal activity including drug introductions, escapes, planned violence, and work and food stoppages.

Ordeal by Water: A torture process in which prisoners were strapped down on their backs and had a funnel forced into their mouths, into which a steady stream of water was poured.

Order of Misericordia: A group founded in 1488 to provide assistance and consolation to offenders condemned to death, accompany them to the gallows, furnish religious services, and provide a Christian burial.

Organic Disorders: A mental disorder caused by damage to the central nervous system.

Organizational Culture: A persistent, patterned way of thinking about the central tasks of, and human relationships in, an organization.

Organizational Smarts: Inmates that enter prison with skills in interpersonal

relations, managing bureaucracies, and common courtesy are said to have organizational smarts.

Organized Crime Syndicates: Sophisticated self-perpetuating organized groups, involved in illegal acts for power and profit. This includes groups like La Cosa Nostra and some prison gangs with inside and outside groups. These groups provide illegal goods and services and also operate legitimate businesses. Their organizational features include the availability of large capital resources, disciplined management, division of labor, and a focus on maximum profit.

Orientation Process: A period during which inmates are provided with information about what is expected of them and what they can anticipate from their institutional experience. This includes being informed about institutional rules and the disciplinary process and being given a copy of the inmate handbook. Also called reception process.

Orwellian: A term derived from the name of George Orwell, the author of *1984*, which detailed the oppressive conditions in a society in which the government was able to monitor the activities of all its citizens.

Out Custody: The second lowest level assigned to an inmate, requiring the second lowest level of security and staff supervision. These inmates may be assigned to less secure housing and be eligible for work details outside the institution.

Outlawry: Those who could not or would not pay blood fines were declared outlaws; they could be sold into slavery or be killed. The only way to remain a part of the community was to pay the fine.

Outlaws: In medieval times men and women who either fled from justice (failed to appear in court to face the charges against them) or had been banished to the wilderness.

Outside Cell Blocks: Cells line the outside wall of each unit with doors that open onto a central corridor and may be several tiers high. Older units may have barred windows, whereas newer units may have windows of special unbreakable materials that allow light in but do not open.

Overclassification: Placement of inmates under more supervision (custody) and control (security) than required.

Overcrowding: The state that exists in correctional facilities when there are too many inmates for the available space, programs, and resources. This condition may force the early release of serious offenders.

Pains of Imprisonment: Describes the deprivations and limits on freedom to which prisons subject inmates.

Paramilitary Model: The structure followed by the Texas Syndicate. The organizational structure is hierarchical; however, it differs from the hierarchical model in that when the leader leaves, a new leader is chosen by a vote.

Parchman Farm: A Mississippi prison farm, noted up until the 1960s for its racists and inhumane conditions.

Parenting Programs: In prison, these are programs that improve parenting skills through a series of educational activities that may include special events involving inmates and their children. These programs include efforts to increase participants' knowledge of child development; instill effective parenting styles and techniques and family communication; strengthen inmate family relationships; and create an understanding of the impact of incarceration on children and other family members.

Parity: In corrections, this term refers to equality in programming and distribution of resources between female and male inmates.

Parole: The conditional release, by an agency that has statutory authority to grant such releases, of inmates from prison to serve the remainder of their sentences under community correctional supervision.

Parole Board: A panel of individuals usually appointed by the governor that makes decisions about the release of inmates. A decision is usually based on an evaluation of the progress made by the inmate while incarcerated, the risk posed to the community by the release, and the inmate's plan for the postprison period.

Parolee: A person on parole status.

Parole Guidelines: Guidelines used by parole authorities in making parole decisions, similar to those used for sentencing. They attempt to gauge accurately the risk the parolee poses to the community.

Parole Officer: An employee of a parole agency whose primary duties include the supervision of parolees.

Participative Organizational Model: This approach allows for input from all members of the organization in the way it is run.

Pedophile: *See* Child Molester.

Peer Tutors: Inmates, usually with a GED or high school diploma, who tutor other inmates with low-level academic skills. They may be specially trained and under the supervision of a certified teacher.

Penal Slavery: A system of imprisonment of both black and white convicts that made them the temporary or lifelong "slaves" of states or of the employers or corporations to whom they were assigned.

Penile Plethysmograph: A device sometimes used in the behavior modification of sex offenders. It measures penile erection.

Penitentiaries: Another name for prisons.

Pennsylvania System: The approach to imprisonment, also called the separate system, developed at the Eastern Penitentiary. It was designed to reform inmates through a program of isolation, work, and penitence.

Penology: The generic term for the organized body of concepts, theories, and approaches centered on the prison and the institutional experience; it describes the study of punishment. This term was used previously to denote what today is described as the study of corrections.

Penry v. Lynaugh: A 1989 decision in which the Supreme Court ruled that the mentally retarded could be executed; they found that mentally disabled adults could not be equated with children.

Pepper Spray (OC): A recently developed nonlethal gas that is becoming more popular among law enforcement and correctional agencies. OC is more effective on the extremely agitated, the mentally ill, or inmates under the influence of drugs.

Perceptual Research: A line of research that asks subjects their belief about how likely they would be to get caught and punished if they broke a specific law and then whether they would commit that crime anyway. The research attempts to study deterrence.

Perimeter Security: The structures and processes, consisting of secure walls, protected windows, and controlled access to the points of entrance and exit, that protect against escape from a prison or jail.

Peripheral Members: Gang members who are generally paranoid about their position in the gang. They are very careful not to say or do the wrong thing.

Perpetrator: The chief actor in the commission of a crime—that is, the person who commits the crime.

Personality Disorders: An inflexible and maladaptive pattern of behavior developed early in life causing significant impairment in overall functioning. The most important of these for the criminal justice system is the antisocial personality disorder.

Philadelphia Society for Alleviating the Miseries of Public Prisons: A reform group in the 18th and 19th centuries in Philadelphia. Today, this organization is known as the Pennsylvania Prison Society.

Piece-Price Prison Industries System: Similar to the contract system except that state officials had full control of the production process. The contractor furnished the raw materials, but prison authorities were responsible for manufacturing the product, which the contractor then sold.

Pillories: A device similar to the stocks, by which an individual could be punished by being secured by his or her wrists and neck. These devices were usually placed in a town's square so that the offender would suffer public humiliation at the hands of his or her fellow citizens.

Plantations: Prisons organized in the manner of pre–Civil War plantations. Also called farm prisons.

Playing the Game: *See* Conning.

Plea: A defendant's formal answer in a criminal proceeding to the charge contained in a complaint, information, or indictment, that he or she is guilty or not guilty of the offense charged.

Pluralistic Prison Environment: Describes the inmate world of the contemporary prison, characterized by ethnic, religious, self-help, special interest, and unauthorized groups.

Podular Direct Supervision: Supervision in jails or prisons with a direct supervision design. This design permanently situates staff among the inmates within each housing unit, thus allowing the most continuous supervision.

Podular Remote Surveillance: Surveillance in jails and prisons with pods housing various numbers of inmates that are arranged to permit observation of activities from a central, protected control room.

Police Role: The role assumed by the police in working with the community, the courts, and parole or probation officers.

Political Prisoners: Individuals imprisoned for engaging in political activities deemed as criminal within the society in which they occur. These acts can range from simple political dissent to murder.

Politicians: Prisoners who generally worked for key officials or occupied positions in the administrative offices and whose position gave them the ability to influence decisions affecting other inmates (e.g., cell and work assignments and access to files and other sources of information).

Population Caps: Limits placed by the courts or by statute on the number of inmates that can be legally housed in a jail, prison, or prison system.

Population Movement: In corrections, the entries and exits of adjudicated persons, or persons subject to judicial proceedings, into or from correctional facilities or programs.

Postconviction Remedy: The procedures by which a person who has been convicted of a crime can challenge in court the lawfulness of that conviction, the penalty received, or the actions of a correctional agency and thus obtain relief in situations where this cannot be done by direct appeal.

Potential Members: An official designation for an inmate suspected of being a gang member. It means that there is insufficient evidence to classify the inmate at this point but that his case should be reviewed within 6 months.

Preliminary Injunction: In corrections, an injunction granted at the beginning of a lawsuit to prevent institutional officials from continuing to engage in certain conduct or keeping an inmate in a designated status that is in dispute. It may be terminated or continued depending on the results of the court decision.

Presentence Investigation Report (PSI): An investigation and report of the defendant by a probation officer designed to help the sentencing judge decide on the most appropriate sentence. It may also be used for other purposes by criminal justice personnel.

Preservice Training: Any form of training occurring before the individual assumes the day-to-day responsibilities of a job.

Pretrial Detainees: Individuals being held in a jail or similar facility while awaiting court processing.

Pretrial Detention: A period of confinement occurring between arrest and any further prosecution.

Pretrial Intervention: *See* Diversion.

Pretrial Status: Any status (e.g., ROR, detention) in which an accused individual finds himself or herself while awaiting court processing.

PRIDE: Prison Rehabilitative Industries and Diversified Enterprise is a not-for-profit corporation that runs Florida's prison industries. It is an example of the "corporate model" used by some jurisdictions to run their prison industry programs.

Primary Prevention: Measures that are taken to eliminate or reduce as many of the criminogenic conditions existing within the community as possible.

Principle of Least Eligibility: The notion that prisoners should not be given programs and services or live under conditions that are better than those of the lowest classes of the noncriminal population in the society.

Prison Administration: The group of individuals that runs the prison—composed of the superintendent and his or her assistants.

Prison Chaplains: He or she is a minister of a particular faith who is typically employed and paid by a jurisdiction to administer, supervise, and plan all religious activities and services at a particular facility and is responsible for ministering to inmates, staff, and families regardless of their religious beliefs or affiliation.

Prison Classification: *See* Classification.

Prisoner: A person in physical custody in a confinement facility or in the physical custody of a criminal justice official while being transported to or between confinement facilities.

Prisoner Litigation Reform Act (PLRA): Legislation that restricts courts' intrusion into the operations of prisons. The PLRA limits inmates' ability to file lawsuits by requiring them to exhaust all other administrative remedies first, mandating that they pay filing fees, and requiring that their awards go to satisfy restitution orders against them. It also restricts courts' ability to place population caps on prisons and, thereby, forcing early release to relieve overcrowding conditions.

Prisoner Movement: A movement, inspired by the changes that occurred in the United States during the 1960s, which focused on reforming prison conditions. It included both free-world and inmate groups.

Prisoner Rights Groups: These groups were influenced by the civil rights movement. They directed their efforts toward reducing the disparities between prisoners and members of conventional society and sought to increase inmates' constitutional rights.

Prison Fellowship (PF): A prison ministry that recruits and trains volunteers and provides teaching, mentoring, and aftercare programs for released inmates.

Prison Furloughs: Short-term, escorted or unescorted trips away from the prison granted for various purposes.

Prison Industry Enhancement Certification Program (PIECP): A provision of the Justice System Improvement Act of 1979 that establishes partnerships between state or local prison industries and the private sector.

Prison Intelligentsia: A group of inmates who during the rehabilitation era took advantage of educational programs to develop their academic skills and eventually came to enjoy reading. They expanded their knowledge by reading in all areas, which provided them with a perspective on the world scene and changed their views of themselves and society. This led them to critically examine the prison system and expose its flaws. This group was very vocal during the prisoner movement era.

Prisonization: The socialization process by which inmates take on (to a greater or a lesser degree) the folkways, mores, customs, and general culture of the penitentiary or prison.

Prison Overcrowding: *See* Overcrowding.

Prison Queens: Inmates who are openly homosexual and manifest their "feminine" characteristics in dress and manner.

Prison Rules: To be considered constitutionally acceptable institutional rules should be clear, be intelligible, and only prohibit behavior that threatens important institutional interests such as order, security, and safety.

Prison Smarts: Inmates who have learned through experience how to manage the prison community's resources and members in a way that allows them to do their time on their own terms.

Prison Stupor: Referred to as prison psychosis, this is a mental escape from the deprivations of prison life.

Prison Toughs: Inmates who manifested a constant hostility toward prison officials, conventional society, and most other prisoners and occasionally hurt or killed other inmates, usually those without prestige or power.

Private Benefit Prison Industry System: A system of prison industry in which a private entity derives profits from its involvement in the industry.

Private Sector Involvement in Corrections: Some jurisdictions contract with companies to provide specific services such as food or to manage or build a facility.

Private Wrongs: In current usage, private wrongs are referred to as torts or civil wrongs. In preliterate times, these included many things that today we consider criminal offenses.

Privileged Communication: Statements made by certain persons in a protected relationship (e.g., priest-penitent, lawyer-client) which the law protects from forced disclosure on the witness stand unless the individual making them waives his or her legal right to secrecy.

Proactive: A term that means to act in anticipation of an event. In corrections, this refers to dealing with and correcting conditions that are known to cause problems before the problems can manifest themselves.

Proactive Management: This approach to management involves trying to anticipate and correct problems before they develop by continually evaluating programs and planning for and creating opportunities for the organization to develop the capacity to pursue its mission.

Probation: A sentence that keeps the convicted offender in the community under supervision by a probation agency and usually requires compliance with legally imposed restrictions and conditions.

Probation Conditions: Conditions (control and treatment) imposed on all probationers as part of their sentences.

Probationer: A person who is placed on probation status.

Probation Officer: An employee of a probation agency whose primary duties include the supervision of probationers and other probation agency functions.

Probation Supervision Fees: Statutory requirements that probationers (and parolees) contribute to their own supervision. These fees average between $20 and $25 per month.

Probation without Adjudication: Allows judges to withhold adjudication in the interests of reducing the penetration of offenders into the criminal justice system. This is similar to the use of deferred prosecution in the federal courts.

Procedural Due Process: Laws that enforce constitutional limits on actions taken by the government or its agencies to enforce criminal laws. In correctional facilities due process does not necessarily involve any specific procedures. Generally, the greater the consequences for inmates, the more extensive the due process requirements are likely to be.

Programmed Contact Devices: Consists of a wristlet or a voice verification unit and a central computer. The device is programmed to call an offender during the hours he or she is to be monitored. The calls can be random. The offender must repeat the words the unit requests.

Prohibitory Act of 1940: Prohibited the interstate transport of all prison-made products except agricultural commodities and goods produced for states and their political subdivisions.

Project Rio: This is a multiagency program operated by the Texas Department of Criminal Justice. While in prison, project inmates are assessed and referred to appropriate academic and/or vocational programs. Upon release they are referred to the Texas Employment Commission to continue training or for job placement.

Prop Friendships: Involve a close relationship between two inmates, one who may be stronger than the other, who will back one another up in violent confrontations.

Proportionality: Requires that the severity of the punishment given the convicted offender match the seriousness of his or her crime.

Protective Custody (PC): Involves the segregation of a variety of inmates who are in serious danger of being harmed for reasons that include their offense (e.g., child molestation), gambling debts, homosexual triangles, or being identified as a snitch.

Protestant Ethic: A moral precept that required that "everyone should work."

Pruno: Also called "Raisin Jack," this is an intoxicating brew made by accumulating sugar, grains, fruit, or potatoes and yeast, and allowing them to ferment for several days to a few weeks.

Pseudofamilies: Adaptive groupings of female inmates that involve familylike relationships. Each individual within the group adopts a role as one of the family members (e.g., father, mother, daughter).

Psychiatric or Psychologic Disability: Any type of mental disturbance or disorder.

Psychopath: *See* Antisocial Personality Disorder.

Psychotic Disorders: Severe emotional disruptions characterized by personality disorganization and significant impairment in normal functioning (e.g., schizophrenia).

Public Humiliation: Publicly shaming offenders as a punishment. This has been used from primitive times to the present.

Public Works and Ways System: Under this system prison labor is used to benefit the governmental entity overseeing the work of the inmates. Inmates are used for construction, repair, and maintenance of prisons or other public structures, roads, and parks.

Public Wrongs: Considered crimes in preliterate societies. There were six basic categories: sacrilege and other offenses against religion, treason, witchcraft, incest and other sex offenses, poisoning, and violations of the hunting rules.

Publisher-Only Rule: A court ruling mandating that inmates can only receive hardback books if they are mailed directly by publishers, book clubs, or bookstores.

Punitive Damages: In a correctional setting, those damages awarded over and above what would barely compensate inmates for their losses when the wrongful act was done intentionally and maliciously or with reckless disregard for the rights of the inmate. The intent is to punish the wrongdoer.

Punks: Young inmates, seduced by gifts or favors, or coerced by threats or force to provide sexual favors to other inmates. *Also see* Kid.

Qualified Immunity: A situation in which correctional workers can be exempted from having to pay damages for their actions when a law is not clearly established, or it was not reasonably recognized at the time that the actions were unconstitutional.

Quasimilitary Model: Auburn-type prisons were organized in military fashion, which included a rigid daily schedule, inmates wearing striped uniforms and being marched to and from all activities, and harsh discipline.

Qur'an: Holy book of the Muslim religion. Also referred to as the Koran.

Radical Groups: Left-wing groups that focused on changing society rather than on helping inmates or changing prison conditions.

Rank-and-File Building Tenders: The head building tender's assistants in Texas prisons.

Rank Men: The lowest level of inmate in the Arkansas prison farms. They were the farm laborers.

Rape: Unlawful sexual intercourse with a person, by force or without legal or factual consent.

Rapist: An individual who uses force or threat to have sexual intercourse with a nonconsenting victim.

Rapos: Also called abnormal sex offenders, these are sex offenders sentenced for incest and child molesting. They are considered repulsive by most inmates.

Rasphouses: Workhouses in which the major form of work involved the rasping of bark off logs to produce materials that could be used in the making of dyes.

Rational Choice Theory: A theory that focuses on the rational decision-making elements that contribute to the decision of whether or not to commit a crime. It recognizes that the degree of reasoning involved varies from offender to offender and from crime to crime. *Also see* Choice Theory.

Rats: Inmates known to inform on others to the staff.

Reactive Management: Waiting until a problem manifests before taking action.

Reasonable Force: Refers to the legally justifiable amount of force that may be used in a given situation, which is determined by the amount and type of resistance displayed.

Reasonableness Test: A judicial criterion that mandates that there be a valid rational connection between a prison rule restricting inmates' rights and the legitimate government interests put forth to justify it or that there be alternative means of exercising this right.

Reception and Diagnostic Centers: Correctional facilities in which inmates are assessed, classified, oriented, and then transferred to the appropriate facilities within the system.

Reception Process: *See* Orientation Process.

Recidivism: The repetition of criminal behavior variously defined in terms of either a rearrest, a reconviction, or a reincarceration.

Recidivist: A person convicted of one or more crimes, and who is alleged to have subsequently committed another crime.

Reckless Endangerment: An offense characterized by the willful disregard for the safety of others.

Reclassification: An ongoing process of monitoring inmates' progress; dealing with problems as they arise; and where appropriate, reassigning inmates based on changes in their behavior and attitudes. Typically, this occurs every 6 months and includes both a reevaluation of an inmate's security and custody status and program and service needs.

Recognizance: A way in which an offender can be released from custody during court proceedings. *Also see* Release on Recognizance.

Reformation: The idea that imprisonment or other types of punishment or treatment will change inmates by instilling a new sense of morality and purpose in them.

Reformatory: A type of prison developed in the late 1800s that was supposed to incorporate the principles advocated at the National Prison Congress meeting. It was for young, first offenders and emphasized training.

Regional Jails: Centralized jail facilities that serve two or more jurisdictions.

Rehabilitation: The process of providing inmates with a variety of services and programs (e.g., education, job training, psychological counseling) while under the supervision of the corrections system; designed to reduce the probability of future criminality and make productive members of society.

Rehabilitative Institution: In corrections, a prison that functions as a treatment facility where the major focus is to treat and "cure" the offender.

Rehabilitative Model: Advocates treatment to change offenders' attitudes and behavior and improve their academic and vocational skills to reduce the likelihood of their reinvolvement in crime.

Reintegration: A correctional approach that emphasizes graduated release programs and the greater use of community facilities and programs to assist offenders released from prison to adjust to life back in the community.

Relapse Prevention: A treatment strategy that prepares the individual to deal with the various circumstances that can lead to resumption of the condition being treated.

Release on Recognizance (ROR): A pretrial release in which the defendant signs a promise to appear in court when asked to but does not pledge anything of value to be forfeited upon nonappearance. Jurisdictions use certain criteria to screen defendants for eligibility. These include severity of the offense, previous conviction for a serious offense, family ties, residence, employment, financial condition, and mental condition. It excludes those charged with certain crimes, previously convicted serious offenders, and those with a previous violation of prerelease conditions.

Religious Freedom Restoration Act (RFRA): Federal legislation requiring that the government show a compelling interest in the restriction of religious expression and employ the least restrictive measurements available when curtailing it.

Religious Organizations: Formal prison groups that exist apart from regularly scheduled religious programming.

Remote Supervision: *See* Podular Remote Surveillance.

Residential Commitment: A sentence of commitment to a correctional facility that requires persons committed to reside there at night but permits them to leave unaccompanied during the day.

Residential Programs: Community-based programs that require the clients to live there while participating in the program.

Resistance: Refers to the actions manifested by a prisoner who is attempting to evade an officer's efforts to control him or her. Resistance varies based on the inmate's state of agitation, propensity to commit violence, mental stability, state of intoxication, and view of the rewards and punishments of resisting.

Resource Brokers: POs acting as referral agents for their clients and also acting as advocates.

Restitution: As a sentence (or part of a sentence), the requirement that the offender repay the victim (or the community), either through money or services, so that the damages or losses caused by the criminal act can be restored.

Restorative Justice: A new criminal justice framework that emerged in the 1990s as a method for reforming the justice system. It focuses on the harm that crime does to the victim and the community and seeks repair of that harm to the victim by the offender.

Restrained Hands-on Doctrine: A modification of the hands-on doctrine adopted in the mid-1970s, which recognized that while inmates do not forfeit all constitutional rights, their rights are not as broad as those enjoyed by nonprisoners. This is because inmates are imprisoned and prison officials need to maintain order, security, and discipline in their facilities, which justifies the imposition of certain restrictions on inmates' rights.

Restraints: Handcuffs, belly chains, leg irons, straitjackets, leather restraints, flex cuffs, and restraint chairs are devices that temporarily bridle inmates. They are used to prevent escapes, to prevent injury to inmates or others, and to protect property.

Retentionists: A term applied to those who favor capital punishment.

Rethermalization Units: A mobile unit that is used to bring food to appropriate serving temperatures.

Retribution: A philosophy underlying punishment that specifies that the punishment is deserved because of the evil done by the perpetrator.

Revocation: A process that involves a termination or modification of an individual's probation or parole status for cause (violation of conditions or arrest for the commission of a crime) and is likely to result either in the imposition of more stringent conditions and supervision or imprisonment.

Ride the Medical Pony: A term connoting the abuse of the prison medical system by inmates who deliberately fake symptoms for secondary gains, including opportunities to complain and receive sympathetic attention; obtain medications, particularly narcotic and sedative drugs; take time off from work details; meet inmates from other housing units; or gain relief during a lockdown.

Right Guys: Big House inmates at the top of the prison hierarchy because they could be depended on to do right according to the inmate code. Their high prestige as thieves, tendency to cooperate with each other, and demeanor of toughness and coolness further enhanced their position.

Right to Treatment: The right of an individual who is institutionalized for the purpose of receiving some form of treatment to receive that treatment.

Risk Prediction Scales: Any scale employed to determine the level of supervision required by an offender by determining the risk that individual poses to those around him or her.

Road Deputies: Sheriff's deputies generally responsible for conducting patrol activities within their jurisdictions.

Road Gangs: Prison or jail inmates who work on highways, parks, and other public or government areas.

Robbery: The unlawful taking or attempted taking of property that is in the immediate possession of another, by use or threatened use of force.

Role Conflict: In corrections, role conflict has typically been associated with the different and conflicting role expectations related to custody and treatment.

Role Dispossession: The separation of inmates from many of the roles they normally occupy in the outside world.

Ruiz v. Estelle: A district court decision that resulted in the most sweeping and detailed order in the history of prison litigation. It found almost all major aspects of the Texas prison system unconstitutional and resulted in a special master being appointed to oversee the remediation of these conditions. *See also* Special Masters.

Russian Knout: *See* Knout.

Sally Ports: Vehicle entrances into prison compounds that consist of double gates, only one of which is open at any time. At high-security facilities a pit or inspection well is used to allow COs to look at the undercarriage of the vehicle on mirrors or creepers used for this purpose. After the search is completed the second gate is opened, allowing the vehicle to enter the prison proper.

Sanctuary: A medieval practice that allowed protection of those accused of crimes who entered a city or a special building, such as a temple or church, which could not be lawfully entered.

Scared Straight: A program begun at the Rahway Prison in New Jersey by the Lifer's group that brought juvenile delinquents into the institution to be confronted with the realities of being in prison.

Schizophrenia: A psychotic disorder.

School Resource Officer: A law enforcement officer who is assigned to junior and senior high schools for purposes of preventing delinquency and diverting youths from contact with the juvenile justice system.

Screws: *See* Hacks.

Script: Nonlegal tender or "money" created for special situations. Some prison systems issue their own "script," which inmates are required to use to buy goods at the prison commissary.

Section 1983 Actions: A term to describe civil rights lawsuits filed by inmates.

Section 1983 of the Civil Rights Act: A part of the Civil Rights Act of 1871 that allowed individuals who were deprived of their rights by state officers, acting under color of state law, irrespective of their actual authority to engage in the behavior in question, to sue them in federal court.

Security: The level of physical barriers to escape required to safely confine inmates.

Security Threat Groups (STGs): Two or more inmates, acting together, who pose a threat to the security or safety of staff or inmates and are disruptive to programs or to the orderly management of the facility.

Security Threat Individual: Any individual who has the potential to or has committed acts that threaten the safety of others and the orderly operations and security of an institution.

Segmentation Vocational Training Programs: Vocational training programs that take a standard course of study and divide it into four equal segments. Each segment teaches a group of related skills and knowledge sufficient to provide employment possibilities.

Selective Incapacitation: A form of incapacitation based on predictions that certain offenders will commit serious offenses at higher rates than others convicted of the same types of crimes and thus should receive longer sentences.

Selective Incorporation: The process by which the due process aspects of the Fourteenth Amendment to the U.S. Constitution were incorporated into other amendments.

Self-Help Groups: Formal prison organizations concerned with the improvement of the life circumstances of prisoners and ex-prisoners. Eighty-one percent of the inmates in these groups were white. Whites lack a common cultural background, and these groups provide a nonethnically based focus for inmates.

Self-Mutilation: Self-inflicted injuries by inmates designed to remove them from the harsh conditions that existed on the Texas prison farms.

Sentence: The punishment specified for a given crime by the legislature of a given political jurisdiction, imposed by one of its courts, and carried out by its correctional system.

Sentence Credits: Time deducted from an inmate's sentence that he or she has already served or on the basis of good-time credits that have been earned by the inmate.

Sentencing Disparity: A situation in which a significant difference exists in the sentences received by similar individuals convicted of similar crimes.

Sentencing Guidelines: Statutory guides that set forth explicit policies and procedures for making decisions about the sentences to be imposed for each crime.

Sentencing Review Procedures: Any set of arrangements employed to reduce sentencing inconsistencies.

Separate But Equal: A doctrine underlying the southern system of segregation of blacks and whites until the middle of the 20th century that justified segregation on the basis that comparable services and facilities existed for both groups. It was eventually declared unconstitutional.

Separation of Powers: A constitutional mandate that specifies distinct functions for each branch of government.

Serious Medical Need: A condition that would have been diagnosed by a physician as requiring treatment or one so obvious even a layperson would easily recognize the need for a doctor's attention.

Seven Steps: One of the earliest of the self-help organizations. Modeled after the 12 steps of the Alcohol Anonymous program, the 7 steps were developed to guide inmates in maintaining their freedom.

Sexual Misconduct: Any type of improper conduct of a sexual nature directed at inmates by correctional staff.

Sexual Safety: A sexist rationalization offered by male officers for not assigning women to direct contact positions in male prisons.

Shadow Board: A pegboard on which tools can be hung that has an outline of each item making it easy to recognize when an item is missing.

Shakedowns: Searches of individuals and their cells conducted at frequent, irregular intervals for the purpose of discovering contraband.

Sham Religious Groups: Groups of inmates claiming to belong to a religious body that does not meet the requirements for constituting a religion. These groups have ulterior motives for wanting to be recognized as a legitimate religious group.

Shivs: Knives made from materials available in the prison, including kitchen utensils, metal from the shops, and even from seemingly harmless items such as toothbrushes.

Shock Incarceration: *See* Shock Probation/Parole.

Shock Probation/Parole: A form of split sentence that begins with an unspecified short period of incarceration in a local jail or a state or federal prison followed by a period of community supervision.

Siberia: An area in the extreme northeast part of Russia that was used as a penal colony.

Sickouts: A form of strike used where strikes are prohibited in which large numbers of officers call in sick on the same day.

Sissy: *See* Kid.

Slaves of the State: The prevailing court view of prison inmates, as enunciated in *Ruffin v. Commonwealth*, from the birth of our nation until the 1900s, that prisoners had no rights guaranteed to them.

Snitch: An inmate informer.

Sociopath: *See* Antisocial Personality Disorder.

Soledad: A California state prison that represented a prototypical correctional facility during the rehabilitation era.

Solitary Confinement: Often called the hole. In the past, prior to court oversight of prison conditions, these were frequently bare, unlit, and unventilated cells used for punishment. Inmates placed there were sometimes stripped and not given blankets, which meant they slept naked on a stone floor and were fed only bread and water. Today, this term is used also to refer to units used for isolating inmates for disciplinary purposes. *Also see* Disciplinary Detention.

Span of Control: Recognizes the limits of supervision by one person and defines the number of persons that person can effectively supervise directly.

Special Diets: Diets that fulfill therapeutic or medical requirements and generally accommodate the special dietary restrictions of legitimate religious groups.

Special Interest Organizations: A type of prison group that was involved in a greater range of activities than many groups. Groups were involved in activities that included fund-raising, lobbying, stock car racing, and other activities. These groups were more likely to receive support from authorities than other groups.

Special Management: In corrections, this refers to specially designed programs to deal with or care for inmates who have conditions that impair their normal functioning.

Special Masters: Masters are persons appointed to act as representatives of the court in some particular action or transaction, including to collect information; to aid the court in deciding whether a constitutional violation occurred; and to assist in developing or monitoring a remedial decree that involves constitutional violations.

Specific Deterrence: The belief that if offenders suffer punishment that outweighs the gains resulting from their crimes, they will presumably not engage in subsequent crimes.

Specific Learning Disabilities: A disability believed to be related to a minimal brain disorder, resulting in perceptual distortions that inhibit proper learning of reading, writing, and other skills.

Spin House: An early Dutch workhouse for women.

Square Johns: Accidental offenders, or those who committed only a few crimes, who were often better educated than most inmates. They were not considered criminals by the inmate population and were oriented to conventional society.

Squares: The adaptive role taken by female inmates who held and followed conventional norms and values.

Staff Personnel: The workers who provide the support services for line workers (e.g., training, communications, accounting).

Staff Subculture: *See* CO Subculture.

State Benefit System: A system that employed inmates for the benefit of the state or its political subdivisions.

State or Public Account Prison Industries System: The state or municipality becomes a manufacturer and the prison becomes an industrial establishment operating in the same manner as any outside free industry. The state markets and profits from the items manufactured.

State-Raised Youths: Individuals literally raised by state agencies because they have spent most of their youth in one or more institutions. They are at home in prison and tend to form tightly knit cliques that threaten and use violence for protection and to increase their power, privileges, and prestige.

State-Use Prison Industries System: Whether managed by the state or a private entity, under this system the sales of the products made by inmates are limited to public institutions, municipalities, and political divisions of the state.

States' Rights: This refers to the fact that states retain any powers not specifically delegated to the federal government by the U.S. Constitution.

States' Sovereign Domain: Those areas of government over which a state has exclusive control.

Steering Committee Model: The organizational structure preferred by the Aryan Brotherhood. A committee comprising an odd number of members who founded the organization governs it. When a committee member dies, the council chooses his replacement.

Stocks: A device similar to a pillory, by which an individual could be punished by being secured by his or her wrists and ankles. These devices were usually placed in the town's public square so that the offender would suffer humiliation at the hands of his or her fellow citizens.

Strap: A leather strap attached to a handle and used for inflicting whippings.

Strategic Intelligence: Focuses on developing a detailed information base about the characteristics of a particular group or individual. For example, with STGs, information is obtained about their members and activities.

Stress: A state of the body caused by undue demands being placed on it by internal and environmental stressors, which can lead to physical and mental disorders.

Strip Searches: Require inmates or visitors to remove all clothing and submit to a visual inspection of the body, including the outer portions of orifices and cavities.

Structured Conflicts: Conflicts between guards and inmates that arise from the differences in their organizational roles, which build in differential power roles.

Study Release: A community release program that allows inmates to go into the community to pursue educational opportunities not available inside the prison or at community residential facilities.

Stun Belt: Used as nonlethal control techniques, these include Taser guns, stun guns, and stun belts. Stun guns can temporarily incapacitate a person when pressed against his or her body and discharged. Stun belts are worn by a prisoner and can be activated by a corrections officer using a remote control.

Stun Guns: *See* Electronic Shocking Devices.

***Sub-Rosa* Inmate Economy:** The inmate black market that provides illegal (i.e., contraband) goods and services.

Substantial (Impermissible) Burden on Religious Freedom: Pressuring an individual to commit an act forbidden by the religion or preventing him or her from engaging in conduct or having a religious experience that the faith mandates. The tenet or belief must be central to the religion's doctrine.

Substantive Due Process: The means by which the rights to life, liberty, and property are applied to issues of crime and punishment.

Substantive Predicates: Language that delineates specific conditions or requirements.

Summary Admission Report: An account of the legal aspects of the inmate's case; a summary of his or her criminal history, demographics, family and personal history data, occupational interests, recreational preferences, and needs; and a summary of the assessments and recommendations made by classification staff.

Superintendent: In corrections, the person responsible for running the entire prison (e.g., implementation of policy; responsibility for all personnel, programs, and activities within the prison). Also called the warden.

Supermax Institutions: Provide the highest level of custody and security. Inmates assigned to these facilities have demonstrated an inability to adjust satisfactorily to general population units at other secure facilities. Inmates are all housed in single secure units. They typically spend 23 hours per day in their cells with 1 hour for recreation. All programming involving staff takes place through the cell doors (e.g., religious and casework services and other programs are provided by correspondence courses or by closed-circuit TV). When inmates are removed from their cells they are often strip searched, always placed in full restraints, and accompanied by more than one CO.

Supremacy Clause: A clause of Article VI of the U.S. Constitution, which declares that all laws made in pursuance of the Constitution and all treaties made under the authority of the United States shall be "the supreme law of the land" and shall enjoy legal superiority over any conflicting provision of a state constitution or law.

Surveillance by Probation/Parole: The process of controlling the offender through supervision.

Suspected Members: An official designation for an inmate suspected of being in a gang. Officials believe these individuals are in a gang but cannot yet sufficiently document or prove it.

Suspended Sentence: A procedure by which a judge can either defer the pronouncement of a sentence or suspend its implementation.

Sweat Box: A torture device consisting of a coffinlike cell with just enough space to accommodate a man standing erect. Generally made of wood or tin, it was completely closed except for a hole 2 inches in diameter at nose level. In the heat of the southern sun, temperature levels in these devices reached 120 degrees or more.

Sympathizers: Inmates who have no desire to join the gang but who share the group's beliefs.

Synanist: A person receiving treatment within a Synanon program.

Synanon: A long-term residential drug treatment program, using the therapeutic community approach, that is still in operation today.

Tactical Intelligence: The daily routine of gathering and processing information. For STGs, this involves focusing on drug

smuggling, escapes, planned violence, work and food stoppages, and other signs of potential problems.

Tactical Response Teams: Teams developed by departments of corrections to conduct planned cell extractions and searches and to take charge of hostage situations. Teams usually comprise snipers, negotiators, and rescuers.

Tanks: The housing units in Texas prison farms or the cell blocks in its prisons.

Technical Violation: The violation of one or more of the conditions of the probation or parole contract, which may result in further sanctions.

Tejanos: The name given Mexican-American inmates raised in Texas.

Telemedicine: Uses advanced video technology to link an inmate in a correctional setting with a physician who could be hundreds of miles away.

Temporary Restraining Order: *See* Preliminary Injunction.

Texas Syndicate: A group started by Texas-born Mexican-American inmates, at San Quentin Prison in California in 1975, to protect themselves from victimization by other California prison gangs. It spread to other California prisons and to Texas prisons, where it became the second largest gang.

Theft: Generally, any taking of the property of another with the intent to permanently deprive the rightful owner of its possession.

Therapee: The person receiving the therapy.

Therapeutic Community Drug Treatment Programs: Highly structured, long-term residential programs that help residents face the fact that they are addicted to drugs and its associated lifestyle. They foster change in their personalities and behavior so they can live drug-free, socially productive lives.

Therapeutic Program: Any program that includes individual and group therapy and counseling under the direction of psychologists and psychiatrists (or other trained counselors and therapists).

Therapeutic Recreation (TR): A recreational program that concentrates on the knowledge of leisure and recreation as they relate to achieving optimal health for inmates. The focus is on helping inmates learn leisure skills that will assist them when they leave prison.

Thompson v. Oklahoma: A 1989 decision in which the Supreme Court ruled that the execution of juveniles under 16 at the time of the offense is cruel and unusual punishment and therefore unconstitutional.

Three Strikes Laws: Anticrime statutes that sentence offenders convicted of three felonies, usually involving violence, to life in prison without the possibility of parole.

Throwaways: Inmates that are considered expendable and are used by a gang to do jobs that involve high risk of injury, death, or apprehension.

Ticket of Leave: A conditional pardon. For example, in Australia during the transportation era convicts given "tickets" were freed from their obligation to work for the government or a master. They could work as free agents or for wages as long as they committed no new crimes and remained in the colony until their sentences ended.

Time Served: The time spent in confinement in relation to conviction and sentencing for a given offense.

Time to Think (TTT): An example of a cognitive skills training program that is one component of the Living Skills Program. This program addresses thinking and social skills such as problem solving, negotiation, communication, creative thinking, management of emotions, values enhancement, and critical reasoning.

Tips: These were crowds or extended social networks of inmates whose association was based on preprison contacts or common subcultural involvement.

Token Economies: A type of behavior modification based on tangible payoffs (points, tokens, etc.) to inmates who manifest certain behavior. Tokens are accumulated over a period of time and can be spent on a variety of goods and privileges. The goal is to eliminate undesirable behavior and create desirable behavior.

Tort: A civil wrong arising from a claim by one party that another party has negligently, maliciously, or deliberately inflicted some sort of injury on him or her.

Total Incapacitation: Any form of punishment that prevents an offender from ever doing the crime again (e.g., capital punishment or life imprisonment without parole).

Total Institutions: A way of describing the environment that characterizes custodial hospitals, boarding schools, and military training bases and prisons. These are places in which large groups of people live and work together around the clock within a circumscribed space and under a tightly scheduled sequence of activities.

Totality of Conditions: A court interpretation indicating that, taken individually, conditions cited may not represent constitutional violations, but when taken together (in "their totality") they may constitute cruel and unusual punishment.

Tough Time Institutions (TTI): Proposed as alternatives to prison for nonviolent offenders who would only serve one-half of their sentence if they successfully completed the program. These would be spartan facilities like boot camps without the military aspects. The program would be characterized by a long day in which activities would include physical conditioning, half a day of work, half a day of program participation (e.g., education, drug treatment), and limited recreational opportunities.

Tracking Devices: Using a geographic grid, these devices can pinpoint an offender's exact location at any given time.

Transfer: In corrections, the movement of a person from one correctional facility or caseload to another.

Transportation: The term used to denote banishment of prisoners to overseas or remote locations.

Treatment Conditions: Conditions tailored to fit the problems and needs of each offender. They may include psychiatric treatment or participation in a training or educational program.

Treatment Programs: Programs such as education and psychological counseling that are intended to remediate inmates' deficiencies that are believed likely to impair their successful functioning in the free society.

Tricking: A term usually associated with prostitution. In women's prison usage it refers to indiscriminate sexual activity, perhaps for economic gain.

Trusty: A jail or prison inmate who has been entrusted with some custodial responsibilities or who performs other services assisting in the operation of the facility.

Trusty-Guards: Inmates in many of the southern prison systems who were given the responsibility of guarding other prisoners. In many instances, they were armed with rifles and were rewarded for shooting escapees. *Also see* Trusty-Shooter.

Trusty-Servants: Trusty inmates who performed household duties in the homes of prison officials.

Trusty-Shooter: An armed trusty guard.

Trusty System: A system under which inmates were given various responsibilities for running a prison.

Truth-in-Sentencing Laws: Laws that require offenders to serve a substantial portion of their sentence.

Tuberculosis: An infectious disease spread by bacteria in the air resulting from coughs or sneezes from infected individuals.

Tucker Telephone: A torture device, previously used in the Arkansas prison system, that consisted of an electric generator taken from a crank-type telephone and wired in sequence with two dry cell batteries. An undressed inmate had electrodes attached to his big toe and his penis. The crank was then turned, sending an electrical charge throughout his body.

Turnkeys: Inmates responsible for opening and closing riot gates.

Type I Minimum Security Facilities: Designated for inmates who have a short period before release, facilitating reintegration into the community. These facilities provide little or no programming.

Type II Minimum Security Facilities: Designed for inmates, posing no security risk, with release or parole dates of 18 months or less. These facilities provide extensive on-site programming.

Typical Prisoner: The "undistinguished" majority of prisoners. Of middle class status in the prison (and typically lower or working class outside), they had no or few skills as a criminal and received little respect.

UCR: *See* Uniform Crime Reports.

Unconditional Releases: In this type of release, which is granted at the expiration of an inmate's sentence, the releasee is free from further correctional supervision.

Underclass: The lowest segment of the poverty group, which is characterized by extreme poverty and little hope of bettering itself.

Underclassification: Placement of inmates under lower levels of supervision and control than required.

Unicor: The federal prison system's industry program.

Uniform Crime Reports: An annual statistical summary of certain types of crimes reported to the police and of persons arrested for these offenses. Published by the Federal Bureau of Investigation.

Unit Management: A form of correctional administration in which a team of correctional workers, including correctional officers, counselors, and others, takes responsibility for managing a particular wing or cell block of a prison.

Unity of Command: Refers to the view that workers should only have to report directly to one boss.

Universal Precautions: Basic medical standards of safety and care to reduce the spread of infectious diseases.

Utilitarian Model: Advocates the use of punishment as a way to affect, control, or change future criminal behavior.

Validated Members: Gang members who have met the criteria for being officially designated as gang members by correctional officials.

Value Clarification: Part of the Leisure Education Model, in which inmates identify their need for praise, belonging, and acceptance. Next, they look at methods for satisfying these values within themselves.

Verbal Direction: Using communication skills to control inmate resistance and obtain compliance.

Veterans Preference System: A system that rewards veterans for their military service by giving them an advantage when applying for government jobs.

Victims Known As *Survivors*: Victims who survived a crime when others did not.

Video Mug Shots: Photographs taken of arrestees at booking. They result from the integration of computer graphics and video.

Vietnam War: A conflict fought on Vietnamese soil from the late 1950s to the

1970s that divided people within the United States. The vocal opposition to the war influenced the prisoner movement. *Also see* Prisoner Movement.

Visitation: The practice of allowing friends or relatives to visit inmates.

Visiting Rules: Institutions typically have rules that specify who can visit, their mode of dress, the items that can be brought in, the frequency and length of the visit, and the extent of contact.

Visitor Centers: Provide a variety of services to the family members of inmates that visit them in prison. These services include transportation, child care, emergency clothing, information on visiting regulations and processes, referral to other agencies and services, emergency food, crisis intervention, and a sheltered area to use before and after visitation.

Voluntary Commitment: Admission to a correctional, residential, or medical facility or program for care or treatment without a court commitment and by personal choice.

Voyeurs: Individuals who achieve sexual arousal and release through secretly looking at nude persons, persons who are disrobing, or persons engaging in sexual activity.

WAIS: The Wechsler Adult Intelligence Scale. An individually administered intelligence test.

Walnut Street Jail: A jail in Philadelphia, Pennsylvania, that was converted to function as the first true prison in the United States.

Walsh-Healy Act of 1936: Prohibited the use of prison labor to fulfill general government contracts that exceeded $10,000.

Wanna-Be's: Young rookie gangs members looking for opportunities to break into the gang's core.

Wanton and Unnecessary: In the correctional context, this means actions of correctional personnel to control or deal with inmates that are characterized by reckless or unreasonable disregard of the rights and safety of others or evil intent

and not required by the circumstances of the situation.

Warden: *See* Superintendent.

Warrant: Any of a number of writs issued by a judicial officer that directs a law enforcement officer to perform a specified act and affords the officer protection from damage if he or she performs it.

Warrantless Searches: A search conducted without a warrant under one of a number of constitutionally permissible circumstances.

Warren Court: The Supreme Court in the 1950s and 1960s when Earl Warren was the chief justice. During this period, constitutional rights were extended to disenfranchised minority groups including accused criminals and prison inmates.

Watts: A black section of Los Angeles, California, that was the scene of widespread rioting during the summer of 1965.

Weekend Sentence: A form of intermittent sentence in which the time is served on weekends.

Wergild: *See* Compensation.

Whipping: Also known as flogging or scourging, this is one of the oldest, most widely used means of corporal punishment. It dates back to Egyptian times.

Windham School District: The nongeographical school district established in Texas specifically for conducting educational programs at Texas Department of Criminal Justice correctional facilities.

Withdrawal: An alternative chosen by many inmates to joining a gang or adopting a convict identity. The inmate withdraws from associating with the larger prison population, thereby guaranteeing his safety.

Wolves: *See* Jockers.

Women's Work: The term applied to work or jobs that have traditionally been done by women (e.g., secretary, cosmetician) which are generally low paying and have little prestige. These have been the most frequently offered training programs at women's prisons.

Workhouses: Penal facilities established in England and other European countries to reform those who were considered to be immoral or living in sin or who had committed minor crimes.

Working Ideologies: The development of officer work styles as a result of the beliefs developed from interactions with other groups in the institution.

Work Release: A community correctional program that allows specially selected inmates to work in the community without direct supervision while still incarcerated either at a prison or, most often, at a community residential facility.

Writ: A court document ordering or forbidding the performance of a specified act.

Writ of Detainer: An official notice from a government agency to a correctional agency noting that the person identified is wanted by the first agency and requesting that he or she not be released or discharged without notifying the first agency and giving it an opportunity to respond.

Yard: A feature of the Big House prison, it was typically enclosed by cell blocks and the prison's exterior wall. It was used by the inmates for recreation.

Yard Man: The chief trusty.

Young Lords: A prison gang that emerged from a street gang in Chicago in 1969. It was revolutionary in nature and guided by Marxist/Leninist/Maoist principles.

Youthful Offender: Offenders who fall somewhere between the ages of 13 and 24. There is little agreement among the various jurisdictions about what the age range should be.

Zidovudine (AZT)/Didanosine: Antiviral medications used for preemptive or early intervention treatment of AIDS.

*Some of the definitions of these terms and concepts are adapted from Search Groups, Inc. (1981). *Dictionary of Criminal Justice Data Terminology*. Washington, DC: U.S. Department of Justice.

References

A judge's view of society's 'losers.' (1988, January 7). *The New York Times.*

Abadinsky, H. (1994). *Probation and parole: Theory and practice* (5th ed.). Englewood Cliffs, NJ: Prentice Hall.

Abadinsky, H. (1997). *Probation and parole: Theory and practice* (6th ed.) Upper Saddle River, NJ: Prentice Hall.

Abbott, J. H. (1991). *In the belly of the beast.* New York: Vintage Books.

Abell, P. (1991). *Rational choice theory.* Aldershot, England: Edward Elgar Publishing Limited.

Acoca, L. (1998). Defusing the time bomb: Understanding and meeting the growing health care needs of incarcerated women. *Crime and Delinquency, 44*(1), 49–69.

Acoca, L., & Austin, J. (1996). *The crisis: The woman offender sentencing study and alternative sentencing recommendations project.* National Council on Crime and Delinquency.

Acoca, L., & Raeder, M. S. (1999). The plight of nonviolent offenders and their children. *Stanford Law and Policy Review.*

Adair, D. N., & Slawsk, T. D. (1991). Looking at the law: Fact-finding in sentencing. *Federal Probation, 55,* 58–72.

ADAM. (1999). *1998 annual report on drug use among adult and juvenile arrestees.* Washington, DC: National Institute of Justice.

Adams Commission. (1989). *The final report of the governor's commission to investigate disturbances at Camp Hill Correctional Institution.* Harrisburg, PA: Author.

Adams, D., & Fischer, J. (1976). The effects of prison residents' community contacts on recidivism rates. *Corrective and Social Psychiatry and Journal of Behavioral Technology Methods, 22,* 21–27.

Adams, K. (1992). Adjusting to prison life. In M. Tonry (Ed.), *Crime and justice: A review of research.* (pp. 275–358). Chicago: University of Chicago Press.

Adams, W. E., Barlow, R. B., Kleinfeld, G. R., Smith, R. D., & Wootten, W. W. (1968). *The western world, volume I: To 1700.* New York: Dodd, Mead & Company.

Adler, F. (1975). *Sisters in crime: The rise of the new female criminal.* New York: McGraw-Hill.

Agresti, D. (Former Director of Institutional Programs, PRIDE, Inc.) (1991). Personal communication.

Agresti, D. (undated). Liberty and justice for all? A question and answer pamphlet about the Death penalty—(compilation of seminar reports). Unpublished manuscript: University of South Florida.

Ahrens, C. (1998, April). Spirituality and health care in prison: Inmates faith may impact their well-being. *Corrections Compendium, 23*(4): 6–7.

Akre, B. S. (1994, September 4). Indian teens banished to islands. *Tampa Tribune/Times,* pp. 1, 7.

Alabama to make prisoners break rocks. (1995, July 28). *New York Times,* p. A5.

Albanese, J. S., Fiore, B. A., Powell, J. H., & Storti, J. R. (1981). *Is probation working?* Washington, DC: University Press of America.

Alexander, E. (1991). Proving "deliberate indifference" in the wake of Wilson v. Seiter. National Prison Project, 6(1), 3–5, 12.

Alexander, J. A., & Austin, J. (1992). *Handbook for evaluating objective prison classification systems.* Washington, DC: U.S. Department of Justice, National Institute of Corrections.

Allen, H. E., Carlson, E. W., & Parks, E. C. (1979, September). *Critical issues in adult probation: Summary.* Washington, DC: U.S. Department of Justice, National Institute of Law Enforcement and Criminal Justice.

Allen, H. E., Eskridge, C. W., Latessa, E. J., & Vito, G. F. (1985). *Probation and parole in America.* New York: The Free Press.

Allen, H. E., & Latessa, E. (1982). Half-way houses and parole: A national assessment. *Journal of Criminal Justice, 10*(2), 153–163.

Allen-Mills, T. (1997, April 20). American criminals sentenced to shame. *New York Times.*

Ambrosio, T. J., & Schiraldi, V. (1997). *From classroom to cell blocks: A national perspective.* Washington, DC: Justice Policy Institute.

Ambrosio, T. J., & Schiraldi, V. (1997). *Striking out: The crime impact of "three strikes laws."* Washington, DC: Justice Policy Institute.

American Association on Mental Deficiency. (1983). *Manual on terminology and classification in mental retardation* (H. J. Grossman, Ed.). Washington, DC: Author.

American Bar Association. (1977). *Joint committee on the legal status of prisoners.* Washington, DC: Author.

American College of Physicians, Human Rights Watch, National Coalition to Abolish the Death Penalty, and Physicians for Human Rights. (1994). *Breach of trust: Physician participation in executions in the United States.*

American Correctional Association. (1980). *Directory of juvenile and adult correctional departments, institutions, agencies & paroling authorities.* Laurel, MD: Author.

American Correctional Association. (1981a, May). *Guidelines for the development of policies and procedures for adult correctional institutions.* Laurel, MD: Author.

American Correctional Association. (1981b). *Standards for adult correctional institutions.* College Park, MD: Author.

American Correctional Association. (1983). *Design guide for secure adult correctional facilities.* Laurel, MD: Author.

American Correctional Association. (1983). *The American prison: From the beginning . . . A pictorial history.* College Park, MD: Author.

American Correctional Association. (1986a). *1985 directory of juvenile & adult correctional departments, institutions, agencies & paroling authorities.* Laurel, MD: Author.

American Correctional Association. (1986b). *A study of prison industry: History, components, and goals.* College Park, MD: National Institute of Corrections.

American Correctional Association. (1989). *Legal issues for correctional officers.* Laurel, MD: Author.

American Correctional Association. (1990a). *Causes, preventive measures, and methods of controlling riots and disturbances in correctional institutions* (3rd ed.). Washington, DC: Author.

American Correctional Association. (1990b). *Standards for adult correctional institutions.* College Park, MD: Author.

American Correctional Association. (1990c). *Causes, preventive measures, and methods of controlling riots and disturbances in correctional institutions* (3rd ed.). Washington, DC: Author.

American Correctional Association. (1992). *Directory of juvenile and adult correctional departments, institutions, agencies and paroling authorities.* Laurel, MD: Author.

American Correctional Association. (1993). *Directory of juvenile & adult correctional departments, institutions, agencies & paroling authorities.* Laurel, MD: Author.

American Correctional Association (1994). *Vital statistics in corrections.* Laurel, MD: Author.

American Correctional Association (1995). *Directory of juvenile & adult correctional departments, institutions, agencies & paroling authorities.* Laurel, MD: Author.

American Correctional Association. (1999). *Juvenile and adult correctional departments, institutions, agencies, and paroling authorities for the years 1982, 1993, 1999.* Lanham, MD: Author.

American Correctional Association. (undated). *Gangs in correctional facilities: A national assessment.* (Contract 91–IJ-CS-0026), [Unpublished report]. Washington, DC: National Institute of Justice, Office of Justice Programs, U.S. Department of Justice.

American Jail Association. (1992). Jail industries column. *American Jails, 6*(5), 96.

American Jail Association. (1992a). Resolutions. *American Jails, 6*(1), 123–130.

American Jails. (1994). Work in American jails; NIJ provides first national profile. *American Jails, 8*(2), 37.

American Probation and Parole Association. (1999). http://www.appa-net.org/issue1.html.

American Psychiatric Association. (1994). *Diagnostic and statistical manual of mental disorders (DSM IV)* (4th ed.). Washington, DC: Author.

Amnesty International. (1989a). *When the state kills . . . The death penalty: A human rights issue.* New York: Author.

Amnesty International. (1989b). *Amnesty International: 1988 report.* New York: Author.

Amnesty International. (1990). *Amnesty International: 1990 report.* New York: Author.

Amnesty International. (1991). *Amnesty International: 1991 report.* New York: Author.

Amnesty International. (1992). *Amnesty International: 1992 report.* New York: Author.

Amnesty International-USA (AIUSA). (1997). *Amnesty International report: 1997.* New York: Author.

Amnesty International-USA (AIUSA). (1999, April). *Abolitionist and retentionist countries.* http:// www.amnestyusa.org/abolish/abret.html.

Amnesty International-USA (AIUSA). (2000a, March). *Death penalty facts in the U.S.* Author.

Amnesty International-USA (AIUSA). (2000b, March). *Methods of execution in the USA.* http:// www.amnestyusa.org/abolish/methus.html.

Anderson, A. F. (1990). AIDS and prisoners' rights laws: Deciphering the administrative guideposts. In M. Blumberg (Ed.), *AIDS: The impact of the criminal justice system* (pp. 211–225). Columbus, OH: Merrill Publishing Co.

Anderson, E. (1978). *A place on the corner.* Chicago: University of Chicago Press.

Andrews, W. (1899). *Bygone . . . punishments.* London: William Andrews & Co.

Angelone, R. (1999). Protective custody. In P. M. Carlson & J. S. Garrett (Eds.), *Prison and jail administration* (pp. 226–245). Gaithersburg, MD: Aspen.

Anglin, M. D., & Hser, Y. (1990). Treatment of drug abuse. In M. Tonry & J. A. Wilson (Eds.), *Drugs and crime* (pp. 393–460). Chicago, IL: University of Chicago Press.

Angolite: The Prison News Magazine. (1981, January/February). Inside Angola: "Religion in prison"—A look at the pulpit behind bars. *Angolite,* pp. 31–56.

Anno, B. J. (1989, December). Prison health care: The state of the states. A paper presented at the Federal Bureau of Prisons conference on Prison Health Care Issues, Washington, DC.

Anno, B. J. (1991a). *Prison health care: Guidelines for the management of an adequate delivery system.* Washington, DC: National Institute of Corrections.

Anno, B. J. (1991b, July). Secretary, National Commission on Correctional Health Care. Personal communication.

Anno, B. J. (1993, December). Chairman, National Commission on Correctional Health Care. Personal communication.

Ansay, S. (1994, January). Personal communication. Gainesville, FL: University of Florida.

Apgar, E. (1998). Satellite tracking: Latest in defendant monitoring. *New Jersey Lawyer* (August 3): 5.

Arax, M. (2000, April). California and the West: Guards on trial in Corcoran shootings blame the prisoners. *Los Angeles Times,* p. 3.

Arax, M. (2000, June). 8 prison guards are acquitted in Corcoran battles. *Los Angeles Times,* p. 1.

Archembeault, W. G., & Archembeault, B. N. (1982). *Correctional supervision management.* Englewood Cliffs, NJ: Prentice-Hall.

Archer, D., Gartner, R., & Beittel, M. (1983). Homicide and the death penalty: A cross-national test of a deterrence hypothesis. *Journal of Criminal Law and Criminology, 74,* 991–1013.

Aric Press. (1986, October 6). Reported by D. Pederson, D. Shapiro, and A. McDaniel. Inside America's toughest prison. *Newsweek*, pp. 46–61.

Arnold, L. (1991). Florida Department of Corrections. Personal communication.

Arvonio, P. (1997). Former warden, East Jersey State Prison. Personal communication.

Assembly Committee on Public Safety. (1997). *Further examination of the* Romero *and* Alvarez *decisions*. Sacramento, CA: Author.

Associated Press. (1997, September 27). Money offered to stop beheading. *Tampa Tribune*, p. 5.

Atherton, E. (1999). Current practices. In C. Hemmens & E. Atherton (Eds.), *Use of force: Current practice and policy* (pp. 54–73). Lanham, MD: American Correctional Association.

Attorney General's Office, S. O. Hawaii. (1989). *Parole and Recidivism*. Honolulu, HI: Hawaii Criminal Justice Data Center.

Auerbach, B. J., Sexton, G. E., Farrow, F. C., & Lawson, R. H. (1988). *Work in American prisons: The private sector gets involved*. Washington, DC: National Institute of Justice.

Austin, D. R. (1996). Introduction and overview. In D. R. Austin & M. E. Crawford (Eds.), *Therapeutic recreation: An introduction* (2nd ed.). Boston: Allyn and Bacon.

Austin, J. (1993). Objective prison classification systems: A review. In American Correctional Association, *Classification: A tool for managing today's offenders* (pp. 108–123). Laurel, MD: American Correctional Association.

Austin, J. (1994, July). Managing offender classification: Is key to proper housing decisions. *Corrections Today, 56*(4), 94–96.

Austin, J., Bloom, B., & Donahue, T. (1992, April). *Female offenders in the community: An analysis of innovative strategies and programs*. Washington, D.C.: National Institute of Corrections, U.S. Department of Justice.

Austin, J., Clark, J., & Henry, D. (1997). *Three strikes and judicial discretion: A review of state legislation*. Washington, DC: National Institute of Justice.

Austin, J., & McVey, A. D. (1989, December). *The impact of the war on drugs*. San Francisco, CA: National Council on Crime and Delinquency.

Ayers, E. L. (1984). *Vengeance and justice: Crime and punishment in the 19th-century American south*. New York: Oxford University Press.

Ayres, M. B. (1988). *Food service in jails*. Alexandria, VA: The National Sheriffs' Association.

Bailey, W. C. (1990). Murder, capital punishment, and television: Execution publicity and homicide rates. *American Sociological Review, 55*, 628–633.

Baird, S. C., Heinz, R. C., & Bemus, J. (1982). *The Wisconsin case classification/staff deployment project: A two year followup report in classification*. College Park, MD: American Correctional Association.

Baldus, D. C., Woodworth, G., & Pulaski, C. A. (1990). *Equal justice and the death penalty: A legal and empirical analysis*. Boston: Northeastern University Press.

Bamford, P. W. (1973). *Fighting ships and prisons: The Mediterranean galleys of France in the age of Louis XIV*. Minneapolis: University of Minnesota Press.

Banished tribal teens sent to prison. (1995, October 2). Tampa Tribune, p. 5, Nation/World.

Banks, A., Porter, J., Tardin, R., Siler, T., & Unger, V. (1977). *Summary, phase I evaluation of intensive probation projects*. Washington, DC: U.S. Government Printing Office.

Barak-Glantz, I. (1986). Toward a conceptual scheme of prison management styles. *The Prison Journal, 61*, 42–60.

Barnes, H. E. (1968). *The evolution of penology in Pennsylvania: A study in American social history*. Montclair, New Jersey: Patterson Smith. (Original work published in 1927).

Barnes, H. E. (1969). *The repression of crime: Studies in historical penology*. Montclair, NJ: Patterson Smith. (Original work published 1926).

Barnes, H. E. (1972). *The story of punishment: A record of man's inhumanity to man* (2nd Edition revised). Montclair, NJ: Patterson Smith. (Original work published 1930).

Barnes, H. E., & Teeters, N. K. (1943). *New horizons in criminology: The American crime problem*. New York: Prentice Hall.

Barnes, H. E., & Teeters, N. K. (1951). *New horizons in criminology* (2nd ed.). Englewood Cliffs, NJ: Prentice Hall.

Barnes, H. E., & Teeters, N. K. (1959). *New horizons in criminology* (3rd ed.). Englewood Cliffs, NJ: Prentice Hall.

Barry, J. V. (1958). *Alexander Maconochie of Norfolk Island: A study of prison reform*. London, England: Oxford University Press.

Barry, J. V. (1972). Alexander Maconochie (1787–1860). In H. Mannheim (Ed.), *Pioneers in criminology* (2nd edition enlarged). Montclair, NJ: Patterson Smith.

Bartollas, C. (1985). *Correctional treatment: Theory and practice*. Englewood Cliffs, NJ: Prentice Hall.

Bartolo, A. (1991). The female offender in the bureau of prisons. In U.S. Department of Justice, *The June 7, 1991 forum on issues in corrections: Female offenders* (p. 2). Washington, DC: U.S. Department of Justice.

Bates, S. (1936). *Prison and beyond*. New York: Macmillan.

Batiuk, E. B. (1997). The state of post-secondary correctional education. *Journal of Correctional Education, 48*(3): 70–72.

Baunach, P. J. (1979). *Mothering behind prison walls*. Paper presented at American Society of Criminology meeting, Philadelphia.

Bayens, G. J., Williams, J., & Smykla, J. O. (1997). Jail type makes a difference: Evaluating the transition from a traditional to a podular direct supervision jail across ten years. *American Jails* (May/June): 35–36, 39.

BCEL. (1992, April). GED pays off. *Newsletter for the Business and Literacy Communities*, p. 8.

Beattie, J. M. (1986). *Crime and courts in England 1660–1800*. Princeton, NJ: Princeton University Press.

Beatty, C. (1997). *Parents in prison: Children in crisis*. Washington, DC: Child Welfare League.

Beccaria, C. (1963). *On crimes and punishments.* (H. Paolucci, Trans.) Indianapolis, IN: Bobbs-Merrill. (Original work published 1764)

Beck, A. J. (1991, April). *Profile of jail inmates, 1989.* Washington, DC: Bureau of Justice Statistics.

Beck, A. J. (2000, April). *Prison and jail inmates at midyear 1999.* Washington, DC: Bureau of Justice Statistics.

Beck, A. J., Bonczar, T. P., & Gilliard, D. K. (1993). *Jail inmates 1992.* Washington, DC: Bureau of Justice Statistics.

Beck, A. J., & Gilliard, D. K. (1995, August). *Prisoners in 1994.* Washington, DC: U.S. Department of Justice.

Beck, A., Gilliard, D., Greenfeld, L., Harlow, C., Hester, T., Jankowski, L., Snell, T., & Stephan, J. (1993, March). *Survey of state prison inmates, 1991.* Washington, DC: U.S. Department of Justice.

Beck, A. J., & Mumola, C. J. (1997). *Prisoners in 1996.* Washington, DC: U.S. Department of Justice.

Beck, A. J., & Mumola, C. J. (1999). *Prisoners in 1998.* Washington, DC: Bureau of Justice Statistics.

Beck, A. J., & Shipley, B. E. (1987). *Recidivism of young paroles.* Washington, DC: U.S. Department of Justice.

Beck, A., & Shipley, B. (1989). *Recidivism of prisoners released in 1983.* Washington, DC: Bureau of Justice Statistics.

Bedau, H. A. (Ed.). (1982). *The death penalty in America* (3rd ed.). New York: Oxford University Press.

Bedau, H. A., & Radalet, M. L. (1987). Miscarriages of justice in potentially capital cases. *Stanford Law Review, 40,* 21–179.

Belenko, S., Peugh, J., Califano, Jr., J. A., Usdansky, M., & Foster, S. E. (1998, October). Substance abuse and the prison population. *Corrections Today,* 82–89.

Belknap, M., Dunn, M., & Holsinger, K. (1997). *Moving toward juvenile justice and youth-serving systems that address the distinct experiences of the adolescent female: A report to the governor.* Columbus, OH: Office of Criminal Justice Services.

Bell, M. (1985). *The turkey shoot: Tracking the Attica coverup,* New York: Grove Press.

Bell, R., Conard, E., Laffey, T., Lutz, J. G., Simon, C., Stakelon, A. E., & Wilson, N. J. (1979). *Correctional educational programs for inmates.* Washington, DC: U.S. Department of Justice.

Bell, R., Conard, E. H., & Suppa, R. J. (1984). The findings and recommendations of the national study on learning deficiencies in adult inmates. *Journal of Correctional Education, 35*(4), 129–137.

Bellamy, J. (1973). *Crime and public order in England in the later middle ages.* London: Routledge & Kegan Paul.

Bellorado, D. (1986). *Making literacy programs work, Vol. 1, A practical guide for correctional educators.* Washington, DC: National Institute of Corrections.

Benestante, J. (1999). Educational specialist, Federal Programs and Grants. Windham School District, Texas Department of Criminal Justice. Personal communication.

Benestante, J. (2000). Personal communication.

Bennett, L. A. (1987, November). What has happened to prison visiting? Current use of a rehabilitative tool. Paper presented at the annual meeting of the American Society of Criminology, Montreal, Canada.

Bennett, L. A. (1989). Correctional administrators' attitudes toward private family visiting. *The Prison Journal, 66,* 110–114.

Bennett, L. A. (undated). *Problems in implementing and operating private prison visiting programs.* Sacramento, CA: Unpublished manuscript.

Berkman, R. (1979). *Opening the prison gates: The rise of the prisoners' movement.* Lexington, MA: Lexington Books.

Berlin, F., & Meinecke, C. F. (1981). Treatment of sex offenders with antiandrogenic medication: Conceptualization, review of treatment modalities, and preliminary findings. *American Journal of Psychiatry, 138,* 601–607.

Bernat, F. P., & Zupan, L. L. (1989). An assessment of personal processes pertaining to women in a traditionally male dominated occupation: Affirmative action policies in prisons and jails. *The Prison Journal,* pp. 64–73.

Besharov, D. J. (1992, July). Sex offenders: Is castration an acceptable punishment? *American Bar Association,* p. 42.

Bien, M. W. (1997). *Monitoring relief and financing litigation.* Prepared for the National Prison Project Litigation Conference.

Black, B. (1991, January/February). Juvenile confinement in Kentucky—A step in the right direction. *American Jails, 4*(5), 32–36.

Black, H. C., Nolan, J. R., & Nolan-Haley, J. M. (1991). *Black's Law Dictionary.* St. Paul, MN: West Publishing Co.

Bloom, B. (1988). *Women behind bars: A forgotten population.* Paper presented at the Academy of Criminal Justice Sciences, San Francisco.

Bloom, B., & Covington, S. (1999). *Gender-responsivity: An essential element in women's programming.* Paper presented at the National Conference on Women Offenders.

Bloom, I., & Steinhart, D. (1993). *Why punish the children?: A reappraisal of the children of incarcerated mothers in America.* San Francisco, CA: National Council on Crime and Delinquency.

Blount, W. R. (1994, July). Department of Criminology, University of South Florida. Personal communication.

Blount, W. R., Danner, T. A., Vega, M., & Silverman, I. J. (1991, Spring). The influence of substance abuse use among adult female inmates. *Journal of Drug Issues, 21*(2), 449–467.

Blumberg, A. (1970). *Criminal justice.* Chicago, IL: Quadrangle Books.

Blumberg, M. (1990). Issues and controversies with respect to the management of AIDS in corrections. In M. Blumberg (Ed.), *AIDS: The impact of the criminal justice system* (pp. 195–210). Columbus, OH: Merrill Publishing Co.

Blumenthal, W. H. (1962). *Brides from Bridewell: Female felons sent to colonial America.* Rutland, VT: Charles E. Tuttle Co.

Bohm, R. (1998). American death penalty: Past, present, and future. In J. R. Acker, R. M. Bohm, & C. S. Lanier (Eds.), *America's experiment with capital punishment: Reflections on the past, present, and future* (pp. 1–21). Durham, NC: Carolina Academic Press.

Bohm, R. M. (1991). American death penalty opinion, 1936–1986: A critical examination of the Gallup polls. In R. M. Bohm (Ed.), *The death penalty in America: Current research* (pp. 113–145). Cincinnati, OH: Anderson Publishing Co.

Bohm, R. M. (1992). Retribution and capital punishment: Toward a better understanding of death penalty opinion. *Journal of Criminal Justice, 20,* 227–236.

Bohn, S. E. (1993, December). Corrections mental health: New techniques and technologies bring basic theories up to date. *Corrections Today, 55*(7), 8, 12.

Bonczar, T. P. (1997). *Characteristics of adults on probation, 1995.* Washington, DC: Bureau of Justice Statistics, U.S. Department of Justice.

Bonczar, T. P., & Beck, A. J. (1997). *Lifetime likelihood of going to state and federal prison.* Washington, DC: Bureau of Justice Statistics.

Bonnie, R. J., Coughlin, A. M., & Jeffries, J. (Eds). (1997). *Criminal law.* Westbury, NY: Foundation Press.

Bonnyman, G. (1993). Reform advances in Tennessee after decades of brutality. *The National Prison Project Journal, 8*(4), 1–5.

Bonta, J., Wallace-Capretta, S., & Rooney, J. (2000). Can electronic monitoring make a difference? An evaluation of three Canadian programs. *Crime and Delinquency, 46*(1): 61–75.

Booth Gardner inks sex predator bill, & then pleads for more prisons. (1990, March 1). *Walla Walla Union Bulletin.* p. 1.

Booth, D. E. (1989). Health status of the incarcerated elderly: Issues and concerns. *Journal of Offender Counseling, Services and Rehabilitation, 13*(2), 193–213.

Boss, D., Schecter, J., & King, P. (1986, March). Food service behind bars. *Food Management,* pp. 83–87, 114, 120–136.

Boston, J. (1990, Fall). Case law report: Highlights of most important cases. *The National Prison Project Journal, 5*(4), 9–16.

Boston, J. (1991, Spring). Case law report: Highlights of most important cases—Crowding/damages/contempt/ pre-trial detainees. *The National Prison Project Journal, 6*(2), 6.

Boston, J. (1993/1994, Winter). Case law report. *The National Prison Project Journal, 9*(1), 13–15.

Boston, J. (1994). Highlights of most important cases. *The National Prison Project, 9*(3), 6–17.

Boston, J. (1995a, June 20). Director of the Prisoners' Rights Project, Legal Aid Society of New York. Personal communication. New York, NY.

Boston, J. (1995b, Sept. 25). Director of the Prisoners' Rights Project, Legal Aid Society of New York. Personal communication. New York, NY.

Boston, J., & Manville, D. E. (1995). *Prisoners self-help litigation manual.* New York: Oceania.

Bottoms, A. E., & Light, R. (1987). Introduction: Problems of long term imprisonment. In A. E. Bottoms & R. Light (Eds.), *Problems of long term imprisonment.* Aldershot, England: Gower Publishing Co.

Bowers, W. (1993). Research on the death penalty. *Law and Society Review,* 27, 157–175.

Bowers, W. J., & Pierce, G. L. (1980). Arbitrariness and discrimination under post-Furman capital statutes. *Crime and Delinquency, 26,* 563–635.

Bowker, L. (1982). *Corrections: The science and the art.* New York: Macmillan.

Bowker, L. H. (1980). *Prison victimization.* New York: Elsevier.

Boyce, R. N., & Perkins, R. M. (1989). *Cases and materials on criminal law and procedure.* Westbury, NY: The Foundation Press, Inc.

Bradley, E. (Reporter). (1986, January 27). *60 Minutes* report on prison gangs. New York: CBS News.

Braithwaite, J. (1998). *Restorative justice.* In M. Tonry (Ed.), *The handbook of crime & punishment* (pp. 323–344). New York: Oxford University Press.

Braithwaite, J. (1999). Life line: An alliance for progress. *Corrections Compendium, 24*(1): 15–17.

Brake, S. C., & Shannon, D. (1997). Using pretreatment to increase admission in sex offenders. In B. K. Schwartz & H. R. Cellini (Eds.), *The sex offender: New insights, treatments, innovations, and legal developments.* Kingston, NJ: Civic Research Institute.

Braly, M. (1967). *On the yard.* Boston: Little Brown and Co.

Braly, M. (1976). *False starts: A memoir of San Quentin and other prisons.* Boston: Little Brown and Co.

Brame, R., & Piquero, A. (1998). The police and the control function. In G. Alpert & A. Piquero (Eds.), *Community policing: Contemporary readings* (pp. 175–199). Prospect Heights, IL: Waveland Press.

Branch-Johnson, W. (1957). *The English prison hulks.* London: Christopher Johnson Publishers, Ltd.

Branham, L. S. (1992). *The use of incarceration in the United States: A look at the present and the future.* Chicago: American Bar Association.

Branham, L. S., & Krantz, S. (1997). *Cases and materials on the law of sentencing, corrections, and prisoners' rights* (5th ed.). St. Paul, MN: West.

Breed, A. (1996). Experienced master offers views on PLRA. *Correctional Law Reporter, 8*(2): 21–22, 26.

Brennan, T. (1987). Classification: An overview of selected methodological issues. In D. M. Gottfredson & M. Tonry (Eds.), *Prediction and classification: Criminal justice decision making.* Chicago: University of Chicago Press.

Brennan, T. (1993). Risk assessment: An evaluation of statistical classification methods. In American Correctional Association, *Classification: A tool for managing today's offenders* (pp. 46–70). Laurel, MD: American Correctional Association.

Brennan, T., & Wells, D. (1992). The importance of inmate classification in small jails. *American Jails, 6*(2), 49–52.

Bright, S. (1994, May). The death sentence not for the worst crime but for the worst lawyer. *Yale Law Journal, 103*: 1835–1883.

Bright, S. (1997a, June 26). *Capital punishment on the 25th anniversary of* Furman v. Georgia. Southern Center for Human Rights.

Britton, D. M. (1997). Perceptions of the work environment among correctional officers: Do race and sex matter? *Criminology*, *35*(1): 85–105.

Bronik, M. J. (1989, Fall). Relieving subpopulation pressures: The Bureau of Prisons' use of private correctional facilities. *Federal Prisons Journal*, 17–21.

Bronstein, A. J. (1985). Prisoners and their endangered rights. *Prison Journal*, *45*(1), 3–17.

Brooks, R. (1969). Domestic violence and America's wars: A historical interpretation. In H. D. Graham (Ed.), *The history of violence in America* (pp. 529–550). New York: Bantam Books.

Brown, C. (1965). *Manchild in the promised land.* New York: Signet Books.

Brown, J. M., & Langan, P. A. (1999). *Felony sentences in state courts, 1996.* Washington, DC: Bureau of Justice Statistics.

Brown, M. (1984). *Executive summary of research findings from the Massachusetts risk/need classification system. Report 5.* Boston, MA: Office of the Commissioner of Probation.

Brown, P. W. (1993). Probation officer safety and mental conditioning. *Federal Probation*, *57*(4), 17–21.

Brown, V. L. (1994, January 17). Session End Report. *New Jersey Lawyer*, p. 4.

Bryan, D. (1994). Dealing with violent inmates: Use of non-lethal force. *Corrections Compendium*, *19*(6), 1–2, 23.

Buchanan, R. A. (1986, Spring). An evaluation of objective prison classification systems. (Contract 84–IJ-CX-K029) [Unpublished report under Grant from National Institute of Justice, U.S. Department of Justice]. Kansas City: Correctional Services Group.

Buchanan, R. A., & Whitlow, K. L. (1987). *Guidelines for developing, implementing, and revising an objective prison classification system.* Washington, DC: National Institute of Justice.

Buchanan, R. A., Whitlow, K. L., & Austin, J. (1986). National evaluation of objective prison classification systems: The current state of the art. *Crime and Delinquency*, *32*(3), 272–290.

Buck, G. (1989). The effectiveness of the "new" intensive supervision programs. *Research in Corrections*, *5*, 64–75.

Buckley, W. F. (1978, September). Humiliating criminals is worth a try. *Tampa Tribune*, p. 11-A.

Buentello, S. (1986). *Texas syndicate: A review of its inception, growth in violence and continued threat to the Texas Department of Corrections* (Confidential and unpublished report). Huntsville, TX: Texas Department of Corrections.

Buentello, S. (1992, July). Combatting gangs in Texas. *Corrections Today*, 58, 59.

Buentello, S. (1997). Assistant director, Security Threat Group Management, Texas Department of Criminal Justice. Personal communication.

Buentello, S. (1999). Assistant director, Threat Security Group Management. Personal communication.

Bureau of Justice Assistance. (1996a). *How to use structured fines (day fines) as an intermediate sanction.* Washington, DC: U.S. Department of Justice.

Bureau of Justice Assistance. (1997). *Crime prevention and community policing: A vital partnership.* Washington, DC: U.S. Department of Justice, Office of Justice Programs.

Bureau of Justice Assistance. (1998). *1996 national survey of state sentencing structures.* Washington, DC: U.S. Department of Justice, Office of Justice Programs.

Bureau of Justice Statistics. (1981, May). *Prisoners in 1980.* Washington, DC: U.S. Department of Justice.

Bureau of Justice Statistics. (1982). *Prisoners 1925–81.* Washington, DC: U.S. Department of Justice.

Bureau of Justice Statistics. (1983, April). *Prisoners in 1982.* Washington, D.C.: U.S. Department of Justice.

Bureau of Justice Statistics. (1984). *State and federal prisoners, 1983.* Washington, DC: U.S. Department of Justice.

Bureau of Justice Statistics. (1984, April). *Prisoners in 1983.* Washington, DC: U.S. Department of justice.

Bureau of Justice Statistics. (1984, November). *The 1983 jail census.* Washington, DC: U.S. Department of Justice.

Bureau of Justice Statistics. (1985). *State and federal prisoners, 1984.* Washington, DC: U.S. Department of Justice.

Bureau of Justice Statistics. (1986). *State and federal prisoners, 1925–85.* Washington, DC: Author.

Bureau of Justice Statistics. (1986, June). *Prisoners in 1985.* Washington, DC: U.S. Department of Justice.

Bureau of Justice Statistics. (1987, December). *Correctional populations in the United States, 1985.* Washington, DC: U.S. Department of Justice.

Bureau of Justice Statistics. (1988a). *Report to the nation on crime and justice* (2nd ed.). Washington, DC: U.S. Department of Justice.

Bureau of Justice Statistics. (1988b, April). *Prisoners in 1987.* Washington, DC: U.S. Department of Justice.

Bureau of Justice Statistics. (1992, May). *Prisoners in 1991.* Washington, DC: U.S. Department of Justice.

Bureau of Justice Statistics. (1996b). *Correctional populations in the United States, 1994.* Washington, DC: U.S. Department of Justice.

Bureau of Justice Statistics. (1997). *Correctional populations in the United States, 1995.* Washington, DC: U.S. Department of Justice, pp. 5, 33, 127.

Bureau of Justice Statistics. (1997). *State and federal prisoners 1995.* Washington, DC: U.S. Department of Justice.

Bureau of Justice Statistics. (1999, April). *Correctional populations in the United States, 1996.* Washington, DC: Author, Table 1.20.

Bureau of the Census. (1993a). *Money income of households, families, and persons in the United States: 1992.* Washington, DC: U.S. Department of Commerce.

Bureau of the Census. (1993b). *Statistical abstract of the United States, 1993.* Washington, DC: U.S. Government Printing Office.

Burger, W. F. (1983). Factories with fences. *Pace Law Review, 4*(1), 1–9.

Burke, J. (1992, Feb. 7). Former prisoners say Russian abuses persist. *The Christian Science Monitor, The World*, p. 6.

Burke, P., & Adams, L. (1991). *Classification of women offenders in state correctional facilities: A hand book for practitioners.* Washington, DC: National Institute of Corrections.

Burlington, B. (1991, Winter). Involuntary treatment: When can mentally ill inmates be medicated against their will? *Federal Prison Journal, 2*(4), 25–29.

Burns, H. (1975). *Corrections organization and administration.* St. Paul, MN: West Publishing Co.

Burns, K. L. (1997). Return to hard time: The Prison Litigation Reform Act of 1995. *Georgia Law Review, 31*: 879–927.

Burrell, G., & Morgan, G. (1979). *Sociological paradigms and organizational analysis.* London: Heineman.

Bursik, R., Grasmick, H., & Chamlin, M. (1990). The effect of longitudinal arrest patterns on the development of robbery trends at the neighborhood level. *Criminology, 25*, 431–450.

Burstein, J. Q. (1977). *Conjugal visits in prison.* Lexington, MA: Heath.

Butterfield, F. (1995, March 23). California's courts clogging under its 'three strikes' law. *The New York Times*, pp. 1A, 9A.

Butterfield, F. (1995, October 5). More blacks in their teens and 20's have trouble with the law. *New York Times*, p. A8.

Buzbee, S. S. (1993, November 20). Prison escapees are in for a shock. *Tampa Tribune*, Sec. A, p. 1.

Byers, J. (1910). Prison labor. In C. R. Henderson (Ed.), *Penal and reformatory institutions: Correction and prevention.* New York: Charities Publication Committee.

Byrd, T., Cochan, J., Silverman, I., & Blount, W. (1998). Behind bars: An assessment of the effects of job satisfaction, job-related stress, and anxiety on jail employees' inclinations to quit. (Publication unknown).

Byrne, C. (1994, March 14). "Childish nonsense" or good politics? A punishing debate. *Washington Star Tribune*, p. 1A.

Byrne, J. (1986, March). The control controversy: A preliminary examination of intensive probation and supervision programs in the United States. *Federal Probation, 50*(1), 4–16.

Byrne, J. (1990). The future of intensive probation supervision and the new intermediate sanctions. *Crime and Delinquency, 36*, 6–41.

Byrne, J., Kelly, L., & Guarino-Ghezzi, S. (1988). Understanding the limits of technology: An examination of the use of electronic monitoring in the criminal justice system. *Perspectives, 12*(2), 30–37.

Byrne, J., Lurgio, A., & Baird, C. (1989). The effectiveness of the "new" intensive supervision programs. *Research in Corrections, 5*, 1–48.

Byrne, J., Lurgio, A., & Petersilia, J. (1992). *Smart sentencing: The emergence of intermediate sanctions.* Newbury Park, CA: Sage Publications.

Byrne, J. M., & Pattavina, A. (1992) The effectiveness issue: Assessing what works in the adult community corrections system. In J. M. Byrne, A. J. Lurgio, & J. Petersilia (Eds.), *Smart sentencing: The emergence of intermediate sanctions.* Beverly Hills: Sage.

Cabana, D. A. (1996). *Death at midnight: The confession of an executioner.* Boston: Northeastern University Press.

Cain, C. (1996, November). Guards fear fallout from state prison smoking ban: Union predicts increase in violence smuggling; restrictions start in '98. *Detroit News.*

Caldwell, R. G. (1947). *Red hannah.* Philadelphia: University of Pennsylvania Press.

Caldwell, R. G. (1965). *Criminology* (2nd ed.). New York: The Ronald Press Co.

California Code of Regulations. (1991). *Division 3. Department of Corrections.* San Francisco, CA: Barclay's Law Publishers.

California judge refuses to apply a tough new sentencing law (1994, July 20). *New York Times*, p. WA9.

Callender, D. (1993). Regional Director, New York Therapeutic Communities, Inc. Personal communication.

Camp, C. G., & Camp, G. M. (1997). *The corrections yearbook: 1997.* South Salem, NY: Criminal Justice Institute, Inc.

Camp, C. G., & Camp, G. M. (1998). *The corrections yearbook: 1998.* South Salem, NY: Criminal Justice Institute, Inc.

Camp, G. M., & Camp, C. G. (1985). *Prison gangs: Their extent, nature, and impact on prisons.* Washington, DC: U.S. Department of Justice, pp. 11, 19.

Camp, G. W., & Camp, C. G. (1985, July). *Prison gangs: Their extent, nature and impact on prisons.* Washington, DC: U.S. Government Printing Office.

Camp, G. W., & Camp, C. G. (1988). *Management strategies for combating prison gang violence.* South Salem, NY: Criminal Justice Institute.

Camp, G. M., & Camp, C. G. (1989, January). *Management of crowded prisons.* Washington, DC: National Institute of Corrections.

Camp, G. M., & Camp, C. G. (1992). *The corrections yearbook 1992: Adult corrections.* South Salem, NY: Criminal Justice Institute.

Camp, G. M., & Camp, C. G. (1994a). *The corrections yearbook: Adult corrections.* South Salem, NY: Criminal Justice Institute.

Camp, G. M., & Camp, C. G. (1994b). *The corrections yearbook 1994: Jail systems.* South Salem, NY: Criminal Justice Institute.

Camp, G. M., & Camp, C. G. (1994c). *The corrections yearbook 1994: Probation and parole.* South Salem, NY: Criminal Justice Institute.

Campaign for an Effective Crime Policy. *Public policy reports: "Three strikes"— Five years later.* Washington, DC: Author.

Campbell, J. S. (2000). Coordinator of Men's Ministries, Kairos, Inc. Personal communication.

Carleton, M. T. (1971). *Politics and punishment: The history of the Louisiana state penal system.* Baton Rouge, LA: Louisiana State University Press.

Carlson, P. M. (1999). Correctional officers today: The changing face of the workforce. In P. Carlson & J. S. Simon (Eds.),

Prison and jail administration: Practice and theory. Gaithersburg, MD: Aspen.

Carp, S. V., & Davis, J. A. (1989). *Design considerations in the building of women's prisons.* Washington, DC: Department of Justice.

Carrol, L. (1974). *Hacks, blacks and cons: Race relations in maximum security prison.* Lexington, MA: Lexington Books.

Carrol, L. (1977). Humanitarian reform and biracial sexual assault in a maximum security prison. *Urban Life, 5*(4), 417–437.

Carroll, L. (1988). Race, ethnicity, and the social order of the prison. In R. Johnson & H. Toch (Eds.), *The pains of imprisonment* (pp. 181–203). Prospect Heights, IL: Waveland Press, Inc.

Carroll, L. (1990). Race, ethnicity, and the social order of the prison. In D. H. Kelly (Ed.), *Criminal behavior: Text and readings in criminology* (2nd ed., pp. 510–527). New York: St. Martin's Press.

Carter, R. M. (1966). It is respectfully recommended. . . . *Federal Probation, 30,* (2), 38–42.

Carter, R., & Wilkins, L. (1976). Caseloads: Some conceptual models. In R. Carter and L. Wilkins (Eds.), *Probation, parole and community corrections.* New York: John Wiley and Sons.

Castro, J. A. (1992, March 9). Judge whose ideas nearly got him killed. *Time,* pp. 12, 16.

Catanese, R., & Hennessey, J. (1989). Fire safety. *Jail Operations Bulletin, 1*(3), pp. 3, 6.

Caulkins, J. P., Rydell, C. P., Schwabe, W. L., & Chiesa, J. (1997). *Mandatory minimum drug sentences: Throwing away the key or the taxpayers' money?* Santa Monica: Rand.

Cavadino, M., & Dignan, J. (1992). *The penal system: An introduction.* London: Sage Publications.

Cavan, R. S. (1962). *Criminology* (3rd ed.). New York: Thomas Y. Crowell Co.

Center on crime, communities, & culture. (1997). Education as crime prevention—providing education to prisoners. *Research Brief—Occasional Paper Series, 2.*

Centerforce. (1993). *Annual report to the legislature; fiscal year 1992/1993.* San Quentin, CA: Author.

Centerforce. (1998). http:// drake.marin.k12.ca.us/Centerforce/visited.html.

Cesarz, G., & Madrid-Bustos, J. (1991). Cultural awareness—New Mexico focuses on ethnic and minority issues. *Corrections Today, 53*(7), 68–71.

Chachere, V., & Lavelle, L. (1993, October 28). Prisons lose bid on new bill: Officials failed to get an exemption on a bill that would expand religious privileges. *Tampa Tribune,* Florida/Metro, p. 1.

Chaiken, J. M., & Chaiken, M. R. (1982). *Varieties of criminal behavior: Summary and policy implications.* Santa Monica, CA: The Rand Corporation.

Chaiken, M. (1989). *Prison programs for drug involved offenders.* Washington, DC: National Institute of Justice.

Chaiken, M., & Johnson, B. (1988). *Characteristics of different types of drug-involved offenders.* Washington, DC: National Institute of Justice.

Chambliss, W. J. (1964). A sociological analysis of the law of vagrancy. *Social Problems, 12,* 67–77.

Champion, D. J. (1990). *Probation and parole in the United States.* Columbus, OH: Merrill Publishing Co.

Champion, D. J. (1998). *Corrections in the United States* (2nd ed.). Upper Saddle River, NJ: Prentice Hall.

Chapman, J. (1980). *Economic realities and female crime.* Lexington, MA: Lexington Books.

Chastang, C. (1993, February 1). Smugglers' blues. *Los Angeles Times,* Metro, p. 3.

Cheatwood, D. (1988). The life-without-parole sanction: Its current status and a research agenda. *Crime and Delinquency, 34,* 43–59.

Cheek, F. E., & Miller, M. D. (1982). *Prisoners of life: A study of occupational stress among state corrections officers.* Washington, DC: American Federation of State, County, and Municipal Employees.

Chenault, P. (1951). Education. In P. W. Tappan (Ed.), *Contemporary corrections.* New York: McGraw-Hill.

Chesney-Lind, M. (1982). Guilty by reason of sex: Young women and the juvenile justice system. In B. Price & N. Sokoloff (Eds.), *The criminal justice system and women* (pp. 77–105). New York: Clark Boardman.

Chesney-Lind, M. (1986). Women and crime: The female offender. *Signs: Journal of Women in Culture and Society, 12,* 78–96.

Chesney-Lind, M. (1987). Female offenders: Paternalism reexamined. In L. L. Crites & W. L. Hepperle (Eds.), *Women, the courts, and equality* (pp. 114–139). Newbury Park, CA: Sage Publications.

Chiricos, T., & Waldo, G. (1970). Punishment and crime: An examination of some empirical evidence. *Social Problems, 18,* 200–217.

Chonco, N. R. (1989). Sexual assaults among male inmates: A descriptive study. *The Prison Journal,* 72–82.

CIA Newsletter. (1994, Spring). Death row inmates join Alabama's correctional industries program. *CIA Newsletter, 11*(2), 3.

Civil Rights Act of 1871 (42 U.S.C. Sec. 1983).

Clark, C. L., Aziz, D. W., & MacKenzie, D. L. (1994, August). *Shock incarceration in New York: Focus on treatment.* Washington, DC: National Institute of Justice.

Clark, D. (1989, July). Chuck Colson: Born again prison reformer. *Corrections Today,* 80, 81, 84.

Clark, D. D. (1991). *Analysis of return rates of the inmate college program participants.* Albany, NY: State of New York Department of Correctional Services.

Clark, M. (1986). Missouri's sexual offender program. *Corrections Today, 48*(3), 84, 85, 89.

Clark, R. J. (1998). Weight training in prison: Pros and cons. *Corrections Today, 59*(2): 16.

Clayton, S. L. (1997, November). Weight lifting in corrections: Luxury or necessity? *On the Line, 20*(5): 1, 3.

Clear, T. (1996). Backfire: When incarceration increases crime. *Journal of the Oklahoma Criminal Justice Consortium, 3*: 7–17.

Clear, T. R. (1988). A critical assessment of electronic monitoring in corrections. *Policy Studies Review, 7*(2): 671–681.

Clear, T. R. (1988). Statistical prediction in corrections. In J. Petersilia (Ed.), *Research in corrections* (Vol. 1, 1–35).

Clear, T., Flynn, S., & Shapiro, C. (1987). Intensive supervision probation: A comparison of three projects. In B. McCarthy (Ed.), *Intermediate punishments: Intensive supervision, home confinement and electronic surveillance.* Monsey, NY: Criminal Justice Press.

Clear, T., & Hardyman, P. (1990). The new intensive supervision movement. *Crime and Delinquency, 36*(1), 42–60.

Clements, C. B. (1979). Crowded prisons: A review of psychological and environmental effects. *Law and Human Behavior, 3,* 217–225.

Clemmer, D. (1958). *The prison community.* New York: Holt, Rinehart & Winston. (Originally published in 1940.)

Clines, F. X. (1994, October 17). A futuristic prison awaits the hard core. *The New York Times,* Sec. A. pp. 1, 12.

Cloward, R. A. (1969). Social control in prison. In. L. E. Hazelrigg (Ed.), *Prison within society: A reader in penology.* Garden City, NY: Anchor Books.

Cohen, F. (1988, November). *Legal issues and the mentally disordered prisoner.* Washington, DC: National Institute of Corrections.

Cohen, F. (1990). Correctional law in the 90's: My murky crystal ball says bodies will be the issue. *Correctional Law Reporter, 1,* 10–12.

Cohen, F. (1993). The legal context for mental health services. In H. J. Steadman & J. J. Cocozza (Eds.), *Mental illness in America's prisons.* Seattle, WA: National Coalition for the Mentally Ill in the Criminal Justice System.

Cohen, F. (1997). The sex offender. In B. K. Schwartz & H. R. Cellini (Eds.), *Registration and scarlet letter conditions.* Kingston, NJ: Civic Research Institute, pp. 30-1–30-5.

Cohen, J. (1983). *Incapacitating criminals: Recent research findings.* Washington, DC: U.S. Department of Justice, National Institute of Justice.

Cohen, L. (1981). *Prisoners in 1990.* Washington, DC: Bureau of Justice Statistics.

Cohen, R. L. (1991, May). *Bureau of Justice Statistics Bulletin: Prisoners in 1990.* Washington, DC: U.S. Department of Justice.

Cohen, S. B. (1991). Behind every good security system stand the people who make it work. *Corrections Today, 53*(4), 86, 88–90.

Cohn, A. W. (1973). The future of correctional management. *Crime and Delinquency, 19,* 323–331.

Cohn, A. W. (1979). The future of correctional management revisited. *Federal Probation, 33,* 10–15.

Cohn, A. W. (1981). The future of correctional management reconsidered. *Criminal Justice Review, 6,* 55–61.

Cohn, A. W. (1987). Behavioral objectives in probation and parole: A new approach to staff accountability. *Federal Probation, 51,* 40–49.

Cohn, A. W. (1991). The future of correctional management. *Federal Probation, 45,* 12–16.

Collins, B. (1998, October/November). *Benjamin:* Another view—second circuit approach may create confusion. *Correctional Law Reporter, 9*(4): 60–61.

Collins, W. C. (1986). *Correctional law 1986: An analysis and discussion of the key issues and developments in correctional law over the past year.* Olympia, WA: Author.

Collins, W. C. (1993). *Correctional law for the correctional officer.* Lanham, MD: American Correctional Association.

Collins W. C. (1997b). *Correctional law for the correctional officer* (2nd ed.). Lanham, MD: American Correctional Association.

Collins, W. C. (2000). Attorney at law and co-editor of *The Corrections Law Reporter.* Personal communication.

Colvin, M. (1982). The 1980 New Mexico prison riot. *Social Problems, 29*(5), 449–461.

Committee for the Revision of the 1954 Manual (1959). *Manual of correctional standards.* New York: The American Correctional Association.

Committee on Internal Security House of Representatives (1973a). *Staff study on revolutionary activity directed toward the administration of penal or corrections systems.* Washington, DC: U.S. Government Printing Office.

Committee on Internal Security House of Representatives (1973b). *Staff study: The National Lawyers' Guild.* Washington, DC: U.S. Government Printing Office.

Condemned man's mask burst into flames. (March). *New York Times,* p. 12A.

Conklin, J. E. (1992). *Criminology.* New York: Macmillan Publishing Co.

Conley, R. W., Luckasson, R., & Bouthilet, G. N. (1992). *The criminal justice system and mental retardation.* Baltimore, MD: Paul H. Brookes Publishing Co.

Connecticut Department of Corrections. (1995, May). *Gang membership.* Wethersfield, CT: Author.

Connecticut Department of Corrections. (1998). Corrections Officer Maintenance Program: Connecticut Department of Corrections. Submitted to the National Institute of Justice.

Connors, E. Lundregan, T. Miller, N., & McEwen, T. (1996). *Convicted by juries, exonerated by science: Case studies in the use of DNA evidence to establish innocence after trial.* Washington, DC: U.S. Department of Justice, Office of Justice Programs, National Institute of Justice.

Conrad, J. P. (1965). *Crime and its correction: An international survey of attitudes and practices.* Berkeley, CA.: University of California Press.

Conrad, J. P. (1981). *Adult offender education programs.* Washington, DC: U.S. Department of Justice.

Conrad, J. P. (1986). Research and development in corrections. *Federal Probation, 1*(3), 74–77.

Conrad, J. P., & Dinitz, S. (1978, September). The state's strongest medicine. Paper presented at the Colloquium on the Criminal Justice System, Columbus, OH.

Contact. (1988a, August). Furlough programs success rate high: Majority furlough lifers. *Corrections Compendium, 13*(3), p. 11.

Contact. (1988b, September–October). Furlough programs success rate high: Majority furlough lifers. *Corrections Compendium, 13*(3), 12–18.

Contact. (1992a, October). Correctional officers, Part I—Numbers, salaries. *Corrections Compendium, 17,* 9–11.

Contact. (1992b, October). Correctional officers, Part II—Requirements, training. *Corrections Compendium, 17,* 12–14.

Cook, I. (1999). Research associate, National Youth Gang Center. Tallahassee, FL. Personal communication.

Cook, P. J., and Slawson, D. B. (1993). Study finds each death penalty cost North Carolina more than $250,000. Durham, NC: Duke University News.

Coombs, E. (1991). The Simon of Cyrene Society: Stretching a helping hand to reformatory visitors. *Corrections Today, 53*(5), 114, 116, 118.

Cooper, W. M. (1870). *A history of the rod in all countries.* London: John Camden Hotten.

Copeland, R. C. (1980, August). *The evolution of the Texas Department of Corrections.* Unpublished master's thesis, Sam Houston State University.

Copley, E. W. (1995, July 3). State prisons inmates have to pay for part of college costs: Federal budget cuts force drops in courses. *State Journal-Register (Springfield, IL),* Local, p. 7.

Cornish, D. B., & Clarke, R. V. (Eds.). (1986). *The reasoning criminal: Rational choice perspectives on offending.* New York: Springer-Verlag.

Correctional Association of New York. (1990, September). *Imprisoned generation: Young men under criminal justice custody in New York State.* New York: Author.

Correctional Educational School Authority. (1988–1989). *Annual report.* Tallahassee, FL: Author.

Correctional Educational School Authority. (1990). *Academic and vocational program completers released from prison during fiscal year 1986–88: Employment, recidivism and cost avoidance.* Tallahassee, FL: Author.

Correctional Law Reporter. (February 1994a). Supreme Court accepts "I didn't know" as defense to failure to protect claim. *Correctional Law Reporter, 5*(2), 17–18, 26–29.

Correctional Law Reporter. (February 1994b). New rules, new law suits: RFRA means litigation and change for corrections. *Correctional Law Reporter, 5*(5), 65–66, 72–73.

Correctional Law Reporter. (February 1994c). What's a warden to do about RFRA? Well, don't just wait to be sued. *Correctional Law Reporter, 5*(5), 69.

Correctional Law Reporter. (1995). Federal district court judge rules that administrative segregation reviews must be "substantive and legitimate." *Correctional Law Reporter, 6*(6): 92.

Correctional Law Reporter. (1996). Habeas Corpus Reform Act may cut inmate petitions. *Correctional Law Reporter, 8*(1): 3.

Correctional Law Reporter. (1996). Many groups tackling problem of litigation—Congress may approve bill trimming court's power. *Correctional Law Reporter, 7*(5): 65–66, 73–77.

Correctional Law Reporter. (1996). Meritorious claims may hide in chaff of "frivolous" inmate lawsuits. *Correctional Law Reporter, 8*(1): 28–31.

Correctional Law Reporter. (1996). Prison Litigation Reform Act and Habeas Reform Law may drastically curtail inmate lawsuits. *Correctional Law Reporter, 8*(1): 1–2, 11–14, 24.

Correctional Law Reporter. (1996). Supreme Court tightens prisoners' right of access to the courts and remedial power of federal courts. *Correctional Law Reporter, 8*(2): 1–2, 28–31.

Correctional Law Reporter. (1998, June/July). Criminal charges, convictions catch correctional staff. *Correctional Law Reporter, 10*(1): 7.

Correctional Law Reporter. (1998, August/September). Force used against inmate who was beating staff member violated no rights of inmate. *Correctional Law Reporter, 10*(2): 21.

Correctional Law Reporter. (1998, October/November). No liability for rape of young, small inmate celled with sex offender. *Correctional Law Reporter, 10*(3): 39.

Correctional Law Reporter. (1999). Court bops gift book ban. *Correctional Law Reporter,* 24.

Correctional Law Reporter. (1999). Most inmate suits decided without trial—Here's how. *Correctional Law Reporter, X*(1), 5.

Correctional Law Reporter. (1999). Ninth circuit approves ban on frontal nudity in inmate magazines. *Correctional Law Reporter,* 35, 47.

Correctional Law Reporter. (1999). State courts not to inherit consent decrees dismissed under PLRA. *Correctional Law Reporter,* 5.

Correctional Law Reporter. (1999). State judge's stun belts defendant, shocks federal judge. *Correctional Law Reporter,* 37, 45.

Correctional law Reporter. (1999, December/January). Do PLRA's attorney fee limits apply to pending pre-PLRA cases? *Correctional Law Reporter, 10*(4): 54.

Correctional Law Reporter. (1999, February/March). Litany of force-related problems plaguing California DOC; raises questions about causes. *Correctional Law Reporter, 10*(5): 65–66.

Correctional Services Group, I. (1985). *Overview of objective prisoner classification.* Unpublished report. Kansas City, MO: Author.

Corrections Alert. (1998). California tests hard labor for parole violators. *Corrections Alert, 5*(5): 9.

Corrections Compendium. (1993, July). Survey: Correctional officer training—Pre-service/curricula hours. Author, pp. 5–15.

Corrections Compendium. (1994a, September). Hiring of correctional officers increasingly more selective—Part I: Numbers and salaries of C.O.s. *Corrections Compendium,* pp. 8–11.

Corrections Compendium. (1994b, September). Hiring of correctional officers increasingly more selective—Part II: Requirements, recruitment and training of C.O.s. *Corrections Compendium,* pp. 11–16.

Corrections Compendium. (1996). Prison violence survey. *Corrections Compendium, 22*(1): 13–25.

Corrections Compendium. (1997). Good time survey. *Corrections Compendium, 22*(1): 3–16.

Corrections Compendium. (1997). Survey of correctional officer training. *Corrections Compendium, 22*(8): 3–16.

Corrections Compendium. (1998). Female offenders: As their numbers grow, so does the need for gender-specific programming. *Corrections Compendium* (3): 23–24.

Corrections Compendium. (1998). Religion behind bars: Survey finds variety of beliefs, activities within correctional institutions. *Corrections Compendium, 23*(4): 8–22.

Corrections Compendium. (1998). Survey of correctional officers. *Corrections Compendium, 21*(8): 16–22.

Corrections Compendium. (1998, May). Mental illness and a chronic condition. *Corrections Compendium,* 1–6.

Corrections Compendium. (1999). Food service management in correctional settings. *Corrections Compendium, 24*(7): 6–19, 21.

Corrections Compendium. (1999a, October). Inmate health care—Part I. *Corrections Compendium,* 8–15.

Corrections Compendium. (1999b, November). Inmate health care—Part II. *Corrections Compendium,* 12–21.

Corrections Professional. (1997, August 8). Arizona DOC closes 34 inmate law libraries. *Corrections Professional, 2*(22): 1–3.

Corrections Professional. (1997, August 22). Where to draw the line with inmate legal access. *Corrections Professional, 2*(23): 1–3.

Corrections Professional. (1999). DOC settles with paralyzed inmate for 2.2 million. *Corrections Professional, 4*(18).

Corrigan, P. (1993, February 9). Police accuse county jail guard of supplying drugs to inmates. *St. Louis Post-Dispatch,* p. 1A.

Costanzo, Mark (1997). *Just revenge; costs and consequences of the death penalty.* New York, NY: St. Martin's Press.

Coste, C. (1976). Prison health care—Part of the punishment? *The New Physician, 25,* 29–35.

Cotton, D. J., & Groth, A. N. (1984). Sexual assault in correctional institutions: Prevention and intervention. In I. R. Stuart (Ed.), *Victims of sexual aggression: Treatment of children, women, and men.* New York: Van Nostrand Reinhold.

Covington, S. (1998). The relational theory of women's psychological development: Implications for the criminal justice system. In R. T. Zuplan (Ed.), *The female offender: Critical perspectives and effective interventions.* Gaithersburg, MD: Aspen.

Cowles, E. L. (1990a, December). Program needs for long-term inmates. In Federal Bureau of Prisons, *Long term confinement and the aging inmate population* (pp. 17–25). Washington, DC: Federal Bureau of Prisons.

Cowles, E. L., (1990b, December). Programming for long-term inmates: Executive summary. In Federal Bureau of Prisons, *Long term confinement and the aging inmate population* (pp. 114–119). Washington, DC: Federal Bureau of Prisons.

Cowles, E. L., Castellano, T. C., & Gramsky, L. A. (1995). "Boot Camp" drug treatment and aftercare intervention: An evaluation review. Washington, D.C.: U.S. Department of Justice.

Cox, B. (2000). Educational specialist, Federal Programs and Grants, Windham School District, Texas Department of Criminal Justice. Personal communication.

Cox, G. H., Jr., & Rhodes, S. J. (1990). Managing overcrowding: Corrections administrators and the prison crisis. *Criminal Justice, 4*(2), 115–143.

Crabtree, J. (1993). A small county jail: Wasecha, Minnesota. *American Jails, 7*(5), 62–66.

Crane. (1995). Crane on corrections: Access to a law library and inmates assisting inmates may not be the best ways of guaranteeing prisoners' right to court access. *Correctional Law Reporter, 7*(5): 67, 79.

Crawford, J. (1988). *Tabulation of a nationwide survey of state correctional facilities for adult and juvenile female offenders.* College Park, MD: American Correctional Association.

Crawford, W. (1969). *Report on the penitentiaries of the United States.* Montclair, NJ: Patterson Smith. (Original work published 1835.)

Crew, B. K. (1991). Sex differences in criminal sentencing: Chivalry or patriarchy? *Justice Quarterly, 8*(1), 59–83.

Cripe, C. A. (1997). *Legal aspects of corrections management.* Gaithersburg, MD: Aspen.

Cromwell, P., Marks, A., Olson, J., & Avary, D. W. (1991). Group effects on decision making by burglars. *Psychological Reports, 69,* 579–588.

Cromwell, P., Olson, J., & Avary, D. W. (1991). *Breaking and entering, an ethnographic analysis of burglary.* Newbury Park, CA: Sage Publications.

Crossette, B. (1997, September 30). UN monitor to investigate U.S. use of death penalty. *New York Times,* p. A8.

Crouch, B. M. (1980). *The keepers: Prison guards and contemporary corrections.* Springfield, IL: Thomas.

Crouch, B. M., & Marquart, J. W. (1989). *An appeal to justice: Litigated reform of Texas prisons.* Austin, TX: University of Texas Press.

Crutchfield, E., Garrette, L., & Worral, J. (1981, February). Recreation's place in prisons: A survey report. *Parks and Recreation,* 35–39, 73.

Culbertson, R., & Ellsworth, T. (1985). Treatment innovations in probation and parole. In L. Travis (Ed.), *Probation, parole and community corrections.* Prospect Heights, IL: Waveland Press.

Cullen, F. T., & Gilbert, K. E. (1982). *Reaffirming rehabilitation.* Cincinnati, OH: Anderson Publishing Co.

Cullen, F. T., Lutze, F. E., Link, B. G., & Wolfe, N. T. (1989). The correctional orientation of prison guards: Do officers support rehabilitation? *Federal Probation, 53,* 33–41.

Cullen, F. T., & Travis, L. F. (1984). Work as an avenue of prison reform. *New England Journal on Criminal and Civil Confinement, 9*(1), 1–20.

Cunniff, M. A. (1987). *Sentencing outcomes in 28 felony courts.* Washington, DC: National Association of Criminal Justice Planners.

Curry, T. H., II. (1993). Dealing with diversity. *Corrections Today, 55*(5), 168–172.

Cusac, A. (1996). Stunning technology: Corrections cowboys get a charge out of their new sci-fi weaponry. (Life in prison). *The Progressive, 60*: 18–22.

Cusson, M., & Pinsonneault, P. (1986). The decision to give up crime. In D. B. Cornish & R. V. Clarke (Eds.), *The reasoning criminal: Rational choice perspectives on offending* (pp. 72–82). New York: Springer-Verlag.

Dale, M. J. (1987). Who are these people and why are they suing us? *American Jails, 1*(3), 23–24.

Dale, M. J. (1989). Inmate medical care: Defining the constitutionally permissible level of care. *American Jails, 3*(2), 61–64.

Dale, M. J. (1991). The female inmate: An introduction to legal rights and issues. *American Jails, 4*(4), 56–58.

Dallao, M. (1996). Fighting prison rape: How to make your facility safe. *Corrections Today, 58*(7): 100–102, 106.

Darnton, J. (1993, February 6). After nearly 4 years, Rushdie has hope. *The New York Times*, p. 4.

Davidson, M. (1995, June 18). Chain-gang debate clangs; Inmates: Work is 'humiliating.' *Arizona Republic*, p. B1.

Davidson, T. R. (1983). *Chicano prisoners: The key to San Quentin.* Prospect Heights, IL: Waveland Press. (Originally published in 1974.)

Davis, E. K. (1978). Offender education in the American correctional system: An historical perspective. *Quarterly Journal of Corrections, 2*(2), 7–13.

Davis, J. R. (1998). Co-corrections in the U.S.: Housing men and women together has advantages and disadvantages. *Corrections Compendium, 23*(3): 1–3.

Davis, S. P. (1990, April). Inmates use of phones in prison "a positive that outweighs negatives." *Corrections Compendium, 15*(3), 9–16.

Davis, S. P. (1991, July). Survey: Number of sex offenders in prison increases 48%. *Corrections Compendium*, pp. 9–19.

Davis, S. P. (1992). Survey: Programs and services for female offenders. *Corrections Compendium*, September (9), pp. 7–20.

Davis, S. P. (1993a). Health care costs—10% of the pie. *Corrections Compendium, 18*(5).

Davis, S. P. (1993b, April). Survey: Work and educational release, 1993. *Corrections Compendium, 18*(4), 5, 22.

De Groot, A. S., Leibel, S. R., & Zierler, S. (1998). A standard of HIV care for incarcerated women: A northeastern United States experience. *Journal of Correctional Health Care, 5*(2), 139–176.

Death Penalty Information Center. (1993). *Sentencing for life: Americans embrace alternatives to the death penalty.* Washington, DC: Author.

Death Penalty Information Center. (1995, March). *Facts about the death penalty.* Washington, DC: Author.

Death Penalty Information Center. (1997a, December). *The death penalty in 1997: Year end report,* Washington, DC: Author.

Death Penalty Information Center. (1997b, November 24). *Facts about the death penalty,* Washington, DC: Author.

Death Penalty Information Center. (1998). *The death penalty in 1998: Year end report December 1998.* Washington, DC: Author.

Death Penalty Information Center. (2000). *Executions in the U.S. from 1930 to 2000.* http:// www.essential.org/dpic.

Death Penalty Information Center. (2000b). *Public opinion about the death penalty.* http:// www. essential.org/dpic.

Death Penalty Information Center. (2000e). *Facts about clemency.* http:// www.essential.org/dpic.

Del Carmen, R., & Vaughn, J. (1986). Legal issues in the use of electronic surveillance in probation. *Federal Probation, 50*(2), 60–66.

deLangy, G. (1854). *The knout and the Russians.* New York: Harper & Brothers, Publishers.

DeLeon, G. (1984). *The therapeutic community: Study of effectiveness.* Rockville, MD: National Institute of Drug Abuse.

DeLeon, G. (1985). The therapeutic community: Status and evolution. *International Journal of Addictions, 20,* 823–844.

DeLeon, G. (1994). Therapeutic communities. In M. Galanter & H. D. Kleber (Eds.), *The American Psychiatric Press textbook of substance abuse treatment.* Washington, DC: American Psychiatric Press.

Delguzzi, K. (1993, May 21). Prison guard accused of smuggling ammo inside. *The Cincinnati Enquirer.*

Dell'Apa, F. (1973). *Educational programs in adult correctional institutions: A survey.* Boulder, CO: The Western Interstate Commission for Higher Education.

DeMaret, W. F. (1991). Time to think: Social/cognitive skills programming in transition in New Mexico. *Journal of Correctional Education, 42*(2), 107–110.

Deming, B. (1966). *Prison notes.* Boston: Beacon Press.

Deutsch, M. (1998). Attorney at law, active in the defense of Attica prisoners for over 20 years. Personal communication.

Deutsch, M. E. (1993). Attorney for the inmate plaintiffs in Attica civil rights suits. Personal communication.

Deutsch, M. E., Cunningham D., & Fink, E. M. (1991). Twenty years later—Attica civil rights case finally cleared for trial. *Social Justice, 18*(3), 13–25.

DeVolentine, J. (1993). Program Director, Florida Correctional Mental Health Institution. Personal communication.

DeVolentine, J. M. (1996/1997). Juvenile justice manager, Florida Department of Juvenile Justice. Personal communication.

DeVolentine, J. M. (1999). Programs manager, Florida Department of Juvenile Justice. Personal communication.

Dickey, W. (1979). The lawyer and the accuracy of presentence reports. *Federal Probation, 43,* 28–38.

Dieter, R. (1996). *Killing for votes: The dangers of politicizing the death penalty process.* Washington, DC: Death Penalty Information Center.

Dieter, R. (1997). *Innocence and the death penalty: The increasing danger of executing the innocent.* Washington, DC: Death Penalty Information Center.

Dieter, R. C. (1995, October). With justice for few: The growing crisis in death penalty representation. Washington, DC: Death Penalty Information Center.

DiIulio, J. J., Jr. (1987). *Governing Prisons.* New York, NY: McMillan.

DiIulio, J. J., Jr. (1991). *No escape.* New York: Basic Books.

Dinitz, S. (1980). Are safe and humane prisons possible? The John Vincent Barry Memorial Lecture, University of Melbourne, Australia.

Dinitz, S., & Huff, C. R. (1988). *The Figgie report part VI: The business of crime: The criminal perspective.* Richmond, VA: Figgie International, Inc.

Dison, J. E. (1991, November). *A brief history of the Arkansas prison system through the mid 1960s.* Paper presented at the annual meeting of the American Society of Criminology, San Francisco.

Ditton, P. M. (1999). *Truth in sentencing in state prisons.* Washington, DC: Bureau of Justice Statistics.

Ditton, P. M. (1999, July). *Mental health and treatment of inmates and probationers.* Washington, DC: Bureau of Justice Statistics, p. 46.

Dobash, R. P., Dobash, R. E., & Gutteridge, S. (1986). *The imprisonment of women.* Oxford, England: Basil Blackwell, Ltd.

Doeran, S., & Hageman, M. (1982). *Community corrections.* Cincinnati, OH: Anderson Publishing Co.

Donaldson, S. (1993, December 29). The rape crisis behind bars. *The New York Times,* p. 11A.

Donnelly, P. G., & Forschner, B. R. Predictors of success in a co-correctional halfway house: A discriminant analysis. In T. Ellsworth (Ed.), *Contemporary community corrections.* Prospect Heights, IL: Waveland Press.

Dooley, E. E. (1981, Winter). Sir Walter Crofton and the Irish or intermediate system of prison discipline. *New England Journal on Prison Law, 72.*

Dorin, D., & Johnson, R. (1979). The premature dragon: George Jackson as model for the new militant inmate. *Contemporary Crises, 3,* pp. 295–315.

Dorman, M. (1995, June 18). On the chain gang. *Newsday,* p. 7.

Dormer, S. G. (1997). Twenty-sixth annual review of criminal procedure: VI. Prisoners' rights. *Georgetown Law Journal, 85*(4): 1561–1615.

Drennon, D. (1999). Classification officer, Federal Bureau of Prisons. Personal communication.

Driven out sex offender returns to town. (1993, August 14). *New York Times-Final,* 1, p. 23.

Drug Court Program Office and Technical Assistance Project. *Looking at a decade of drug courts.* Washington, DC: U.S. Department of Justice, Drug Courts Program Office.

Duffee, D. (1980). *Correctional management.* Englewood Cliffs, NJ: Prentice Hall.

Dugan, B. (1998). Juveniles in adult jails: More kids in jail. Presentation at American Jail Association Training Conference, April 29, 1988. *American Jails, 12*(4): 79–85.

Dugger, R. L. (1988, June). The graying of America's prisons: Special care considerations. *Corrections Today,* pp. 26–28.

Dugger, R. L. (1990). Life and death in prison. *The Prison Journal, 70*(1), 112–114.

Dumond, R. W. (1992). The sexual assault of male inmates in incarcerated settings. *International Journal of Sociology, 20:* 135–157.

Dwyer, D. C., & McNally, R. B. (1993, June). Public policy, prison industries, and business: An equitable balance for the 1990s. *Federal Probation,* 30–36.

Earle, A. M. (1969). *Curious punishments of bygone days.* Montclair, NJ: Patterson Smith. Originally published 1896.

Earley, P. (1992). *The hot house: Life inside Leavenworth Prison.* New York: Bantam Books.

Edwards, E. M., Granfield, J., & Onnen, J. (1997). *Evaluation of pepper spray.* Washington, DC. National Institute of Justice.

Edwards, T. (1999). The aging inmate population. *SLC special series report.* Longmont, CO: NIC.

Egan, T. (1994, February 15). It's not as simple as it seems. *The New York Times,* p. 1.

Ehrlich, I. (1975). The deterrent effect of capital punishment: A question of life and death. *American Economic Review, 65:* 397–417.

Eigenberg, H. (1990, July). Male rape: An empirical examination of correctional officers' attitudes toward rape in prison. *The Prison Journal,* 39–56.

Eigenberg, H. M. (1994). Rape in male prisons: Examining the relationships between correctional officers' attitudes toward male rape and their willingness to respond to acts of rape. In M. Braswell, R. H. J. Montgomery, & L. X. Lombardo (Eds.), *Prison violence in America* (2nd ed.). Cincinnati, OH: Anderson.

Ekirch, A. R. (1987). *Bound for America: The transportation of British convicts to the colonies 1718–1775.* Oxford: Clarendon Press.

Ellis, A. (1980). An overview of the clinical theory of rational-emotive therapy. In R. Greiger, & J. Boyd (Eds.), *Rational-emotive therapy: A skills based approach.* New York: Van Nostrand Reinhold.

Ellis, J. W., & Luckasson, R. A. (1985). Mentally retarded defendants. *George Washington Law Review, 53*(3–4), 483.

Embert, P. S., & Kalinich, D. B. (1988). *Behind the walls.* Salem, WI: Sheffield Publishing Co.

Empey, L. (1967). *Alternatives to incarceration.* Washington, DC: U.S. Department of Health, Education and Welfare, Office of Juvenile Delinquency and Youth Development.

EMT Associates, Inc. (1985). *Evaluation of the M-2 sponsors program.* Sacramento, CA: Author.

EMT Associates, Inc. (1987). *Evaluation of the M-2 sponsors program: Final report.* Sacramento, CA: Author.

Engleman, L. (1995, June/July). Take two prisoners and call me in the morning. *CorrecCare*, 3.

Erwin, B. (1987). *Evaluation of intensive probation supervision in Georgia*. Atlanta, GA: Department of Offender Rehabilitation.

Erwin, B. (1990). Old and new tools for the modern probation officer. *Crime and Delinquency, 36*(1), 61–74.

Exum, J. G., Jr., Turnbull, H. R., III, Martin, R. and Finn, J. W. (1992). Point of view: Perspectives on the judicial, mental retardation services, law enforcement, and correctional systems. In R. W. Conley, R. Luckasson, & G. N. Bouthilet (Eds.), *The criminal justice system and mental retardation: Defendants and victims* (pp. 8–16). Baltimore, MD: Paul H. Brookes Publishing Co.

Fabiano, E. A. (1991). How education can be correctional and how corrections can be educational. *Journal of Correctional Education, 42*(2), 100–106.

Fagan, T. J., Wennerstrom, D., & Miller, J. (1996). Sexual assault of male inmates: Prevention, identification, and intervention. *Journal of Correctional Health Care, 3*(1): 49–63.

Farbstein J., & Wiener, R. (1989, June 1). *A comparison of corrections "direct" and "indirect" supervision correctional facilities. Final report Grant GG-1*. Washington, DC: U.S. Department of Justice, National Institute of Corrections.

Farkas, M. A. (1997). The normative code among correctional officers: An exploration of components and functions. *Journal of Crime and Delinquency, 20*(1): 23–36.

Farkas, M. A., & Rand, R. L. (1999). Sex matters: A gender-specific standard for cross-gender searches of inmates. *Women and Criminal Justice, 10*(3): 31–55.

Faucheaux, R. (1994, March). Analysis: The politics of crime. *Campaigns and Elections, Inc., 15*(4), 5.

Fayol, H. (1916). General and industrial management. In J. M. Shafritz, & J. S. Ott (Eds.), *Classics of organizational theory* (4th ed., 1996, pp. 52–65). New York: Harcourt Brace.

Federal Bureau of Investigation. (1994). *Crime in the United States 1993 (Uniform Crime Report)*. Washington, DC: U.S. Department of Justice.

Federal Bureau of Investigation. (1997). *Crime in the United States 1996*. Washington, DC: U.S. Department of Justice.

Federal Bureau of Investigation. (1998). *Crime in the United States 1997*. Washington, DC: U.S. Department of Justice.

Federal Bureau of Investigation. (1999). *Crime in the United States, 1998*. Washington, DC: U.S. Department of Justice.

Federal Bureau of Prisons. (1988). *Program statement: Firearms and badges*. Washington, DC: Author.

Federal Bureau of Prisons. (1994). *State of the Bureau 1993*. Washington, DC: U.S. Department of Justice.

Federal Bureau of Prisons. (1995). *Common fare: Religious diet program*. Washington, DC: U.S. Department of Justice.

Federal Bureau of Prisons. (1995). *Sexual assault prevention/intervention programs for inmates*. Washington, DC: Author.

Federal Bureau of Prisons. (1998). *State of the bureau: Accomplishments*. Washington, DC: Author.

Federal Bureau of Prisons. (undated). *A working manual of day-to-day procedures for field chaplains*. Washington, DC: Author.

Feinman, C. (1986). *Women in the criminal justice system*. New York: Praeger.

Fickenauer, J. O. (1988). Public support for the death penalty: Retribution as just deserts or retribution as revenge? *Justice Quarterly, 5*, 81–100.

Finger, M. (1993, February 26). A judge's sentence may be, write one. *The New York Times*, p. B10.

Fink, M. J., Goodman, A. K., Hight, E., Miller-Mack, E., & De Groot, A. (1998). Critical prevention, critical care: Gynecological and obstetrical aspects of comprehensive HIV prevention and treatment among incarcerated women. *Journal of Correctional Health Care, 5*(2): 201–223.

Finn, P. (1989). Decriminalization of public drunkenness: Response of the healthcare system. *Journal of Studies on Alcohol, 46*, 7.

Finn, P. (1997). Sex offender community notification. *Research in action*. Washington, DC: National Institute of Justice.

Finn, P. (1998, June). *Texas project RIO*. Washington, DC: U.S. Department of Justice.

Finn, P., & Newlyn, A. K. (1993). *"Miami's Drug" court—a different approach*. Washington, DC: National Institute of Justice.

Finn, P., & Sullivan, M. (1988). *Police response to special populations*. Washington, DC: National Institute of Justice.

Fisher, I. (1994, January). Why '3-strike' sentencing is a solid hit this year. *The New York Times*, p. A16.

Fisher, M., O'Brien, E., & Austin D. T. (1987). *Practical law for jail and prison personnel*. St. Paul, MN: West Publishing Co.

Fishman, J. F. (1934). *Sex in prison: Revealing sex conditions in American prisons*. New York: National Library Association.

Fishman, L. T. (1990). *Women at the wall*. Albany, NY: State University of New York Press.

Flanagan, T. J. (1989). Prison labor and industry. In L. Goodstein & D. L. MacKenzie (Eds.), *The American prison*. New York: Plenum Press.

Flanagan, T. J. (1991, Spring). Long-term prisoners: Their adaptation and adjustment. *Federal Prison Journal*, 45–51.

Flanagan, T. J. (1996). Community corrections in the public mind. *Federal Probation, 60*(3): 3–9.

Flanagan, T. J. (1996). Reform or punish: Americans' views of the correctional system. In T. J. Flanagan & D. J. Longmire (Eds.), *Americans view crime and justice*. Thousands Oaks, CA: Sage.

Flanagan, T. J., Hindelang, M. J., & Gottfredson, M. R. (1980). *Sourcebook of criminal justice statistics—1979*. Washington, DC: U.S. Department of Justice.

Flanagan, T. J., & Longmire, D. R. (Eds.). (1996). *Americans view crime and justice: A national public opinion survey*. Thousand Oaks, CA: Sage.

Flanagan, T. J., Thornberry, T. P., Maguire, K. E., & McGarrell, E. F. (1988). *The effect of prison industry employment on offender behavior: Final report of the prison industry research project*.

Albany, NY: State University of New York, Hindelang Criminal Justice Research Center.

Fleisher, M. S., & Rison, R. H. (1999). Gang management in corrections: An organizational strategy. In P. Carlson & J. S. Simon (Eds.), *In prison and jail administration.* Gaithersburg, MD: Aspen.

Florida Auditor General Department of Corrections. (1994, March 4). *Performance audit of the prison industries program administered by Prison Rehabilitative Industries and Diversified Enterprises, Inc.* Tallahassee, FL: Author.

Florida Corrections Commission. (1997, June). *Execution methods used by states* (supplement).

Florida Department of Corrections. (1982, March). *Policy and procedure directive: Chaplaincy services.* Tallahassee, FL: Author.

Florida Department of Corrections. (1988). *Annual report 1987/88.* Tallahassee, FL: Author.

Florida Department of Corrections. (1991). *Annual report 1989/90.* Tallahassee, FL: Author.

Florida Department of Corrections. (1991, November 22). *Rules of the Department of Corrections: Use of force—rule No. 33-3.0066.* Tallahassee, FL: State of Florida.

Florida Department of Corrections. (1993). *Annual report 1991/92.* Tallahassee, FL: Author.

Florida Department of Criminal Justice Standards and Training Commission. (1999). *Use of force/levels of resistance matrix, basic recruit training program.* Tallahassee, FL: Author.

Florida Department of Juvenile Justice. (1997). *Annual Report 1996–1997.* Tallahassee: Author.

Florida Department of Law Enforcement. (1990). *School resource officer student guide.* Tallahassee, FL: Author.

Florida TaxWatch Inc. (1989). *PRIDE—Is Florida's prison industries experiment succeeding.* Tallahassee, FL: Author.

Florida TaxWatch Inc. (1991). *Making our correctional education investment pay off.* Tallahassee, FL: Author.

Flynn, E. E. (1992). The graying of America's prison population. *The Prison Journal, 72*(1&2), 77–98.

Flynn, F. T. (1951). Employment and labor. In P. W. Tappan (Ed.), *Contemporary correction.* New York: McGraw-Hill.

Fogel, C. I. (1991). Mothers in prison. *American Academy of Nurses.*

Fogel, C. I. (1993). Hard time: The stressful nature of incarceration for women. *Issues in Mental Health Nursing, 14*: 367–377.

Fogel, C. I. (1998). Associate professor, School of Nursing, University of North Carolina. Personal communication.

Fogel, D. (1979). *We are the living proof: The justice model for corrections.* Cincinnati, OH: Anderson Publishing Co.

Fong, R. (1990). The organizational structure of prison gangs: A Texas case study. *Federal Probation, 54*(1), 36–43.

Fong, R. S., & Buentello, S. (1991, March). The detection of prison gang development: An empirical assessment. *Federal Probation,* pp. 66–69.

Fong, R. S., Vogel, R. E., & Buentello, S. (1992). Prison gang dynamics: A look inside the Texas Department of Correc-

tions. In P. J. Benekos & A. V. Merlo (Eds.), *Corrections: Dilemmas and directions.* Cincinnati, OH: Anderson Publishing Co.

Fong, R. S., Vogel, R. E., & Buentello, S. (1995). Blood-in, blood-out: The rationale behind defecting from prison gangs. *Journal of Gang Research, 2*(4): 48.

Fong, R. S., Vogel, R. E., & Buentello, S. (1996). Prison gang dynamics: A research update. In J. M. Miller & J. P. Rush (Eds.), *Gangs: A criminal justice approach.* Cincinnati, OH: Anderson.

Fong, R. S., Vogel, R. E., Little, R. E. & Buentello, S. (1991). Prison violence and disruption: An analysis of hispanic, black and white prison gangs. Paper presented at the annual meeting of the Academy of Criminal Justice Sciences, Nashville, TN.

Former prison guard admits accepting bribes from inmates. (1993, July 9). United Press International.

Foster, C. D., Siegel, M. A., & Jacobs, N. R. (Eds.). (1992). *Capital punishment: Cruel and unusual?* Wylie, TX: Information Plus.

Fox, J. (1996). *Trends in juvenile violence: A report to the attorney general of the United States on the current and future rates of juvenile offending.* Boston, MA: Northeastern University.

Fox, J. G. (1982). *Organizational and racial conflict in maximum security prisons.* Lexington, MA: Lexington Books.

Fox, J., Radalet, M., & Bonsteel, J. (1990). Death penalty opinion in the post-Furman years. *New York University Review of Law and Social Change, 18*, 499–528.

Fox, V. (1956). *Violence behind bars.* Westport, CT: Greenwood Press.

Fox, V. (1983). *Correctional institutions.* Englewood Cliffs, NJ: Prentice Hall.

Frank, J., & Applegate, B. K. (1998). Assessing juror understanding of capital sentencing. *Crime and Delinquency, 44*(3): 412–433.

Frase, R. S. (1993, February). Prison population growing under Minnesota guidelines. *Overcrowded Times, 4*(1), p. 1.

Freedman, E. (1981). *Their sisters' keepers: Women's prison reform in America, 1830–1930.* Ann Arbor, MI: University of Michigan.

Freeman, R. M. (1997). Remembering the Camp Hill riot. *Corrections Today, 59*(1), 56–59.

Freeman, R. W., & Johnson L. (1982). Health related knowledge, attitudes and practices of correctional officers. *Journal of Prison and Jail Health, 2*(2), 125–138.

Friedrichs, D. (1989). Comment—Humanism and the death penalty. *Justice Quarterly, 6*, 197–211.

Friel, J. (1984). Staff perceptions of prisoner life tasks in a Canadian penitentiary. *Canadian Journal of Criminology, 26*(3), 355–357.

From thief to cell block sex slave: A convict's testimony. (1997, Oct. 19). *New York Times,* sec. 4, p. 7.

Funke, G., Wayson, B., & Miller, N. (1982). *Assets and liabilities of correctional industries.* Lexington, MA: Lexington Books.

Gaes, G. (1990a, December). Fact finding information. In Federal Bureau of Prisons, *Long term confinement and the aging inmate population* (pp. 5–12). Washington, DC: Federal Bureau of Prisons.

Gaes, G. (1990b, December). Long term inmates—A preliminary look at their programming needs and adjustment patterns. In Federal Bureau of Prisons, *Long term confinement and the aging inmate population* (pp. 82–93). Washington, DC: Federal Bureau of Prisons.

Gaes, G. (1998). Correctional treatment. In M. Tonry (Ed.), *The handbook of crime & punishment* (pp. 712–738). New York: Oxford University Press.

Gaffigan, S. J. (1994). *Understanding community policing.* Washington, DC: U.S. Department of Justice, Office of Justice Programs, Bureau of Justice Assistance.

Gailium, M. (1997, July). Telemedicine takes off. *Corrections Today*, 68–70.

Gainey, R. R., & Payne, B. K. (2000). Understanding the experience of house arrest with electronic monitoring: An analysis of quantitative and qualitative data. *International Journal of Offender Therapy and Comparative Criminology, 44*(1): 84–96.

GAO. (1997). *Drug courts: Overview of growth, characteristics, and results.* Washington, DC: General Accounting Office.

GAO. (1999). *Women in prison: Issues and challenges confronting the U.S. correctional system.* Washington, DC: General Accounting Office.

Garcia, S. A., & Steele, H. V. (1988). Mentally retarded offenders in the criminal justice system and mental retardation services systems in Florida: Philosophical, treatment and placement issues. *Arkansas Law Review, 41*(4), 809–859.

Gardner, E. (1992). Regional jails. *American Jails, 6*(2), 45–47.

Gardner, R. (1981). Guard stress. *Corrections Magazine*, 7, 6–14.

Garey, M. (1985). The cost of taking a life: Dollars and sense of the death penalty, pp. 1253–1255, 1269.

Garibaldi, M., & Moore, M. (1981, April). The treatment team approach. *Journal of Physical Education and Recreation, 52*(4), 28–32.

Garner, B. (Ed.). (1999). *Blacks law dictionary* (7th ed.). St. Paul, MN: West.

Garrett, D. G. (1993, November 15). Pretrial Programs Director, State Attorney's Office, Duval County, Florida. Personal communication.

Garrett, J. S. (1999). Compliance with the constitution. In P. M. Carlson (Eds.), *Prison and jail administration* (pp. 321–326). Gaithersburg, MD: Aspen Publishers, Inc.

Geerken, M. R., & Hayes, H. D. (1993). Probation and parole: Public risk and the future of incarceration alternatives. *Criminology, 31*(4), 549–564.

Geerken, M., Miranne, A., & Kennedy, M. B. (1993). *The New Orleans offender study: Development of official databases.* Washington, DC: National Institute of Justice.

Gelb, B. (1992, November). The effectiveness of prison tactical teams. *Corrections Compendium, 17*(11): 2–4.

Gendreau, P. (1996). The principles of effective intervention with offenders. In A. Harland (Ed.), *Choosing correctional options that work.* Thousand Oaks: Sage.

General Accounting Office. (1990a). *Death penalty sentencing: Research indicates pattern of racial disparities.* Washington, DC: Author.

General Accounting Office. (1990b). *Intermediate sanctions: Their impacts on prison crowding, costs and recidivism are still unclear.* Washington, DC: Author.

General Accounting Office. (1991). *Mentally ill inmates: Better data would help determine protection and advocacy needs.* Washington, DC: Author.

General Accounting Office. (1993). *Prison inmates: Better plans needed before felons are released.* Washington, DC: Author.

Gettinger, S. (1978, March). The Windham school district. *Corrections Magazine*, pp. 14–15.

Giallombardo, R. (1966). *Society of women: A study of a women's prison.* New York: Wiley.

Gibbs, J. (1968). Crime, punishment and deterrence. *Social Science Quarterly, 48*, 515–530.

Gilbert, M. (1997). Associate professor, University of Texas, San Antonio. Personal communication.

Gilbert, M. (1999). Personal communication.

Gilbert, M. J. (1993, March). *Discretionary workstyle preferences among correctional officers: Implications for correctional training and management.* Paper presented at the annual meeting of the Academy of Criminal Justice Sciences, Kansas City, MO.

Gilbert, M. J. (1995, March 27). Assistant Professor, The University of Texas at San Antonio. Personal communication.

Gilbert, M. J. (1997). The illusion of structure: A critique of the classical model and the discretionary power of correctional officers. *Criminal Justice Review, 22*(1): 49–64.

Gillaspy, J. A. (1997, May). It's lights! Beginning Aug. 1, the DOC will ban cigarettes and other tobacco products for inmates and employees alike. *Indianapolis Star*, p. A01.

Gilliard, D. (1999). *Prison and jail inmates at midyear 1998.* Washington, DC: Bureau of Justice Statistics.

Gilliard, D. K. (1993). *Prisoners in 1992.* Washington, DC: U.S. Department of Justice.

Gilliard, D. K., & Beck, A. J. (1994, June). *Prisoners in 1993.* Washington, DC: U.S. Department of Justice.

Gillin, J. L. (1935). *Criminology and penology.* New York: D. Appleton-Century Company.

Gilpin, A. B. (1997). Sexual offenders to be broadcast. *Tampa Tribune* (August 19), pp. 1, 3.

Glaberson, W. (1991, December 9). Violence at Attica Prison echoes in the courtroom. *The New York Times*, pp. A1, A17.

Glaser, D. (1954). *A reformulation and testing of parole prediction factors.* Unpublished doctoral dissertation, University of Chicago.

Glaser, D. (1969). *The effectiveness of a prison and parole system.* Indianapolis, IN: The Bobbs-Merrill Co.

Glaser, D. (1971, November–December). Politicalization of prisoners: A new challenge to American penology. *American Journal of Correction, 33,* 6–9.

Glasser, W. (1965). *Reality therapy.* New York: Harper and Row.

Gleason, S. E. (1978, June). Hustling: The "inside" economy of a prison. *Federal Probation, 42*(2), 32–40.

Glick, B., & Sturgeon, W. (1998). *No time to play: Youth offenders in adult correctional systems.* Lanham, MD: ACA.

Glick, R., & Neto, V. (1977). *National study of women's correctional programs.* Washington, DC: U.S. Government Printing Office.

Gluckstern, N. B., Neuse, M. A., Harness, J. K., Packard, R. W., Patmon, C., & Coleman, M. (1979). *Health care in correctional institutions.* Washington, DC: U.S. Department of Justice.

Glueck, S., & Glueck, E. (1974). *Of delinquency and crime.* Springfield, IL: Thomas.

Gobert, J. J., & Cohen, N. P. (1981). *Rights of prisoners.* Colorado Springs, CO: Shepard's/McGraw-Hill.

Gobert, J. J., & Cohen, N. P. (1992). *Rights of prisoners: 1992 cumulative supplement.* Colorado Springs, CO: Shepard's/McGraw-Hill.

Godwin, C. (1999). Personal communication. Tallahassee, FL: Florida Department of Corrections.

Godwin, C. (2000). Personal communication.

Goetting, A. (1982, September). Conjugal association in prison: A world view. *Criminal Justice Abstracts,* pp. 406–416.

Goffman, E. (1961). *Asylums: Essays on the social situation of mental and other inmates.* New York: Anchor Books.

Goldfarb, R. (1973). *Jails: The ultimate ghetto.* Garden City, NY: Anchor Press/Doubleday.

Goldkamp, J. S., & Weisland, D. *Assessing the impact of Dade County.* Washington, DC: National Institute of Justice.

Goldstein, H. (1990). *Problem oriented policing.* New York: McGraw Hill.

Gondles, J. A. (1997). Kids are kids, not adults. *Corrections Today,* 6.

Gottfredson, D. M., & Tonry, M. (1987). *Prediction and classification: Criminal justice decision making.* Chicago, IL: University of Chicago Press.

Gottlieb, D. J. (1985). The legacy of Wolfish and Chapman: Some thoughts about "big prison case" litigation in the 1980s. In I. D. Robbins (Ed.), *Prisoners and the law.* New York: Clark Boardman Co. Ltd.

Gottlieb, D. J. (1991). A review and analysis of the Kansas sentencing guidelines. *Kansas Law Review, 39,* 65–89.

Gottlieb, D. J. (1993, June). Kansas adopts sentencing guidelines. *Overcrowded Times, 4,* pp. 1, 10–12.

Gould, J. (1981, June). How to keep prisoners from returning to lockup. *Today—University of Florida, 6*(3), 21–23.

Gould, L. A., MacKenzie, D. L., & Bankston, W. (1991). *A comparison of models of parole outcome.* Paper presented at the annual meeting of the American Society of Criminology, San Francisco.

Gover, A. R., Styve, G. J. F., & MacKenzie, D. L. (1999). *Boot camp programs: Correctional issues and concerns.*

Gowdy, V. (1993). *Intermediate sanctions.* Washington, DC: National Institute of Justice, U.S. Department of Justice.

Grasmick, H., & Bursik, R. (1990). Conscience, significant others and choice: Extending the deterrence model. *Law and Society Review, 24,* 837–861.

Greek, C. (1992). Drug control and asset seizures: A review of the history of forfeiture in England and colonial America. In T. Mieczkowski (Ed.), *Drugs, crime and social policy.* Boston: Allyn and Bacon.

Greene, J. (1992). The Staten Island day-fine experiment. In D. C. McDonald (Ed.), *Day fines in American courts: The Staten Island and Milwaukee experiments.* Washington, DC: U.S. Department of Justice, Office of Justice Programs.

Greenfeld, L. (1985). *Examining recidivism.* Washington, DC: U.S. Government Printing Office.

Greenfeld, L. A., & Minor-Harper, S. (1991, March). *Women in prison.* Washington, DC: Bureau of Justice Statistics.

Greenfeld, L. A., & Stephan, J. J. (1993). *Capital punishment 1992.* Washington, DC: U.S. Department of Justice.

Greenfeld, L. W. (1999). *Sex offenses and offenders: An analysis of data on rape and sexual assault.* Washington, DC: U.S. Department of Justice, Bureau of Justice Statistics.

Greenfeld, L. W., & Snell, T. L. (1999). *Women offenders.* Washington, DC: U.S. Department of Justice, Bureau of Justice Statistics.

Greenhouse, L. (1998). High court refuses to hear challenges to "Megan's Laws." *New York Times* (February 24), pp. A1, A20.

Greenwood, P. (1982). *Selective incapacitation.* Santa Monica, CA: Rand.

Grier, W. H., & Cobbs, P. M. (1969). *Black rage.* New York: Bantam Books.

Grieser, R. (1997). Manager of planning, Federal Prison Industries. UNICOR, Research and Activation Branch. Personal communication.

Grieser, R. C. (1988, August). Model approaches: Examining prison industry that works. *Corrections Today,* pp. 174–178.

Grieser, R. C., Miller, N., & Funke, G. S. (1984, January). *Guidelines for prison industries.* Washington, DC: U.S. Department of Justice, National Institute of Corrections.

Gross, S. R. (1966). The risk of death: Why erroneous convictions in capital cases. *Buffalo Law Review, 44*(2): 469–500.

Grossman, J. (1984). *Bedford Hills mothers follow-up.* Albany: New York State Department of Correctional Services.

Grossman, J. (1984, March). *An examination of the trends of female new commitments: 1960–1982.* Report prepared for the New York State Department of Correctional Services.

Groth, N. A. (1979). *Men who rape: The psychology of the offender.* New York: Plenum Press.

Grunhut, M. (1972). *Penal reform: A comparative study.* Montclair, NJ: Patterson Smith. (Original work published 1948)

Gryta, M. (1998, October). Man convicted of rape after prison release. *Buffalo News,* p. 5B.

Gunn, B. (1979). *Identification & control of drugs in correctional institutions.* Sacramento, CA: California Department of Corrections.

Gustafson, A. (1993, January 5). Law would allow indefinite imprisonment of sex predators. *The Salem Statesman Journal.*

Gustafson, J. I. (1994, August). Specialist, National Institute of Corrections. Personal communication.

Guynes, R. G., & Grieser, R. C. (1986, January). Contemporary prison industry goals. In American Correctional Association (Eds.), *A study of prison industry: History, components, and goals.* Washington, DC: National Institute of Corrections.

Hackett, J., Hatry, H. P., Levinson, R. B., Allen, J., Chi, K., and Feigenbaum, E. D. (1987). *Issues in contracting for the private operation of prisons and jails.* Washington, DC: U.S. Department of Justice.

Hafiz, A. (1993). Chaplain, Federal Correctional Institution Terminal Island. Personal communication.

Hafiz, A., & Hamidullah, M. (undated). Practicing Islam in prison. In Federal Bureau of Prisons, *African American work group report.* Washington, DC: U.S. Department of Justice.

Hager, J. (1992). Proactive jail management. *Jail Managers Bulletin, 2*(9).

Hahn, P. H. (1994, August). A standardized curriculum for correctional officers: History and rationale. Paper presented at the American Congress on Corrections, St. Louis, MO.

Haigler, K., Harlow C. W., O'Connor P. E., & Campbell, A. (1994, October). *Literacy behind bars: Profiles of the prison population from the National Adult Literacy Survey.* Washington, DC: U.S. Department of Education, Office of Education Research and Improvement.

Hairston, C. F. (1988, March). Family ties during imprisonment: Do they influence future criminal activity? *Federal Probation, 52*(1), 48–52.

Hairston, C. F. (1990). Men in prison: Family characteristics and parenting views. *Journal of Offender Counseling, Services and Rehabilitation, 14*(1), 23–29.

Hairston, C. F., & Hess, P. M. (1989). Regulating parent-child communication in correctional settings. In J. Mustin & B. Bloom (Conference Directors), *The First National Conference on the Family and Corrections* (pp. 29–32). Richmond, KY: Training Resource Center, Department of Correctional Services, Eastern Kentucky University.

Hairston, C. F., & Lockett, P. W. (1987). Parents in prison: New directions for social services. *Social Work, 32*(2), 162–164.

Halford, S. C. (1984). Kansas co-corrections concept. *Corrections Today, 46,* 44–46.

Hall, M. (1990, December). *Special needs inmates: A survey of state correctional systems.* Boulder, CO: National Institute of Corrections.

Halleck, S., & Herski, M. (1962). Homosexual behavior in an institution for adolescent girls. *American Journal of Orthopsychiatry, 32,* 911–917.

Haly, K. (1980). Mothers behind bars: A look at the parental rights in incarcerated women. In S. K. Datesmen & F. Scarpitti (Eds.), *Women, crime and justice.* New York: Oxford University Press.

Hambrick, M. (1992, Winter). The correctional worker concept: Being connected in the 90's. *Federal Prison Journal,* 11–14.

Hambrick, M. C. (1988, December). Correctional recreation: Get your program off and running. *Corrections Today,* 134, 136.

Hammett, T. M. (1988a). *Precautionary measures and protective equipment: Developing a reasonable response.* Washington, DC: National Institute of Justice.

Hammett, T. M. (1988b). *AIDS in correctional facilities: Issues and opinions* (3rd ed.). Washington, DC: National Institute of Justice.

Hammett, T. M., Harmon, P., & Maruschak, L. M. (1999, July). *1996–1997 update: HIV/STDs, and TB in correctional facilities.* Washington, DC: National Institute of Justice.

Hammett, T. M., & Harrold, L. (1994, January). *Tuberculosis in correctional facilities.* Washington, DC: U.S. Department of Justice, National Institute of Justice.

Hammett, T. M., Harrold, L., Gross, M., & Epstein, J. (1994). *1992 update: AIDS in correctional facilities: Issues and opinions.* Cambridge, MA: Abt Associates.

Hammett, T. M., & Lynne, H. (1994). *1992—Tuberculosis in correctional facilities.* Cambridge, MA: Abt Associates.

Hammett, T. M., & Moini, S. (1990). *Update on AIDS in prisons and jails.* Cambridge, MA: U.S. Department of Justice.

Hammons, T. (2000). Retired classification manager, Federal Bureau of Prisons. Personal communication.

Haney, C. (1984). On the selection of capital juries: The biasing effects of the death-qualification process. *Law and Social Behavior, 8:* 7–30.

Haney, C., Banks, C., & Zimbardo, P. (1977). Internal dynamics in a simulated prison. In R. G. Leger (Ed.), *The sociology of corrections: A book of readings.* New York: Wiley, pp. 65–92.

Hankins, W. E. (1973, July 24 & 25). Testimony before the Committee on Internal Security of the House of Representatives. Hearings on revolutionary activities directed toward the administration of penal or correctional systems. Washington, DC: U.S. Government Printing Office.

Hanson, R. A., & Daley, H. W. K. (1995). *Challenging the conditions of prisons and jails.* Washington, DC: Bureau of Justice Statistics, p. 17.

Harer, M. D., & Steffensmeir, D. J. (1996a). Race and prison violence. *Criminology, 34*(3): 323–355.

Harland, A. (1992, Summer). Toward the rational assessment of economic sanctions. In National Institute of Corrections (Eds.), *Topics in community corrections.* Washington, DC: National Institute of Corrections.

Harlow, C. W. (1992, July). *Drug enforcement and treatment in prisons, 1990.* Washington, DC: U.S. Department of Justice.

Harlow, C. W. (1993). *HIV in U.S. prisons and jails.* Washington, DC: U.S. Department of Justice.

Harlow, C. W. (1994). *Comparing federal and state prison inmates, 1991.* Washington, DC: U.S. Department of Justice.

Harlow, C. W. (1998, April). *Profile of jail inmates, 1996.* Washington, DC: Bureau of Justice Statistics.

Harries, K., & Cheatwood, D. (1997). *The geography of execution: The capital punishment quagmire in America.* Lanham, MD: Rowman & Littlefield Inc.

Harris, L. A. (Spring 1997). The ABA calls for a moratorium on the death penalty: The task ahead reconciling justice with politics. *Focus on Law Studies. Commission on College and University Legal Studies of the American Bar Association, XII*(2): 2.

Hart, S. (1998). Correctional services administrator, STG Intelligence Officer, Florida Department of Corrections. Personal communication.

Hart, S. (1999). Personal communication.

Hart, S. (2000). Personal communication.

Harter, B., & Oehler, B. (1997). *Educating the older offender: Four lesson plans for establishing educational programming for the elder male offender in a correctional setting.* Paper presented at the 52nd Correctional Education Association International Conference. Houston, TX.

Hassine, V. (1997). *Life without parole: Living in prison today.* Los Angeles: Roxbury.

Hawkins, C. W. (1999). Chaplain, Inspectional Services Division, Hillsborough County Sheriff's Department, Tampa FL. Personal communication.

Hawkins, G. (1976). *The Prison.* Chicago: University of Chicago Press.

Hawkins, G. (1983). Prison labor and prison industries. In M. Tonry & M. Norval (Eds.), *Crime and justice, an annual review of research* (Vol. 5). Chicago, IL: University of Chicago Press.

Hawkins, S. (1996, August). Death at midnight . . . hope at sunrise. *Corrections Today,* 31.

Hayes, L. M., & Rowan, J. R. (1988). *National study of jail suicides: Seven years later.* Alexandria, VA: National Center on Institutions and Alternatives.

Hecht, F. (1992). Substance abuse program development—A direct supervision approach. *American Jails, 6*(4), 53–55.

Heffernan, E. (1972). *Making it in prison: The square, the cool, and the life.* New York: Wiley.

Hemmens, C., & Atherton, E. (1999). *Use of force: Current practice and policy.* Lanham, MD: American Correctional Association.

Henderson, J. D., & Phillips, R. L. (1990, November). *Protective custody management in adult correctional facilities: A discussion of causes, conditions, attitudes and alternatives.* Washington, DC: American Correctional Association.

Henderson, J. D., Rauch, W. D., & Phillips, R. L. (1997). *Guidelines for the development of a security program* (2nd ed.). Lanham, MD: American Correctional Association.

Henriques, Z. W. (1996). Imprisoned mothers and their children. Separation-reunion syndrome. *Women and Criminal Justice, 8*(1): 77–95.

Hepburn, J. R. (1987). The prison control structure and its effects on work attitudes. *Journal of Criminal Justice, 15,* 49–64.

Hepburn, J. R., & Knepper, P. E. (1993). Correctional officers as human service workers: The effect on job satisfaction. *Justice Quarterly, 10*(2), 315–335.

Herbeck, D. (1993, October 17). Jail aide held in connection with drug scam: Cocaine seized in sting. *The Buffalo News, Section—Local.*

Heuer, G. (1993). Direct supervision. *American Jails, 7*(4), 57–60.

Hill, G. (1997). Correctional officer training traits and skills.

Hills, A., & Karcz, S. (1990, May). Literacy survey. *ASFDCE National Agenda,* pp. 6–7.

Hillsman, S. T., & Greene, J. A. (1988). European "day fines" as method for improving the administration of monetary penalties in American criminal courts. *American Probation and Parole Association Perspectives,* pp. 35–38.

Hillsman, S. T, Mahoney, B., Cole, G. F., & Auchter, B. (1987). Fines as criminal sanctions. Washington, DC: U.S. Department of Justice, National Institute of Justice.

Hippchen, L. J. (1978). Trends in classification philosophy and practice. In L. J. Hippichen (Ed.), *Handbook on correctional classification: Treatment and reintegration.* Washington, DC: American Correctional Association.

Hirliman, T. (1982). *The hate factory.* Agoura, CA: Paisano Publications, Inc.

Hirst, J. B. (1983). *Convict society and its enemies.* Sydney, Australia: George Allen & Unwin.

Hold, D. J. (1998). Teacher, Windham School District, Texas Department of Criminal Justice. Personal communication.

Holeman, H., & Krepps-Hess, B. J. (1983, January). *Women correctional officers in the California Department of Corrections.* Sacramento, CA: California Department of Corrections.

Holmes, S. A. (1991, September 30). Frustrated by federal courts, A.C.L.U. looks to states on individual rights. *The New York Times,* p. A14.

Holmes, S. A. (1994, March 4). As Farrakkan groups land jobs from government, debate grows. *The New York Times,* pp. 1A, 10A.

Holt, K. E. (1981–82). Nine months to life—The law and the pregnant inmate. *Journal of Family Law, 20*(3), 523–543.

Holt, N., & Miller, D. (1972). *Explorations in inmates family relationships.* Sacramento, CA: California Department of Corrections.

Holt, R., & Phillips, R. (1991). Marion: Separating fact from fiction. *Federal Prison Journal, 2*(1), 29–35.

Hopper, C. B. (1969). *Sex in prison: The Mississippi experiment in conjugal visiting.* Baton Rouge, LA: Louisiana State University Press.

Hopper, C. B. (1989). The evolution of conjugal visiting in Mississippi. *The Prison Journal, 66,* 103–109.

Hormachea, C. R. (1981, April). Recreation programming for local jails. *Journal of Physical Education and Recreation, 52*(4), 45–46.

Houston, J. (1995). *Correctional management: Functions, skills and systems.* Chicago: Nelson-Hall Publishers.

Houston, J. G. (1999). *Correctional management* (2nd ed.). Chicago: Nelson Hall.

Houston, R., & Koch, J. (1993, March). *Work release adjustment: Predicting a headache.* Paper presented at the annual meeting of the Academy of Criminal Justice Sciences, Kansas City, MO.

Howard, J. (1792). *The state of prisons in England and Wales with preliminary observations and an account of some foreign prisons and hospitals* (4th ed.). London, England: J. Johnson, C. Dilly, and T. Cadell. (Reprinted by Patterson Smith, Montclair, NJ: 1973).

Howser, J., Grossman, J., & MacDonald, D. (1984). Impact of family reunion program on institutional discipline. *Journal of Offender Counseling, Services and Rehabilitation, 8*(1/2), 27–36.

Hubbard, R. L., Marsden, M. E., Rachal, J. V., Harwood, H. J., Cavanaugh, E. R., & Ginzberg, H. M. (1989). *Drug abuse treatment: A national study of effectiveness.* Chapel Hill, NC: University of North Carolina Press.

Huft, A. G., Fawkes, L. S., & Lawson, W. T. (1992). Care of the pregnant offender. *Federal Prisons Journal, 3*(1), 49–53.

Hughes, H. H. (1973, March 29 & May 1). *Testimony before the Committee on Internal Security of the House of Representatives. Hearings on revolutionary activities directed toward the administration of penal or correctional systems.* Washington, DC: U.S. Government Printing Office.

Hughes, R. (1987). *The fatal shore.* New York: Alfred A. Knopf.

Hull, J. D. (1993, August 2). A boy and his gun. *Time,* pp. 20–27.

Human Rights Watch. (1977). *Cold storage: Super-maximum security confinement in Indiana.* New York: Author.

Hunt, G., Reigel, S., Morales, T., & Waldorf, D. (1996). Changes in prison gangs and the case of the "Pepsi Generation." In Paul Cromwell (Ed.), *In their own words: Criminals on crime.* Los Angeles, CA: Roxbury.

Hunter, R. J., Crew, B. K., Sexton T., & Lutz, G. M. (1997). *Management strategies for long-term inmates.* Cedar Falls, IA: University of Northern Iowa, College of Social and Behavioral Sciences.

Hussey, F. A., & Duffee, D. E. (1980). *Probation, parole and community field service: Policy, structure and process.* New York: Harper and Row.

Ibrahim, Y. M. (1989, February 16). Khomeini's judgment: Iranian leader's instruction to kill writer may reflect a calculation rooted in politics. *The New York Times,* pp. 1, 7.

Immarigeon, R., & Chesney-Lind, M. (1990). *Women's prisons: Overcrowded and overused.* A paper presented at the American Society of Criminology, Baltimore, MD.

Inbau, F. E., Thompson, J. R., Zagel, J. B., & Manak, J. P. (1984). *Criminal law and its administration* (4th ed.). Mineola, NY: The Foundation Press.

Inciardi, J., Martin, S. S., Butzin, C. A., Harper, R. M., & Harrison, L. D. (1997). An effective model of prison-based treatment for drug-involved offenders. *Journal of Drug Issues, 27*(2): 261–278.

Independent Research Consortium. (1989). *Current description, evaluation and recommendations for treatment of mentally disordered criminal offenders.* San Francisco, CA: Standard Consulting Corp.

Ingley, G. S. (2000). Executive director, Correctional Industries Association. Personal communication.

Ingley, G. S., & Cochran, M. E. (1999). Ruinous or fair competition?: The correctional industries public policy debate. *Corrections Today, 61*(6): 82–85, 98.

Innes, C. A. (1988, January). *BJS special report: Profile of state prison inmates, 1986.* Washington, DC: U.S. Government Printing Office.

Innes, C. A., & Greenfeld, L. A. (1990, July). *Violent state prisoners and their victims.* Washington, DC: U.S. Department of Justice.

Institute of Medicine, Committee for the Substance Abuse Coverage Study. (1990). *Treating drug problems.* Washington, DC: National Academy Press.

Irwin, J. (1970). *The felon.* Englewood Cliffs, NJ: Prentice Hall.

Irwin, J. (1980). *Prisons in turmoil.* Boston: Little Brown.

Irwin, J. (1985). *The jail: Managing the underclass in American society.* Berkeley, CA: University of California Press.

Irwin, J., & Austin, J. (1994). *It's about time: America's imprisonment binge.* Belmont, CA: Wadsworth Publishing Co.

Irwin, J., &. Austin, J. (1997). *It's about time: America's imprisonment binge* (2nd ed.). Belmont, CA: Wadsworth.

Irwin, J., & Cressey, D. (1962). Thieves, convicts, and the inmate culture. *Social Problems, 10,* 145–147.

Isele, W. P. (1977). *Legal obligations to the pre-trial detainee.* Chicago, IL: American Medical Association.

Isele, W. P. (1979). Constitutional issues of the prisoner's right to health care. In N. B. Gluckstern, M. A. Neuse, J. K. Harness, R. W. Packard, C. Patmon, & M. Coleman (Eds.), *Health care in correctional institutions.* (pp. 3–23). Washington, DC: U.S. Department of Justice.

Ives, G. (1970). *A history of penal methods: Criminals, witches, lunatics.* Montclair, NJ: Patterson Smith. (Original work published 1914)

Jackson, J. E. (1992, November). *Female and minority officers' attitudes toward treatment programs in the Texas correctional system.* Paper presented at the annual meeting of the American Society of Criminology, San Francisco.

Jacobs, J. B. (1974). Street gangs behind bars. *Social Problems, 21*(3), 395–409.

Jacobs, J. B. (1976). Stratification and conflict among prison inmates. *Journal of Law and Criminology, 6,* 476–482.

Jacobs, J. B. (1977). *Stateville: The penitentiary in mass society.* Chicago: University of Chicago Press.

Jacobs, J. B. (1978). What prison guards think: A profile of the Illinois force. *Crime and Delinquency, 24,* 185–196.

Jacobs, J. B. (1980). The prisoner rights movement and its impact, 1960–1980. In N. Morris & M. Tonry (Eds.), *Crime and justice: An annual review of research* (Vol. 2), Chicago: University of Chicago Press.

Jacobs, J. B., & Kraft, L. S. (1978). Integrating the keepers: A comparison of black and white prison guards in Illinois. *Urban Life, 7*, 304–318.

Jacobs, J. B., & Retsky, H. G. (1975). Prison guards. *Urban Life, 4*, 5–29.

James, G. (1994, December 29). Computer replaces Rabbi's picture. *The New York Times*, p. A15.

James, J. T. L. (1975). The halfway house movement. In G. R. Perlstein & T. R. Phelps (Eds.), *Alternatives to prison: Community based corrections*. Pacific Palisades, CA: Goodyear Publishing Co.

Jankowski, L. (1991). *Probation and parole 1990*. Washington, DC: U.S. Department of Justice, Bureau of Justice Statistics.

Jankowski, L. (1992). *Correctional populations in the United States, 1990*. Washington, DC: U.S. Department of Justice, Bureau of Justice Statistics.

Janofsky, M. (1998). Delaware driver's licenses to note sex offenders. *New York Times* (April 21), p. A15.

Jemelka, R. P., Rahman, S., & Trupin, E. W. (1993). Prison mental health: An overview. In H. J. Steadman & J. J. Cocozza (Eds.), *Mental illness in America's prisons*. Seattle, WA: National Coalition for the Mentally Ill in the Criminal Justice System.

Jenkins, H. D. (1999). Education and vocational trainings. In P. Carlson & J. S. Simon (Eds.), *Prison and jail administration: Practice and theory* (pp. 89–93). Gaithersburg, MD: Aspen.

Jewell, D. L. (1981, February). Behind the leisure eight ball in maximum security. *Parks and Recreation*, pp. 41–45, 77.

Johns, D. R. (1971). Alternatives to conjugal visiting. *Federal Probation, 36*(1), 48–52.

Johnson, C. (1993). Director of Instruction, Windham School District, Texas Department of Criminal Justice. Personal communication.

Johnson, C. (1994). Director of Instruction, Windham School District, Texas Department of Criminal Justice. Personal communication.

Johnson, D. (February 6, 1989). Iowa inmates granted right to read porn. *The Tampa Tribune*, Sec. A, pp. 1, 4.

Johnson, E. L. (1968). *Crime, correction, and society*. Homewood, IL: Dorsey Press.

Johnson, H. A. (1988). *History of criminal justice*. Cincinnati, OH: Anderson Publishing Co.

Johnson, L. (1998). Training development coordinator, Food Services Specialty, Virginia Department of Corrections. Personal communication.

Johnson, P. M. (1993a). Corrections should take the lead in changing sentencing practices. *Corrections Today, 52*, 54–55, 130–131.

Johnson, R. (1976). *Culture and crisis in confinement*. Lexington, MA: Lexington Books.

Johnson, R. (1987). *Hard time: Understanding and reforming the prison*. Monterey, CA: Brooks/Cole.

Johnson, R. (1990). *Death work: A study of the execution process*. Pacific Grove, CA: Brooks/Cole.

Johnson, R. (1993b, Spring). A history of correctional training: A national perspective. *Journal of Correctional Training*, Spring, pp. 12–17.

Johnson, R. (1996). Hard time: Understanding and reforming prison (2nd ed.). Belmont, CA: Wadsworth.

Johnson, R. (1998). *Death work: A study of the modern execution process*. Belmont CA: West/Wadsworth.

Johnson, R., & Dorin, D. (1978). Dysfunctional ideology: The black revolutionary in prison. In D. Szabo & S. Katzenelson (Eds.), *Offenders and corrections*. Lexington, MA: DC Heath.

Johnson, R., & Price, S. (1981). The complete correctional officer: Human service and the human environment of prison. *Criminal Justice and Behavior, 8*(3), 343–373.

Johnson, R., & Toch, H. (1982). *The pains of imprisonment*. Beverly Hills, CA: Sage Publications.

Johnston, D. (1995). Effects of parental incarceration. In K. Gabel, & D. Johnston (Eds.), *Children of incarcerated parents*. New York: Lexington Books.

Johnston, N. (1969). Introduction to Crawford, W. Report on the Penitentiaries of the United States. Montclair, NJ: Patterson Smith.

Joint Legislative Committee. (1983). *Laws of Florida, Chapter 83–131*. Tallahassee, FL: State of Florida.

Jones, D. A. (1976). *The health risks of imprisonment*. Lexington, MA: DC Heath.

Jones, M., & Ross, D. L. (1997). Is less better?: Boot camp, regular probation, and rearrest in North Carolina. *American Journal of Criminal Justice, 21*(2): 147–161.

Jones, S. T. (1992, October). Evaluating correctional officer training: Is it working? *Corrections Compendium*, pp. 1, 4–8.

Jones, W. R. (1989). Mentally ill offenders. *American Jails, 3*(3), 47–56.

Jones-Brown, P. (1992). Most female offenders incarcerated for non-violent drug and alcohol related offenses. *Corrections Compendium, 27*(8), p. 11.

Jorgenson, J. D., Hernandez, S. H., & Warren, R. C. (1986). Addressing the social needs of families of prisoners: A tool for inmate rehabilitation. *Federal Probation, 50*, 47–52.

Josi, D. A., & Sechrest, D. K. (1998). *The changing correctional officer: Policy implications for the 21st century*. Boston: Butterworth-Heinemann.

Jurik, N. C., Halemba, G. J., Musheno, M. C., & Boyce, B. V. (1987). Educational attainment, job satisfaction, and the professionalization of correctional officers. *Work and Occupations, 14*(1), 106–125.

Justice Policy Institute. (2000). Two million Americans behind bars. Press release. Washington, DC: Author.

Kahn, B. (1978, June 14). *Prison gangs: A briefing document for the Board of Corrections.* Sacramento, CA: State Board of Corrections.

Kairos, Inc. (1997). Kairos recidivism study: Florida Department of corrections—Chaplaincy services. *God's special time: The newsletter of Kairos Prison Ministry, 21*(4): 2.

Kairos, Inc. (1999a). *Kairos outside manual, 1999.* Winter Park, FL: Author.

Kairos, Inc. (1999b). *The Kairos horizon program project.* Daytona Beach, FL: Author.

Kairos, Inc. (2000, January). *God's speed: Special time. The newsletter of Kairos prison ministry.* Orlando, FL: Author.

Kalinich, D. B. (1986). *Power, stability, & contraband: The inmate economy.* Prospect Heights, IL: Waveland Press.

Kalinich, D. B., & Stojkovic, S. (1987). Prison contraband systems: Implications for prison management. *Journal of Crime and Justice, 10*(1), 1–21.

Kalinich, D. B., Stojkovic, S., & and Klofas, J. (1988). Toward a political-community theory of prison organization. *Journal of Criminal Justice, 16*, 217–230.

Kamper, C. (1995). Post-traumatic stress reaction in children of imprisoned mothers. In K. Gabel & D. Johnston (Eds.), *Children of incarcerated parents.* New York: Lexington Books.

Kane, T., & Saylor, W. (1983). *Security designation: A validation study.* Washington, DC: U.S. Bureau of Prisons.

Kansas Statutes Annotated, Section 59-29A01 et seq. (1994).

Kansas v. Hendricks (1997). 521 U.S. 117 S.Ct. 2072.

Kantrowitz, N. (1996). *Close control: Managing a maximum security prison—the story of Regan's Stateville Penitentiary.* Guilderland, New York: Harrow and Heston.

Kaplan, J., & Waltz, J. R. (1987). *Evidence: Cases and materials* (6th ed.). Mineola, NY: The Foundation Press.

Karacki, L. (1987, May). *An assessment of the high security operation at USP-Marion, Illinois.* Washington, DC: Federal Bureau of Prisons.

Kassebaum, G. W., Ward, D. A., & Wilner, D. M. (1971). *Prison treatment and parole survival: An empirical assessment.* New York: John Wiley & Sons.

Kaye, A. (1996, Spring). Comment: Dangerous places: The right to self-defense in prison and prison conditions jurisprudence. *University of Chicago Law Review, 63,* 693.

Keating, J. M. (1990, Fall). How to work with special masters. *National Prison Project Journal, 5*(4), 1–3.

Keil, T. J., & Vito, G. F. (1991). Kentucky prosecutor's decision to seek the death penalty: A LISREL model. In R. M. Bohm (Ed.), *The death penalty in America: Current research.* Cincinnati, OH: Anderson Publishing Co.

Keller, O. J., & Alper, B. S. (1970). *Halfway houses: Community-centered correction and treatment.* Lexington, MA: Heath Lexington Books.

Kelly, J. A., & Murphy, D. A. (1992). Psychological interventions with AIDS and HIV: Prevention and treatment. *Journal of Consulting and Clinical Psychology, 60,* 576–585.

Kendig, N. (1998). Tuberculosis control in prisons. *International Journal of Tuberculosis and Lung Diseases, 2*(9): 557–563.

Kennedy, D. B. (1994). Rethinking the problem of custodial suicide. *American Jails, 7*(6), 41–45.

Kenney, L. (1999). *Intermediate sanctions for women offenders: Project overview and analysis—1991–1999.* Washington, DC: National Institute of Corrections.

Kerle, K. (1993). Jails and minorities—An editorial. *American Jails, 7*(2), 5.

Kimme, D. A. (1986, Winter). The nature of new small jails. *American Jails.*

Kindel, T. C. (1993, July). Live from San Quentin: Planning is the key to handling media interest in an execution. *Corrections Today,* 65–66, 68–69.

King, K. (1995). Administrative Assistant to the Assistant Director for Administration, Federal Bureau of Prisons. Personal communication.

Kising, J. (1996, December). Courts rediscover shame. *Denver Post,* p. G-13.

Kittrie, N. M., & Zenoff, E. H. (1981). *Sentencing, sanctions and corrections: Law, policy and practice.* Mineola, NY: The Foundation Press.

Klaas, J. (1999, September). Three-strikes is missing the mark. *Tampa Tribune,* p. 15 (Nation/World).

Klein, A. (1997). Howard judge orders teenage vandal to write a book report. *Washington Post,* p. B06.

Klepper, S., & Nagin, D. (1989). Tax compliance and perceptions of the risks of detection and criminal prosecution. *Law and Society, 23,* 209–240.

Klofas, J. M. (1991). Disaggregating jail use: Variety and change in local corrections over a ten year period. In J. A. Thompson & G. L. Mays (Eds.), *American jails: Public policy issues* (pp. 40–58). Chicago: Nelson-Hall Publishers.

Knight, B. B. (1986). *Prisoners' rights in America.* Chicago, IL: Nelson-Hall Publishers.

Knowles, F. (1994, May 17). Sergeant, Hillsborough County Sheriff's Office, Tampa, FL, Detention Division. Personal communication.

Koban, L. A. (1983). Parents in prison: A comparative analysis of the effects of incarceration on the families of men and women. *Research in Law, Deviance and Social Control, 5,* 171–183.

Koeninger, R. C. (1951, April). What about self-mutilation? *Prison World.*

Korn, R. K., & McCorkle, L. W. (1959). *Criminology and penology.* New York: Holt, Rinehart and Winston.

Krajick, K. (1978, March). Profile Texas. *Corrections Magazine,* pp. 5–8, 10–25.

Krajick, K. (1980a, June). At Stateville, the calm is tense. *Corrections Magazine, VI*(3), 6–9.

Krajick, K. (1980b, June). The menace of the supergangs. *Corrections Magazine, VI*(3), 11–12.

Kramer, S., Bench, L., & Erickson, S. (1999). Psychologists, Benchmark Behavioral Health Systems. Personal communication.

Krantz, S. (1988). *The law of corrections and prisoners' rights in a nutshell* (3rd ed.). St. Paul, MN: West Publishing Co.

Krantz, S., & Branham, L. S. (1991). *The law of sentencing, corrections and prisoners' rights.* (4th ed.). St. Paul, MN: West Publishing Co.

Kratcoski, P. C. (1989, November). *Adjustment of older inmates in long term correctional institutions.* Paper presented at the meeting of the American Society of Criminology, Reno, NV.

Kratcoski, P. C., & Babb, S. (1990). Adjustment of older inmates: An analysis by institutional structures and gender. *Journal of Contemporary Criminal Justice, 6*(3), 139–156.

Kratcoski, P. C., & Pownall, G. A. (1989). Federal Bureau of Prisons programming for older inmates. *Federal Probation, 53*(2), 28–35.

Krauss, C. (1994, November 13). No crystal ball needed on crime. *The New York Times,* Sec. E, p. 4.

Krauth, B., & Smith, R. (1988, October). *An administrator's overview: Questions and answers on issues related to the incarcerated male sex offender.* Washington, DC: U.S. Department of Corrections.

Kruttschnitt, C. (1981). Social status and sentences of female offenders. *Law and Society Review, 15* (2), 247–265.

Kruttschnitt, C. (1982). Respectable women and the law. *Sociological Quarterly, 23,* 221–234.

Kruttschnitt, C. (1984). Sex and criminal court dispositions: The unresolved controversy. *Journal of Research in Crime and Delinquency, 21*(3), 213–232.

Kuether, F. B. (1951). Religion and the chaplain. In P. W. Tappan (Ed.), *Contemporary correction* (pp. 254–265). New York: McGraw-Hill.

Labaton, S. (1993, June 29). Justices restrict ability to seize suspects' goods. *The New York Times,* pp. A1, A8.

Lacayo, R. (1992, March 23). Sentences inscribed on flesh. *Time,* p. 54.

Landress, H. (1999). Vice president of planning, Gulf Coast Jewish and Family Services. Personal communication.

Langan, P. A. (1991, May). *Race of prisoners admitted to state and federal institutions, 1926–1986.* Washington, DC: U.S. Department of Justice.

Langan, P. A., & Cunniff, M. A. (1992). *Recidivism of felons on probation, 1986–1989.* Washington, DC: U.S. Department of Justice.

Langan, P. A., & Dawson, J. M. (1993). *Felony sentences in state courts, 1990.* Washington, DC: U.S. Department of Justice, Bureau of Justice Statistics.

Langan, P. A., & Solari, R. (1993). *National Judicial Relocating Program, 1990.* Washington, DC: Bureau of Justice Statistics.

Lange, A. (1986). *Rational-emotive therapy—A treatment manual.* Rockville, MD: National Institute of Mental Health.

Latessa, E. J., & Allen, H. E. (1999). *Corrections in the community* (2nd ed.). Cincinnati: Anderson.

Latessa, E., & Allen, H. (1982). Halfway houses and parole: A national assessment. *Journal of Criminal Justice, 10*(2), 153–163.

Laurence, J. (1960). *A history of capital punishment.* New York: The Citadel Press.

Laws, D. R. (1985). *Prevention of relapse in sex offenders.* Washington, DC: National Institute of Mental Health.

Lay, D. P. (1990, October 22). Our justice system, so called. *The New York Times,* p. A19.

Layson, S. K. (1986). United States time-series regressions with adaptive expectations. *Bulletin of the New York Academy of Medicine, 62,* 589–600.

Leflore, L., & Holston, M. A. (1990). Perceived importance of parenting behaviors as reported by inmate mothers: An exploratory study. *Journal of Offender Counseling, Services and Rehabilitation, 14*(1), 5–21.

LeGrande, R. M. (1994). Executive Director, Louisiana Junior Chamber of Commerce. Personal Communication.

Leibert, J. A. (1965). *Behind bars: What a chaplain saw in Alcatraz, Folsom and San Quentin.* Garden City, NY: Doubleday and Co.

Leibowitz, M. J. (1991). Regionalization in Virginia. *American Jails, 5*(5), 42–43.

Leone, M. C., & Kinkade, P. T. (1996). Prison privatization and conjugal visitation: A nexus of opportunity? In G. L. Mays & T. Gray (Eds.), *Privatization and the provision of correctional services.* Cincinnati, OH: ACJS/Anderson Monograph Series, pp. 103–117.

Lester, D., & Van Voorhis, P. (1997). Psychoanalytic therapy. In P. Van Voorhis & D. L. D. Braswell (Eds.), *Correctional counseling and rehabilitation* (3rd ed.) (pp. 109–125). Cincinnati: Anderson.

Levin, D. J., Langan, P. A., & Brown, J. M. (2000, February). *State court sentencing of convicted felons, 1996.* Washington, DC: BJS.

Levinson, M. R. (1982). Special masters: Engineers of court ordered reform. *Corrections Magazine, 7*(4), 7–18.

Levinson, R. (1980, September). Security designation system: Preliminary results. *Federal Probation,* 26–30.

Levinson, R. (1999). *Unit management in prisons and jails.* Lanham, MD: American Correctional Association.

Levinson, R. B., & Gerard, R. E. (1986, July). Classifying institutions. *Crime and Delinquency, 32*(3), 272–290.

Levinson, R. B., & Green III, J. J. (1998). *New boys on the block: Under 18-year-olds in adult prisons.* Lanham, MD: American Correctional Association.

Levinson, R., & Williams, J. (1979, March). Inmate classification: Security/custody considerations. *Federal Probation,* 37–43.

Lewis, O. F. (1967). *The development of American prisons and prison customs, 1776–1845.* Montclair, NJ: Patterson Smith. (Original work published in 1922.)

Lewis, O. L. (1996). *The development of American prisons and prison customs, 1776–1845.* Montclair, NJ: Patterson Smith. (Original work published in 1922.)

Libstag, K. (1993). Licensed Psychologist, The Vermont treatment program for sexual aggressors. Personal communication.

Libstag, K. (1994). Licensed Psychologist, The Vermont treatment program for sexual aggressors. Personal communication.

Lichtblau, E., & Leonard, J. (1999, July). U.S. prisons to study "stun belt" concerns; corrections officials agree to review objections raised by Amnesty International, which calls electroshock restraint devices high-tech torture. *Los Angeles Times,* p. 8.

Lieb, R. (1996). *Washington's sexually violent predator law: Legislative history and comparisons with other states.* Olympia, WA: Washington Institute for Public Policy.

Liebow, E. (1967). *Tally's corner: A study of Negro streetcorner men.* Boston: Little, Brown.

Likert, R. (1961). *New patterns of management.* New York: McGraw-Hill.

Lillis, J. (1993a, November). Incarcerated sex offenders total nearly 100,000. *Corrections Compendium, 28*(11), pp. 7–16.

Lillis, J. (1993b, November). Family visitation evolves. *Corrections Compendium, 28*(11), pp. 1–4.

Lillis, J. (1993c, July). Survey: Corrections training budget approaches $57 million. *Corrections Compendium, 28*(7), pp. 4, 15.

Lillis, J. (1994a, July). Sentencing guidelines determine penalties in 19 systems: Survey summary. *Corrections Compendium, 29*(7), pp. 7–14.

Lillis, J. (1994b, June). Prison escapes and violence remain down. *Corrections Compendium, 29*(6), pp. 6–21.

Lillis, J. (1994c, January). Female inmates: A current overview. *Corrections Compendium, 29*(1), pp. 6–13.

Lillis, J. (1994d, February). Programs and services for female inmates. *Corrections Compendium, 29*(2), pp. 6–13.

Lillis, J. (1994e, March). Education in U.S. prisons: Part one. *Corrections Compendium, 29*(3), pp. 5–6.

Lillis, J. (1994f). Education in U.S. prisons: Part one. *Corrections Compendium, 29*(3): 10–16.

Lillis, J. (1994f, March). Education in U.S. prisons: Part two. *Corrections Compendium, 29*(3), pp. 10–16.

Lilly, J. R., Ball, R., & Wright, J. (1987). Home incarceration with electronic monitoring in Kenton County, Kentucky: An evaluation. In B. McCarthy (Ed.), *Intermediate punishments: Intensive supervision, home confinement and electronic surveillance.* Monsey, NY: Criminal Justice Press.

Lima, P. (1998, August). Tampa man is guilty in rape charges in Pinellas sex case. *Tampa Tribune,* p. 3.

Lincoln, C. E. (1973). *The Black Muslims in America.* Chicago, IL: University of Chicago Press.

Linder, C. L., & Savarese, M. (1984, June). The evolution of probation. *Federal Probation, 48*(2), 3–10.

Lindsey, R. (1986, June 28). Bingham cleared in 1971 shootout. *The New York Times,* pp. 1, 8.

Linebaugh, P. (1992). *The London hanged: Crime and civil society in the eighteenth century.* New York: Cambridge University Press.

Lipson, S. (1990, December). Aging inmates: The challenge for corrections. In Federal Bureau of Prisons, *Long term confinement and the aging inmate population* (pp. 47–49). Washington, DC: Federal Bureau of Prisons.

Lipton, D. S. (1994). The correctional opportunity: Pathways to drug treatment for offenders. *Journal of Drug Issues, 24*(1–2), 331–348.

Lipton, D. S. (1995). *The effectiveness of treatment for drug abusers under criminal justice supervision.* Washington, DC: National Institute of Justice.

LIS, Inc. (1991, September). Smoke-free jails: Collected resources. Boulder, Colorado: U.S. Department of Justice, National Institute of Corrections.

LIS, Inc. (1995). *Offenders under age 18 in state correctional systems: A national picture.* Longmont, CO: U.S. Department of Justice, National Institute of Corrections Information Center.

LIS, Inc. (1997). *Environmental scan: Working papers.* Longmont, CO: U.S. Department of Justice, National Institute of Corrections Information Center.

Litras, M. F. X. (2000). *Civil rights complaints in U.S. district courts, 1990–1998.* Washington, DC: Bureau of Justice Statistics.

Lockwood, D. (1980). *Prison sexual violence.* New York: Elsevier.

Lombardi, G., Sluder, R. D., & Wallace, D. (1997, June). Mainstreaming death-sentenced inmates: The Missouri experience and its legal significance. *Federal Probation, 61*(2): 3–10.

Lombardo, L. X. (1981). *Guards imprisoned: Correctional officers at work.* New York: Elsevier.

Lombardo, L. X. (1989). *Guards imprisoned: Correctional officers at work* (2nd ed.). Cincinnati: Anderson.

London, R. (1991, February 8). Strategy on sex crimes is prison, then prison. *The New York Times,* Law, p. 16.

Lopez, M., & Chayriques, K. (1994). Billing prisoners for medical care blocks access. *National Prison Project Journal, 9*(2), 1–2.

Lopez, M., & Cheney, C. (1992, Summer). Crowded prisons and jails unable to meet needs of mentally ill. *National Prison Project Journal, 8*(3), 15–16.

Lotke, E. (1996). Sex offenders: Does treatment work? *Corrections Compendium, 21*(5).

Low, P. W., Jeffries, J. C., Jr., & Bonnie, R. J. (1986). *Criminal law: Cases and materials* (2nd ed.). Mineola, NY: The Foundation Press.

Lucas, R. (1999). Captain, Hillsborough County Jail Division, Tampa FL: Personal communication.

Luise, M. A. (1989). Solitary confinement: Legal and psychological considerations. *New England Journal on Criminal and Civil Confinement, 15*(2), 301–324.

Lund, L., & Collins, W. C. (1997). *Session 5: Prison Litigation Reform Act.* Large Jail Network Conference.

Lurgio, A. (1990). Intensive probation supervision: An alternative to prison in the 1980s. *Crime and Delinquency, 36*(1), 3–6.

Lyon, J. (1996). *Research in brief: Long-term inmates.* Albany, NY: State Department of Corrections.

Maahs, J., & Pratt, C., & Hemmens, C. (1999). Current use-of-force policies, practices, and procedures: Results of a national survey. In C. Hemmens & E. Atherton (Eds.), *Use of force: Current practice and policy* (pp. 37–53). Lanham, MD: American Correctional Association.

MacDonald, D. (1980, May). *Follow-up survey of post-release criminal behavior of participants in family reunion program.* Albany, NY: New York Department of Correctional Services.

MacDonald, D., & Bala, G. (1986, March). *Follow-up study sample of family reunion participants.* Albany, NY: New York Department of Correctional Services.

MacDonald, J., & Gifford, R. (1989). Territorial cues and defensible space theory: The burglar's point of view, *Journal of Environmental Psychology, 9,* 193–205.

Mackay, D. (1985). *A place of exile: The European settlement of New South Wales.* Melbourne: Oxford University Press.

MacKenzie, D. L. (1993, November). Boot camp prisons in 1993. *National Institute of Justice Journal,* 21–28.

MacKenzie, D. L, Shaw, J., & Gowdy, V. (1993). *An evaluation of shock incarceration in Louisiana.* Washington, DC: National Institute of Justice.

MacKenzie, D. L., & Souryal, C. (1994, November). *Multisite evaluation of shock incarceration.* Washington, DC: National Institute of Justice.

Maghan, J. (1981). Guarding in prison. In D. Fogel, & J. Hudson (Eds.,) *Justice as fairness.* Cincinnati, OH: Anderson Publishing Co.

Maghan, J. (1994, July). Measuring training. *Corrections Compendium,* pp. 1–3.

Maghan, J. (1994, September 30). Vice President, International Association of Correctional Officers. Personal communication.

Maguire, K., & Pastore A. (Eds.). (1996). *Sourcebook of criminal justice statistics, 1995.* Washington, DC: U.S. Department of Justice, Bureau of Justice Statistics.

Maguire, K., & Pastore, A. (Eds.). (1997). *Sourcebook 1996.* Washington, DC: Bureau of Justice Statistics.

Maguire, K., & Pastore, A. L. (Eds.). (1999). *Sourcebook of criminal justice statistics, 1998.* Washington, DC: Bureau of Justice Statistics.

Maguire, M., & Pastore, A. L. (1994). *Sourcebook of criminal justice statistics, 1993.* Washington, DC: U.S. Department of Justice.

Maguire, M., Pastore, A. L., & Flanagan, T. L. (1993). *Sourcebook of criminal justice statistics, 1992.* Washington, DC: U.S. Department of Justice.

Mair, G. (1988). *Probation day centres.* London, England: HMSO Books.

Maitland, A. S., & Sluder, R. D. (1996). Victimization in prison: A study of factors related to the general well-being of youthful inmates. *Federal Probation, 60*(2): 24–31.

Malcolm X. (1965). *The autobiography of Malcolm X.* New York: Grove Press.

Malcolm, A. H. (1989, May 3). Tainted trials stir fears of wrongful executions. *The New York Times,* p. 9.

Males, M., Macular, A., & Taq-Eddin. *Striking out: The failure of California's "three strikes and you're out" law.* Washington, DC: Justice Policy Institute.

Malloy, T. E., & Mays, G. L. (1984). The police stress hypothesis. *Criminal Justice and Behavior, 11*(2): 197–224.

Maltz, M. D. (1984). *Recidivism.* Orlando, FL: Academic Press.

Mann, C. (1984). *Female crime and delinquency.* Birmingham, AL: University of Alabama Press.

Mann, T. (1999). General manager, Labor Line, an affiliate of PRIDE of Florida. Personal communication.

Mann, T. (1999). PRIDE in the name of jobs: A new approach to offender job placement. *Corrections Today 61(6),* 110–112, 131.

Mann, T. (2000). General manager, Labor Line, an affiliate of PRIDE of Florida. Personal communication.

Marble, G. (1988, June). Chaplain ministers to Texas death row. *Corrections Today,* pp. 96–97.

March, J. (1995, Sept. 11). Public Affairs Officer, Washington Attorney General's Office. Personal communication.

Marchese, J. D. (1990). Emergency preparedness planning for jail officers. *Jail Operations Bulletin, 2*(9).

Marciniak, L. M. (1999). The use of day reporting as an intermediate sanction: A study of offender targeting and program termination. *Prison Journal, 79*(2): 205–225.

Marke, J. J. (1988). Prisoner's right of access to law libraries. *New York Law Journal, 200*(118), 4–5.

Markley, C. W. (1973). Furlough programs and conjugal visiting in adult correctional institutions. *Federal Probation, 37*(1), 19–26.

Markman, S., & Cassell, P. (1988). Protecting the innocent: A response to the Bedau-Radalet study. *Stanford Law Review, 41,* 121–170.

Marlatt, G., & Gordon, J. (1980). Determinants of relapse: Implications for the maintenance of change. In P. O. Davis & S. M. Davidson (Eds.), *Behavioral medicine: Changing health styles.* New York: Brunner/Mazel.

Marlette, M. (1990a). An essential part of corrections: Drug treatment programs for inmates. *Corrections Compendium 15*(6), pp. 1, 5–20.

Marlette, M. (1990b). Furloughs tightened—Success rates high. *Corrections Compendium, 15*(1), pp. 1, 6–8.

Marquart, J. W. (1986). Prison guards and the use of physical coercion as a mechanism of prisoner control. *Criminology, 24*(4), 347–366.

Marquart, J. W. (1990). Prison guards and the use of physical coercion as a mechanism of prisoner control. In D. H. Kelly

(Ed.), *Criminal behavior: Text and readings in criminology* (2nd ed., pp. 528–544). New York: St. Martin's Press.

Marquart, J. W., & Crouch, B. M. (1984). Coopting the kept: Using inmates for social control in a southern prison. *Justice Quarterly, 1*(4), 491–509.

Marquart, J. W., Ekland-Olson, S., & Sorensen, J. R. (1989). Gazing into the crystal ball: Can jurors accurately predict dangerousness in capital cases? *Law & Society Review, 23*(3).

Marquart, J. W., & Sorensen, J. R. (1988). Institutional and postrelease behavior of *Furman*-commuted inmates in Texas. *Criminology, 26*(4): 677, 692–693.

Marques, J. K., Day, D. M., Nelson, C., & Miner, M. H. (1989). *The sex offender treatment and evaluation project.* Sacramento, CA: Department of Mental Health.

Marriott, M. (1994, March 5). 'Manhood' classes at Mosque: Hope, discipline and defiance. *The New York Times*, pp. 1A, 8A.

Marshall, I. H., & Horney, J. (1991). *Motives for crime and self-image among a sample of convicted felons.* Paper presented at the annual meeting of the American Society of Criminology, San Francisco.

Marshall, R. (1999, May). *Preliminary opinion on the economics of inmate labor participation.* Paper presented at the National Symposium on the Economics of Inmate Labor Force Participation, Washington, DC.

Marshall, W. L., Jones, R., Ward, T., & Johnson, P. (1991). Treatment outcome with sex offenders. *Clinical Psychology Review, 11*, 465–485.

Martin, R., & Zimmerman, S. (1990, December). A typology of the causes of prison riots and an analytical extension to the 1986 West Virginia riot. *Justice Quarterly, 7*(4), 711–738.

Martin, S. J., & Eckland-Olson, S. (1987). *Texas prisons: The walls came tumbling down.* Austin, TX: Texas Monthly Press.

Martinez, R., & Wetli, C. V. (1982). Santeria: A magico-religious system of Afro-Cuban origin. *The American Journal of Social Psychiatry II, 3*(Summer), 32–38.

Martinson, R. (1975). What works?—Questions and answers about prison reform. *Public Interest, 35*, 22–54.

Maruschak, L. M. (1999). *DWI offenders under correctional supervision.* Washington, DC: U.S. Department of Justice, Bureau of Justice Statistics.

Maruschak, L. M. (1999, November). *HIV in prisons 1997.* Washington, DC: Bureau of Justice Statistics.

Marzulli, J. (1999, January). Parolee in new uproar—He's charged in two slayings since his release. *Daily News (New York)*, p. 1.

Maslach, C. (1982). *Burnout: The cost of caring.* Englewood Cliffs, NJ: Prentice Hall.

Maslach, C., & Jackson, S. E. (1981). The measurement of experienced burnout. *Journal of Occupational Behavior, 2*, 99–113.

Mason, G. L. (1990). Indeterminate sentencing: Cruel and unusual punishment, or just plain cruel. *New England Journal on Criminal and Civil Confinement, 16*(1), 89–120.

Matson, S., with Lieb, R. (1996, July). *Sex offender registration: A review of state laws.* Olympia, WA: Washington State Institute for Public Policy.

Matson, S., with Lieb, R. (1996, November). *Community notification in Washington State: 1996 survey of law enforcement.* Olympia, WA: Washington State Institute for Public Policy.

Matson, S., with Lieb, R. (1996, October). *Megan's law: A review of state and federal legislation.* Olympia, WA: Washington State Institute for Public Policy.

Mauer, M. (1994, July). 3 strikes and you're out. *Corrections Compendium*, pp. 15–16.

Mauer, M. (1995). *Intended and unintended consequences of racial disparities in imprisonment.* Washington, DC: The Sentencing Project.

Mauer, M., & Huling, T. (1995). *Young black Americans and the criminal justice system.* Washington, DC: The Sentencing Project.

Mayer, C. (1986). Legal issues surrounding private operation of prisons. *Criminal Law Bulletin*, pp. 309–325.

Mayer, C. (1989). Survey of case law establishing constitutional minima for the provision of mental health services to psychiatrically involved inmates. *New England Journal of Criminal and Civil Confinement, 15*(2), pp. 243–275.

Mays, G. L., & Winfree, L. T. (1998). *Contemporary corrections.* Belmont, CA: West/Wadsworth.

Mays, G. L., Fields, C. B., & Thompson, J. A. (1991). Preincarceration patterns of drug and alcohol use by jail inmates. *Criminal Justice Policy Review, 5*(1), 30–52.

McBride, D., & VanderWaal, C. (1997). Day reporting centers as an alternative for drug using offenders. *Journal of Drug Issues, 27*(2): 379–397.

McCall, G. (1981, April). Leisure restructuring. *Journal of physical education and recreation, 52*(4), 38–39.

McCall, G. (1988, December). The history of the NCRA 1966 through 1988; 22 years of growth. *Correctional Recreation Today, 3*(4), 9–10.

McCall, G. (1993, December). Associate Professor, Department of Recreation, University of Florida. Personal communication.

McCall, G. (1996). Corrections and social deviance. In D. Austin & M. E. Crawford (Eds.), *Therapeutic recreation: An introduction* (2nd ed.). Boston: Allyn and Bacon.

McCarthy, B. (1985, March). Mentally ill and mentally retarded offenders in corrections. In New York State Department of Corrections (Ed.), *Source book on the mentally disordered prisoner* (pp. 13–30). Washington DC: National Institute of Corrections.

McCarthy, B. R., & McCarthy, B. J. (1991). *Community based corrections* (2nd ed.). Pacific Grove, CA: Brooks/Cole.

McCarthy, J. (1998). Transition to accreditation. *American Jails, 12*(4).

McCartt, J., & Mangogna, T. (1973). *Guidelines and standards for halfway houses and community treatment centers.* Washington, DC: U.S. Government Printing Office.

McClain, P., Sheehan, B., & Butler, L. (1998). Prisoner's right: Substantive rights retained by prisoners. *Georgetown Law Review*, 1972.

McClone, J. (1998). Superintendent, Ohio Central School System. Personal communication.

McCollum, S. G. (1992). Mandatory literacy: Evaluating the Bureau of Prisons' long standing commitment. *Federal Prisons Journal*, *3*(2), 33–36.

McConville, S. (1985, October). *Prison gangs*. Symposium conducted at the annual meeting of the Midwestern Criminal Justice Association, Chicago.

McCorkle, R. C. (1992). Institutional violence: How do inmates cope? *Forum on Corrections Research*, *4*(3): 9–11.

McCorkle, R. C. (1992). Personal precautions to violence. *Criminal Justice and Behavior, 19*(2): 161–173.

McDonald, D. C. (1992). Introduction: The day fine as a means of expanding judges' sentencing options. In D. C. McDonald (Ed.), *Day fines in American courts: The Staten Island and Milwaukee experiments*. Washington, DC: U.S. Department of Justice, Office of Justice Programs.

McDonald, D., Hassol, A., & Carlson, K. (1999, July). Can telemedicine reduce spending and improve prisoner health care? *National Institute of Justice Journal*, 20–25.

McEntee, G. W. (1993, July). President's column. *AFSCME Public Employee, 58*(5), 3.

McFarland, S. G. (1983). Is capital punishment a short term deterrent to homicide? A study of the effects of four recent American executions. *Journal of Criminal Law and Criminology, 74*, 1014–1032.

McGaha, J., Fichter, M., & Hirschburg, P. (1987). Felony probation: A reexamination of public risk. *American Journal of Criminal Justice, 11*, 1–9.

McGillis, D. *Community mediation: Developments and challenges*. Washington, DC: Office of Justice Programs.

McGinnis, K. L. (1990) Programming for long-term inmates. *Prison Journal, 70*(1), 119–120.

McGrath, R. J., & Carey, C. H. (1987). Treatment of men who molest children—A program description. *Journal of Offender Counseling, 7*(2), 23–33.

McGregor, D. (1960). *The human side of enterprise*. New York: McGraw-Hill.

McKelvey, B. (1977). *American prisons: A history of good intentions*. Montclair, NJ: Patterson Smith.

McMillian, T. (1985). Habeas Corpus and the Burger court. In I. P. Robbins (Ed.), *Prisoners and the law*. New York: Clark Boardman Co.

McShane, M. D., & Krause, W. (1993). *Community corrections*. New York: MacMillan Publishing Co.

McShane, M. D., Williams, F. P., & Wagoner, C. P. (1992, January). Prison impact studies: Comments on methodological rigor. *Journal of Crime and Delinquency, 38*(1), 105–120.

Megargee, E. I. (1971). Population density and disruptive behavior in a prison setting. In A. Cohen, G. Cole, & R. Bailey (Eds.), *Prison violence*. Lexington, MA: DC Heath.

Meier, K. J. (1987). *Politics and the bureaucracy*. Monterey, CA: Brooks/Cole.

Metzgar, S. (1996). Electronic fence secure for but prison jobs. p. B2.

Millard, P. (1988, July). Inside Marion: Warden Gary Hennan talks about BOP's most secure prison. *Corrections Today*, pp. 92–94, 96–98.

Miller, F. W., Dawson, R. O., Dix, G. E., & Parnas, R. I. (1976). *Criminal justice administration*. Mineola, NY: The Foundation Press.

Miller, F. W., Dawson, R. O., Dix, G. E., & Parnas, R. O. (1991). *Criminal justice administration: Cases and materials* (4th ed.). Westbury, NY: Foundation Press.

Miller, N., & Grieser, R. C. (1986). The evolution of prison industries. In American Correctional Association (Eds.), *A study of prison industry: History, components, and goals*. Washington, DC: National Institute of Corrections.

Miller, R. (2000). President of CRS Inc. Personal communication.

Miller, S., Dinitz, S., & Conrad, J. P. (1982). *Careers of the violent few: The dangerous offender and criminal justice*. Lexington, MA: Lexington Books.

Minnesota Department of Corrections. (1997). *Background: Restorative justice*. St. Paul, MN: Author.

Minnesota Department of Corrections. (1997). *Minnesota sex offender screening tool*. St. Paul, MN.

Minnesota Statutes. (1993). Criminal sentences, conditions, duration, appeals: Supervised release term. *Minnesota Statutes 244.05*, St. Paul, MN.

Mitsubishi Electronics Inc. (1990). The comprehensive tools for breath alcohol monitoring in home detention programs. Sunnyvale, CA: Author.

Modlin, B. (1991, Fall). Naked men and uniformed women: The erotic element in cross gender supervision. *Odyssey*, pp. 67–78.

Montes, M. (1996). Technical advances in parole supervision. *Corrections Today*, (July): 88, 90–91.

Mooney, M. (1996, February). Fear as inmates kick butts. *Daily News*, p. 14.

Moore, J. W. (1978). *Homeboys: Gangs, drugs, and prison in the barrios of Los Angeles*. Philadelphia: Temple University Press.

Moos, M. C. (1942). *State penal administration in Alabama*. Tuscaloosa, AL: Bureau of Public Administration, University of Alabama.

Morain, D. (1986, September 26). Inmate convicted in prison killings gets retrial. *Los Angeles Times*, Part 1, p. 3.

Morash, M., Bynum, T. S., & Koons, B. A. (1996). *Women offenders: Programming needs and promising approaches*. Washington, DC: National Institute of Justice.

Morgenbesser, L. (1984). Psychological screening mandated for New York correctional officer applicants. *Corrections Today, 46*, 28–29.

Moriarty, D. (1991). Jail training—Preparing officers for today's inmates. *Corrections Today, 53*(7), 72–75.

Morris, D. W. (1974). The university's role in prison education. In A. Roberts (Ed.), *Readings in prison education.* Springfield IL: Charles C. Thomas.

Morris, N., & Tonry, M. (1990). *Between prison and probation: Intermediate punishments in a rational sentencing system.* Oxford, England: Oxford University Press.

Morris, S. M., Steadman, H. J., & Veysey, B. M. (1997, March). Mental health services in United States jails: A survey of innovative practices. *Criminal Justice and Behavior, 24*(2): 3–19.

Morse, W. (Ed.). (1940). *The attorney general's survey of release procedures.* Washington, DC: U.S. Government Printing Office.

Morton, J. B. (1992a, August). *An administrative view of the older inmate.* Washington, DC: National Institute of Corrections.

Morton, J. B. (1992b, August). Women in corrections: Looking back on 200 years of valuable contributions. *Corrections Today,* pp. 76–87.

Morton, J. B. (1998). Programming for women offenders. In J. B. Morton (Ed.), *Complex challenges, collaborative solutions: Programming for adult and juvenile offenders.* Lanham, MD: American Correctional Association.

Moses, M. (1996). *Keeping incarcerated mothers and their daughters together.* Washington, DC: National Institute of Justice.

Moses, M. C. (1993, August). Girl scouts behind bars: New program at women's prison benefits mothers and children. *Corrections Today,* pp. 132–135.

Moses, M. C. (1996). *Project re-enterprise: A Texas program.* Washington, DC: National Institute of Justice.

Mouzakitis, C. M. (1981). Inquiring into the problem of child abuse and juvenile delinquency. In R. J. Hummer & Y. E. Walker (Eds.), *Exploring the relationship between child abuse and delinquency.* Montclair, NJ: Allanheld.

Moynahan, J. (1992). An American gaoler in London: A self guided tour American gaolers may take of gaol-related pubs in and around the central London district. *American Jails, 6*(4), 79–86.

Mullen, R. (1991, September). Therapeutic communities in prison: Dealing with toxic waste. *Proceedings for the 14th World Conference on Therapeutic Communities.*

Mumola, C. J. (1999, January). *Substance abuse and treatment: State and federal prisoners, 1997.* Washington, DC: National Institute of Justice.

Mumola, C. J. (2000, January). *Veterans in prison or jail.* Washington, DC: BJS.

Muraskin, R. (1989). *Disparity of correctional treatment: Development of a measurement instrument.* Unpublished doctoral dissertation, City University of New York.

Murphy, S. P. (1992, June 30). Weld proposal on sex criminals will be challenged, lawyers say. *The Boston Globe,* pp. 17–18.

Murphy, W. D., & Von Minden, S. (1981, April). Hard time and free time. *Journal of Physical Education and Recreation, 52*(4), 50–52.

Murray, C., & Cox, L. (1979). *Beyond probation: Corrections and the chronic delinquent.* Beverly Hills, CA: Sage Publications.

Murton, T., & Hyams, J. (1969). *Accomplices to the crime: The Arkansas prison scandal.* New York: Grove Press.

Mushlin, M. (1993). *Rights of prisoners* (2nd ed.). Colorado Springs, CO: Shepard's/McGraw-Hill.

Mushlin, M. (1997). *Rights of prisoners: Supplement to volume 2.* (2nd ed.). St. Paul, MN: West Group.

Mushlin, M. (1998). *Rights of prisoners: Cumulative supplement to volume 1.* (2nd ed.). United States: McGraw-Hill.

Mushlin, M. (1998a). *Rights of prisoners—1998 cumulative supplement to volume 2* (2nd ed.). St. Paul MN: West Group.

Mushlin, M. (1998b). *Rights of prisoners: Supplement to volume 1* (2nd ed.). Eagen, MN: West Group.

Mustin, J. W., & Bee, C. W. (1992). *Directory of programs serving families of adult offenders.* Washington, DC: U.S. Department of Justice.

Myers, M. A. (1998). *Race, labor, & punishment in the new South.* Columbus, OH: Ohio State University Press.

NAACP Legal Defense Fund. (2000, January). *Death row USA.* New York: Author, pp. 24–25.

Nacci, P. L., & Kane, T. R. (1983, December). The incidence of sex and sexual aggression in federal prisons. *Federal Probation, 47*(4), *31–36.*

Nacci, P. L., & Kane, T. R. (1984, March). Sex and sexual aggression in federal prisons: Inmate involvement and employee impact. *Federal Probation, 48*(1), 46–53.

Nadel, B. (1993, July). Architectural group addresses state's TB problem. *CorrectCare, 7*(3), 4.

Nagel, W. G. (1973). *The new red barn: A critical look at the modern American prison.* New York: Walker and Co.

Nagin, D. S. (1998). Deterrence and incapacitation. In M. Tonry (Ed.), *The handbook of crime & punishment* (pp. 345–368). New York: Oxford University Press.

Nathan, V. M. (1978). The use of masters in institutional litigation. *The University of Toledo Law Review, 10*, 419–464.

National Advisory Commission on Civil Disorders. (1968). *Report.* New York: Bantam Books.

National Commission on Correctional Health Care. (1992). *Standards for health services ill prisons.* Chicago: Author.

National Correctional Recreation Association. (undated). *National mission statement, policy statement, personnel standards, facility standards for correctional recreation.* Author.

National Criminal Justice Association. (1997). *Sex offender community notification.* Washington, DC: Author.

National Institute of Corrections. (1981). *Prison classification: A model systems approach.* Washington, DC: Department of Justice.

National Institute of Corrections. (1983, May). *Handbook for special masters: Judicial version.* Washington, DC: U.S. Department of Justice.

National Institute of Corrections. (1987, July). *Guidelines for the development of a security program.* Washington, DC: U.S. Department of Justice.

National Institute of Corrections. (1991). *Management strategies, in disturbances and with gangs/disruptive groups.* Washington, DC: U.S. Department of Justice.

National Institute of Corrections. (1997, September). *Prison medical care: Special needs populations and cost control.* Longmont, CO: Author.

National Institute of Corrections. (1998, September). *Hospice and palliative care in prisons.* Longmont, CO: Author.

National Institute of Justice. (1994). *Oleoresin capsicum: Pepper spray as a force alternative.* Washington, DC: U.S. Department of Justice.

National Institute of Justice. (1999, March). *Telemedicine can reduce correctional health care costs: An evaluation of a prison telemedicine network.* Washington, DC: Author.

National Prison Hospice Association. (2000). http//:www.nhpa.org.

National Prison Project Journal. (1994/95, Winter). Status Report: State prisons and the courts, January 1, 1995. Author, 10(1), p. 5.

Needels, K. E. (1996). *What uncensored data tell us about censoring: Prediction recidivism rates from a long-term follow-up.* Princeton, NJ: Mathematical Policy Research, Inc.

Nelson, C. (1974). *A study of homosexuality among women inmates at two state prisons.* Ph.D. dissertation, Temple University, Philadelphia.

Nelson, E. K., Ohmart, H., & Harlow, N. (1978). *Promising strategies in probation and parole.* Washington, D.C.: U. S. Government Printing Office.

Nelson, R. W. (1988). The origins of the podular direct supervision concept: An eyewitness account. *American Jails, 2*(1), 8–16.

Nelson, V. F. (1933). *Prison days and nights.* Garden City, NY: Garden City Publishing Co.

Nesbit, C. A. (1992). The female offender: Overview of facility planning and design issues and considerations. *Corrections Compendium, 27*(8), 1, 5–7.

Neto, V. V. (1989). Prison visitors: A profile. In J. Mustin & B. Bloom (Conference Directors), *The First National Conference on the Family and Corrections* (pp. 33–39). Richmond, KY: Training Resource Center, Department of Correctional Services, Eastern Kentucky University.

Neto, V., & Banier, L. M. (1983). Mother and wife locked up: A day with the family. *The Prison Journal, 63*(2), 124–141.

New York State Department of Correctional Services and the New York Division of Parole (1998). *Seventh annual shock legislative report.* Albany, NY: Author.

New York State Department of Correctional Services. (1988, April). Grandmas' key helpers at Arthur Kill. In *Inmate family service programs* (pp. 14, 22). Albany, NY: Author.

New York State Department of Correctional Services. (1993, October). *Bedford Hills Correctional Facility Children's Center fact sheet.* Bedford Hills, NY: Author.

New York State Special Commission on Attica. (1972). *Official Report.* New York: Bantam Books.

New York Times. (1999, May 29). Hepatitis C is found rife among inmates. *New York Times,* p. A12.

Newman, D. J. (1975). *Introduction to criminal justice.* Philadelphia: J. B. Lippincott Co.

Newman, G. (1978). *The punishment response.* New York: J. B. Lippincott Co.

NIC Information Center. (1998). *Use of physical restraints/restraint chair: Policies and procedures from various jail facilities.* Longmont, CO: Author.

Nicolai, S. (1981, April). Rehabilitation and leisure in prisons. *Journal of Physical Education and Recreation, 52*(4), 33–35.

Ninth Circuit Gender Bias Task Force. (1993, July). *The final report of the 9th Circuit Gender Bias Task Force.*

Nobel, J. B. (1997). Ensuring meaningful jailhouse legal assistance: The need for a jailhouse lawyer-inmate privilege. *Cardoza Law Review,* 1569–1607.

Northham, G. (1985, April). America's new generation prisons: Can we learn any lessons from death row? *The Listener,* pp. 5–7.

Nossiter, A. (1994, September 17). Making hard time harder, states cut jail TV and sports. *The New York Times,* pp. 1a, 10a.

Nunnellee, D. (1994, November 12). Public Information Officer, Texas Department of Criminal Justice. Personal communication.

O'Bryan, S. H. (1997). Closing the courthouse door: The impact of the Prison Litigation Reform Act's physical injury requirement on the constitutional rights of prisoners. *Virginia Law Review, 83:* 1189–1224.

Office of Justice Program. (1998, October). *State efforts to reduce substance abuse among offenders.* Washington, DC: Author.

Office of Juvenile Justice and Delinquency Prevention. (1997). *1996 national youth gang survey.* Washington, DC: U.S. Department of Justice.

Office of National Drug Control Policy. (1990). *Understanding drug treatment.* Washington, DC: The White House.

Ohlin, L. E. (1951). *Selection for parole.* New York: Russell Sage Foundation.

Oppenheimer, H. (1975). *The rationale of punishment.* Montclair, NJ: Patterson Smith. (Original work published 1913.)

Oshinsky, D. M. (1996). *Worse than slavery: Parchman Farm and the ordeal of Jim Crow justice.* New York: The Free Press.

O'Toole, M. (1997). Jails and prisons: The numbers say they are more different than assumed. *American Jails, 10*(4): 25–29.

Owen, B. (1985). Race and gender relations among prison workers. *Crime and Delinquency, 31,* 147–159.

Owen, B. (1998). *In the mix: Struggle and survival in a women's prison.* New York: State University of New York Press.

Palm Beach County Sheriff's Office. (1987). Palm Beach County's in-house arrest work release program. In B. McCarthy (Ed.), *Intermediate punishments: Intensive supervision, home confinement and election surveillance.* Monsey, NY: Criminal Justice Press.

Palmer, J. W. (1977). *Constitutional rights of prisoners*. Cincinnati, OH: Anderson Publishing Co.

Palmer, J. W. (1991). *Constitutional rights of prisoners*. Cincinnati, OH: Anderson Publishing Co.

Palmer, J. W. (1999). *Constitutional rights of prisoners* (6th ed.). Cincinnati: Anderson.

Palmer, T. (1978). *Correctional intervention and research*. Lexington, MA: Lexington Books.

Palmer, T. (1992). The re-emergence of correctional intervention. Newbury Park, CA: Sage Publications.

Parent, D., Dunworth, T., McDonald, D., & Rhodes, W. (1997). *Key legislative issues in criminal justice: Intermediate sanctions*. Washington, DC: National Institute of Justice, U.S. Department of Justice.

Parent, D., & Snyder, B. *Police-corrections partnerships*. Washington, DC: National Institute of Justice.

Parent, D. G. (1989). *Shock incarceration: An overview of existing programs*. Washington, DC: U.S. Department of Justice.

Parent, D. G. (1990a, May). *Residential community corrections: Developing an integrated policy*. Washington, DC: U.S. Department of Justice.

Parent, D. G. (1990b, September). *Day reporting centers for criminal offenders: A descriptive analysis of existing programs*. Washington, DC: U.S. Department of Justice.

Parent, D. G. (1990c). *Recovering correctional costs through offender fees*. Washington, DC: U.S. Department of Justice.

Parent, D. G., Wentworth, D., Burke, P., & Ney, B. (1994). *Responding to probation and parole violators*. Washington, DC: U.S. Department of Justice.

Parker, W. (1975). *Parole*. College Park, MD: American Correctional Association.

Parrish, D. (2000). Colonel/Commander, Jail Division, Hillsborough Sheriffs Office. Personal communication.

Parry, L. A. (1975). *The history of torture in England*. Montclair, NJ: Patterson Smith. (Original work published 1934.)

Parsonage, W. H. (1990). *Worker safety in probation and parole*. Longmont, CO: National Institute of Corrections.

Pataki, G. E. (1996, August). The death penalty brings justice. *Corrections Today*.

Paternoster, R. (1991). Prosecutorial discretion and capital sentencing in North and South Carolina. In R. M Bohm (Ed.), *The death penalty in America: Current research*. Cincinnati, OH: Anderson Publishing Co.

Patrick, A. L. (1986). Private sector—Profit motive vs. quality. *Corrections Today, 48*(2), 68–71.

Patrick, W. J. (1994, January 21). Senior Deputy Director for Administration, Federal Bureau of Prisons. Personal communication.

Pearson, F. (1987). Taking quality into account: Assessing the benefits and costs of New Jersey's intensive supervision program. In B. McCarthy (Ed.), *Intermediate punishments: Intensive supervision, home confinement and electronic surveillance*. Monsey, NY: Criminal Justice Press.

Pearson, F., & Harper, A. (1990). Contingent intermediate sanctions: New Jersey's intensive supervision program. *Crime and Delinquency, 36*(1), 75–85.

Peed, C. (1989). Inmate classification procedures. *Jail Operations Bulletin, 1*(6).

Peltz, M. E. (1986, March). *When brotherhood leads to violence, Managing inmate gangs in the Texas prison system*. Paper presented at the annual meeting of the Southwestern Sociology Association, San Antonio, TX.

Pelz, B. (2000). Prison gangs vs. incarcerated street gangs. *Corrections: A comprehensive view* (2nd ed.). Belmont, CA: Wadsworth.

Pepper, B., & Hendrickson, E. L. (1996, March). Working with seriously mentally ill substance abusers. In A. J. Lurigio (Ed.), *Community corrections in America: New directions and sounder investment for persons with mental illness and co-disorders*. Seattle, WA: National Coalition for Mental Health and Substance Abuse in the Justice System.

Perkins, C. (1992). *National corrections reporting program, 1986*. Washington, DC: U.S. Department of Justice.

Perkins, C. (1993). *National corrections reporting program*, 1990. Washington, DC: U.S. Department of Justice.

Perkins, C. (1994, Feb.). *National corrections reporting program, 1991*. Washington, DC: U.S. Department of Justice.

Perkins, C. (1994, October). *National corrections reporting program, 1992*. Washington, D.C.: U. S. Department of Justice.

Perkins, C. A., Stephan, J. J., & Beck, A. J. (1995, April). *Jails and jail inmates 1993–94*. Washington, DC: Bureau of Justice Statistics.

Pertman, A. (1997, April). Security envelops Rushdie at Amherst. *Boston Globe*, p. A1.

Peters, H. A. (1993, November 1). Caution on prison religious freedom. *Chicago Tribune*, p. 18.

Peters, R. H. (1993). Drug treatment in jails and detention settings. In J. Inciardi (Ed.), *Drug treatment and criminal justice* (pp. 44–80). Newbury Park, CA: Sage Publications.

Peters, R. H., & Bartoi, M. G. (1997, April). *Screening and assessment of co-occurring disorders in the justice system*. Delmar, NY: Policy Research, Inc., National GAINS Center.

Peters, R., Kearns, W. D., Murin, M., & Dolante, D. (1992). Effectiveness of in-jail substance abuse treatment: Evaluation results from a national demonstration program. *American Jails, 6*(l), 98–104.

Petersilia, J. (1983). *Racial disparities in the criminal justice system*. Santa Monica, CA: Rand Corp.

Petersilia, J. (1987). *Expanding options for criminal sentencing*. Santa Monica, CA: Rand Corp.

Petersilia, J. (1988). *House arrest: Crime file study guide*. Washington, DC: U.S. Department of Justice, National Institute of Justice.

Petersilia, J. (1990). Conditions that permit intensive supervision to survive. *Crime and Delinquency, 36*(1), 126–145.

Petersilia, J. (1998). Probation and parole. In M. Tonry (Ed.), *The handbook of crime & punishment* (pp. 563–587). New York: Oxford University Press.

Petersilia, J., Greenwood, P., & Lavin, M. (1978). *Criminal careers of habitual felons*. Washington, DC: U.S. Department of Justice, National Institute of Law Enforcement and Criminal Justice.

Petersilia, J., Honig, P., & Hubay, C. (1980). *Prison experience of career criminals*. Washington, DC: National Institute of Justice.

Petersilia, J., & Turner, S. (1988, June). Research perspectives—Minorities in prison. *Corrections Today, 50*(3), 92–95.

Petersilia, J., & Turner, S. (1990). Comparing intensive and regular supervision for high-risk probationers: Early results from an experiment in California. *Crime and Delinquency, 36*(1), 87–111.

Petersilia, J., & Turner, S. (1993). *Evaluating intensive supervision Probation/parole: Results of a nationwide experiment*. Washington, DC: U.S. Department of Justice.

Petersilia, J., Turner, S., Kahan, J., & Peterson, J. (1985). *Granting felons probation: Public risks and alternatives*. Santa Monica, CA: Rand Corporation.

Petersilia, J., Turner, S., & Peterson, J. (1986). *Prison versus probation in California: Implications for crime and offender recidivism*. Santa Monica, CA: Rand Corporation.

Peterson, R. D., & Bailey, W. C. (1991). Felony murder and capital punishment. *Criminology, 29*, 367–395.

Pettigrove, F. G. (1910). State prisons of the United States under separate and congregate systems. In C. R. Henderson (Ed.), *Penal and reformatory institutions*. New York: Russell Sage Foundation.

Philliber, S. (1987). Thy brother's keeper: A review of the literature on correctional officers. *Justice Quarterly, 4*, pp. 9–37.

Phillips, R. L., & McConnell, C. R. (1996). *The effective corrections manager: Maximizing staff performance in demanding times*. Gaithersburg, MD: Aspen.

Physicians for Human Rights. (1993). *Cruel and inhuman treatment: The use of four-point restraints in the Onondoga County public safety building*. Boston: Author, p. 60.

Pike, L. O. (1968). *A history of crime in England, illustrating the changes of the laws in the progress of civilization*. (Vols. 1–2). Montclair, NJ: Patterson Smith. (Original work published in 1873–76.)

Pisciotta, A. (1994). *Benevolent repression: Social control and the American reformatory-prison movement*. New York: New York University Press.

Pisciotta, A. W. (1983, October). Scientific reform: The 'new penology' at Elmira, 1876–1900. *Crime & Delinquency, 29*(4), 613–630.

Pollack, R. (1979). The ABCs of prison education. *Corrections Magazine, 5*(3), 60–66.

Pollock, J. (1986). *Sex and supervision: Guarding male and female inmates*. New York: Greenwood Press.

Pollock-Byrne, J. (1990). *Women, prison and crime*. Pacific Grove, CA: Brooks/Cole.

Pompi, K., & Resnick, J. (1987). Retention in a therapeutic community for court referred adolescents and young adults. *American Journal of Drug and Alcohol Abuse, 13*(3), 309–326.

Poole, E., & Regoli, R. M. (1980). Work relations and cynicism among prison guards. *Criminal Justice and Behavior, 7*, 303–314.

Porporino, F. J. (1990). Difference in response to long-term imprisonment: Implications for the management of long-term offenders. *The Prison Journal, 70*(1), 35–44.

Porter, B. (1982, December). California prison gangs: The price of control. *Corrections Magazine, VIII(6)*, 6–19.

Porter, C. (2000). Personal communication.

Porter, R. F., & Porter, J. G. (1984). Survey of attitudes of incarcerated felons on dropping out of public schools. *Journal of Correctional Education, 35*, 80–82.

Pospichal, T. (1991). Division Manager, UNICOR, Plans and Policies, Federal Bureau of Prisons, Personal communication.

Potter, J. (1979, Sept.). Guards' unions: The search for solidarity. *Corrections Magazine, 5*, pp. 25–35.

Potter, J. (1980, Sept.). Should women guards work in prisons for men? *Corrections Magazine, 6*, pp. 30–38.

Powell, J. C. (1970). *The American Siberia or fourteen years experience in a southern convict camp*. Montclair, NJ: Patterson Smith. (Original work published in 1891.)

Powell, R. L. (1993). City shock—Corrections XXI. *American Jails, 7*(5), 9–13.

Powers, E. (1959, July–August). Halfway houses: A historical perspective. *American Journal of Correction, 21*(4), 20–22, 35.

President's Commission on Law Enforcement and Administration. (1967). *The challenge of crime in a free society*. Washington, DC: Bureau of Justice Statistics.

President's Commission on Organized Crime. (1986, April). *The impact: organized crime today*. Washington, DC: U.S. Government Printing Office.

Prettyman, E. B. (1981). The indeterminate sentence and the right to treatment. In D. Fogel & J. Hudson (Eds.), *Justice as fairness: Perspectives on the justice model*. Cincinnati, OH: Anderson Publishing Co.

PRIDE Enterprises. (1999). *Annual report*. Tallahassee, FL: PRIDE.

Prison guard gets 55 months in contraband caper. (1992, October 30). United Press International.

Program Services Office. (1983). *Probation classification and service delivery approach*. Los Angeles, CA: Los Angeles County Probation Department.

Project. (1991). Twentieth annual review of criminal procedure: United States Supreme Court and Courts of Appeals 1989–1990, Part VI: Prisoners' rights. *Georgetown Law Journal, 79*(4), 1253–1305.

Project. (1992). Twenty-first annual review of criminal procedure: United States Supreme Court and Courts of Appeals 1990–1991, Part VI: Prisoners' rights. *Georgetown Law Journal, 80*(4), 1677–1734.

Project. (1994). Twenty-third annual review of criminal procedure: United States Supreme Court and Courts of Appeal 1992–1993, Part VI: Prisoners' rights. *Georgetown Law Review, 82*(3), 1365–1419.

Project. (1997). Twenty-sixth annual review of criminal procedures: Part VI. Prisoner rights United States Supreme Court and Courts of Appeal. *Georgetown Law Journal.*

Propper, A. (1976). *Importation and deprivation perspectives on homosexuality in correctional institutions: An empirical test of their relative efficacy.* Ph.D. dissertation, University of Michigan, Ann Arbor.

Propper, A. (1982). Make believe families and homosexuality among imprisoned girls. *Criminology, 20*(1), 127–139.

Protests force sex offender to move. (1993, July 20). *The New York Times*, p. 8.

Prout, C., & Ross, R. N. (1988). *Care and punishment: The dilemmas of prison medicine.* Pittsburgh, PA: University of Pittsburgh Press.

Public Health Service. (1976). Community-based correctional programs. In R. Carter and L. Wilkins (Ed.), *Probation, parole and community corrections.* New York: John Wiley and Sons.

Public whipping proposed. (1989, January 29). *Tampa Tribune,* p. 2A.

Pugh, R. B. (1968). *Imprisonment in medieval England.* London: Cambridge University Press.

Purdum, T. S. (1997). Registry laws tar sex crime convicts with broad brush. *New York Times* (July 1), pp. A1, A11.

Quinlan, J. M. (1990, December). Welcome. In Federal Bureau of Prisons, *Long term confinement and the aging inmate population* (pp. 7–8). Washington, DC: Federal Bureau of Prisons.

Quinlan, J. M. (1993, December). News of the future: Carving out new territory for American corrections. *Federal Probation, 57*(4), 59–63.

Rachin, R. (1972). So you want to open a halfway house. *Federal Probation, 36*(1), 30–37.

Radelet, M. L., Bedau, H. A., & Putnam, C. E. (1992). *In spite of innocence: Erroneous convictions in capital cases.* Boston: Northeastern University Press.

Rae-Dupree, J. (1991, Dec. 13). He's putting his faith behind bars. *Los Angeles Times*, Sec. B, p. 3.

Rafter, N. H. (1985). *Partial justice: State prisons and their images, 1800–1935.* Boston, MA: Northeastern University Press.

Rafter, N. H. (1990). *Partial justice: Women, prisons and social control* (2nd ed.). New Brunswick, NJ: Transaction Publishers.

Rafter, N. H., & Stanko, E. A. (1982). *Judge, lawyer, victim, thief: Women, gender roles and criminal justice.* Boston: Northeastern University Press.

Ralph, P., Hunter, R. J., Marquart, J. M., & Merianos, D. (1996). Exploring the differences between gang and nongang prisoners. In C. R. Huff (Ed.), *Gangs in America* (2nd ed.). Thousands Oaks, CA: Sage.

Randall, C. (1994). Director, Prison Industries, California Youth Authority. Personal communication.

Rasche, C. (2000). Professor, Department of Criminal Justice, University of North Florida. Personal communication.

Rasmussen, D. W. *An evaluation of juvenile justice innovations in Duval County, Florida.* Tallahassee, FL: Florida State University.

Reed, S. O. (1993). The plight of jail deputies in a sheriff's office. *Sheriff, 48*(1), 10–13.

Reform. (1988). Major outcome study of "Stay'n Out." *Reform—National Program to Develop Comprehensive Prison Drug Treatment, 1*(3), pp. 1, 11.

Reindollar, R. W. (1999, July/August). HCV, inmates, and corrections professionals. *American Jails*, 21–24.

Renzema, M., & Skelton, D. (1990). *Final report: The use of electronic monitoring by criminal justice agencies, 1989.* Washington, DC: U.S. Department of Justice.

Reuters Limited. (1994, March 1). *Florida politicians mull castration for rapists.* Tallahassee, FL: Author.

Reynolds, M. O. (1992, December). *Why does crime pay?* Dallas, TX: National Center for Policy Analysis.

Rhine, E. E., Smith, W. R., & Jackson, R. W. (1991). *Paroling authorities: Recent history and current practices.* Laurel, MD: American Correctional Association.

Rice, M., Harris, G., Varney, G., & Quinsey, B. (1989). *Violence in institutions: Understanding, prevention and control.* Toronto, Canada: Aogrefe and Huber.

Richardson, E. (1998, September). Sometimes, evidence of guilt isn't everything. *New York Times*, p. A27.

Rickards, C. (1968). *The man from devil's island.* New York: Stein and Day.

Rifkin, M. (1995). Farmer v. Brennan: Spotlight on an obvious risk of rape in a hidden world. *Columbia Human Rights Law Review, 26*(2), 273–307.

Riggs, C. (1989, Fall). Chaplaincy in the 1990s: A changing calling. *Federal Prisons Journal*, pp. 4–6.

Rinehart, E. (1990, May 16). Budget cuts may threaten programs to educate inmates. *The Tampa Tribune*, Sec. A, pp. 1, 13.

Rison, R. (1996). Retired prison warden with 35 years of experience who administered five federal prisons. Personal communication.

Rison, R. (2000). Personal communication.

Robinson, J., Wilkins, L. T., Carter, R. M., & Wahl, A. (1969). *The San Francisco project: A study of federal probation and parole.* Berkeley, CA: University of California, School of Criminology.

Robitscher, J. (1980). *The power of psychiatry.* Boston, MA: Houghton Mifflin.

Roehl, J., & Ray, L. (1986, July). *Toward the multi-door courthouse—Dispute resolution intake and referral.* Washington, DC: U.S. Department of Justice, National Institute of Justice.

Rolph, J. E., & Chaiken, J. M. (1987). *Identifying high-rate serious criminals from official records.* Washington, DC: U.S. Department of Justice.

Rosazza, T. (1993, Summer/Fall). Career development: The new frontier. *The Journal of Correctional Training*, pp. 10–11.

Rosecrance, J. (1988). Maintaining the myth of individualized justice: Probation presentence reports. *Justice Quarterly, 5*(2): 235–256.

Rosenthal, A. M. (1989, May). Into the heart of the Gulag. *Reader's Digest*, pp. 71–75.

Ross, D. L. (1989). *A model policy on the use of non-deadly force in corrections: Based on a comprehensive analysis of correctional non-deadly force policies nationwide.* Big Rapids, MI: Criminal Justice Institute, Ferris State University.

Ross, H. L., McCleary, R., & LaFree, G. (1990). Can mandatory jail laws deter drunk driving? The Arizona case. *Journal of Criminal Law and Criminology, 81,* 156–167.

Ross, H., & McKay, B. (1981). The correctional officer: Selection through training. In R. Ross (Ed.), *Prison guard/correctional officer: The use and abuse of the human resources of prisons* (pp. 259–272). Toronto, Canada: Butterworth.

Ross, P. H., & Lawrence, J. E. (1998). Health care for women offenders: Specialized services, needs will challenge correctional administrators into the next century. *Corrections Today, 60*(7): 122–126, 128–129.

Ross, R. R. (1980). *Socio-cognitive developments in the offender: An external review of the UVIC program at Matsqui Penitentiary.* Ottawa, Canada: The Solicitor General.

Ross, R. R., & Fabiano, E. (1982). *Effective correctional treatment: Cognitive components.* Ottawa, Canada: Department of Criminology.

Ross, R. R., & Fabiano, E. (1986). *Female offenders: Correctional afterthoughts.* Jefferson, NC: McFarland and Co.

Ross, R. R., Fabiano, E., & Eweles, C. (1988). Reasoning and rehabilitation. *The International Journal of Offender Therapy and Comparative Criminology, 32,* 29–35.

Rothman, D. J. (1971). *The discovery of the asylum; Social order and disorder in the New Republic.* Boston: Little Brown.

Rothman, D. J. (1980). *Conscience and convenience: The asylum and its alternatives in progressive America.* Boston: Little Brown.

Roulet, E. (1993, October). *Bedford Hills Correctional Facility fact sheet.* Unpublished manuscript, New York State Department of Corrections, Bedford Hills, NY.

Rowan, J. R. (1991). Beware the halo effect of mental health personnel when they say "not suicidal." Recommended: A national policy change. *American Jails, 4*(5), 24–27.

Rowan, J. R. (1996). Research perspectives: Who is safer in male maximum security prisons? *Corrections Today, 58*(2): 186–189.

Royko, M. (1995, March 10). Life sentence fits the crime: Being a jerk. *The Tampa Tribune,* Nation/World, p. 13.

Rubin, S. (1973). Law *of criminal correction.* St. Paul, MN: West Publishing Co.

Rudin, J. P. (1998). Teaching undergraduate business management courses on campus and in prison. *Journal of Correctional Education, 49*(3): 100–105.

Rusche, G., & Kirchheimer, O. (1967). *Punishment and social structure.* New York: Russell and Russell. (Original work published in 1939.)

Rutherford, A. (1985, September). The new generation of prisons. *New Society, 20,* pp. 408–410.

Ryan, T. A. (1984). *Adult female offenders and institutional programs: A state of the art analysis.* Washington, DC: National Institute of Corrections.

Ryan, T. A. (1990, November). Literacy training and reintegration of offenders. *Forum on Corrections Research.*

Ryan, T. A., & Woodard, J. C. (1987). *Correctional education: A state-of-the-art analysis.* Washington, DC: National Institute of Corrections.

Ryan, T., & Plummer, C. C. (1999). Jail accreditation: A panacea or problem? *Corrections Today, 61*(2).

Sabath, M. J., & Cowles, E. L. (1990). Using multiple perspectives to develop strategies for managing long-term inmates. *The Prison Journal, 70*(1), 58–72.

Saenz, A. B., & Reeves, T. Z. (1989, July). Riot aftermath: New Mexico's experience teaches valuable lessons. *Corrections Today,* pp. 66, 67, 70, 88.

Salter, A. C. (1988). *Treating child sex offenders and victims: A practical guide.* Newbury Park, CA: Sage Publications.

Samolinski, C. J. (1998). Chiles signs sexual predators law. *Tampa Tribune* (May 20), pp. 5–6.

Samuels, H. (1991). Criminal histories and addiction addressed in a rehabilitative setting. *American Jails, 5*(4), 33–38.

Sanchez, C. S. (1993, August). Teaching inmates thinking skills. *Corrections Today,* pp. 162–165.

Sands, B. (1964). *My shadow ran fast.* New York: Signet Books.

Sandys, M., & McGarrell, E. F. (1994, December). Attitudes toward capital punishment among Indiana legislators: Diminished support in light of alternative sentencing options. *Justice Quarterly, 11*(4).

Santaour, M. B. (1990). Mentally retarded offenders: Texas program targets basic needs. *Corrections Today, 52*(1), 52, 92, 106.

Santos, M. G. (1995). Facing long-term imprisonment. In T. J. Flanagan (Ed.), *Long-term imprisonment: Policy science and correctional practice.* Thousands Oaks, CA: Sage.

Saylor, W. G., & Gaes, G. G. (1992). Prison work has measurable results on post-release success. *Federal Prisons Journal, 2*(4), 32–36.

Scalia, J. (1997). *Prisoner petitions in the federal courts, 1980–96.* Washington, DC: Bureau of Justice Statistics.

Schafer, N. E. (1989). Prison visiting: Is it time to review the rules? *Federal Probation, 53,* 25–30.

Schafer, N. E. (1991). Prison visiting policies and practices. *International Journal of Offender Therapy and Comparative Criminology, 35*(3), 263–275.

Schafer, N. E., & Dellinger, A. B. (1993a). Jail classification: Is it time to include women? (Part I). *American Jails, 7*(4), 31–35.

Schafer, N. E., & Dellinger, A. B. (1993b). Jail classification: Is it time to include women? (Part II). *American Jails, 7*(5), 33–38.

Schafer, S. (1969). *Theories in criminology: Past and present philosophies of the crime problem.* New York: Random House.

Schafer, S. (1976). *Introduction to criminology.* Reston, VA: Reston Publishing Co.

Schafer, S. (1977). *Victimology: The victim and his criminal.* Reston, VA: Reston Publishing Co.

Schailer, R. (1995, November 22). Florida's latest chain gangs toil on prison grounds. *Tampa Tribune.* Florida/Metro, p. 3.

Schiraldi, V., & Ambrosio, T. (1997). *Striking out: The crime impact of "three strikes laws."* Washington, DC: Justice Policy Institute.

Schmidt, A. (1989). Electronic monitoring. *Journal of Contemporary Criminal Justice, 5*(3), 133–140.

Schmidt, A., & Curtis, R. (1987). Electronic monitors. In B. McCarthy (Ed.), *Intermediate punishments: Intensive supervision, home confinement and electronic surveillance* (pp. 137–152). Monsey, NY: Criminal Justice Press.

Schneider, V., & Smykla, J. O. (1991). A summary analysis of executions in the United States, 1608–1987: The Espy file. In R. M. Bohm (Ed.), *The death penalty in America: Current research.* Cincinnati, OH: Anderson Publishing Co.

Schramek, L. (1993, March). If not government, then who? Private sector corrections. *Corrections Compendium, 28*(3), p. 1.

Schulze, R. R. (1991). Assistant Chaplaincy Administrator, Federal Bureau of Prisons. Personal communication.

Schwartz, B. K. (1995). Characteristics and typologies of sex offenders. In B. K. Schwartz, & H. R. Cellini (Eds.), *The sex offender: Corrections, treatment, and legal practice.* Kingston, NJ: Civic Research Institute.

Schwartz, B. K., & Cellini, H. R. (Eds.). (1988, February). *A practitioner's guide to treating the incarcerated male sex offender: Breaking the cycle of sexual abuse.* Washington, DC: U.S. Department of Justice.

Schwartz, I. M. (1991). Removing juveniles from adult jails: The unfinished agenda. In J. A. Thompson & G. L. Mays (Eds.), *American jails: Public policy issues* (pp. 216–226). Chicago: Nelson-Hall Publishers.

Schwartz, M. C., & Weintraub, J. F. (1974, Dec.). The prisoner's wife: A study in crisis. *Federal Probation, 26,* 20–26.

Schweber, C. (1984). Beauty marks and blemishes: The coed prison as a microcosm of integrated society. *The Prison Journal, 64*(1), 3–15.

Schwitezgebel, R. K., Pahnke, W. N., & Hurd, W. S. (1964). A program of research in behavioral electronics. *Behavioral Science, 9,* 233–238.

Sciacca, K. (1991). Integrated treatment approach for severely mentally ill individuals. *New Directions for Mental Health Services, 50,* Chapter 6.

Scott, G. R. (1938). *The history of corporal punishment.* London: T. Werner Laurie Ltd.

Seashore, M. J., Haberfeld, S. I., Irwin, J., & Baker, J. (1976). *Prisoner education: Project Newgate and other college programs.* New York: Praeger Publishers.

Seiter, R. P., Carlson, E. W., Bowman, H. H., Granfield, J. J., & Beran, N. J. (1977, January). *National evaluation program, Phase 1 report: Halfway houses.* Washington, DC: U.S. Department of Justice, National Institute of Law Enforcement and Criminal Justice.

Sellers, S. M. (1997). The Antiterrorism and Effective Death Penalty Act changes the focus of the habeas corpus debate. *New Jersey Law Review,* 35.

Sellin, J. T. (1976). *Slavery and the penal system.* New York: Elsevier.

Sellin, T. (1930). The house of correction for boys in the Hospice of Saint Michael in Rome. *Journal of the American Institute of Criminal Law and Criminology, 20,* 533–553.

Senese, J. W., Wilson, J., Evans, A. O., Aguirre, R., & Kalinich, D. B. (1992). Evaluating jail reform: Inmate infractions and disciplinary response in a traditional jail and a podular direct supervision jail. *American Jails, 6,* 14–23.

Serrill, M., & Katel, P. (1980). New Mexico: The anatomy of a riot. *Corrections Magazine, 6*(2), 6–24.

Sexton, G. E., Farrow, F. C., & Auerbach, B. J. (1985, August). *The private sector and prison industries.* National Institute of Justice Research in Brief.

Shane-Dubow, S., Brown, A. P., & Olsen, E. (1985). *Sentencing reform in the United States: History, content and effect.* Washington, DC: U.S. Government Printing Office.

Shapiro, P., & Votey, H. (1984). Deterrence and subjective probabilities of arrest: Modeling individual decisions to drink and drive in Sweden. *Law and Society Review, 18,* 111–149.

Sharp, D. (1995). Boot camps—punishment and treatment. *Corrections Today, 57*(3), special pullout between pp. 80–81.

Shaw, A. G. L. (1966). *Convicts and the colonies.* London: Faber and Faber.

Shaw, R. D. (1990). *The jail/prison ministry and stress.* Unpublished doctoral dissertation, State University of New York at Albany.

Sheehan, S. (1978). *A prison and a prisoner.* Boston: Houghton Mifflin.

Shelton, E. (1985). The implementation of a life coping skills program within a correctional setting. *Journal of Correctional Education, 36,* 41–45.

Shenon, P. (1994, April 1). Flogging upheld for U.S. youth in Singapore. *The New York Times,* p. A5.

Sherman, L., & Berk, R. (1984). The specific deterrent effects of arrest for domestic assault. *American Sociological Review, 49,* 261–272.

Shichor, D., & Sechrest, D. K. Three strikes as public policy: Future implications. In D. Shichor & D. K. Sechrest (Eds.), *Three strikes and you're out: Vengeance as public policy.* Thousand Oaks, CA: Sage.

Shorstein, H. L. (1998). State attorney, Fourth Circuit Court of Florida. Personal communication.

Shusman, E. J., Inwald, R., & Landa, B. (1984). Correction officer job performance as predicted by the IPI and the MMPI. *Criminal Justice and Behavior, 11*(3), 309–329.

Sigler, R. (1988). Role conflict for adult probation and parole officers: Fact or myth? *Journal of Criminal Justice, 16*(2): 121–129.

Silberman, C. E. (1978). *Criminal justice, criminal violence.* New York: Vintage Books.

Silberman, M. (1995). *A world of violence.* Belmont, CA: Wadsworth Publishing Co.

Simmons, C., Cochran, J. K., & Blount, W. R. (1997). The effects of job-related stress and job satisfaction on probation officers' inclinations to quit. *American Journal of Criminal Justice, 21*(2): 213–229.

Simms, B. E., Farley, J., & Littlefield, J. R. (1987). *Colleges with fences: A handbook for improving corrections education programs*. Columbus, OH: National Center for Research in Vocational Education.

Simon, R. J. (1975). *Women and crime*. Lexington, MA: D. C. Heath/Lexington Books.

Simon, R. J., & Simon, J. D. (1993). Female guards in men's prisons. In R. Muraskin & T. Alleman (Eds.), *It's a crime: Women and justice* (pp. 226–259). Englewood Cliffs, NJ: Regents/Prentice-Hall.

Simpson, D. D., & Sells, S. B. (1988). Legal status and long term outcomes for addicts in the DARP follow-up project. In C. G. Leukefeld, & F. M. Tims (Eds.), *Compulsory treatment of drug abuse: Research and clinical practice*. Rockville, MD: National Institute of Drug Abuse.

Singer, R. G., & Statsky, W. P. (1974). *Rights of the imprisoned: Cases, materials and directions*. Indianapolis, IN: Bobbs-Merrill.

Skolnick, H. (1994). Assistant Director, Prison Industries, Nevada Department of Corrections. Personal communication.

Slaying suspects on early release. (1993, September 23). *Bradenton Herald*, Sec. B, p. 6.

Sluder, R. D., & Sapp, A. D. (1994). Peering into the crystal ball to examine the future of America's jails. *American Jails, 7*(6), 81–87.

Sluder, R. D., Sapp, A. D., & Langston, D. C. (1994, June). Guiding philosophies for probation in the 21st century. *Federal Probation, 58*(2), 3–10.

Smart, C. (1979). The new female criminal: Reality or myth? *British Journal of Criminology, 19*(1), 50–57.

Smith, A. E. (1963). *Colonists in bondage: White servitude and convict labor in America, 1607–1776*. Chapel Hill, NC: The University of North Carolina Press. (Original work published in 1947.)

Smith, D., & Gartin, P. (1989). Specifying specific deterrence: The influence of arrest in future criminal activity. *American Sociological Review, 54*, 94–105.

Smith, L. (1994, July). Department of Criminology, University of South Florida. Personal communication.

Smith, L., & Akers, R. (1993). A comparison of Florida's community control and prison: A five year survival analysis. *Journal of Research in Crime and Delinquency, 30*(3), 267–292.

Smith, R. R. (undated). *American prisoner home furloughs*. Unpublished manuscript, West Virginia College of Graduate Studies: West Virginia Institute of Justice Studies.

Smith, W. E. (1989, February 27). Hunted by an angry faith: Salman Rushdie's novel cracks open a fault line between east and west. *Time*, pp. 28–32.

Smykla, J. O. (1980). *Coed prisons*. New York: Human Sciences Press.

Smykla, J. O. (1987). The human impact of capital punishment: interviews with families of persons on death row. *Journal of Criminal Justice, 15*: 331-347.

Snell, T. (1998, December). *Capital punishment 1997*. Washington, DC: Bureau of Justice Statistics.

Snell, T. (1999, December). *Capital punishment 1998*. Washington, DC: Bureau of Justice Statistics.

Snell, T. L. (1993, August). *Correctional populations in the United States, 1991*. Washington, DC: U.S. Department of Justice.

Snell, T. L. (1995, January). *Correctional populations in the United States, 1992*. Washington, D.C.: U.S. Department of Justice.

Snell, T. L., & Morton, D. C. (1992, March). *Prisoners in 1991*. Washington, DC: Bureau of Justice Statistics.

Snell, T. L., & Morton, D. C. (1994, March). *Survey of state inmates, 1991: Women in prison*. Washington, DC: Bureau of Justice Statistics.

Solari, R. (1992). *National judicial reporting program, 1988*. Washington, DC: U.S. Department of Justice, Bureau of Justice Statistics.

Solomon, E. (1990). Administrator of Chaplaincy Programs, Texas Department of Criminal Justice. Personal communication.

Solomon, E. (1991). Administrator of Chaplaincy Programs, Texas Department of Criminal Justice. Personal communication.

Solomon, L., & Camp, A. T. (1993). The revolution in correctional classification. In American Correctional Association, *Classification: A tool for managing today's offenders* (pp. 1–16). Laurel, MD: American Correctional Association.

Soonchan, I. (2000). Inmates rebuild lives after Hurricane Floyd. *On the Line, 23*(1): 1–2.

Sorensen, J., & Wrinkle, R. D. (1996). No hope for parole: Disciplinary infractions among death-sentenced and life-without-parole inmates. *Criminal Justice and Behavior, 23*: 542–552.

Sorkin, L. G. (1998). The trilogy of federal statutes. In *National conference on sex offender registries*. Washington, DC: Bureau of Justice Statistics, pp. 16–17.

Souryal, C., & MacKenzie, D. (1993, March). *Shock incarceration and recidivism: An examination of boot camp programs in four states*. Paper presented at the annual meeting of the Academy of Criminal Justice Sciences, Kansas City, MO.

Souryal, S. S. (1997). Romancing the stone or stoning the romance: Ethics of community-based corrections. In P. F. Cromwell & R. G. Dunham (Eds.), *Crime & justice in America*. Upper Saddle River, NJ: Prentice Hall, pp. 342–353.

Southwick, K. (Aug. 2, 1992). Use Norplant, don't go to jail: Judges, social workers and medical professionals debate the ethic. *The San Francisco Chronicle*, pg. 13/Z1.

Speckman, R. (1981, April). Recreation in prison—A panacea? *Journal of Physical Education and Recreation, 52*(4), 46–47.

Spierenburg, P. (1991). *The prison experience: Disciplinary institutions and their inmates in early modern Europe.* New Brunswick, NJ: Rutgers University Press.

Staff. (1990). "Vigilantism" threatens sex offender law. *Walla Walla Union-Bulletin* (October 30), pp. 1–2.

Stanton, A. (1980). *When mothers go to jail.* Lexington, MA: Lexington Books.

Star Tribune Editorial. (1996, May). Our perspective: Frank Wood—He worked to keep people out of prison. *Star Tribune.*

State of Minnesota. (1998, August). *IV. Sentencing guidelines grid.* http://www.corr.state.mn.us.

Steadman, H. J., Fabisiak, S., & Dvoskin, J. (1987). A survey of mental disability among state prison inmates. *Hospital and Community Psychiatry, 38,* 1086–1090.

Steadman, H., & Veysey, B. M. (1997). Providing services for jail inmates with mental disorders. *American Jails, 11*(2): 23.

Steele, W. W., & Thornburg, J. (1988). Jury instructions: A persistent failure to communicate. *North Carolina Law Review, 67:* 77–109.

Steffensmeier, D. (1992, December). More PA prisoners did not reduce violent crime. *Overcrowded Times, 3*(6), 1, 7–9.

Steffensmeier, D., & Allan, E. (1998). The nature of female offenders: Patterns and explanation. In R. Zaplan (Ed.), *Female offenders: Critical perspectives and effective interventions.* Gaithersburg, MD: Aspen Publishers, Inc.

Steffensmeier, D., Kramer, J., & Streifel, C. (1993). Gender and imprisonment decisions. *Criminology, 31*(3), 411–446.

Stein, M. A. (1990, April 24). High court won't restore conviction of former Panther. *Los Angeles Times,* Part A, p. 3.

Stephan, J. (1989, December). *Prison rule violators.* Washington, DC: Bureau of Justice Statistics.

Stephan, J. J. (1997). *Census of state and federal correctional facilities, 1995.* Washington, DC: U.S. Department of Justice, Bureau of Justice Statistics.

Stephan, S., Brien, P., & Greenfeld, L. A. (1994, December). *Capital punishment 1993.* Washington, DC: U.S. Department of Justice, Bureau of Justice Statistics.

Stephen, S. (1992, May). *Census of state and federal correctional facilities, 1990.* U. S. Department of Justice, Bureau of Justice Statistics, Washington, DC: U. S. Government Printing Office.

Steurer, S. J. (1991). Inmates helping inmates: Maryland's peer tutoring reading academies. *Yearbook of Correctional Education,* pp. 133–139.

Steurer, S. J. (1995, August). Executive Director, Corrections Education Association. Personal communication.

Stevens, D. J. (1997). Origins and effects of prison drug gangs in North Carolina. *Journal of Gang Research, 4*(2): 23–35.

Steward, D. (1999). Senior psychologist, Corrections Mental Health Institution, Chattahoocee, FL. Personal communication.

Stokes, J. F. (1991, July). President, Judy Ford Stokes & Associates Inc., Atlanta, GA, Food Management and Design Consultants. Personal communication.

Stokes, J. F. (1993, December). President, Judy Ford Stokes & Associates Inc., Atlanta, GA, Food Management and Design Consultants. Personal communication.

Stokes, J. F. (1998). President, Judy Ford Stokes & Associates, Inc. Food management and design consultants, Atlanta, GA. Personal communication.

Stokes, J. F., & Associates. (1985). *Control food services: Costs and courts.* Atlanta, GA: Author.

Stokes, J. F., & Associates. (undated). *Your kitchen can pay for itself!* Atlanta, GA: Author.

Stoltz, B. A. (1978). *Prisons as political institutions—What are the implications for prison ministry?* College Park, MD: American Correctional Association.

Stone, A. (1994, March 10). Whipping penalty judged too harsh—by some. *USA Today,* Sec. A, p. 3.

Stout, B. D., & Clear, T. R. (1992, Winter). Federal prison chaplains: Satisfied in ministry but often undervalued. *Federal Prisons Journal,* pp. 8–10.

Straley, N., & Morris, S. (1994). New legal standard set on religious rights of prisoners. *The National Prison Project Journal, 9*(4), 2–5.

Stratton, J. (1973, March 29 and May 1). *Testimony before the Committee on Internal Security of the House of Representatives. Hearings on revolutionary activities directed toward the administration of penal or correctional systems.* Washington, DC: U.S. Government Printing Office.

Straus, M., Gelles, R., & Steinmetz, S. (1980). *Behind closed doors: Violence in the American family.* New York: Anchor.

Streib, V. L. (1992, January 17). *Capital punishment for female offenders: Present female death row inmates and death sentences and executions of female offenders, January 1, 1973 to December 31, 1991.* Unpublished paper, Cleveland State University, Marshall College of Law, Cleveland, OH.

Streib, V. L. (1996). *Executing women, children, and the retarded: Second class citizens in capital punishment.* Paper presented at the annual meeting of the American Society of Criminology in Chicago, November 23, 1986.

Streib, V. L. (1999). *Death penalty for female offenders: January 1, 1973 to June 1999.* http:// law.onu.edu./faculty/streib/ femdeath.

Streib, V. L. (1999). *The juvenile death penalty today: Death sentences and executions for juvenile crimes for female offenders: January 1, 1973 to June 1999.* http.law.onu.edu./faculty/streib/ femdeath.

Stumbo, N. J., & Little, S. L. (1990). *Camp celebration: Incarcerated mother and their children camping together.* Springfield, IL: Illinois Department of Corrections.

Styles, S. (1991, Summer). Conditions of confinement suits: What has the Bureau of Prisons learned? *Federal Prisons Journal,* pp. 41–47.

Sullivan, L. E. (1990). *The prison reform movement: Forlorn hope.* Boston: Twayne Publishers.

Sun-Sentinel. (1995, June 9). Standard chain gangs not in Florida's plans: Alabama study instructive for prison chief, p. 16A.

Suro, R. (1990, October 1). As inmates are freed, Houston feels insecure. *The New York Times,* p. A16.

Survey identifies relevant issues in support of '95–'96 priorities. (1995, Nov.). *On the Line, 18*(5), p. 1.

Sutherland, E. H. (1924). *Criminology.* Philadelphia: J. B. Lippincott Co.

Sutherland, E. H., & Cressey, D. R. (1966). *Principles of criminology* (7th ed.). New York: J. B. Lippincott Co.

Suttles, G. D. (1968). *The social order of the slum: Ethnicity and territory in the inner city.* Chicago: University of Chicago Press.

Sweet, R. W., Jr. (1991). Juvenile jailing: Federal compliance. *American Jails, 5*(1), 92–96.

Sykes, G. M. (1956). *Crime and society.* New York: Random House.

Sykes, G. M. (1958). *The society of captives: A study of a maximum security prison.* Princeton, NJ: Princeton University Press.

Sykes G. M., & Messinger, S. L. (1960). The inmate social system. In D. R. Cressey, G. H. Grosser, R. McCleery, L. E. Ohlin, G. M. Sykes, S. L. Messinger, & R. A. Cloward (Eds.), *Theoretical studies in social organization in the prison.* New York: Social Science Research Council.

Szasz, T. (1970). *The manufacture of madness.* New York, NY: Harper and Row.

Takas, M., & Hammett, T. M. (1989). *Legal issues affecting offenders and staff.* Washington, DC: National Institute of Justice.

Tannenbaum, F. (1924). *Darker phases of the south.* New York: Putnam.

Tappan, P. W. (1960). *Crime, justice and correction.* New York: McGraw-Hill.

Task Force on Corrections. (1967). Task force report: Corrections. Washington, D.C.: President's Commission on Law Enforcement and the Administration of Justice, U.S. Government Printing Office.

Task Force on Corrections. (1973). *Corrections.* Washington, DC: National Advisory Commission on Criminal Justice Standards and Goals.

Task Force on the Courts. (1973). Task force report: Courts. Washington, DC: National Advisory Commission on Criminal Justice Standards and Goals.

Taylor, J. M. (1996). Violence in prison. *Corrections Compendium, 21*(6): 1–3.

Taylor, S. (1993, August 23). "Taking issue" in the drug wars: Small minds go after small fry; can Reno muster the courage to end mandatory-minimum madness? *The Connecticut Law Tribune,* p. 14.

Taylor, S. J. (April 23, 1987). Court, 5–4, rejects racial challenge to death penalty. *The New York Times,* pp. 1, 13.

Taylor, W. B. (1978, Spring). Alexander Maconochie and the revolt against the penitentiary. *Southern Journal of Criminal Justice, 3*(1).

Taylor, W. B. (1984, March). *In pursuit of profit: Observation on convict labor in Mississippi 1907–1934.* Paper presented at the annual meeting of the Academy of Criminal Justice Sciences, Chicago.

Taylor, W. B. (1993). *Brokered justice: race, politics, and the Mississippi prisons, 1798–1992.* Columbus, OH: Ohio State University Press.

Taylor, W. B. (1997). Professor, Department of Criminal Justice, University of Southern Mississippi. Personal communication.

Taylor, W. B. (1998). *Down on Parchman Farm.* Columbus, OH: Ohio State University Press.

Teeters, N. K. (1970). The passing of Cherry Hill: Most famous prison in the world. *The Prison Journal, 50*(1), 3–12.

Telander, R. (1987, October). Sports behind the walls. *Sports Illustrated,* pp. 82–88.

Teller, F. E., & Howell, R. J. (1981). Older prisoners: Criminal and psychological characteristics. *Criminology, 18,* pp. 549–555.

Terry, D. (1994, March 3). Farrakhan: Fiery separatist in a somber suit. *The New York Times,* pp. 1A, 8B.

Terry, W. C. (1981). Police stress: The empirical evidence. *Journal of Police Science and Administration, 9*: 61–75.

Tewksbury, R. (1989). Fear of sexual assault in prison inmates. *The Prison Journal,* pp. 62–71.

Texas Department of Corrections. (1977). *Texas Department of Corrections: 30 years of progress.* Huntsville, TX: Author.

Texas Department of Corrections. (1985, July). *Administrative directive: Religious policy statement.* Huntsville, TX: Author.

Texas Department of Corrections. (1986, January). *Basic job analysis for the position of Chaplain II.* Huntsville, TX: Author.

Texas Department of Criminal Justice. (1993). *Annual report 1993.* Austin, TX: Author.

Thalheimer, J. (1975). *Cost analysis of corrections standards: Halfway houses* (Vol. 1). Washington, DC: National Institute of Law Enforcement and Criminal Justice.

Thibaut, J. (1982). To pave the way to penitence: Prisoners and discipline at the Eastern State Penitentiary 1829–1835. *Pennsylvania Magazine of History and Biography, 106,* 187–221.

Thigpen, M. L., & Hunter, S. M. (1997). Prison medical care: Special needs populations and cost control. *Special issues in corrections.* Longmont, CO: NIC.

Thomas, C. W. (1990). Prisoners' rights and correctional privatization: A legal and ethical analysis. *Business & Professional Ethics Journal, 10*(1), 3–45.

Thomas, C. W. (1993, Winter). Are "doing well" and "doing good" contradictory goals of privatization? *Large Jail Network Bulletin,* pp. 3–7.

Thomas, C. W. (1994, April). Growth in privatization continues to accelerate. *Corrections Compendium,* pp. 5–6.

Thomas, C. W., & Logan, C. H. (1991). *The development, present status, and future potential of correctional privatization in America.* A paper presented at the Conference of the American Legislative Exchange Council held in Miami, FL, March 23, 1991.

Thomas, C. W., & Petersen, D. W. (1977). *Prison organization and inmate subcultures.* Indianapolis, IN: Bobbs-Merrill Co.

Thomas, J. (1988). *Prisoner litigation: The paradox of the jailhouse lawyer.* Totowa, NJ: Rowman and Littlefield.

Thomas, J., Aylward, A., Casey, M. L., Moton, D., Oldham, M., and Wheetley, G. W. (1985). Rethinking prisoner litigation: Some preliminary distinctions between habeas corpus and civil rights. *The Prison Journal, 65,* 83–106.

Thornberg, D. (1990). Opening remarks by the Attorney General of the United States. Presented at the National Drug Conference.

Thornberry, T. P., & Call, J. E. (1983). Constitutional challenges to prison overcrowding: The scientific evidence of harmful effects. *Hastings Law Journal, 35,* 313–351.

Three guards arrested in contraband bust. (1993, June 12). *The Times-Picayune,* Metro, p. B2.

Thurman, Q. C., & Mueller, D. G. (1996). Community based gang prevention and intervention programs: An evaluation of the Neutral Zone. *Crime and Delinquency, 42*(2): 279–295.

Time. (1990, May 21). A shocking way to go. *Time.*

Tischler, E. (1998). Smoking bans have supporters, detractors. *On the Line, 21*(1): 1, 3.

Tittle, C., & Rowe, A. (1974). Certainty of arrest and crime rates: A further test of the deterrence hypothesis. *Social Forces, 52,* 455–462.

Toch, H. (1977a). *Living in prison: The ecology of survival.* New York: The Free Press.

Toch, H. (1977b). *Police, prisons, and the problem of violence.* Washington, DC: Government Printing Office.

Toch, H. (1978). Social climate and prison violence. *Federal Probation, 42*(4), 21–25.

Toch, H. (1982). The disturbed disruptive inmate. *Journal of Psychiatry and Law,* 327–349.

Toch, H., & Adams, K. (1987). The prison as dumping ground: Maintaining disturbed offenders. *Journal of Psychiatry and Law,* 539–553.

Todd, J. C. (1993). Accreditation byline: Ohio county finds accreditation offers solutions for small jails. *Corrections Today, 55*(4): 164–165.

Tonry, M. (1990). Stated and latent features of ISP. *Crime and Delinquency, 36*(1), 174–191.

Tonry, M. (1992). Mandatory penalties. In M. Tonry (Ed.), *Crime and justice: A review of research* (Vol. 16, pp. 243–273). Chicago: The University of Chicago Press.

Tonry, M. (1996). *Sentencing matters.* New York: Oxford University Press.

Tonry, M. (1998). Introduction: Crime and punishment. In M. Tonry (Ed.), *The handbook of crime & punishment* (pp. 3–30). New York: Oxford University Press.

Tonry, M., & Will, R. (1988). *Intermediate sanctions: Preliminary report.* Washington, DC: National Institute of Justice.

Torbet, P., Gable, R., Hurst, H., Montgomery, I., Szymanski, L., & Thomas, D. (1996, July). *State responses to serious and violent juvenile crime.* Washington, DC: National Center for Juvenile Justice.

Torrey, E. F., Steiber, J., Ezekiel, J., Wolfe, S., Sharfstein, J., Noble, J. E. & Lauric, M. (1992). *Criminalizing the seriously mentally ill—The abuse of jails as mental hospitals.* Washington, DC: National Alliance of the Mentally Ill.

Tracey, A. (1993, August). Literacy volunteers share a belief in rehabilitative effect of education. *Corrections Today,* pp. 102–109.

Tracy, P. E., Wolfgang, M. E., & Figlio, R. M. (1985). *Delinquency in two birth cohorts: Executive summary.* Washington, DC: U.S. Department of Justice.

Trout, C., & Meko, J. A. (1990, Spring). The uses of intelligence: Every staff member is a vital part of the network. *Federal Prison Journal,* pp. 16–21.

Tucker, K. (1998). Letter from Karla Faye Tucker to Governor George W. Bush. *American Statesmen.*

Turley, J. (1990). Alternative solutions. In U.S. Department of Justice, Federal Bureau of Prisons, (Ed.). *The December 7, 1990 forum on issues in corrections—Long term confinement in the aging inmate population.* Washington, DC: U.S. Department of Justice.

Turner, A. (1997, May). Doing time smokeless; prison tobacco ban is hailed but all smoke hasn't cleared. *Houston Chronicle,* p. 1.

Turner, S., & Petersilia, J. (1996). *Work release: recidivism and corrections costs in Washington State.* Washington, DC: National Institute of Justice, U.S. Department of Justice.

Turner, W. B. (1979, June). When prisoners sue: Prisoner section 1983 suits in federal courts. *Harvard Law Review, 92,* 610–63.

U.S. Department of Justice. (1986, September). *Program statement: Inmate recreation programs.* Washington, DC: Author.

U.S. Department of Justice. (1988, March). *Report to the nation on crime and justice.* Washington, DC: Author.

U.S. Department of Justice. (1989). *The December 12, 1989 conference on issues in corrections.* Washington, DC: Author.

U.S. Department of Justice. (1990, September). *A survey of intermediate sanctions.* Washington, DC: Author.

U.S. Department of Justice. (1994, September 11). *Probation and parole populations reach new highs.* Washington, DC: Author.

U.S. Department of Justice. (1997, December). *Capital punishment 1996.* Washington, DC: Bureau of Justice Statistics.

U.S. Department of Justice. (undated). *Federal prison industries: Meeting the military's needs when quality really counted.* Washington, DC: Federal Bureau of Prisons.

U.S. Department of Justice, Bureau of Justice Statistics. (1980). *Capital punishment 1979: National prisoner statistics.* Washington, DC: Author.

U.S. Department of Justice, National Institute of Corrections. (1993). *Podidar Direct Supervision Jails Information Packet.* Washington, DC: Author.

United Nations. (1951). *Probation and related matters.* New York: Author.

United Nations. (1970). Probation and related measures. *United Nations, IV,* 15–26.

University of Illinois Law Forum. (1980). *Prieser v. Rodriguez in retrospect.* In D. P. Robbins (Ed.), *Prisoners' rights source book,* New York: Clark Boardman Co.

Useem, B., Camp, C. G., & Camp, G. M. (1996). *Resolution of prison riots: Strategies and policies.* New York: Oxford University Press.

Van Balaan, S. (1998). Chaplaincy administrator, Federal Bureau of Prisons. Personal communication.

Van Balaan, S. (1999). Personal communication.

Van Den Haag, E. (1975). *Punishing criminals: Concerning a very old and painful question.* New York: Basic Books.

Van der Slice, A. (1936, June). Elizabethan house of correction. *Journal of Criminal Law and Criminology, 27,* 45–67.

Van der Zee, J. (1985). *Bound over: Indentured servitude and American conscience.* New York: Simon and Schuster.

Van Voorhis, P. (1993). Psychological determinants of the prison experience. *The Prison Journal, 73(1),* 72–101.

Van Yelyr, R. G. (1942). *The whip and the rod.* London: Gerald G. Swan.

Vasquez, D. B. (1993). Trauma treatment: Helping prison staff handle the stress of an execution. *Corrections Today,* 70–71.

Vaughn, M. S., & Carroll, L. (1998, March). Separate and unequal: Prison versus free-world medical care. *Justice Quarterly, 15(1):* 3–40.

Vaughn, M. S., & del Carmen, R. V. (1993, April). Research note: A national survey of correctional administrators in the United States. *Crime and Delinquency, 39(2),* 225–239.

Vaughn, M. S., & Sapp, A. D. (1989, Fall/Winter). Less than utopian: Sex offender treatment in a milieu of power struggles, status positioning, and inmate manipulation in state correctional institutions. *The Prison Journal,* pp. 73–89.

Velimesis, M. I. (1981). Sex roles and mental health of women in prison. *Professional Psychology, 12(1),* 128–135.

Veneziano, L., Veneziano, C., & Tribolet, C. (1987). Special needs of inmates with handicaps: An assessment. *Journal of Offender Counseling Services and Rehabilitation, 12(1),* 61–72.

Vera Institute of Justice. (1977). *Felony arrests: Their prosecution and disposition in New York City's courts.* New York: Author.

Verhovek, S. H. (1998a, January). As woman's execution nears Texas squirms. *New York Times,* pp. A1, A16.

Verhovek, S. H. (1998b, February). Her final appeal exhausted, Tucker is put to death. *New York Times,* pp. A1, A17.

"Vigilantism" threatens sex offender law. (1990, October 30). *Walla Walla Union Bulletin,* p. 1.

Vild, D. R. (1992, July). *A comparative study of state academics for basic correctional officer training.* Unpublished report to the Arizona Department of Corrections.

Vito, G., & Allen, H. (1981). Shock probation in Ohio: A comparison of outcomes. *International Journal of Offender Therapy and Comparative Criminology, 25,* 70–76.

Vito, G. F., & Wilson, D. G. (1985). Elderly inmates. *Federal Probation, 49(1),* 18–24.

Vogel, B. (1996). Arizona DOC closes 34 inmate law libraries. *Corrections Professional, 1(21):* 1–6.

Volunteer Today. (1993, Summer). Islamic volunteers work to meet diverse needs. *Volunteer Today,* p. 4.

Von Hirsch, A. (1998). Penal theories. In M. Tonry (Ed.), *The handbook of crime & punishment* (pp. 559–582). New York: Oxford University Press.

Wagner, D., & Baird, C. (1993, January). *Evaluation of the Florida Community Program.* Washington, DC: National Institute of Justice Journal.

Wagner, G. (1999). Accreditation: The pathway to excellence. *Corrections Today, 61(6):* 26.

Waldo, G., & Chiricos, T. (1974). *Work as a rehabilitation tool: An evaluation of two state programs, final report.* Washington, DC: U.S. Department of Justice.

Waldo, G., & Griswold, D. (1979). Issues in the measurement of recidivism. In L. Sechrest, S. O. White, & E. D. Brown (Eds.), *The rehabilitation of criminal offenders: Problems and prospects.* Washington, DC: National Academy of Sciences.

Walker, J. T. (1994). *Police and correctional use of force: Parity or parody.* Paper presented at the annual meeting of the Academy of Criminal Justice Sciences, Chicago.

Walker, P. N. (1973). *Punishment: An illustrated history.* New York: Arco Publishers.

Wallerstein, A. M. (1989, Spring). New generation/direct supervision correctional operations in Bucks County. *American Jails, 1(1),* 34–36.

Walsh, E. R. (1997). The sex offender. In B. K. Schwartz & H. R. Cellini (Eds.), *Megan's laws—Sex offender registration and notification statutes and constitutional challenges.* Kingston, NJ: Civic Research Institute.

Walters, G. (1994). *The criminal lifestyle: Patterns of serious criminal conduct.* Newbury Park, CA: Sage Publications.

Walters, S. (1990). *Factors affecting the acceptance of female prison guards by their male counterparts.* Unpublished manuscript, University of Wisconsin-Platteville.

Ward, D., & Kassebaum, G. (1965). *Women's prison: Sex and social structure.* Chicago: Aldine-Atherton.

Ward, D. A. (1987). Control strategies for problem prisoners in American penal systems. In A. E. Bottoms & R. Light (Eds.), *Problems of long-term imprisonment.* Aldershot, England: Gower Publishing Co.

Washington, P. A. (1989). Mature mentally ill offenders in California jails. *Journal of Offender Counseling, Services and Rehabilitation, 13(2),* 161–173.

Wees, G. (1996). Sex offenders in state and federal prisons top 100,000 mark. *Corrections Compendium, 41*(5).

Wees, G. (1996). Violence on the rise in U.S. prisons. *Corrections Compendium, 21*(6): 9–11.

Wees, G. E. (1996a). Inmate population expected to increase by 43% by 2002. *Corrections Compendium, 21*(4): 1–4.

Wees, G. (1996b). Survey summary: Inmate population projections. *Corrections Compendium, 21*(4): 10–11.

Weinstein, M. (1989, June). Executive Director, State Attorney's Office, Duval County, FL. Personal communication.

Weir, E., & Kalm, L. (1936). *Crime and religion: A study of criminological facts and problems.* Chicago: Franciscan Herald Press.

Weis, B. (1985, March). *The Cleveland prosecutor mediation program.* Washington, DC: National Institute of Justice.

Weisheit, R. (1985). Trends in programs for female offenders: The use of private agencies as service providers. *International Journal of Offender Therapy and Comparative Criminology, 29*(1), 35–42.

Welch, R. (1990, December). The arts in prison. *Corrections Compendium, 15*(10), 1, 5–6.

Welling, A. D. (1997). Executive director, National Major Gang Task Force. Personal communication.

Welling, A. D. (1999). Personal communication.

Wells, C. (1993). *Manatee initiate boot camp.* Bradenton, FL: Manatee County Sheriff's Office.

Wenk, E. A., Robison, J. D., & Smith, G. W. (1972). Can violence be predicted? *Crime and Delinquency, 9,* 171–196.

Westcott, K. (1995, November 10). Legislative Liason, Coalition Against STOP, National Prison Project. Personal communication.

Wetli, C. V., & Martinez, R. (1981). Forensic sciences aspects of santeria, a religious cult of African origin. *Journal of Forensic Sciences, 26*(3), 506–514.

Wetli, C. V., & Martinez, R. (1983). Brujeria: Manifestations of Palo Mayombe in South Florida. *Journal of Florida Medical Association, 70*(8), 629–634.

Wexler, H. K. (1994). Progress in prison substance abuse treatment: A five year report. *Journal of Drug Issues, 24* (1&2), 349–360.

Wexler, H. K., Falkin, G. P., & Lipton, D. S. (1990). Outcome evaluation of a prison therapeutic community for substance abuse treatment. *Criminal Justice and Behavior, 17*(1), 71–92.

Wexler, H. K., & Lipton, D. S. (1993). From reform to recovery: Advances in prison drug treatment. In J. Inciardi (Ed.), *Drug treatment and criminal justice* (pp. 209–227). Newbury Park, CA: Sage Publications.

Wexler, H. K., & Williams R. (1986). The Stay'N Out therapeutic community: Prison treatment for substance abusers. *Journal of Psychoactive Drugs, 19*(3), 221–230.

What are prisons for? (1982, Sept. 13). *Time Magazine,* pp. 38–41.

White, R. M., & Abeles, R. P. (1990, November 26). *The behavioral and social research program at the National Institute on Aging: History of a decade.* Bethesda, MD: National Institute on Aging, Behavioral and Social Research Program.

Whitehead, C. H., & Bloom, C. (1993). *Criminal procedure: An analysis of cases and concepts.* (3rd ed.). Westbury, NY: Foundation Press.

Whitehead, J. (1985). Job burnout in probation and parole: Its extent and intervention implications. *Criminal Justice and Behavior, 12*: 91–110.

Whitehead, J. (1987). Probation officer job burnout: A test of two theories. *Journal of Criminal Justice, 15*(1): 1–16.

Whitehead, J. T. (1989). *The effectiveness of felony probation.* A paper presented at the annual meeting of the American Society of Criminology, Reno, NV.

Whitehead, J. T. (1991). The effectiveness of felony probation. *Justice Quarterly, 4,* 525–543.

Who's Who in Jail Management. (1994). Hagerstown, MD: American Jail Association.

Wicker, T. (1975). *A time to die.* NY: Quadrangle/The New York Times Press.

Wickersham Commission Reports. (1931). *Report on penal institutions, probation, and parole.* Washington, DC: U.S. Government Printing Office.

Wicks, R. J. (1980). *Guard! Society's professional prisoner.* Houston, TX: Gulf Publications.

Wilkerson, I. (1987, April 29). Detroit crime feeds on itself and youth. *The New York Times,* Sec. Y, pp. 1, 14.

Wilkerson, I. (1988, March 1). Two decades of decline chronicled by Kerner follow-up report. *The New York Times,* p. 5.

Wilkinson, K., & Brehm, D. (1992). Overcrowding—A cooperative approach. *American Jails, 6*(1), 89–91.

Williams, J. E. H. (1970). *The English penal system in transition.* London: Butterworth & Co.

Wilson, D. W. (1948). *My six convicts.* New York: Rinehart and Co.

Wilson, J. Q. (1975). *Thinking about crime.* New York: Basic Books.

Wilson, J. Q. (1989). *Bureaucracy: What government agencies do and why they do it.* New York: Basic Books.

Wilson, J. Q., & Kelling, G. L. (1982). The police and neighborhood safety: Broken windows. *Atlantic Monthly,* 29–38.

Wilson, M. (1931). *The crime of punishment.* New York: Jonathan Cape Harrison & Smith.

Wilson, R. (1980). Who will care for the mad and bad? *Corrections Magazine, 6*(1), 5–9, 12–17.

Windham School System. (1986). *Windham school system: The national leader in correctional education.* Huntsville, TX: Texas Department of Criminal Justice.

Windham School System. (1987). *Annual performance report.* Huntsville, TX: Texas Department of Criminal Justice.

Windham School System. (1989). *Meeting the challenge: Innovative educational programming.* Huntsville, TX: Author.

Windham School System. (1991–1992). *Annual performance report*. Huntsville, TX: Texas Department of Criminal Justice.

Wines, E. C., & Dwight, T. (1867). *Report on the prisons in the United States and Canada*. Albany, NY: Van Benthuysen.

Wines, F. H. (1895). *Punishment and reformation: A historical sketch of the rise of the penitentiary system*. New York: Thomas Crowell.

Winfree, L. T. J., Awmiller, M. M., & Devenny, G. G. (1996). *Criminal histories and prison-inmate attitudes toward sexual behavior: A comparison of incarcerated sex-offenders and other prisoners*. Paper presented at the annual meetings of the Academy of Criminal Justice Sciences.

Winterfield, L. A., & Hillsman, S. T. (1991). *The effects of instituting means-based fines in a criminal court: The Staten Island day-fine experiment*. New York: Vera Institute of Justice.

Winterfield, L. A., & Hillsman, S. T. (1993). *The Staten Island day-fine project*. Washington, DC: National Institute of Justice, U.S. Department of Justice.

Wolfgang, M. E., Figlio, R. M., & Sellin, T. (1972). *Delinquency in a birth cohort*. Chicago: University of Chicago Press.

Wolford, B. I. (1987). Correctional education: training and education opportunities for delinquent and criminal offenders. In C. M. Nelson, R. B. Rutherford, and B. I. Wolford, Columbus, OH: Merrill Publishing Co.

Wood, A. W., & Waite, J. B. (1941). *Crime and its treatment: Social and legal aspects of criminology*. New York: American Book Company.

Wood, F. (1985, Summer). Oak Park Heights sets high supermax standards. *The National Prison Project Journal*, pp. 3–6.

Wood, F. (1998). Retired commissioner, Minnesota Department of Corrections. Personal communication.

Wooden, W. S., & Parker, J. (1982). *Men behind bars: Sexual exploitation in prison*. New York: Plenum.

Woodruff, L. (1993, September/October). Occupational stress for correctional personnel, Part 1. *American Jails*, pp. 15–20.

Wormser, R. (1991). *Lifers: Learn the truth at the expense of our sorrow*. Englewood Cliffs: NJ: Julian Messner.

Worzella, C. (1992). The Milwaukee Municipal Court day fine project. In D. C. McDonald (Ed.), *Day fines in American courts: The Staten Island and Milwaukee experiments*. Washington, DC: U.S. Department of Justice, Office of Justice Programs.

Wright, C. D. (1899). Prison labor. *The Catholic University Bulletin, V*(4), 403–423.

Wright, D. T., & Mays, G. L. (1998). Correctional boot camps, attitudes, and recidivism: The Oklahoma experience. *Journal of Offender Rehabilitation, 28* (1&2): 71–87.

Wright, J. H., Jr. (1991). Life without parole: The view from death row. *Criminal Law Bulletin, 27*, 334–367.

Wright, K. (1991). Successful prison leadership. *Federal Probation, 55*(3), 5–7.

Wright, K. N., & Saylor, W. G. (1991). Male and female employees' perceptions of prison work: Is there a difference? *Justice Quarterly, 8*(4), 505–524.

Wunder, A. (1995, July). Prison tactical response teams. *Corrections Compendium, 20*(7): 4.

Wunder, A. (1995, August). Prison tactical response teams. *Corrections Compendium, 20*(8): 4.

Wunder, A. (1995a, May). Inmate phone use: Calling collect from America's prisons and jails. *Corrections Compendium, 20*(5), 6–7.

Wunder, A. (1995b). Corrections systems must bear the burden of new legislation. *Corrections Compendium, 20*(3), 4–20.

Yablonsky, L. (1965). *The tunnel back: Synanon*. New York: The Macmillan Co.

York, M. (1992, April 28). D.C. jail officers admit smuggling: Drug sting caught seven guards. *The Washington Post*, p. B1.

Zamble, E., & Porporino, F. (1988). *Coping, behavior, and adaptation in prison inmates*. New York: Springer-Verlag.

Zane, T. (1987, September). Personal communication.

Zang, N. L. (1998). Special administrator, Michigan Department of Corrections. Personal communication.

Zedlewski, E. W. (1987). *Making confinement decisions*. Washington, DC: National Institute of Justice.

Zelenka, D. J. (1993, July). South Carolina victim advocate helps address families' concerns. *Corrections Today*, 80, 82.

Zimmer, L. (1986). *Women guarding men*. Chicago: The University of Chicago Press.

Zimmerman, J. (1999, May). Twenty-eighth annual review of criminal procedure: Substantive rights retained by prisoners. *Georgetown Law Journal*.

Zimring, F. E., & Hawkins, G. J. (1973). *Deterrence*. Chicago: University of Chicago Press.

Zupan, L. L. (1991). *Jails: Reform and the new generation philosophy*. Cincinnati, OH: Anderson Publishing Co.

Table of Cases

For Further Reference

Altizer v. Deeds, 191 F.3d 540 (4th Cir. 1999)

Austin v. James, second amended complaint, No 95-t-637-N (M.D., Al filed Sept. 19, 1995)

Banks v. Hanvener, 234 F.Supp. 27 (D.C. Cir. 1964)

Benjamin v. Coughlin, 905 F.2d 571 (2d Cir. 1990)

Benjamin v. Jacobson, 124 F.3d 162 (2d Cir. 1997)

Benjamin v. Jacobson, WL 18840 (2d Cir. 1999)

Benjamin v. Sielaff, 752 F.Supp. 140 (S.D. N.Y. 1990)

Berry v. City of Muskogee, 900 F.2d 1489 (10th Cir. 1990)

Name Index

Subject Index

Photo Credits

4 AP/Wide World Photos; 6 © Joseph Sohm/Corbis; 9 © Cary Wolinsky/Stock Boston; 14 © Jim Pickerell/Stock Boston; 22 AP/Wide World Photos; 25 © A. Ramey/Photo Edit; 28 © George Cohen/Impact Visuals; 33 AP/Wide World Photos; 39 © Corbis; 49 AP/Wide World Photos; 53 AP/Wide World Photos; 57 © Bettmann/Corbis; 71 © Corbis; 73 Bettmann/Corbis; 77 Liaison/Hulton Getty; 80 © Historical Picture Archive/Corbis; 87 Liaison/Hulton Getty; 88 Culver Pictures; 90 © Corbis; 96 American Correctional Association; 101 Culver Pictures; 103 © Bettmann/Corbis; 105 American Correctional Association; 120 American Stock/Archive Photos; 124 © Earl Dotter/Impact Visuals; 135 © Nick Sapieha/Stock Boston; 140 AP/Wide World Photos; 155 AP/Wide World Photos; 181 © Bill Swersey/Liaison Agency; 184 © A. Ramey/Photo Edit; 185 © Andrew Lichtenstein/Corbis Sygma; 196 © Gale Zucker/Stock Boston; 199 © Lester Sloan/Woodfin Camp & Associates; 205 AP/Wide World Photos; 214 © Rod Rolle/Liaison Agency; 224 AP/Wide World Photos; 227 © A. Ramey/Photo Edit; 236 © A. Ramey/Photo Edit; 245 © William Greenblatt/Gamma Liaison; 254 Robert Durell/Los Angeles Times; 255 Robert Durell/Los Angeles Times; 258 © John Eastcott/Yva Momatiuk/Stock Boston; 269 © Norman Bergsma/Corbis Sygma; 277 © Daniel Laine/Corbis; 287 © Gary Wagner/Stock Boston; 289 © A. Ramey/Photo Edit; 295 © Andrew Lichtenstein/Corbis Sygma; 304 © Joel Gordon; 311 © Marilyn Humphries/Impact Visuals; 318 © Joel Gordon; 321 AP/Wide World Photos; 330 AP/Wide World Photos; 334 © Joel Gordon; 340 © Bob Daemmrich/Stock Boston; 353 © John Chiasson/Liaison Agency; 359 © A. Ramey/Photo Edit; 364 © Gerd Ludwig/Woodfin Camp & Associates; 374 © Andrew Lichtenstein/Corbis Sygma; 383 © Joel Gordon; 386 © Andrew Lichtenstein/Impact Visuals; 395 © Raymlond Gehman/Corbis; 399 AP/Wide World Photos; 414 AP/Wide World Photos; 423 © Alain McLaughlin/Impact Visuals; 428 © Joel Gordon; 433 © Andrew Lichtenstein/Corbis Sygma; 449 (both) © Andrew Lichtenstein/Corbis Sygma; 452 ©Alain McLaughlin/Impact Visuals; 455 © Joel Gordon; 457 © A. Ramey/Woodfin Camp & Associates; 467 © Jack Kurtz/Impact Visuals; 472 © David Young-Wolff/Photo Edit; 476 © John Chiasson/Liaison Agency; 483 © Tannenbaum/Corbis Sygma; 487 © Brooks Kraft/Corbis Sygma; 489 © Joel Gordon; 495 © John Chiasson/Liaison Agency; 503 © Andrew Lichtenstein/Corbis Sygma; 511 AP/Wide World Photos; 516 © A. Ramey/Stock Boston; **Feature Box images:** "Program Focus;" © Ed Eckstein/Corbis; "Close Up;" © Joel Gordon; "Consider This;" © Gary Wagner/Stock Boston; "Historical Perspective;" Culver Pictures; "In Their Own Words;" AP/Wide World Photos